Dictionary of Literary Biography

1 *The American Renaissance in New England,* edited by Joel Myerson (1978)

2 *American Novelists Since World War II,* edited by Jeffrey Helterman and Richard Layman (1978)

3 *Antebellum Writers in New York and the South,* edited by Joel Myerson (1979)

4 *American Writers in Paris, 1920-1939,* edited by Karen Lane Rood (1980)

5 *American Poets Since World War II,* 2 parts, edited by Donald J. Greiner (1980)

6 *American Novelists Since World War II, Second Series,* edited by James E. Kibler Jr. (1980)

7 *Twentieth-Century American Dramatists,* 2 parts, edited by John MacNicholas (1981)

8 *Twentieth-Century American Science-Fiction Writers,* 2 parts, edited by David Cowart and Thomas L. Wymer (1981)

9 *American Novelists, 1910-1945,* 3 parts, edited by James J. Martine (1981)

10 *Modern British Dramatists, 1900-1945,* 2 parts, edited by Stanley Weintraub (1982)

11 *American Humorists, 1800-1950,* 2 parts, edited by Stanley Trachtenberg (1982)

12 *American Realists and Naturalists,* edited by Donald Pizer and Earl N. Harbert (1982)

13 *British Dramatists Since World War II,* 2 parts, edited by Stanley Weintraub (1982)

14 *British Novelists Since 1960,* 2 parts, edited by Jay L. Halio (1983)

15 *British Novelists, 1930-1959,* 2 parts, edited by Bernard Oldsey (1983)

16 *The Beats: Literary Bohemians in Postwar America,* 2 parts, edited by Ann Charters (1983)

17 *Twentieth-Century American Historians,* edited by Clyde N. Wilson (1983)

18 *Victorian Novelists After 1885,* edited by Ira B. Nadel and William E. Fredeman (1983)

19 *British Poets, 1880-1914,* edited by Donald E. Stanford (1983)

20 *British Poets, 1914-1945,* edited by Donald E. Stanford (1983)

21 *Victorian Novelists Before 1885,* edited by Ira B. Nadel and William E. Fredeman (1983)

22 *American Writers for Children, 1900-1960,* edited by John Cech (1983)

23 *American Newspaper Journalists, 1873-1900,* edited by Perry J. Ashley (1983)

24 *American Colonial Writers, 1606-1734,* edited by Emory Elliott (1984)

25 *American Newspaper Journalists, 1901-1925,* edited by Perry J. Ashley (1984)

26 *American Screenwriters,* edited by Robert E. Morsberger, Stephen O. Lesser, and Randall Clark (1984)

27 *Poets of Great Britain and Ireland, 1945-1960,* edited by Vincent B. Sherry Jr. (1984)

28 *Twentieth-Century American-Jewish Fiction Writers,* edited by Daniel Walden (1984)

29 *American Newspaper Journalists, 1926-1950,* edited by Perry J. Ashley (1984)

30 *American Historians, 1607-1865,* edited by Clyde N. Wilson (1984)

31 *American Colonial Writers, 1735-1781,* edited by Emory Elliott (1984)

32 *Victorian Poets Before 1850,* edited by William E. Fredeman and Ira B. Nadel (1984)

33 *Afro-American Fiction Writers After 1955,* edited by Thadious M. Davis and Trudier Harris (1984)

34 *British Novelists, 1890-1929: Traditionalists,* edited by Thomas F. Staley (1985)

35 *Victorian Poets After 1850,* edited by William E. Fredeman and Ira B. Nadel (1985)

36 *British Novelists, 1890-1929: Modernists,* edited by Thomas F. Staley (1985)

37 *American Writers of the Early Republic,* edited by Emory Elliott (1985)

38 *Afro-American Writers After 1955: Dramatists and Prose Writers,* edited by Thadious M. Davis and Trudier Harris (1985)

39 *British Novelists, 1660-1800,* 2 parts, edited by Martin C. Battestin (1985)

40 *Poets of Great Britain and Ireland Since 1960,* 2 parts, edited by Vincent B. Sherry Jr. (1985)

41 *Afro-American Poets Since 1955,* edited by Trudier Harris and Thadious M. Davis (1985)

42 *American Writers for Children Before 1900,* edited by Glenn E. Estes (1985)

43 *American Newspaper Journalists, 1690-1872,* edited by Perry J. Ashley (1986)

44 *American Screenwriters, Second Series,* edited by Randall Clark, Robert E. Morsberger, and Stephen O. Lesser (1986)

45 *American Poets, 1880-1945, First Series,* edited by Peter Quartermain (1986)

46 *American Literary Publishing Houses, 1900-1980: Trade and Paperback,* edited by Peter Dzwonkoski (1986)

47 *American Historians, 1866-1912,* edited by Clyde N. Wilson (1986)

48 *American Poets, 1880-1945, Second Series,* edited by Peter Quartermain (1986)

49 *American Literary Publishing Houses, 1638-1899,* 2 parts, edited by Peter Dzwonkoski (1986)

50 *Afro-American Writers Before the Harlem Renaissance,* edited by Trudier Harris (1986)

51 *Afro-American Writers from the Harlem Renaissance to 1940,* edited by Trudier Harris (1987)

52 *American Writers for Children Since 1960: Fiction,* edited by Glenn E. Estes (1986)

53 *Canadian Writers Since 1960, First Series,* edited by W. H. New (1986)

54 *American Poets, 1880-1945, Third Series,* 2 parts, edited by Peter Quartermain (1987)

55 *Victorian Prose Writers Before 1867,* edited by William B. Thesing (1987)

56 *German Fiction Writers, 1914-1945,* edited by James Hardin (1987)

57 *Victorian Prose Writers After 1867,* edited by William B. Thesing (1987)

58 *Jacobean and Caroline Dramatists,* edited by Fredson Bowers (1987)

59 *American Literary Critics and Scholars, 1800-1850,* edited by John W. Rathbun and Monica M. Grecu (1987)

60 *Canadian Writers Since 1960, Second Series,* edited by W. H. New (1987)

61 *American Writers for Children Since 1960: Poets, Illustrators, and Nonfiction Authors,* edited by Glenn E. Estes (1987)

62 *Elizabethan Dramatists,* edited by Fredson Bowers (1987)

63 *Modern American Critics, 1920-1955,* edited by Gregory S. Jay (1988)

64 *American Literary Critics and Scholars, 1850-1880,* edited by John W. Rathbun and Monica M. Grecu (1988)

65 *French Novelists, 1900-1930,* edited by Catharine Savage Brosman (1988)

66 *German Fiction Writers, 1885-1913,* 2 parts, edited by James Hardin (1988)

67 *Modern American Critics Since 1955,* edited by Gregory S. Jay (1988)

68 *Canadian Writers, 1920-1959, First Series,* edited by W. H. New (1988)

69 *Contemporary German Fiction Writers, First Series,* edited by Wolfgang D. Elfe and James Hardin (1988)

70 *British Mystery Writers, 1860-1919,* edited by Bernard Benstock and Thomas F. Staley (1988)

71 *American Literary Critics and Scholars, 1880-1900,* edited by John W. Rathbun and Monica M. Grecu (1988)

72 *French Novelists, 1930-1960,* edited by Catharine Savage Brosman (1988)

73 *American Magazine Journalists, 1741-1850,* edited by Sam G. Riley (1988)

74 *American Short-Story Writers Before 1880,* edited by Bobby Ellen Kimbel, with the assistance of William E. Grant (1988)

75 *Contemporary German Fiction Writers, Second Series,* edited by Wolfgang D. Elfe and James Hardin (1988)

76 *Afro-American Writers, 1940–1955,* edited by Trudier Harris (1988)

77 *British Mystery Writers, 1920–1939,* edited by Bernard Benstock and Thomas F. Staley (1988)

78 *American Short-Story Writers, 1880–1910,* edited by Bobby Ellen Kimbel, with the assistance of William E. Grant (1988)

79 *American Magazine Journalists, 1850–1900,* edited by Sam G. Riley (1988)

80 *Restoration and Eighteenth-Century Dramatists, First Series,* edited by Paula R. Backscheider (1989)

81 *Austrian Fiction Writers, 1875–1913,* edited by James Hardin and Donald G. Daviau (1989)

82 *Chicano Writers, First Series,* edited by Francisco A. Lomelí and Carl R. Shirley (1989)

83 *French Novelists Since 1960,* edited by Catharine Savage Brosman (1989)

84 *Restoration and Eighteenth-Century Dramatists, Second Series,* edited by Paula R. Backscheider (1989)

85 *Austrian Fiction Writers After 1914,* edited by James Hardin and Donald G. Daviau (1989)

86 *American Short-Story Writers, 1910–1945, First Series,* edited by Bobby Ellen Kimbel (1989)

87 *British Mystery and Thriller Writers Since 1940, First Series,* edited by Bernard Benstock and Thomas F. Staley (1989)

88 *Canadian Writers, 1920–1959, Second Series,* edited by W. H. New (1989)

89 *Restoration and Eighteenth-Century Dramatists, Third Series,* edited by Paula R. Backscheider (1989)

90 *German Writers in the Age of Goethe, 1789–1832,* edited by James Hardin and Christoph E. Schweitzer (1989)

91 *American Magazine Journalists, 1900–1960, First Series,* edited by Sam G. Riley (1990)

92 *Canadian Writers, 1890–1920,* edited by W. H. New (1990)

93 *British Romantic Poets, 1789–1832, First Series,* edited by John R. Greenfield (1990)

94 *German Writers in the Age of Goethe: Sturm und Drang to Classicism,* edited by James Hardin and Christoph E. Schweitzer (1990)

95 *Eighteenth-Century British Poets, First Series,* edited by John Sitter (1990)

96 *British Romantic Poets, 1789–1832, Second Series,* edited by John R. Greenfield (1990)

97 *German Writers from the Enlightenment to Sturm und Drang, 1720–1764,* edited by James Hardin and Christoph E. Schweitzer (1990)

98 *Modern British Essayists, First Series,* edited by Robert Beum (1990)

99 *Canadian Writers Before 1890,* edited by W. H. New (1990)

100 *Modern British Essayists, Second Series,* edited by Robert Beum (1990)

101 *British Prose Writers, 1660–1800, First Series,* edited by Donald T. Siebert (1991)

102 *American Short-Story Writers, 1910–1945, Second Series,* edited by Bobby Ellen Kimbel (1991)

103 *American Literary Biographers, First Series,* edited by Steven Serafin (1991)

104 *British Prose Writers, 1660–1800, Second Series,* edited by Donald T. Siebert (1991)

105 *American Poets Since World War II, Second Series,* edited by R. S. Gwynn (1991)

106 *British Literary Publishing Houses, 1820–1880,* edited by Patricia J. Anderson and Jonathan Rose (1991)

107 *British Romantic Prose Writers, 1789–1832, First Series,* edited by John R. Greenfield (1991)

108 *Twentieth-Century Spanish Poets, First Series,* edited by Michael L. Perna (1991)

109 *Eighteenth-Century British Poets, Second Series,* edited by John Sitter (1991)

110 *British Romantic Prose Writers, 1789–1832, Second Series,* edited by John R. Greenfield (1991)

111 *American Literary Biographers, Second Series,* edited by Steven Serafin (1991)

112 *British Literary Publishing Houses, 1881–1965,* edited by Jonathan Rose and Patricia J. Anderson (1991)

113 *Modern Latin-American Fiction Writers, First Series,* edited by William Luis (1992)

114 *Twentieth-Century Italian Poets, First Series,* edited by Giovanna Wedel De Stasio, Glauco Cambon, and Antonio Illiano (1992)

115 *Medieval Philosophers,* edited by Jeremiah Hackett (1992)

116 *British Romantic Novelists, 1789–1832,* edited by Bradford K. Mudge (1992)

117 *Twentieth-Century Caribbean and Black African Writers, First Series,* edited by Bernth Lindfors and Reinhard Sander (1992)

118 *Twentieth-Century German Dramatists, 1889–1918,* edited by Wolfgang D. Elfe and James Hardin (1992)

119 *Nineteenth-Century French Fiction Writers: Romanticism and Realism, 1800–1860,* edited by Catharine Savage Brosman (1992)

120 *American Poets Since World War II, Third Series,* edited by R. S. Gwynn (1992)

121 *Seventeenth-Century British Nondramatic Poets, First Series,* edited by M. Thomas Hester (1992)

122 *Chicano Writers, Second Series,* edited by Francisco A. Lomelí and Carl R. Shirley (1992)

123 *Nineteenth-Century French Fiction Writers: Naturalism and Beyond, 1860–1900,* edited by Catharine Savage Brosman (1992)

124 *Twentieth-Century German Dramatists, 1919–1992,* edited by Wolfgang D. Elfe and James Hardin (1992)

125 *Twentieth-Century Caribbean and Black African Writers, Second Series,* edited by Bernth Lindfors and Reinhard Sander (1993)

126 *Seventeenth-Century British Nondramatic Poets, Second Series,* edited by M. Thomas Hester (1993)

127 *American Newspaper Publishers, 1950–1990,* edited by Perry J. Ashley (1993)

128 *Twentieth-Century Italian Poets, Second Series,* edited by Giovanna Wedel De Stasio, Glauco Cambon, and Antonio Illiano (1993)

129 *Nineteenth-Century German Writers, 1841–1900,* edited by James Hardin and Siegfried Mews (1993)

130 *American Short-Story Writers Since World War II,* edited by Patrick Meanor (1993)

131 *Seventeenth-Century British Nondramatic Poets, Third Series,* edited by M. Thomas Hester (1993)

132 *Sixteenth-Century British Nondramatic Writers, First Series,* edited by David A. Richardson (1993)

133 *Nineteenth-Century German Writers to 1840,* edited by James Hardin and Siegfried Mews (1993)

134 *Twentieth-Century Spanish Poets, Second Series,* edited by Jerry Phillips Winfield (1994)

135 *British Short-Fiction Writers, 1880–1914: The Realist Tradition,* edited by William B. Thesing (1994)

136 *Sixteenth-Century British Nondramatic Writers, Second Series,* edited by David A. Richardson (1994)

137 *American Magazine Journalists, 1900–1960, Second Series,* edited by Sam G. Riley (1994)

138 *German Writers and Works of the High Middle Ages: 1170–1280,* edited by James Hardin and Will Hasty (1994)

139 *British Short-Fiction Writers, 1945–1980,* edited by Dean Baldwin (1994)

140 *American Book-Collectors and Bibliographers, First Series,* edited by Joseph Rosenblum (1994)

141 *British Children's Writers, 1880–1914,* edited by Laura M. Zaidman (1994)

142 *Eighteenth-Century British Literary Biographers,* edited by Steven Serafin (1994)

143 *American Novelists Since World War II, Third Series,* edited by James R. Giles and Wanda H. Giles (1994)

144 *Nineteenth-Century British Literary Biographers,* edited by Steven Serafin (1994)

145 *Modern Latin-American Fiction Writers, Second Series,* edited by William Luis and Ann González (1994)

146 *Old and Middle English Literature,* edited by Jeffrey Helterman and Jerome Mitchell (1994)

147 *South Slavic Writers Before World War II,* edited by Vasa D. Mihailovich (1994)

148 *German Writers and Works of the Early Middle Ages: 800–1170,* edited by Will Hasty and James Hardin (1994)

149 *Late Nineteenth- and Early Twentieth-Century British Literary Biographers,* edited by Steven Serafin (1995)

150 *Early Modern Russian Writers, Late Seventeenth and Eighteenth Centuries,* edited by Marcus C. Levitt (1995)

151 *British Prose Writers of the Early Seventeenth Century,* edited by Clayton D. Lein (1995)

152 *American Novelists Since World War II, Fourth Series,* edited by James R. Giles and Wanda H. Giles (1995)

153 *Late-Victorian and Edwardian British Novelists, First Series,* edited by George M. Johnson (1995)

154 *The British Literary Book Trade, 1700–1820,* edited by James K. Bracken and Joel Silver (1995)

155 *Twentieth-Century British Literary Biographers,* edited by Steven Serafin (1995)

156 *British Short-Fiction Writers, 1880–1914: The Romantic Tradition,* edited by William F. Naufftus (1995)

157 *Twentieth-Century Caribbean and Black African Writers, Third Series,* edited by Bernth Lindfors and Reinhard Sander (1995)

158 *British Reform Writers, 1789–1832,* edited by Gary Kelly and Edd Applegate (1995)

159 *British Short-Fiction Writers, 1800–1880,* edited by John R. Greenfield (1996)

160 *British Children's Writers, 1914–1960,* edited by Donald R. Hettinga and Gary D. Schmidt (1996)

161 *British Children's Writers Since 1960, First Series,* edited by Caroline Hunt (1996)

162 *British Short-Fiction Writers, 1915–1945,* edited by John H. Rogers (1996)

163 *British Children's Writers, 1800–1880,* edited by Meena Khorana (1996)

164 *German Baroque Writers, 1580–1660,* edited by James Hardin (1996)

165 *American Poets Since World War II, Fourth Series,* edited by Joseph Conte (1996)

166 *British Travel Writers, 1837–1875,* edited by Barbara Brothers and Julia Gergits (1996)

167 *Sixteenth-Century British Nondramatic Writers, Third Series,* edited by David A. Richardson (1996)

168 *German Baroque Writers, 1661–1730,* edited by James Hardin (1996)

169 *American Poets Since World War II, Fifth Series,* edited by Joseph Conte (1996)

170 *The British Literary Book Trade, 1475–1700,* edited by James K. Bracken and Joel Silver (1996)

171 *Twentieth-Century American Sportswriters,* edited by Richard Orodenker (1996)

172 *Sixteenth-Century British Nondramatic Writers, Fourth Series,* edited by David A. Richardson (1996)

173 *American Novelists Since World War II, Fifth Series,* edited by James R. Giles and Wanda H. Giles (1996)

174 *British Travel Writers, 1876–1909,* edited by Barbara Brothers and Julia Gergits (1997)

175 *Native American Writers of the United States,* edited by Kenneth M. Roemer (1997)

176 *Ancient Greek Authors,* edited by Ward W. Briggs (1997)

177 *Italian Novelists Since World War II, 1945–1965,* edited by Augustus Pallotta (1997)

178 *British Fantasy and Science-Fiction Writers Before World War I,* edited by Darren Harris-Fain (1997)

179 *German Writers of the Renaissance and Reformation, 1280–1580,* edited by James Hardin and Max Reinhart (1997)

180 *Japanese Fiction Writers, 1868–1945,* edited by Van C. Gessel (1997)

181 *South Slavic Writers Since World War II,* edited by Vasa D. Mihailovich (1997)

182 *Japanese Fiction Writers Since World War II,* edited by Van C. Gessel (1997)

183 *American Travel Writers, 1776–1864,* edited by James J. Schramer and Donald Ross (1997)

184 *Nineteenth-Century British Book-Collectors and Bibliographers,* edited by William Baker and Kenneth Womack (1997)

185 *American Literary Journalists, 1945–1995, First Series,* edited by Arthur J. Kaul (1998)

186 *Nineteenth-Century American Western Writers,* edited by Robert L. Gale (1998)

187 *American Book Collectors and Bibliographers, Second Series,* edited by Joseph Rosenblum (1998)

188 *American Book and Magazine Illustrators to 1920,* edited by Steven E. Smith, Catherine A. Hastedt, and Donald H. Dyal (1998)

189 *American Travel Writers, 1850–1915,* edited by Donald Ross and James J. Schramer (1998)

190 *British Reform Writers, 1832–1914,* edited by Gary Kelly and Edd Applegate (1998)

191 *British Novelists Between the Wars,* edited by George M. Johnson (1998)

192 *French Dramatists, 1789–1914,* edited by Barbara T. Cooper (1998)

193 *American Poets Since World War II, Sixth Series,* edited by Joseph Conte (1998)

194 *British Novelists Since 1960, Second Series,* edited by Merritt Moseley (1998)

195 *British Travel Writers, 1910–1939,* edited by Barbara Brothers and Julia Gergits (1998)

196 *Italian Novelists Since World War II, 1965–1995,* edited by Augustus Pallotta (1999)

197 *Late-Victorian and Edwardian British Novelists, Second Series,* edited by George M. Johnson (1999)

198 *Russian Literature in the Age of Pushkin and Gogol: Prose,* edited by Christine A. Rydel (1999)

199 *Victorian Women Poets,* edited by William B. Thesing (1999)

200 *American Women Prose Writers to 1820,* edited by Carla J. Mulford, with Angela Vietto and Amy E. Winans (1999)

201 *Twentieth-Century British Book Collectors and Bibliographers,* edited by William Baker and Kenneth Womack (1999)

202 *Nineteenth-Century American Fiction Writers,* edited by Kent P. Ljungquist (1999)

203 *Medieval Japanese Writers,* edited by Steven D. Carter (1999)

204 *British Travel Writers, 1940–1997,* edited by Barbara Brothers and Julia M. Gergits (1999)

205 *Russian Literature in the Age of Pushkin and Gogol: Poetry and Drama,* edited by Christine A. Rydel (1999)

206 *Twentieth-Century American Western Writers, First Series,* edited by Richard H. Cracroft (1999)

207 *British Novelists Since 1960, Third Series,* edited by Merritt Moseley (1999)

208 *Literature of the French and Occitan Middle Ages: Eleventh to Fifteenth Centuries,* edited by Deborah Sinnreich-Levi and Ian S. Laurie (1999)

209 *Chicano Writers, Third Series,* edited by Francisco A. Lomelí and Carl R. Shirley (1999)

210 *Ernest Hemingway: A Documentary Volume,* edited by Robert W. Trogdon (1999)

211 *Ancient Roman Writers,* edited by Ward W. Briggs (1999)

212 *Twentieth-Century American Western Writers, Second Series,* edited by Richard H. Cracroft (1999)

213 *Pre-Nineteenth-Century British Book Collectors and Bibliographers,* edited by William Baker and Kenneth Womack (1999)

214 *Twentieth-Century Danish Writers,* edited by Marianne Stecher-Hansen (1999)

215 *Twentieth-Century Eastern European Writers, First Series,* edited by Steven Serafin (1999)

216 *British Poets of the Great War: Brooke, Rosenberg, Thomas. A Documentary Volume,* edited by Patrick Quinn (2000)

217 *Nineteenth-Century French Poets,* edited by Robert Beum (2000)

218 *American Short-Story Writers Since World War II, Second Series,* edited by Patrick Meanor and Gwen Crane (2000)

219 *F. Scott Fitzgerald's* The Great Gatsby: *A Documentary Volume,* edited by Matthew J. Bruccoli (2000)

220 *Twentieth-Century Eastern European Writers, Second Series,* edited by Steven Serafin (2000)

221 *American Women Prose Writers, 1870–1920,* edited by Sharon M. Harris, with the assistance of Heidi L. M. Jacobs and Jennifer Putzi (2000)

222 *H. L. Mencken: A Documentary Volume,* edited by Richard J. Schrader (2000)

223 *The American Renaissance in New England, Second Series,* edited by Wesley T. Mott (2000)

224 *Walt Whitman: A Documentary Volume,* edited by Joel Myerson (2000)

225 *South African Writers,* edited by Paul A. Scanlon (2000)

226 *American Hard-Boiled Crime Writers,* edited by George Parker Anderson and Julie B. Anderson (2000)

227 *American Novelists Since World War II, Sixth Series,* edited by James R. Giles and Wanda H. Giles (2000)

228 *Twentieth-Century American Dramatists, Second Series,* edited by Christopher J. Wheatley (2000)

229 *Thomas Wolfe: A Documentary Volume,* edited by Ted Mitchell (2001)

230 *Australian Literature, 1788–1914,* edited by Selina Samuels (2001)

231 *British Novelists Since 1960, Fourth Series,* edited by Merritt Moseley (2001)

232 *Twentieth-Century Eastern European Writers, Third Series,* edited by Steven Serafin (2001)

233 *British and Irish Dramatists Since World War II, Second Series,* edited by John Bull (2001)

234 *American Short-Story Writers Since World War II, Third Series,* edited by Patrick Meanor and Richard E. Lee (2001)

235 *The American Renaissance in New England, Third Series,* edited by Wesley T. Mott (2001)

236 *British Rhetoricians and Logicians, 1500–1660,* edited by Edward A. Malone (2001)

237 *The Beats: A Documentary Volume,* edited by Matt Theado (2001)

238 *Russian Novelists in the Age of Tolstoy and Dostoevsky,* edited by J. Alexander Ogden and Judith E. Kalb (2001)

239 *American Women Prose Writers: 1820–1870,* edited by Amy E. Hudock and Katharine Rodier (2001)

240 *Late Nineteenth- and Early Twentieth-Century British Women Poets,* edited by William B. Thesing (2001)

241 *American Sportswriters and Writers on Sport,* edited by Richard Orodenker (2001)

242 *Twentieth-Century European Cultural Theorists, First Series,* edited by Paul Hansom (2001)

243 *The American Renaissance in New England, Fourth Series,* edited by Wesley T. Mott (2001)

244 *American Short-Story Writers Since World War II, Fourth Series,* edited by Patrick Meanor and Joseph McNicholas (2001)

245 *British and Irish Dramatists Since World War II, Third Series,* edited by John Bull (2001)

246 *Twentieth-Century American Cultural Theorists,* edited by Paul Hansom (2001)

247 *James Joyce: A Documentary Volume,* edited by A. Nicholas Fargnoli (2001)

248 *Antebellum Writers in the South, Second Series,* edited by Kent Ljungquist (2001)

249 *Twentieth-Century American Dramatists, Third Series,* edited by Christopher Wheatley (2002)

250 *Antebellum Writers in New York, Second Series,* edited by Kent Ljungquist (2002)

251 *Canadian Fantasy and Science-Fiction Writers,* edited by Douglas Ivison (2002)

252 *British Philosophers, 1500–1799,* edited by Philip B. Dematteis and Peter S. Fosl (2002)

253 *Raymond Chandler: A Documentary Volume,* edited by Robert Moss (2002)

254 *The House of Putnam, 1837–1872: A Documentary Volume,* edited by Ezra Greenspan (2002)

255 *British Fantasy and Science-Fiction Writers, 1918–1960,* edited by Darren Harris-Fain (2002)

256 *Twentieth-Century American Western Writers, Third Series,* edited by Richard H. Cracroft (2002)

257 *Twentieth-Century Swedish Writers After World War II,* edited by Ann-Charlotte Gavel Adams (2002)

258 *Modern French Poets,* edited by Jean-François Leroux (2002)

259 *Twentieth-Century Swedish Writers Before World War II,* edited by Ann-Charlotte Gavel Adams (2002)

260 *Australian Writers, 1915–1950,* edited by Selina Samuels (2002)

261 *British Fantasy and Science-Fiction Writers Since 1960,* edited by Darren Harris-Fain (2002)

262 *British Philosophers, 1800–2000,* edited by Peter S. Fosl and Leemon B. McHenry (2002)

263 *William Shakespeare: A Documentary Volume,* edited by Catherine Loomis (2002)

264 *Italian Prose Writers, 1900–1945,* edited by Luca Somigli and Rocco Capozzi (2002)

265 *American Song Lyricists, 1920–1960,* edited by Philip Furia (2002)

266 *Twentieth-Century American Dramatists, Fourth Series,* edited by Christopher J. Wheatley (2002)

Dictionary of Literary Biography Documentary Series

1 *Sherwood Anderson, Willa Cather, John Dos Passos, Theodore Dreiser, F. Scott Fitzgerald, Ernest Hemingway, Sinclair Lewis,* edited by Margaret A. Van Antwerp (1982)

2 *James Gould Cozzens, James T. Farrell, William Faulkner, John O'Hara, John Steinbeck, Thomas Wolfe, Richard Wright,* edited by Margaret A. Van Antwerp (1982)

3 *Saul Bellow, Jack Kerouac, Norman Mailer, Vladimir Nabokov, John Updike, Kurt Vonnegut,* edited by Mary Bruccoli (1983)

4 *Tennessee Williams,* edited by Margaret A. Van Antwerp and Sally Johns (1984)

5 *American Transcendentalists,* edited by Joel Myerson (1988)

6 *Hardboiled Mystery Writers: Raymond Chandler, Dashiell Hammett, Ross Macdonald,* edited by Matthew J. Bruccoli and Richard Layman (1989)

7 *Modern American Poets: James Dickey, Robert Frost, Marianne Moore,* edited by Karen L. Rood (1989)

8 *The Black Aesthetic Movement,* edited by Jeffrey Louis Decker (1991)

9 *American Writers of the Vietnam War: W. D. Ehrhart, Larry Heinemann, Tim O'Brien, Walter McDonald, John M. Del Vecchio,* edited by Ronald Baughman (1991)

10 *The Bloomsbury Group,* edited by Edward L. Bishop (1992)

11 *American Proletarian Culture: The Twenties and The Thirties,* edited by Jon Christian Suggs (1993)

12 *Southern Women Writers: Flannery O'Connor, Katherine Anne Porter, Eudora Welty,* edited by Mary Ann Wimsatt and Karen L. Rood (1994)

13 *The House of Scribner, 1846–1904,* edited by John Delaney (1996)

14 *Four Women Writers for Children, 1868–1918,* edited by Caroline C. Hunt (1996)

15 *American Expatriate Writers: Paris in the Twenties,* edited by Matthew J. Bruccoli and Robert W. Trogdon (1997)

16 *The House of Scribner, 1905–1930,* edited by John Delaney (1997)

17 *The House of Scribner, 1931–1984,* edited by John Delaney (1998)

18 *British Poets of The Great War: Sassoon, Graves, Owen,* edited by Patrick Quinn (1999)

19 *James Dickey,* edited by Judith S. Baughman (1999)

See also DLB 210, 216, 219, 222, 224, 229, 237, 247, 253, 254, 263

Dictionary of Literary Biography Yearbooks

1980 edited by Karen L. Rood, Jean W. Ross, and Richard Ziegfeld (1981)

1981 edited by Karen L. Rood, Jean W. Ross, and Richard Ziegfeld (1982)

1982 edited by Richard Ziegfeld; associate editors: Jean W. Ross and Lynne C. Zeigler (1983)

1983 edited by Mary Bruccoli and Jean W. Ross; associate editor Richard Ziegfeld (1984)

1984 edited by Jean W. Ross (1985)

1985 edited by Jean W. Ross (1986)

1986 edited by J. M. Brook (1987)

1987 edited by J. M. Brook (1988)

1988 edited by J. M. Brook (1989)

1989 edited by J. M. Brook (1990)

1990 edited by James W. Hipp (1991)

1991 edited by James W. Hipp (1992)

1992 edited by James W. Hipp (1993)

1993 edited by James W. Hipp, contributing editor George Garrett (1994)

1994 edited by James W. Hipp, contributing editor George Garrett (1995)

1995 edited by James W. Hipp, contributing editor George Garrett (1996)

1996 edited by Samuel W. Bruce and L. Kay Webster, contributing editor George Garrett (1997)

1997 edited by Matthew J. Bruccoli and George Garrett, with the assistance of L. Kay Webster (1998)

1998 edited by Matthew J. Bruccoli, contributing editor George Garrett, with the assistance of D. W. Thomas (1999)

1999 edited by Matthew J. Bruccoli, contributing editor George Garrett, with the assistance of D. W. Thomas (2000)

2000 edited by Matthew J. Bruccoli, contributing editor George Garrett, with the assistance of George Parker Anderson (2001)

2001 edited by Matthew J. Bruccoli, contributing editor George Garrett, with the assistance of George Parker Anderson (2002)

Concise Series

Concise Dictionary of American Literary Biography, 7 volumes (1988-1999): *The New Consciousness, 1941-1968; Colonization to the American Renaissance, 1640-1865; Realism, Naturalism, and Local Color, 1865-1917; The Twenties, 1917-1929; The Age of Maturity, 1929-1941; Broadening Views, 1968-1988; Supplement: Modern Writers, 1900-1998.*

Concise Dictionary of British Literary Biography, 8 volumes (1991-1992): *Writers of the Middle Ages and Renaissance Before 1660; Writers of the Restoration and Eighteenth Century, 1660-1789; Writers of the Romantic Period, 1789-1832; Victorian Writers, 1832-1890; Late-Victorian and Edwardian Writers, 1890-1914; Modern Writers, 1914-1945; Writers After World War II, 1945-1960; Contemporary Writers, 1960 to Present.*

Concise Dictionary of World Literary Biography, 10 volumes projected (1999-   ): *Ancient Greek and Roman Writers; German Writers; African, Caribbean, and Latin American Writers; South Slavic and Eastern European Writers.*

Dictionary of Literary Biography® • Volume Two Hundred Sixty-Six

Twentieth-Century American Dramatists
Fourth Series

Dictionary of Literary Biography® • Volume Two Hundred Sixty-Six

Twentieth-Century American Dramatists
Fourth Series

Christopher J. Wheatley
Catholic University of America

A Bruccoli Clark Layman Book

ST. PHILIP'S COLLEGE LIBRARY

Detroit • New York • San Diego • San Francisco • Cleveland • New Haven, Conn. • Waterville, Maine • London • Munich

PS
350
T96
2003

Dictionary of Literary Biography, Volume 266
Twentieth-Century American Dramatists

Advisory Board
John Baker
William Cagle
Patrick O'Connor
George Garrett
Trudier Harris
Alvin Kernan
Kenny J. Williams

Editorial Directors
Matthew J. Bruccoli and Richard Layman

Senior Editor
Karen L. Rood

© 2003 by Gale. Gale is an imprint of The Gale Group, Inc., a division of Thomson Learning, Inc.

Gale and Design™ and Thomson Learning™ are trademarks used herein under license.

For more information, contact
The Gale Group, Inc.
27500 Drake Rd.
Farmington Hills, MI 48331-3535
Or you can visit our Internet site at
http://www.gale.com

ALL RIGHTS RESERVED
No part of this work covered by the copyright hereon may be reproduced or used in any form or by any means—graphic, electronic, or mechanical, including photocopying, recording, taping, Web distribution, or information storage retrieval systems—without the written permission of the publisher.

For permission to use material from this product, submit your request via Web at http://www.gale-edit.com/permissions, or you may download our Permissions Request form and submit your request by fax or mail to:

Permissions Department
The Gale Group, Inc.
27500 Drake Rd.
Farmington Hills, MI 48331-3535
Permissions Hotline:
248-699-8006 or 800-877-4253, ext. 8006

Fax: 248-699-8074 or 800-762-4058

While every effort has been made to ensure the reliability of the information presented in this publication, The Gale Group, Inc. does not guarantee the accuracy of the data contained herein. The Gale Group, Inc. accepts no payment for listing; and inclusion in the publication of any organization, agency, institution, publication, service, or individual does not imply endorsement of the editors or publisher. Errors brought to the attention of the publisher and verified to the satisfaction of the publisher will be corrected in future editions.

LIBRARY OF CONGRESS CATALOGING-IN-PUBLICATION DATA

Twentieth-century American dramatists. Fourth series / edited by Christopher J. Wheatley.
  p. cm.—(Dictionary of literary biography ; v. 266)
"A Bruccoli Clark Layman book."
Includes bibliographical references and index.
   ISBN 0-7876-6010-8
   1. American drama—20th century—Bio-bibliography—Dictionaries.
   2. Dramatists, American—20th century—Biography—Dictionaries.
   3. American drama—20th century—Dictionaries.
   I. Wheatley, Christopher J., 1955–   . II. Series.

PS350 .T96 2002
822'.5--dc21   2002010077

Printed in the United States of America
10 9 8 7 6 5 4 3 2 1

Contents

Plan of the Series xiii
Introduction xv

Edward Albee (1928–) 3
   Lincoln Konkle

George Pierce Baker (1866–1935) 27
   Mark Hodin

George Cram Cook (1873–1924) 37
   Colette Epplé

Rachel Crothers (1870–1958) 43
   Glenda Frank

Mart Crowley (1935–) .57
   Kathleen M. Gough

William de Mille (1878–1955) 66
   Brian M. Amend

Margaret Edson (1961–) 75
   Martha Greene Eads

Edna Ferber (1885–1968) 79
   Angela Courtney

Harvey Fierstein (1954–) 88
   James Fisher

Horton Foote (1916–) .98
   Charles S. Watson

Charles Fuller (1939–) 110
   Çiğdem Üsekes

Philip Kan Gotanda (1951–) 116
   Magdalena Mączyńska

A. R. Gurney (1930–) .128
   Robert F. Gross

Moss Hart (1904–1961) .143
   Mary L. Cutler

Harry Kondoleon (1955–1994) 158
   Robert F. Gross

Leslie Lee (1935–) 165
   Sara J. Ford

Charles Ludlam (1943–1987) 171
   Robert F. Gross

Emily Mann (1952–) .178
   Christina S. McGowan

Arthur Miller (1915–) 185
   Stephen A. Marino

Marsha Norman (1947–) 210
   Pamela Monaco

OyamO (Charles F. Gordon)
(1943–) 225
   Jasmin L. Lambert

John Pielmeier (1949–) 231
   Bridget Brennan

Miguel Piñero (1946–1988) 238
   Jon D. Rossini

Paul Rudnick (1957–) 245
   Martha Greene Eads

Wallace Shawn (1943–) 255
   William C. Boles

Neil Simon (1927–) 269
   Susan Koprince

Samuel Spewack (1899–1971)
and Bella Cohen Spewack
(1899–1990) 288
   Donald E. Whittaker

Cheryl L. West (1957–) 297
   Tracey L. Walters

Elizabeth Wong (1958–) 306
   Elizabeth Kim

Books for Further Reading 317
Contributors 321
Cumulative Index 325

Plan of the Series

... Almost the most prodigious asset of a country, and perhaps its most precious possession, is its native literary product—when that product is fine and noble and enduring.

Mark Twain*

The advisory board, the editors, and the publisher of the *Dictionary of Literary Biography* are joined in endorsing Mark Twain's declaration. The literature of a nation provides an inexhaustible resource of permanent worth. Our purpose is to make literature and its creators better understood and more accessible to students and the reading public, while satisfying the needs of teachers and researchers.

To meet these requirements, *literary biography* has been construed in terms of the author's achievement. The most important thing about a writer is his writing. Accordingly, the entries in *DLB* are career biographies, tracing the development of the author's canon and the evolution of his reputation.

The purpose of *DLB* is not only to provide reliable information in a usable format but also to place the figures in the larger perspective of literary history and to offer appraisals of their accomplishments by qualified scholars.

The publication plan for *DLB* resulted from two years of preparation. The project was proposed to Bruccoli Clark by Frederick G. Ruffner, president of the Gale Research Company, in November 1975. After specimen entries were prepared and typeset, an advisory board was formed to refine the entry format and develop the series rationale. In meetings held during 1976, the publisher, series editors, and advisory board approved the scheme for a comprehensive biographical dictionary of persons who contributed to literature. Editorial work on the first volume began in January 1977, and it was published in 1978. In order to make *DLB* more than a dictionary and to compile volumes that individually have claim to status as literary history, it was decided to organize volumes by topic, period, or genre. Each of these freestanding volumes provides a biographical-bibliographical guide and overview for a particular area of literature. We are convinced that this organization—as opposed to a single alphabet method—constitutes a valuable innovation in the presentation of reference material. The volume plan necessarily requires many decisions for the placement and treatment of authors. Certain figures will be included in separate volumes, but with different entries emphasizing the aspect of his career appropriate to each volume. Ernest Hemingway, for example, is represented in *American Writers in Paris, 1920–1939* by an entry focusing on his expatriate apprenticeship; he is also in *American Novelists, 1910–1945* with an entry surveying his entire career, as well as in *American Short-Story Writers, 1910–1945, Second Series* with an entry concentrating on his short fiction. Each volume includes a cumulative index of the subject authors and articles.

Since 1981 the series has been further augmented by the *DLB Yearbooks*, which update published entries, add new entries to keep the *DLB* current with contemporary activity, and provide articles on literary history. There have also been nineteen *DLB Documentary Series* volumes which provide illustrations, facsimiles, and biographical and critical source materials for figures, works, or groups judged to have particular interest for students. In 1999 the *Documentary Series* was incorporated into the *DLB* volume numbering system beginning with *DLB 210: Ernest Hemingway*.

We define literature as the *intellectual commerce of a nation*: not merely as belles lettres but as that ample and complex process by which ideas are generated, shaped, and transmitted. *DLB* entries are not limited to "creative writers" but extend to other figures who in their time and in their way influenced the mind of a people. Thus the series encompasses historians, journalists, publishers, book collectors, and screenwriters. By this means readers of *DLB* may be aided to perceive literature not as cult scripture in the keeping of intellectual high priests but firmly positioned at the center of a nation's life.

DLB includes the major writers appropriate to each volume and those standing in the ranks behind them. Scholarly and critical counsel has been sought in

*From an unpublished section of Mark Twain's autobiography, copyright by the Mark Twain Company

deciding which minor figures to include and how full their entries should be. Wherever possible, useful references are made to figures who do not warrant separate entries.

Each *DLB* volume has an expert volume editor responsible for planning the volume, selecting the figures for inclusion, and assigning the entries. Volume editors are also responsible for preparing, where appropriate, appendices surveying the major periodicals and literary and intellectual movements for their volumes, as well as lists of further readings. Work on the series as a whole is coordinated at the Bruccoli Clark Layman editorial center in Columbia, South Carolina, where the editorial staff is responsible for accuracy and utility of the published volumes.

One feature that distinguishes *DLB* is the illustration policy—its concern with the iconography of literature. Just as an author is influenced by his surroundings, so is the reader's understanding of the author enhanced by a knowledge of his environment. Therefore *DLB* volumes include not only drawings, paintings, and photographs of authors, often depicting them at various stages in their careers, but also illustrations of their families and places where they lived. Title pages are regularly reproduced in facsimile along with dust jackets for modern authors. The dust jackets are a special feature of *DLB* because they often document better than anything else the way in which an author's work was perceived in its own time. Specimens of the writers' manuscripts and letters are included when feasible.

Samuel Johnson rightly decreed that "The chief glory of every people arises from its authors." The purpose of the *Dictionary of Literary Biography* is to compile literary history in the surest way available to us—by accurate and comprehensive treatment of the lives and work of those who contributed to it.

The *DLB* Advisory Board

Introduction

Hundreds of playwrights have been produced on twentieth-century American stages. Not all can be included even in a multivolume series—nor could contributors be found for them if they could. Selecting which authors to include leads to larger questions of canonicity in American drama. Debate about canons of American drama involves distinctions between drama and theater (play as text versus play as performed), the different grounds for academic and popular approval, and judgments about aesthetic merit and ideology.

Debates about the canon of Western literature and philosophy reached their peak in the late 1980s and early 1990s but have quieted greatly since then. In academic usage the canon signifies works that are typically regarded as representing the enduring examples of aesthetic and cultural achievement. Virgil Nemoianu, in his article "Literary Canons and Social Value Options" (in *The Hospitable Canon,* 1991), introduces an important distinction between the "canon" and the "curriculum": the latter works are taught in class and included in anthologies for reasons that include the aesthetic but may also involve the political and practical. The canon, on the other hand, comes into existence because of the popularity of a work over time, its ability "to carry the burden of hundreds or indeed thousands of meanings," and as a point where high and low culture can meet: William Shakespeare, after all, was popular before he was praised by any intellectual elite.

For both academics and theater professionals, the relationship between the curriculum and the canon is dynamic; that which is not in print cannot be taught (and that which is not taught will quickly fall out of print in most cases). A fifteen-week semester often demands that the instructor eliminate interesting works from the schedule to include those he or she regards as more important for a variety of reasons. A theater season is also a kind of curriculum. Paying customers are necessary to defray the expenses of production, but producers and directors also seek to include a variety of voices, including minorities and those who speak for the disenfranchised. Works that are unpopular in terms of house receipts have a serious handicap when it comes to being produced in the future, but even "classics" are difficult to mount if there is not some perceived preexistent audience desire: Thomas Middleton's *The Changeling* (1622) is a brilliant play and one that compares favorably with many of Shakespeare's tragedies, but because it does not hold the place in the curriculum that a play such as *Coriolanus* does, it is much less often produced.

In 1988 E. D. Hirsch argued in *The Dictionary of Cultural Literacy* that a shared knowledge of myths and facts was necessary for basic communication and for social and economic progress: "We help people in the underclass to rise economically by teaching them how to communicate effectively beyond a narrow social sphere, and that can only be accomplished by teaching them shared, traditional culture." Here, the canon is used for curricular purposes, but Hirsch's treatment of plays unconsciously reveals the tension between performance and text in drama. Tennessee Williams makes Hirsch's dictionary because he is "famous for his plays, which portray violent passions in ordinary people." Further, *A Streetcar Named Desire* (1947) gets its own entry as "a play by Tennessee Williams about the decline and tragic end of Blanche DuBois, a Southern belle who, as she puts it, has 'always depended on the kindness of strangers.'" But while Williams's Blanche is, in Hirsch's view, an important shared element of American culture, apparently Stanley in the same play is not, although any comic can get a laugh by howling "Stella! Stella!" in imitation of Marlon Brando, who premiered the role. As a character who can be read about, Blanche matters. The play in performance, no matter how famous the performer, is ephemera—one hundred years from now, few will know who Brando was or what the importance of "The Method" (a style of actor training based on the work of Russian director Konstantin Stanislavsky, 1863–1938) was and how it affected American drama. This separation illustrates the inherently problematic status of drama in canon formation. Plays come to life on stage, but canons are largely concerned with the printed page. This phenomenon is a recurring one: in the early nineteenth century some critics held that Shakespeare was more fully realized in reading than in performance.

In 1981 the *Dictionary of Literary Biography* published the two-volume *Twentieth-Century American Drama-*

tists, First Series. The editor, John MacNicholas, in his preface referred to the developing canon of American drama:

> After Eugene O'Neill's astonishingly productive period in the 1920s, it was clear to people in other countries as well as in the United States that American drama had finally come of age. For an American playwright to be seriously considered for a Nobel Prize was hardly imaginable prior to the productions of *The Emperor Jones* [1920], *Desire Under the Elms* [1924], and *Mourning Becomes Electra* [1931]. Today, of course, works such as *Our Town* [Thornton Wilder, 1938], *A Streetcar Named Desire* [Tennessee Williams, 1947], and *Who's Afraid of Virginia Woolf?* [Edward Albee, 1962] are known to an international audience.

It would be difficult to argue with MacNicholas's choice of major playwrights. If you asked an Irish or Polish scholar of American literature in the early twenty-first century who the canonical American playwrights are, he or she would probably respond O'Neill, Arthur Miller, Williams, probably Albee, and maybe Wilder. This recognition does not mean that other American dramatists are not produced elsewhere in the world. In fact, Martin Sherman (*DLB 228*) and Naomi Wallace (*DLB 249*) are examples of American playwrights who have had most of their plays premiere in England, where their critical reputation is much higher than it is in the United States. But when exam questions are set in secondary schools and universities in Europe, O'Neill, Miller, Williams, Albee, and Wilder are likely to be the American playwrights for whom the students are responsible. The canon shapes the curriculum.

However, even in the plays MacNicholas chose to illustrate the importance of American drama to the world stage, one can see where a disagreement about the canon would start. O'Neill won the Nobel Prize in literature in 1936 for his experiments in dramatic form, among which are those listed by MacNicholas: expressionism in *The Emperor Jones,* modernized Greek tragedy in *Mourning Becomes Electra,* and poetic, psychological drama in *Desire Under the Elms*. These plays have more in common with European movements in drama than they do with O'Neill's contemporaries on Broadway. Yet, most American drama scholars today would argue that O'Neill's best plays are his realist dramas written after he had come to be regarded as a fading figure on the American stage: *The Iceman Cometh* (1946), *A Long Day's Journey into Night* (written between 1939 and 1941, first produced 1956), and *A Moon for the Misbegotten* (written 1943, first produced 1947). The latter plays not only are more representative of the domestic realism that is the dominant mode of American drama but also demonstrate O'Neill's gift for dramatic structure at his best, while his more experimental plays look somewhat dated compared to those of the theatricalist playwrights of the European stage such as Samuel Beckett, Luigi Pirandello, or Eugène Ionesco.

Nevertheless, MacNicholas's implied canon has held up quite well, especially when contrasted with John Houseman's foreword to the same *DLB* volume. Houseman says of post–World War I theater, "It furnished a rich and fertile field for hacks of all sorts but also for such vital playwrights as Sidney Howard, Maxwell Anderson, Philip Barry, George Kelly, and George Kaufman and his sundry collaborators." Some of these playwrights are still produced. Barry's *Holiday* (1928) in particular has been revived successfully. Moreover, Kaufman's collaborations remain staples of the American theater: two of his plays written with Moss Hart, *You Can't Take It With You* (1936) and *The Man Who Came to Dinner* (1939), are regularly presented both in summer stock and at regional theaters, while one of his collaborations with Edna Ferber, *The Royal Family* (1927), was revived successfully in London in October of 2001. But all of these playwrights' reputations have clearly declined since publication of Houseman's foreword. Even while the plays of Kaufman and his collaborators hold the stage, their optimism and patriotism limit their appeal to critics, who are more likely to elevate plays that criticize American capitalism and bourgeois liberalism.

Houseman, born in Bucharest and educated in England, was one of the most influential directors of the twentieth century; consequently, his judgments about who were important playwrights should not be taken lightly. Yet, in this case the passage of a mere twenty years has lessened the reputations of Kelly, Howard, and Anderson, whether justly or not, to such an extent that their work is more likely to be encountered in the library rather than on the stage. Some of this decline is a consequence of the plays. Anderson's poetic drama requires training in how to speak verse, which places special demands upon the performers. But to some extent—and it is difficult to describe why—some plays, because of their themes or subjects, become "dated," and theater professionals no longer are willing to risk time and money on mounting a revival. Plays do not become dated because they are concerned with the issues of their own time. George Pierce Baker taught many of the most important playwrights, designers, and directors of the first half of the twentieth century in his English 47 course at Harvard, including O'Neill and Barry, and he stressed that "No play can have a lasting popularity which neglects the prejudices, tastes, above all the ideals of its day. That we find delight in Shakespeare's plays to-day does not alter the fact that had he written for us he could not have written exactly as he did for the Elizabethans." At some point with lesser playwrights audiences and readers become unwilling to try to understand the references that are no longer a part of contemporary culture.

Kaufman was the consummate theatrical craftsman, turning out scripts that were written to be performed rather than critically analyzed, and his work is thus revived frequently. As such, he is the polar opposite of T. S. Eliot. That is not to say that Eliot's plays are not dramatically viable; Murder in the Cathedral (1935) has been staged successfully many times. But academics read and teach Murder in the Cathedral because Eliot is one of the premier poets of the twentieth century. On one level, his poetic reputation creates his dramatic reputation. Modernism, the twentieth-century literary movement that prized formal experimentation, ranks higher in critical esteem than the wisecracks of Kaufman and Hart. Eliot's high modernist style, dense and allusive, requires a great deal of critical explication and hence is the perfect subject matter for an academic industry that requires both publication and a demonstrable expertise in critical analysis to justify professorial salaries.

A contemporary example of how literary practice diverges from popular esteem would be the works of Neil Simon. Few American playwrights have had a surer feel for what audiences want or a better knack for the one-liner, while his plays have grown in emotional range and become historical documents of the American middle class in the twentieth century. But Simon's plays do not really require any critical explanations: an audience understands perfectly well what Simon has to say. Simon's plays may be studied as examples of the well-made play, or for ethnic humor, but they do not represent new dramatic forms or subjects.

The complexity of making claims about the canon of American drama is illustrated in the case of Simon by the distance between critical and practical judgment. Even in highly regarded regional theaters that receive various government and private subsidies, 50 percent or more of revenue must come from ticket sales. Simon and Kaufman command respect from producers and artistic directors because their plays draw audiences. Eliot's drama is the subject of ongoing critical discussion carried out in scholarly journals and books. Thus, Simon and Eliot have two different audiences and are thus members in two different canons of American drama. A third kind of drama, with its own criteria for achievement, would be the avant-garde theater, represented in this volume by Charles Ludlam and Harry Kondoleon. Their works tend to be presented in small venues (even coffeehouses) and represent a theater community that regards both Eliot and Simon as too mainstream to be interesting. In particular, Ludlam's Ridiculous Theatrical Company parodies a world of popular culture that is not merely the antithesis of Eliot's pantheon of literary tradition but is even below the tone of Simon's mainstream success. Ludlam's motto, "If one is not living a mockery of one's own ideals, one has set one's ideals too low," introduces plays that humorously borrow from nineteenth-century melodrama and bad television. While these plays have never achieved widespread success or critical acclaim, they have carved out a niche Off-Off-Broadway and in small theater groups around the country.

The "musty" Christian humanism of dead white males and the post-structuralist play of living ones are almost equally irrelevant to the instruction in diversity and political challenge to the existing social order that Paul Lauter calls for in Canons and Contexts (1991); in short, what Nemoianu refers to as the curriculum. The virtues of commercially successful playwrights are not infrequently the virtues that Lauter proposes as an alternative to those promulgated by the academic establishment in the middle of the twentieth century. Rachel Crothers was a constant presence on Broadway for more than three decades, from The Three of Us (1906) to Susan and God (1937), and, like Kaufman, a consummate theater professional—she directed most of her own plays. The Cambridge Guide to American Theater (1996) quotes an unnamed source calling her "The Neil Simon of her Day." Crothers is a playwright of the stage, and much of her vigor is lost in the reading.

Leslie Lee and OyamO (Charles F. Gordon) are a part of the expansive canon that Lauter favors. Minority playwrights depict experiences that the New York stage prior to the late 1950s either tended not to present or modified for the large audiences needed for the Broadway theaters (the sensationalism of the stage version of Langston Hughes's Mulatto in 1935 was at the instigation of the producer—Hughes was unhappy about it, but the play was a resounding success). In the second half of the twentieth century, smaller theaters allowed for plays unlikely to achieve mass appeal because of their focus on the oppression of people of color; the Negro Ensemble Company under Douglas Turner Ward, for instance, produced Lee's play about African American history, Colored People's Time (1982). The academy and arts foundations have also worked toward the inclusion of minority voices in drama. Although OyamO was master electrician for the Negro Ensemble Company (among many other practical theater experiences), he has also been awarded Rockefeller and Guggenheim fellowships that financially made it possible for him to write, and he has had faculty appointments as well. Still, while the existence of small theaters and financial awards makes it possible for more playwrights to have their work staged, the whole theatrical enterprise has remained precarious.

Unpredictable circumstances play a role in both the canonical and curricular status of playwrights. Elmer Rice is in danger of falling out of the typical American drama course despite his significant achievements. The example of Rice indicates why there actually was a point to the widespread critical debates that surrounded the canon. In the 1990s the canon was expanded as more women and minority writers were added, and by tacit agreement the entire debate was allowed to drop. However, the problems of limited classroom time and active stages did not go away. If as an example of early-twentieth-century American drama one teaches Crothers's *He and She* (1911), then perhaps William Vaughan Moody's *The Great Divide* (1906) falls off the schedule. If an instructor thinks the frontier is a defining element in American culture, the latter play is more important and stays on the syllabus. Alternately, if one is interested in neglected women playwrights, the former play gets taught. What gets taught has some effect on what gets produced in the long run, although it should not be overstated. The fairly limited number of plays that get revived is to some degree an aesthetic judgment: no one wants to produce a bad play except for comic effect. But the fact that the same plays get revived over and over may be partially because those are the plays the theater professionals know.

In short, one cannot ignore the kind of debates about critical reputation that Northrop Frye, in *Fables of Identity: Studies in Poetic Mythology* (1963), dismissed as belonging to the "history of taste" and related to an aesthetic stock market: "That wealthy investor Mr. Eliot, after dumping Milton on the Market, is now buying him again; Donne has probably reached his peak and will begin to taper off; Tennyson may be in for a slight flutter but the Shelley stocks are still bearish." Shifting critical reputations affect what is available to teach.

Nelson Presley's review in *The Washington Post* (17 January 2002) of a revival of Albee's *Tiny Alice* observes that:

> With its hints of an alternate universe and an unexplained crew of schemers, "Tiny Alice" is a little too pretentious and ultimately ambiguous to do more than tantalize audiences. But it does tantalize; it's powerful and strange, and you can see why the Washington Shakespeare Company would want to have a go at it.

An unknown playwright judged to be pretentious would not be produced. Albee's career illustrates how reputations ebb and flow. In the late 1950s and throughout the 1960s, Albee was critically acclaimed and sometimes commercially successful. But by the early 1970s (and despite winning a Pulitzer Prize for *Seascape* in 1975) he had largely disappeared from the important American venues as a consequence of his abstract and private dramas, a tendency that was apparent in his work from the beginning but that came to dominate it. He has experimented with a variety of forms and styles throughout his career, with apparent indifference to public taste. The success of the more accessible *Three Tall Women* in 1991 has restored him to his place at or near the top of the hierarchy of American playwrights, mostly by simply reminding the critics and public of his existence.

Political changes can marginalize plays that were once regarded as groundbreaking. Mart Crowley's *The Boys in the Band* (1968), perhaps the first openly gay play to be a hit, ran for more than two years, was produced in venues on both sides of the Atlantic, and was made into a movie. A year later in the East Village of New York, patrons of the gay Stonewall Bar rioted against police mistreatment. Suddenly *The Boys in the Band* appeared dated: not a play about the conflicts in the lives of gay characters, but itself an example of how gay men had internalized the homophobia of society. The play is surely more complex than it was then caricatured by gay activists, but the self-loathing of the characters did not appeal to subsequent playwrights who emphasized gay pride. Harvey Fierstein's characters struggle with their homosexuality, but that is an indictment of society; only characters implicitly criticized within the plays would talk about homosexuality as a "sin," as a character in *The Boys in the Band* does. Yet, in another sense, both playwrights, despite many critical claims for the universality of their themes, are tied to their sexual orientation in a way that gay playwrights such as Albee and Williams are not.

If Fierstein and Crowley are playwrights identified by sexual orientation, Horton Foote and Paddy Chayefsky are playwrights whose achievements as such tend to be forgotten because of their success in other media. Like Neil Simon, both were important writers in the Golden Age of television for shows such as the *Philco-Goodyear Television Playhouse*. They are even more closely associated with movies. Foote is nonetheless an important playwright because of his realist nine-play cycle about his fictional town of Harrison, Texas. Accomplished as both playwrights are, there is nothing distinctively theatrical about their work, yet both have significant achievements in more than one medium, and their canonical status is a function of versatility.

Some playwrights remain known for a single play. One wonders what will happen to the reputation of a playwright such as Margaret Edson, for example. Her play, *Wit* (1995), was a genuine dramatic phenomenon of the late 1990s. Her only published work, the play won the Pulitzer Prize and several other awards and was staged to acclaim all over the United States. Edson has stated, however, that she has no particular desire to write another play. In this respect she is like Donald Coburn, author of *The Gin Game,* Pulitzer Prize winner for 1979, who also has written no plays since that initial triumph. In the absence of a body of work, the individual achievement must be extraordinary for an author to be remembered, and only time will tell whether *Wit* will still be dramatically vital in twenty years. It may be, simply because the central character is a great "star" part.

Harold Bloom writes in *The Western Canon* (1994): "There has never been an official American literary canon, and there never can be, for the aesthetic in America always exists as a lonely, idiosyncratic, isolated stance. 'American Classicism' is an oxymoron, whereas 'French Classicism' is a coherent tradition." In the seventeenth century, French critics could actually determine the shape of drama based on rules they had deduced from Aristotle and classical drama, the so-called unities: a play should have a single plot taking place at a single location and represent a time span of less than twenty-four hours. No such proscriptive canon is possible anymore, because an American playwright must seek a distinctive voice simply to be heard amid the enormous American theatrical enterprise. So many new plays are produced in the United States every year that for any one of them to stand out, something striking must be present: a great part, a previously ignored community given a voice on stage, a lyrical prose style, or a gift for dramatic construction.

Although there are no formal characteristics that sum up the American canon, there are continuities. Most of the best plays tend to be examples of domestic realism: O'Neill's *A Long Day's Journey into Night,* Miller's *The Crucible* (1953), Williams's *A Streetcar Named Desire,* and Albee's *Who's Afraid of Virginia Woolf?* are some examples. Some continuities are a consequence of one of the chief sources of American vitality: immigration. Bella Cohen was born in Transylvania in 1899, the same year her eventual husband, Samuel Spewack, was born in the Ukraine. Raised in the United States, they both became journalists and then successful playwrights. The contemporary playwright Elizabeth Wong is the daughter of Chinese immigrants. Like the Spewacks, she became a successful journalist before becoming a widely praised playwright. The American theater is enriched by the diverse experiences of those who write for it.

Nemoianu also argues that, ultimately, neither the critics nor popular acclaim are the determining factors in what makes a work canonical. There is an essential continuity in the canon in the way writers respond to some works creatively. In A. R. Gurney's prolific career, previous authors sometimes provided a starting point for a new play; *The Bridal Dinner* (1965) plays off the second act of Wilder's *Our Town; The Dining Room* (1982) reconsiders Wilder's *The Long Christmas Dinner* (1931); and *What I Did Last Summer* (1983) pays homage to O'Neill's *Ah, Wilderness!* (1933). Oscar Hammerstein and Richard Rodgers's *Flower Drum Song* (1958) has at times been criticized as a patronizing portrayal of Asian Americans. In 2001, however, the important Asian American playwright David Henry Hwang's adaptation received strongly positive notices. As playwrights such as Gurney and Hwang have shown, at its best the theater creates a community that can endure over time.

—*Christopher Wheatley*

Acknowledgments

This book was produced by Bruccoli Clark Layman, Inc. Karen L. Rood is senior editor. Tracy Simmons Bitonti was the in-house editor, assisted by Charles Brower.

Production manager is Philip B. Dematteis.

Administrative support was provided by Ann M. Cheschi and Carol A. Cheschi.

Accountant is Ann-Marie Holland.

Copyediting supervisor is Sally R. Evans. The copyediting staff includes Phyllis A. Avant, Brenda Carol Blanton, Caryl Brown, Melissa D. Hinton, Philip I. Jones, Rebecca Mayo, Nancy E. Smith, and Elizabeth Jo Ann Sumner.

Editorial associates are Michael S. Allen, Michael S. Martin, and Catherine M. Polit.

Permissions editor and database manager is Amber L. Coker.

Layout and graphics supervisor is Janet E. Hill. The graphics staff includes Zoe R. Cook and Sydney E. Hammock.

Office manager is Kathy Lawler Merlette.

Photography supervisor is Paul Talbot. Photography editor is Scott Nemzek.

Digital photographic copy work was performed by Joseph M. Bruccoli.

Systems manager is Marie L. Parker.

Typesetting supervisor is Kathleen M. Flanagan. The typesetting staff includes Patricia Marie Flanagan, Mark J. McEwan, and Pamela D. Norton. Freelance typesetter is Wanda Adams.

Walter W. Ross did library research. He was assisted by Jo Cottingham and the following other librarians at the Thomas Cooper Library of the University of South Carolina: circulation department head Tucker Taylor; reference department head Virginia W. Weathers; reference department staff Brette Barron, Marilee Birchfield, Paul Cammarata, Gary Geer, Michael Macan, Tom Marcil, Rose Marshall, and Sharon Verba; interlibrary loan department head John Brunswick; and interlibrary loan staff Robert Arndt, Hayden Battle, Alex Byrne, Bill Fetty, Marna Hostetler, and Nelson Rivera.

Dictionary of Literary Biography® • Volume Two Hundred Sixty-Six

Twentieth-Century American Dramatists
Fourth Series

Dictionary of Literary Biography

Edward Albee
(12 March 1928 -)

Lincoln Konkle
College of New Jersey

See also the Albee entry in *DLB 7: Twentieth-Century American Dramatists.*

PLAY PRODUCTIONS: *The Zoo Story,* Berlin, Schiller Theater, 28 September 1959; New York, Provincetown Playhouse, 14 January 1960;

The Sandbox, New York, Jazz Gallery, 15 April 1960;

The Death of Bessie Smith, Berlin, Schlosspark Theater, 21 April 1960; New York, York Playhouse, 1 March 1961;

Fam and Yam, Westport, Conn., White Barn Theatre, 27 August 1960; New York, Theatre de Lys, 25 October 1960;

The American Dream, New York, York Playhouse, 24 January 1961;

Who's Afraid of Virginia Woolf? New York, Billy Rose Theatre, 13 October 1962;

The Ballad of the Sad Café, adapted from Carson McCullers's novella, New York, Martin Beck Theatre, 30 October 1963;

Tiny Alice, New York, Billy Rose Theatre, 29 December 1964;

Malcolm, adapted from James Purdy's novel, New York, Shubert Theatre, 11 January 1966;

A Delicate Balance, New York, Martin Beck Theatre, 12 September 1966;

Everything in the Garden, adapted from Giles Cooper's play, New York, Plymouth Theatre, 29 November 1967;

Box and *Quotations from Chairman Mao Tse-Tung,* Buffalo, Studio Arena Theatre, 6 March 1968; New York, Billy Rose Theatre, 30 September 1968;

All Over, New York, Martin Beck Theatre, 27 March 1971;

Seascape, New York, Shubert Theatre, 26 January 1975;

Counting the Ways, London, National Theatre, 6 December 1976; Hartford, Conn., Hartford Stage Company, 28 January 1977; New York, Signature Theatre Company, 5 November 1993;

Listening, Hartford, Conn., Hartford Stage Company, 28 January 1977; New York, Signature Theatre Company, 5 November 1993;

The Lady from Dubuque, New York, Morosco Theatre, 31 January 1980;

Lolita, adapted from Vladimir Nabokov's novel, New York, Brooks Atkinson Theatre, 19 March 1981;

The Man Who Had Three Arms, Chicago, Goodman Theatre, 4 October 1982; New York, Lyceum Theatre, 5 April 1983;

Finding the Sun, Greeley, Colo., University of Northern Colorado, 10 May 1983; New York, Signature Theatre Company, 4 February 1994;

Marriage Play, Vienna, English Theatre, 17 May 1987; Houston, Alley Theatre, 8 January 1992; New York, Signature Theatre Company, 1 October 1993;

Three Tall Women, Vienna, English Theatre, 14 June 1991; Woodstock, N.Y., River Arts Repertory, 30 July 1992; New York, Vineyard Theatre, 27 January 1994;

The Lorca Play, Houston, Alley Theatre, 24 April 1992;

Fragments, Cincinnati, Ensemble Theatre, 10 October 1993; New York, Signature Theatre Company, 8 April 1994;

The Play about the Baby, London, Almeida Theatre, 1 September 1998; Houston, Alley Theatre, 11 April 2000; New York, 1 February 2001;

Occupant, New York, Signature Theatre Company, 5 February 2002;

Edward Albee (photograph by Jerry Speier; courtesy of Edward Albee)

The Goat, or Who is Sylvia? New York, John Golden Theatre, 10 March 2002.

BOOKS: *The Zoo Story, The Death of Bessie Smith, The Sandbox* (New York: Coward-McCann, 1960); republished with the addition of *The American Dream* as *The Zoo Story and Other Plays* (London: Cape, 1962);

The American Dream (New York: Coward-McCann, 1961; London: S. French, 1962);

Who's Afraid of Virginia Woolf? (New York: Atheneum, 1962; London: Cape, 1964);

Tiny Alice (New York: Atheneum, 1965; London: Cape, 1966);

A Delicate Balance (New York: Atheneum, 1966; London: Cape, 1968);

Box and Quotations from Chairman Mao Tse-Tung: Two Inter-Related Plays (New York: Atheneum, 1969; London: Cape, 1970);

All Over (New York: Atheneum, 1971; London: Cape, 1972);

Seascape (New York: Atheneum, 1975; London: Cape, 1976);

Counting the Ways and Listening, Two Plays (New York: Atheneum, 1977);

The Lady from Dubuque (New York: Atheneum, 1980);

Selected Plays of Edward Albee (Garden City, N.Y.: Doubleday, 1987);

The Sandbox and The Death of Bessie Smith (with Fam and Yam) (New York: Plume, 1988);

Finding the Sun (New York: Dramatists Play Service, 1994);

Edward Albee's Marriage Play (New York: Dramatists Play Service, 1995);

Three Tall Women (New York: Dutton, 1995);

Fragments: A Sit-Around (New York: Dramatists Play Service, 1995);

Tony Rosenthal, by Albee and Sam Hunter (New York: Rizzoli, 2000);

The Play about the Baby (New York: Dramatists Play Service, 2002).

Editions and Collections: *The American Dream and The Zoo Story* (New York: Signet, 1961);

The Plays, 4 volumes (New York: Atheneum, 1981–1982);

Who's Afraid of Virginia Woolf? (New York: Signet, 1983).

PRODUCED SCRIPTS: *A Delicate Balance,* motion picture, American Film Theatre, 1973;

Listening, BBC Radio Three, 28 March 1976.

OTHER: Introduction to *Three Plays by Noel Coward* (New York: Dell, 1965), pp. 3–6;

"Which Theatre Is the Absurd One?" in *American Playwrights on Drama,* edited by Horst Frenz (New York: Hill & Wang, 1965), pp. 168–174;

"Albeit!" in *The Off-Broadway Experience,* edited by Howard Greenberger (Englewood Cliffs, N.J.: Prentice Hall, 1971), pp. 52–62.

SELECTED PERIODICAL PUBLICATIONS–UNCOLLECTED: "Some Notes on Non-Conformity," *Harper's Bazaar,* 95 (August 1962): 104;

"Critics Are Debasing Audience Taste," *Dramatists Guild Quarterly,* 2 (Spring 1965): 9–14;

"Creativity and Commitment," *Saturday Review,* 49 (4 June 1966): 26;

"The Decade of Engagement," *Saturday Review,* 53 (24 January 1970): 19–20.

Early in the twentieth century, American theater critics and drama scholars wondered where the native modern dramatists were–the American equals to Henrik Ibsen, August Strindberg, and Anton Chekhov–and why the United States had failed to produce a theater tradition as literary and artistic as those of Great Britain, France, and Scandinavia. By the end of the century the first question, at least, could be answered: Eugene O'Neill was the first great American dramatist, followed by Thornton Wilder, Tennessee Williams, Arthur Miller, and Edward Albee. Subsequently, scholars have made the case that Albee, having sustained a career in the American theater for more than six decades, has joined Williams as a serious challenger to O'Neill's status as the great American playwright. Comprising more than twenty-five plays, his body of work is as extensive as Williams's, as varied in subject and form as O'Neill's, as experimental as Wilder's, and as reflective on American society as Miller's.

Albee has won three Pulitzer Prizes in three different decades, as well as many other awards, and his drama is the subject of many book-length studies and hundreds of articles published in scholarly journals. He is the most intellectual of the major American playwrights, and his dialogue is the most articulate and witty. His first full-length play, *Who's Afraid of Virginia Woolf?* (1962), has been so critically and commercially successful that even people who do not go to the theater know of it. It also continues to be widely taught in high-school and college English and theater courses. Beginning with *The Zoo Story* (1959), Albee's plays have been translated, produced, and published abroad as often as at home. Early in his career he was labeled as part of the theater of the absurd, the postwar European movement that includes such dramatists as Eugene Ionesco, Samuel Beckett, and Harold Pinter; however, this classification is inaccurate. Although Albee's dramaturgy and theatrical style in certain plays have resembled Ionesco's and Beckett's, the worldview expressed in his plays is never as fatalistic and nihilistic as theirs. Rather, he espouses an existentialist vision from which he criticizes individuals and American society as a whole with biting satire. As a critic of American society, he is in the tradition of Jonathan Edwards, Henry David Thoreau, and Sinclair Lewis; as a stylist and experimenter with form, he follows Henry James, T. S. Eliot, and John Barth; and as a writer of Juvenalian satire and black humor, he compares favorably with Mark Twain and Kurt Vonnegut. Albee can also be read within the contemporary context of postmodernism, in that a few of his plays are pastiches that borrow from other literary works and popular culture, and they manifest a reflexivity on the nature of theater and drama itself.

Alienation is a key concept to existentialism and existentialist literature, but the alienation in Albee's plays stems not from his reading of the works of Albert Camus or Jean-Paul Sartre but from the most significant formative event of his life: he was given up for adoption shortly after his birth on 12 March 1928 in Washington, D.C. Although Albee knew by the age of six that he was adopted, he learned the circumstances only after his adoptive mother's death in 1989. His biological father, whose name is unknown, had abandoned Albee's mother, Louise Harvey, and she gave up her son, Edward Harvey, to an adoption agency two weeks after his birth. When he was eighteen days old, Reed and Frances Albee became his foster parents, bringing him to their home in Larchmont, New York. They officially adopted him on 1 February 1929 and changed his name to Edward Franklin Albee III. This initial abandonment and the stormy relationship with his adoptive parents, who ultimately threw him out of the house and disinherited him, underlie the fundamental and particular sense of alienation and displacement in Albee's drama. He has said that he felt like an outsider from the beginning, even within his own family.

The Albees belonged to an old American family that had immigrated to Maine in the seventeenth century; an ancestor was one of the original minutemen in the Revolutionary War. Albee's grandfather Edward Franklin Albee Jr. was cofounder and partner with B. F. Keith in a chain of vaudeville theaters located throughout the United States. Consisting of more than four hundred theaters, the Keith-Albee circuit, which later merged with other theaters to form the Radio-Keith-Orpheum Corporation (RKO), made the elder Albee millions, which were inherited by his son. Reed Albee worked as an assistant general manager in his father's company until he retired the year he and his

Albee in Greenwich Village, circa 1955–1958, sitting at the stolen typewriter on which he wrote his first produced play, The Zoo Story *(photograph © Bettmann/CORBIS)*

wife adopted their son. Reed had married Frances Cotter in 1925, a year after his first marriage of ten years ended in divorce; it was the first marriage for "Frankie," who was twelve years younger than Reed. She was tall and imposing, he short and dapper. He bought and showed thoroughbred horses; she rode them and won ribbons in competitions. Frances was working in a department store in Manhattan when she and Reed met; she came from a family of upstate New York farmers who apparently were not a significant part of young Edward Albee's life, except for her mother, "Grandma Cotter," who eventually came to live with the Albees.

According to Albee, his mother was emotionally cold and domineering, while his father was distant and uninvolved in his son's rearing. Albee's closest adult relationships were with his nanny, Anita Church, and with Grandma Cotter. The affluence of his family facilitated his exposure to culture: his nanny introduced him to opera and classical music; the library in the Albees' large Tudor house contained the classics of world literature (though Edward was scolded for removing the volumes, which were intended for show and not actual reading). He was driven in a limousine to see Broadway productions deemed appropriate for his age–for example, *Jumbo* (1935) with Jimmy Durante, *On Your Toes* (1936) by Richard Rodgers and Lorenz Hart, and *Hellzapoppin'* (1941)–and famous entertainers, such as Ed Wynn, were frequent guests in his parents' home. The Albees lived in an upper-class neighborhood of Larchmont, in Westchester County, New York; they were members of the country club and the yacht club, and they employed servants. Albee has said that he rebelled early against their snobbery and prejudice, and he later satirized these traits in characters that resembled his adoptive parents socioeconomically as well as psychologically.

Albee was expelled from three private preparatory schools: Rye Day School in New York, the Lawrenceville School in New Jersey, and Valley Forge Military Academy in Pennsylvania. He found his niche at Choate in Wallingford, Connecticut, however, where he wrote a play, a novel, poems, and short stories in the manner of those published in *The New Yorker,* which was an early inspiration (especially the work of James Thurber). Some of these juvenilia were published in the school literary magazine, and one poem was published in a Texas literary magazine,

Kaleidograph, in 1945. Albee has said that he decided as a young child he was a writer; his teachers at Choate encouraged him in that pursuit. After graduation he matriculated at Trinity College in Hartford, Connecticut, where he published in the literary magazine and acted in a couple of plays but was expelled in his second year for not attending required courses and chapel. In that same year, 1947, he left home after a fight over his late-night drinking, ending all contact with his adoptive parents for twenty years.

Albee spent the 1950s living in Greenwich Village in a series of apartments and working a variety of odd jobs (for example, a telegram delivery person) to supplement his monthly stipend from a trust fund left for him by his paternal grandmother. He met and became involved with William Flanagan, who had come east from Detroit to study music and was the music critic for the *Herald Tribune* and other publications. In 1952 Albee moved in with Flanagan, beginning his first long-term homosexual relationship. Although he had previously had a few heterosexual experiences and had even been unofficially engaged to a socialite whose parents were friends of his parents, Albee had also had homosexual experiences as early as age thirteen and frequented gay bars while he was in college. Flanagan was more than a lover to the young Albee; he was also an artistic and intellectual mentor. He was the leader of a group of young composers and musicians who socialized together and sometimes with painters, sculptors, and other artists in the Village who were part of various avant-garde movements. According to Albee's biographer Mel Gussow, Greenwich Village in the 1950s was like Paris in the 1920s, when Ernest Hemingway, F. Scott Fitzgerald, and other writers, artists, and intellectuals lived, wrote, and socialized on the Left Bank. Flanagan and his entourage, of which the only writer was Albee, attended the theater, art exhibits, and other cultural events, as well as frequenting lower-Manhattan nightspots. During this time Albee saw O'Neill's *The Iceman Cometh* (1946) and Eliot's *The Cocktail Party* (1949) on Broadway.

In his early adulthood Albee was still bent on becoming a writer, though not making much progress. On his first trip abroad to Italy and France with Flanagan, he searched for inspiration and wrote a great deal, but nothing came to fruition. He submitted work to *The New Yorker* but was rejected. Over a ten-year period Albee wrote, according to Gussow, "nine plays, dozens of stories, and more than 100 poems," none of which were published or produced. During the early part of the 1950s he was concentrating on poetry, but after showing his poems first to W. H. Auden and then to Wilder, whose *Our Town* (1938) and *The Skin of Our Teeth* (1942) he had seen on Broadway, Albee took Wilder's advice and started writing plays, of which a few survive in manuscript. C. W. E. Bigsby, writing in *A Critical Introduction to Twentieth-Century American Drama* (1984), and Gussow, the only two critics who have read these apprentice plays and commented on them in print, have agreed with Albee that they lack his distinctive voice, especially his sense of humor, which was first heard in *The Zoo Story* in 1959. The well-known story of how Albee wrote his first produced play has him approaching his thirtieth birthday with a sense of desperation that he would never be a published writer. Thus, he "liberated" a typewriter from the Western Union office where he worked and wrote *The Zoo Story* (which for years he claimed was his first play) in three weeks as a birthday present to himself. Although it took some time to get the play on the stage, both Albee and Flanagan knew that Albee had taken a giant step forward. Gussow reports that on listening to a staged reading of *The Zoo Story* at the Actors Studio, novelist Norman Mailer stood up and proclaimed it the best one-act play he had ever seen.

Certainly *The Zoo Story* is the quintessential Off-Broadway one-act play; it requires for production only two actors, a park bench, and two props (a book and a fake knife), which is not far from Molière's claim that all he needed to create theater was a platform and a passion or two. The passion in Albee's play is provided by the protagonist, Jerry, a loner in his thirties who lives in a run-down tenement. The antagonist is Peter, a middle-aged New Yorker who works for a publishing firm. The setting is Central Park, specifically, a bench where Peter comes every Sunday afternoon to read. Jerry appears to be wandering through the park and stops to strike up a conversation with Peter, though it becomes more of an interrogation. Jerry gets Peter to reveal that he is married with children and pets and is in every way a typical middle-class American, though unhappy because he is so dominated by his domestic and socioeconomic situation that his weekly pilgrimage to the park bench is his only refuge, his only self-gratification. Through Jerry's many witty comments and a long monologue he titles "The Story of Jerry and the Dog," which is about how he tried to befriend his landlady's watchdog, he attempts to foster in Peter a self-awareness that will awaken him from the passivity and alienation of his life. Peter, however, is too entrenched in his conventional middle-class existence to come to the epiphany Jerry tries to inspire. Thus, Jerry provokes him to assist in Jerry's self-martyrdom by throwing himself onto the knife he has given Peter in a fight for the bench, which Peter regards as the one thing in his life that he possesses for himself. Dying on the bench, Jerry has displaced Peter not only from the bench and his Sunday routine but also from the com-

George Maharis and William Daniels in the 1960 New York production of The Zoo Story *(from Mel Gussow,* Edward Albee: A Singular Journey, *1999)*

placent solipsism of a life lived without making conscious choices. Albee attempts to teach this existential lesson in virtually all of his plays.

The Zoo Story was initially staged in 1959 in Berlin with German actors speaking a German translation of Albee's dialogue. Critics' reactions to this first production and the subsequent American premiere in 1960 were mostly positive, but as Albee himself has noted for years and Gussow's biography confirms, his plays have always received mixed reviews, rather than the usual description of his career as going from universal acclaim for early works to condemnation for later ones. Critics praised *The Zoo Story* for the dramatic intensity of its agon and for the witty dialogue spoken by Jerry, whom some saw as a beatnik, in his attempt to educate Peter, the representative of the American bourgeoisie.

Albee has said that Peter and Jerry manifest different parts of his own personality, his Larchmont self and his Greenwich Village self, making the play something of a psychomachia (a battle within one's soul). Scholars have analyzed Albee's carefully written text for its criticism of conformity and the isolation caused by a materialistically based class structure, its portrait of the psychology of the "sane" insider versus the "insane" outsider, and its allegory of the Passion, with Jerry as a modern Jesus making Peter a disciple through the telling of parables ("Jerry and the Dog") and a self-crucifixion. Generically, *The Zoo Story* has been classified as tragedy, satire, and theater of the absurd. The last designation, however, which has been applied by critics such as Martin Esslin and Nelvin Vos, is clearly inaccurate with regard to *The Zoo Story* since its setting, action, and characterization are conventionally realistic, unlike those of Beckett and Ionesco. Furthermore, the philosophical outlook of *The Zoo Story* is not nearly as pessimistic as that of a Beckett play, as evidenced by Jerry's success in making contact, in finally communicating with someone through the "bars" of isolation and alienation, even though it requires the sacrifice of his own life. In the theater of the absurd the attempt to communicate or to engage in any meaningful act is always futile.

The excellence of *The Zoo Story* as a literary work is also attested to by its frequent appearance in anthologies of American literature, American drama, and world drama and by the number of scholarly articles written on it: according to the *MLA Bibliography*, among Albee's plays only *Who's Afraid of Virginia Woolf?* is the focus of more critical studies. *The Zoo Story* is also Albee's second-longest running play (*Who's Afraid of Virginia Woolf?* again ranks first), with 582 performances Off-Broadway before Off-Broadway was recognized as where the new, serious American dramas were to be found. Thus, from every perspective, *The Zoo Story* was a success and launched Albee's career as a professional playwright in spectacular fashion: it won him the Obie (the Off-Broadway equivalent of the Tony Award) and other awards; got him an agent at William Morris, by whom he is still represented; partnered him with his longtime producer, Richard Barr; and earned him fame if not fortune, the latter coming with the enormous commercial success of *Who's Afraid of Virginia Woolf?* a few years later. He was regaled as "a savior of the American theater" and was grouped with Jack Richardson and Jack Gelber as a trio of radical new American playwrights who constituted the beginning of the Off-Broadway movement.

In Albee's personal life, right before he left for the German premiere of *The Zoo Story*, he and Flanagan separated, and soon after his return from Europe he began living with Terrence McNally, a young actor who later became a playwright himself. While he was abroad Albee saw plays by Bertolt Brecht, Jean Genet, and Brendan Behan. His grandmother Cotter died at age eighty-three, before *The Zoo Story* was produced in New York; he later dedicated *The Sandbox* (1960) to her. Now that he was financially secure, having received the $100,000 principal of the trust fund left for him by his paternal grandmother when he turned thirty, Albee no longer needed to work odd jobs and could write full-time.

Albee's second play, *The Death of Bessie Smith* (1960), was another one-act, the inspiration for which was the description on the back of an album cover of the circumstances of the blues singer's death. In contrast to *The Zoo Story*, with its simple two-character agon that follows the Aristotelian unities, *The Death of Bessie Smith* is an episodic play of eight scenes in five locations, interweaving two story lines that converge in the last scene. The less developed of the two plots concerns Jack, the traveling companion of Bessie Smith (who does not appear in the play). In scene 1 he brags to a friend he meets in a bar in Memphis, Tennessee, that he is driving the great singing legend to New York City to revive her career. In scene 3 he tries to rouse Bessie (offstage) from an alcohol-induced heavy sleep and the audience hears them depart in a car. Following a passage of narration taken from the album cover, Jack and Bessie are in a car accident in which her arm is nearly severed from her body. In scene 7 he has brought her to a whites-only hospital, where a bigoted nurse responds to his plea for help only with a racial epithet. The second plot of *The Death of Bessie Smith* involves a nurse who works at another whites-only hospital. She is first introduced in scene 2 in a mutually wounding battle for power with her father, who is a stereotypical Southern bigot. In the fourth scene she humiliates an African American orderly at the hospital for his attempts to assimilate into the dominant Southern Caucasian culture. Scene 5 is a brief telephone conversation between the two nurses at their respective hospitals, and scene 6 depicts the sensual relationship between the nurse and an intern, but it mirrors the earlier scene with her father as a struggle for control in the relationship. Finally, in scene 8, Jack enters the hospital, again pleads for help for Bessie and again receives a racist response from the nurse; but the intern, who is more liberal, goes out to help Bessie, only to return in a few moments, revealing that she was already dead.

Clearly, one of the themes of *The Death of Bessie Smith* is racism: how it is passed from one generation to the next, how it infects the workplace, and how it causes suffering and death. Scholars, however, have given more attention to what receives dramatic emphasis in the play, the nurse's unhappiness resulting from unfulfilled relationships with her father, her lover, and her coworkers. She concludes a long speech of complaints by yelling that she, not one of the African American characters, is tired of her skin and wants out of it. Like *The Zoo Story*, *The Death of Bessie Smith* premiered in Germany before being performed in the United States; it was not as well received by critics as *The Zoo Story*, nor have scholars regarded it as a successful work. Probably the greatest difference between *The Death of Bessie Smith* and *The Zoo Story* and most of Albee's later plays is that it employs little humor to make its points. What humor there is in *The Death of Bessie Smith* is mostly where one character cruelly mocks another, such as when the nurse makes fun of an orderly for bleaching his skin. *The Death of Bessie Smith* does show, however, that early in his professional career Albee was committed to experimenting with dramatic form and writing on different subjects.

The year 1960 was a watershed for Albee, with three plays performed in New York: *The Zoo Story*, *The Sandbox*, and *Fam and Yam*; a fourth, *The American Dream*, was mounted in the first month of 1961, and *The Death of Bessie Smith* opened on 1 March. Back in 1958 Albee had shown *The Zoo Story* to several theatrical professionals to enlist their help in getting it produced, including William Inge, who was at the time the most successful American playwright being produced on Broadway. After visiting him in his Manhattan apartment without receiving any pledge of assistance, Albee wrote *Fam and Yam*, a brief dramatic sketch based on their meeting. In it YAM, the "Young American Playwright," interviews FAM, the "Famous American Playwright," for a magazine article about the state of the professional theater, which in YAM's view is a disaster because of the theater owners, the producers, the critics, and the commercial playwrights (such as Inge) themselves. *Fam and Yam* was published in the September 1960 issue of *Harper's Bazaar* before being staged first in Connecticut and then in New York. Interestingly, the sketch shows the inaccuracy of the accepted version of how Albee's career unfolded, specifically, how his war with the critics began—at the press conference he held on 22 March 1965 following the befuddled reviews of *Tiny Alice* (1964). In *Fam and Yam* he was already attacking the theater establishment. That attack, narrowed to focus on the critics, was continued, again in print, in the preface to *The American Dream*, dated 24 May 1961 in the Signet edition of *The American Dream and The Zoo Story*. Perhaps his attacks account in part for the mixed reviews even of plays (*The Zoo Story*, *The American Dream*, *Who's Afraid of Virginia Woolf?*) that are now universally acclaimed as masterworks of drama.

Albee's next project after *The Death of Bessie Smith* was *The American Dream*, which, according to Gussow, was a reconceptualization of "The Dispossessed," one of his apprentice plays from the 1950s. While working

Uta Hagen, Arthur Hill, George Grizzard, and Melinda Dillon in the 1962 New York production of Who's Afraid of Virginia Woolf? *(Harvard Theatre Collection)*

on *The American Dream* he received a commission from a festival in Spoleto, Italy, to write a short play; rather than begin something new, Albee excerpted four of the characters from *The American Dream,* putting them in a different setting and circumstance; the result was *The Sandbox*. This approach to the composition process has been typical in Albee's career: he thinks about a play over a period of time (sometimes years), and when he is able to imagine the characters in a situation different from the one in the play he is working on and can predict what they would say and do, he knows he is ready to begin writing.

With a playing time of only fourteen minutes and a set consisting only of chairs for two characters and a musician and a child's sandbox, *The Sandbox* is a minimalist theatrical piece, though still structured around conflict between characters. Modeled after Albee's maternal grandmother, Grandma, the major character, is carried onstage by Mommy and Daddy, her daughter and son-in-law, who bear some resemblance to Albee's adoptive parents. After they unceremoniously dump her into the sandbox, Grandma utters some gibberish and throws sand at Mommy, then tells the audience about how she raised Mommy, only to be mistreated when she and Daddy took Grandma in after her husband died. Mommy complains to Daddy about Grandma's throwing sand, but she politely waits for Grandma's death, which is signified by a few offstage rumbles and a blackout. The lights come back up to reveal Grandma burying herself in sand; she plays dead as Mommy and Daddy stop for a last look before exiting the stage. Then the Young Man, a bodybuilder who has been doing calisthenics during the play, comes over to Grandma and announces that he is the Angel of Death and has come for her. This allegorical identity is meant to be underscored in production by special lighting that casts shadows of the Young Man's arms in motion so that an effect of beating wings is created. As Gussow points out, even this element has a tinge of autobiography: for his job as a Western Union messenger Albee functioned as a kind of angel of death, since the telegrams he delivered were often death notices.

Because *The Sandbox* and *The American Dream* share all the same characters but one and treat similar themes, it is difficult to analyze the former without referring to the latter. As in *The Sandbox,* Grandma is the major character in *The American Dream;* she has the most volition of any of the characters as well as the most lines, and she is the only likable character in the play. The action is more fully developed, and thus the playing time of *The American Dream* is double that of *The Sandbox*. *The American Dream* takes place in Mommy and Daddy's apartment and consists of several exchanges between Mommy and Daddy, Grandma, Mrs. Barker (who is an adoption agency worker and "chairman" of Mommy's woman's club), and the Young Man (who is a drifter and apparently the twin of the first "bumble" Mommy and Daddy received from the adoption agency). In contrast to *The Sandbox,* in *The American Dream* Grandma is in control of her destiny. Although Mommy frequently threatens to call "the van man" to take Grandma away, Grandma stages her own escape from the apartment and the play with the prize money she won from a baking contest. Before she leaves, Grandma meets the Young Man, whom she calls the American Dream. Realizing he would be a perfect replacement for Mommy and Daddy's first child (with whom they were so dissatisfied that they gradually killed him in a series of punitive dismemberments), Grandma suggests to Mrs. Barker that she should present the Young Man to Mommy and Daddy and should explain Grandma's disappearance by saying that she was taken away by the van man. Finally, Grandma closes the play by telling the audience, in effect, the moral of the story.

The Sandbox and *The American Dream* have generated a good deal of scholarly discussion as to their meaning. While some see the plays as satirizing the materialism, consumerism, and lack of morality in the American dream, others see one or both plays as immoral and nihilistic. Indeed, these two plays come the closest to justifying the label of Albee as belonging to the theater of the absurd. Of *The American Dream* Esslin said, "Albee has produced a play that clearly takes up the style and subject matter of the Theatre of the Absurd." Albee has admitted that the plays are something of an homage to Ionesco, specifically *The Bald Soprano* (1950). As in the plays of Beckett and Ionesco, in *The Sandbox* and *The American Dream* there is virtually no plot, the characters are one-dimensional types, and much of the dialogue is insipid to the point of almost being meaningless. Also, the stage settings for the two plays are so simple as to be abstract, and realism is dispensed with when Grandma "breaks the fourth wall" by directly addressing the audience. However, even though *The Sandbox* and *The American Dream* resemble Beckett and Ionesco's dramaturgy and theatrical style, they are still not as pessimistic as those playwrights' works. By the end of both plays, Grandma is free of the oppression of Mommy and Daddy, and she stage-manages the conclusion of *The American Dream* so that, as she says, "everybody's got what he wants . . . or everybody's got what he thinks he wants." Her self-determination in *The American Dream* and her acceptance of death in *The Sandbox* belie a worldview that sees all human action as meaningless. Some Albee scholars (for example, Gilbert Debusscher, Ronald Hayman, Anne Paolucci) do classify these plays as absurdist; yet, for every article or book chapter taking this position, one can also find others taking the opposite (for example, those by Michael E. Rutenberg, Bigsby, and Matthew C. Roudané).

The critic's inclusion of Albee in the theater of the absurd may well stem from the pairing of *The Zoo Story* in its premieres both in Berlin and New York with Beckett's *Krapp's Last Tape* (1958). Had *The Zoo Story* been produced along with *The Death of Bessie Smith* or another one-act play by an author not considered an absurdist, the label might never have been applied to Albee. He even questioned the validity of Esslin's characterization of the theater of the absurd as a movement in his own essay, "Which Theatre Is the Absurd One?" first published in *The New York Times Magazine* on 25 February 1962. In an imaginary scene that takes place in Paris, Albee lampoons the idea that the absurdist playwrights are doing anything new by having Beckett and Genet join Ionesco at a Left Bank café; after exchanging greetings, Ionesco asks, "Well, what's new in The Theatre of the Absurd?," to which Beckett responds "Oh, less than a lot of people think," and they all laugh. Albee goes on to praise those playwrights as the avant-garde, but interestingly he offers a definition of the theater of the absurd that is based on "existentialist and post-existentialist philosophical concepts," which would seem to indicate that Albee distinguishes between existentialist and absurdist worldviews. Since existentialism by strict definition (or, at least, Sartre's definition) need not be pessimistic in its outlook, even if retaining Camus's view that the modern human condition is absurd (literally, out of tune or harmony), then Albee, by his own definition, need not subscribe to the more pessimistic, even nihilistic point of view dramatized by Beckett and Ionesco in order to consider himself part of the theatrical avant-garde.

Regardless of how Albee or *The American Dream* and *The Sandbox* are classified, clearly both plays criticize Mommy and Daddy for their cruelty toward their child and Grandma, representing the mistreatment within American society of both the young and the old. *The American Dream* and *The Sandbox* have been viewed as an attack on the American family for its sterility, lack of communication, and the emasculation of the hus-

Sudie Bond and Ben Piazza in the 1961 New York production of The American Dream *(Zodiac)*

bands by the wives, which led to claims that Albee was a misogynist. His defense has been that his portraits of men are as equally unflattering as his portraits of women. Finally, a few critics have even seen the disruptions of the theatrical illusion, mainly by Grandma—who addresses the audience as well as backstage technicians, when they miss the lighting cue, and the musician—as metatheater that satirizes the employment of such effects (dramatic lighting, sentimental music) in conventional theater. This reflexivity later becomes one of the defining elements of postmodernism; thus, Albee can be seen as part of that movement almost from the beginning of his career.

Though *The Sandbox* did not have a long run, the following year it was performed on television with plays by Beckett and Ionesco, again perpetuating the association of Albee with the theater of the absurd. *The Sandbox* incorporated music by Flanagan written especially for the piece, which was his and Albee's second collaboration; their first, a song with lyrics by Albee and music by Flanagan, had been performed in Carnegie Hall in 1959. Their third collaboration was the opera *Bartleby*, adapted from Herman Melville's 1853 short story "Bartleby, the Scrivener" with music by Flanagan and libretto by Albee. *Bartleby* was initially paired onstage with *The American Dream*, but it was so poorly received that the producers quickly replaced it with a dance piece until the first American production of *The Death of Bessie Smith* could be mounted to play with *The American Dream*. *The American Dream* was the first play staged by the production team that became Albee's favorite: Richard Barr and Clinton Wilder producing and Alan Schneider directing. *The American Dream* opened in January 1961, had a healthy run of 370 performances, and has often been revived along with various combinations of the other three early one-act plays. Riding the swell of the success of 1960 and early 1961, Albee went on a cultural-exchange program to South America, along with the production of *The Zoo Story,* which was actually assailed on the floor of the U.S. Senate as filthy, not the last time an Albee play was branded with that label. While Albee was in Brazil, Reed Albee, his adoptive father, died; Albee did not attend the funeral. On his return to the United States, he continued writing his first full-length play, which he had begun working on the previous year; *Who's Afraid of Virginia Woolf?* was finished by January 1962. As with his one-acts, there was praise from readers for the new work in manuscript, but it did not immediately find a theater or the backing to stage it.

Despite its three-hour-plus performance time, *Who's Afraid of Virginia Woolf?* is easier to summarize than some of the one-act plays. A college professor and his wife entertain a new faculty member and his wife late into the night and early the next morning, during which there are many arguments, secrets revealed, attempted adultery, and finally a purgation of illusion that may benefit both couples. In the first act, "Fun and Games," the audience gets to know both couples. As the act opens, George, a history professor at a New England liberal arts college, and his wife, Martha, have just returned home from a faculty party given by Martha's father, who is the president of the college. Martha has invited Nick, a new biology professor, and his wife, Honey, over for a nightcap. Although George is unhappy about having to entertain guests at such an hour, and he and Martha spend most of the play fighting, the opening scene of the play before Nick and Honey enter shows that they are a comfortable middle-aged couple who like to drink and tease each other. The act culminates with Martha humiliating George by telling the younger couple how he arrived at the college with great promise but had not risen through the ranks, much to the disappointment of her and her father, who was hoping to groom his son-in-law as his successor. When George interrupts her by dancing with Honey and singing "Who's afraid of Virginia

Woolf, Virginia Woolf, Virginia Woolf," as Martha had done at the faculty party, Honey is suddenly sick to her stomach and rushes out.

In the second act, "Walpurgisnacht," George tries to give Nick advice, to make contact much like Jerry attempted with the dog and then Peter, but the younger man scorns this attempt at mentoring, having accepted Martha's assessment of George as a failure. Nick, who is also drunk, has revealed family secrets—for example, he and Honey were married when they thought she was pregnant and that one of the compensations for marrying her was her father's money. George uses this information as ammunition for a "game" he calls "Get the Guests" after Martha has played "Humiliate the Host" by revealing an even more sensitive secret: Martha's father prevented George from publishing an ostensibly fictional work that was actually autobiographical, about a son accidentally killing both of his parents in separate incidents. George thinly disguises Nick and Honey's story as his proposed second novel, thus humiliating Nick, who swears revenge, and Honey again has to run to the bathroom. Martha and Nick get back at George by dancing seductively together in front of him and then go upstairs, presumably to have sex. Honey returns and accidentally reveals to George that she is afraid to go through labor and has been preventing herself from getting pregnant; George receives inspiration for getting back at Martha when he throws a book at the door chimes in his anger at her going upstairs to the bedroom with Nick.

Act 3 is titled "The Exorcism," which was a working title for the play at one point. As George forces Martha and the guests to play one last game, "Bringing Up Baby," two things are exorcised: Honey's fear of having a baby, and George and Martha's imaginary son, whom Nick and Honey and the audience have assumed was real. When George has Martha recite a speech about their son, something she has obviously done before with George in a game to make up for their not being able to have children, he kills off their fictional offspring by announcing that the doorbell rang and he was given a telegram reporting their son's death. Martha weeps for him as if he were their real child, demonstrating the degree to which she had begun to lose the distinction between what is real and what is illusion. It is subtly suggested in the final moments of the play that the net result of the night will be a coming together of George and Martha and, perhaps, also of Nick and Honey with the likelihood of a real child having, in effect, been conceived on the night of their visit with a sterile couple.

Who's Afraid of Virginia Woolf? has been the subject of more than a hundred conference papers, journal articles, and book chapters written by scholars. The most prominent theme in these analyses revolves around love, sex, and marriage. In reading the play as a dramatization of the war between the sexes, some Albee scholars compare *Who's Afraid of Virginia Woolf?* to the Swedish dramatist August Strindberg's *Dance of Death* (1900); however, most comparisons are to Albee's own earlier work, especially *The American Dream,* with George and Martha often seen as fleshed-out versions of Mommy and Daddy. Some studies view Martha as a domineering, castrating Mommy to George's weaker, emasculated Daddy, which is used to support the charge of misogyny against Albee, but other studies have rebutted these claims by pointing out that George is a much stronger, more animated character than Daddy or the intern in *The Death of Bessie Smith*. In fact, for all his athletic build and threats of force, Nick fits the emasculated male figure better than George, for in the course of the play he takes orders from all three of the other characters. Nick has also been compared to the Young Man in *The American Dream* as a personification of the corruption of liberal ideals of progress and their being supplanted by materialistic and technological advances. Furthermore, though Nick and Honey are often characterized as younger versions of George and Martha, despite the pain George and Martha inflict on one another, their relationship is more honest and caring than the other couple's. Scholars point out that although both couples are childless, it is by choice—Honey's—that the younger couple is sterile, whereas George and Martha were infertile. The theme of sterility also works on a symbolic level, with George and Martha again representing not only the older generation but also the United States itself, as their names—with their echo of George and Martha Washington, another barren couple—suggest. Albee has admitted to choosing their names for their allegorical import, as well as Nick's name, which derives from the premier of the Soviet Union at the time, Nikita Khruschev.

Like William Shakespeare's best plays, *Who's Afraid of Virginia Woolf?* works on many levels. For example, scholars have found a plethora of signifiers of the decline of Western civilization in the play, some of which include the allusion to fallen or destroyed cities, such as Carthage and Gomorrah; an allusion to Oswald Spengler's book *Decline of the West* (1918); George's punning declension "Good, better, best, bested"; and his assertions about history versus biology. George's jeremiad against Nick's genetic engineering research, though exaggerated to a scenario resembling something out of Aldous Huxley's *Brave New World* (1932), warns of the dangers to individualism in the face of social-scientific determinism, such as created by the totalitarian state in the Soviet Union. Whether the tone of the outlook for either couple or the West is optimistic or pessimistic is widely debated

*Jessica Tandy, Rosemary Murphy, and Hume Cronyn
in the 1966 New York production of*
A Delicate Balance *(Photofest)*

in Albee scholarship. Another motif that also supports the interpretation that *Who's Afraid of Virginia Woolf?* is more hopeful on the literal and allegorical levels is the religious symbolism found in the language and action of the play. Recalling the underlying Christian elements in *The Zoo Story,* some scholars interpret George's killing off of the imaginary son as a crucifixion that will bring about the resurrection of George and Martha's marriage, as well as the possibility for new life with the exorcism of Honey's fear of childbearing. George's role of priest as he reads the Requiem Mass in Latin during Martha's recitation is also crucial to this explication of the play. Allusions to Greek mythology (such as Oedipus and Jason and Medea), however, have been interpreted as countering the redemptive reading. The one theme virtually all studies of *Who's Afraid of Virginia Woolf?* agree on is the illusion-versus-truth dichotomy or the fear of facing up to reality, which is suggested by elements such as the imaginary son, Honey's hysterical pregnancy, and the games the couples play. Albee himself said early on that he wrote *Who's Afraid of Virginia Woolf?* partly as an answer to O'Neill's *The Iceman Cometh,* which, he says, favors maintaining illusions, while Albee thinks it best to dispel them. Other themes discussed in the scholarship on *Who's Afraid of Virginia Woolf?* include the pattern of climactic deaths in Albee's plays, repeated here in the imaginary son's death; the failure to communicate through language; and the closeted homosexual characters, which Albee has repudiated. On this issue Albee has said that he has never denied being gay but he has not been compelled to write about gay characters and issues except in *Finding the Sun* (1983) and in *The Goat, or Who is Sylvia?* (2002). He has stated that there are gay writers and writers who happen to be gay, and that he belongs to the latter category.

Although *Who's Afraid of Virginia Woolf?* has been canonized as one of the great American plays, the critics' early reviews were mixed; that is, they were generally either all praise or all pan, with few in between. Those who criticized the play focused on the implausibility of the imaginary child, the risqué language, and the bitterness of the characters; according to Gussow, some reviewers even called it "a deep cesspool" or "sick." Those who championed the play pointed to its sheer theatricality, its emotional power, and its biting, wildly funny satire. It won the New York Drama Critics Circle Award for best play and five of the six Tony Awards for which it was nominated: best play, production, director (Alan Schneider), actor (Arthur Hill), and actress (Uta Hagen). It was denied the Pulitzer Prize, however, because the board of directors did not want to give the award to a "dirty" play. John Gassner and John Mason Brown, the widely respected drama critics who recommended *Who's Afraid of Virginia Woolf?* for the prize, resigned from the Pulitzer committee in protest, and no award in drama was given that year. The play was commercially successful, however, running for 664 performances. With his earnings Albee purchased a house in Montauk on Long Island and with his producers formed "The Playwrights Unit," a workshop that helped young playwrights by staging their early dramatic works. More than one hundred plays were produced by Barr, Clinton, and Albee between 1963 and 1971, many of them by beginning playwrights who have gone on to have successful careers in the theater, including Sam Shepard, John Guare, Lanford Wilson, and Amiri Baraka. Also around this time, Albee started lecturing at colleges. The culmination of the hype over *Who's Afraid of Virginia Woolf?* was Albee meeting President John Kennedy at the White House. Thus, he had become a "FAM" with his first full-length play. *Who's Afraid of Virginia Woolf?* went on to even greater success when Ernest Lehman adapted it for the screen, directed by Mike Nichols and starring Richard Burton and Elizabeth Taylor, who won an Academy Award for best actress in 1967. According to Gussow, the movie was reviewed even more favorably than the play. Albee was relieved that Hollywood had not completely subverted his intention, though he lamented the lack of humor in the movie version.

Not content to rest on his laurels, in 1963 Albee wrote his next play, an adaptation of Carson McCullers's novella *The Ballad of the Sad Café* (1951). The play was the first of four adaptations he has written in his career and may have been his undoing, in Gussow's estimation. McCullers's story is an example of the Southern grotesque. It concerns Miss Amelia, a six-foot-tall, cross-eyed woman who opens a café in a small town, how she uses and rejects the handsomest man in the county, Marvin Macy, after he falls in love with her, and then how she falls in love with a hunchbacked dwarf named Cousin Lymon. Marvin returns from prison bent on revenge, which comes in the form of Cousin Lymon apparently falling in love with him. The climax of the story is a boxing/wrestling match between Miss Amelia and Marvin, which Cousin Lymon helps Marvin win, and then they run off together, leaving Miss Amelia heartbroken by the hunchback's betrayal. Albee made his adaptation as faithful to McCullers's plot and characters as possible, adding only a few townspeople and a narrator to solve the problem of jumping over large periods of time and providing exposition that would be tedious in dialogue. Even with Alan Schneider directing and Colleen Dewhurst starring, however, the play was a relative failure, running for 123 performances and receiving negative reviews.

Later in 1963 Albee went on another cultural exchange, this time to the Soviet Union, along with John Steinbeck and his wife. Visiting Poland, Hungary, and Czechoslovakia, as well as the Soviet Union, they met with writers, painters, and university students. While in Eastern Europe, they heard President Kennedy had been assassinated. When Albee returned, he and McNally broke up, and he began living with William Pennington, an interior decorator. By December of 1964 he had his second original, full-length play on the stage, *Tiny Alice*. Albee's reputation in the theatrical world was such that his plays could now attract the biggest name actors. *Tiny Alice* starred John Gielgud and Irene Worth, who had played George and Martha in the London production of *Who's Afraid of Virginia Woolf?*, and was directed by Schneider. *Tiny Alice* did not fare much better than *The Ballad of the Sad Café*, however, either critically, though it did win the New York Drama Critics Circle Award, or commercially, running for only 167 performances. The reason for its failure, according to the critics, was that the play was too confusing both philosophically and dramatically.

Acccording to Ruby Cohn, Albee has described *Tiny Alice* as "a metaphysical dream play" and a "double mystery play" in the sense of both "a metaphysical mystery and, at the same time, a conventional 'Dial M for Murder'–type mystery." The action revolves around three characters, known only as Lawyer, Butler, and Miss Alice, who bring Brother Julian, an assistant to a cardinal of the Catholic Church, to Miss Alice's castle-like mansion ostensibly for the purpose of negotiating a two-billion-dollar grant to the Church. It soon becomes apparent to Julian that he is being tested or tempted by the worldliness of the rich woman, and at the end of the second act she succeeds in seducing him. The third act begins shortly after their wedding, with Butler, Lawyer, and Miss Alice getting ready to close up the house and leave, but not, as Julian thinks, for his and her honeymoon. They try to persuade him that he has actually married not Miss Alice but Alice, who lives in a dollhouse-like scale model of the castle in the library, which is where much of the action of *Tiny Alice* takes place. When Julian refuses to believe there is anything in the model and starts to leave, Lawyer shoots him. After the others leave, Julian accepts God or Alice, a name that means "truth," and dies against the model in a crucifixion pose. Simultaneously, something moves from the model into the outer world of the mansion, as signified by the stage darkening in shadow and the audience hearing a loud heartbeat and breathing.

After perplexed reviews and diminishing audiences, Albee called a press conference at the theater to offer his explanation of what *Tiny Alice* was about and to assert that audiences were not confused until the critics told them they should be. Albee has since made several statements about the meaning of the play, the most succinct of which is that it is about Brother Julian's need for martyrdom; in a more philosophical explanation he says that "*Tiny Alice* examines the relationship or nonrelationship of man and God," who exists or whom man created. In other words, Albee is applying his illusion-versus-reality theme to religious faith and providing the audience with an existential choice as to what they believe they have witnessed onstage: the hallucination of a dying man or the physical manifestation of Alice or God. Although *Tiny Alice* was not successful as a theatrical production, it has sparked many scholarly attempts to interpret it as a literary text. These readings are many and varied, focusing on the Platonic relationship between the macrocosm and the microcosm as symbolized by the mansion and the model, the conflation of religious and sexual ecstasy, a homosexual nightmare, an examination of sanity versus insanity, and the corruption of organized religion.

In 1965 Frances Albee suffered a heart attack, moving Albee to contact his mother after almost twenty years of estrangement. He began a relationship with her that lasted until her death twenty years later. They did not grow close emotionally, despite seeing each other regularly at the openings of his plays or visits to his Montauk house, but it did prove beneficial to Albee at least professionally when he later wrote *Three Tall Women* (1991), based on stories his mother told him about her life. His next project, *Malcolm,* was adapted from the James Purdy novel of the same title. Opening in January 1966, it closed after only seven performances, his third commercial failure in a row. Reminiscent of Beckett's *Waiting for Godot* (1953), Melville's "Billy Budd" (1924), and Albee's own *The Zoo Story,* the play is about an innocent youth who has been sitting on a park bench for months, waiting for his father to return. In the course of the play he is exploited by various people attracted to his unspoiled nature. Through it all the boy remains naive and bewildered by the people and places he is taken to, until finally he dies from too much sex and alcohol. All the discussion of whether Malcolm's father exists or ever existed lends itself to an allegorical reading, but this more serious theme was not enough to win the play support from critics or in subsequent years from scholars. Later in the same year Albee was hired as a "script doctor" for a musical adaptation of Truman Capote's *Breakfast at Tiffany's* (1958), but with only one week to revamp the book he could not change its fate, and it closed during previews.

After a string of disappointments, Albee's career took an upswing with his third original full-length play, *A Delicate Balance,* which won him his first Pulitzer Prize in drama, though it had a limited run of 132 performances beginning in September 1966. *A Delicate Balance* starred Jessica Tandy and her husband, Hume Cronyn, as Agnes and Tobias, an upper-class couple bearing a resemblance to Albee's adoptive parents. The autobiographical origin of the play is further evidenced by the similarity between Agnes's alcoholic sister Claire and Albee's Aunt Jane, as well as Julia, Agnes and Tobias's grown daughter, who resembles one of Albee's cousins. The action occurs in the living room of Agnes and Tobias's well-appointed house from Friday night through Sunday morning. There are two disturbances of the balance, which is already delicate because of the conflict between Agnes and Claire, who lives with her sister and had an affair with Tobias years ago: first, their daughter, Julia, has left her fourth husband and is returning home; and, second, their best friends, Harry and Edna, arrive at their door wanting to be taken in after fleeing their own house when they realized they were afraid but could not say of what. Thus, the conflict between Agnes and Claire over the latter's heavy drinking that begins the play is replaced by a conflict based on the question of who has the right to live in the house. Does Claire, in denial of being an alcoholic but still Agnes's sister? Does Julia, unable to sustain a marriage long enough to establish an independence from her parents, but still Agnes and Tobias's daughter? Do Harry and Edna, abandoning their own home because of a sudden, sourceless terror, but still Agnes and Tobias's best friends and Julia's godparents? These serious issues notwithstanding, in *A Delicate Balance* Albee returned to the kind of humorous satirical drama that had characterized his early successes, *The Zoo Story, The American Dream,* and *Who's Afraid of Virginia Woolf?* The reviews of *A Delicate Balance* were mixed, as always, mostly because critics found the unexplained terror of Harry and Edna implausible, and some believed the Pulitzer was an attempt to make up for not having awarded it to *Who's Afraid of Virginia Woolf?* However, the success of the 1996 revival, winning Tonys for best play, director, and actor, confirmed the acclamation of the original production. *A Delicate Balance* has fared somewhat better with scholars, who have found in it Albee's typical themes of alienation, the corruption of the family and the American dream, people's preference for illusion over reality, language that does not facilitate communication, and existentialism. For Albee, the play is about the failure to participate fully in one's own life, with the consequence that when faced with a crisis of values, it is too late for Tobias and Agnes to change. *A Delicate Balance* was to date the most realistic of his plays, dramaturgically speaking. Despite the family being upper-class, their values, beliefs, and experience are solidly middle-class, mainstream American. *A Delicate Balance* was filmed in 1973 with an impressive cast, including Katharine Hepburn, Paul Scofield, Kate Reid, Lee Remick, and Joseph Cotton; Tony Richardson was the director. As with the movie version of *Who's Afraid of Virginia Woolf?,* Albee has pronounced aspects of it interesting but again laments the missing humor.

By this point in his career Albee had written at least one play a year and had a play produced every year since 1959. The 1967 project was *Everything in the Garden,* his third adaptation, though he had not planned to write another adaptation at this time. His production team had intended to bring British playwright Giles Cooper's play to New York, revising it only with an American setting. In working on it, however, Albee found himself rewriting so much of it that he eventually felt it had become his own play. Although the original is a British work, the plot is reminiscent of two American stories, Nathaniel Hawthorne's "Young Goodman Brown" (1835) and Stephen Vincent Benét's "The Devil and Daniel Webster" (1936). Jenny and Richard are a middle-class couple living above their means, having a house and garden in an affluent neighborhood, sending their son to a prestigious boarding school, and socializing at the country club. Richard is a modestly salaried research

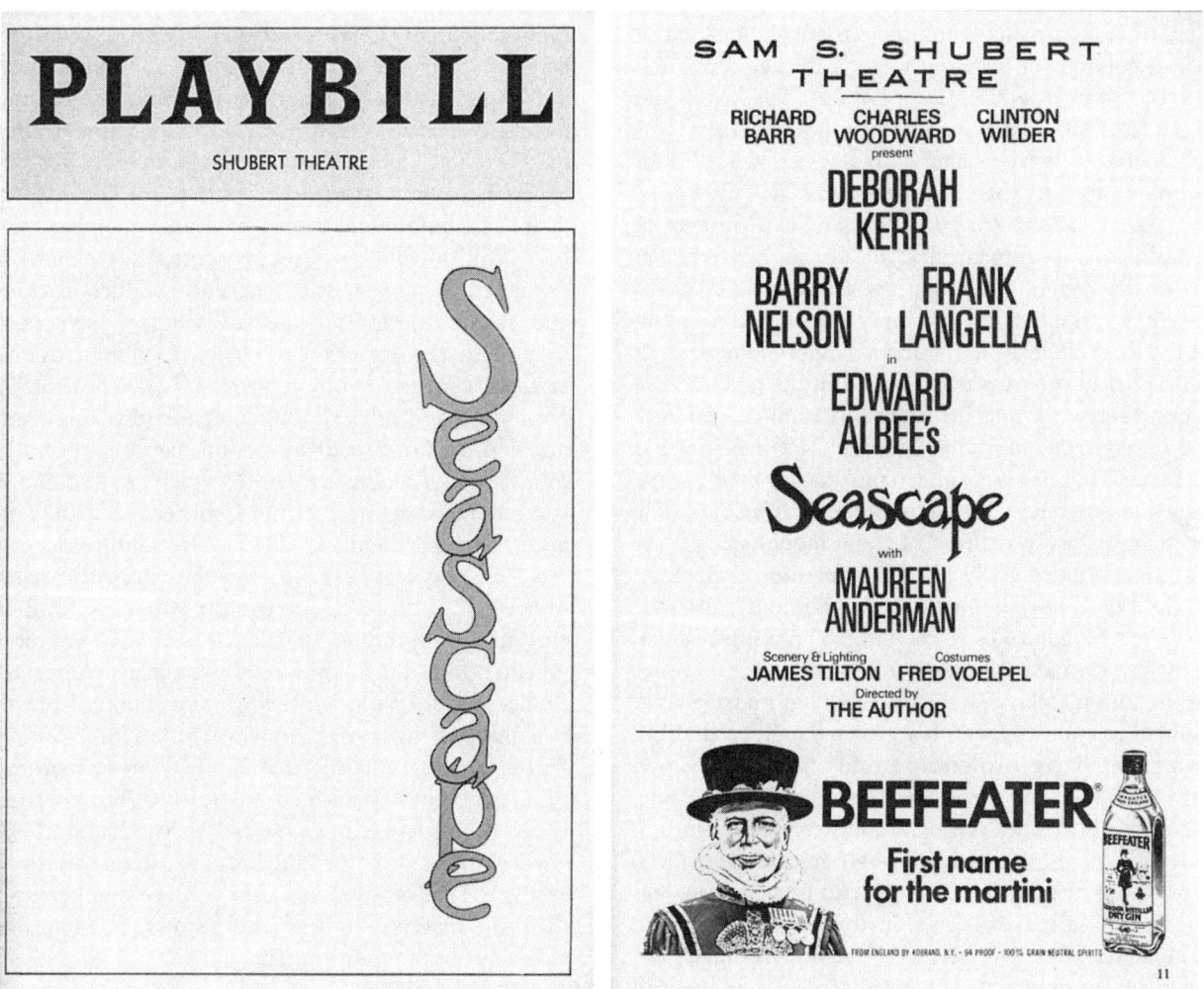

Cover and title page for the 1975 New York production of the second play for which
Albee won a Pulitzer Prize (Bruccoli Clark Layman Archives)

chemist who refuses to let his wife work despite their tight finances. The solution appears at their door one day in the form of Mrs. Toothe, who turns out to be a madam for a high-class house of prostitution. She hires Jenny, and suddenly there are stacks of cash around the house. Richard is horrified when he finds out the source of the extra income, but at a party they throw on impulse before he learns the truth, it is revealed that all of their upper-class friends have already been living the high life thanks to the wives' employment with Mrs. Toothe. *Everything in the Garden* is narrated by Jack, a neighbor who got his wealth the old-fashioned way—he inherited it. He genuinely likes Jenny and Richard, but when he stumbles on the truth about all the couples' improved fortunes, the men are forced to kill him to protect their wives and their privileged lifestyles. Returning from his grave in the garden as a ghost, Jack bears no ill will toward Jenny and Richard who, ironically, will be even richer because he had made them his beneficiaries. This story of the corruption of innocence and of the revelation that none are innocent is meant to represent society as a whole since, the play implies, everyone is compelled to sell their souls in some way. *Everything in the Garden* ran for eighty-four performances and was mostly panned by critics. In their studies of Albee's work, scholars have ignored it or only mentioned it briefly. Those few who do comment on it agree with the theater critics who found such plot elements as all of Jenny's friends being prostitutes, the husbands' accepting their wives prostituting themselves, and the murder of Jack unbelievable. They also disliked Jack's halting the action from time to time to comment on the characters and events to the audience.

Albee's next stage venture was no more commercially or critically successful than his adaptations, but it speaks volumes of his integrity as a theater artist. *Box* and *Quotations from Chairman Mao Tse-Tung* (1968) are interrelated plays that perhaps show that Albee was influenced by Beckett's later works, which were shorter and more abstract than his earlier ones. *Box* and *Quotations from Chairman Mao Tse-Tung* are experiments in nonmimetic and nonnarrative theater and drama. *Box* has no characters or action, just a disembodied voice speaking a monologue, with only the outline of a box on the stage. The Voice laments the decline of art, the technological progress that resulted in the invention of nuclear weapons, and the failure to eliminate poverty and hunger. *Quotations from Chairman Mao Tse-Tung* has characters but no action; it consists of three monologues intertwined with the monologue from *Box*. The most dramatically realistic of these monologues is by the Long-Winded Lady, who is named for a character in *The New Yorker*, the first of two such homages to the magazine Albee makes in his plays. The Long-Winded Lady is a wealthy widow taking an ocean cruise; throughout the play she speaks about her marriage, her strained relationship with her grown daughter, and her own falling overboard on a previous cruise, which perhaps was the lady's unconscious attempt at suicide. Ostensibly she is addressing a minister who reclines in a deck chair; he indicates through gestures and facial expressions that he is listening, except when he falls asleep, but he never speaks in the play. The second monologue is delivered by an actor costumed and made up to resemble communist revolutionary and Chinese ruler Chairman Mao. He delivers excerpts from "The Little Red Book," that is, *Quotations from Chairman Mao Tse-Tung;* he does not make any speeches other than the aphorisms and political and economic points from the book. The third monologue is by the Old Woman; she recites a ballad titled "Over the Hill to the Poor House," which tells the story of a woman who marries, bears children, works hard to raise them, is widowed, and then is turned away by her grown children when she comes to them for help. Then there is the monologue from *Box* that begins after the alternating delivery pattern of the other three monologues has been established.

Albee's production notes to *Box* and *Quotations from Chairman Mao Tse-Tung* explain that, ideally, the two short plays should be produced together, with *Box* performed first, then *Quotations from Chairman Mao Tse-Tung,* then a reprise of *Box*. He calls this arrangement an experiment with musical structure and an exercise in counterpoint. That is, rather than a play based on narrative, Albee wrote two pieces in which speeches function like notes in a symphony, and the actors are musical instruments. Following the musical analogy, the four monologues at times harmonize with regard to certain motifs and the overall theme—the decline of morality and the value of life in modern civilization—but each has its own melody that often contradicts one or more of the others. The intended effect can only truly be experienced in performance, but in reading the text Albee's intention—and genius—is clear.

Critics and audiences were, as would be expected, perplexed, and the 1968 production closed after twelve performances, but scholars have taken interest in this experimental work exhibiting Albee's aesthetic courage. Paolucci, in *From Tension to Tonic: The Plays of Edward Albee* (1972), compares the interrelated plays to his Off-Broadway period, particularly to *The Sandbox* and *The American Dream,* which are also interrelated, somewhat abstract, and concerned with dying both on the personal and societal levels. Other scholars saw the plays as a return to the absurdist school because of its abstractness, like the late works of Beckett, or as a product of the 1960s, the two pieces together forming a kind of protest play. Albee had challenged dramatic and social conventions from the beginning of his career, however; therefore, *Box* and *Quotations from Chairman Mao Tse-Tung* are the product of a playwright dedicated to pushing the theatrical envelope. *Box* and *Quotations from Chairman Mao Tse-Tung* is also the production most deserving of the aesthetic label postmodern, since Albee synthesizes in them the writing of others with his own, taking artifice as his material rather than life.

Furthermore, more than any other play of Albee's, *Box* and *Quotations from Chairman Mao Tse-Tung* show the influence of his former partner, Flanagan, who was a composer and the leader of a coterie of musical artists with whom Albee socialized when he first came to Greenwich Village. Shortly after *Box* and *Quotations from Chairman Mao Tse-Tung* were produced, Flanagan suffered a drug- and alcohol-induced heart attack and died. Although it had been ten years since Albee and Flanagan separated, the playwright had continued to send the composer drafts of his plays for comment. Gussow says that with Flanagan's death Albee lost "his most reliable and forthright critic." The following year Albee sponsored a memorial for Flanagan and announced that he would establish a writers' colony in Montauk to be named the William Flanagan Memorial Creative Persons Center. The colony has since served as a place where writers, musicians, and artists could come for a month in the summer to work on their projects.

The death of Flanagan perhaps also inspired Albee's next play, *All Over* (1971), which has as its subject the gathering of family and friends around a

Patricia Kilgarriff, Robert Drivas, and Wyman Pendleton in the 1982 Chicago production of The Man Who Had Three Arms *(photograph by George Kamper)*

wealthy man on his deathbed. Unlike *Box* and *Quotations from Chairman Mao Tse-Tung*, *All Over* is conventionally realistic theater and drama: all the characters are three-dimensional, even if of a type, and none of them breaks the fourth wall. The set is simply a bedroom with a curtain behind which the doctor and nurse attend to the dying man. While it is possible that the deaths of Flanagan and other friends (for example, Steinbeck) and national figures (such as Martin Luther King Jr. and Robert Kennedy) inspired the writing of *All Over*, death has been a motif in Albee's plays from the beginning. In fact, most of them up to this point climaxed in the death, real or symbolic, of a character–Jerry, Bessie Smith, Grandma, George and Martha's imaginary son, Julian, and Malcolm–though some of them die offstage or unseen, as is the case of the unnamed wealthy man in *All Over*. Even the plays that do not climax in a death have characters talk about the death of someone important to them: in *A Delicate Balance* it is Teddy, Agnes and Tobias's son who died as a child; in *Quotations from Chairman Mao Tse-Tung* it is the Long-Winded Lady's and the Old Woman's husbands. This apparent preoccupation with death, however, is Albee's existentialist charge to his audience to appreciate life and to choose to live it fully. Given his return to realism and his own voice, which had last been heard in *A Delicate Balance* (a few of the characters in *All Over* resemble characters in *A Delicate Balance,* and the wives in each play were originally played by the same actress, Jessica Tandy), one would expect the critics and theatergoers to have responded more favorably, but there may have been too much ill will built up from the string of *Tiny Alice, The Ballad of the Sad Café, Malcolm, Everything in the Garden,* and *Box* and *Quotations from Chairman Mao Tse-Tung*. *All Over* closed after forty-two performances and was nominated for only one Tony Award, for best supporting actress. Critics and scholars alike point to the lack of action and an overreliance on the donnée of a deathbed watch.

Originally, *All Over* was titled "Death" and was conceived along with a companion play to be called "Life." After many revisions, "Life" appeared on Broadway in 1975 under the title *Seascape*. Although it was no more commercially successful than most of his plays following *Who's Afraid of Virginia Woolf?*, running for only sixty-five performances, it did win him his second Pulitzer Prize. *Seascape* was also a significant step in Albee's career because it was the first time that he directed the original production of one of his plays. As far back as 1967 when he was thinking about "Life" and "Death," he stated that it was about evolution; later he revised that to being about whether or not evolution had taken place. *Seascape* was written in the study of Albee's house on the eastern point of Montauk, which overlooks a long stretch of beach and the Atlantic Ocean; this "birthplace" is manifested in the setting of the play, which is the seashore. The first act introduces the audience to a newly retired couple, Nancy and Charlie, who disagree over how their retirement should be spent. He thinks they have earned a rest and wants to lie around doing nothing in particular. She objects strenuously to this plan, seeing it as a return to an infantile state. The resolution of their conflict is precipitated by the arrival of two green-skinned, human-sized lizards, with whom Charlie and Nancy converse during the second act. Albee admits that the lizards "are a metaphor, but they must be as real as possible." He gives them conventional names, Leslie and Sarah, and makes them speak and act as a married couple much like Charlie and Nancy. Ostensibly, the lizards represent a less-evolved life-form; however, given that Charlie's first impulse on seeing them is to find a weapon, and his earlier contentment with living in a vegetative state, it is uncertain which species is really the more evolved. Nancy has a passion for living, both when she is trying to cajole Charlie into activity in the first act and into cohabitation with Leslie and Sarah in the second act. In the most optimistic ending of any of Albee's plays, Leslie and Sarah, who have become discouraged about their prospects on land, start to return to the ocean depths; their decision rouses Charlie out of his lethargy that began the play. He pleads with them to stay, and he and Nancy offer to help the sea creatures adapt to their new environment; *Seascape* ends with Leslie accepting their offer by saying, "Begin."

Reviews were mixed for both the writing and the direction, with many of them extreme in their condemnation of Albee, but *Seascape* is more highly regarded in scholarship, which analyzes its themes of animal versus human, spiritual and moral evolution, and the difficulty of communication (though this time it is successful). Leslie and Sarah are a metaphor for the Other; they have been interpreted as the animal world, emotion, and the id. Perhaps on a political level, they symbolize minorities marginalized in Anglo-American culture, or the Communist bloc. In terms of genre, *Seascape* can be classified as Albee's first true comedy rather than satire (Grandma dubs *The American Dream* a comedy, but clearly it is more in the spirit of Ben Jonson than Molière), not only because of the "happy" ending but also the warmth of the characterization and the implication that evolution will, or at least can, go on.

If one had to account for the more optimistic tone of *Seascape* by what was happening in Albee's personal life, an informed guess would be the beginning of the longest and most stable relationship of his life. After breaking up with Pennington in 1971, Albee met Jonathon Thomas, a Canadian artist, and not long after, they began living together. Albee credits Thomas with saving him from drinking himself to death, a problem that at times during the 1960s and 1970s was out of control and may have been a factor in his professional decline. At the end of 1975 Albee fulfilled a lifelong dream: he had a poem published in *The New Yorker*. In 1976 he directed a Broadway revival of *Who's Afraid of Virginia Woolf?* starring Colleen Dewhurst, who had previously appeared in two of his plays (*The Ballad of the Sad Café* and *All Over*). According to Gussow, the reviews for this production were the "closest Albee has come to a unanimously favorable press." In 1977 he bought a loft in Tribeca and redecorated it with his growing collection of paintings and sculpture. In that same year two short plays, *Listening* and *Counting the Ways,* had their American debut. The plays premiered in England, since *Listening* was commissioned by the BBC as a radio drama, and *Counting the Ways* was written as a curtain-raiser.

Albee subtitled *Counting the Ways* "A Vaudeville," which it resembles with its lighthearted tone and rapid-fire exchange of dialogue between characters named She and He without any narrative context. *Counting the Ways* is essentially a dramatization of Elizabeth Barrett Browning's question in her poem "How Do I Love Thee?" He and She count the ways in good humor, even with outright silliness; for example, Albee has He eat the rose petals from the flower he is using for the "she loves me, she loves me not" routine. *Listening* is a much darker, more disturbing play that takes place on the grounds of a mental institution. The characters include a cook at the institution, the psychiatrist with whom he was once sexually involved, and her patient; they are identified in the cast of characters simply as the Man, the Woman, and the Girl. Some scholars claim that this Albee trait of writing type characters (often indicated by not giving characters names) began later in his career, but recalling Mommy, Daddy, and Grandma from *The American Dream* and *The Sandbox,* one should recognize this as a consistent feature of his dramaturgy. The conversation among the three characters revolves around the patient and her behavior in interacting with the Woman and other patients. The Man finds the Woman's treatment of the Girl to be unsympathetic and controlling; his judgment is proven true at the end of *Listening* when the Girl reveals that she has slit her wrists and asks if it is done right, as in a story the Woman had told earlier of someone attempting suicide. There has not been much scholarly analysis of this play, but the few who have commented on *Listening* compare it to *Tiny Alice* with regard to Julian's story of having spent six years in a mental institution. Scholars see both *Counting the Ways* and *Listening* as dealing with the difficulty of communicating because of the imperfection of language, a familiar Albee theme.

In 1980 Albee returned to the full-length form with *The Lady from Dubuque,* which he has said stems from an idea he had in 1960 for a play called "The Substitute Speaker." A later inspiration was reading Elisabeth Kubler-Ross's book *On Death and Dying* (1969). The title of his new play was another allusion to *The New Yorker;* the original editor, Harold Ross, had described the magazine as not being written for the little old lady from Dubuque, by which he meant a provincial, unsophisticated reader. Elizabeth, who is identified in the play as "the lady from Dubuque," is closer to Ross's ideal reader than the actual New Yorkers in the play, in that she is quite sophisticated and cosmopolitan with refined manners. According to Gussow, Albee has said, "If *The New Yorker* is written for anyone, it's written for her." This appropriation of a character from popular culture is another example of Albee's postmodernism.

As with Leslie and Sarah in *Seascape,* Elizabeth, the lady from Dubuque, does not actually appear in the two-act play until right before intermission. The first act establishes the main character as Sam, a forty-year-old man who is struggling to deal with his wife, Jo, who is dying of cancer. On the night *The Lady from Dubuque* takes place, Sam and Jo have friends over to help distract them from their crisis. The play opens with the three couples–Jo and Sam, Edgar and Lucinda, and Fred and Carol–playing Twenty Questions. Sam's question "Who am I?" becomes the philosophical issue of the play: how identity is determined–by who one is or what one does (the existential issue of essence versus existence)–is what Sam, and to a lesser degree the other characters, are forced to consider and decide. During the game and after, the characters interact in a way that is reminiscent of George and Martha's verbal dueling in *Who's Afraid of Virginia Woolf?* Jo's attacks on the others, especially Lucinda, who is supposedly her best friend, is attributable to the intense pain she occasionally feels in the late stage of her disease; even her pain medication does not give her relief for long. Rather than understand her plight, however, the others, even Sam, chastise Jo for her lashing out. There is one tender exchange between Sam and Jo when they are briefly alone. Clearly they love each other, but Sam is feeling as much pity for himself in losing his wife as he is for Jo, who is dying young and suffering terribly at the end.

In the second act Jo gets one thing she wants: the comfort of her mother in her time of need. When Jo's mother is discussed in act 1, it comes out that she and Jo are estranged. Thus, the next morning (the beginning of act 2), when Sam comes downstairs and finds Elizabeth, who claims to be Jo's mother as well as the lady from Dubuque, the audience does not know what to believe, nor do Sam's friends, who have returned. Sam knows that Elizabeth and her companion, Oscar, a middle-aged, distinguished-looking African American man, are not, as they say, "relatives come to call." Therefore, just as act 1 began with Sam's refrain of "Who am I?," act 2 begins with his repeatedly asking, "Who are you?" His friends have no basis for determining if Elizabeth is who she claims to be, but they believe her over Sam's objections, especially once Jo comes downstairs and accepts Elizabeth's offer of the comfort a mother gives to a frightened child. Sam cannot let go of his incredulity and outrage at the hoax the intruders are perpetrating, which requires Oscar, dressed in Sam's nightgown, to stand in for him, carrying Jo upstairs to die, which she longs for as a release from the pain wracking her body. Albee's point would seem to be that because Elizabeth gives Jo the comfort she needs in her dying hour, she is, for all intents and purposes, Jo's mother. In short, what one does answers the question of who one is.

The mystery of Elizabeth and Oscar's presence was one of two aspects of *The Lady from Dubuque* that confused audiences and critics; the other was Albee's having all the actors break the fourth wall and address the audience directly. For example, during the game of Twenty Questions Jo turns to the audience and tells them who Sam is. Then throughout the first act all of the characters occasionally speak to the audience as casually as if they had been doing so all their lives. In the second act, only Elizabeth and Oscar, for the most part, address the audience. This device would seem to dispel the illusion that the audience is watching real people, thus precluding expectations of realistic drama, perhaps to negate the breaking of the willing suspension of disbelief that would have occurred when Elizabeth and Oscar make their entrance. Thomas P. Adler, in "The Pirandello in Albee: *The Lady from Dubuque*" (1987), compares this theatrical technique to that of Luigi Pirandello's in such plays as *Six Characters in Search of an Author* (1921) to point out the ambiguity between life and art, between what is real and what is illusion. In the few published analyses of *The Lady from Dubuque,* Albee is criticized for repeating himself, for example, with Elizabeth and Oscar as angels of death like the Young Man in *The Sandbox,* and the verbal warfare lubricated by late-night drinking in *Who's Afraid of Virginia Woolf?* Lincoln Konkle's study of *The Lady from*

Dubuque excavates an underlying Christian allegory such as has been found in *The Zoo Story* and *Who's Afraid of Virginia Woolf?*, reading Elizabeth and Oscar as having come to separate the sheep, or the saved (Jo), from the goats, or the damned (the others), on Judgment Day. A dream of a nuclear war described by Elizabeth at the end of the play warns the audience that the imminence of death, whether on the macrocosmic or microcosmic scale, compels people to live their lives in such a way that they have no regrets at the end of life.

The Lady from Dubuque closed after only twelve performances, the first of three commercial and critical failures during the 1980s that in effect banished Albee from Broadway and the New York theater scene for a decade. The second was an adaptation of Vladimir Nabokov's 1955 novel *Lolita* in 1981. According to Albee, between the Nabokov family, the producers, and the actor playing Humbert Humbert making changes in the script almost daily through rehearsal, what was performed eleven times on stage was not his work; he considers the original draft of a two-part version to be his *Lolita,* but that has not been published. Faring even worse than *Lolita,* his original play *The Man Who Had Three Arms* opened first in Chicago in 1982 and then in New York in 1983 but received scathing reviews and closed after sixteen performances. Most critics saw the story of a man who once enjoyed great wealth and fame from growing a third arm in the middle of his back and then losing everything when it went away as Albee's autobiographical lament at the loss of his talent and critical favor. When the title character, called HIMSELF, attacks the audience at his lecture for their fickle nature, it sounds like Albee is attacking his audience and the theater critics. As it was later published, *The Man Who Had Three Arms* ends with HIMSELF noticing he has a foot growing from his back, almost as if Albee had a premonition of the resurrection of his career in the 1990s.

Finding the Sun, written in 1983 on commission from the University of Northern Colorado and first staged there in a production directed by the author, already showed signs of Albee's comeback. Like his other two plays set at the beach, *The Sandbox* and *Seascape,* it is almost as if the warmth of the realistic setting imbues the play with warmth toward the characters and human folly. This long one-act play dramatizes four pairs of characters (three couples and a mother and son) arriving at the beach for a day of basking in the life-giving sun. Abigail and Benjamin and Cordelia and Daniel are two young couples in their twenties and thirties but unhappily paired, for Benjamin and Daniel are truly in love but prevented by society, in the form of Daniel's father, from being together. The marriages are for show only. The third couple is Henden (age seventy), Daniel's father, and Gertrude (age sixty), his second wife. Edmee and Fergus, a mother in her forties and her sixteen- year-old son, do not know the others initially, but through conversations casually struck up they make their acquaintance. Fergus is one of Albee's most delightful characters; his youthful innocence, curiosity, and precocious self-awareness charms the other characters.

Finding the Sun does not have a strong plot, but the dialogue is so sharply written, full of insights and humor, and the characters are realized fully enough despite the one-act length, that the play sustains interest and is genuinely moving. The theatrical style is realistic for the majority of the play, though Albee does allow three of the characters to address the audience in soliloquies of modest length. Two of them, Henden and Fergus, represent the two ends of the ages of man, giving *Finding the Sun* a compassionate wisdom encompassing the human life span. Although the play is grounded firmly in the literal, there are double meanings in the language (for example, sun/son) that form motifs. *Finding the Sun* did not have its New York premiere until 1994 during the Albee season at the Signature Theatre Company, where it appeared in a limited run along with *The Sandbox* and *Box* under the title *Sand*. There are few published comments by critics or scholars on *Finding the Sun;* of what there is, the evaluation is mixed, with the complaint about the lack of action and too many characters for a one-act play being repeated. From the perspective of Albee's career overall, *Finding the Sun* is significant in that it was his only play up to that time to include gay (or, at least, bisexual) characters whose sexuality was an explicit issue.

In 1984 and 1985 Albee wrote two short plays that have never been published or produced in New York, *Walking* and *Envy,* but were performed once each at, respectively, the University of California, Irvine, and McCarter Theatre in Princeton, New Jersey. The McCarter Theatre was also the site of the East Coast premiere of *Marriage Play,* in the month after its American premiere at the Alley Theatre in Houston on 8 January 1992. The play was commissioned by the English Theatre in Vienna, where it had its world premiere in 1987. It was the opening production of the Signature Theatre Albee season in the fall of 1993 and not well received by critics. *Marriage Play* is a one-act even longer than *Finding the Sun* but with only two characters, Jack and Gillian, a married couple in their fifties. The play opens with Jack informing Gillian he is leaving her; the ensuing reflection on their thirty years of making love, raising children, and growing old analyzes where things might have gone wrong, what men and women want from marriage, and the difficulty of communicating when neither partner listens to the other. Given that

Cover and title page of the program for the 2002 New York production of Albee's play about a man who falls in love with a goat (Bruccoli Clark Layman Archives)

their argument escalates into an actual wrestling match in their living room, there is an obvious comparison to George and Martha in *Who's Afraid of Virginia Woolf?*; however, Gerald C. Weales, in his review in *Commonweal* (10 April 1992), says they are closer to Agnes and Tobias of *A Delicate Balance*. *Marriage Play* was also produced at the Alley Theatre in Houston, where Albee has been a writer-in-residence at the University of Houston since the late 1980s, teaching a course in playwriting and occasionally directing his and others' plays. The Alley Theatre commissioned *The Lorca Play,* about the Spanish playwright Frederico Garcia Lorca, which Albee wrote and directed there in 1992, but it has not been produced in New York or published.

In 1989 Albee's mother died, which was a significant event in more ways than one. First, he learned that she had changed her will so that he was no longer the primary beneficiary as he had been after their reconciliation. Albee saw this change as a final rejection, probably caused by his mother's refusal to accept his homosexuality. Second, Albee found his adoption papers in her personal possessions, revealing his birth name and a few details of his abandonment. Third, and most important, Albee felt free and perhaps compelled to write about his adoptive family, not to take revenge, but as an exorcism. He began writing his most autobiographical play in 1990, finished it at the end of the year, and directed its world premiere in Vienna in mid 1991. *Three Tall Women* had its U.S. premiere in Woodstock, New York, in 1992, then opened Off-Broadway in January 1994. Act 1 of *Three Tall Women* introduces three women without names (designated A, B, and C in the program and script): a rich dowager in her early nineties and in frail health, her middle-aged caregiver, and a young lawyer from the firm that handles the old woman's financial affairs. The old woman tells the other two stories of her marriage that are variously risqué, moving, and funny. Her prejudices and dominating personality repulse them, but they sympathize with her losses—of her husband, her son (through estrangement), and her health. At the end of act 1 they realize she has had a stroke. Act 2 begins with the old woman in bed wearing an oxygen mask, then the actresses playing the caregiver and lawyer appear in different costume (dresses and jewelry) and acting in a somewhat different manner. As they talk about themselves to each other, it becomes evident that they are the old woman at the ages corresponding to the ages of the characters they played in the first act. This is confirmed when the actress playing the old woman enters in dress and jewelry, now able to move and speak freely, rather than crippled with illness and old age as in act 1. Through the rest of the play the three incarnations of Albee's mother discuss their life, going into more depth with their marriage and stormy relationship with their son (Albee) who comes to pay his respects at the bedside of the comatose old woman (a life-like mannequin in the second act). Each of the three tall women thinks her perspective—young adulthood, middle age, near the end—must be the best time of life, so that although the play ends with their/her death, represented as a chorus of expelled breath, the play is, finally, an affirmation of life.

Three Tall Women was a phenomenal success. Directed by Laurence Sacharow and starring Myra Carter and Marion Seldes, it ran for 582 performances, won the New York Drama Critics Circle Award and the Pulitzer Prize (Albee's third), and was hailed as the playwright's second coming by the critics—even those who had condemned his plays in the past. Most of the praise focused on Carter's bringing to life the main character based on Albee's mother, with one review calling her performance sublime. A few of the reviews picked up on the exorcism of the playwright's demons but also acknowledged that Albee wrote the play in a way that transcends the personal and becomes universal. They also praised the nonrealistic dramaturgy of the second act that allows the woman to converse with herself at three different ages. Perhaps the most notable thing about Albee's portrait of his mother and her struggles in life is its sympathy and yet absolute honesty. Even Albee was surprised that he could be so objective, finding some respect for her in spite of all the pain he suffered at her hands. The London production of *Three Tall Women* was also successful, winning Dame Maggie Smith and Albee the Evening Standard Awards for best actress and play respectively. In 1994 he was given an Obie Award for Sustained Achievement in the American Theatre.

The rest of the 1990s proved as productive if not as successful for Albee. The Albee season at the Signature Theatre culminated with *Fragments,* a full-length play commissioned by Ensemble Theater of Cincinnati, where it had its premiere in 1993. Reviews of the 1994 New York production were mixed; some went back to the old claim of Albee's having lost his talent. His interest in music is visible in its original subtitle, "A Concerto Grosso," which is a composition for a small group of solo instruments. Albee changed this subtitle in the published version to "A Sit-Around," presumably to emphasize the improvisational nature of the dialogue. *Fragments* appears to dramatize a group therapy session with eight participants, half men and half women, who range in age from twenty to sixty-five. They have no names, identified in the script and program only by gender and number, for example, Man 3. The eldest man is apparently the therapist (or the conductor of the concerto), but he also shares his concerns and is comforted by the group, as are the others. Each character is a fragment, telling fragments of his or her life that range widely in kinds of experience. The play begins and ends with each character sharing a proverb they get from a book or make up themselves; if there has been any development in any of them, it would have to be found by comparing the proverbs they offer in the two acts. In *Fragments* Albee is again examining how people live their lives awake or asleep, actively or passively, and if there is any help in attempting to communicate through the alienation and isolation they are born into or choose.

In 1996 *A Delicate Balance* was revived successfully, the first Broadway production of an Albee play in thirteen years; it ran for a modest 186 performances and won Tonys for best revival, direction, and actor (George Grizzard, who originated the role of Nick in *Who's Afraid of Virginia Woolf?*). The London production of *A Delicate Balance* was also successful. Later that year at the Kennedy Center Honors in Washington, D.C., Albee was feted by President Bill Clinton and friends and colleagues in the theatrical profession. In 1998 Albee's *The Play about the Baby* premiered in London to mixed reviews. The American premiere was at the Alley Theatre in Houston in April 2000. *The Play about the Baby,* which opened in New York on 1 February 2001, is a short two-act play that might be considered a thematic sequel to *Who's Afraid of Virginia Woolf?* or a reprise of *The Lady from Dubuque.* In the first act a young married couple, the Girl and the Boy, is happy until a mysterious older couple, the Man and the Woman, arrives and takes away their newborn baby. Before the Man and the Woman begin to interact with the Girl and the Boy, they individually address the audience and one another, telling stories, stating opinions, and asking rhetorical questions. In the second act they force the young couple, now bereft of their happy innocence as well as their baby, to resign themselves to the belief that the baby never existed. Albee is asking the old question: what is truth and what is illusion? The coming of the older couple to the young family would seem to be Albee's dramatization of the suffering that life ultimately brings to everyone. When the Boy begs the Man for more time before they are initiated into the hard lessons of life, the Man replies, "Time's up." Gussow describes the play as "an absurdist comedy with farcical overtones about paternity, maternity, and how the imagination can act to control reality." The reception of *The Play about the Baby* was so mixed that it appeared both on best-of-the-year-in-theater and worst-of-the-year-in-theater lists.

Despite promptings from some critics at various points in his career, Albee has refused to retire from the American theater. Judging by interviews, he has no intention of slowing down. Two new Albee plays had their world premieres in New York in 2002: *Occupant* and *The Goat, or Who is Sylvia?* The first is Albee's homage to American sculptor Louise Nevelson, who was a good friend and inspiration to him early in his career. There are only two characters in this two-act play: Nevelson (played by Anne Bancroft) and an anonymous interviewer who could be an art critic, graduate student, or Albee himself. The interviewer asks about Nevelson's life before she became an artist, her years of struggle for recognition once she had taken up sculpture, and finally her life after she had, in Albee's view, sculpted herself into the artist-as-artwork à la Salvadore Dali or Andy Warhol. Nevelson delivers extended responses, most in the form of stories, some humorous and some sad. *Occupant* is not so much a play with a conflict-driven plot as it is a series of parables about art, life, and their ultimate meaning. In fact, one hears echoes of Albee's existentialist philosophy in more than one of Nevelson's speeches.

The Goat, or Who is Sylvia? was Albee's first play on Broadway after the disastrous 1983 production of *The Man Who Had Three Arms*. In interviews before the premiere, Albee warned that *The Goat* would be his most controversial play ever because it deals ostensibly with bestiality. (Its real theme is the mercurial nature of love.) Once again Albee focuses on a middle-aged Manhattan couple, Martin and Stevie (played by Bill Pullman and Mercedes Ruehl). Martin is an award-winning architect who is experiencing his "two-thirds-life" crisis. He is having difficulty accepting his son Billy's homosexuality, and he has fallen in love with a goat named Sylvia. He discovered the animal when he was driving around rural New York in search of a house to buy so that he and Stevie can leave the city for a more pastoral life. Martin's passion for Sylvia is not merely Platonic; he reveals that he has known his beloved in the biblical sense. This absurd premise is written and staged in a conventionally realistic style, which may account for some of the negative reaction from critics. Martin tries to explain his actions first to his best friend Ross, then to Stevie, and finally to Billy. The first half of this play is filled with humor, as all four characters deliver one-liners in reference to Martin's interspecies affair. In the second half Stevie responds to Martin's attempt to make her understand how such a thing could happen by breaking most of the knickknacks, vases, and artwork in their living room. Finally she utters an animal-like howl of pain and leaves with the promise to hurt Martin as he has hurt her. The end of *The Goat* vividly alludes to an ancient Greek ritual that gave birth to classical tragedy. In Greek fertility rites a goat, as a predecessor to the tragic hero, was sacrificed to Dionysus, the god of the vine, wine, and intoxication bordering on madness. The final tableau of Albee's play shows a grief-stricken Martin bending over the bloody goat, which Stevie, also covered in blood, has killed and carried into the apartment to place at her husband's feet. Although the critics were divided in their assessment, *The Goat* won the 2002 Tony and Drama Desk Awards for best new play, as well as the New York Drama Critics Circle Award and the Outer Critics Circle Award for best play of the year. In his acceptance speech during the live broadcast of the Tony Awards, Albee thanked his producers for having faith that Broadway was ready for a play about love.

Edward Albee's career has spanned six decades, during which he has written nearly thirty plays, three of which were awarded Pulitzer Prizes, and won many other awards not only for his plays but also for his support of other artists through the Playwrights Unit and the Flanagan Center. He has received many honorary doctorates at esteemed universities at home and abroad, and his plays have been produced all over the world. Albee has also had a great impact on the American theater, with many drama critics and scholars crediting him with practically inventing Off-Broadway single-handedly and influencing many young playwrights who went on to their own success. Gussow says, "One could trace a direct path from *The Zoo Story* to David Mamet," and he cites Guare as acknowledging the debt of post-1960 American playwrights to Albee. Even the British playwright Tom Stoppard, whose works are also known for their challenging intellectual content, says he was more influenced by Albee than John Osborne, the British playwright whose works were acclaimed in the 1950s. Albee's plays are almost certainly the most intellectual of those by the major American playwrights O'Neill, Wilder, Williams, Miller, and himself. He has enjoyed success but not made that his priority, so that he could expand the possibilities of theater and drama and continue to pose tough moral and philosophical questions to his audiences. His plays have been taught in English classes in high schools and colleges and have inspired literary scholars to write copious analyses of his texts. The plays of Albee will surely continue to be performed, read, and studied well into the new millennium.

Interviews:

Philip C. Kolin, ed., *Conversations with Edward Albee* (Jackson & London: University Press of Mississippi, 1988).

Bibliographies:

Charles Lee Green, *Edward Albee, an Annotated Bibliography, 1968–1977* (New York: AMS Press, 1980);

Richard Tyce, *Edward Albee: A Bibliography* (Metuchen, N.J.: Scarecrow Press, 1986);

Scott Giantvalley, *Edward Albee: A Reference Guide* (Boston: G. K. Hall, 1987).

Biography:

Mel Gussow, *Edward Albee: A Singular Journey* (New York: Simon & Schuster, 1999).

References:

Thomas P. Adler, "The Pirandello in Albee: *The Lady from Dubuque*," in *Edward Albee: Modern Critical Views*, edited by Harold Bloom (New Haven, Conn.: Chelsea House, 1987), pp. 131–140;

Richard E. Amacher, *Edward Albee*, revised edition (Boston: Twayne, 1982);

American Drama, special Albee issue, 2, no. 2 (Spring 1993);

Lee Baxandall, "The Theatre of Edward Albee," *Tulane Drama Review*, 9 (1965): 19–40;

C. W. E. Bigsby, *Albee* (Edinburgh: Oliver & Boyd, 1969);

Bigsby, *A Critical Introduction to Twentieth-Century American Drama*, volume 2: *Tennessee Williams, Arthur Miller, Edward Albee* (Cambridge: Cambridge University Press, 1984), pp. 249–329;

Bigsby, ed., *Edward Albee: A Collection of Critical Essays*, Twentieth Century Views (Englewood Cliffs, N.J.: Prentice-Hall, 1975);

Ruby Cohn, *Edward Albee,* Pamphlets on American Writers, no. 77 (Minneapolis: University of Minnesota Press, 1969);

Gilbert Debusscher, *Edward Albee: Tradition and Renewal*, translated by Anne D. Williams (Brussels: American Studies Center, 1967);

Patricia De La Fuente, ed., *Edward Albee, Planned Wilderness: Interviews, Essays, and Bibliography*, Living Author Series, no. 3 (Edinburg, Tex.: Pan American University, 1980);

Edward Albee, video, edited and presented by Melvyn Bragg, London Weekend Television in association with RM Arts, Films for the Humanities, 1996;

Martin Esslin, *The Theatre of the Absurd* (Garden City, N.Y.: Doubleday, 1961), pp. 225–227;

Scott Giantvalley, "Albee's Titles," *Explicator,* 46 (1988): 46–47;

Ronald Hayman, *Edward Albee* (New York: Ungar, 1971);

Foster Hirsch, *Who's Afraid of Edward Albee?* (Berkeley, Cal.: Creative Arts, 1978);

Philip C. Kolin and J. Madison Davis, eds., *Critical Essays on Edward Albee* (Boston: G. K. Hall, 1986);

Gerry McCarthy, *Edward Albee* (New York: St. Martin's Press, 1987);

Anne Paolucci, *From Tension to Tonic: The Plays of Edward Albee* (Carbondale: Southern Illinois University Press, 1972);

Matthew C. Roudané, *Understanding Edward Albee* (Columbia: University of South Carolina Press, 1987);

Roudané, *Who's Afraid of Virginia Woolf? Necessary Fictions, Terrifying Realities*, Twayne's Masterwork Studies, no. 34 (Boston: Twayne, 1990);

Michael E. Rutenberg, *Edward Albee: Playwright in Protest* (New York: Avon, 1969);

Anita Marie Stenz, *Edward Albee: The Poet of Loss* (The Hague & New York: Mouton, 1978);

Nelvin Vos, *Eugene Ionesco and Edward Albee: A Critical Essay* (Grand Rapids, Mich.: Eerdmans, 1968);

Julian N. Wasserman, ed., *Edward Albee: An Interview and Essays,* Lee Lecture Series (Houston: University of St. Thomas, 1983).

Papers:

Manuscripts of Edward Albee's unpublished plays, novels, stories, and poems are archived in the New York Public Library at Lincoln Center.

George Pierce Baker
(4 April 1866 – 6 January 1935)

Mark Hodin
Canisius College

BOOKS: *The Principles of Argumentation* (Boston: Ginn, 1895; Boston & London: Ginn, 1898);

The Revolving Wedge: A Football Romance in One Act, by Baker and Thornton M. Ware (Boston: Baker, 1896);

The Development of Shakespeare as a Dramatist (New York & London: Macmillan, 1907);

Peterborough Memorial Pageant (Concord, N.H.: Rumford Press, 1910);

A Pageant of Hollis Hall, 1763–1913. Given 14 June, 1913, in Celebration of the One Hundred and Fiftieth Anniversary of the Building of the Hall (Cambridge, Mass.: Harvard University Press, 1913);

Dramatic Technique (Boston: Houghton Mifflin, 1919);

The Pilgrim Spirit: A Pageant in Celebration of the Tercentenary of the Landing of the Pilgrims at Plymouth, Massachusetts, December 21, 1620 (Boston: Marshall Jones, 1921);

Control: A Pageant of Engineering Progress (New York: American Society of Mechanical Engineers, 1930).

OTHER: *Specimens of Argumentation: Modern*, edited by Baker (New York: Holt, 1893; revised, 1897);

John Lyly, *Endymion, the Man in the Moon; Played before the Queen's Majesty at Greenwich on Candlemas Day, at Night, by the Children of Paul's*, edited, with an introduction, by Baker (New York: Holt, 1894);

William Shakespeare, *Shakspere's A Midsummer Night's Dream*, edited, with an introduction, by Baker, Longmans' English Classics (New York: Longmans, Green, 1895);

The Forms of Public Address, edited by Baker (New York: Holt, 1904);

Charles Dickens and Maria Beadnell: Private Correspondence, edited by Baker (Boston: Bibliophile Society, 1908);

"Drama: General Introduction," in *Lectures on the Harvard Classics*, edited by William A. Neilson (New York: Collier, 1914), pp. 369–386;

George Pierce Baker, 1920 (photograph by The Marshall Studio)

Plays of the 47 Workshop, First Series, edited by Baker, Harvard Plays, no. 1 (New York: Brentano's, 1918);

Plays of the Harvard Dramatic Club, edited by Baker, Harvard Plays, no. 2 (New York: Brentano's, 1918);

Plays of the Harvard Dramatic Club, edited by Baker, Harvard Plays, no. 3 (New York: Brentano's, 1919);

Modern American Plays, edited by Baker (New York: Harcourt, Brace & Howe, 1920);

Plays of the 47 Workshop: Second Series, edited by Baker, Harvard Plays, no. 4 (New York: Brentano's, 1922);

Plays of the 47 Workshop: Third Series, edited by Baker, Harvard Plays, no. 5 (New York: Brentano's, 1922);

Plays of the 47 Workshop: Fourth Series, edited by Baker, Harvard Plays, no. 6 (New York: Brentano's, 1925);

Yale One-Act Plays, volume 1, edited by Baker (New York & London: S. French, 1930).

SELECTED PERIODICAL PUBLICATIONS–UNCOLLECTED: "Brother Filippo," *New England Magazine,* 1 (February 1890): 630–639; (March 1890): 73–85;

"The Young French Dramatist: His Public as Contrasted with the American," *Boston Evening Transcript,* 9 April 1902, p. 16;

"The American Public and the Theatre: An Attempt to Analyze Public Taste," *Boston Evening Transcript,* 7 June 1902, p. 19;

"A Subsidized Theatre," *Boston Evening Transcript,* 10 September 1902, p. 16;

"*Hamlet* on an Elizabethan Stage," *Shakespeare Jahrbuch,* 41 (1905): 296–301;

"The Mind of the Undergraduate," *Educational Review,* 30 (1905): 189–200;

"What Parents Can Do for the Theater," *Ladies' Home Journal,* 29 (November 1912): 24, 92, 93;

"The 47 Workshop," *Century,* 101 (1921): 417–425;

"The Theatre and the University," *Theatre Arts Monthly,* 9 (February 1925): 98–108.

An innovator in university theater study, George Pierce Baker's pedagogy shaped the production and reception of modern drama in the United States. His famous course in dramatic technique at Harvard University, known as English 47, trained some of the most influential theater practitioners of the period–including Eugene O'Neill, Robert Edmond Jones, Kenneth Macgowan, and Hallie Flanagan–and the graduate program he instituted at Yale became a model for theater studies in the United States. Throughout his career as a teacher and a scholar, Baker insisted that the academic study of dramatic literature center on performance issues.

George Pierce Baker Jr. was born in Providence, Rhode Island, on 4 April 1866 into circumstances not unfavorable for raising a professor of dramatic literature. A cultivated and prosperous physician, Baker's father, George Pierce Baker, had been a student of Oliver Wendell Holmes at Harvard, and he nurtured his son's passion for theatrical performance, while insisting upon the liberal training necessary for successful university life. Baker's mother was Lucy Cady Baker. As a youth Baker distinguished himself in rhetoric and elocution at the prestigious Mowry and Goff's School in Providence; at home he produced meticulous performances of plays for neighborhood audiences in a miniature "toy theater." Later, a spare bedroom in the Baker house was furnished into a stage where Baker performed dramatic pieces, in costume, to the delight of family friends. By his early teens he had become an avid theatergoer in Providence, a city especially well positioned to pick up the best touring companies as they traveled regionally in combination shows. Clippings included in Baker's theater scrapbook from these years suggest as much a budding critic as stagestruck fan; several entries follow critical controversies and trends, especially questions of realism on the stage.

As an undergraduate at Harvard, Baker committed himself to formal literary study, shifting from a pre-medical track after his freshman year. Going to plays remained Baker's favorite form of leisure at college; and, with the encouragement of Barrett Wendell, then a beginning teaching assistant at Harvard, Baker began to explore academically his enthusiasm for theatrical performance in a paper on Henry Irving and a series of essays on historical contexts of Shakespearean performance. By his senior year Baker was conducting research for a possible monograph on John Lyly, a project that would eventually lead to his first academic work of drama criticism, an edition of *Endymion* published in 1894.

Despite the prescience of such class work, the undergraduate Baker would never have considered himself a drama specialist, nor would he have regarded his academic studies as training for a teaching career; rather, he aspired to be a literary figure in the traditional sense, a professional author and editor. He wrote light verse (publishing a poem in *Life* in November 1844) and served as editor-in-chief of the *Harvard Monthly,* increasing the circulation of the literary review significantly during his tenure. In 1887, after graduating Phi Beta Kappa, with eminence in English, philosophy, and history, Baker had planned to move to New York City and begin work as a literary editor. When no job offers came, he was devastated. A year later, Baker settled for a position as an instructor at Harvard; as it turned out, he worked there for the next thirty-seven years.

Baker's responsibilities were initially to teach freshman rhetoric classes and assist in forensics, and it was primarily in such fields that he first made his reputation as a scholar and teacher. By his second year he was offering his own course, called "Argumentative Composition," and from the class materials he published his first book, *Specimens of Argumentation: Modern,* in 1893. Two years later, he completed *The Principles of Argumentation,* a text that soon became a standard in the expanding field of forensics. As universities such as Harvard struggled to adapt traditional curricula for training their students for professions in law and business, Baker's courses and publications were especially welcome, and for such contributions he was promoted to assistant professor in 1895.

In these years Baker became distinguished in the eyes of Harvard president Charles W. Eliot in another way as well. He fell in love with Eliot's niece, Christina Hopkinson, who was studying at Radcliffe College. The two were married in 1893 at Eliot's summer house in Mt. Desert, Maine. Together they raised four sons: John Hopkinson Baker, born in 1894; Edwin Osborne Baker, born in 1896; Myles Pierce Baker, born in 1901; and George Pierce Baker III, born in 1903.

As Baker gained standing in the English department as a rhetorician, he was also developing a reputation at Harvard as a drama specialist. He appeared as an actor in local amateur theatrical troupes, including the Cambridge Social Dramatic Club, and participated in private literary societies, such as The Mermaid, which included Barrett Wendell and George Santayana. In addition, he invited students to his own living room to discuss modern drama and playwriting, a coterie that came to be known as "Baker's Dozen."

Baker also sent several original plays to producers in the 1890s. Inspired by the success of his Harvard classmate and friend Clyde Fitch, Baker wrote mostly one-act comedies of contemporary social manners he called "comediettas." In *My Nihilist* (1891–1892), for instance, a socialite and amateur actor plays a joke on a younger woman who has been reading about Nihilism, when he masquerades as a demented Russian. Other plays were even more explicitly located in the college milieu, including *The Revolving Wedge: A Football Romance in One Act* (1896) and *Office Hours from 1 to 3* (1901), both written with Thornton M. Ware, who had studied drama with Baker at Harvard. Not able to place these or any of his "comediettas" with commercial producers, Baker eventually stopped writing plays altogether.

At the same time, however, Baker was beginning to incorporate his passion for theatrical performance directly into his literary scholarship and teaching at Harvard. Indeed, Baker's place as a founder of university theater studies followed

Program for the "Elizabethan" Shakespeare production that Baker directed in 1904 (Harvard Theatre Collection)

directly from such struggles to place drama in the field of English literature.

Baker's literary biography is significant not because it manifests a not-so-uncommon division between professional and literary ambition; what makes his career important is how it eventually broke down such an opposition, and how Baker was able to incorporate his passion for theatrical performance directly into his literary scholarship and teaching. An initial step in this process was Baker's English 14 class, the course in English drama he took over from Wendell in 1890–1891. In this survey of drama to 1660, Baker especially emphasized production aspects of the plays, stressing historical developments in theatrical production and arguing for a gradual evolution in English drama from the simple morality of medieval plays to the more complex human studies of Renaissance drama. Crucial to this evolutionary approach was the implication that contemporary drama was part of this academic history, and in 1895–1896 Baker added "The Development of the Drama in the Nineteenth Century" as the concluding unit of the English 14 class he was teaching at Radcliffe. Eventually this section was expanded to a full course, English 39, "The Drama from 1642 to the Present Day," which included academic analysis of contemporary plays by Oscar Wilde, Arthur Wing Pinero, and Henry Arthur Jones. Baker's idea to teach playwriting emerged directly from questions posed by such modern drama study.

As a scholarly adjunct to this emerging drama curriculum, Baker edited a series of English dramatic texts. In 1895 Baker completed an edition of *A Midsummer Night's Dream* for Longmans' English Classics, and in 1902 he was made general editor of The English Drama from Its Beginnings to the Present Day section of the Belles-Lettres Series published by D. C. Heath. Modeled on the popular Mermaid Series, the volumes were pocket-sized and had a user-friendly scholarly apparatus, including a biographical introduction, textual footnotes, and a glossary. In his capacity as general editor, Baker not only provided scholarly work for drama specialists working in literature departments across the country, he also provided class materials for the drama courses they were starting to teach. In all, Baker supervised the publication of twenty-three volumes in the series, including editions of plays by Francis Beaumont and John Fletcher, Thomas Heywood, and Thomas Middleton.

In light of such struggles to define himself a scholar of dramatic literature, Baker's most important academic achievement was his 1907 monograph, *The Development of Shakespeare as a Dramatist*. Prior to the publication of the book, Baker had already established himself an authority on Shakespeare's stage; he spoke on the subject around the country, delivering a series of prestigious Lowell Institute Lectures and giving a slide presentation, "London and Its Theatres in Shakespeare's Time," at colleges and high schools. The most significant of these extracurricular activities, however, was the "Elizabethan" production of *Hamlet* (1600–1601) Baker directed in 1904 at Harvard. Working with architecture professor Langford Warren, Baker drew on historical documents to reconstruct the look of an Elizabethan performance space in the Sanders Theatre at Harvard, even staging an "audience" of students in historical costume. Significantly, Baker considered the production experience to be of scholarly value, claiming that his experiment should settle critical disagreement over the makeup of Shakespeare's stage; such space, Baker concluded, was entirely flexible and must have been reconfigured continually according to practical need.

In much the same way, *The Development of Shakespeare as a Dramatist* proposed that Shakespeare's artistry could be appreciated fully only by grounding his literary production in the conditions of the Elizabethan stage. Baker offers such an argument to mend what he sees as a rift in Shakespeare criticism between "uncritical" approaches that celebrate Shakespeare's originality by isolating him from his contemporaries and "hypercritical" studies that appreciate Shakespeare's accommodation of popular taste but do so in order to question his integrity as a literary artist. Rather, Baker argues that Shakespeare's artistic genius became manifest only when he achieved technical mastery within the Renaissance theater situation: "No play can have a lasting popularity which neglects the prejudices, tastes, above all the ideals of its own day. That we find delight in Shakespeare's plays to-day does not alter the fact that had he written for us he could not have written exactly as he did for the Elizabethans." The first two chapters elaborate this context, providing a snapshot of the London theater scene in the 1590s, a presentation Baker had already polished from his public lectures and from years of classroom teaching. Reviewers found this section of the book particularly authoritative and welcome.

A bit more controversial was Baker's case for Shakespeare's development as an artist. Beginning with essentially a poet's sensibility, Shakespeare became a dramatist, Baker argues, only through toil as a professional playwright. First, Shakespeare learned the fundamentals of plot construction and became a competent "worker in melodrama and farce-comedy" by appealing to "the prejudices and tastes of his public" for action and broad character types. Next, Shakespeare's drama began to transcend the work of his contemporaries through an interest in complex characterization, particularly in the Chronicle-based plays. Lines from the conclusion of *Richard II* (circa 1595) are juxtaposed with relevant quotations from their source in Raphael Holinshed's *The Chronicles of England, Scotland, and Ireland* (1577) to show how "Shakespeare metamorphoses the dry lines of history into human documents, quickens them into human figures." By thus working to transform historical lives into viable drama, Shakespeare became especially drawn to the struggle of individuals against forces of nature and society; and it was primarily

Scene from The Pilgrim Spirit, *a pageant Baker wrote to celebrate the three-hundredth anniversary of the landing of the* Mayflower *at Plymouth Rock (Harvard Theatre Collection)*

from this playwriting work, Baker theorizes, that Shakespeare discovered tragedy as the theatrical mode to express his artistic genius. At his most skillful, Shakespeare was able to "serve two masters at once": "By crowding his plays with story, he strove to keep his audience attentive even as his scenes developed states of mind in some central figure or figures." In doing so Shakespeare provided the "perfect illustration of the right relation of the dramatist to his public." Baker writes:

> Considering his audience, regarding it, Shakespeare moulded his material so that while it delighted them as much or more than the work of his contemporaries, he yet accomplished, in characterization what most interested him, and by poetry, philosophical comment, and ideality lifted his audience to an unwonted level of artistic appreciation.

Baker's conception of Shakespeare as a technically proficient playwright with an artistic conscience soon become the ideal of English 47, the course in dramatic technique that made Baker one of the best-known English professors in the country. When asked to explain the place of playwriting instruction in the English curriculum, Baker liked to characterize the development as an inevitable step in the process of teaching dramatic literature at the university level. He had for years supervised informal student workshops among his "Baker's Dozen" group, but in order to incorporate playwriting legitimately into his classroom, he needed to connect the process of composition directly to the historical and theoretical orientation of his dramatic literature courses. The opportunity presented itself especially in English 39, the class in "The Drama from 1642 to the Present Day" Baker started teaching in 1895; as students studied dramatic literature in terms of contemporary theater, they began asking if they could submit an original play in place of a final paper. In 1903, as an experiment, he offered students in his English 39 section at Radcliffe a playwriting option; the assignment was so successful that Baker proposed for the next year English 46, "The Forms of the Drama: Practice in Dramatic Composition." Significantly, Baker chose Radcliffe as the place to first institute his class; not only was drama central to the campus culture—the Idler theater club was already famous in Cambridge for its productions—but Baker also believed his classroom activities would be under less scrutiny at the "Annex." In 1905 he proposed a version of the class for Harvard, designating it an elective for advanced literature; after some opposition, the course was approved for the curriculum as English 47, "English Composition—The Technique of the Drama: Lectures and Practice."

With an initial enrollment of ten, the first English 47 class would have been relatively inconspicuous if it had not been for the fact that Edward Sheldon's course work that semester included *Salvation Nell*, his acclaimed drama of slum life. When the play, which featured Minnie Maddern Fiske, became a popular and critical success on Broadway in 1908, it was publicized that the author was a Harvard student who had studied playwriting under Professor Baker. From this moment English 47 was invariably seen as a class in professional training, and the prospect of Broadway success made the course one of the most popular electives at Harvard—and one of its most controversial. As other English 47 plays gained favorable commercial productions, many graduate students were drawn to Harvard to take Baker's course, most famously O'Neill, Philip Barry, and Thomas Wolfe.

Admission to English 47 required Baker's permission, and he asked students to submit a manuscript in order to evaluate their promise and sincerity. (O'Neill's letter of application to Baker is now legendary: "With my present training I might hope to become a mediocre journey-man playwright. It is just because I don't wish to be one, because I want to be an artist or nothing, that I am writing to you.") In 1910 Baker established a graduate fellowship in dramatic composition in association with the MacDowell Club of New York, specifying that the award be made only for students primarily engaged in playwriting rather than in historical research. In order to accommodate an expanding cohort of playwrights at Harvard, in 1915 Baker added 47a, "The Technique of the Drama," a variable-credit class for students who "have taken Course 47 with distinction" and wished to continue with their playwriting studies under Baker's direction.

At the core of English 47 was a sequence of writing assignments designed to get students to understand the difference between narrative fiction and drama and then elaborate a dramatic situation drawn from their own environment and experience. Initially, students were asked to adapt short stories, first by boiling down the action of the story before rewriting it in play form. Nearly half of this year-long course was spent writing and rewriting such scenarios. The composition of original one-act plays followed, again beginning with scenarios, and the class concluded with each student attempting a full-length version of their play.

Baker explained his emphasis on scenario writing by telling his pupils that professional script readers reject promising submissions that lack clear and decisive dramatic action. In addition to guiding their composition process, writing scenarios also helped students practice a rhetorical form that Baker knew would be useful for making contact with producers and agents. Through analysis of several examples of actual scenarios, he explained how an effective scenario is both clear, like an architect's plan for building a house, and compelling, written in such a way as to arouse and maintain the reader's interest throughout.

In the classroom Baker's approach was detached and authoritative, always warmly encouraging of student effort but often relentless in his criticism of individual play scripts. Typically his method was to read student manuscripts aloud, ask each member of the class for comment, and then present a detailed critique of the manuscript. Rarely did he offer specific suggestions for revision except to highlight particularly successful or promising aspects of a particular student work in question.

Although he was committed to giving pupils their choice of subject and approach, Baker steered them away from writing thesis plays and toward developing social comedies. The problem with problem plays, he told his students, was that they tended to be flawed technically; too often, characters in such dramas were merely mouthpieces for their author's point of view. By suggesting comedy, Baker was encouraging students to think first in terms of a familiar dramatic situation rather than a specific idea or message.

As they worked to dramatize these contemporary situations, Baker asked his writers to be like good public speakers, decisive and perfectly clear at each step: first, action must always be illustrative of character and conflict; next, audience interest should be maintained continually through suspense and build toward a climax near the final curtain. Despite insisting upon such grounding in the well-made structure, Baker told his students that, in the final analysis, the value of their work would be judged by the complexity of its characterization. Farce and melodrama may stimulate the emotions through physical action, but comedy and tragedy compel a

The Yale University Theater, designed by Baker and built under his supervision after he became head of the new Yale theater program in 1925

deeper emotional response by revealing the complex "mental states" of individuals.

Baker was forthright with students that he could not teach them the kind of human perceptiveness necessary for such characterization; what he could do was help them express such a personal vision effectively in a theater. As he put it, he would help them make the "dramatic" "theatric." As a scholar of the drama and not a playwright, Baker illustrated this process for students through various historical examples—not, as he said, for models to imitate or for theories to emulate, but rather in order to show various cases of what successful playwrights have done in actual practice and perhaps in doing so illuminate the proper relationship between the dramatist and the public.

In *Dramatic Technique* (1919), the book drawn from his playwriting lectures, Baker addresses this issue by distinguishing three kinds of dramatic technique: universal, special, and individual. Most of the book considers realizations of the universal, those basics that make a play a play. Special technique refers to the dominant style or practice of a period, following the preferences and tastes of audiences, such as Elizabethan or Restoration. Within such contexts, the great dramatist exerts so-called individual technique, "a particular temperament" that engages with "problems of the drama peculiar to a special time." Thus, Baker explains, imitating great playwrights of the past never really works; the individual technique is both weak and removed from its original connection to the "special" situation. Masterworks therefore should be used not as models but as case studies for seeing how the universals were realized effectively in certain circumstances. After such study, the playwright may be ready to find ways of bringing his individual perspective to bear on the special technical issues of his day. "Insisting on saying what he wishes to say, he must learn to speak in terms his audience will readily understand." However, "Though presentation of a chosen subject should be flexible, the central purposes, human and artistic, of the play should be maintained inflexibly." A writer who aims to "please the public even in its most unthinking mood" is "not a dramatist"; he is "merely a hack playwright, bribed by the hope of immediate gain into slavish obedience to the most unthinking part of the public."

Because of Baker's fundamental ambivalence about commercially successful drama, his greatest struggles came from attempts to link English 47 plays to the theater marketplace. For the most part such work was informal, as Baker used connections to get English 47 manuscripts considered for possible production, often calling on former students in positions of power in the theater industry. One such relationship was solidified in the John Craig Prize, an award given annually to the most promising play developed in English 47. In association with Horace Baxter Stanton, who studied forensics under Baker as an undergraduate and later audited English 47, John Craig, the manager of the Castle Square Theatre in Boston, instituted the award in 1910, offering a prize of $500 ($250 for the winning playwright and $250 for support of the drama collections at Harvard). Most important, each winning play received a professional production at the Castle Square. By securing a place for himself on the judging committee, Baker was able to exert some control over which English 47 plays were considered exemplary, but it soon became evident that the impetus behind Craig's generous support of Harvard playwriting was shrewdly commercial. Indeed, the first award winner, Florence Lincoln's *The End of the Bridge,* was so popular in its Boston debut that Craig toured the show nationally for years. In 1913 the third prize winner, Fred Ballard's *Believe Me, Xantippe!* became a profitable vehicle for John Barrymore, also earning Craig substantial income.

Well aware that his class could itself become commercialized in the marketplace, and frustrated by the limitations imposed by such conditions, Baker continually tried to establish a production space for English 47 where students would be free to experiment without restriction. His main goal was to institute a Harvard Theater, furnished with a stage equipped to accommodate new techniques in the continental stagecraft, a small auditorium, lecture rooms, and a library. On his own initiative Baker asked Langford Warren to draw plans for such a structure, and he actively solicited donations to support its construction and maintenance. Baker's rationale for such a theater was primarily pedagogical; as a kind of practical laboratory, the theater would allow playwriting students to test for themselves the effectiveness of their manuscripts on stage.

President A. Lawrence Lowell and the Harvard Corporation saw the issue differently; they found the prospect of a Harvard theater unsettling, evidently for reasons having to do with the already conspicuous successes of English 47 plays. At first they asked Baker to focus on raising an endowment for a chair in dramatic writing before proceeding further on funding the theater; then he was told to abandon the project altogether.

Baker's disappointment was eventually reversed in 1925 when, approaching retirement, he was asked to direct the new theater program at Yale, and he oversaw the construction and operation of a university theater built along the lines of his original Harvard design. Indeed, much of Baker's groundbreaking work to integrate theater studies at Yale involved giving curricular shape to work he had already been doing with students in an extracurricular capacity at Harvard. The most significant forerunner in this regard was the 47 Workshop, an informal group of students and faculty organized in 1912 for producing and critiquing English 47 works-in-progress. Baker, who was unofficial leader of the group, envisioned the performance space for the workshop, located in a large room in Massachusetts Hall, as a place set aside for student experimentation and learning, and he insisted that all rehearsals and productions be closed to the general public.

Yet, Baker did not consider the 47 Workshop itself a form of alternative theater; rather, he saw its experimentation as part of a wider process of developing working playwrights and commercially viable plays. English 47 student Philip Barry's sensationally successful *You and I* (1923) was reworked extensively during the workshop process, for instance. Above all, Baker explained, the 47 Workshop underscored for his playwriting students the central lessons of English 47:

> If he has shifted scenery, he will make few, if any, unnecessary demands for elaborate and heavily constructed pieces. When he has had his part in the handling of stage properties, he will not call for them to an unnecessary extent, nor will he clutter his stage with what is artistically undesirable. When he has assisted in lighting, he will be less likely to ask the light man to provide an atmosphere and the subtler gradations of feeling which it is his business to provide by his text. Studying rehearsals, he will better understand the value of the spoken word and will come to see why it is not wise, as a rule, merely to sketch in his characters. . . . Indeed, he will learn a hundred and one details as to the absolute essentiality [*sic*] of writing with actors in mind rather than for a reading public.

Baker's workshopping philosophy was soon the standard practice in many little-theater groups and university theaters nationwide, and it was at the core of the theater studies program he instituted at Yale.

When a minor fire damaged the Massachusetts Hall facilities of the 47 Workshop in the spring of 1924, and President Lowell decided that the building would be renovated as a dormitory, Baker announced that the 47 Workshop would suspend its operations until proper facilities were obtained; many saw the announcement as Baker's signal that his retirement from Harvard was imminent. Around the same time, Everett Meeks, dean of the Yale School of Fine Arts, was initiating a search for candidates to head the graduate school of drama Edward Harkness had agreed to finance. Baker's lack of support at Harvard was well known, and he emerged as the leading candidate. In November 1924 Baker accepted the position, explaining in a press release that his relations with the Harvard administration "were of the most pleasant and congenial sort. However, the University authorities could not see their way to extend the work. Yale offered the opportunity and I accepted it." The quotation that received a wider circulation in the press was from Baker's former student Heywood Broun: "Yale: 47; Harvard: 0."

As he began work at Yale, Baker was immediately surrounded by loyal disciples; indeed, many students entering the first class were transfers from Harvard, and the principal instructors Baker hired to teach production classes—Hubert Osborne for directing, Stanley McCandless for lighting, and Donald Oenslager for scenic design—had all been former students at Harvard. Baker continued to teach his courses in playwriting (English 47 became Drama 47), but his official duties became increasingly administrative, as chairman of the Yale Department of Drama, as director of the Yale University Theatre, and as the first president of the National Theatre Conference. In 1925 Baker was elected to the American Academy of Arts and Letters, and in 1927 he received a gold medal from the National Institute of Social Sciences. As a nationally recognized academic leader he articulated his vision of collaborative theater studies widely at a moment when many university programs were in the process of forming; he did so particularly succinctly in "The Theatre and the University," published in *Theatre Arts Monthly* in February 1925, an article that could rightly be called his manifesto. In the piece Baker essentially summarizes the key methods and philosophies he developed for years at Harvard in English 47 and the 47 Workshop—the need to expose students to various forms and styles but discourage them from "imitating," the need for a laboratory theater that can accommodate both student experimentation and practical training, and, most emphatically, the great value of the collaborative workshop process, especially for the student dramatist: "He prepares intelligently for each complementary worker to do his part—though he does not attempt to do the work for him. He becomes one of a corps—a commanding officer, if you like—and not an individual insisting on pet ideas who complicates a group."

Baker's emphasis on the playwright as "a commanding officer" at times set him apart from students and colleagues more committed to the so-called New Stagecraft and its primary emphasis on the director and scenic effects. Indeed, although he continued to guide student playwrights through the workshop process, Baker discovered that his most promising students at Yale were doing work in production rather than playwriting. (One of Baker's last students, for instance, was Elia Kazan.) To understand Baker's contribution, however, solely in terms of the important dramatists he nurtured—Sheldon, O'Neill, Barry, Sidney Howard—is to miss the scope of his influence on the making of modern American drama.

Robert Edmond Jones, whose scenic style came to define the look of modern American theater, had been Baker's student; so had Hallie Flanagan, who administrated the Federal Theatre Project. Walter P. Eaton, Robert Benchley, Heywood Broun, Kenneth Macgowan, and John Mason Brown all became influential theater critics after taking Baker's Harvard courses. In the *Theatre Arts Monthly* (February 1925), McCandless illustrated the broad scope of Baker's influence: on a map of the United States he plotted more than one hundred of Baker's former students who had since assumed leadership positions in the modern theater as teachers, critics, directors, and producers.

Among the most influential in this constellation were Theresa Helperin, Lee Simonson, and Maurice Wertheim, three Bakerites who helped form and manage the Theatre Guild, the producing organization that brought many modern plays to Broadway throughout the 1920s and 1930s. In many ways the success of the Theatre Guild at making the production of modern theater commercially viable confirmed one of Baker's central principles: the quality of dramatic literature in a given period inevitably follows from the sort of drama demanded by its audience. It was the civic responsibility of the cultivated classes, he argued, to take the lead in reforming public taste. Baker modeled this behavior as president of the Boston Drama League and through his participation in the historical pageantry movement. (*The Pilgrim Spirit,* the pageant he wrote and directed in 1921 to celebrate the tercentenary of the Mayflower landing, featured a cast of more than one hundred residents of the Plymouth community performing on a stretch of beach before thousands of spectators nightly.) In many articles and public lectures over the course of his career, Baker insisted that the problem with American theater was not so much that it was commercial, but that local audiences did not more actively demand their preferences as consumers. In "What Parents Can Do for the Theater" (1912), for instance, he told *Ladies' Home Journal* readers: "You have no right to expect a manager to run his theater at a loss. Make it worth his while to give standard plays, and you won't have to complain of the manager."

In the classroom George Pierce Baker told his students that to be legitimate dramatists they needed to study dramatic technique and remain true to their artistic conscience; from the logic of this pedagogy followed a broader model for theatergoing, one authorized by "education" and the insistence on "standards." It was perhaps, above all, Baker's capacity to negotiate commercial and academic spaces that best explains why so many found his ideas inspiring. As Baker's biographer Wisner Kinne put it: "To the inhabitants of the Yard, he might seem some secret envoy from the footlights; but to the denizens of Broadway he was obviously a professor incognito."

In May 1933 Baker retired from Yale, and on 6 January 1935 he died. A week later *The New York Times* published a public letter from Eugene O'Neill expressing his thanks for Baker's support and guidance. In February, at a tribute held for Baker during the Third National Theatre Conference, former student Sidney Howard observed that even playwrights who had never taken English 47 referred to Baker as their mentor. According to Kinne's biography, Howard asked the assembly, "I wonder if we can know how much he dominated this whole generation of American dramatists." Indeed, modern drama scholars who pursue Howard's query will find that the influence of Baker's pedagogy was far-reaching and vital.

Biography:

Wisner Kinne, *George Pierce Baker and the American Theatre* (Cambridge, Mass.: Harvard University Press, 1954).

References:

John Mason Brown, "The Four Georges: G. P. Baker at Work," *Theatre Arts Monthly,* 17 (1933): 537–551;

Dorothy Chansky, "The 47 Workshop and the 48 States," *Theatre History Studies,* 18 (1998): 135–146;

Barrett Clark, Brown, and others, *George Pierce Baker: A Memorial* (New York: Dramatists Play Service, 1939);

Walter Prichard Eaton, "Baker's Method of Making Playwrights," *Bookman,* 49 (1919): 478–480;

William Hutson, "Elizabethan Stagings of *Hamlet*: George Pierce Baker and William Poel," *Theatre Research International,* 12 (1987): 253–260;

Percy MacKaye, *The Civic Theatre in Relation to the Redemption of Leisure* (New York & London: Kennerley, 1912), pp. 207–223;

Stanley McCandless, "A Map of These United States Showing the Influence of the Work of George Pierce Baker (1890–1924)," *Theatre Arts Monthly,* 9 (1925): 106–108;

Lafayette McLaws, "A Master of Playwrights," *North American Review,* 200 (1914): 459–467;

Louis Sheaffer, *O'Neill: Son and Playwright* (Boston: Little, Brown, 1968), pp. 294–310;

Boyd Smith, "The University Theatre, as It Was Built, Stone upon Stone," *Theatre Arts Monthly,* 17 (July 1933): 521–534.

Papers:

George Pierce Baker's papers are held at the Harvard Theatre Collection, Houghton Library, Harvard University, and Sterling Library, Yale University.

George Cram Cook
(7 October 1873 – 14 January 1924)

Colette Epplé
Catholic University of America

PLAY PRODUCTIONS: *Suppressed Desires,* by Cook and Susan Glaspell, Provincetown, Mass., Lewis Wharf Theatre, 1 August 1915;

Change Your Style, Provincetown, Mass., Lewis Wharf Theatre, 9 September 1915;

The Athenian Women, New York, Playwright's Theatre, 1 March 1918;

Tickless Time, by Cook and Glaspell, New York, Playwright's Theatre, 20 December 1918;

The Spring, New York, Playwright's Theatre, 31 January 1921.

BOOKS: *Company B of Davenport* (Davenport, Iowa: Democrat Company, 1899);

In Hampton Roads: A Dramatic Romance, by Cook and Charles Eugene Banks (Chicago: Rand McNally, 1899);

Roderick Taliaferro: A Story of Maximilian's Empire (New York & London: Macmillan, 1903);

The Chasm: A Novel (New York: Stokes, 1911);

The Spring: A Play (New York: Shay, 1921; London: Benn, 1925);

Suppressed Desires, by Cook and Susan Glaspell (Boston: Baker, 1924);

Tickless Time: A Comedy in One Act, by Cook and Glaspell (Boston: Baker, 1925);

Greek Coins, edited by Glaspell (New York: Doran, 1925).

OTHER: *The Provincetown Plays,* edited by Cook and Frank Shay (Cincinnati: Kidd, 1921).

George Cram Cook

During his life George Cram Cook was a farmer, aristocrat, author, socialist, scholar, soldier, politician, professor, and literary editor, but he is most noted for his role in the theater. He was a founder of the Provincetown Players, an experimental theater group that rebelled against the stilted, commercialized, mainstream Broadway theater. The Provincetown Players' goal was to establish an American theater that could nurture young playwrights. The group is noted as a leading force in the early-twentieth-century American "little theater" movement. Cook not only helped found the theater but also was a major artistic force; in addition to directing, designing, and acting for many productions, he also wrote several plays. Cook's dramas concerned an abiding desire to fuse the past with the present and had a tendency to satirize modern popular trends.

The son of Edward and Ellen Hubbard Cook, George Cram "Jig" Cook was born on 7 October

1873 in Davenport, Iowa. The Cooks were a wealthy Midwestern family who had lived in Iowa from the time the land was opened for settlement. Cook had one sibling, a brother named Ruel. Cook studied classics at the University of Iowa and Harvard University, and from 1894 to 1896 he continued his education by traveling throughout Europe, studying in Heidelberg, Geneva, and Florence. After graduating with a B.A. from Harvard, he taught Greek at the University of Iowa and Stanford University. When war was declared against Spain, he joined the American army, becoming a corporal in Company B, Fiftieth Regiment, Iowa Volunteer Infantry. He was discharged on 10 September 1898 without seeing any military action: his regiment never proceeded beyond Camp Cuba Libre.

Before Cook moved into the theatrical milieu, he was known for his work as a novelist. He intended his books to preserve moments from history for posterity. He published his first book in 1899, *Company B of Davenport,* a nonfiction account of his time as a soldier; in an explanatory note, he wrote: "The purpose of this writing is to give some notion of the kind of life we led in Uncle Sam's Volunteer Army." His next literary endeavor was a Civil War novel titled *In Hampton Roads: A Dramatic Romance* (1899). His third novel, published in 1903, *Roderick Taliaferro: A Story of Maximilian's Empire,* was likewise an historical romance, but it was set in Emperor Maximilian's Mexico. These novels illustrate a melodramatic flair that appears in some of Cook's plays.

When the war ended he returned to Iowa and attempted to settle into a conventional life; he married Sara Herndon Swain in 1902, but their marriage was short-lived. After they divorced, in 1908 he married Mollie A. Price, with whom he had two children, Nilla and Harl. During this time he began writing for the *Friday Literary Review* of the *Chicago Evening Post.* Between May 1911 and August 1912 he contributed some thirty articles to the *Friday Literary Review.* He was also deeply involved in politics, founding the Monist Society of Davenport. In 1911 he wrote his final novel, *The Chasm,* in which the conflict lies within the protagonist as he faces a moral battle—much like the one Cook was fighting—between his Nietzschean philosophy and his socialist ideology.

While pursuing his career in writing and his interest in politics, Cook was exposed to Ireland's Abbey Theatre group, which performed in Chicago during its first tour of the United States in 1911. When Cook saw the Abbey tour he was inspired by the group's dedication to developing a distinctive Irish theater; he realized what a national theater devoted solely to the advancement of a country's artistic development could do. He was acutely aware of the void in American theater, which was dominated at the time by uninspiring, flashy melodramas. His desire was to revolutionize the vacuous mainstream American theater by providing a place for new playwrights to experiment and grow, much like the one the Abbey Theatre created.

In April of 1913, after his second divorce, Cook married author Susan Glaspell, whom he had met through the Monist Society and with whom he had been romantically involved throughout his second marriage. In search of a more liberating environment, which they could not find in the early-twentieth-century Midwest society, the couple moved to New York City. However, he still had ties to Chicago, as he continued to be employed as an associate for the *Chicago Evening Post*–a position he held until 1915. By this time Cook had his own column titled "New York Letters," a section of the paper containing news from the New York literary and theatrical worlds. He was a prolific writer, contributing 118 columns in a total of 135 issues.

When Cook and Glaspell moved to New York they gravitated toward Greenwich Village, which was famous for its avant-garde, progressive inhabitants. During this time he began working in another genre: drama. Cook and Glaspell wrote their first one-act play, *Suppressed Desires* (initially subtitled *A Freudian Comedy in Two Scenes*), in 1915. Even though he and Glaspell were noted figures in the New York literary community, they were unable to get their play produced. The first amateur performance occurred in the parlor of fiction writer Neith Boyce and her husband, Hutchins Hapgood, on 15 July 1915.

Suppressed Desires, a satire on the popular fad of psychoanalysis, dramatizes the attraction, bordering on obsession, of one woman to this new, fashionable form of therapy. Henrietta Brewster is captivated by the merits of psychoanalytic treatment. Much to the annoyance of her husband, Stephen, she continually convinces others to try the treatment in order for them to free themselves from societal conventions, which, according to the psychology books littering the kitchen table, keep them from being free to claim their true selves. She persuades her sister, Mabel, who is visiting from Chicago, to visit a psychoanalyst, Dr. Russel. During her session he helps Mabel unearth her "true" feelings by interpreting a dream she had that involved a rooster. From this dream, Dr. Russel makes Mabel believe she has suppressed her desire for Stephen Brewster: "Step-hen Be Rooster." To humor his wife, Stephen also goes to Dr. Russel, who interprets one of Stephen's dreams as a representation of suppressed desires for Mabel, and he

Scene from the 1918 Provincetown Players production of Cook's play The Athenian Women *(The Fales Library and Special Collections, Elmer Holmes Bobst Library, New York University)*

encourages Stephen to immediately leave his wife to avert insanity. Amused by this instruction, Stephen returns to tell Henrietta of Dr. Russel's "diagnosis." This information quickly cures Henrietta's obsession with psychoanalysis: "Look at all I've done for psychoanalysis—and—what has psychoanalysis done for me?" Concerned with her own sanity, Mabel turns to Stephen asking what she should do about her desire; he places his arm around her and gently tells her to "go right on suppressing it."

Moving from its humble beginning in the Hapgoods' parlor, *Suppressed Desires* was produced for a wider audience in August at the Lewis Wharf Theatre, a converted fish house in Provincetown. The play was produced four times before it attracted critical attention; it was finally reviewed during a 1918 production by the Washington Square Players. A 24 January 1918 *New York Times* article praised the play as "keenly written and a joy throughout." Heywood Broun's 30 January 1917 *New York Tribune* review stated, "the skill of the authors lies in the wide appeal which they have given a special subject. There are those who have never heard of Freud or of psychoanalysis, but the humor of the play can be discovered without the aid of a compass, or a complex, for that matter." Alan Dale's 24 January 1918 *New York American* review praised the play because it "proved to be genuinely funny." But on 24 January 1918 Phillip Moeller of *The World* criticized it as a "a thin satire of the 'Isms'." Of the theme he noted, "The same idea has already been done to death." Overall, he said, it was "several degrees worse than mediocre." For the most part, however, reactions were positive.

Cook's next play, *Change Your Style,* was also produced at the Lewis Wharf Theatre, on 9 September 1915. *Change Your Style* is another satire, this time set in Provincetown. It is a biting commentary on the trends in modern art schools, with a particular attack on academia. This type of denunciation of contemporary academic instruction is a common motif in Cook's writings.

The protagonist in *Change Your Style,* Marmaduke Marvin Jr., is a student torn between conflicting schools of art. Marmaduke wants to study with Mr. Bordfeldt, the head of a postimpressionist art school, much to the distaste of Marvin Sr., who wants his son to study with Mr. Crabtree, the head of a more traditional school of art. Marvin Sr., a banker, believes that Marmaduke will have a better chance making a living at selling more traditional work.

Although Marmaduke produces many paintings, he is unable to sell them because of their Cubist style. He soon finds himself unable to pay his bills. Then Myrtle Dart, a rich patron who is renting a room in his building, buys one of his paintings for one hundred dollars, which is enough to pay Marmaduke's overdue rent. Dart buys the artwork to decorate her room in order to enhance her meditations, as she believes it depicts "the spiritual form of the navel." However, Dart returns the picture and demands her money back when she discovers that it was originally meant to be "the eye of God." Keeping him from financial ruin, Marmaduke's landlord, Mr. Josephs, buys the painting believing it will be of value—not for its artistic mastery, but for the interesting story of how it was bought and sold. Ultimately, the banal art from Crabtree's school wins because of its continued economic success.

Although Cook and Glaspell's plays were received positively, it was not until the next winter in New York that they formed an actual theater company: on 5 September 1916 the Provincetown Players came into being. On the suggestion of one of the ensemble's most famous writers, Eugene O'Neill, the theater located on 139 Macdougal Street was named the Playwright's Theatre. (In 1918 they moved to larger quarters at 133 Macdougal Street, later known as the Provincetown Playhouse.) Cook helped create the group's constitution and was elected president. The lessons he learned as an audience member at the Abbey Theatre tour four years earlier inspired the Provincetown Players' mission.

Like others of his generation, Cook was deeply affected by the horrors of World War I. During the Provincetown Players' fifth season, 1918–1919, he wrote an unpublished manifesto reflecting his philosophical ideology regarding the place of art in a civilization ripped apart by war:

> One faculty, we know, is going to be of vast importance to the half-destroyed world—indispensable for its rebuilding—the faculty of creative imagination. . . . The social justification which we feel to be valid now for makers and players of plays is that they shall help to keep alive in the world the light of imagination. Without it the wreck of the world that was cannot be cleared away, and the new world shaped.

Always socially conscious, he integrated his beliefs into his dramaturgy.

In March 1918 the Provincetown Players produced Cook's new play, *The Athenian Women,* their first full-length play. It reflected Cook's continuing preoccupation with the historic parallels between ancient and modern times; he said that he was able to write about the Peloponnesian War because he lived through World War I. His interest in antiquity—particularly a passion for Greece—helped fashion *The Athenian Women.* He took the themes presented comically in Aristophanes' *Lysistrata* (411 B.C.) as the basis for a drama that showed the depravity of war, capable of destroying everything virtuous. In a review for the *New York Tribune* (4 March 1918) Broun said that the play was lacking because of "the too obvious attempt to state present-day problems in terms of Greece." Later in his life Cook translated *The Athenian Women* into modern Greek and produced it in one of Greece's ancient theaters.

In December of 1918 Cook and Glaspell teamed up again for their next play, *Tickless Time,* a one-act comedy that satirizes the young intelligentsia. In attempts to return to "truth," Ian Joyce, the protagonist, buries all the clocks in his house and replaces them with a homemade sundial. For Ian, the sundial is "more than a sun-dial. It's a first-hand relation with truth. A personal relation." His wife, Eloise, is swept up by Ian's mania, as she likewise wants to live in a firsthand relation with truth, casting aside her own, and all of society's, dependence upon machines. While their enthusiasm is able to convert their neighbor, Mrs. Stubbs ("a Native"), their maid, Annie (originally played by Edna St. Vincent Millay), is not so easily swayed. Annie serves as Ian's foil, illustrating the impracticality of his notions—after all, as Annie points out, a sundial is useless at night. Through Ian's interactions with Annie and other members of the town, he realizes that the world is not ready for his brilliance; dejected by society's lack of understanding, Ian buries the sundial because "It cannot live in this world where no one wants truth of feeling about truth. This is a world for clocks." On 23 December 1919 Broun praised the play in the *New York Tribune* because the theme was "capitalized most amusingly"; but, he noted, the "play suffers slightly from being allowed to run just a shade too long."

Cook's final publicly produced play (he wrote one short unpublished verse play titled "Darkness") was *The Spring* (1921). Again, the theme of the past infiltrating the present dominates the play, which juxtaposes the Native American lifestyle of Cook's home state of Iowa with modern academia. *The Spring,* a full-length play including a prelude, was his most experimental. The prelude is set at Namequa's Spring on Rock River in October of 1813, as the Sauk chief, Black Hawk, rescues an American scout, Elijah Robbins, and takes him into the tribe as his son. The rest of the play occurs a hundred years later. The scout's grandson, Ira Robbins, is a teacher in the psychology department of a local university. He has an unconventional theory about the transmittance of knowledge from past generations to the present. He invites the chairman of the department, William Chantland, and his daughter Esther out to his home for the weekend. There Esther has a supernatural experience: looking into the spring she sees the events that took place in the prelude and later produces some writing in a Native American idiom. Robbins believes that she has transmitted knowledge from his dead father about the Native American legends. This view tallies with Robbins's theories, but it alienates him from Chantland, who believes the theories to be too fantastical to warrant any scholarly attention. Chantland has the support of the established psychological community. He threatens to fire Robbins if the young man does not acquiesce to Chantland's beliefs. In traditional melodramatic fashion, Robbins, the hero, who is presented as morally superior, sets off to rescue Esther, the fair maiden, from the clutches of her closed-minded father. Cook attacks academia by showing its inability to accept new ideas.

After being produced by the Playwright's Theatre, *The Spring,* along with Glaspell's *The Verge* (first performed in 1921) and O'Neill's *Diff'rent* (first performed in 1920) and *Emperor Jones* (first performed in 1920), was moved uptown to the Princess Theatre on Broadway on 21 September 1921. The critical reactions to Cook's play were mixed: in *The Provincetown: A Story of the Theatre* (1931) his contemporaries Helen Deutsch and Stella Hanau described it as "interesting, but it suffered, characteristically, from too overcrowded and metaphysical a theme, and from the fact that Jig's half-thoughts, so pregnant when spoken in his beautiful voice, with the weight of his unuttered associations behind them, were unfinished and aborted in the mouths of actors." On 15 October 1921 a critic for the *Independent* acknowledged the experimental qualities of *The Spring* but noted it was "often unpalatable . . . driven to the use of the most childish and naive of melodramatic effects." This critique was kind compared to Alexander Woollcott's 6 February 1921 *New York Times* review of the first production, in which he stated that Cook "has been so absorbed in his heroine as a psychic sensitive that he has almost lost sight of her as a woman. It is, therefore, a small wonder if the average insensitive out front, while mildly interested in what visions this heroine sees in the bubbling waters of the spring, is also quite indifferent as to whether or not she falls into those waters and stays there." Woollcott criticized the dependence of the play upon an esoteric theme rather than on dramatic power, which he said was "like offering lemon extract as a refreshing drink or pure oxygen in place of air." However, a 1 October 1921

Susan Glaspell and Cook in Delphi, Greece, circa 1922–1923

article in *The Dramatic Mirror and the Theatre World* touted *The Spring* as "an altogether fascinating piece of playwriting."

Cook viewed the migration of a growing number of Provincetown Players' plays to uptown New York theaters as the demise of the group he helped found. According to Glaspell's *The Road to the Temple* (1926), he believed that this type of move was detrimental to their theater because it filled the "atmosphere of Provincetown Players with up-town point of view of money and notoriety" and "prevents our giving an equal chance to the unknown or little-known playwrights, whose need is greater":

We exist to cause the writing of the best plays that can be written in the United States, and to give each play the best possible start in life. This includes inspiring playwrights. If in any way we decrease the force of the desire to write true plays, we defeat the purpose for which we exist.

In 1922, during a proposed one-year interim break for the Provincetown Players, Cook and Glaspell traveled to his beloved Greece. However, the break turned into the end of the original Players; the group disbanded and re-formed under the direction of O'Neill, Kenneth Macgowan, and Robert Edmond Jones.

Cook and Glaspell turned their vacation to Greece into a relocation. Cook, now christened Kyrios Kouk by the locals, adopted Greece as his home, making the lifestyle of the Greek goatherds of Mount Parnassus his own. Cook was held in such high regard that when he died on 14 January 1924, the Greek government made a special tribute to him. In an unprecedented gesture, the government allowed for one of the stones from the remains of the Temple of Apollo to be removed and made into the marker for his grave in Delphi. Glaspell published Cook's final work, *Greek Coins,* a collection of his poetry, in 1925.

George Cram Cook was a theater visionary, generous collaborator, astute satirist, and ardent Hellenist. In her sentimental memoir of Cook, *The Road to the Temple,* Glaspell wrote: "He was the aristocrat who was something of a snob; he was a vegetable man and revolutionist. But just as, though at one time the mystic, and again the passionate evolutionist, in it all was the poet richly aware of life."

References:

Helen Deutsch and Stella Hanau, *The Provincetown: A Story of the Theatre* (New York: Farrar & Rinehart, 1931);

Susan Glaspell, *The Road to the Temple* (London: Benn, 1926; New York: Stokes, 1927);

Leona Rust Egan, *Provincetown as a Stage* (Orleans, Mass.: Parnassus Imprints, 1994);

Robert Károly Sarlós, *Jig Cook and the Provincetown Players: Theatre in Ferment* (Amherst: University of Massachusetts Press, 1982).

Rachel Crothers
(12 December 1870 – 5 July 1958)

Glenda Frank
Fashion Institute of Technology, State University of New York

See also the Crothers entry in *DLB 7: Twentieth-Century American Dramatists.*

PLAY PRODUCTIONS: *Elizabeth,* New York, Madison Square Theatre, 18 April 1899;
Criss-Cross, New York, Madison Square Theatre, 20 April 1899;
Mrs. John Hobbs, New York, Madison Square Theatre, April 1899;
The Rector, New York, Savoy Theatre, 3 April 1902;
Nora, New York, Savoy Theatre, September 1903;
The Point of View, New York, Manhattan Theatre, 1904;
The Three of Us, New York, Madison Square Theatre, 17 October 1906;
The Coming of Mrs. Patrick, New York, Madison Square Theatre, 6 November 1907;
Myself-Bettina, New York, Daly's Theatre, 5 October 1908;
A Man's World, New York, Comedy Theatre, 8 February 1910;
The Herfords, Boston, 1911; produced again as *He and She,* New York, Little Theatre, 12 February 1920;
Revenge, or the Pride of Lillian Le Mar, New York, Lyceum Theatre, 25 February 1913;
Ourselves, New York, Lyric Theatre, 13 November 1913;
Young Wisdom, New York, Criterion Theatre, 5 January 1914;
The Heart of Paddy Whack, New York, Grand Opera House, 25 November 1914;
Old Lady 31, New York, Thirty-ninth Street Theatre, 30 October 1916;
Mother Carey's Chickens, by Crothers and Kate Douglas Wiggin, New York, Cort Theatre, 25 September 1917;
Once upon a Time, New York, Fulton Theatre, 15 April 1918;
A Little Journey, New York, Little Theatre, 26 December 1918;
39 East, New York, Broadhurst Theatre, 31 March 1919;

Rachel Crothers (Billy Rose Theatre Collection, New York Public Library for the Performing Arts)

Nice People, New York, Klaw Theatre, 2 March 1921;
Everyday, New York, Bijou Theatre, 16 November 1921;
Mary the Third, New York, Thirty-ninth Street Theatre, 5 February 1923;
Expressing Willie, New York, Forty-eighth Street Theatre, 16 April 1924;
A Lady's Virtue, New York, Bijou Theatre, 23 November 1925;
Venus, New York, Masque Theatre, 26 December 1927;
Let Us Be Gay, New York, Little Theatre, 21 February 1929;
As Husbands Go, New York, John Golden Theatre, 5 March 1931;

Caught Wet, New York, John Golden Theatre, 4 November 1931;

When Ladies Meet, New York, Royale Theatre, 6 October 1932;

Susan and God, New York, Plymouth Theatre, 7 October 1937.

BOOKS: *Criss-Cross* (New York: Dick & Fitzgerald, 1904);

The Rector (New York & London: S. French, 1905);

The Three of Us (New York: Rosenfield, 1906);

A Man's World (Boston: R. G. Badger, 1915);

A Little Journey (New York: S. French, 1923);

Mary the Third, "Old Lady 31," A Little Journey (New York: Brentano's, 1923);

Expressing Willie, Nice People, 39 East (New York: Brentano's, 1924);

The Heart of Paddy Whack (New York: S. French, 1925);

Mother Carey's Chickens, by Crothers and Kate Douglas Wiggin (New York: S. French, 1925);

Once upon a Time (New York: S. French, 1925);

Six One-Act Plays (Boston: Walter H. Baker, 1925)—comprises *The Importance of Being Clothed, The Importance of Being Married, The Importance of Being Nice, The Importance of Being a Woman, Peggy,* and *What They Think;*

Let Us Be Gay (New York & London: S. French, 1929);

Everyday (New York: Co-national Plays, 1930);

As Husbands Go (New York & London: S. French, 1931);

Caught Wet (New York & London: S. French, 1932);

When Ladies Meet (New York & London: S. French, 1932);

He and She (Boston: Walter H. Baker, 1933);

Susan and God (New York: Random House, 1938).

PRODUCED SCRIPT: *Splendor,* motion picture, Samuel Goldwyn Productions, 1935.

OTHER: "To the American Theatre," in *Mary the Third, "Old Lady 31," A Little Journey* (New York: Brentano's, 1923);

"The Construction of a Play," in *The Art of Playwriting: Lectures Delivered at the University of Pennsylvania on the Mask and Wig Foundation,* by Crothers, Jesse Lynch Williams, Langdon Mitchell, Lord Dunsany, and Gilbert Emery (Philadelphia: University of Pennsylvania Press, 1928), pp. 115–134;

"Why Did I Write *Susan and God,*" in *Susan and God: A Magazine of the Play,* Shubert Archive, n.d.

SELECTED PERIODICAL PUBLICATIONS–UNCOLLECTED: "Troubles of a Playwright," *Harper's Bazaar,* 45 (January 1911): 14, 46;

"Woman and the Theatre," *Boston Evening Transcript,* 14 February 1912;

"Future of the American Stage Depends on Directors," *New York Times Magazine* (3 December 1916): 13;

"The War and the Women of Our Stage," *New York Times,* 27 May 1917, VIII: 5;

"The Producing Playwright," *Theatre Magazine,* 27 (January 1918): 34;

"The Arts of the Theatre," *New York Times,* 2 February 1919, IV: 2;

"Looks to Stage to Mend Present Day Morals," *New York Herald Tribune,* 24 April 1921;

"Here Is the 'How,' 'Why' and 'When'" of 'Mary the Third,'" *New York Tribune,* 25 (February 1923);

"Notes on the Usages of Charity," *New York Herald Tribune,* 30 Nov 1932;

"Whence Came Susan?" *New York Times,* 7 November 1937, p. 3.

Rachel Crothers was a celebrated presence on the Broadway stage for almost four decades. As a director and producer she required complete control of her productions. As a playwright she was distinctive in keeping the spotlight on women and the issues that concerned them. She offered the American public the latest feminist ideas and plots in which attractive young women struggled with critical life decisions. She identified her work as a mirror of women's progress, a "Dramatic History of Women" and "Comédie Humaine de la Femme." Crothers's war work and support of other theater workers went beyond the call of duty, and she received many awards. Her plays, especially the earlier ones with the clearest feminist themes, enjoyed a minor revival in the 1980s and 1990s, although most of them have since gone out of print.

Rachel Crothers was born on 12 December 1870 in Bloomington, Illinois, the youngest of seven children. Her parents, Eli Kirk Crothers and Marie Louise de Pew, were both physicians who embodied the pioneer spirit. Her mother was the first woman doctor in central Illinois. She began her medical studies at the age of thirty-nine, several years after Rachel was born. In addition to running a large medical practice, her father was a founder and second president of the McLean County Medical Society and a prominent businessman. Abraham Lincoln, a family friend, defended the physician in Crothers's only lawsuit.

The family was generally indifferent to the arts, which Crothers ascribed to the conservative, religious atmosphere in the home, although her appreciation of the theater developed early. Exact dates are difficult to ascertain. Crothers repeatedly gave 1878 as her birth date, but her death certificate records 1870, and a Rachael is listed as the nine-year-old daughter of Eli

Crothers directing Ruth Holb Boucicault, two stagehands, Charles Richman, John Sainpolis, Mark Short, Helen Ormsby, Mary Mannering, and Ernest Perrin in a rehearsal for the 1910 production of A Man's World
(Billy Rose Theatre Collection, New York Public Library for the Performing Arts)

and Maria Carothers in the 1880 census for Bloomington. Among Crothers's papers in the Theatre Collection of the Museum of the City of New York is a program from her first play, "Every Cloud Has a Silver Lining; or, The Ruined Merchant," a five-act melodrama, which she remembered writing at the age of twelve. She and May Fitzwilliams, a friend, staged it in her back parlor. She wrote and directed short plays with morals for the Sunday school classes she instructed and was active in the Bloomington Dramatic Club.

After graduation from Normal University High School in 1891, she studied elocution at the New England School of Dramatic Instruction in Boston. She returned to Bloomington to teach for three years, perhaps in response to the death of her father in 1893. In 1896 she continued her studies at the Stanhope-Wheatcroft School of Acting in New York, and the next semester she was hired as an instructor. She remained affiliated with the school for more than four years, writing and producing one-act plays with the students while also pursuing a career on the stage. In 1897 she debuted with E. H. Sothern's acting troupe.

These experiences served her well when she began her playwriting career with showcase productions of one-act plays, among them *Criss-Cross* (1899), in which a New Woman writer is torn between love and duty; *The Rector* (1902), in which a clergyman chooses as his wife an impractical woman; and *Nora* (1903), in which an actress battles her husband's rich family to keep her son. Other one-act plays that were produced include *Elizabeth* (1899), *Mrs. John Hobbs* (1899), and *The Point of View* (1904). A review of *The Rector* in *The New York Times* encouraged Crothers, who was demonstrating a growing command of character and construction. These apprenticeship dramas prepared her well for her first full-length work, *The Three of Us* (1906), which ran for 227 performances and had many regional productions.

Crothers's career can be divided into three phases, all reflections of the times and her growing interest in what younger women were thinking. The early plays, those written between 1906 and 1912, focus on the "New Woman," who is professional, competent, and attractive. Although these plays might end in marriage, they were essentially about women living independently of men. In the middle period, from 1913 to 1924, the New Woman was replaced by the "New Girl," an attractive young woman, sometimes a flapper, who voices radical ideas about marriage. Often she has an outraged father, an overwhelmed boyfriend, and genuine complaints. Marriage is the subject of the third phase in Crothers's career, dating from 1925 to 1937. The woman protagonists in the plays of this period are restless and reconsider their choices, sometimes tempted by a career, another man, or the challenge of living with a difficult husband. As the early problem plays became comedies of manners, Crothers adopted the technique of working out the plot beforehand, although the ideas were embodied in living human beings.

Her dramatic structure rarely varied. In the beginning of the play she would establish the values and lifestyle of her always appealing protagonists. In the middle of the play she would present provocative points of view and often heated debates, but at the end her protagonists would conform to the mores of the dominant culture, satisfying contemporary sentiments and ensuring a long run. In the novice plays it seems that she is speaking her mind about women's issues. Later she became more circumspect and the plays more commercially oriented. The New Woman plays did not enjoy long runs, which may have tempered her dramaturgy; Crothers was always an astute businesswoman who conceived of theater as both a forum and a source of income that would enable her to continue her career. She felt a strong antipathy toward the Little Theater movement—the genesis of the not-for-profit theater—because, as she suggested in her essay "The Construction of a Play" (published in *The Art of Playwriting*, 1928), it overemphasized the literary and failed to show professional proficiency; yet, as she wrote in "Future of the American Stage Depends on Directors" (*The New York Times Magazine*, 3 December 1916), she was excited by European experimental scenography, which was leaving behind the era of photographic realism and entering a new era of imagination.

Rhy MacChesney in *The Three of Us* is Crothers's first New Woman. She arrives on stage pulling a large trunk and tossing her keys like a boy. With both parents dead, Rhy works the family mine and rears her two younger brothers. Louis Berresford, a stranger, has purchased a seemingly worthless mine from a neighbor. Stephen Townley, who owns an adjacent mine, has just discovered a rich vein and confides in Rhy. His vein is connected to a neighbor's played-out mine, so to protect his interest, he advises a friend to buy the neighbor's property and become his partner. After Louis Berresford, a stranger, secures the neighbor's property first, Townley believes Rhy has betrayed him. To clear her name, she visits Berresford secretly at night to discuss the matter. Berresford attempts to blackmail her by threatening to reveal the visit publicly and ruin her reputation. She easily refutes him, but when Townley catches them together and insists she marry Berresford, the problem shifts from Berresford's individual villainy to a general social stricture. Recognizing the danger to her freedom. Rhy again asserts her independence and innocence in rousing words: "If I were a man you wouldn't dare treat me like this. . . . My honor! Do you think it's in your hands? It's in my own. . . . I don't need you—either of you." In the end she is reconciled with Townley, whom she loves, and they plan to marry.

The controversy over the demands that Rhy marry Berresford—a man she does not love—to atone for her impropriety sparked lively reviews and columns as the work moved across the country. Rhy's protest had been heard: a woman who does a man's work is still subject to a double standard. Critics found the American themes, dialogue, and local color so authentic that they were astonished to discover that the young author was not from Nevada. After its New York run, the play moved to London with Ethel Barrymore as Rhy.

Crothers's next two plays failed. *The Coming of Mrs. Patrick* (1907) is a tangled domestic melodrama about a nurse who heals the dysfunctional lives of everyone in a wealthy household. *Myself-Bettina* (1908) marked a significant step in Crothers's career. It was purchased by Maxine Elliott as a stage vehicle. Elliott suggested that Crothers direct the play herself, a practice the playwright continued for the rest of her career. The drama also introduced symbolic polarities present throughout the playwright's subsequent work: the United States represents a bastion of conservative conformity; Europe, an escape to a more liberal atmosphere. The plot once more revolves around a double standard. Having studied voice in Europe, Bettina, upon her return, can clearly see the moralistic penchant of the well-meaning clergyman she had thought of marrying and the judgmental rigidity of his sister, who keeps house for him. Bettina tries to reason with him, without success. When she discovers that her half sister is being forced into a loveless marriage because of a brief fling, Bettina uses her inheritance to send her to Europe to study music while Bettina renews her romance with the minister. It is noteworthy that, unlike Rhy in *The Three of Us*, the sister is not innocent; nevertheless, she is rescued from the conventional solution. The play ran for thirty-two performances at Daly's Theatre in New York.

A Man's World (1910) ran for only seventy-one performances at Collier's Comedy Theatre in New York but has become a feminist classic because its protagonist, Frank Ware, remains a role model, staunch in her values from curtain to curtain. (Crothers gave masculine names to the protagonists of several of her plays as a sign of their determination and problem-solving skills.) Frank not only supports herself as a writer but is also raising a boy, Kiddie. In the first scene several of her bohemian neighbors are gathered in her apartment, caring for the child and awaiting her return. When she arrives, the men offer to bring her dinner and fetch her slippers in a half-comical role reversal. Frank has been visiting a poor section of town, interviewing women as research for her next novel, and making plans to establish a settlement house. *The Beaten Path,* Frank's first novel, about the poverty that forces women into prostitution, was so authentic and well written that the critics believed the writer had to be a man.

She is being courted by Malcolm Gaskell, whom she finds attractive. When she discovers that he is the father of the illegitimate child she is rearing, she asks him to accept his paternity. Frank and her father had given shelter to Kiddie's mother in Europe. After the mother's death the novelist accepted responsibility for him, but her neighbors believe he is her child. Gaskell argues that a woman must remain pure, but society has to accommodate men's stronger needs. "This is a man's world," he informs Frank. "Man sets the standard for woman. He knows she's better than he is and he demands that she be—and if she isn't, she's got to suffer for it. That's the whole business in a nutshell."

When Gaskell demands that Frank send Kiddie away, she refuses in a fiery speech that posits a single code of behavior for male and female alike. Alan Dale, writing for the *New York American* (10 February 1910), observed that "Miss Crothers . . . had the courage of her convictions . . . in a woman's world and declined to end her play in a man's world." Other critics compared the play negatively to works by male playwrights such as Eugène Brieux and accused Crothers of giving way to moods instead of the logic that would have permitted Frank to accept Gaskell.

A Man's World also depicts the competition, backbiting, poverty, and mutual support of an artists' community. Among the resident artists are two dramatic foils. Lione Brune, an opera singer, is ambitious and coldly pragmatic. "Men are pigs of course," she tells Frank. "They take all they can get and don't give any more than they have to. It's a man's world—that's the size of it. . . . I never believed before that you really meant all this helping women business. What's the use? You can't change anything to save your neck." Thirty-seven-year-old Clara Oakes is a defeated woman, a mousy miniaturist, whose wealthy relatives do not even attend her exhibition. She confesses that she would accept any man who proposed just to get the bills paid, but she also protests the gender inequality. "If I were a man," she argues, "the most insignificant runt of a man—I could persuade some woman to marry me . . . and could have a home and children and hustle for my living and life would mean something." Frank reminds Clara how much she has to offer, especially as an instructor and mentor to the women in the settlement house. Feminist bonding is achieved through action and the involvement of the full community. The realism in situation and staging, the many confrontations, and the lively dialogue remain characteristic of Crothers's plays.

The opposition to women's equality was formidable. Crothers made it the subject of the last play in this group, which played briefly in Boston and Albany in 1911 as *The Herfords* opened in New York as *He and She* on 12 February 1920. It presents a worst-case scenario for the New Woman who tries to have it all. Ann and Tom Herford are sculptors with their own studios. She is "intensely feminine"; he is confident and energetic. Both enter a major contest, and Ann's design wins the $100,000 prize, while Tom's is awarded second place. Despite family criticism Ann is determined to complete the project, not only for herself but also as a representative of the talent and perseverance of all women. Then they receive news that their teenage daughter plans to leave school and marry the chauffeur from her boarding school.

Ann is blamed. She is attacked for selfishness and slackness in her responsibilities by Tom's assistant, who believes women and their work are inferior by nature, and by Tom's unmarried sister, who cannot understand how a woman can desire more than a husband and family. The worst denunciation comes from her father, Dr. Remington, whose misogyny is unadulterated by any affection for his daughter. He argues that men and women have biologically determined roles in life and that to blur that distinction causes chaos. Further, he quotes an adage: "A woman, a dog and a walnut tree—the more you beat 'em, the better they be." Ann's friend Ruth Creel, a professional journalist who ended her engagement when her fiancé insisted she leave her career after marriage, offers firm support, but she soon disappears from the play. Ann, who feels that she has neglected her daughter by becoming engrossed in her work, decides to cede the prize to her husband and dedicate herself to Millicent.

*Roman Bohnen and Catharine Doucet in the 1931
New York production of* As Husbands Go
*(Billy Rose Theatre Collection, New York
Public Library for the Performing Arts)*

The play was particularly important to Crothers. Although the 1911 productions were failures, she struggled for nine years to have it staged on Broadway. When Viola Allen resigned during the Boston preview, Crothers decided to play Ann herself and received praise for the passion of her performance. In both 1911 and 1920, when the play opened at the Little Theatre on Broadway, it caused an uproar, yet it ran for only twenty-eight performances in New York. Kenneth Macgowan, in an article for *The Globe* (13 February 1920), wrote that "'He and She' will delight that shrinking body of persons who would like to keep woman in her proper hemisphere." In his review in the *New York Tribune* (13 February 1920), an outraged Heywood Broun called *He and She* antifeminist. The author of a 29 February 1920 article titled "The Modern Woman's Career Can Find No Sympathy on Stage" protested that as many children suffer from excessive maternal affection as from neglect and that it makes no difference who removes the open safety pin that is sticking into the child. Alan Dale in the *New York American*, (13 February 1920), on the other hand, saw the drama as an attack on male selfishness. Mixed reactions greeted revivals in the 1970s and 1980s, but the general consensus was that women were still struggling with the conflicting responsibilities of family and career.

In the second phase of Crothers's career, the plays conflate conventions found in both comedies of manners and problem plays. Although their theme is intellectual freedom, it is couched in plots that emphasize sexual and familial relationships. Unlike the earlier protagonists, these young women still have to learn that with freedom comes responsibility.

The transitional play is a heavy-handed melodrama, *Ourselves* (also titled "The Social Evil" and "When It Strikes Home" in drafts), which ran only twenty-nine performances after its premiere. It is interesting for the insight it provides into Crothers's feminism. The dramatic revelations are all designed to educate the two lead characters about power relationships between the sexes. Act 1 is set in a reformatory where the inmates tell their stories of crime and victimization to Beatrice Barrington, a wealthy reformer. She decides to bring Molly, a "bit of human jetsam," home for one month. A better life seems assured when Molly rejects her abusive pimp, but she is no match for Beatrice's sophisticated brother, who seduces her. When Irene, his pregnant wife, uncovers the affair, Beatrice ejects Molly from her home. Irene is not placated, however, and rejects her husband, holding him equally responsible for the adultery. Beatrice recognizes her own bias against women and forgives Molly, although she terminates their friendship. Molly begins to understand the weakness that has cost her respect and independence.

The dramatist's research included visits to criminal court and interviews at Bedford State Reformatory for Women, where she later staged the play to a deeply affected audience. When she returned to the theme of freedom and responsibility for her next few plays, Crothers decided to mount more-upscale productions, casting richer and more headstrong ingenues in trendy costumes and closing with their engagements. There is an exciting hint of danger in the flapper lifestyle and in their questioning of morality. For the opening scene of *Nice People* (1921), which is set in a plush living room on Fifth Avenue, the stage directions read: "The girls are exquisite in their youth and freshness, finely bred animals of care, health and money–dressed with daring emphasis of the prevailing fashion, startling in their delicate nakedness and sensuous charm." These elements became a winning formula, enabling Crothers to explore ideas and engage in subtle social criticism.

Young Wisdom (1914) is about trial marriages. As with other plays of this period, as the plot reaches its happy ending, the title is transformed from the ironical to the descriptive. Victoria has returned from college with many "advanced" ideas. Her younger sister, nineteen-year-old Gail, is worried about her approaching marriage. She decides that she and her fiancé and Victoria and her boyfriend should elope and set up house. Although the men are shocked, they concur. An automobile accident interrupts their journey. When Max Norton, an artist who rescues them, discovers their plan, he lectures them instead of offering support, which leads to heated discussions of contemporary issues. In act 3 the conflict accelerates as the five return home and are confronted by the girls' authoritarian father, Judge Claffenden. Max and Gail discover a mutual attraction and agree to marry. Van Horn, Gail's fiancé, relieved not to have married such a freethinker, offers to drive them to a minister. Crothers added extra appeal to the play by casting Mabel and Edith Taliaferro as the Claffenden sisters.

Like many other artists during World War I, Crothers turned her energies to public service. In 1917 she became the founder and first president of the Stage Women's War Relief. In addition to providing entertainment for hospitalized service personnel, the organization raised a record amount of funds and became a vehicle for equal opportunity in the labor market for women. According to producer John Golden, during her presidency almost $7 million was raised. It also guided underemployed theater women to business training and theater administration positions by urging managers to make them available.

After the war Crothers's success continued. The three-act drama *A Little Journey* (1918) played 252 performances and was nominated for a Pulitzer Prize. The protagonist is the self-indulgent Julie Rutherford, who suddenly finds herself destitute when her doting aunt loses her assets. Her boyfriend voices his regrets that he can offer no assistance because all he has is his allowance of $6,000 a year. Lacking skills and training, she decides to journey from New York to Nevada to find her brother. As she travels west, her despair deepens. At the end of act 2 her decision to commit suicide is interrupted by a train wreck, which makes her realize the insignificance of her plight. Proving to be adept at ministering to the wounded and calming fears, she resolves to shoulder responsibility and adopts the illegitimate son of a fellow passenger who was killed. Jim, a recovering alcoholic who has established a communal work camp in Nevada, is deeply touched and proposes. For Crothers, as Colgate Baker noted in the *New York Review* (17 March 1923), Julie represented a large class of girls whom she called victims of the American social system because they were brought up to expect a man to take charge of their lives. This play was an opportunity for Crothers to return to the New Woman of the early period and to create in the West a setting for her protagonist to assert her autonomy. By closing the play with an implied romance between Julie and Jim, however, Crothers conveys a different message: the protection of a good man through marriage, not independence, is the ultimate reward.

A Little Journey offers a microcosm of lively character types. Lois C. Gottlieb, Crothers's biographer, read the comedy as a commentary on the state of American civilization. She interpreted the train as emblematic of U.S. involvement in World War I.

In *Nice People* the modern young woman's rebellion is more deliberate. The characters are now the self-indulgent rich, swilling scotch and scoffing at Prohibition, smoking, wearing skimpy, high-fashion dresses, and beginning their evening activities after 10:00 P.M. Teddy, a twenty-year-old heiress, decides to punish her father for disciplining her. She convinces Scotty, who has proposed, to make a midnight excursion to her country home. A storm also drives Billy, a veteran from the West, to seek shelter in the farmhouse. The next morning, when the handyman and later Teddy's family discover she has spent the night in a house with two bachelors, her father insists she marry Scotty. He disowns her when she refuses. At a loss she takes up residence in the country. Billy becomes her hired hand, and within a few months, they have discovered a sense of fulfillment in a simpler life built upon shared work. When her former friends visit, they are as bewildered by the change as she is repelled by their postures. Billy proposes with the condition that she reject her father's money. She refuses, reconsiders, and, with a delicate feminist touch, takes the reins and proposes to him.

The play ran 242 performances and was included in Burns Mantle's *The Best Plays 1920–21*. Most critics were amused by the comedy; delighted by the cast, which included Tallulah Bankhead, Katharine Cornell, and Francine Larrimore in their first major roles; and attracted by the lively, thought-provoking arguments. Rabbi Stephen Wise used the play as an illustration of modern vice, however, calling upon his congregation to retain high standards.

Walter Abel and Frieda Inescort in the 1932 New York production of When Ladies Meet
(Billy Rose Theatre Collection, New York Public Library for the Performing Arts)

(Crothers, in fact, would have concurred to some extent with Wise's assessment. In a 15 March 1931 *New York Herald Tribune* interview she asserted that the stage "can preach a sermon that people who have forgotten the way to churches stop and listen to. A transcendent power–yet we waste it." Evoking the classical definition of comedy as a corrective for human faults in "Looks to Stage to Mend Present Day Morals" (*New York Herald Tribune*, 24 April 1921) she further argued that the dramatized example can "persuade a girl of the 'nice people' type that she is giving an exhibition of bad taste and you'll find that she quickly reforms.") In a 29 April 1923 article for the *Morning Telegraph*, Agnes Smith observed that the playwright "has come to be our world court for regulating the manners and morals of the younger generation."

The theme of self-determination from *A Little Journey* is repeated in *Mary the Third* (1923), and again Crothers closes with a romantic pairing. The play is an historical triptych; the minimalist set for the proposals to all three generations of women named Mary is the same mahogany sofa in the living room. There are two scenes in the prologue: the first Mary seduces a formerly rejected suitor when she discovers that he has inherited a fortune; then her daughter, also named Mary, chooses the pragmatic egotist Robert over the poetic Richard, whom she loves. The three acts of the play bring together the grandmother, mother, and daughter as "Mary the Third" considers the institution of marriage. Throughout, Mary's struggles to reconcile her romanticism with the recognition that she needs a cool head and criteria on which to base her decision.

Act 1 opens with the manipulative grandmother criticizing her daughter for permissiveness with her two children. Because Mary's brother is spoiled, the audience assumes that she, too, is irresponsible. Although bitter, the mother is a voice of reason. She responds to the grandmother's warning that every aspect of life is full of danger, and for her it is "being swamped by the hateful ugliness of–respectable–

everyday life." When the daughter—boyishly slender, scantily dressed, vital, and eager—is introduced, she and her friends are planning an unchaperoned camping trip to discover which of her two boyfriends is the best prospect for "perfect" love. She wants to know them when they are not in their best clothing and on their best behavior. She posits avoiding the "disappointing experiment" of marriage by practicing free love before "lifetime mating."

Despite familial objections, Mary and her friends depart in the middle of the night. Mary's appetite for excitement is clear as she urges the driver to accelerate, but by four that morning they have all returned to Mary's house. Stricken by conscience, she invents an attack of appendicitis. She overhears her mother and father having a caustic argument and learns how hurtful their marriage has become. She insists her mother divorce, only to discover her mother's economic dependence, and she vows never to find herself in that situation. She accepts Lynn, one of her suitors, and they promise to work hard at their marriage but to separate once the love departs. Yet, as the play ends, they are still talking about "the most wonderful love that was ever in the world."

The implication is that the other Marys erred, but the youngest Mary has the right attitude to create a successful marriage. She is Crothers's ideal Modern Girl, which the playwright described in a 22 May 1923 interview with Ruth Brownlow as "the best thing women have turned out. She is thinking for herself and refusing to follow the orthodox stuff that has been handed down to her. . . . She takes things not for what they have been, but for what they are or can be. She will have something very fine and sensible to give her children."

Career development and financial independence are motifs that Crothers addresses repeatedly in her work. Her basic premises were clear, but they proved to be problematic in their application in plays such as *He and She*. In discussing *A Little Journey* for an interview with *Hearst's Magazine* in August 1919, she said, "There isn't a situation in life which a girl cannot face with more courage and more success if she actually can earn her living. It takes away the horror of being an 'old maid.' . . . It tremendously reduces the necessity of enduring an unhappy marriage and above all it helps to keep happy marriages, because of the evident fact that if a woman can take care of herself, her husband respects her the more."

In *Expressing Willie* (1924), the last of the Modern Girl plays and Crothers's favorite comedy, the playwright reverses the trajectory by moving a country girl into sophisticated society with absurd results. Willie Smith, as his name implies, is an ordinary man from the Midwest who has had astonishing success marketing toothpaste. With his conspicuous consumption and all-out attempts to flatter the smart set, he is a parody of the nouveau riche. His down-to-earth mother invites the "utterly drab" Minnie Whitcomb, an awkward, introverted music teacher and old friend, to the mansion in an attempt to bring him back to himself. Minnie literally trips over her own feet. Willie is taken with Mrs. Frances Sylvester, a much-divorced fortune hunter.

The play was both a nod of respect to and a parody of pop Freudianism. The sophisticates talk the jargon, telling Willie he has hidden greatness. Taliaferro, a painter and one of the weekend guests, convinces Minnie that she needs to liberate her spirit. Her repressions melt, and by act 3 she has developed the confidence to demonstrate how well she has mastered the piano and how attractive she is. The night before, the rivals each visit Willie's bedroom. Minnie, in her plain robe, hides in the closet when Frances, in expensive lingerie, arrives and tries to seduce Willie. Upset at the scene, Minnie bursts out of the closet, and Frances, distressed, becomes abusive to Willie. His eyes opened, the millionaire declares his love for Minnie, who encourages him to return to Frances. "I must be *free*," she informs him. "We speak a different language. My music—my art—my inner life don't mean anything to you." Having won the heart of the toothpaste baron, she overshoots the mark and rejects him for the idea of expressing herself through art, and so the romantic comedy ends in irony. Critics and audiences agreed in their praise. The comedy ran 281 performances.

Crothers occasionally directed scripts by other people—*The Book of Charm* (1925) by John Kirkpatrick, for example, and Caroline Francke's *Exceedingly Small* (1927). She suffered significant financial losses when she directed and produced Zoë Akins's drama *Thou Desperate Pilot* (1927), however, which probably curtailed her enthusiasm for producing other playwrights' work.

While many of Crothers's plays responded to American crises, her transitional dramas often were prescient, preceding historical traumas. Just before World War I, she abandoned the New Woman for the flapper and her middle-class sisters, and just as the stock market was about to crash, she left the well-to-do homes of these daring single women to focus on married life.

In the first of the marriage comedies, *Let Us Be Gay* (1929) and *As Husbands Go* (1931), with their questions of sexual freedom and European permissiveness, her touch was light. The former is a transition play, with the divorced protagonist a conflation of the flapper and the New Woman. Kitty takes back

Cover and cast list for the first production of Crothers's last play
(Bruccoli Clark Layman Archives)

her maiden name, becomes a successful businesswoman and single parent, and plays the field. Instead of romance and excitement, however, she finds loneliness. When she and Bob Brown, her former husband, meet unexpectedly at Mrs. Boucicault's Westchester house, he is surprised at her brittle gaiety and her appeal to men. He threatens to take the children away from her, but she laughs him off. A series of coincidences brings them together and they talk. In the end he asks her to take him back. At first she refuses, but finally she agrees to try marriage again.

The comedy offered Crothers the opportunity to explore the theme of the double standard once again and employ her successful box-office formula of sexual experimentation leading to reform. Mrs. Boucicault, a septuagenarian who had suffered through her husband's infidelities for decades but urged her daughter to divorce three times, defines the core question of the comedy: "Women are getting everything they think they want, but are they any happier than they were when they used to stay at home—with their romantic illusions—and let men fool them?" *Let Us Be Gay* was included in Mantle's *The Best Plays of 1928-29* and made into a movie featuring Norma Shearer and Marie Dressler in 1930.

Paris is the setting for the prologue to *As Husbands Go*. Lucile Lingard and Emmie Sykes, both middle-aged housewives, flirt with two charming European men. Five weeks later the men have followed them home to Dubuque, Iowa, and the comedy begins. Even in this heavily manipulated play with its standard dramatic devices—a drunken scene, an anxious woman, a letter, and a mysterious disappearance—laughter and poignancy derive from character and situation.

Using two protagonists enabled Crothers to devise various resolutions in the play. Charles Lingard, when confronted by a sophisticated rival, a British writer, neither sulks nor bullies. To his wife's surprise, he takes him fishing, the men discover that they like each other, and then they get drunk together. The skittish Emmie, on the other hand, is a widow. The monocled dandy Hippolitus Lomi is far from the American image of the romantic groom, especially after he confesses that if Emmie had no money he would not have proposed. She accepts his honesty and defies Peggy, her shrewish teenage daughter, with unexpected firmness. She tells Lucile: "Why shouldn't I have some fun?–I'm not as old as Methuselah you know. *Hippie* knows. *He* sees things in me. Things I'd forgotten I *had*–have come out. I'm darned sick of just being Peggy's mother." Despite the negative critiques, Mantle included it in *The Best Plays of 1930-31*. It ran for 148 performances in 1931, and 131 performances in a 1933 revival.

Crothers finished her career with two of her finest plays, *When Ladies Meet* (1932) and *Susan and God* (1937). The first is the story of an affair from the perspective of the other woman, Mary Howard, a successful novelist in her thirties who seems to have it all: a career, an expensive Greenwich Village apartment, and a sophisticated lifestyle. She has been having an affair with her publisher, Rogers Woodruff, and not only believes that he will divorce his wife but also that the wife will gracefully release him when she learns that he and Mary have a perfect relationship. Her beliefs echo the romantic idealization voiced by the youngest Mary in *Mary the Third*. Although Mary Howard has no compunction about the affair or a weekend rendezvous with Woodruff at her friend Bridget Duke's Connecticut estate, she is redeemed by her naiveté.

The plot complications are created by Mary's friend Jimmie Lee. He arranges for Woodruff to be delayed and for his wife, Claire, to visit the country home as Jimmie's cousin. Mary and Claire admire each other at first sight and share confidences, although without naming names. Claire begins to realize that Mary is her husband's latest affair–just before Woodruff enters Mary's room. Claire confronts him, admitting that she has known about his affairs, and exits. Mary demands that Woodruff announce to his wife his intentions to marry her. When he refuses, she begins to understand his deception. Neither woman is able to hide behind the stereotypes they had developed–the dull housewife and the loose woman–to salvage their self-respect and are forced to see Woodruff clearly. Bolstered by their respect for each other, they terminate their relationships with him. The play was well received, and the Dramatists Guild of the Authors' League awarded it the Roi Cooper Megrue Prize for comedy.

This genuine and rare onstage portrait of women bonding is affecting and rings true, but the males are stick figures. In his review for the *New York Sun* (7 October 1932) Richard Lockridge, decidedly a Crothers enthusiast, pointed out that "the inability to get her men in three dimensions seldom does any particular harm to any particular one of Miss Crothers's plays. If Miss Crothers knew but half as much about men as she knows about women, she would be one of our most important playwrights, as she is now quite our most amusing." Brooks Atkinson, writing in *The New York Times* (16 October 1932), saw the problem as more intricate: "if her characters . . . suddenly decided to 'follow after their own . . . desire' probably Mary Howard, novelist, would take Rogers Woodruff, publisher, away from his wife for good, all and evil." Crothers, he continues, subordinates her characters "to the wisdom and tolerance of her ideas. What makes 'When Ladies Meet' so satisfying for an evening in the theatre and for a tiff over the coffee cups . . . is the gusto of Miss Crothers's thinking." The 1933 motion-picture version of the play starred Myrna Loy, Robert Montgomery, and Alice Brady.

Crothers spent several unhappy months in 1934–1935 in Hollywood and asked that her name be withdrawn from the movie adaptation of *No More Ladies* (1935), based on A. E. Thomas's play. She was happier with *Splendor* (1935), an adaptation of her "House of Larrimore," an unproduced stage play.

She was delighted to return to Broadway with the production of *Susan and God,* which was named the outstanding play of the season by the Theatre Club. Although the setting is familiar, Susan Trexel is a complex, fascinating creation. The play opens at Irene Burroughs's elegant country house; Susan's rich, sophisticated friends are awaiting her return from England, where she encountered a new, evangelical religion. An alcoholic husband who adores her and an awkward, homely daughter who spends most of the year in boarding school have left her dissatisfied with her marriage. She has given herself wholeheartedly to this new faith. When she arrives, she insists that her friends confess their failings to each other to "save" them from living unexamined lives. They find her annoying, especially when she homes in on uncomfortable issues. They play a practical joke on her, convincing her that she has healing power. The only convert she makes is Barry, her husband, who swears he will remain sober if only she will return home.

The results are visible in act 3. With her mother's new interest, Blossom has become popular and attractive. Barry has kept his word, but Susan encourages him to spend time with Charlotte, a golfing friend, while she coordinates a conference in Newport for the new movement. The logistical conflict between the conference and her daughter's birthday forces her to make a choice. There is a slight dramatic crisis when Barry vanishes upon learning that Susan plans to testify to his transformation not as proof of his love but as a demonstration of her healing powers. After much pacing and tension, Susan realizes how much she cares for him, and Barry, who had been driving aimlessly for hours, returns.

Critics read Susan as immature, spoiled, and delusional, a woman who follows trends to escape from her problems. Stark Young, writing in the *New Republic* (27 October 1937), was the only commentator to believe that Susan's conversion was genuine. Modern readers find it easier to perceive her need to engage in work–rather than play tennis and drink like her friends–as a hunger for recognition beyond her role of wife and mother. This interpretation links the play to *He and She,* but the nature of Susan's pursuit permits a great deal of ambiguity.

The impetus for the comedy had little to do with gender roles and shows how distant Crothers's vision was from such issues. In an article titled "Why Did I Write *Susan and God,*" published in *Susan and God: A Magazine of the Play,* the author explained her distress over global discord, "private fights . . . raging in various places on the earth . . . death in the morning and evening and night . . . more capitulation to evil." A "radiant" character, "prattling in a new way about old truths," God, and the Bible, entered Crothers's "house," and she decided to create a play. She believed all that Susan–"foolish and wise, selfish and generous"–says, "though not quite as she says it," and had the reformer argue that only a return to goodness would stop war. The comedy was a popular success, with a run of 288 performances. Some of the appeal was Gertrude Lawrence's interpretation of the role of Susan, her $5,000 wardrobe for the production, and Jo Mielziner's set. It was made into a movie with a screenplay by Anita Loos and, as *The New York Times* reported on 8 June 1938, was the first play to be televised. It grossed more than $1 million.

Crothers seemed indefatigable as she juggled theatrical success with public service. From 1932 to 1951 she was the president of the Stage Relief Fund, a creation of the United Theatre Relief Committee, which was formed during the Great Depression. In 1940 she helped found and direct the British War Relief Society's American Theatre Wing, with two thousand members nationally. The organization is best known for its Stage Door Canteens, established in 1942 to assist wounded veterans.

A prolific playwright, Crothers also has a body of minor work. *The Heart of Paddy Whack* (1914) is a romantic comedy set in Ireland. *Old Lady 31* (1916) is a highly sentimental play redeemed by Crothers's stage savvy: it features three romances (two geriatric, one young), much bickering, and cross-dressing. This story of an indigent elderly couple who avoid separation when the husband becomes the thirty-first boarder at a woman's home offered aging actors such meaty roles that she could find few young performers who did not suffer by comparison. *Mother Carey's Chickens* (1917), adapted by Crothers and Kate Douglas Wiggin from Wiggin's 1910 novel, is a sentimental comedy about an indigent widow who returns with her family to her maternal home and finds happiness. The 1938 movie version featured Ruby Keeler and Walter Brennan. *Once upon a Time* (1918) is the story of a westerner who travels east to market his invention, which cost him ten years of privation and dedication. Although he is duped by corrupt businessmen, he rediscovers a lost love and is content. The title of the play is almost self-mocking in its evocation of fairy-tale conventions. *39 East* (1919), a light comedy that ran for 160 performances, earned critical sneers for celebrating the naiveté of an ingenue who, fumbling through show business, is rescued by an fellow roomer in her boardinghouse, but Crothers liked the play. Her papers include detailed plans for turning the work into a musical. *Everyday* (1921) is another romantic comedy about love restoring value to a competitive world. *Venus* (1927) is a formulaic science-fiction fantasy about aviators who have returned from a planet where the inhabitants practice gender equality. To duplicate this arrangement on Earth, a group of volunteers take an experimental injection that renders males feminine and females masculine–with bizarre results. *Caught Wet* (1931) is both a comedy of manners and a whodunit, complete with missing pearls and two dramatic blackouts. "Bill Comes Home" (1945), about a shell-shocked veteran, and "My South Window" (1950) remain unproduced and in manuscript.

Crothers's writing was highly controlled. She would begin her dialogue only when she was sure how the play would end, opening late in the story line and trusting that the thesis would circumscribe the actions of the characters. Driven by dramatic inevitability, her plays necessarily climb and advance, so that the end of one act always pushes into the next. She was disciplined, writing quickly from 8:00 A.M. until noon, then revising more calmly in the afternoon, all on unlined yellow paper. She advised young playwrights to visit the theater constantly and to keep revising. Even though she claimed Anton Chekhov, J. M. Barrie, and George Bernard Shaw as influences, she believed that the box office ruled supreme, as she related in "The Theatre–The Greatest of All Arts," an undated clipping in the Schubert Archive: Broadway's approval was the measure of a play's success.

The confluence of minds and tastes yielded a judgment she considered fair because it *is* the consensus of a heterogeneous mass. There was no finer measure for the theatre professional.

Atkinson admired Crothers more as a director than a playwright. Claiming she was "the best director we have," he wrote that she could coach the performances of their careers from accomplished actors such as Walter Able. "When Miss Crothers," he wrote, "does her best work . . . the Hudson does not burst into flame. But everyone who loves the theatre feels in the royalest humor." She judged staging a play superior to writing one and argued that the true vision of a work could only be realized when the playwright was the director. In a 4 March 1931 interview with Marion Clyde McCarroll for the *New York Evening Post,* she compared directing to conducting an orchestra.

She was forward-looking, a strong proponent of the New Stagecraft and its practitioners, whom she felt brought a new creative enthusiasm to the production. She eliminated superfluous ornamentation and selected lines and colors carefully, so the set could interpret the mood. She eschewed special effects for lighting and sound. "More and more," she said during a 1919 interview titled "Miss Crothers Argues for the New Scenic Art," a clipping from the Schubert Archive, "we know that the imagination of the audience is kindled as much by suggestion in stage settings as it is by suggestion in acting, and that the more feeling of beauty we arouse in the audience and the less of absolute material we put on the stage the greater our achievement."

In a ceremony at the White House, Eleanor Roosevelt presented the playwright with the 1938 Chi Omega National Achievement Award, an honor granted to American women of notable accomplishments in the professions, public affairs, arts, letters, business and finance, or education. John Golden, with whom she had produced many plays, was a speaker at the occasion and praised her indomitable spirit: "She began at a time when dramatists were cheap and women dramatists barely tolerated." In her own acceptance speech she defined the Stanhope-Wheatcroft years as "an experience of inestimable value because the doors of the theatre are very tightly closed to women in the work of directing and staging plays." At other times she mentioned her gratitude to Mrs. Wheatcroft and Maxine Elliott. She told writer Djuna Barnes in an interview for *Theatre Guild Magazine* (May 1931): "I should have been longer about my destiny if I had had to battle with men alone."

Nine years later, in 1940, Ida Tarbell included her in a list of the "Fifty Foremost Women of the United States." She was elected to the National Institute of Arts and Letters and was a founding member of PEN. She belonged to the Society of American Dramatists and the Authors' League of America. Considered an expert on the American woman, she was much in demand as a speaker.

Crothers never married. She died at Roadside, her fifty-acre estate in Redding, Connecticut, on 5 July 1958 from a heart ailment.

Although she created no masterpiece, Rachel Crothers's body of work forms a major contribution to American drama. One reason for her neglect is that most of the plays are out of print. She was a key playwright, director, and producer during the decades that created contemporary American drama, however. As a writer she persisted in keeping the American woman center stage, although her own conservatism and the nature of her genre kept her from championing many of the freedoms gained by the feminists of her time. She added new dimensions to the quintessential American theme of the independent girl, which stretches from the writings of Alexis de Tocqueville and Henry James through Eugene O'Neill and F. Scott Fitzgerald to playwrights Beth Henley and Wendy Wasserstein. As a director, she proved that a woman could be a successful creative force in the theater at a time when even theater management positions for women were rare. She championed the New Stagecraft and developed the talents of the finest American performers and designers. Crothers did not have the vision of Henrik Ibsen, the satirical daring of Shaw, or the tragic insight of Tennessee Williams. Her themes were too small for greatness. She wanted commercial success and learned quickly to tailor the plays to audience expectations, but her dramaturgy, bold, language, and confrontational scenes make her a writer's writer. She was a consummate woman of the theater.

Interviews:
Ada Patterson, "Woman Must Live Out Her Destiny," *Theatre,* 11 (May 1910): 134, 136, xxiv;

"A Little Journey," *Hearst's Magazine,* August 1919;

"Miss Crothers Argues for the New Scenic Art," clipping, 1919, Shubert Archive;

Ruth Brownlow, "Rachel Crothers Gives Her Views of the Problems Faced Today by the Modern Girl," *New York Evening Telegram,* 22 May 1923, p. 18;

Marion Clyde McCarroll, "Directing a Play Is Like Directing an Orchestra, Says Rachel Crothers Rehearsing Her 23rd Production," *New York Evening Post,* 4 March 1931;

Henry Albert Phillips, "Rachel Crothers Talks of Her Plays," *New York Herald Tribune,* 15 March 1931, VIII: 2, 5;

Djuna Barnes, "The Tireless Rachel Crothers," *Theatre Guild Magazine,* 8 (May 1931): 17–18;

Charlotte Hughes, "Women Play-makers," *New York Times Magazine,* 4 May 1941, pp. 10–11, 27.

Bibliography:

Colette Lindroth, *Rachel Crothers: A Research and Production Sourcebook* (Westport, Conn.: Greenwood Press, 1995).

References:

Irving Abrahamson, "The Career of Rachel Crothers in the American Drama," dissertation, University of Chicago, 1956;

Helen Krich Chinoy and Linda Walsh Jenkins, eds., *Women in American Theatre: Careers, Images, Movements* (New York: Crown, 1981), pp. 137–144;

Eleanor Flexner, *American Playwrights, 1918–1938: The Theatre Retreats from Reality* (Freeport, N.Y.: Books for Libraries Press, 1966), pp. 239–248;

Lois C. Gottlieb, *Rachel Crothers* (Boston: Twayne, 1979);

Brenda Murphy, "Feminism and the Marketplace: The Career of Rachel Crothers," in *The Cambridge Companion to American Women Playwrights,* edited by Murphy (Cambridge & New York: Cambridge University Press, 1999), pp. 82–97;

Arthur H. Quinn, "Rachel Crothers and the Feminine Criticism of Life," in his *A History of the American Drama From the Civil War to the Present Day,* volume 2 (New York: Appleton-Century-Crofts, 1936), pp. 50–61;

Yvonne Shafer, *American Women Playwrights, 1900–1950* (New York: Peter Lang, 1995), pp. 15–35;

Agnes Smith, "Rachel Crothers—Her Own World Court," *Morning Telegraph,* 29 April 1923, p. 3.

Papers:

The Crothers Collection at the Bloomington Public Library in Bloomington, Illinois, includes clippings related to Rachel Crothers from the *Bloomington Daily Pantagraph,* dated from 1893 through 1932. The Illinois State Normal University Library houses three volumes of scrapbooks, as well as typescripts, clippings, and correspondence. The McLean County Museum of History of Bloomington houses clippings and other historical documents relating to the Crothers family. The Theatre Collection of the Museum of the City of New York houses typescripts, letters, clippings, awards, memorabilia, and "The Box in the Attic," an unpublished draft of Crothers's autobiography. The Billy Rose Theatre Collection and the Burnside-Frohman Collection of the New York Public Library for the Performing Arts house clippings, photographs, programs, and typescripts; the Robinson Locke Collection houses scrapbooks of clippings filed under performers' names. The Shubert Archive of New York City houses typescripts, contracts, photographs, programs, clippings, correspondence, and press releases.

Mart Crowley
(21 August 1935 –   )

Kathleen M. Gough
University of California, Berkeley

See also the Crowley entry in *DLB 7: Twentieth-Century American Dramatists.*

PLAY PRODUCTIONS: *The Boys in the Band,* New York, Theatre Four, 14 April 1968; London, Wyndham's, 11 February 1969;

Remote Asylum, Los Angeles, Ahmanson Theatre, 1 December 1970;

A Breeze From the Gulf, New Hope, Pa., Bucks County Playhouse, February 1973; New York, Eastside Playhouse, 15 October 1973;

The Spirit of It All [Avec Schmaltz], Williamstown, Mass., Williamstown Theatre Festival, 11 August 1984;

For Reasons That Remain Unclear, Olney, Md., Olney Theatre, 12 November 1993;

The Men from the Boys [staged reading], Sag Harbor, N.Y., Bay Street Theatre, 23 October 1999.

BOOKS: *The Boys in the Band* (New York: Farrar, Straus & Giroux, 1968; London: Secker & Warburg, 1969);

A Breeze From the Gulf (New York: Farrar, Straus & Giroux, 1974);

Three Plays (Los Angeles: Alyson Publications, 1996)—includes *The Boys in the Band, A Breeze From the Gulf,* and *For Reasons That Remain Unclear.*

PRODUCED SCRIPTS: *The Boys in the Band,* motion picture, Cinema Center Films, 1970;

There Must Be a Pony, adapted from James Kirkwood Jr.'s novel, television, 5 October 1986;

Bluegrass, adapted from Borden Deal's novel, television, 28 February 1988;

People Like Us, adapted by Crowley and Kathleen A. Shelley from Dominick Dunne's novel, television, 13 May 1990;

Remember, adapted by Crowley, Shelley List, Jonathan Estrin, and John Herzfeld from Barbara Taylor Bradford's novel, television, 24 October 1993;

Hart to Hart: Harts in High Season, television, 24 March 1996.

Mart Crowley (*from John L. DiGaetani,* A Search for Postmodern Theater, *1991)*

OTHER: Kay Thompsen, *Eloise Takes a Bawth,* edited by Crowley (New York: Simon & Schuster, 2002).

On 14 April 1968 Mart Crowley's *The Boys in the Band* opened Off-Broadway at Theatre Four on West 55th Street. It was the first successfully produced American play that openly and unapologetically portrayed gay characters and gay lifestyles. Clive Barnes, writing for *The New York Times* (15 April 1968), said it "is not a play about a homosexual, but a play that takes the homosexual milieu, the homosexual way of life, totally for granted and uses it as a valid basis for human experience." Prior to the production of *The Boys in the Band*, plays that addressed homosexuality did so by incorporating the incidental gay character functioning on the periphery of society, by making homosexuality the "big surprise in the third act," or, as Stanley Kauffmann wrote in his landmark *New York Times* editorial "Homosexual Drama and Its Disguises" (23 January 1966), by disguising homosexuality under the auspices of heterosexual relationships (as portrayed in the plays of purported homosexual dramatists Tennessee Williams, Edward Albee, and William Inge). Kauffmann posited that if the homosexual "is to write of his experience, he must invent a two-sex version of the one-sex experience that he really knows. It is we who insist on it, not he." Yet, Crowley did what no other playwright had attempted: he challenged the normative response to how homosexuality is perceived in society and on stage by portraying his characters not as liminal figures constantly moving between two worlds but as central figures whose lives are presented with no explanation and no apology. The playwright was seemingly indifferent to how his play would be received by both gay and straight audiences; but as its Off-Broadway revival in 1996 shows, the work continues to draw attention more than three decades later. In its "end-of-the-century" issue (8 June 1998) *Time* magazine called *The Boys in the Band* one of "six landmarks of (modern) Drama," praising the play for giving "honest expression to the sensibilities tht so often inform (gay) theatre today." Crowley has written five other plays since *The Boys in the Band*, as well as many television treatments and screenplays. *The Boys in the Band*, however, remains Crowley's seminal work.

Edward Martino Crowley was born on 21 August 1935 in Vicksburg, Mississippi, to Edward Joseph Crowley and Pauline Husbands Crowley. He grew up an only child in a middle-class, Southern Catholic family. His father owned a tavern and poolroom. His mother suffered from a mental disorder, became addicted to pills and liquor, and was in and out of mental institutions later in her life. Little is written about Crowley's early life except what can be found, fictionalized yet thinly disguised, in his plays (most notably *A Breeze From the Gulf,* 1973). Although Crowley dramatizes the many "demons" that haunted his past, using description that can be torturous and claustrophobic, he is also capable of revealing the humor of otherwise destructive situations. "My parents were remarkably funny people," he recalled in an unpublished 1999 interview. He believes the family's humor about their own shortcomings was what saved all of them from sudden death.

In 1953 Crowley graduated from St. Aloysius School, where he had attended both grammar and high school, and left Vicksburg to enroll at The Catholic University of America in Washington, D.C. He joined the drama department in the School of Speech and Drama; as quoted in a personal interview, he knew he "wasn't an actor, didn't have the personality for a director, but had a talent for scene design." It was years before his interests turned to playwriting. During Christmas break in 1955, however, Crowley had a brief encounter that proved to be portentous. Some family friends who ran the restaurant "Doe's Eat Place" in Greenville, Mississippi, told Crowley that some movie people had come in to eat and that they were in town filming Tennessee Williams's *Baby Doll* (1956). When Crowley found out that Elia Kazan was directing the movie, he drove to Greenville to meet him. Kazan was so taken with Crowley that he wrote a pass on a napkin so that Crowley could watch the shoot, and the director told the young man that when he finished school he should come to New York, and Kazan would see what he could do about helping Crowley find work.

After graduating from Catholic University in 1957 Crowley did move to New York, where he found work as a production assistant on various movies, including the 1960 adaptation of John O'Hara's 1935 novel *Butterfield 8,* with Elizabeth Taylor. One night shortly after production for *Butterfield 8* had started, Crowley was walking home from the set and encountered Kazan, who recognized Crowley as well and asked him why he had not called. Kazan had just formed New Town Productions and was preparing to shoot *Splendor in the Grass* (1961), and he offered Crowley a job. Crowley gave notice to *Butterfield 8* and served as the sole production assistant for *Splendor in the Grass,* which starred Natalie Wood and Warren Beatty. Wood became a faithful friend and confidante to Crowley until her death.

After wrapping up *Splendor in the Grass,* Kazan planned to disband New Town Productions. Since Crowley needed to find work, Wood suggested that if he were serious about being a writer he should come with her to Los Angeles. She offered him a job as her personal assistant, a place to live in the apartment above her garage, and help in getting an agent for his writing through the William Morris Agency.

After the filming of *Splendor in the Grass* was completed, Crowley left New York and flew to Los Angeles. The time between 1960 and 1967 was full of projects for him, but most soon fell apart. His first screenplay for 20th Century-Fox, titled "Cassandra at the Wedding," was adapted from a novel of the same title by Dorothy Baker. Two weeks into filming, tensions between the director and actors shut down the project, and the movie was never produced.

Next, there was an offer to rewrite a television pilot for star Bette Davis. The movie diva liked his writing; however, she was not willing to commit to the long hours needed to shoot a weekly television series. This project also disbanded, and Crowley was once again without work. He was offered a job writing for a small spin-off movie Western titled "Fade-In"; however, he was so unhappy with the project that he fought to get his name taken off the credits.

In the midst of these failed projects Crowley also had his mind on Kauffmann's editorial "Homosexual Drama and Its Disguises," which had appeared in *The New York Times*. In a 1993 interview Crowley recounted that at the time he was thinking: "'Well, why *doesn't* someone write a play in which there are gay men who are just gay men?' And then I said, 'Well, why not me?'" Crowley admitted he "had nothing to lose . . . No one I knew had written this 'uncloseted' play. Some people wouldn't speak to me anymore. Some wouldn't understand it. And most would think I was nuts. But I was broke and depressed."

In the summer of 1967, desperate and in need of cash, Crowley sublet his apartment and lived off the money while house-sitting for friends in a Beverly Hills mansion. He had a vague idea of a play he wanted to write, so he started scribbling notes in bed one morning. In five weeks Crowley had finished all but the last scene of *The Boys in the Band*.

One New York agent told Crowley she was embarrassed by the play and could not send it out with her name on it. Then Richard Barr decided to produce it at a playwright's workshop that he was running with Albee in the Village. Robert Moore was chosen as the director. The initial run was extended from five to seven days, and the play was moved to Theatre Four, where it remained for almost three years, thus becoming one of the most successful nonmusicals of the twentieth century.

Crowley had first thought of setting the play in a gay bar and calling it "The Birthday Party," but Harold Pinter had used the title first. Crowley then decided on setting the party in a living room and calling it *The Boys in the Band*. The play opens in a fashionable New York apartment where Michael, a man in his early thirties, is preparing a birthday party for his friend Harold. As John Loughery writes in *The Other Side of Silence: Men's Lives and Gay Identities: A Twentieth Century History* (1998), "The party is the excuse to bring together several men who don't so much represent a cross-section of gay life in New York as a plausibly diverse circle of friends and acquaintances."

Program cover for the 1969 London production of the play
Time *magazine called one of the "six landmarks" of twentieth-century drama (Bruccoli Clark Layman Archives)*

Michael, loosely based on Crowley, is the bitchy party host and a self-proclaimed spoiled brat. He is a guilt-ridden lapsed Catholic who blames his problems on his parents, who he believed never let him grow up—particularly his mother, who made him into her "girlfriend dash lover." Similarly, Michael's former boyfriend Donald tries to work through his relationship with his own mother, who he believed loved him more when he failed and is thus the cause of his failure at this point. Hank, a teacher, and Larry, an artist, are a couple struggling with Larry's proclivity toward an "open" relationship and Hank's desire for monogamy. Bernard, the most stable of the group and also the most difficult to figure out, is the only African American at the party. He seems to be silenced throughout much of the play, and the audience is given little information about how he views his place in a society that is both homophobic and racist. Harold, the birthday boy, is the most outwardly self-loathing; he hates his appearance and refers to himself as an "ugly, pockmarked Jew fairy."

Emory, a decorator, is perhaps the most interesting and complex character. In light of the Stonewall uprising in the East Village (in which a mob led mostly by drag queens rebelled against the deplorable treatment of the gay community by attacking the police who had raided the Stonewall Inn bar) fourteen months after the premiere of *The Boys in the Band*, Crowley's creation of Emory seems most prescient. Emory is certainly the most effeminate and seems to represent the stereotype of how society defines all gay men. Yet, he is also the most self-actualized. When Michael self-loathingly discusses his "sin," Emory quickly replies, "It depends on what you think sin is." He realizes he should not have to be ashamed of his identity, but society has failed to understand how heterosexuality has been, historically, constructed as the "norm" and homosexuality as deviant.

When Alan, Michael's straight friend from college, arrives at the party quite by accident (possibly seeking advice for marital woes), he makes each man confront his own hatred—of himself and of the society that fosters their feelings of shame. At the end of act 1 Alan punches Emory while yelling "I'll kill you, you goddamn little mincing swish! You goddamn freak! FREAK! FREAK!"

In an attempt to "out" Alan as gay and seek revenge for his outburst, Michael presses his guests to participate in a party game in which everyone must "call on the telephone the *one person* we truly believe we have loved." After the others have made calls that have left them humiliated or depressed, Michael forces Alan to make a call. He gives Alan the number of a college friend whom he believes Alan loved but broke away from when he found out the friend was gay. Alan, however, calls his wife, Fran, to say he loves her and that he is returning home. After the others leave, Michael realizes he has gone too far in taunting Alan, and his own self-hatred returns. In perhaps the most often-quoted phrase of the play, Michael says to Donald, "who is it that once said 'you show me a happy homosexual and I'll show you a gay corpse?'" The play ends with Donald asking Michael if he knew why Alan had wanted to talk to him. Michael says maybe it was because he had left Fran. When Donald says, "I wonder why he had left," Michael recollects, "As my father said to me when he died in my arms, 'I don't understand any of it. I never did.'"

Although the play ends on a somber note, it is not a tortured portrait of gay life. Ultimately the play is not so much a study of gay male life in the 1960s as it is the story of six friends who experience pain and frustration but are not without laughter. As Loughery argues, "For all the gloom that underlies Harold's ill-fated birthday party, no one—including Michael—is really any more lost or self-absorbed than countless other malcontents of American realist drama." Moreover, although in a moment of frustration Michael spouts off the line about the "gay corpse," he is also the one who earlier replies to Harold's jokes about suicide: "It's not always like it happens in plays, not all faggots bump themselves off at the end of the story."

There were many skeptics who believed that the public would not be ready for a play like *The Boys in the Band*. Even some of Crowley's best friends thought it would be a tough sell. Yet, a play that even two years earlier would have seemed impossible to produce was, by 1968, lauded as one of the best plays of the season. After opening night Barnes remarked that *The Boys in the Band* made Albee's *Who's Afraid of Virginia Woolf* (1962) "look like a vicarage tea party" and stated that "the power of the play . . . is the way in which it remorselessly peels away the pretensions of its characters and reveals a pessimism so uncompromising in its honesty that it becomes in itself an affirmation of life." Rex Reed, also writing for *The New York Times* (12 May 1968), observed that "the 'boys' in Mart Crowley's band are human beings and, like human beings, they have fun, too. They don't kill themselves or want to get married or spend the rest of their lives tortured by conscience. The only way they 'pay' is to know who they are. Then they go to bed with a hangover and start all over again, like life." The play was applauded nationwide, and in 1969 Crowley was awarded the first Los Angeles Drama Critics Circle Award.

Although *The Boys in the Band* achieved artistic and commercial success quickly, after the Stonewall uprising it was called "a period piece." Crowley's depiction of gay life as he experienced it was attacked from both inside and outside the gay community. In fact, Barnes, who had praised the play at its opening, stated two years later in *The New York Times* (18 April 1970) that he "did not believe that all homosexuals are nearly as miserable as Mr. Crowley would have us believe." In just two years critics and audiences had gone from viewing *The Boys in the Band* as a drama based on the specific experiences of a small pocket of individuals to making it a macrolevel sociological study of gay male life. In 1970, with the release of the movie version of *The Boys in the Band,* for which Crowley wrote the screenplay, there were demonstrations in Los Angeles outside the production studio. In *The Other Side of Silence,* Loughery writes, "One sign captured the essence of all the grievances: '*The Boys in the Band:* Best Gay Movie of 1947.' It was the temper of the times [that] demanded that Crowley's characters be taken as representatives of their kind rather than quirky, suffering individuals; straight audiences were still too eager to see the homosexual as grotesque in a category of his own, and gays wanted role models."

Just after *The Boys in the Band* completed its run in New York, Crowley's next play, *Remote Asylum*, premiered at the Ahmanson Theatre in Los Angeles on 1 December 1970. The action of the play is based on the life that Crowley observed among his friends and acquaintances in Hollywood while he was working as Wood's personal secretary. The play takes place in a contemporary mansion on the island of Acapulco and dramatizes the lives of five rather unlikable characters: Dinah, a movie star; Tom, her tennis-pro lover; Irene, an aging harridan; Ray, Irene's terminally ill husband; and Michael—the same guilt-ridden gay Southern Catholic who appears in *The Boys in the Band,* although this incarnation of the character seems to predate, in age and temperament, the Michael of the first play.

All of the characters seem to have made this physical journey to the island in lieu of a far less definitive and more metaphorical venture that they wish or need to take. Dinah needs the love of her two children, who are now with their father; Tom needs his former wife; Irene needs the companionship of her terminally ill and seemingly mute husband, Ray; and Michael needs to come to terms with both his past and his sexuality. Yet, the play does not really leave the audience with much to think about. In the end Ray dies, and everyone decides to leave the island, but it is not clear what, if anything, has been resolved.

The problems with the play as a text are related to the problems of its production. Two weeks into a five-week rehearsal, the director, José Quintero, resigned because of illness. Edward Peron replaced him and took on the arduous task of pulling together the fragmented direction and the script into a cohesive whole. Looking at the script twenty-five years later, Crowley said that it still showed marks of hurried revisions, of cutting and pasting—that "it is a script in need of a good editor." To date, there is no definitive edition of *Remote Asylum,* and it will probably remain unpublished.

Because *Remote Asylum* was following the success of *The Boys in the Band,* its opening was covered as if it were a New York debut, and Dick Adler, a drama critic from *The New York Times,* was sent to Los Angeles to report on the premiere. Adler noted in his 13 December 1970 review that *Remote Asylum* was "an event that did nothing to enrich the reputation of anyone concerned." Dan Sullivan of the *Los Angeles Times* (3 December 1970) stated that "the impulse it most consistently obeys is to be soap opera, the dull psychoanalytic kind where the action must stop for a discussion of one's castrating mother, one's too-soon-dead father, one's unfortunate luck at not being invited to parties as a little girl." The fact that the opening received nationwide attention was "unheard of at the time," says Crowley. In a period when *The New York Times* rarely covered theater outside of New York, and the theater scene was more regional, the widespread disparaging coverage of *Remote Asylum*—which was still a work in progress—virtually ensured the demise of the play. The play continued, unrehearsed, for seven weeks with a "trapped audience" at the Ahmanson, where ticket sales were on a subscription basis. Producers refused to continue any further financial backing, and the play has never been performed again.

Although it is clear from both the reviews and interviews with Crowley that the play was fraught with trouble from the beginning, there is another factor in its downfall. However underprepared the play was, it had attracted a prominent cast, including Anne Francis, William Shatner, Arthur O'Connell, and Nancy Kelly; with those names on the marquee along with Crowley's, it would have been difficult to keep curious theatergoers away. The necessary discretion needed for the successful launching of any new production was overshadowed by the economics of show business. There was simply too much hype surrounding the project. Thus, the early success of *The Boys in the Band* ultimately impeded the success of *Remote Asylum*.

The experience of *Remote Asylum* both infuriated and paralyzed Crowley; he recollects that he went into a decline for almost three years: "I had a difficult time even writing my own name again." But *The Boys in the Band* remained a huge success both nationally and internationally. It was produced all over the world and gained additional audiences with the movie version in 1970. In a *New York Times* review (18 March 1970) Vincent Canby shares many of the same criticisms as the protesters. He states, "watching the film version of 'The Boys in the Band,' which opened yesterday at the Loew's State I and Tower East theaters, I experienced the same sensation I'd had when I saw the Off Broadway play two years ago. It was a feeling of time disorientation, as if, in 1970, I were looking at a well-made Broadway play from the late thirties or early forties, something on the order of Clare Booth's 'The Women' or Joseph Fields's 'The Doughgirls.'" Although the depression following the failure of *Remote Asylum* was real, there was still considerable cash flow from the success of *The Boys in the Band*. Thus, "suffering pangs of failure," Crowley left for Paris, where he took an apartment for three months before heading to the south of France, where he could "drink a lot and think a lot." During this time he knew

Dust jacket for the play in which Crowley drew on his life with his parents in Vicksburg, Mississippi (Richland County Public Library)

he wanted to write an autobiographical play about his family, but the idea was painful. His mother was still alive, and he did not know if he could write the play he wanted to write. He returned from France empty-handed and spent the next two years in New York.

In 1973 he left New York for San Juan, Puerto Rico, where he stayed for three months. During this time he wrote *A Breeze From the Gulf*–a fictionalized autobiography of his life with his parents in Vicksburg, in the form of a memory play. Before its New York opening, *A Breeze From the Gulf* had a workshop production in Bucks County, Pennsylvania, that Crowley said was "superior to the New York production." The Bucks County production was staged with a scaled-down, minimalist set: "All that was really needed were levels and lights, the elaborate staging and scene design in New York took away from the play." *A Breeze From the Gulf* opened at the Eastside Playhouse in New York on 15 October 1973 under the direction of John Going, a longtime friend and former classmate of Crowley's at Catholic University. After six weeks in this Off-Broadway playhouse, the show closed.

The play, which takes place over two acts and ten years, is fashioned similarly to Williams's *The Glass Menagerie* (1945) in its use of "memory" as a thematic trope and in the development of the character Michael, who appears to share as many similarities with Tom Wingfield from *The Glass Menagerie* as he does with the author's own life. This time Michael is younger, and the play depicts his relationship with his parents, Loraine and Teddy Connelly. As the stage notes indicate, "because of the convention of the play, because he 'remembers' the two characters, he is outside of time even though he appears in the scene."

Act 1 begins when Michael is fifteen years old. Teddy has just bought a house for his family, and this house–which embodies the family's isolation from society and Michael's consequent claustrophobia–is where the entire play takes place. Teddy is a successful businessman and an alcoholic, while Loraine is a dope fiend and controlling mother with a penchant for romanticism that resembles Amanda Wingfield's in *The Glass Menagerie*. Therefore, Michael is subjected to a life he would never choose for himself. This sense of alienation is also indicated by the fact that Michael lacks even an accent that would place him in this small town in Mississippi. The stage notes indicate that from the beginning Michael walks through the play like "a stranger in a foreign country." Much like Tom in *The Glass Menagerie* and like Crowley himself, Michael finds solace only in movie houses and movie magazines.

Clearly, Teddy's alcoholism and his devout Catholicism are both sources for many of the wounds he inflicts on his family and himself; yet, Michael's relationship with Loraine is the one that provides the connections between Michael in *A Breeze From the Gulf* and the older Michael in *The Boys in the Band* who says that his mother made him into "her girlfriend dash lover." Michael's conversations with Loraine make it clear not only that she bathed with him past the age when it would be acceptable but also that he has to share a bedroom with her. Michael is the only thing Loraine thinks she can control, and she does her best to keep a tight rein on him.

In the last scene of act 1, Teddy, in a drunken rage, "grabs Loraine by both her arms and hurls her aside with such force that she is thrown to the floor. She screams." Michael, who up until this point has appeared quite docile and ineffective, "backs in Teddy's room, grabs the gin bottle, and cracks it over his [Teddy's] skull, crushing the bottle." With the sobs of the characters the scene goes to blackout.

Michael is in his early twenties and has just returned home from college when act 2 begins. Because he has had the opportunity to leave home and attend college in Washington, D.C., he finds it impossible to live in a world of lies when he returns home for summer vacation. Although in fits of angry dialogue Michael rages against the personal hell to which his parents have subjected him, the years have not been kind to Teddy or Loraine either. Loraine is in a sanatorium, which she continues to drift in and out of during the course of the play. Teddy now has health problems as well, presumably brought on from years of drinking. When he tells Michael "what your mother and I do to ourselves has nothing to do with *you*," Michael shouts back "But it does! I am included whether you want me to be or not! All the three of us do is torture each other. You call this home? A home to come home to? It's a nightmare!" When Teddy finally collapses of a heart attack, Michael tries to assuage his father's fear and his own by asking Teddy to pray the act of contrition with him. Teddy dies in Michael's arms as he says, "I don't understand any of it. I never did."

In the final scene of the play Michael is once again taking Loraine back to the sanatorium because of her addictions. Although harsh and hurtful words are exchanged between mother and son, Michael apologizes for his attack, and Loraine begs his forgiveness: "Please believe me when I say I never meant to hurt you—of all people. Or anyone, for that matter. And I *want* you to get as far away from all this as you can. There's no need of you grievin' your life away over my shortcomings." Just as with Teddy, there appears to be a reconciliation that does not bring about a sense of peace as much as it does the beginning of an understanding. Beneath all of the hurt that the individual family members inflict on each other, the intention was love. Father, mother, and son were all trying to come to grips with a world that had delivered more disappointment than hope.

The reviews after the play opened at the Eastside Playhouse were ambivalent—critics wanted to praise the honesty of the play while discussing its lack of form. Barnes wrote in *The New York Times* (16 October 1973) that "it had some extremely strong performances and a great deal of fierce family writing in it. There were some scenes—all played to explosion point—that had considerable power, and the play ended far better than it began. Yet, it had the air of a work in progress." Walter Kerr remarked in the same newspaper (21 October 1973) that it "is so honestly written, and so perfectly performed that you cling to it for dear life, as though the very act of clinging might finally give it a shape."

With two consecutive plays that were commercially unsuccessful Crowley "really didn't have any ideas for anything." He realized he was getting pigeonholed as a naturalistic writer and decided to try an experimental play under the working title "Parted Curtains," but agents and producers were wary of taking it on. He stayed in New York for another year before getting a job for Columbia Pictures, writing a script titled "Jane," which was to star Faye Dunaway. This project took Crowley to London for six months, but the picture was never made.

By 1979 Crowley left again for Paris. Shortly after his arrival, Wood and her husband, Robert Wagner, came for a visit. Wagner was starting the television series *Hart to Hart,* which was having difficulty taking shape. He encouraged Crowley to return to Los Angeles and work on it. Crowley agreed to try out the project, so he moved back to Los Angeles and into the apartment above Wood's garage and started to rewrite scripts. Crowley started as head story writer and executive script consultant, and after three episodes took over as sole producer. He went on to produce the series to critical acclaim for five years and ninety episodes. In 1981 Crowley was awarded the Arts and Entertainment Alumni Achievement Award from Catholic University for his work on stage and in movies and television.

After five years of producing *Hart to Hart* Crowley decided it was time to move on to another project, and he returned to playwriting. His next play, titled *Avec Schmaltz,* had its staged reading in the New Play Series at the Williamstown Theatre Festival in Williamstown, Massachusetts, on 11 August 1984, under the new title *The Spirit of It All,* a result of rewriting incurred by his experience at Williamstown. The play, which takes place between Connecticut and New York, dramatizes the life of a strong-willed divorced mother of two, Kit, played by Marsha Mason, who is trying to rebuild her life with a new lover, Nick, played by Frank Hankey; however, her former husband, played by James Naughton, is not completely out of the picture. Overall, it is a domestic drama in which a family must work to overcome their shortcomings and start over on different ground.

The cast also included Kiefer Sutherland as the son and Kevin Spacey as Colin, a family friend. The play was optioned by Warner Bros. for seven months under the title "Dance a Little Closer," and it seems to read better as a television treatment than a stage play. But neither project was ever produced, and the script remains unpublished.

Shortly following the staged reading of *Avec Schmaltz,* Crowley returned to screenwriting and in 1986 wrote the television-movie adaptation of James

Kirkwood Jr.'s 1960 novel, *There Must Be a Pony,* starring Wagner and Elizabeth Taylor. Crowley continued writing for television through the early 1990s when, once again, he returned to the stage, this time with *For Reasons That Remain Unclear,* which premiered at the Olney Theatre in Olney, Maryland, on 12 November 1993. Going returned as the director. Along with *The Boys in the Band* and *A Breeze From the Gulf* it completes Crowley's autobiographical trilogy—a trilogy published by Alyson Publications in 1996. Like the other two works, this tale, according to Crowley in the preface to his collected plays, was "pushed and pulled, fictionalized and dramatized and, yes, personalized." Crowley said in the same source that *For Reasons That Remain Unclear* was "the way I dreamt I'd exorcise my demons. And by finally being able to consider what happened and invent a way to put it down, I think I accomplished that."

The full-length (ninety-minute) one-act play takes place in Rome, where Patrick, a young screenwriter, encounters Conrad, a Catholic priest who had sexually molested him at the age of nine. Patrick recognizes Conrad immediately; however, the priest does not remember Patrick. When the latter invites Conrad back to his hotel room for a drink, the past relationship between the two men slowly begins to unfold.

Although their initial connection is unclear to the audience, it quickly becomes apparent that Patrick holds some sort of grudge against the priest. Patrick begins by offering some information about himself, but also corners Conrad into answering questions about his own background and his reasons for entering the priesthood. When Patrick mentions that he is from "a little cow track" in Mississippi, Conrad cannot believe the coincidence. He tells Patrick that he had been a teacher in Mississippi. When Patrick's silence over the nostalgic revisiting of the past turns icy and he admits obsessing over the events of his past, Conrad retorts, "in some cases I think it's better to forget and move on," to which Patrick replies, "The past, for me, is not a darkened stage whose players have vanished and are forgotten." From that point the play escalates toward revelations that Conrad could never have anticipated.

After Conrad has had more than a few drinks and is subtly suggesting his willingness for a sexual encounter with Patrick, the tables turn. As Patrick's fury toward the priest grows more evident, Conrad gets frightened and tries to leave. When Patrick reveals to Conrad his real identity, Conrad yells, "why have you come back?! To get even?" Patrick yells in turn: "Ask your all-knowing God that! Ask Him why, after all these years, He's permitted this curious little collision in the mad mix-up of streets in this ancient holy town!" Bewildered and scared, Conrad does not know if the encounter will turn violent. But for Patrick, an act of violence would be "too predictable" considering the situation. Instead, in an unpredictable move—one quite unexpected in the contemporary sensationalist tales of priests molesting young boys—Crowley gives the audience something far more profound when Patrick tells Conrad: "ask your God why He permitted you to be the first person to teach me what I thought was love?! *Love!*—For the first time in my life! And for the last time in my life!" Conrad then admits what he was going to tell Patrick earlier: that he, too, had been sexually abused by his mother. Yet, he admits that it makes no difference and that he still cannot comprehend why he did what he did. Patrick tells him not to bother, because "You can try, and all you'll get is a giant explosion, like the first blast of the universe. Something you simply cannot explain. In the end, whatever you figure out, whatever you really *crack,* just reassembles into a question mark as soon as you turn your head."

Crowley's complex dramatizations of these two characters avoids the usual stereotyping of such a scenario. In another unexpected move, Patrick forgives Conrad, who leaves with a sense that he has been absolved. Patrick, however, is the one most affected by the forgiveness, because he is the one who has been living with resentment and anger all of these years. When he does absolve Conrad, it is understood that he will also be able to release that veil of anger and hatred and move forward.

Although the reviews for *For Reasons That Remain Unclear* were mixed, they were generally favorable. Lloyd Rose of *The Washington Post* (17 November 1993) wrote that "as ripped-from-the-headlines as a TV movie of the week, Crowley's script is almost as predictable. The surprise is that in the middle of the overwrought writing and dramatic posturing, there's real pain. . . . Crowley is more honest, and wiser about human nature than many playwrights." Although *For Reasons That Remain Unclear* never went on to a New York production, it continues to be performed at regional and university theaters around the country.

Perhaps it was the Broadway revival of *The Boys in the Band* at the WPA Theatre in June 1996 that rekindled Crowley's interest in his first and most famous (and infamous) play and incited him to try to write a sequel. By 1996 the fickle political climate had changed once again. This time, however, the climate proved positive for restaging *The Boys in the Band*. Historical distance from the early post-Stonewall criticism ensured that the play, according to Ben Bratley in *The New York Times* (21 June 1996), was no longer "the political embarrassment it was once vilified as being." Crowley said in a 1999 unpublished interview that the death of a friend on whom the character Larry from *The Boys in the Band* is based also made him start to think about writing a play that revisits the lives of the original characters. This sequel, *The Men from the Boys,* had its first staged reading on 23 October 1999 at the Bay Street Theatre in Sag Harbor, New York. The play is expected to open at the New Conservatory Theate Center in San Francisco on 26 October 2002.

Starting with the success of *The Boys in the Band* in 1968, Crowley's life and his work were placed at the center of political controversy. Despite Crowley's achievements as a screenwriter, television producer, and author of a variety of plays that cannot easily be pigeonholed as "gay drama," his first play marked him, categorically, through the rest of his career. "Gay playwright" and "homosexual spokesperson" were two of the labels that seemed to stick after the opening of *The Boys in the Band.* Yet, however limiting this categorization may seem to the playwright, who still resides in Los Angeles, *The Boys in the Band* was lauded as the start of the gay liberation movement in drama, and it certainly opened the floodgates for playwrights such as Terrence McNally, William Hoffman, Larry Kramer, and Harvey Fierstein, whose work would hardly be possible if it were not for *The Boys in the Band.* Years after seeing Crowley's controversial play, Neil Simon, as quoted in an interview with Richard Kramer for *The New York Times,* said that "'*The Boys in the Band* did for plays what *Oklahoma!* did for musicals.' . . . He went on to say that at the time he'd never seen such honesty on stage before." Mart Crowley has left an indelible mark not only as a leader in the gay liberation movement in drama but also as a creator of some compelling characters in American theater.

Interviews:

John L. DiGaetani, "Mart Crowley," in his *A Search for Postmodern Theater: Interviews with Contemporary Playwrights* (New York: Greenwood Press, 1991), pp. 48–53;

Richard Kramer, "A Play of Words about A Play," *New York Times,* 31 October 1993, II: H1+.

References:

James W. Carlsen, "Images of the Gay Male in Contemporary Drama," *Gayspeak: Gay Male and Lesbian Communication,* 16 (1981): 165–174:

Joe Carrithers, "The Audiences of *The Boys in the Band,*" *Journal of Popular Film and Television,* 23 (Summer 1995): 64–70;

John Loughery, "The Boys in the Band," in his *The Other Side of Silence: Men's Lives and Gay Identities: A Twentieth Century History* (New York: Holt, 1998), pp. 291–302.

William de Mille
(25 July 1878 – 5 March 1955)

Brian M. Amend
Lynchburg College

PLAY PRODUCTIONS: *The Forest Ring,* by de Mille and Charles Barnard, New York, Carnegie Lyceum, 20 December 1900;

Forest Flower, New York, Empire Theatre, 13 March 1902;

Strongheart, New York, Hudson Theatre, 30 January 1905;

The Genius, by de Mille and Cecil B. DeMille, New York, Bijou Theatre, 3 October 1906;

Classmates, by de Mille and Margaret Turnbull, New York, Hudson Theatre, 29 August 1907;

The Warrens of Virginia, New York, Belasco Theatre, 3 December 1907;

The Royal Mounted, by de Mille and Cecil B. DeMille, New York, Garrick Theatre, 6 April 1908;

The Land of the Free, by de Mille and Cecil B. DeMille, New Haven, Grand Opera House, 28 September 1910;

The Woman, New York, Theatre Republic, 19 September 1911;

Rollo: A Play of the Future, New York, Twelfth Night Club, 6 January 1912;

The Squealer, New York, Union Hall, 17 March 1913;

Food: A Tragedy of the Future, New York, Princess Theatre, 13 April 1913;

Poor Old Jim, New York, Odeon Theatre, 15 September 1913; New York, Waldorf Theatre, 9 May 1929;

After Five, by de Mille and Cecil B. DeMille, New York, Fulton Theatre, 29 October 1913.

BOOKS: *The Genius,* by de Mille and Cecil B. DeMille (New York: S. French, 1904);

Strongheart (New York: Rosenfield, 1904?);

The Truth of the Unreal: Notes on Certain Principles Underlying Stagecraft (New York: American Academy of Dramatic Arts, 1906);

Deceivers (New York: S. French, 1913);

Votes for the Fairies; The Christmas Spirit (New York: John Martin's House, 1913);

Food: A Tragedy of the Future (New York & London: S. French, 1914);

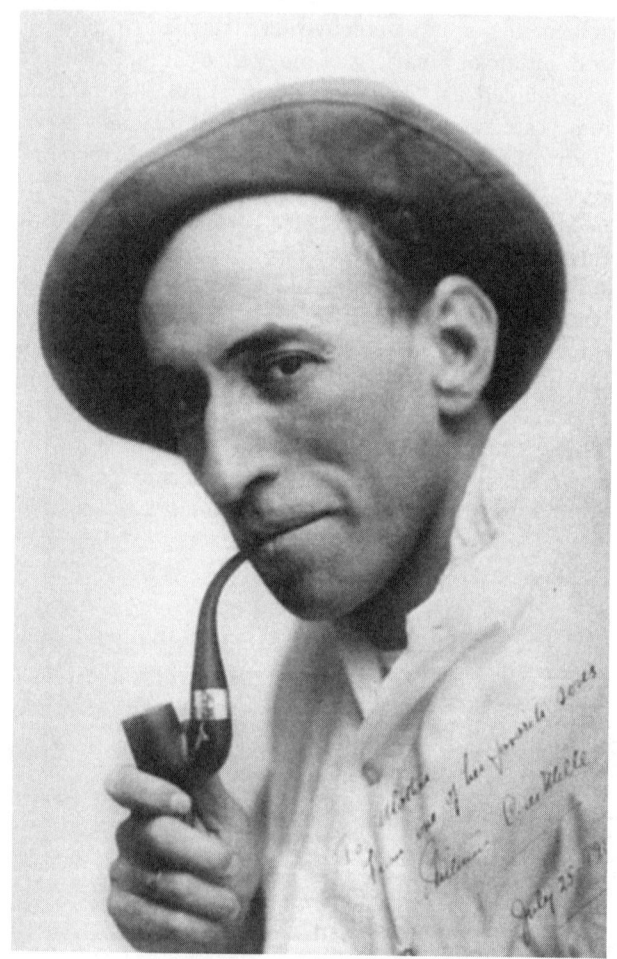

William de Mille, 1917 (from Anne Edwards, The DeMilles: An American Family, *1988)*

The Forest Ring (New York: Doran, 1914);

In 1999: A Problem Play of the Future (New York: S. French, 1914);

Poor Old Jim (New York: S. French, 1914);

The Forest Ring: A Play in Three Acts, by de Mille and Charles Bernard (New York & London: S. French, 1921);

My Country—So What? (New York: S. French, 1932);

Hollywood Saga (New York: Dutton, 1939).

PRODUCED SCRIPTS: *Classmates,* motion picture, Biograph / Klaw & Erlanger, 1914;

Cameo Kirby, motion picture, adapted by de Mille and Clara Beranger from the play by Booth Tarkington and Harry Leon Wilson, Jesse L. Lasky Feature Play Company, 1914;

After Five, motion picture, adapted from the play by de Mille and Cecil B. DeMille, Jesse L. Lasky Feature Play Company, 1915;

Carmen, motion picture, adapted from the novel by Prosper Mérimée, Jesse L. Lasky Feature Play Company, 1915;

The Explorer, motion picture, adapted from the novel by W. Somerset Maugham, Jesse L. Lasky Feature Play Company, 1915;

The Goose Girl, motion picture, adapted from the novel by Harold MacGrath, Jesse L. Lasky Feature Play Company, 1915;

The Governor's Lady, motion picture, adapted from the play by Alice Bradley, Jesse L. Lasky Feature Play Company, 1915;

The Puppet Crown, motion picture, adapted from the novel by MacGrath, Jesse L. Lasky Feature Play Company, 1915;

The Secret Orchard, motion picture, adapted from the play by Channing Pollock Sr., Jesse L. Lasky Feature Play Company, 1915;

Temptation, motion picture, adapted from the story by Hector Turnbull, Jesse L. Lasky Feature Play Company, 1915;

The Warrens of Virginia, motion picture, adapted from de Mille's play, Jesse L. Lasky Feature Play Company, 1915;

The Wild Goose Chase, motion picture, Jesse L. Lasky Feature Play Company, 1915;

The Woman, motion picture, adapted from de Mille's play, Jesse L. Lasky Feature Play Company, 1915;

Young Romance, motion picture, adapted from de Mille's play, Jesse L. Lasky Feature Play Company, 1915;

The Blacklist, motion picture, by de Mille and Marion Fairfax, Jesse L. Lasky Feature Play Company, 1916;

Joan the Woman, motion picture, by de Mille and Jeanie MacPherson, Cardinal Film / Paramount, 1916;

Maria Rosa, motion picture, adapted from the play by Wallace Gilpatrick, Ángel Guimerá, and Guido Marburg, Jesse L. Lasky Feature Play Company / Paramount, 1916;

The Ragamuffin, motion picture, Jesse L. Lasky Feature Play Company, 1916;

The World and the Woman, motion picture, by de Mille and Philip Lonergan, Pathé Exchange, 1916;

The Woman God Forgot, motion picture, by de Mille and Macpherson, Artcraft Pictures, 1917;

We Can't Have Everything, motion picture, adapted from the novel by Rupert Hughes, Artcraft Pictures, 1918;

For Better, for Worse, motion picture, adapted by de Mille and Macpherson from the play by Edgar Selwyn, Famous Players-Lasky, 1919;

Why Change Your Wife? motion picture, by de Mille, Sada Cowan, and Olga Printzlau, Artcraft Pictures, 1920;

The Warrens of Virginia, motion picture, adapted from de Mille's play, Fox Film, 1924;

The Splendid Crime, motion picture, by de Mille and Violet Clark, Famous Players-Lasky, 1926;

The Doctor's Secret, motion picture, adapted from the play by J. M. Barrie, Paramount-Famous Players-Lasky, 1929;

The Forest Ring, motion picture, adapted by de Mille from his and Charles Barnard's play, 1930;

Captain Fury, motion picture, by de Mille, Jack Jevne, and Grover Jones, Hal Roach / United Artists, 1939.

OTHER: *The Warrens of Virginia,* in *Monte Cristo as Played by James O'Neil and Other Plays,* edited by J. B. Russak (Princeton: Princeton University Press, 1941);

"Mickey Mouse versus Popeye," in *Hollywood Directors, 1914-1940,* compiled by Richard Koszarski (New York: Oxford University Press, 1976), pp. 295-298.

SELECTED PERIODICAL PUBLICATIONS–UNCOLLECTED: "The Drama and the University," *Columbia Alumni News,* 3, no. 12 (December 1911): 214-216;

"DeMille and the Movies," *Columbia Alumni News* (1914): 614;

"Our Commercial Drama," *Yale Review,* 4 (January 1915): 316-329;

"Movies Improve as Faults Are Recognized," in "Reviews and Interviews," edited by B. Raymond, *Columbia Spectator,* 6 January 1919;

"No More Adaptations: Famous Director Declares Himself Emphatically in Favor of the Original Story, Written for the Screen," *Photoplaywright,* 12 (February 1921): 34;

"The Audience and the Motion Pictures," *Drama,* 11 (July 1921): 344-346;

"The Motion Pictures from the Inside," *Story World and the Photodramatist* (March 1923): 51-59;

"Bigoted and Bettered Pictures," *Scribner's Magazine,* 76 (September 1924): 231–236;

"Prudes and Pictures," *Scribner's Magazine,* 81 (March 1927): 311–316;

"Talkie Technique," *American Cinematographer,* 9 (March 1929): 17;

"The Screen Speaks," *Scribner's Magazine,* 85 (April 1929): 367–373;

"Mores Are Not Made by Law," *Robert Wagner's Weekly,* 5 (4 July 1931);

"What's Wrong with These Pictures: A Distinguished Director Tells of Hollywood Suffering from Too Much Organization and Efficiency," *Liberty,* 10 (4 March 1933): 42–46;

"O Kay Mr. Wagley: A Famous Director Spins the Blithe Yarn—Which Maybe You Haven't Heard—of Rosie, Mr. Halloran's Hippo, and a $40,000 Foible in Filmland," *Liberty,* 12 (17 August 1935);

"Plow the Plays Under," *Stage,* 2 (June 1936): 36;

"Without the Fourth Wall," *Stage,* 2 (July 1936): 22;

"A Letter to David Belasco from William deMille," *Stage,* 2 (August 1936): 55;

"A Letter to Samuel Goldfish from William de Mille," *Stage,* 13 (1936).

William de Mille decided on a career in drama while attending Columbia University at the turn of the twentieth century. He pursued success in the New York theater world with vigor and received considerable acclaim until a variety of factors drew him into motion-picture production in 1914. Even there, the plays he had written and produced influenced the now-better-known contributions he made in Hollywood.

Anne Edwards reports in *The DeMilles: An American Family* (1988) that about the time William Churchill de Mille was born, on 25 July 1878, his father, Henry Churchill de Mille, was beginning to teach at Columbia Grammar School, and his mother, Beatrice de Mille, was establishing herself as a promoter of her husband's writing by selling one of his short stories to *Leslie's Weekly.* (She later performed a similar role for her sons.) By the time William's only brother, Cecil B. DeMille, was born in 1881, Henry was close to venturing into playwriting.

Henry de Mille died unexpectedly of typhoid in early 1893 at age thirty-nine. Edwards writes that his deathbed wish for his sons not to enter theater life succumbed immediately to exigency: "Daily for six weeks after Henry's death, Beatrice sat fourteen-year-old Bill down at his father's desk while the two attempted to complete Henry's play *The Promised Land.*" This attempt to shore up the family's finances was unsuccessful but may have prepared de Mille for his decision in his senior year of college at Columbia University to drop his engineering major and instead major in drama. Edwards notes that this choice was encouraged by his mother.

After graduating from Columbia University in 1900, de Mille studied at the American Academy of Dramatic Arts, from which he received a diploma in 1901. About this time, he also began reading German drama, which—according to Catherine Walker—he first encountered when he traveled to Germany in 1895 to study at a Realschule for a year. According to Edwards, de Mille derived from reading the German playwright Arthur Schnitzler "a quiet cynicism and a reminiscent moodiness" as well as a conviction that "the best stories were told simply and humanly." This last aspect of de Mille's work is frequently and briefly noted by movie historians, usually as an aside in a narration of his brother Cecil's motion-picture career. Kevin Brownlow's encapsulated assessment, coming at the end of a chapter on Cecil, is typical both in its brevity and its admiration: William, Brownlow states, "cared more for psychological reality than melodramatic action, and his style was as different from Cecil's as a miniaturist's from an epic painter."

By the time Cecil DeMille left for Hollywood in 1914, William de Mille was a well-established and popular New York playwright. He had been for some time following in the footsteps of their father, who enjoyed with his frequent collaborator, David Belasco, considerable popular success in the New York theater of the late nineteenth century. De Mille's first play, *The Forest Ring,* which he wrote with Charles Barnard, is a fairy tale in three acts, written for a young audience. It was first produced on 20 December 1900 at the Carnegie Lyceum. De Mille later reworked *The Forest Ring* as a novel, published in 1914. The play tells the story of a circle of fairies whom animals, but almost no humans, can see. When hunter Hank Struble falls asleep in a wooded area of the Adirondack Mountains where the fairies dwell, various animals petition the leader of the fairies, Arbutus, to slay Hank because he has captured three bear cubs and is currently hunting their mother, Ursa. Arbutus instead sends a dream to Hank that frightens him into leaving. Hank wants to marry Sabrina Watson, whose niece, Jane Adams, is one of the few people who can see the fairies. Hank finally relinquishes his rifle and repents of his hunting lifestyle after he nearly shoots Sabrina and her son, who have gone into the woods to help Ursa. Through magic, Arbutus opens the cubs' kennel, releasing them and reuniting them with their mother. The play provides early evidence of de Mille's interest in using dramatic situations—in this case a fairy tale—to comment on social and ethical concerns. The writers received high marks from critics, who noted that the play they had

Advertisement for de Mille's 1907 play, in which a young Union officer puts loyalty to his cause above his love for a Confederate general's daughter (Theatre Collection, Museum of the City of New York)

constructed was suitable for young audiences in its capacity both to instruct and delight.

On 30 March 1903 de Mille married Anna George, daughter of economist Henry George, formulator and advocate of the single-tax concept, which de Mille supported. The de Milles had two daughters, Agnes (born in 1905), who became a well-known choreographer, and Margaret (born in 1908).

De Mille's first major stage breakthrough, *Strongheart*, which premiered at the Hudson Theatre on 30 January 1905, tells the story of an American Indian varsity football player at Columbia University who struggles to overcome, among other difficulties, racial prejudice. At the climax of the play, Soangataha, nicknamed Strongheart, has won Dorothy Nelson's hand in marriage. As a result, however, he is rejected by his best friend–Dorothy's brother, Frank–and his teammate and friend Dick Lovingston. A messenger from Strongheart's tribe arrives to inform him that his father has died and that he is now his people's chief. The tribe will not accept a white woman as the chief's wife, though, and since his people have paid for Strongheart's education out of their scant resources, he feels the need to return to them, abandoning Dorothy. The play ends with Strongheart crying: "Oh great spirit of my fathers, I call to you for help, for I am in the midst of a great desert. Alone."

Gerald Bordman comments that "other plays had touched on the Indian in the white man's world, but none to date as skillfully as de Mille's." Bordman credits the fact that the play ran for just under one hundred performances in large part to the actor playing the lead character, Robert Edeson, for whom William wrote the play. De Mille's dramatic portrayal of an Indian in a Columbia University production of *The Governor's Vrouw* by Henry Harrison and Melville Cane, and the Indian themes of other plays de Mille had a hand in writing or publishing, led the critic Jules Eckert Goodman, writing in the *Bookman* (February 1907), to conclude that de Mille was committed to writing quintessential American dramas. Goodman quotes de Mille's prediction of a great revolution in American drama that

> will mean the era of national mental activity, and the era of great literature and especially of great drama, because the drama more than any other form of literature reflects the mind of the people. It must reflect the mind of the people to be patronized. Consequently I am glad that my life has fallen in this period, for the chances are that my generation will do some of the biggest work in the history of the country. The great American play? It will be written, but it will be the best of a series of great American plays.

The Genius, on which de Mille collaborated with his brother, Cecil, had only thirty-five performances after its New York premiere at the Bijou Theatre on 3 October 1906, but his next play, *Classmates,* written with Margaret

Turnbull, was quite successful. The play premiered at the Hudson Theatre on 29 August 1907, ran for 102 performances, and then toured outside of New York. Theatergoers must have enjoyed the exploits of two West Point classmates, from different levels of society in the same North Carolina town and in love with the same girl. Edeson again played the lead, this time as Irving Duncan, who is engaged to Sylvia Randolph, played by Flor Juliet Bowley. Sylvia is from the same privileged social set as Bert Stafford (Wallace Eddinger), who is in love with her. When Bert insults Irving, Irving responds with a blow that blinds his friend and leads to his expulsion. Bert resigns from school and leaves for an expedition to the Amazon, where he becomes lost. Sylvia breaks off her engagement with Irving, and when Irving resolves to find his alienated friend, she sends with him a message that she loves Bert. Irving finds Bert, who, after his return, reveals his petty nature to Sylvia. She then realizes that Irving is her true love.

The success of *Strongheart* and *Classmates* might have prompted Belasco to produce de Mille's *The Warrens of Virginia*. According to J. B. Russak's preface to the play in *Monte Cristo as Played by James O'Neil and Other Plays* (1941), after an out-of-town tryout opened at the Lyric Theatre in Philadelphia on 18 November 1907, positive reviews encouraged its production in New York, where it continued to receive positive reviews and receipts, running for 190 performances. According to Russak, the play had more than 300 performances in and outside of New York. Edwards points out that the "fifteen-month run and many touring companies" of the play cemented de Mille's reputation and solidified his financial standing. Set in Virginia during the U.S. Civil War, the play focuses on the relationship between a Federal officer, Lieutenant Ned Burton (played by C. D. Waldron in the original New York production), and Agatha Warren (played by Charlotte Walker), the daughter of a Confederate general (played by Frank Keenan). Burton, who has courted Agatha before the war, stops Agatha and the Warren family's black servant, Sappho, who are trying to smuggle silver to the Confederate lines in a picnic basket. Reminding Burton of their old ties, Agatha tries to persuade Burton to let her through, but he refuses, telling her that times have changed. Later, Burton agrees to take advantage of his connection to the Warrens by using a visit to their house to plant false information about Union plans. The result is a successful ambush of the Confederate forces that leads to their surrender at Appomattox. Realizing the fraud Burton has perpetrated, General Warren threatens to execute him, but Burton escapes with his life if not with Agatha's forgiveness. Act 4 takes place in the rose garden outside the Warren house five years after the end of the war. When Burton returns to ask again for forgiveness and for Agatha's hand, General Warren asks Sappho to fetch his shotgun. Sappho intentionally delays, and in the interim, General Warren hears Burton's response to Agatha's refusals. Genuinely moved, he declares: "Young man—I don't like a hair in yo' head—But my daughter—Aggie—Look heah—you come back some mo'—"

If critics concurred, as Bordman reports, that the play "was no great shakes but that Belasco's consummate staging raised it to something approaching high theatrical art," they were less kind to de Mille's collaboration with Cecil on *The Royal Mounted*, first produced at the Garrick Theatre on 6 April 1908. A critic reviewing the play for *Theatre* magazine in May of that year proclaimed the piece a "commercial play filled with situations interesting to the idle, yet empty as a play can well be." The melodrama, the review continued, offered "too many effects without adequate of [sic] sufficiently worked out causes," and the playwrights evidenced "the serious error of believing that Business is the soul of play writing." Richard de Mille argues that William de Mille had nothing to do with the writing of the play but let his younger sibling use his name to give "his struggling brother a boost." (The biological son of William de Mille and Lorna Moon, with whom William began an affair in 1919, Richard de Mille was adopted in secrecy by Cecil DeMille and his wife, Constance.) Richard cites as evidence of this authorship the contradiction in the beginning of the play when Rosa Larabee warns her brother Sam of a telegram sent downriver notifying Canadian authorities of Jed Brown's death; at this point in the play only Rosa and Sam know Brown is dead. (Sam has killed Brown to prevent him from raping Rosa.) As Richard de Mille comments, "If Jed Brown's body wasn't discovered till Sergeant Radly found it in a snow bank, who would have sent a telegram down river to the Mounties?" The movie version of the play, Cecil DeMille's *Northwest Mounted Police* (1940), resolved this dramatic flaw so that the story was, according to Richard de Mille, "as William would have wanted it to be." The stage production of *The Royal Mounted* was not successful with critics or audiences. The play lasted only four weeks and thirty-two performances.

Belasco's production of de Mille's next solo project, *The Woman*, which premiered on 19 September 1911, was a success. Amid many glowing reviews, the reviewer for the *Bookman* in 1911 was even careful to note that "no detraction is intended from the merits of his authorship when we call attention to the advantage that his play has reaped from the superlative production that it has received at the hands of his more experienced adviser." Belasco's considerable talents and reputation were in this case perceived as complementing a strong script. The play begins in the "Amen Corner" of the West Corridor of the Hotel Keswick in Washington, D.C. Wanda Kelly sits in the telephone operator's booth in the center of the lobby, privy to and sometimes commenting upon the business that occurs

Merrieworld, the house in Sullivan County, New York, that William and Anna de Mille bought in 1909

both onstage and through the wires. At one point Wanda explains, "the phone girl is a sort of fate. . . . Oh, I tell you, it's hard not to interfere sometimes when you've got the whole world under your two hands." Her decisions in this regard become crucial when a cadre of corrupt lobbyists and politicians led by Jim Blake, representative from Illinois, and his son-in-law Mark Robertson, representative from New York, contrive to blackmail Matthew Standish, a congressman who opposes a bill that will put large sums of money into the pockets of Blake, Robertson, and their political cronies. With the bill close to a vote, they confront the skilled and powerful Standish, an icon of moral purity, with their knowledge of a one-time liaison he had before he was married. As the blackmail plot progresses, with the apparent collusion of Wanda, it is revealed to the audience that Standish's female acquaintance is Robertson's wife. Bordman comments: "This first-act curtain brought gasps from the audience."

In the second act Wanda reneges on her tacit agreement with Blake and tries to warn Grace Robertson to avoid the danger awaiting her. Grace insults and puts off Wanda because she thinks the young telephone operator is scheming in order to get Grace to speak on her behalf to her father regarding Wanda's interest in Grace's brother Tom. Standish, for his part, tries to convince Grace to head off public trouble by revealing their private fling to her husband, rejecting her requests to lie to save her honor. Grace responds: "And if I had married you, after I had ceased to love you, you'd have owed me everything, wouldn't you? If I'd have wrecked your life you'd have protected me against the world, wouldn't you? But because I wouldn't add a blasphemous marriage to my other sin, you owe me nothing." Standish states that he cannot compromise his loyalty to his party and the people he represents, however, even though it will cost Grace her reputation. As Jim Blake takes the phone to relay the damning information to the press, Wanda unplugs the connection, which leads Blake and his cohorts to remove her to a separate room where they cross-examine and threaten her with imprisonment for disconnecting their call. When the congressmen discover that both Grace and Wanda know who the woman in question is, they try to coax the one and pressure the other to reveal her. It gradually becomes clear to the men that Grace is the woman involved in the liaison, which she is unable to deny. The lawmakers and lobbyists realize their defeat and tell their cronies on Capitol Hill that there is no scandal with which to tar Standish and that the bill will therefore pass. As act 3 ends, Wanda receives a call from Tom Blake and–from her side of their conversation–the audience infers that he has proposed to her.

The Woman attracted both critical acclaim and box-office receipts, lasting through 247 performances. Focusing on the moment in the play when Standish refuses to allow consideration for Grace's reputation to override his commitment to political virtue, the *Boston Transcript* reviewer opined on 28 December 1912 that the "old theatrical formula . . . failed for the first time." That is, Standish's decision contradicts the traditional view that a woman's "good name" must be defended at all costs. The paper explained that this portion of the drama demonstrated "why Mr. de Mille had written this strong, clear modern play"–that is, to give expression to "the new morality" of his age. The paper quoted the pronouncements of the playwright: "Every age has its own code of morality, and a wide gulf separates them one from another." The morality of his age, he declared, was shifting, so that a man's actions were no longer considered solely in terms of the consequences to only one man or (in this case) woman. Instead, "thanks to our awakening social conscience," the propriety of an act in a given situation would be determined on the basis of how it affected society as a whole.

De Mille's concern with the morality of theater, both as an art and as a business, was a common theme in both the playwright's magazine articles and his public speeches. His popularity as an essayist and public speaker followed him to Hollywood, where he continued to discuss the morality of theater, more broadly conceived. In articles such as "Bigoted and Bettered Pictures" (*Scribner's Magazine*, September 1924), he argued against censorship of movies, writing that audiences influenced movies rather than vice versa. In another essay, "Mickey Mouse versus Popeye"–first published in the November 1935 issue of the *Forum* and republished in *Hollywood Directors, 1914-1940* (1976), compiled by Richard Koszarski–de Mille argued satirically that a recent poll showing that cartoon fans preferred Popeye to Mickey Mouse indicated a growing tendency toward fascism in American youth, since a preference for Popeye's brusque and muscular problem-solving style resulted from a growing predisposition toward violence. De Mille argued frequently that plays and movies should strive simultaneously for the values of artistic distinction and popular entertainment, that they should be produced without the interference of heavy-handed censors, and that the audience influenced art more than art influenced the audience.

De Mille used not only his long plays and his prose to reflect on questions of import. His one-act dramas tend to consider social questions quite starkly. For instance, *Rollo: A Play of the Future*, also called *In 1999: A Problem Play of the Future*–which premiered at the Twelfth Night Club on 6 January 1912–involves the conflict between Rollo and his wife, Jean, who leaves one October evening in 1999 for a night in Manhattan, as Rollo sits knitting an outfit for their infant son. The husband protests his provider's abandonment, to which she gives what the audience would recognize as stock male responses about working hard and needing to socialize. After Jean leaves, Florence enters and tries to seduce the husband, arguing that Jean provides for his financial but not his emotional needs. When Jean reenters near the end of the act, Rollo is in Florence's lap, Florence quieting with a kiss Rollo's objections to leaving Jean. In an outburst of rage Jean commands Rollo to leave their home at once, eliciting his lamentation:

> How easy it is to be just–with your woman's justice–You say I've broken my marriage vow–well what of your own? You promised to love and protect me and you haven't done it–it's the old story–one law for the woman–another for the man–Oh–I know what you'll say–Custom–always custom–One member of the household must be pure and spotless–Yes, but why must it be the *man?*–tell me that? Why must it be the man?

Jean responds: "Civilization decrees it–and custom demands it–The laws of society were not made by you or me–They are stronger than we are because they are founded on wisdom and logic–." Catherine Walker calls the play "a satiric farce on the current feminist movement."

On 13 April 1913 another one-act play by de Mille, *Food: A Tragedy of the Future*, premiered at the Princess Theatre. Bordman comments on the reception of the one-act plays that were the specialty of the Princess: "Good notices kept playgoers coming until the hot weather chased them away." The domestic drama *Food* occurs fifty years into the future, when the world suffers from two debilitating evils: famine and inflation. The couple who occupy the stage are about to sit down to a dinner of crackers, which they will wash down with beads of milk delivered through a dropper. The wife relates that their doctor has informed her that she will die unless she eats an egg. The husband furiously protests the cost of such a prescription, prompting the wife to complain that he is putting money above her health. When the husband leaves the room, the audience finds that she once had a true love whom she did not marry because her current spouse had at the time better financial prospects. That true love, now an officer of the Food Trust, arrives at the door carrying an egg to be delivered to a billionaire. She begs him for the egg, enticing him with promises of rekindling their dormant passion. The husband enters, eavesdrops, grabs the egg, and dashes it to the floor.

A happier ending and a lighter situation lend humor to the one-act play *Poor Old Jim,* first produced at the Odeon Theatre in New York on 15 September 1913 and revived at the Waldorf Theatre on 9 May 1929, after de Mille had become a successful Hollywood writer and director. "Poor Old Jim" is the refrain that Jim's wife, Marie, and his doctor, Paul, repeat as they play a trick on Jim, pretending not to see, hear, or notice him in order to convince him that he is dead. The two have contrived the plot to scare Jim out of his alcoholism. As Jim begins to believe he is dead, Paul acts at wooing Marie for marriage. With Jim's jealousy aroused, Paul renders him unconscious with a cloth soaked in chloroform. When Jim comes to, Paul tells him that he has been dead for two hours and would still be so if the good doctor had not massaged Jim's heart. Jim grabs Marie and answers Paul: "Yes, and you tried to take advantage of a dead man, didn't you? . . . And you think you'll have lots more chances when I'm at the club, don't you? Well, you won't, because I've given up the club."

In the three-act comedy *After Five* (1913), the negative reception of which—according to de Mille's daughter, Agnes, in her autobiography, *Dance to the Piper* (1952)—contributed to his exodus to Hollywood, the main character, Ted Ewing, contemplates ending his life. He has lost not only his own money in the stock market but also that of his fiancée, Nora Hildreth. His desperation leads him to hatch a plot with a thug who is trying to get money from the bankrupt Ted. Ted persuades the man to murder him after Ted can manage to purchase a sizable life insurance policy. The comic overtones of Ted's suicidal failures, and then his struggles to stay his own murder when the stock market bounces back, did not win the approval of critic or audience. Rigdon reports that the play was performed only thirteen times.

Alexander Walker, in *The Shattered Silents: How the Talkies Came to Stay* (1979), reports that de Mille, already by 1929 a successful silent-movie director, enlisted in the sound revolution with alacrity: He "rushed over to Paramount and applied to learn all he could about the new technique in the sound department under Roy Pomeroy, who had been his own assistant only a year or two earlier." In 1914, when Cecil first left for the West Coast, however, de Mille was hesitant to switch from writing for the dramatic stage to writing for the silent screen. In his 1939 memoir, *Hollywood Saga,* he recounts his reply to Cecil's suggestion that de Mille relocate with him to Hollywood: "'Boy,' I replied with lilting humor, 'there have been times when I wasn't sure of my name; times when I didn't know whether I was awake or asleep; times when I was all confused as to whether the sun rose in the east or the west; but this one time I am sure with the deepest cer-

De Mille and his brother, Cecil B. DeMille, at Lasky Studio in Hollywood, October 1914 (from William de Mille, Hollywood Saga, *1959)*

tainty a human being can feel: I do *not* want to go in with you.'" He recalls too that the "quarter of the original Lasky Company," which his brother offered to him for $5,000, "could have sold about four years later for something over two million."

After the failure of *After Five,* however, de Mille reconsidered his decision not to go to Hollywood. The critical censure of the play might have been a contributing factor, but De Mille provided a different explanation of his decision. In *Hollywood Saga* he stated that his viewing of *The Squaw Man* (1914), the first motion picture Cecil produced, led him to a new vision of the moving picture as the most democratic of all art forms. In "The Audience and the Motion Pictures," published in *Drama* (July 1921), de Mille offered more subtle reasons for his journey westward:

It was given to us (for of that little group I count myself one) to be the pioneers of a new art. I welcomed the opportunity as the only chance I should ever have to be an old master, because, in the drama where I had been working for years, the previous fellows were a little strong for me. I did not think I could eclipse Shakespeare, or Moliere, or Sophocles. I did not think these gentlemen were going to turn over in their graves through fear of the competition of my work; but when we considered the motion pictures, how different the view. If there were any old masters in motion pictures, they were all old friends of mine. To be sure we differed among ourselves as to which of us were really the 'old masters', but at least we were all in the running. Greater fellows might come after us, but they were not in front of us. So, wishing to be an 'old master', I took this as the one opportunity.

As a Hollywood writer and director, de Mille turned many of his plays into movies. Although he arrived in California belatedly, he commanded and maintained the respect of the industry from the time he started a scenario department for Jesse L. Lasky's Famous Players Company until after his departure from the Hollywood scene in the late 1930s. From October 1929 to October 1931 he served as president of the Academy of Motion Picture Arts and Sciences, in which capacity he preached to young hopefuls to steer clear of Hollywood because it had, like much of the world at that time, few opportunities for those seeking jobs. He closed his motion-picture career with the publication of *Hollywood Saga,* which offers fascinating details and anecdotes of the earliest days of the movie colony. On 13 August 1928, three days after his divorce from Anna George de Mille became final, de Mille married Clara Beranger. In 1946 he founded the drama department at the University of Southern California, where Beranger also lectured. In 1953 he retired from the university, where his reputation for exacting students' best work combined with his family name to intimidate and inspire students.

In his memoir de Mille writes that drama "has never been the art of the few, but the art of the many." Though he aspired to be remembered as a popular and important playwright and motion-picture artist, the exploits of his director brother, his choreographer daughter, and even to some extent his playwriting father have overshadowed de Mille's thought and work. Not only his individual accomplishments have been obscured, but also his more general impact on theater and movies. As Catherine Walker argues, de Mille was instrumental, along with such luminaries as Percy MacKaye, in forging a distinctly American drama that did not slavishly imitate or rehash Continental themes and styles. Walker's thesis provides a readable and informative introduction to de Mille's work in the New York theater world with some discussion of his role in early Hollywood. Her thesis benefits from a personal interview with de Mille as well as the opportunity the playwright provided her to peruse his personal files at his home in Playa del Rey, California, in 1938. Sumiko Higashi has argued that de Mille's presence in Hollywood contributed in part to the legitimization of the screenplay as an art form.

Shortly after his death in Playa del Rey on 5 March 1955, William de Mille's ashes were interred at the Cecil B. DeMille Memorial in Hollywood Cemetery. Subsequently, his memory has more often been evoked by Cecil's and Agnes's autobiographical works than by his own *Hollywood Saga.*

Interviews:

"A Columbia Playwright," *Columbia Alumni News,* 2, no. 36 (Boating Number), pp. 187–188;

"Grand Opera on the Screen," *News Movie* (January 1935): 33.

Biographies:

Agnes de Mille, *Dance to the Piper: Memoirs of the Ballet* (Boston: Little, Brown, 1952);

Cecil B. DeMille, *The Autobiography of Cecil B. DeMille,* edited by Donald Hayne (Englewood Cliffs, N.J.: Prentice-Hall, 1959);

Anne Edwards, *The DeMilles: An American Family* (New York: Abrams, 1988);

Richard de Mille, *My Secret Mother, Lorna Moon* (New York: Farrar, Straus & Giroux, 1998).

References:

Gerald Bordman, *American Theatre: A Chronicle of Comedy and Drama, 1869–1914* (New York: Oxford University Press, 1994);

Kevin Brownlow, *The Parade's Gone By* (New York: Bonanza, 1968);

Sumiko Higashi, *Cecil B. DeMille and American Culture: The Silent Era* (Berkeley: University of California Press, 1994);

"Playwriting Epidemic in De Mille Family," *New York Sun,* 5 May 1905;

Alexander Walker, *The Shattered Silents: How the Talkies Came to Stay* (New York: Morrow, 1979);

Catherine Walker, "William de Mille's Contribution to American Drama as a Commercial Playwright (1900–1914)," M.A. thesis, University of Washington, 1939.

Papers:

Manuscripts, clippings, and reviews related to William de Mille's life and work can be found at the New York Public Library at Lincoln Center, including the Library's Manuscript and Rare Books Division.

Margaret Edson
(4 July 1961 -)

Martha Greene Eads
Valparaiso University

PLAY PRODUCTIONS: *Wit,* Costa Mesa, Cal., South Coast Repertory, 25 January 1995; New Haven, Conn., Long Wharf Theatre, 31 October 1997; New York, Manhattan Class Company, 17 September 1998; New York, Union Square Theatre, 7 January 1999.

BOOK: *Wit* (New York: Faber & Faber, 1999).

Although she insists that her true vocation is teaching kindergarten, Margaret Edson has distinguished herself as a dramatist on the basis of her debut play. *Wit,* which premiered in Costa Mesa, California, in 1995, won several awards before moving to the East Coast. After a short run in New Haven, Connecticut, *Wit* moved to New York and took the 1999 Pulitzer Prize for drama. Edson also earned the Berilla-Kerr Award, Helen Merrill Award, Dramatists Guild Award, John Gassner Playwriting Award, and George Oppenheimer Playwriting Award for her play. A teacher in Atlanta, Georgia, Edson says that she has no further dramatic or literary ambitions.

Margaret Ann Edson was born on 4 July 1961 in Washington, D.C., the middle child of Peter Edson, a newspaper columnist, and Joyce Winnifred Edson, a medical social worker. The family lived in Washington, where Edson attended public school until the fourth grade, when she enrolled at the Sidwell Friends School. As a child, Edson enjoyed staging neighborhood plays and later performed in several high-school drama productions, but she never aspired to a career in the theater.

From 1979 to 1983 Edson attended Smith College in Northampton, Massachusetts, where she earned a bachelor's degree in history. Having developed an interest in monasticism during college, she spent a year in a Dominican convent in Rome and held a series of odd jobs, including selling hot dogs on the street in Iowa City, Iowa, and ice cream in Washington, D.C. From 1984 to 1986 she worked as a unit clerk in the AIDS/oncology unit of a Washington-area research hospital.

Margaret Edson (courtesy of the author)

In an unpublished 8 February 2000 interview she explained that in September 1991 she decided to "get serious . . . and get a Ph.D." She completed her master's degree in literature at Georgetown University in 1992, writing her thesis on teaching with poetry. While pursuing graduate study at Georgetown, she volunteered for her church as an English as a Second Language tutor and subsequently enrolled in a local program to bring people from other professions into public education. Instead of pursuing her Ph.D. in literature, Edson focused on teaching children to read.

While developing her teaching career, Edson sent the script of *Wit* to, she claims, "every theater in the country." She finally received an acceptance letter from the South Coast Repertory in Costa Mesa, California, in 1995. Director Martin Benson cut the play significantly, compressing it from two acts to one. Edson approved Benson's decision, saying that the cuts "made the play more like itself." The South Coast Repertory production of *Wit* won six Los Angeles Drama Critics Circle Awards, including the prize for best world premiere. *Wit* moved from the West to the East Coast under the direction of Derek Anson Jones, a former classmate of Edson at the Sidwell Friends School. Jones directed the play at the Long Wharf Theatre in New Haven, Connecticut (where it won three Connecticut Drama Critics Circle Awards, including best play), and at the Manhattan Class Company in New York before taking it to the Union Square Theatre on 7 January 1999. Under his direction the play won New York Drama Critics Circle, Drama Desk, Drama League, Outer Critics Circle, and Lucille Lortel Awards. Jones prepared the show for a national tour before dying of AIDS complications on 17 January 2000.

Edson's earlier encounters with AIDS and cancer patients in Washington had shaped *Wit*. Describing her work as a hospital unit clerk, Edson told Jim Lehrer in a 14 April 1999 interview, "Since it was such a low-level job, I was able to really see a lot of things first hand. I was sort of unnoticed because I was so insignificant. And so I was able to witness a lot, both the actions of the care-givers and reactions of the patients." That experience equipped her to create a convincing depiction of one cancer patient's treatment. The protagonist of *Wit*, Vivian Bearing, is a fifty-year-old poetry professor in the final stages of ovarian cancer. Specializing in John Donne's poetry, Vivian is proud of her scholarly accomplishments and masterful command of language. As a cancer patient, however, she finds that her academic authority has little value. As death approaches, Vivian learns that human connection can be even more meaningful than intellectual activity.

When the play opens, Vivian greets the audience with a dignity that belies her incongruous costume. Wearing two hospital gowns, one tied in front and the other in back, her bald head topped by a baseball cap, she informs viewers, "I am a professor of seventeenth-century poetry, specializing in the Holy Sonnets of John Donne." In flashbacks to her classroom, she ridicules a student for his inability to answer her questions and refuses to grant his classmate a deadline extension for a paper. At the hospital, however, she is at others' mercy. Aside from rare instances of collegiality with Dr. Kelekian, her senior physician, she suffers daily assaults to her self-worth. From the medical technicians who administer her cancer treatment to Jason Posner, the research fellow who directs it, the hospital staff sees Vivian as little more than a research rat. Only her nurse, Susie Monahan, seems capable of recognizing Vivian as a suffering fellow human.

Although Vivian is at first dismissive of Susie as being "never very sharp to begin with," she eventually comes to rely on her for emotional support as well as medical care. While administering Popsicles and sympathy, Susie also proves herself to be an intelligent and skilled nurse. She respects Vivian enough to talk honestly with her about her impending death, hinting that Jason and his colleagues are likely to prolong her life in order to continue their research. Formerly an avid researcher herself, Vivian realizes that she is too tired to continue assisting others in their scholarly pursuits and requests a "do not resuscitate" order.

As Vivian comes to terms with her own death, she also begins to examine her life. She finds herself identifying with her young doctor, formerly her student. Even though Jason had performed well in one of her literature courses as an undergraduate, Vivian finds herself dissatisfied with his work as her doctor. She muses, "So. The young doctor, like the senior scholar, prefers research to humanity. At the same time, the senior scholar, in her pathetic state as simpering victim, wishes the young doctor would take more interest in personal contact." Edson underlines the contrast between Jason and Susie by having the nurse speak soothingly to the sleeping Vivian as she inserts a catheter. As he stands by, the research fellow scoffs, "Like she can hear you." Just before the play ends, Jason and Susie clash openly when he orders a Code Blue for the dying Vivian. Facing humiliation before his colleagues when Susie cancels his order, Jason collapses. As his catastrophe takes place on one part of the stage, Vivian's triumph emerges on another. Susie lifts her blanket, and Vivian rises from the bed and sheds her cap, her hospital bracelet, and those hated gowns. Edson's stage notes indicate, "*The instant she is naked, and beautiful, reaching for the Light–Lights out.*"

Although many theater critics have acknowledged the emotional impact of that conclusion, Emma Thompson and Mike Nichols altered it in their 2001 television adaptation of *Wit* for Home Box Office (HBO). In the HBO production, Bearing (played by Thompson) dies only to reappear on the screen in close-up, her health (and hair) restored, and she recites Donne to television viewers as she had to her students when she was at the height of her teaching powers. This adjustment to the script reduced the effectiveness of the production, as did the difficulty of conveying the humor that had enlivened stage productions of *Wit,* but the HBO motion picture nevertheless earned the 2001 Emmys for best telefilm and best directing for a miniseries, movie, or special.

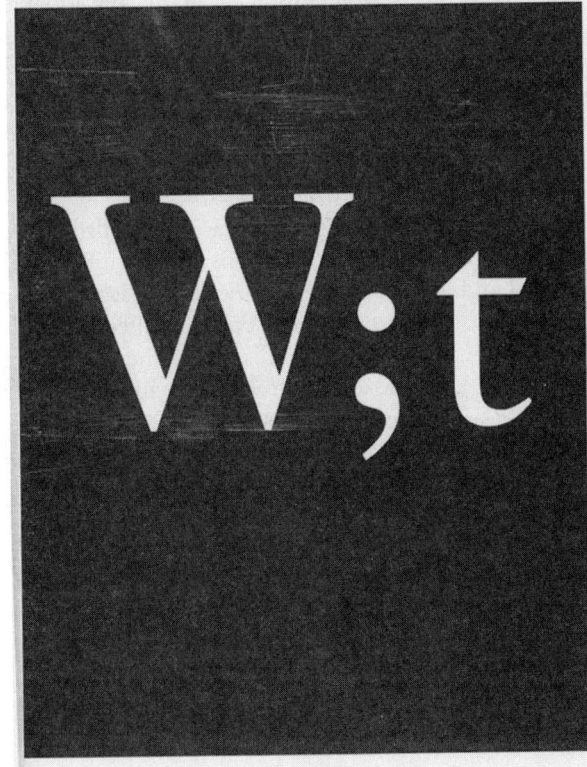
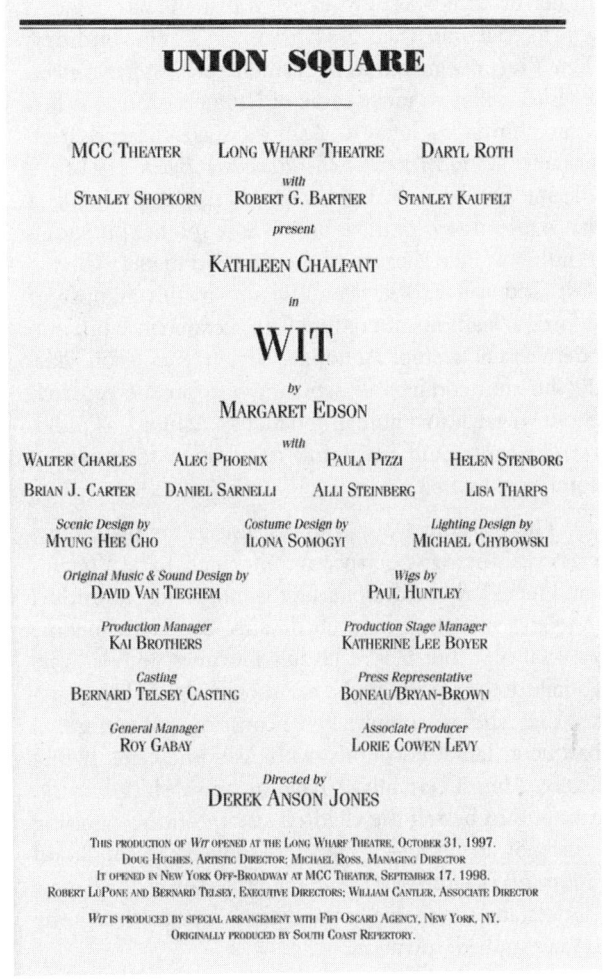

Program cover and title page for the 1999 New York production of the play that won the 1999 Pulitzer Prize for Drama (courtesy of Margaret Edson)

Most critics write about *Wit* as an academic play or a medical drama. For example, Bernie Bregman, in a 1999 article for the British medical journal *Lancet*, lauded Edson for having shown that professionals trained in the liberal arts can be just as heartless as the worst bedside physician. *Wit*, he explained, challenges the "false dichotomy of arts and science, revealing to us what anyone who has spent enough time in academia knows: the cold intellectuality that precludes empathy is a function of the scholar, not the discipline." Michael Phillips, critic for the *Los Angeles Times* (28 January 2000), praised Edson for having "written specifically and eloquently of an educator's life." Similarly, Rosette Lamont described the play as "a celebration of a life dedicated to the art of literature."

Edson has marveled publicly that so few reviewers have recognized the spiritual element in *Wit*. "The play is about redemption," she told *American Theatre* writer Adrienne Martini, "and I'm surprised no one mentions it." Carol Iannone, who accused Edson of failing to appreciate Donne's work, was so pained by the treatment of religious experience in *Wit* that she wrote, "Why can't a contemporary playwright appreciate that something real goes on in religious thought?" In a 1999 interview for *Books and Culture*, however, Betty Carter asked Edson about Christian material in *Wit*, prompting the playwright to reply: "It's a very religious play, and you're the first person who's ever said that to me. People always want to talk about the medicine, want to talk about the punctuation, and so I compliment you and thank you for that."

One of the most spiritually significant scenes in *Wit* occurs shortly before Vivian's death. Minutes after Susie has inserted Vivian's catheter, eighty-year-old E. M. Ashford, the dying woman's academic mentor and only visitor, enters the hospital room. During her brief encounter with her protégée, Ashford explains that she has come to town to celebrate her great-grandson's fifth birthday. When Vivian begins to weep from the pain of her cancer, her visitor offers to recite some of Donne's poetry. When Vivian shows no interest, Ashford reads instead from Margaret Wise Brown's *The Runaway Bunny* (1942), a book she has brought for her great-grandson. "Look at that," Ashford says of the rabbit, whose mother pursues it faithfully. "A little allegory of the soul. No matter where it hides, God will find it. See, Vivian?" In this glimpse of Ashford, *Wit* affirms not only religious experience but also academic scholarship. Although Vivian and Jason illustrate the shortcomings of scholars who pursue research without regard for human relations, Ashford is kind, down to earth, and insightful, in addition to being an accomplished scholar.

The placement of Ashford's visit in the play, however, reveals her wise perspective ultimately to be Vivian's own. The elderly professor's visit is most likely a product of Vivian's morphine-induced dreams, coming sometime after 4:00 A.M. but before Jason's morning rounds. Vivian's failure to respond to the insertion of the catheter suggests that she is completely unconscious; therefore, a subsequent, literal encounter with Ashford seems highly unlikely. Almost certainly, Vivian dreams Ashford's visit, recounting to herself the children's story and recognizing its spiritual significance. Through some faint childhood memory of *The Runaway Bunny*, the professor finally begins to understand the theme of the difficult Donne poetry she had long studied: salvation.

Edson claims not to see Donne as a spiritual authority; when Carter asked whether she likes Donne's poetry, she replied:

> It's very fun to get yourself educated to a level where you can get it. But it takes a lot of hard work, and the fun of catching it is greater than the benefit of the insight to be gained. So the points that are made about it in the play are that it's complex and difficult, but the complexity doesn't necessarily lead you to a higher level of insight. The poems are complex for their own sake.... [Donne] wasn't trying to reveal any truth or even pursue any truth. He was just trying to be witty and clever.

Similarly, Edson distances herself from religious orthodoxy, although she does identify herself as Christian. "If you're completely united with God," she told Carter, "you don't need religion." Despite her protestations, Edson has created in *Wit* something other than a mere critique of Donne's religious poetry and of advanced literary scholarship. Vivian's vocation ultimately finds affirmation in the example Ashford provides, and the dying woman's apparent acceptance of the message of *The Runaway Bunny* and her subsequent reaching for the light at the end of the play reveal a strong spiritual sensibility.

Edson moved to Atlanta, Georgia, in 1998, when her partner, Linda Merrill, an art historian, accepted a position at the High Museum. (The couple have a son, Timothy Edson Merrill.) Edson began teaching at Centennial Place Elementary School and now teaches kindergarten at John Hope Elementary School. Even though *Wit*, her first and only produced play to date, won a Pulitzer Prize, Edson says, "I don't know if I'll ever do another play. If there's something I want to say, then I'll do it. But the thing I'm most proud to be is a teacher."

While determining the measure of Edson's literary influence on the basis of one play is difficult, the critical and popular success of *Wit* marks it as a significant twentieth-century work. The careful consideration of vocational and theological issues in the play, and its candid and compassionate account of cancer treatment, make it instructive as well as compelling. Kathleen Chalfant, who played Vivian Bearing in the New York production only a year after losing her brother to cancer, spoke for many when she told *People* magazine, "I am immensely grateful to the play. It helped teach me how to help my brother at the end of his life."

Interviews:

"Play Right: *Wit* Author Margaret Edson Loves Teaching Kindergarten," *People* (5 April 1999): 179;

Jim Lehrer, "Love and Knowledge," *NewsHour with Jim Lehrer,* 14 April 1999 <http://www.pbs.org/newshour/bb/entertainment/jan-june99/edson_4-14.html>;

Betty Carter, "John Donne Meets *The Runaway Bunny*," *Books and Culture* (September–October 1999): 24–26;

Adrienne Martini, "The Playwright In Spite of Herself," *American Theatre,* 16 (October 1999): 22–25.

References:

Bernie Bregman, "Blame the Scholar, Not the Discipline," *Lancet* (6 March 1999): 851;

Martha Greene Eads, "Unwitting Redemption in Margaret Edson's *Wit*," *Christianity and Literature,* 51 (Winter 2002): 241–254;

Carol Iannone, "Donne Undone," *First Things,* 100 (February 2000): 12–14;

Rosette Lamont, "Coma Versus Comma: John Donne's Holy Sonnets in Edson's *Wit*," *Massachusetts Review,* 40 (Winter 1999–2000): 569–575;

Pamela Renner, "Science and Sensibility," *American Theatre,* 16 (April 1999): 34–36;

Toby Zinman, "Illness as Metaphor," *American Theatre,* 16 (April 1999): 25.

Edna Ferber
(15 August 1885 – 17 April 1968)

Angela Courtney
Fairfield University

See also the Ferber entries in *DLB 9: American Novelists, 1910–1945; DLB 28: Twentieth-Century American-Jewish Fiction Writers;* and *DLB 86: American Short-Story Writers, 1910–1945, First Series.*

PLAY PRODUCTIONS: *Our Mrs. McChesney,* by Ferber and George V. Hobart, New York, Lyceum Theatre, 19 October 1915;

$1200 a Year, by Ferber and Newman Levy, Baltimore, 1920;

The Eldest, Newark, N.J., Recital Hall, 9 January 1924;

Minick, by Ferber and George S. Kaufman, New York, Booth Theatre, 24 September 1924;

The Royal Family, by Ferber and Kaufman, New York, Selwyn Theatre, 28 December 1927;

Dinner at Eight, by Ferber and Kaufman, New York, Music Box Theatre, 22 October 1932;

Stage Door, by Ferber and Kaufman, New York, Music Box Theatre, 22 October 1936;

The Land Is Bright, by Ferber and Kaufman, New York, Music Box Theatre, 28 October 1941;

Bravo! by Ferber and Kaufman, New York, Lyceum Theatre, 11 November 1948.

BOOKS: *Dawn O'Hara: The Girl Who Laughed* (New York: Stokes, 1911; London: Methuen, 1925);

Buttered Side Down (New York: Stokes, 1912; London: Methuen, 1926);

Roast Beef Medium: The Business Adventures of Emma McChesney (New York: Stokes, 1913; London: Methuen, 1920);

Personality Plus: Some Experiences of Emma McChesney and Her Son, Jock (New York: Stokes, 1914);

Emma McChesney & Co. (New York: Stokes, 1915);

Fanny Herself (New York: Stokes, 1917; London: Methuen, 1923);

Cheerful, By Request (Garden City, N.Y.: Doubleday, Page, 1918; London: Methuen, 1919);

Half Portions (Garden City, N.Y.: Doubleday, Page, 1920);

Edna Ferber, 1936 (from Julie Goldsmith Gilbert, Ferber, *1978)*

$1200 a Year, by Ferber and Newman Levy (Garden City, N.Y.: Doubleday, Page, 1920);

The Girls (Garden City, N.Y. & Toronto: Doubleday, Page, 1921; London: Heinemann, 1922);

Gigolo (Garden City, N.Y.: Doubleday, Page, 1922; London: Heinemann, 1923);

Old Man Minick, by Ferber, and *Minick,* by Ferber and George S. Kaufman (Garden City, N.Y.: Doubleday, Page, 1924; London: Heinemann, 1924);

So Big (Garden City, N.Y.: Doubleday, Page, 1924; London: Heinemann, 1924);

The Eldest: A Drama of American Life (New York: D. Appleton, 1925);

Edna Ferber

Show Boat (Garden City, N.Y.: Doubleday, Page, 1926; London: Heinemann, 1926);

Mother Knows Best: A Fiction Book (Garden City, N.Y.: Doubleday, Page, 1927; London: Heinemann, 1927);

The Royal Family, by Ferber and Kaufman (Garden City, N.Y.: Doubleday, Doran, 1928; London: S. French, 1929);

Cimarron (Garden City, N.Y.: Doubleday, Doran, 1930; London: Heinemann, 1930);

American Beauty (Garden City, N.Y.: Doubleday, Doran, 1931; London: Heinemann, 1931);

Dinner at Eight, by Ferber and Kaufman (Garden City, N.Y.: Doubleday, Doran, 1932; London: Heinemann, 1933);

They Brought Their Women (Garden City, N.Y.: Doubleday, Doran, 1933; London: Heinemann, 1933);

Come and Get It (Garden City, N.Y.: Doubleday, Doran, 1935; London: Heinemann, 1935);

Stage Door, by Ferber and Kaufman (Garden City, N.Y.: Doubleday, Doran, 1936; London: Heinemann, 1937);

Nobody's in Town (Garden City, N.Y.: Doubleday, Doran, 1938; London: Heinemann, 1938);

A Peculiar Treasure (New York; Doubleday, Doran, 1939; London: Heinemann, 1939);

The Land Is Bright, by Ferber and Kaufman (Garden City, N.Y.: Doubleday, Doran, 1941);

No Room at the Inn (Garden City, N.Y.: Doubleday, Doran, 1941);

Saratoga Trunk (Garden City, N.Y.: Doubleday, Doran, 1941; London: Heinemann, 1942);

Great Son (Garden City, N.Y.: Doubleday, Doran, 1945; London: Heinemann, 1945);

One Basket: Thirty-One Short Stories (New York: Simon & Schuster, 1947);

Your Town (Cleveland: World, 1948);

Bravo! by Ferber and Kaufman (New York: Dramatists Play Service, 1949);

Giant (Garden City, N.Y.: Doubleday, 1952; London: Gollancz, 1952);

Ice Palace (Garden City, N.Y.: Doubleday, 1958; London: Gollancz, 1958);

A Kind of Magic (Garden City, N.Y.: Doubleday, 1963; London: Gollancz, 1963).

Generally known as a novelist who deftly illustrated American life and culture in her popular fiction, Edna Ferber was always drawn to the stage. As a child she wanted to act, but she later realized that her talents were in the written word and achieved her dreams of a life in the theater by writing for the stage. Her most successful plays were written in collaboration with the "Great Collaborator" George S. Kaufman, with whom she worked on six successful Broadway plays. Ferber brought to her dramatic works the ability to astutely and accurately depict her subjects with a lovingly critical eye, giving the stage unforgettable characters whom she never tired of seeing revived.

Edna Ferber was born on 15 August 1885 in Kalamazoo, Michigan, to Jacob Charles and Julia Neumann Ferber. Jacob Ferber had immigrated to America from Oylso, Hungary, when he was seventeen and was soon joined by the rest of his family. Julia Ferber was an American, born in Milwaukee, Wisconsin. Edna Ferber's father was a shopkeeper in Kalamazoo, Michigan, but he had bigger dreams for his family. In 1888 the Ferbers moved to Chicago in anticipation of the 1893 World's Fair, hoping to open a general store that would eventually reap the benefits from the influx of tourists to the city. After living with Julia Ferber's family in Chicago for about a year, however, the Ferbers became displeased with their prospects there, and Jacob turned his sights to Ottumwa, Iowa, a small town that he felt was in need of a store like the one he had run in Kalamazoo. In Ottumwa, where the Ferbers lived from 1890 until 1897, young Edna Ferber first encountered sustained anti-Semitism against her family. The family store did not prosper, and eventually the Ferbers became embroiled in a lawsuit brought by a former employee whom they had accused of stealing from the store. The Ferbers were found guilty of slander and forced to pay thousands of dollars to the employee, who—Edna Ferber always maintained—truly had stolen from the family store. Soon after this blow, Ferber's father began to lose his vision, and the family began preparing for yet another move.

Despite their unhappiness in Ottumwa, in her first autobiography, *A Peculiar Treasure* (1939), Ferber credited her time there with fostering her interest in creative endeavors. The family eagerly attended any theatrical production that came to town and sought out opportunities to experience the arts. During these years Ferber became a voracious reader, reading a book a day. She also developed an affinity for performing public recitations.

On leaving Ottumwa in 1897, the Ferbers went back to live with Julia's family in Chicago, where they were more comfortable because the city had more Jewish families than Ottumwa. Yet, their lives remained difficult; and later the same year the Ferbers decided to relocate to Appleton, Wisconsin. There they took part in the life of the Jewish community, attending services and participating in other events. Ferber and her sister, Fannie, put on plays at home. Throughout her years at Ryan High School in

*Ferber with her frequent collaborator, George S. Kaufman
(from Malcolm Goldstein,* George S. Kaufman, *1979)*

Appleton, Edna Ferber participated in school theater productions and recitation and declamation contests, winning the Wisconsin state declamatory contest in her senior year. As Ferber's father became increasingly incapacitated by his loss of vision, her mother began to take on his responsibilities as the provider for the family. She ran the store and made the business deals that kept the family on steady financial ground. In her mother Ferber found an inspiration for many of her fictional characters.

After graduating from high school in 1903, seventeen-year-old Edna Ferber became the first female reporter for the *Appleton Daily Crescent*. She aspired to attend the School of Elocution at Northwestern University but saw that hope fade as her father's health continued to decline. As the youngest and newest reporter on the staff, she was given mundane assignments, but she made the best of them. The people she encountered on her daily rounds provided a good deal of the background for her later stories.

Ferber remained at the *Daily Crescent* for two years before she was fired by a new editor who did not approve of female reporters. The editors of the *Milwaukee Journal*, however, had seen her work and were favorably impressed, especially by her coverage of the Wisconsin Federation of Women's Clubs, which had its annual meeting in Appleton. From amid stories by many seasoned out-of-town reporters, the Federation had singled out Ferber's coverage for the *Daily Crescent* as the best, most accurate, and most issue oriented. In 1909, after three years at the *Milwaukee Journal*, Ferber, who was suffering from anemia, had a nervous breakdown and returned home for a long period of rest. In the fall of the same year the family returned to Chicago, and her ailing father died.

Soon after this family upheaval, Ferber started writing fiction. Her first published story, "The Homely Heroine," appeared in the November 1910 issue of *Everybody's Magazine*. Shortly thereafter she finished her first novel, *Dawn O'Hara: The Girl Who Laughed* (1911), generally regarded as beautified autobiography. Ferber had been unhappy with the work and discarded the completed manuscript, but her mother had retrieved it and encouraged her daughter to submit it to a publisher. Over the next five years Ferber exploited one of her most popular characters, Emma McChesney, in a series of short-story collections. Modeled in part on Ferber's mother, Emma is a young divorced mother, a strong woman who sells petticoats as a means of supporting her teenage son. In 1912 Ferber moved to New York City, where she lived for most of the remaining years of her life. She started out by working for *American* magazine, continuing to strive to prove herself worthy of employment and respect in the male-dominated world of journalism. In the same year she covered the Democratic National Convention in Chicago, where she met the prominent journalist William Allen White, who became not only her friend but also a lasting and supportive influence in her life.

In 1914 Joseph Brooks acquired the dramatic rights to the Emma McChesney stories, and—while Ferber was taking a prewar tour of Europe—he put the dramatization in the hands of Charlotte Thompson. On Ferber's return, however, Ethel Barrymore's manager Charles Frohman asked Ferber to dramatize the work herself. She joined forces with George V. Hobart to adapt stories for Broadway as *Our Mrs. McChesney* (1915). She and Hobart often disagreed over how to dramatize the stories, with Ferber usually holding out for a more realistic representation of life than Hobart's version. Ferber, who had always been fascinated by the stage, attended rehearsals, watching the production take shape. Under the shadow of Frohman's death on the ocean liner *Lusitania*, which was sunk by a German U-boat on 7 May 1915, the production opened on 19 October of that year, with Ethel Barrymore as its star. It ran for 151 performances. Though the production was well received both popularly and critically, Ferber's first collaboration was not completely satisfactory to her, and only when she began working with George S. Kaufman did she feel pleased with her plays. While the story of a hard-working woman in a man's world was not necessarily a new one, despite Ferber's reservations *Our Mrs. McChesney* was well done. Ferber employed the same theme in her 1917 novel, *Fanny Herself*, again showing the influence of Julia Ferber. Like her, the title character of *Fanny Herself* is a hardworking midwestern Jewish woman who is the backbone of her family.

During World War I, Ferber became a war correspondent for the Red Cross, but she was forced to give up the job after she was refused entry into France because of her father's Hungarian birth. She tried to write war-related short stories but was not comfortable with the subject. In fact, she was never able to write fiction on assigned topics. She redirected her efforts to writing articles for the war effort and traveling throughout the country speaking to promote American participation.

In 1919 Newman Levy contacted Ferber with an idea for a play and a request for collaboration. Although working with a partner on his idea rather than her own ran counter to Ferber's creative grain, she was eager to return to the theater and agreed to work on the play, *$1200 a Year*. Produced by Sam Harris, the play opened in Baltimore in 1920 and closed in the same week. Nevertheless, Ferber and Levy enjoyed working together, and Ferber began to see the potential of collaborative dramatic efforts. The theme of the play is the disparity in wages between well-paid laborers and poverty-level academics, whose yearly salary is mentioned in the title. At the center of the play is a professor turned mill worker turned labor activist, who is torn between his moral devotion to academic ideals and the practical reality of poverty. While the play is entertaining, it ends with an all-too-convenient intervention by Hollywood, eager to make the professor's life into a movie, thus eliminating the threat of bankruptcy and the impending crash of laborers' wages. Despite the poor professional performance of the play, Ferber remained fond of it, and it was later produced in small theaters and by amateur acting groups.

Once the war had ended in 1918, Ferber had begun traveling regularly to Europe. During the 1920s she lived in both New York and Chicago. She enjoyed life in New York but still felt connected to the Midwest, where her family remained. She sold her novel *Fanny Herself* to Universal in 1921, and it was produced as a movie later that year with the title *No Woman Knows*.

In 1923 Ferber read in *The New York Times* that the Provincetown Players were producing a play titled *The Eldest*. Because she had published a short story with the same title, the announcement piqued her curiosity. She had the director send her a summary of the play and discovered that it was indeed a dramatization of her story. She immediately disallowed the production but dramatized the work herself for the Provincetown Players. Quickly rehearsed and staged, her version opened in Newark on 9 January 1924 and was generally ignored by the critics. Lacking the fast-paced wit that characterizes later Ferber-Kaufman collaborations, *The Eldest* is decidedly humorless.

That same year Ferber worked for the first time with George S. Kaufman, who contacted her just after *The Eldest* was produced. Though Ferber wanted to dramatize her short story "The Gay Old Dog," Kaufman selected "Old Man Minick" from Ferber's 1922 collection, *Gigolo,* and his choice prevailed. Ferber did not feel "Old Man Minick" could make the transition to the stage, and—despite its subsequent success—she apparently remained unconvinced of its stageworthiness throughout her life. In spite of such reservations Ferber was enthusiastic about working with Kaufman and did not let this difference of opinion stand in the way of their partnership. Their collaborative enterprise remained intact off and on for the next twenty-five years, and her friendship with Kaufman was close and lasting. They usually worked at her apartment, except for a rare move in search of a quieter locale. Although rumors abound about her unrequited love for Kaufman, Ferber never indicated that they were anything more than friends and writing partners. In *A Peculiar Treasure* she explained that once they established their work pattern, it never changed. Their first play was written quickly and was readily approved by producer Winthrop Ames. Although Ferber was not entirely displeased with the cast, she felt that some characters were miscast. She was proud, however, that this production rejected the then-standard practice of using white actors in blackface to portray black characters. Instead, an African American actress from Harlem was given the part of the black maid. Ferber apparently enjoyed her participation in the production; yet, she felt a bit out of her element when it came to rewrites and other practical alterations.

Minick (1924) opened on Broadway at the Booth Theatre on 24 September and was relatively well received by the critics. Stark Young, critic for *The New York Times,* said that the play provoked an "affectionate and happy response" from the audience but asserted that it needed "more plot, or more complication of incident, or at least more intense motive" (25 September 1924). The play, which ran for 154 performances, centers on the conflicts and emotions that emerge after the recently widowed Minick moves in with his son and daughter-in-law, an arrangement that pleases no one, while each thinks it is good for the others. Comic mishaps illustrate the impracticality of reversing parent-child relationships in adulthood. The play benefits from Ferber's abili-

Otto Kuruger and Haidee Wright in the 1927 New York production of The Royal Family *(Billy Rose Theatre Collection, New York Public Library for the Performing Arts)*

ties to create believable and sympathetic characters who fit easily into Kaufman's well-constructed plot. During the production of *Old Man Minick,* Ferber traveled to the three theaters in Connecticut where the play had tryout productions before its Broadway opening—including a theater in New London that had apparently gone unused for several years and had become home to a small bat colony. In *A Peculiar Treasure* she recalled how the bats were awakened when the show began, shocking the actors and the audience. The show finished to a smaller audience than the one with which it began. In the postmortems for this particular performance, Ames suggested working on a showboat, thus planting the seed for one of Ferber's most successful novels.

In 1924 Ferber also wrote *So Big,* a novel about another strong woman who provides for her family. This novel was a popular and critical success, garnering her rave reviews as well as a Pulitzer Prize. A silent-movie version was released that same year, and sound versions were made in 1932 with Barbara Stanwyck and in 1953 with Jane Wyman.

Around the time of their first collaboration, Ferber and Kaufman became part of the Algonquin Round Table, a group of writers and theater people who lunched at the Algonquin Hotel in New York. Known for its witty repartee, the group also included Dorothy Parker, Robert Benchley, Alexander Woollcott, Harpo Marx, *New Yorker* editor Harold Ross, columnists Franklin Pierce Adams and Heywood Broun, and playwrights Marc Connelly and Robert Sherwood—as well as less-frequent attendees such as Louis Bromfield and Noel Coward, both of whom developed long friendships with Ferber.

Still intrigued by the idea of a showboat, Ferber did extensive research on this American phenomenon and even spent time with a theater family on a working showboat. In 1926 she published *Show Boat,* a novel about a family who runs a showboat on the Mississippi River. The following year Jerome Kern and Oscar Hammerstein 2nd turned the novel into an extremely successful musical. Ferber's novel has been translated into several foreign languages, and there have been four movie versions of the play. The stage musical opened at the Ziegfeld Theatre on 27 December 1927, and it was followed the next night by the premiere at the Selwyn of Ferber and Kaufman's collaboration *The Royal Family.* Ferber was actively involved in watching the progress of both productions, dividing her time between the two theaters. *Show Boat* ran on Broadway until May 1929, went on tour, and then reopened on Broadway in May 1932, soon after the end of the touring production.

Ferber and Kaufman's *The Royal Family* is about several generations of an acting family. Though Ferber maintained that these characters were not based on the Barrymores, many similarities exist, and there was much speculation. She did concede that John Barrymore served as inspiration for many characteristics but not for one character. Ferber and Kaufman worked together daily for eight months on *The Royal Family* and turned out a play that purportedly required no rewriting during rehearsals. Nevertheless, the play was problematic, especially because the role of Julie Cavendish was almost impossible to cast. Not only was Cavendish an aging actress, but Ethel Barrymore found the character personally offensive and turned down the part in no uncertain terms, refusing to speak to Ferber for five years. Then Ferber offered to play Julie Cavendish, but Ann Andrews was finally cast in the role. Although her girlhood dream of appearing onstage as a professional actress was not realized with the premiere production of *The Royal Family,* Ferber did play Fanny Cavendish for a week when the play was staged again almost thirteen years later. After this experience she never again wanted to act. The original production of *The Royal Family* ran for 343 performances. It was a popular success, but the response of her friend Brooks Atkinson, who called it only "steady entertainment" (*The New York Times,* 29 December 1927), was rather typical of the critics' reaction.

Once *Show Boat* and *The Royal Family* were running, Ferber took a trip to Kansas to visit friends. While there she conceived the idea of writing a novel about Oklahoma and toured the state for research purposes. The result was *Cimarron* (1930), a novel now generally considered one of her best works. At the time critics and Oklahomans criticized her apparent unfamiliarity with her subject, but the book was otherwise well received and sold well. While Ferber intended *Cimarron* to be an attack on Americans' stereotypical view of womanhood, she feared it was read as an approving, sentimentalized view of the American West.

In 1931 Ferber was awarded an honorary doctor of letters degree by Columbia University. Since her collaboration with Kaufman on *The Royal Family* in 1927, the two had occasionally discussed the possibility of working on another play. The idea for *Dinner at Eight* (1932) kept coming up, but the two writers repeatedly rejected it. The premise was good, they felt, but it would be impossible to stage, because it would require too many scenes and too much character development of a large cast. Finally Ferber convinced Kaufman that they could pull it off and create a play that would be popular despite its similarities to the 1930 Broadway hit *Grand Hotel.* Once they began writing in spring 1931, *Dinner at Eight* was completed by June. In *A Peculiar Treasure* Ferber described writing the play as a pleasant experience for both partners.

Faced again with a character in her forties, Ferber and Kaufman found casting a chore. Kaufman directed the play, and Ferber was again involved in the production, attending almost every rehearsal. This production was special to Ferber because her niece, Janet Fox, was cast as the maid, and Ferber had high hopes for her performance. The play used eleven scenes and seven settings, all accommodated on a revolving stage. The plot was complex, yet built around the simple premise of a dinner party. Throughout the play, the audience is introduced to individual guests and their personal demons, with everything building to a final climax. Running for 232 performances, *Dinner at Eight* was an astounding success. Atkinson called it "an extraordinarily engrossing piece of work . . . a reflective drama,

Program cover, with a photograph of Margaret Sullavan, and cast list for the first New York production of the play Ferber and Kaufman set in a boardinghouse for aspiring actresses (Bruccoli Clark Layman Archives)

detached and observant" (*The New York Times,* 24 October 1932). Soon after its opening in New York, producer Charles Cochrane wanted to stage it in London. Ferber went to England to oversee rehearsals and contracted a life-threatening strain of influenza, spending most of the rehearsal time in bed.

Ferber and Kaufman's next collaborative effort was *Stage Door,* which opened on Broadway on 22 October 1936 and ran for 159 performances. While it was not a huge success like *Dinner at Eight,* the play did earn a positive critical reception. The play focuses on young women living at the Footlights Club, an overcrowded boardinghouse for aspiring actresses. Ferber and Kaufman depict a stressful and often unrewarding life in which the girls are faced with remaining faithful to their art or cheapening it with offers from Hollywood. One girl leaves New York for the lure of Hollywood, and another commits suicide after being cut from a play, while Terry, the heroine, remains true to herself and eventually gets the part and her man. The critics were divided on their assessment of *Stage Door*. Brooks Atkinson called it at once "ingeniously fashioned" and yet noted the "emptiness which the expert dialogue and direction do not wholly conceal" (*The New York Times,* 23 October 1936). Overall, the performance, acting, and directing were applauded, while the play itself was judged as less notable than Ferber and Kaufman's earlier efforts. Nevertheless, in 1937 the play was made into a successful movie, which led to a friendship between Ferber and Katharine Hepburn, who played the lead.

Throughout the 1930s Ferber continued to publish short stories and novels, as well as *A Peculiar Treasure* (1939). This autobiography is more interesting for what it fails to mention than for what it actually discusses—especially when the book is read in light of others' accounts of her life and personality. She avoided discussing her romantic life, or lack thereof, and glossed over the rage and disdain that other relatives said she felt toward her mother and sister. Ferber had not wanted to write the book but did so because of popular demand.

In 1940 Ferber was considering an idea for a play that would take place in the health spa and horse-racing resort of Saratoga Springs, New York. She sold actors Lynn Fontaine and Alfred Lunt on the idea and then set out to convince Kaufman to write the play with her. They took an unfortunate wintertime exploratory trip to Saratoga Springs, a trek so unpleasant to Kaufman that Ferber stopped trying to sway him. Instead she wrote the novel *Saratoga Trunk* (1941), a work that was relatively well received even though Ferber was not pleased with it during the writing process. It was eventually made into a successful 1945 movie and a relatively unsuccessful 1959 musical. Ferber played no part in either adaptation.

Another Ferber-Kaufman collaboration, *The Land Is Bright,* opened on 28 October 1941. The two had difficulty getting started on this play, whose title comes from a poem by Arthur Clough, and it was ultimately a money loser. The reviews were not scathing, nor were they glowing. A melodrama about three generations of a wealthy American family over a span of fifty years, *The Land Is Bright* was deemed entertaining and harmless fun. *The New York Times* praised it mildly as a "rousing drama" that examines American society (29 October 1941). The play opened fewer than two months before the Japanese bombed Pearl Harbor and ran for only seventy-nine performances. Ferber believed the play was simply not right for American society at the time.

As an American Jew, Ferber was hit hard by the atrocities of World War II and lent her talents and her time to the Writers' War Board, producing propaganda fiction and encouraging the American public to invest in war bonds. The Writers' War Board wrote stories and articles illustrating various aspects of the war effort. While Ferber participated willingly, she found it difficult to have someone else assigning her subject matter. Ferber also served as a war correspondent, receiving a temporary commission in the U.S. Army Air Force and traveling to Europe with her niece Mina.

In 1948 Ferber and Kaufman collaborated on their last play, *Bravo!* While it was not poorly received, their public and the critics apparently expected more from Ferber and Kaufman than what *Bravo!* offered. The play opened on 11 November and ran for only two months, forty-four performances, even with financial help from Ferber. The play focuses on the experiences of several immigrants–many well respected in their native countries–trying desperately to succeed and to fit in with American culture in New York City. Ferber envisioned the play as a comedy, but Kaufman considered this theme an odd idea for comic treatment. The result was an uncomfortable combination of comic tone and bleak situation. The characters include a Hungarian playwright and his actress wife, a former prince who works at an automat, and a would-be émigré trying to hide a period of institutionalization so that she will be allowed to enter the United States. The play has a happy but unsatisfying ending. Atkinson called the play "warm and sympathetic," but nevertheless faulted it for a shallowness that leaves the audience knowing little about the characters (*The New York Times,* 12 November 1945).

Julia Ferber died in 1950, at the age of nearly ninety. Soon after her mother's death, Edna Ferber sold her Connecticut home, Treasure Hill, and moved into a New York apartment, where she lived for the rest of her life. *The Royal Family* was revived on 11 January 1951 at the City Center in New York, almost a quarter of a century after its premiere.

In 1952 Ferber published *Giant,* which fell victim to the same criticism as most of her regional fiction. Texans, like Oklahomans years earlier, felt she was insufficiently knowledgeable about them. Despite such umbrage, the book was well received and later became a movie starring James Dean, Elizabeth Taylor, and Rock Hudson. Ferber apparently became quite close to both leading men during the making of the movie and was saddened by the death of Dean in a car accident in September 1955. Released in 1956, *Giant* was Dean's final movie, and it did well, both monetarily and critically.

Ferber visited Alaska to research her 1958 novel, *Ice Palace,* which was credited with helping the successful drive for Alaskan statehood. Critics were not impressed, but the novel was made into a movie.

Near the end of the 1950s, Ferber regained the musical-stage rights to *Saratoga Trunk,* which she had leased for its movie adaptation, and she was soon besieged with requests from directors and producers who wanted to make the novel into a Broadway musical. Ferber had worked with Moss Hart and Richard Rodgers and Hammerstein years earlier in an unsuccessful attempt to adapt the novel into a play, and now she was naturally cautious about allowing someone else to proceed. Ultimately she was worn down by Robert Fryer, who had convinced Alan Jay Lerner and Frederick Loewe to adapt the novel. After they pulled out of the agreement because of exhaustion and ill health, Fryer got Morton Da Costa to direct and adapt the story. He was joined by lyricist Johnny Mercer and composer Harold Arlen. Ferber was unhappy when Da Costa did not follow through on an agreement that she would be allowed to edit and rewrite his work. The resoundingly unsuccessful show opened in December 1958 and closed the following February.

This ill-fated production was Ferber's final foray into the theater. When George S. Kaufman died in 1961, Ferber lost not only a friend but also her only congenial collaborator.

During the 1960s Ferber had many health problems. In 1963 she had surgery on her eyes to alleviate problems caused by glaucoma and cataracts. For roughly the last decade of her life, she suffered from a condition called trigeminal neuralgia, or tic douloureux, which caused intermittent, extreme facial pain. The only cure was cutting facial nerves, which would render one side of her face completely paralyzed. Ferber elected to live with the pain. This affliction went away in 1965, giving her a few months of apparent good health before she was diagnosed with cancer. During this time she was trying to begin a novel on the American Indian. Ferber's literary production during her final years was scattered and of comparatively low quality. Her final book was *A Kind of Magic* (1963), her second autobiography. Like *A Peculiar Treasure,* this book seems to gloss over unhappy or disturbing events. During her later years Ferber was filled with a great disdain and animosity toward her sister, Fannie. According to Ferber's niece, Julie Goldsmith Gilbert, while the two continued to visit one another regularly, the visits were tainted with ill will and explosive scenes, mostly initiated by Ferber.

Edna Ferber died on 17 April 1968 after a long battle with cancer. Some of her acquaintances regarded her as hard and cold, or manipulative and powerful, while others considered her sweet and lonely. Clues to all these aspects of her personality may be found in her autobiographies. She was demanding of herself and expected her friends and family to live up to similar standards. She was wealthy and overly generous; yet, when she was crossed she could, and would, hold a grudge for many years. She lived her life on her own terms.

Edna Ferber's novels are usually described as entertainments for the general reader rather than as literary masterpieces. Her greatest talent seems to have been her skill as an observer, having learned from her early years as a reporter how to depict accurately what she saw. Her plays allowed her to show a playfulness that is not apparent in her prose fiction. She was skilled at drawing keen portraits that revealed characters' personalities, idiosyncrasies, faults, and strengths. Like her novels, her plays were written to appeal to the tastes of her time, and were rewarded both critically and popularly. More important, the theater allowed her an active role in giving her characters material shape.

Biography:

Julie Goldsmith Gilbert, *Ferber: A Biography* (Garden City, N.Y.: Doubleday, 1978).

Reference:

Robert Karoly Sarlos, *Jig Cook and the Provincetown Players* (Amherst: University of Massachusetts Press, 1982).

Papers:

The principal collection of Edna Ferber's papers is at the State Historical Society of Wisconsin.

Harvey Fierstein
(6 June 1954 -)

James Fisher
Wabash College

PLAY PRODUCTIONS: *In Search of the Cobra Jewels,* New York, Playwrights' Workshop Club at Bastiano's, 2 October 1972;

Freaky Pussy, New York, New York Theatre Ensemble, 15 February 1974;

Flatbush Tosca, adapted by Fierstein from Giacomo Puccini's opera *Tosca,* New York, New York Theatre Ensemble, 22 May 1975;

The International Stud, New York, Theater for the New City, Fall 1976; New York, La MaMa Experimental Theatre Club, 2 February 1978;

Fugue in a Nursery, New York, La MaMa Experimental Theatre Club, 1 February 1979;

Widows and Children First! New York, La MaMa Experimental Theatre Club, 24 October 1979;

Torch Song Trilogy, New York, Richard Allen Center, 16 October 1981; New York, Greenwich Village Actors Playhouse, 15 January 1982; transferred to Little Theatre, 10 June 1982—comprises *The International Stud, Fugue in a Nursery,* and *Widows and Children First!*

Spookhouse, New York, Circle Repertory Projects, 15 March 1982; London, Hampstead Theatre Club, 1987;

La Cage aux Folles, libretto adapted by Fierstein from Jean Poiret's play, music and lyrics by Jerry Herman, Boston, Colonial Theatre, June 1983; New York, Palace Theatre, 21 August 1983;

Safe Sex, New York, La MaMa Experimental Theatre Club, 8 January 1987; New York, Lyceum, 5 April 1987—comprises *Manny and Jake, Safe Sex,* and *On Tidy Endings;*

Forget Him, New York, St. Clement's Church, August 1988;

Legs Diamond. The Almost Totally Fictitious Musical Hystery of Legs Diamond, libretto by Fierstein and Charles Suppon, music and lyrics by Peter Allen, New York, Mark Hellinger Theatre, 26 December 1988.

Harvey Fierstein (courtesy of the author)

BOOKS: *Torch Song Trilogy* (New York & London: S. French, 1979; New York: Gay Presses of New York, 1981)—comprises *The International Stud, Fugue in a Nursery,* and *Widows and Children First!;*

La Cage aux Folles (New York: S. French, 1987);

Safe Sex (New York: Atheneum, 1987; New York & London: S. French, 1987)—comprises *Manny and Jake, Safe Sex,* and *On Tidy Endings;*

The Sissy Duckling (New York: Simon & Schuster, 2002).

PRODUCED SCRIPTS: *Tidy Endings,* adapted by Fierstein from his *On Tidy Endings,* television, HBO, 14 August 1988;

Torch Song Trilogy, motion picture, New Line Cinema, 1988;

The Sissy Duckling, television, HBO, 21 September 1999;

"Amos and Andy," *Common Ground,* television, Showtime, 29 January 2000.

RECORDING: *This Is Not Going to Be Pretty: Live at the Bottom Line,* performed by Fierstein, New York, Plump Records, 1995.

OTHER: *Torch Song Trilogy,* in *The Best Plays of 1981–82,* edited by Otis L. Guernsey (New York: Dodd, Mead, 1983), pp. 181–200;

La Cage aux Folles, in *The Best Plays of 1983–84,* edited by Guernsey (New York: Dodd, Mead, 1984);

Forget Him, in *Out Front: Contemporary Gay and Lesbian Plays,* edited by Don Shewey (New York: Grove, 1988);

Robert Patrick, *Untold Decades. Seven Comedies of Gay Romance,* introduction by Fierstein (New York: St. Martin's Press, 1988);

Safe Sex, in *The Way We Live Now: American Plays & The AIDS Crisis,* edited by M. Elizabeth Osborn (New York: Theatre Communications Group, 1990).

John Glines, the Off-Off-Broadway producer of Harvey Fierstein's landmark play *Torch Song Trilogy* (1981), summed up Fierstein's importance to the development of American drama in the last decades of the twentieth century: "What Harvey proved was that you could use a gay context and a gay experience and speak in universal truths," Glines told *New York Times* interviewer Leslie Bennetts in 1983. A few others, particularly Mart Crowley, author of the groundbreaking play *The Boys in the Band,* had anticipated Fierstein in this regard, but no prior gay-themed play equaled the commercial and critical success of *Torch Song Trilogy.* Following the success of *Torch Song Trilogy,* theaters in the United States were flooded with dramas, comedies, and musicals in which the gay experience—from the personal dilemmas of coming out of the closet to the tragedies of AIDS—is set centrally into the fabric of human existence. Fierstein, who told James Grant in 1994 that he "can't really read or write. I read at a snail's pace, and forget what I'm reading all the time because my mind wanders, and I can't write a decent sentence grammatically," led the way for dramatists such as Larry Kramer, Terrence McNally, Craig Lucas, and Tony Kushner to extend his pioneering vision of what the gay experience means to both gays and straights in negotiating a shared future.

Harvey Forbes Fierstein was born on 6 June 1954 in the Bensonhurst section of Brooklyn, New York, son of handkerchief manufacturer Irving Fierstein and Jacqueline Harriet Gilbert, a school librarian. He began working as a drag performer around 1970, featured as a 270-pound teenage transvestite specializing in Ethel Merman impersonations. He made his professional debut at Club 82 and the La MaMa Experimental Theatre Club in 1971 prior to earning a Bachelor of Fine Arts degree from the Pratt Institute in 1973. Fierstein told *New York Times* interviewer Bennetts that "A drag queen's life is not a long life, and I've lost so many friends who have died over the years—from drugs, from suicide, from stupidity, from pain, because they could not find themselves or their place in the world." Drag, he believed, could be a way for a gay man to be himself. Fierstein also acted in plays, beginning with Andy Warhol's *Pork* in 1971, playing, he later recalled, an "asthmatic dyke."

While at Pratt, Fierstein began writing plays, including *In Search of the Cobra Jewels* (1972), *Freaky Pussy* (1974), and *Flatbush Tosca* (1975), the last two of which were produced by the New York Theatre Ensemble. Fierstein's 1975 play "Cannibals Just Don't Know No Better" remains unproduced, but Fierstein's playwriting began to gain attention within a few years of his graduation from Pratt. He received a Ford Grant, a Rockefeller playwright-in-residence grant to work with the La MaMa Experimental Theatre Workshop in 1979, and a Creative Artists Public Services grant in 1982.

Fierstein's breakthrough as a dramatist came with *Torch Song Trilogy,* which is actually a collection of three separate one-act plays—*The International Stud* (1976), *Fugue in a Nursery* (1979), and *Widows and Children First!* (1979)—held together by a central character, Arnold Beckoff, Fierstein's alter ego. Arnold is a Jewish gay man who works as a drag queen and is in search of a meaningful love relationship; Arnold believes, as Fierstein underscores in all of his dramatic work, that the need for love is independent of gender or the moral conceptions and constraints of any era. Actor Brian Kerwin, who appeared in the screen version of *Torch Song Trilogy,* saw similarities between Arnold and Fierstein: "A lot of people wonder about Harvey because he's such a character and an odd duck. There is something sweet and very gentle about the man. It's that thing that you see with so many tough, brusque, big talkers. There's definitely something in there that you can see has been, or could easily be, hurt" (*Out,* Octo-

Program cover for the 1983 touring production of the plays for which Fierstein won two Tony Awards (courtesy of Harvey Fierstein)

ber 1994). This duality is certainly present in Arnold, who remains indomitable and hopeful in the face of personal tragedy and disappointments.

In *The International Stud* Arnold, working as a drag act (under the name "Virginia Hamm," after having discarded prior stage names including "Kitty Litter" and "Bang Bang LaDesh"), is left by Ed, his bisexual lover, for a woman. As Arnold notes with equal parts bemusement and wistfulness:

> I think my biggest problem is being young and beautiful. It is my biggest problem because I have never been young and beautiful. More importantly, I will never be young and beautiful. Oh, I've been beautiful. And God knows I've been young. But never the twain have met. Not so's anyone would notice anyway.

Despite his seemingly outrageous persona, Arnold succinctly states his desire for a loving relationship, although there are many failed affairs in his past:

> In my life I have slept with more men than are named and/or numbered in the Bible (Old and New Testaments put together). But in all those beds not once has someone said, "Arnold, I love you . . ." that I could believe. So, I ask myself, "Do you really care?" And the only honest answer I can give myself is, "Yes, I care." I care because . . . [*catches himself*] I care a great deal. But not enough.

Ed cannot quite let go of his relationship with Arnold when he becomes intimately involved with Laurel, in what Arnold calls "a sudden burst of heterosexuality." Tellingly, Arnold's concern is for fairness to Laurel, a vulnerable and intelligent young woman, who apparently does not know about Ed's bisexuality. Arnold asks Ed, "Don't you think she has a right to know what she's letting herself in for? [*no response*] What's the matter? Catch your tongue in the closet door?" Ed continues to ignore Arnold's warnings and pretends to be proud of his move into the "straight" world, but Arnold insists, "How can sleeping with a woman make you proud of yourself if you know you'd rather be with a man? How can you ever get any respect from anyone if you won't be yourself? There's no you to respect!" In spite of the warnings, Ed goes to Laurel; Arnold, feeling abandoned, turns to impersonal sexual encounters at a gay bar. Ed later returns to visit Arnold in his dressing room, and, in tears, insists that "I'm so scared. I need you." As the play ends, Arnold is left pondering how to handle the situation with Ed.

In *Fugue in a Nursery* Arnold and his current lover, Alan, are invited to the country home of Ed and Laurel, who now live together. Laurel has learned of Ed's bisexuality, and the play begins when she calls to invite Arnold and Alan to visit. Arnold resists going, but Alan insists they do, and the rest of the play takes place in and around a huge circular bed that serves as all of the rooms in Ed's farm house. Laurel, hoping to get a sense of Ed's true feelings for Arnold, pretends to be excited about the visit: "Imagine being hostess to your lover's ex and his new boyfriend. Now if that isn't civilized then what is? It's downright Noel Coward." Arnold, however, remains wary. He is especially sensitive about the age difference between himself (nearly forty) and Alan (eighteen). Ed is not pleased about Alan's presence, referring to him as "that damned kid" ruining what "was going to be a beautiful weekend." The foursome pairs off in different groupings, allowing Fierstein to explore differences between gay and straight views of love and sex. Arnold and Ed reminisce about their relationship and have a fleeting sexual encounter that leads to confrontations between the two pairs of lovers, with new understanding in both relationships. Laurel later visits Arnold at the club, where she hears him sing a torch song; he explains that his affection for such songs is "about taking all that misery and making it into something. . . . Anyway, the audiences like it. I guess getting hurt is one thing we all have in common." As the play ends, Arnold and Alan have solidified their relationship, considering themselves "As married as two men can illegally get," and Laurel contemplates the possibility of marriage with Ed.

In *Widows and Children First!*, set five years later, Arnold is trying to cope with the murder of Alan, who has been beaten to death by antigay thugs, and to find approval from his mother, "Ma," in his desire to raise David, a troubled gay teenager he and Alan had applied to adopt. Ed is sleeping on Arnold's couch while he and Laurel, who have been married, are going through a separation, and Arnold elicits Ed's support in facing his widowed mother, who has not fully faced Arnold's sexuality. As Arnold puts it, when Alan died, "I was expected to observe the same vow of silence about him as she had about my father. So we've learned to make meaningful conversation from the weather, general health and my brother's marital status. I never even told her how Alan was killed." Fierstein depicts Arnold's anxiety about his mother's judgment in both comic and serious ways. After some verbal sparring, Arnold goes off to take a shower and Ma unexpectedly meets David, who has skipped school to meet her, although Arnold has yet to explain to Ma why David is living with him. When David announces, "I'm his son," Ma takes the news badly, accusing Arnold of making a crazy choice; but Arnold replies, "Adopting David is not a crazy thing. It's a wonderful thing that I'm very proud of." When Arnold compares his feelings about missing Alan to Ma's for her late husband, she explodes with rage: "What loss did you have? You fooled around with some boy . . . ? Where do you come to compare that to a marriage of thirty-five years?" Arnold loses his temper, as well:

> Listen, Ma, you had it easy. You have thirty-five years to remember, I have five. You had your children and friends to comfort you, I had me! My friends didn't want to hear about it. They said, "What're you gripin' about? At least you had a lover." 'Cause everybody knows that queers don't love. How dare I? You had it easy, Ma. You lost your husband in a nice clean hospital, I lost mine out there. They killed him there on the street. Twenty-three years old laying dead on the street. Killed by a bunch of kids with baseball bats.

Resolving not to talk about Alan, Arnold and Ma continue trying to resolve their differences over David. Ma sarcastically wonders what Arnold knows about raising children, to which he replies, "What's to know? Whenever I have a problem I simply imagine how you would solve it, and do the opposite."

When Ma finds out that David is a gay teen placed with Arnold, who, it is hoped, will provide a positive role model, Ma concludes that "The world has gone completely mad and I'm heading south for the summer." Arnold tells her that he has made himself independent so "I don't have to ask anyone for anything. There is nothing I need from anyone except love and respect. And anyone who can't give me those two things has no place in my life." Ma prepares to leave, while Arnold has too much to drink, confessing to Ed that "what I want more than anything is to have exactly the life she had." Ed wants to get back together with Arnold, but Arnold is not sure what to do and is concerned about Laurel; he confesses to Ma in a final attempt to reconcile with her that he misses Alan deeply. Touched, Ma advises that his feelings for Alan "won't ever go away," that remembering "becomes part of you, like wearing a ring or a pair of glasses." Ma leaves, and Arnold is left to ponder his future as he listens to a radio playing "I Will Never Turn My Back on You," which David has requested for Arnold.

Following Off-Broadway productions of each of the plays, they were joined together under the title *Torch Song Trilogy* for a large-scale production starring Fierstein, Matthew Broderick, Estelle Getty, Diane Tarleton, Paul Joynt, and Joe Crothers, under the direction of Peter Pope. *Torch Song Trilogy* opened on 16 October 1981 at the Richard Allen Center in a production by The Glines, a group organized to promote the work of gay writers, before extending its run by moving on 15 January 1982 to the Greenwich Village Actors Playhouse. Its final move was an important one, to Broadway in June 1982 at the Little Theatre, where it had a successful run. Mel Gussow, writing in *The New York Times* (1 November 1981), called *Torch Song Trilogy* and Fierstein's central performance "an act of compelling virtuosity." Walter Kerr, also writing in *The New York Times* (27 June 1982), was less impressed and felt that the play and performance were crippled by too much self-mockery: "The quality of the jokes varies, but that's not the point. The point is that there's no knowing the joker. His defenses are, and remain, impenetrable." Few others shared Kerr's criticisms; *Wall Street Journal* critic Edwin Wilson, for example, stressed that Fierstein "transcends the homosexual emphasis of the evening and makes Arnold a person with whom everyone can empathize" (30 June 1982). John Simon concurred, noting in *New York Magazine* (14 December 1981) that Fierstein's "ultimate achievement is the perfect blend of hard justice and warm empathy with which he embraces all characters, his own alter ego included." Clive Barnes, in his *New York Post* review (15 July 1982), called *Torch Song Trilogy* "a devastatingly comic play with just the right resonances," and in a long essay in *Theater*, Kim Powers writes that Fierstein not only "invited outsiders into this society, he has

Jay Garner, Merle Louise, George Hearn, and Gene Barry in the 1983 New York production of La Cage aux Folles *(photograph by Kenn Duncan)*

armed them with the codes of social conduct with which to create a utopian future."

The strong commercial success of *Torch Song Trilogy* made it a rarity, as few new nonmusical plays were being produced on Broadway in the last decades of the twentieth century. Fierstein won two Antoinette Perry (Tony) Awards in 1981 (for both his writing and acting), and in 1983 he also received an Oppenheimer Award, Dramatists Guild Hull-Warriner Award, and Drama Desk Awards for writing and acting, as well as the Los Angeles Drama Critics Circle Award in 1984. *Torch Song Trilogy* appeared when the magnitude of the AIDS crisis was just being fully grasped, and Fierstein, like many of his contemporaries, felt personal losses and the full societal significance most painfully. Fierstein told Joe Pollack in 1989 that the gay community's "response to AIDS has been, to a great extent, with love and help for one another. The straight community has responded with hate and fear, with demands for isolation, with threats." As an "out" celebrity, Fierstein became more engaged in the political and charitable causes surrounding the AIDS crisis, and the subject of AIDS became more central to his work as a dramatist.

The acclaim for *Torch Song Trilogy* eased the way for other Fierstein projects. Although *Spookhouse* (1982) had been written earlier, Fierstein, because of his relative obscurity, was not able to produce it in New York until after the success of *Torch Song Trilogy*. Opening on 15 March 1982 as a Circle Repertory Project, *Spookhouse* had a brief run, incurring bad reviews and otherwise garnering little significant critical attention. A grim comedy about a lower-class family residing in the "spookhouse" at Coney Island, the play focuses on Connie, a fortune teller, who battles with a gay social worker, Sam, as he tries to get her to care for her incorrigible son, who lies in the hospital with a broken back. In *The New Yorker* (14 May 1982) critic Edith Oliver called *Spookhouse* "less a play than a cluster of monologues" and added, "It would be tempting to dismiss the show as rubbish and leave it at that were it not for some skill in the writing and delineation of the characters." Reviewer Irving Wardle, however, writing in *The Times* (London, 23 April 1987), felt that Fierstein achieved "an unstoppable eruption of wounded, mendacious, viciously funny Manhattan defiance from Connie."

On the heels of the success of *Torch Song Trilogy* (as well as the modest reception of *Spookhouse*), Fierstein again won a Tony Award in 1984, this time for his libretto for *La Cage aux Folles* (1983), a lavish musical comedy based on the popular 1978 French screen farce of the same name, which, in turn, had been based on Jean Poiret's 1973 play (Fierstein was not involved with the 1996 movie *The Birdcage*, which was also suggested by the same source). With music and lyrics by Jerry Herman, who had previously written such landmark musicals as *Hello, Dolly!* (1964), *Mame* (1966), and *Mack & Mabel* (1974), and direction by Arthur Laurents, *La*

Cage aux Folles was a major hit, running for 1,761 performances in New York. It won six Tony Awards in all, and its New York run was followed by lengthy tours and popular productions around the world.

La Cage aux Folles is set at a transvestite nightclub run by Georges (played in the original Broadway production by Gene Barry) and starring his longtime lover, Albin (George Hearn, in a Tony Award–winning performance). Georges and Albin have raised Georges's son, who is about to marry a young woman from a staid family but fears that if they meet the flamboyant Albin and learn of the relationship of Georges and Albin, the engagement will fall apart. The son insists that Albin absent himself during the meeting with his fiancée's parents, but Albin instead comes in full drag pretending to be the boy's "mother," with a series of comic confusions ensuing. The son finally comes to the realization that Albin has, in fact, been his real parent, and all ends happily. *La Cage aux Folles* was the first Broadway musical to feature a gay couple in leading roles, but mainstream audiences embraced the show. Fierstein told *Washington Post* interviewer Joyce Wadler in 1984 that "It's just fun to see the real people be the gays and the farcical characters be straights. It's the opposite of what I've seen all my life."

Critics were generally enthusiastic about *La Cage aux Folles,* although Frank Rich, writing in *The New York Times* (22 August 1983), found it merely a "splashy entertainment" that "hums along in its unabashedly conventional way." In *Women's Wear Daily* (22 August 1983) reviewer Howard Kissel commented on the lack of preachiness about homosexual issues in the show, noting that it "is not a parochial show about a special kind of love. It has a warmth and tenderness we have not experienced in the musical theater since *Ballroom.*" Edwin Wilson, reviewing for *The Wall Street Journal* (26 August 1983), found *La Cage aux Folles* to be "pure fun," and in *Newsweek* (29 August 1983) Jack Kroll applauded the "campy brashness" of Fierstein's libretto.

Fierstein next turned his attention to another trilogy, *Safe Sex,* which was first produced in 1987 at the La MaMa Experimental Theatre. In the mode of *Torch Song Trilogy,* it is made up of three one-act plays—*Manny and Jake, Safe Sex,* and *On Tidy Endings*—all connected by the theme of showing the impact of AIDS on both homosexuals and heterosexuals. *Manny and Jake* depicts an AIDS sufferer debating new dating rules with a potential new lover; *Safe Sex* dramatizes a man who fears intimacy and uses his HIV status to continue his isolation; and *On Tidy Endings,* regarded by most critics as the best of the three plays, offers an intense encounter between the widow and gay lover of a man who has recently died of AIDS.

Fierstein told Glenn Collins in a 5 April 1987 *New York Times* article that "Everyone assumed that *Torch Song* was autobiographical, when it wasn't, very. But *Safe Sex* is much more autobiographical, more real." *Safe Sex* also revealed a playwright angered by the slow response of straight American society to the AIDS crisis, and the play was intended to address all members of society. As Fierstein told Collins, "This is a show about living in the era of AIDS, and it's something all people, not just gays, will have to deal with."

Safe Sex moved to the Lyceum Theatre on Broadway in a Shubert Organization production starring Fierstein, Anne De Salvo, and John Wesley Shipp, but it closed after only nine performances and twenty-two previews. Fierstein was bitter about the quick closing, feeling that the play was not given a fair chance by the Shubert Organization to find its audience. Critics of *Safe Sex* were mixed about the worth of the play, with many finding it less compelling than *Torch Song Trilogy.* Rich, writing in the *New York Times* (6 April 1987), found it "most forceful when its creator's anger burns through his other personas as saint and class clown," noting that this anger was most evident in a speech describing "two decades of American sociosexual history" in which, "his voice and face quivering with rage," Fierstein challenges "the conscience of any heterosexual who has latently decided to 'court' homosexuals for selfish reasons alone." In the *Boston Globe* (20 March 1989) critic Kevin Kelly wrote that *Manny and Jake* and *Safe Sex* were "purple embarrassments," but that *On Tidy Endings* was "taut, funny, eloquent" in its "questions about human connections," and most reviewers shared this view.

As the 1980s drew to a close, Fierstein's playwriting began to take a back seat to his work as an actor, although he kept his hand in as a dramatist. His one-act *Forget Him* sparked little interest when it had a brief August 1988 run at St. Clement's Church in New York, and another musical, *Legs Diamond,* written with Charles Suppon and featuring music and lyrics by Peter Allen, who also starred in the show, was a disappointment. *Legs Diamond,* which opened on 26 December 1988 at the Mark Hellinger Theatre in New York, garnered Fierstein an Ace Award in 1988, but reviewers were generally dismissive, and the production had a short run.

Following his narration of the documentary *The Times of Harvey Milk* in 1984 and his performance in the supporting role of Bernie Whitlock in the mildly successful screen comedy *Garbo Talks* (1984) starring Anne Bancroft, Fierstein did little acting on-screen until he played Arnold in the 1988 movie version of his own *Torch Song Trilogy.* Costarring Bancroft, Kerwin, Broderick, and Karen Young, the motion picture received a

Fierstein, Ricky Addison Reed, and Anne De Salvo in the 1987 Lyceum Theatre production of On Tidy Endings, *one of the three one-act plays in Fierstein's* Safe Sex *(photograph by Peter Cunningham)*

respectful response. Janet Maslin, writing in *The New York Times* (14 December 1988), felt that the movie fell short of the stage version of *Torch Song Trilogy,* noting that everything "is delivered at top volume. Miss Bancroft, playing in a manner that might seem scenery-chewing in another context, is exactly right in what she does here. And Mr. Fierstein matches her arm-wave for arm-wave, grimace for grimace, decibel for decibel." While *Boston Globe* reviewer Michael Blowen found it a "tepid adaptation" (7 July 1989), *Washington Post* critic Rita Kempley felt that Fierstein gave "a nakedly honest performance," and that "the themes are universal" (23 December 1988). The ephemeral nature of these plays was understood by Fierstein, who commented to Terry Dolan in 1993 that "More than any other work with which I have involved myself, these plays are this moment. They could not have existed two years ago, and probably would not be written two years hence."

In the late 1980s and early 1990s, Fierstein began to appear with greater frequency in movies, although occasionally generating controversy in the gay community over whether his typically over-the-top roles were breakthroughs or "just another gay friend used for comic relief," as James Grant suggested in *Out Magazine*. Fierstein's many appearances include supporting roles in movies such as *Mrs. Doubtfire* (1993) starring Robin Williams, Woody Allen's *Bullets Over Broadway* (1994), and the blockbuster *Independence Day* (1996); he also provided the voice of Yao in Disney's animated *Mulan* (1998) and appeared as an interviewee discussing Hollywood's view of gays in the acclaimed documentary *The Celluloid Closet* (1995). Fierstein has had roles in many smaller movies and on television, including appearances on *The Larry Sanders Show* (1997) and as a voice on the popular animated series *The Simpsons* (1990).

characters on a network situation comedy in the short-lived CBS series *Daddy's Girls,* starring Dudley Moore. Again, questions about Fierstein accepting what, to some, appeared to be a stereotypical role, generated a strong reaction from him. When Grant asked about the issue, Fierstein responded:

> I think *stereotype* is an unnecessarily vicious word. I think we have hated ourselves so much—we've hated our feminine side and we've hated our mannerisms—when we see that reflected, we go out of our minds. So when someone says to me, "You play a stereotype," I say, "No, I don't. . . . I play a specific gay man who *does* exist."

The failure of *Daddy's Girls,* owing equally to audience disinterest and to network fears of the gay content, did not change Fierstein's view, and he undoubtedly paved the way for DeGeneres's controversial "coming out" on her series four years later. Fierstein also acted in television movies, including an adaptation of his short play *On Tidy Endings,* shown in 1988 on HBO as *Tidy Endings,* costarring Stockard Channing. *Los Angeles Times* critic Don Shirley thought the characters were "too exemplary" but that *Tidy Endings* was "a passionate appeal for conciliation and respect in the face of the plague" (13 August 1988). It won four ACE awards for cable excellence, including one for Fierstein's writing. In 1999 Fierstein appeared in a supporting role in the critically disparaged television movie *Double Platinum,* costarring Diana Ross and Brandy.

From the mid 1990s, Fierstein turned his attentions more fully toward his successful acting career in movies, television, and in cabaret. In large theaters such as the Mark Taper Forum in Los Angeles or on smaller nightclub stages, Fierstein frequently performs a live show of comedy and songs. A live performance was released in 1995 on a compact disc under the title *This Is Not Going to Be Pretty;* the album demonstrates Fierstein's reconnection with his roots in drag and Off-Off-Broadway theater. *Los Angeles Times* critic Daryl H. Miller wrote of a 1998 performance that "Fierstein seemed to channel the spirits of Marlene Dietrich, Joan Crawford, Nina Simone and Lenny Bruce," and that he won a standing ovation from an enthusiastic audience (20 February 1998). Another successful venture for Fierstein was his authorship of *The Sissy Duckling,* which debuted as an animated program for HBO in 1999 before its publication as a children's book in 2002. It was widely praised for its sensitive and humorous approach to explaining "difference" to children.

In January 2000 Fierstein contributed a one-act screenplay to a Showtime television movie called *Com-*

Fierstein in a publicity photograph for his 1995 album, This Is Not Going to Be Pretty *(photograph © 1995 by Jeff Babitz)*

Fierstein made a highly publicized appearance as an out-of-the-closet old boyfriend of Rebecca Howe on the long-running television situation comedy *Cheers* in 1992. In 1998 he appeared as himself in an episode of the controversial situation comedy *Ellen,* when its star, comedienne Ellen DeGeneres, came out of the closet publicly at the same time her television character did. In 1994 Fierstein had played one of the first openly gay mon Ground, which featured three playlets chronicling gay life from the 1950s to the present; Pulitzer Prize–winning playwrights Paula Vogel and McNally wrote the other two. Fierstein's effort, "Amos and Andy," deals with gay marriage in the present. James Le Gros played Amos, a gay young man seeking to make permanent his sixteen-year relationship with his lover Andy; Ed Asner played his disapproving, conservative father, who finally comes to partial terms with his son's decision, although he shows up for the wedding ceremony wearing his military uniform. In the *Los Angeles Times* (29 January 2000) Miller called Fierstein's playlet "a shambles from the start," but Tom Shales, writing in the *Washington Post* (29 January 2000), stressed that Fierstein "knows how to tell a story with a moral and keep the moral from becoming a thick wet blanket." *The New York Times* critic Walter Goodman felt that "Amos and Andy" was "the slightest effort but the most successful, owing to some smart Fierstein dialogue and his turn as a gay florist" (28 January 2000).

Whether Fierstein will produce more stage drama is unclear at the beginning of the twenty-first century, but his impact is undeniable. In comparison with the white-hot anger of Kramer's indictments of American society's apathy toward gays in the crucible of the AIDS crisis in *The Normal Heart* (1985), or Kushner's toweringly moral and highly theatrical *Angels in America* plays (first performed in 1990 and 1991), Fierstein's work may seem relatively conventional in structure and more personally based in its view of gay life in America. However, working within a familiar Broadway style, Fierstein offers a conciliatory and forgiving tone in his drama, but one burnished by a level of anger and defiance meant to inspire progress in the relations between the gay and straight communities. As Fierstein told John Coulbourn in 1999, "You don't turn the world, but you do help shape it."

Interviews:

Michiko Kakutani, "Fierstein and *Torch Song*: A Daring Climb From Obscurity," *New York Times,* 14 July 1982, p. C17;

Leslie Bennetts, "Harvey Fierstein's Long Journey to the Tony and Beyond," *New York Times,* 26 June 1983, II: 3;

Joyce Wadler, "*Torch Song* Memories; Playwright Harvey Fierstein, In Life and Art," *Washington Post,* 19 September 1984, p. B1;

Joe Pollack, "Fierstein's Quest for Love and Respect," *St. Louis Post-Dispatch,* 22 January 1989, p. 6F;

Peter Goddard, "A 'Gayer, Braver' *Torch Song;* Harvey Fierstein Dismisses Critics Who Say Film Watered Down His Broadway Hit," *Toronto Star,* 9 February 1989, p. C1;

Patrick Brennan, "Romancing Rebecca; Bringing Gays to Sitcoms," *Washington Post,* 19 April 1992, p. Y5;

Hal Boedeker, "Gay Playwright Cheers Sitcom Role," *Toronto Star,* 23 April 1992, p. B7;

Terry Dolan, "Passing Time: Harvey Fierstein's Plays Are Anchored in a Moment," *Buffalo News,* 16 April 1993, "Gusto" section, p. 24;

Tom Orr, "After 17 Years, Fierstein Still Carrying That *Torch Song,*" *Seattle Times,* 28 April 1994, p. E1;

Greg Quill, "Harvey Fierstein Has Critics on Their Knees with Laughter," *Toronto Star,* 22 July 1994, p. B9;

Janine Dallas Steffan, "Wild About Harvey–Fierstein's Back in Town for Two Nights of Cabaret–And Partying," *Seattle Times,* 22 July 1994, p. D3;

James Grant, "Haaarvey! On the Verge of a Network Breakthrough," *Out* (October 1994): 72–75;

Mike Steele, "Tonies to TV, Feisty Fierstein Blazes Trail as Gay Icon," *Minneapolis Star Tribune,* 4 November 1994, p. 1E;

Peter Stack, "Harvey Fierstein Fires Away. Actor Chides Critics, Scolds Closet Gays on Eve of Show at Solo Mio," *San Francisco Chronicle,* 14 September 1997, p. 58;

Carol K. Dumas, "As Play Turns 20, a Rekindled *Torch,*" *Boston Globe,* 18 July 1999, p. B11;

Deborah Orr, "Edinburgh Festival: The Star-Spangled Stand-Up; Harvey Fierstein, Legendary Actor and Drag Queen, Talks to Deborah Orr," *Independent* (London), 8 August 1999, p. 4;

John Coulbourn, "Harvey Holds Torch: Activist, Actor, Playwright Part of Proud Voices," *Toronto Sun,* 12 October 1999, p. 33.

References:

Susan Heller Anderson and David W. Dunlap, "New York Day By Day: Shelter for AIDS Victims," *New York Times,* 15 December 1984, I: 27;

Rob Baker, *The Art of AIDS. From Stigma to Conscience* (New York: Continuum Books, 1994);

Fred A. Bernstein, "Wouldn't You Be Proud?" *People Weekly* (12 May 1986): 95–96+;

Leo Bersani, *Homos* (Cambridge, Mass.: Harvard University Press, 1995);

"Best Chest," *People Weekly* (15 July 1985): 100–104;

"Broadway's Funny Boy Takes Broadway On a Gay Mad Whirl," *People Weekly* (26 December 1983 – 2 January 1984): 60–61;

Andrea Chambers, "Harvey Fierstein, the Gay Torchbearer, Could Be Queen of the Tonys," *People Weekly* (6 June 1983): 82–83;

Gerald Clarke, "No One Opened Doors for Me," *Time*, 121 (20 June 1983): 80;

John M. Clum, *Acting Gay: Male Homosexuality in Modern Drama*, revised edition (New York: Columbia University Press, 1994);

Jodi R. Cohen, "Intersecting and Competing Discourses in Harvey Fierstein's *Tidy Endings*," *Quarterly Journal of Speech*, 77 (May 1991): 196–207;

Alexander Doty, *Making Things Perfectly Queer: Interpreting Mass Culture* (Minneapolis: University of Minnesota Press, 1993);

"The 42 Most Underrated and Overrated People in American Arts and Letters," *Saturday Review* (March/April 1985): 31–35;

William Green, "*Torch Song Trilogy:* A Gay Comedy with a Dying Fall," *Maske und Kothurn*, 30, no. 1–2 (1984);

Gregory D. Gross, "Coming Up for Air: Three AIDS Plays," *Journal of American Culture*, 15 (Summer 1992): 63–67;

Ernest James Hall II, "Harvey Fierstein: A Prophetic Voice in the Gay Community," M.A. thesis, University of Nevada, 1998;

Caryn James, "Fierstein Keeps On Joking, On Camera and Off," *New York Times*, 28 May 1988, I: 14;

Peter Johnson and Jefferson Graham, "Fierstein, Carrying Torch for Gay Network Sitcom," *USA Today*, 22 April 1992, p. 3D;

Wayne Kostenbaum, *The Queen's Throat: Opera, Homosexuality, and the Mystery of Desire* (New York: Poseidon, 1993);

Peter Lehman, *Running Scared: Masculinity and the Representation of the Male Body* (Philadelphia: Temple University Press, 1993);

Emmanuel S. Nelson, *AIDS: The Literary Response* (New York: Twayne, 1992);

Edith Oliver, "Boo!" *New Yorker*, 60 (14 May 1984): 131;

Kim Powers, "Fragments of Trilogy: Harvey Fierstein's *Torch Song*," *Theater*, 14 (Spring 1983): 63–67;

David Román, *Acts of Intervention. Performance, Gay Culture, and AIDS* (Bloomington & Indianapolis: Indiana University Press, 1998);

Román, "'It's My Party and I'll Die If I Want To!': Gay Men, AIDS, and the Circulation of Camp in U.S. Theatre," *Theatre Journal*, 44 (October 1992): 305–328;

Douglas Sadownick, "Curtain Rises on Broadway AIDS Discrimination Case," *Los Angeles Times*, 31 July 1989, part 6, p. 3;

Jay Scott, "Dignity in Drag," *Film Comment*, 25 (January/February 1989): 9–12+;

David R. Shaw, "Re-Presenting AIDS: A Bakhtinian Analysis of Passion, Play, and Carnival in Harvey Fierstein's *Safe Sex*," M.A. thesis, University of North Carolina at Chapel Hill, 1994;

Kath Weston, *Families We Choose: Lesbians, Gays, Kinship* (New York: Columbia University Press, 1991).

Horton Foote
(14 March 1916 -   )

Charles S. Watson
University of Alabama

See also the Foote entry in *DLB 26: American Screenwriters.*

PLAY PRODUCTIONS: *Wharton Dance,* New York, American Actors Company, fall 1940;

Texas Town, New York, Humphrey-Weidman Studio Theater, April 1941;

Out of My House, New York, Humphrey-Weidman Studio Theater, January 1942–comprises *Night after Night, Celebration, The Girls,* and *Behold a Cry;*

Only the Heart, New York, Provincetown Playhouse, 6 December 1942; New York, Bijou Theatre, 4 April 1944;

The Chase, New York, Playhouse Theatre, 15 April 1952;

The Trip to Bountiful, New York, Henry Miller's Theatre, 3 November 1953;

The Traveling Lady, New York, Playhouse, 27 October 1954;

Tomorrow, adapted from William Faulkner's story, New York, Herbert Berghof Playwrights Foundation, April 1968;

Gone with the Wind, adapted from Margaret Mitchell's novel, libretto by Foote, music and lyrics by Harold Rome, London, Drury Lane Theatre, 1972;

Lily Dale, New York, Ensemble Studio Theatre, 1977 [reading]; New York, Samuel Beckett Theatre, 20 November 1986;

Courtship, New York, Herbert Berghof Playwrights Foundation, 5 July 1978;

Night Seasons, New York, Herbert Berghof Playwrights Foundation, 1978; Teaneck, N.J., American Stage Company, 26 February 1993;

In a Coffin in Egypt, New York, Herbert Berghof Playwrights Foundation, 1980; revised as *A Coffin in Egypt,* Sag Harbor, N.Y., Bay Street Theatre, 17 June 1998;

Valentine's Day, New York, Herbert Berghof Playwrights Foundation, 1980;

Horton Foote, 2001 (photograph by Marion Ettlinger)

Blind Date and *The Man Who Climbed the Pecan Trees,* Los Angeles, Loft Studio, 1982;

The Road to the Graveyard, New York, Herbert Berghof Playwrights Foundation, 1982; New York, Ensemble Studio Theatre, May 1985;

The Roads to Home, New York, Manhattan Punch Line Theatre, 25 March 1982–comprises *A Nightingale, The Dearest of Friends,* and *Spring Dance;*

The Old Friends, New York, Herbert Berghof Playwrights Foundation, 27 July 1982;

Cousins, Los Angeles, Loft Studio, 1983;

Harrison, Texas, New York, Herbert Berghof Playwrights Foundation, 7 July 1985–comprises *The One-Armed Man, The Prisoner's Song,* and *Blind Date;*

The Widow Claire, New York, Circle in the Square, 17 December 1986;

Land of the Astronauts, New York, Ensemble Studio Theatre, May 1988;

The Habitation of Dragons, Pittsburgh, Pa., Pittsburgh Public Theater, 20 September 1988;

Dividing the Estate, Princeton, N.J., McCarter Theatre, 28 March 1989;

Talking Pictures, Sarasota, Fla., Asolo Theater, 14 April 1990;

The Young Man from Atlanta, New York, Signature Theatre, 27 January 1995; New York: Longacre Theatre, 27 March 1997;

Laura Dennis, New York, Signature Theatre, 10 March 1995;

The Death of Papa, Chapel Hill, N.C., Playmakers Repertory Company, Paul Green Theatre, 8 February 1997;

The Day Emily Married [Indian Fighters], Silver Spring, Md., Silver Spring Stage, 30 May 1997;

Vernon Early, Montgomery, Alabama Shakespeare Festival, 26 May 1998;

The Last of the Thorntons, New York, Signature Theatre, 2000;

The Carpetbagger's Children, Houston, Alley Theatre, 1 June 2001; Minneapolis, Guthrie Theater, 3 August 2001; Hartford, Conn., Hartford Stage, September 2001; New York, Mitzi E. Newhouse Theater, 7 March 2002;

Getting Frankie Married–and Afterwards, Costa Mesa, Cal., South Coast Repertory, 29 March 2002.

BOOKS: *Only the Heart* (New York: Dramatists Play Service, 1944);

The Chase (New York: Dramatists Play Service, 1952);

The Trip to Bountiful (New York: Dramatists Play Service, 1954);

The Traveling Lady (New York: Dramatists Play Service, 1955);

The Chase [novel] (New York: Rinehart, 1956);

Harrison, Texas: Eight Television Plays (New York: Harcourt, Brace, 1956)–comprises *A Young Lady of Property, John Turner Davis, The Tears of My Sister, The Death of the Old Man, Expectant Relations, The Midnight Caller, The Dancers,* and *The Trip to Bountiful;*

The Midnight Caller (New York: Dramatists Play Service, 1959);

Roots in a Parched Ground (New York: Dramatists Play Service, 1962);

Three Plays (New York: Harcourt, Brace & World, 1962)–comprises *Old Man, Tomorrow,* and *Roots in a Parched Ground;*

Old Man and Tomorrow, adapted from William Faulkner's stories (New York: Dramatists Play Service, 1963);

To Kill a Mockingbird, adapted from Harper Lee's novel (New York: Harcourt, Brace & World, 1964);

The Roads to Home (New York: Dramatists Play Service, 1982);

Courtship (New York: Dramatists Play Service, 1984);

Tomorrow and Tomorrow and Tomorrow, edited by David G. Yellin and Marie Connors (Jackson: University Press of Mississippi, 1985);

Blind Date (New York: Dramatists Play Service, 1986);

1918 (New York: Dramatists Play Service, 1987);

Courtship, Valentine's Day, 1918: Three Plays from the Orphans' Home Cycle (New York: Grove, 1987);

Lily Dale (New York: Dramatists Play Service, 1987);

Valentine's Day (New York: Dramatists Play Service, 1987);

The Widow Claire (New York: Dramatists Play Service, 1987);

The Road to the Graveyard (New York: Dramatists Play Service, 1988);

Roots in a Parched Ground, Convicts, Lily Dale, The Widow Claire: The First Four Plays of the Orphans' Home Cycle (New York: Grove, 1988);

Cousins (New York: Dramatists Play Service, 1989);

The Death of Papa (New York: Dramatists Play Service, 1989);

Cousins and The Death of Papa: The Final Two Plays of the Orphans' Home Cycle (New York: Grove, 1989);

The Man Who Climbed the Pecan Trees (New York: Dramatists Play Service, 1989);

To Kill a Mockingbird, Tender Mercies, and The Trip to Bountiful: Three Screenplays (New York: Grove, 1989);

Horton Foote's Three Trips to Bountiful, edited by Yellin and Barbara Moore (Dallas: Southern Methodist University Press, 1993);

Four New Plays (Newbury, Vt.: Smith & Kraus, 1993)–comprises *The Habitation of Dragons, Night Seasons, Dividing the Estate,* and *Talking Pictures;*

The Young Man from Atlanta (New York: Dramatists Play Service, 1995; New York: Dutton, 1995);

Laura Dennis (New York: Dramatists Play Service, 1996);

Night Seasons (New York: Dramatists Play Service, 1996);

Talking Pictures (New York: Dramatists Play Service, 1996);

The Young Man from Atlanta (New York: Plume, 1996);

Getting Frankie Married–and Afterwards and Other Plays (Lyme, N.H.: Smith & Kraus, 1998)–comprises

The Day Emily Married, Tomorrow, A Coffin in Egypt, Laura Dennis, Vernon Early, and *Getting Frankie Married—and Afterwards;*

Farewell: A Memoir of a Texas Childhood (New York: Scribner, 1999);

The Last of the Thorntons (Woodstock, N.Y.: Overlook Press, 2000; revised, New York: Dramatists Play Service, 2001);

Beginnings: A Memoir (New York: Scribner, 2001).

Editions and Collections: *A Young Lady of Property* (New York: Dramatists Play Service, 1983)—comprises *A Young Lady of Property, The Dancers, The Oil Well, The Old Beginning, Death of the Old Man,* and *John Turner Davis;*

Selected One-Act Plays of Horton Foote, edited by Gerald C. Wood (Dallas: Southern Methodist University Press, 1989)—comprises *The Old Beginning, A Young Lady of Property, The Oil Well, The Death of the Old Man, The Tears of My Sister, John Turner Davis, The Midnight Caller, The Dancers, The Man Who Climbed the Pecan Trees, A Nightingale, The Dearest of Friends, Spring Dance, Blind Date, The Prisoner's Song, The One-Armed Man, The Road to the Graveyard,* and *Land of the Astronauts;*

Collected Plays (Lyme, N.H.: Smith & Kraus, 1996)—comprises *The Trip to Bountiful, The Chase, The Traveling Lady,* and *The Roads to Home;*

The Orphans' Home Cycle (New York: Grove, 1999).

PRODUCED SCRIPTS: *Only the Heart, Kraft Television Theatre,* NBC, 21 January 1948;

The Old Beginning, Philco-Goodyear Television Playhouse, NBC, 23 November 1952;

The Trip to Bountiful, Philco-Goodyear Television Playhouse, NBC, 1 March 1953;

A Young Lady of Property, Philco-Goodyear Television Playhouse, NBC, 5 April 1953;

The Oil Well, Philco-Goodyear Television Playhouse, NBC, 17 May 1953;

Expectant Relations, Philco-Goodyear Television Playhouse, NBC, 21 June 1953;

The Death of the Old Man, television, *First Person Playhouse,* NBC, 17 July 1953;

The Tears of My Sister, television, *First Person Playhouse,* NBC, 14 August 1953;

John Turner Davis, Philco-Goodyear Television Playhouse, NBC, 5 November 1953;

The Dancers, Philco-Goodyear Television Playhouse, NBC, 7 March 1954;

The Roads to Home, television, *U.S. Steel Hour,* ABC, 26 April 1955;

The Traveling Lady, television, *Studio One,* CBS, 22 April 1957;

Old Man, adapted from William Faulkner's story, television, *Playhouse 90,* CBS, 20 November 1958; revised, *Hallmark Hall of Fame,* 9 February 1997;

Tomorrow, adapted from Faulkner's story, television, *Playhouse 90,* CBS, 7 March 1960;

To Kill a Mockingbird, adapted from Harper Lee's novel, motion picture, Universal, 1962;

Baby, the Rain Must Fall, motion picture, Columbia Pictures, 1965;

Tomorrow, adapted from Faulkner's story, motion picture, Filmgroup Productions, 1972;

Tender Mercies, motion picture, Universal, 1983;

The Trip to Bountiful, motion picture, Island Pictures, 1985;

1918, motion picture, Guadalupe Productions, 1985;

On Valentine's Day, motion picture, Guadalupe Productions, 1986;

Courtship, motion picture, Guadalupe Productions, 1987;

Convicts, motion picture, MCEG Productions, 1990;

Of Mice and Men, adapted from John Steinbeck's novel, motion picture, M-G-M, 1992;

The Habitation of Dragons, Turner Network Television, 8 September 1992;

Lily Dale, Showtime Television, 9 June 1996;

Alone, Showtime Television, 21 December 1997.

OTHER: "Flight," in *Television Plays for Writers,* edited by A. S. Burack (Boston: The Writer, Inc., 1959), pp. 107–147;

"On First Dramatizing Faulkner" and "Tomorrow: The Genesis of a Screenplay," in *Faulkner, Modernism and Film: Faulkner and Yoknapatawpha,* edited by Evans Harrington and Ann J. Abadie (Jackson: University Press of Mississippi, 1979).

SELECTED PERIODICAL PUBLICATIONS—UNCOLLECTED: *Emily, Kansas City Review,* 15 (Summer 1949): 263–266;

"The Trip to Paradise," *Texas Monthly* (December 1987): 140–149, 182–183.

Horton Foote's long, distinguished career in American playwriting started in the late 1930s and has continued without interruption to the beginning of the twenty-first century. Although he has become known for the variety of his works for the media—including the screenplay adaptation of Harper Lee's 1960 novel, *To Kill a Mockingbird,* for which Foote won an Academy Award in 1962, and his pioneering contributions to the Golden Age of television—his development as a playwright shows his most meaningful writing. He has put his best efforts into drama, particularly his epic nine-play *Orphans' Home Cycle* (composed during the 1970s), and he received a Pulitzer Prize for *The Young Man from Atlanta* (1995). Foote's career is also marked by steady advancement in the dramatization of his fictional town of Harrison, Texas, a sustained achievement unequaled by contemporary dramatists.

Albert Horton Foote Jr. was born on 14 March 1916, in Wharton, Texas, the eldest son of Albert Horton Foote, a haberdasher and cotton farmer, and Harriet (Hallie) Gautier Brooks, daughter of a civic leader. He was descended from the prominent Horton family; his great-great-grandfather was Albert Clinton Horton, a wealthy planter elected lieutenant governor in 1845 when Texas became a state. Foote graduated from high school in 1932 and studied acting at the Pasadena Playhouse from 1933 to 1935. For two years (1937–1939) he attended the Tamara Daykarhanova Theatre School in New York, where he was trained by Russian actors in the Stanislavsky method. He joined the American Actors Company in 1938, met Tennessee Williams, and began to write plays for that company. The main themes he began to develop are courage and adjustment to change; other subjects of interest include country music, Victorian customs, returning home, marital infidelity, oil fever, and the decline of the upper class. Foote has adhered to the style of the realistic play, which he learned from Henrik Ibsen. His intensely personal plays include some social criticism but are mainly family dramas. Foote married Lillian Vallish in 1945. They had four children: Hallie, Horton Jr., Walter, and Daisy.

Foote's first play was *Wharton Dance* (1940), about small-town gossip; the aim was to depict the varied cultures of America. Robert Coleman of the *New York Mirror* praised the piece. In 1940 Foote composed *Texas Town* (performed in 1941), which derides the oppressive life in a small town and recounts the oil fever sweeping Texas. Foote was quite pleased by Brooks Atkinson's review in *The New York Times*. Atkinson called the play "an engrossing portrait of small town life" and thought Foote highly "inventive" as a playwright but inadequate as an actor in the lead part of Ray Case, a young man eager to leave town and find something better.

Foote's best writing in this play occurs with Pap, Judge, and Digger Neal—the old men who gather daily at a drugstore; these scenes demonstrate his talent for salty dialogue. Pap and Judge deride the campaign of the governor but nevertheless attend his rally, where they enjoy the string band and rendition of "Beautiful Texas" but not the political rhetoric. Judge praises his crony Digger for standing up to a ruthless creditor, Damon, whose mortgage foreclosure will force an old black man named Hannah to leave his home. When Digger and Hannah hear that Judge has taken over

Foote in about 1935, while he was studying acting at the Pasadena Playhouse (Southern Methodist University Archive)

their mortgage, the two of them break down and cry together. Judge remembers fondly "the ole days" of the town and does not welcome the signs of progress: "Paved streets, brick buildings, chamber of commerce"–and no more saloons. Judge and his cronies furnish the comic relief in the play, which Foote handles to good effect.

Foote's next play was a collection of one-acts, *Out of My House* (1942). Under the heading "Those Southern Blues," Atkinson wrote in *The New York Times* (8 April 1942) that the first three segments lacked luster, but that the fourth, *Behold a Cry,* was "vibrant and glowing" and "bitterly realistic." Foote has noted that because of Atkinson's favorable recognition of *Texas Town,* all nine of the daily reviewers in New York attended the opening of *Out of My House*. Many praised *Behold a Cry,* but none so enthusiastically as Atkinson, who felt that Foote had done his best writing thus far.

Only the Heart (1942), like *Texas Town,* is the story of an individual's search for self through fleeing the confinement of small-town life. Julie Borden leaves Richmond, Texas, and begins a new life in Houston. She is accompanied by her husband, Albert, who chooses love for his wife over loyalty to his mother-in-law. This play, like the drama of Ray Case in *Texas Town,* ends with hope for a better life. Despite the importance of the young couple, the play is dominated by the mother, Mamie Borden, a new woman of Texas; she is onstage almost continually and gives the play its principal interest. She had been anticipated in *Texas Town* by a comic woman, also named Mamie, who proudly reported her oil strike to women in the drugstore. In *Only the Heart* Mamie speaks country Texan and displays the type of dry humor that Foote continued to cultivate in later work. Foote thinks the dream of oil, whether realized or not, is a will-o'-the-wisp, and oil fever is a recurrent motif in his plays. In *Only the Heart* there is a strike, and Mamie can look forward to astronomical wealth. Still, the oil money does not bring her happiness. The title of the play is from Heinrich Heine: material prosperity abounds, but "only the heart is withered and sere."

Only the Heart was Foote's first play to transfer to Broadway, and the critical reception was mostly negative. The dislike went from tepid to harsh as the play moved from the Provincetown Playhouse in 1942 to the Bijou Theatre in 1944. Writing about the first production, Lewis Nichols called Foote "the minnesinger of Texas morals, attitudes, and family life" (*The New York Times,* 7 December 1942). When Nichols reviewed *Only the Heart* on Broadway, however, he had nothing good to say. The company had an advantage in its original, less-formal production by not trying to be too professional, which it lost by moving uptown. In *The New York Times* (5 April 1944) Nichols censured the play for being "talky, old fashioned, and dull." Of six reviews on the same date, only two could be called favorable. Burton Rascoe of the *New York World-Telegram* said young people could be saved from many a disaster by attending the performance. He called the play "absorbingly interesting and satisfying." Ward Morehouse of the same paper said Foote revealed a talent for both construction and characterization. Some critics compared Mamie Borden to the domineering mother in Sidney Howard's *The Silver Cord* (1926), in which the blood-sucking matriarch wrecks the lives of her two sons. Most of the evaluations, however, were strongly negative. Howard Barnes of the *New York Herald-Tribune* called *Only the Heart* "a dreary domestic drama." John Chapman of the *New York Daily News* said that not since Tallulah Bankhead in *The Little Foxes* (1939) had he seen a woman he would so like to "bat down." Not amused by actress June Walker's dialect as Mamie, he said she could be from "Texas, Iowa, or the Erie Canal."

Foote's next important play, *The Chase* (1952), deals with a major subject in an original way. It is the story of a Texas sheriff who, unlike the stereotype, wants to save a criminal's life, not end it by killing him. Sheriff Hawes seeks to end the chase after a fugitive who has been in trouble his entire life. Hawes knows that killing the escaped prisoner will not end the chase for others like him but only perpetuate it. In this anti-Western, written in 1948, Foote spells out his dissent from contemporary movie trends. After World War II, Hollywood was trying to regain its dwindling audiences. There was a return to the popular genre of the Western in John Ford's cavalry trilogy, starring that hard-riding, fast-shooting hero, John Wayne. The first movie was *Fort Apache* (1948), followed by *She Wore a Yellow Ribbon* (1949) and *Rio Grande* (1950), all of which glorified the violent repression of the Indians. Relentless killing was the way to solve the problem of those who broke the law in this country. Foote, however, refuses to justify the use of violence to exterminate the criminal.

The Chase, which ran for thirty-one performances, was more successful on Broadway than *Only the Heart.* However, the critics failed to see it as more than a Western on stage. Reviewers who liked the play gave most of their praise to the actors. Jim O'Connor of the *New York Journal* (16 April 1952) enjoyed the "excitement" and acclaimed the stage debut of John Hodiak as Sheriff Hawes. John Chapman in the *New York Daily News* called it "a psychological western." Influential critics such as Walter Kerr and George Jean Nathan reacted negatively; the latter considered the play warmed-over melodrama. Also strongly disapproving was Atkinson, who was beginning to find Foote's plays not to his taste after praising the early ones highly; he had favorable comment only for the character studies, which had a literary flavor. He felt the Western without the ethical point would have been preferable. Atkinson wrote in *The New York Times* (16 April 1952) that by the middle of act 3, little drama was left in this "melodrama." A later analysis of *The Chase* by Marion Burkhart in *Commonweal* (26 February 1988) recognized Foote's attempt to discredit violence. She observed that the play is a gloss, unconscious or not, on *High Noon* (1952), a popular Western starring the epitome of Texas belligerence, Gary Cooper. Burkhart argued that the movie justifies violence, while in the play, the sheriff is admirable because he does not want to shoot the criminal, Bubber, but wants instead to return him to prison. In *The Chase* Foote revealed himself as a dramatist able to look critically at American values; he recognized a more humane approach to handling crime. Sheriff Hawes understands what not to do: no more whippings or public executions outside the law. As a compassionate man of law who wants to reform criminals, he will start early with young offenders and communicate with them.

Program for the 1953 Broadway stage production of one of the plays that Foote wrote for the Philco-Goodyear Television Playhouse; *Lillian Gish played the lead in both versions (Bruccoli Clark Layman Archives)*

After failing to write a commercially successful play for the Broadway theater, Foote turned to television during its Golden Age years, beginning in 1952. Paddy Chayefsky and Reginald Rose were also among the talented writers for television during this period. Fred Coe, the enterprising producer, mounted ten television plays by Foote. These were later published in *Harrison, Texas: Eight Television Plays* (1956).

Of these plays, *A Young Lady of Property* (broadcast in 1953) and *The Trip to Bountiful* (1953) were the most highly acclaimed, and *Expectant Relations* (1953) is less successful than the others. *A Young Lady of Property* depicts a teenager, Wilma, who is anxious about her future. Her mother has died and bequeathed to her a valuable piece of property in Harrison, and her father is going to remarry. Wilma realizes that the property gives her status and would provide security for the future. Her father tells Sybil Leighton, the woman he is to marry, that he plans to sell the property himself. When Wilma learns of this intent, she throws herself on the mercy of her future stepmother, who sympathizes with Wilma and lets her keep the property. They become good friends. Then, Wilma decides she does not want to be rich and remains in Harrison; she overcomes her fear of the future. This teleplay received a favorable review in *Variety* (8 April 1953). It also attracted the keen interest of Bette Davis, who was considered a highly intelligent critic of plays. *A Young Lady of Property* has remained popular, given often by amateur and professional companies.

The Trip to Bountiful, first performed on the *Philco-Goodyear Television Playhouse,* is arguably Foote's best work in the Golden Age of television. It transferred to the Broadway stage in 1953 with Lillian Gish reprising her television role as Mrs. Carrie Watts, and it was a critical success. The play presents Mrs. Watts, an elderly lady who lives in Houston in a cramped apartment with her shrewish daughter-in-law and son. She suffers from the pains of urban life and yearns to return to her rural home in Bountiful. At almost every attempt she is blocked by

Jessie Mae, her comic but heartless daughter-in-law; but she finally escapes and heads home. Jessie Mae is an example of the giddy Southern wife, similar to Tennessee Williams's women. She is totally selfish and at the end arrives in Bountiful with her ineffectual husband, Ludie, who is becoming stronger, to take his mother back to Houston. But this admirable lady has regained her courage to endure the trials of her life: through her archetypal return home she has been reborn. The roles of Mrs. Watts, Jessie Mae, and Ludie are provocative character studies. In 1985 the play became a motion picture, with one of Foote's most successful screenplays. Foote is one of the leading playwrights to turn his original conceptions into movies faithful to the originals. *The Trip to Bountiful* movie is true to his picture of a troubled old woman, desolate in an urban hell. It retains essentially the realism, social comment, and exploration of the central subject of returning home that was expounded in the play. Geraldine Page, as Mrs. Watts, won the Academy Award for Best Actress. Since its success as an independent movie, it has been shown on television and performed often as a play. In the fall of 1999 the television version with Gish, which is preserved in the Museum of Modern Art, was broadcast again on Showtime.

Foote's next play was *The Traveling Lady* (1954), which shows his interest in country music. Henry Thomas, who sings with a string band, has married Georgette, but he soon gets into trouble and kills a man in a fight. His problems originate in childhood when Miss Kate, his foster mother, whipped him without mercy. When he is released from the penitentiary, Georgette joins him in Harrison, his hometown, but Henry cannot face the reality of his shattered life. He now works for Mrs. Tillman, a prohibitionist; he steals her silver and tears the flowers off the grave of Miss Kate. Taken again to prison, he sings for his young daughter, Mary Rose. Georgette has met a neighbor, Slim Murray, and at the end leaves with him for the Rio Grande Valley. The play received encouraging reviews but had a short run. Atkinson, in *The New York Times* (28 October 1954), called the play a pleasure in a theater populated by "decadent people who don't understand anything" and thought the emotional scenes worth the "languors" in between. Foote adapted it for the screen in 1965 as *Baby, the Rain Must Fall*, starring Steve McQueen as Henry Thomas. It was a financial success.

After a long absence from the theater while he worked on screenplays, including the Oscar-winning adaptation of *To Kill a Mockingbird,* Foote returned to his first love to compose his monumental epic of Harrison, Texas. He wrote the bulk of *The Orphans' Home Cycle* in the 1970s, after his parents died. The title of the cycle is taken from Marianne Moore's poem "In Distrust of Merits" (1944): "All the world's an orphans' home." The first of the nine plays is *Roots in a Parched Ground* (1962), which takes place during 1902 and 1903 and introduces protagonist Horace Robedaux, based on Foote's father, when Horace is only a boy. Horace is abandoned by his mother after his father's early death, making him a semi-orphan. This play depicts the decline of the aristocracy in Texas. The Robedaux (based on the Footes) and the Thorntons (based on the Hortons) are destroying themselves by quarreling.

Convicts (published in 1988) is set in 1904. Horace works at a store on the plantation of Soll Gautier, a relic of the Old South, who is cruel to his convict labor. He has murdered one of them and fears retaliation. This play shows the Old South at its nadir. Horace, however, survives the lower depths of the plantation system. Soll promises $11.50 to Horace for his services, with which the boy plans to buy a monument for his father's grave, but the old man never pays him. Horace meets an upstanding black man named Ben Johnson (played by James Earl Jones in the 1990 movie version, for which Foote wrote the screenplay), who befriends him. Johnson foresees the end of this evil place, saying the cane will go and the people as well, white and black. At the end the old Confederate Soll dies and releases his grip–literal and figurative–on Horace. A reviewer for *Variety* did not like the uncinematic nature of the movie but rated it a vivid microcosm of the decadent plantation.

Lily Dale (produced in 1986) takes place in Houston in 1910 and focuses on Horace. He is a young man who must confront rejection by his stepfather, Pete Davenport, who coldly insults Horace and will not help him find a job. Horace falls ill in Pete's house from a psychosomatic fever. He overcomes it with the help of his mother, Corella, and his own determination. Horace also faces the dislike of his selfish sister, Lily Dale. This girl, who is younger than Horace, is dating a businessman, Will Kidder. She is afraid of sex and childbirth. While Horace loves their father, Lily refuses to remember him. Eventually Horace and Lily make peace. Lily asks forgiveness for the way she has treated him, and Horace recognizes his antagonism toward Pete. This play was successful onstage. It was presented at the Samuel Beckett Theatre from November 1986 to February 1987, with Mary Stuart Masterson as Lily Dale. The work was praised by the New York critics and made into a television movie. *Variety* called it "absorbing, uninterrupted theater."

The Widow Claire (performed in 1986) takes place in 1912, an age of reckless socializing, as Horace goes courting. Many popular songs of the day, such as "Waltz Me Around Again, Willie," are featured. The play serves as a bridge between youth and marriage.

After his return to Harrison, Horace, who has been working as a traveling salesman, lives in a boardinghouse full of dissolute young men, but he avoids their ways. He wants to attend business school in Houston and become manager of a dry-goods store. Unlike the others, Horace shows respect to women. He is dating the widow Claire Ratliff, who has two small children. Val, a violent suitor, knocks Horace out in a fight. Eventually Claire marries a middle-aged bachelor, whom her children adore. The play opened on 17 December 1986 at the Circle in the Square and closed on 26 April 1987. Matthew Broderick originated the part of Horace (and was later replaced by Eric Stoltz), and Hallie Foote, the playwright's daughter, played Claire. Frank Rich, the well-known New York critic, said the play had the poignancy of a naturalistic American short story from that era.

Courtship (performed in 1978) is a one-act play based on the lives of Foote's parents. It tells how a strong-willed daughter rebels against her father. This play takes place in 1915 at the height of the Victorian Age in Texas. Henry Vaughn is a patriarch opposed to his daughter Elizabeth's boyfriend, Horace, because he dances, drinks, and gambles: "We don't like *him*." Mrs. Vaughn agrees with her husband and tries to keep Elizabeth from "slipping out" with Horace. In spite of all they can do, Elizabeth continues to see him, wearing the ring he gave her on a necklace concealed under her clothing. When her parents confront her, the ring drops to the ground. Laura, Elizabeth's timid sister, asks her if she will marry him. Elizabeth answers, "If he asks me." This concise play confirmed Foote's reputation as an outstanding playwright of the one-act form.

Valentine's Day (performed in 1980) takes place on Christmas Eve, 1916. Elizabeth and Horace were married the previous Valentine's Day. This play shows the consequence of their elopement and the reconciliation with Elizabeth's parents. Mr. and Mrs. Vaughn come to visit the couple, who are living in a rented single room. Elizabeth's father at first disparages their quarters, which cannot be a real home. After a short while, however, he recognizes it as a home because he finds peace and contentment there. Other residents of the boarding house contrast with the happy marriage of Elizabeth and Horace. George Tyler, who married Horace's aunt, is remorseful because he did not marry his first love and stabs himself. Little Bobby Pate has lost his wife because his mother disapproved of the marriage; in her eyes, his wife was "common." A supportive figure who boards in the house is Ruth Amos, who sang "Oh, Promise Me" at the wedding of Elizabeth and Horace. Accompanying Mr. and Mrs. Vaughn on their visit is Brother (played by Matthew Broderick), the

Hallie Foote in the title role and Eric Stoltz as Horace Robedaux in the 1986 New York production of The Widow Claire *(photograph by Susan Cook)*

black sheep of the family and a casualty of Victorian strictness. He clashes constantly with his father.

1918 (published in 1987) dramatizes the flu epidemic of that year, which had as large an impact on Harrison as World War I had. Horace and Elizabeth's young daughter dies; Horace almost succumbs; and T. Abell, Horace's uncle, dies. The drama ends hopefully with the birth of a son, Horace Jr., to Elizabeth and Horace; the model for this development was Foote himself. Independent movie versions of *Courtship, Valentine's Day,* and *1918* were made into a five-part series titled *The Story of a Marriage* and shown on the television series *American Playhouse* in April 1987. Foote's daughter Hallie played Elizabeth. A critic for *Public TV Reviews* (1987) called it "an admirable achievement," and *TV Guide* rated it "excellent."

Cousins (performed in 1983) takes place in 1925 and satirizes the assumed close kinship of middle-class white Southerners. The worst example shown is Lewis

Higgins, based on a cousin in the line that stole the inheritance from the Thorntons. This intoxicated man enters Horace's store in Harrison but ignores his third cousin. A defender of females, regardless of their morality, Lewis killed his own cousin for insulting two women. A few virtuous cousins respect the values of kinship. Gordon Kirby is the son of Horace's Aunt Inez. He invites Minnie Curtis, a cousin on the alienated Robedaux side, to his house for a meal of fried chicken. These two practice the best qualities of kinship: kindness and forgiveness. Peggy Feury gave a full production of this play at her theater in California.

The last play of the cycle, *The Death of Papa,* was first performed on 8 February 1997 at the Paul Green Theatre, Chapel Hill, with Matthew Broderick and Hallie Foote. The time is 1925, and the patriarch, Henry Vaughn, a civic leader of the New South, has died. The focus, however, is on Brother Vaughn, who represents the end of the aristocratic class in the New South. It has declined greatly after World War I, unable to adjust to modern commercialism. Brother continues to suffer failures in his life: he cannot get along with the tenants on the farms inherited from his father; he drinks and is cheated by Mr. Borden, an unprincipled man of modern business; and worst of all, on the way to take passage as a worker on a ship to Germany, he stabs a man to death. A lenient Texas jury, however, gives him a suspended sentence. Horace Jr., the grandson, loves reading, which is foolishness to his grandmother Corella, an example of Texas anti-intellectualism. Horace Sr. defends his son's interest. Foote shows himself to be a perspicacious social historian through this cycle of nine plays, an imposing achievement.

While he worked on his plays, Foote did not entirely abandon screenwriting. The motion picture *Tender Mercies* (1983), with Robert Duvall, became one of Foote's most successful original screenplays. Foote and Duvall were also the producers. This movie portrays an older country music singer, Mac Sledge, who is battling to recover from a slumping career, alcoholism, and his divorce from Dixie Scott, also a country singer. The cause of the singer's failure is not oppressive society but his own faults. With the help of his second wife, Rosa Lee, and her strong Christian faith, which Mac adopts, he faces reality and looks forward to a better life. Rosa Lee thanks God for his "tender mercies" in sending her Mac. More openly religious than other works by Foote, this one shows that wealth does not bring happiness: the daughter of Dixie and Mac is killed in a car accident. *Tender Mercies* received favorable reviews and was a popular success. In the *New Republic* (31 March 1986) Stanley Kaufman acclaimed it as "one of the best screen plays in years." Foote had more freedom in writing this screenplay because it was produced by EMI, an independent British company. Directed by Bruce Beresford, an Australian, it won Foote an Oscar for best screenplay; Duvall also won for best actor.

Foote had returned to New York in the 1980s after residing in New England. He found the New York stage receptive to short plays because of the high costs of production, and he wrote several one-acts for Off-Broadway theaters. He was welcomed back by his supporters and by the critics. In these plays, taking place in the 1920s and 1930s, he analyzed the disintegration of families.

A trilogy of one-acts, *The Roads to Home* (different from the 1955 teleplay with that title), was first performed in 1982 at Manhattan Punch Line Theatre. In *A Nightingale* Annie Gayle Long, who often sings mournfully, has moved to Houston from Harrison. Unhappily married, she visits her friends Mabel and Vonnie, staunch Baptists who advise prayer to solve her emotional problems. Annie, on the other hand, says she needs mercy and tenderness. In the second play, *The Dearest of Friends,* Annie has gone to an asylum in Austin. Her friends talk about her as they travel to Harrison, which Mabel has praised so much. On the way Eddie, Vonnie's husband, falls for Rachel Gibson, a friend, and asks for a divorce. Mabel condemns him and warns her husband not to think of such a thing. In *Spring Dance* Annie is at the asylum, her new home, where she talks with two inmates, Greene Hamilton and Dave Dushon. She refuses the former's invitation to dance because that would make her divorce irrevocable. The trilogy was repeated at Lamb's Little Theatre in 1992. Clive Barnes, in *The New York Times* (1992), called it a "light play not to be taken lightly." Hallie Foote starred as Annie Gayle, and Jean Stapleton played Mabel.

Continuing his depiction of the antihome, Foote wrote *The Man Who Climbed the Pecan Trees.* First performed at the Loft Studio in Los Angeles in 1982, it was revived at the Ensemble Studio Theatre of New York in July 1988. Alcoholic Stanley Campbell works at the newspaper; when he is drunk, his wife writes the editorials. She locks him out and will not let him see his son. Then he goes to his mother's house next door and regresses to climbing pecan trees and singing plaintively "In the gloaming, / Oh, my darlin.'" Walter Goodman, reviewing the Ensemble Studio production in *The New York Times* (14 July 1988), praised the character of the doting mother (played by Lois Smith) and said the dialogue convincingly established a real place in the 1930s.

The Road to the Graveyard was performed in 1982 and revived in 1985 at the Ensemble Studio Theatre. This Gothic play also describes the disintegration of an old family. Residing on the road to the graveyard, India blames her mother's ills on this location. India's

Cover and title page from the program for the 2002 New York production of Foote's play, in which three sisters recount their memories of their father, who fought in the Union Army and settled in Texas after the Civil War (courtesy of Horton Foote)

pathetic brother, a film operator at "The Gem," wants to get married, but their mother, Miss Lilly, opposes his choice because his intended is a Cajun. Though invited, his fiancée, Bertie Dee, does not arrive for the supper. Sonnie gets sick and snatches an invisible rabbit out of the air in an effort to please Miss Lillie. Rich, in *The New York Times* (27 November 1985), saw unbearable turbulence beneath a surface peace in "this overpowering play."

Land of the Astronauts is Foote's last one-act of the 1980s. This satire of the Space Age was first presented at the Ensemble Studio Theatre in May 1988. In the manner of Flannery O'Connor, whom he admires, Foote introduces displaced persons who have no real homes. Phil Massey moves to Houston because he wants to be an astronaut. He leaves his wife, Lorena, and young daughter, Mabie Sue, in a Harrison motel run by the Taylor family. Son Taylor is in bed with a psychosomatic backache because his father keeps dipping his hand in the cashbox. Son's strong wife works at the reservation desk and is kind to Lorena and her daughter. Buster Duncan, a deputy for the female sheriff, drives to Baytown to fetch Phil. When Phil returns to the motel room, he and Lorena talk honestly about their lives. She reminds him that if he left Earth he would have to come back sometime or he would die. The truth versus illusion theme appears in another guise in this one-act. Phil wishes to find a place without worries, a desire that reflects the emptiness of his life. With the help of his wife he returns to reality and agrees to make this motel room his "home." Foote gave a dramatic reading of this play at the Sewanee Writers' Workshop.

In the late 1980s Foote also produced several full-length plays across the Hudson in cities such as Pittsburgh and Sarasota, Florida. The best of these is *The Habitation of Dragons* (performed in 1988), which deals with the subject of marital infidelity in American life and invites comparison with Greek tragedy. The hero, Leonard Tolliver, is a powerful man with a wife and two sons. He experiences a classic reversal of fortune when both sons are drowned in the Colorado River while on an outing with Wally Smith, Leonard's brother-in-law. Margaret, Leonard's wife, is in love with Wally and wants a divorce. Leonard is beset by the dragons of the title, which in his case are guilt and bitterness; ultimately he rises above them.

Leonard asks the question that recurs in many plays by Foote: is God punishing him for his sins? The answer is an emphatic "No." Bernice, the fiancée of Leonard's brother, George, gives the answer when asked, "I don't know why it happened." The predicament of Leonard is resolved when he grants his wife forgiveness. He is assisted by his Uncle Virgil, who recounts a story about a preacher who kept repeating the word "forgiveness" to a man. Leonard says that his heart will mend in time. George Anderson in the *Pittsburgh Post Gazette* (29 September 1988) called *The Habitation of Dragons* "a genuinely American tragedy." Foote turned the play into a screenplay for Turner Network Television, broadcast on 8 September 1992 and featuring Hallie Foote and Horton Foote Jr. A critic in *Variety* (1992) said it was overwrought but stunning drama.

During the 1994–1995 season, Foote was the selected playwright-in-residence at the Signature Theatre Company in New York, which produced four of his full-length works. He received a Critics Circle Special Achievement Award for this Signature Series of his plays. The best, *The Young Man from Atlanta,* won the Pulitzer Prize for drama in 1995. This play is set in 1950 and returns to the characters of Will and Lily Dale Kidder, presenting the plight they face when their only son, Bill, drowns in Florida. Bill had been living in Atlanta with Randy Carter, with whom he had a homosexual attachment. Randy (who never appears on stage) comes to Houston and avows that Bill's death was an accident, which Lily Dale accepts; but Will considers Randy a liar and holds that Bill committed suicide. Will has also just lost his job at the age of sixty-four and has to take a lesser one, adding financial difficulties to their emotional ones. He and his wife ultimately decide they will not investigate their son's death further. Will declares to Lily Dale that they will make it: "We always have."

After its world premiere at the Signature Theatre in 1995, the play was given a tryout in Chicago in January 1997 with Rip Torn as Will and Shirley Knight as Lily Dale. In New York the play opened at the Longacre Theatre on Broadway in March 1997. Clive Barnes called it "a rare thing, a living play about living, and it brings luster to Broadway" (*New York Post,* 28 March 1997). Foote has been accused of being undramatic, low-key, and noncommittal, an opinion Atkinson, despite early compliments, leveled at him. An appreciation of Foote's quiet manner and understated humor is an acquired taste. But the subtext in plays such as *The Young Man from Atlanta* is powerful and insistent. At the end of his career Foote proved he could still fashion a serious melodrama with interesting characters and a provocative theme.

With Foote's plays one acquires a more nuanced understanding of small-town Texas—the Confederate heritage, the agricultural economy, and the centrality of religion, especially the Baptist dominance. His depictions of Southern women are also interesting. While fellow Southerner Tennessee Williams depicted high-strung, neurotic women, Foote runs him a close second in capturing the idle, gabby wife, such as Jessie Mae or Lily Dale. The self-centeredness and tendency to hysteria appear strongly in all of these women, who reflect the psychological neuroses and often hilarious talkativeness of Southern women. Foote is a "social writer" in the sense that he records impartially the mores and sentiments of a distinct society. He strives above all for objectivity. He aims for truth, like Ibsen, always being careful not to tip the scales, as he narrates the annals of his family, his father especially, and his hometown. By recognizing the truth of their lives, audiences gain a better understanding of complex human beings, with all their faults and redeeming traits.

Although Foote is best known as a screenwriter, that is not his own preference. Without doubt Foote has consistently given his best effort to serious plays for the theater. Awards and recognition for his achievements include the Evelyn F. Burkey Award from the Writers Guild of America; the William Inge Lifetime Achievement Award, 1989; the Lucille Lortel Award for an individual body of work, 1995; election to the Theatre Hall of Fame, 1996; election to the American Academy of Arts and Letters, 1998; and the National Medal of Arts, 2000.

The word "retirement" is not in Horton Foote's vocabulary. In his eighties, he has continued to work in a variety of genres. He wrote the screenplay for the television movie *Alone,* which was presented on Showtime on 21 December 1997. This story of an elderly Texas farmer (played by Hume Cronyn) recovering from the death of his wife is not autobiographical but has its origins in the loss of Foote's wife in 1992. He has also written two volumes of autobiography: *Farewell: A Memoir of a Texas Childhood* (1999) recalls his early years in Wharton, while *Beginnings: A Memoir* (2001) continues his story from his arrival in Pasadena to the productions of his first plays and his marriage. In June 2000 Foote directed *When They Speak of Rita*, a play written by his daughter Daisy Foote and featuring Hallie Foote in the title role, at Primary Stages Off-Broadway. And as always, he is writing plays, including *The Last of the Thorntons* (2000), *The Carpetbagger's Children* (2001), and *Getting Frankie Married–and Afterwards* (2002). His place in American drama has long been secure.

Interviews:

Gerald C. Wood and Terry Barr, "'A Certain Kind of Writer': An Interview with Horton Foote," *Literature/Film Quarterly*, 14, no. 4 (1986): 226–237;

Ronald L. Davis, "Roots in a Parched Ground: An Interview with Horton Foote," *Southwest Review*, 73 (Summer 1988): 298–318;

Laurin R. Porter, "An Interview with Horton Foote," *Studies in American Drama*, no. 2 (1991): 177;

Wood, "Horton Foote: An Interview," *Post Script*, 10 (Summer 1991): 3–12.

References:

Terry Barr, "The Ordinary World of Horton Foote," dissertation, University of Tennessee, 1986;

Rebecca Luttrell Briley, *You Can Go Home Again: The Focus on Family in the Works of Horton Foote* (New York: P. Lang, 1993);

Marion Castleberry, "Voices from Home: Familial Bonds in the Works of Horton Foote," dissertation, Louisiana State University, 1993;

Charles S. Watson, "Beyond the Commercial Media: Horton Foote's Procession of Defeated Men," *Studies in American Drama 1945–Present*, 8 (1993): 175–187;

Watson, *The History of Southern Drama* (Lexington: University Press of Kentucky, 1997);

Gerald C. Wood, *Horton Foote and the Theater of Intimacy* (Baton Rouge: Louisiana State University Press, 1999);

Wood, ed., *Horton Foote: A Casebook* (New York: Garland, 1998).

Papers:

The main archive of Horton Foote's papers is the Horton Foote Collection held by the DeGolyer Library, Southern Methodist University, Dallas, Texas.

Charles Fuller
(5 March 1939 -)

Çiğdem Üsekes
Western Connecticut State University

See also the Fuller entry in *DLB 38: Afro-American Writers After 1955: Dramatists and Prose Writers.*

PLAY PRODUCTIONS: *The Village: A Party,* Princeton, N.J., McCarter Theater, November 1968; produced as *The Perfect Party,* New York, Tambellini's Gate Theater, 20 March 1969;

The Rise [*Brother Marcus*], Philadelphia, Afro-American Arts Theatre, 1968;

The Sunflowers, Philadelphia, Afro-American Arts Theatre, 1969—comprises *Ain't Nobody Sarah, But Me; Cain; Indian Giver; J. J.'s Game; The Layout;* and *The Sunflower Majorette;*

An Untitled Play, Philadelphia, Afro-American Arts Theatre, 1970;

In My Many Names and Days, New York, New Federal Theatre, September 1972;

The Candidate, New York, New Federal Theatre, April 1974;

In the Deepest Part of Sleep, New York, St. Marks Playhouse, 4 June 1974;

First Love, New York, Billie Holiday Theatre, June 1974;

The Lay Out Letter, Philadelphia, Freedom Theatre, Spring 1975;

The Brownsville Raid, Waterford, Conn., 1975; New York, Theater DeLys, 5 December 1976;

Sparrow in Flight, based on a concept by Rosetta LeNoire, book by Fuller, music by Larry Garner, New York, AMAS Repertory Theatre, 2 November 1978;

Zooman and the Sign, New York, Theatre Four, 7 December 1980;

A Soldier's Play, New York, Theatre Four, 10 November 1981;

We, New York, Theatre Four, 1988—comprises *Sally* and *Prince;*

Eliot's Coming, in *Urban Blight,* based on an idea by John Tillinger, book by Fuller, music by David Shire, lyrics by Richard Maltby Jr., New York, Manhattan Theatre Club, 18 May 1988;

Charles Fuller, circa 1988 (from David Savran, *In Their Own Words,* 1988)

Jonquil, New York, Theatre Four, January 1990;
Burner's Frolic, New York, Theatre Four, February 1990.

BOOKS: *A Soldier's Play* (New York: Hill & Wang, 1982);
Zooman and the Sign (New York: Doubleday, 1982).

PRODUCED SCRIPTS: *Roots, Resistance, and Renaissance* (12-part series), WHYY-TV, Philadelphia, 1967;
Mitchell, WCAU-TV, Philadelphia, 1968;
Black America, WKYW-TV, Philadelphia, 1970–1971;
"The Black Experience," WIP Radio, Philadelphia, 1970–1971;

"The Sky is Gray," adapted from Ernest J. Gaines's story, *American Short Story Series,* television, PBS, 1980;

A Soldier's Story, motion picture, Columbia Pictures, 1984;

A Gathering of Old Men, adapted from Gaines's novel, television, CBS, 10 May 1987;

Zooman, television, Showtime, 19 March 1995;

The Wall (segment "The Badge"), television, Showtime, 24 May 1998;

Love Songs, television, Showtime, 25 April 1999.

OTHER: "Black Writing is Socio-Creative Art," *Liberator,* 7 (January 1967): 8–10;

The Rise, in *New Plays from the Black Theatre: An Anthology,* compiled by Ed Bullins (New York: Bantam, 1969), pp. 247–304.

The second African American playwright to be awarded the Pulitzer Prize, Charles Fuller is well known for his social plays, which probe into what he calls "the madness of race in America." His primary mission as a writer is to rectify stereotypes of African Americans; as he told David Savran in a 1988 interview: "It's very important for me as a black writer to change how Western civilization—which includes black people—perceives black people. That's at the heart of what I do." Most of his plays are grounded in history, with an understanding that history itself is in need of revision and can benefit from a new perspective. Fuller explained to interviewer Frank White III in 1983 that he prefers a military setting for his plays because it enables "men to confront men. You can't call a man a fool whose principal function is to defend this country." In these settings Fuller draws from his father's experiences in the navy during World War II and his own in the army, a personal history the playwright does not otherwise discuss.

Charles Henry Fuller Jr. was born on 5 March 1939 in Philadelphia, Pennsylvania, to Charles H. and Lillian Anderson Fuller. He grew up in a bustling household; in addition to Charles Jr. and his two biological sisters, his parents took in a total of twenty foster children over the years, eventually adopting two. Charles Fuller Sr. worked as a printer, and he kindled in young Charles an early appreciation for the written word when he asked his son to proofread some of his work. Fuller was first drawn to the theater at age thirteen when he attended a Yiddish play. Although he did not understand a word of it, he was thrilled; as he told Herbert Mitgang in a 1982 interview, "it was live theater, and I felt myself responding to it." At Roman Catholic High School, he became close friends with Larry Neal, who later emerged as an important poet, dramatist, and critic. Neal introduced him to great literature, and since both were avid readers, they competed to be the first to read every book at the local public library. This endeavor revealed to them how deep-rooted negative stereotypes of blacks were in literature. Fuller and Neal began writing to correct such stereotypes.

After graduating from high school in 1956, Fuller attended Villanova University, where he majored in English, hoping to become a professional writer. One of his professors discouraged him from pursuing a literary career, citing the challenges facing African American writers at the time. As a result, Fuller dropped out of Villanova in 1958 and enlisted in the army the following year. For the next few years, he served as a petroleum-lab technician in Japan and South Korea. After his discharge in 1962, he returned to Philadelphia and married Miriam A. Nesbitt, a high-school teacher and registered nurse; the couple has two sons (Charles III and David). During the 1960s, Fuller held various positions in Philadelphia as a bank loan collector, a counselor for minority students at Temple University, and a city housing inspector in Ludlow. Between 1965 and 1968, he attended night classes at La Salle College and continued to write short stories that mostly consisted of dialogue. Fuller's first dramatic enterprise was cofounding the Afro-American Arts Theatre in Philadelphia in 1967; he codirected it until 1971. Fuller described the project to Savran as a community rebuilding effort: "At that time I wasn't really writing plays, but skits connected to community issues. I was interested in how you save your community." Through his work at the Afro-American Arts Theatre, Fuller was discovered by the managers of the McCarter Theater in Princeton, New Jersey, who commissioned him to write *The Village: A Party,* his first long play, for the 1968–1969 season.

Fuller's first professionally produced work, *The Village* depicts a utopian community founded by five interracial couples; problems surface when their black leader falls in love with a woman of his race. The play opened at the McCarter Theater and in 1969 moved Off-Broadway to Tambellini's Gate Theater for a brief run under the new title *The Perfect Party.* It won mixed praise from critics, who appreciated its presentation of a complex racial problem but denounced its weak ending. However, Dan Sullivan, writing for *The New York Times* (13 November 1968), stressed that "The play's originality and urgency are unquestionable and so is the talent of the playwright." Years later, Fuller claimed to Mitgang that this early effort "was one of the world's worst interracial plays."

Wanting to be a part of the theater scene in New York City, Fuller moved there in 1969. His next two

Charles Brown, Peter Friedman, Stephen Zetleer, and Cottel Smith in the 1981 Negro Ensemble Company production of A Soldier's Play (photograph by Bert Andrews)

plays—*In My Many Names and Days* (1972), a fifty-year family history, and *The Candidate* (1974), a play about a black man running for mayor—were both performed at the New Federal Theatre. Fuller's long association with the Negro Ensemble Company began in 1974 with *In the Deepest Part of Sleep*. But the play, which examined the relationships of a mentally disturbed woman with her family, failed. Fuller told Mitgang, "I decided then that I wanted to do something bigger and beyond myself, something historical, that would stand *outside* normal black theater. I wanted to open up black theater so that it couldn't be labeled that easily." The result was *The Brownsville Raid* (1975), Fuller's first real hit and his first play to use a military setting.

The Brownsville Raid was first produced in Waterford, Connecticut, in 1975 and opened at Theatre DeLys on 5 December 1976 where it ran for 112 performances. Based on a true incident, the play dramatizes events surrounding the 1906 shooting spree in Brownsville, Texas, of which soldiers from an all-black company stationed nearby were falsely accused. When the murder investigation yielded no results, the entire regiment (167 men in all) was dishonorably discharged without a trial by President Theodore Roosevelt. The play and the playwright received immediate recognition. According to Martin Gottfried in *The New York Post* (1976), "The power of his play lies in the realization of his characters that they have placed their faith in an Army, an America that would betray them the first chance it got."

During the 1970s Fuller received several fellowships and grants—from the Rockefeller Foundation (1975), the National Endowment for the Arts (1976), and the Guggenheim Foundation (1977–1978)—as well as the Creative Artist Public Service Award (1974). Fuller's next play to be performed by the Negro Ensemble Company, *Zooman and the Sign* (1980), won two Obie Awards (for best playwright and best actor) and an Audelco Award for best playwright. *Zooman and the Sign* came out of the same community-focused theatrical tradition Fuller had helped to forge at the Afro-American Arts Theatre in Philadelphia, and his goal this time was to draw attention to the violence in black communities. In a 13 April 1982 *New York Post* article, he stated: "I went around to see about getting lawyers for this kid who had just killed another kid. The boy was just as calm as could be. So that's where *Zooman* came from." The play begins with black teenager Zooman's indifferent admission of accidentally murdering a black girl, Jinny Tate: "I just killed somebody. Little girl, I think." When Jinny's father, Reuben, realizes that his daughter's murderer is going free because his neighbors will not identify the guilty one, he hangs a conspicuous sign on his front porch condemning all members of the community: "THE KILLERS OF OUR DAUGHTER JINNY ARE FREE ON THE STREETS BECAUSE OUR NEIGHBORS WILL NOT IDENTIFY THEM!" In the end, as Zooman is trying to tear down the sign, he is killed by Jinny's great-uncle. The play closes with another sign: "HERE, LESTER JOHNSON WAS KILLED. HE WILL BE MISSED BY FAMILY AND FRIENDS. HE WAS KNOWN AS ZOOMAN."

Zooman and the Sign was a critical success because of Fuller's ability to transcend flat characterization. According to Frank Rich, "In *Zooman and the Sign,* there are no real villains, only victims. Every character is locked into the same cycle of terror, and it's a nightmare only courage can end" (*The New York Times,* 8 December 1980). Gerald Weales, in *The Georgia Review* (Fall 1981), commended the dramatist's complex outlook on society and individuals in *Zooman and the Sign:* "Without excusing Zooman with the once fashionable assumptions about society as the real criminal, Fuller presents a character who has found his own unhappy, insufficient response to a world that he has known only in the physical and spiritual ruins around him." Violence often marks the confrontations among blacks or between blacks and whites in Fuller's plays, and *Zooman and the Sign* exemplifies the violence that permeates Fuller's dramatic world.

The sudden heart-attack death of his close friend Larry Neal in January 1981 prompted Fuller to write a play in his memory; it was finished in four months. *A Soldier's Play* opened on 10 November 1981 and ran for 481 performances. His most successful play to date, it won Fuller the 1982 Pulitzer Prize, the New York Drama Critics Circle Award, the Outer Critics Circle Award, and the Theatre Club Award. Loosely modeled after Herman Melville's *Billy Budd* (1924), the play is structured as a murder mystery that focuses on racial prejudices. Set in 1944 in a segregated military camp in Louisiana, the dramatic action revolves around the investigation by Captain Davenport, a black lawyer sent down from Washington, into the murder of Technical Sergeant Vernon Waters. As Walter Kerr pointed out in *The New York Times* (6 December 1981), "Its particular excitement, however, doesn't really stem from the traditional business of tracking down the identity of the criminal. It comes instead from tracking down the identity of the victim."

Indeed, in order to find out who killed the sergeant, the audience first has to discover who the sergeant was. A series of flashbacks discloses that Waters believed in advancing his race by eliminating blacks he considered to be in the way of their social progress (whom he refers to as "geechies"). However, Waters falls apart when C. J. Memphis, a "geechy" he has helped put behind bars, kills himself. The sergeant's self-disgust and self-hatred are revealed in his final words: "They still hate you!" Although he has worked, even killed, for whites, he realizes that he can never be like them or one of them. Arguably Fuller's most compelling character, Sergeant Waters and his actions confirm Richard Hornby's claim that "In Fuller's plays, the focus is on the injuries blacks do to blacks, which always result ultimately from the racist infrastructure in which they find themselves."

A Soldier's Play is more than a mystery; it challenges both the onstage and the offstage investigators (the audience) to examine their own racial prejudices, as the usual suspects range from the Ku Klux Klan to two white racist officers. A twist in the narrative thwarts such expectations and reveals the person responsible for the murder of Waters to be one of the victim's own black soldiers, Peterson, who kills the sergeant to avenge the death of Memphis. The play ends with black soldiers overjoyed at the news of their being shipped off to fight Adolf Hitler's troops. According to Rich in *The New York Times* (27 November 1981), this ending continues the vicious circle of self-hatred and self-destruction: "this aspiration is just another version of Waters's misplaced ambition to deny his blackness by emulating whites—and just as likely to end in tragic, self-annihilating doom." Proving Rich's theory, Davenport informs the audience that "The entire outfit—officers and enlisted men—was wiped out in the Ruhr Valley during a German advance."

A Soldier's Play was almost universally celebrated. Despite its immense critical and popular success, Fuller refused to let the show move to Broadway, in part to keep ticket prices down. His screen adaptation of the play, *A Soldier's Story* (1984), was directed by Norman Jewison and featured most of the original cast, including Adolph Caesar (as Waters) and Denzel Washington (as Peterson). The movie was nominated for three Academy Awards: best supporting actor (Caesar), best picture, and best adapted screenplay. It drew large and diverse audiences to the movie theaters and won the 1985 Edgar Allan Poe Mystery Award.

Fuller continued to receive prestigious awards and honors during the 1980s: honorary doctorates from La Salle College (1982), Villanova University

Maureen Silliman, William Mooney, and Hattie Winston in the 1988 Negro Ensemble Company production of Prince, *the second part of a six-play cycle called* We *(photograph by Bert Andrews)*

(1983), and Chestnut Hill College (1985) and the Hazelitt Award from the Pennsylvania State Council on the Arts (1984). He has taught at various institutions such as Yale University, Hunter College, and (until 1993) Temple University. He has also lectured widely in the United States, Canada, and Europe.

Fuller's next theater project was a cycle, *We: A History in Five Plays* (later expanded to six plays), which portrays the experiences of the newly freed slaves between 1863 and 1900. For his *We* series, which has overlapping characters, Fuller read an estimated 120 books on the Civil War era. *Sally* and *Prince* were produced under the joint title of *We* in 1988 at Theatre Four by the Negro Ensemble Company, followed by *Jonquil* and *Burner's Frolic* in 1990. The fifth and sixth plays have not yet been produced. Fuller's objective in this cycle is to rewrite American histories of the Civil War and postbellum periods from an African American vantage point. Fuller argues that because most African Americans from this period did not know how to read and write, history has been written from the perspective of the literate, white majority, and therefore, it excludes the black perspective. It is now time, Fuller told Savran, to "reexamine these events, to define ourselves rather than to be defined." Fuller concludes, "If you lead people to rethink the past, that may change how they perceive black people in the future." Despite its impressive objective, Fuller's *We* cycle has stirred little excitement among critics, who have often found the individual plays disappointing.

The most celebrated aspect of Fuller's drama is his complex characterization. Fuller stressed to Savran that "Even the worst man has something in him that is admired and loved by somebody else. If you understand that, you can't in a play describe characters" simplistically. While critics also applaud Fuller's multidimensional white characters, the dramatist's main goal has been to create complex black characters. He said in a 1982 interview with Stanley Crouch: "I feel my job is to get away from all the old images. My development, and the development of black theater is an attempt to send an arrow into the literature of America, to make a hole large enough for our humanity to move through." However, Amiri Baraka, a leading African American writer, has denounced Fuller's later plays, especially *Zooman and* the Sign and *A Soldier's Play*, which, he argues, condemn blacks and portray them as "the problem" and as "animals." Responding to such criticisms, Fuller says his goal is not to depict blacks unrealistically—violence, after all, does take place in the black community, and African Americans should assume responsibility for it. He told White, "I can't see how any growing people would want to be continually portrayed as sweet and innocent."

In spite of his all-too-human characters with their fair share of good and evil, and in spite of the element of violence in his plays, Fuller's drama does not, according to most critics, present a desperate outlook on race relations in America. Esther Harriott claims, for example, that "Even though his plays are about the anguish of racism in American life, they are hopeful. The hope is his heroes' belief in the possibility of making a difference." Whether they can make a difference is questionable, though. Fuller likes writing about "complex situations that do not admit easy resolution," according to David Savran, and the dramatist himself admits that "stories have gray endings. We don't simply close the door and step into a new life."

Since 1990 Fuller has devoted more attention to writing for television and movies, because they allow him to reach large audiences. His television scripts include "The Sky is Gray" (1980), based on an Ernest J. Gaines story; *A Gathering of Old Men* (1987), adapted from a Gaines novel; *Zooman* (1995); and *Love Songs* (1999). However, he reassures his audiences that he is committed to the theater.

Charles Fuller's main contribution to American theater has been his social commitment. He believes dramatists are morally responsible for putting onstage the truth as they see it: "People are benefitted by the truth, no matter how ugly it is. Anything that we are misled by or misinformed about or afraid to confront limits us." True to his artistic credo, Fuller has offered a fresh look at race relations in America, one that refuses to point the finger at any one group or institution. Instead, he challenges audiences to acknowledge their responsibility for and involvement in the race problem and to take action to remedy it.

Interviews:

Herbert Mitgang, "Playwright Traces the Long Road to a Hit," *New York Times*, 11 January 1982, p. C13;

Stanley Crouch, "Talent, Luck, and the Sleeping Yo-Yo of American Social Progress—A Conversation with Charles Fuller," *Vogue* (October 1982): 186;

Frank White III, "Pushing beyond the Pulitzer," *Ebony* (March 1983): 116–118;

Sharyn Kane and Richard Keeton, "The Writing Life," *Writer's Digest*, 64 (March 1984): 24–25;

Glen Duffy, "No More Blues for Uncle Charles," *Philadelphia*, 75 (October 1984): 112+;

Maralyn Lois Polak, "Charles Fuller: He Grew Up with Words," in her *The Writer as Celebrity: Intimate Interviews* (New York: M. Evans, 1986), pp. 116–120;

David Savran, "Charles Fuller," in his *In Their Own Words: Contemporary American Playwrights* (New York: Theatre Communications Group, 1988), pp. 70–83;

Esther Harriott, "Interview with Charles Fuller," in *American Voices: Five Contemporary Playwrights in Essays and Interviews* (Jefferson, N.C.: McFarland, 1988), pp. 112–125;

Dennis Kucherawy, "Charles Fuller: Haunted by History," *Theater Week* (12–18 December 1988): 8–17;

Graham N. Nesmith, "Charles Fuller: Steadfast," *American Theatre*, 16 (October 1999): 99–101.

References:

Nilgün Anadolu-Okur, *Contemporary African American Theater: Afrocentricity in the Works of Larry Neal, Amiri Baraka, and Charles Fuller* (New York: Garland, 1997), pp. 127–171;

Amiri Baraka, "The Descent of Charlie Fuller into Pulitzerland and the Need for African-American Institutions," *Black American Literature Forum*, 17 (Summer 1983): 51–54;

Steven R. Carter, "The Detective as Solution: Charles Fuller's *A Soldier's Play*," *Clues*, 12 (Spring–Summer 1991): 33–42;

William W. Demastes, "Charles Fuller and *A Soldier's Play*," in his *Beyond Naturalism: A New Realism in American Theatre* (New York: Greenwood Press, 1988), pp. 126–136;

Esther Harriott, "Charles Fuller: The Quest for Justice," in *American Voices: Five Contemporary Playwrights in Essays and Interviews* (Jefferson, N.C.: McFarland, 1988), pp. 101–111;

Richard Hornby, "Minority Theatre," *Hudson Review*, 42 (Summer 1989): 283–289;

Linda K. Hughes and Howard Faulkner, "The Role of Detection in *A Soldier's Play*," *Clues*, 7 (Fall–Winter 1986): 83–97;

Don Kunz, "Singing the Blues in *A Soldier's Story*," *Literature/Film Quarterly*, 19, no. 1 (1991): 27–34;

Leo Sauvage, "Plays that Got Away," *New Leader* (12–26 July 1982): 21;

Gary P. Storhoff, "Reflections of Identity in *A Soldier's Story*," *Literature/Film Quarterly*, 19, no. 1 (1991): 21–26;

Gerald Weales, "American Theater Watch, 1981–1982," *Georgia Review* (Fall 1982): 517–526.

Philip Kan Gotanda
(17 December 1951 –)

Magdalena Mączyńska
Catholic University of America

PLAY PRODUCTIONS: *The Avocado Kid or Zen in the Art of Guacamole,* Los Angeles, East West Players, November 1979;

A Song for a Nisei Fisherman, San Francisco, Asian American Theatre Company, 15 August 1980;

Bullet Headed Birds, San Francisco, Asian American Theatre Company, 11 March 1981;

American Tattoo [staged reading], Berkeley, Cal., Berkeley Repertory Theatre, March 1982;

The Dream of Kitamura, San Francisco, Asian American Theatre Company, 19 June 1982;

Jan Ken Po, by Gotanda, David Henry Hwang, and R. A. Shiomi, San Francisco, Asian American Theatre Company, 21 March 1986;

The Wash, San Francisco, Eureka Theatre Company, February 1987;

Yankee Dawg You Die, Berkeley, Cal., Berkeley Repertory Theatre, 19 March 1988;

Fish Head Soup, Berkeley, Cal., Berkeley Repertory Theatre, 6 March 1991;

Day Standing on Its Head, New York, Manhattan Theatre Club, 20 December 1993;

in the dominion of the night, by Gotanda and Dan Kuramoto, San Francisco, Asian American Theatre Company, 14 December 1994;

Ballad of Yachiyo, Berkeley, Cal., Berkeley Repertory Theatre, 8 November 1995;

Beans, in *Pieces of the Quilt,* San Francisco, Magic Theatre, 1996;

The Sisters Matsumoto, Seattle, Seattle Repertory Theatre / San Jose Repertory Theatre / Asian American Theatre Company, 4 January 1999;

Yohen, Los Angeles, East West Players / Robey Theatre Company, 13 January 1999;

floating weeds, San Francisco, Campo Santo and Intersection Theater, 29 November 2001;

Under the Rainbow [informal reading], San Francisco, Locus Arts, 20 March 2002—comprises *white manifesto and other perFumed tales of self-entitlement* and *natalie wood is dead;*

Philip Kan Gotanda (photograph from the dust jacket for Fish Head Soup and Other Plays, *1995)*

The Wind Cries Mary, adapted from Henrik Ibsen's *Hedda Gabler,* San Jose, Cal., San Jose Repertory Theatre, 19 October 2002.

BOOKS: *The Wash* (New York: Dramatists Play Service, 1991);

Yankee Dawg You Die (New York: Dramatists Play Service, 1991);

Day Standing on Its Head (New York: Dramatists Play Service, 1994);

Fish Head Soup and Other Plays (Seattle: University of Washington Press, 1995);

Ballad of Yachiyo (New York: Theatre Communications Group, 1996).

PRODUCED SCRIPTS: *The Wash,* motion picture, American Playhouse, 1988;

The Kiss, motion picture, Fish Head Films / National Asian American Telecommunications Association, 1992;

Drinking Tea, motion picture, Joe Ozu Films, 1996;

Life Tastes Good, motion picture, Joe Ozu Films, 1999.

Philip Kan Gotanda is known primarily as a playwright, but he is also the author of songs, screenplays, and spoken-word performances. Not limiting himself to the role of writer, Gotanda participates in the production process in the capacities of musician, director, producer, actor, and performer. The breadth of his artistic interests is reflected in the stylistic and genre variety of his plays: from quasi musicals to realistic family dramas and biting satires. In spite of this diversity, the playwright's works are united by a common thematic concern—an examination of the complex relationships between the lives of individuals and their sociohistorical circumstances. In the words of Michael Omi, in his introduction to Gotanda's *Fish Head Soup and Other Plays* (1995), Gotanda's plays "reveal a deep appreciation for both history and biography, and for the intimate connection between the two." This connection is explored through careful studies of small, closely knit groups of characters.

Gotanda's preferred microcosm is the Japanese American family; his preferred protagonist is the Japanese American in search of an identity. Though deeply rooted in the Asian American experience, the playwright's work is often characterized as universal, even archetypal. In a 1994 interview with Judith Weinraub, Gotanda commented: "The more truthfully you tell a story, the more detailed it is, the more it is driven by a truthful cultural psychology, the more it opens up, the more human it becomes.... In fact it becomes more universal." Paradoxically, Gotanda's refusal to divest his plays of their culturally specific settings gives his work both its local flavor and its acclaimed universality.

Gotanda was born on 17 December 1951 in Stockton, California. His mother, Catherine Matsumoto, came from a wealthy Stockton family and worked as a teacher at a local school. His father, Wilfred Itsuta Gotanda, was born on the island of Kauai, Hawaii, and established a medical practice in Stockton after receiving a degree in medicine at the University of Arkansas. Catherine Matsumoto and Wilfred Gotanda were both living in Stockton when Japan attacked the United States in 1941. Together with thousands of other Japanese Americans, they were sent to an internment camp in Rohrer, Arkansas. Although Philip Gotanda had not yet been born at the time of the encampment, he believes it to be a formative, traumatic element of the Japanese American experience. The camps became an important theme in several of his plays. In an interview with Robert B. Ito, Gotanda commented on this influence: "My parents' camp experience continues to inform my work and life both on a conscious and on an unconscious level. I've exploited themes of its psychic scar in *American Tattoo* (1982), the subsequent internalized racism being passed on from generation to generation in *Fish Head Soup* (1991), and its immediate psychological aftermath in *Sisters Matsumoto* (1999)." Gotanda's parents married in Stockton after returning from the camp. They had three sons, of whom Philip is the youngest.

Gotanda's first creative interest was music. He listened to his brothers' records and found himself drawn to rock, which inspired him to learn to play the guitar, begin writing songs, and create a band. He kept playing through his college years and beyond, performing original music centered on Asian American subjects. Faced with a lack of interest in his work on the part of mainstream commercial record companies, Gotanda performed in small clubs in Los Angeles, Santa Barbara, and San Francisco. He also auditioned as singer for the jazz-fusion group Hiroshima, whose leader, Dan Kuramoto, later became Gotanda's artistic collaborator. Shared musical interests also lay at the basis of the playwright's collaboration with David Henry Hwang, who helped Gotanda form a band and went on to direct several of his early plays at San Francisco's Asian American Theatre Company.

Gotanda began his college education in 1969 at the University of California, Santa Cruz, with the intention of majoring in psychology. He soon became interested in the Asian American Political Alliance, a group dedicated to fighting racism and supporting the anti-Vietnam War effort. In 1970 Gotanda decided to spend a year in Japan, where he studied pottery under the late master Hiroshi Seto in the village of Machiko and took Japanese classes at the International Christian University. In the country of his grandparents' birth, Gotanda experienced both an exhilarating, previously unknown sense of racial anonymity and an acute awareness of his American identity. Omi quotes Gotanda as observing: "In Japan, I had a somewhat mystical experience. For the first time in my life, I experienced a sense of racial anonymity. I was living without the burden of racism.... What an extraordinary feeling." Upon returning from Japan, Gotanda pursued a B.A. in Asian Studies at the University of California, Santa Barbara. This conscious academic pursuit of Asian aesthetics, rather than any kind of innate Japanese "essence," is the source of his experiments with Eastern theatrical techniques and Eastern art in general.

After his 1973 graduation, Gotanda spent two years writing and performing music. He also enrolled at the Hastings College of Law in San Francisco, partly in response to his parents' wish that he acquire a profession, partly because he saw the possibility of helping his community through class-action suits and impact litigation. Gotanda graduated in 1978 but never took his bar exam. While clerking at North Beach–Chinatown Legal Aid in San Francisco, he sent his first play to the actor Mako at East West Players (Los Angeles) and received an invitation. *The Avocado Kid or Zen in the Art of Guacamole* opened in November 1979. Gotanda's theatrical career had been launched.

The Avocado Kid or Zen in the Art of Guacamole is a rock musical. The play is rooted in Gotanda's art of songwriting, as noted by Omi: "Interestingly, Gotanda's initial foray into playwriting came about because of what he perceived as the limitations of the song format. He was never satisfied with the simple rendering of a song." Gotanda based his first play on "Momotaro the Peach Boy," a traditional Japanese children's tale about a boy living inside a peach. In Gotanda's version, the protagonists are a set of outcasts who come to discover the power of friendship. The play is youthful and aggressive, showing close affinities to rock music and popular culture in general and pointing in the direction Gotanda's dramatic art took in his subsequent works. Following its Los Angeles production, *The Avocado Kid or Zen in the Art of Guacamole* moved to the Asian American Theatre Company in San Francisco, where it opened on 16 May 1981 and closed on 28 June. Eric Hayashi of the Asian American Theatre commented to interviewer Jan Breslauer on Gotanda's early work: "There was a great depth to his work. It was startling to see a young playwright writing with that kind of structure."

Gotanda's second play, *A Song for a Nisei Fisherman,* premiered on 15 August 1980 and closed on 21 September at the Asian American Theatre Company. From the perspective of Gotanda's later work, the play can be read as the opening part of a Japanese American family trilogy, continued by *The Wash* (performed in 1987) and *Fish Head Soup*. Always interested in the stories of his elders, Gotanda based *A Song for a Nisei Fisherman* on the generational and private experiences of his father. The biographical elements are combined with fiction and history to create a poignant tale of a Japanese American life.

The central character of *A Song for a Nisei Fisherman* is Itsuta "Ichan" Masumoto, a Nisei (second-generation Japanese American) man who wants to become a doctor. His ambition is juxtaposed with both the racism of American society (from Caucasian taxi girls to relocation-camp officials) and the pressures of Itsuta's family, preoccupied with their fishery business. The five segments of the play are "Catching Fish," "Cleaning Fish," "Cooking Fish," "Eating Fish," and, once again, "Catching Fish," providing the framework against which Itsuta's life unfolds. Yet, characteristically, Gotanda abandons the demands of chronology: events are presented in a series of scenes, often remembered, allowing the viewers to piece together the complete tale of Itsuta's childhood, college years, courtship, marriage, camp experience, fatherhood, and retirement. *A Song for a Nisei Fisherman* explores the theme of emotional isolation central to Gotanda's work: Itsuta does not know how to express his feelings, and he fails to communicate with his wife and Sansei (third-generation Japanese American) sons. Only in the last scene does the ghost-haunted protagonist try to achieve a belated closeness with his parents, wife, and elder child.

Gotanda had not abandoned his earlier interest in music. The action of *A Song for a Nisei Fisherman* is accompanied by a singer, as well as several players on Western and traditional Japanese instruments, including the *shakuhachi* (Japanese flute) and *taiko* (Japanese drum). Nevertheless, Gotanda's second play is a development toward a more strictly dramatic form; moving beyond the musical format of *The Avocado Kid or Zen in the Art of Guacamole*, the playwright has created a play that, in the words of Omi, leaves audiences "with an understanding of a man and a generation."

In 1981 the Asian American Theatre Company staged Gotanda's second musical, *Bullet Headed Birds* (11 March – 26 April), a contemporary story of a songwriter in search of a new sound. Accompanied by the author's original music performed by an onstage rock band (the Bullet Headed Birds of the title), the play is a combination of the poetic, the comic, and the surreal. Haunted by the Suicide Shadow, a mysterious mime figure who emerges from a typewriter and invades the protagonist's dreams, as well as other shadowy forces, the protagonist strives to preserve his innocence and integrity and finally finds the sound he was seeking in "All-American Asian Punk," Gotanda's own brand of music. The play was also performed by the Pan Asian Repertory Theatre in November 1981 in New York, where it was noted for its excellent sound as well as its departure from the naturalistic mode characteristic of other Pan Asian productions. Mel Gussow, in *The New York Times* (25 November 1981), compared *Bullet Headed Birds* to the early work of Sam Shepard, confirming Gotanda's position as a young experimental playwright.

In March 1982 Gotanda's exploration of the trauma of Japanese American internment camps, *American Tattoo,* was read at the Berkeley Repertory Theatre. That same year, the punk-rock fantasy *The Dream of Kitamura* was performed from 19 June through 25 July by the Asian American Theatre Company. The latter play is a story of a married couple's foray into crime, followed by a sense of guilt and an overpowering fear of retribution. Reviewers noted an affinity between the thematic concerns of *The Dream of Kitamura* and such classics of the Western theatrical tradition as *Oedipus Rex, Hamlet,* and *Macbeth.* The fears of the protagonists—Rosjanin and his wife, Zuma—are surrealistically centered on Kitamura, the haunting mythical avenger. One of the two guards hired to defend the couple turns out to be a witness to their crime, while the other guard is revealed as the lost child of the victim. The story is eclectically based on tales collected from the author's family and friends as well as on Gotanda's own experiences, including a dream; in 1996 he told Misha Berson, "I dreamt my brother and I were these samurai guards protecting my father from a fierce monster. That's the whole basis of the play, though I added a lot of other crazy stuff." The strength of *The Dream of Kitamura* lies, again, in its freedom from the constraints of naturalism. Such liberty, however, may also lead to accusations of vacuity; *Los Angeles Times* (4 March 1983) reviewer Lawrence Christon remarked about the appearance of Kitamura's images, "Gotanda's 'Dream-Drama' tag doesn't remove the suspicion that for too long a time there is nothing behind them." Criticisms notwithstanding, Gotanda had succeeded in establishing his early style—upbeat, surreal, closely bound to the aesthetics of rock, and unmistakably Japanese American.

Gotanda's association with such renowned Asian-American theatrical venues as East West Players and the Asian American Theatre Company, in addition to facilitating his debut, provided the young playwright with a cultural milieu. Gotanda is a Sansei, and his work belongs to a broader movement toward the artistic self-definition of ethnic Asians in the United States. At the time of the 1979 production of *The Avocado Kid or Zen in the Art of Guacamole,* this movement was already well advanced. As Misha Berson put it, "clearly, the time had to arrive for Asian Americans to begin telling their own stories in their own authentic voices. The pent-up frustrations of this 'silent' minority emptied in the 1960s and early 1970s, in the wake of the black movement for civil rights and ethnic pride." Gotanda is keenly conscious of this broader sociocultural context of his work. Describing his first alliance with East West Players, he wrote in an autobiographical essay contributed to Berson's book: "All this grew out of a much larger Asian-American movement happening in California. From its early days it was a cultural movement—people were involved in printmaking, street poetry, publications, music, filmmaking. As the Blacks and Hispanic Americans emerged, so did we."

The cultural emergence of Asian Americans entailed a struggle not only against institutional racism but also against stereotypes of Asians disseminated by the media: the asexual detective Charlie Chan, the scheming villain Fu Manchu, the cowardly-but-loyal servant, the meek China Doll, or the erotically threatening Dragon Lady. Gotanda's work, like the work of his fellow artists, exposes the limitations of such stereotypes. In contrast to the prevalent, clichéd representations of Asian lives, Gotanda's plays draw on lived experience, bringing together recorded voices, friends' anecdotes, and fragments of family history. The problems of his characters are problems of people bridging two cultures, constantly switching between linguistic and behavioral codes, threatened by the racism of their own compatriots. In his songs, plays, and motion pictures, Gotanda explores what it means to be an American of Asian descent.

Cultural hybridity is also visible in Gotanda's artistic method. Although his plays include elements of Japanese theater and culture, they are also firmly rooted in the Western tradition. The result is a distinctive style that is neither of the East nor of the West. Gotanda makes use of such elements as traditional Japanese music, puppets, masks, and *shoji* screens—Japanese screens made of translucent rice paper extended over a light wood frame, which allow for an interesting play of light and shadow. But he also employs a Chekhovian naturalistic style, draws on the theater of the absurd, and alludes to American cinematography, German Expressionism, and Surrealist painting. In his work, Eastern and Western modes come together seamlessly. Asked by interviewer Nina Siegal about the use of puppets in *Ballad of Yachiyo* (performed in 1995), Gotanda replied: "I'm not Japanese, I'm Japanese American, and when I do use those elements, or that aesthetic, I approach it more from that perspective." Like his characters, the artist's methods spring from a fusion of cultures.

Gotanda's entrance into mainstream American theater came with the production of *The Dream of Kitamura* at the Theatre of the Open Eye in New York in 1985, and of *A Song for a Nisei Fisherman* and *The Wash* as part of the "New Theatre for Now" series at the Mark Taper Forum in Los Angeles in 1991. *The Wash,* Gotanda's sixth play, had premiered in February 1987 at the Eureka Theatre Company in San Francisco, and was made into a well-received motion picture in 1988 (screenplay by Gotanda, directed by Michael Toshiyuki

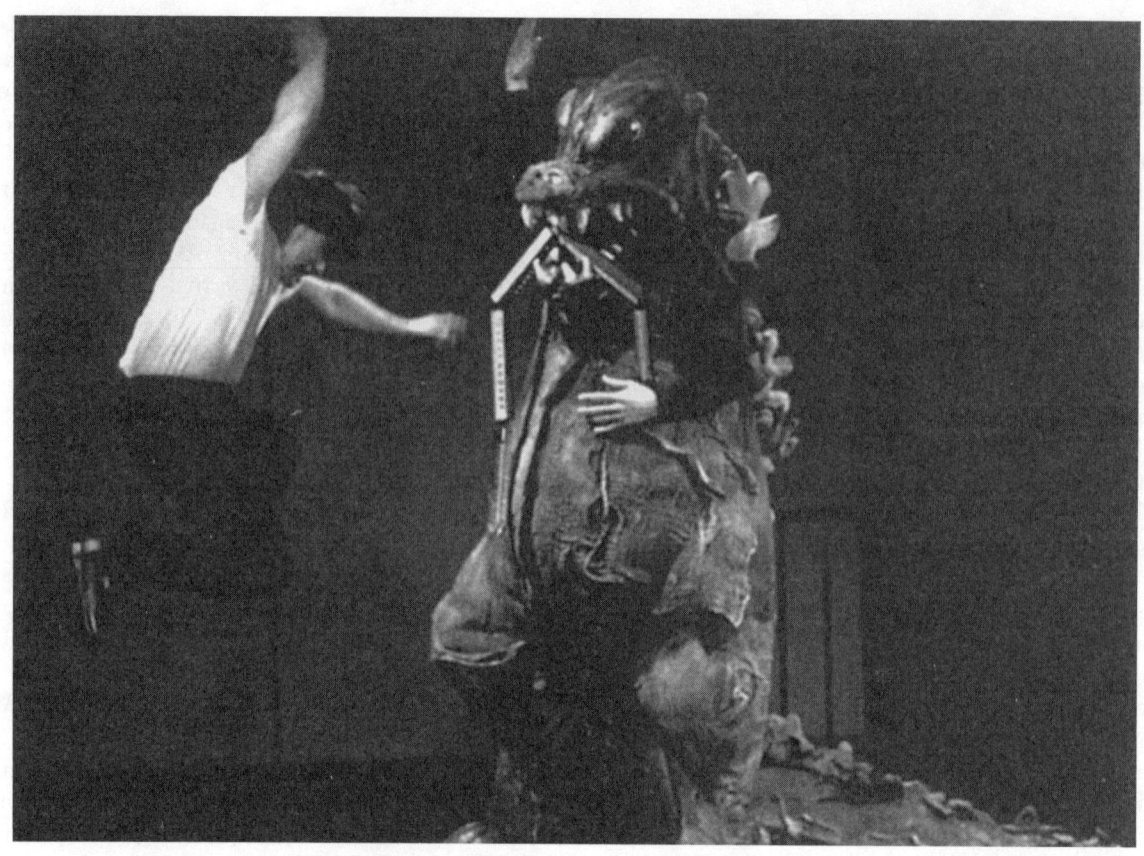

Kelvin Han Yee and Sab Shimono in the 1988 Berkeley production of
Yankee Dawg You Die *(photograph by Fred Speiser)*

Uno). The play continues the story of the Nisei generation begun in *A Song for a Nisei Fisherman*. When gathering materials for his work, Gotanda frequently conducts and records interviews with people belonging to the group he wishes to portray, a strategy Omi called "collecting voices." While *A Song for a Nisei Fisherman* was based on the experiences of Gotanda's father and other Nisei men, for *The Wash* the playwright collected female voices. The work was inspired by the story of a Nisei wife who, in a gesture of self-assertion extremely rare in her generation, decided to leave her husband and begin a new life.

The protagonists of *The Wash*, Nobu and Masi Matsumoto, are an elderly couple whose marriage is falling apart. At the beginning of the play, Masi is no longer living with her husband, but she still returns weekly to pick up Nobu's laundry, replacing stacks of his dirty shirts with the clean ones she has brought with her. In spite of the fact that this ritual is all that remains of the Matsumoto marriage, Nobu refuses to acknowledge his wife's newly found independence. He stubbornly persists in his patriarchal frame of mind, unable to face the fact that his own egocentrism and emotional as well as sexual coldness drove his wife away in the first place. The same stubbornness prevents him from seeking romance with the widow Kiyoko or from bonding with his daughter Judy and her child. What alienates Nobu from Judy even further is that she married a black man: Japanese attitudes toward other nationalities and races are a theme that Gotanda had already broached in *A Song for a Nisei Fisherman* (when the fisherman resented his son's moving in with a Chinese girl) and to which he returned in later plays.

Another theme characteristic of Gotanda's work and central to *The Wash* is the emotional and sexual life of elderly people. Eroticism is a constant, if never quite overt, presence in the play. It is a crucial aspect of Masi's newly found happiness, to which, as she needs to remind herself frequently, she does have a right. In the final scene of the play, Masi leaves the clothes she has washed at Nobu's place but does not pick up the dirty pile. Her liberation is symbolically completed. Nobu, on the other hand, remains locked in his stubbornness. He is not, however, a mere flat "type" of the emotionally blocked Nisei patriarch: in a moment of rare tenderness Nobu picks up his grandson and secretly sings him a Japanese lullaby. Such ambiguity and unpredictability give Gotanda's characters their roundness and appeal.

Reviewing the 1990 Manhattan Theatre Club performance of *The Wash* in *The New York Times* (18 November 1990), David Richards found "subtle fascination" in "the lengths to which the characters go to avoid saying what lies heavily on their hearts and to pretend that the gathering unpleasantness doesn't exist." Richards's review also emphasized the impressionistic character and vignette-based structure of the play, while in *The New Yorker* (19 November 1990) Edith Oliver praised *The Wash* as "so entertaining and modest and trustworthy" that it "opens up a whole world for many of us, and could well become a classic." *Los Angeles Times* (19 January 1991) reviewer Don Shirley commended the play as a "spare, subtle marital drama," but found the movie version of *The Wash* more convincing than the Mark Taper Forum stage rendering (6 January – 16 February 1991). Shirley criticized the lack of specificity in the play: "Gotanda's story is so 'universal' that it never becomes as distinctive as it should." In a published response to Shirley's review (printed in the 4 February 1991 *Los Angeles Times*), Gotanda and his brother Neil Gotanda commented disapprovingly on the ideological underpinnings of the reviewer's critique: "Unlike the movie, the play does not contain exotic and foreign-looking visual cues. Did Shirley conclude, then, that there was nothing Japanese American in the play? His review reflects a dismissal of anything that doesn't fit into his apparent conception of Japanese Americans." Gotanda's response exemplifies the playwright's passionate polemical involvement with questions of ethnic and national identity.

Following *The Wash*, Gotanda briefly departed from his preoccupation with family life in order to address the question of institutional racism. The dramatic satire *Yankee Dawg You Die* opened on 19 March 1988 at the Berkeley Repertory Theatre and closed on 10 April. The protagonists are a pair of Japanese American actors—one an enthusiastic beginner, the other a seasoned pro—whose views on artistic responsibility and personal integrity are transformed in the course of a troubled friendship. The story revolves around dilemmas faced by Asian American actors working in a racist movie industry. Vincent Chang's brilliant career has been maintained for years at the price of accepting demeaning, stereotypical Asian roles. His readiness to compromise is initially scorned by the idealistic younger actor Bradley Yamashita. At the end of the play, however, Vincent accepts a role in an independent Japanese American production, while Bradley, eager to forward his career, cannot find it in himself to refuse a lucrative but stereotypical assignment. *Yankee Dawg You Die* gives the older generation of Asian American actors their due, showing that their compliance with Hollywood standards was a more complex affair than most young critics are willing to admit.

Yankee Dawg You Die abounds in quotations from popular cinema. The play is punctuated with Vincent's monologue from his 1940s role as Sergeant Moto, the "Jap soldier," with his compulsory "Asian" accent. Godzilla is evoked as Vincent and Bradley work on a project for the Asian American Theater. Omi also noted allusions to *Bad Day at Black Rock* (1955), *Year of the Dragon* (1985), and the celebrated actress Anna Mae Wong.

In his discussion of *Yankee Dawg You Die* in *Theatre Journal*, James S. Moi praised the successful rendering of the contrast between the protagonists, as well as Gotanda's sensitivity to "the depth of the Asian-American desire to find role models" and his use of "what could be called 'jarring' contemporary language" to "demythologize the stereotypical portrayals of Asians." Moi, however, proposed the disturbing thesis that, instead of countering racism, plays such as *Yankee Dawg You Die* or Hwang's *M. Butterfly* (1988) "provide a good evening's entertainment and then float as exotic Oriental fetishes," reinforcing a "new order of stereotypical representations created by Asian-Americans." Less suspiciously, reviewer John Beaufort in the *Christian Science Monitor* (25 May 1989) called Gotanda's play a "funny, touching, and at times astringent study" of racial stereotyping. In *The New Yorker* (29 May 1989) Mimi Kramer praised the first act of *Yankee Dawg You Die* for keeping the viewers in suspense as to "which of the actors has the moral ascendancy" as well as for its "sprightly and stimulating" character. Kramer criticized the second act as "aimless and poorly structured," speculating that the play would have been better off without its latter half. A similar critique was made by John Simon of *New York* magazine (28 June 1989); he complained that the second act "falls flat." In the same vein, Frank Rich's review in *The New York Times* (15 May 1989) noted with regret that "the men's delicate symbiosis becomes diagrammatic in Act II." Nevertheless, Rich commended the "piquant comedy" for being "anything but preachy." In Rich's words, "Mr. Gotanda is a polemicist who sees both sides of a question, a writer whose grievances are balanced by a wicked sense of humor."

Gotanda's next work, *Fish Head Soup*, continues the theme of the Japanese American nuclear family explored in *A Song for a Nisei Fisherman* and *The Wash*. The play premiered on 6 March 1991 at the Berkeley Repertory Theatre and closed on 14 April after twenty-eight performances. Unlike Gotanda's earlier family plays, *Fish Head Soup* focuses on the lives of the younger generation—the Sansei. The opening scenes present a household of mentally and emotionally crippled individuals: a withdrawn father (Papa Iwasaki) traumatized by the death of his son Matt; a mother (Dorothy Iwasaki) dissatisfied with her work as a waitress and involved in an affair with a white lover obsessed with "Oriental" femininity; and a son (Victor) who cannot free himself from the burden of memories from Vietnam, where he fought as an American soldier against other Asians. To this home the younger brother, Matt, returns to reveal the secret of his supposed drowning. The shocked family learns that Matt had staged his death in an attempt to escape the burden of his Asian identity. Now, having undergone an ethnic change of heart, Matt wants to produce an independent motion picture about the real life of Japanese Americans, and he hopes to boost his budget by mortgaging the family house. As Matt's egocentrism is added to the ills of his brother and parents, the picture of a dysfunctional Japanese American family becomes complete.

The true source of the Iwasakis' dysfunction is the internalized racism that poisons all the members of the family. Matt's shame at being Asian led him to simulate death by drowning, causing the derangement of his father's mind. Dorothy agrees to continue a humiliating liaison with a man who takes her to seedy hotels and asks her to dress up in traditional kimonos—a garment both uncomfortable and alien to her—in order to fulfill his particular brand of "ethnic" sexual appetite. Dorothy's belief in the marginality of her race is also apparent in her reaction to her younger son's cinematographic project. She doubts that a movie about Japanese Americans could be of interest to the general viewer. The play focuses particularly on the confrontations between the two brothers, with the prodigal son wanting to overthrow the status quo, and his older sibling trying to defend the peaceful if unsatisfactory existence they have all grown to lead. Finally, a mystical reconciliation is achieved by means of a traditional Japanese meal of fish head soup, which the father prepares and all partake of at the family table.

John Stanley's review in the *San Francisco Chronicle* (3 March 1991) emphasized the continuity of this play with Gotanda's earlier family dramas, as well as its importance as a "forum for exploration" of racism in its many forms. Stanley quoted Gotanda talking about the anger he feels as a person of color living in a racist society: "I prefer to explore my own feelings through literature and public forum. This is a very passionate area of interest for me." The Breslauer interview also quoted Hayashi, who called *Fish Head Soup* Gotanda's "most O'Neill-ish play," adding that Gotanda "doesn't candy-coat anything." In the *International Examiner* (4 October 1994) Dan Sato described *Fish Head Soup* as "a brilliant, ambitious play about the subtle effects of racism" and, even more forcefully, "one of the finest contemporary American dramas." *Fish Head Soup* marked the end of a stage in Gotanda's career. Following its production, the artist decided to take a year off in order to rethink the directions his work should take in the future. "I reached a point where the writing I was doing felt like a straitjacket. Theatre had stopped being fun for me," confessed the playwright in his interview with Breslauer.

In 1992 Gotanda worked on a short movie, *The Kiss*, his second cinematographic project after the movie version of *The Wash*. *The Kiss*, which Gotanda wrote, directed, and produced, as well as starred in, is a thirteen-minute 16mm black-and-white short. It tells the story of an introverted, cowardly office nerd, Wilfred Funai, who is unexpectedly confronted with a life-and-death situation when a gay coworker starts choking during a work meal. The protagonist's intervention reveals his hitherto concealed heroic potential. *The Kiss* was presented at several festivals, including the Sundance Film Festival, and the Edinburgh, Budapest, Berlin, and San Francisco film festivals. It received San Francisco's Golden Gate Award in 1994.

Gotanda's foray into motion pictures did not mean a neglect of the theater. His tenth play, *Day Standing on Its Head*, premiered on 20 December 1993 and closed on 13 February 1994 at the Manhattan Theatre Club in New York. The work is a Surrealist exploration of the personal and political life of Harry Kitamura, a middle-aged Japanese American law professor. In fragmented, dream-like sequences, Harry revisits his old loves and sexual attractions, as well as his political past as a pro-Maoist Yellow Guard student activist. Both sets of memories are fraught with guilt and frustration. Harry dwells on his failure to satisfy his wife and on his troubled desires for two young women, Lisa and Nina. His former political involvements are exposed as a cruel boyish game, involving a dog corpse delivered to the opponent's door. Worst of all, when Harry tries to write an article about his past as a student activist, he experiences a severe writer's block symbolic of his overall psychological impotence. The protagonist's sense of helpless frustration is highlighted by a series of surreal occurrences: in the middle of a peaceful Sunday afternoon, he suddenly starts sinking into a chair to the point of disappearance; his arm slowly vanishes in a dream; he is addressed by movie characters and troubled by menacing visitations from the past. *Day Standing on Its Head* is an uncanny, Kafkaesque exploration of midlife crisis.

The first play following Gotanda's own months-long writer's block, *Day Standing on Its Head* was greeted with mixed feelings. In his review for *The New York Times* (26 January 1994) Ben Brantley criticized the banality of the protagonist's dilemmas, which "seem entirely too close to self-help books promoting the search for 'the child within.'" In a similar vein, *The New York Times* (5 February 1994) reviewer Vincent Canby summed up the plot as a "not very interesting journey to self-awareness," while David A. Rosenberg in *Back Stage* (11 February 1994) called the drama "irritating and faintly embarrassing" as well as "didactic and familiar." While the somewhat autobiographical content seemed to disappoint the reviewers, *Day Standing on Its Head* received praise for its formal originality. Brantley commended the structural concept of "casting the quest for self knowledge in the form of a hallucinogenic detective story," while Susan Chira, in another *New York Times* review (23 January 1994), emphasized the youthfully experimental character of the piece, which she referred to as "deliberately raw and sprawling." A revised draft of *Day Standing on Its Head* was produced by the Asian American Theatre Company, premiering on 29 March 1994.

After branching out into movies and exploring new territories in drama, Gotanda decided to return to his earliest artistic fascination—music. In 1994 the Asian American Theatre Company produced a spoken-word performance, *in the dominion of the night,* created by Gotanda in collaboration with Kuramoto and his fictional group, the new orientals. The performances ran from 14 to 18 December 1994. *in the dominion of the night* is centered on the enigmatic figure of Joe Ozu, already known to Gotanda's audiences from *Day Standing on Its Head,* in which he figured as an oneiric guide to the protagonist. In *in the dominion of the night* Ozu is "a writer who can't write very well, lives in a small apartment South of Market or in the Tenderloin, doesn't have much money, maybe drinks a little too much." Gotanda takes on the role of Ozu, while Kuramoto enacts the persona of Mr. Moto in this film-noir-inspired combination of jazz, poetry, and improvisation.

In his review in the *San Francisco Examiner* (13 December 1994) Steven A. Chin praised the "raw, inspired poetry" as well as the experimental energy of *in the dominion of the night.* Reviewer F. Kathleen Foley, in the *Los Angeles Times* (26 January 1995), called the performance "a perfect marriage of poetic, oblique narrative with driving contemporary music." Foley noted both the parodic potential of the play and the disquieting nature of the images surfacing in Ozu's stream of consciousness. In her words, the playwright "disarms us with laughter, then disturbs us with his imagery." Foley commended the performance for its nonlinear poetry, reminiscent of the Beat artists, and for its great jazz.

Following Gotanda's experiment in performance art, his most lyrical play, *Ballad of Yachiyo,* premiered at the Berkeley Repertory Theatre. *Ballad of Yachiyo* opened on 8 November 1995 and closed on 23 December after fifty-nine performances. The play dramatizes a young girl's sexual awakening, drawn against the background of traditional Japanese tea-drinking and pottery-making ceremonies. The model for Yachiyo was the playwright's aunt who, while still in her teens, moved to a neighboring town to acquire some social polish, became pregnant by a married man, and committed suicide by poisoning. Because Yachiyo's name was never again spoken in the family, it was only by accident that Gotanda learned of his aunt's existence. The secret of her story deeply moved and intrigued the playwright. He kept Yachiyo's photograph on his desk for ten years, searching for a way to render her brief life. He finally wrote the play at the bedside of his wife, Diane Emiko Takei, as she was recovering from surgery.

Gotanda's Yachiyo is a passionate and strong character. She is not portrayed as an innocent victim of a seduction. On the contrary, Yachiyo initiates her sexual relationship with Hiro Takamura, the master of the house to which she had been sent in order to learn the social skills required of an accomplished bride—tea making and flower arrangement. Yachiyo's initiation into the world of sexuality and shame is symbolically reflected in the ritual of the tea ceremony. When the young girl first tastes the beverage offered by her hostess, Hiro's neglected spouse, Okusan, she finds the taste too bitter to enjoy. With time, however, Yachiyo learns to appreciate the bitterness, a transformation mirroring her new maturity.

Whereas the story of Yachiyo's love is central to the play, art constitutes another highly significant theme. The art of pottery making is Hiro's passion and profession. Hiro's father had been a distinguished potter, and the son strives in vain to achieve the parent's excellence. As a result of his repeated failures, Hiro suffers from an anxiety further aggravated by a midlife crisis and feelings of artistic exhaustion. The artist's brief affair with Yachiyo brings about a rejuvenation of his spirit. As a result, he is finally able to create pieces of great beauty. However, the other fruit of their passion—the child in Yachiyo's womb—has to be rejected. At the end of the play, Hiro turns away from his short-term muse toward his renewed creative strength, and Yachiyo returns home to take her life and that of her unborn child.

Steven Winn observed in the *San Francisco Chronicle* (10 November 1995) that *Ballad of Yachiyo* "balances the affectionate realism of his early family play *The Wash* with the more fantastical strains of *Fish Head Soup* and *Day Standing on Its Head.*" Winn praised the tenderness of the drama and the "vertiginous power" of its

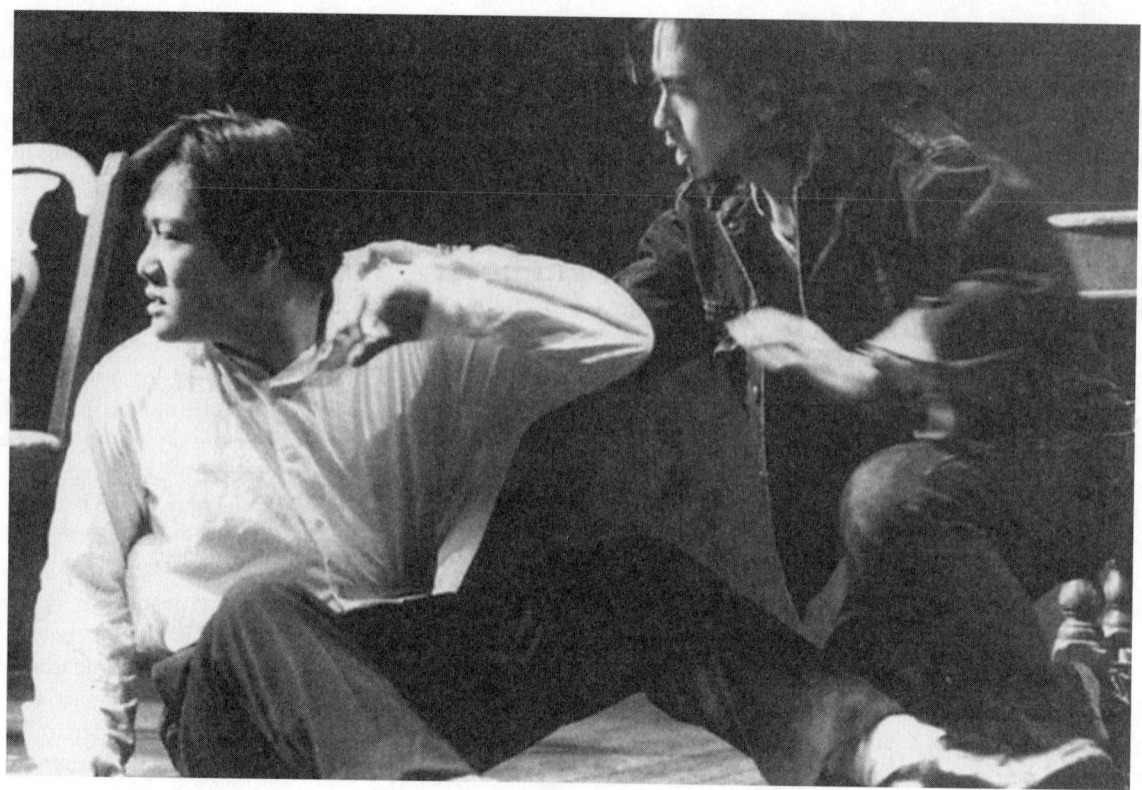

Yee and Stan Egi in the 1991 Berkeley production of
Fish Head Soup *(photograph by Ken Friedman)*

finale, but criticized its "slim characterizations, extraneous plot lines and static dialogue." *Los Angeles Times* reviewer Laurence Winer also noted the strengths and shortcomings of the work: "*Yachiyo* is not a perfect play. Some scenes are rich and utterly specific, others embrace the generic. Some characters are precisely etched, others wander in out of stock" (15 January 1996). Gotanda's writing, according to the review, is "confident, but uneven." Winer's overall evaluation, however, is positive; *Ballad of Yachiyo,* in his assessment, is "a compelling tale" and "a haunting story." Dennis Harvey noted in *Variety* (4 December 1995) that Gotanda's play "seems unpleasantly balanced between a modern psychological complexity and something more mythic and elemental." In Harvey's view, "the two strains never quite meld." Nevertheless, Harvey commended the "fine craftsmanship," "superb" writing, and the "engrossing" as well as entertaining character of Gotanda's "complexly structured effort." Apart from general, if not unqualified, critical acclaim, *Ballad of Yachiyo* brought its author a 1996 PEN/West award.

In 1996 Gotanda returned to moviemaking with his thirty-minute 16mm color short *Drinking Tea,* screened at the Sundance Film Festival that year. *Drinking Tea* is a story of an estranged middle-aged couple, Mary and Kan Ogawa, unable to deal with the loss of their child. In the course of the movie Kan gradually comes to terms with the reality of death—his long-gone son's, his elderly friend Sumi's, and his own. Kan's development is orchestrated against the background of tea making, pouring, and serving performed by three women: Mary, her sister Cookie, and Sumi. *Drinking Tea* is delicate and lyrical, as when Kan takes care of the dying Sumi and becomes the sharer of her last sensuous pleasures—the smell of fresh cut flowers, or the soothing touch of a wet towel on a pained body. Relying on a sparse cast and a muted atmosphere, the movie is another exercise in Gotanda's subtle art of understatement.

Gotanda's fourteenth play, *The Sisters Matsumoto,* is, like a lot of his work, loosely based on the playwright's own family history. The play, which opened on 4 January 1999 and ran until 13 February at the Seattle Repertory Theatre, is set in post–World War II Stockton. The protagonists are three Japanese American sisters from a well-to-do local family, much like that of Gotanda's mother; but the story, although grounded in historical fact and biography, is fictitious. The play takes a close look at a Japanese American family's post-camp attempts at reconstructing their lives. Predictably, ideas concerning the future shape of these lives vary significantly. The three sisters hold diverging opinions on several issues, including love, family, progress, tradition, and Japanese American identity. The middle sister, Chiz, wants to become part of the mainstream American culture; the youngest, Rose, is sweet and nostalgic; and Grace, the eldest, is the mother figure, both rational and traditionalist.

The war and the camp experience are a constant presence in the play. Gotanda touches upon such painful subjects as ethnic hatred, incarceration, and the sacrificing of Japanese American soldiers as cannon fodder by their American leaders. *The Sisters Matsumoto,* however, tackles not only the subject of race but also the problems of social class. The protagonists come from a wealthy and privileged home, but after their return from internment they are forced to face the prospect of poverty. Thus, the play provides both an analysis of the Japanese American community's struggles within a racist dominant culture, and an examination of the complex class and power relationships within the minority community itself. The burden of social problems tackled in *The Sisters Matsumoto* at times weighs down the story. The play has been criticized for being too rhetorical and message ridden. Berson complained in the *Seattle Times* (12 January 1999) that, "the show oozes messages from every pore" and that its "relationships are studies in class tension." Lynn Jacobson expressed a similar sentiment in *Variety* (1 February 1999): "Midway through, the sheer weight of exposition becomes a burden." Both Berson and Jacobson, however, acknowledged the importance of *The Sisters Matsumoto* in addressing the Japanese American community's postcamp dilemmas. "Gotanda's treatment of the subject is informative and conscientious," admitted Jacobson. The production at the Seattle Repertory Theatre was accompanied by an exhibition documenting the historical period examined in the play.

The premiere of *The Sisters Matsumoto* was directed by Sharon Ott, Gotanda's longstanding artistic collaborator. Ott's earlier productions of Gotanda's work included *The Wash,* which was staged at the Manhattan Theatre Club (23 October–18 November 1990) and the Mark Taper Forum (17 January–16 February 1991), and *Ballad of Yachiyo* and *Yankee Dawg You Die* at Berkeley Repertory Theatre. *Ballad of Yachiyo* also opened Ott's career at Seattle Repertory, where the director moved after leaving Berkeley. Gotanda appreciates Ott's cinematographic style, as well as her ability to "weed out the sentimentality and melodrama" present in his texts, while "strengthening the structure and developing the characters." Ott, in turn, in an 11 July 2001 interview, commended Gotanda for the elegance and range of his style, as well as for creating "one of the largest bodies of Asian-American themed work" and playing "an important role in shaping and sustaining the Asian-American arts movement in this country." In Ott's words, "Mr. Gotanda has successfully worked to bring this underrepresented American perspective to the stages of larger mainstream venues while maintaining his support of the smaller ethnic specific theatres."

The first production of *The Sisters Matsumoto* was a collaboration between the San Jose Repertory Theatre, the Seattle Repertory Theatre, and the Asian American Theatre Company. Gotanda's fondness for such joint projects results from the fact that they introduce an element of community-building dialogue. Jean Schiffman wrote in *American Theatre* (February 1999) that "such productions, in the playwright's opinion, can be crucial means of working out the dialectics of contemporary American theatre." The staging of Gotanda's next work, *Yohen,* was also a collaboration.

Yohen was produced by the East West Players and the African American Robey Theatre Company. It opened on 13 January 1999 and closed on 5 February. The play takes place in 1986 in California and recounts the story of an interracial marriage between African American James and his Japanese war bride, Sumi (originally played by Danny Glover and Nobu McCarthy). The plot is structured around James's attempts to reconcile with his wife, who, exasperated by her spouse's lethargic ways, decides to start a new life, enrolls in art classes, and starts looking for fresh romance. James's repeated returns to the home Sumi had asked him to leave result in a series of confrontations during which the history of the troubled marriage is gradually revealed. The personal conflicts between the spouses are closely interwoven with their racial differences. Developing themes subtly present in several of Gotanda's earlier plays, *Yohen* addresses the problem of relationships between two minority races, as well as the question of mature love and sexuality. As in *Ballad of Yachiyo,* Gotanda makes metaphorical use of pottery–in Japanese ceramics, *yohen* means a type of imperfection occasionally produced by the heat of the kiln. Because of their unpredictability, the deformed pieces attract scholars and connoisseurs alike. Both the capriciousness of *yohen* and its lack of perfection have symbolic significance in Gotanda's play.

In the *Los Angeles Times* (15 January 1999) Kathleen Foley compared the "happy imperfection" and the "distinct and odd" beauty of *yohen* to the protagonists' marriage. In Foley's view the play asks the question: "When is a marriage beautifully imperfect and when is it merely defunct?" Foley's overall evaluation of *Yohen* is rather critical. In her opinion the "potentially powerful scenario sinks under the weight of staccato reminiscences and cumbersome segues." Thus, "despite moments of humor and lyrical power, Gotanda's drama fails to adequately address the philosophical dilemma it poses. Choppy and poorly structured, the play is not, one fears, truly 'yohen.'" Polly Warfield, reviewing the play for *Back Stage West* (21 January 1999), proposed yet another reading of the symbolic meaning of the pottery, comparing the changes wrought on the vessels in the kiln to the changing lives of the protagonists: "Change is what this play is about—its necessity, its difficulty, the pain and displacement of it." Warfield called the play "insightful" and "multi-layered," a "brilliant" fulfillment of the "bright promise implicit in East West's 1979 premiere staging of Gotanda's playful and tuneful early work *The Avocado Kid*." The review also underlined the importance of Sumi's ethnic and national complexity; for Warfield, Sumi represents "an America that is becoming—a place like no other that ever has been, of disparate elements fired in a crucible into a yohen asymmetrical but uniquely strong and beautiful." The multiracial character of *Yohen* attracted a variety of audiences, as noted by *Theatre Journal* (December 1999) reviewer San Metzger: "The show brought in the most diverse crowd of spectators I have ever seen in two years at EWP."

In addition to the premieres of *The Sisters Matsumoto* and *Yohen*, in 1999 Gotanda released his feature-length 35mm color movie, *Life Tastes Good*. The motion picture was written and directed by the playwright, who was also the coproducer (together with Dale Minami). *Life Tastes Good* was screened at Sundance as well as at the San Francisco Asian Film Festival, the Hawaii and Seattle International Film Festivals, the Dublin Film Festival, and the Toronto Reel and Los Angeles Asian International Film Festivals. Gotanda's first feature is the neo-noir tale of Harry Sado, an aging money launderer, whose story is framed by a narrative involving a pair of San Francisco detectives. The emotional center of the movie is an unlikely family reunion between Harry and his estranged children. Not limiting himself to family affairs, Harry is also involved in a developing romance with a mysterious widow and a death-and-life battle with his former partner in crime. In *Variety* (8 March 1999) reviewer Dennis Harvey called *Life Tastes Good* "gracefully executed," "deliberately paced," and "stylish," but complained about the pat familiarity of the material. According to Harvey, the "delicacy of mood . . . seems a bit squandered on characters that aren't drawn richly enough to move us and situations that feel hermetically contrived." Harvey nevertheless praised Gotanda's feature for its quirky humor and meticulous craftsmanship. Other reviews emphasized the originality of the movie as well as its genuine comic value.

Yet another of Gotanda's many 1999 projects was the development of his official website (http://www.philipkangotanda.com). The site offers an informal, irregularly updated journal titled *floating weeds*, featuring the author's eclectic reflections on such matters as film theory, chicken wings, and the stock market. The author also uses the site to publish his poems and plays. Gotanda documented the beginnings of this innovative procedure in the 21 November 1999 entry: "One thought is that I'll publish my new play, *floating weeds*, in installments over a period of time on this website. That'd be cool. I don't think anyone has ever done that. Sort of like debuting an album or movie, online."

A production of the play *floating weeds* was launched in 2001 by Campo Santo and Intersection Theater in San Francisco. It ran from 29 November to 23 December. *floating weeds* is an unflinching group portrait of four twenty- and thirty-somethings trying to stay afloat in a tough urban world. As the characters enter into varied emotional and erotic entanglements with one another, their flaws and vulnerabilities become painfully apparent. Responsible but insecure Gloria tries to take care of her mentally disturbed brother Earl, as well as of her slacker boyfriend Benny, whose days are filled with pathetic schemes to scam money off unwitting strangers. Gloria also carries the burdens of past and present sexual abuse and a memory of an unrevealed crime. Gloria's friend Sarah is afflicted not only with hypochondria and kleptomania but also with an unwanted power of attracting men. All four protagonists strive to preserve a sense of dignity in a world where self-worth is at least as hard to find as a decent job. In his enthusiastic review (quoted in the 6 December 2001 entry on Gotanda's website), Mark de la Viña called *floating weeds* "gruff, deeply disturbing and very funny." De la Viña emphasized the continuity of this play with Gotanda's previous work, with which it shares "a beautifully rendered, understated text." Finally, de la Viña underlined the significance of *floating weeds* as a new turn in Gotanda's writing, which, according to the review, has been "re-energized" by the playwright's association with Campo Santo and the Intersection.

Gotanda's next projects include *The Wind Cries Mary* (an adaptation of Henrik Ibsen's *Hedda Gabler* [1890]) scheduled for October 2002 at San Jose Repertory, and *Under the Rainbow* (2002), a play of two one-acts: *white manifesto and other perFumed tales of self-entitlement* and *natalie wood is dead*. The first of these one-acts explores the controversial issue of white male obsession with "Oriental" femininity, a theme Gotanda had already broached in *Fish Head Soup*. According to the artist's website, *white manifesto and other perFumed tales of self-entitlement* offers an "offensively provocative look" at the matter. *natalie wood is dead* examines the toxic relationship between an aging actress determined to stay young and attractive as long as she can and her much less assertive thirty-something daughter, unable and unwilling to live up to her mother's Hollywood standards of perfection. The play is an unflinching analysis of an unhealthy mother-daughter relationship as well as of the inhuman demands of the glamour industry. *Under the Rainbow* had an informal reading on 20 March 2002 at Locus Arts in San Francisco.

In addition to his work as playwright, Gotanda has directed several theatrical productions, including the world premiere of *Uncle Tadao* by R. A. Shomi, *The House of Sleeping Beauties* by David Henry Hwang, and his own *Fish Head Soup*. Gotanda's rich and varied artistic achievement has earned prestigious prizes and scholarships, including three Rockefeller Playwright Awards, the Guggenheim Foundation scholarship, the Lila Wallace–Reader's Digest Writer's Award, the PEW-TCG National Theatre Artist Award, three National Endowment for the Arts Artist Grants, Gerbode and McKnight Foundation fellowships, and the Theatre Communication Group / National Endowment for the Arts Directing Fellowship. He is an associate artist at the Seattle Repertory Theatre. He lives in San Francisco with his wife and collaborator, Takei, who is actively involved in directing, producing, and acting in his plays and movies.

Throughout his career, Philip Kan Gotanda has gained the position of a role model in the Asian American community as a leading playwright, director, actor, musician, and cofounder of the Asian American Musicians Organization. Always willing to expand the range of his artistic interests, the playwright maintains strong connections with the emerging generations of ethnic Asian artists. He remains acutely sensitive to what is cutting edge in Asian American art and deeply interested in the new directions within a culture that he has helped to create.

Interviews:

Jan Breslauer, "Swimming Against the Tide," *Los Angeles Times,* 3 January 1993, Calender section, pp. 3, 74;

Judith Weinraub, "Three Questions for Phillip Kan Gotanda: His Japanese American Spin on 'The Wash'," *Washington Post,* 3 April 1994, pp. G2:4;

Nina Siegal, "Choice and Chance," *American Theatre,* 13 (February 1996): 26;

Misha Berson, "Role Model on a Roll: Philip Kan Gotanda's Work Grabs Mainstream Attention and Inspires Younger Artists," *Seattle Times,* 10 October 1996, pp. D1, D5;

Robert B. Ito, "Philip Kan Gotanda," in *Words Matter: Conversations with Asian American Writers,* edited by King-Kok Cheung (Honolulu: University of Hawaii Press / Los Angeles: UCLA Asian American Studies Center, 2000), pp. 173–185.

References:

Misha Berson, ed., *Between Worlds. Contemporary Asian American Plays* (New York: Theatre Communications Group, 1990), pp. 30–35;

James S. Moi, "David Henry Hwang's *M. Butterfly* and Philip Kan Gotanda's *Yankee Dawg You Die:* Repositioning Chinese American Marginality on the American Stage," *Theatre Journal,* 42 (March 1990): 48–56.

A. R. Gurney
(1 November 1930 –   )

Robert F. Gross
Hobart and William Smith Colleges

PLAY PRODUCTIONS: *Three People,* New Haven, Yale School of Drama, March 1956;

Turn of the Century, New Haven, Yale School of Drama, March 1957;

Love in Buffalo, New Haven, Yale School of Drama, 1958;

The Bridal Dinner, Cambridge, Mass., Massachusetts Institute of Technology Community Players, 1962;

The Rape of Bunny Stuntz, New York, Cherry Lane Theatre, December 1962;

The Comeback, Cambridge, Mass., Image Theater Workshop, May 1964;

The Open Meeting, Boston, Atma Coffee House Theatre, January 1965;

The David Show, Tanglewood, Mass., Boston University Playwrights Workshop, 1966; New York, Players Theatre, 31 October 1968; revised one-act version produced with *The Golden Fleece* as *Tonight in Living Color,* New York, Actors Playhouse, 10 June 1969;

The Golden Fleece, New York, Van Dam Theatre, 1967; Los Angeles, Mark Taper Forum, 1968;

The Love Course, Boston, Theatre Company of Boston, 1970; London, King's Head Theatre, July 1974;

Scenes from American Life, Tanglewood, Mass., Boston University Summer Workshop, 1970; Buffalo, N.Y., Studio Arena Theatre, fall 1970; New York, The Forum [Lincoln Center Theater], 26 March 1971;

The Problem, London, King's Head Theatre, 1970; New York, Soho Repertory Theatre, 19 January 1973;

The Old One-Two, Waltham, Mass., Brandeis University, 1972; London, King's Head Theatre, 1975;

Children, adapted from John Cheever's short story "Goodbye, My Brother," London, Mermaid Theatre, 8 April 1974; New York, Manhattan Theatre Club, 20 October 1976;

Who Killed Richard Cory? New York, Circle Repertory Company, 10 March 1976; revised as *Richard*

A. R. Gurney (from John L. DiGaetani, A Search for a Postmodern Theater, *1991)*

Cory, Williamstown, Mass., Williamstown Theatre Festival, 2 July 1984;

The Wayside Motor Inn, New York, Manhattan Theatre Club, 3 November 1977;

The Middle Ages, Los Angeles, Mark Taper Forum Lab, 1977; Stamford, Conn., Hartman Theatre, 8 January 1978; New York, Ark Theater, March 1982; transferred to Theater at St. Peter's Church, 23 March 1983;

The Golden Age, London, Greenwich Theatre, spring 1980; revised, Washington, D.C., Kennedy Center, fall 1983; New York, Jack Lawrence Theatre, 12 April 1984;

The Dining Room, New York, Playwrights Horizons, 24 February 1982;

What I Did Last Summer, Dennis, Mass., Cape Playhouse, 9 August 1982; New York, Circle Repertory Company, 6 February 1983;

The Perfect Party, New York, Playwrights Horizons, 2 April 1986; transferred to Astor Place Theatre, 24 June 1986;

Sweet Sue, Williamstown, Mass., Williamstown Theatre Festival, July 1986; New York, Music Box, 8 January 1987;

Another Antigone, San Diego, Old Globe Theatre, March 1987; New York, Playwrights Horizons, 11 January 1988;

White Walls, in *Urban Blight,* music by David Shire, lyrics by Richard Maltby Jr., New York, Manhattan Theatre Club, 18 May 1988;

The Cocktail Hour, San Diego, Old Globe Theatre, 2 June 1988; New York, Promenade Theatre, 20 October 1988;

Love Letters, New Haven, Long Wharf Theater, 3 November 1988; New York, Promenade Theatre, 13 February 1989; transferred to Edison Theatre, 31 October 1989;

The Snow Ball, Hartford, Conn., Hartford Stage Company, 9 February 1991; San Diego, Old Globe Theatre, 4 May 1991;

The Old Boy, New York, Playwrights Horizons, 6 May 1991; revised, San Diego, Old Globe Theatre, 18 January 1992;

The Fourth Wall, Westport, Conn., Westport Country Playhouse, 3 August 1992;

Later Life, New York, Playwrights Horizons, 23 May 1993; transferred to Westside Theatre / Upstairs, August 1993;

A Cheever Evening, New York, Playwrights Horizons, 6 October 1994;

Sylvia, New York, Manhattan Theatre Club, 23 May 1995; transferred to John Housman Theater, 29 September 1995;

Overtime, San Diego, Old Globe Theatre, 15 July 1995; New York, Manhattan Theatre Club, 5 March 1996;

Let's Do It! music by Cole Porter, New Haven, Conn., Long Wharf Theatre, March 1996;

Labor Day, San Diego, Old Globe Theatre, 12 February 1998; New York, Manhattan Theatre Club, 1 June 1998;

Far East, Williamstown, Mass., Williamstown Theatre Festival, 26 July 1998; New York, Mitzi E. Newhouse Theater, 11 January 1999;

Darlene and *The Guest Lecturer,* New Brunswick, N.J., George Street Playhouse, 18 October 1998;

Strawberry Fields, music by Michael Torke, Cooperstown, N.Y., Glimmerglass Opera, Alice Busch Opera Theatre, 27 July 1999; New York, New York City Opera at Lincoln Center, fall 1999;

Ancestral Voices, New York, Mitzi E. Newhouse Theater, 18 October 1999;

Human Events, New Brunswick, N.J., George Street Playhouse, 2 February 2001;

Buffalo Gal, Williamstown, Mass., Williamstown Theatre Festival, July 2001; Buffalo, N.Y., Studio Arena Theatre, March 2002.

BOOKS: *Around the World in Eighty Days,* adapted from Jules Verne's novel, by Gurney [as Peter Gurney] and Gilbert Leibinger (Chicago: Dramatic Publishing, 1962);

The Rape of Bunny Stuntz (New York: S. French, 1964);

The Comeback (New York: Dramatists Play Service, 1965);

The Golden Fleece (New York: S. French, 1967);

The David Show (New York: S. French, 1968);

The Problem (New York: S. French, 1968);

The Open Meeting (New York: S. French, 1968);

The Love Course (New York: S. French, 1969);

Scenes from American Life (New York: S. French, 1970);

The Old One-Two (New York: S. French, 1971);

The Gospel According to Joe (New York: Harper & Row, 1974);

Children (London: S. French, 1975; New York: Dramatists Play Service, 1977);

Who Killed Richard Cory? (New York: Dramatists Play Service, 1976);

Entertaining Strangers (Garden City, N.Y.: Doubleday, 1977; London: Allen Lane, 1979);

The Middle Ages (New York: Dramatists Play Service, 1978);

The Wayside Motor Inn (New York: Dramatists Play Service, 1978);

The Dining Room (Garden City, N.Y.: Doubleday, 1982; London: S. French, 1982);

What I Did Last Summer (New York: Dramatists Play Service, 1983);

The Snow Ball [novel] (New York: Arbor House, 1984);

The Golden Age (New York: Dramatists Play Service, 1984);

Richard Cory (New York: Dramatists Play Service, 1985);

The Perfect Party (New York: Dramatists Play Service, 1986);

Sweet Sue (New York: Dramatists Play Service, 1987);

Another Antigone (New York: Dramatists Play Service, 1988);

The Cocktail Hour (New York: Dramatists Play Service, 1989);
Love Letters (New York: Dramatists Play Service, 1989);
The Old Boy (Garden City, N.Y.: Fireside Theatre, 1992);
The Snow Ball (New York: Dramatists Play Service, 1992);
A Cheever Evening (Garden City, N.Y.: Fireside Theatre, 1994);
Later Life (New York: Dramatists Play Service, 1994);
Sylvia (Garden City, N.Y.: Fireside Theatre, 1995);
Overtime (New York: Dramatists Play Service, 1996);
The Fourth Wall (New York: Dramatists Play Service, 1996);
Darlene and The Guest Lecturer (New York: Broadway Play Publishing, 1999);
Far East (New York: Broadway Play Publishing, 1999);
Labor Day (New York: Dramatists Play Service, 1999);
Ancestral Voices (New York: Broadway Play Publishing, 2000);
Human Events (New York: Broadway Play Publishing, 2001);
Buffalo Gal (New York: Broadway Play Publishing, 2002).

Editions and Collections: *Four Plays* (New York: Avon, 1985)—comprises *Scenes from American Life, Children, The Middle Ages,* and *The Dining Room;*
The Cocktail Hour and Two Other Plays: Another Antigone and The Perfect Party (New York: Plume, 1989);
Love Letters and Two Other Plays: The Golden Age and What I Did Last Summer (New York: Plume, 1990);
Public Affairs (New York: S. French, 1992)—comprises *The Love Course* and *The Open Meeting;*
Later Life and Two Other Plays: The Snow Ball and The Old Boy (New York: Plume, 1994);
Collected Plays, 5 volumes (Lyme, N.H.: Smith & Kraus, 1995–2001)—comprises volume 1, *Nine Early Plays 1961–1973* [*The Comeback, The Rape of Bunny Stuntz, The Golden Fleece, The David Show, The Problem, The Love Course, The Open Meeting, The Old One-Two,* and *Scenes from American Life*]; volume 2, *1974–1983* [*Children, Richard Cory, The Middle Ages, The Wayside Motor Inn, The Dining Room,* and *What I Did Last Summer*]; volume 3, *1984–1991* [*The Cocktail Hour, The Golden Age, The Perfect Party, Another Antigone, Love Letters, The Old Boy,* and *Sweet Sue*]; volume 4, *1992–1999* [*Sylvia, Labor Day, Darlene, The Guest Lecturer, Far East,* and *Ancestral Voices*]; and volume 5, *1991–1995* [*The Snow Ball, The Fourth Wall, Later Life, A Cheever Evening,* and *Overtime*].

PRODUCED SCRIPTS: "3 by Cheever: O Youth and Beauty," adapted from John Cheever's short story, television, *Great Performances,* PBS, 31 October 1979;
"The Hit List," television, *Trying Times,* PBS, 1989;
Love Letters, television, ABC, 12 April 1999;
Far East, television, PBS, 20 May 2001.

OTHER: *Three People,* in *The Best Short Plays of 1955–56,* edited by Margaret Mayorga (Boston: Beacon, 1956), pp. 231–243;
Turn of the Century, in *The Best Short Plays of 1957–58,* edited by Mayorga (Boston: Beacon, 1958), pp. 1–21;
Eugene O'Neill, *Four Plays by Eugene O'Neill,* introduction by Gurney (New York: Signet, 1998);
Thornton Wilder, *The Collected Short Plays of Thornton Wilder,* volume 2, edited by A. Tappan Wilder and Donald Gallup, introduction by Gurney (New York: Theatre Communication Group, 1998).

SELECTED PERIODICAL PUBLICATIONS–UNCOLLECTED: *The Bridal Dinner: A Play in Three Acts, First Stage: A Quarterly of New Drama,* 4, no. 1 (1965): 33–56;
"Pushing the Walls of Dramatic Form," *New York Times,* 27 July 1986, II: 1, 6;
"A Guide to Australia's Good Women," *New York Times,* 6 September 1987, VII: 5;
"The Dinner Party," *American Heritage,* 39 (1988): 69–71;
"Where the Final Act is Only the Beginning," *New York Times,* 27 October 1991, II: 5.

A. R. Gurney is one of the few major playwrights to emerge in the 1960s and maintain a flourishing stage career four decades later. His plays continue to be performed widely Off-Broadway and in resident, summer stock, community, and academic theaters across the United States, as well as enjoying some international recognition. Although he is often dismissed by academic critics as an epigone, he is the only playwright of his generation to continue the tradition of high comedy. In contrast to leading American playwrights of the 1950s and 1960s, who generally took a psychosexual approach to character, Gurney concentrates on class as the major determinant of behavior. Rather than providing detailed individual character portraits, he often constructs representative social types and depicts their efforts to cope with change. Believing that women are adapting better than men, Gurney frequently contrasts women who are invigorated by new prospects with men who are beset with crises of self-worth and find themselves looking to the past for consolation. Focusing on these men, Gurney imbues his plays with a sharp

Remak Ramsay, Pippa Pearthree, W. H. Macy, Lois de Banzie, Ann McDonough, and John Shea in the 1982 Playwrights Horizons production of The Dining Room
(from Gurney, The Dining Room, *1982)*

sense of anomie, despite the charm and civilized repartee that so often animates them.

Albert Ramsdell Gurney Jr. was born on 1 November 1930 in Buffalo, New York, to Marion Spaulding and Albert Ramsdell Gurney. The second of three children, he grew up in the upper-middle-class WASP world of private schools, ballroom-dancing classes, and country clubs, a milieu often depicted in his plays. He soon acquired the nickname "Pete" because he disliked being called "Junior," and at age eight he announced at the dinner table that he would not follow in his father's line of work, which was investment banking and real estate. After prep school at St. Paul's School, he attended Williams College, where he decided to major in English. As a student he organized two musical reviews. After graduation in 1952 he entered the navy as a commissioned officer; one of his responsibilities was arranging entertainments, revues, and variety shows for those on board ship. While stationed in Japan, he became romantically involved with a Japanese woman, a relationship that ended in part because of strong familial objections. This event, alluded to in several of Gurney's plays, eventually became the basis for *Far East* (1998).

Opposing further parental objections, he entered the Yale School of Drama in 1955 to study playwriting. Two years later he married Mary Goodyear, with whom he has raised four children: George, Amy, Evelyn, and Benjamin. His first significant project at Yale was an adaptation of a John Cheever story, showing an affinity that has lasted throughout his career, including the later Cheever adaptations *Children* (1974) and *A Cheever Evening* (1994). He also continued his interest in musical theater, writing a musical adaptation of John Fletcher's comedy *The Wild Goose Chase* (circa 1621). Of the two published one-act plays from the Yale years, *Three People* (1956) is an uncharacteristically harsh drama about a young academic couple with a brain-damaged child, but *Turn of the Century* (1957) already shows the thematic concerns of the mature playwright. An elderly matriarch has spent her estate and is now rapidly working through the assets of her three sons, imagining that she is still living in an opulent world of Victorian splendor. When she announces her plans to rent an Italian villa and take the entire family there, the tension between illusion and reality becomes unbearable for one of the daughters-in-law. "We haven't got enough money to keep three maids in the kitchen while the homemade rolls grow stale and the butter melts on the silver butter plates, and stains the lovely, lovely lace tablecloth," she cries. "We haven't got enough money." This confrontation, however, merely sends the mother more firmly into fantasies of the past, and she makes a crazed, genteel exit.

After receiving his M.F.A. in playwriting in 1958, Gurney supported himself as a teacher, working at Belmont Hill School for two years before moving on to teach humanities and literature at the Massachusetts Institute of Technology. Although only one of his full-length plays, *Another Antigone* (1987), has focused on college life, a few of them (*The Perfect Party* [1986], *The Fourth Wall* [1992], and *The Guest Lecturer* [1998]) include comic portraits of academics with intense theatrical aspirations. Gurney's years of teaching are most clearly reflected in the fondness for myth, classical literature, and allusions to dramatic literature found throughout his plays. Although he enjoyed the classroom, he found the conflicting rhythms of academic and theatrical life increasingly jarring, especially during the intensity of rehearsals, and he quit teaching full-time after the success of *The Dining Room* in 1982. From 1982 to 1984 he taught part-time and then was given an extended leave of absence until his official retirement from MIT in 1996.

His one-acts *The Comeback* (1964), *The David Show* (1966), and *The Golden Fleece* (1967) are all retellings of legendary material and show Gurney's fondness for playing with literary sources. In them, Gurney casts a disillusioned and satiric light on the privileged and glamorous in contemporary America by presenting them in the stories of Odysseus and Penelope (*The Comeback*), David and Bathsheba (*The David Show*), and Jason and Medea (*The Golden Fleece*). In *The Comeback*, for example, Odysseus returns home to Ithaca only briefly before going on an absurd quest that he knows will lead to his death. Penelope stays home, an aging party girl who is eager to entertain her suitors.

In these early one-acts Gurney flirts with absurdism but never entirely abandons realistic grounding. In *The Problem* (1970) the sexual games of the married couple seem indebted to Harold Pinter's *The Lover* (1963), but Gurney avoids the existential anxiety that haunts Pinter's play in favor of a broader social satire. *The Rape of Bunny Stuntz* (1962) probes more deeply, as the unexpected presence of a silent, unshaven intruder at Bunny's club meeting gradually reveals the desperation of her suburban existence and leads her to suicide. This Pinteresque quality rarely resurfaces in Gurney's work, with the exception of *Darlene* (1998), which shows another desperate suburban wife whose desire for a more passionate life flares up when she finds a note, which is either a salacious sadomasochistic fantasy or a terrifying, murderous threat, on the windshield of her car.

Thornton Wilder is a significant influence on Gurney's first published full-length play, *The Bridal Dinner* (1962). The play is a lively variation on the second act of Wilder's *Our Town* (1938), at the same time more broadly comic and more troubled. A bridal dinner, made up of figures as typical as any found in Grovers Corners, quickly degenerates into a series of comic sketches, debates, and brief lectures on modern matrimony. In one of the earliest of Gurney's many metatheatrical gestures, the occasion is a play in the mind of its playwright, the Toastmaster, who taunts the guests: "You are to be considered flesh and blood, but you are really only figments of my teeming brain." The Toastmaster wreaks havoc with the impending nuptials by introducing a series of reservations about marriage, until the characters rebel and go ahead with the marriage all the same. Their triumphant rebuttal, however–"You can't talk about love," they conclude, "You've got to live love!"–sounds a touch facile in the light of all that has gone before it, as if the playwright lacks the courage of his convictions when it comes to imagining alternatives to the status quo. In its presentation and its seemingly irreverent approach to married life, which finally capitulates to traditional values, *The Bridal Dinner* looks back to such plays as J. B. Priestley's *Ever Since Paradise* (1947) and forward to Stephen Sondheim's *Company* (1970).

The Bridal Dinner introduces what becomes a major motif in later Gurney plays–the equation of a gathering, often a dinner party, as an image of the theatrical experience, and, on a more mythic level, an image of community. In this play the Toastmaster is a conflicted figure, simultaneously bringing the comic society to life in his imaginings and separating them by introducing impediments to the marriage. As he loses control of his play he retreats from the wedding celebration in disillusionment, the one figure who cannot be included in the comic resolution.

Gurney's New York debut, with a two-act version of *The David Show,* was hardly auspicious. Running for a single performance, the play was castigated by Clive Barnes in *The New York Times* (1 November 1968) as "Monstrous, pretentious and, perhaps most of all, vain"–a pronouncement that made the playwright physically ill. Although later reviews have rarely been as vicious, Barnes leveled an accusation that has resurfaced during Gurney's career–that his attempts at broad humor are sophomoric. In this case the use of biblical material to spoof television and the modern obsession with image struck Barnes as an annoyingly arch and facile juxtaposition. Trimmed back to a one-act play, however, teamed with *The Golden Fleece*, and reviewed by a different critic from *The New York Times* (11 June 1969) the following year, *The David Show* fared much better.

In 1970 Gurney seemed poised to make a major breakthrough in the New York theater with *Scenes from American Life*. A series of satiric vignettes, performed by an ensemble of eight actors playing a host of roles with piano accompaniment, it chronicles upper-middle-class life in Buffalo from 1930 to the not-so-distant future, in which American life has degenerated into a dystopia of urban terrorism, detention camps, evening curfews, and secret police. The rise of this state, the playwright implies, is not because of the loss of WASP power but instead stems directly from strains of insularity, greed, philistinism, and racism inherent in WASP ideology. In one scene, a mother badgers a daughter who wants to

Debra Mooney, Stephen Pearlman, Charlotte Moore, June Gable, and John Cunningham in the 1986 Astor Place Theatre production of The Perfect Party (photograph by Peter Cunningham)

attend college into submission, arguing that a debutante ball is far preferable. In another, father and son come to blows as they argue whether the son should voluntarily go to prison for defying the new police state. The wit in the play, its ingenious use of doubling, and its deep pessimism about America in the wake of the Vietnam War struck a responsive chord in audiences and led to the playwright's winning the Drama Desk Award. Although Edith Oliver, writing for *The New Yorker* (3 April 1971), found the episodic form of the play "elusive," she praised Gurney for his skill in writing for actors and noted the distinctive mixture of "satire and valedictory" that has so often distinguished the attitude of Gurney to his characters.

A change in the artistic directorship of the Lincoln Center Theater shortly after *Scenes from American Life* meant that the theater was less sympathetic to Gurney's WASP milieu, and Gurney did not have another play performed there until 1999. In fact, no other theater in New York made any serious commitment to his work for some time, and Gurney's career until 1982 was largely sustained by productions in American regional theaters and London. The 1970s were a decade of creative experimentation, in which Gurney tried his hand at different theatrical genres and published two of his three novels, *The Gospel According to Joe* (1974) and *Entertaining Strangers* (1977).

Children (1974), Gurney explains in volume two of his *Collected Plays* (1997), was his first attempt to move from full-length works with episodic structures to a well-made play. Its London premiere received a glowing review from Sandy Wilson in the May 1974 issue of *Plays and Players;* Wilson found its domestic realism and well-made structure a pleasant relief from the experimental dramas that he felt had deluged the London stage. A free expansion of John Cheever's short story "Goodbye, My Brother" (1953), it takes Cheever's exploration of the tension between two brothers with different views of life and reworks it into a melodramatic domestic tale that foreshadows some of Gurney's own concerns. While the mother in Cheever's short story is a deftly sketched minor character, a shallow old patrician rapidly sinking into alcoholism, Gurney refashions her as a hopeful and insightful widow on the verge of a long-deferred marriage to her true love. While the climactic outbreak of violence between the siblings is presented in Cheever's story as the result of years of tension between an optimistic but somewhat deluded brother and a truth-telling malcontent, Gurney precipitates the violence by having the malcontent, Pokey, falsely assert that the mother had committed adultery years ago. Pokey is presented as the only family member who reacted to their father's death with overt grief, and Gurney presents his anger as less an inheritance from the New England Puritans, as Cheever had, and more as a strongly Oedipal situation. The mother, who significantly is the only character in the play not to have a proper name, ultimately renounces her opportunity for romantic happiness in favor of being a mother to her adult children, who, she comes to realize, have never quite matured. The tension between passion and social role runs throughout Gurney's work.

Perhaps the most revealing play of the 1970s is *Who Killed Richard Cory?* (1976), another of Gurney's examinations of anomie masked by middle-class success and respectability. A dramatic elaboration of Edwin Arlington Robinson's poem "Richard Cory" (1897), it explores the final summer of an elegant, wealthy, kind, and widely admired pillar of the community. Deciding to stay in town while his wife and children go off for their usual summer vacation, he drifts, has an affair, reads books on anthropology, and suffers from a deep-seated and obscure crisis. The fluid structure of the play, its sparse staging, presentational style, and evocation of an eastern city populated by naive, typical figures all show the strong influence of Wilder, as does the dramatic strategy of showing contemporary life through the filter of myth, with Cory finally identified with the sacrificed king in James Frazer's *The Golden Bough* (1890–1915). The reserved and understated depiction of a devastating inner crisis in the life of its protagonist, however, is distinctly Gurney's. Revised later as *Richard Cory* (1984), this work shows the playwright giving mythic resonances to two of his most persistent motifs—male menopause and the decline of WASP ascendancy.

Gurney's consciously comic and ironic treatment of mythic patterns beneath a thin veneer of realism echoes the concerns Northrop Frye brought to literary criticism in the 1950s with his *Anatomy of Criticism* (1957). Often the male protagonists of Gurney's plays are scapegoats, variously subjected to ridicule, ostracism, and symbolic castration. Gurney's most extravagant use of sacrificial myth has been *The Guest Lecturer* (1998), a weirdly exuberant one-act play that, he admits, took him more than two decades to write. A bloody and bawdy farce, it introduces a young academic who appears as the annual lecturer for a drama society, only to learn that he is to be castrated, strangled, and consumed, just as his predecessors have been. Luckily, he is resourceful enough to persuade the community to consider that mimesis may be preferable to the real thing.

The Wayside Motor Inn (1977) shows Gurney at his closest to Alan Ayckbourn. Taking the anonymity of the modern motel room as its starting point, the play superimposes five different sets of inhabitants, each moving through the room, oblivious to the others. There is a college couple meeting for a tryst, a businessman and hippie waitress negotiating what proves to be an abortive romance, a married couple going through the emotional maelstrom of an impending divorce, a domineering and insecure father who is badgering his son to attend Harvard, and an elderly couple visiting their children and grandchildren. Like Ayckbourn, Gurney is deft at exploiting the theatrical potential of his premise. Unlike Ayckbourn, however, his tone is warmer, even at times sentimental, and his characters are less idiosyncratic and more representative of social types.

The Middle Ages (1977) has proved one of the most vital of Gurney's plays of the 1970s and one of his most theatrically durable works. Set in that bastion of WASP privilege, the men's club, *The Middle Ages* is a robust romantic comedy with considerable comic energy that stems from its audacious hero, Barney, rebelling against the restraints of his family's decorous life in Buffalo—only to reveal, somewhat sentimentally, that his father's approval is what he has wanted all along. In his life of arrested development, Barney recalls Pokey in *Children,* but his manic energy of rebellion distinguishes him from all of Gurney's other characters. At the end, Barney buys the club and dreams of opening it to all those who have been traditionally excluded from it—a quintessential Gurneyan gesture of utopian aspirations. Premiering at the Mark Taper Forum Lab in 1977, the play did not go to New York until after the Off-Broadway success of *The Dining Room,* but then both play and production were warmly praised—"a poisoned quiche of a play," Jack Kroll called it in his 4 April 1983 review for *Newsweek.*

The Dining Room proved to be a major step forward in Gurney's career. Adopting a device from Wilder's *The Long Christmas Dinner* (1931), it uses a WASP dining room to show the history of its owners; but while Wilder uses the device to heighten the audience's sense of temporality, showing characters aging before viewers' eyes and exiting to their deaths, Gurney uses it to explore the values of a social class from its heyday through its decline. Similar to *Scenes from American Life* in its episodic and nonchronological structure,

Susan J. Coon and Christopher Wells in the 1991 Hartford Stage Company production of The Snow Ball, *which Gurney adapted from his 1984 novel (photograph by Ken Howard)*

as well as its extensive use of doubling (six actors play more than fifty roles), *The Dining Room* is more nostalgic, gently comic, and altogether free of the dystopian elements that darkened its predecessor. Widely performed in both professional and amateur theaters across the United States, *The Dining Room* has contributed to Gurney's greatly oversimplified reputation as a nostalgic dramatist who looks with fondness and gentle humor at the world of WASP ascendancy. Although Gurney described the play as a Marxist/feminist critique of WASP ascendancy, Bruce McConachie has criticized *The Dining Room* for evoking nostalgia for the heyday of the class. In her 1 March 1982 review for *The New Yorker,* Oliver avoided ideological extremes, once again sensing an ambivalence in Gurney's attitude, "occasionally rueful but never elegiac." David Trainer, the director of the first production, felt the vision of the play was universal; he observed, "the play appealed because everybody who ever had dinner with their parents understood what was going on. It was a basic human experience; eating with your parents and being instructed about tradition and life."

With the New York production of Gurney's next play, he briefly had three plays running Off-Broadway, but *What I Did Last Summer* (1982) ran into trouble with its director and leading lady and never gained much recognition. In his 14 April 1983 review for *New York* John Simon dismissed it as trivial and tepid, while Oliver's 21 February 1983 review for *The New Yorker* pronounced the lead character unrealistically drawn. Inspired by the playwright's memory of himself as a fourteen-year-old, working for a vigorous female nonconformist who lived in a converted pigsty and had the idea he should become a painter ("I was terrible," Gurney admits), *What I Did Last Summer* is an American pastoral with just enough uneasy truth to keep it from lapsing into sentimentality. Caught between a loving but restrictive family and the futile countercultural diatribes of his bohemian mentor, the young hero finds writing as a way of dealing with both conflict and the inevitable losses that come with life.

While both *The Dining Room* and *What I Did Last Summer* have their nostalgic moments, *The Golden Age* (1980) focuses critically on nostalgia as a theme. The Golden Age of the title is the Jazz Age, both as idealized by a young academic and remembered more accurately by an old woman who lived through it. The play first appeared in a workshop in 1979, followed by a London production the following year, starring Constance Cummings. Not until 1984 did a revised version come to New York, starring Irene Worth. Inspired by Henry James's *The Aspern Papers* (1888), the play is set in contemporary New York, where a legendary socialite tempts an obsessed scholar with the possibility that she possesses a manuscript of F. Scott Fitzgerald's *The Great Gatsby* (1925), including a lost chapter detailing Jay Gatsby and Daisy Buchanan's sexual affair. Using this manuscript as bait, she tries to manipulate the scholar into marrying her emotionally troubled granddaughter. The result is a disturbing mixture of wit and ruthlessness that increases as the play unfolds. Nostalgia is unmasked as a form of false consciousness, easily manipulated to selfish ends. In *The New Yorker* (23 April 1984) Brendan Gill criticized the play for an "essential unpleasantness," which remained despite the skilled efforts of the cast, while Simon, in his 23 April 1984 review in *New York*, found the plot improbable and the tone uncertain.

With *The Perfect Party* (1986) Gurney's mood turned lighthearted again, and he once more found critical favor–Frank Rich, in his 3 April 1986 review for *The New York Times*, called this piece Gurney's "funniest, meanest and most theatrical play yet." Rich found the comic flair of the play an advance over the playwright's usual cautiousness. Returning to the identifications of a social gathering with theater and America first suggested in *The Bridal Party*, Gurney's comic protagonist resolves to vindicate ailing WASP culture by throwing the perfect cocktail party, only to attract a vicious and sexually voracious reporter from a New York newspaper, eager to write a critical review. In hopes of winning his adversary over, the host invents and impersonates an evil twin brother with an outrageous Italian accent and even more outrageous sexual notoriety, who succeeds in seducing the reporter. Both party and seduction rate no better than a "7" in the reporter's postparty review, but the hero's wife salvages the event by concocting a far more casual social affair, free from Anglo-Saxon performance anxieties. A success in its 1986 Off-Broadway run, *The Perfect Party* shows Gurney's ability to transform his usual themes of anomie, obsolescence, and failure into effervescent humor. The high artifice and metatheatrical games of the play led Richard Hornby to wonder in the Autumn 1986 *Hudson Review* if critics had not done Gurney a disservice by linking him with Cheever and John Updike, when his real peers were Oscar Wilde, George Bernard Shaw, Ayckbourn, and Christopher Hampton.

Another Antigone was originally designed as a companion piece to *The Perfect Party*, and Playwrights Horizons considered producing both, with either George Grizzard or Remak Ramsay playing both male leads in rotating repertory, but abandoned the project as too expensive. Updating legendary material to present-day America, Gurney makes Antigone an ambitious student who defies her professor's traditional ways and conservative prejudices. Professor and student ultimately clash over questions of Jewish identity and anti-Semitism. The play draws on Gurney's dismay when his novel *Entertaining Strangers* was perceived by some of his colleagues as anti-Semitic. Fearing that this volatile material might once again give offense, Gurney gave a draft of *Another Antigone* to two Jewish playwrights to read before moving forward. The problem with the play, however, was not so much offensiveness as it was banality. Lacking the satirical edge that energized Gurney's earlier retellings of mythology, *Another Antigone* was criticized as merely a sentimental diminution of tragic material. The title of Erika Munn's 26 January 1988 review for the *Village Voice* succinctly summed up critical response: "The Whining Room."

Sweet Sue (1986) has been Gurney's only play to enjoy a Broadway run. First conceived as a reworking of the story of Phaedra in contemporary dress, using the device of having two actors playing each character, it held out promise of fleshing out the haunted figure of suburban female desperation first outlined in *The Rape of Bunny Stuntz*. Somehow, however, it considerably lightened into a superficial and somewhat antiseptic romantic comedy, telling the story of a woman's affair with the roommate of her collegiate son. The characters were so simple that critics found the doubling less revealing than gimmicky. Despite poor reviews, however, *Sweet Sue* ran for six months, in part because of the marketable casting of Mary Tyler Moore and Lynn Redgrave as the two aspects of the protagonist, even though, as Simon pointed out in *New York* on 19 January 1987, Moore was unable to tailor her television acting technique to the demands of the stage, while Redgrave overacted.

The Cocktail Hour (1988), applauded by many reviewers as Gurney's most sophisticated and self-aware work yet, won a Lucille Lortel Award in 1989 and was praised as a "masterpiece" of high comic

Programs for the premiere and a later New York production of Gurney's 1993 play inspired by Henry James's 1903 story "The Beast in the Jungle" (courtesy of A. R. Gurney)

writing by Feingold in the *Village Voice* (15 June 1993). Harking back to the premiere of *Scenes from American Life*, which had so upset the playwright's father as a betrayal of friends and family that he found it hard to speak to his son for over a year, it had a clear autobiographical dimension. Using its playwright-protagonist's return to his parents' home in Buffalo to persuade them to agree to the production of a play he has written about them as its premise, the play explores the conflicting demands of artistic expression and domestic renunciation. In a clever bit of wish fulfillment, the playwright is able to have his cake and eat it too: the protagonist agrees not to have the play he has brought home produced—but that play is the one the audience is watching. Deciding that the best way to write about his parents would be to use the American high comic mode of Philip Barry and S. N. Behrman, Gurney draws the parents as figures like those often played by the high comic actors Alfred Lunt and Lynn Fontanne, even overlapping their speeches in an allusion to that famous performance signature of the Lunts.

Love Letters (1988) began as a short story that was rejected for publication by *The New Yorker*. When Gurney and actress Holland Taylor presented it as a reading at the New York Public Library, its acceptance by the audience made Gurney wonder if it had a future, not as a fully staged play, but as a piece to be read in public. Using the Promenade Theatre during the run of *The Cocktail Hour*, *Love Letters* was staged on Sunday and Monday evenings, using only a table and two chairs. As a reading, it did not require much rehearsal time, so the producers were able to contract a notable succession of actors to appear briefly in the two roles, including Kathleen Turner, Edward Herrmann, Elaine

Stritch, Jason Robards, Julie Harris, and Christopher Walken. Following its initial success in New York, *Love Letters* has been performed around the world with great success, partly because its simplicity allows it to be quickly rehearsed and inexpensively mounted. But its appeal goes much deeper than that. The decades of correspondence between the ultimate insider Andrew Makepeace Ladd III and the rebellious and troubled Melissa Gardner work with conciseness and suggestive force. Like the young hero of *What I Did Last Summer*, Andrew embraces writing as a way of keeping his bearings in a world of conflicts, but Melissa points out the limitations of his solution, and Gurney dramatizes how writing can be as much a flight from the messiness of existence as an engagement in it. Most reviewers found the play a disappointment after the sophistication of *The Cocktail Hour*, with Simon in *New York* (18 September 1989) objecting to the contrivances that keep the characters in correspondence, and Katharine Dieckmann in a *Village Voice* review (12 September 1989) finding Melissa yet another stage heroine made to pay for her pleasure. But there was general consensus that *Love Letters* "played" well.

The minimalism of *Love Letters* was followed by one of Gurney's most elaborate projects, a dramatization of his 1984 novel, *The Snow Ball*. It was originally imagined as a play (Gurney has said that if he imagines a story with entrances and exits, it is a play; if not, it is narrative), but he reworked it as a novel because he thought it was too big and demanding to find a producer, only to have director Jack O'Brien encourage him to make a play of it. When Cooper Jones, a familiar Gurneyan male at loose ends with life, takes on the project of christening the renovated Cotillion Room in Buffalo's George Washington Hotel by reviving the "Snow Ball" of his youth and working against all odds to reunite the dance team of Kitty and Jack, he is attempting not only another "perfect party" but also a Proustian triumph over time. Reminiscent of Sondheim's *Follies* (1971) in its use of a reunion to play youthful dreams off of mature disappointments, *The Snow Ball* has a gentleness and graceful resignation that contrasts strongly with Sondheim's more acerbic vision. The deft dancing collaboration of Kitty, an heiress from Buffalo's social elite, and Jack, an ambitious Irish American, becomes a fragile image of liberal American aspirations, with class and ethnicity momentarily vanishing in the artistic celebration of a common culture. Along with O'Brien and choreographer Graciela Daniele, Gurney worked, as he explained in an interview with Tim Sanford, to make it not only a play with dancing in it, but a play about dancing—and its place in the imagination of an era. The result was a large and demanding production that, for producers, fell uncomfortably between drama and musical theater. A second stage adaptation of a Gurney novel—*Human Events* (2001), based on *Entertaining Strangers*—fared no better.

Gurney's response to the AIDS pandemic, *The Old Boy* (1991), is an uncharacteristically bitter and morally earnest work. In *The New York Times* (21 October 1991) Rich praised the work for its stormy confrontations, instead of the usual Gurneyan indirection, and was glad to find that Gurney had moved beyond asking for sympathy for his male WASP protagonist and instead was examining the people hurt by his privileges. Sam, an aspiring politician, returns to his prep school to deliver the commencement address, only to learn that Perry, a good friend from his school days, has committed suicide because he was suffering from AIDS. Gone is any sense of nostalgia or benign amusement. The school is drawn as a place of philistinism, self-delusion, and moral blindness—snobbish, sexist, and homophobic. In flashbacks, Sam relives the way he brutally imposed heterosexual norms on his friend and eventually conspired to couple him with a girlfriend Sam was eager to discard. By admitting his guilt in a highly emotional commencement address, he sabotages his promising career. The dialogue bristles with anger at a world dominated by greed and ambition.

The Off-Broadway run of *The Old Boy* was cut short when some of the key actors left the cast to honor television commitments; but the opportunity for a second production developed at the Old Globe the following year, for which Gurney did extensive rewriting. He remains, however, unhappy with the result. In volume three of his *Collected Plays* (2000) he judged the climactic speech "articulate, well-meaning, and something of a bore." It may be that the commencement speech cannot possibly fulfill the expectations that have been set for it, but the play still includes some of Gurney's most passionate writing and harshest insights. More than any other play yet, *The Old Boy* shows Gurney driven to write without retreating into his considerable ability to charm.

In 1993 *Later Life* premiered at Playwrights Horizons. A particular favorite of the playwright's, it is one of his most elegantly constructed and moving pieces, finding him "almost perfectly on form," in Feingold's judgment (*Village Voice*, 15 June 1993). The mixture of high comic tone and melancholy insight equals *The Cocktail Hour* in thoughtful sophistication, and the production, directed by Don Scardino and distinguished by the nuanced performance of Charles Kimbrough as the protagonist, led to a critical and popular success. Suggested by Henry James's short story "The Beast in the Jungle" (1903), *Later Life* compresses James's action from many years to a single meeting on a terrace during one of Gurney's signature parties. While his protag-

Page from an early draft for Sylvia, *Gurney's 1995 play about a middle-aged man's attachment to his dog; in this draft the dog's name is Mary (Collection of A. R. Gurney)* onist, Austin, exhibits a paralysis similar to that of James's John Marcher, his foil, Ruth, has none of the passive, sibylline quality of May Bartram. Rather, she is a woman who has immersed herself in life with an intensity bordering on self-destruction. Austin and Ruth are joined on the terrace by a series of guests, all of whom are played by two actors—a series of variations on the theme of second chances in life, as each of them suggests a different attitude toward aging.

The Scardino-Gurney collaboration continued the following season with *A Cheever Evening,* and once again, a light comic veneer was applied to material that was often at base disturbing. Fluidly assembled from seventeen short stories (sometimes presented in their entirety, sometimes as short fragments), the play opens with an invitation to nostalgia for the world of Cheever's WASPs but quickly modulates in tone to a much more desperate world. It was cast with accomplished comic actors, and reviewers Jan Stuart (*New York Newsday,* 13 October 1994) and Richard Corliss (*Time,* 17 October 1994) both concluded that the darker aspects of Cheever's vision were being sacrificed in favor of easy laughs. Reading Gurney's adaptation of "The Enormous Radio" (1953), which is the first story to be presented, one sees that the elimination of most of Cheever's descriptions and the quickening of the tempo (the printed version of Gurney's adaptation is less than half the length of the published story) results in what could easily become a comic sketch in the style of James Thurber. If the material is not to be trivialized by this reduction, actors, directors, and designers need to fill in some of the material Gurney excised and sometimes resist the tempo that Gurney's dialogue suggests.

In contrast to the bleakness of *The Old Boy,* the finely tuned melancholy of *Later Life,* and the underlying desperation of *A Cheever Evening,* Gurney's three farces of the early 1990s—*The Fourth Wall, Sylvia* (1995), and *Overtime* (1995)—show a return to comic buoyance, but at the cost of nuance and a pervasive sense of strained ingenuity. *The Fourth Wall* echoes *The Perfect Party* in its ingenious love of theatricality, as its protagonist comes to believe that she is a sadly limited character in a realistic play, and eagerly breaks through the theatrical "fourth wall" to make contact with a more varied America. But although this metatheatrical romp has gone largely unnoticed, *Sylvia* has become one of Gurney's more widely performed works. While *The Snow Ball* showed a middle-aged man reacting to a sense of loss by immersing himself in nostalgia, *Sylvia* shows a similar figure becoming obsessed with a stray dog that he has brought home. By having the dog, Sylvia, played by a woman, Gurney is able to work new variations on the old "Seven-Year Itch" theme once so common in sex comedies. In this play the protagonist's menopausal dilemma is invoked as a premise and never deeply explored, while the focus is on exploring the possibilities of actor-as-dog. *Sylvia* has provoked the most strongly divided responses of any Gurney play. For some, it is an amusing, ingenious, and affectionate examination of middle-class, urban dog ownership. For others, it is a precious, gimmicky play that exhibits misogynistic impulses by having a woman play, among other things, a bitch who has just been spayed. Both Jeremy Gerard, who enjoyed the play immensely (*Variety,* 29 May 1995), and Donald Lyons, who called its title character "aggressively obnoxious" (*Wall Street Journal,* 26 May 1995), found the ending weak and evasive.

In *Overtime* Gurney took on the challenge of putting a diverse and multicultural party onstage, rather than relegating it to the wings, as he had so often done before. A fanciful sequel to *The Merchant of Venice* (1600), it can also be seen as a continuation of *The Perfect Party,* in which the husband's attempt at old-style WASP ritual is replaced by his wife's plan for a far more casual, multicultural shindig. Portia's estate at Belmont becomes the site of a social experiment in diversity. Complicating the Jewish/Gentile opposition of William Shakespeare's play, Gurney adds an African American Gratiano, an Irish American Bassanio, a gay Italian American Antonio, and a Latina Nerissa. Reviewers generally agreed with Barnes, who observed in his 6 March 1996 review for *The New York Post* that the play extended a rather thin and self-conscious conceit to exhausting lengths.

The melancholy of *Later Life,* however, returned with increasing poignancy as the decade came to an end. *Labor Day* (1998), a sequel that replays the premise of *The Cocktail Hour,* shows its protagonist once again writing a play but this time about his wife and children. It is a gentle play that mingles domestic affection with an acute sense of mortality and estrangement, as the playwright looks at his personal and professional life after undergoing cancer treatment, but its strength is undermined by lengthy discussions of the problems of play development in the American theater. In *New York* (15 June 1998) Simon accurately observed the structural weaknesses of the play: it relies on too many offstage characters and never ties together the domestic and show-business plots.

In *Far East* (1998), extensively revised while in rehearsal, Gurney returned to his ill-fated Japanese romance. The appropriation of techniques from the traditional Japanese theater seems little more than window dressing, however, and the overall banishment offstage of the Japanese characters makes the cross-cultural engagement central to the plot seem thin. Feingold (*Village Voice,* 19 January 1999) rightly observed that it was

Charles Kimbrough and Sarah Jessica Parker in the 1995 Manhattan Theatre Club production of Sylvia
(photograph by Joan Marcus)

Madama Butterfly (1904) without Cio-San. At the same time, the pain of the central characters rings true, and the critique of the narrowness of American life recalls the indignation and pathos of *The Old Boy* and *Scenes from American Life*.

Strawberry Fields (1999), one of an omnibus of three one-act operas set in Central Park (with libretti by Gurney, Wendy Wasserstein, and Terence McNally), was the most popular piece of the three. Composer Michael Torke created a melodious and accessible score to Gurney's libretto, which told the story of an elderly woman who sits on a bench in Central Park, believing that it is a box at the opera. This patrician, regressing to a vanished time of grandeur and happiness, harks back to the matriarch in Gurney's student-written *Turn of the Century*, but in this play the tone is more generous and lyrical. In a representative gesture, the playwright corrects the stereotype of opera as essentially elitist by recalling that Giuseppe Verdi was a great populist and linking him with John Lennon. As the voices of the old lady, a graduate student, and fans of Lennon intertwine in an ensemble, Gurney comes closer than ever to finding a ritual expression of his hopes for a more varied and inclusive American culture, one that can embrace both loss and change.

In *Ancestral Voices* (1999) Gurney returned to the concept of a play to be read aloud, rather than fully staged, which had served him so well in *Love Letters*. The play began as a partly autobiographical novel that failed to find a publisher, and which later refused to accommodate itself to Gurney's sense of dramatic form. Director Dan Sullivan experimented with the possibilities of staging the play more fully, only to meet with Gurney's objection that the props kept getting in the way of the story he was trying to tell. First read aloud at the Mitzi Newhouse Theater on "dark nights" during the run of *Far East*, *Ancestral Voices* returns to Gurney's Buffalo, with a youthful narrator (born the same year as the playwright) who observes the decline of his beloved grandparents counterpointed with the decline of his hometown. When eight-year-old Eddie's grandmother separates from her husband and takes a lover, Eddie hopes for, and even makes some awkward attempts at, reconciling his grandparents, but without success. Eddie sees his grandmother enter into an unpleasant and isolating second marriage and his "Gramps" descend into a deep period of mourning from which he never recovers. Although occasionally lightened by typical Gurney vignettes of growing up in Buffalo, *Ancestral Voices* is a deeply melancholy piece, in which the grandfather is one of the most depressed and passive of Gurney's obsolescent WASP males, and the grandmother is one of the most melancholy of the Gurney women who strike out for freedom and self-realization in the modern world. Peter Marks, in *The New York Times* (20 October 1999), praised the play for its subtlety and the "rueful maturity with which it is recounted by a man gazing back over the decades."

A. R. Gurney has described himself as an "experimentalist," but it would be more apt to describe him as a traditionalist. Even his most self-consciously metatheatrical work is strongly rooted in the realistic tradition of the Broadway theater that flourished in Gurney's youth and seems tame (though no less engaging) when in the context of postmodern performance. His strengths as a playwright derive from the realistic, well-made play. He excels in drawing emotionally repressed characters in detail, exploring indirect means of communicating emotional life, observing the power of class as a determinant of character, and accepting the limitations of this tradition as inherent in the medium, rather than historically determined. Because of his conservatism, he has tended to be passed over by theater critics and historians who see the development of modern theater as a narrative of innovation and revolt, and his theatrical expertise, sympathetic portraits, and ability as a deft chronicler of his time have been largely ignored. If anything, Gurney has been undervalued, and it may be that his theatrical life will endure beyond that of some of his more experimental contemporaries, and his reputation grow. Without being an uncritical traditionalist, he has fashioned thoughtful and emotionally varied interpretations of old forms, crafting them to meet the challenges of a new age.

Interviews:

Leslie Bennetts, "His Obsession is Culture in Decline," *New York Times,* 30 May 1982, II: 4–5;

Jerry Tallmer, "What the Pig Woman Did for A. R. Gurney," *New York Post,* 5 February 1983: 15;

John L. DiGaetani, "A. R. Gurney," in his *A Search for a Postmodern Theater: Interviews with Contemporary Playwrights* (Westport, Conn.: Greenwood Press, 1991), pp. 113–120;

Tim Sanford, Interview with A. R. Gurney, Playwrights Horizons, May 1993, New York Public Library for the Performing Arts, Theatre Collection;

Jackson R. Bryer, "A. R. Gurney," in *The Playwright's Art: Conversations with Contemporary American Dramatists,* edited by Bryer (New Brunswick, N.J.: Rutgers University Press, 1995), pp. 86–101;

André Bishop, "A Conversation with A. R. Gurney," Lincoln Center Theater Platform Series, 20 January 1999 <http://www.lct.org/calendar/platform_detail.cfm?id_event=52191835>.

References:

Edward M. Cohen, *Working on a New Play: A Play Development Handbook for Actors, Directors, Designers and Playwrights* (New York: Prentice Hall, 1988);

Karl Levett, "A. R. Gurney, Jr., American Original," *Drama,* 149 (Autumn 1983): 6–7;

Bruce McConachie, "*The Dining Room:* A Tocquevillian Take on the Decline of WASP Culture," *Journal of American Drama and Theatre,* 10 (1998): 39–50.

Papers:

A. R. Gurney's papers are at the Sterling Library, Yale University, New Haven, Connecticut.

Moss Hart
(24 October 1904 – 21 December 1961)

Mary L. Cutler
University of North Dakota

See also the Hart entry in *DLB 7: Twentieth-Century American Dramatists*.

PLAY PRODUCTIONS: *The "National" Revue,* New York, 26 June 1922;

The Hold-up Man, by Hart and Edward Eliscu as Robert Arnold Conrad, Rochester, N.Y., Lyceum Theater, 23 November 1924; revised as *The Beloved Bandit,* Youngstown, Ohio, 17 September 1925; revised as *Anything Might Happen,* one-act version, Brooklyn, N.Y., 28 May 1927;

Jonica, by Hart and Dorothy Heyward, adapted from Heyward's *Have a Good Time, Jonica,* music by Joseph Meyer, lyrics by Billy Moll, New York, Craig Theatre, 7 April 1930;

No Retreat, Easthampton, N.Y., 16 July 1930;

Once in a Lifetime, by Hart and George S. Kaufman, New York, Music Box Theatre, 24 September 1930;

Face the Music, libretto by Hart, music by Irving Berlin, New York, New Amsterdam Theatre, 17 February 1932;

As Thousands Cheer, sketches by Hart, songs by Berlin, New York, Music Box Theatre, 30 September 1933;

The Great Waltz, by Hart, lyrics by Desmond Carter, New York, Center Theatre, 22 September 1934;

Merrily We Roll Along, by Hart and Kaufman, New York, Music Box Theatre, 24 September 1934;

Jubilee, libretto by Hart, music and lyrics by Cole Porter, New York, Imperial Theater, 12 October 1935;

You Can't Take It With You, by Hart and Kaufman, New York, Booth Theatre, 14 December 1936;

I'd Rather Be Right, by Hart and Kaufman, music by Richard Rodgers, lyrics by Lorenz Hart, New York, Alvin Theatre, 2 November 1937;

The Fabulous Invalid, by Hart and Kaufman, New York, Broadhurst Theatre, 8 October 1938;

The American Way, by Hart and Kaufman, New York, Center Theatre, 21 January 1939;

Moss Hart

The Man Who Came to Dinner, by Hart and Kaufman, New York, Music Box Theatre, 16 October 1939;

George Washington Slept Here, by Hart and Kaufman, New York, Lyceum Theatre, 18 October 1940;

Lady in the Dark, libretto by Hart, music by Kurt Weill, lyrics by Ira Gershwin, New York, Alvin Theatre, 23 January 1941;

Winged Victory, New York, 44th Street Theatre, 20 November 1943;

Christopher Blake, New York, Music Box Theatre, 30 November 1946;

Light Up the Sky, New York, Royale Theatre, 18 November 1948;

The Climate of Eden, adapted from Edgar Mittelholzer's novel *Shadows Move Among Them,* New York, Martin Beck Theatre, 13 November 1952.

BOOKS: *Once in a Lifetime,* by Hart and George S. Kaufman (New York & Toronto: Farrar & Rinehart, 1930; London: Gollancz, 1932);

Merrily We Roll Along, by Hart and Kaufman (New York: Random House, 1934);

You Can't Take It With You, by Hart and Kaufman (New York: Farrar & Rinehart, 1937; London: Barker, 1938);

I'd Rather Be Right, by Hart and Kaufman (New York: Random House, 1937);

The Fabulous Invalid, by Hart and Kaufman (New York: Random House, 1938);

The American Way, by Hart and Kaufman (New York: Random House, 1939);

The Man Who Came to Dinner, by Hart and Kaufman (New York: Random House, 1939; London: English Theatre Guild, 1945);

George Washington Slept Here, by Hart and Kaufman (New York: Random House, 1940);

Lady in the Dark (New York: Random House, 1941);

Six Plays by George S. Kaufman and Moss Hart, by Hart and Kaufman (New York: Random House, 1942);

Winged Victory: The Air Force Play (New York: Random House, 1943);

Christopher Blake (New York: Random House, 1947);

Light Up the Sky (New York: Random House, 1949);

The Climate of Eden, adapted by Hart from Edgar Mittelholzer's *Shadows Move Among Them* (New York: Random House, 1953);

Act One: An Autobiography (New York: Random House, 1959; London: Secker & Warburg, 1960).

PRODUCED SCRIPTS: *Flesh,* dialogue by Hart, motion picture, M-G-M, 1932;

The Masquerader, dialogue by Hart, motion picture, United Artists, 1933;

Broadway to Hollywood, by Hart, Willard Mack, and Edgar Allan Woolf, motion picture, M-G-M, 1933;

Frankie and Johnnie, by Hart and Lou Goldberg, adapted from Jack Kirkland's story, motion picture, Republic Pictures, 1936;

Winged Victory, motion picture, 20th Century-Fox, 1944;

Gentleman's Agreement, adapted by Hart from Laura Z. Hobson's novel, motion picture, 20th Century-Fox, 1947;

Hans Christian Andersen, adapted by Hart from Myles Connolly's story, motion picture, RKO, 1952;

A Star Is Born, adapted by Hart from Dorothy Parker, Alan Campbell, and Robert Carson's screenplay, motion picture, Warner Bros., 1954;

Prince of Players, adapted by Hart from Eleanor Ruggles's book, motion picture, 20th Century-Fox, 1955.

SELECTED PERIODICAL PUBLICATIONS–UNCOLLECTED: "Men at Work," *Stage,* 14 (November 1936): 58–61;

"Graduate Academy," *Theatre Arts,* 34 (April 1950): 54–55;

"How a Lady Kept a Playwright in the Dark," *Theatre Arts,* 36 (November 1952): 80–82;

"My Most Interesting Work: 'Climate of Eden'," *Theatre Arts,* 38 (May 1954): 32–33.

Edna Ferber wrote in a 1936 article for *Stage* that beyond Moss Hart's "elan there is a fine playwright with still finer potentialities; a dignified and dimensional human being with insight, sympathy, and understanding considerably beyond his years." In the same article Ferber dashed the popular opinion that Hart's rise in the theater had been on a fast track and instead asserted that his talent and career were "founded on a solid basis of endeavor, study, ambition, and heartbreaking preliminary work." Although Hart's intimates were aware of his several idiosyncrasies, they also recognized his immense gifts as a playwright, director, author, actor, and producer.

Hart's theatrical gifts were acknowledged in his day, as he and collaborator George S. Kaufman won the Roi Cooper Megrue Prize from the Dramatists Guild for their first joint effort, *Once in a Lifetime* (1930). These two authors, one of the most famous playwriting teams in the history of the American theater, also won the 1937 Pulitzer Prize in drama for *You Can't Take It With You* (1936). Hart received praise for his first Broadway performance as Smithers in a 1926 production of Eugene O'Neill's *The Emperor Jones* (1920) and other acting roles, including turns as Oswald in a 1926 production of Henrik Ibsen's *Ghosts* (1881) and Beverly Carleton and Sheridan Whiteside in later productions of *The Man Who Came to Dinner* (1939). He was also awarded the 1943–1944 Donaldson Award for outstanding achievement in the theater as best director for *Winged Victory* (1943) and a 1957 Antoinette Perry (Tony) Award for his direction of the stage version of *My Fair Lady*. Hart's autobiography, *Act One* (1959), has been judged by some theater historians and literary figures as a highly informative treatise on 1920s American theater.

Moss Hart was born on 24 October 1904 in New York City to Barnett and Lillian Solomon Hart. In

Hart with his collaborator George S. Kaufman

addition to his parents and younger brother, Bernard (who became a producer of Hart's works), Hart's family included his grandfather—a colorful, explosive, perennially out-of-work cigar maker and supposed colleague of labor leader Samuel Gompers—and Hart's unstable but theatergoing Aunt Kate, whom Hart credits with inspiring his art. In *Act One* Hart poignantly relates how poverty, dysfunctional behavior, and deep-seated emotional pain consumed his family. Only later, when he provided financial stability for his relatives, did home life become less strained. Yet, Hart biographer Steven Bach opines that Hart never was really intimately connected with his family. Finances forced Hart to quit school before the eighth grade and find work as a delivery boy, clerk, and fur-storage-vault worker, and finally as a clerk and floorwalker for the National Cloak and Suit Company. For a National Cloak and Suit Company affair Hart created his first musical and comedy revue in 1922.

Although in 1923 Hart's first full-length play, "Oscar Wilde," was sold but not produced by a silent-movie producer, Hart claims his career began when he was a delivery boy, office worker, and a script reader in the theatrical agency of Augustus Pitou, a producer of "road shows" in the 1920s. Hart in 1924 used the pseudonym "Robert Arnold Conrad" to write a script with fellow aspiring author Edward Eliscu for his employer. Although Hart confessed his authorship, Pitou produced *The Hold-up Man* (renamed *The Beloved Bandit* in 1925); it played Rochester, New York, and Chicago but did not fill Pitou's dwindling coffers, and Hart was let go.

Unemployment encouraged Hart to join a group of theatrical hopefuls whose coffee drinking and theater gossip united them; although they were unknowns at the time, several eventually became famous theater makers during the Golden Age of New York theater. Through networking Hart became involved as an actor, then as a director and a playwright, with such groups as the Labor Temple Players, Young Men's Hebrew Association Masquers, Brooklyn Jewish Center, Hampton Players, and a variety of Brooklyn and

New Jersey theater groups, all participants in the Little Theater movement.

During this same time period Hart also began a long association as a theater director with several famed summer resort camps, known as the "Borscht Circuit." In both camp and city venues Hart staged plays by George Bernard Shaw, Eugene O'Neill, John Galsworthy, and George Kelly, along with his own plays, while he wrote and directed musical comedy sketches and revues as well. Some of the plays he wrote in this era assumed some status in the New York theater, including *Anything Might Happen* (a 1927 one-act version of *The Beloved Bandit*), *Jonica* (1930), and *No Retreat* (1930). Also during this period Hart won the role of the Cockney trader, Smithers, in Charles Gilpin's revival of *The Emperor Jones;* in *Act One* Hart remarked that Gilpin's erratic, alcoholic behavior on stage challenged and improved Hart's acting ability.

Along with his amateur directing and playwriting career, Hart attempted to have his works read by significant people in the theater. He received several rejections, but a script reader suggested that Hart's best writing lay in his comedy, a comment that inspired Hart to write the script that eventually became *Once in a Lifetime*. Hart was introduced first to producer Jed Harris and then to the Sam Harris group, who eventually connected Hart with one of his playwriting idols, Kaufman, upon whose playwriting Hart modeled his own. Kaufman liked Hart's play and consented to work with him, thus beginning their legendary collaboration and enduring friendship. Hart's work with Kaufman introduced a rich and significant chapter in Hart's career.

Even in their first collaboration, *Once in a Lifetime*, the themes they employed are ones that scholar Cheryl Frederic-Nuzzo perceives in most of the playwrights' collaborations: "topicality, optimism, patriotism, and sentimentality," as well as "the situation of the arts in America." These themes can also be found in Hart's solo works. Frederic-Nuzzo opines that the duo's renowned use of satire was effective because they seemed to "build people up with one hand and slap them down with the other. The softening effect in the humor derives from the authors' identification with the American people and their empathic ability to read the public mood, thus knowing when reassurance was needed and when clear-eyed cynicism was needed." Frederic-Nuzzo asserts that in their playwriting, Hart "contributed the warmth (or sentimentality) evident in the collaboration."

In *Once in a Lifetime* the playwrights focus on the state of American arts. They incorporate current events and accompanying environmental details such as the Hollywood "talkies" and New York-Hollywood settings. Optimism is expressed throughout the text, as the protagonists' success story illustrates that good people are rewarded despite the vicissitudes of life.

The plot in *Once in a Lifetime* depicts a 1930s three-person vaudeville act seeking to survive the end of vaudeville. They scheme to offer elocution lessons to the Hollywood studio stars. In Hollywood the trio pose as speech experts but fail to solve studio dilemmas. Their none-too-bright straight man ingratiates himself with the fickle studio chiefs, and when they make him the new studio boss, he sees that his old partners are reinstalled.

Once in a Lifetime had a respectable run of 305 performances and received a wide measure of critical acclaim. Heywood Broun stated in *The Nation* (8 October 1930): "I cannot imagine anybody's having more fun in a theater than can be had at *Once in a Lifetime*," although he added, "Perhaps an accurate estimate of this gorgeous fooling should include the acknowledgement of one flaw . . . there is a very inferior love story dodging about in the piece." Also in *The Nation* (8 April 1931) Mark Van Doren wrote: "there is genius in it of an extraordinarily opulent sort; the invention is great, and the dialogue, while free and full, is managed with a vicious economy." Brooks Atkinson exclaimed in *The New York Times* (25 September 1930): "It is a hard, swift satire–fantastic and deadly, and full of highly charged comedy lines." He concluded: "It is all swift, shrieking and lethal. It is merciless and fairly comprehensive. . . . the best scenes all the way through are so outrageously fantastic."

The tremendous number of revisions the playwrights gave the script until the Broadway opening are legendary and reveal Broadway protocol of that era. Kaufman honored Hart in his final-curtain speech, given at the New York opening, by informing the audience that "80% of this play is Moss Hart."

In the 1930s Hart pursued his own playwriting career beyond his collaborations with Kaufman. He also used his talents for musical productions and revues and wrote comedy sketches in collaboration with other greats of the Golden Age of Broadway. In 1932 Hart and Irving Berlin wrote the musical *Face the Music* (165 performances) concerning New York City politics; "Let's Have Another Cup of Coffee" came from this opus. Richard Dana Skinner, writing for *Commonweal* (2 March 1932), felt "the revue, as a whole is pretentious beyond its real abilities." Although Atkinson had reservations about this satiric amalgam of "politics, show business, and the depression" in musical comedy form, he offered: "as for Mr. Hart, who is well remembered as co-author of *Once in a Lifetime,* he can look after himself as a wit. There is an undercurrent of genuine humor in his most poisonous barrages" (*The New York Times,* 18 February 1932).

Advertisement for Hart's first collaboration with Kaufman, a 1930 play about a failing vaudeville trio who schemes to teach elocution to Hollywood stars (Theatre Collection, University of Wisconsin)

In 1933 Berlin also collaborated with Hart on *As Thousands Cheer,* a topical revue concerning social problems. It featured the song "Easter Parade," Ethel Waters's rendition of "Heat Wave," and a sketch concerning the lynching of African Americans. The revue ran for four hundred performances; in *Commonweal* (29 October 1933) Skinner called this work "an excursion into verbal clowning of a pretty low order." Conversely, Atkinson in *The New York Times* (2 October 1933) proclaimed that all the collaborators "have created a superb panorama of entertainment: By being topical it is a revue in the genuine meaning of that word. By being excellent in quality it is enormously exhilarating. Among the thousands who cheer, count this column as one of the noisiest." Atkinson even chose to single out Hart's work: "Mr. Hart has never tuned his wit with such economical precision."

In 1934 Hart wrote an operetta, *The Great Waltz,* depicting the father-and-son rivalry of Johann Strauss Sr. and Jr., thereby employing the theme from his earlier work *No Retreat.* The Strausses' music was given lyrics by Desmond Carter. Hassard Short's famed designs received credit for the success of this production, which ran for 298 performances. Critic Gilbert W. Gabriel minced no words in the *New York American* (30 September 1934) as he called the production a "musical play . . . of some sentimental charm . . . turned into a monstrously beautiful bore." Gabriel also opined that

"*The Great Waltz* could have been a gracious little chamber piece. It has been turned into a convention of overstuffed stage effects." The production had some modest defenders, such as Atkinson in *The New York Times* (30 September 1934), who defined the work as an "operetta in good taste," also noting: "Moss Hart has told a simple, romantic operetta story. . . . Although the book is neither original nor distinguished, it is a workmanship job of music drama architecture."

This decade of Hart's collaborations with Kaufman remains the stuff of legend. In 1934 the duo wrote their second joint effort, titled *Merrily We Roll Along.* Nearly fifty years later the Stephen Sondheim-Hal Prince duo based their 1981 musical of the same name upon the Kaufman-Hart text. Neither production was critically well received, regardless of the ingenuity of the time-reversal device. The Sondheim-Prince 1981 version closed even earlier than did Kaufman and Hart's, but the contemporary musical duo has attempted several different revisions of this work during their careers. Frederic-Nuzzo's perceived themes of optimism, sentimentality, and topicality are evident in *Merrily We Roll Along,* and the musical is another of Kaufman and Hart's observations of the arts.

Merrily We Roll Along begins in the then-current time of 1934; the main character, Richard Niles, has found great success as a playwright, is troubled by his second wife, and is flirting with another starlet. Then time reverses, and Niles's career and life are depicted as regressing from high ideals to meaningless relationships and banal writing. Niles's friends, eccentric artist Johnny Crale and would-be writer Julia Glenn, proceed "backward" over the course of the play, from losing Niles to the day they first meet. Significant events are dramatized in reverse order: loss of friendships, second marriages, first marriages, writing for money, writing for art, all the way back to Niles's own commencement valedictory, in which he promotes the ideals of genuineness and friendship.

Merrily We Roll Along ran for 155 performances; Burns Mantle selected it for *Best Plays of 1934–1935*. Detractors such as Clifton Fadiman in *Stage* (December 1934) observed that the production "seemed flashy with the surface sheen of the Broadway which it claims to show up." Joseph Wood Krutch quipped in *The Nation* (17 October 1934): "It is ingenious and clever and ever so well oiled. . . . it is not very alive." Atkinson, however, heaped high praise upon it in *The New York Times* (1 October 1934), calling it "the first resolute, mature-minded drama of the season." He continued: "*Merrily We Roll Along* is a skillful piece of playwriting and staging. But it is also a fine one that dares to stand on principle. After this declaration of ethics it will be impossible to dismiss Mr. Kaufman and Mr. Hart as clever jesters with an instinct for the stage." Regardless of the mixed nature of the reviews, the ingenuity of the time-reversal device should not be slighted, for it invites effective audience reflection.

In 1935 Hart worked with Cole Porter on the musical *Jubilee,* in which Hart imagined the British royal family "slumming it"; the play ran for 169 performances and features "Begin the Beguine" and "Just One of Those Things." Atkinson in *The New York Times* (14 October 1935) heralded the short-lived musical as a "rapturous masquerade" and "an aristocrat of American festivals to music." Critic Grenville Vernon wrote less effusively in *Commonweal* (25 October 1935): "while Cole Porter and Moss Hart have done their part, they have done other shows that were equally as fine." Despite several positive critiques, the revue failed to maintain a long run and was possibly too esoteric for widespread appeal.

Hart and Kaufman teamed in 1936 on their most endearing and enduring piece, *You Can't Take It With You,* which many critics have proclaimed the duo's best, with Broadway revivals, movie and television versions, and productions in all manner of theatrical venues. The optimism, sentimentality, offbeat patriotism, and even topicality of the play seem to work effectively in any era.

The cast of characters in *You Can't Take It With You* is headed by Grandpa Sycamore, who one day walked away from Wall Street to entertain himself with snakes, commencement speakers, and his loving family. Grandpa's clan features his amateur-playwright daughter, Penny; his fireworks-making son-in-law; a ballet dancing/candy making granddaughter; the normative office-worker granddaughter, Alice; and former Russian royalty and dance masters, African American servants, and "guests" who showed up and never left. Although family members each do his or her own thing, love and acceptance are the rule. When Alice becomes engaged to her boss, Tony Kirby (the big boss's son), there is a glitch, and Tony's traditional family and the Sycamores clash. Impressed by Alice's loving relatives, Tony intentionally mistakes the date for their intended meeting, so that his overly formal parents might encounter the Sycamores at their most eccentric. The evening ends in chaos, and a union between Alice and Tony looks bleak; but Grandpa saves the day by proving the rightness of following one's dreams.

You Can't Take It With You and its lucrative run of 837 performances allowed Hart to spend his profits on entertaining and on buying and decorating new homes. Bach states that most critics were "delighted" by the work. Atkinson wrote in *The New York Times* (15 December 1936): "Moss Hart and George S. Kaufman have written their most thoroughly ingratiating comedy." Some critics, such as Fadiman, questioned the legitimacy of Grandpa's preaching about riches of the spirit with his apparently comfortable standard of living; in *Stage* (March 1937) Fadiman posited, "The whole point of the play (though the authors may not realize it) is that if you have an income of three to four thousand dollars a year for which you don't have to work . . . then, and only then, can you afford to hang around and develop lovable eccentricities." Other critics, such as Krutch, considered the play "pervaded by a humanity, an amiability, and a gaiety wholly delightful" (*The Nation,* 26 December 1936). Bach asserts that every situation comedy on television owes a debt to this play. Although there was some debate about the decision, *You Can't Take It With You* won the 1937 Pulitzer Prize in drama.

Also in 1937 Hart and Kaufman opened *I'd Rather Be Right,* an interesting amalgam of vaudeville, musical comedy, and sermon, with music and lyrics by Richard Rodgers and Lorenz Hart. Highly topical and satiric, but optimistic and patriotic, its tone is like Hart's musical revues written for his camp jobs. *I'd Rather Be Right,* set in Depression-era days, depicts Franklin D. Roosevelt (a portrayal originated by George M. Cohan) encountering a young couple, Peggy and Phil, as they are questioning whether marriage is possible in such insecurity. Roosevelt renews

Monty Woolley, as Sheridan Whiteside, and Gordon Merrick in the original 1939 New York production of Hart and Kaufman's The Man Who Came to Dinner *(photograph by Charles Hulse)*

his resolve to find a solution to America's problems, so that the couple might marry. In his attempts to alleviate the Depression, this version of Roosevelt runs up against many of the same problems the actual president did, such as presidential term limits and Supreme Court scrutiny. Ultimately, Roosevelt and his comically drawn cabinet cannot find a suitable solution; yet Roosevelt encourages the young couple: "Take your life and live it. You'll manage. People have done it before. You'll come through somehow," a message of Hart-Kaufman optimism.

Bach states that *I'd Rather Be Right* "became the longest running topical show of the 1930s," and he observes that this work was not the typically biting satire for which the playwrights were known. Along this same line, Vernon wrote in *Commonweal* (19 November 1937): "It is not the wittiest of the Kaufman-Hart musicals. . . . but it none the less makes an enjoyable evening." Even Atkinson wrote a less-than-enthusiastic review for *The New York Times* (3 November 1937): "In fact, every one has conspired to make *I'd Rather Be Right* a clever and generally likable musical comedy. But it is not the keen and brilliant political satire most of us have been fondly expecting." Instead critics heralded Cohan's performance and his return to Broadway, a factor that might have accounted for the success of the production.

During this period Hart also contributed sketches to two additional revues: *The Show Is On* (1936) and *Sing Out the News* (1938). In both of these shows Hart worked with several luminaries of the Great White Way. *The Show Is On* (237 performances) was a lampoon of show business; musical contributors were Rodgers, Lorenz Hart, Arthur Schwartz, Howard Dietz, George and Ira Gershwin, Harold Arlen, and E. Y. "Yip" Harburg. The show was directed by Vincente Minnelli and starred Beatrice Lille and Bert Lahr. Hart and Kaufman produced the show with Max Gordon—the first of many productions by these three theater makers—and Hart is noted for his sketch titled "Mr. Gielgud Passes By." Patrick Alan Farmer notes that the show "received generally favorable reviews."

Sing Out the News (105 performances) was a revue initially written by Charles Friedman with composer/lyricist Harold Rome. Bach relates that during the "journey from the Labor Stage [the rehearsal space] to the Music Box [where it premiered] something got lost, and Moss and Kaufman quietly took over the writing" but attempted to keep that fact hidden. Bach describes the tone of the revue as "frankly leftist and antifascist." The production was short-lived, and the Gordon-Kaufman-Hart production team lost money on the project.

In 1938 the two playwrights attempted to take another look at the situation of the arts in America in *The Fabulous Invalid*. Frederic-Nuzzo claims that Kaufman and Hart's concern for the American theater is only outdone by their belief in the American dream. The play chronicles the history of the fictive Alexandria Playhouse, reflecting the accompanying changes in American theater. The playwrights assert that, although there have been rough times for the theater, it will survive—the same message they wrote for the country in *I'd Rather Be Right*.

The Fabulous Invalid begins with fifty scenes from Broadway hits from 1899 to 1929; the Alexandria is converted to a movie theater, then a burlesque house, and finally turned back into a theater by young, idealistic artists. The production was not financially successful, possibly because mass audiences were not overly interested in the subject matter. Its run lasted sixty-five performances, the shortest of Kaufman and Hart's collaborations.

Critics could not doubt the sincerity of the playwrights' message but found their technique unsuitable, such as Atkinson, when he defined the production in *The New York Times* (10 October 1938) as "a handsome show that has grown out of an attractive impulse to serve the theater. But it has taken the authors into a branch of writing they have not mastered yet." Other voices were more deprecating, such as Krutch in *The Nation* (22 October 1938), who asserted: "Probably the authors, with so much material and so much scenery on their hands, despaired of getting a word in edgewise and finally, losing interest in the whole business, decided that anything would do." Other critics, such as Vernon in *Commonweal* (21 October 1938), might have praised the playwrights' "tender, nostalgic, sentimental" reverence for the theater but not their technique of dramatizing this type of work.

In 1939 the Hart-Kaufman team wrote another highly patriotic play, *The American Way*. The device of topicality is quite evident as the play dramatizes the buildup to World War I, the interwar years, and other historic events, interwoven into small-town life. *The American Way* is the saga of three generations of immigrant German Americans. Throughout hardships, births, loves, war, and losses, the patriarch of the clan, Martin (a role originated by Frederic March), remains staunch in his belief in "the American way." Martin opens a furniture shop in Ohio, and because of his craftsmanship, sense of fair play, and love of his family, becomes a leading citizen. The drama ends sentimentally, as three decades later, Martin is killed while speaking out against a Fascist rally to which his disillusioned grandson has been lured. The grieving, guilt-ridden grandson swears he will never forget his grandfather's sacrifice. As is typical of many Hart-Kaufman plays, the authors employ a wide range of settings—from the docking of a New York ship to country clubs and factories.

The show ran for 244 performances, and Mantle included it in *The Best Plays of 1938–1939*. Critics chose to praise the patriotism of the production. Atkinson offered in his review for *The New York Times* (23 January 1939): "Like all cyclopean shows, it has some leaden moments . . . when the material is a little flimsy and the story-telling less firmly directed." However, he continued, "the earnest convictions of the authors and the actors . . . is both solemn and stirring. . . . it is a first primer in Americanism worth the storm of bravos."

Supporters of this production, such as Damon Runyon (writing for *The Daily Mirror*, 9 February 1939), labeled it "swell entertainment." Runyon continued: "We had been told that there is a great patriotic message in the show, but we must have muffed most of it in contemplation of the sheer entertainment values of the thing." Yet, Broun dismissed *The American Way* when he posited in the *New York World-Telegram* (24 January 1939) that the playwrights "were commissioned to write a sort of American *Cavalcade* in honor of the approaching World's Fair. With the best intentions in the world and with some degree of skill Mr. Kaufman and Mr. Hart have endeavored to fulfill this assignment. It seems to me that they have fallen flat on their faces." Broun did suggest that the size of the theater in which the play was staged might have been daunting. Overhead and the huge cast salaries resulted in a financial loss.

Later in 1939 the playwriting duo opened what is their most popular satire, *The Man Who Came to Dinner*. Frederic-Nuzzo asserts of their writing that with the Depression over, their style decreased both in "sentimentality and their use of environmental detail," as well as did their emphases on patriotism and optimism. Many of these techniques recur in Hart's solo work, but in *The Man Who Came to Dinner* the effective uses of satire and farce prevail. Name-dropping and portrayals of well-known figures in this play are consistent with the authors' musical revues, for *The Man Who Came to Dinner* satirizes Alexander Woollcott, Dorothy Parker, Noel Coward, and Harpo Marx. Frederic-Nuzzo claims that the theme of internationalism, represented through the different characters, was a device the playwrights used to express how they felt the country should respond to the approaching World War II; other critics simply define the play as a well-written farce.

In *The Man Who Came to Dinner* radio personality Sheridan Whiteside breaks his leg in small-town Ohio and inflicts himself upon the kindly Midwestern Stanley family. Tyrannical and outspoken, Whiteside is constantly critiquing people and things, and he rules the Stanley roost during his convalescence. He endears the underdogs to him by advising them to follow their dreams, treats the Stanleys like servants in a hotel, and creates chaos while he specializes in verbal destruction. The zany cast includes a long-suffering nurse, the bewildered Stanleys, a wisecracking secretary who falls in love with a local, and even a Marx brother. The fast-paced humor and door-slamming exits, plus these odd characters, offer a sophisticated farce.

Atkinson offered praise in *The New York Times* (22 October 1939): "it is the funniest comedy of this season, and is likely to remain so long after the competition has grown stiffer." He continued, "Mr. Hart and Mr. Kaufman have put together a fantastic piece of nonsense, with enough plot to serve and a succession of witty rejoinders to keep it hilarious." Krutch, however, in *The Nation* (28 October 1939), found fault: "It is funny without being gay, and it leaves no pleasant chuckles behind." Writing for *The New Republic* (1 November 1939), Stark Young reported that "the mounting freshness of the patter, emotional reactions and character-drawing in the first act fills the whole theatre with laughter, acid fumes, and really native entertainment."

The play is legendary, running for 739 performances in New York, with a run in London and a Western U.S. tour, and it was made into a classic 1942 motion picture with Monty Woolley, Bette Davis, and Jimmy Durante. It is included in *Best Plays of 1939–1940*. Nearly sixty years after its debut, the play remains a "choice" Kaufman and Hart text.

In 1940 Hart collaborated with Kaufman for the last time on a full-length play with *George Washington Slept Here*. Although patriotism is somewhat illustrated in the issue of heritage appreciation, and sentimentality is present in the issue of home ownership, farce dominates this work. *George Washington Slept Here* involves an oddly matched husband and wife who, at the husband's

The actress, singer, and later television personality Kitty Carlisle, whom Hart married in 1946

insistence, move to a dilapidated historic country home. There are complications galore: money problems, rising costs, rural living, eccentric relatives, and the invasion of summer-stock actors. The family survives it all and comes to love their new home.

Critics seemed to believe that the Kaufman-Hart collaboration should have ended before *George Washington Slept Here* was written. The play ran for 173 performances, and critical reviews were scathing. Even perennial supporter Atkinson felt the play "is a labored and empty enterprise. . . . Mr. Kaufman and Mr. Hart have gone through the motions of playwriting without taking much fresh enjoyment in what they are doing" (*The New York Times,* 19 October 1940). George Freedley commented in *The Morning Telegraph* (20 October 1940): "You can't expect the Messrs. Kaufman and Hart to ring the bell every time, and *George Washington Slept Here* . . . is certainly one of their misses." John Anderson of the *New York Evening Journal* (19 October 1940) surmised: "it seems always on the verge of being shatteringly funny and never completely succeeds. The material appears to be there but the invention is lacking to give the play viewpoint and comic force." Even Mantle, in the *Daily News* (19 October 1940), called the play

"Class B Kaufman-Hart," although he managed a partial compliment: "But their Class B is a shade better than a majority of their contemporaries' Class A."

Critics questioned the "odd couple" in this play; however, the wisecracking woman character became a favorite in Hart's later works. Hart and Kaufman were pursuing other, more interesting projects during the writing time of *George Washington Slept Here,* and some critics indicate that these pursuits might have distracted them too much.

At this point in his career Hart's self-doubts about his talents (without Kaufman's) could no longer be ignored. His psychiatrist, Lawrence S. Kubie, a highly influential figure in Hart's life, along with Hart's friends, advised him to break off his playwriting partnership with Kaufman. The two nevertheless remained good friends throughout their lives, neighbors at their summer homes in Bucks County, Pennsylvania, coproducers, advisers on each other's projects, business cohorts, and occasionally writers together for revues and fund-raisers. Hart gave the eulogy at Kaufman's funeral in 1961.

Hart's 1941 musical with Kurt Weill, *Lady in the Dark,* is often considered his first "solo" work. Some critics stated that the theme of the musical concerned women's innate desire to be dominated by stronger male figures, but the work also has the potential to illustrate that women should make healthy choices of partners in relationships and should not forgo career desires. The script confronts notions of gender equality and women's professional needs. Farmer heralds Hart's work as a "milestone in the development of the American musical."

In *Lady in the Dark* Liza Elliott, a successful but "unfashionable" editor of a fashion magazine, ends up in a psychiatrist's office discussing not only her career but also her relationships with men, particularly a needy married man. Also in Liza's life is her independent, brash assistant editor, for whom Liza reciprocates a covert attraction. As a catalyst to the plot, a young, suave, but needy actor attempts to woo Liza and proposes marriage. Liza shares her fantasies and dreams in therapy sessions, which Hart dramatizes. Therapy and her dreams allow her to realize that her romances are with inadequate partners. When the brash assistant is leaving for a better job, Liza makes him a counteroffer, a position as co-editor; he accepts, and they more openly express their attractions.

Gertrude Lawrence played the title character of *Lady in the Dark;* the original cast also included Danny Kaye (Hart's "find"), Macdonald Carey, and Victor Mature. The production ran for 467 performances. Bach records that "the New York and national press were of one voice in praising the production and the star" but did not include Hart. Vernon's review of the production for *Commonweal* (7 February 1941) exemplifies this point: "The story itself is not important, and Mr. Hart's writing not particularly imaginative, but it gives an opportunity to Miss Lawrence to prove once again that she is the most versatile actress on the stage today." Young proclaimed in *The New Republic* (10 February 1941): "The play is somewhat pretentious. The psychoanalysis theme has by now got to the point in the theatre where it must be either significant, or else clever, or novel and fresh. *Lady in the Dark* achieves very little in any of these directions." In *The New York Times* (2 December 1941) Atkinson lauded the production as "a masterpiece," "a fine, fresh-minded musical play, notable for its taste and artistic integrity," and "a feather in the cap of the American theatre." Even Krutch wrote supportively in *The Nation* (8 February 1941) that "*Lady in the Dark* is a superlatively 'good show.'" He stated the scenes "are astonishingly right" and "achieve more completely than any recent musical comedy or operetta I can remember that mysterious thing called style."

As a financial proposition *Lady in the Dark* was lucrative, and the sale of the motion-picture rights to Paramount set a record. Along with *George Washington Slept Here,* Hart's *Lady in the Dark* is featured in Mantle's *Best Plays of 1940–1941.* Although the musical has not found an audience in later eras, the songs "My Ship" and "The Saga of Jenny," written by Weill and Berlin for this production, are featured in the Julie Andrews movie *Star!* (1968) and on soprano Dawn Upshaw's album *I Wish It So* (1994).

In 1943 Hart wrote his next play, *Winged Victory.* Filled with patriotic fervor, *Winged Victory* concerns the experiences of several new recruits to the air force during World War II–Allen, Frankie, Pinky, Irving, and their buddies. These characters from small- and big- town America have dreamed of flying and serving their country. Hart dramatizes the selection process of flight training, as well as the flyers' relationships, marriages, partners, growing families, and bonding with one another.

Winged Victory received great emotional praise from theater critics and friends for its patriotic themes; it was included in *Best Plays 1943–1944.* Bach notes that the opening-night audience gave a fifteen-minute, tearful ovation to the production, and he remarks that reviews were more "testimonials" than reviews. Lewis Nichols stated in *The New York Times* (28 November 1943) that the production "gives a cross section of America at war, one which is moving, inspiring, and stimulating." Nichols lauded Hart's work comprehensively and proclaimed that "he has done something of which he should be proud–as should the theatre."

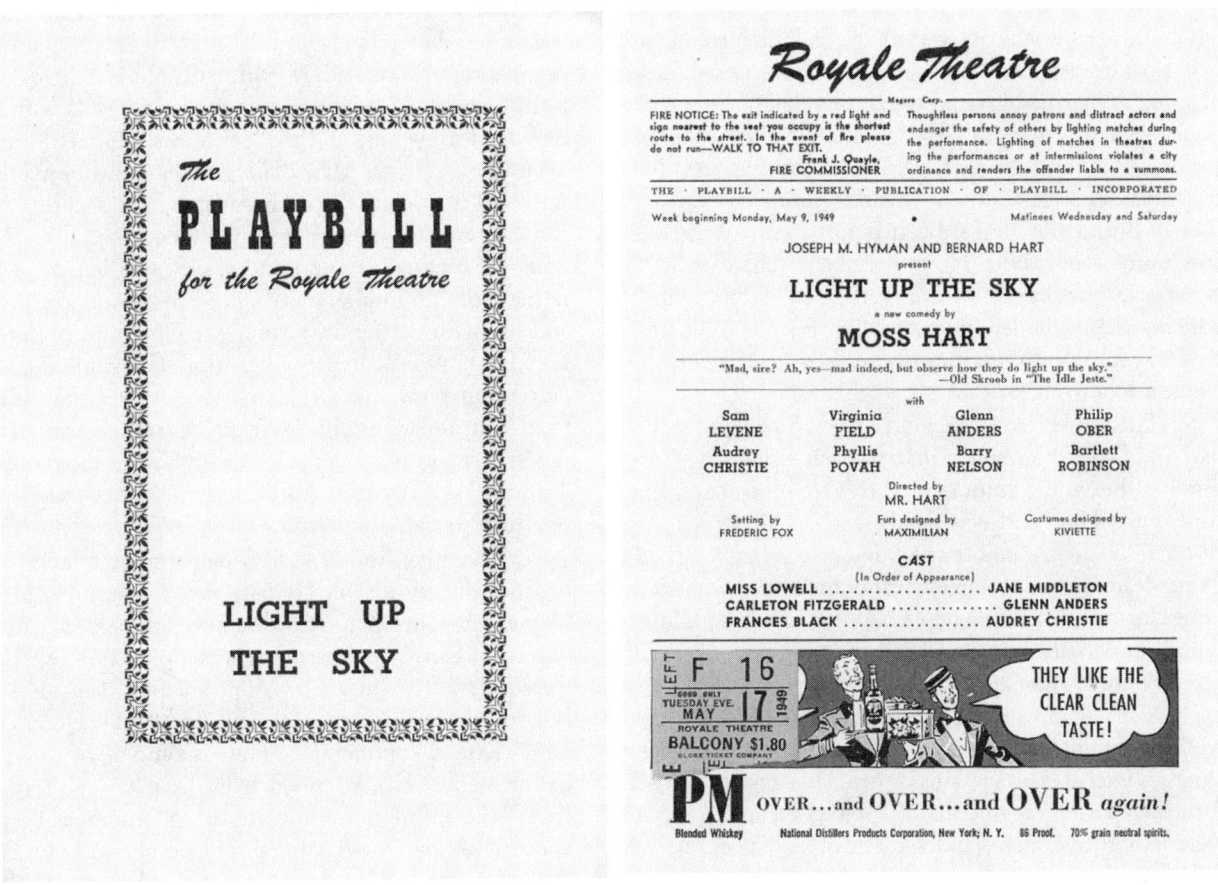

Program cover and title page for the 1948 New York production of Hart's farce about the first production by a truck driver turned playwright (Bruccoli Clark Layman Archives)

Rosamond Gilder also wrote a patriotic critique for *Theatre Arts* (January 1944): "The play is a remarkable achievement, for it succeeds in making articulate the modern miracle—the miracle of creation, almost overnight, of one of the world's greatest air forces, the miracle of the rising up of an easy-going, careless and carefree generation in defense of an ideal."

Other voices were critical, such as that of Louis Kronenberger, who labeled the piece "popular theater" in his review for the New York *P.M. Daily* (22 November 1943). While recognizing its appeal, Kronenberger bemoaned: "it has nothing to say. It is simply emotional entertainment." Margaret Marshall, in *The Nation* (4 December 1943), similarly wrote: "As a play it is feeble and at times boring. There are touching episodes, and the G.I. cast itself makes an irresistible appeal to the affections. But for all one's willingness to be moved, the deeper emotions are not tapped, and one ends by wishing that Mr. Hart knew less about air transport and more about human nature."

Winged Victory ran for 212 performances and was made into a movie in 1944. The original cast featured actors and service personnel, such as Private Barry Nelson, Private First Class Edmond O'Brien, Staff Sergeant Peter Lind Hayes, Private Karl Malden, Sergeant Kevin McCarthy, Private Lee J. Cobb, and Private Red Buttons, plus other actors, designers, and producers serving in the air force. Hart conducted his research for this play by undergoing eight weeks of flight training, and he also staged the play, for which he received the Donaldson Award. Hart donated his time and all income from this project, including fees from Darryl F. Zanuck for the motion-picture rights, to the Army Emergency Relief Fund.

This decade was significant not only in Hart's professional life but also in his personal life. After a courtship he married Catherine "Kitty" Carlisle (née Catherine Conn) in 1946. They had met earlier when she was pursuing a career as a singer and actress on stage and in movies; Carlisle is also known for her appearance as a panelist on the long-running television show *To Tell the Truth?* beginning in the 1950s and for her arts advocacy in New York City in subsequent decades.

There are many details of Hart's personal life that have not been revealed by Hart or his intimates. However, Bach's research indicates that Hart maintained meaningful friendships and romantic relationships with both women and men. Bach writes of Hart that his "sexuality had never been rigidly this or that and that he functioned sexually at various times in various ways." But in the 1940s, Bach reports, Hart wanted a commitment in his life. His influential psychiatrist, who is known to have discouraged Hart's and other patients' same-gender intimacies (as did the American Psychiatric Association in this era), was urging Hart to commit to a woman.

Therefore, in 1946 Hart (then forty-two years old) and Carlisle agreed to marry. Bach writes that Carlisle had heard the rumors of Hart's involvements; she confronted Hart and was satisfied when he denied the rumors. A strong emotional bond was what both of them desired, Bach suggests, and they were married until Hart's death. The couple had two children, Christopher and Catherine, and lived in New York City, in Bucks County, and later in California.

Also significant in Hart's personal life were his widely known depressions and his reliance upon psychiatry. Bach reports: "Moss's dramatic mood swings from incapacitation to feats of copious creative output were almost certainly manifestations of manic-depressive disorder. The pattern was one he suffered all his life and was probably genetic in origin. The vacillations from ebullience to contemplation of suicide had been occurring since his early twenties." Chronic insomnia and accompanying ingestion of sleeping pills also added to Hart's difficulties. For relief, Hart relied upon psychiatrists. In those years, psychiatrists (and society in general) did not believe manic depression was a chemical imbalance, and treatments included sleeping pills, aversion or shock therapy, and transference. Kubie, in particular, is also said to have sought out celebrity patients such as Hart.

Regardless of the challenges facing Hart, in 1946 he managed not only to get married but also to write an atypically serious drama. *Christopher Blake* is the story of a couple's divorce as seen from the perspective of a twelve-year-old boy. Critics frequently state that the theme of *Christopher Blake* concerns divorce hurting children; however, the play comprehensively demonstrates the feelings of all parties involved–mother, father, and this wise twelve-year-old, who comes to appreciate his parents as mere humans. Undoubtedly Hart's psychological leanings prompted him to create such characters. Hart once again used the flashback and fantasy techniques employed in *Lady in the Dark*.

The plot of *Christopher Blake* centers on the lad's decision about which parent he will reside with. Upon questioning by Christopher, both parents relate their individual difficulties with their marriage. For example, Mr. Blake, to cope with his wife's disinterest, developed a relationship with another woman. He pleads with his wife for forgiveness and pledges he will do anything to keep the marriage. Mrs. Blake, rather than forgive her husband, recognizes that she married for security and feels she must now seek her own identity. Christopher makes a mature decision and chooses to live with his father, for his mother needs her independence. Interspersed with the family's story are Christopher's guilt/revenge fantasies: he imagines himself committing suicide upon receiving the Nobel Peace Prize; becoming rich, but forsaking his destitute parents; and being unfairly sentenced in a nightmarish trial for the crime of "causing" the divorce. All of these fantasies were written for elaborate stagings.

The play ran for 114 performances and was coproduced by Joseph Hyman and Bernard Hart, the playwright's brother. Reviews were mostly negative; Farmer records, "critics thought the play was overproduced" and that such a lavish production was not warranted for this theme. In *The Nation* (21 December 1946) Krutch commented, "Here is a movie transferred to the stage." He described what he felt was its main flaw: "the effort is to find more and more elaborate ways of saying what could be said simply and of realizing in greater and greater physical detail what could be implied or suggested." Young added in the *New Republic* (16 December 1946): "There are some excellent ideas in all this, many effective motifs and considerable human feeling. But the scenes on the whole drag and run from a good deal of dramatic intensity to the tedious and banal." In *Commonweal* (20 December 1946) Kappo Phelan wrote: "the stress on large engineering, in order to accomplish the piece, is awfully damn silly I think." In the *New York Daily News* (21 December 1946) John Chapman even titled his review "Christopher Blake Suffers From the Curse of an Aching Hart," to which Hart wrote a public rebuttal. Bach mentions a 1983 revival that spawned negative notices for a "dated" and melodramatic text.

Yet, the play was included in *Best Plays of 1946–1947,* and Atkinson supported Hart in *The New York Times* (2 December 1946): "Mr. Hart has wholly succeeded in his basic theme of dramatizing the spiritual agony of a helpless boy victimized by the personal limitations of his parents; and *Christopher Blake* does credit to his maturity as a writer about people." Warner Bros. purchased the motion-picture rights and made *The Decision of Christopher Blake* (1948) with Alexis Smith as the boy's mother. As evidence both of Hart's largesse and the difficulties of the production, Hart decided to forgo his royalties.

In 1948 Hart returned to familiar turf, a comic look at the situation of the arts. *Light Up the Sky* is reminiscent of Kaufman days and the blockbusters *You Can't Take It With You* and *The Man Who Came to Dinner*. Many issues in this play relate to Hart's own career, and the familiar elements of sentimentality, optimism, and topicality are quite evident. *Light Up the Sky* concerns the opening night of a play written by an intense truck-driver-turned-playwright. His leading lady, Irene Livingston, is a renowned diva; the director is Carleton Fitzgerald, a highly emotional artiste; and the producer is Sidney Black, a nontheater moneymaker. Supporting these characters are two wisecracking, worldly women characters, the actress's mother and the producer's wife, plus an uninitiated secretary and an older, wiser playwright.

The plot of *Light Up the Sky* is that of a sophisticated and funny farce. Act 1 occurs just before the opening night of their production, and act 2 depicts the moments after the final curtain; precurtain praise and generosity change to sniping, sedition, and sarcasm. The trucker-playwright, ever the idealist, asks only to make the necessary revisions so the show can go on, but the others are convinced all is doomed. When the reviews are positive, however, the crew suddenly reverts to their gushing, effusive selves, but both playwrights lecture the rest about the true nature of art and artists. After the budding playwright sets new boundaries with these fickle theater folk, the cycle repeats as Hart's curtain falls.

Light Up the Sky, a humorous look at the theater, is complete with stereotypical stage personalities, humorous dialogue, farcical plot, and somewhat of a message. This production ran for a healthy 216 performances. Some critics were harsh; Phelan wrote in *Commonweal* (3 December 1948), "I think there was a play here, if we ever could have learned what the 'play' in the play was about; but the author has studiously avoided this point." Harold Clurman in *The New Republic* (6 December 1948) called it "a play that is a hit by design. . . . there is so little actual human substance or particularization that one cannot speak seriously of any theme, thesis or point of view." However, in *The New York Times* (19 November 1948) Atkinson praised this "whirlwind lampoon" as "funnier than anything the dramatic stage has spawned this season," adding that the jokes "bound off the rafters in an evening of honest, merchantable laughter." John Mason Brown was most complimentary in *The Saturday Review* (11 December 1948): "theatre people—are Mr. Hart's plot, and they prove plot enough. . . . He writes wittily and maliciously, with an easy professional touch."

Hart's brother, Bernard, was coproducer of *Light Up the Sky*, and Hart was convinced that this cast was the best one he had directed—with Nelson, Sam Levene, Virginia Field, and Philip Ober. The play was also included in the retitled *Burns Mantle Best Plays of 1948–1949*. Hart's revisions of the play were extensive, and he faced potential lawsuits (although none materialized) over characterizations that resembled well-known theater personalities.

In 1952 Hart wrote his last play, *The Climate of Eden*, which was an adaptation of *Shadows Move Among Them*, Edgar Mittelholzer's 1951 novel. *The Climate of Eden* was an unlikely work for Hart, as its issues are corporal punishment, nudity, premarital sexuality, incest, and miscegenation. Although the story line includes these highly sensational issues, the subtext concerns identity, acceptance, tolerance, and spirituality. Mittelholzer's psychologically based story undoubtedly appealed to Hart, who wrote scenic effects resembling his earlier fantasy techniques.

The Climate of Eden is concerned with the British missionary family of Reverend Harmston, who receives their tormented cousin, Gregory, into their home in British Guiana. This missionary family is far from typical, for they have adopted many of their parishioners' beliefs and traditions. While Gregory proceeds to fall in love with the minister's daughter, their "child of nature," Mabel, his malaise is discovered to emanate from supposedly killing his wife. Gregory's love for Mabel causes his guilt about his wife to resurface. After a highly erratic attempt to kill Mabel, Gregory confesses that his wife committed suicide, probably from Gregory's blaming her for his own failures and infidelities. (Bach suggests that Gregory's infidelities were with male lovers.) With Mabel's and the family's acceptance, Gregory finally faces his own culpability in his wife's pain and is absolved by the family. Subplots among other characters reinforce the themes of self-knowledge, self-acceptance, and acceptance by others.

The Climate of Eden, coproduced by Bernard Hart and featuring a young Rosemary Harris, ran for a disappointing twenty performances in 1952. In his widely read essay on the play, "My Most Interesting Work: 'Climate of Eden,'" published in *Theatre Arts* in May 1954, Hart wrote that he loved the piece and its many challenges. Critics offered damning reviews, which mostly criticized the character of Gregory and the actor portraying him, Lee Montague, as well as the extensive scope of the play. The critic for *Time* (17 November 1952) commented that the play "is unusual in itself and more unusual for Moss Hart" and continued: "obviously written with seriousness and care, 'Climate' has interesting scenes and characters, striking turns of behavior and speech. One reason for its lack of sustained interest may be that it tackles too much for one

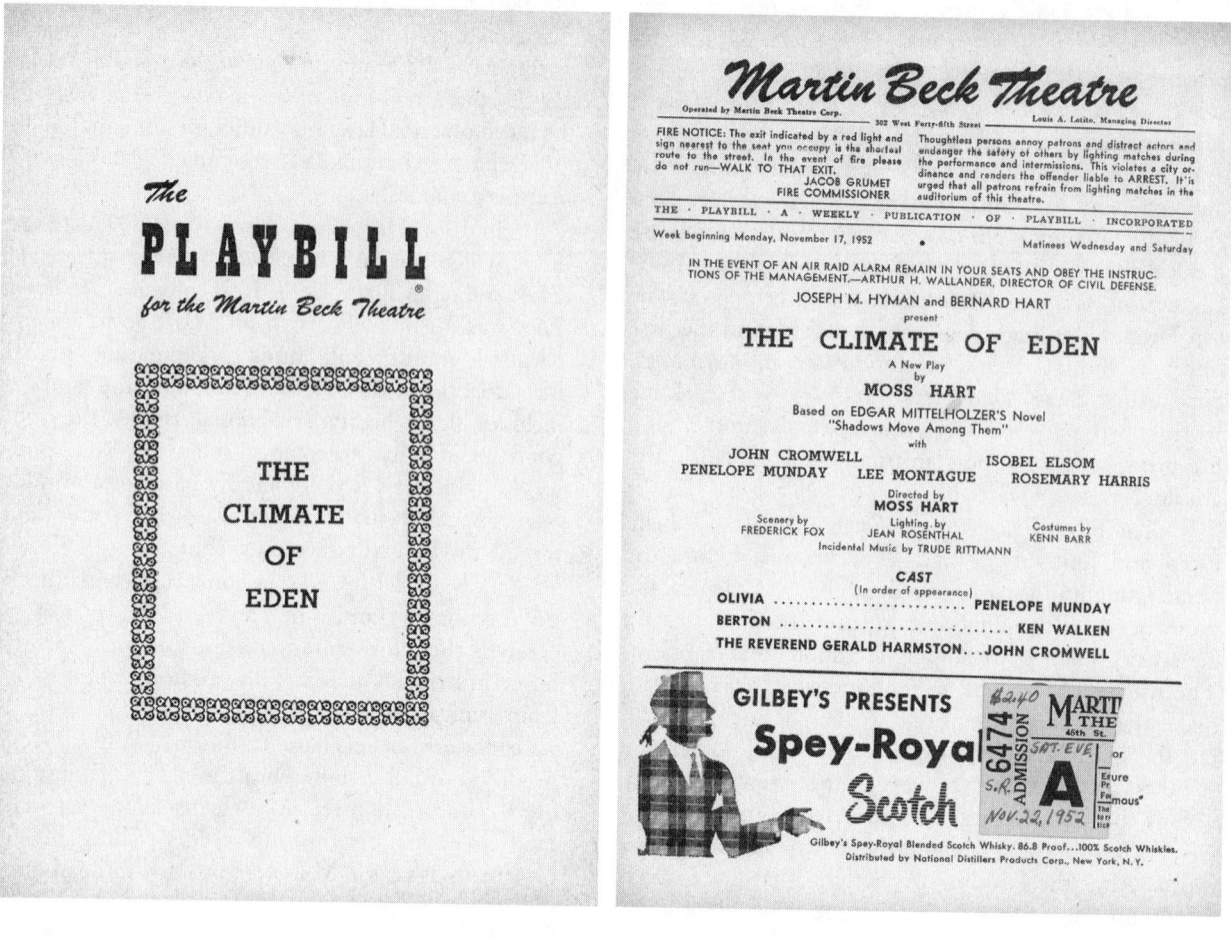

Program cover and title page for Hart's last play, which includes references to corporal punishment, nudity, premarital sex, incest, and miscegenation (Bruccoli Clark Layman Archives)

evening." Richard Hayes said in *Commonweal* (5 December 1952): "I am at a loss to comprehend at what points the talent which produced *Once in a Lifetime* is inferior to that responsible for this exotic *fleur d'ennui*."

Others, however, recognized the finer points of the play. Marshall wrote in *The Nation* (22 November 1952) that the production was "Not a very likely story but a pleasant fantasy full of relevant and amusing commentary on the world as it is." Although she, too, criticized Montague, Marshall added: "he serves as foil to a group of delightful characters," and she ended her review by stating that the characters produce "from beginning to end, a state of intense excitement as catching as it is convincing." Atkinson stated in *The New York Times* (16 November 1952) that the play "has an artistic vitality that has to be reckoned with. It is original and inspiring." He even proclaimed Hart's "abrupt transition from popular comedy to a serious drama with the skill of a professional." Upon seeing a 1953 revival of the play, Richard Watts Jr. even revised his initial comments, calling the play "a theatrical work of unusual freshness and imagination, one of the finest things its author has done for the stage" (*New York Post*, 27 December 1953). *The Climate of Eden* was included in the 1954 *Theatre Arts* issue, and later critics felt that Hart's play was worthy of further attention; it was included in *Best Plays of 1952–1953* by editor Kronenberger. Farmer reports that Hart attended some revivals of the play in subsequent years to reassess his work.

Beyond Hart's playwriting of the 1940s and 1950s, he also wrote revues, directed others' works, and wrote screenplays. He contributed sketches to two revues, *Seven Lively Arts* (1944) and *Inside USA* (1948). Hart directed Jerry Chodorov and Joe Fields's *Junior Miss* (adapted from Sally Benson's sketches) in 1941; Ben Hecht's *We Will Never Die*, described as a memorial to "the Two Million Murdered Jews of Europe," in 1943; Norman Krasna's *Dear Ruth* in 1944; Robert

Turney's *The Secret Room* in 1945; Berlin and Robert E. Sherwood's *Miss Liberty* in 1949; Chodorov and Fields's *Anniversary Waltz* (starring Carlisle) in 1954; and Alan Jay Lerner and Frederick Loewe's award-winning *My Fair Lady* (adapted from Shaw's 1913 play *Pygmalion*) in 1956. Hart's fascination with Hollywood and movie scripts often lured him to California; in the later 1940s and the early 1950s he wrote several memorable movie scripts, including the screenplay for director George Cukor's rendition of *Winged Victory* (1944); the Oscar-winning *Gentleman's Agreement* (1947), adapted by Hart from Laura Z. Hobson's novel; the Kaye vehicle *Hans Christian Andersen* (1952), based on Myles Connolly's story; the Judy Garland remake of the 1937 movie *A Star Is Born* (1954); and *Prince of Players* (1955), based on Eleanor Ruggles's book.

Hart's passion for his art extended beyond the proscenium, for Hart also distinguished himself in his service to the profession. He served as president of the Dramatists Guild from 1947 to 1955 and as president of the Authors' League from 1955 to 1961. He worked to oppose Hollywood's blacklist, assisted negotiations during the 1960 Actors' Equity strike, and supported increased state financing of the arts. Hart contributed to establishing an American Graduate Academy of Theatre; his concepts about training actors would securely link young actors with the profession, and his proposed training program imitated European models.

After Hart's first heart attack in 1954 he tried to slow his pace down, but he experienced a second attack while directing Lerner and Loewe's *Camelot* in 1960 and could not finish the rehearsal process. However, when he was released, Hart revamped the production, even after its opening, and he afforded his collaborators another Broadway hit. Although he attempted to pare down his life once again, at age fifty-seven Hart was stricken by a third heart attack and died on 21 December 1961.

Anyone who contemplates the whole of Moss Hart's career ponders why he does not rank higher in the annals of the American theater. Possibly his abilities in so many areas limit his recognition in any one venue. That he enjoyed and was respected for directing both his own and others' works are merits reserved for only a few. Farmer and Bach credit Hart's collaborative style of directing as influential to several Broadway hits. Some of his movie scripts are still considered classics. Additionally, Hart found time for activism in the arts and service to his profession. Above all, Hart's playwriting, with and without Kaufman, will be remembered for its depth, humor, and passion.

Biography:
Steven Bach, *Dazzler: The Life and Times of Moss Hart* (New York: Knopf, 2001).

References:
Patrick Alan Farmer, "Moss Hart: American Playwright/Director," dissertation, Kent State University, 1980;

Edna Ferber, "A Rolling Moss Gathers Considerable Heart," *Stage,* 14 (December 1936): 41–43;

Cheryl Frederic-Nuzzo, "The Social Philosophy of George S. Kaufman and Moss Hart as Revealed by Recurring Themes and Devices within Their Plays," dissertation, Florida State University, 1993.

Papers:
Collections of Moss Hart's papers are in the State Historical Society of Wisconsin, Center for Film and Theatre Research; in the Moss Hart Papers, Dore Schary Papers, Edna Ferber Papers, George S. Kaufman Papers, Kitty Carlisle Papers, and Walter Kerr Papers, Lincoln Center Library of the Performing Arts, New York Public Library; at the Museum of the City of New York; and in the George S. Kaufman Papers at the Library of Congress, Manuscript Division.

Harry Kondoleon
(26 February 1955 – 16 March 1994)

Robert F. Gross
Hobart and William Smith Colleges

PLAY PRODUCTIONS: *The Côte d'Azur Triangle,* New York, Actors Studio, May 1980;

The Brides, music by Gary S. Fagin, Stockbridge, Mass., Lenox Art Center, July 1980; New York, Cubiculo Theatre, May 1981;

Rococo, New Haven, Yale Repertory Company, 14 January 1981;

Andrea Rescued, Self-Torture and Strenuous Exercise, The Côte d'Azur Triangle, and *The Fairy Garden,* New York, Double Image Theatre, 2 June 1982;

Clara Toil, Waterford, Conn., Eugene O'Neill Playwriting Conference, July 1982;

Slacks and Tops, in *Triple Exposure,* New York, Manhattan Theatre Club, 8 March 1983;

Christmas on Mars, New York, Playwrights Horizons, 2 June 1983;

The Vampires, Seattle, Empty Space Theatre, January 1984; New York, Astor Place Theatre, 11 April 1984;

Linda Her and *The Fairy Garden,* New York, Second Stage, 31 May 1984;

Anteroom, New York, Playwrights Horizons, 20 November 1985;

Play Yourself, Norfolk, Virginia Stage Company, 8 March 1988; New York, New York Theatre Workshop, 19 July 2002;

Poet's Corner, New York, Theatre for the New City, 19 May 1988;

Zero Positive, New York, Public Theater, New York Shakespeare Festival, 1 June 1988;

Love Diatribe, New York, Circle Repertory Company, 14 December 1990;

The Houseguests, New York, Theatre for the New City, 28 May 1993;

Saved or Destroyed, Cleveland, Working Theater, 27 May 1994; New York, Rattlestick Theater, 20 November 2000;

The Little Book of Professor Enigma, New York, Theater for the New City, 19 December 1994;

Half Off, New York, Theatre for the New City, 4 February 1997.

BOOKS: *Christmas on Mars* (New York: Dramatists Play Service, 1983);

Rudy on Ruby and Nadine, Wedge Pamphlet 9 (New York: Wedge Press, 1983);

Slacks and Tops (New York: Dramatists Play Service, 1983);

The Vampires (New York: Dramatists Play Service, 1984);

Anteroom (New York: Dramatists Play Service, 1985);

The Côte d'Azur Triangle (New York: Vincent FitzGerald, 1985); republished as *Points along the Côte d'Azur Triangle* (Boston: Harcus Gallery / New York: Vincent FitzGerald, 1985);

The Fairy Garden (New York: Dramatists Play Service, 1985);

Linda Her, and, The Fairy Garden: Two Short Plays (New York: Dramatists Play Service, 1985);

Andrea Rescued: An Act of Faith (Montclair, N.J.: Caliban Press, 1987);

The Death of Understanding: Love Poems (Montclair, N.J.: Caliban Press, 1987);

The Whore of Tjampuan (New York: Performing Arts Journal Publications, 1988);

Zero Positive (New York: Dramatists Play Service, 1989);

Love Diatribe (New York: Dramatists Play Service, 1991);

The Houseguests (New York: Dramatists Play Service, 1993);

Diary of a Lost Boy (New York: Knopf, 1994);

Saved or Destroyed (New York: Dramatists Play Service, 2002).

Collection: *Self Torture and Strenuous Exercise: Selected Plays* (New York: Theatre Communications Group, 1991)—comprises *Self Torture and Strenuous Exercise, Slacks and Tops, Christmas on Mars, The Vampires,* and *Anteroom.*

OTHER: *The Brides,* in *Wordplays 2: An Anthology of New American Drama,* edited by Bonnie Marranca and Gautam Dasgupta (New York: Performing Arts Journal Publications, 1982), pp. 97–114;

Harry Kondoleon, 1985 (from Harcus Gallery, Boston,
Points along The Côte d'Azur Triangle, 1985)

Self Torture and Strenuous Exercise, in *Best Short Plays 1984,* edited by Ramon Delgado (Radnor, Pa.: Chilton, 1984), pp. 203-225;

The Fairy Garden, in *Out Front: Contemporary Gay and Lesbian Plays,* edited by Don Shewey (New York: Grove, 1988), pp. 419-447;

Zero Positive, in *The Way We Live Now: American Plays and the AIDS Crisis,* edited by M. Elizabeth Osborne (New York: Theatre Communications Group, 1990), pp. 205-279;

Linda Her, in *Plays in One Act,* edited by Daniel Halpern (Hopewell, N.J.: Ecco Press, 1991), pp. 259-266.

Harry Kondoleon's idiosyncratic mixture of whimsy, religiosity, and rage made him one of the most distinctive dramatists to emerge in the New York theater of the 1980s. Although his plays only occasionally found favor with mainstream reviewers, they attracted a relatively small but enthusiastic following who found in them an ingenious expression of spiritual desperation amid affluence and privilege. Kondoleon was not yet forty when he died of AIDS; his play *Zero Positive* (1988) and his novel *Diary of a Lost Boy* (1994) remain two of the most eloquent expressions of the earlier years of the epidemic.

Kondoleon was born on 26 February 1955 and raised in Queens, New York, the son of Sophocles Kondoleon, a public accountant, and Athena Cola Kondoleon, a secretary. He had one older sister, Christine. As a student at Hamilton College in Clinton, New York, he quickly established himself as a talented dramatist, winning the school's Wallace Bradley Playwriting Prize four years in a row. After graduating from Hamilton in 1977, he entered the M.F.A. program in playwriting at the Yale School of Drama, where he soon distinguished himself with a one-act play titled *The Côte d'Azur Triangle* (1980). The story of an American ménage à trois who travel to the French Riviera, stylishly dressed in black swimwear and sunglasses, only to lapse into joyless promiscuity before being devoured by sea monsters, this early work exhibits the combination of high chic and spiritual desolation that marks much of Kondoleon's writing. "The dullness of the Côte d'Azur," the prologue announces, "Reveals to these three Americans / The dullness and impossibility of love."

Sheila Dabney, Caitlin O'Heaney, Pamela Reed, and Susan Bommaert in the 1980 Stockbridge production of The Brides *(photograph by Clemens Kalischer)*

Their hedonistic vacation on the Riviera turns into an experience of interminable confinement, from which the lovers call upon God to manifest himself and put an end to their suffering. Not since T. S. Eliot's verse comedies had an American playwright so skillfully combined high comedy, verse drama, and spiritual concerns. Though Kondoleon soon abandoned verse drama, his continued fusion of high comic veneer and deep spirituality continued throughout his career.

The Côte d'Azur Triangle, along with *The Brides* (1980), a jaded take on modern heterosexual courtship as a fairy tale gone sour, won Kondoleon the Kazan Award in Playwriting at Yale. One of Kondoleon's teachers, John Guare, saw an affinity between the fledgling playwright and Ronald Firbank, a novelist of cruel preciosity, whose work he urged his student to read. But Kondoleon, perhaps fearing exposure to an accomplished predecessor as a possible threat to his own creative expression, carefully avoided his teacher's advice.

The Yale Repertory Company had sufficient faith in the young playwright to premiere his first full-length play, *Rococo,* for twelve performances in 1981, though this comic treatment of artistic affectation failed to please even Kondoleon's admirers. His one-acts, however, quickly began to attract interest Off-Off-Broadway. *Andrea Rescued* (1982) is the bloodiest and most aggressive of the lot, with its heroine married to a savage attack dog. *Linda Her* (1984), a compressed piece of highly atmospheric writing, conveys a wistful mood, as a man ponders the death of a woman he had a crush on in nursery school. Its companion piece, *Slacks and Tops* (1983), a dream-like play that rapidly accelerates into a frenetic nightmare, shows a similar concern with domestic entrapment and fantasies of escape. *Self-Torture and Strenuous Exercise* (1982), a somewhat strident comedy of two highly self-absorbed and neurotic couples, takes an unexpected, but for Kondoleon, characteristic turn into spiritual concerns at its climax, in which protagonist Alvin reports having had a vision of God on Park Avenue, which filled him with a sense of shame. Not

Jayne Haynes, John Vickery, Paul Guilfoyle, Elizabeth Berridge (on Guilfoyle's shoulders), Graham Beckel, and Anne Twomey in the 1984 New York production of The Vampires *(photograph by Martha Swope)*

even a manifestation of the divine, however, seems able to jolt the other characters in the play out of their fundamental narcissism.

Next to *The Côte d'Azur Triangle*, *The Fairy Garden* (1982) is Kondoleon's most accomplished and substantial one-act play. Like *The Brides,* it combines fairy-tale elements with contemporary anomie. In a 1982 interview with Don Shewey, Kondoleon explained that he added certain elements to the play merely to entertain. He knew audiences liked to hear actors sing, so he added a song; he knew audiences liked watching actors take their clothes off, so he included a male stripper. In *The Fairy Garden,* couples, both gay and straight, restlessly and unsuccessfully pursue happiness, which even the magic ministrations of a self-interested fairy cannot help them achieve. Finally, the protagonist, Roman, says "I want the world to disappear," and the fairy (and Kondoleon) grant the wish in a lyrical and effective theatrical image. No less desperate at base than the other one-acts, *The Fairy Garden* succeeds at keeping that desperation in tension with high comic banter, amusing plot complications, and a palpable desire to charm. Kondoleon's one-acts earned him a 1983 Obie Award for "most promising playwright" and a George Oppenheimer/Newsday Award for Best New American Playwright the same year.

Kondoleon's first full-length play to gain a production in New York City, *Christmas on Mars* (1983), shares the charm of *The Fairy Garden,* though critics found themselves at a loss to describe the play to their readers. Writing in the *Village Voice* (14 June 1983) Michael Feingold may have been the most accurate when he called it "a sort of hyper-realist repainting of a MAD Comix version of *A Doll's House* and *Private Lives.*" The play tells the story of Audrey, a bitter and insecure yuppie who finds herself pregnant by her lover Bruno, a shallow and unsuccessful male model. Her pregnancy generates a hope that improbably unites her with Bruno, her emotionally distant mother, and a hysterical airline steward who has a crush on Bruno. In this Christmas for emotionally crippled Manhattanites, an unexpected pregnancy touchingly elicits all the spiritual longing associated with the coming of the Christ child.

But Kondoleon's eccentric charm gave way to anger—at moral laxity, hypocrisy, and self-indulgence—in 1984 with *The Vampires,* his most intricately plotted and violent play. Although Ed, an aspiring but completely untalented playwright, and his brother Ian, a vain and malicious drama critic, share a history of competition and mutual betrayal, and their spouses despise each other, the two couples unite to brutally assault an intruder who threatens to reveal how their negligent behavior led to the death of a child. The murdered man rises from his coffin, however, as flashes of lightning and crashes of thunder serve as the prelude to an imminent Last Judgment. Dismissed as self-indulgent and obscure by more than one reviewer, the play foreshadows the rage manifested in later Kondoleon pieces such as *Poet's Corner* (1988) and *The Houseguests* (1993).

With *Anteroom* in 1985, however, Kondoleon returned to sophisticated charm. The play is a high

John Glover and Carol Kane in the 1984 New York production of The Fairy Garden
(photograph by Stephanie Saia)

comedy set in a mansion in Southampton. Parker, a scheming aesthete, connives for his friend Wilson to work as a domestic servant for his wealthy, tranquilizer-popping Aunt Fay and dreams of getting his hands on her fortune. His plans, however, grow increasingly bizarre, and he is finally carted off to a mental institution by his father, while Wilson is unceremoniously dragged back home by his working-class mother. The combination of clever repartee and cynical manipulation in the play encouraged critical comparisons of Kondoleon with Joe Orton, but Parker's schemes are far more outlandish and naive than anything found among Orton's savvy predators. Showing Kondoleon at his most lighthearted, *Anteroom* won higher praise from the mainstream critics than any of his earlier plays, who found much to admire in Elizabeth Wilson's stylish and assured portrayal of Aunt Fay.

In 1987 Kondoleon began making forays into literature outside the theater. *The Death of Understanding*, a brief volume of eleven poems, is a sort of *Symphonie Fantastique* (1830) in lyric form. Charting the end of an unhappy love affair, it culminates in images of self-destruction and the demonic. Kondoleon's first novel, *The Whore of Tjampuan* (1988), draws on the author's experiences in Bali as a Guggenheim fellow. Within the structure of a rambling, picaresque novel, Kondoleon follows his usual cast of affluent and desperately neurotic drifters on their journeys around the world. Protagonist Frank escapes his slovenly, reclusive, and hypochondriacal parents and travels to Bali, where he meets a variety of eccentrics and tries to deal with the spiritual malaise at the core of his existence. He leaves Bali and continues to drift, becoming in turn a caterer, male prostitute, and patient in a psychiatric hospital. At long last he finds spiritual peace caring for a retired nurse, now an invalid, who claims that she could see the souls of dying patients hovering above their hospital beds. *The Whore of Tjampuan* goes beyond the plays in its articulation of happiness gained through the practice of patience, good works, and a profound desire to become "infinitely alluring to God." Kondoleon had plans to dramatize the novel, using a variety of styles from traditional Balinese theater to Western realism and expressionism, but the project was never completed.

Poet's Corner, a tirade-filled feud between an estranged husband and wife, inspired by the marriage of Sylvia Plath and Ted Hughes, failed to win much attention, while *Zero Positive,* first performed at the Public Theater in 1988, was widely anticipated as Kondoleon's breakthrough to a larger audience and greater recognition. The rocky rehearsal period, however, led to an uncertain production that closed in little more than a week. The rehearsals began with Reed Birney in the role of Himmer and Mark Linn-Baker directing. But, in the middle of previews, Kondoleon found the production far too gloomy and insisted that Birney be fired. Previews were canceled; Birney was replaced by David Hyde Pierce; and Linn-Baker quit, to be replaced by Kenneth Elliott, a director whose forte was considered camp comedy. The result was an oddly cold and unmoving production, though Feingold was able to see beyond the production to the script itself, which he judged to be an important achievement (*Village Voice,* 14 June 1988).

A drama of mourning, family, and friendship in the shadow of AIDS, *Zero Positive* is one of Kondoleon's most compassionate plays. In the aftermath of his mother's death, Himmer learns that he is HIV-positive. Having discovered *The Ruins of Athens,* a death-haunted (and often unintentionally humorous) play written by his mother, Himmer decides to give it a premiere and to use the final scene of death by poisoning as a way of staging his own suicide. His plans are foiled, however, when his father drinks the poison instead. No play of Kondoleon's sounds more despairing in summary than *Zero Positive,* and yet the character interactions are largely free of the vicious narcissism and anger that are found in so many of his other plays.

Love Diatribe (1990) is one of Kondoleon's most charming plays and quickly found a warm reception. The play is a domestic comedy in which two adults return to their parents' home and learn to overcome their bitterness and self-absorption through the arrival of a mischievous stranger, disguised as a foreign-exchange student, who appears with a magical elixir. The production history of *Love Diatribe,* however, repeated the backstage unpleasantness of *Zero Positive* and showed Kondoleon's increasing frustration with directors who, he believed, did not know how to present his plays to their best advantage. The program for the production listed Jorge Cacheiro as director, but the playwright complained about problems with the ensemble and pacing and took over during the final rehearsals, with the approval of the Circle Repertory Company artistic director. Cacheiro was unimpressed with Kondoleon's directorial choices, telling Alex Witchel that the end result

Elizabeth Wilson, Mitchell Lichtenstein, and Colin Fox in the 1985 production of Anteroom *(photograph by Gerry Goodstein)*

was more naturalistic and less farcical than the script required (*The New York Times,* 28 December 1990); but the production was, on the whole, well received.

Kondoleon's bile soon reemerged, however, with *The Houseguests.* The play begins with a situation similar to Edward Albee's *Who's Afraid of Virginia Woolf?* (1962). Vera and John, a couple whose marriage has deteriorated into a nonstop barrage of insults, briefly join forces to humiliate their naive summer houseguests, Manny and Gale. Finally realizing that they have all reached a desperate impasse in their relationships, the couples agree to exchange spouses and head off in separate directions for the next six months, then reunite. At the reunion, each of them has suffered a mishap. Vera is in a body cast; Manny is almost deaf; Gale is blind; and John has lost his hands and feet. Through their vehement expressions of disgust, anger, and fear, they reach a nadir at which they accomplish the first tentative steps toward regeneration. As the play comes to an end, they timidly speak the word "love" together. Although the malice and desperation of Kondoleon's foursome was too intense to attract a wide audience, it won an Obie Award as one of the best productions of the 1992–1993 season.

Kondoleon's second novel, "Vivi Jump: (The Fin-de-Siécle Girl)," the story of an unemployed actress, remains unpublished. His third and final novel, *Diary of a Lost Boy,* is Kondoleon's most significant published work, one in which he gives his spiritual concerns their most extended treatment. Mirroring Georges Bernanos's classic Roman Catholic novel *Journal d'un curé de campagne* (1936; *The Diary of a Country Priest,* 1937) in its title, structure, and thematic concerns, *Diary of a Lost Boy* is the first-person narrative of a young man dying of AIDS and his attempts to attain emotional detachment from the world. Once again, it is populated with Kondoleon's usual egomaniacs, neurotics, and sexual obsessives, but the satiric edge is softened by the concern these narcissists show for Hector, the dying protagonist, and his affection for them. Hector's observations, though rich in the amusing details and satiric touches one expects from Kondoleon, are also suffused with an interest in mysticism, as evidenced by his frequent quotations from the medieval German mystic Meister Eckhart. In its balance of humor and pathos, social commentary and religious insight, *Diary of a Lost Boy* may well be Kondoleon's best achievement, as well as his most personal. It is difficult to read Hector's final words, "Please do not feel sorry for me–I go some place thrilling," without feeling the farewell of the thirty-nine-year-old author.

By the time *Diary of a Lost Boy* was published, Kondoleon was a patient at St. Vincent's Hospital and quite ill with AIDS; yet, he went out in an ambulette, despite his doctor's warnings, to briefly attend a party celebrating the publication of the book. Although Frank Rich, drama critic for *The New York Times,* did not attend the party, he wrote a piece about it for the paper (3 February 1994), celebrating both the author's quiet heroism and the novel. Kondoleon, however, was not pleased. Believing that Rich's unfavorable reviews of his plays had virtually ruined his career in the New York theater, he accused Rich of exploiting the AIDS crisis merely to publicly dramatize his own sensitivity (quoted by George Rush in the *New York Daily News,* February 1994). A little more than a month later, on 16 March 1994, Kondoleon died, leaving behind three plays that have been produced posthumously: *Saved or Destroyed* (1994), *The Little Book of Professor Enigma* (1994), and *Half Off* (1997). Of these three, *Saved or Destroyed*–a Pirandellian fantasy in which a cast of disillusioned, bitter, and frightened actors rehearse a play about a typically neurotic Kondoleon family–has met with the greatest acclaim. Although its premiere in Cleveland largely went unnoticed, its New York production as part of a 2000 retrospective of Kondoleon's work mounted by New York's Rattlestick Theater, was praised by Ben Brantley of *The New York Times* (24 November 2000) as "essential viewing for any lover of theater." The success of *Saved or Destroyed,* directed by playwright Craig Lucas, has been followed by the New York premiere of *Play Yourself,* also directed by Lucas. Kondoleon's reputation, like those of Firbank and Orton, continues to survive through the efforts of a coterie of admirers who are attuned to his distinctive sensibility–one concocted of wit, desperation, rage, and deep desire for spiritual illumination.

Interviews:

"Wild about Harry: An Interview with Playwright Harry Kondoleon, Author of *Zero Positive,*" *New York Native,* 6 June 1988, p. 25;

"Playwright, Lost," *Theatre Week,* 4 April 1994, p. 22.

References:

Glenn Collins, "Harry Kondoleon Is Dead at 39: Wrote of the Desolation of AIDS," *New York Times,* 17 March 1994, p. D21;

Don Shewey, "Homage to a Theatrical Comet of the 80's," *New York Times,* 19 November 2000;

Sonia Taitz, "Theater: A Meditation on Death Gets a New Life," *New York Times,* 15 May 1988, II: 5.

Papers:

Some typescripts and correspondence relating to Harry Kondoleon can be found at the Yale University Libraries and the Billy Rose Theatre Collection at the New York Public Library. A revised playscript of *Play Yourself* is in the Eileen Heckart Collection, Jerome Lawrence & Robert E. Lee Theatre Research Institute, Ohio State University.

Leslie Lee
(November 1935 -   )

Sara J. Ford
Inver Hills Community College

PLAY PRODUCTIONS: *Elegy to a Down Queen*, New York, La MaMa Experimental Theatre Club, 11 March 1970;

Cops & Robbers, New York, La MaMa Experimental Theatre Club, 29 January 1971;

As I Lay Dying, a Victim of Spring, New York, New Dramatists, 1972;

The Night of the No-Moon, New York, New Dramatists, 1973;

Between Now and Then, New York, New Dramatists, 6 February 1975; New York, Billie Holiday Theatre, 25 March 1983;

The First Breeze of Summer, New York, St. Marks Playhouse, 2 March 1975; New York, Palace Theatre, 10 June 1975;

The War Party, New York, New Dramatists, 1975; New York, Theatre Four, 7 October 1986;

The Book of Lambert, New York, American Theater Experiment at St. Clements Church, 26 May 1977;

Nothin' Comes Easy, New York, Village Gate, 1978;

Colored People's Time, New York, Cherry Lane Theatre, 29 March 1982;

The Wig Lady, New York, American Folk Theatre at the Samuel Beckett Theatre, 1983;

Golden Boy, New York, Billie Holiday Theatre, 1984;

Willie, New York, American Folk Theatre at the Samuel Beckett Theatre, 1984;

Phillis, New York, Apollo Theatre, 30 October 1986;

Martin Luther King, Jr., New York, Brooklyn Center for the Performing Arts, 6 January 1987;

Hannah Davis, New Brunswick, N.J.: Crossroads Theatre, March 1987;

Black Eagles, New Brunswick, N.J.: Crossroads Theatre, 24 February 1990; New York, City Center Stage I, 2 April 1991;

Ground People, New York, American Place Theater, May 1990;

The Rabbit Foot, New Brunswick, N.J.: Crossroads Theatre, 1991; Los Angeles, Los Angeles Theatre Center, May 1991;

Take Your Spirit North, St. Louis, Grandel Theatre, 18 March 1998.

BOOKS: *The Day after Tomorrow* (New York: Scholastic Book Services, 1974);

The First Breeze of Summer (New York: S. French, 1975);

Colored People's Time: A History Play (New York: S. French, 1983);

Between Now and Then (New York: S. French, 1984);

The Rabbit Foot (New York: S. French, 1991);

Black Eagles (New York & London: S. French, 1992).

PRODUCED SCRIPTS: *The First Breeze of Summer*, television, PBS, 28 January 1976;

"Almos' a Man," adapted from Richard Wright's story, television, *The American Short Story*, PBS, 1977;

Summer Father, television, *Vegetable Soup*, PBS, 1978;

"The Killing Floor," adapted from Elsa Rassbach's story, television, *American Playhouse*, PBS, 10 April 1984;

Go Tell It on the Mountain, adapted by Lee and Gus Edwards from James Baldwin's novel, television, *American Playhouse*, PBS, 14 January 1985;

"Langston Hughes," television, *Voices and Visions*, PBS, 1988;

The Massachusetts 54th Colored Infantry, by Lee and Jacqueline Shearer, television, *The American Experience*, PBS, 14 October 1991;

The Road to Freedom: The Vernon Johns Story, story by Lee and Kevin Arkadie, screenplay by Arkadie, television, 15 January 1994;

Born to Trouble: Adventures of Huckleberry Finn, by Lee and Jill Janows, television, PBS, 26 January 2000;

Ralph Bunche: An American Odyssey, adapted by Lee and William Greaves from Brian Urquhart's book, television, PBS, 2 February 2001.

Throughout a playwriting career that has spanned nearly thirty years, Leslie Lee has explored the history and implications of race in the United States. His plays illustrate the often overlooked history of Afri-

Vondie Curtis-Hall, Adam Wade, Brian Wesley Thomas, and Tico Wells in a 1986 production at Theatre Four in New York City of The War Party (1975), *one of the plays in which Leslie Lee explores the tensions of racial identity (photograph by Bert Andrews)*

can Americans, racially turbulent periods in American history, tensions both within and beyond black communities, and the complexity of racial identity.

Leslie E. Lee, who has refused to divulge his birth date to interviewers, was born in November 1935 in Bryn Mawr, Pennsylvania, one of nine children. His father ran a small plastering business. As a child Lee was often bedridden, suffering from the bone disease osteomyelitis. His condition kept him from participating in physical games with his six sisters and two brothers, and in a 1998 interview with Judith Newmark he recalls spending his time talking with his mother, reading, and writing plays for his siblings. Though active in literary pursuits at an early age, Lee went on to earn a bachelor of science degree from the University of Pennsylvania. He worked as a medical technician at the Valley Forge Army Hospital, a bacteriologist for the Pennsylvania State Department of Health, and a cancer researcher for more than three years before entering the theater program at Villanova University with a Rockefeller grant in 1966 and beginning his long and prolific career as a playwright. Lee's roommate at Villanova was David Rabe, who had recently returned from Vietnam and was embarking on his own career in playwriting. This relationship led to Lee's direction of an early version of Rabe's 1976 Vietnam drama, *Streamers*.

The first of Lee's plays to reach a wide audience and garner substantial critical attention was *The First Breeze of Summer*, first produced at the St. Marks Playhouse in New York in 1975 and published that year by Samuel French. The two-act play was expanded from his earlier work *Elegy to a Down Queen*, which was originally produced in 1970 at La MaMa Experimental Theatre Club in New York. *The First Breeze of Summer* focuses on three generations of an African American family and their struggle with racism, their hopes for a brighter future, and their memories of the past. The play explores the tension between the power of tradition and acceptance of change that had been at the center of his earlier plays, particularly the 1970 *Cops & Robbers*. One of the two central stories of the more accomplished *First Breeze of Summer* involves two sons coming into adulthood, at odds with their father's expectations for their professional lives and with each other. The younger, Louis, aims at transcending the trap of manual labor that he feels degrades his father and brother, and he studies to become a doctor. The story that runs parallel to that of the young men involves their grandmother, a pillar of Christian faith and the center of her adoring family. Her character is steeped, for much of the play, in stereotype, not just for the audience, but for the other members of her family who apparently have not considered her all-too-human history. Interspersed throughout the play are flashback scenes that illustrate her past—which includes three children born out of wedlock, each to a different father. The climax of the play centers on Louis's newfound understanding and condemnation of his grandmother's past and her own defense of that history.

A highly autobiographical play, *The First Breeze of Summer* illustrates the complex human limitations imposed on individuals and their relationships by a racist culture. In doing so, it challenges oversimplified visions of African American history and a few of the stereotypes that often accompany such histories. *The First Breeze of Summer* also raises the themes of black identity and the tension between working-class and middle-class values, suggested by the struggle between Louis and his father, though these themes are largely undeveloped. Most critical reviews of the 1975 production of the play were favorable, among them Mel Gussow's for *The New York Times* (23 April 1975), which credited the play with Lee's arrival as a playwright. Other critics praised Lee's ability to illustrate with clarity complex racial issues, particularly for a white audience, and the final note of hope: the play ends with the characters standing to face a welcome breeze, the first in a long time to offer much-needed relief from the heat. Lee's play also met with some accurately placed criticism. Marianne Evett, reviewing a performance in Cleveland for *The Plain Dealer* (7 February 1996), argued that the issues raised in the characters of Louis and his father are overshadowed and underdeveloped in the face of the dramatic implications of the grandmother's flashbacks. Scott Collins, writing for the *Los Angeles Times* (22 July 1994), argued that the play relies on some "unfortunate stereotypes of whites." Nevertheless, *The First Breeze of Summer* raises some of the issues that became central to Lee's career as a playwright; and, in its dismantling of the stereotypical character of the grandmother through the revelation of a sensual and emotionally complex history, the play also challenges oversimplifications of understanding race in America. In this play, as in his other, less significant plays from the 1970s, among them *Between Now and Then* (1975) and *The War Party* (1975), Lee illustrates the pressures brought on the individual by his or her racial identity. At the same time, he explores the tensions inherent in personal relationships both within and across racial lines.

Another prominent theme in Lee's work is African American history. In a 1991 article in *The New York Times,* Emil Wilbekin cites Lee's desire to "educate his audience about African-American history and culture and the human condition." In *Colored People's Time,* originally produced in 1982, Lee offers thirteen vignettes, each presenting a story set in a different time period. The historical moments he focuses on are well known, though what the play offers is a deeper understanding of the implications those moments had for the black men and women who experienced them. In one scene slaves share a crude understanding of Christian myth and plan secretly to start a new church with which to foster and promote their faith. In another a young black man with dreams of education survives by donning blackface and playing minstrel street shows for the small change he receives from an amused white passerby. Other vignettes feature three black characters and a Jewish store owner, all victims of race riots in Chicago; the excitement and skepticism with which Marcus Garvey's politics were greeted in the African American community; and a Depression-era poet who rents a dirty bed in an infested apartment building, only to be forced from his sleep by an overflowing toilet that the landlords have refused to repair. Throughout the play Lee shows that racial divisions limit human potential and create wasted and unfulfilled lives. The vignettes are framed by the reading of one character, Brooks, who is browsing through the collected and preserved clippings that his father has kept in scrapbooks and boxes in the attic. The vignettes that make up the bulk of the play pay homage to African Americans who have sacrificed in the past; they remind Brooks, and Lee's audiences, of the suffering, determination, confusion, and compromise that existed at the center of the African American struggle for survival and dignity, from slavery to the Civil Rights movement.

Colored People's Time does not offer significant enlightenment about what the major historical events in African American history have been, for Lee brings to the stage little that is new in that regard. The play lacks significant character development, as most characters are onstage only for a few minutes and are not involved in sustained or dynamic relationships. What the play does offer, however, is a worthwhile illustration of some of the human consequences of these historical events. Sheila Simmons of *The Plain Dealer* (9 February 1995) in Cleveland argued that the play is successful precisely because it shows audiences not what happened, but what it might have been like for those who were there. Viewers learn what it was like to be a couple in love and a part of the Northern Migration; a working woman supporting the Montgomery bus boycott by walking to work; or an affectionate couple at great odds

William Christian and Ray Anthony Thomas as World War II Tuskegee airmen in Lee's Black Eagles, *produced in 1990 at the Crossroads Theatre in New Brunswick, New Jersey (photograph by Eddie Birch)*

with one another over the political movements of their day. Though often noting the lack of character development, critics reviewed the play favorably, in general, citing the importance of the lessons it teaches.

Following *Colored People's Time,* Lee's playwriting career continued to be marked most significantly by his attention to the historical complexity that is race in America. His 1986 *Phillis* tells of the life of Phillis Wheatley, an American slave and poet; and *Martin Luther King, Jr.,* appearing the next year, offers another biography, this time for a juvenile audience. *Hannah Davis* (1987) examines a variety of racial and economic issues faced by a contemporary and affluent African American family. *Ground People* (1990) examines the life and struggles of poor black Southern sharecroppers in the 1920s.

Another play steeped in African American history, and the play to garner the most critical attention for Lee to date, is *Black Eagles* (1990), which premiered at the Crossroads Theatre in New Brunswick, New Jersey. In it, Lee recounts the story of a regiment of black pilots from Tuskegee, Alabama, who fought in World War II. Rather than humanizing a story his audience already knew, as in *Colored People's Time, Black Eagles* tells a story that had largely been forgotten. Lee has spoken about his desire in writing this play "to rectify a wrong, and the wrong is that nobody knows about the Tuskegee airmen." The play takes place at a Washington reception for Colin Powell, the first African American to serve as Chairman of the Joint Chiefs of Staff for the U.S. military. Gathered to help celebrate Powell's achievements are the surviving Tuskegee pilots, who recount their experiences through a series of flashbacks that illustrate the struggles of the airmen in a racially segregated U.S. Air Force. The men are fighting for a country that offers them neither the dignity nor the recognition their military exploits would otherwise ensure them.

The characters in *Black Eagles* speak about their experience of the double standard placed upon black soldiers in the U.S. military: they were not allowed to participate in the kind of combat that would bring them the most opportunity for valor, and yet a lack of accomplishment fueled the racist argument that kept them from such positions. If they defied expectations by engaging in combat, their actions were seen as a breach of orders and an inability to follow through with their assignments. The characters in Lee's play also struggle with the segregation that keeps them from celebrating their victories in the all-white officers' club. Not until nearly the end of the war were the Tuskegee fliers allowed to engage in air combat, and when they did, they proved to be remarkable pilots. Throughout the war they never lost a bomber, and by the end of the war they had destroyed or damaged four hundred enemy aircraft. Lee reenacts the heroism and the mistreatment of the Tuskegee airmen in a play that suggests that Powell's trail has been blazed by men such as these, men whose stories have not always been told.

One of the Black Eagles in the play, Buddy, has an affair with an Italian woman; in the scenes devoted to this relationship, Lee explores the effect World War II had on black soldiers who experienced, while in Europe, what it was like to exist in a culture that was not structured according to a racial hierarchy. Clearly this experience adds to the characters' understanding of American racial politics and makes problematic their role in war.

Critical reviews of *Black Eagles*, though not overly enthusiastic about the play itself, overwhelmingly support his choice of subject matter, arguing that the story has significant dramatic potential and needs to be told. Many reviewers, however, pointed to the play as something of a missed opportunity, often focusing above all on the lack of interesting character development. Writing a review for *The Plain Dealer* (4 February 1993) of a Cleveland performance, Evett observed that the "characters are sketchily drawn types." David Sheward, who reviewed the New York production of the play, argued that the Tuskegee airmen of Lee's play are "uncomfortably close to their white counterparts in innumerable World War II flyboy movies.... they remain stock figures rather than fleshed-out human beings" (*Back Stage*, 10 May 1991). Lee's soldiers are static, identified by a single characteristic. Nevertheless, if the aim of *Black Eagles* is to fill in the gaps in audiences' limited understanding of American history by recounting a significant moment involving the Tuskegee airmen, Lee's play is successful.

The Rabbit Foot, written just after *Black Eagles* and produced at the Crossroads Theatre in 1991, also explores—with greater attention to character development—the importance of the experiences of black soldiers who, while fighting wars overseas, became involved in interracial relationships that were not defined by the American racial hierarchy. Its willingness to present dynamic characters and its establishment of complex social relationships make *The Rabbit Foot* a much more interesting play than *Black Eagles*. In this play Reggie, a young black sharecropper, has just returned from World War I. He was in France, where he had an affair with a French woman. Returning to his wife in rural Mississippi, he argues with her about the identity of this woman. His wife, Berlinda, is horrified that he has been with a "white lady." Reggie argues adamantly that "she wasn't no white woman, she was French." Reggie has had a relationship not based on race, and so he no longer finds the adjectives "black" or "white" to be relevant. His wife, having seen no such cultural mores, retains her belief in the "whiteness" of the French woman, insisting upon the only identity markers she has ever known. Reggie's experiences in Europe allow Lee to illustrate the absurdity of racially defined relationships. *The Rabbit Foot* also develops an interesting gender conflict. Throughout the play female characters remain unable to exercise the autonomy the male characters have and offer powerful arguments about this gender divide. Reggie's wife identifies her suffering with that of other African American women in the rural South: "We women folk die early, birthin' chil'ren and workin' our fingers to the bone. I wish I could be a man for just a little while."

The Rabbit Foot is set in 1920, a year in the middle of the Northern Migration, during which tens of thousands of African Americans moved from the rural South to northern industrial cities following promises of higher wages and better living conditions. Reggie and his wife struggle while deciding whether to move north. Berlinda receives letters from a relative in Chicago and believes the North holds promises of opportunity. Her husband, inspired by his experiences in Europe, is at first determined to stay in the South, organize black laborers, and fight for institutional and social change. Woven together with the story of Reggie and Berlinda is a parallel narrative, focusing on the traveling black entertainment troupe whose name gives Lee's play its title. The story involves tensions between its struggling, alcohol-dependent members, who bemoan their difficulties and argue, like Reggie and Berlinda, about the benefits of heading north. The leader of the troupe, Singin' Willie Ford, is an older man who believes that blacks should stay in the South and remain loyal to what they know. At the beginning of the play, he and Reggie seem alike in their commitment to staying in the South, but Reggie's eventual decision to head north underscores how different the two characters are. At the end of the play Singin' Willie Ford is a destitute man, clinging to a way of life as a black entertainer in an American South that is changing too rapidly to support him.

Though reviewers often commented on the disjointed nature of *The Rabbit Foot*, arguing either that Lee tried to accomplish too much or that the two major stories in the play are not woven together tightly enough, others praised its complexity and Lee's willingness to develop the character of Reggie in interesting ways. In its development of multiple themes and its willingness to engage carefully in its historical period, *The Rabbit Foot* demonstrates that the decision for many African Americans to move north was fraught with difficulties; that although black men might gain a new perspective on race through their military experiences, they still faced insurmountable problems at home; and that black women were still mired in a racial and gender-based ideology and an economic trap they were often powerless to transcend. Lee's play offers a complex view of the quickly changing rural South of the early 1920s.

Like *The Rabbit Foot*, Lee's later work explores black life in America with a greater willingness to delve into issues more complicated and more controversial than those tackled in earlier plays. Most significantly, *Take Your Spirit North* (1998), which premiered at the Grandel Theatre in St. Louis, has at its center the trial of a black teenager accused of killing a Jewish teenager. The play focuses on Paul Massey, the defendant's attorney, and Paul's wife, Leila, who has known the boy as a thug and disagrees with her husband's decision to rally in support of the boy, a decision in keeping with the sentiments of a larger black community. The play raises questions about the integrity of a black community that focuses only on who is accused of a particular crime rather than paying close attention to what might have actually happened. It is a play about the limitations of group loyalty so determined that it overlooks fundamental moral principle.

Lee's career has never been limited strictly to playwriting. He is the author of a work of juvenile fiction, *The Day after Tomorrow* (1974). He adapted Richard Wright's short story "Almos' a Man" (1940) in 1977 and James Baldwin's *Go Tell It on the Mountain* (1953) in 1985 for television productions. Lee is also the author of "Langston Hughes" (1988), a documentary exploring the work of that great poet, and "The Killing Floor," a 1984 television adaptation about black labor in the Chicago stockyards during World War I. The latter was presented at major film festivals and awarded first prize by the National Black Film Consortium in 1984.

Lee also wrote scripts for the soap opera *Another World* in 1982 and 1983 and a television miniseries, *Summer Father,* in 1978.

Nevertheless, Leslie Lee has made his most significant contribution as a playwright, and he has focused most of his professional energies in that direction. He is the recipient of several awards and grants, including the Shubert Foundation Playwriting Grant, the Isabelle Strickland Award for excellence in the fields of arts and human culture, a National Endowment for the Arts Playwriting Grant, a Eugene O'Neill Playwriting Fellowship, an Obie Award, a Tony nomination, and a John Gassner Medallion for playwriting. Lee's drama career has consistently reflected his belief that, as he told Newmark, "there is no place for the writer who is interested purely in aesthetics. . . . the modern writer is obliged to take a moral stand." His early work offers an important contribution to a still-lacking understanding of African American history, and much of his later work offers an interesting perspective on the complex and timely issues of racial identity and the pressures that require African American communities to embrace change.

References:

Mel Gussow, "Sharing of Life's Riches Is Way of Black Writer," *New York Times Biographical Source,* 6 (April 1975): 469–470;

Judith Newmark, "'We Have to Talk': Playwright Leslie Lee Spreads His Message of Understanding in 'Spirit North,' Onstage at the St. Louis Black Repertory Company," *St. Louis Post-Dispatch,* 26 March 1998, p. G1;

Emil Wilbekin, "World War II's Black Pilots Fought on Two Fronts," *New York Times,* 21 April 1991, p. 10H.

Charles Ludlam
(12 April 1943 – 28 May 1987)

Robert F. Gross
Hobart and William Smith Colleges

PLAY PRODUCTIONS: *Big Hotel,* New York, Gate Theatre, 1966;

Conquest of the Universe, New York, Bowery, September 1967;

When Queens Collide, New York, Gate Theatre, October 1967; restaged as *Conquest of the Universe, or When Queens Collide,* New York, One Sheridan Square, 1979;

Turds in Hell, by Ludlam and Bill Vehr, New York, Gate Theatre, 1968;

The Grand Tarot, New York, various venues, including Gotham Art Theater, 1969;

Bluebeard, New York, Christopher's End, transferred first to La MaMa Experimental Theatre Club, then Performing Garage, spring 1970;

Eunuchs of the Forbidden City, Berlin, Reichskaberet, summer 1971; New York, Theatre for the New City, March 1972; transferred to Performing Garage, May 1972;

Corn, New York, Thirteenth Street Theatre, 23 November 1972;

Camille: A Tear Jerker, New York, Thirteenth Street Theatre, 2 May 1973;

Hot Ice, New York, Evergreen Theater, 7 February 1974;

Stage Blood, New York, Evergreen Theater, 11 November 1974;

Caprice, New York, Provincetown Playhouse, 15 April 1976; Los Angeles, Sacred Fools Theater Company, 18 October 2001;

Der Ring Gott Farblonjet, New York, Truck and Warehouse Theatre, 27 April 1977;

Utopia, Incorporated, New York, One Sheridan Square, 17 November 1978;

The Ventriloquist's Wife, New York, Reno Sweeny's, 26 December 1978;

Anti-Galaxie Nebulae, by Ludlam, Vehr, and Everett Quinton, New York, One Sheridan Square, 1978;

The Enchanted Pig, New York, One Sheridan Square, 24 April 1979;

Charles Ludlam (photograph by Henry Groskinsky; from the dust jacket for The Complete Plays of Charles Ludlam, *1989)*

A Christmas Carol, adapted from Charles Dickens's novel, New York, One Sheridan Square, 1 December 1979;

Reverse Psychology, New York, One Sheridan Square, 14 September 1980;

Love's Tangled Web, New York, One Sheridan Square, 7 June 1981;

Secret Lives of the Sexists, New York, One Sheridan Square, 9 February 1982;

Exquisite Torture, New York, One Sheridan Square, 6 October 1982;

Le Bourgeois Avant-Garde, New York, One Sheridan Square, 12 April 1983;

Galas, New York, One Sheridan Square, 13 September 1983;

The Mystery of Irma Vep, New York, One Sheridan Square, 2 October 1984;

How to Write a Play, New York, One Sheridan Square, 1984;

Salammbô, New York, One Sheridan Square, 7 November 1985;

The Artificial Jungle, New York, One Sheridan Square, 21 September 1986;

Medea, New York, One Sheridan Square, 7 November 1987.

BOOKS: *Stage Blood* (New York: S. French, 1979);

The Artificial Jungle: A Suspense Thriller (New York: S. French, 1987);

Bluebeard: A Melodrama in Three Acts (New York & London: S. French, 1987);

The Mystery of Irma Vep: A Penny Dreadful (New York: S. French, 1987);

The Ridiculous Theatrical Company Presents Medea: A Tragedy (New York: S. French, 1988);

The Enchanted Pig: A Fairy Tale for the Disenchanted (New York: S. French, 1989);

Love's Tangled Web (New York & London: S. French, 1989);

Reverse Psychology (New York & London: S. French, 1989);

Ridiculous Theatre: Scourge of Human Folly: The Essays and Opinions of Charles Ludlam, edited by Steven Samuels (New York: Theatre Communications Group, 1992).

Editions and Collections: *The Complete Plays of Charles Ludlam,* edited by Steven Samuels (New York: Perennial Library, 1989)—comprises *Big Hotel, Conquest of the Universe, Turds in Hell, The Grand Tarot, Bluebeard, Eunuchs of the Forbidden City, Corn, Camille, Hot Ice, Stage Blood, Jack and the Beanstalk, Isle of the Hermaphrodites, Caprice, Der Ring Gott Farblonjet, The Ventriloquist's Wife, Utopia, Incorporated, The Enchanted Pig, A Christmas Carol, Reverse Psychology, Love's Tangled Web, Secret Lives of the Sexists, Exquisite Torture, Le Bourgeois Avant-Garde, Galas, The Mystery of Irma Vep, Medea, How to Write a Play, Salammbô,* and *The Artificial Jungle;*

The Mystery of Irma Vep and Other Plays (New York: Theatre Communications Group, 2001)—comprises *The Mystery of Irma Vep, Camille, Galas, Stage Blood,* and *Bluebeard.*

Actor, director, designer, puppeteer, and playwright—Charles Ludlam was as versatile a theater artist as could be found in twentieth-century America. As a gay man, he was one of the most influential and celebrated theater artists to emerge from the liberating energies of the Stonewall era and the first wave of gay liberation. Current queer theater and performance remains strongly indebted to his work. As a theater experimenter, he preceded much of the poststructuralist theatrical theorizing with his own parodic, densely intertextual, and self-consciously ironic theater pieces. His appetite for literature and performance is reflected on each page of his plays—from Christopher Marlowe to Antonin Artaud, from Aristophanes to George Abbott. A self-proclaimed traditionalist in theatrical matters, he brought a rich knowledge and understanding of the theater to his own inventive work.

Ludlam was born on 12 April 1943 in Floral Park, Long Island, the second of the three sons of Joseph William and Marjorie Braun Ludlam. A disaffected and uncommitted student in high school, he had a great appetite for dramatic literature and appeared at his best in the school theatricals. His high-school drama teacher arranged for him to work as an intern with a local summer-stock company in 1958. Although the director of the company told him that his effeminate mannerisms would keep him from having a career as an actor, Ludlam enjoyed the theatrical atmosphere, the energy that it took to mount a new production every two weeks, and the more liberated sexual mores of the company. Soon after, he discovered the Living Theatre, where productions of Luigi Pirandello's 1930 play *Tonight We Improvise* and Jack Gelber's *The Connection* (1959) led him to idolize Julian Beck and Judith Malina. In imitation, he soon founded his own company, where he and his fellow students performed plays by Nikolai Nikolaevich Evreinov, August Strindberg, and Eugene O'Neill.

An acting scholarship took him to Hofstra University, where the professors tried to encourage him to pursue directing and playwriting instead of acting. While a student, he wrote his first play, a semi-autobiographical and expressionist piece called "Edna Brown," which he later destroyed.

Upon finishing his B.A. in dramatic literature in 1965, he moved to New York City and soon found himself in the world of experimental theater and movies. He first made an impression when he went on, without preparation, as Lupe Velez's lesbian lover in José Rodriguez-Soltero's underground movie *The Life, Death and Assumption of Lupe Velez* (1967), starring the noted female impersonator Mario Montez. Roles with John Vaccaro's Play-House of the Ridiculous soon followed. Ludlam later credited Vaccaro with freeing him as an actor, allowing him to follow his instincts—however low, campy, or outrageous. Ludlam's major epiphany

Ludlam as Norma Desmond in his first play, Big Hotel, produced at the Gate Theatre in New York City in 1966 (photograph by Diane Dorr-Dorynek)

came when he assumed a wig for a production of Ronald Tavel's *Screen Test* (1966) at the Play-House of the Ridiculous. Ludlam later explained in *Ridiculous Theatre: Scourge of Human Folly* (1992) that upon donning the wig, he found himself spontaneously assuming the role of Norma Desmond, the crazed silent-movie actress in Billy Wilder's *Sunset Boulevard* (1950), as if it were second nature to him. His performance of Norma was a great success, much to the annoyance of Vaccaro, who said that he found Ludlam's style far too campy and homosexually identified.

When house playwright Tavel left the company after a run-in with the notoriously volatile Vaccaro, Ludlam found himself writing for the Play-House of the Ridiculous, even though he preferred to act. His first play, *Big Hotel* (1966), loosely inspired by the 1933 movie *International House,* collected such diverse figures as Lupe Velez, Mata Hari, Svengali, Santa Claus, and Bartok's Miraculous Mandarin in a highly episodic succession of camp and ribald scenes. His next script for Vaccaro, *Conquest of the Universe* (1967), took Marlowe's *Tamburlaine the Great* (1587–1588) into outer space, with Marlowe's hero conquering the solar system and forcing Bajazeth, the king of Mars, to be his sex slave. During the rehearsal period for this play, tensions between Vaccaro and Ludlam grew, with Vaccaro finally taking the play out of Ludlam's hands and firing him as an actor in it. Ludlam and his adherents in the Play-House broke with Vaccaro and founded the Ridiculous Theatrical Company, explaining that, although Vaccaro had the Play-House, he and his fellow actors *were* the Company. The new company revived *Big Hotel* and presented a new version of *Conquest of the Universe,* titled *When Queens Collide* (1967), while Vaccaro produced *Conquest of the Universe* with a cast of performers from Andy Warhol's circle.

The form of these and other early plays was casual. The action would suddenly stop to spotlight popular performers, drag queens, and local personalities. No attempts were made to impose a coherent ensemble style. Performance venues changed frequently, as did the casts, and a single performance could run as long as three to four hours. At this stage in his career, Ludlam reveled in the fact that no two performances were similar, often by chance. Ludlam's exploration of chance elements became most complex with *The Grand Tarot* (1969), in which scenes were written to correspond to cards in the tarot deck, with the order of scenes for any given performance determined by the order in which the cards were dealt out that night. The project remained fragmentary, and in his "Confessions of a Farceur," published in *Ridiculous Theatre,* Ludlam spoke of returning to it, finding in its twenty-two miniature dramas "infinite plot." Such experiments gained Ludlam and his company their first Obie Award in 1969, for distinguished achievement in the Off-Broadway theater.

But Ludlam was tiring of these loosely constructed entertainments, and his next play set off in a new direction. *Bluebeard* (1970) had a small cast, a single set, and a comparatively well-made plot. Suggested by H. G. Wells's *The Island of Doctor Moreau* (1896), it tells of a mad doctor who, bored with the sexual possibilities of male and female, dreams of creating "the third genital." *Bluebeard* was more successful, both with audiences and reviewers, than any previous Ludlam play. A European tour for the company and a Guggenheim Fellowship in playwriting for Ludlam were marks of growing recognition.

The tour, however, was filled with ups and downs. The company's greatest success was the Berlin premiere of a new epic, *Eunuchs of the Forbidden City* (1971), based on the life of the last empress of China; but the rejections outweighed the ovations, and the company came home divided, exhausted, and poor. Only grants from the National Endowment for the Arts and the New York State Council for the Arts gave the company new energy. A New York production of *Eunuchs of the Forbidden City* was followed by *Corn* (1972), a musical with Marlene Dietrich's character Lola Lola from the 1930 movie *The Blue Angel* turned into a country-and-western entertainer amid the Hatfields and McCoys.

In 1973 Ludlam attained a new level of critical and popular success with *Camille: A Tear Jerker,* in which he starred as the doomed courtesan Marguerite Gautier. Guided by the well-made structure of Alexandre Dumas *fils*'s 1852 drama *La Dame aux camélias,* Ludlam restrained the extent of both his allusions and his ribaldry. His revision strove both to entertain the audience with the comic potential of the period tale and to move them as well. Allowing his hairy chest to show in Marguerite's low-cut gowns, he did not use female impersonation as a way of deceiving the audience. Instead he invited them to enter into the complex relationship between male actor and female character, as well as introducing gay issues within an ostensibly heterosexual romance. Ludlam's performances in *Corn* and *Camille* won him his second Obie and led to a second tour of Europe.

Ludlam considered machismo in his next role, a tough New York City cop named Tank Irish in *Hot Ice* (1974); the part was as much of an exercise in drag as Marguerite. *Hot Ice* showed the playwright returning to a more farcical tone and bawdy humor. The play is a reworking of the 1949 gangster movie *White Heat,* with the unicycle-riding Euthanasia Police in pursuit of an illicit cryogenics ring. Ludlam avoided drag altogether in *Stage Blood* (1974), a mystery of backstage life concerning a down-at-the-heels troupe preparing to perform *Hamlet* (circa 1602). Neither production elicited the popular enthusiasm of *Camille,* however, and Ludlam believed much of his audience was disappointed that he had not created new female-impersonation vehicles along the lines of *Camille.*

Ludlam's 1975 "Manifesto: Ridiculous Theatre, Scourge of Human Folly," originally published in *The Drama Review,* lays out a theoretical framework for his work. Its first axiom, "If one is not a living mockery of one's own ideals, one has set one's ideals too low," underlies much of Ludlam's theatrical practice—his habit of casting against gender, physical type, and character type; his creation of larger-than-life characters with transgressive desires; and his development of a style of writing and performance in which the excesses of pathos and comic bathos intertwine. The manifesto and Ludlam's other essays (collected in the 1992 volume) show his vision of the theater to be a consciously Nietzschean revaluation of values, in which cultural artifacts that have been rejected as kitsch or base—whether nineteenth-century melodramatic acting, comic vaudeville turns, or B-movies—are readopted for theatrical use, just as transgressive activities, such as Bluebeard's search for the third genital or Max Mortimer's Cryogenics Foundation, provide the central energies for the plots. In Ludlam's plays, the excessive dreams and ambitions of the characters find their equivalent in theatrical excesses. Ludlam linked his Nietzschean heroes of the Ridiculous to the heroes of Artaud's Theatre of Cruelty and claimed that his own theatrical work was far closer to Artaud's theories than most avant-garde artists. Cruelty, Ludlam argued, derived from the fact that people come to the theater to witness suffering, whether in comedy or tragedy. The impossible yearnings of his Ridiculous protagonists lead inevitably to suffering, in both its pathetic and bathetic dimensions.

In the late 1970s, Ludlam took on an almost bewildering variety of projects. *Caprice* (1976) is a modern comedy in the Restoration mode about the fashion industry. *Isle of the Hermaphrodites* (1976), included in *The Complete Plays of Charles Ludlam* (1989), was the book for an unperformed musical comedy on the unlikely subject of the St. Bartholomew's Day Massacre. *Der Ring Gott Farblonjet* (1977) fuses Friedrich Wilhelm Nietzsche, Richard Wagner, and Yiddish humor in a condensed comic rewriting of *Der Ring des Nibelungen* (1863). Momentarily retreating from epic undertakings, he wrote *The Ventriloquist's Wife* (1978), a two-person ventriloquism routine to be performed in nightclubs. *Utopia, Incorporated* (1978), a fantasy about two marijuana dealers who get lost in the Bermuda Triangle, spins an extravagant tale rife with contradictions and dialogue abounding in puns. In between all these major projects, Ludlam somehow found the time to write three plays for children (his Obie-winning *Professor Bedlam's Educational Punch and Judy Show*, 1975; *Jack and the Beanstalk*, 1976; and *The Enchanted Pig*, 1979), a science-fiction puppet serial (*Anti-Galaxie Nebulae*, 1978), and an opera libretto for composer Peter Golub ("The Production of Mysteries," 1980). He also mounted a revival of *Conquest of the Universe* and a surprisingly straightforward adaptation of *A Christmas Carol* (1979), with Ludlam in the role of Ebenezer Scrooge.

This period was also marked by two important developments in the Ridiculous Theatrical Company and in Ludlam's life. *Caprice* was the theatrical debut of Everett Quinton, who became not only an important member of the troupe but also Ludlam's partner and the artistic director of the company after Ludlam's death. The 1978 premiere of *Utopia, Incorporated* marked the achievement of one of Ludlam's dreams: a permanent residence for his company. The theater at One Sheridan Square in Greenwich Village remained the home of the Ridiculous Theatrical Company for several years after Ludlam's death, and New York City renamed the street in front of the theater "Charles Ludlam Lane" in 1988.

During the 1980s the Company began simplifying its methods. It had abandoned repertory for long runs. Ludlam wrote four farces of modern life, which had smaller casts, less exotic settings, and more modest ambitions than his earlier works—*Reverse Psychology* (1980), *Love's Tangled Web* (1981), *Secret Lives of the Sexists* (1982), and *Le Bourgeois Avant-Garde* (1983). These farces, though less ostentatious in their intertextuality, are still clearly loving homages to their dramatic predecessors. For example, *Secret Lives of the Sexists* combines the plot device of men impersonating women in order to infiltrate an exclusively female domain, drawn from Aristophanes' *Thesmophoriazousai* (Women at the Thesmophoria, 411 B.C.) and Avery Hopwood's *Ladies' Night* (1920), with the story of a fallen woman

Ludlam and Bill Vehr in Camille: A Tear Jerker *(1973), Ludlam's version of the 1852 Alexandre Dumas fils tragedy* La Dame aux camélias *(photograph by John Stern)*

struggling to regain her respectability with the secret aid of her son-in-law, taken from Oscar Wilde's *Lady Windermere's Fan* (1892). But the dialogue of these farces is far less crammed with quotations and intertextual references than the earlier work, and the plotting is far tighter.

Ludlam was not, however, content to stay with a single genre for long. After the third of his farces, he briefly returned to drag and high romance with *Exquisite Torture* (1982). Like *Camille*, the play took a Greta Garbo vehicle as its starting point—the 1932 movie adaptation of Luigi Pirandello's *Come tu mi vuoi* (1930; *As You Desire Me*, 1931). Unlike *Camille*, however, the play was filled with baroque turns of plot and surreal imagery. Ludlam wrote in *Ridiculous Theatre* that he enjoyed it when his audience was divided about how to respond emotionally, but such division usually led to cooler reviews and smaller houses. Audiences, for the most part, preferred Ludlam when he was working as a pure farceur or camp female impersonator.

Ludlam satisfied his followers' taste for camp impersonation with *Galas* (1983), his fanciful dramati-

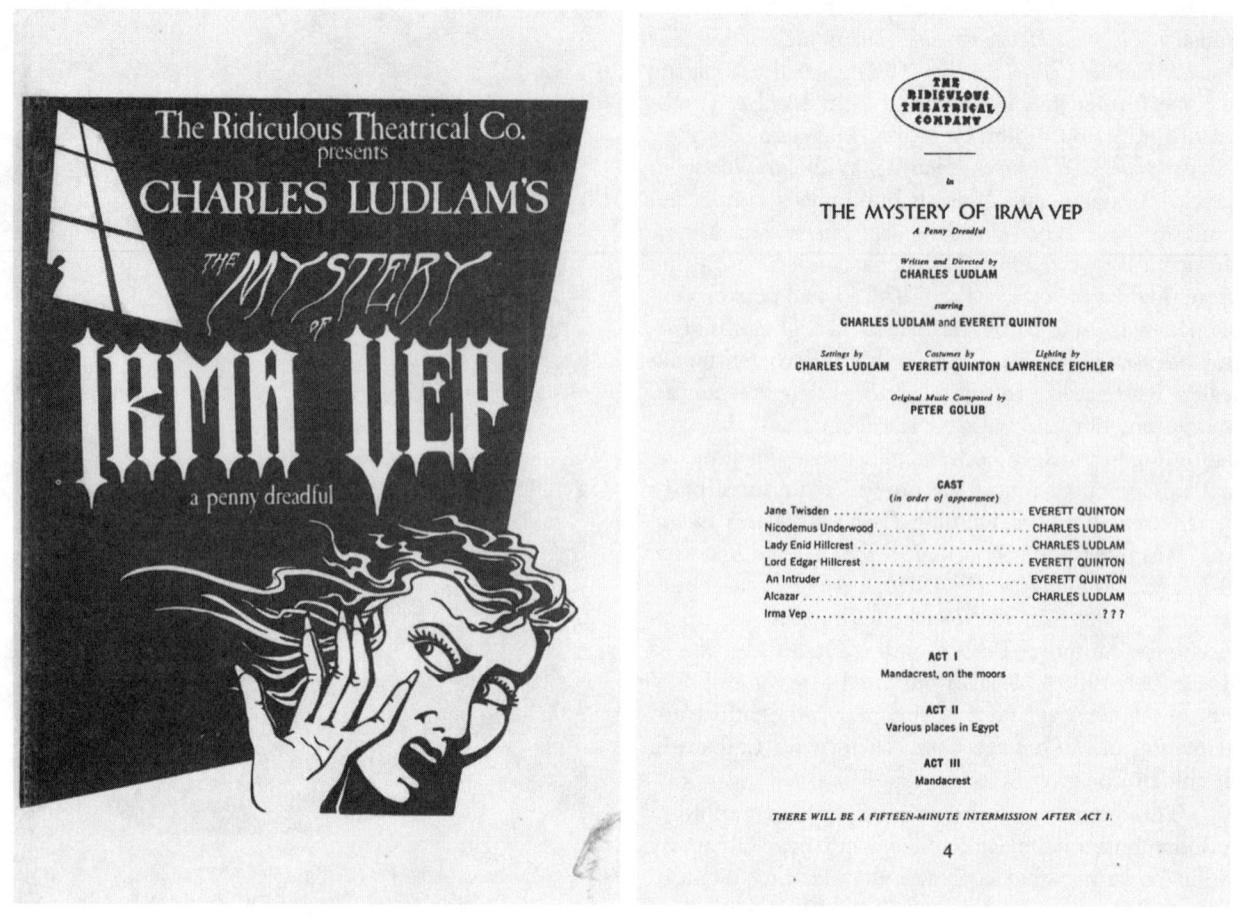

Cover and cast list for the 1987 acting edition of the 1984 farce that has become the most widely performed of Ludlam's plays (Thomas Cooper Library, University of South Carolina)

zation of the life of prima donna Maria Callas, and the desire for ingenious farce with *The Mystery of Irma Vep* (1984), a comic tour de force of quick-change in which two actors play all eight roles. The theatrical inventiveness of *The Mystery of Irma Vep,* coupled with its small cast, has helped to make it the most widely performed and enthusiastically accepted of all of Ludlam's plays. Free of the nudity, mimed copulation, overt sexual references, and scatological humor of *Conquest of the Universe* and *Bluebeard,* and even the sexual frankness of the farces, it has proved a major work in the introduction of queer theatrical techniques into the American theatrical mainstream.

Any suspicions, however, that Ludlam had capitulated to the values of the commercial theater were quickly dispelled by his flamboyantly transgressive 1985 adaptation of Gustave Flaubert's 1852 novel *Salammbô.* Ludlam's *Salammbô,* subtitled *An Erotic Tragedy,* was his audacious response to the conservatism of the Ronald Reagan era and, for a gay audience wracked by the AIDS pandemic, an affirmation of queer desire. Starring in the title role of the Priestess of the Moon, who is consumed with a forbidden desire for a handsome barbarian, Ludlam decorated the stage with bodybuilders of impressive dimensions and limited acting skills, and he provoked controversy by casting a three-hundred-pound actress in the role of Hanno, a decadent and leprous official. Coming in the wake of the popular acceptance of *The Mystery of Irma Vep, Salammbô* received the most consistently negative response of all of Ludlam's later work and yet was perhaps the most thorough application of his dramatic theories to the stage.

Ludlam's last completed play, *The Artificial Jungle* (1986), a film-noir spoof, returned to the less controversial world of engaging parody that most critics and many audience members preferred from him. Ludlam also gained further acceptance from the mainstream that year: he was invited to direct Johann Strauss's *Die Fledermaus* (1874) at the Santa Fe Opera and *Titus*

Andronicus (1594) for the New York Shakespeare Festival and appeared in the motion pictures *The Big Easy* and *Forever, Lulu,* both released in 1987. His parody *Der Ring Gott Farblonjet* was even under consideration for a Broadway production. But Ludlam, at the height of his recognition, was diagnosed with AIDS at Thanksgiving in 1986, and he died on 28 May of the following year.

Charles Ludlam's distinctive theatrical sensibility ran counter to most of the American theater of his time. He rejected the dominance of realistic dramaturgy with its reliance on Stanislavskian acting, on the one hand, and the theatrical minimalism of the Absurdists on the other. Both styles, he observed, limited the expressive potential of the stage. In pursuit of a more richly theatrical style of performance, he drew on the often-denigrated genres of farce and melodrama, as well as popular entertainments such as burlesque, vaudeville, and cabaret performance. Rejecting the contemporary tendency to create theater from personal experience and observation of daily life, Ludlam preferred well-worn plots and stock characters, finding archetypal resonances in highly artificial devices. He recommended that dramatists should turn to Carlo Gozzi's list of the thirty-six dramatic situations for inspiration rather than their own lives. His emphasis on artifice was not escapism but an attempt to critique and expand the limits of American life through a creative refashioning of its cultural detritus. He continues to be admired as a skilled farceur and inspired camp performer, but the bolder and more transgressive implications of his work remain to be more widely considered.

Interviews:

Robert Heide, "From the Ridiculous to the Sublime: Talking with Charles Ludlam," *New York Native,* 27 October 1986, pp. 49–53;

Gautam Dasgupta, "Theatre and the Ridiculous: A Conversation with Charles Ludlam," in *Theatre of the Ridiculous,* edited by Dasgupta and Bonnie Marranca, revised and expanded edition (Baltimore: Johns Hopkins University Press, 1998), pp. 77–91.

References:

Martin Andrucki, "'Ah, the Old Questions, the Old Answers . . .': Postmodernism and Poetic Justice in the Plays of Charles Ludlam," *Text and Performance Quarterly,* 10 (October 1990): 294–305;

Stefan Brecht, *Queer Theatre* (New York: Methuen, 1986), pp. 76–106;

Gregory Bredbeck, "The Ridiculous Sound of One Hand Clapping: Placing Ludlam's 'Gay' Theatre in Space and Time," *Modern Drama,* 39 (March 1996): 64–83;

James Leverett, "Old Forms Enter the New American Theater: Shepard, Foreman, Kirby, and Ludlam," *New York Literary Forum,* 7 (1980): 107–122;

Rick Roemer, *Charles Ludlam and the Ridiculous Theatrical Company: Critical Analyses of 29 Plays* (Jefferson, N.C.: McFarland, 1998);

Calvin Tomkins, "Charles Ludlam," *New Yorker,* 52 (15 November 1976): 55–98;

Robert Thomas Wharton, "The Working Dynamics of the Ridiculous Theatre Company: An Analysis of Charles Ludlam's Relationship with His Ensemble from 1967 to 1981," dissertation, University of Florida, 1986.

Papers:

Charles Ludlam's papers are collected in the New York Public Library, Rare Books and Manuscripts Division.

Emily Mann
(12 April 1952 -   )

Christina S. McGowan
Fairfield University

PLAY PRODUCTIONS: *Annulla Allen: Autobiography of a Survivor (A Monologue),* Minneapolis, Guthrie 2 at the Guthrie Theater, 16 March 1977; revised as *Annulla, An Autobiography,* St. Louis, Repertory Theatre of St. Louis, 20 March 1985; Brooklyn, N.Y., New Theatre of Brooklyn, 10 November 1988;

Still Life, Chicago, Goodman Studio Theatre, 23 October 1980; New York, American Place Theatre, 19 February 1981;

Execution of Justice, Louisville, Actors Theatre of Louisville, 22 February 1984; New York, Virginia Theatre, 13 March 1986;

Nights and Days [staged reading], adapted from Pierre Laville's play, New York, New Dramatists, 19 October 1984;

Betsey Brown, adapted from Ntozake Shange's novel, book by Shange and Mann, music by Baikida Carroll, lyrics by Shange, Mann, and Carroll, Philadelphia, Forum Theater–WHYY, 30 March 1989;

Miss Julie, adapted from August Strindberg's play, Princeton, McCarter Theatre, 13 February 1993;

Having Our Say: The Delany Sisters' First 100 Years, adapted from the book by Sarah L. Delany and A. Elizabeth Delany with Amy Hill Hearth, Princeton, McCarter Theatre, 7 February 1995; New York, Booth Theatre, 6 April 1995;

Greensboro: A Requiem, Princeton, McCarter Theatre, 6 February 1996;

The House of Bernarda Alba, adapted from Federico García Lorca's play, Princeton, McCarter Theatre, 24 October 1997;

Meshugah, adapted from Isaac Bashevis Singer's novel, Princeton, McCarter Theatre, 23 October 1998;

The Cherry Orchard, adapted from Anton Chekhov's play, Princeton, McCarter Theatre, 31 March 2000;

Uncle Vanya, adapted from Chekhov's play, Princeton, McCarter Theatre, 29 April 2002.

Emily Mann (photograph by Joan Marcus; courtesy of Emily Mann)

BOOKS: *Still Life: A Documentary* (New York: Theatre Communications Group, 1979);
Annulla, An Autobiography (New York: Theatre Communications Group, 1985);
Execution of Justice (New York: S. French, 1986);
Having Our Say: The Delany Sisters' First 100 Years: A Play (New York, Dramatists Play Service, 1996);

Testimonies: Four Plays (New York: Theatre Communications Group, 1997)—comprises *Annulla, An Autobiography, Still Life, Execution of Justice,* and *Greensboro: A Requiem;*

The House of Bernarda Alba: A Drama about Women in Villages of Spain (New York: Dramatists Play Service, 1999);

The Cherry Orchard, adapted from Anton Chekhov's play (New York: Dramatists Play Service, 2000).

PRODUCED SCRIPTS: *Having Our Say: The Delany Sisters' First 100 Years,* TeleVest and Columbia Tri-Star Television, CBS, 18 April 1999;

Execution of Justice, television, Justice Productions, 1999.

OTHER: Roy Harris, *Eight Women of the American Stage: Talking about Acting, Roy Harris with Mary Alice, Judith Ivey, Cherry Jones, Mary McDonnell, Donna Murphy, Sarah Jessica Parker, Gwen Verdon, Joanne Woodward,* foreword by Mann (Portsmouth, N.H.: Heinemann, 1997);

Political Stages: Plays That Shaped a Century, edited by Mann and David Roessel (New York: Applause Theatre & Cinema Books, 2002).

SELECTED PERIODICAL PUBLICATIONS– UNCOLLECTED: "Nature morte d'Emily Mann," *L'Avant-Scene,* 753/754 (July 1984): 78–93;

"Nights and Days," *L'Avant-Scene,* 765 (March 1985): 38–54;

"Execution of Justice," *American Theatre,* 2 (November 1985): 1–20.

Using newspaper accounts, trial transcripts, television-news reports, and interviews, Emily Mann has created a "theatre of testimony." This term, coined by the late Barney Simon, director of the Market Theatre in South Africa, describes a form of drama that employs documentary materials to deal with controversial social and political subjects such as the Holocaust, the Vietnam War, homophobia, racism, and domestic abuse. Through testimony and oral history, audiences can hear all sides of a story and experience different views of an event. David Savran credits Mann "for bringing a new level of political dialogue and a new kind of contemporary history play to the American theatre." Mann challenges her audiences to confront subjects that are often painful, an approach that some critics have found a refreshing change from the escapist theater of the past.

Emily Betsy Mann was born in Boston, Massachusetts, on 12 April 1952 to Arthur and Sylvia (Blut) Mann. She has one older sister, Carol. Sylvia Mann was a reading specialist, while Arthur Mann was a professor of American history with an expertise on race and ethnicity. In 1966 Arthur Mann accepted a position at the University of Chicago, and the family moved to the Hyde Park neighborhood on the South Side of the city, where the university is located. Hyde Park was integrated, and some of the Manns' neighbors included members of the Black Panthers as well as the noted African American historian John Hope Franklin, who was Arthur Mann's close friend. Emily Mann's upbringing was intellectual, and dinnertime conversations usually centered on questions of civil rights and social issues. In a 1996 interview with Mary Houlihan-Skilton, Mann commented, "I was instilled with an incredible sense of social responsibility and history. In a lot of ways, Hyde Park in those early years formed the themes for what I have written and for what I continue to write."

Mann's interest in theater began at a young age, sparked by her attendance at a Yiddish theater production of *The Dybbuk* when she was seven and at a performance of the musical *Fiorello!* somewhat later. Mann attended Radcliffe College of Harvard University, where she studied playwriting with William Alfred. After she received her A.B. degree in 1974, she won a directing fellowship to the Guthrie Theatre in Minneapolis and attended the University of Minnesota, where in 1976 she received an M.F.A. in theater arts. After earning her master's degree, Mann served as associate director of the Guthrie Theatre (1978–1979), resident director at the Brooklyn Academy of Music (1981–1982), and director of the workshop for play development of New Dramatists in New York City (1984–1991). She has also directed productions of her own plays and those of others at theaters across the country. Since 1990 she has been the artistic director of McCarter Theatre in Princeton, New Jersey, the recipient of a 1994 Tony Award for Outstanding Regional Theatre. On 12 August 1981 Mann married actor Gerry Bamman, by whom she has one son, Nicholas Isaac. Mann and Bamman are now divorced.

Mann's first play, *Annulla Allen: Autobiography of a Survivor (A Monologue)*—first staged in 1977 and later revised for production in 1985 as *Annulla, An Autobiography*—was inspired by an experience she had during a visit home in 1974. She discovered on her father's desk a stack of transcribed interviews collected for the oral-history project of the American Jewish Committee. One interview was a young woman's talk with her mother about how she survived in the Treblinka concentration camp. When Mann expressed her desire to turn it into a play, her father strongly urged her not to do so, insisting that the story belonged to the woman and that Emily should find her own material. That summer, Mann and her college roommate traveled to Poland

Peter Friedman, Nicholas Kepros, and Gerry Bamman in the 1986 New York production of Execution of Justice *(photograph by Gerry Goodstein)*

and England on a grant to compile oral histories of the roommate's family. In London they met with the roommate's aunt, Annulla Allen, who had escaped the Nazis during World War II. When they asked Allen why she survived, she told them a story that evolved into Mann's play.

The first version, *Annulla Allen,* includes only Annulla's voice; in the second, Mann added her reactions to the story as the "Young Woman's Voice." A Holocaust survivor, Allen told her niece and Mann the story of how she saved herself by passing as an Aryan and tricked the Nazis into releasing her husband from the Dachau concentration camp. Mann included details of her own life story as a Jew and her own Jewish community which she learned from the older woman, who, as Mann describes her in the play, "had the language." While Mel Gussow criticized Mann for a "strict adherence to documented evidence" that "impeded her sense of theater" and saw a need for "additional structuring and clarification" in her writing (*The New York Times,* 2 November 1998), other critics called Mann's reliance on Annulla's words an important addition to the testimonies of a time that should never be forgotten. Mann directed the premiere of the play on the Guthrie 2 stage of the Guthrie Theater in 1977. The revised version opened at the Repertory Theatre of St. Louis in 1985. That same year, the play was selected for publication in the Theatre Communication Group Plays in Process series.

While Mann opposed the Vietnam War, her father supported it. Her second play, *Still Life,* first staged in 1980, is her answer to her father. During the summer of 1978, Mann interviewed three people in Minnesota: Mark, a Vietnam veteran, Cheryl, his wife, and Nadine, his mistress. From 140 hours of tape transcribed as eight hundred pages of interview material, Mann distilled a ninety-page documentary drama. In the play the three characters sit at a table in front of a screen that displays haunting images of the war. The setting resembles a courtroom, and—with the characters delivering monologues to the audience instead of speaking to each other—the audience becomes the jury. From the characters' words one realizes that all three are victims trying to deal with the devastating effects of the war and to adjust to life after it. *Still Life* premiered at the Goodman Studio Theatre in Chicago on 23 October 1980, and in 1981 it moved to the American Place Theatre in New York, where under Mann's direction it won six Obie (Off-Broadway) Awards including the awards for distinguished playwriting, distinguished directing, and best production. The play was also presented at the Avignon Festival and won the Fringe First Award for best play at the Edinburgh Festival. Despite such honors, the reviews for *Still Life* were not all positive; several critics called her characters self-involved, unlikable, and unsympathetic and complained that their monologues were long and monotonous. Yet, many others considered *Still Life* one of the best homecoming plays ever written. Like *Annulla, An Autobiography, Still Life* was published in the Theatre Communication Group Plays in Process series.

Still Life has had many successful productions. The directors at the Eureka Theatre in San Francisco were especially impressed by the play and offered to commission Mann's next work. Tony Taccone, then artistic director at the Eureka, suggested that Mann might dramatize the trial of former city supervisor Dan White for the 1978 murders of San Francisco mayor George Moscone and Harvey Milk, an openly homosexual city supervisor. Armed with a Guggenheim Fellowship (1983), Mann was able to do extensive research, using trial transcripts, newspaper articles, and extensive interviews as the backbone of her script. The result was Mann's most ambitious play to date, *Execution of Justice* (1984), which has a cast of twenty-three actors playing forty-two roles.

After resigning from the board of supervisors, Dan White had reconsidered his decision and asked for his job back. When Moscone appointed someone else, White killed Moscone and Milk in a fit of rage. The defense used the "Twinkie defense," saying White had been binging on junk food; he was found guilty of manslaughter under "diminished capacity." The verdict outraged the San Francisco homosexual community, and riots broke out in the city.

Mann's play is set in a courtroom and once again uses the audience as a jury. In addition to excerpts from the trial transcripts, Mann included material from interviews with people she labels "uncalled witnesses" to provide viewpoints that were not offered at the actual trial. Because Mann took such an evenhanded approach, allowing the audience to hear from all sides, many theatergoers have felt confused at the conclusion of the play, which has inspired argument and controversy. Mann has compared her play to the work of Bertolt Brecht, telling David Goetz, "I think his strongest work is where he didn't tell you what to think at the end" (*San Francisco Examiner*, 14 March 1984). Slides, clips from documentaries, and recorded sounds and music give the play intensity. Critics have found this high-tech format both effective and distracting. As with Mann's earlier plays, reviewers have had mixed opinions about *Execution of Justice*. Many critics have admired Mann's approach to a contemporary, controversial issue; some, however, considered the story of Dan White not worth retelling.

Execution of Justice was originally scheduled to open at the Eureka, but after that theater was firebombed, the play had its premiere at the Actors Theatre of Louisville as part of the 1984 Humana Festival of New American Plays, where it was cowinner of the Great American Play Contest. *Execution of Justice* was subsequently produced at many other regional theaters and made its Broadway debut in 1986, under Mann's direction. The many awards Mann received for the play include a Bay Area Critics Award, the Helen Hayes Award, a Playwriting Award from the Women's Committee of the Dramatists Guild, a Burns Mantle Yearbook Best Play Citation, and a Drama Desk nomination.

Following *Execution of Justice,* Mann translated and adapted Pierre Laville's play *Nights and Days,* about a released convict and his new life. She performed a staged reading at the New Dramatists in New York in 1984.

In 1989 Mann collaborated with Ntozake Shange and composer Baikida Carroll on the rhythm-and-blues musical *Betsey Brown,* which was adapted from Shange's novel of the same name. Premiering at the Forum Theater–WHYY in 1989, the two-act play with twenty-eight songs focuses on an African American teenager and the struggles of her middle-class family in St. Louis during the early years of the Civil Rights movement in the late 1950s. Harry Harris called *Betsey Brown* a work that "promises to emerge as a candidate for frequent revival" (*Variety*, 12–18 April 1989). Harris and critic Clark Groome (*Chestnut Hill Local*, 6 April 1989) applauded the forceful and daring story line but agreed that the play suffered from too much exposition and appeared awkward at times.

Mann's best-known and most widely praised play is *Having Our Say,* her stage version of the best-selling memoir of Sarah L. Delany and A. Elizabeth Delany. The play had its world premiere at the McCarter Theatre in 1995 before its successful run on Broadway at the Booth Theatre and a national tour. For this play Mann received two Joseph Jefferson Awards and the Hull-Warriner Award as well as nominations for two Antoinette Perry (Tony) Awards (best play and best director), an Outer Critics Circle Award, and a Drama Desk Award. *Having Our Say* chronicles the lives of two elderly African American sisters, beginning with their childhood in Raleigh, North Carolina, where they were brought up in a family of ten children, all of whom

SADIE
Poor Mr. Miliam. When Grandma died, we saw him -- he sat in Grandma's kitchen with his head in his big hands and he said, "What I loved most in this world is lying in the other room." So Bessie and I ~~came from Raleigh~~ stayed, cooked and kept him company.

BESSIE
In the morning, he would go out and shoot a squirrel for his breakfast. He ~~always~~ used to say: "those little ones are mighty tasty."

SADIE
Grandma had predicted Mr. Miliam would not last long without her, and she was right. Despite our efforts to keep him happy, he died just two years after Grandma.

BESSIE
The will was challenged by some white nephew of his who was just furious over the fact that our Mama, "this colored woman," should get those 68 acres and that money...even if she was Mr. Miliam's daughter!

SADIE
Mama gave $500 to the nephew to keep the fellow happy. She didn't want to be sued. But she did what Mr. Miliam would have wanted.

BESSIE and SADIE (together)
She hung onto that land.

SADIE
And to this day, it is still in our family.

BESSIE
Those white relatives are just waiting for us to mess up, just once with those taxes. Be one day late. But we haven't. Not in 85 years. And we won't. (BESSIE stands.) That land is

BESSIE and SADIE (together)
(shaking hands)
ours.

(BESSIE crosses for glass of water at dining room table.)

BESSIE
Our Mama was always a bit embarrassed that her parents were not --could not have been-- legally married. She was determined that she was going to have a legal marriage someday, or not get married at all!

① In current production, Gloria says: "So Mama gave the nephew $500.00 to keep the fellow happy..."

② In the morning, Mr. Miliam would go out... good.

Page from the revised typescript for Having Our Say
(Collection of Emily Mann)

Program cover and title page for Mann's dramatization of a popular autobiography by two African American sisters (Collection of Emily Mann)

went on to become successful professionals. Their father, who was born a slave and later became an Episcopal bishop, always stressed the importance of a good education. Sadie became the first black domestic-science teacher in the New York City school system, and Bessie became a dentist.

Mann's two-and-a-half-hour, three-act play was hailed by audiences and critics, who praised the way in which Mann conveyed the special bond between the two sisters. In *Having Our Say* Mann used an approach similar to the one she used in the first version of *Annulla Allen*. Instead of just adapting the book, she interviewed the sisters and used material from those meetings in the play as well. Just as Annulla tells her story of the Holocaust from her kitchen while making chicken soup, the Delany sisters talk about their experiences of racism while in their kitchen preparing a dinner in honor of their late father's birthday. After a successful run on Broadway, Mann's adaptation aired on CBS television on 18 April 1999.

Mann's next play, *Greensboro: A Requiem* (1996), dramatizes the events of 3 November 1979 in Greensboro, North Carolina, where members of the Ku Klux Klan killed five people and wounded eight at an anti-Klan rally organized by members of the Communist Workers' Party. The tragedy was given little press coverage because it occurred one day prior to the capture of the American hostages in Iran, and media attention became almost entirely focused on that international event. An all-white jury acquitted the defendants in the 1980 trial, and in 1984 they were found not guilty on federal charges. In a civil suit brought by survivors, however, the Greensboro police, who did nothing to intervene, and the Klan were found jointly liable.

Taking dialogue directly from trial transcripts, interviews, television coverage, and newspaper articles,

Mann created *Greensboro: A Requiem,* a play in two acts with a cast of eleven actors playing more than thirty roles, which premiered at the McCarter Theatre in 1996. By including voices from both sides and letting the audience act as jury and draw its own conclusions, she again provoked discussion, achieving the kind of reaction for which she had hoped. Critics such as Gretchen C. Van Benthuysen (*Asbury Park Press,* 13 February 1996) and Robert L. Daniels (*Variety,* 26 February –3 March 1996) praised Mann for dramatizing an important historical event but had reservations about her documentary approach. Some critics called the language of the play commonplace, repetitious, and undramatic and found themselves distracted by the projections, fluorescent and flashing lights, and sounds from two turntables in the McCarter production.

Since becoming artistic director at the McCarter Theatre in 1990, Mann has adapted several works for production there, including August Strindberg's play *Miss Julie* (1993), Federico García Lorca's play *The House of Bernarda Alba* (1997), Isaac Bashevis Singer's novel *Meshugah* (1998), and Anton Chekhov's plays *The Cherry Orchard* (2000) and *Uncle Vanya* (2002). In 1994, just days after accepting the Tony Award for Outstanding Regional Theatre on behalf of the McCarter Theatre, Mann learned that she had multiple sclerosis. In a 2000 interview with Maria LoBiondo, Mann explained that she sees a "blessing in the curse. In some ways it has been a rebirth . . . with fewer hours in the day, my work has improved." Emily Mann has made, and continues to make, a substantial contribution to American theater, both as a playwright and as a director. Her distinctive documentary style in dramatizing often-controversial historical events has brought a renewed political consciousness to the American theater.

Interviews:

Leigh Buchanan Bienen, "Emily Mann," in *Speaking on Stage: Interviews with Contemporary American Playwrights,* edited by Philip C. Kolin and Colby H. Kullman (Tuscaloosa: University of Alabama Press, 1996), pp. 205–215;

Mary Houlihan-Skilton, "Playwright Has Her Say: Emily Mann Gives a Voice to History," *Chicago Sun-Times,* 25 February 1996, SHO 12;

Melissa Salz Bernstein, "Emily Mann: Having Her Say," *American Drama,* 6 (Spring 1997): 81–99;

Maria LoBiondo, "Profile: Emily Mann, Artistic Director of McCarter Theatre," *Patron Magazine,* 16 March 2000 <http://www.princetonol.com/patron/index.shtml>.

Bibliography:

Philip C. Kolin and Daniel LaNelle, "Emily Mann: A Classified Bibliography," *Studies in American Drama,* 4 (1989): 223–266.

Reference:

David Savran, *Danger: Present Tense Theatre* (Providence, R.I.: Paradigm Press, 1988).

Arthur Miller
(17 October 1915 –   )

Stephen A. Marino
Saint Francis College

See also the Miller entry in *DLB 7: Twentieth-Century American Dramatists.*

PLAY PRODUCTIONS: *The Man Who Had All the Luck,* New York, Forrest Theatre, 23 November 1944;

All My Sons, New York, Coronet Theatre, 29 January 1947;

Death of a Salesman, New York, Morosco Theatre, 10 February 1949;

An Enemy of the People, adapted from Henrik Ibsen's play, New York, Broadhurst Theatre, 28 December 1950;

The Crucible, New York, Martin Beck Theatre, 22 January 1953;

A View from the Bridge, one-act version and *A Memory of Two Mondays,* New York, Coronet Theatre, 29 September 1955;

A View from the Bridge, revised two-act version, London, Comedy Theatre, 11 October 1956;

After the Fall, New York, ANTA Washington Square Theatre, 23 January 1964;

Incident at Vichy, New York, ANTA Washington Square Theatre, 3 December 1964;

The Price, New York, Morosco Theatre, 7 February 1968;

The Creation of the World and Other Business, New York, Shubert Theatre, 30 November 1972; revised as *Up from Paradise,* Ann Arbor, Mich., Powell Center for the Performing Arts, 23 April 1974;

The Archbishop's Ceiling, Washington, D.C., Eisenhower Theatre, Kennedy Center for the Performing Arts, 30 April 1977;

The American Clock, adapted from Studs Terkel's *Hard Times,* Charleston, S.C., Spoleto Festival Dockside Theater, 24 May 1980; New York, Biltmore Theatre, 20 November 1980;

2 by A.M., New Haven, Long Wharf Theatre, 26 October 1982—comprised *Elegy for a Lady* and *Some Kind of Love Story;*

Arthur Miller in Manchester, 1989
(photograph by Michael Arron)

Danger: Memory! New York, Mitzi E. Newhouse Theater, 23 January 1987—comprised *Clara* and *I Can't Remember Anything;*

The Last Yankee, one-act version, New York, Ensemble Studio Theatre, June 1991; revised two-act version, New York, Manhattan Theatre Club, 21 January 1993;

The Ride Down Mt. Morgan, London, Wyndham's Theatre, 11 October 1991; Williamstown, Mass., Williamstown Theatre Festival, July 1996; New York, Joseph Papp Public Theater, November

1998; New York, Ambassador Theater, 9 April 2000;

Broken Glass, New Haven, Long Wharf Theatre, March 1994; New York, Booth Theatre, 24 April 1994;

Mr. Peters' Connections, New York, Signature Theatre Company, 28 April 1998;

Resurrection Blues, Minneapolis, Guthrie Theater, 9 August 2002.

BOOKS: *Situation Normal* (New York: Reynal & Hitchcock, 1944);

Focus (New York: Reynal & Hitchcock, 1945; London: Gollancz, 1949);

All My Sons (New York: Reynal & Hitchcock, 1947);

Death of a Salesman (New York: Viking, 1949; London: Cresset, 1949);

An Enemy of the People, adaptation of Henrik Ibsen's play (New York: Viking, 1951);

The Crucible (New York: Viking, 1953; London: Cresset, 1956);

A View from the Bridge: Two One-Act Plays (New York: Viking, 1955)—includes *A Memory of Two Mondays;*

A View from the Bridge: A Play in Two Acts, revised edition (New York: Dramatists Play Service, 1957; London: Cresset, 1957);

The Misfits (New York: Viking, 1961; London: Secker & Warburg, 1961);

Jane's Blanket (New York: Crowell-Collier / London: Collier-Macmillan, 1963);

After the Fall (New York: Viking, 1964; London: Secker & Warburg, 1965);

Incident at Vichy (New York: Viking, 1965; London: Secker & Warburg, 1966);

I Don't Need You Any More: Stories (New York: Viking, 1967; London: Secker & Warburg, 1967); revised as *The Misfits: And Other Stories* (New York: Scribners, 1987);

The Price (New York: Viking, 1968; London: Secker & Warburg, 1968);

In Russia, by Miller and Inge Morath (New York: Viking, 1969; London: Secker & Warburg, 1969);

The Creation of the World and Other Business (New York: Viking, 1973);

In the Country, by Miller and Morath (New York: Viking, 1977);

The Theater Essays of Arthur Miller, edited by Robert Martin (New York: Viking, 1978); revised and expanded, edited by Martin and Steven R. Centola (New York: Da Capo, 1996);

Chinese Encounters, by Miller and Morath (New York: Farrar, Straus & Giroux, 1979);

Playing for Time: A Screenplay (New York: Bantam, 1981);

The American Clock (New York: Dramatists Play Service, 1982);

Elegy for a Lady (New York: Dramatists Play Service, 1982);

Some Kind of Love Story (New York: Dramatists Play Service, 1983);

Up from Paradise, book and lyrics by Miller, music by Stanley Silverman (New York: S. French, 1984);

The Archbishop's Ceiling (London: Methuen, 1984; New York: Dramatists Play Service, 1985);

Salesman in Beijing, by Miller and Morath (New York: Viking, 1984);

Danger: Memory! (London: Methuen, 1986; New York: Grove, 1987)—comprises *I Can't Remember Anything* and *Clara;*

Timebends: A Life (Franklin Center, Pa.: Franklin Library, 1987; New York: Grove, 1987; London: Methuen, 1987);

The Golden Years and The Man Who Had All the Luck (London: Methuen, 1989);

Everybody Wins: A Screenplay (New York: Grove Weidenfeld, 1990; London: Methuen, 1990);

The Last Yankee (New York: Dramatists Play Service, 1991; revised and expanded, London: Methuen, 1993; New York: Penguin, 1994);

The Ride Down Mt. Morgan (London: Methuen, 1991; New York: Penguin, 1992);

Homely Girl: A Life (New York: Peter Blum, 1992); republished as *Plain Girl: A Life* (London: Methuen, 1995);

Broken Glass (New York: Penguin, 1994);

The Crucible: Screenplay (New York: Penguin, 1996; London: Methuen, 1996);

Mr. Peters' Connections (New York: Penguin, 1999);

Echoes Down the Corridor: Collected Essays 1944–2000, edited by Steven R. Centola (New York: Viking, 2000);

On Politics and the Art of Acting (New York: Viking, 2001).

Editions and Collections: *Arthur Miller's Collected Plays,* volume 1 (New York: Viking, 1957; London: Cresset, 1958); republished as *Plays: One* (London: Methuen, 1988);

The Portable Arthur Miller, edited by Harold Clurman (New York: Viking, 1971);

Arthur Miller's Collected Plays, volume 2 (New York: Viking, 1981; London: Secker & Warburg, 1981); republished as *Plays: Two* (London: Methuen, 1988);

Two-Way Mirror (London: Methuen, 1984)—comprises *Elegy for a Lady* and *Some Kind of Love Story;*

The American Clock and The Archbishop's Ceiling: Two Plays (New York: Grove, 1989);

Plays: Three (London: Methuen, 1990);

Plays: Four (London: Methuen, 1994);

Homely Girl, A Life, and Other Stories (New York: Viking, 1995);

Plays: Five (London: Methuen, 1995);

The Portable Arthur Miller, edited by Christopher Bigsby (New York: Penguin, 1995).

PRODUCED SCRIPTS: *The Misfits,* motion picture, United Artists, 1961;

Fame, television, NBC, 30 November 1978;

Playing for Time, adapted from Fania Fénelon's *The Musicians of Auschwitz,* television, CBS, 30 September 1980;

Everybody Wins, adapted from Miller's play *Some Kind of Love Story,* motion picture, Orion, 1990;

The Crucible, motion picture, 20th Century-Fox, 1996.

OTHER: *The Pussycat and the Expert Plumber Who Was a Man* and *William Ireland's Confession,* in *One Hundred Non-Royalty Radio Plays,* edited by William Kozlenko (New York: Greenburg, 1941), pp. 20–30, 512–521;

The Man Who Had All the Luck, in *Cross-Section,* edited by Edwin Seaver (New York: L. B. Fischer, 1944), pp. 486–552;

Grandpa and the Statue, in *Radio Drama in Action,* edited by Erik Barnouw (New York: Farrar & Rinehart, 1945), pp. 265–281;

That They May Win, in *The Best One-Act Plays of 1944,* edited by Margaret Mayorga (New York: Dodd, Mead, 1945), pp. 45–60;

The Story of Gus, in *Radio's Best Plays,* edited by Joseph Liss (New York: Greenburg, 1947), pp. 303–319;

"I Think about You a Great Deal," in *Václav Havel: Living in Truth,* edited by Jan Vladislav (London: Faber & Faber, 1986), pp. 263–265.

SELECTED PERIODICAL PUBLICATIONS–UNCOLLECTED:

FICTION

"It Takes a Thief," *Collier's,* 119 (8 February 1947): 23, 75–76;

"Kidnapped?" *Saturday Evening Post,* 242 (25 January 1969): 40–42, 78–82;

"Ham Sandwich," *Boston University Quarterly,* 24, no. 2 (1976): 5–6;

"White Puppies," *Esquire,* 90 (July 1978): 32–36;

"1928 Buick," *Atlantic,* 242 (October 1978): 49–51;

"Bees," *Michigan Quarterly Review,* 29 (Spring 1990): 153–157;

"Bulldog," *New Yorker* (13 August 2001): 72–76;

"The Performance," *New Yorker* (22–29 April 2002): 176–188.

NONFICTION

"Should Ezra Pound Be Shot?" *New Masses* (25 December 1945): 6;

"Subsidized Theatre," *New York Times,* 22 June 1947, II: 1;

"Picking a Cast," *New York Times,* 21 August 1955, II: 1;

"Global Dramatist," *New York Times,* 21 July 1957, II: 1;

"My Wife Marilyn," *Life,* 45 (22 December 1958): 146–147;

"A New Era in American Theater?" *Drama Survey,* 3 (Spring 1963): 70–71;

"Lincoln Repertory Theater–Challenge and Hope," *New York Times,* 19 January 1964, II: 1, 3;

"With Respect for Her Agony–But with Love," *Life,* 56 (7 February 1964): 66;

"How the Nazi Trials Search the Hearts of All Germans," *New York Herald Tribune,* 15 March 1964, p. 24;

"Our Guilt for the World's Evil," *New York Times Magazine,* 3 January 1965, pp. 10–11, 48;

"*After the Fall:* An Author's View," *New Haven Register,* 25 April 1965, p. 9;

"The Writer as Independent Spirit: The Role of P.E.N.," *Saturday Review,* 49 (4 June 1966): 16–17;

"Literature and Mass Communication," *World Theatre,* 15 (1966): 164–167;

"Writers in Prison," *Encounter,* 30 (June 1968): 60–61;

"On the Shooting of Robert Kennedy," *New York Times,* 8 June 1968, p. 30;

"The War between Young and Old, or Why Willy Loman Can't Understand What's Happening," *McCall's,* 97 (July 1970): 32;

"Banned in Russia," *New York Times,* 10 December 1970, p. 47;

"When Life Had at Least a Form," *New York Times,* 24 January 1971, p. 17;

"Politics as Theater," *New York Times* (4 November 1972): 33;

"Miracles," *Esquire,* 80 (September 1973): 112–115, 202–204;

"Our Most Widespread Dramatic Art Is Our Most Unfree," *New York Times,* 26 November 1978, II: 33;

"A Playwright's Choice of 'Perfect' Plays," *New York Times,* 14 January 1979, II: 10;

"Every Play Has a Purpose," *Dramatists Guild Quarterly,* 15 (Winter 1979): 13–20;

"Clurmania," *Nation* (26 May 1979): 606;

"Arthur Miller on McCarthy's Legacy," *Harper's,* 269 (July 1984): 11–12;

"Arthur Miller Speaks Out on the Election," *Literary Cavalcade* (November 1984): 4–5;

"The Theater Must Be Bread, Not Cake," *U.S. News and World Report* (11 January 1988): 54–55;

"Arthur Miller on Rushdie and Global Censorship," *Authors' Guild Bulletin* (Summer 1989): 5;

"Death in Tiananmen," *New York Times,* 10 September 1989, IV: 31;

"In the Ayes of the Beholder: With Congress Debating Obscenity in Federally Funded Art, What Will Happen to Free Expression?" *Omni,* 13 (February 1991): 10;

"The One Thing That Keeps Us from Chaos," *New Choices for Retirement Living* (October 1994): 22–25;

"Why I Wrote *The Crucible,*" *New Yorker,* 21 (28 October 1996): 158–164;

"On Broadway, Notes on the Past and Future of American Theater," *Harper's* (March 1999): 37–47;

"My New York," *New York* (18 December 2000): 122;

"Writers on Writing: Shattering the Silence, Illuminating the Hatred," *New York Times,* 22 October 2001, p. E1.

Arthur Miller is one of the major dramatists of the twentieth century. He has earned this reputation during a more than sixty-year career in which he wrote his first plays as an undergraduate at the University of Michigan in the 1930s; achieved critical success with dramas such as *All My Sons* (1947), *Death of a Salesman* (1949), *The Crucible* (1953), and *A View from the Bridge* (1955) in the 1940s and 1950s; served as president of the International Association of Poets, Playwrights, Editors, Essayists and Novelists (PEN) and as a delegate to two Democratic conventions in the 1960s and 1970s; produced a critically acclaimed autobiography, *Timebends: A Life,* in 1987; and premiered new plays on Broadway and in London in the 1990s. In the twenty-first century Miller remains as active as at the beginning of his career, having published a collection of essays, *Echoes Down the Corridor* (2000), and completed a new play, *Resurrection Blues* (2002). Recipient of the New York Drama Critics Circle Award for *All My Sons, Death of a Salesman,* and *A View from the Bridge,* the Pulitzer Prize for *Death of a Salesman,* Tony Awards for *Death of a Salesman, The Crucible,* and Lifetime Achievement (1999), and the Olivier Award for *Broken Glass* (1994), Miller clearly ranks with the other truly great figures of American drama such as Eugene O'Neill, Tennessee Williams, and Edward Albee.

Arthur Asher Miller was born on 17 October 1915 in Manhattan, the second son of Isadore and Augusta Barnett Miller. His older brother, Kermit, was a businessman, and his younger sister is the actress Joan Copeland. The Millers–his father a Jewish immigrant from Poland, his mother born on the lower East Side of Manhattan to Polish Jewish émigrés–were wealthy from their coat and suit factory, a family business that his father had built up. The Millers lived in upper-middle-class splendor on East 112th Street in a large apartment that Miller describes in *Timebends* as "at the edge of Harlem, six stories above the glorious park, from whose windows we could see downtown, even down to the harbor it seemed." The family owned a chauffeur-driven, seven-passenger "National" automobile and a summer bungalow on the beach in Far Rockaway. However, Isadore Miller's business collapsed, even before the stock-market crash of 1929; the family relocated to Brooklyn in 1928, when Arthur was thirteen. The move was clearly a step down, and the family settled in the Midwood section of the borough in a little six-room house on East Third Street, where Arthur shared a bedroom with his maternal grandfather.

The move to Brooklyn and the onset of the Depression were the most defining events of Miller's youth. Many critics have discussed the autobiographical elements of Miller's work, and his experiences as a teenager and young man in Brooklyn during the Depression are evident in many of his plays. The Brooklyn of Miller's youth, despite the size and population of the borough, was still relatively rural and undeveloped, and Miller's recollections emphasize the pastoral aspect. In *Timebends* Miller recounts the life of his "two pioneer uncles," Manny Newman and Lee Balsam, both salesmen whom Miller later used as prototypes for Willy Loman. They had moved their families to Brooklyn after World War I, almost ten years earlier than his own family. Miller describes the Midwood area as "so empty they could watch their kids walking all the dozen blocks to the school across the scrubby flatlands." Miller often describes the physical transformation of Brooklyn in the era between the world wars, when he witnessed a quick and dramatic change to the wholly urban environment of today.

Miller attended James Madison and Abraham Lincoln High Schools in Brooklyn, where he was an average student and played on the second squad of the Lincoln football team. In 1932 Miller graduated from Lincoln. His poor grades and his family's finances kept him out of college. For two years Miller worked in a succession of odd jobs as a deliveryman for his father, as an on-air tenor for a Brooklyn radio station, and as a stock clerk in the warehouse of an auto-parts supplier, an experience he turned into his 1955 one-act play *A Memory of Two Mondays*. During this time Miller first encountered anti-Semitism, which became a major theme of his later work. After saving the $500 minimum bankbook balance to assure the school he would not become an indigent ward of the state, Miller finally entered the University of Michigan at Ann Arbor in 1934.

Miller worked his way through the university with jobs washing dishes three times a day and feeding three floors of mice in a genetics laboratory. But he maintained a full academic schedule and immersed himself in university life, which then had the reputation of being a hotbed of 1930s leftist political radicalism. He wrote for the student newspaper and majored in English. However, Miller's years at Michigan are most notable as the start of his playwriting career. Miller had known little about the theater, but during these formative years he became aware of German expressionism, August Strindberg, and Henrik Ibsen, who was a major influence on him. Miller read one-act protest plays about miners and stevedores and was markedly affected by the social protest work of Clifford Odets. As a result, Miller twice won the annual $250 Avery Hopwood Award (which Miller called the college's Nobel Prize) for *Honors at Dawn* in 1936 and *No Villain* in 1937; a third play, *The Great Disobedience,* placed second in 1938, the year he finished his A.B.

After graduation Miller joined the Federal Theater Project, which employed promising young playwrights at a living wage of $23 per week. He expected to have *The Golden Years,* a drama about Montezuma II and Hernán Cortés, produced, but Congress curtailed the program. This play, which was not produced until a 1987 British radio and television version, was written in response to the growing power of Adolf Hitler and was an early demonstration of Miller's lifelong interest in the social relevance of drama.

At this time, because a high-school football injury had made him ineligible for the draft, he also wrote half-hour radio plays for DuPont's Cavalcade of America, the Columbia Workshop, and U.S. Steel. These radio plays exhibit themes that are evident in later Miller masterpieces. For example, in the radio playlet *The Pussycat and the Expert Plumber Who Was a Man* (1941) one character states: "The one thing a man fears next to death is the loss of his good name. Man is evil in his own eyes, my friends, worthless, and the only way he can find respect for himself is by getting other people to say he's a nice fellow." This proclamation foreshadows similar cries by such Miller characters as Willy Loman, John Proctor, and Eddie Carbone, who value the worth of their names in the eyes of the world.

To assist the war effort and earn some money, Miller worked in the Brooklyn Navy Yard for two years while continuing to work on his plays. In 1940 he married Mary Grace Slattery, a fellow student and a Catholic, whom he had met at the University of Michigan. They settled in Brooklyn Heights and had two children, Robert and Jane. In early 1943, Miller left the Navy Yard to conduct background research for the screenplay of *The Story of G.I. Joe* (1945), adapted from columns by American war reporter Ernie Pyle. Miller used his research for a book of reportage called *Situation Normal* (1944), his first published book, in which he

Miller in Brooklyn Heights during the 1940s
(photograph © Dan Weiner)

tried to see a higher purpose operating among soldiers about the aims of World War II.

Miller then turned to his first play produced on Broadway, *The Man Who Had All the Luck* (1944). In 1940 he had written a 360-page novel about a man for whom everything turns out perfectly and who therefore comes to believe he has no control over his own destiny. Failing to find a publisher for the novel, Miller rewrote it as a play, publishing it in *Cross-Section* (1944), a volume of new American writing that included works by other then-unknowns such as Norman Mailer and Ralph Ellison. The play opened at the Forrest Theatre on 23 November 1944 to almost universally negative reviews, and the critics punned unmercifully on the title. It closed after four performances.

Miller has called *The Man Who Had All the Luck* "an argument with God." He says that the crux of the play is: "How much of our fate do we make and how much is accident?" The so-called fantasy relates the story of David Beeves (Frieber in the published version), a young, self-taught garage mechanic, who is successful at everything he attempts and benefits from an unbroken series of fortunate events: his garage becomes a success when the state builds a highway next to it; he is rescued from an inability to repair a valuable automobile by the sudden appearance of an expert mechanic; the father of the girl he loves refuses to allow the marriage but is killed in a timely automobile accident; even David's apparent sterility is overcome when his injured wife gives birth to a healthy son. But instead of reveling in his streak of good luck, David becomes haunted by it, coming to believe that his good fortune must be paid for.

David's good luck is contrasted with the story of his brother, Amos, in whom David's father has invested all his hopes and dreams of turning him into a star baseball player. Their father has taught Amos how to pitch in the cellar of their house, and the result is a technically perfect pitcher who is unable to cope in a real game with men on base. David cannot fathom why his brother, despite his efforts, has failed while David has succeeded. David is further challenged by Shory, a wheelchair-bound character who harangues him with his insistence on man's inability to control his fate.

David challenges his fate by staking his wealth on a mink-breeding ranch. The results seem calamitous when a sudden, violent hailstorm and poisoned feed threaten the animals. His wife insists that David should allow the animals to die, for only then will he be free of his fear and accept responsibility for his own actions. The mink survive because David picks the silkworms (fatal if ingested) off the fish he is feeding them, and he, perhaps, realizes he has some measure of control in his life.

Although a critical failure, *The Man Who Had All the Luck* clearly included strains of plot and themes that Miller used in his later successful plays. The rivalry of two brothers is a major component of *All My Sons, Death of a Salesman, The Price* (1968), and even *The Creation of the World and Other Business* (1972), in which Cain and Abel struggle in the first fraternal battle. Similarly, David's acceptance of responsibility for his actions is a key for other major characters. In his introduction to volume one of his *Collected Plays* (1957) Miller acknowledged the critical failure of *The Man Who Had All the Luck* but realized its importance as a seminal text:

> The play was impossible to fix because the overt story was only tangential to the secret drama the author was unconsciously trying to write. But in writing of the father-son relationship and the son's search for his relatedness there was a fullness of feeling I had never known before; a crescendo was struck with a force I could almost touch. The crux of *All My Sons*, which would not be written until nearly three years later, was formed; and the roots of *Death of a Salesmen* were sprouted.

In recent years critics and theater companies have recognized the importance of Miller's first Broadway play. In 1988 a successful staged reading of *The Man Who Had All the Luck* was given in New York, which led to the publication of a new version in 1989.

Disappointed by the reception of *The Man Who Had All the Luck* and convinced he would never write another play, in 1945 Miller wrote and published a novel, *Focus,* one of the first important American works about anti-Semitism. The novel was successful, selling ninety thousand copies. The title possesses literal and figurative meanings for the main character, Lawrence Newman. The Gentile Newman, the personnel manager of a large company that refuses to hire Jews, is forced to wear glasses because of failing eyesight. Although the glasses help him see clearly, his co-workers suddenly view him differently. The glasses make him look like a Jew, and he becomes the object of discrimination and persecution. His colleagues suspect his real name is Neuman, and he is removed to a back desk. He quits and cannot find another job because of his appearance. Moreover, he becomes an outcast to his neighbors, and his wife, a worker for an anti-Semitic organization, is also accused of being a Jew. His neighbors plan an assault against a Jewish grocer who serves their community. But Newman, emboldened by identification with a man he now sees as a fellow Jew, defends the grocer Finkelstein with a baseball bat against the attack. *Focus* tackles a subject that Miller made a major part of his dramatic canon: all humanity shares a responsibility for the suffering of the Jews. The novel was adapted into a motion picture in 2001, starring William H. Macy and Laura Dern.

Despite the success Miller had with the novel form, he was determined to write another play and decided if it were not a hit, he would give up playwriting altogether. The result of Miller's self-ultimatum was *All My Sons,* his first Broadway hit and critically acclaimed drama. Miller formed the idea for the play from a story his Midwestern mother-in-law told him about a family in her neighborhood that had been destroyed when the daughter discovered her father had been selling faulty machine parts to the army and reported him to the authorities. Miller decided to transform the daughter into a son, and a play was born.

The drama focuses on Joe Keller, a small factory owner, finally forced to confront his legal and moral crime of knowingly selling defective airplane parts during World War II, which resulted in the deaths of twenty-one pilots. Joe has denied his part in the crime by blaming his business partner, who has been in jail for three years, while Joe has reestablished his successful business. When his cover-up unravels, he can no longer deny the truth, and when he ultimately realizes the ramifications of his crime for his family and society, he kills himself.

Keller's two sons and wife also struggle with the repercussions of his crime. Three years earlier, the pilot son, Larry, deliberately crashed his plane out of shame and guilt after discovering his father's culpability. The other son, Chris, survived the war and witnessed the sacrifices men make for each other. Chris suppresses his suspicions of Joe's crime, works in his plant, and plans to marry Ann Deever, Larry's fiancée and daughter of Joe's jailed business partner. But Chris is shattered when the truth is revealed, and he confronts his own and his father's accountability for denying the crime. The mother, Kate, consciously denies her husband's crime and son's death; although she has known the truth from the beginning, she uses astrology and religion to create the illusion that Joe is innocent and Larry is merely missing in action and coming back.

Miller writes in his *Collected Plays* introduction that *All My Sons* is "designed to bring a man into the direct path of the consequences he has wrought." Miller judges that Joe is a threat to society because "his cast of mind cannot admit that he, personally, has any viable connection with his world, his universe, his society." *All My Sons* established Miller as a realistic social playwright in the Ibsenesque tradition, a reputation that has stuck with him throughout his career. Clearly, *All My Sons* is a "well-made" play with a long exposition, careful attention to plot detail, the device of a concealed letter, hidden truths, and secrets. Many critics have seen parallels to Ibsen's *The Wild Duck* (1884) with its emphasis on the revelation of past action.

With the production of *All My Sons* Miller began his professional and personal association with the motion-picture and stage director Elia Kazan. *All My Sons* ran for 328 performances and received the New York Drama Critics Circle Award. Universal Pictures purchased the movie rights, turning it into a movie with Edward G. Robinson and Burt Lancaster in 1948. Miller was beginning to reap the benefits of his success financially and artistically: he bought a house in Brooklyn Heights, and royalty income gave him a new freedom to create. After researching life in the Italian criminal underworld on the docks, waterfronts, and piers of Red Hook, Brooklyn, which he later used as the raw material for *A View from the Bridge,* Miller turned to writing his masterpiece, *Death of a Salesman*.

Death of a Salesman had been gestating in Miller for some time. When Miller was seventeen he wrote a story (rediscovered by his mother during the original production of the play) called "In Memoriam," based on his experiences with a Jewish salesman when he was working for his father a few months after graduating high school. Miller also had written a play about a salesman and his family during his time at the University of Michigan. Miller was particularly influenced by the memory of his uncle Manny Newman. In *Timebends* Miller relates how Manny, who later committed suicide, raised his two sons to be competitive alter egos with Miller. Thus, the prototypes of Willy, Biff, and Hap were born.

Miller wanted this play to differ from the tight composition of *All My Sons*. By the spring of 1948 he felt that he could find the form of the play but that he would have to write it in one sitting. He retreated to his country house on four hundred acres in Connecticut, which he had bought the year before, and built a workshop where he could block out the world while he wrote the play. As he labored physically, he contemplated everything he had in his head about the play: the name of the salesman's family, Loman; a death; and the first two lines: "Willy" and "It's alright. I came back." When the tiny ten-by-twelve-foot cabin was completed, Miller sat down one April morning and began. He wrote all day until dark, had dinner, and then went back to his desk until the middle of the night. He had finished act 1. When he lay down to sleep, he realized he had been weeping; his eyes and throat hurt from talking out the lines, shouting, and laughing. It took him six more weeks to complete act 2.

Miller sent the completed play to Kazan, who immediately recognized its merit and together with Miller began the casting of what is now widely considered to be one of the greatest American plays of the twentieth century. Lee J. Cobb played the original Willy Loman, while Mildred Dunnock portrayed his wife, Linda. Kazan also enlisted the services of designer Jo Mielziner, who had created the set for Williams's *A Streetcar Named Desire* (1947). Miller, Kazan, and Mielziner collaborated to produce innovative staging and a revolutionary set that became legendary in the American theater.

Death of a Salesman depicts the last twenty-four hours in the life of Willy Loman, a sixty-three-year-old traveling salesman, who for thirty-six years has plied his trade all over New England. Willy has come to realize that he is a failure and is contemplating suicide. At the same time, he is haunted by an unresolved conflict with his son, Biff, over the latter's discovery of Willy's adultery with a woman in a Boston hotel room. Biff, at thirty-four years old, is a fallen football hero who has flunked out of school, stolen himself out of every job he has had, and led an unsettled existence. As the play opens, he has been ranching out West but has come home to Brooklyn on one of his infrequent visits. A younger son, Hap, is mired in a dead-end merchandise job in a New York department store and wallows in whores and booze. Linda is the seemingly long-suffering,

Arthur Kennedy, Karl Malden, Beth Merrill, Ed Begley, and Lois Wheeler in the 1947 New York production of All My Sons *(photograph © Eileen Darby)*

supportive wife and mother but also conveys a strength that neither her husband nor sons possess.

In *Death of a Salesman* Miller created a form that was deliberately opposite to a straight realistic play such as *All My Sons*, in which one event creates the necessity for the next. As Miller explains in his *Collected Plays* introduction, he conceived *Death of a Salesman* with the "concept that nothing in life comes next, but that everything exists together and at the same time within; that there is not a past to be 'brought forward' in a human being, but that he is his past at every moment and the present is merely that which his past is capable of noticing and smelling and reacting to." Working in an expressionistic style that has become known as "subjective realism," Miller simultaneously depicted both the real time of the play and the internal workings of Willy's mind, especially as he recalls events of the past. Miller called these scenes "imaginings," and they are not flashbacks but rather what Miller describes in the *Collected Plays* introduction as "a mobile concurrency of past and present," because linear time is broken down in the play. The overall effect is to convey the dislocation of time in Willy's mind, because as Miller has noted, "In his desperation to justify his life Willy Loman has destroyed the boundaries between then and now."

The original working title for *Death of a Salesman* was "The Inside of His Head." Miller's first idea for the set was of an enormous face, the height of the proscenium arch, which would open so that the audience would see the inside of a man's head, where all the action of the play would occur. Mielziner took this image and designed the now-famous set with a series of three platforms, for the kitchen and two bedrooms, without walls. The Boston hotel room, Howard's office, and the yard scenes were played in the open space downstage. Moreover, Mielziner created surrealistic apartment buildings surrounding and encroaching on the Loman house. Lighting and music helped convey the instantaneous changes in time and place. Furthermore, plaintive, haunting flute music punctuated Willy's musings throughout the play.

When the play opened on 10 February 1949 at the Morosco Theatre, the critical reaction was overwhelming. It ran for 742 performances and won a Tony Award, the New York Drama Critics Circle

Award, and the Pulitzer Prize. Within a year of its premiere, *Death of a Salesman* was playing in every major city in the United States and within a few years began its incredible run of international productions. Brenda Murphy has concluded that since the first production there has never been a time when *Death of a Salesman* was not being performed somewhere in the world.

The enduring universal appeal of *Death of a Salesman* to audiences, theater critics, and scholars lies in its focus on the American Dream as a central theme. For thirty-six years as a traveling salesman Willy Loman has fought to achieve the success that the American Dream promises, and he has accrued the tangible products that signify the dream. However, the intangibles—personal satisfaction, self-worth, and economic security—have eluded him, and the play captures the dramatic moments when Willy confronts this failure. Perhaps this recognition is why most audiences have identified with Willy. When Linda tries to convey to her sons that Willy is "a human being and a terrible thing is happening to him," audiences realize that the same can happen to them.

Willy's failure is based largely on his flawed understanding of what constitutes the American Dream; he confuses his material and spiritual values so that he no longer can differentiate between reality and illusion, as illustrated in his imaginative longings for the idyllic past. He alternately believes that personal appearance, being liked, and contacts are the ways to succeed in the material world. Willy has spent his career with these beliefs but has never been a successful "hot shot" salesman with big commissions. He, therefore, has struggled to make the payments on the tangible items that exemplify the dream: his home, the car, the refrigerator. In addition, Willy possesses spiritual flaws; his adultery and condoning of stealing and cheating signify his moral failings. Willy has transmitted his flawed beliefs to his sons, and as a result both men are failures too. Neither is able to perform the hard work necessary to achieve financial success and personal fulfillment. In contrast, the Lomans' next-door neighbor, Charley, and his son, Bernard, have integrated the material and spiritual; they have succeeded financially through integrity, humility, and studiousness.

Death of a Salesman has been analyzed as a play that critiques the role of capitalism in American society. Certainly, the play illustrates Willy's lifelong dream for economic success while he struggles to compete in the American economic system. At the end of the play, in a "Requiem," Hap expresses Willy's striving for the American Dream in a climactic metaphor that is at the heart of Willy's struggle: "It's the only dream you can have—to come out number one man." Willy's drive to achieve that status illustrates the workings of an American capitalist system based on competition. Although the dream possesses the potent allure of seeming attainable for all, its enchantment masks the competition that in reality does not guarantee its achievement by everyone. Willy himself declares in the first scene that "The competition is maddening," and the play details how he is literally maddened as he fails at his dream to be number one. The very products of the American capitalist system seem arrayed against Willy: his car breaks down, and the refrigerator consumes belts like a "goddamn maniac." But ultimately Willy fails to realize that he actually is competing against himself: that he is responsible for his own failure.

Willy's sons also desire the American Dream. Throughout the play, Hap and Biff detail their relative disappointment in what they have accomplished in life: Biff is torn between his love of the outdoors and his desire for economic success in the city, while Hap is stuck selling in a department store. Both men seek financial success and personal contentment, but they are as confused as Willy about how to achieve these things. By the end of the play, only Biff seems to have become aware of his failings, as he tries to tell Willy to take his "phony dream and burn it." On the other hand, Hap decides to stay in the city in an attempt to show that Willy Loman did not die in vain. As the bearer of Willy's legacy, Hap makes the same mistakes as Willy—especially in perverting spiritual and material values. But Hap does not understand that Willy exalts the acquisition of material possessions without regard for personal conduct, misunderstands the legitimate methods for attaining success, and corrupts his humanity.

Perhaps one of the most intriguing analyses of *Death of a Salesman* has been whether Willy Loman is a tragic hero, and therefore, whether the play is a modern tragedy. Critics have argued on both sides: that Willy's death is merely the pathetic demise of a small man, and conversely, that Willy's death is the consequence of his noble action. A few weeks after the production opened, Miller wrote an op-ed piece for *The New York Times* titled "Tragedy and the Common Man" (27 February 1949) in which he made the case for Willy as a modern tragic hero. Miller maintains that modern literature did not require characters to be royalty or leaders and therefore fall from some great height to their demise, as in the tragedies of other eras. Rather, Miller insists: "I think that the tragic feeling is evoked when we are in the presence of a character who is ready to lay down his life, if need be, to secure one thing—his sense of personal dignity. From Orestes to Hamlet, Medea to Macbeth, the underlying struggle is that of the individual attempting to gain his 'rightful' position in his society." Thus, Miller argues that a lowly man such as Willy could be considered a tragic hero. (Miller chuckled at those critics who emphasized Loman as a pun for "low man"; he actually took the name from a 1933 movie, *The Testament of Dr. Mabuse*.) "Tragedy and the Common Man" is now widely considered to be an important part of twentieth-century literary criticism. It stands as the first of a large body of dramatic criticism that Miller has produced over a span of fifty years, the most significant output of such writing since George Bernard Shaw.

Since the original production there have been many notable revivals of *Death of a Salesman* both in the United States and around the world. A New York revival in 1975 featured George C. Scott as Willy; Dustin Hoffman led a stellar 1984 Broadway production with John Malkovich as Biff; and the Goodman Theater of Chicago mounted a fiftieth-anniversary production that opened on 11 February 1999 at the Eugene O'Neill Theater. That show won Tony Awards for Brian Dennehy as Willy, Linda Franz in a redefining role as Linda, and for Best Play Revival. Miller also won a Tony for Lifetime Achievement. International audiences have never lost their attraction to the quintessentially American struggle of Willy Loman. In 1950 audience members in Vienna wept; Japanese audiences responded with empathy to Willy's fall; and the 1983 Beijing production, which Miller directed, caused tears in the Communist Chinese audiences.

In 1950 Miller wrote an adaptation of Ibsen's 1882 play, *An Enemy of the People,* a version that reinforced in the critics' eyes Miller's significant debt to the Norwegian playwright. The play concerns itself with Peter Stockmann, a doctor who refuses to allow his town a permit to build a spa when he discovers the unhealthy quality of the water supply. Stockmann literally becomes the enemy of the townspeople, who turn their wrath on him, one of their most respected citizens, because his decision threatens their profit-making ability. Although *An Enemy of the People* was a commercial failure, closing after thirty-six performances, critics have seen this play as an important transition for Miller. In it he signaled his return to a thematic interest that he had expressed in *All My Sons:* one's responsibility to self and society.

Miller certainly saw political relevance in *An Enemy of the People,* for in 1950 the United States was embarking on a period of political and social upheaval that had a lasting effect on Miller's career and personal life. Miller said in the preface to the play that "Its central theme is, in my opinion, the central theme of our social life today. Simply it is the question of whether the democratic vision of the truth ought to be a source of guilt at a time when the mass of men condemn it as a dangerous and devilish lie." During these times, Miller witnessed the rise of the hearings conducted by Wisconsin senator Joseph McCarthy and the establishment of the House Un-American Activities Committee (HUAC), which was revived after World War II in response to the "Red Scare" threat from the Soviet Union and the fall of China to a Communist government. People were called before these committees and made to account for suspected radical pasts, and the targets of these accusations were often high-profile celebrities whose appearances would guarantee major publicity. In the next few years Miller's friends and colleagues became targets, and eventually Miller did too. Thus, in the preface to *An Enemy of the People,* he explained that in Peter Stockmann's principled stand against his entire town, Miller saw the universal theme that "there never was nor will there ever be an organized society able to countenance calmly the individual who insists that he is right while the vast majority is absolutely wrong." With these events in mind, he turned to *The Crucible*.

Miller became interested in writing about the 1692 Salem witch trials when he read Marion Starkey's book *The Devil in Massachusetts* (1949). In April 1952 Miller decided to write a play about the events in Salem because he saw a "living connection between myself and Salem, and between Salem and Washington." Miller planned an exploratory trip to Massachusetts to research the original court records. The day before he was to leave, he received a phone call from Kazan, who had been subpoenaed by the HUAC. Kazan and Miller met in Connecticut, where Kazan told Miller that he had decided to cooperate and testify about other celebrities Kazan had encountered at Communist Party meetings years earlier. Kazan's decision caused a breach in his personal and professional relationship with Miller that lasted until the next decade.

In Salem, Miller examined the court records and became struck by the testimony about a farmer, John Procter (Miller changed the spelling in his play), his wife, Elizabeth, and their servant girl Abigail Williams, who accused Elizabeth, but not John, of witchcraft. Months before the witchcraft hysteria had begun, Abigail had been dismissed from service by Elizabeth. Miller perceived that Abigail had personal motives against the Procters. Thus, Miller decided to wrap his historical play about the Salem trials around what he viewed as the personal story of John's adultery with Abigail, Elizabeth's discovery of it, and Abigail's vengeance. When Miller left Salem, he heard a news report of Kazan's testimony before the HUAC: he had "named names." In the next few months the playwright Odets, who had a major influence on Miller, was called before the committee; he, too, named names. Cobb, the original Willy

Mildred Dunnock, Lee J. Cobb, Arthur Kennedy, and Cameron Mitchell in the 1949 New York production of Death of a Salesman *(photograph © Eileen Darby)*

Loman, was called, and he also succumbed to the pressure. Miller was struck by the power of the state to force men to testify and further implicate others. This power became a central focus of the play Miller was about to write.

Miller constructed *The Crucible* in four acts. Act 1 details the start of the hysteria, when a group of girls led by Abigail Williams, Reverend Parris's niece, is caught dancing naked and conjuring spirits in the woods. From the outset Miller shows how under the guise of witchcraft the personal conflicts simmering in Salem among the villagers quickly surface. Reverend Hale, an expert on demonic arts, arrives to discover the truth of the sorcery in Salem. At the center of the action is the personal vengeance of Abigail Williams, who was dismissed as servant girl after Elizabeth Proctor discovered Abigail's adultery with John. The dramatic high point of act 1 is when Hale examines Tituba, Parris's Barbados slave, after Abigail accuses her of bewitching her. In fear, Tituba confesses to consorting with the devil and names villagers she claims to have seen with the devil. Abigail leads the girls in a general outcry against the others.

Act 2 focuses on the tension in the marriage between John and Elizabeth as a result of his adultery. Weeks have passed since the initial accusations, which have spread to include Salem's most prominent citizens, including Rebecca Nurse and Martha Corey. Hale arrives at the Proctor farmhouse to examine the Proctors' religious beliefs, and the marshals arrest Elizabeth, who has been accused of bewitching Abigail. John resolves to go to court.

Act 3 takes place in the anteroom of a Salem village meetinghouse that has been turned into a court to accommodate the trials. In this act the power of the theocratic state is represented by Judge Hathorne and by the deputy governor Danforth, who is thought to be somewhat representative of McCarthy and of HUAC chairman Francis E. Walters. Miller depicts a court with absolute power, willing to crush any dissent from its mission to discover evil in Salem village. Giles Corey, Francis Nurse, and John Proctor come to obtain their wives' freedom. Danforth wields his unjust power when John presents him with a deposition of Salem citizens who attest to the good character of Rebecca, Martha, and Elizabeth. Parris sees this document as an attack on the court, and Danforth calls for these innocent citizens' arrest and examination. Miller shows how the scantiest evidence can accuse and convict people, not only in Salem in 1692 but also in the United States in the 1950s. Proctor calls Abigail a whore and confesses his adultery. Abigail denies the charge and threatens Danforth, while Elizabeth is brought in to confirm John's accusation. Having no knowledge that John has confessed, Elizabeth lies to protect him, and he is arrested. Hale finally comes to an awareness of the hypocrisy of the trials, realizing that private vengeance fuels many of the witchcraft accusations.

Act 4 occurs in late fall, months after the initial accusations; the hysteria has subsided, and there is a growing resentment against the trials, especially at the impending hanging of reputable citizens. Hale is going among the prisoners encouraging them to falsely confess to save their lives. John admits that he wants to confess, since as a sinner he is not worthy to mount the gibbet with good women such as Martha and Rebecca. Elizabeth admits culpability for prompting his adultery because of her coldness. John decides to confess, which delights the magistrates who look to use him as an example. However, John's confession breaks down when Rebecca is brought in. Proctor refuses to name others, then refuses to hand over his signed confession because his name will be posted on the church door. He admits his confession is a lie, and he is sent to his hanging with Elizabeth proclaiming his goodness to Hale.

The Crucible marked a notable change in the style of language Miller used. In his previous work Miller was mostly known for his use of colloquial dialect, the so-called common man's language. In *The Crucible* Miller created a vernacular that suggests the archaic forms of the seventeenth-century Puritan dialect but at the same time approaches the level of poetry with its use of metaphors particular to Puritan society. In fact, Miller has shown a keen interest in verse drama and reported that he initially wrote much of *Death of a Salesman* and all of *The Crucible* in verse and later converted them to prose.

The Crucible raises several complicated themes and issues. Like *An Enemy of the People* and *All My Sons*, the play is about moral choices when an individual confronts the pressures imposed by society. John Proctor is a character whose individual conscience does not allow him to succumb to the will of others, even an autocratic state. Proctor's sense of sin, guilt, and shame over his adultery at first impedes his ability to see himself as good, but Elizabeth ultimately helps him find his moral compass. The play shows how the goodness of individual conscience defeats its opposite: the evil of state-sponsored fanaticism. Some critics have also pointed out the significance of marriage and adultery in *The Crucible* and how these topics are a major focus of Miller's other plays.

The original production of *The Crucible* was not a hit with audiences or critics, who, Miller noted, felt uncomfortable with the subject and theme, given the parlous current events in the country. He reports that on opening night, people with whom he had close professional relationships passed him by as if he were invisible. The reviews were respectable, as Miller has wryly observed: "the kind that bury you decently." However, the show played for 197 performances, a decent run, and won a Tony Award. It proved popular in Europe, and Miller was planning to attend the Brussels opening in 1954 when the State Department denied him a passport because he was believed to be involved in Communist activities. In 1958, well after the Communist hysteria had died down, *The Crucible* was revived Off-Broadway to plaudits and ran for more than 600 performances.

For Miller's next play, *A View from the Bridge*, he turned to a subject that had interested him earlier–the Italian immigrant society of the Brooklyn docks. In 1950, when Miller had been researching the criminal underworld of the dockside for an unmade movie titled "The Hook," a lawyer who had been trying to fight the corruption and unionize the workers told him the story of a longshoreman who had informed immigration authorities about two brothers who were related to him and living illegally in his house. The man had done so in order to break up the relationship between his niece and one of the brothers, but his action made him a pariah in his neighborhood. Local gossip held that he had been killed by one of the brothers.

In "Tragedy and the Common Man" Miller had maintained that it was possible for tragedies to be written about modern characters, and he clearly set his dramatic sights on achieving this goal in *A View from the Bridge*. But he also was clearly interested in further exploring the themes of betrayal, informing, and adultery, which he had illustrated in *The Crucible*. By the time he was writing the one-act version of *A View from the Bridge*, Miller had embarked on an affair with Marilyn Monroe, was about to divorce his wife, and was becoming a target of the HUAC.

The one-act version opened in New York in 1955 together with *A Memory of Two Mondays*. The production had a disappointing run, closing after 149 performances, though Miller won his third New York Drama

Critics Circle Award. A year later, Miller revised and expanded the play to two acts and premiered it in London. Evaluation of the differences between these versions has focused almost exclusively on how Miller, in response to criticism of the sketchiness of the characters in the one-act, enlarged the psychological motivations of the principal characters–Eddie Carbone, a Brooklyn longshoreman; his wife, Beatrice; and her niece, Catherine–in order to emphasize the social consequences of the central action: Eddie's desire for Catherine. Most literary criticism focuses almost exclusively on the two-act version, which is the published version.

Eddie and Beatrice have raised Catherine since she was a child. When the play begins, Catherine is seventeen and on the verge of becoming a woman. Eddie's affection as an uncle/stepfather has changed into a physical and emotional attraction, which neither Eddie nor Catherine fully perceives, but of which Beatrice is aware. Eddie's emotion is transformed into jealousy when Catherine falls in love and wants to marry Rodolpho, one of two Italian illegal immigrants, cousins of Beatrice who are living in the Carbones' Red Hook apartment. Eddie impugns Rodolpho's masculinity and tells Catherine that Rodolpho is only using her to obtain citizenship. After Eddie discovers the young couple coming out of a bedroom, he informs to immigration authorities–a deed abhorrent to the social codes of the Sicilian American community–who arrest Rodolpho and his brother, Marco, who publicly accuses Eddie of snitching. Out on bail, Rodolpho intends to marry Catherine, and Marco comes to vindicate his and his brother's honor. Eddie wants Marco to apologize in front of the neighborhood for his accusation because he wants his "name" back. When Marco strikes him, Eddie pulls a knife, which Marco turns back on Eddie, killing him.

In the writing and production of the one-act version of *A View from the Bridge*, Miller wanted to make a tragedy of Eddie Carbone's story; so he created an outside narrator, the lawyer Alfieri, who functions as a Greek chorus, both as character and commentator. Alfieri's speeches to the audience directly connect Eddie to what Miller sees as the mythic level of the play: Eddie's larger universal fate, his destiny to enact the tragic action. Moreover, the New York production used sparse staging to achieve the "skeletal" quality of the mythic story, because as Miller wrote in the introduction to the two-act version, "nothing existed but the purpose of the tale."

Miller admits that the meaning of Eddie's fate remained a mystery to him even after writing the one-act play. In revising for the London production, Miller sought to place Eddie more in relation to his Sicilian American society. As he explains in the two-act introduction, he realized that "The mind of Eddie Carbone is not comprehensible apart from its relation to his neighborhood, his fellow workers, his social situation. His self-esteem depends upon their estimate of him, and his value is created largely by his fidelity to the code of his culture." For the London production the set was more realistic; additional actors played Eddie's neighbors. Miller ultimately judged that "once Eddie had been placed squarely in his social context, among his people, the myth-like feeling of the story emerged of itself, and he could be made more human and less a figure, a force."

The most provocative issues that *A View from the Bridge* raises are incest and sexuality. From the outset, Eddie's attention to Catherine is depicted as more than fatherly affection. The girl is not his blood niece but Beatrice's, although he has raised her as his own daughter, which further complicates his borderline incestuous desire for her. When the cousins arrive, Catherine's immediate attraction to Rodolpho is obvious, and Eddie's jealousy turns into an attack: he is repulsed by what he perceives as Rodolpho's effeminate nature.

Eddie's conflicting sexual impulses are one of the most intriguing aspects of the play. The one-act version downplays Eddie's apparent impotency, which is central in the two-act version, in which Beatrice asks him, "When am I going to be a wife again, Eddie?" They have not slept together in more than three months, which heightens the sexual conflicts. Although he is unable to perform with Beatrice, he clearly desires Catherine, but at the same time he does not want her virginity violated. Furthermore, Eddie has possible sexual feelings for Rodolpho, whose masculinity Eddie assaults because he seems both repulsed and attracted by Rodolpho's femininity. Yet, Eddie clearly is portrayed as completely unconscious of his desires.

One of the most controversial actions in *A View from the Bridge* occurs in the first scene of act 2, when Eddie returns home a few days before Christmas to find that Rodolpho and Catherine have been intimate in his own home. Eddie is drunk and beyond rage, and he wants to expel Rodolpho. When Catherine attempts to leave, Eddie grabs her and kisses her on the mouth, a visible sign of his unconscious desire for her. Then, when Rodolpho intervenes, Eddie pinions him and kisses him on the mouth. Eddie acts out of rage, but he clearly needs to humiliate Rodolpho. Eddie later uses Rodopho's unwillingness to fight back as further proof of his effeminacy. Yet, the complication is that Eddie may also have unconscious homosexual desire for Rodolpho. After this incident, he informs to the immigration authorities, which brings the vengeance of Marco on him.

Program cover for the 1955 New York production of Miller's controversial play about a Brooklyn longshoreman's attraction to his wife's niece (Bruccoli Clark Layman Archives)

In late 1955 and early 1956 Miller's troubles with the government over his suspected leftist activities increased. While he had been working on "The Hook," an investigator from the HUAC warned the city administration about being associated with Miller for his political opinions. In turn, the American Legion and the Catholic War Veterans successfully applied pressure to stop the movie because of Miller's "Communist ties."

Also during this period, Miller had divorced Mary Slattery and in 1956 married Monroe. The seemingly unlikely marriage caused a media sensation, and Miller suspected that the publicity would draw the attention of the HUAC, whose influence had been waning. Miller was subpoenaed, and the hypocrisy of the committee was evident to him when his lawyer told him that chairman Walters had proposed that the hearing could be canceled if Monroe agreed to be photographed shaking hands with him.

In Miller's testimony he answered the committee's questions about his association with political groups, and he gave his opinions on freedom of speech, Communist conspiracies, and figures such as Kazan and the poet Ezra Pound. At the end of his testimony Miller was asked about his attendance at a meeting of Communist writers a decade earlier. Miller admitted his presence but refused to give the names of others in attendance. He was warned that he would be in contempt of Congress for refusing to answer since he had chosen not to claim the Fifth Amendment protection against self-incrimination. He still refused and therefore was cited.

Miller was allowed a six-month visa to accompany Monroe to England, where she was to make a movie with Laurence Olivier while Miller oversaw production of the two-act version of *A View from the Bridge*. Miller returned to stand trial for contempt of Congress and was found guilty on two counts. His sentencing was deferred for an appeal, and in 1958 the U.S. Court of Appeals overturned his conviction. In 1957 his *Collected Plays* appeared.

Meanwhile, Miller had become completely engrossed in his marriage to Monroe. He worked on a few projects, but it was, he admits, an unproductive period for him since he devoted much of his time to the emotional support that he knew Monroe needed. After Monroe suffered a miscarriage, he revised a short story he had written, "The Misfits," into a screenplay for her. When Miller was in Nevada establishing residency for his divorce from Slattery, he had accompanied a group of cowboys who were rounding up mustangs to sell for dog food. The mustangs, too small to ride, were called "misfits." Miller created for Monroe the part of Roslyn, a dance-hall girl who identifies with the mustangs. Monroe and Miller's marriage was clearly faltering during the making of the movie. Her emotional insecurity, inconsistent work habits, and the untoward influence of Lee and Paula Strasberg, whose Actor's Studio Monroe had attended, caused an irreparable rift. Miller and Monroe divorced in early 1961, and a year later she was dead, apparently from an overdose of barbiturates.

Miller's first play in nine years, *After the Fall*, premiered with the new Lincoln Center Repertory Company in 1964. The play was a result of a concatenation of events for Miller since his marriage to Monroe ended. In 1962 Miller married Ingeborg Morath, a renowned photographer whom he had met on the set of *The Misfits*. Their daughter, Rebecca, was born in 1963, the same year Miller published a children's book, *Jane's Blanket*. Miller also had been thinking about Albert Camus's *The Fall* (1956), a novel about a man who was unable to forget that he had not tried to stop a girl from jumping to her death in a river. Miller was intrigued by the character's obsession and by his lack of moral responsibility. Miller had tackled the theme before in *All My Sons* and *The Crucible*, but he wanted to write a new play about this issue. Since the bombing of

Hiroshima, Miller also had been thinking about writing a play about the men who had created the bomb, including physicist J. Robert Oppenheimer. The creative process of the scientists whose noble intentions had inadvertently unleashed an awful power into the world fascinated him. Miller became intrigued by the question: "Why was one responsible if one had no evil intention?" He began drafting a verse play about Oppenheimer in which blame, guilt, and responsibility were major themes. Miller and Morath then took a trip to Austria and Germany, where Miller attended the Nazi trials that were then being held in Frankfurt, which he covered for the *New York Herald Tribune*. His experience in court solidified the formation of *After the Fall*, for he realized the theme of his play–the paradox of denial–was at the heart of Germany and the aftermath of the war. Thus, *After the Fall*, like *The Crucible*, is about how individuals and nations confront guilt, denial, and responsibility.

In *After the Fall* Miller returned to the expressionistic dramatic structure he had used in *Death of a Salesman*. The action of *After the Fall* occurs entirely in the mind, thoughts, and memory of the protagonist, Quentin. The form of these plays puts Miller at odds with his persistent critical reputation as a realistic playwright in the Ibsenesque tradition. The nonrealistic play, in which the conflicts are staged as occurring inside characters' heads, actually has been a dominant method in Miller's dramaturgy. American critics, in particular, have had difficulty perceiving Miller as a nonrealistic playwright.

Miller has said that the dramatic structure of *After the Fall* is based on psychoanalysis. He structured the scenes and the characters, who remain on the stage, to appear as almost free associations popping into Quentin's head. Quentin speaks to an unidentified Listener– a friend, perhaps, or an analyst–someone he is going to tell about a decision he must make. In this fashion he examines his entire life: his guilt and responsibility in his relationship with his parents, his two failed marriages to Louise and Maggie, and his doubts about marrying a third time to Holga. But Miller moves the play beyond Quentin's personal story and shows how guilt and responsibility also operate in history, particularly in the Holocaust and McCarthyism. The tower of a concentration camp dominates the set, designed by Mielziner, and indicates the guilt of the survivor. Similarly, Quentin confronts the guilt of betrayal when one of his friends, Mickey, modeled after Kazan, is subpoenaed to testify before the HUAC and tempted to betray his friends and colleagues.

Critical reaction to *After the Fall* was mixed. In addition to the critics' difficulty with the unconventional stage design, there was a chorus of negative reaction to the portrayal of Maggie, who was judged to resemble too closely Monroe, who had already become an iconic figure in American culture. Many critics focused on the personal elements and mostly ignored the theme and implications of the play, thus obscuring the fact that *After the Fall* is a major drama in Miller's canon. Miller believes that the play was bound to fail since it was produced so soon after Monroe's death. He praises the direction of Kazan, with whom Miller had partially reconciled, especially his casting of Jason Robards as Quentin and Barbara Loden as Maggie.

Despite the controversy, *After the Fall* played to consistently high attendance during its fifty-nine performances. Therefore, Miller was commissioned to write another play for the Lincoln Center Repertory. *After the Fall* is the first Miller play to blatantly tackle a Jewish subject, and he decided to address this topic again in *Incident at Vichy* (1964), which premiered only eleven months later. The roots of the play came from a psychiatrist friend of Miller's who had hidden in Vichy, France, during World War II. Miller combined this story with one of an old friend of Morath's, an Austrian prince who had suffered during the war because he refused to cooperate with the Nazis.

Incident at Vichy takes place in a room where men suspected of being Jews are detained before questioning; the interrogation determines either their release or further incarceration in a concentration camp. The characters discuss the fate that awaits them if they cannot prove their identity papers are valid. The play also depicts the characters' uncertainty about their detention: they are not completely sure why they have been arrested, in what building they are being detained, and whether racial laws are being applied. However, underlying their uncertainty is the real fear that everyone in the room has been detained because he is "Peruvian"–the euphemism for Jew. The prisoners are called individually into an adjacent room where their credentials are checked. However, the identity check is an examination not only of their papers but also of what, at that time, physically identified a Jew–whether he is circumcised.

Two of the more important characters in the play are the major, a Nazi officer assisting with the roundup, and the Gentile Austrian prince Von Berg. The major has been assigned to the examination of Jews in Vichy, a detail that he admits "takes a little getting used to." When two of the detainees attempt to escape down a hall, they encounter the major returning from a walk he took in order to escape the unpleasant proceedings. The major is drunk, and he begins a dramatic confrontation with Leduc, one of the escapees. The major drinks to create an oblivion that allows him to escape from, and fortifies him for, the unpleasant examinations of the detainees. More important, the stupor allows him to escape the truth about the larger meaning of what is being enacted in the room, in Vichy, and in all of Europe—events that are, he admits, inconceivable to him. The major believes that the war represents a dramatic shift in man's perception of his humanity, a crucial thematic focus of the play. He asks Leduc if there can be persons any more when there is no such thing as love and respect in a world at war. The major wants to maintain his dignity as a "man of honor," but his hunger to survive "others'" sadism is just as strong as any other man's—Gentile or Jew—so he does what he must in order to survive and loses his humanity in the process.

Von Berg is the most important character in the play, which depicts his growing awareness of his responsibility as an aristocrat, as a Gentile, and as a human being for the atrocities in Europe. Von Berg has lived the war years consumed in his aristocratic lifestyle; he has ignored his cousin's role in the purging of Jewish doctors in Vienna; he has left Austria rather than resist. By the end of the play he recognizes his own identification with Jews—a theme Miller first used in *Focus*. Von Berg's decisive action to give his pass, which frees him, to Leduc signifies the recognition of a moral hunger within himself to identify with Jews as human beings suffering persecution. Miller has said that Von Berg's act of sacrifice represents "the step from guilt to responsibility to action."

Incident at Vichy received a decidedly mixed critical reception, closing after ninety-nine performances. Then Miller broke with the governing board of Lincoln Center in a policy dispute; he felt that the company was not developing a true repertory theater similar to that in Europe. He published a collection of short stories, *I Don't Need You Any More*, in 1967, and then returned to Broadway in 1968 with his next play, *The Price*. Once again he was dramatizing conflicts he had explored in previous plays—including the struggle between two brothers—and the themes of personal responsibility and regret.

The Price is about two estranged brothers who meet in the attic of their deceased father's brownstone, which is being demolished, to settle on a price with an appraiser for its contents. Victor is a police officer who years earlier had given up his dream of becoming a scientist in order to care for his elderly, widowed father, who had apparently lost everything in the Depression; Victor's brother, Walter, is a successful surgeon who has forsaken the family years ago. During the course of the play both brothers, along with Victor's wife, battle over their regrets, frustrations, and responsibility for the choices they made years ago—the "price" they now realize they paid. At the climax of the play Victor blames Walter for not giving him the $500 he needed to finish school and earn his degree. When Walter insists that Victor could have abandoned their father and finished school regardless, Victor rejects that as impossible. Then Walter reveals the huge secret of the play: that the father had more than $4,000 in savings about which he never told Victor. Moreover, Victor admits he knew that his father was not completely destitute.

The Price explores how both brothers confront their responsibility for decisions they made years ago about their father and each other, and the dramatic tension of the play is how Victor and Walter finally account for those decisions. As in *All My Sons* and *Death of a Salesman*, *The Price* illustrates how one must ultimately face the consequences for past actions. Each brother brings to the attic his version of the past: Walter believes that he actually wished to lend Victor the money, and Victor believes he sacrificed his career to care for the father. Each man has his illusions and rationalizations shattered and ultimately comes to understand his personal responsibility, primarily through the probing of the comic character Gregory Solomon, the ninety-year-old appraiser, whose wisdom provokes the brothers to their awareness.

Perhaps the most intriguing personality in *The Price* is Victor and Walter's dead father—an absent character who looms quite large in the play. The memory of his past actions—especially his financial failure during the Depression—has haunted Victor and Walter all these years. The play takes place in an attic filled with the accumulation of furniture, clothes, and castoffs that have been stored for decades. The junk in the attic signifies the psychological detritus not only of the father but also of Walter and Victor. The ever wise Solomon, after bargaining for a price with the brothers, perceives that they can never completely exorcise the father's memory.

The Price was well received by the critics and audiences, running for 428 performances, the longest for a Miller play since *Death of a Salesman*. Although it seems an apolitical play, Miller has indicated that it is connected to the turbulent times in which it was produced. Perhaps the critical response was rooted in questioning America's responsibility in Vietnam in 1968. During the 1960s Miller was as engaging a political figure as during the McCarthy era. He actively protested against the Vietnam War, served as a delegate from Connecticut to the Democratic National Convention in 1968 (and again in 1972), and assumed the presidency of PEN, an organization dedicated to protecting the rights of artists and writers throughout the world. He also produced a book of reportage, *In Russia* (1969), with photographs by Morath.

In the 1970s Miller produced three plays that reflected his continuing interest in morality, politics, and the Depression. In 1972 he staged the offbeat *The Creation of the World and Other Business* at the Shubert Theatre in New York. The play is difficult to categorize. It is a seriocomic retelling of the story of Genesis that focuses particularly on Adam and Eve, Cain and Abel, and God and Lucifer. The play revolves around a debate between God and Lucifer about the nature of good and evil, using the biblical stories as illustrations and counterpoints. The overall effect was uneven, and the critical reaction was so negative that the production closed after twenty performances. Despite the bad notices, Miller remained committed to this play and wrote a musical version, *Up from Paradise,* which was produced at the University of Michigan in 1974.

In 1977 Miller published another book of reportage, *In the Country,* with photographs by Morath. In the same year, partially disgusted with Broadway critics, Miller premiered his next production, *The Archbishop's Ceiling,* for a limited run at the Kennedy Center in Washington, D.C., a location entirely fitting for the politically charged play. Miller details in the introduction to *The Archbishop's Ceiling* how he was moved to write the play after his 1970s experiences visiting Eastern European countries behind the Iron Curtain, where he found himself in living rooms that had almost certainly been bugged by the regimes. However, similar spying that had occurred in the United States in the 1970s also influenced Miller: the microphones in the White House, the Watergate break-in, and domestic espionage. Although bugging became the occasion for the play, power—on all its political, social, legal, personal, artistic, and moral levels—was the predominant theme.

The Archbishop's Ceiling takes places in an unnamed Eastern European country where daily life involves living in homes where the ceilings may have been electronically bugged. Miller illustrates the power that this surveillance gives to the state and the way citizens handle this power. The plot centers on the authorities' confiscation of the manuscript of Sigmund, the country's greatest writer, who is faced with jail or expulsion. Adrian, an American novelist, has come to investigate reports that Marcus, another author who is collaborating with the government, and Maya, a woman who has had relationships with all three writers, have compromised other writers in the bugged room where the play takes place, the former residence of the archbishop.

In his introduction to the published text Miller pointed to the metaphoric significance of the microphones planted alongside the angels on the ceiling: "What happens, in short, when people know they are—at least most probably, if not certainly—at all times talk-

Miller and Marilyn Monroe, to whom he was married from 1956 to 1961 (from Miller, Timebends: A Life, *1987)*

ing to Power, whether through a bug or a friend who is really an informer? Is it not something akin to accounting for oneself to a god? After all, most ideas of God see him as omnipresent, invisible, and condign in his judgments; the bug lacks only mercy and love to qualify, it is conscience shorn of moral distinctions." In the Iron Curtain country where the play takes place, God's power, as symbolized by the angels, has been replaced by political power.

The tension of the plot arises from exactly how each character contends with power in its many forms. Maya, Marcus, and Sigmund fear the clearly defined power of the state, but each responds in his or her own way. Maya, in particular, is the major focus of the conflicts, because she often connects not only to the power of the state but also to other powers—the power of emotions and the power of the writer. Maya has been involved intimately with Marcus, Adrian, and Sigmund, each of whom uses his manipulative power as a writer and as a man to create as suppressive a hold on Maya as the government.

Both Maya and Adrian are contending with political power—he as an American writer publicizing the truth about life behind the Iron Curtain, she as a possible collaborator with the regime. But as former lovers, they equally contend with the power of their emotional hold on each other. Their relationship is complicated further by Adrian's having used Maya as a character in his latest work.

Marcus has become a tool of political power. He has given parties to compromise writers for the state, and as Maya reveals, that is exactly what they are attempting this night. However, Marcus is a complicated character not entirely without sympathy. He has suffered past political persecution as a writer, having spent six years in a labor camp. Moreover, Maya is clear that Marcus has lost his creative power as a writer. However, Marcus knows that real moral power comes from the pen, and he forces political power against writers such as Sigmund, whose creative power, Marcus knows, is more forceful than the state's political power. When the play moves toward its climax in the return of Sigmund's manuscript, in Maya's revelation that the ceiling is bugged, and in Sigmund's decision not to leave his country in exile, each character is forced to confront the suffering and knowledge gained in dealing with political power.

Sigmund is the most crucial character at the end because he suffers in gaining knowledge of all the levels of power in the play. Most important, Sigmund becomes endowed with the power that is beyond politics and religion: moral power. Marcus ultimately recognizes Sigmund's great power as a writer and moral human being when he decides to stay and suffer the consequences of political power.

Although *The Archbishop's Ceiling* received mostly unfavorable reviews, many scholars have viewed it as marking a major new phase in Miller's work for the way the play creates both a reality and unreality for its characters. In 1978 *The Theater Essays of Arthur Miller* was published. During this period he also wrote two screenplays for television—*Fame*, a 1978 comedy for the Hallmark Hall of Fame, and *Playing for Time* (1980), the adaptation of Fania Fénelon's Holocaust memoir—and he produced another book of reportage, *Chinese Encounters* (1979), with photographs by Morath.

Miller returned to the Great Depression for the subject matter of his next work in 1980. In *The American Clock*, Miller chronicles his family's experiences during the 1920s and 1930s, creating the Baum family and combining their episodes with the traumatic events of other actual Americans whom Miller had read about in Studs Terkel's *Hard Times* (1970). The play premiered at the Dockside Theater in Charleston, South Carolina, in May 1980 at the Spoleto Festival and opened on Broadway the following fall to lukewarm reviews. It closed after twelve performances. Miller revamped the play for a 1986 London production, the same version that enjoyed a successful New York revival for the Signature Theater Company in 1997.

The form of *The American Clock* is one of the more spectacular in Miller's dramatic canon. The cast includes forty-six named characters, plus extras who in the revised version remain on the stage the entire time. The plot offers a kaleidoscope of individual stories of economic loss, political turmoil, and social upheaval caused by the Depression, including thinly disguised episodes from Miller's family experiences. The play shows how the individual stories are an integral part of the landscape of the entire American society. All of the action is punctuated by the music of the era, performed by a live band onstage and sung by the characters. Miller also wrote a song for the production. The overall effect is to show Americans' steely determination, innate sense of hope for recovery, and the promise of prosperity in the future.

During the 1980s Miller continued to be engaged in politics: supporting the Polish Solidarity movement, protesting Israel's West Bank settlements, and continuing to defend the rights of artists and writers under repressive governments such as Turkey and the Soviet Union. Miller's railing against the Tiananmen Square massacres was particularly relevant since he had directed an acclaimed version of *Death of a Salesman* in Beijing in 1983.

In 1981 the second volume of his *Collected Plays* was published. Miller also increasingly criticized the state of the American theater, particularly of Broadway. Miller saw the creeping commercialization of Broadway, where the musical was becoming the dominant form, as a condition that made it difficult for serious dramas to be produced and remain viable. During this decade Miller did not produce a new full-length play on Broadway and instead wrote pairs of one-acts. In 1982 *Elegy for a Lady* and *Some Kind of Love Story* appeared at the Long Wharf Theatre in New Haven, Connecticut, under the title *2 by A.M.*, later published in 1984 as *Two-Way Mirror*. In 1986 Miller published a second pair of one-act plays, *Clara* and *I Can't Remember Anything*, under the title *Danger: Memory!*, which subsequently premiered at the Mitzi E. Newhouse Theater of Lincoln Center the next year.

Despite Miller's criticism of the legitimate theater, revivals of his work achieved tremendous popularity on Broadway in the 1980s. In 1983 the two-act version

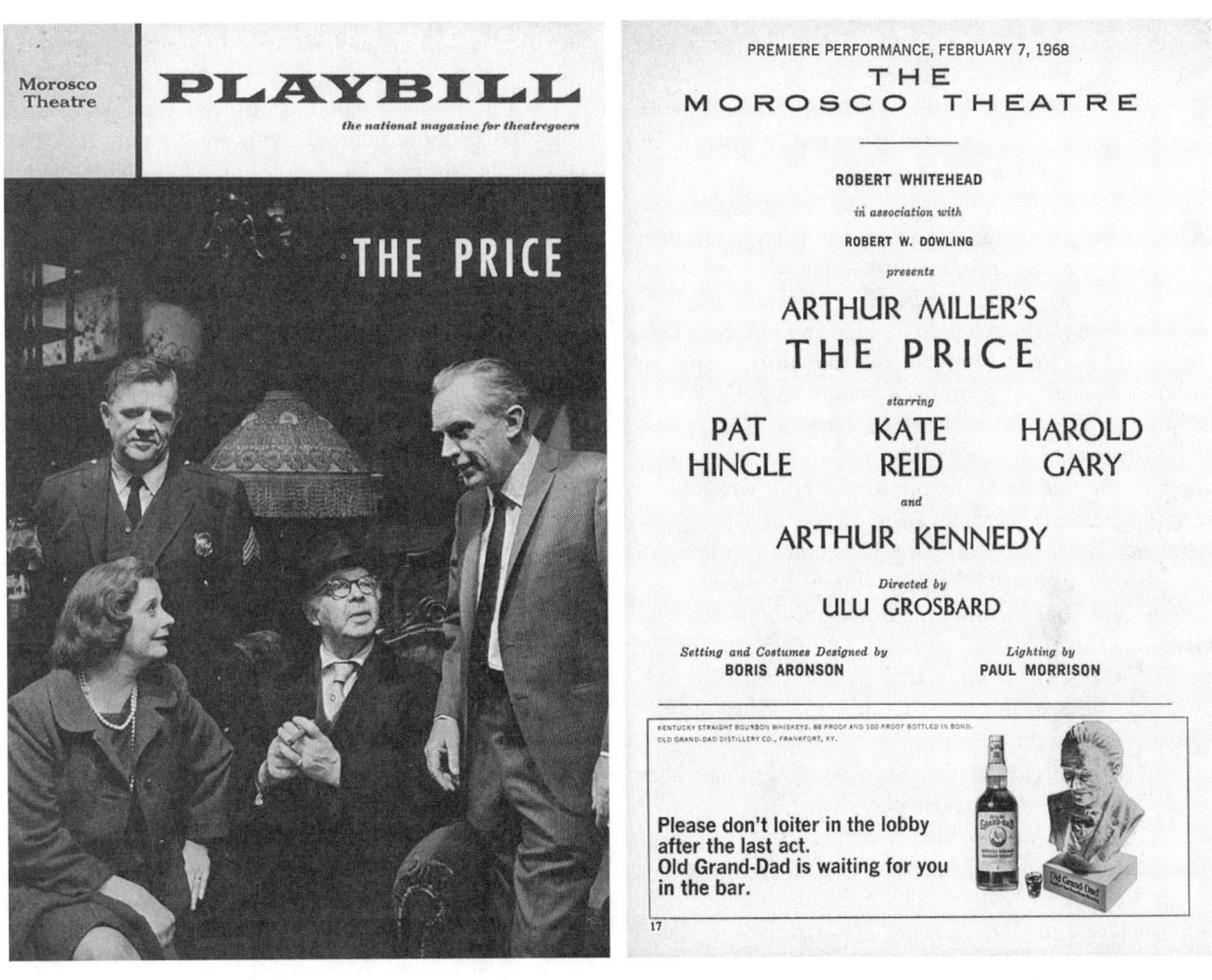

Program cover and title page for the original production of Miller's play about two estranged brothers settling their father's estate (Bruccoli Clark Layman Archives)

of *A View from the Bridge* played on Broadway for the first time to strong reviews, with Tony LoBianco receiving a Tony Award as Eddie Carbone. The 1984 revival of *Death of a Salesman* with Hoffman and Malkovich introduced the play to a new generation of audiences, and the critics rediscovered its importance as a classic American play. A year later, twenty-five million people watched the television version of this production. In 1987 a production of *All My Sons* received a Tony Award for Best Revival.

Miller received the Kennedy Center Honors for Lifetime Achievement in 1984. During this decade he also produced a book-length account of his direction of *Death of a Salesman* in China, *Salesman in Beijing* (1984), and wrote a screenplay version of *Some Kind of Love Story*, which was released as the movie *Everybody Wins* (1990). However, the capstone of his prose writing was the 1987 publication of his autobiography, *Timebends*, in which Miller challenges the conventional form of the biography by deconstructing chronological time and bending it across the sweep of his life experiences. Roger Shattuck, in a front-page *New York Times Book Review* article (8 November 1987), judged it "a work of genuine literary craftsmanship and social exploration."

The 1990s were a period of unparalleled creative activity for a playwright of Miller's age. He wrote three full-length plays, a one-act, a screenplay for *The Crucible*, and a novella, and he continued to write essays and political tracts while overseeing revivals of his work around the world. Miller's first full-length play of the decade, *The Ride Down Mt. Morgan* (1991), was the first Miller play not to premiere in the United States, because at the time Miller found American theater inhospitable to serious new dramas. After the London premiere, the American debut did not occur until the Williamstown Theatre Festival in Massachusetts in

1996. A production with Patrick Stewart ran Off-Broadway in the fall of 1998, and Stewart reprised his role in a Broadway production in 2000.

In *The Ride Down Mt. Morgan* Miller once again returned to the dramatic form of having the characters' crucial conflicts occur inside their heads, blurring even more the line between reality and unreality in the minds of the protagonists. Lyman Felt is an unabashed bigamist, a wealthy insurance executive who, ten years before the play begins, married a younger woman, Leah, without divorcing his older first wife, Theo. Moreover, he has unashamedly maintained ties with both families, shuttling between lives in New York City and upstate New York. When the play begins, Lyman has crashed his Porsche on Mount Morgan in a snowstorm in the middle of the night, and both wives have been inadvertently summoned to the hospital. Lyman's literal ride down the mountain—the euphemism for the car crash—stops his wild ride through his double life, forcing him to confront the tragic results when the wives meet in the waiting room. The entire action of the play takes place while Lyman is in bed; through flashbacks he is forced to confront the morality of having two wives and two lives.

Many critics have discussed how *The Ride Down Mt. Morgan* is a much trickier play than *Death of a Salesman* or *After the Fall* in discerning how the past and present occur inside a character's head. In her essay "From Loman to Lyman: The Salesman Forty Years On," included in *"The Salesman Has a Birthday": Essays Celebrating the Fiftieth Anniversary of Arthur Miller's Death of a Salesman* (2000), Susan C. W. Abbotson points out that while "the scenes which spring from Willy's mind are well signposted in *Salesman*, Miller makes it far harder to recognize any reality in *The Ride Down Mt. Morgan* . . . it is impossible to say for sure if any of the encounters take place anywhere other than in Lyman's mind." The nonrealistic staging of this unconventional play caused little controversy among critics and audiences in America, but audiences of the original London production had difficulty distinguishing between what was real and imaginary. Though Miller made this distinction clearer in the American productions, Abbotson questions further, "is Lyman's crash and hospitalization even real, or just the product of a guilty conscience?" She even suggests that perhaps his whole bigamous relationship is a figment of his imagination.

Miller's one-act play *The Last Yankee* was given a studio production in 1991, then revised and expanded in 1993 to premiere at the Manhattan Theatre Club. The play is set in a mental hospital, where two women are suffering from clinical depression. Patricia is married to Leroy Hamilton, the "last Yankee" of the title, who is descended from Alexander Hamilton and plies his trade as a carpenter, which she views as inadequate for survival in the modern world. The second woman, Karen, has similar anxieties; her husband, Frick, is a successful businessman, but his drive repulses her. The play is tightly structured, with conversations between the husbands in the waiting room, dialogue between the women in the ward, and discussion among all four, climaxing in the release of Patricia from the hospital and the inability of Karen to leave. Critics have viewed this play as offering a kind of redemption in Patricia's apparent recovery, but despair at Karen's continued inability to accept reality.

In *Broken Glass* (1994), Miller's first full-length play on Broadway since *The American Clock,* Miller again explores the subject of the Holocaust. *Broken Glass* takes place in Brooklyn in 1938, and its central concern is with the cause of Sylvia Gellburg's paralysis: her hysteria about the persecution of Jews in Germany after Kristallnacht. However, her condition is also symptomatic of an emotional and sexual paralysis between her and her husband, Phillip. Moreover, Miller connects the world of the European Jew at the beginning of the Holocaust to the Gellburgs' shattered world. The conflict with her husband and the persecution of the Jews literally and figuratively cripple Sylvia. Miller has stated that her paralysis also signifies the world's political paralysis at stopping the Holocaust.

The play is complicated by Phillip's identity as a Jew. He works as the head of the mortgage department at a large New York bank—the only Jew in such a position. At the same time, he separates himself from his identity as a Jew, bristling when his name is mistaken for "Goldberg" and even insisting his ancestors came from Finland. Phillip's denial of his Jewishness is, of course, markedly contrasted with Sylvia's powerful identification with the persecuted Jews in Nazi Germany.

The sexual conflicts of Sylvia and Phillip also complicate the action. Sylvia tells Dr. Hyman, who is treating her, that she and Phillip have not had sex in more than twenty years, since the birth of their son. Hyman is an important character, as the play details his unorthodox and not wholly professional treatment of Sylvia. Hyman becomes aware of Sylvia's sexual anxieties and uses his own sexual attraction in an attempt to cure her paralysis. Thus, Hyman acts as a sexual foil to Phillip, whose impotency symbolizes his own kind of paralysis.

The broken glass of the title is a crucial unifying image, with literal and figurative meanings. Of course, Sylvia's anxiety ostensibly refers to Kristallnacht—the night of glass—the literal smashing of the stores and synagogues in Germany in 1938 that began the Nazi pogrom against the Jews. Also, the broken-glass imagery suggests the breaking of the glass at a Jewish wed-

William Atherton and Joan Copeland in the 1980 New York production of
The American Clock *(Rivka Photos)*

ding ceremony, itself a reminder of historical Jewish loss: the destruction of the temple in Jerusalem. Sylvia and Phillip's marriage is clearly as shattered as glass, and the play ultimately depicts Phillip as the cause of Sylvia's paralysis and the destruction of their marriage. Indeed, Sylvia is frightened by Phillip. He is capable of Nazi-like violence, as the play shows when he and Sylvia discuss his impotency.

In *Broken Glass* Miller continually relates Sylvia's condition to the larger social themes. In one scene, Sylvia turns her attention to the newspapers scattered on her bed and repeats: "What is going to become of us?" and "What will become of us!" Of course, Sylvia's cry operates on two levels: she is literally referring to what will become of her, Hyman, and Phillip, but the "us" also refers to humankind and the paralysis of the entire world in the face of Hitler's ascendance. She screams, "But why don't they run out of the country! What is the matter with those people! Don't you understand . . . ? . . . This is an *emergency!* What if they kill those children! Where is Roosevelt! Where is England! Somebody should do something before they murder us all!"

Broken Glass was mostly well received, although some critics found it melodramatic. It ran for sixty-four performances. Miller received a Tony nomination for Best Play and an Olivier Award as Best Play of the Year for the London production. In 1995 Miller wrote the screenplay for the 1996 movie version of *The Crucible,* for which he received an Academy Award nomination. Also in 1996 a revised and expanded edition of *The Theater Essays of Arthur Miller* was published.

The Signature Theater Company in New York devoted its entire 1997–1998 season to producing Miller plays: *The American Clock, I Can't Remember Anything,* and *The Last Yankee.* For the final play of the season, Miller wrote a new full-length play, *Mr. Peters' Connections,* which starred Peter Falk. Miller once again uses the form of going "inside the head" of a character; however, this time he obliterates the thin line between reality and unreality, past and present, that he kept somewhat visible in previous plays. In this play the "connections" of the title are literally the synapses between the moments of memory in Mr. Peters's life; Miller explains in a preface to the published version that the play is "taking place inside Mr. Peters' mind, or at least on its threshold, from where it is still possible to glance back toward daylight life or forward into misty depths." Some characters are dead; others are alive. The play is set in a broken New York structure, and audiences are often unsure of where they are or how they got there. The whole play

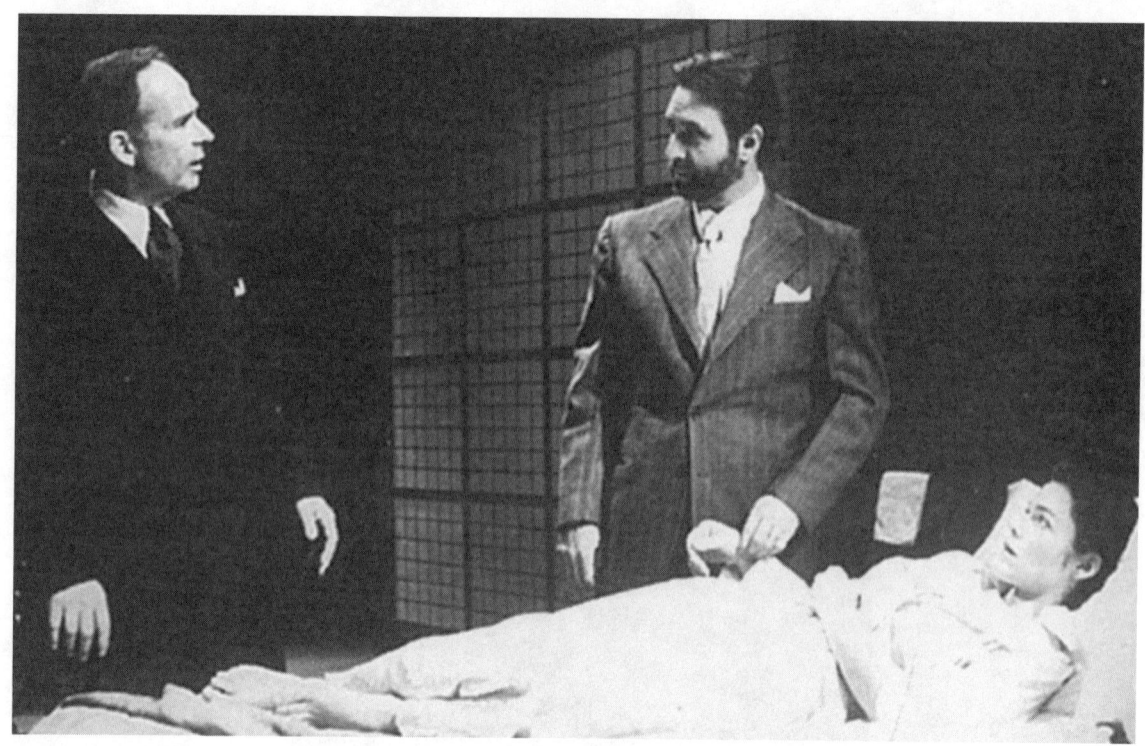

Ron Rifkin, Ron Silver, and Amy Irving in the 1994 Long Wharf Theatre production of Broken Glass *(photograph by T. Charles Erickson)*

involves Mr. Peters's searching for the plaintive, haunting "subject" of his life.

In 1995 Miller received the William Inge Theatre Festival Award for distinguished achievement in the American theater. On the occasion of his eightieth birthday that October, tributes were held at the National Theatre in London and Town Hall in New York. In 1998 Miller received the Lillian Gish Award for notable contribution to the arts. During this time, Miller's career has also undergone a reevaluation by literary critics. His plays have long been examined from the perspective of social criticism, realism, politics, and psychology, but later critics are analyzing his work from feminist and cross-cultural perspectives and are exploring their theatrical innovation and figurative language.

Miller celebrated his eighty-fifth birthday with the publication of *Echoes Down the Corridor,* a collection of his nontheater essays of the previous fifty years on subjects as diverse as growing up in Brooklyn, attending the University of Michigan, meeting Lucky Luciano in Sicily, attending the Russian Opera, walking across the Brooklyn Bridge, and directing *Death of a Salesman* in Beijing. Many of the essays cover Miller's extensive political views and activities. In 2001 Miller gave the annual Jefferson Lecture in Washington, D.C., and typically caused a stir with his controversial comments on the disputed election between Al Gore and George W. Bush. In November 2001 Miller received the Medal for Distinguished Contribution to American Literature at the National Book Awards. Broadway revivals of *The Crucible* and *The Man Who Had All the Luck* opened in 2002. His play, *Resurrection Blues,* premiered at the Guthrie Theater in Minneapolis in August 2002–evidence that Arthur Miller is continuing the pace that has made him one of the major figures of the American theater.

Interviews:

Ira Wolfert, "Arthur Miller, Playwright in Search of His Identity," *New York Herald Tribune,* 25 January 1953, IV: 3;

"Conversation at St. Clerans between Arthur Miller and John Huston," *Guardian* (25 February 1960): 6;

Barry Hyams, "A Theatre: Heart and Mind," *Theatre: The Annual of the Repertory Theater of Lincoln Center,* 1 (1964): 56–61;

Sheridan Morley, "Miller on Miller," *Theatre World,* 61 (March 1965): 4, 8;

Joseph Gruen, "Portrait of a Playwright at Fifty," *New York* (24 October 1965): 12–13;

Joan Barthel, "Arthur Miller Ponders *The Price,*" *New York Times,* 28 January 1968, II: 1, 5;

Ronald Hayman, "Arthur Miller," in his *Playback* (London: Davis-Poynter, 1973), pp. 7–22;

"Symposium: Playwriting in America: Joyce Carol Oates, Arthur Miller, Eric Bentley," *Yale Theater,* 4 (1973): 8–27;

Mel Gussow, "Arthur Miller Returns to Genesis for First Musical," *New York Times,* 17 April 1974, p. 37;

Albert Unger, "Arthur Miller Talks of His Holocaust Drama," *Christian Science Monitor,* 19 September 1980, p. 19;

James Atlas, "The Creative Journey of Arthur Miller Leads Back to Broadway and TV," *New York Times,* 28 September 1980, II: 1, 32;

Kevin Kelly, "Arthur Miller Emerges Again on Several Fronts," *Boston Globe,* 12 October 1980, pp. 81–82;

"Learning from a Performer: A Conversation with Arthur Miller," *Gamut,* 1 (1982): 9–23;

Jennifer Allen, "Miller's Tale," *New York* (24 January 1983): 33–37;

Christopher S. Wren, "Willy Loman Gets China Territory," *New York Times,* 7 May 1983, p. 13;

Richard Christiansen, "Arthur Miller's Verdict on Willy: He Has Elements of Nobility," *Chicago Tribune,* 15 January 1984, XIII: 19;

Gussow, "Arthur Miller: Stirred by Memory," *New York Times,* 1 February 1987, II: 1, 30;

Matthew C. Roudané, ed., *Conversations with Arthur Miller* (Jackson: University Press of Mississippi, 1987);

C. W. E. Bigsby, ed., *Arthur Miller and Company: Arthur Miller Talks about His Work in the Company of Actors, Designers, Directors, Reviewers, and Writers* (London: Methuen, 1990);

Janet Balakian, "A Conversation with Arthur Miller," *Michigan Quarterly Review,* 29 (Spring 1990): 158–170;

Balakian, "An Interview with Arthur Miller," *Studies in American Drama, 1945–Present,* 6 (1991): 29–47;

Matt Wolf, "An Exile of Sorts Finds a Welcome," *New York Times,* 13 October 1991, p. H6;

James Kaplan, "Miller's Crossing," *Vanity Fair* (November 1991): 218–221, 241–248;

Steven R. Centola, *Arthur Miller in Conversation* (Dallas: Northouse & Northouse, 1993);

Robert Simonson, "Values, Old and New: Arthur Miller and John Tillinger on *The Last Yankee,*" *Theater Week* (18–24 January 1993): 13–18;

Douglas Century, "Miller's Tale of 'Tribalism': The Playwright Returns to His Roots," *Forward* (22 April 1994): 1, 10;

Carol Strickland, "Arthur Miller's Latest Message to Humanity," *Christian Science Monitor,* 26 April 1994, p. 12;

Angela Lambert, "An Intellect at Ease," *Independent* (2 August 1994): 17, 19;

David Nathan, "Loman's Land," *Jewish Chronicle* (5 August 1994): 25;

Susan Cheever, "The One Thing That Keeps Us from Chaos," *New Choices for Retirement Living* (October 1994): 22–25;

Centola, "*The Last Yankee:* An Interview with Arthur Miller," *American Drama,* 5 (Fall 1995): 78–98;

Michael Ratcliffe, "Miller's Crossing," *Observer Review* (15 October 1995): 7;

Gussow, "A Rock of the Modern Age, Arthur Miller Is Everywhere," *New York Times,* 30 November 1996, pp. 17, 19;

Peter Applebome, "Present at the Birth of a Salesman," *New York Times,* 29 January 1999, pp. 1, 3;

Douglas Feiden, "Miller's Time," *Daily News,* 11 November 1999, pp. 56–57;

William R. Ferris, "Morality and the Public Role of the Artist," *Humanities,* 22 (March–April 2001): 4–11.

Bibliographies:

Martha Eissenstat, "Arthur Miller; A Bibliography," *Modern Drama,* 5 (May 1962): 93–106;

Harriet Ungar, "The Writings of and about Arthur Miller: A Check List 1936–1967," *Bulletin of the New York Public Library,* 74 (February 1970): 107–134;

Tetsumaro Hayashi, *An Index to Arthur Miller Criticism,* second edition (Metuchen, N.J.: Scarecrow Press, 1976);

George H. Jensen, *Arthur Miller: A Bibliographical Checklist* (Columbia, S.C.: Faust, 1976);

John H. Ferres, *Arthur Miller: A Reference Guide* (Boston: G. K. Hall, 1979);

Hayashi, *Arthur Miller and Tennessee Williams, Research Opportunities and Dissertation Abstracts* (Jefferson, N.C. & London: McFarland, 1983);

Christopher Bigsby, *File on Miller* (London: Methuen, 1988),

Stefani Koorey, *Arthur Miller's Life and Literature: An Annotated and Comprehensive Guide* (Lanham, Md.: Scarecrow Press, 2000).

References:

Susan C. W. Abbotson, "Issues of Identity in *Broken Glass:* A Humanist Response to a Postmodern World," *Journal of American Drama and Theatre,* 11 (Winter 1999): 67–80;

Abbotson, *Student Companion to Arthur Miller* (Westport, Conn.: Greenwood Press, 2000);

I. Altena and A. M. Aylwin, *Notes on Arthur Miller's Death of a Salesman* (London: Eyre Methuen, 1976);

Barclay Bates, "The Lost Past in *Death of a Salesman*," *Modern Drama*, 11 (1968): 164–172;

Santosh K. Bhatia, *Arthur Miller: Social Drama as Tragedy* (New York: Humanities Press, 1985);

C. W. E. Bigsby, *A Critical Introduction to Twentieth-Century American Drama*, volume 2: *Tennessee Williams, Arthur Miller, Edward Albee* (Cambridge: Cambridge University Press, 1984);

Bigsby, ed., *The Cambridge Companion to Arthur Miller* (Cambridge & New York: Cambridge University Press, 1997);

Bigsby, ed., *Modern American Drama, 1945–1990* (Cambridge & New York: Cambridge University Press, 1992), pp. 72–125;

Harold Bloom, ed., *Arthur Miller* (New York: Chelsea House, 1987);

Bloom, ed., *Arthur Miller: Death of a Salesman* (New York: Chelsea House, 1988);

Bloom, ed., *Arthur Miller's All My Sons* (New York: Chelsea House, 1988);

Bloom, ed., *The Crucible: Modern Critical Interpretations* (New York: Chelsea House, 1999);

Bloom, ed., *Modern Critical Views: Arthur Miller* (New York: Chelsea House, 1987);

Bloom, ed., *Willy Loman* (New York: Chelsea House, 1991);

Jean-Marie Bonnet, "Society vs. the Individual in Arthur Miller's *The Crucible*," *English Studies*, 63 (1982): 32–36;

Enoch Brater, "Ethnics and Ethnicity in the Plays of Arthur Miller," in *From Hester Street to Hollywood*, edited by Sarah Blacher Cohen (Bloomington: Indiana University Press, 1983), pp. 123–136;

Richard T. Brucher, "Willy Loman and *The Soul of a New Machine*: Technology and the Common Man," *Journal of American Studies*, 17 (1983): 325–336;

Neil Carson, *Arthur Miller* (New York: St. Martin's Press, 1982);

Steven R. Centola, ed., *The Achievement of Arthur Miller: New Essays* (Dallas: Contemporary Research, 1995);

Harold Clurman, "Director's Notes: *Incident at Vichy*," *Tulane Drama Review*, 9 (Summer 1965): 77–90;

Robert Corrigan, ed., *Arthur Miller: A Collection of Critical Essays* (Englewood Cliffs, N.J.: Prentice-Hall, 1969);

Donald P. Costello, "Arthur Miller's Circles of Responsibility: *A View from the Bridge* and Beyond," *Modern Drama*, 36 (1993): 443–453;

Gordon W. Couchman, "Arthur Miller's Tragedy of Babbit," *Educational Theatre Journal*, 7 (1955): 206–211;

John D. Engle, "The Metaphor of Law in *After the Fall*," *Notes on Contemporary Literature*, 9 (1979): 11–12;

Richard I. Evans, *Psychology and Arthur Miller* (New York: Dutton, 1969);

John H. Ferres, ed., *Twentieth Century Interpretations of The Crucible* (Englewood Cliffs, N.J.: Prentice-Hall, 1972);

Philip Gelb, "*Death of a Salesman*: A Symposium," *Tulane Drama Review*, 2 (1958): 63–69;

Alice Griffin, *Understanding Arthur Miller* (Columbia: University of South Carolina Press, 1996);

Leah Hadomi, "Fantasy and Reality: Dramatic Rhythm in *Death of A Salesman*," *Modern Drama*, 31 (1988): 157–174;

Karl Harshburger, *The Burning Jungle: An Analysis of Arthur Miller's Death of a Salesman* (Washington, D.C.: University Press of America, 1979);

Gary P. Hendrickson, "The Last Analogy: Arthur Miller's Witches and America's Domestic Communists," *Midwest Quarterly*, 33 (1992): 447–456;

Edward Isser, "Arthur Miller and the Holocaust," *Essays in Theatre*, 10 (1992): 155–164;

Walter Kerr, *Thirty Plays Hath November: Pain and Pleasure in the Contemporary Theater* (New York: Simon & Schuster, 1969), pp. 214–220;

Helen Wickam Koon, ed., *Twentieth Century Interpretations of Death of a Salesman: A Collection of Critical Essays* (Englewood Cliffs, N.J.: Prentice-Hall, 1983);

Stephen Marino, "Arthur Miller's 'Weight of Truth,'" *Modern Drama*, 38 (Winter 1995): 488–495;

Marino, "Religious Language in Arthur Miller's *All My Sons*," *Journal of Imagism*, 3 (Fall 1998): 9–28;

Marino, ed., *"The Salesman Has a Birthday": Essays Celebrating the Fiftieth Anniversary of Arthur Miller's Death of a Salesman* (Lanham, Md.: University of America Press, 2000);

Robert A. Martin, "Arthur Miller: Public Issues, Private Tensions," *Studies in the Literary Imagination*, 21 (1988): 97–106;

Martin, ed., *Arthur Miller: New Perspectives* (Englewood Cliffs, N.J.: Prentice-Hall, 1982);

James J. Martine, *The Crucible: Politics, Property, and Pretense* (New York: Twayne, 1993);

Martine, ed., *Critical Essays on Arthur Miller* (Boston: G. K. Hall, 1979);

Walter J. Meserve, ed., *The Merrill Studies in Death of a Salesman: A Collection of Critical Essays* (Columbus, Ohio: Merrill, 1972);

Edmund S. Morgan, "Arthur Miller's *The Crucible* and the Salem Witch Trials: A Historian's View," in *The Golden Hind, Papers in Literature and History, 1650–1800*, edited by John M. Wallace (Berkeley: University of California Press, 1985), pp. 171–186;

Leonard Moss, *Arthur Miller*, second edition (New York: Twayne, 1980);

Brenda Murphy, "Arthur Miller: Revisioning Realism," in *Realism and the American Dramatic Tradition*, edited by William W. Demastes (Tuscaloosa: University of Alabama Press, 1996), pp. 189–202;

Murphy, *Miller: Death of a Salesman* (Cambridge: Cambridge University Press, 1995);

Murphy and Abbotson, *Understanding Death of a Salesman* (Westport, Conn.: Greenwood Press, 1999);

Terry Otten, *The Temptation of Innocence in the Dramas of Arthur Miller* (Columbia: University of Missouri Press, 2002);

N. Bhaskara Panikkar, *Individual Morality and Social Happiness in Arthur Miller* (Atlantic Highlands, N.J.: Humanities Press, 1982);

Henry Popkin, "Arthur Miller: The Strange Encounter," *Sewanee Review*, 68 (1960): 34–60;

James A. Robinson, "*All My Sons* and Paternal Authority," *Journal of American Drama and Theatre*, 2 (Winter 1990): 38–54;

Matthew C. Roudané, ed., *Approaches to Teaching Miller's Death of a Salesman* (New York: Modern Language Association, 1995);

David Savran, *Communists, Cowboys, and Queers: The Politics of Masculinity in the Work of Arthur Miller and Tennessee Williams* (Minneapolis: University of Minnesota Press, 1992);

Wendy Schissel, "Re(dis)covering the Witches in Arthur Miller's *The Crucible*, A Feminist Reading," *Modern Drama*, 37 (1994): 461–473;

June Schlueter, "Power Play: Arthur Miller's *The Archbishop's Ceiling*," *CEA Critic*, 49 (1986-1987): 134–138;

Schlueter, ed., *Feminist Readings of Modern American Drama* (London & Toronto: Associated University Presses, 1989);

Schlueter and James K. Flanagan, eds., *Arthur Miller* (New York: Ungar, 1987);

John S. Shockley, "*Death of a Salesman* and American Leadership: Life Imitates Art," *Journal of American Culture*, 17 (Summer 1994): 49–56;

Gerald Weales, ed., *Arthur Miller, Death of a Salesman: Text and Criticism* (New York: Viking, 1967);

Weales, ed., *The Crucible: Text and Criticism* (New York: Viking, 1971);

Dennis Welland, *Miller: The Playwright*, second edition (New York: Methuen, 1983);

Arvin R. Wells, "The Living and the Dead in *All My Sons*," *Modern Drama*, 7 (1964): 46–51;

Sidney H. White, *Guide to Arthur Miller* (Columbus, Ohio: Merrill, 1970);

William Wiegand, "Arthur Miller and the Man Who Knows," *Western Review*, 21 (1956): 85–103.

Papers:

Collections of Arthur Miller's papers can be found at the American Academy of Arts and Letters, New York; the Museum of Television and Radio, New York; the Billy Rose Theatre Collection, New York Public Library for the Performing Arts; the University of Michigan, Ann Arbor; the Harry Ransom Humanities Research Center, University of Texas, Austin; and at the Viking Press in New York.

Marsha Norman

(21 September 1947 -   )

Pamela Monaco
Mississippi Valley State University

See also the Norman entry in *DLB Yearbook: 1984.*

PLAY PRODUCTIONS: *Getting Out,* Louisville, Ky., Actors Theatre of Louisville, 3 November 1977; Los Angeles, Mark Taper Forum, 6 February 1978; New York, Phoenix Theatre, 19 October 1978; London, Emlyn Williams Theatre, 15 April 1989;

Third and Oak, Louisville, Ky., Actors Theatre of Louisville, 22 March 1978–comprises *The Laundromat* and *The Pool Hall;*

Circus Valentine, Louisville, Ky., Actors Theatre of Louisville, 1 February 1979;

The Holdup, Louisville, Ky., Actors Theatre of Louisville, 15 August 1980; Saratoga, N.Y., Circle Repertory Company, summer 1982; San Francisco, American Conservatory Theatre, 12 April 1983;

'night, Mother [staged reading], New York, Circle Repertory Theatre, November 1981; Cambridge, Mass., American Repertory Theatre, 10 December 1982; New York, John Golden Theatre, 31 March 1983; London, Hampstead Theatre, 4 March 1985;

Traveler in the Dark, Cambridge, Mass., American Repertory Theatre, 2 February 1984; Los Angeles, Mark Taper Forum, 24 January 1985; New York, York Theatre Company, 1990;

Sarah and Abraham, Louisville, Ky., Actors Theatre of Louisville, 19 March 1988; New Brunswick, N.J., George Street Playhouse, 7 February 1992;

The Secret Garden, libretto by Norman, music by Lucy Simon, adapted from Frances Hodgson Burnett's novel, Norfolk, Virginia Stage Company, 1990; New York, St. James Theatre, 25 April 1991;

D. Boone, Louisville, Ky., Actors Theatre of Louisville, 26 February 1992;

The Red Shoes, New York, Gershwin Theatre, 16 December 1993;

Lunch with Lynn, New York, Ensemble Studio Theatre, 1994;

Marsha Norman, 1991 (photograph © Susan Johann)

Trudy Blue, Louisville, Ky., Actors Theatre of Louisville, 19 March 1995; New York, MCC Theater, 2 December 1999;

140, in *Love's Fire,* with plays by Eric Bogosian, William Finn, John Guare, Tony Kushner, Ntozake Shange, and Wendy Wasserstein, Minneapolis, Guthrie Theater Lab, 1 January 1998; London,

Barbican Center, 1998; New York, Joseph Papp Public Theater, 19 June 1998;

RCA, in *Fit to Print,* Sag Harbor, N.Y., Bay Street Theatre, August 1999;

Sisters, Sacramento, Cal., Broadway Playhouse, 7 November 1999.

BOOKS: *The Jumbo Jelly Bean Journal* (Louisville, Ky.: Courier-Journal/Louisville Times, 1975);

Getting Out (Garden City, N.Y.: Doubleday, 1979);

Third and Oak–The Laundromat (New York: Dramatists Play Service, 1980);

'night, Mother (New York: Hill & Wang, 1983; London: Faber & Faber, 1984);

Third and Oak–The Pool Hall (New York: Dramatists Play Service, 1987);

The Holdup (New York: Dramatists Play Service, 1987);

The Fortune Teller (New York: Random House, 1987; London: Collins, 1988);

The Secret Garden (New York: Theatre Communications Group, 1992; London: S. French, 1993).

Collections: *Four Plays* (New York: Theatre Communications Group, 1988)–comprises *Getting Out, Third and Oak, The Holdup,* and *Traveler in the Dark;*

Collected Plays (Lyme, N.H.: Smith & Kraus, 1997)–comprises *Loving Daniel Boone, Sarah and Abraham, Getting Out, Third and Oak, Traveler in the Dark, Circus Valentine,* and *The Holdup.*

PRODUCED SCRIPTS: *It's the Willingness,* television, PBS, 1978;

"In Trouble at Fifteen," television, *Skag,* NBC, 1980;

The Laundromat, television, HBO, 1 April 1985;

'night, Mother, motion picture, Universal, 12 September 1986;

Third and Oak: The Pool Hall, television, A&E, 1989;

Face of a Stranger, based on Mary Stuart's article "My Shadow," television, CBS, 29 December 1991;

A Cooler Climate, adapted from Zena Collier's novel, television, Showtime, 22 August 1999;

The Audrey Hepburn Story, television, ABC, 27 March 2000;

Custody of the Heart, adapted from Barbara Delinsky's book, television, Lifetime, 2000.

OTHER: *Trudy Blue,* in *Humana Festival '95: The Complete Plays,* edited by Marisa Smith (Newbury, Vt.: Smith & Kraus, 1995).

SELECTED PERIODICAL PUBLICATIONS–UNCOLLECTED: "Why Do Good Men Suffer?" *Kentucky English Bulletin,* 13 (Spring 1964): 12–16;

"How Can One Man Do So Much? And Look So Good? A Meditation on a Mystery," *Vogue* (February 1984): 356–358;

"Articles of Faith: A Conversation with Lillian Hellman," *American Theatre,* 1 (May 1984): 10–15;

"Lillian Hellman's Gift to a Young Playwright," *New York Times* (26 August 1984): II: 1+;

"Life without Excellence Doesn't Go Anywhere, It Just Wanders Around," *Ms.* (January 1985): 84+;

"Writing Plays Is an Act of Faith," *New York Times* (23 June 1985): II: 1+;

"Ten Golden Rules for Playwrights," *Writer* (September 1985): 13+;

"TV Families," *Ms.* (July/August 1987): 38+;

"Why Do We Need New Plays? And Other Difficult Questions," *Dramatists Guild Quarterly,* 24 (Winter 1987): 18+.

Marsha Norman's first published essay, "Why Do Good Men Suffer?" (1964), written while she was in high school, was awarded first place in a local writing contest and subsequently published in the *Kentucky English Bulletin.* This early essay about Job suggests Norman's concern with the suffering of humans and an interest in philosophical issues and in man's struggles with faith and independence, themes she continues to develop in her plays. Yet, despite her talent and interest in writing, Norman never considered a career as a playwright, for she found few role models for such a career choice. She told Elizabeth Stone in 1983: "As a girl growing up in Kentucky, I had no models, no one like I am today. One of the great joys to me about my success is that no girl who grows up in Kentucky ever has to wonder about that again." Since the beginning of her playwriting career in 1977 with the production of *Getting Out* by the Actors Theatre of Louisville (ATL), Norman has become one of the predominant female voices in contemporary American theater. Her rise from regional theater typifies the experience of many current playwrights, but her themes and concerns with bringing to the stage the voices of the unheard or overlooked in American society are distinctly her own. Her later predilection for musical theater reflects the powerful role economics plays in the offerings of contemporary theater, yet even her choice of topics suggests her refusal to cater completely to modern tastes.

Norman was born Marsha Williams on 21 September 1947 to Billie and Bertha Williams, who raised their four children in a fundamentalist Methodist home in the suburbs of Louisville, Kentucky. Billie Williams sold insurance before changing to a career in real estate, while Norman's mother stayed at home. Because of the tight rein the parents kept on the children's activities, Norman had few friends, finding companionship instead through her interests in reading and music and in her imaginary

Susan Kingsley and Lynn Cohen in the 1977 Actors Theatre of Louisville production of Getting Out *(photograph by David S. Talbott)*

friend, Bettering. Her musical gifts were such that she considered studying music at Juilliard, but she accepted instead a scholarship to study philosophy at Agnes Scott College, a private women's college outside Atlanta. After graduation in 1969, she married Michael Norman and returned to Louisville to embark on a teaching career, first at Kentucky Central State Hospital, working with children with problems. In 1971 she received a master's degree in education from the University of Louisville, but by 1972 she had turned to teaching movie classes for the Kentucky Arts Commission. While at the commission, Norman made movies with children, worked to bring artists into classrooms, and spent her summers studying in New York at the Center for Understanding Media. Concurrently, she wrote book reviews for the *Louisville Times*, created a Sunday newspaper supplement for children called *The Jellybean Journal*, and wrote for the remedial-reading program produced by Kentucky Educational Television. She and Michael Norman divorced in 1974.

Jon Jory, then the artistic director of the ATL, was instrumental in cultivating Norman as a playwright. In 1977 he commissioned Norman to write a play for ATL, requesting that it be a play about a social issue and suggesting the topic of busing in Louisville. Norman wrote instead *Getting Out,* a play that derived in part from her experiences teaching disturbed children; she told *Contemporary Authors* (1994): "there was one girl in particular, a 13-year-old, who was absolutely terrifying. She's the kind of kid you would not for your life be locked up in a room with for 10 minutes." This girl inspired Norman's creation of Arlie, the violent, rebellious youth who becomes Arlene Holsclaw, a parolee who must adjust to life and freedom after spending eight years in prison for robbery, kidnapping, and manslaughter. The play takes place during Arlene's first twenty-four hours of freedom and utilizes a type of split protagonist by representing Arlene's past through Arlie, the uncontrollable younger self who committed the crimes that landed Arlene in jail. To illustrate the two sides of the character's personality, Norman uses two actresses on the stage simultaneously.

Arlie is a foulmouthed, violent child. Her first monologue describes killing frogs by throwing them on the street for cars to run over while tormenting a neighboring child, a time she recalls as having the most fun in her life. Arlie grew up with a disinterested mother and incestuous father who silenced her with threats. Once in prison, Arlie terrorizes all until she is placed in solitary confinement. Her transformation comes through the caring of the chaplain, who gives her a Bible inscribed with her full name and assures her that she can change: "Arlie was my hateful self and she was hurtin me and God would find some way to take her away." When the chaplain is transferred, Arlie suffers a nervous breakdown and stabs herself with a fork in an attempt to kill the delinquent part of herself.

Freed from prison, Arlene discovers the challenges in "getting out." Initially keeping Arlie at bay, Arlene confronts three people from her past who taunt her: her mother; her former pimp, who tries to lure her back into her old life; and the prison guard who has brought her home but is interested only in seducing her. Only a former-convict neighbor seems to offer friendship without an expectation of payback. Arlene soon discovers that "getting out" means negotiating a release from the psychological prisons that curtail personal freedom. Arlene's transformation develops as she learns to use speech instead of violence as a way to assert herself and through her recognition that Arlie is a necessary part of her. The play ends with the two speaking together as they recall a memory.

The play premiered at the ATL in November 1977 for 12 performances as part of a "Festival of New American Plays" and won high praise from local critics. Norman was named playwright in residence for the 1978–1979 season at ATL as word of this startling first work spread. In February 1978, for 54 performances, the Mark Taper Forum featured *Getting Out* as part of its "New Theatre For Now" series, and then in October the Phoenix Theatre on Broadway presented it with many of the original cast members and director Jory. The play was revived in May 1979 for the Off-Broadway Theatre De Lys for a run of 237 performances. The American Theatre Critics Association voted it best new regional play, and Norman won the John Gassner New Playwright Award (1979), the Outer Critics Circle Award (1979), the first George Oppenheimer-Newsday Playwright Award (1979), a National Endowment for the Arts grant (1978), and a grant from the Rockefeller Foundation (1979) that funded her playwright-in-residence position at the Mark Taper Forum in 1979 and 1980. *Getting Out* was made into a television movie in 1994, with a screenplay by Eugene Corr and Ruth Shapiro and starring Rebecca De Mornay.

The New York critics lavished praise on the new play and the new playwright. Writing for *Newsweek* (28 May 1979), Jack Kroll called it "exhilarating with the energy of truth, of compassion, of empathy, of a sincerity that becomes luminous and exciting." Others praised it for its energy, its structure, its language, and the almost documentary style of the play that reserves judgment and does not resort to maudlin appeals. Others, however, complained that the flashback technique was hackneyed, poorly written, unmoving, and repetitive at times. Although some praised the play for its sociological examination, others complained that the writing was awkward and the characters clichéd. Clive Barnes, in the *New York Post* (16 May 1979), found the play technically and emotionally impressive, although he considered the ending disappointing. Nonetheless, he declared that "Miss Norman can write of people and scenes with the solemn accuracy of a recording angel, and she has a spirit and humor that is going to carry her far."

Norman's debut play includes themes and devices that recur throughout her dramatic canon. Norman told Mel Gussow in 1983 that she tries to give voice to the unheard in society, "making visual people that are rarely seen and never heard." Her characters are generally ordinary people who face moments of crisis; her plays, she says, "explore life at its most basic level." Generally, the people of whom she writes are women who have been silenced through abuse, social conditions, or family structure. Arlene and many of Norman's other protagonists find their voices in their quests for self-definition and autonomy. The dilemma often faced is the desire for autonomy as the characters also seek connection within the family. Arlene, for example, seeks to change her relationship with her mother and reclaim her son as she struggles to begin her life anew. Although the protagonists are not always successful, they do confront the family specter that has haunted them. Of primary interest is the familial bond between mother and daughter.

The success of *Getting Out* convinced Norman to continue to write for the theater. While playwright in residence at ATL, she wrote *Third and Oak* (1978), which consists of two one-act plays, *The Laundromat* and *The Pool Hall*. Each illustrates the minimalist qualities of Norman's writing: one setting, small casts, and a limited time period. In *The Laundromat* two women, Alberta and DeeDee, meet at three in the morning as they wash piles of clothes that reveal their differences. Alberta, a matronly woman from an affluent neighborhood, comes in with her clothes neatly folded and with the correct change and amount of laundry detergent. She is reserved and restrained. DeeDee, young enough to be Alberta's daughter, is talkative, brash, and of a different social class. Her clothes spill out as easily as her talk. In the time it takes to wash a load of laundry, audiences learn that Alberta is a lonely widow who has come to finally wash her dead husband's clothes. Alberta poignantly expresses her inability to let go: "I found our beach ball when I cleaned out the basement. I can't let the air out of it. It's his breath in there." DeeDee is just as lonely in her marriage to a man who has taken up with another woman. Leslie Kane notes that Norman develops the play through the use of two types of silences: the reserved character who will not speak about feelings, and the loquacious character who uses speech as a way to avoid painful issues. By the end of the play these two dissimilar women share their mutual dread of being alone, and in so doing each begins the process of letting go, of a dead spouse or a dead marriage, although the ambiguity of the ending does not allow audiences to know how successful the women will be. As always, Norman stresses the necessity of confronting painful truths if self-definition and freedom from confinement are to be achieved. In a 1985 interview with Beth Ungar, Norman called this play a "tribute to those encounters between strangers that can be so meaningful, that can make a big difference in the way you live. There are things a stranger can tell you that you will never listen to from somebody you know."

The Pool Hall takes place in a poolroom in a run-down building in Louisville. The elderly owner, Willie, has one customer, a local disc jockey named Shooter who is the son of one of Willie's old friends, a pool hustler who committed suicide. Shooter is married to the daughter of another of Willie's good friends. Willie functions as a surrogate father, although not just for an hour but for a lifetime. Each is unwilling to admit the deep emotional bonds that tie them together: Willie offers advice and friendship to Shooter as he tries to keep the younger man honest and happy, while Shooter, leery that Willie will,

Program cover and title page for the 1983 New York production of the play for which Norman won a Pulitzer Prize (Bruccoli Clark Layman Archives)

like so many others, leave him, does not allow Willie to get too close.

Third and Oak was a success when it played for twenty-six performances during the 1978 season at ATL. The two plays function as parallel conversations that work well as character studies. Each play can stand alone, despite the gratuitous link Norman adds by having Shooter and DeeDee appear in both. Of the two, The Laundromat is the stronger play, as evidenced by its frequent solo productions around the country. At least part of the difference in popularity may be attributed to the fact that The Laundromat develops themes involving women. None of Norman's plays featuring male protagonists has been as successful as those written about women. Critics have often found Norman's male-centered plays thin and underdeveloped. Third and Oak is also one of only two Norman plays that is color specific with respect to the actors. Shooter and Willie are African American men, and part of The Pool Hall revolves around Shooter's flirtation with DeeDee, a white woman. Race is briefly brought up in The Laundromat, but in neither play is the hinted conflict developed adequately.

Each play was made separately into a movie. In April 1985 HBO premiered The Laundromat, directed by Robert Altman and starring Carol Burnett and Amy Madigan. In November 1989 Arts and Entertainment network showed Third and Oak: The Pool Hall, starring James Earl Jones and Mario Van Peebles, as the first of the series American Playwrights Theatre: The One-Acts. As with the other movie versions of her plays, neither was overly successful. Indeed, the traits that contribute to Norman's success as a playwright—her focus on language over stage movement, action, or scene changes, and her subtle development of character—do not work as well in a medium devoted to short attention spans and glitzy special effects. Norman acknowledges the need for different media, however, and knows that movies and television will reach far more people than theater and more effectively reach the very people she writes about.

In November 1978 Norman married Dann C. Byck Jr., of the Byck department store chain, a founding member of the ATL who later served as a producer for 'night, Mother (1981). As successful as Third and Oak was for ATL, Norman's next play, Circus Valentine, was poorly received and ran for only eleven performances in February 1979. Norman called this event the first disaster of her writing life. The play tells the story of a failing circus family who travel from town to town to set up their withering act in shopping-center parking lots. The generational conflict common to Norman's plays is present in the desire of daughter Trina Valentine to attempt the triple somersault that was the trademark of her aunt, an action the family opposes. For the first time, the cast includes more than three characters and requires multiple set changes, but the issues of hopelessness and confinement persist. The focal point of the play is the issue of the offstage Siamese twins, the star attraction of the circus, who wish to be surgically separated after the ringmaster, Fred Valentine, suggests it to them—an operation that would end the family business. In order to have the operation, the twins need financial support from the family, and Fred decides to give them the money:

> I told the twins about the surgery and asked them what they thought. And do you know what they said? They said the only reason they were staying together was because of me. Because I was kind to them. Because we play pinochle. Because I never laughed at them. . . . Well, I was not about to be the reason that they stayed together. And I didn't know how I thought we'd get out of this. I didn't think about it. It didn't seem important. What I did for them, that seems important, I think it's the only important thing I ever did.

The operation would literally bring the twins autonomy, from each other and the family. But the family is tied to the past and tradition in ways that stifle everyone, all for the supposed good of the greater whole.

As with her earlier plays, Norman's setting is simultaneously public yet confining. A prison, pool hall, laundromat, and parking lot are all public venues that are, in different ways, cultural icons of life in America; but unlike the other settings, the parking lot is both more open and claustrophobic at the same time, for the circus family is on display as they are confined to their performing roles. At the same time, Norman suggests that the changes in American society extract a high price on the marginalized. The play ends enigmatically, the fate of the circus family uncertain.

The characters are not developed fully enough, however, to create interest in their fates. The success of the play was also not helped by the fact that it was part of a festival that included the premiere of Beth Henley's Crimes of the Heart (1979). Norman was unprepared for reviews that suggested she was a flash-in-the-pan talent who had written a disaster. As Norman told Allan Wallack in Newsday (8 May 1983), "People hated that play more than they ever imagined they would hate anything." The devastation temporarily prevented Norman from writing: "It took me about two years to recover from it and regain my confidence. . . . but the most wonderful result of failure was that ultimately I felt strengthened by it—that they had hated the play and I survived. That they had said everything awful that could be said. And I *still* wanted to write."

Norman's next play, The Holdup (1980), also was traumatic. Commissioned by Gordon Davidson under a Rockefeller Grant, the play was rejected by Davidson because he found it silly. ATL workshopped the play during the summer of 1980; the Circle Repertory Company in New York ran a production of it in Saratoga in 1982; and the American Conservatory Theatre in San Francisco mounted it in April 1983. This play is atypical of Norman's work, although it does suggest her storytelling approach to playwriting. In this case, the play derives from stories Norman's grandfather told her. The Holdup is in the Western "holdup play" tradition and relies heavily on the American mythologizing of the West and the American frontier.

The play takes place in the fall of 1914 in a remote location in New Mexico. A small, mostly male cast symbolizes the past and the present through their response to the changes in civilization. The brothers Henry and Archie Tucker are alone at their cookshack. Into their midst comes the Outlaw, a desperado who is looking for food and a woman named Lily, whom he has not seen in almost a quarter of a century. Henry, obsessed with the untamed old West, challenges the Outlaw to a gunfight, during which Henry is killed. The Outlaw, who questions whether society is changing for the better given the declining morality, tries to kill himself but is nursed back to health by Archie and Lily, the characters who eagerly embrace all that is modern. By the conclusion of the play Archie and the Outlaw have each come to see the values expressed by the other. The play reveals that one must know and appreciate the past, for it molds the future.

The Holdup suggests a correlation to Sam Shepard that is not apparent in other works. Like Shepard, Norman romanticizes the West in this play and suggests that changing civilization does not always bring changes for the better. Robert Cooperman notes the number of myths Norman utilizes in the play, from the frontier myth to the mythologies of war. Norman uses Archie to represent those Americans who equate war with progress. By the end of the play, however, Archie has moderated his

Cover for Norman's first collection, published in 1988 (Collection of Tracy Simmons Bitonti)

views and seems less starry-eyed about the advent of war. Lily is a strong, independent woman who does not rely on a man for self-worth. Lily lives the message Norman's earlier heroines are learning: that one can be a nurturer, but one does not have to have a man to define oneself. Unlike Norman's earlier female characters, Lily is not on a journey to self-actualization; she has arrived.

Reviews were neutral at best. According to Norman, many complained that she tried to be too funny, as if she were attempting to become a Neil Simon. The review in *The San Francisco Chronicle* (14 April 1983) noted that Norman once again proved to be a master of dialogue but complained that the material seemed thin and the characters abruptly changed. Also noted was that Archie, representing the future, was too morally self-righteous.

Norman's ability to write despite negative reviews paid off with her internationally acclaimed play *'night, Mother,* a work Norman wrote when she was angry. She had moved to New York after she was hired to write the book and lyrics for the musical *Orphan Train* and was ecstatic over finally having the opportunity to write a musical, a lifelong goal. When she was abruptly fired and replaced by an eighteen-year-old, she used that anger to write *'night, Mother*. This two-character, one-act play received a staged reading at the Circle Repertory in November 1981 before its premiere at the American Repertory Theatre in Cambridge, Massachusetts, in December 1982. Directed by Tom Moore and starring Anne Pitoniak as Mama and Kathy Bates as Jessie, *'night, Mother* won Norman a Pulitzer Prize in 1983, after it had opened on Broadway at the John Golden Theatre on 31 March 1983 and had run for 388 performances; it also received a Tony nomination and received the Susan Smith Blackburn Prize, the Elizabeth Hull–Kate Warriner Award, and the Dramatists Guild Award. The play has been translated into thirty-two languages and is performed around the world.

Set in the living room and kitchen of a plain house on a country road, isolated from other homes, the play takes place on the harrowing evening that will be the last night of Jessie's life. Jessie tells her mother, Thelma Cates, that she plans to kill herself that night. Jessie tells Mama, not in order to be persuaded to change her mind, but because she wants Thelma to understand this decision and not blame herself. Although the play is structured around Jessie's announcement of her plan, it is not just a suicide story. *'night, Mother* is about the fraught relationships between mother and daughter and about an individual's right to define herself.

The stage directions indicate several important ideas of the play, which is performed without intermission. The house must be removed from the surrounding community, and the living room should be cluttered with homey things, yet "Under no circumstances should the set and its dressing make a judgment about the intelligence or taste of Jessie and Mama." Two parts of the set are especially important: one is Jessie's bedroom door, "an ordinary door that opens onto absolute nothingness"; the other is the importance of clocks set to real time. Time is crucial in this play, as in most of Norman's plays. In this case, the reminder of the passage of time reinforces Norman's belief that theater is a type of "jury duty" in which audiences are judges and witnesses. The door symbolically represents Jessie's concept of herself, as it reminds viewers of the unknown of death. The juxtaposition of the ordinary and the profound provides the structure of the play. In this humble setting a discussion of life and death will ensue, but even that topic will be discussed alongside talk of candy, manicures, and hot chocolate. The calmness with which Jessie announces her decision belies the years of anger and frustration that have led to this evening. The audience is torn between identification with Thelma's attempts to stop Jessie and respect for Jessie's ability finally to take control over her own life. Norman believes the universal appeal of the play comes from parents' recognition that their children are "only on loan" to them, and people's "sense that our lives are given to us and that, particularly in regards to our parents, we have . . . an unpayable debt." On one point she is adamant: 'night, Mother is not a play advocating suicide; rather, "it's about giving up what is not yours."

Ultimately, 'night, Mother is about imprisonment and how to "get out." Jessie lives an isolated, predictable existence. Her father died; her husband left her; and her juvenile-delinquent son moved out after stealing from her. Unbeknownst to Jessie, she suffers from epilepsy. She only knows that she passes out, and she uses these episodes as a reason to shun jobs and friends. Trying to protect Jessie, Mama never explained her illness—just one of the many ways Jessie's power over her own life is denied. Never having control over her life, Jessie will take charge of her death. Jessie, using a metaphor of a bus ride, tries to explain to Mama that there is nothing in particular that has driven her to this decision other than the knowledge that nothing will ever change: "I can get off right now if I want to, because even if I ride fifty more years and get off then, it's the same place when I step down to it. Whenever I feel like it, I can get off. As soon as I've had enough, it's my stop. I've had enough."

One of the last acts of communion between the women is the sharing of hot cocoa, something that neither woman likes but shares as a ritual from the past. Norman frequently uses a food motif to suggest the insatiable hunger that drives her protagonists. Sitting at the kitchen table, Mama uses every tactic she can think of to try to change Jessie's mind, finally using guilt and telling Jessie that she cannot kill herself because she is Mama's child. The play ends with the gunshot as Mama pounds on the bedroom door and then asks forgiveness: "Jessie, Jessie, child . . . Forgive me, I thought you were mine."

Reviews praised 'night, Mother for its painfully honest portrayal of the mother-daughter relationship, her dialogue, and her subject matter. Frank Rich, in The New York Times (12 January 1983), proclaimed it a "totally realistic" and "shattering" play that works because Norman is "too honest a writer" to make judgments or paint her characters as fools. Her greatest achievement, however, is that she "brings both understanding and dignity to forgotten and tragic American lives." Kroll, writing for Newsweek (3 January 1983), declared the play "a hammerblow of truth, a flash of unsparing light" that "detonates with startling quietness, showering us with truth, compassion and uncompromising honesty." Howard Kissel, however, complained in Women's Wear Daily (1 April 1983) that the play was not particularly moving, and Barnes criticized it in the New York Post (1 April 1983) for attempting to make the irrational appear rational and found it "neither so interesting nor so convincing" as Henrik Ibsen's Hedda Gabler (1890), which shares a similar ending. Stanley Kauffmann disliked the play, saying in the Saturday Review (September–October 1983) that its "pervasive flaw" is "manipulation. To put it another way, if the play were true—true to Norman's characters as she wants us to think of them, it wouldn't exist."

Several feminist critics have objected to what they see as the portrait of a weak woman who cannot face reality and thus chooses instead to end her life. Jenny Spencer argues that one reason for the differing reaction to the play is its focus on the development of female identity, which itself has come under scrutiny. Are audiences to understand Jessie's suicide as a courageous act of self-determination, or is it an escape that signals defeat? Jill Dolan and William W. Demastes have also written about what Dolan refers to as "the gender-biased politics of reception," noting the "media response polarized around gender differences."

Norman is often asked if the suicide of a friend prompted the play, but she will only say that the loss of a friend compelled her to write both 'night, Mother and her next play, Traveler in the Dark (1984). The most frequent comment Norman receives about 'night, Mother is "thank you" from friends and family who have lost a loved one to suicide. The portrayal of epilepsy has also garnered attention for the play. While it was in production in New York, doctors working on their continuing education were given recertification credit for attending a special performance of the play, and the Epilepsy Society recognized Norman for bringing attention to the illness.

Norman told Gussow that winning the Pulitzer Prize was "like someone just came into my room in my mind where I work and embroidered a big 'P' on the back of my typing chair. It may not change my life, but it will feel good to know it's back there." The experience did, of course, change things. All future plays would be compared to 'night, Mother, and most would be criticized as not as powerful. Except for musicals, Norman has not had another play produced on Broadway since 'night, Mother.

Norman's next play was produced in February of 1984 at the American Repertory Theatre in Cambridge. Traveler in the Dark concerns the loss of faith suffered by Sam, a brilliant surgeon, who has returned home to bury his beloved nurse and friend, Mavis, whom he could not save from cancer. Norman summarized the play in a Los Angeles Times article (January 1985) as "the incredible longing for God while saying, 'I do not want it to be me.'" The examination of the familial bond this time involves a father and a son, but this play brings the entire family into crises of both family and faith. Norman's concern with

Dave Florek, Skip Sudduth, Catherine Christianson, and Gladden Schrock in the 1992 Actors Theatre of Louisville production of D. Boone *(photograph by Richard Twigg)*

the suffering of good people is explored philosophically in this play.

Sam was raised by Everett, an evangelical preacher, in an atmosphere of revival meetings with an angry, vengeful, omnipresent God. As a youth, Sam participated in these revivals, but following the death of his mother, he rejected religious teaching as fraudulent, and thus rejected his father, too. He turned to science and faith in the human mind to provide answers, but the death of Mavis has challenged his sense of self. No longer considering himself a brilliant, miracle-working surgeon, Sam responds to his loss of faith in himself and science by rejecting his family and asking his wife, Glory, for a divorce. As Sam restores the garden he has not touched since his mother's death, Sam and Everett finally explore their differences as they discuss the existence of God. When Sam accepts his own limitations and the human condition, he ceases trying to be God and vows to restore his family.

The play did not receive favorable reviews. Kroll complained in *Newsweek* (27 February 1984) that the action seemed contrived to support Norman's "urgent need to dramatize a crisis of faith." Reviewing the 1990 York Theatre Company revival, Don Nelson in the *New York Daily News* (23 January 1990) and Brian Bradley in *Backstage* (2 February 1990) observed that the play seemed structured around minilectures. Barnes, noting Norman's seeming preoccupation with death, found the play cliché-ridden and trivial, suggesting that "seriousness needs a mythic quality to enable it to be taken seriously" (*New York Post*, 23 January 1990). Nearly every review commented that Sam was too unlikable a character to care about.

Norman's second marriage ended shortly after the disappointing critical reception of *Traveler in the Dark*. In 1987 she married Tim Dykman, an artist with whom she has two children, Angus and Katherine. Norman temporarily turned away from what she described to Hilary DeVries in the *Chicago Tribune* in 1987 as "the brutality of theater" and worked on a novel and screenplays for Hollywood. The idea for her only novel, *The Fortune Teller*, published that year, came to her while passing fortune-telling shops in New York. Norman began work on it as a play, but the large cast of characters precluded it from a stage production. Additionally, she said in *The New York Times Book Review* (24 May 1987), she "wanted to be able to include things like fire engines and sex, things you can't do onstage." *The Fortune Teller* is the story of Fay Morgan, a clairvoyant who helps police solve a case involving twenty-seven missing children. Using her psychic powers to help locate the children, she sees visions of her own child, a teenage daughter, seeking the comfort of a good-for-nothing man. Despite her success in helping save the lives of other children, Fay fails to keep her own daughter safe from the hardships of life. The novel failed to receive favorable reviews, often being compared, once again, to 'night, Mother. Norman, however, found more enjoyment from writing the novel than she had from writing plays because she was more in control: "I didn't have to write lines and worry that an actor or the audience might not understand my intent."

During this period Norman also wrote screenplays. In 1978 she wrote *It's the Willingness,* a Depression-era story set in Kentucky, for PBS, and in 1980 her script "In Trouble at Fifteen" was an episode of the NBC series *Skag*. Although Norman has written many screenplays, few have been produced. She was successful, however, in getting 'night, Mother made into a movie, for which she wrote the screenplay. Starring Anne Bancroft and Sissy Spacek, the movie was considerably altered from the original play in ways that weakened the project. For example, although Jessie remains in the house, Thelma is seen with friends and relatives, thus negating the sense of isolation of the house and the characters. The multiple rooms and the scenes of outdoors do not convey the claustrophobic feeling created by the play, and the compression of time is lost by having the action take place over more than ninety minutes. No attempt is made to suggest the illusion of real time. Most significant to many was the deletion of Thelma's line as she stands by Jessie's door following the gun blast. Paul Attanasio in the *Washington Post* (13 October 1986) felt that the play could only move people effectively in the theater, for the power comes from being with "two people talking in a room" and "the fact that you're watching flesh and blood and spittle and sweat 10 rows away." Norman's unproduced scripts include adaptations of Gay Talese's *Thy Neighbor's Wife* (1980) for United Artists and his *The Bridge* (1964) about the Verazzano-Narrows Bridge. She also wrote the 1979 screenplay "The Children with Emerald Eyes" for Columbia, about a woman who works with disturbed children.

Norman's return to the theater was with the play *Sarah and Abraham*, first performed as a workshop piece as part of the 1988 Festival of New American Plays at ATL. Norman was attracted to the concept for several reasons. Movies and television, she says, have taken over the "domestic dispute territory" and develop social-issue topics better than theater. Consequently, theater needs to concentrate on the kinds of things not possible in the other media, such as musicals or stories such as *Sarah and Abraham*.

Since the workshop, the play has been professionally produced at the George Street Playhouse in New Brunswick, New Jersey, in 1992. The play is set in a regional theater where a group of actors have gathered to improvise and then perform the biblical story of Sarah and Abraham. Through the device of a play within a play, Norman intertwines the lives of the actors and actresses with the imagined lives of Sarah, Abraham, and Hagar. Cliff and Kitty (Abraham and Sarah) are members of the theater run by Jack (God), who has recruited former company member and successful movie star Monica (Hagar) to return for the play. As Kitty and Cliff's marriage falls apart, various love triangles develop, and Kitty becomes pregnant with Jack's child. Meanwhile, with the help of scholar Virginia Mason, the company reinterprets the biblical tale with a feminist perspective. Because of the success of the play within the play, the company has the chance to go to New York, and Cliff finally has his opportunity to become the star that his wife has always been. Kitty, however, decides to abandon her career in order to stay at home to raise her child.

The play is more comic than most of her previous work. *Sarah and Abraham* explores the development of myths that come from male sources as she posits the possibility of other interpretations. The structure of the play also allows Norman to explore the relationships among actors and the demands of life in the theater. With sensitivity Norman acknowledges a man's plight of living within the shadow of his wife's success, just as she asserts that a woman's right to choose also means the right to choose a child over the pursuit of a career. There is some disagreement as to whether Kitty's choice marks the play as feminist or antifeminist. Gerald Weales argued in *Commonweal* (10 April 1992) that the "assumption" in the play, that a woman is wiser to choose to bear a child than pursue fame, is antifeminist; but others see the reclaiming of women's multiple roles as a feminist statement. As with the discussion about feminist issues with respect to *'night, Mother,* Norman prefers not to engage in the debate, although she contended to Esther Harriott in 1988, "If it's feminist to care about women's lives, yes, I'm a feminist. I don't have political points to make, although they certainly are made by the plays."

The shift in Norman's writing toward plays with a greater mythic quality or fairy-tale aspect coincides with the shift toward musical theater. Her interest in musicals is lifelong, and her first play, unpublished, was a musical for children about Thomas Edison. But this change in focus was at least partially fueled by anger. At a writer's conference in 1981 Norman defined serious theater as that which gives an audience food for thought after the end of the play—but she declared serious theater dead in America. Unlike English theater, American society will not support plays that are not immensely popular and profitable, so in order for playwrights to make a living in America today, they must abandon serious theater. Although one can name several successful American playwrights who write straight plays, Norman contends she cannot make a living from that type of writing today, and she blames theater critics for some of this problem. A popular musical, on the other hand, will generate income for years. Because she has not given up writing straight plays, one can assume that musicals allow her the luxury of writing other plays as she continues her work with regional theaters in America.

In 1989 Skidmore College offered a staged reading of the play that brought Norman the kind of success she had not known since *'night, Mother*. The musical *The Secret Garden* then had its opening as a trial production in 1990 in Norfolk, at the Virginia Stage Company, before moving to the St. James Theatre in New York in April 1991, where it ran for almost two years and more than 450 performances. Based on the classic 1911 children's novel by Frances Hodgson Burnett, the show was anxiously awaited by all who loved the book and hoped the musical would do it justice. In what is believed to be a Broadway first, the entire creative team was female: Heidi Landesman produced and designed the set (she had designed

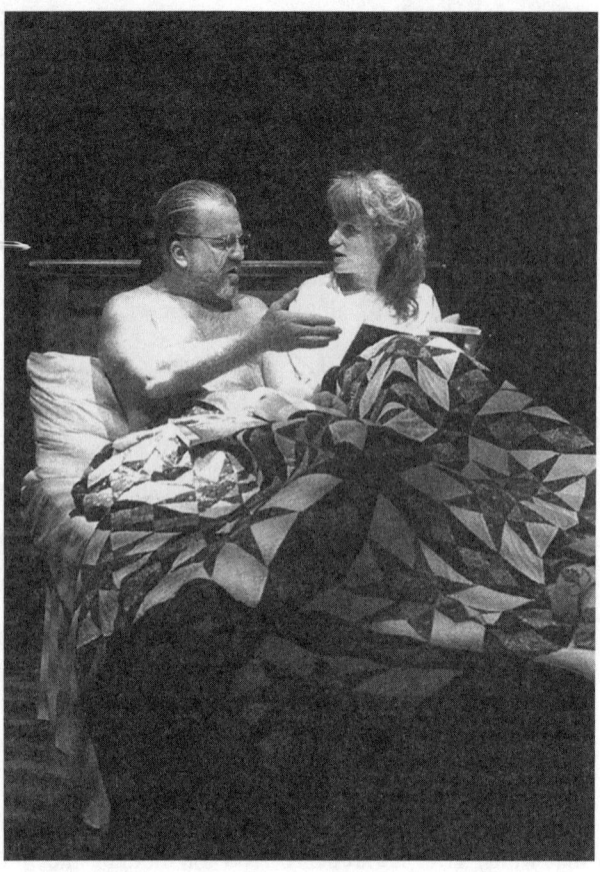
Leo Burmester and Joanne Camp in the 1995 Actors Theatre of Louisville production of Trudy Blue *(photograph by Richard Twigg)*

sets for both *'night, Mother* and *Traveler in the Dark*); Susan Schulman directed; Lucy Simon wrote the music; and Norman wrote the book and lyrics, for which she won Tony Awards. The play received fourteen Drama Desk nominations, and Norman won the award for book in 1991. Never having read the original, Norman felt free to make changes, and she did. Most of the changes stem from the desire to create a musical that would appeal to children but would not be a children's play.

The plot follows a Cinderella pattern. Mary Lennox, child of the British Raj, is orphaned in India when her parents die in a cholera epidemic. Mary returns to the Yorkshire home of her uncle, Nevil Craven. Mary is an unpleasant girl who, never having been given much attention or love, does not know how to give it to others. Her uncle, a hunchback, has become almost a hermit after the death of his beloved wife, Lily, who died in childbirth. Colin, Nevil's son, rarely sees his father, who only visits at night. The garden, a favorite place of Lily, has been locked and left untended. The only people with whom Mary finds a connection are the housekeeper and a country rustic, who tell Mary about the garden and some of the secrets of the house. In a classic story of death and rebirth, Mary restores the garden and in the process restores the family to health.

Most of the changes emanate from the decision to make the story less about Colin and more about Mary and Nevil. In addition, Norman expanded the role of Archibald Craven, who appears only in the beginning and end of the novel, into an almost classic villain. Archibald's presence adds to the fairy-tale quality, but the addition of another adult character and the increased development of Nevil's character may have been ways to attract the interest of major stars (Mandy Patinkin played Nevil in the Broadway production). These changes suggest connections to *Traveler in the Dark* with respect to a father-son relationship; the loss of nurturing parents, especially a mother; the fairy-tale motif; and the dead garden. Other changes include a parade of frequently appearing ghosts and the almost complete omission of the garden itself.

The changes in the story reflect the creators' vision of the project as a story about the discovery of one's powers as a human being. Norman stated to Patti Watts, "The stories I like are the ones where people are trying to solve their problems, and this is what's happening in *The Secret Garden*. . . . It was very important to me that the male view be represented in this piece." The increased attention to the adult situation reflects a subtle shift in Norman's work following motherhood. As in later plays, she seems more attuned to the parental aspect of familial bonds.

Although reviews were mixed, audiences loved the play. Rich complained in *The New York Times* (26 April 1991) that he "had trouble locating the show's pulse," and represented many who complained about the short shrift given to the garden itself: "The actual stage time devoted to this show's equivalent of Oz is brief, and the climactic, moving song about the garden's transforming powers . . . never arrives." Many commented on the appeal of the show to intelligence and artistry over feeling. The presence of the ghosts particularly irritated some critics, who felt that death was overemphasized. Others, however, such as David Patrick Stearns in *USA Today* (30 April 1991), praised the play "as the most adult new musical of the season" that is unafraid "to be genuine." Jan Stuart, in *New York Newsday* (26 April 1991), felt that the Gothic touch, particularly the ghosts, "cut deep into the jugular of an orphaned child's dreams, reflecting the various anxieties of abandonment, guilt, and retribution surrounding the aftermath of a parent's death." The play continues to be revived across the United States.

In 1992 Norman's play *D. Boone,* since retitled *Loving Daniel Boone,* was staged as part of the Humana Festival of New American Plays produced by ATL. The play had been commissioned by the Honorable Order of Kentucky Colonels to celebrate Kentucky's bicentennial. The play concentrates on Flo, a cleaning woman in a history museum, who has fallen in love with Daniel Boone. With few prospects for a contemporary lover, Flo time-travels to the past in order to assist Boone and other frontiersmen when Boone is captured by the Indians and the settlement at Boonesborough looks to be at the point of collapse. Accompanying Flo on this mythical journey are a curator, Mr. Wilson; Rick, a married mechanic attempting to woo Flo; and Hilly, a recently hired cleaning person. The journey tests everyone: Hilly must fight the past and a dead romantic hero to win Flo, who must learn to trust and believe in another. Norman commented in an interview with Linda Ginter Brown that Flo wants someone she can believe in, but modern men suffer by living in a nonchivalrous age, so to "love men that are around now is to redefine heroism." For Norman, this redefining means not fixating on one's personal past either: "Look at those available to us instead of comparing everyone to a past ideal." By the end of the play, Hilly and Flo plan to marry. Hilly has been successful with Flo because he accepts her as she is, as she does him, and is willing to risk everything to be with her: "I don't know, Florence. Maybe everything I've got. Maybe my job. Maybe my whole way of lookin' at things. Maybe you're gonna drive me crazy. Or maybe it'll be wonderful. . . . I don't know what you'll cost me, Florence. And I do not care . . . Florence Adams, I love you." Literally and metaphorically, Hilly has learned Flo's name: "I think you are the first man I ever knew who actually heard what I said."

In several ways this play harks back to Norman's first play, as it also shows new developments in her interests. Like *Getting Out*, this play manipulates time through the juxtaposition of past and present, but it goes beyond the first play by forcing audiences to reconsider representations of history and considerations of gender. Flo, like Arlene, is in the process of reinventing herself, in which the act of naming oneself signifies a separation between past and present. But unlike in her early plays, Norman's interest is squarely with the modern male. By this time, Norman says, she was no longer interested in domestic drama and wished to break away from the traditionally structured play. The few reviews called it a pleasant entertainment but questioned whether Norman's manipulation of history helped or hurt the creative process.

The success of *The Secret Garden* was equaled by the failure of Norman's next musical, *The Red Shoes* (1993), adapted from the 1948 movie. Set in the 1920s, *The Red Shoes* tells the story of Victoria Page, who joins the ballet company of Boris Lermontov with the ambition to be a star ballerina. Meeting and falling in love with a composer, Victoria finds herself caught between her love of performance and the love of a man as she tries to acquiesce to the demands of both the composer and the director. Unable to cope, she kills herself. The creative team, headed by first-time Broadway producer Martin Starger, originally reunited Norman, Schulman, and Landemans and included the legendary composer Jule Styne. Before the show opened, however, the original director and others had been fired over creative differences. Starger wanted the play to be faithful to the motion picture, whereas Norman and others wanted to update to a more feminist version, allowing Victoria to have friends and changing the suicide to an accident. "I didn't want to write an ending where a girl couldn't choose between two men and jumped in front of a train," explains Norman; "It was a lapse, not a girl going crazy. It was the idea that you could die in the perfection of your craft . . . that our passion and self-sacrifice . . . is what is so ennobling and grand about us as artists." Ultimately, Norman said, the show failed because of the "amateurism of the producer and the director." Norman tried to remove all connections between herself and the show, and the lyricist brought in to work with her, Bob Merrill, worked under the pseudonym Paul Stryker.

The show finally opened on Broadway after six weeks of previews and was called "the pink slips" because of all the personnel turmoil. Most critics were puzzled by the decision to attempt to redo a movie onstage without creating something new, prompting John Simon to note in *New York Magazine* (3 January 1994) that any stage-musical adaptation "must add a valid new dimension in order to justify itself." Most reviewers commented that the dancing was decent but the music and book were weak. The show became one of Broadway's great failures; it opened on 16 December 1993 and closed three days later, losing $8 million in the process.

The disaster of *The Red Shoes* has not kept Norman from writing other musicals, although none has been produced. At one point The Circle Repertory considered a production of her musical "Winter Shakers," about the nearly defunct religious group, but that plan fell through. Another unproduced effort is based on the evangelist Aimee Semple McPherson, who appealed to Norman because of her gifts of healing and preaching. Norman's interest in religion and theological concerns obviously plays a role in the choice of her subjects, but more important is her desire to continue to bring unheard voices to the American stage. McPherson and the Shakers share the unconventionality that has marginalized them in American history. Norman has also worked on a musical version of Emily Brontë's *Wuthering Heights* (1847).

Trudy Blue was first produced by ATL in 1995 and Off-Broadway at the MCC Theater in December 1999 with Polly Draper as the lead. In some ways, this play may be the most autobiographical of Norman's works, at least with respect to the genesis of the play. After the *Red Shoes* disaster, Norman became, as she recalls it, "deathly ill." The doctor prescribed many tests and declared that Norman had aggressive lung cancer with two years left to live. Norman consulted other doctors and was told they could not make a diagnosis for two weeks. Before it was discovered that the first doctor had been looking at the wrong test results, Norman took stock of her life and determined that she was not as attached to life as she would like to be. Part of the outcome of this realization was *Trudy Blue*, in which her protagonist realizes that it is not wrong to pursue pleasure or to put oneself before others.

The published play and the produced version are quite different, but in each the protagonist is a writer, Ginger, who has created the character Trudy Blue in one of her novels. Ginger has learned she has cancer and has only a few months to live. Her conversations with her husband take place in real time, but most of the other conversations are dreams, flashbacks, or interactions with people only seen in her mind's eye. Some of the people she communicates with are dead, including her mother. By abandoning a linear sequence for a plot that allows the tangible and intangible, the real and the imagined, to exist simultaneously, Norman allows Ginger to replay memories and events as the character confronts her mortality. Norman explained to Simi Horwitz that the play should be understood to be taking place within a single moment as Ginger reviews her life and seeks to understand it. In addition to suffering from cancer, Ginger is afflicted with a condition Norman terms "living in her head" that prevents her from successfully interacting with the real people in her life. Instead, the voices of ghosts, imagined relationships, and fictional characters hinder her. According to Norman, the goal of the play is to "present a geography of nerve endings" but to do so with comedy.

Like Flo in *Loving Daniel Boone*, Ginger has created an ideal relationship in her mind that impedes her relationship with her husband, and although this relationship is not based on the past, it serves as a warning against creating a mythical ideal lover. *Trudy Blue* also shares the device of the alter ego used so effectively in *Getting Out*, but in this play the alter ego is the fictional creation of Trudy, who does what Ginger wishes she could do. Ginger attempts to learn from Trudy how to be more self-assured. The mother-daughter relationship continues to be of interest to Norman, but this time the relationship is told from the mother's point of view, perhaps reflecting the difference in Norman's own life now that her mother is deceased, and she is the mother of a daughter. Norman points to another connection to *Getting Out*: in each play the protagonist is trapped in a prison, but in this case the prison is of Ginger's own creation, and she is ambivalent about really wanting to break free of these confines.

Some reviewers praised Norman for the concept but found the play flawed and difficult to follow. Others noted that the play failed to follow up on the concept and was moving only at the end, suggesting that the issue of illness should be developed earlier. One reviewer commented that it and Margaret Edson's *Wit* (first performed in 1995) premiered in New York at the same theater; both plays concern women of letters facing death from cancer, but *Wit* had greater appeal to both audiences and critics. Anita Gates, writing for *The New York Times* (3 December 1999), however, called *Trudy Blue* "beautiful" and "a vivid and stirring reminder of just what a fine observer of the interior life she [Norman] is." The play ran for three weeks before closing, although an opening on Broadway was anticipated.

Norman collaborated on another project, which had its premiere in January 1998. *Love's Fire* was commissioned by The Acting Company and was performed for its twenty-fifth anniversary at the Joseph Papp Public Theater. Acting Company director Mark Lamos and dramaturge Anne Cattaneo chose seven playwrights—Eric Bogosian, William Finn, John Guare, Tony Kushner, Norman, Ntozake Shange, and Wendy Wasserstein—who were each given a Shakespearean sonnet and asked to write a short play that the sonnet inspired. Norman's contribution, *140*, is described as a drama in the style of *La Ronde* (the 1950 movie based on Arthur Schnitzler's 1903 play *Reigen*) in which a woman castigates her beloved for his unfaithfulness, setting in motion a chain reaction as the lover must confront his new lover with suspected infidelities, and so forth. The concept for *Love's Fire* was original, but the collection of plays was uneven; most reviews were lukewarm. Stearns praised the idea in *USA Today* (25 June 1998) as "theatre as cocktail party" and found Norman's "secular daisy chain . . . eloquent."

Love's Fire was not the first time Norman contributed to a group project play. In 1994 the Ensemble Studio Theatre presented five one-acts by Edward Allen Baker, Guare, Norman, Jacqueline Reingold, and Regina Taylor. Norman's contribution, *Lunch with Lynn*, is a fifteen-minute depiction of lunchtime meetings between a novelist and three different friends. In August 1999 Norman contributed a ten-minute play, *RCA*, a futurist satire on television news, to Sag Harbor's Bay Street Theatre *Fit to Print* festival of short plays. In 1998 Norman was also chosen as one of ten American playwrights commissioned by the American Playwrights Project, with the goal of producing ten new plays over two years.

Norman has written several television screenplays, including *Face of a Stranger* (1991), starring Gena Rowlands and Tyne Daly, and *A Cooler Climate* (1999), with Judy Davis and Sally Field. The movies share a common theme of women of different backgrounds becoming friends. In March 2000 Norman's *Audrey Hepburn Story*, an ABC miniseries, premiered. Norman focused on the period from Hepburn's childhood through her career breakthrough with *Breakfast at Tiffany's*, saying the dramatic interest is how Hepburn achieved her transformation to a successful movie start.

Norman's next play, Sisters, premiered at the Broadway Playhouse, Sacramento, California, in November 1999. The two-character play focuses on the developing relationship between two African American women who are forced to get to know one another when a snowstorm traps them in the office building where Olivia works as a corporate executive and Cassie works as a cleaning woman. Though separated by class and education, the women discover their experiences of being black in a white environment give them something in common. Over the course of the evening, they share their frustration and concerns over jobs and family, discovering there is more to bring them together than to separate them. The plot structure, the use of two women from different classes, and the African American characters suggest similarities to Third and Oak. Concentrating on a black female corporate executive and a cleaning woman, Norman again brings to the stage voices often not heard in American society.

Since 1994 Norman has served as codirector with Christopher Durang of the playwriting program at Juilliard, where she helps emerging dramatists develop. One of the best feelings, Norman said in a speech at the Southern Writers' Conference, was when a student told her that seeing a production of Getting Out made her want to write: "That's what's really good. I passed the torch. That's what I will feel good about at the end of life." All playwrights, she feels, are "this battalion, marching, valiant soldiers on the front lines, and we must not step on the mines. We are trying as best we can to clear the path, to tell you what's out there."

Marsha Norman has always resisted being labeled a feminist playwright, and much has been written on whether she writes feminist theater. Similarly, some critical work has attempted to define Norman as a Southern playwright. More profitable inquiries may be in locating her place in contemporary American drama. As Norman told John L. DiGaetani in 1991, her plays are about people in "solitary confinement" who do not "have the sophistication to disguise what they are feeling, or rationalize their behavior. I'm not interested in how people cover things up; I'm interested in how people get through the day."

Interviews:

Kathy Henderson, "'night, Mother's Marsha Norman Talks about Her Pulitzer Prize Winning Play," Playbill (May 1983): 22+;

Otis R. Guernsey, "Five Dramatists Discuss the Value of Criticism," Dramatists Guild Quarterly, 21 (March 1984): 11–25;

Robert Brustein, "Conversations with . . . Marsha Norman," Dramatists Guild Quarterly, 21 (September 1984): 9–21;

Beth Ungar, "Talking with Marsha Norman," Cableview (April 1985): 67;

Sherilyn Beard, "An Interview with Marsha Norman," Southern California Anthology, 3 (1985): 11–17;

Alvin P. Sanoff, "Tarot Cards Catch the Eye of a Master Writer," U.S. News and World Report (8 June 1987): 78;

Kathleen Betsko and Rachel Loenig, "Marsha Norman," in their Interviews with Contemporary Women Playwrights (New York: Beech Tree Books, 1987), pp. 324–342;

David Savran, "Marsha Norman," in his In Their Own Words: Contemporary American Playwrights (New York: Theatre Communications Group, 1988), pp. 178–192;

John L. DiGaetani, "Marsha Norman," in his A Search for a Postmodern Theatre: Interviews with Contemporary Playwrights (New York: Greenwood Press, 1991), pp. 245–251;

Linda Ginter Brown, "Update with Marsha Norman" and "More with Marsha Norman," in Marsha Norman: A Casebook, edited by Brown (New York: Garland, 1996), pp. 163–196, 197–220;

Simi Horwitz, "Living in Your Head: Recipe for Disaster," Back Stage (26 November 1999): 17;

Blake Green, "Feeling Blue: Playwright Speaks Ill, and Well, of Her New Show," Newsday (1 December 1999): B3.

Bibliography:

Irmgard H. Wolfe, "Marsha Norman: A Classified Bibliography," Studies in American Drama, 1945–Present, 3 (1988): 149–175.

References:

C. W. E. Bigsby, Contemporary American Playwrights (Cambridge: Cambridge University Press, 1999), pp. 210–251;

Sally Browder, "'I Thought You Were Mine': Marsha Norman's 'night, Mother," in Mother Puzzles: Daughters and Mothers in Contemporary American Literature, edited by Mickey Pearlman (New York: Greenwood Press, 1989), pp. 109–113;

Janet Brown, "Getting Out, 'night, Mother," in her Taking Center Stage: Feminism in Contemporary U.S. Drama (Metuchen, N.J.: Scarecrow Press, 1991), pp. 60–77;

Brown and Catherine Barnes Stevenson, "Fearlessly 'Looking Under the Bed': Marsha Norman's Feminist Aesthetic in Getting Out and 'night, Mother," in Theatre and Feminist Aesthetics, edited by

Karen Laughlin and Catherine Schuler (Rutherford, N.J.: Fairleigh Dickinson University Press, 1995), pp. 182–199;

Katherine H. Burkman, "Demeter Myth and Doubling in Marsha Norman's 'night, Mother," in *Modern American Drama: The Female Canon,* edited by June Schlueter (Rutherford, N.J.: Fairleigh Dickinson University Press, 1990), pp. 254–263;

Susan L. Carlson, "Women in Comedy: Problem, Promise, Paradox," *Themes in Drama,* 7 (1985): 159–172;

Helen Krich Chinoy and Linda Walsh Jenkins, *Women in American Theatre: Careers, Images, Movements* (New York: Crown, 1981), pp. 186–190;

Stephanie Coen, "Marsha Norman's Triple Play," *American Theatre,* 8 (March 1992): 22–26;

William W. Demastes, "Jessie and Thelma Revisited: Marsha Norman's Conceptual Challenge in 'night, Mother," *Modern Drama,* 36 (March 1993): 109–119;

Demastes, "New Voices Using Realism: Fuller, Henley, and Norman," in his *Beyond Naturalism: A New Realism in American Theatre* (New York: Greenwood Press, 1988), pp. 125–154;

Jill Dolan, "Bending Gender to Fit the Canon: The Politics of Production," in *Making a Spectacle: Feminist Essays on Contemporary Women's Theatre,* edited by Lynda Hart (Ann Arbor: University of Michigan Press, 1989), pp. 318–341;

Dolan, *Feminist Spectator as Critic* (Ann Arbor: University of Michigan Press, 1991), pp. 19–40;

Jeanie Forte, "Realism, Narrative, and the Feminist Playwright: A Problem of Reception," *Modern Drama,* 32 (1989): 115–127;

Brendan Gill, "Portrait of the Artist as a Young Saint," *New Yorker* (11 April 1983): 109–112;

Merle Ginsberg, "*Getting Out*'s Marsha Norman: 'I'm Not Young and I'm Not Sweet,'" *Village Voice* (16 August 1979): 15+;

Louis K. Greiff, "Fathers, Daughters, and Spiritual Sisters: Marsha Norman's *'night, Mother* and Tennessee Williams' *The Glass Menagerie,*" *Text and Performance Quarterly,* 9 (1989): 224–228;

Mel Gussow, "Women Playwrights: New Voices in Theatre," *New York Times Magazine* (1 May 1983): 22+;

Janet Haedicke, "Margins in the Mainstream: Contemporary Women Playwrights," in *Realism and the American Dramatic Tradition,* edited by Demastes (Tuscaloosa: University of Alabama Press, 1996), pp. 203–217;

Esther Harriott, *American Voices: Five Contemporary Playwrights in Essays and Interviews* (Jefferson, N.C.: McFarland, 1988);

Lynda Hart, "Doing Time: Hunger for Power in Marsha Norman's Plays," *Southern Quarterly,* 25 (Spring 1987): 67–79;

Leslie Kane, "The Way Out, The Way In: Paths to Self in the Plays of Marsha Norman," in *Feminine Focus: The New Women Playwrights,* edited by Enoch Brater (New York: Oxford University Press, 1989), pp. 225–274;

Helene Keyssar, *Feminist Theatre: An Introduction to Plays of Contemporary British and American Women* (New York: Grove, 1985), pp. 148–166;

Linda Kintz, *The Subject's Tragedy: Political Poetics, Feminist Theory, and Drama* (Ann Arbor: University of Michigan Press, 1992), pp. 195–238;

Jill McDonnell, "Diverse Similitude: Beth Henley and Marsha Norman," *Southern Quarterly,* 25 (1987): 95–104;

Madonne Miner, "'What's These Bars Doin' Here?': The Impossibility of *Getting Out,*" *Theatre Annual,* 40 (1985): 115–134;

Laura Morrow, "Orality and Identity in *'night, Mother* and *Crimes of the Heart,*" *Studies in American Drama, 1945–Present,* 3 (1988): 23–39;

Timothy Murray, "Patriarchal Panopticism, or The Seduction of a Bad Joke: *Getting Out* in Theory," *Theatre Journal* (October 1983): 376–388;

Margaret Rubik, "A Sisterhood of Women: Marsha Norman's *Getting Out* and *The Laundromat,*" *Gramma,* 2 (1994): 141–147;

John Simon, "Theatre Chronicle: Kopit, Norman, and Shepard," *Hudson Review,* 32 (Spring 1979): 78–88;

Raynette Halvorsen Smith, "*'night, Mother* and *True West:* Mirror Images of Violence and Gender," *Themes in Drama,* no. 13: *Violence in Drama,* edited by James Redmond (Cambridge: Cambridge University Press, 1991), pp. 277–289;

Jenny Spencer, "Norman's *'night, Mother:* Psycho-Drama of Female Identity," *Modern Drama,* 30 (September 1987): 364–375;

Elizabeth Stone, "Playwright Marsha Norman: An Optimist Writes about Suicide, Confinement, and Despair," *Ms.* (12 July 1983): 56–59;

Kate Stout, "Marsha Norman: Writing for the 'Least of our Brethren,'" *Saturday Review,* 9 (September–October 1983): 28–33;

Richard Wattenberg, "Feminizing the Frontier Myth: Marsha Norman's *The Holdup,*" *Modern Drama,* 33 (1990): 507–517;

Patti Watts, "Staged for Success: Four Award Winning Women Come Together to Turn a Classic Book into a Broadway Musical," *Executive Female,* 14 (March–April 1991): 24+.

OyamO
(Charles F. Gordon)
(7 September 1943 –   )

Jasmin L. Lambert
College of William and Mary

PLAY PRODUCTIONS: *The Resurrection of Lady Lester,* New Haven, Yale Repertory Theatre, 1981;

The Temple of Youth, by OyamO, Lisa Rifkin, Alex Simmons, and The Bronx Creative Arts for Youth Theatre Company, The Bronx, N.Y., Studio Theatre at Lehman College, 23 January 1987;

Let Me Live, New York, Working Theater, 1990;

One-Third of a Nation, adapted from Arthur Arent's play, Fairfax, Va., Federal Theatre Festival, Black Box Theatre, George Mason University, 1 May 1991;

I Am a Man, New York, Working Theater, 1992;

In Living Colors, Fairfax, Va., George Mason University Center for the Arts, 1992–1993 season;

Dancing on the Brink, East Palo Alto, 31 May 1995;

Pink and Say, adapted from Patrick Polacco's children's book, Seattle, Seattle Children's Theatre, 1996;

Famous Orpheus, Ann Arbor, Performance Network, 1996; Rochester, N.Y., Geva Theatre, 30 May 1998;

Boundless Grace, adapted from Mary Hoffman's book, Minneapolis, Children's Theatre Company, 16 January 1998;

The White Black Man (Mundele Ndombe), Waterford, Conn., Eugene O'Neill Theater Center, 17 July 1998;

Liyanja, Ann Arbor, Trueblood Theatre, University of Michigan, November 1998;

Kickin' Summit, in *Free Market,* New York, Working Theater, June 2001;

Harry and the Streetbeat, Philadelphia, Philadelphia Theatre Company, February 2001.

BOOKS: *The Star That Could Not Play* (New York: OyamO Ujamaa, 1974);

OyamO (Charles F. Gordon; courtesy of the author)

Hillybilly Liberation: A Grossly Understated Prayer of the Theatrical Spectacles, Social Positions and Poetry (New York: OyamO Ujamaa, 1976);

The Resurrection of Lady Lester: A Poetic Mood Song Based on the Legend of Lester Young (New York: Theatre Communications Group, 1981);

I Am a Man: Powa ta da Peepas (New York: Applause Books, 1995).

FROM "I AM A MAN" RED 27

You ain't da kinda man who care about his wife and chilrens. You ain't dat kinda man atall.

JONES

Don't you tell no lie neither! Dem chilrens ain't never been hungry and day got clothes on day back and a shack over day heads. Don't tell me I don't care about mah chilrens. I ain't gon' hear dat!

ALICE MAE

You ain't gon' hear nothin' nobody say now. You think you a big leader or somethin'. Thomas Oliver Jones, President of Local 1733. Hmph! I was witchu when you was hustling pool in the poolhalls, when you was out on the streets scheming. When day used to call you Ollie da Octopus 'cause you had hands in every hustle on the streets. See, don't talk no stuff to me. I know what happened. I done read you for years. I know plenty 'bout you, especially yo' promises. I'm still waitin' on a decent house wit a yard. I been waiting 15 years. Look like we go from bad to worse and worser and all you think about is a buncha mens totin' garbage. Das fine and noble, Ollie, but look at the garbage I been totin' all dese years! Yo garbage!

JONES

Alright, you want me tell ya I ain't no saint? I ain't neva met nobody wit two legs dat was. A man cain't do everything right, cain't satisfy everybody all da time. (soliloquy to the audience) I done eat dirt too, but I still ain't dirt. I'm just a man. Dem bunca mens totin' garbage stayed by me when day fired me in '63. Rememba? We ain't had two pennies ta rub tagetha. Rememba?

Pages from the revised typescript for OyamO's 1992 play about the 1968 Memphis sanitation workers' strike (Collection of OyamO)

Rememba when da mens took up collection every week, branged us groceries, branged us clothese, paid da light bill, an' whatinsoeva we needed? While I'm wuckin' any kinda job I could git, includin' hustlin' when I had ta, dem garbage totin' mens toted you all ova town ta do ya shoppin'. Day come by when da chilrens git sick. Day show me day respeck us, loved us. Day remember how hard I fight fah dem. I love da union, sho! 'Cept fah Jesus, it's da bes' hope a black workin' man got in da South right now. Mah grandaddy chop cotton when he a young man. He makin' fifty cents a day. Long come World War I an' he git hired in the Birmingham Steel Mills 'cause day cain't git no white folks no moe. He wuck in the Birmingham Steel Mills fah thirty yeahs, all in the Depression an' straight up through da Second World War. He was a good wucka. Alright, long come da time fah him ta retire, git a small pension, git his socha se-cure-ty. Den President Roosevelt end da Second World War. Heah come da foe'man talkin' 'bout, say "Lemual, you don't kept this job thirty years. Why you oughtta be rich by now. Time you let anotha man have a chance." Foe'man taken 'n hired his nephew, let grandaddy go. Grandaddy hada go chop cotton fah thirty moe yeahs foe he died in da field wit a hoe in his hands. (Back to Alice Mae) Dis union bidness somethin' I hafta do. I ain't no rich man kin buy mah way into history books, an' I ain't no scholar kin talk his way into dem. Da union is what I got, it's what all black mens got. Maybe it's all da chance we got ta earn respeck. You been wantin' me ta quit dis union, but I cain't quit it.

ALICE MAE

OTHER: *Breakout,* in *Black Drama Anthology,* edited by Woodie King and Ron Milner (New York: New American Library, 1972).

OyamO is a critically acclaimed playwright who focuses on the struggles of people of color in America, people whose voices are often ignored. Seeking to bring to life figures of the past who are not always familiar to contemporary audiences, he focuses his plays on politics, race, gender, and the American class structure. OyamO began writing in the 1960s, during the height of the Civil Rights movement, and he has continued to write plays aimed at educating his audiences and inspiring them to engage in social action. He believes that a successful play and theatrical experience is defined by audience response, that theater must "grab" theatergoers and entertain them. He has written a new play almost every year since the late 1960s, but not all of them have been produced or published.

Charles F. Gordon was born on 7 September 1943 in Elyria, Ohio, to Earnest Gordon, a steelworker, and Bennie Gordon, a housewife. Soon after his son's birth, Earnest Gordon went to fight in World War II, and Bennie Gordon moved with her infant son to Lorain, Ohio, to be close to her family. In *Hillybilly Liberation* (1976) OyamO describes his early life as a time filled with the women who were raising him: his mother, his maternal grandmother, and his godmother. The only significant male influence in his life was his grandfather, the Reverend Benjamin Franklin, whom he admired for his loving disposition and gentle manner.

While attending Admiral King High School in Lorain, Ohio, during the early 1960s, Gordon wrote articles for his high-school newspaper and letters to the editor of the local newspaper. After graduating from high school in 1962, he worked for a while to raise money for college and then enrolled in fall 1963 at Miami University in Oxford, Ohio. Dismayed by the conservatism of the university, he dropped out after two and a half years of study. After leaving school he served in the U.S. Naval Reserve and engaged in political activism, participating frequently in antiwar demonstrations and voter-registration drives in the South. He then decided he could make a larger societal impact if he shared his political ideology with multiracial American audiences and moved to New York City to pursue a career in the theater. In New York during the late 1960s, he changed his name to OyamO, based on some Harlem youths' misreading of his "Miami University of Ohio" T-shirt.

Though his primary goal was to write plays, OyamO felt that to understand that craft he ought to study acting first: "I wanted to see the problems the actor faces on the stage and in 'real life.'" His participation in acting workshops at the New Lafayette Theatre in Harlem provided him with the opportunity to work with rising African American playwrights of the Black Revolutionary theater movement, such as Ed Bullins and Amiri Baraka (then known then as LeRoi Jones). While OyamO was attending acting classes, Ernest Baxter, the resident lighting designer at the New Lafayette Theatre, offered him the opportunity to earn some money as an assistant lighting technician, and he eventually became a full-time lighting assistant. Also during the 1960s, OyamO worked as the master electrician for the Negro Ensemble Company (NEC), founded in 1967 by playwright Douglas Turner Ward.

As OyamO continued to write, he drifted away from acting classes and into a new writing workshop led by Bullins, who had become playwright in residence at the New Lafayette Theatre in 1967. This group later became well known as the Black Theater Workshop. OyamO's relationship with Robert Macbeth, artistic director at the New Lafayette Theatre, eventually deteriorated, and OyamO was fired from his position at the theater. He continued attending Bullins's workshop until 1970, when he and a few other members of the Black Theater Workshop founded the Black Magicians Theatre Company.

During the late 1960s OyamO married and became a father. He also took courses at New York University and Brooklyn College before enrolling at the College of New Rochelle, from which he earned a B.A. in 1970.

During the early 1970s OyamO moved to Buffalo, New York, to be playwright in residence at the Afro-American Cultural Center. In 1972 he was awarded a Rockefeller playwright-in-residence grant, and in 1972–1974 his activities were funded by a Creative Public Service Program Grant. Until 1978 he traveled throughout New York State as a visiting playwright and a scholar, worked as a script reader for the New York Shakespeare Festival. He also returned periodically to New York City to continue his work with the Black Magicians Theatre Company, which dissolved in 1977 because of internal conflicts among company members. Toward the end of this period he became the director of Street Theater at the Eastern Correctional Institute in Napanoch, New York.

In 1978 OyamO was accepted in the M.F.A. playwriting program at the Yale School of Drama, which recognized him in 1980 as its outstanding graduate student. He also served on the search committee that selected the well-known Broadway director Lloyd Richards as the new dean of the School of Drama. Richards encouraged OyamO to continue writing about the African American experience. One result was a play about the well-known tenor saxophonist Lester Young, *The Resurrection of Lady Lester,* which premiered at the Yale Repertory Theatre in 1981.

In 1979, while still at Yale, OyamO began teaching theater courses at the College of New Rochelle. He earned his M.F.A. from Yale in 1981, and in 1982 he was invited

Cover and cast list for the 1998 play for which OyamO won an award from the O'Neill Playwrights Conference (courtesy of OyamO)

to serve as playwright in residence for a year at Emory University. The following year he returned to teach at the College of New Rochelle, and he spent the rest of the 1980s working as adjunct professor, instructor, guest lecturer, or playwright in residence at Princeton University, the University of Iowa Playwrights' Workshop, and at the New Dramatists in New York City. While in New York in 1983–1984 he also worked with the Frank Silvera Writers' Workshop, and in 1985 he was awarded another Rockefeller playwright-in-residence grant.

In 1989 OyamO accepted a teaching position at the University of Michigan, where he is currently an associate professor of theater and English as well as playwright in residence. While at the University of Michigan, OyamO has received a grant from the Office of Vice President for Research and the Minority Faculty Development Fund, a Guggenheim Fellowship, a McKnight Foundation fellowship, and three National Endowment for the Arts fellowships.

Not unlike the plays of August Wilson, OyamO's work blends the African and African American narrative voice with elements of surrealism, expressionism, and realism—as well as with music, dance, and poetry. His characters include well-known historical figures, such as Lester Young and Martin Luther King Jr., as well as unknown men and women, the common man or Everyman searching for meaning amid the mixed messages of racism and the mythology of the American Dream.

This theme is the focus of OyamO's *In Living Colors,* a ritualistic theatrical presentation, including song and dance, on the lifestyle of the Gullah-speaking African Americans living on the Sea Islands of South Carolina and their search for a means to survive without abandoning their traditions and culture. The play has been produced during the 1992–1993 season of the George Mason University Center for the Arts and in Detroit at the Charles H. Wright Museum of African American History, where it opened on 28 January 1999.

OyamO returned to the theme of the common man's search for knowledge in a socially complex world in *Let Me Live*, which had its world premiere at the Working Theater in New York during the 1990–1991 season. Based on the autobiography of labor activist Angelo P. Herndon, the play is set in 1932 and focuses on eight men who have been thrown together in cellblock number seven of a Georgia prison. These eight men of African descent narrate their life stories, which are filled with tales of broken dreams and unfulfilled aspirations. These "Everyman" figures rely on each other for a philosophical understanding of chaotic lives overshadowed with racial oppression and poverty. *Village Voice* reviewer Scott Poulson-Bryant described the play as "ostensibly about the political plight of real-life '30s labor activist Angelo P. Herndon, but actually about the constant negotiation of power that defines a black man in the racist U.S. of A." (22 January 1991). The 1998 production of this play at the Goodman Theatre in Chicago was also well received.

OyamO's most critically acclaimed play to date is *I Am a Man*, which was commissioned by the Working Theater in New York and staged there during its 1992–1993 season. In this play OyamO's Everyman is T. O. Jones, a sanitation-union president leading the 1968 strike in Memphis, during which Martin Luther King Jr. was assassinated. The play focuses not on King but on black working-class characters who figuratively represent all humankind and its innate struggle to find meaning in life and to conquer its environment. Wilborn Hampton of *The New York Times* admired OyamO's "unflinching aim at the often vitriolic feuds between the militant and nonviolent arms of the civil rights movement and the liberal Jews who marched beside them" (20 May 1993). The play was also produced in Chicago at the Goodman Theatre in 1994, and in 1995 at the University of Michigan and the Arena Theatre in Washington, D.C. Reviewing the play for the *Chicago Tribune* (3 May 1994), Sid Smith praised OyamO's focus on "ordinariness and how, even in the midst of revolution, most remain helplessly on the periphery." In the *Washington Post* (10 March 1995) Lloyd Rose lauded OyamO's representation of the broad range of speaking styles that compose "the American voice." Other positive assessments include those of Lawrence Bommer (*Chicago Tribune*, 29 April 1994) and Ellis Cose (*Newsweek*, 13 February 1995).

In 1995 OyamO accepted an invitation from Stanford University to write a play chronicling the history of African Americans, Native Americans, and Latinos living in Palo Alto, California. Set in East Palo Alto during the precolonial era, *Dancing on the Brink* is narrated by an Ohlone Indian chief who tells his dreams about the future of Palo Alto to members of his community.

The following year, the Seattle Children's Theatre commissioned OyamO to write a stage adaptation of Patrick Polacco's children's book *Pink and Say*. Set during the Civil War, the play is about the relationship of two young boys, one an African American and the other a white American. OyamO has also adapted Mary Hoffman's *Boundless Grace* for the Minneapolis Children's Theatre. OyamO's version of the book is a musical that chronicles a young girl's journey into maturity as she comes to terms with her parents' divorce.

OyamO is also working on motion-picture and television projects. HBO has optioned the rights to *I Am a Man* and invited OyamO to work on a program for their Famous Black American Anthology series. He is also under contract with Tri-Star Pictures to work on a movie titled *Ota Benga, The Pygmy in the Zoo*.

OyamO is a talented playwright who insightfully reconstructs and weaves together the lives and voices of African Americans who find hope and wisdom in their search to understand the disorder and prejudice of the modern world. Through his focus on the Everyman, OyamO seeks to edify and entertain his audiences about the lives of people of color and other marginalized individuals.

References:

Wallace Bridges, *Black Theatre*, Bridges Web Service <www.bridgesweb.com>;

Jim Snyder, "Playwright With a 'Wild Side,'" *Chronicle of Higher Education*, 41 (14 April 1995): A6.

Papers:

The Schomburg Center for Research in Black Culture has a collection of OyamO's papers.

John Pielmeier

(23 February 1949 -   )

Bridget Brennan
Catholic University of America

PLAY PRODUCTIONS: *Soledad Brother,* adapted from George Jackson's book, University Park, Pennsylvania State University, May 1971;

A Chosen Room, Minneapolis, 1976;

Agnes of God, Louisville, Actors Theatre of Louisville, 7 March 1980; New York, Music Box Theatre, 30 March 1982;

Chapter Twelve: The Frog, Louisville, Actors Theatre of Louisville, 11 May 1980;

Courage, Louisville, Actors Theatre of Louisville, March 1983; New York, Lamb's Club, 1984;

A Gothic Tale, Louisville, Actors Theatre of Louisville, November 1983;

Cheek to Cheek, Louisville, November 1983;

The Boys of Winter, New York, Biltmore Theatre, 1 December 1985;

Jass [staged reading], Waterford, Conn., Eugene O'Neill Theater Center, 1985;

Evening, Cincinnati, 1986;

In Mortality, Louisville, 1987;

Sleight of Hand, New York, Cort Theatre, 3 May 1987;

Pillow Talk, Louisville, Actors Theatre of Louisville, 1989;

Willi: An Evening of Wilderness and Spirit, Seattle, A Contemporary Theatre (ACT), September 1991;

Young Rube, music and lyrics by Matthew Selman, St. Louis, Repertory Theatre of St. Louis, September 1993;

Voices in the Dark, Seattle, ACT, 20 October 1994; New York, Longacre Theatre, 12 August 1999;

Steeplechase [workshop production], New Harmony, Ind., New Harmony Project, May 2000.

BOOKS: *Agnes of God* (Garden City, N.Y.: Doubleday, 1982);

Haunted Lives: Three Short Plays (New York: Dramatists Play Service, 1984);

Impassioned Embraces: Pieces of Love and Theatre (New York: Dramatists Play Service, 1989);

Voices in the Dark (New York: Broadway Play Publishing, 2000).

PRODUCED SCRIPTS: *Choices of the Heart,* television, NBC, 1983;

Agnes of God, motion picture, Columbia Pictures, 1985;

The Shell Seekers, television, based on Rosamund Pilcher's novel, ABC, 1989;

The Stranger Within, television, CBS, 1990;

An Inconvenient Woman [miniseries], television, based on Dominick Dunne's novel, ABC, 1991;

Through the Eyes of a Killer, television, as Solomon Isaacs, based on Christopher Fowler's "The Master Builder," CBS, 1992;

Last P.O.W.?–The Bobby Garwood Story, television, story by Pielmeier and Edward Gold, teleplay by Pielmeier, ABC, 1993;

Reunion, television, by Pielmeier and Ronald Bass, based on Linda Gray Sexton's *Points of Light,* CBS, 1994;

Original Sins, television, CBS, 1995;

Forbidden Territory: Stanley's Search for Livingstone, television, CBS, 1997;

Mysteries of Egypt, motion picture, by Pielmeier and Bruce Neibaur, Destination Cinema, 1998;

The Rescuers–Stories of Courage: Two Families–We Are Circus, television, Showtime, 1998;

The Happy Face Murders, television, Showtime, 1999;

Flowers for Algernon, television, based on Daniel Keyes's novel, CBS, 2000;

Dodson's Journey, television, based on James Dodson's *Faithful Travelers,* CBS, 2001;

Submerged, television, based on Peter Haas's *The Terrible Hours,* by Peter Haas, by Pielmeier and Edward Khmara, NBC, 2001;

Sins of the Father, television, based on a *Texas Monthly* article by Pamela Colloff, fX Network, 2002;

Living with the Dead [miniseries], television, based on James Van Praagh's *Talking to Heaven,* CBS, 2002.

John Pielmeier achieved critical and commercial success on Broadway in 1982 with his play *Agnes of God,* which earned a Tony for actress Amanda Plum-

John Pielmeier (photograph by Susan Johann; courtesy of John Pielmeier)

mer and a Tony nomination for actress Geraldine Page. The motion-picture adaptation of the play brought Pielmeier further acclaim when both Anne Bancroft and Meg Tilly received Oscar nominations. While he has yet to achieve another major success on Broadway, three more of his plays have been well received in regional theaters. Pielmeier has written a melodrama, a musical, a mystery, a thriller, and several adaptations for the stage. Perhaps the one thing that remains constant in his work is his reluctance to provide easy answers for his audiences, believing that questions are far more important than any answers man is capable of providing.

The son of Len and Louise (Blackburn) Pielmeier, John Leonard Pielmeier was born in Altoona, Pennsylvania, on 23 February 1949. He demonstrated a passion for and understanding of drama at an early age, when he began amusing his family by writing and performing plays, and his main career goal after high school was to become a movie actor. Len Pielmeier, who had entered into the family grocery business somewhat reluctantly himself, supported his son's decision to pursue a different career. In 1966 Pielmeier enrolled at the Catholic University of America with plans to study speech and drama, and his positive experience in the drama program made him decide to shift his focus from movie work to stage acting. He gave little thought to writing plays, but he did take a playwriting course. After receiving his B.A. in 1970, Pielmeier decided to delay going to New York in search of acting jobs in order to attend graduate school.

He applied for the M.F.A. acting program at Pennsylvania State University because its proximity to his family home would allow him to be close to his ailing father. After his application for the acting program was rejected, he applied and was accepted for the M.F.A. playwriting program at Penn State, where he was named a Shubert Fellow. He good-naturedly credits this series of events for his future success as a playwright.

At the end of Pielmeier's first year at Penn State, one of his instructors asked him to do a stage adaptation of *Soledad Brother* (1970), a collection of prison letters by Black Panther George Jackson. Performed twice as part of a student showcase called the Five O'Clock Theater, Pielmeier's play met with great enthusiasm from the student audience, as well as a *New York Times* critic who happened to be in attendance. In her review Anne Fremantle called *Soledad Brothers* "a starkly vivid contemporary drama" (20 June 1971). Pielmeier had less initial success with his next effort, *A Chosen Room*, which the drama department refused to accept as his final project. Pielmeier left Penn State in 1973 without receiving his M.F.A., but after the play was successfully produced in Minneapolis in 1976, the department reconsidered its decision, and Pielmeier received an M.F.A. from Penn State in 1978.

After leaving school, Pielmeier acted in productions at various regional theaters, including the Actors Theatre of Louisville, the Guthrie Theatre in Minneapolis, the Milwaukee Repertory Theater, and Center Stage in Baltimore. After attending the O'Neill Playwrights Conference as an actor, Pielmeier traveled back to New York, where he was then living, and began writing a play to submit for performance at the conference the following year. When this script did not make the final cut, Pielmeier was undeterred and started another play, which was inspired by a headline that read "Nun Strangles Baby." This play, *Agnes of God*, was given a staged reading at the O'Neill Playwrights Conference in 1979 and went on to be cowinner of the 1979 Great American Play Contest sponsored by the Actors Theatre of Louisville, where the play had its first full-scale professional production in March 1980. In March 1982 it opened on Broadway for a successful seventeen-month run. During that time Pielmeier married poet Irene O'Garden on 9 October 1982.

The title character in *Agnes of God* is a young nun who has been accused of giving birth to a baby in secret, strangling it, and dumping its body. Agnes claims to have no knowledge of the baby's conception, birth, or murder. During psychological testing to determine her fitness to stand trial, a court-appointed psychiatrist, Dr. Martha Livingstone, who has become convinced that Agnes did not kill her baby, tries to discover the identity of the baby's father and the extent of Agnes's knowledge about the murder. Mother Superior Miriam Ruth serves as a mediator between the two and hopes that there is a miraculous explanation for how the innocent, child-like Agnes could have become pregnant. The play ends as the hypnotized Agnes confesses to the murder of her child. The question of the identity of the baby's father is left unanswered.

Although the play is ostensibly about Agnes, it also focuses on the struggles of Dr. Livingstone and Mother Miriam to come to terms with their own spiritual beliefs. The play questions modern conceptions of science and religion, explores the theme of innocence, and investigates whether a belief in miracles is possible in the modern world. Dr. Livingstone is torn between a belief in the possibility that Agnes could have conceived a child without having had sexual intercourse and her firm, pragmatic faith in science. Mother Miriam summarizes Dr. Livingstone's dilemma as one that plagues all people living in modern times:

> Two thousand years ago, some people believe, a man was born without a father. Now no intelligent person today accepts that without question. We want answers, yes, that's the nature of science, but look at the answers we provide. An angel came to a woman in a shaft of light, hysterical parthenogenesis.

The audience is left wondering about the possibility of an immaculate conception. At the same time it must face the reality that an innocent person is capable of a hideous crime. In a 1984 interview with Trevor Thomas, Pielmeier explained his intentions in this regard:

> I've always been fascinated by innocence. I find it compelling and mysterious. If this nun were in some way spiritually, mentally innocent—and yet capable of committing a horrible crime—well, I became fascinated by the duality. . . . I wanted to write a play that simply asked questions, because I don't think answers are as important.

Mother Miriam expresses Pielmeier's sentiments when she chastises the doctor for needing concrete answers: "You'll never find the answer to everything, Doctor. . . . The wonder of science is not in the answers it provides but in the questions it uncovers."

Reviewers praised Pielmeier's humorous treatment of serious subject matter and his provocative, thought-provoking premise. Yet, many critics found it impossible to avoid comparisons between this play and Peter Shaffer's Tony Award–winning play *Equus*, which had a successful three-year New York run in 1974–1977, finding that Pielmeier's play lacked the depth and sophistication of language of Shaffer's play about a seemingly innocent individual who has committed a horrifying crime. Reviewing *Agnes of God* for *The New York Times* (31 March 1982), Frank Rich wrote of Pielmeier's "promise" but asserted that the playwright had not "figured out how to meld melodramatic and spiritual concerns."

Pielmeier's *Courage*, which premiered at the Actors Theatre of Louisville in March 1983, is a monodrama in which the speaker is James M. Barrie, the author of *Peter Pan* (1904). Using as his framework Barrie's 1922 commencement address at St. Andrew's

Program cover and title page for the 1982 New York production of Pielmeier's play about a young nun accused of murdering her newborn infant, with Carrie Fisher replacing Amanda Plummer in the title role (Bruccoli Clark Layman Archives)

Academy in Edinburgh, Pielmeier wrote a play in which his character describes his life and works. The play was performed in 1984 as part of a showcase at the Lamb's Club in New York, where it met with positive reviews. Herbert Mitgang of *The New York Times* praised its "rich language" (14 May 1984), and other critics called the drama a moving portrait of Barrie.

In addition to working on stage plays and adapting *Agnes of God* for the screen, Pielmeier also started writing for television, beginning with *Choices of the Heart* (1983), about American missionaries who died in El Salvador. This teleplay garnered many positive reviews, earning Christopher and Humanitas Awards in 1984—as well as a Writers Guild of America nomination—and paving the way for more work in television.

In 1985 Pielmeier mounted his second Broadway show, *The Boys of Winter*. Its genesis was ABC producer Bernie Sofronski's suggestion that Pielmeier write a play based on Lt. William Calley Jr.'s participation in the My Lai massacre (16 March 1968), during which Calley and men under his command killed some three hundred innocent Vietnamese civilians—women, children, and old people. Found personally responsible for forcing some villagers into a ditch and killing them with machine-gun fire, Calley was convicted of murder and sentenced to life in prison. Initially, Pielmeier was not interested in writing about Calley, but he did want to write a play about the special relationships shared among men during wartime. During his research for that play, however, Pielmeier became intrigued by Calley's seeming normalcy. As Pielmeier explained to Nina Darnton in 1985, "I decided to write a play about a man whom I felt for who committed an atrocity. It's probably one of the themes that connects this play with *Agnes of God*, the theme of innocence with blood on one's hands."

Pielmeier felt some initial trepidation about writing on the Vietnam War because he did not serve in it.

To compensate for his lack of firsthand knowledge, he did a great deal of research and made sure that his young cast—which included Ving Rhames, Wesley Snipes, and Matt Dillon—underwent instruction about the war and military life. They read books by veterans, viewed movies and documentaries about the war, and attended a mock version of boot camp.

The Boys of Winter opens after Lt. Bonney, a Native American who is loosely based on Calley, has murdered seven innocent Vietnamese villagers in retaliation for the deaths of soldiers in his platoon. The play consists of discussions among the dead soldiers that reveal the comradery of men at war, and a soliloquy by each of the dead soldiers and Bonney, in which each man tries to explain Bonney's motivation for killing innocent people. The soliloquies are presented in the manner of testimony, with each of the dead soldiers presumably saying what he would have said if he were alive to serve as a witness at Bonney's court-martial.

In the attempt of *The Boys of Winter* to examine what could cause a seemingly normal soldier to commit an atrocity, many critics saw an effort to remove most of the blame from Calley and place it squarely on Americans who supported the Vietnam War. Although Pielmeier was given some credit for developing an analogy between mistreatment of Native Americans and that of the Vietnamese, most critics found the play to be inferior to other Vietnam War plays such as David Rabe's *Streamers* (1976) and John DiFusco's *Tracers* (1980). Some reviewers described Pielmeier's play as a reworking of stories that had already been told more convincingly by other writers. Writing for the *New York Post* (2 December 1985), Clive Barnes commented, "the reality seemed second hand, the pain once removed, and the sentiments more literary and perhaps moralistic than is usually called for by the immediacy of pain." While they felt that Pielmeier successfully explored the theme of "innocence with blood on one's hands" in *Agnes of God*, many critics considered it inappropriate in the context of My Lai because they believed that the murderer should share a large part of the blame. Writing for *The New York Times* (2 December 1985) Frank Rich was critical of the various "excuses" made by Bonney's men and complained about "moral rigor mortis infecting the men's arguments." As a result of such negative reviews, the play was a commercial flop, running for just nine performances. Yet, Pielmeier has a fondness for *The Boys of Winter*, characterizing it as his "most personal" play.

Pielmeier returned to Broadway in 1987 with *Sleight of Hand*, in which he tried to "attack the thriller form head-on." Through a twisted and complicated plot, *Sleight of Hand* dramatizes the love triangle among an evil magician, his dancer girlfriend, and her stage director. Mixing magic and mystery, *Sleight of Hand* was enlivened by the infusion of magic tricks but riddled with problems. The play ran for only nine performances, and later Pielmeier said the play did not represent his best efforts.

Affected by the harsh reviews of *The Boys of Winter* and *Sleight of Hand*, Pielmeier retreated from the Broadway scene. In his 1999 interview with Gregory Bossler, he explained, "After these experiences, I stopped writing for the theater. It was emotionally and mentally debilitating and discouraging. It took me a long time to start writing again." He turned his attention to the more lucrative and less critical world of television. As he told Joe Pollack in 1993, "I was kind of burned out and frustrated. Broadway can be difficult. A writer just isn't as involved in television. It's a job, with less control, but I understand that and it works satisfactorily."

When he was again ready to concentrate on stage plays, Pielmeier created *Willi*, a one-man show based on the life of Willi Unsoeld, in whom Pielmeier had become interested when he was asked to write a movie script about Unsoeld, but instead—with a commission from A Contemporary Theatre (ACT) in Seattle—he developed a one-man show. Using Unsoeld's speeches, Pielmeier created a monologue in which his character recalls his personal and professional life. Pielmeier performed the play himself when it was staged at ACT in 1991.

As he told Bossler in 1999, Pielmeier believes that one can learn a great deal from Unsoeld's life philosophy:

> Willi would go around the country and give lectures on wilderness, the spirituality of wilderness, and the importance of risk-taking in life. He talked a lot about risk-taking. I think we have to do that in our lives to learn, to progress, and to understand what being alive is all about. . . . I guess if there's any piece of mine that typifies me, what I am attracted to, and what I try to do in my writing, it's *Willi*.

As in *Agnes of God*, a bare stage and the use of only a few props in *Willi* keep the audience's focus on the words and thoughts of the character. Pielmeier has classified *Agnes of God* as a "play of the mind," and the same could be said for *Willi*. Stage adaptations such as *Courage* or *Willi* allow Pielmeier to exercise his skill at bringing to life other people's stories.

Willi was well received by critics. Jim Kjeldsen, writing in *The Seattle Post-Intelligencer* (21 September 1991), credited Pielmeier with creating "an evocative and sometimes stunning portrayal of the late climber." The reviewer for the *St. Louis Dispatch* (23 January 1994) praised Pielmeier's acting: "Pielmeier performs

Program cover and title page for the New York premiere of Pielmeier's thriller about a radio-show therapist being stalked at her isolated cabin (courtesy of John Pielmeier)

splendidly, moving from comedy to drama and back again with ease."

Pielmeier's next major project was working with composer Matthew Selman on a musical about cartoonist Rube Goldberg, who won a Pulitzer Prize in 1947 and was well known for his humorous sketches of complicated "inventions." The project had begun as a collaboration between Selman and Goldberg's son George W. George, who wanted to write a musical about his father's struggle to become an artist despite family objections. The pairing did not work, and Selman suggested that Pielmeier take the son's place. After George agreed, Selman and Pielmeier worked together at The Gathering at Bigfork, a playwrights' laboratory in Montana where Pielmeier was in residency from 1991 to 1994. *Young Rube* made its debut at the Repertory Theatre of St. Louis in September 1993.

Mixing humor and sorrow, *Young Rube* chronicles Goldberg's struggle to become an artist, even bringing to life some of his cartoon characters as it explores the development of the artist. In fact, as Pielmeier told Pollack in 1993, the play is "really about what makes an artist an artist." Reviewers again praised Pielmeier's ability to create a poignant portrait of a man's life, while Pollack hailed Pielmeier's "great talent for humor, with one-liners, bad puns, and a full arsenal of spoofs."

At the same time that Pielmeier was working on *Young Rube*, he began work on his second thriller, *Voices in the Dark*, the play that eventually marked his return to Broadway. Jeff Steitzer, the artistic director of ACT, commissioned the play in 1991, and Pielmeier began work on it in 1992. He directed the first production, which opened at ACT in October 1994. The play later had a tryout run at the George Street Playhouse in New Brunswick, New Jersey, and opened on Broadway in August 1999.

Voices in the Dark is in some ways a conventional stage thriller in the tradition of Patrick Hamilton's *Gas Light* (1938; produced in the United States as *Angel Street,* 1941), Frederick Knott's *Dial M for Murder*

(1952), and Ira Levin's *Deathtrap* (1978). The audience is alternately shocked and scared as it watches the unfolding fate of Lil, a talk-show therapist who is trapped in a remote cabin in the Adirondacks. All violence happens offstage, allowing the audience to dwell on what the playwright calls a "malevolent force." In an interview with Michael Kuchwara (*Washington Times,* 4 September 1999) Pielmeier explained the appeal of the thriller: "The heart of *Voices in the Dark*—what essentially gave me the idea for the play—is that the malevolent force is what we don't see. It's what we hear. I think the scariest moments in thrillers are the moments before we see the malevolent force." David Stearns, reviewing the play for *USA Today* (18 April 1999), credited Pielmeier with depicting the "senseless grotesqueness" of violence rather than creating a "gratuitous blood bath." Stearns also saw the play as "a covert commentary on how TV can breed emotional detachment from violence and what an impact that can have on the mentally disturbed." *The New Yorker,* however, called *Voices in the Dark* "a truly thrilling stage thriller" (6 September 1999), and the Mystery Writers of America gave it the 1999 Edgar for best play.

Other reviewers were less impressed than Stearns, though many seemed to aim their negative remarks less at Pielmeier than at the thriller or the genre as a whole. Most critics seemed to share the idea that the thriller genre was passé and that it lacked the dignity and depth necessary for Broadway success. Pielmeier disagreed, telling Bossler that the thriller is "absolutely the most challenging form to write for the theater." Most of the specific criticism of the play centered on the somewhat convoluted plot. Reviewing the New Brunswick production for *Variety* (4 May 1998), Robert Daniels commented, "If the plot seems filled with holes, and leaves too many questions unresolved, the play provides enough chilling moments to warrant more than a few gasps and screams." The play ran for a respectable sixty-four performances.

Pielmeier now spends most of his time writing for television and the movies, but he continues to write new plays. Summarizing the theme of his stage work for Bossler in 1999, the playwright said, "If my plays are about anything, it's about being alive and understanding the thrill of being alive, the thrill of surviving, and the thrill of being so present in a moment that it illuminates the mystery just for a flash."

Interviews:

Trevor Thomas, "The Headline that Became a Play," *Los Angeles Times,* 14 February 1984, VI: 6;

Nina Darnton, "Young Actors, Their Own Truths About Vietnam," *New York Times,* 24 November 1985, II: 4;

Joe Pollack, "On the Road with 'Rube': A 'New' Musical's Long Journey to Production," *St. Louis Post-Dispatch,* 9 September 1993, p. G1;

Michael Kuchwara, "Making an Effective Thriller Can Be a Tense Job," *Washington Times,* 4 September 1999, D5;

Gregory Bossler, "Writers and Their Work," *Dramatist,* (September/October 1999): 14–23.

Miguel Piñero

(19 December 1946 – 17 June 1988)

Jon D. Rossini
Texas Tech University

PLAY PRODUCTIONS: *All Junkies,* New York, 1973;

Straight from the Ghetto, by Piñero, Neil Harris, and others, New York, 1973;

Short Eyes, New York, Riverside Church theater, January 1974; New York, Vivian Beaumont Theater, 23 May 1974;

Sideshow, New York, 30 May 1974;

The Guntower, New York, Nuyorican Theatre Festival in association with the New York Shakespeare Festival, Public Theater, 12 August 1976;

The Sun Always Shines for the Cool, New York, Booth Theatre, 1976;

Eulogy for a Small-Time Thief, New York, Ensemble Studio Theatre, November 1977;

Paper Toilet, Los Angeles, circa 1979;

Cold Beer, New York, 1979;

NuYorican Nights at the Stanton Street Social Club, New York, Nuyorican Poets Café, 1980;

Playland Blues, New York, Henry Street Settlement theater, 1980;

A Midnight Moon at the Greasy Spoon, New York, Theatre for the New City, 1981;

Cold Beer, Gun Tower, Paper Toilet, Tap Dancing & Bruce Lee Kicks, and *Sideshow,* Miguel Piñero Festival of One-Act Plays, Los Angeles, Nosotros Theatre, April 1992;

Outrageous: Three One-Acts (Sideshow, Cold Beer, Paper Toilet), New York, Nuyorican Poets Café, December 1995.

BOOKS: *Short Eyes: A Play* (New York: Hill & Wang, 1975);

La Bodega Sold Dreams (Houston: Arte Público Press, 1980);

The Sun Always Shines for the Cool, A Midnight Moon at the Greasy Spoon, Eulogy for a Small-Time Thief (Houston: Arte Público Press, 1983);

Outrageous: One-Act Plays (Houston: Arte Público Press, 1986).

Miguel Piñero (photograph by Arlene Gottfried; from the cover for Outrageous: One-Act Plays, *1986)*

Collection: *Piñero: Selected Writings of Miguel Piñero, Poet, Playwright, and Outlaw* (Houston: Arte Público Press, 2001).

PRODUCED SCRIPTS: *Short Eyes,* motion picture, Film League, 1977;

"Por Nada," television, *Baretta,* by Piñero and Chris Lucky, ABC, 23 November 1977;

"The Gadjo," television, *Baretta,* story by Piñero and Ray Hutcherson, ABC, 30 March 1978;

"Smuggler's Blues," television, *Miami Vice,* NBC, 1984;

A Midnight Moon at the Greasy Spoon, radio, *KCRW Playhouse,* KCRW-FM, Los Angeles, 7 November 1988.

OTHER: *Nuyorican Poets: An Anthology of Puerto Rican Words and Feelings,* edited by Piñero and Miguel Algarín (New York: Morrow, 1975);

Playland Blues [acts 1 and 3], in *Action: The Nuyorican Poets Café Theater Festival,* edited by Algarín and Lois Elaine Griffith (New York: Simon & Schuster, 1997), pp. 140–197.

Although it is not uncommon to speak metaphorically about a writer as criminally transgressive, it is less common to encounter one, such as Miguel Piñero, with an actual criminal history. Piñero is best known for his 1974 play *Short Eyes,* a prison drama that won a New York Drama Critics Circle Award and an Obie in 1974 and was eventually made into a movie. To presuppose that his criminal history is the only driving force in Piñero's work is unfair and limiting, but to ignore its influence on his plays neglects his entire artistic formation as a playwright. His dramatic language and situations reflect his experiences in *Loisaida*–the Lower East Side of Manhattan. His experiences on the street and in prison helped to shape his identity as an actor, in life as well as in the theater and on the screen. Although Piñero would have resisted making the connection between life and acting too easy, the idea of play in his work illustrates the fragile distinction between the way of being someone on the streets and the way of playing someone on the stage or screen.

Like other Puerto Ricans who left their island for New York in the 1950s, the Piñero family, who moved to the mainland United States when Miguel was four, did not achieve their dream of economic mobility. The future playwright was born on 19 December 1946 in Guarabo, Puerto Rico, and his parents, Miguel Angel Gomez Ramos and Adelina Piñero, brought him and his younger sister, Elizabeth, to New York City in 1950. In 1954 his father abandoned the family while his mother was pregnant with her fifth child. With no source of income, she and her children spent some time living on the streets, and Miguel began stealing food for his family. Talking about his difficult and abbreviated childhood to Mel Gussow in 1974, Piñero described the presence of "rats, roaches, bedbugs, flies, winos and dope fiends." He attended four different schools, three public and one parochial, but most of his education occurred as a result of his own reading, his time in correctional schools and facilities, and life on the street. The Lower East Side shaped much of his artistic production. During his youth, he was in trouble with the law for various property crimes and drug possession, and he spent time at the Otisville State Training School for Boys. Involved in gangs, he began participating in more elaborate thefts and rumbles. One of these conflicts led to threats on his life and the decision to move to Brooklyn. In Brooklyn he and three friends began a series of robberies (more than one hundred according to Piñero), which came to an end when he was caught in a jewelry store. Serving time at Riker's Island Prison in 1964, he began a lifelong addiction to drugs, especially heroin. After his first stay in Riker's, he joined the Job Corps and was sent for training to Camp Kilmer, New Jersey, hoping–he told Gussow–"to get an education–but the Job Corps was Dope City, Skag Town." He returned to New York City and became affiliated with the Young Lords, a Puerto Rican group that in many ways paralleled the Black Panthers. He was soon back in Riker's, this time on drug-possession charges, despite attempts to kick the habit, including a stint at Phoenix House in a drug-rehabilitation program. After he completed his second term at Riker's, his mother placed him in Manhattan State Hospital, where he managed to earn his high-school equivalency diploma.

Piñero's life as a writer did not really begin until his incarceration at Ossining Correctional Facility (Sing Sing) for armed robbery in 1971. The sentence at Sing Sing was the longest he had ever faced, and he began his writing career by producing letters for his fellow inmates. His first literary work was "Black Woman with a Blonde Wig On," which he later included in *Straight from the Ghetto* (1973) and in *La Bodega Sold Dreams* (1980). The poem drew wanted and unwanted attention. Marvin Felix Camillo, director of The Family, a theatrical group of former inmates, submitted the poem to a contest, and it won a prize, but when a newspaper report mentioned the award the warden became concerned about "contraband" being taken from the prison and nearly put Camillo in jail. Working initially with Clay Stevenson and later Camillo in various prison writing workshops, Piñero began to develop his self-conception as a writer. Knowledge of Piñero's poetry, a much smaller body of work than his drama, is crucial for understanding his theater. Though his plays are not written in verse, they are often street poetry. Their language is the gritty idiom of the street and many of their structural flaws are overcome by the beauty of his characters' poetic monologues.

When Piñero left Sing Sing on parole in June 1973 he had a place to go–The Family. Within its protective structure he developed his award-winning 1974 play *Short Eyes.* Set in a "house of detention," the play focuses on a small group of inmates who try to maintain their codes of conduct within the realities of incarceration. *Short Eyes* dramatizes the transformations these inmates undergo after the arrival in their midst of Clark

Davis, a man accused of child molestation. The title of the play comes indirectly from the slang term for this crime. As Piñero told Norma Alarcón McKesson in 1974, the slang for pornography is "short heist," but "Los puertorriqueños couldn't say the 'h' in heist so it became eyes." From a different level of society, and one of only two white inmates in the group, Davis is guilty of molesting a child, although he is found innocent of this particular charge. The other prisoners kill him—not only because of their disgust with his particular crime but also because of his refusal to adapt to the living conditions in prison.

The real crisis of the play is not Davis's death but the moral dilemma of the prisoners' responsibility and complicity. By killing another human being, they lose their own humanity. The guards who deal regularly with the prisoners are happy to ignore the mistreatment of Davis. Only one of the prisoners, Juan, a Puerto Rican old-timer attempting to maintain a sense of moral values even in prison, knows for a fact of Davis's guilt, having learned of it through an unsolicited confession, and Juan is the only one who refuses to participate in the murder. Although his noninvolvement may be read as a product of an increased intimacy with Davis, it seems more about self-preservation. That is, Juan does not want to stain his soul with this crime. He will not go against his code; nor will he unburden the other prisoners of their guilt by conveying Davis's confession. He refuses to do so because, regardless of Davis's guilt, they have also committed a heinous crime. Reviewers, including Walter Kerr of *The New York Times* (27 March 1974), called *Short Eyes* "promising" but "not yet freed from its initial debt to life." This tendency to see the play as a "quasi-documentary" comes not only from the audience's knowledge of the playwright's experiences, but also from the initial performances, in which former inmates acted out scenes of prison life. Eventually made into a well-received movie (1977), *Short Eyes* was the first play by a Puerto Rican to make it on Broadway, and this work has had a tremendous influence on both Puerto Rican writers and dramatists dealing with prison issues.

With the success of *Short Eyes* Piñero was able to support himself and continued to work with kids from the streets, helping them to find security and an artistic voice. As he said to Nat Hentoff in May 1974, theater workshops were "a way to stay human in prison," and the activity "helps make you aware of who you are, what you can be." Though he was beginning to receive opportunities to lecture at prestigious universities, including Rutgers and Princeton, his primary commitment was to Puerto Ricans and their artistic voices. He worked with Miguel Algarín to found the Nuyorican Poets Café and helped edit an anthology of poetry by Puerto Ricans in New York. The term *Nuyorican* helps explain Piñero's artistic sensibilities. It suggests the realities of Puerto Rican life in New York City, a bilingual, bicultural existence that demands a constant negotiation between languages and cultures to maintain one's identity.

An important example of how Piñero tried to help youths that had been in his position—as he told Hentoff, to "instill pride and confidence in their own intelligence so that they can feel there are things they can do instead of hustling"—is *Sideshow* (1974). An early, shorter version of Piñero's full-length show *Playland Blues* (1980) and first performed by former hustlers and members of The Young Family, the play gives the audience a sense of street life as a kind of performance. In *Sideshow* a group of street kids decide to put on their own play about a social worker placing difficult teenagers in various living situations and their attempts to adapt. Surrounding the drama they create "for fun" is the drama they live on the streets. As Piñero told Carlos Morton in 1974, "The question I would like to ask myself is: Why did these kids quit hustling just to work on my show?" Theater is an avenue in which to try out different versions of the self. Rather than seeing theater as removed from the world, Piñero saw it as showing realities that many audiences would prefer to forget. The central shocking event, the knifing death of a young pimp, is interpreted in various ways by other characters. Referring in part to the carnival freak show, Piñero tries to show his audiences that these human "freaks," young kids who have been labeled and then ignored in various ways, are not what they have been tagged. Their ways may be destructive, but their culture must be understood as a genuine, though difficult and dangerous, way of life. Piñero did not try to glamorize their lifestyle, but he took it seriously and left calls for reform to others. In the words of Henry Clearnose, named for his glue-sniffing habit (and played by Piñero's younger brother Carlos Noel in the first production), "Oh, I wish everyone would stop saying how much they care and love." Reviewing a 1992 revival of the play, T. H. McCulloh called it "a bit dated" but "a joy to watch" (*Los Angeles Times,* 3 April 1992).

Produced at the 1976 New York Shakespeare Festival, Piñero's one-act play *The Guntower* is again set in a prison, but this time the focus is on two guards in a tower. After Simmon Johnson's feeling of alienation is established, he shifts into a flashback to Vietnam, showing how he is displaced from society at several levels. Prison guards, the play reveals, are the same as the men who served in the military, looking for action and yet troubled by it, obeying orders because that is the only way to process what they are doing. When German Rosado joins Simmon in the tower, the audiences sees the possibilities of this space, the power

Bruce Waite, Chino Melao, and Ramon Franco in a 1979 New York production of Piñero's 1976 play
The Sun Always Shines for the Cool *(photograph by Bert Andrews)*

made possible by a location that allows a person to look down on others. German refuses Simmon's friendship precisely because Simmon does not recognize the creative power of his position—being able to see everything, abstract from it, and create. Power, sexuality, the ability to define oneself, and confusion about relationships and one's identity come to the fore in this world turned upside down, in which every action is surrounded by potential danger.

Piñero's next full-length play, *The Sun Always Shines for the Cool* (1976), explores the lives of players, operators, drug dealers, and thieves as they come together in a bar owned by a man named Justice. The question of being a *player* (a word that has separate meanings on the street and in the theater) has in part to do with knowing how to make a play (do a particular job or carry out a particular interaction) and how to treat other players with respect. The play focuses on Viejo's attempts to reach his daughter, Chile Girl, to whom he has not been a particularly good father. Chile Girl feels that Viejo has abandoned her, and in a sense he has, for he has spent time in jail. At the same time, Viejo does what he can to protect her from the world he knows so well by making her lover, Cat Eyes, admit to his intentions to transform her into a prostitute. As he has done the same thing to his own sister, it is not surprising that he would do the same thing to the woman he "loves." Viejo's suicide at the conclusion, his final "play," not only garners respect, it also impugns Cat Eyes's status within this world and educates Chile Girl in the skills necessary to interpret the motives of the people around her.

Justice's bar operates on a model in which the hierarchy of a self-selecting community is predicated on an individual's ability to garner and grant respect. A scene in which Viejo is in bed with a prostitute conveys a clear sense of the relationship between language and respect. Viejo gets upset because she calls him "old man," which is the translation of his name but entirely inappropriate to the situation. This insistence on respect for Viejo is in part based on Piñero's experiences in Sing Sing, where a fellow inmate called El Viejo helped the young writer get a job as a clerk so that he could have access to a typewriter. (The same man also provided an important line in *Short Eyes*: Juan's statement to another inmate that he has "placed himself above understanding.") Reactions from critics were mixed. Joseph McLellan insisted that there were "minor technical problems" and "melodrama" in the play, but it had "a convincing atmosphere and dramatic power that make the problems seem unimportant" (*The Washington Post*, 9 June 1977).

The theme of *Eulogy for a Small-Time Thief* (1977) is the problem of the player who does not really know his place in the world and thinks he can manipulate it to his liking. The setting is Philadelphia, where Piñero had moved in late 1975 to play the role of God in *Steambath* by Bruce Jay Friedman. In *Eulogy for a Small-Time Thief* David Dancer (called Panama in the original stage production) is playing host to a couple of working stiffs he has brought to meet Elaine and Rita, girls recruited by his girlfriend's younger sister. This foray into procuring turns out disastrously when one of the men turns out to be Elaine's father. In this play about assumptions, hiding, and various forms of self-delusion, two sisters fight over David, and only one of them, Rosemarie, is smart enough to realize his worthlessness. The younger sister, Nicole, thinks naively that love will conquer all. She does not understand that David relies on Rosemarie, who is much smarter than he is, and he is perfectly aware of his dependence. He considers Rosemarie his girl and Nicole only a fling. Nicole's revealing her pregnancy to her elder sister has the unfortunate effect of sending Rosemarie away, and David is left to die at the hands of an acquaintance who has been hired to kill him. David has brought the hit on himself by scamming money from a deal and using it to purchase a farm that he envisions as an idyllic paradise. Yet, the play and this world do not allow his retirement. David's death reveals how seldom he was ever in control. There is no space for romanticizing in the play, no real loyalty or connection. As with Nicole and David, there is really nothing but lust (a reality she does not recognize). David's death is a shock, but the true focus is on how the various characters deal with their recognition of their lack of control. Reviewers such as Richard Eder criticized "a forced and narrow manipulation" of "plots and characters" but said they "seem authentic" (*The New York Times*, 28 November 1977).

While maintaining a base in Philadelphia, Piñero returned to New York in 1976 to work on the movie version of *Short Eyes*, explaining to Leticia Kent that "I haven't given up on New York—I've just gone to Philadelphia to find new energies for myself." During the filming he and Tito Goya, a member of The Family who also worked on the original stage production of *Short Eyes*, were accused of armed robbery and were arraigned in the same building where they were filming. The charges were dismissed in 1978, but the attention the case garnered forced some people to speculate that Piñero had a "need" to get back to prison. For the motion-picture version Piñero played the role of Go-Go (a part created for the movie). Although the reviews for the movie were mixed, Piñero's performance was well received.

Piñero married Juanita Lovette Ramirez in 1977, and the two adopted a child, Ismael Castro. Their marriage ended in 1979, and Piñero moved to Los Angeles, where he played small roles in several movies, including *The Jericho Mile* (1979), *Times Square* (1980), *Fort Apache, The Bronx* (1981), and *Alphabet City* (1984). Having written episodes of *Baretta* in 1977–1978 and acted in an episode of that show as well as in a 1973 *Kojak* episode, he later wrote the "Smuggler's Blues" episode (1984) for *Miami Vice*.

He also wrote several one-act plays, including *Paper Toilet* and *Cold Beer,* both staged around 1979 and collected along with *The Guntower* (first produced in 1976), *Irving* (unproduced), and *Tap Dancing & Bruce Lee Kicks* (produced in 1992) in *Outrageous* (1986), a title that fits these plays well. *Paper Toilet* takes place in a subway men's room and involves a series of events framed by the voice of a man asking for toilet paper from inside a stall. The opposition of law and order versus chaos, sex, and violence is first demonstrated by a vice cop snaring a man for "soliciting for the purpose of an unnatural sex act" in a manner verging on entrapment. The toilet is a site for illicit acts that must be policed. This need is illustrated even more clearly in the second episode, as two young boys run into the toilet to count the money they have acquired from the theft of a purse. They vent their frustration with finding only 59¢ by stealing the man's pants and his money. Before they can leave, their first victim arrives, and they begin a fight, which is broken up by the police. The vice cop seems less concerned about the robbery than about the presence of the female purse-snatching victim in a men's bathroom. Suddenly the law becomes the instrument of protecting the sanctity of the men's bathroom from female invasion. Seeing this transgression as the beginning of the breakdown of gender differences—and thus society—the vice cop feels compelled to create a charge against the woman. While the other characters question the vice cop's sanity, Piñero was clearly using his comedy as a subversive examination of the role of the law in protecting individual privacy and maintaining sexual boundaries. Reviewing a 1995 revival of the play, Lisa Kennedy called it "a little too extended" (*The Village Voice,* 5 December 1995).

Like the later one-act *Tap Dancing & Bruce Lee Kicks, Cold Beer* examines the role of the dramatist and writer through an alter-ego protagonist. *Cold Beer* is a snapshot of the difficult creative process of the bohemian artist, Mike the "beerbelly poet," who vibrantly transgresses by urinating on the neighbor's dog, which has deservedly been cursed with the name "Poopoo." Though no sustained creation takes place in *Cold Beer,* Piñero's vision of his own role as an artist is clarified by the metaphor of a different way of writing that questions the mainstream and is confrontational but comprehensible. Playing with the possibilities of theater, Piñero has Mike encounter real and imagined characters, and both sorts find their way into his story.

Irving is an exploration of a Jewish man's "coming out" party, made slightly more difficult by the presence of his bisexual lover as his sister's date. In many ways a stereotypical exploration of Jewish identity, it is clearly also an examination of the transformation of children as they move away from their parents.

A full-length reworking of *Sideshow,* the 1980 *Playland Blues* attempts to explore the lives of seventeen youthful players, mostly prostitutes, each with his own way of getting by. The older men (in their twenties) have moved from being hustlers to drug pushers because they cannot market their bodies as they did before. The death of the oldest hustler, Pepper, whose attempts to unite the men and thus solidify their power, forces at least some of the men to re-evaluate their positions. Pepper's partner, Louie, eventually decides to leave street life, taking responsibility for the baby he has fathered and its mother, Nellie. Hector ends up going off with Mike, an older man who has tried to help the young hustlers. Unlike Henry Clearnose at the end of *Sideshow,* Hector has found a relationship that offers a future.

A Midnight Moon at the Greasy Spoon (1981) is different from Piñero's previous work, what Mel Gussow has called "a sympathetic slice of working-class life, a play about idealism and disillusionment" (*The New York Times,* 27 April 1981). Piñero wrote the play in response to a request that he try something new. In the published version (1983) Joe and Gerry, both in their sixties, run a café in Times Square with the help of Dominick, a young Greek immigrant who is thirty years their junior. At the start of the play Dominick has just returned

Paperback cover for Piñero's 1986 collection, which includes Paper Toilet, Cold Beer, The Guntower, Irving, and Tap Dancing & Bruce Lee Kicks
(Bruccoli Clark Layman Archives)

from his wedding, which was arranged to change his immigration status. With a large cast ("as many customers as can effectively be included"), this loosely episodic work deals with various characters' setbacks, providing them opportunities to wax poetic about their lives. Joe, the man who never made it on Broadway as an entertainer, has located his business on the street in order to be there one way or another. Dominick's eventual replacement in the café, necessary because the woman he married turns out not to be a U.S. citizen, is Zulma, a woman who has finally given up her dream of making it in show business and has resigned herself to working on Broadway in the restaurant. Her fate is but one example of the failure of all the dreams in this world, and the succession of failures ends with Joe's death at the conclusion of the play.

Tap Dancing & Bruce Lee Kicks is set in an "inner-city tenement building" where "the holiday spirit is not as joyful as it was back in Dayton, Ohio in 1903." The play is bilingual, beginning with a couple speaking to one another in Spanish, but as they yell to their neighbors they switch to English. One of the neighbors is Mike, the writer figure who appears in several plays. As a stand-in for Piñero, Mike offers a pragmatic worldview and also the possibility of transforming life into art. In this play Mike is working on a story about David Dancer, the subject of Piñero's *Eulogy for a Small Time Thief,* and Mike reads an excerpt from his story that expresses the desire "to capture all the sounds that invade his privacy. They painted a picture only a Michelangelo could create." Another apartment has been converted to a shooting gallery for heroin, whose operators discuss the "tapping" of Mike's typewriter downstairs and insist that the typewriter has an almost religious significance for a writer. The association of typing and tap dancing highlights the artistry of the writing process. The second part of the title plays off the karate idea, suggesting the splitting of a good product into too many parts. The name *Bruce Lee* in the title brings to mind an expertise at chopping and separating, while *Kicks* refers not only to a karate action but also the experience produced by drugs. As a reflection on the artistic process, the play articulates the difficulty of capturing the real sense, or poetry, of any segment of society. Piñero shows his audience the difficulty of pursuing his creative agenda.

"A Lower East Side Poem," a poem recited by a character in *Playland Blues* and collected in *La Bodega Sold Dreams,* is perhaps Piñero's clearest expression of the motivation and direction of his life as an artist. In the first stanza he wrote:

Just once before I die

I want to climb up on a

tenement sky

to dream my lungs out till

I cry

then scatter my ashes thru

the Lower East Side.

At the time of his death from cirrhosis of the liver in 1988, Piñero was working on a new play for Joseph Papp and the New York Shakespeare Festival: the unfinished "Every Form of Refuge Has Its Price," set in an intensive-care unit. He also left unfinished a play called "The Cinderella Ballroom." In the introduction to *Action: The Nuyorican Poets Café Theater Festival* (1997), Lois Elaine Griffith remembered Piñero this way: "It was 1973 when Miguel Piñero taught me about theater. Miky could stand on a street corner, gather a crowd him, and spit out a poem that induced action from an audience—an audience completely unaware that their response was creating drama about the intensity of everyday life."

Interviews:

Carlos Morton, "Social Realism on Aston Place: The Latest Piñero Play," *Revista Chicano-Riqueña,* 2, no. 1 (1974): 33–35;

Mel Gussow, "From Prison, 'Nowhere Being Nobody,' A Young Playwright Emerges to Fame," *New York Times,* 27 March 1974, pp. 45, 68;

Nat Hentoff, "Piñero: I Wanted to Survive," *New York Times,* 5 May 1974, II: 1, 8;

Norma Alarcón McKesson, "An Interview with Miguel Piñero," *Revista Chicano-Riqueña,* 2, no. 4 (1974): 55–57;

Leticia Kent, "Playwright Miguel Piñero Brings His 'Eyes' To the Tombs," *New York Times,* 23 January 1977, II: 1, 13, 29;

Guy Trebay, "Talking Heads: Miguel Piñero—Promise Dies Hard," *Village Voice,* 15–21 April 1981, p. 63.

Biography:

Piñero [motion picture], written and directed by Leon Ichaso, Miramax, 2001.

References:

Michael Roy Hames-Garcia, "Justice and the Politics of Freedom: Writings by United States Prisoners and Their Advocates," dissertation, Cornell University, 1998;

Steven Edward Hart, "The Family: A Theatre Company Working with Prison Inmates and Ex-Inmates," dissertation, City University of New York, 1981;

Nicolás Kanellos and Jorge Huerta, eds., "Nuevos Pasos: Chicano and Puerto Rican Drama," *Revista Chicano-Riqueña,* 7, no. 1 (1979): 173–174;

Roger S. Platizky, "Humane Vision in Miguel Piñero's *Short Eyes,*" *Americas Review,* 19 (Spring 1991): 83–91;

Ariel Ruiz, "Raza, sexo y politica en *Short Eyes* de Miguel Piñero," *Americas Review,* 15 (Summer 1987): 93–102;

Robert Vorlicky, *Act Like a Man: Challenging Masculinities in American Drama* (Ann Arbor: University of Michigan Press, 1995), pp. 133–154.

Papers:

Typescripts for Miguel Piñero's *The Guntower* and *All Junkies* are in the Billy Rose Theatre Collection at the New York Public Library for the Performing Arts.

Paul Rudnick

(29 December 1957 -)

Martha Greene Eads
Valparaiso University

PLAY PRODUCTIONS: *Poor Little Lambs,* New York, Theater at St. Peter's Church, 14 March 1982;

Cosmetic Surgery, Chicago, Immediate Theatre Company, 1983;

Arts and Leisure, Louisville, Ky., Actors Theatre, 1 November 1983;

Raving, New York, Ensemble Studio Theatre, 5 May 1984;

I Hate Hamlet, New York, Walter Kerr Theatre, 8 April 1991;

Jeffrey, New York, WPA Theatre, 20 January 1993; transferred to Minetta Lane Theatre, 6 March 1993;

The Naked Truth, New York, WPA Theatre, 16 June 1994; revised as *The Naked Eye,* Cambridge, Mass., American Repertory Theatre, 10 May 1996;

Mr. Charles, Currently of Palm Beach, New York, Ensemble Studio Theatre, 11 May 1998;

The Most Fabulous Story Ever Told, Williamstown, Mass., Williamstown Theatre Festival, 1 July 1998; New York, New York Theater Workshop, 14 December 1998; transferred to Minetta Lane Theatre, 2 February 1999;

Rude Entertainment, New York, Greenwich House Theater, 3 October 2001—comprised *Mr. Charles, Currently of Palm Beach; Very Special Needs;* and *On the Fence.*

BOOKS: *Social Disease* (New York: Knopf, 1986);

I'll Take It (New York: Knopf, 1989);

I Hate Hamlet (Garden City, N.Y.: Fireside Theatre, 1991);

If You Ask Me: The Collected Columns of America's Most Beloved and Irresponsible Critic, as Libby Gelman-Waxner (New York: St. Martin's Press, 1994);

Jeffrey (New York: Plume, 1994; New York: Dramatists Play Service, 1995);

The Most Fabulous Story Ever Told (New York: Dramatists Play Service, 1999);

Paul Rudnick (photograph by David Rogers; from the dust jacket for Social Disease, *1986)*

The Most Fabulous Story Ever Told; and, Mr. Charles, Currently of Palm Beach: Two Plays (Woodstock, N.Y.: Overlook Press, 2000).

PRODUCED SCRIPTS: *Sister Act,* by Rudnick and others, as Joseph Howard, motion picture, Touchstone, 1992;

Addams Family Values, motion picture, Paramount, 1993;

Jeffrey, motion picture, Orion, 1995;

The First Wives' Club, uncredited contributions by Rudnick to screenplay by Robert Harling, based on Olivia Goldsmith's novel, motion picture, Paramount, 1996;

In & Out, motion picture, Paramount, 1997;

Isn't She Great, motion picture, Universal, 2000;
Marci X, motion picture, Paramount, forthcoming 2003.

SELECTED PERIODICAL PUBLICATION—
UNCOLLECTED: "If Sex Has Lost Its Shock Value, How About God?" *New York Times,* 6 December 1998, pp. 2, 7.

Paul Rudnick has been a significant contributor to American popular culture at the turn of the millennium. His work as a screenwriter has included such movies as *Sister Act* (1992), *Addams Family Values* (1993), *Jeffrey* (1995), and *In & Out* (1997), while his accolades as a dramatist have included an Obie (Off-Broadway) Award, an Outer Critics Circle Award, and a John Gassner Award. Rudnick possesses the ability to lampoon serious religious, political, and social institutions and practices without appearing mean-spirited. He sends up even his own gay community by making the most of stereotypes in such plays as *Jeffrey* (1993), *The Most Fabulous Story Ever Told* (1998), and *Mr. Charles, Currently of Palm Beach* (1998). Beneath the surface of much of Rudnick's humorous work, however, lie questions about the nature and inevitability of suffering; the obligation humans have to care for one another; and the persistence and significance of sexual, racial, and religious stereotyping.

Paul Rudnick was born on 29 December 1957 in Piscataway, New Jersey, to Norman Rudnick and Selma Klahr Rudnick. His parents' lifelong interest in the theater helped guide Rudnick's career; as he recounted in a 1996 interview with Shawn René Graham, he declared in an essay at the age of five that he was a playwright, before even having seen his first play. In an unpublished 26 September 2000 interview, Rudnick joked about how his parents' collection of playbills and original cast albums shaped his theological views as well as his professional goals. His notion of God, he reported, comes from the album cover illustration for *My Fair Lady* (1956) on which a caricature of George Bernard Shaw operates marionettes resembling Julie Andrews and Rex Harrison. Describing his home as "deeply Reformed Jewish," Rudnick quipped that he and his older brother, Evan, "did have a real sense of worship for gift wrap and ribbon and whatever came from Hasbro and Mattel." He nevertheless noted that he, like many twentieth-century American children of Jewish descent, grew up in the shadow of the Holocaust: "There was always the sense that you had better deal with Judaism, with your Jewish heritage, because other people will be," he said.

Rudnick studied drama at Yale University, which he credits for much of his later success. "I may have been writing badly, but it was a way to learn something," he explained to Graham; "I would make these enormous mistakes but I learned how not to make the same mistake twice." Graduating in 1977, he moved to New York to write. His first produced play, chronicling the adventures of a Yale all-male singing group over the course of a year, was *Poor Little Lambs,* which opened at the Theater at St. Peter's Church in New York on 14 March 1982. Starring Kevin Bacon and Bronson Pinchot, *Poor Little Lambs* was optioned in Hollywood but never produced. Although he called the story "trite," Frank Rich reported in *The New York Times* (16 March 1982) that the play revealed Rudnick's "terrific ear for undergraduate locker-room chatter" and his "killer instinct for wisecracks."

Rudnick's second play, *Cosmetic Surgery,* was a one-act in which three characters (one of them male) chat in the women's restroom of a restaurant; it was part of the Chicago Immediate Theatre Company's 1983 lineup. Rudnick's next two one-acts were about critics: *Arts and Leisure,* which opened at the Actors Theatre in Louisville, Kentucky, on 1 November 1983, and *Raving,* which opened in New York at the Ensemble Studio Theatre on 5 May 1984. Starring Nathan Lane and Jack Gilpin, *Raving* focused on the reactions of three playwrights to a newcomer dramatist's rave review and spoofed both creative writers and critics. Mel Gussow of *The New York Times* (1 June 1984) dismissed it as "a forced exercise in theatrical backbiting." In his afterword to a 1997 edition of his novel *Social Disease* (1986) Rudnick describes this period of his life as his "early career as a triumphantly unsuccessful playwright," noting that he discarded several of his first scripts. "I had made the common mistake of writing plays not out of some necessary inspiration, but because I longed to be a playwright," he confesses; "This is like becoming an actor because you lust to see your caricature on the wall at Sardi's."

Turning his attention from drama to fiction, Rudnick spoofed the Manhattan club scene in his 1986 novel, *Social Disease.* In his afterword to the 1997 edition, Rudnick calls the book an account of his own early years in New York and "far too obvious an homage to Evelyn Waugh." Written just before AIDS became an epidemic, *Social Disease* celebrates an urban culture of youthful hedonism. Christopher Schemering of the *Washington Post* (10 June 1986) called the book "offensive, hilarious, charming, and, yes, even alarming," and praised its satire for having "the snap of a bullwhip." While he objected to Rudnick's "aggressive refusal to include the kind of characters, story or plot required to make

William Thomas Jr., Bronson Pinchot, Kevin Bacon, David Naughton, Miles Chapin, Blanche Baker, Page Mosley, Albert Macklin, and Gedde Watanabe in the 1982 New York production of Poor Little Lambs *(photograph by Gerry Goodstein)*

this work a 'novel' in any sense of the word," *Los Angeles Times* (8 June 1986) critic John H. Mankiewicz conceded that "there's no getting around Rudnick's solid talent" and compared him favorably to Jay McInerney and Bret Easton Ellis.

Rudnick's second novel, *I'll Take It* (1989), offers an account of a Yale-educated Jewish man's journey with female relatives to rob a New England shopping outlet. Reviewing the book for *The New York Times* (11 June 1989), Susan Isaacs acknowledged the political incorrectness of linking Jewish women to compulsive shopping but nevertheless called *I'll Take It* "an amusing, warmhearted book that will appeal to anyone who has an uncritical love of family and shiny objects." Rudnick's third book, *If You Ask Me: The Collected Columns of America's Most Beloved and Irresponsible Critic* (1994), is a volume of movie reviews first published in the late 1980s and early 1990s in *Premiere* magazine under the name Libby Gelman-Waxner.

Rudnick also took up screenwriting in the 1980s, completing a script titled *Sister Act* in 1987. Although Rudnick had Bette Midler in mind for the leading role, Touchstone bought the script and cast Whoopi Goldberg as Delores Van Cartier, a gangster's moll who witnesses a mob hit and subsequently takes refuge in a convent. The Touchstone picture differed so much from Rudnick's original script that the playwright eventually shared credit for the 1992 movie with other writers under the joint pseudonym Joseph Howard. The movie won the NAACP Image Award for Motion Picture of the Year and was one of the ten top-grossing pictures of 1992, and Goldberg's performance earned her a Golden Globe Award nomination and the Image Award for Best Actress in a Motion Picture.

Rudnick also collaborated on the 1991 screenplay for *The Addams Family*, based on *New Yorker* cartoonist Charles Addams's characters. Having been the subjects of a popular 1964–1966 television series, Gomez and Morticia Addams (played in the movies by Raul Julia and Anjelica Huston) and their relatives were familiar figures to movie audiences. With the success of *The Addams Family*, Rudnick was hired to write the screenplay for a sequel, *Addams Family Values*. Reviewer Desson Howe complained in the *Washington Post* (19 November 1993) that Rudnick "earns easy money with the jokes but doesn't strain himself to provide anything else like, say, character." *The New York Times* review (19 November 1993) was more positive; Janet Maslin praised the sequel as having "a cast and visual conception that were perfect in the first place, and a screenplay by Paul Rudnick that specializes in delightfully arch, subversive humor." *Addams Family Values*, she asserted, has "less novelty than its predecessor but more of a plot."

Rudnick had not abandoned playwriting as his screenwriting career developed. *I Hate Hamlet,* his first commercially successful play, opened at the Walter Kerr Theatre in New York on 8 April 1991. Living in a Greenwich Village apartment once owned by John Barrymore had inspired Rudnick to write a Noel Coward–like comedy about Andrew Rally, a young television performer to whom Barrymore's ghost gives acting lessons. The original cast included Evan Handler as Rally, Nicol Williamson as Barrymore, and Celeste Holm as Lillian Troy, Rally's agent and Barrymore's former flame. Adam Arkin, who played Rally's friend Gary Peter Lefkowitz, earned a Tony Award nomination for best supporting actor. As Barrymore, Williamson won not only rave reviews but also notoriety when he struck Handler in an onstage sword-fight. Although Williamson complained that his role had been badly written, the critics' response to the play was positive. In the *Christian Science Monitor* (23 April 1991) John Beaufort called *I Hate Hamlet* "a good-natured ghost comedy with its heart in the right place and its finger pressed firmly on the laugh button."

Rudnick's next New York dramatic success was *Jeffrey,* for which he received the Obie Award, the Outer Critics Circle Award, and the John Gassner Award for outstanding new American play. *Jeffrey* opened on 20 January 1993 at the WPA Theatre and moved to the Minetta Lane Theatre on 6 March of the same year. Starring John Michael Higgins in the title role, *Jeffrey* was directed by Christopher Ashley and traces the path of a gay New Yorker who resolves to forego sex in response to the AIDS epidemic. In his introduction to the play, Rudnick admits that he felt uncertain about viewers' reactions to the work:

> I had no idea how audiences would respond to *Jeffrey,* whether they'd be willing to accept repartee and big-time Gershwin amour amid the nightmare of AIDS. But I knew that any portrait of Manhattan life in the nineties would have to be a blend of the highest farce and the most devastating tragedy, laced with the gay style that has allowed a ravaged community to survive with its wisecracks and wardrobes intact.

The critics marveled at the success of his formula. *Los Angeles Times* (30 September 1993) reviewer Sylvie Drake mused, "A *comedy* about *AIDS?* Yes, but a comedy with a breezy subtext that is consistently hilarious and, surprisingly, consistently serious. Heavy-duty stuff, so breezy and palatable that it dazzles with its ability to demonstrate how you can take away the power of AIDS to intimidate when you make people laugh at pain without trivializing the tragedy."

Rudnick launches the play with a slide show of New York scenes, accompanied by a George Gershwin score, before introducing Jeffrey, his thirty-something protagonist. In the first of several surrealistic sequences, Rudnick shows Jeffrey in bed with a series of men: a lover who looks to him as a maternal figure; a bored male prostitute; a masked, gloved, and Saran-wrapped hypochondriac; and someone who simply is not attracted to him. After the rapid sequence of encounters, Jeffrey confesses to the audience that although he is obsessed with sex, he will give it up. "Sex," he asserts, "is too sacred to be treated this way. Sex wasn't meant to be safe, or negotiated, or fatal."

Having declared his intentions, however, Jeffrey faces many challenges. The most difficult arises from his gym encounter with the devastatingly attractive Steve. Jeffrey rebuffs Steve early in the play, but when his happily paired friends Sterling and Darius urge him to take a chance on love, he accepts Steve's dinner invitation. Before their date, however, Steve tells Jeffrey that he is HIV positive.

In spite of the encouragement of a female evangelist who tells him that "where you don't have love, illness makes a home," Jeffrey cancels his date with Steve. He subsequently undergoes a beating by homophobes, attends a meeting for sexual compulsives, holds both an imagined and a real conversation about his sexuality with his conservative Midwestern parents, and fends off Father Dan, a lecherous gay priest. Although he resists the priest's advances, Jeffrey does talk with him about his own despair. "Why did He do this?" he demands. "Why did God make the world this way, and why do I have to live in it? You're a priest—you have to tell me! Don't you?" Father Dan suggests that God is in music, in sex, in friendship, and in "the very best in all of us. The kindness. The heavy petting. The eleven o'clock numbers." The only "real blasphemy," he declares, is "the refusal of joy! Of a corsage and a kiss!"

Confused by Father Dan's remarks, Jeffrey continues his frustrating quest for happiness. He considers returning to his family in Wisconsin, learns that Steve has taken a new lover, and visits the hospital where Darius is dying of AIDS. When Sterling tells him that Darius had described Jeffrey as the saddest person he ever knew, Jeffrey asks the older man if he really thinks it is worth risking the sadness of losing a lover as Sterling is losing Darius. "Yes," Sterling says simply. Darius tells Jeffrey, "Go dancing. Go to a show. Make trouble. Make out. Hate AIDS, Jeffrey. Not life. . . . Just think of AIDS as . . . a guest

Program cover and title page for the 1991 New York production of Rudnick's play about a television actor haunted by the ghost of John Barrymore (Bruccoli Clark Layman Archives)

that won't leave. The one we all hate. But you have to remember . . . it's still our party."

In the final scene Mother Teresa and Jeffrey enter the observation deck of the Empire State Building. She helps him don a sports jacket and, before exiting, hands him a red balloon tied to the railing. When Steve enters and tells Jeffrey that he is romantically available again, Jeffrey asks him if they could have sex. Although Steve hesitates, their flirtation resumes, this time with both men aware of the risks they face. They bat the balloon back and forth before kissing as the lights dim.

The stage success of *Jeffrey* led to Rudnick's adapting the play for the screen. The Orion motion picture, also directed by Ashley, was released in 1995, with Steven Weber as Jeffrey, Michael T. Weiss as Steve, Patrick Stewart as Sterling, and Nathan Lane as Father Dan. Several critics observed that despite its funny moments, the movie did not have the appeal of the play. In his review for *USA Today* (4 August 1995) Tom Green noted that breaking the action into titled chapters made the movie choppy, reducing "what moved gleefully on the stage . . . to annoying stops and starts on film." Writing for the *San Francisco Chronicle* (16 February 1996), Edward Guthmann agreed, indicating that the movie "never matches the gleeful, irreverent mischief it had on stage." Nevertheless, his review described Rudnick as "one of the funniest writers in America. . . . He's an expert joke writer, has a flawless ear for brittle urban dialogue and manages to poke fun at the free-floating absurdity of our times without scrimping on respect for his characters."

Another of Rudnick's plays from the period received a second treatment when it returned to the stage two years later. Having first opened on 16 June 1994 at the WPA Theatre in New York, *The Naked Truth* underwent revisions and began a second run as

The Naked Eye at the American Repertory Theatre on 10 May 1996. Both productions starred Mary Beth Peil as Nan Bemiss, a sexually repressed socialite who finds liberation through her encounter with a controversial gay photographer patterned after Robert Mapplethorpe. The other characters include Nan's husband, a philandering senator on the campaign trail; their daughter; and his mistress. Rudnick uses the characters' interactions at a gala art exhibition to explore such subjects as hypocrisy, the relationship between art and politics, and the desire for love.

Hypocrisy was also a theme in Rudnick's next motion picture, *In & Out,* which depicts the coming out of high-school English teacher Howard Brackett, portrayed by Kevin Kline. When a former-student-turned-movie-star thanks him during the televised Academy Awards for serving as a gay role model, Howard begins to question his sexual identity. Inspired by Tom Hanks, who thanked his own gay drama teacher in his Academy Award acceptance speech for *Philadelphia* (1993), Rudnick uses a similar situation to challenge stereotypes of "gay" and "straight" behavior. Howard manfully coaches track, but he loves Broadway musicals and Barbra Streisand. When a handsome if sleazy journalist (played by Tom Selleck) comes to town to cover the story, Howard struggles to convince the journalist, his own fiancée and parents, his students and colleagues, and even himself that he is heterosexual.

Although the subject matter of the movie was still controversial at the time of its release, Rudnick's playful handling of it yielded a box-office success. Jay Carr, writing in the *Boston Globe* (19 September 1997), called the movie "a funny but compromised comedy," explaining that "*In and Out* retreats to the level of sitcom after promising something stronger that most audiences would have no difficulty accepting. Still, it's hard to begrudge *In and Out* what will certainly be mainstream success. You'll certainly laugh at the heads-up performances. But you'll also be aware of the film's limitations."

Anything Rudnick held back in *In & Out* surfaced in his next stage play, *Mr. Charles, Currently of Palm Beach.* The fourteen-page one-act, which first opened at the Ensemble Studio Theatre in New York on 11 May 1998, featured Peter Bartlett as the effeminate Mr. Charles, a cable-channel talk-show host. Mr. Charles reads viewers' letters asking him about the origins of homosexuality, cures for AIDS, gays in the military, rearing "gay-positive children," and gay theater. Although his answers are frequently flippant, Mr. Charles reveals a certain desperation. He jokes about being "so deeply homosexual" that he can turn someone gay "just with a glance." Claiming that he was asked to leave New York, he explains that his prissy manner embarrasses other gays. "This is because, on certain occasions," he says, "I take what I call—a nelly break." He demonstrates by squealing and gesturing, embodying the stereotype of the camp homosexual.

His lover Shane, whom Mr. Charles calls his "ward," is a handsome young man of limited intelligence. Shane appears briefly on the program, dancing, exiting, and then returning in a Robin costume and military fatigues to illustrate Mr. Charles's fantasies. Shane asks Mr. Charles to use his powers to make more gays. Rudnick's script then offers two endings for the play. In the first, Mr. Charles "zaps" the baby of his studio receptionist. In the second, he turns his attention to the camera, "making a hissing noise, zapping the viewing audience." In both, his dramatic finale is his confession that his carefully coiffed hair is not a hairpiece: he mouths "it's mine!" as his theme music plays and the lights fade. Peter Marks of *The New York Times* (21 May 1998) praised both Rudnick's clever quips and Bartlett's comic performance but asserted that Rudnick's goals were ultimately serious: "*Mr. Charles* is a politically incorrect swipe at the orthodoxy of any political, social or ethnic group that demands everyone swim with the tide. That Mr. Charles, because his manner is passe, should feel himself an outcast in the gay world, the one in which he sought comfort, is an outrage. Make the gay world safe for sashaying."

Rudnick's next play, *The Most Fabulous Story Ever Told,* was even less politically correct. Opening first at the Williamstown Theatre Festival in Massachusetts on 1 July 1998, the show moved to the New York Theater Workshop on 14 December 1998, and then to the Minetta Lane Theatre on 2 February 1999. Using a daring mix of sex and religion, *The Most Fabulous Story Ever Told* uses biblical stories as a framework for considering gay and lesbian relationships. The first act introduces Adam and Steve and Jane and Mabel—Rudnick's alternatives to Adam and Eve. In the second act he brings the two couples from the ancient Mideast to twentieth-century Manhattan.

Rudnick wrote in an article for *The New York Times* (6 December 1998) that working on the play showed him how deeply reluctant Americans are to talk openly about religious faith: "God suddenly struck me as a final taboo.... Chronic depression, infertility and incest are now talk show staples; God is relegated to the far reaches of cable, as a form of evangelical home shopping." He asserts that despite its controversial sexual content, *The Most Fabulous Story Ever Told* has more to do with religion than with sex. Rudnick credits religious conservatives with inspiring him to write the play, as he explains in his introduction:

John Michael Higgins and Tom Hewitt in the 1993 WPA Theatre production of Jeffrey *(photograph by William Gibson)*

The Most Fabulous Story Ever Told was sparked by the fundamentalist remark, "God made Adam and Eve, not Adam and Steve"; this is about as blithe as fundamentalists tend to get. Sometime around 1996, a thought occurred to me—well, what if God had started things off with two guys, and the first lesbians as well, Jane and Mabel? Certainly, my version of biblical matters could be every bit as absurd as the King James take. Creation tales tend toward the delirious; I quickly realized that mere Bible satire was not particularly satisfying, and would grow wearisome for a full-length play; what I wanted to do was explore larger matters of faith through a frame of biblical events.

Questions of faith, he suggested to interviewer Steven Winn in 2001, serve as a profound and exciting subject for theater: "These are the questions that cut across all the educational, gender, race and religious boundaries. It's more deeply personal than just about anything." In *The Most Fabulous Story Ever Told* Rudnick considers all these questions—as well as asking what humans should do if they realize that God is simply the projection of their own longings.

Rudnick opens his play by reenacting the Creation as the opening of a play; a character called the Stage Manager first cues the houselights and then moves on to light itself: "Monday, go. Light, go. I love this. . . . First sunset, go. . . . Tuesday, go. Oceans, go." Adam and Steve, wearing only jockstraps, enter from opposite sides of the stage and greet each other warmly. After a speedy exchange of pleasantries, the earnest and idealistic Adam asks Steve,

Where did we come from? How did we get here? Who made us, and who made this garden, and why? Are we the only ones here, are we meant to be together, are there things we're supposed to do, how will we know, will our relationship be good for the both of us, will we be together forever, what's forever, and is this all part of some plan, or did it just happen?

Masking the seriousness of these questions by putting them on the lips of a giddy, nearly naked man, Rudnick then explores them throughout the play.

Adam and Steve "invent" gay sex before Adam is addressed by an actor seated in the audience, playing the role of Father Joseph Markham. Although Father Joseph rebukes him for his behavior, other actors in the audience defend Adam and try to advise him. When the action resumes onstage, Adam and Steve soon meet their lesbian counterparts, Jane and Mabel. Both couples work to maintain satisfying relationships, struggling over their eviction from the Garden of Eden and later over conflicting views of spirituality, whether to have children, and whether to remain monogamous. Aboard the ark during the Flood (cued by the Stage Manager), Adam and Steve quarrel over Adam's faith in God, and Steve and Jane each succumb to the charm of a lecherous animal.

The first humans the four meet after the Flood are two cookie-cutter heterosexual couples. The homosexual couples are horrified to learn the details of human reproduction, prompting Jane to declare it "unnatural" and the heretofore agnostic Steve to say, "That is just not what God intended!"

Rudnick's version of the Old Testament continues with an elaborately robed and made-up Pharaoh who informs Adam, Steve, Jane, and Mabel that he has enslaved a huge population of homosexuals to build his pyramids. Pharaoh also confesses that he is in love with Brad, a young Jewish man he saved as an abandoned baby. Brad enters, a Moses figure wearing a yarmulke and prayer shawl. Pharaoh tests both couples' love, prompting Adam and Steve to quarrel again and antagonizing Brad. As various members of the cast storm offstage, Pharaoh and one of his Amazons dance to a recording of "gay slaves" singing a Broadway show tune. The first act ends after Mabel prays for a miracle and conceives, resulting in a Nativity scene. Adam and Steve reenter, dressed in robes as "wise guys," and reconcile. A ringing cell phone prompts the Stage Manager to announce, "Two thousand years, go." Adam removes his robe to reveal contemporary clothing and turns to watch the Nativity scene, on which snow is falling. The Stage Manager calls, "Intermission, go."

The second act takes place in Adam and Steve's 1990s Manhattan loft, decorated with holiday kitsch. The two men prepare to host a holiday party, neither of them remembering their first-act lives. While he looks forward to entertaining, Adam is worried about Steve, now undergoing AIDS treatment. Comic relief comes in conversations the couple have with their guests: a pregnant Jane; Mabel; Cheryl Mindle, a naive Mormon who teaches elementary school with Adam; Trey Pomfret, a cynical and effeminate homosexual who has been volunteering as Santa Claus in a homeless shelter; Kevin Markham, a gay go-go dancer; and Rabbi Sharon, a wheelchair-bound lesbian television preacher. Rudnick uses this diverse ensemble to send up a host of twentieth-century American groups: wealthy, white, straight liberals; black welfare mothers; campy gay men; Mormons; televangelists; the disabled; and lesbians. Despite the offensiveness of his stereotyping, Rudnick hits his targets. His portrayal of Rabbi Sharon, for example, who offers customized religious services for money, is a critique of late-twentieth-century Americans' desire to "shop" for everything–even faith.

Rabbi Sharon performs Jane and Mabel's wedding ceremony and then takes on the antireligious Steve in a theological debate. Accusing him of indulging in self-pity, Sharon asserts that she, too, has suffered and has raged at God. Having come to terms with injustice, she points out that "sometimes God delivers." Steve's AIDS-drug cocktail, she suggests, is a kind of miracle. Adam concurs, pointing out that Steve had nearly died and that Mabel had miscarried the previous Christmas. "And tonight," he says, "Look at Jane. Look at you." Soon afterward, Jane's water breaks, and the cast comes together to deliver her daughter.

After the excitement fades and their guests leave, Adam and Steve tidy their apartment. Pressed by Adam, Steve admits that his AIDS-drug cocktail has stopped working. Again they argue about spiritual issues, but Steve placates Adam by giving him a cashmere Armani sweater and asking, "So–do you feel better now? About my dying? And losing your faith?" Adam laughs helplessly at the ridiculousness of the question and then stands, cursing God. Steve affirms his action, but Adam admits that he cannot stop looking for meaning:

> I need . . . a story. . . . I can't believe in the Virgin Mary, not anymore. But I can believe–in Jane and Mabel. And I can't believe in the baby Jesus. But I can believe in our baby. . . . And I won't tell her about the Garden of Eden. But I will tell her about Central Park. . . . And the day we met.

Their reverie yields to the Stage Manager's calling "Central Park, go," prompting the reenactment of their first meeting in an Edenic-looking Central Park. As the Stage Manager calls for the curtain, Adam sees her and demands to know if she is really God: "I still need to know! Have you really made everything happen? You have to tell me!" She replies, "No I don't. I don't have to tell you anything. What do you want from me? I've been doing my job, and now I'm into overtime. . . . No! I'm done! That's it! I'm outta here." She exits, calling for a taxi, leaving Adam and Steve to their own devices. Adam calls a

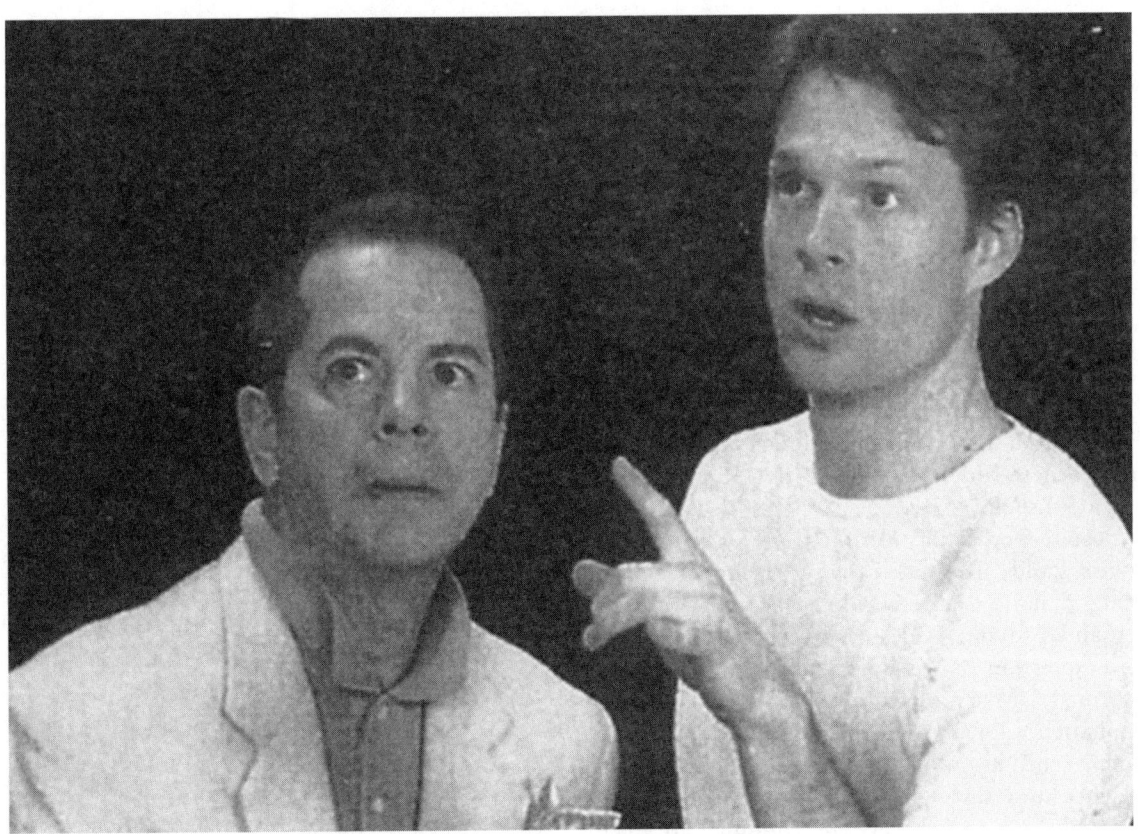

Peter Bartlett in the title role and Ross Gibbi as Shane in the 1998 Ensemble Studio Theatre production of Mr. Charles, Currently of Palm Beach *(photograph by Carol Rosegg)*

sound cue, and a romantic blues version of "Have Yourself a Merry Little Christmas" plays as he and Steve embrace. Suddenly becoming aware of the audience, they opt for privacy. With "a mixture of sexual anticipation and great good humor," Adam calls, "Curtain, go!," and the play ends.

Some critics have been dissatisfied with the relatively lighthearted conclusion of the play. In *USA Today* (15 December 1998) reviewer David Patrick Stearns complained, "When Adam realizes Steve is going to die, Steve makes him feel markedly better by giving him a cashmere sweater. This trivializes love, death, AIDS and gays, all in one brief stroke." Ben Brantley of *The New York Times* (15 December 1998) disagreed, asserting,

> It says much about "Fabulous" that the opening of a Christmas present, an Armani sweater, is allowed to alleviate the sting of a tragic revelation without cheapening the scene's sadness. For Mr. Rudnick, paradise, or unquestioning happiness, can be fleetingly glimpsed in a variety of phenomenons, from the miracle of birth to an item of designer clothing. And in laughter, there is something like the memory of Eden.

Reviewers seem more interested in the sweater than in the most provocative assertion of the final scene: if God exists at all, S/He is gone and had nothing to say to humankind before leaving. Rudnick anticipated being asked about his religious convictions, confessing in the introduction: "When I wrote MOST FABULOUS, I knew that people would ask me if I believed in God. The play is my answer, but that's a little easy. I think I believe in the transcendence of art, in that perishable moment when an audience and a performer and a play work together, when laughter and technique and emotion create a conspiracy of pleasure." Rudnick told Winn, "I revere comedy. If anything, that's my religion."

Rudnick's earlier comedy *Mr. Charles, Currently of Palm Beach* ran again with two other one-acts as *Rude Entertainment* at New York's Greenwich House Theater on 3 October 2001, fulfilling the prophecy in Marks's original review of *Mr. Charles, Currently of Palm Beach:* "A couple more of similar caliber and Mr. Rudnick has an irresistible evening of one-acts." The newer plays were *Very Special Needs,* about gay adoption, and *On the Fence,* a conversation among

Eleanor Roosevelt, Paul Lynde, and Matthew Shepard. While reviewers generally liked *Mr. Charles, Currently of Palm Beach,* they questioned whether the other two were of its caliber. Brantley called *Very Special Needs* not "much more than a throwaway revue sketch" and asserted that the important questions *On the Fence* raises "tend to hang in the air. They may resonate, but they don't develop into anything else" (*The New York Times,* 4 October 2001). In the *New York Press* (10 October 2001) critic Mimi Kramer charged that *On the Fence* "breaks every rule of dramaturgy Rudnick has always subscribed to, and seems to go against everything he represents. It's obvious, sentimental, politically correct and most uncharacteristically earnest—almost like something Rudnick had written at gunpoint."

Despite her dismissal of *On the Fence,* Kramer otherwise holds Rudnick's work in high regard, asserting that he "writes brilliant, witty plays that bother and provoke and surprise an audience and make us question our assumptions and send us out transformed." Many of Rudnick's fans would stop short of such a lofty assessment, simply praising his one-liners and his ability to depict contemporary popular culture through various media. From his apartment in New York City, he continues to write regular magazine columns as Gelman-Waxner as well as play and movie scripts. His 2000 movie *Isn't She Great,* starring Midler and Lane, treated the life of novelist Jacqueline Susann, and his works in progress include scripts for "The First Wives' Club 2" and a remake of the 1975 movie *The Stepford Wives.* His movie *Marci X,* about a Jewish American princess who inherits her father's hard-core rap music business, stars Lisa Kudrow and Damon Wayans and is scheduled to open in movie theaters in 2003. In tackling stereotypes about wealthy Jewish women and African American rappers, Paul Rudnick will undoubtedly continue to challenge audiences to question their assumptions about race, class, and religion while making them laugh.

Interviews:

M. G. Lord, "The Ghost of Hamlets Past; In *I Hate Hamlet,* It Isn't Enough That the Actor Hates the Role: He's Haunted by John Barrymore, Too," *Newsday,* 7 April 1991, II: 15;

Janny Scott, "Paul Rudnick; Changing the Way America Thinks about Gays," *Los Angeles Times,* 25 April 1993, p. M3;

William Grimes, "At the Movies with Paul Rudnick," *New York Times,* 16 November 1994, p. C1;

Karin Winegar, "*Premiere* Movie Critic Leads a Double Life," *Minneapolis Star Tribune,* 30 April 1995, p. 1F;

Douglas J. Rowe, "Writer of Gay Movie Applauds Long Lineups," *Toronto Star,* 10 October 1995, p. E7;

Shawn René Graham, "The Naked Interview," 1 May 1996 <http://www.amrep.org/past/naked/naked1.html>;

Steven Winn, "Playwright Paul Rudnick Says He Found Religion More Controversial Than Sex," *San Francisco Chronicle,* 13 May 2001, p. 38.

Wallace Shawn
(12 November 1943 -   )

William C. Boles
Rollins College

PLAY PRODUCTIONS: *Our Late Night,* New York, Public Theater, 9 January 1975; London, New Ambassadors Theatre, 20 October 1999;

A Thought in Three Parts, London, Joint Stock Company, 28 February 1977;

The Mandrake, translation of Niccolò Machiavelli's play *La Mandragola,* New York, Public Theater, November 1977;

Marie and Bruce, London, Royal Court Theatre Upstairs, 13 July 1979; New York, Public Theater, 8 January 1980;

My Dinner with André, by Shawn and André Gregory, London, Royal Court Theatre Upstairs, November 1980;

The Hotel Play, New York, La MaMa Experimental Theatre Club, 12 August 1981;

Aunt Dan and Lemon, London, Royal Court Theatre, 27 August 1985; New York, Public Theater, 21 October 1985;

The Fever, New York, an apartment near Seventh Avenue, January 1990; New York, Public Theater, 17 November 1990; London, Royal Court Theatre Upstairs, 7 January 1991;

The Designated Mourner, London, Royal National Theatre, Cottesloe Theatre, 18 April 1996; New York, 21 South William Street, May 2000.

BOOKS: *The Mandrake,* translation of Niccolò Machiavelli's play *La Mandragola* (New York: Dramatists Play Service, 1978);

Marie and Bruce (New York: Grove, 1980; New York: Dramatists Play Service, 1980);

My Dinner with André: A Screenplay, by Shawn and André Gregory (New York: Grove, 1981);

The Hotel Play (New York: Dramatists Play Service, 1982);

Our Late Night (New York: Targ, 1984; London: Royal Court Theatre, 1999);

Aunt Dan and Lemon (New York: Grove, 1985; London: Methuen, 1985; New York: Dramatists Play Service, 1986);

Wallace Shawn (photograph by Bobbi Hazeltine)

The Fever (New York: Farrar, Straus & Giroux, 1991; London: Faber & Faber, 1991; New York: Dramatists Play Service, 1992);

The Designated Mourner (New York: Farrar, Straus & Giroux, 1996; London: Faber & Faber, 1996).

Editions and Collections: *My Dinner with André: A Screenplay and Marie and Bruce* (London: Methuen, 1983);

Plays One (London: Faber & Faber, 1997)—comprises *A Thought in Three Parts, Marie and Bruce, Aunt Dan and Lemon,* and *The Fever;* republished as *Four Plays* (New York: Noonday, 1998).

PRODUCED SCRIPTS: *My Dinner with André,* by Shawn and André Gregory, motion picture, Troma Films, 1981;

The Designated Mourner, motion picture, BBC and Greenpoint Films, 1997.

RECORDING: *The Fever* (excerpt), read by Shawn, in *First Words,* audiocassette, Gang of Seven, 1992.

SELECTED PERIODICAL PUBLICATIONS–UNCOLLECTED: "Summer Evening," *Plays and Players* (April 1977): 16–19;

"Some Notes on Louis Malle and *My Dinner with André,*" *Sight and Sound* (Spring 1982): 118–120;

"Tall, Dark, and Obsessed" [interview of Bruce Wagner], *Interview,* 19 (March 1989): 76, 126;

"Guatemala Noché: A Conversation with Francisco Goldman," *Village Voice* (21 July 1992): 90–93;

"The Foreign Policy Therapist," *Nation* (3 December 2001): 23.

Since his comedic cameo as Diane Keaton's former husband in Woody Allen's *Manhattan* (1979), the short, balding, lisping, seemingly always rumpled Wallace Shawn has made an indelible mark on American movie culture. William Goldman's *The Princess Bride* (1987) offered Shawn his most recognizable role as Vizzini, the "inconceivable" villain who abducts Princess Buttercup, screams invectives at his rhyming cohorts, and ultimately falls victim to his own intellect in a battle of wits over a poisoned drink. Shawn's acting career encompasses more than fifty movies, many television appearances, and a variety of theatrical roles. Yet, unknown to most of America, this talented character actor is also a three-time Obie (Off-Broadway) Award winner and one of the most divisively received, politically agitating, and theatrically challenging playwrights of the contemporary era.

Wallace Shawn was born in New York City on 12 November 1943 to William Shawn, editor in chief of the *New Yorker* magazine from 1952 to 1987, and Cecille Lyon Shawn, a journalist. Growing up, Shawn lacked for nothing financially, socially, or academically, as his family belonged to the upper crust of New York City literary society. He told John Lahr in a 1996 interview: "I was raised with the absolute understanding that I was a very special little being. A little king." In his plays he skewers the hollowness of the social-set parties he witnessed as a child and unveils the dark sexual longings lurking beneath the aristocratic veneer. In 1990, through private performances of his play *The Fever,* he returned to Manhattan living rooms similar to the ones he visited as a child, challenging the inhabitants to realize their own culpability in the economic, social, and political oppression of the poor.

While in fifth grade at the Dalton School in Manhattan, Shawn wrote and performed his first play, which was about Socrates. In an interview with David Savran, Shawn noted the influence of this experience on his future careers as playwright and actor: "People were quite moved by this play and looked at me in a different way. I don't think it would take Sigmund Freud to figure out that this was positive reinforcement, a pleasant, even wonderful experience, and I'm sure the rest of my life has been an attempt to crawl along behind that experience and repeat it." Shawn continued writing plays as well as musical puppet shows (including one about the decline of China's dynasties) with his younger brother, Allen, who later became a composer. William Shawn told Don Shewey that the puppet shows "weren't hasty or haphazard productions. . . . They were quite ambitious," including "an adaptation of *Paradise Lost* that went on for hours."

While Shawn wrote and performed plays at school and home, he also attended the theater, seeing José Quintero's productions of Eugene O'Neill's *The Iceman Cometh* (1946) and *Long Day's Journey into Night* (1956); Eugène Ionesco's *The Bald Soprano* (1950), *The Lesson* (1951), and *The Chairs* (1952); and Alan Schneider's production of Samuel Beckett's *Endgame* (1957). Shawn also read everything by O'Neill. However, his literary diligence was not limited to drama: at the age of fifteen he read James Joyce's *Ulysses* (1922).

In college, politics replaced drama as Shawn's main intellectual pursuit, since he wanted to be a diplomat or work in government service. He confessed to Shewey: "When I went off to college, I felt the world was in such a bad way that everyone should devote themselves to ending the arms race and preventing nuclear war and solving the problems of global poverty." He attended Harvard University, graduating in 1965 with a B.A. in history. After graduation he taught English in India for a year on a Fulbright scholarship. He then enrolled in Magdalen College at Oxford University, where he received a B.A. in philosophy, politics, and economics in 1968 and an M.A. in 1975. At Oxford, Shawn returned to drama, entering a playwriting competition, which he did not win. Shawn's educational experience as well as the year in India seriously challenged his notion that being a diplomat would be the most effective means to rectify the wrongs in the world. Instead, he realized the powerful influence that an artist wields. He told Shewey: "the problems of the world are caused largely by things that are inside people's heads, and it's entirely possible that by altering people's consciousness a writer or a musician might do something that would improve the world situation."

John Ferraro, James Lally, Shawn, and Tom Costello in the 1977 Public Theater production of The Mandrake *(photograph by Sy Friedman)*

With this epiphany Shawn returned to New York City in 1968 to be a playwright. Before his first play was finally produced in 1975, he supported himself through a variety of positions, including teaching Latin, drama, and English, working as a shipping clerk for a dress company, and operating a Xerox machine. In 1971 he took a sabbatical from the work world, immersing himself in the study of acting, so that he could become a better playwright.

In his first attempts Shawn struggled to compose a producible play. Between 1967 and 1971 he wrote five plays, but only one ever had a professional production, occurring ten years after it was written. However, W. D. King, author of *Writing Wrongs* (1997), the only book-length study of Shawn's work, stresses that the unproduced and unpublished works "are distinctly modernist in their violation of expectations about plot and form, in their allusiveness, and, especially, in their fragmentary quality."

"Four Meals in May" (1967), written during a holiday in Italy, was the piece he entered in the playwriting competition at Oxford. The play focuses on five people—a grandfather, father, son, mother, and former fiancée—during different meals. Shawn told Shewey that he thought "Four Meals in May" was "the answer to the war in Vietnam. I thought they would rename the country after me when people saw that play!" However, the people who read it reacted "as if they'd been given a handful of blank pieces of paper."

He followed "Four Meals in May" with "The Old Man" (1969), which he wrote in Ireland. The fragmented monologue of an elderly man in a hospital is comprised of forty-four segments that detail his physical suffering as well as his recollection of fond and painful memories. King wrote that this work "goes immediately to the outer limits of what anyone might identify as a play." Shawn's next two attempts, *The Hotel Play* (1970) and "The Family Play" (1970), were written in the West Indies. *The Hotel Play* was eventually produced in 1981. "The Family Play," originally called "A Play in Seven Scenes," deals with the sexual competition of two young sisters for the attention of a visitor in their home. King described it as "a play of the happy home gone nightmarishly bad when the children verge on adulthood."

Having exhausted his savings, Shawn required financial assistance to go away to write his next play. He sold 1 percent of his future playwriting profits to six friends for $400 each, allowing him to stay in a $4-a-night hotel room in Cedar Falls, Iowa, where he wrote "The Hospital Play" (1971). Shawn has remarked that "The Hospital Play" was the only play he ever wrote that showed compassion. King, however, thought it was "an incredibly gruesome and unbearable play, a hopeless and hideous monster." He called it "the inscription of what should not be a play, a story in which nearly everyone dies for no good reason, with weeping, vomiting, no hero, a little sex but no hope, and it is no wonder that it survives now only as a hundred yards of photocopy."

Despite the problems inherent in his efforts, these early plays proved to be important precursors to his later plays. While only one of these plays eventually received a full-scale production, Shawn was honing his distinctive theatrical voice that refused to follow the conventional rules of playwriting. His reliance on fragmentation and dismissal of plot and character development became essential to the success of his later plays. By removing the usual theatrical conventions, Shawn forced his audience out of the voyeuristic safety of the darkened theater and directly into the tempestuous world of his characters and their thoughts.

Written in 1970 in Bequia in the West Indies, *The Hotel Play,* paradoxically inspired by Shawn's experience of being the only guest in an island hotel, features one of the largest casts for a one-act play. The La MaMa Experimental Theatre Club production in 1981 featured seventy-seven performers. In his prefatory note to the play, Shawn eschewed the use of double and triple casting, encouraging future productions to single-cast the play as well. Shawn argued, "I don't in general find it all that fascinating or amusing to see actors proving their versatility by playing many different roles in one evening. It reminds me that I'm in the theatre, rather than allowing me the more interesting impression that in some odd way I'm watching life unfold even though I'm looking at actors on a stage." Following Equity rules, the house was limited to ninety-nine seats and each actor received $100 for the three-week run. The cast included actors, writers, and artists such as Griffin Dunne, Elizabeth McGovern, Wendy Wasserstein, Christopher Durang, Dominick Dunne, Linda Hunt, Ed Bullins, Ann Beattie, Deborah Eisenberg (a writer and Shawn's longtime companion), and Shawn himself.

The one-act play, comprised of five sections, is virtually plotless. The single thread linking the entire piece is a hotel clerk. Almost all seventy-seven members of the cast appear in the second and fourth sections, set in the communal space of the hotel dining room. In both sections the audience randomly eavesdrops on varied conversations. The morning section includes a man going hunting, squabbling couples, single and married travelers on the make, and tourists planning their sightseeing itinerary. The evening scenes become more protracted, angry, and rambunctious as the characters are now exhausted, drunk, hot, nauseated, and sexually frustrated. Throughout both scenes the clerk routinely tends to the guests.

The first, third, and fifth sections prominently feature the clerk and his relationship with three different women. In the first section a young female tourist reluctantly departs from the clerk's room only to be replaced a few hours later by a different young female tourist. The third section shows the clerk surprising a woman coming out of her shower as he attempts to fix a light in her room, while in another room a couple try to have an affair but are farcically interrupted by every male member of the woman's family. The fifth and final section returns to the clerk and the girl he left in his room that morning. He unsuccessfully tries to seduce her, and as she picks up a razor, a blackout occurs. In the next scene, her bloody, lifeless body lies in a heap on the floor as the clerk calmly calculates the supplies needed by the hotel. The play ends with him describing the damaging wind outside his window that is blowing everything away. All the while he ignores the girl's body.

Frank Rich of *The New York Times* (28 August 1981) had a mixed reaction to the production. He wrote that because Shawn "is willing to go for broke to realize his vision—and honorably refuses to make any concessions to so-called good taste—he at times achieves a pungent, heightened form of reality that remakes the meaner alienations of modern life into ferocious comedy." However, Rich continued, "the incendiary, even dangerous, cataclysms of *The Hotel Play* are too few and scattered." While its structure is exceedingly random and problematic, *The Hotel Play* highlights many characteristics of his writing: fractured random conversations; the sometimes violent, sometimes comic, and almost always dark sexuality of his characters; the absence of closure on any of the relationships and situations; underdeveloped characters; and the emotional, social, and communicative disconnectedness between characters.

While some of Shawn's unproduced plays did receive the occasional workshop, *Our Late Night* (1975) was the first of Shawn's early plays to receive a full-

Cast of the 1980 Public Theater production of Marie and Bruce
(photograph by Martha Swope)

scale production. The one-act play went through a two-and-a-half-year production process, receiving its first rehearsal in September 1972, its first performance workshop in the spring of 1974, and then finally its premiere in January 1975 at the Public Theater, directed by André Gregory, who has continued to collaborate with Shawn on theatrical and cinematic projects.

Set in a penthouse sporting a fantastic view of an unnamed city, *Our Late Night* presents various conversations at an upscale cocktail party. Rather than depicting the stereotypical chitchat of high society, Shawn uses the cocktail talk to reveal the underbelly of the upper class in terms of their broodingly violent sexual needs. For example, a guest named Tony describes the effect of the tropics on his libido: it takes several encounters not only with his wife and through self-stimulation but also with a large, repellent, sweaty, mustached and bearded local woman to temporarily sate his uncontrollable needs. It is a mesmerizing and painful monologue about the insatiability of the male libido as well as the complete victimization of Tony to his sexual urges. But besides featuring Shawn's brutally accurate and hilariously painful depiction of the troubled male sexual psyche, the piece also depicts the chasm of compassion between individuals. The response of another guest, Jim, to Tony's tale of sexual anguish is: "My God—and to think that I planned to go to the tropics on my vacation!" True, Jim's reaction shows Shawn's comic skill, but it also displays Jim's utter disregard for Tony's suffering. An honest revelation of self is ignored, replaced with a selfish concern about future vacation plans. Nothing else in the play makes Shawn's view of these cocktail-party gatherings and the people who attend them clearer. The second half of the play continues the fractured conversations, only they now become even more graphic in their discussions of sex and relationships, as if Tony's confession gave license to the others to unveil their own prurient desires.

While the play won Shawn his first Obie, the reaction of the audience and critics was mixed. Some audience members found Tony's monologue especially provoking. Joseph Papp, who produced *Our Late Night*, remarked to Lucinda Franks: "The audience went crazy at that scene. . . . Some were shouting and one man got up and walked around in a menacing way—they didn't even know they were doing it. Wally was looking around the theatre, very perplexed—he didn't realize he had gotten rid of his own sexual mania and given it to everybody else." Gregory told Lahr: "Somebody tried to hit an actor. People would scream 'Shut up!' and 'Stop it!' It was very scary in the audience. I think what they were offended by was their own shadow—that Wally was seeing something under the surface of Americans." Clive Barnes's review in *The New York Times* (10 January 1975) did not express the same outrage. However, he did note: "One has rarely seen such pornographic decadence with, guiltily, so much going for it. This is the most obscene show in town. . . . However, the obscenity does have a wit to it, and even some insights on modern society, satirically exaggerated as those insights might be." Even though British audiences ultimately appreciated Shawn's work more than American audiences did, *Our Late Night* did not premiere in England until 1999, when Caryl Churchill, author of *Cloud Nine* (1979) and *Top Girls* (1981), directed the play as a "production without décor" at the New Ambassadors Theatre in conjunction with the Royal Court Theatre.

Before his next play, *A Thought in Three Parts* (1977), was produced, Shawn wrote the libretto to *In the Dark*, an opera, in collaboration with his brother, Allen, who composed the music. It was produced at the Lenox Arts Center in Massachusetts in 1976. The piece depicts a couple on their first date and what happens later that night in the darkness.

Impressed with *Our Late Night,* Papp commissioned Shawn to write another play, which became *A Thought in Three Parts*. It was workshopped in 1976 at the Public Theater and received negative feedback. Shawn told Strand, "Oh, it was a disaster. It was unspeakable how much they didn't like it." Papp did not extend the production beyond the originally scheduled workshop run. Instead, *A Thought in Three Parts* premiered in London, performed by the Joint Stock Company. Unsurprisingly, the explicit sexuality provoked an outcry in London about onstage obscenity. Even though the Lord Chamberlain had been removed from his censorship role over London theaters in the previous decade, the sex scenes caused an uproar similar to the reaction of audiences to the stoning of a baby in Edward Bond's *Saved* (1965).

A Thought in Three Parts opens safely enough with "Summer Evening," which takes place in an unnamed foreign hotel room where Sarah and David, an American couple, are on holiday. Their conversation covers mundane things such as the dresses Sarah purchased and whether they should get something else to eat. However, their asides reveal the real status of their relationship. Neither communicates his or her true desires about their sexual relationship. At one point David says: "Quietly I watch her dress, undress. Incredible, incredible, she has no idea the trembling in my heart as I lie in bed and watch her clothing, falling to the floor, softly to the chair." Sarah reveals her own desires: "It's strange, there's nothing, there isn't anything I wouldn't, I wouldn't, I wouldn't do for pleasure." When they directly speak to one another, they try to express themselves, but invariably back away from revealing the truth of their desires. The scene ends in darkness as the two retire to bed, just barely touching, the status of their unarticulated needs unresolved.

"The Youth Hostel," the second piece, provoked the controversy. Throughout it the characters perform a variety of sexual acts involving an array of combinations of men, women, and groups. One critic counted more than thirty orgasms in the piece. While one might argue (and many did) that Shawn was writing pornography for the stage, "The Youth Hostel," like Tony's monologue in *Our Late Night,* subverts prudish perspectives about sex. One way Shawn accomplishes this undermining is through the language of the play. The characters all speak as if they belong in an English primer. Their simplistic sentence structure provides a comic base, subverting the graphic nature of their desires. Even more compelling, Shawn explores the fleeting temporality of sexual pleasure through the absence of emotional connection between the various partners. Shallowly, they think that the next orgasm will finally provide them with the fulfillment they seek, removing the pain they are feeling; but as soon as they climax, their disgust with themselves and their partner(s) invariably returns. The scene actually features more expressions of hatred than pleasure. By placing "The Youth Hostel" directly after "Summer Evening," Shawn effectively captures the implicit complications of sexuality and relationships. Neither the married couple nor the youths can find contentment in sex or through the presence of another individual. Instead, like Tony in *Our Late Night* and future Shawn characters, they are condemned to suffer.

The play ends with the short monologue "Mr. Frivolous," which focuses on a lonely man at breakfast who, like Beckett's Krapp, is lost in his memories of past relationships with his priest and a former lover who never returns to him. The reflective monologue contrasts with the energy of the preceding two pieces, and its subject matter enriches Shawn's depiction of the difficulty of relationships.

The public outcry in England over the sexual explicitness of "The Youth Hostel" stirred governmen-

Cover for the 1981 screen adaptation of the 1980 play that Shawn crafted from several months of conversations between him and director André Gregory (University of South Carolina, Union)

tal reactions. On the second night of the Joint Stock production, vice-squad members sat in the audience to judge whether the play was obscene. In Parliament, Lord Nugent called on the government to protect the public from such explicit work. Joint Stock found their finances under investigation (specifically the spending of government grants), while Shawn briefly believed he was going to be deported. Despite the hullabaloo, the play finished its run.

Plays and Players, a London theater weekly, responded to the controversy by publishing part of the script. Oddly, however, they printed the tame "Summer Evening" rather than the troublemaking "The Youth Hostel." Next to the script they reprinted excerpts from some of the scathing reviews. Among the comments: John Barber of *The Daily Telegraph* wrote, "Squalid squirming on beds, accompanied by the obligatory oohs and aahs, becomes monotonous sooner than might be believed possible"; B. A. Young of *The Financial Times* called the piece "tedious, illiterate material"; and Irving Wardle of *The Times* said the play offered "most winsome and inexpert dialogue." However, the magazine also republished a letter to the editor of *The Guardian,* written by some British playwrights, including Churchill and David Hare, expressing their support for Shawn: "We believe him to be a writer of outstanding talent exploring love and sex with great linguistic and theatrical insight. On the whole he has received only mindless and prudish abuse. We want to express our support for our gifted colleague and hope the public will ignore the grubby obstacles put in their way to a pleasurable evening."

Despite the reception of London audiences to his first full-length play, Shawn continued to favor London over New York audiences, resulting in several of his plays premiering there. Shawn told Patrick McGrath: "The indifference and lack of interest from people in the audience in New York over a period of decades has been painful to me," but in London "They will go, and they are prepared to listen. They aren't immediately angry as soon as the play has begun."

Even though Papp could not produce *A Thought in Three Parts,* he asked Shawn to translate Niccolò Machiavelli's 1518 comedy *La Mandragola,* which became *The Mandrake* (1977). The play, set in Venice, details the machinations of Callimaco, recently returned from Paris, in his efforts to sleep with Lucrezia, married to an overprotective, foolish, and older husband, Professor Nicia. Helping Callimaco in his quest are Ligurio, a parasitic follower, and Brother Timothy, a priest. Through a complicated scheme of deceptions and disguises, Callimaco successfully dupes Nicia and receives the passionate affections of Lucrezia.

Machiavelli's play is an amusingly perceptive work about the foibles of humanity and the apparent ease people have in relinquishing their values in order to acquire what they desire. Nicia, for example, allows Callimaco to sleep with his wife, thinking that he will have heirs from their coupling, and Brother Timothy betrays his vows to the church for money. Shawn's translation maintains the spirit of Machiavelli throughout, but he also retains his own distinctive syntactic, fragmented phrasing, which smoothly blends with the deceptive nature of the characters.

The Mandrake was an important financial success for Shawn, whose need for income at that time was making him think about becoming a taxi driver, even though his driving skills were spotty. Not only did the production play for six months—it was only scheduled to be a three-week workshop—but also Shawn was cast as Callimaco's servant as well as the speaker of the Prologue, receiving positive reviews for both. In addition, his performances caught the eye of a casting agent, who had Shawn audition for Woody Allen. The director cast him in *Manhattan,* which began his movie career. After a decade of struggling in various full-time low-paying jobs to support his writing, he finally landed a lucrative part-time occupation that would provide him with the financial stability to write.

Marie and Bruce (1979) continued Shawn's partnership with Papp. In this case, Shawn turned his dramatic eye on the strained marriage of Marie and Bruce, who, unlike Sarah and David in "Summer Evening," express their true feelings to one another, resulting in a brutal verbal and psychological war. The play covers one day in their marriage, and in Marie, Shawn has created one of the most vindictive and foul-mouthed wives in American drama. At the opening, as Bruce sleeps, Marie informs the audience that she is going to leave him. She says: "Yesterday morning this fucking pig woke me up from a good night's sleep to ask me—to ask me where his God damned horrible piece-of-shit two-hundred-year-old typewriter was. I threw your typewriter *out,* you God damned fucking incredible pig!" The brutality of Marie's attack (and Louise Lasser's stunning performance) struck critics immediately. A few years after the production Shewey finally asked Eisenberg, Shawn's longtime companion, the question that had lingered in many minds: whether the brutal relationship was modeled on their own. "It doesn't come from nowhere," she responded.

After the breakfast scene, in which Bruce is a figure of placating pitifulness, the couple attends an evening cocktail party that once again presents the conversations of various partygoers. Unlike *Our Late Night,* their discussions are not the centerpiece of the play, but instead complementary background noise to the continuing struggle of Marie and Bruce. In the public space of the party, Marie's verbal browbeating of Bruce disappears, and he now possesses the controlling power of the relationship as she admits that she finds him attractive. While he relishes the social aspects of the party and his temporary public power, Marie perches sickly on a couch, eventually falling asleep.

After the party, they go to dinner, where they overhear a man graphically describe the difficulty of emptying his bowels. Bruce's attempt to halt the man's story only results in the man cowing Bruce into silence. The couple then returns home and goes to bed. Yet, the final moments suggest that Marie will not leave her husband. Instead, they are trapped in a Sartre-like relationship. No exit exists for either of them. In a sense, Shawn has written a play depicting David's definition of love in "Summer Evening": "Well, it's quite like hatred . . . an intense focus on the other person." Marie and Bruce, despite the divisiveness of their relationship, need each other to survive. They only have one another. Shawn makes this fact clear in two monologues in which they describe what they did after breakfast and before the party. In each monologue Bruce and Marie distance themselves from others. Marie befriends a dog (that eventually leaves her) and falls asleep in a park, overcome by the heat and the aroma of the flowers, while Bruce, after failing miserably to pick up a woman at a bar, sits in a hotel room, staring vicariously into the apartment across the way. While their relationship may be characterized by their intense hatred for one another, the absence of anyone else is enough to warrant their staying married.

Before playing in New York, *Marie and Bruce* opened in London. After seeing the New York production, Jack Kroll praised the work in *Newsweek* (18 February 1980), noting that it "sees, hears, smells and tells more about the way we really live now than any American play in years." Robert Brustein, writing for *New Republic* (5 April 1980), thought the play was "one of the most savage assaults yet on the failure of the American promise" and Lasser's performance was "more overpowering than anything I have seen in the theater this year."

Shawn's next project, *My Dinner with André* (1980), once again reunited him with Gregory. Shawn, struggling with his writing process, and Gregory, seeking a new format of artistic expression, decided to meet two to three times a week and record their conversations. The process began in December of 1978 and continued for three to four months. Using a grant from PBS, they had their conversations transcribed, producing more than 2,200 pages of material. Shawn then took a year to create a script culled from all their talks. The conversational basis of the piece provided Shawn a freedom with the creative process that he had previously lacked. His foreword to the screenplay conveys the glee he felt at the process: "my script would be based on our real conversations, and I would use his words and his ideas—It wouldn't just be me!" All the elements he needed were right there at his disposal, freeing him from having to rely on his own creative inspiration.

The script interested the director Louis Malle, and he encouraged them to perform it on the stage first to solidify their performances. Even though Shawn and Gregory had actually said all the words in the script, Malle pressed them to treat their lines as actors would. Shawn wrote in "Some Notes on Louis Malle and *My Dinner with André*" (1982):

> André and I instinctively started off just trying to be just like ourselves, and Louis immediately realized that if we kept on doing that, it would be much better to hire two actors to play us, because any good actor would attempt to *interpret* his character, to show what was going on beneath his character's façade, while we were merely reproducing the façade.

In November of 1980 Shawn and Gregory performed the script at the Royal Court Theatre Upstairs in London before filming the movie in Richmond, Virginia, in December of 1980.

At the start of the movie Wally reveals how uncomfortable he is in meeting André for dinner, since he has not seen him for many years and has no idea what they will talk about. He decides to prod André with questions, making him talk, so he can avoid participating in the conversation. More than half of the movie focuses on André's adventures, which include his experimentation with alternative theatrical outlets in Poland with Jerzy Grotowski, his struggle with a Japanese Buddhist monk who inserts himself a bit too much into André's family life, and his own symbolic death and resurrection on Long Island, New York.

Eventually, Wally begins to emerge from his uncomfortable social shell and he engages with his dinner companion as they discuss the merits of the contemporary theater (as might be expected when a playwright/actor talks with a director/actor) and their differing perspectives about life. One of the most memorable exchanges they have—and the one to have a rippling effect on Shawn's later work—concerns an electric blanket. André dismisses its importance and value, arguing the electric blanket distances people from being human as they avoid the cold as well as the potential warmth to be found from another body. He tells Wally: "turn on that electric blanket, and it's like taking a tranquilizer, or it's like being lobotomized by watching television." Wally, though, prefers the electric blanket precisely because it provides warmth in his cold apartment and comfort from the brutal world around him. He tells André: "I'm trying to protect myself, because really there are these abrasive beatings to be avoided, everywhere you look." While seemingly an insignificant object, the electric blanket represents each man's philosophical approach to life. André wants nothing to separate himself from the reality of the world, as shown by his various adventures, while Wally finds comfort a necessary requirement against the reality of the world, as shown by his initial distress at having to participate in the conversation with his friend. When they finally come up for air, they realize that they are the last ones in the restaurant. As André pays the bill, their conversation ends. Wally, who at first was pessimistic about the encounter, now looks forward to telling Debbie about his dinner with André.

The movie was a critical and a financial success. However, more importantly, the experience was fundamental to Shawn's development as a playwright. Gay Brewer has rightly called *My Dinner with André* "the crucial work dividing Shawn's *oeuvre*." While Shawn continued to buck against the structural conventions of the theater by refusing to provide closure, clear characterization, or even a plot in his plays, his ideas began showing a maturation in their focus, politicization, and argument. Specifically, Shawn seized on the concept of comfort, and in his next two plays he challenged and subverted the idea of "being comfortable" in order to display the oppressive repercussions such a state has on society.

Shortly after *My Dinner with André* opened, *The Hotel Play* was produced. In 1983 Shawn wrote another libretto (with his brother composing the music) for a piece called "The Music Teacher," which details the title character's struggles through various sexual escapades, including an obsession with one of his female students, and ultimately his own sexual identity. It was never produced.

Of all of Shawn's plays, *Aunt Dan and Lemon* (1985) has received the most critical attention and been the most anthologized. Part of its continuing success resides in its ability to provoke divisive opinions from audience members, reviewers, and literary critics. The play is either praised for its evocative power in challenging the contented, comfortable apathy of society or vilified for the logic of its final monologue, which rationalizes the slaughtering of the Jews by the Nazis.

Continuing his usual structural devices, Shawn composed *Aunt Dan and Lemon* out of fragments, including flashback memories, short random scenes, monologues, and incomplete conversations, while bookending these components with two lengthy monologues by Lemon, a sickly, anorexic, vegetable-and-fruit-juice-drinking loner born in 1960. As a child, Lemon lived a sheltered life, never actually doing anything, only listening to other people's conversations. Her cherished memories are not based on her own life experiences but instead on the stories told to her by Aunt Dan, an American lecturer at Oxford who befriends Lemon's father and mother. Her father is overworked, overstressed, and solidly business oriented (Shawn played him in the original New York production), and her mother is a liberal thinker who argues ineffectively with Aunt Dan about how much compassion Henry Kissinger actually possesses.

Lemon recounts her memories of her eleventh summer, when Aunt Dan would tell her bedtime stories about such topics as adulterous relationships with her professors; her respect for Kissinger, including a chance sighting of Kissinger at a club; and the sexual exploits of her friends. At the center of Aunt Dan's stories, and therefore Lemon's memories, exists the smoky, sexy figure of Mindy, who always needs money. Through Aunt Dan's stories (and their enactments on stage) Mindy first coerces £60,000 from a man who wants to sleep with her and then becomes a killer for hire, strangling a man after enticing him to her room for sex. Lemon's last memory is of visiting the cancer-ridden Aunt Dan on her deathbed.

Lemon's final monologue returns the audience to the present. Based on her reading about the Nazi death camps, Lemon argues that the Nazis were not wrong in persecuting the Jews. They were merely trying to improve their quality of life by exterminating the people who they believed were a threat. She contends that the Nazis were doing what the human race has done every day of its existence. The only characteristic that differentiated the Nazis from all the others was that they lacked compassion, echoing the same word at the heart of Lemon's mother's argument with Aunt Dan about Kissinger. Lemon continues by equating the Nazis' extermination of the Jews with killing criminals in a violent society, slaughtering the Indians, or killing cockroaches. Essentially, she argues that the comforts people have, the contentment they feel with their lives, depend upon others being exterminated. After all, some group has to pay for this comfortable quality of life.

While Lemon's argument effectively angers the audience, it also challenges the way that a play works. Few playwrights have ever indicted the audience so slyly and yet so brutally. Sylviane Gold of *The Wall Street Journal* noted this quality in her 20 November 1985 review: "Going to the theater is itself an act of trust, an affirmation of our common humanity, and for a playwright to tell us that we are all killers is to subvert the very meaning of theater." Ross Wetzsteon in *American Theatre* (September 1997) also remarked on the power of the concluding argument, "The audience, in short, is entrapped. No one can leave the theatre feeling the kind of complacent compassion so common in traditional drama. No one can go home thinking the theatre isn't part of the world we actually live in."

While several critical articles have discussed *Aunt Dan and Lemon,* perhaps none better acknowledges the strengths and weaknesses of Shawn's play than the conversation between Bonnie Marranca, Johannes Birringer, and Gerald Rabkin transcribed in *Performing Arts Journal* (1986). While Rabkin agreed with Wetzsteon about Shawn's effectiveness in forcing "the audience to accept a certain kind of complicity" in the oppression of others, Marranca and Birringer questioned Shawn's technique. Marranca seized on an argument that many continue to make, namely that "there is no differentiation between the kinds of killings that are spoken about. There must be a difference between killing criminals, Indians, Jews, or cockroaches. Lemon's point of view is faulty in that all kinds of killing are equated—you simply can't link killing cockroaches and Nazi philosophy." Birringer questioned the structural framework of presenting the politics of the play through Aunt Dan and Lemon: "The performance trivializes the issue by making us understand one continuous irony in the play, namely the monstrous views put forth by two relatively nice women who seem so innocent in what they're saying although it is outrageous." Despite, or perhaps because of, the divided reaction, *Aunt Dan and Lemon* continues to be Shawn's most produced play; a 1999 revival in London at the Almeida Theater starred Glenne Headly as Lemon and Miranda Richardson as Aunt Dan.

While five years passed before his next play, *The Fever* (1990), was performed, Shawn's political awareness continued to develop. His personal interest in America's political oppression of others compelled him to visit Central America, and upon his return he wanted to convey the essence of the experience but found it difficult. He told Wetzsteon in a *Village Voice* profile:

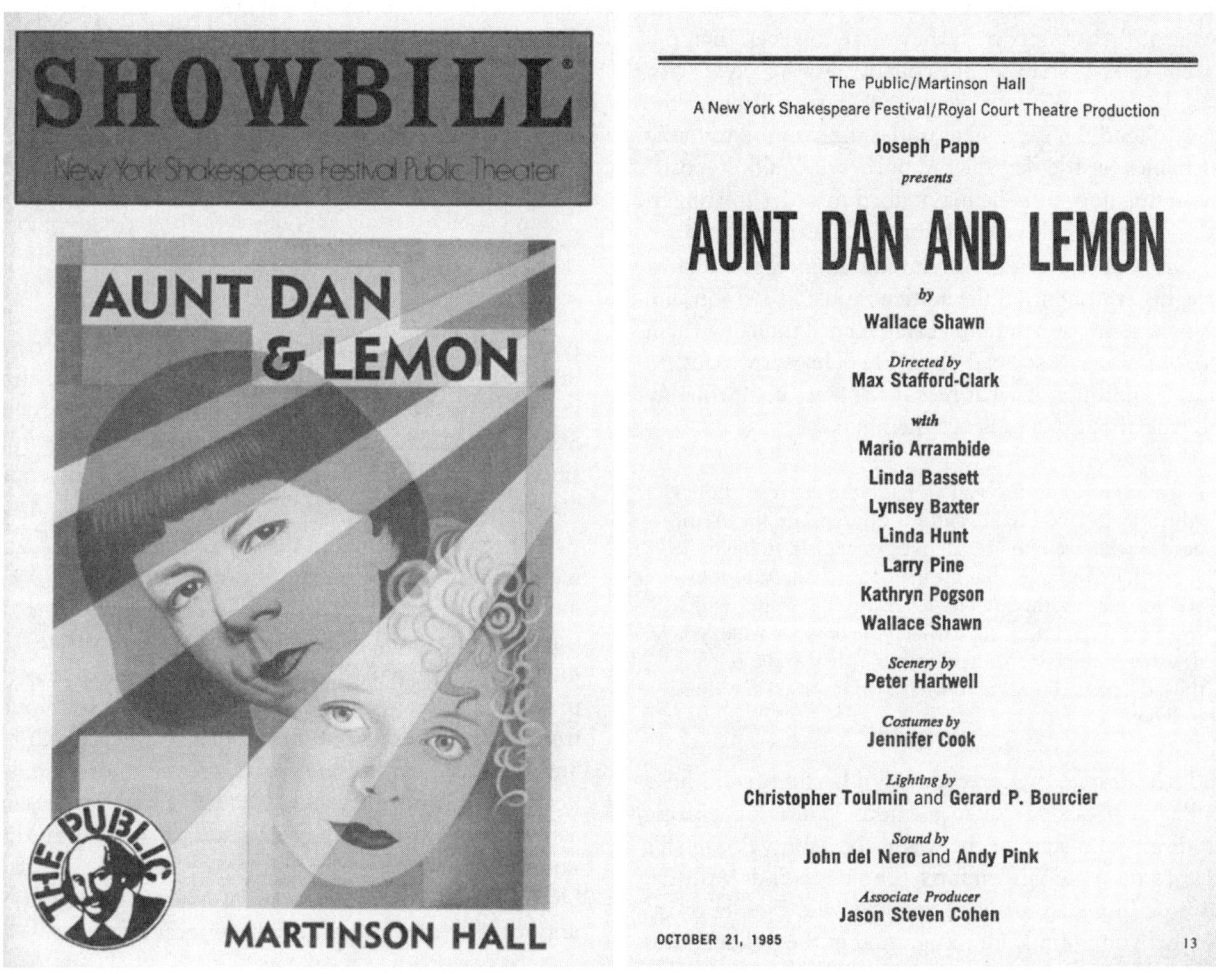

Program cover and title page for the U.S. premiere of Shawn's most frequently anthologized play (Bruccoli Clark Layman Archives)

I worked very hard for a very long time trying to find a way to communicate things that can't be communicated in casual conversation, things that I couldn't communicate in articles giving what would be considered explicit political opinions. I wanted to find a form that would allow me to express the feelings and perceptions that *underlie* political opinions.

The form he finally chose was something familiar: the monologue. *The Fever* is a lengthy monologue set in an unnamed country and delivered by an unnamed character that describes his epiphany about his upper-class life and its connection to the oppression of the poor.

Rather than using a theater, Shawn first performed the piece in New York City living rooms. After more than seventy private performances Shawn transferred the monologue to the Public Theater. In keeping with the spirit of his living-room performances, Shawn refused all the theatrical trappings. There were no ushers, programs, costumes, theatrical lighting, props, reserved seats, or curtain call.

The main contention of the narrator's argument, based on his perusing of Karl Marx, is that the condition, plight, and oppression of the poor is based on the need of the upper class to maintain their current level of material comfort and consumption, while not acknowledging all those persons who handled the items before they arrived in their upper-class homes. Before his economic epiphany, which occurs as he lies vomiting on his bug-infested hotel bathroom floor, the narrator admits to having been an aesthete, enjoying his parties, books, and music. However, in this unnamed country he finally sees for the first time what he had ignored before: the faces of the poor and their continual suffering. He realizes that their wretched condition of illiteracy and poverty continues unchecked precisely because of the willful oppression by the privileged class. They keep the poor ignorant, not wanting them to realize the power of their numbers. If they were to rebel, then the current class system would collapse. As he says: "We need the poor. Without the poor to get the fruit off the trees, to tend the excrement under the ground, to bathe our babies on the day they're born, we couldn't exist." The status quo must be maintained in order for upper-class society to enjoy its comfortable, clean existence.

At the end of this 100-minute monologue Shawn turns his argument on the audience, just as Lemon did, posing a series of conditional statements, indicting them into the abusive societal structure. He is speaking to himself, although if what he says is true, it is probably also true about the audience members:

> if it's appropriate for you to have the share of things which in fact you have, and it's appropriate for all the people who are like you all over the world to have the share that *they* have, that means that it's not *in*appropriate for all of the others to have the share which remains. You know that what you have is what you deserve, and that means that what they have is what they deserve. They have what's appropriate for them to have.

And yet, despite the forcefulness of his argument, he is conflicted about his own position. While recognizing the disgraceful state of the world, he acknowledges his reliance on material comforts. The piece ends with the narrator in a state of flux, caught in the middle of his horrific, vomit-inducing recognition of the political situation and his own difficulty in giving up his past life. The play ends with the metaphor of him voluntarily falling from a great height, but he never lands. Instead, he admits that he is still falling. He has relinquished his initial privileged viewpoint of the world, but he has yet to face the hard ground of reality. He exists in limbo struggling with his own place amid the harsh political nature of the world.

The Fever won Shawn his third Obie and once again provoked divided reactions about the political effectiveness of the play as well as questions about Shawn's motives for writing and performing it. Some critics merely saw the piece as a public airing of his own guilt about his privileged upbringing. In *The New York Times* (29 November 1990) Rich called the play "an orgy of self-flagellation that even Woody Allen might find a bit rich." While he conceded that the play was "charged with intelligence and a desire to do good," Rich ultimately judged that the work is "rendered nearly inert by its author's solipsism." Kevin Kelly of *The Boston Globe* remarked in his 12 April 1991 review: "To be polite about it, *The Fever* is blather parsed through one man's politically correct anguish, and as exploitative in its own way as all the robber barons Brecht ever wrote about." Wetzsteon, though, held a different position and argued in his *Village Voice* profile:

> Shawn is a passionate provocateur. Far from trying to get the members of the audience to identify with *his* emotional life, he's trying to get them to reevaluate their *own*. Far from luxuriating in self-absorbed escapism or self-lacerating guilt of self-absorbing confession, he's attempting to elicit *our* self-satisfaction, to challenge *our* self-satisfaction, to trigger *our* self-doubt.

After the run at the Public, Shawn then performed the piece at the Royal Court Theatre Upstairs before returning to New York for performances at Second Stage, La MaMa, and Lincoln Center. *The Fever* has since had several interpretations by male and female actors.

Brewer commented that *The Fever* was "the culmination of Shawn's work and the purification of his most important themes." However, he continued, "it is his least theatrical play, as if its realization demonstrates the difficulty of Shawn's future in theatre." With his next project, *The Designated Mourner* (1996), Shawn moved from class oppression to the conflict between highbrow and lowbrow culture and produced his most conventional play, featuring two richly defined characters and a story with closure. The end result, according to Marranca in "The Solace of Chocolate Squares: Wallace Shawn in Mourning" (2000), was "one of the most important works for the theatre in recent decades."

The Designated Mourner is set in an unspecified time period as three characters remark not only on the political unrest in their unnamed country but also on the violent repercussions it has on their own lives. The title character, Jack, who claims, "You can sum me up in about ten words: a former student of English literature who—who—who went downhill from there!" is married to Judy, the daughter of Howard, a famous essayist and poet who is the lightning rod for the familial and political conflicts of the play. As a young man, Howard wrote an essay humanizing the lower-class, lowbrow citizens of the country and questioning his government's political oppression of them. Shortly thereafter, Howard started writing poetry, realizing that government officials do not read or understand poetry. However, the essay he wrote criticizing his government would never be forgotten or forgiven.

Over the course of the play Jack reveals how he came to be involved with and then distanced himself from Judy, Howard, and the liberal intellectuals of their social group. Jack admits he never felt comfortable with Judy's close relationship with her father, and he felt continually cowed by his father-in-law. As the country's political unrest worsens and Howard becomes ill, Jack's discomfort increases and he decides to leave. Judy refuses to go with him.

Through Jack, Shawn highlights his thematic interest in the conflict between highbrow and lowbrow culture. Living in Howard's house, Jack, by extension, was a supporter and protector of highbrow culture, even though he never completely understood any of it. Jack has to decide whether to maintain his highbrow status or join the lowbrows. In his hotel room, he makes his decision. Rather than ignoring the couple making love in the room next door and continuing to read his book of poetry, he gives in to his voyeuristic primal urge and masturbates. When all are finished, he then chooses to read some magazines about the lives of actresses rather than his poetry. Afterward he chooses to watch television, ultimately displacing not only the book of poetry but also all that Judy, Howard, and his previous life had represented. Later, he displays his badge of membership in lowbrow society by urinating and defecating on a book.

Shortly after Jack leaves, Judy and Howard are imprisoned for five years before being released. Howard is murdered in his own home after his release, and Judy is later publicly executed for being the daughter of an "enemy to the government." With Judy's death Jack realizes that he has become the designated mourner, the lone person who remembers a group that no longer exists. Jack notes that all the people who could read and understand John Donne are gone, and the one person left to remember the liberal intelligentsia of the country is a porn-reading journalist completely enmeshed in and subsumed by lowbrow culture. Shawn suggests that the deaths of Judy, Howard, and the others represent the death of the arts, as lowbrow culture has won out. While the play is set in an unnamed country, many critics have suggested that *The Designated Mourner* is a warning about the waning power and presence of culture in the United States.

The tone and style of *The Designated Mourner* dramatically departs from Shawn's previous accusations aimed at the audience's culpability. Instead of recriminations, the play ends somberly with the recognition of the extermination of highbrow culture and its liberal protectors. Shawn told McGrath: "Because even these weak liberals who don't know what to do, who either lack the ideas or the courage to actually make anything of the sympathy that they feel for others–if you get rid of them, if they are actually removed from the world, the prospects could be even worse." Instead of leaving the theater angry, the audience exits with a sense of loss as well as a feeling of repulsion at what has replaced highbrow culture: Jack and his kind.

The premiere of *The Designated Mourner* in London at the Cottesloe Theatre featured Mike Nichols in

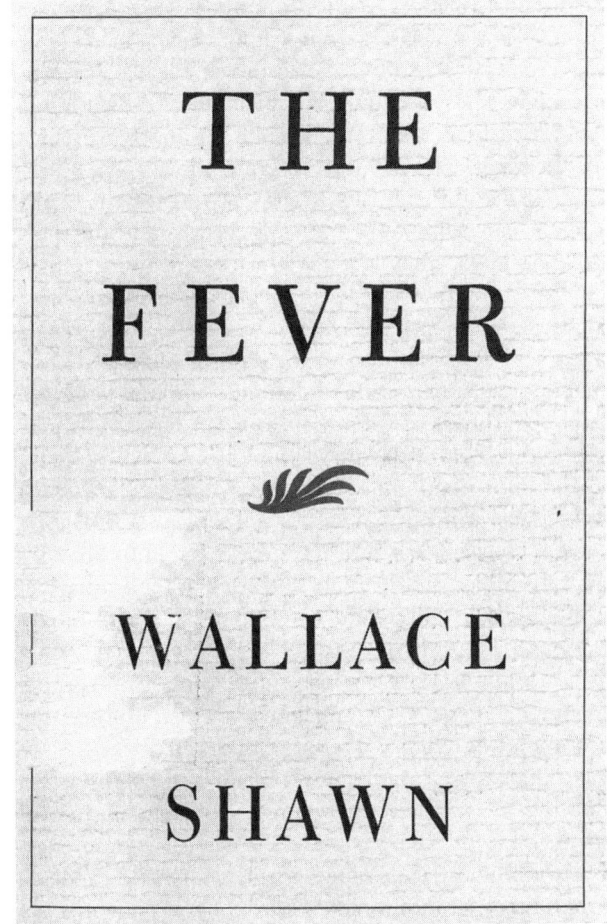

Paperback cover for Shawn's 1990 monologue about the narrator's awareness of the oppression of the poor classes by the privileged (Richland County Public Library)

the role of Jack. Nichols, returning to the stage after a twenty-year absence, found the play intriguing. He told Lahr: "There's nothing more fun than scaring the shit out of an audience. And I think *The Designated Mourner* really scares the shit out of an audience." Benedict Nightingale commented in *The Times* (London) (26 April 1996): "This is a playwright who does not just tell you what it is like to be arrested at night by goons or to fall morally apart and become an aimless yet weirdly contented ghost of yourself. He has the originality to make you feel it." Immediately after the play closed, the BBC made a movie version, which McGrath called "an action movie for brainy people."

Four years later the play made its New York City premiere, directed by Gregory and featuring Shawn as Jack and Eisenberg as Judy. The audience size was limited to thirty, and the play was performed on the fourth and fifth floors of an abandoned building. Bruce Weber's review in *The New York Times* (15 May 2000) described the effect of the decomposing performance space: "You feel as though you're sealed in a vault, suggestive of the stifling world the characters describe, or maybe the execution chamber whose image chills the play's final minutes." And he ultimately summed up the work by writing: "Overall it means to be the kind of art—difficult, unsettling and out of the mainstream, but with an embracing heart—that the play itself declares endangered." Marranca's discussion of the play in *Performing Arts Journal* aptly summed up Shawn's status in the theatrical world: "he has created one of the few examples of the kind of serious intellectual drama of the sustained dramatic voice and compelling psychosocial dimension that has virtually disappeared from theatre in this country, where plays sound more and more like television, magazines or self-empowerment manuals." *The Designated Mourner, Aunt Dan and Lemon,* and *The Fever* exemplify Shawn's maturation as an artist and skill at creating drama that is not only intellectually entertaining but also politically and culturally provocative.

In his *American Theatre* profile, Wetzsteon complimented Shawn by calling him "the uncompromising scourge of our stage." For more than thirty years Wallace Shawn has unrelentingly held firm to his belief that the arts can best effect political change because of their ability to alter the consciousness of its audience. By continually challenging the values people hold, he forces them to question the nature of governments, the traps of materialism, the nature of relationships, and their own role in the cycle of social, economic, and political oppression. In doing so, his plays and their ideas, he contends, can change perspectives and, in turn, the world.

Interviews:

David Savran, "Wallace Shawn," in his *In Their Own Words: Contemporary American Playwrights* (New York: Theatre Communications Group, 1988), pp. 207–222;

Mark Strand, "The Man Behind the Voice: Interview of Wallace Shawn," *Interview,* 19 (March 1989): 72–75, 124, 126;

Patrick McGrath, "Wallace Shawn," *Bomb,* 59 (Spring 1997): 24–27;

Ross Wetzsteon, "Shawn on Shawn: A Kind of Sense," *American Theatre* (September 1997): 15.

References:

Gay Brewer, "He's Still Falling: Wallace Shawn's Problem of Morality," *American Drama,* 2 (Fall 1992): 26–58;

Lucinda Franks, "The Shawns—A Fascinating Father-and-Son Riddle," *New York Times,* 3 August 1980, II: 1, 25;

W. D. King, *Writing Wrongs: The Work of Wallace Shawn* (Philadelphia: Temple University Press, 1997);

John Lahr, "The Dangling Man," *New Yorker* (15 April 1996): 45–51;

Bonnie Marranca, "The Solace of Chocolate Squares: Wallace Shawn in Mourning," *Performing Arts Journal,* 2 (September 2000): 38–46;

Marranca, Johannes Birringer, and Gerald Rabkin, "The Controversial 1985-86 Theatre Season: A Politics of Reception," *Performing Arts Journal,* 10 (1986): 7–33;

Don Shewey, "The Secret Life of Wally Shawn," *Esquire* (October 1983): 90–97;

Ross Wetzsteon, "Wallace Shawn, Subversive Moralist," *American Theatre* (September 1997): 12–14, 16–17;

Wetzsteon, "Wally Shawn: The Holy Fool of the American Theater?" *Village Voice* (2 April 1991): 35–37.

Neil Simon
(4 July 1927 -)

Susan Koprince
University of North Dakota

See also the Simon entry in *DLB 7: Twentieth-Century American Dramatists.*

PLAY PRODUCTIONS: *Catch a Star!* by Simon, Danny Simon, and others, New York, Plymouth Theatre, 6 November 1955;

New Faces of 1956, by Simon, Danny Simon, and others, New York, Ethel Barrymore Theatre, 14 June 1956;

Come Blow Your Horn, New Hope, Pa., Bucks County Playhouse, August 1960; New York, Brooks Atkinson Theatre, 22 February 1961;

Little Me, adapted from Patrick Dennis's novel, music by Cy Coleman, New York, Lunt-Fontanne Theatre, 17 November 1962;

Nobody Loves Me, New Hope, Pa., Bucks County Playhouse, 1962; produced again as *Barefoot in the Park,* New York, Biltmore Theatre, 23 October 1963;

The Odd Couple, New York, Plymouth Theatre, 10 March 1965; revised, female version, New York, Broadhurst Theatre, 11 June 1985;

Sweet Charity, adapted from Federico Fellini's screenplay *Nights of Cabiria,* music and lyrics by Coleman and Dorothy Fields, New York, Palace Theatre, 29 January 1966;

The Star-Spangled Girl, New York, Plymouth Theatre, 21 December 1966;

Plaza Suite, New York, Plymouth Theatre, 14 February 1968;

Broadway Revue, by Simon and others, New York, Bloomgarden Theatre, November 1968;

Promises, Promises, adapted from Billy Wilder and I. A. L. Diamond's screenplay *The Apartment,* music by Burt Bacharach, lyrics by Hal David, New York, Shubert Theatre, 1 December 1968;

Last of the Red Hot Lovers, New York, Eugene O'Neill Theatre, 28 December 1969;

The Gingerbread Lady, New York, Plymouth Theatre, 13 December 1970;

Neil Simon (from Neil Simon, Rewrites: A Memoir, *1996)*

The Prisoner of Second Avenue, New York, Eugene O'Neill Theatre, 11 November 1971;

The Sunshine Boys, New York, Broadhurst Theatre, 20 December 1972;

The Good Doctor, adapted from Anton Chekhov's short stories, music by Peter Link, lyrics by Simon, New York, Eugene O'Neill Theatre, 27 November 1973;

God's Favorite, New York, Eugene O'Neill Theatre, 11 December 1974;

California Suite, New York, Eugene O'Neill Theatre, 10 June 1976;

Chapter Two, New York, Imperial Theatre, 4 December 1977;

They're Playing Our Song, book by Simon, music by Marvin Hamlisch, lyrics by Carole Bayer Sager, New York, Imperial Theatre, 11 February 1979;

I Ought to Be in Pictures, New York, Eugene O'Neill Theatre, 3 April 1980;

Fools, New York, Eugene O'Neill Theatre, 6 April 1981;

Brighton Beach Memoirs, New York, Alvin Theatre, 27 March 1983; transferred to the 46th Street Theatre, 26 February 1985;

Biloxi Blues, New York, Neil Simon Theatre, 28 March 1985;

Broadway Bound, New York, Broadhurst Theatre, 4 December 1986;

Rumors, New York, Broadhurst Theatre, 17 November 1988;

Lost in Yonkers, New York, Richard Rodgers Theatre, 21 February 1991;

Jake's Women, New York, Neil Simon Theatre, 24 March 1992;

The Goodbye Girl, music by Marvin Hamlisch, lyrics by David Zippel, New York, Marquis Theatre, 4 March 1993;

Laughter on the 23rd Floor, New York, Richard Rodgers Theatre, 22 November 1993;

London Suite, New York, Union Square Theatre, 10 April 1995;

Proposals, New York, Broadhurst Theatre, 6 November 1997;

Hotel Suite, New York, Gramercy Theatre, 15 June 2000—selected one-acts from *Plaza Suite, California Suite,* and *London Suite;*

The Dinner Party, New York, Music Box Theatre, 19 October 2000;

45 Seconds from Broadway, New York, Richard Rodgers Theatre, 11 November 2001.

BOOKS: *Adventures of Marco Polo: A Musical Fantasy,* by Simon and William Friedberg (New York: S. French, 1959);

Heidi, adapted by Simon and Friedberg from Johanna Spyri's novel (New York: S. French, 1959);

Come Blow Your Horn (London & New York: S. French, 1961; Garden City, N.Y.: Doubleday, 1963);

Barefoot in the Park (New York: Random House, 1964; London & New York: S. French, 1967);

The Odd Couple (New York: Random House, 1966; London: S. French, 1966; revised, female version, New York: S. French, 1986);

Sweet Charity (New York: Random House, 1966);

The Star-Spangled Girl (New York: Random House, 1967);

Plaza Suite (New York: Random House, 1969);

Promises, Promises (New York: Random House, 1969);

Last of the Red Hot Lovers (New York: Random House, 1970);

The Gingerbread Lady (New York: Random House, 1971);

The Prisoner of Second Avenue (New York: Random House, 1972);

The Sunshine Boys (New York: Random House, 1973);

The Good Doctor (New York: Random House, 1974);

God's Favorite (New York: Random House, 1975);

California Suite (New York: Random House, 1977);

Chapter Two (New York: Random House, 1979);

They're Playing Our Song (New York: Random House, 1980);

I Ought to Be in Pictures (New York: Random House, 1981);

Fools (New York: Random House, 1981);

Brighton Beach Memoirs (New York: Random House, 1984);

Biloxi Blues (New York: Random House, 1986);

Broadway Bound (New York: Random House, 1987);

Rumors (New York: Random House, 1990);

Lost in Yonkers (New York: Random House, 1991);

Neil Simon's Lost in Yonkers: The Illustrated Screenplay of the Film (New York: Newmarket Press, 1993);

Jake's Women (New York: Random House, 1994);

Laughter on the 23rd Floor (New York: Random House, 1995);

London Suite (New York: S. French, 1996);

Rewrites: A Memoir (New York: Simon & Schuster, 1996);

Proposals (New York: S. French, 1998);

The Play Goes On: A Memoir (New York: Simon & Schuster, 1999);

The Odd Couple I and II: The Original Screen Plays (New York: Simon & Schuster, 2000).

Editions and Collections: *The Comedy of Neil Simon* (New York: Random House, 1971); republished as *The Collected Plays of Neil Simon, Vol. 1* (New York: Plume, 1986);

The Collected Plays of Neil Simon, Vol. 2 (New York: Random House, 1979);

The Collected Plays of Neil Simon, Vol. 3 (New York: Random House, 1991);

Neil Simon Monologues: Speeches from the Works of America's Foremost Playwright, edited by Roger Karshner (Rancho Mirage, Cal.: Dramaline, 1996);

The Collected Plays of Neil Simon, Vol. 4 (New York: Touchstone, 1998);

Neil Simon Scenes: Scenes from the Works of America's Foremost Playwright, edited by Karshner (Rancho Mirage, Cal.: Dramaline, 2000).

PRODUCED SCRIPTS: *After the Fox,* by Simon and Cesare Zavattini, motion picture, United Artists, 1966;
Barefoot in the Park, motion picture, Paramount, 1967;
The Odd Couple, motion picture, Paramount, 1968;
The Out-of-Towners, motion picture, Paramount, 1970;
Plaza Suite, motion picture, Paramount, 1971;
The Heartbreak Kid, adapted from Bruce Jay Friedman's short story, motion picture, 20th Century-Fox, 1972;
Last of the Red Hot Lovers, motion picture, Paramount, 1972;
The Trouble with People, television, NBC, 12 November 1972;
The Sunshine Boys, motion picture, M-G-M, 1975;
The Prisoner of Second Avenue, motion picture, Warner Bros., 1975;
Murder By Death, motion picture, Columbia, 1976;
The Goodbye Girl, motion picture, Warner Bros., 1977;
The Good Doctor, adapted from Anton Chekhov's short stories, television, PBS, 8 November 1978;
The Cheap Detective, motion picture, Columbia, 1978;
California Suite, motion picture, Columbia, 1978;
Chapter Two, motion picture, Columbia, 1979;
Seems Like Old Times, motion picture, Columbia, 1980;
Only When I Laugh, adapted from *The Gingerbread Lady,* motion picture, Columbia, 1981;
I Ought to Be in Pictures, motion picture, 20th Century-Fox, 1982;
Max Dugan Returns, motion picture, 20th Century-Fox, 1983;
The Slugger's Wife, motion picture, Columbia, 1985;
Brighton Beach Memoirs, motion picture, Universal, 1986;
Plaza Suite, television, ABC, 1987;
Biloxi Blues, motion picture, Universal, 1988;
The Marrying Man, motion picture, Hollywood Pictures, 1991;
Neil Simon's "Broadway Bound," television, ABC, 23 March 1992;
Lost in Yonkers, motion picture, Columbia, 1993;
The Sunshine Boys, television, CBS, 1995;
Jake's Women, television, CBS, 3 March 1996;
London Suite, television, NBC, 15 September 1996;
The Odd Couple II, motion picture, Paramount, 1998;
Laughter on the 23rd Floor, television, Showtime, 26 May 2001.

Neil Simon is a master of comedy and one of the most popular dramatists in the history of the American theater. His plays, which range from light romantic comedy and farce to drama, have entertained Broadway audiences for nearly four decades and have also been a mainstay for regional and amateur theater companies. Simon has furnished the books for hit musicals such as *Sweet Charity* (1966) and *Promises, Promises* (1968), has adapted more plays to movies than any other American dramatist, and has written ten original screenplays. Although ignored in the past by most literary scholars, Simon has begun to attract more serious critical attention, particularly since winning the Pulitzer Prize in drama in 1991 for *Lost in Yonkers.* Summing up the Pulitzer drama jury's decision, critic Douglas Watt wrote that *Lost in Yonkers* was "a mature work by an enduring (and often undervalued) American playwright."

The second son of Mamie and Irving Simon, Marvin Neil Simon was born in the Bronx, New York, on 4 July 1927 and grew up in Washington Heights, Manhattan, during the Great Depression. His parents had a stormy marriage; his father (a garment salesman) abandoned the family frequently during Simon's boyhood, causing serious financial strain as well as emotional turmoil. "I think part of what has made me a comedy writer," Simon told Richard Meryman in 1971, "is the blocking out of some of the really ugly, painful things in my childhood and covering it up with a humorous attitude."

Following his graduation at age sixteen from DeWitt Clinton High School in the Bronx, Simon enlisted in the Army Air Force Reserve training program at New York University. In 1945 he was assigned to Lowry Field, Colorado, where he attended the University of Denver and worked as sports editor for the military publication *Rev-Meter.* Simon later used his experience in the army as material for *Biloxi Blues* (1985), the second play in his semi-autobiographical Brighton Beach trilogy.

After his discharge as a corporal in 1946, Simon launched his career in show business with his brother, Danny, writing comedy for producer/writer Goodman Ace of CBS. For the next decade Danny and "Doc" Simon (a nickname originating from Simon's childhood impersonations of the family doctor) collaborated in writing comedy sketches for radio (*The Robert Q. Lewis Show*) and for television series such as the *Phil Silvers Show* and Sid Caesar's *Your Show of Shows.* Eventually ending his partnership with his brother, Simon continued to write comedy for television until the opening of his first Broadway play, *Come Blow Your Horn,* in 1961. Because he initially learned his craft during the Golden Age of television comedy, Simon came to the theater with a gift for writing gags and one-liners and an instinctive knowledge of what would make an audience laugh.

A hallmark of Simon's comedy is its Chekhovian mixture of humor and poignancy. As the playwright explained to Paul D. Zimmerman in 1970, "My view is 'how sad and funny life is.' I can't think of a humorous

Mildred Natwick, Elizabeth Ashley, Kurt Kasznar, and Robert Redford in the 1963 Biltmore Theatre production of Barefoot in the Park *(Theatre Collection, Museum of New York City)*

situation that does not involve some pain." His early plays, though lighthearted, actually deal with serious themes—marital conflict, incompatibility, the midlife crisis—and as Simon has matured as a playwright, he has addressed subjects as troubling as alcoholism, homophobia, and the dysfunctional family. Yet, he cannot imagine writing a play that is altogether devoid of humor: in a 1979 *Playboy* interview he said, "It's not that I want to make people laugh, it's just that I see humor in even the grimmest of situations. And I think it's possible to write a play so moving it can tear you apart and *still* have humor in it."

Simon's comic vision is directly related to his Jewish heritage and to the tradition of Jewish humor that he embraces. As Peter L. Hays writes in "Neil Simon and the Funny Jewish Blues" (1997), Jewish humor typically uses laughter as a defense mechanism—as a way of deflecting anxiety, pain, and humiliation. Frequently, such humor is self-deprecating or self-pitying, displaying the attitude that "everything happens to me." In *Brighton Beach Memoirs* (1983), for example, Simon's young protagonist tells the audience that he hates his name: "How am I ever going to play for the Yankees with a name like Eugene Morris Jerome? You have to be a Joe . . . or a Tony . . . or a Frankie . . . If only I was born Italian . . . All the best Yankees are Italian . . . My mother makes spaghetti with ketchup, what chance do I have?" Although Simon did not focus explicitly on Jewish characters in his comedies until the 1980s, there has always been a distinct Jewishness to his humor—not only a penchant for self-satire but also a desire to take a serious (or even painful) subject and present it in a comical manner.

The most pervasive theme in Simon's plays is that of marriage and divorce—a theme he has examined for almost forty years, from his story of newlyweds Corie and Paul Bratter in *Barefoot in the Park* (1963) to his portrait of three divorced couples in *The Dinner Party* (2000). Repeatedly making use of the "problem marriage" plot (a variant of the classic boy-meet-girl story

Program cover and title page for Simon's 1965 Broadway success (Bruccoli Clark Layman Archives)

line established by the ancient Greek playwright Menander), Simon explores issues such as infidelity, fear of aging, and the difficulty of finding an enduring love. Affirming his traditional values throughout his comedies, he asserts his basic faith in the institution of marriage and his belief in the primacy of family. Simon does so despite the troubled marriage of his own parents and despite his personal experience with divorce (from his second wife, actress Marsha Mason, in 1982 and from his third wife, Diane Lander, in 1988 and again a decade later). Simon's happy first marriage to dancer Joan Baim in 1953 ended twenty years later when she died of cancer. In September 1999 he married actress Elaine Joyce.

Recounting Simon's experience of leaving his parents' home for the first time, Simon's first comedy, *Come Blow Your Horn*, focuses on the theme of coming of age. Two brothers, Alan and Buddy Baker, are pictured as Simon's original "odd couple." Thirty-three-year-old Alan, modeled on Danny Simon, is presented as a smooth-talking ladies' man; whereas twenty-one-year-old Buddy, based on the playwright, is portrayed as a diffident, sexually inexperienced youth. The plot revolves around the brothers' attempt to share an apartment and to free themselves from the control of their parents, particularly their father, Harry Baker, a despotic manufacturer of wax fruit who is also their boss at work.

After three weeks of living together as roommates, Alan and Buddy essentially exchange identities. By act 3 Buddy has turned into a rakish bachelor, staying out late at night and dating glamorous women. Alan, on the other hand, has lost his earlier brashness, becoming more responsible at work and proposing marriage to his first serious girlfriend, Connie Dayton. Because Alan's rite of passage involves an acceptance of the traditional values of his parents, his reconciliation in act 3 with his father, Harry, is crucial to the dramatic action. Also important is Harry's final willingness to accept Buddy's departure from home, a grudging acknowledgment that his younger son, too, is coming into manhood.

Critics found Simon's first play slender in plot and overly dependent on stock characters (the swinging bachelor, the bimbo), but they were uniformly impressed by the amusing portrait of the tyrannical Harry and by Simon's gift for witty dialogue. Enjoying a Broadway run of 677 performances, *Come Blow Your Horn* marked an auspicious beginning to Simon's theatrical career.

Simon continued his autobiographical approach to playwriting in the romantic comedy *Barefoot in the Park* (1963), in which he affectionately recalled his marriage to his first wife, Joan, and their life together in a "one-room, five-story walk-up" in Greenwich Village. Rather than adopting the traditional "boy-meets-girl" framework of romantic comedy, Simon employed his favorite variation of that story line–the "problem marriage" plot–portraying the troubles of a pair of newlyweds, Corie and Paul Bratter, who, though deeply in love with each other, are opposite in temperament, and who must eventually learn the delicate art of compromise. *Barefoot in the Park* proved to be a major critical and commercial hit for Simon, running on Broadway for 1,532 performances.

Like the Baker brothers in *Come Blow Your Horn*, Corie and Paul are pictured as an odd couple. Corie is carefree, fun-loving, and romantic–someone who delights in mischievous pranks and in walking barefoot in the park in the winter. Paul, on the other hand, is reserved, conservative, and pragmatic–a serious young lawyer who has just taken on his first case. Also included in the play are Ethel Banks (Corie's mother) and Victor Velasco (a flamboyant neighbor), who serve as reflector characters to the newlywed couple. Like Paul, Mrs. Banks is subdued and cautious; she suffers from a bad back and worries that if she takes a pleasure cruise, she will fall off the ship. Victor, on the other hand, shares Corie's impulsive, adventuresome nature, enjoying exotic foods as well as skiing, mountain climbing, and the company of women.

The conflicts that emerge from these pairings of opposites form the dramatic action of Simon's comedy. A blind date between Mrs. Banks and Victor turns into a fiasco, and near the end of act 2 Corie even declares that she and Paul should get a divorce, since the two of them "have absolutely *nothing* in common." The play ends in traditional comedic fashion, however, with a reconciliation between the newlyweds as well as between Mrs. Banks and Victor–all of whom learn about the need for compromise. As Edythe M. McGovern writes, "Each of the four characters has altered his behavior so that it has become less polarized, less radical, less extreme. Each person has gravitated toward a moderation which seems to be the playwright's ideal."

Simon's next big hit, *The Odd Couple* (1965), was a natural outgrowth of *Barefoot in the Park,* since it, too, focused on the themes of incompatibility and adaptability. Simon employed the same "problem marriage" framework found in his previous comedy, cleverly altering it to depict a pair of heterosexual males, Felix Ungar and Oscar Madison, who have separated from their spouses and who have decided to share an apartment together. The friends quickly discover, however, that they are no better off in this new domestic union than they were with their wives. In act 3, after the men have reached a state of open warfare, an exasperated Oscar finally kicks his roommate out of his apartment, crying, "It's all over, Felix. The whole marriage. We're getting an annulment!"

Although Felix and Oscar are in many respects realistically drawn (they are based primarily on Simon's brother, Danny, and a theatrical agent named Roy Gerber), Simon exaggerates his characters' differences so that the two men–played by Walter Matthau and Art Carney in the Broadway premiere–are absurdly incompatible. Oscar is sloppy, irresponsible, and carefree–a fun-loving man who enjoys the weekly poker game with his buddies. Felix, on the other hand, is compulsively neat, fussy, and high-strung–a frustrated "housewife" who takes pleasure in cooking and cleaning and who likes to serve dainty sandwiches to his guests. The other poker players–Speed, Roy, Murray, and Vinnie–function as a sort of Greek chorus and a voice for moderation. In act 1 the men complain about Oscar's slovenly apartment, with its litter, its broken air conditioner, and its stench of garbage. In act 2, however, they are equally distressed when Felix transforms Oscar's apartment into a scene out of *House and Garden,* even disinfecting the playing cards. "Look," says Roy, "I've been sitting here breathing Lysol and ammonia for four hours! Nature didn't intend for poker to be played like that."

In an effort to produce a happy ending in act 3, Simon pushes his previously inflexible protagonists to change a little too much: the shy and neurotic Felix is suddenly willing to move in with Oscar's British neighbors, the Pigeon sisters, while the inveterate slob Oscar, claiming that his home is not a pigsty, warns the poker players not to drop their cigarette butts on his rug. But despite a few weaknesses in its final act, *The Odd Couple* was hailed by critics as a hilarious and original comedy. A tremendous success on Broadway, with a run of 965 performances, the play was later adapted into one of the best movie versions of Simon's comedies and also into a popular ABC television series. As Robert K. Johnson observed, "Oscar Madison and Felix Ungar–

Program cover and title page for the 1968 New York production of Simon's collection of one-act plays that take place in the same hotel room (Bruccoli Clark Layman Archives)

and Simon's whole concept of 'the odd couple'—have become as much a part of our cultural folklore as Babbitt, Superman, Holden Caulfield, and Archie Bunker."

In 1985 Simon created a new female version of *The Odd Couple*. Oscar and Felix were replaced by characters named Olive and Florence; the British Pigeon sisters became the Spanish Costazuela brothers; and the poker game was switched to the more feminine contest of Trivial Pursuit. Although the revised play has its entertaining moments—especially in the scenes involving the Costazuela brothers—it does not comment as humorously on sexual stereotypes. As critics pointed out, it is still more amusing for a man to be a gourmet cook and compulsive housekeeper than it is for a woman.

The Star-Spangled Girl (1966) is, by Simon's own admission, one of his weakest plays, primarily because its subject matter is not drawn from the material of his own life. Superficially addressing the topic of 1960s radicalism, the play describes two young leftists, Andy Hobart and Norman Cornell, who are struggling in San Francisco to publish a protest magazine called *Fallout* and who both become infatuated with Sophie Rauschmeyer, a conservative, all-American girl who believes that their magazine is subversive. First pursued relentlessly by Norman, Sophie realizes in the end that her heart actually belongs to Andy, and she even becomes more tolerant of his radical politics. Although some of the dialogue is humorous, critics generally agreed that Simon's comedy was weakened by a contrived plot, artificial characters, and an unsound premise. Reviewing *The Star-Spangled Girl* for *The New York Times* (22 December 1966), Walter Kerr quipped: "Neil Simon . . . hasn't had an idea for a play this season, but he's gone ahead and written one anyway."

Simon's early experience writing comedy sketches for television sharpened his interest in the one-act play—a format that he first employed to advan-

Simon with stars Sam Levine and Jack Albertson on opening night of the 1972 New York production of The Sunshine Boys (from Simon, Rewrites: A Memoir, 1996)

tage in *Plaza Suite* (1968). With the one-act play, Simon noted, "you can get straight to the big scenes, the crucial moments, the immediate laughs." Composed of three playlets, all taking place in the same suite of the famous New York hotel, *Plaza Suite* is unified not only by its setting but also by its commentaries on love and marriage.

The first playlet, "Visitor from Mamaroneck," features Karen and Sam Nash, a middle-aged couple who, as they celebrate their twenty-third anniversary, are experiencing marital difficulties. Karen is desperately trying to recapture the romance of their honeymoon, whereas Sam appears to be interested only in his work. When Sam reveals that he is going through a midlife crisis and is having an affair with his young secretary, Karen struggles to maintain her dignity, while at the same time pleading with her husband not to leave her. Although it includes some witty lines (especially from Karen, who uses humor as a defense mechanism), this first sketch is clearly more serious than Simon's previous works, even concluding with an open ending in which the couple's marriage hangs in the balance.

"Visitor from Hollywood" also deals with the issue of infidelity, describing how a suave movie producer, Jesse Kiplinger, attempts to seduce his former high-school sweetheart, Muriel Tate. Disillusioned with the Hollywood scene—particularly after three different wives have been unfaithful to him—Jesse returns to New York in hopes of reliving his youth and of making love to an innocent woman. In order for the seduction of Muriel to be successful, both characters must adopt a persona: Jesse must play the role of the self-confident Hollywood producer, pretending to relish his celebrity status; and Muriel (who has actually turned into a disgruntled housewife and problem drinker) must play the part of the all-American girl next door. Although both characters ultimately get what they want in this sexual encounter, the comedy itself is tinged by sadness, as the relationship between Jesse and Muriel is shown to be superficial, loveless, and banal.

An unabashed farce, "Visitor from Forest Hills" takes the traditional ending to romantic comedy—a wedding—and turns it into a private nightmare. Roy and Norma Hubley discover that their daughter, Mimsey, has locked herself in the hotel bathroom on her wedding day, refusing to get married. As the guests downstairs in the Green Room grow restless, Roy and Norma become increasingly upset, bickering with each other and resorting to outlandish strategies to persuade their daughter to come out of the bathroom. While Norma worries about being embarrassed by a canceled wedding, Roy is obsessed with his possible financial losses, at one point yelling, "Mimsey! This is your father. I want you and your four-hundred-dollar wedding dress out of there in five seconds!" The only person who can finally extricate the girl from the bathroom is her fiancé, who knocks on the door and calmly says, "Mimsey? . . . This is Borden . . . Cool it!" Despite its hilarious situation and its physical humor, "Visitor from Forest Hills" deals with serious themes such as marital conflict and lack of communication. *Plaza Suite*, as a whole, does not endorse the optimistic view of marriage found in Simon's earlier comedy *Barefoot in the Park*.

Inspired by the sexual revolution of the 1960s, *Last of the Red Hot Lovers* (1969) focuses on the midlife crisis of forty-seven-year-old Barney Cashman, the portly, uncouth owner of a fish restaurant who feels that his life is slipping away from him and who is strongly tempted to commit adultery. Barney proves to be a clumsy ladies' man, however, and his three seduction attempts (one in each act) all end in failure. Part of the problem is Barney's choice of potential lovers. Elaine Navazio, in act 1, is interested only in casual sex and not in a deeper romantic attachment. Bobbi Michele, in act 2, is emotionally unbalanced and only wants to tell wild stories about her sexual past. Finally, Jeanette Fisher, in act 3, is pictured as "probably the singularly most depressed woman on the face of the Western Hemisphere." In the end Barney invites his wife, Thelma, to his mother's apartment (the incongruous setting for all of his romantic trysts), revitalizing his own marriage and proving that, even if he is not ready to join the sexual revolution, he is essentially a "decent, gentle, and loving" man.

Although *Last of the Red Hot Lovers* was a popular success, some reviewers criticized Simon's use of a pattern plot, in which the main action (the attempted seduction) is repeated three times. Claiming that "the laughs grow fewer" as the play progresses, Kerr viewed this comedy as a group of redundant one-acts and argued that it was time for Simon to write a full-length play again, "with four and five and six people bumping into each other from time to time, and with the second and third acts standing on, instead of alongside, the first" (*The New York Times*, 4 January 1970). Clive Barnes, however, praised Simon's ability to blend the comic with the poignant, asserting that in Barney Cashman, Simon had created "a character who is far from a figure of farce, but has the sluggish blood of disappointment running through his veins" (*The New York Times*, 12 December 1969).

In *The Gingerbread Lady* (1970) Simon made an even more overt effort to combine tragedy with comedy, writing a drama about an alcoholic, self-destructive singer reminiscent of Judy Garland. Recently released from a sanitarium, the protagonist, Evy Meara, uses wisecracks to cover up her lack of self-esteem and sense of personal failure. She jokes about her alcoholism, her promiscuity, and her incompetence as a mother but admits that she has "only one more chance at this human-being business . . . and if I blow it this time, they'll probably bury me in some distillery in Kentucky." Evy's self-destructive habits are exacerbated by her choice of companions—a group of weak, dependent people who serve as enablers in Evy's tragic battle with alcoholism. Jimmy Perry is a gay actor who, at age forty-one, still cannot find success in the theater. Toby Landau is a middle-aged former beauty queen who is narcissistic and absorbed with her own personal problems. And Lou Tanner, Evy's former lover, is an unsuccessful musician who is physically abusive. The only positive character, Evy's selfless and affectionate daughter, Polly, likewise becomes an enabler by acting as her mother's caretaker rather than placing the responsibility for Evy's addiction on Evy herself. It is no surprise, therefore, when the heroine goes on another alcoholic binge, and her life begins to spiral out of control.

The Gingerbread Lady lasted for only 193 performances on Broadway, largely because audiences were not comfortable with its dark subject. Even a new tacked-on ending, in which Evy is given more hope for a lasting recovery, failed to satisfy theatergoers, who were expecting to be entertained by a typical Neil Simon comedy. Nor was the play well received by the critics. Martin Gottfried argued in *Women's Wear Daily* (15 December 1970) that this latest effort by Simon was "trivial, plotless, characterless," and he urged the playwright not to abandon his comic sense but to explore it in greater depth. Kerr was especially disappointed by the skeletal plot of the play and its lack of fully developed characters, maintaining that the audience never really comes to know Evy Meara at all: "She is a woman who drinks, and that is that" (*The New York Times*, 20 December 1970).

In 1981 Simon adapted *The Gingerbread Lady* into the movie *Only When I Laugh*, which starred his second

Program cover and title page for the 1977 New York production of the play Simon based on his experiences after the death of his first wife and his marriage to actress Marsha Mason (Bruccoli Clark Layman Archives)

wife, Marsha Mason. Demonstrating that he could learn from his mistakes, he radically altered the movie version, using less than half of the material from his play script. He gave Evy a new name (Georgia Hines), a new career (actress), and more admirable qualities than she had displayed in the stage play (for example, she is not sexually promiscuous). Because Georgia receives more support from her friends and because she is not as self-lacerating as Evy, the hopeful ending of the movie makes better sense than the tacked-on conclusion to Simon's drama.

In another dark comedy, *The Prisoner of Second Avenue* (1971), Simon attempts for the first time to engage in serious social commentary, describing the urban angst of his protagonist, Mel Edison, who is beleaguered by big-city problems such as noise, crime, unemployment, and pollution. At forty-seven, Mel has been fired from his job as an advertising executive and is desperately worried about how he is going to support his wife, Edna, and his two college-age daughters. After the couple's apartment is burglarized, stripping them of their possessions, Mel becomes depressed and paranoiac, eventually suffering a nervous breakdown.

Simon uses exaggeration—and even slapstick humor—to make his protagonist's situation funny, turning Mel's New York angst into comic suffering. Especially amusing are Mel's tirades against his neighbors: he bangs loudly on the wall, causing it to crack; he exchanges insults on the terrace with his upstairs neighbor, who douses him with a bucket of water; and he buys a shovel with the intention of flinging snow down on his new enemy from fourteen floors above. Trapped in an urban jungle in which neighbors are doing battle with each other, Mel and Edna can only endure by fighting back, adopting a harsh survivor's mentality.

Employing the device of a voice-over newscast, Simon also makes it clear that Mel's problems are shared by other embattled New Yorkers. The newscaster reports on muggings, robberies, strikes, water shutoffs, rat infestations, and even an accident in which a Polish freighter crashed into the Statue of Liberty. As Michael Woolf has noted, such newscasts—though exaggerated for comical effect—help to depict the city "as an irrational landscape and the experience of the Edisons as more than personal misfortune. They are victims of a world close to a kind of absurd disintegration."

Running on Broadway for 788 performances, *The Prisoner of Second Avenue* received mixed critical reviews. Some critics faulted the play for its flimsy plot and one-dimensional characters, while others declared it hilarious and true to life. Barnes, noting the serious direction in which Simon's comedy had moved, wrote in *The New York Times* (12 November 1971): "Now his humor has a sad air to it; it is all the more deliciously funny for that undercurrent of discontent."

In *Rewrites: A Memoir* (1996) Simon recalls an encounter at the Astor Hotel in New York with an aging vaudeville star named Willie Howard, whose show-business career was long behind him: "The look and dress of Willie Howard, the seediness and sadness of his room, and the improbability that he would ever work much again stayed with me for years and finally became the model in my mind for what later would be *The Sunshine Boys*." Both a popular and critical success, *The Sunshine Boys* (1972) pays tribute to the bygone art of vaudeville, focusing on two old comedians, Willie Clark and Al Lewis, who have been estranged for eleven years but who reunite in an effort to reprise their classic comedy act for a CBS television special. Ben Silverman, Willie's nephew and agent, serves not only as his uncle's caregiver but also as a peacemaker between the retired vaudevillians.

Like *Barefoot in the Park* and *The Odd Couple*, *The Sunshine Boys* explores the theme of incompatibility. Although Willie Clark and Al Lewis were a famous comedy team for more than forty years, the two men never managed to get along with each other and have not even been on speaking terms since Al retired from show business eleven years ago. So great is the antipathy between the pair (especially after Willie changes one of the lines in their classic vaudeville routine and Al resumes his annoying habits of spitting at Willie and poking him in the chest) that the comedy sketch for CBS is never taped, and Willie suffers a heart attack. The play concludes with a partial reconciliation between the former partners, who, by coincidence, will be moving to the same actors' retirement home in New Jersey.

Simon with (clockwise from upper left) Madeline Kahn, Louise Fletcher, Eileen Brennan, Ann-Margret, Mason, and Stockard Channing, the stars of his 1978 screenplay The Cheap Detective *(photograph © 1978 Rastar Films, Inc.)*

Simon also focuses on the theme of old age—a new subject for him. In a humorous, yet poignant, manner he depicts the age-related problems of his protagonists: Willie has high blood pressure, is forgetful, and is not really capable of living independently anymore; Al suffers from diabetes, asthma, arthritis, poor vision, and hardening of the arteries. Whereas Al seems to have accepted his old age, living quietly with his daughter in New Jersey, Willie rails against his forced retirement from show business and fights for self-respect. According to McGovern, Simon speaks in this play of the universal need for human dignity and the difficulty of fulfilling that need "when one is old, isolated, and dependent."

Most critics agreed that Simon was at the top of his form with *The Sunshine Boys*. Whereas they had previously faulted the playwright for his overreliance on gags and one-liners, in this play the jokes seem organic to its structure. Fashioning humor out of the misfortunes of his characters and drawing upon a rich theatrical past, Simon created what Gottfried in *Women's Wear*

Daily (22 December 1972) described as "a melancholy valentine to American vaudeville."

Simon recalled in a 1991 interview with Jackson R. Bryer that at a performance in New Haven of his next work, *The Good Doctor* (1973), a woman approached the playwright during intermission, telling him disappointedly, "It's just not Neil Simon." Indeed, *The Good Doctor* represents a major shift from Simon's typical New York setting and contemporary urban characters. A collection of sketches based on early stories by Anton Chekhov, the play is also the first of Simon's dramas to depart from the realistic tradition, making use of a metatheatrical structure. Three men and two women perform all twenty-six parts in *The Good Doctor*—a device that adds coherence to the vignettes. Unifying the play as well is the character of the Writer, who serves as a narrator, takes parts in some of the sketches, and breaks through the imaginary "fourth wall" onstage to speak directly to the audience. The Writer's monologues about the craft of writing itself—in which he discusses writer's block, his sense of alienation, and his endless compulsion to write—can be seen as preparation for the self-reflexivity of some of Simon's later plays.

Referring both to Chekhov (who composed these stories when he was a young medical student) and to Simon (whose nickname is "Doc"), the title *The Good Doctor* suggests a strong affinity between the two playwrights. According to Simon, his comedies ultimately have the same purpose as that declared by Chekhov for his own life's work: "to show people how absurdly they live their lives." Some of the sketches in *The Good Doctor* are critical of government bureaucracy and social stratification (such as "The Sneeze," in which a civil servant accidentally sneezes on a high government official while attending the theater); others are farcical depictions of human misery (such as "Surgery," in which an inexperienced dentist tries to extract a tooth from a panicky patient). One of the most effective sketches, "The Seduction," presents a character who is adept at seducing other men's wives and who brazenly offers the audience a "practical demonstration." On the whole, *The Good Doctor* cannot be considered one of Simon's stronger plays, but it is an interesting dramatic experiment, demonstrating the author's willingness to take certain risks with his playwriting.

In July 1973 Simon's first wife, Joan, died of cancer at the age of thirty-nine. She and Simon had been married for nearly twenty years and were raising two daughters, Ellen and Nancy. (Simon later adopted Bryn, the daughter of his third wife, Diane Lander.) Devastated by grief, Simon wrote *God's Favorite* (1974)—a comic retelling of the biblical story of Job. As Simon explained in a 1991 interview, "I could not understand the absurdity of a thirty-nine-year-old beautiful, energetic woman dying so young." The play was Simon's "railing at God to explain to me why He did this thing."

God's Favorite tells the story of Joe Benjamin, a wealthy New York businessman who has achieved the American dream, but whose faith in God is tested as he endures one catastrophe after another: his factory burns down; his mansion is destroyed; his family briefly deserts him; his son is blinded; and he is beset by a host of physical ailments. Despite its somber subject, the play is often farcical and amusing—especially during scenes involving Sidney Lipton, the myopic, wisecracking messenger from God, who claims that he has been in the presence of the Almighty, but that "there's always a big light over Him—the glare is murder."

Lasting for only 119 performances on Broadway, *God's Favorite* was neither a popular nor a critical success. Reviewers believed that the characters (with the exception of Sidney Lipton) were poorly defined and that the play was weakened by an excess of one-liners. Some critics even found this black comedy sacrilegious. One of the playwright's least successful dramas, *God's Favorite* nonetheless demonstrates Simon's continued commitment to experimentation and his determination to mix pathos with broad comedy.

In *California Suite* (1976) Simon returned to the crowd-pleasing format of *Plaza Suite,* presenting four playlets set in the same suite of the Beverly Hills Hotel, alternating between more-serious drama and farce. The first sketch, "Visitor from New York," involves a divorced couple who are meeting in Los Angeles to determine who will get custody of their teenage daughter. Not only does a parental battle take place, but there is also a clash between East and West Coast cultures. Hannah Warren is a die-hard New Yorker who makes fun of her former husband's new California lifestyle, while Bill Warren accuses Hannah of East Coast elitism. In the end, the couple's shared love for their daughter enables them to arrive at a tentative solution to the custody issue, but this first playlet also explores the pain and insecurity masked by the pair's clever repartee.

"Visitor from Philadelphia," like most farces, centers on a hilariously improbable situation: a middle-aged man, Marvin Michaels, awakens in his hotel room to find an intoxicated call girl in his bed—a surprise present from his brother the previous evening. When Marvin's wife, Millie, arrives at the hotel, Marvin tries desperately to divert her attention and to prevent her from seeing the unconscious body of the prostitute. In contrast to many bedroom farces, which attack the institution of marriage, Simon's sketch ultimately reaffirms his traditional family values. Marvin (who is basically a decent man) confesses his sins; his wife forgives

Program cover and title page for the 1983 New York production of the first play in Simon's trilogy about semi-autobiographical protagonist Eugene Jerome (Bruccoli Clark Layman Archives)

him; and their fifteen-year marriage is saved. But he is not allowed to escape from this episode unscathed: "I am now going into Beverly Hills," announces Millie, "and spend every cent you've got."

The third playlet, "Visitors from London," describes the troubled relationship of a British couple, Diana and Sydney Nichols, who have come to Hollywood in order to attend the Academy Awards ceremony. Diana is extremely nervous about her nomination for best actress, fearing that she will lose to one of her rivals. But her real insecurities stem from her marriage. In scene 2 the audience learns that Sydney is bisexual and that part of the reason he has traveled to California is to meet new sexual partners. When the couple make love at the end of the playlet, Diana asks Sydney not to fantasize about anyone else and to focus on her: "Look at *me* tonight," she begs. "Let it be *me* tonight."

One of Simon's best short pieces, "Visitors from London" is basically a high comedy in the manner of Noel Coward. Simon not only makes use of witty, sophisticated dialogue but also engages in social satire–ridiculing the hypocrisy and crassness of Hollywood. Noting that Jack Nicholson actually wore black patent leather tennis shoes to the Oscars ceremony that night, for example, Sydney declares, "they're not civilized out here, it's as plain as that." As in most high comedies, Simon presents a serious character study–emphasizing the human qualities of his protagonists. He depicts a married couple who stay together because they genuinely need each other but whose relationship brings considerable pain.

California Suite concludes with the farcical "Visitors from Chicago," a playlet describing two married couples–Mort and Beth Hollender and Stu and Gert Franklyn–whose friendship has become severely strained while they vacation together. Following a series of mishaps, Mort and Stu lose their tempers, exchange insults, and eventually resort to physical attacks—transforming the suite at the Beverly Hills Hotel into a war zone. Although *California Suite* as a whole lacks the coherence of *Plaza Suite*, the play does emphasize a theme found in many of Simon's comedies: the need for reconciliation. The couples in the first three sketches all move toward some kind of rapprochement or accommodation with each other, and in "Visitors from Chicago" the combatants, in their own bizarre way, also seek to declare a truce: "We came here friends and we're leaving friends," insists Mort, with a stranglehold on Stu. "Now, tell me we're friends, you bastard!"

Simon's next offering, *Chapter Two* (1977), is an autobiographical work expressing Simon's sorrow over the death of his wife, Joan, and his mixture of joy and guilt about his marriage a few months later to Marsha Mason. The play describes a recently widowed writer, George Schneider, who falls in love with and marries a divorced actress named Jennie Malone, but who suffers from emotional problems as he tries to adjust to this second marriage. Although Simon offers a realistic portrait of bereavement, his play is still a romantic comedy, including a great deal of humorous repartee as well as an optimistic ending. *Chapter Two* is a notable example of the playwright's talent for blending the amusing with the poignant.

In act 1 Simon follows the classical boy-meets-girl plot of romantic comedy, concentrating on George's whirlwind courtship of Jennie and building up to the couple's wedding. In act 2 Simon shifts to his familiar "problem marriage" framework, focusing on George's emotional turmoil and his continued attachment to his deceased wife. After a disappointing honeymoon and a major confrontation with Jennie, George separates from his bride. But he returns to her at the end of the play, deciding that it is time to begin "chapter two" of his life.

Critics were divided in their response to Simon's play. Some objected to the subplot involving an attempt at adultery between George's brother, Leo, and Jennie's friend Faye Medwick. Others believed that Simon's serious scenes in act 2 were inferior to the comedy of act 1 and that the play itself was overly long. Several reviewers, however, expressed the opinion that Simon had written a touching drama about love and loss and that *Chapter Two* was one of his best works to date.

Simon's next comedy, *I Ought to Be in Pictures* (1980), is a rather simplistic study of a father-daughter relationship. Libby Tucker, a nineteen-year-old girl from New York, has traveled to West Hollywood to visit her father, screenwriter Herb Tucker, who deserted his family sixteen years earlier. Libby claims that she has come to California to become a Hollywood actress, but her real reason is to establish a relationship with her father—something that she manages to accomplish during her two-week stay with Herb. Although entertaining at times, the play is weakened by its sentimentality and by its overidealization of Libby, who seems to provide the answer to all of her father's problems, including his writer's block. The theme of abandonment, which is important in Simon's dramatic canon, is treated more skillfully in other works.

Simon's desire to experiment with his craft is evident in *Fools* (1981), a humorous, fairy-tale-like romance modeled after Joseph Stein's *Fiddler on the Roof* (1964) and the stories of Sholom Aleichem. Set in 1890 in a fictional Ukrainian village, the play depicts the efforts of schoolteacher Leon Tolchinsky to remove a curse that has rendered all of the villagers stupid, and to marry Sophia Zubritsky, the dim-witted beauty with whom he has fallen in love. Filled with jokes about human stupidity, the play offers little insight beyond the simple notion that love conquers all. As Ellen Schiff has noted, Simon also "bleaches out" his Yiddish sources and "de-ethnicizes the folk material, ignoring the patent implication that these simple characters are Jews." Probably better suited to Off Broadway, *Fools* was neither a popular nor a critical success, closing on Broadway after forty performances.

With *Brighton Beach Memoirs* (1983) Simon resumed his autobiographical approach to playwriting, warmly recalling his boyhood in New York City during the Depression. The first of Simon's dramas to use explicitly Jewish characters, this comedy is a memory play in the manner of Tennessee Williams's *The Glass Menagerie* (1944). Played by Matthew Broderick in the Broadway premiere, the adolescent Eugene Jerome, who hopes to become a writer someday, speaks directly to the audience, revealing his family's assorted problems: financial insecurity resulting from his father's and brother's job losses; health issues such as father Jack's heart attack, Aunt Blanche's asthma, and her daughter Laurie's heart condition; and sibling rivalry between Eugene and his brother, Stanley, as well as between Eugene's mother, Kate, and her sister, Blanche. But the protagonist presents these problems from a comic perspective, and by the end of the play it is clear that the Jerome family will survive. According to Simon, it is the idealization of the family that has made *Brighton Beach Memoirs* one of his most widely performed plays; he told Bryer in 1991, "It's like looking back on your family album and seeing it better than it was."

The play also focuses on Eugene's coming of age—a theme that is explored further in the final two plays of the Brighton Beach trilogy, *Biloxi Blues* (1985) and *Broadway Bound* (1986). In *Brighton Beach Memoirs*

Kate Burton, Paxton Whitehead, Jeffrey Jones, and Brooks Ashmanskas in the 1995 New York production of London Suite (photograph by Carol Rosegg)

Eugene's rite of passage includes an increased awareness of his sexuality (illustrated primarily by his erotic feelings toward his pretty cousin Nora), as well as a maturing sense of himself as a writer. Keenly observant, Eugene makes notes in his journal (or "secret memoirs") about the idiosyncracies of his family, and he also uses writing as a way of expressing his innermost thoughts. One of the most appealing aspects of the play is Eugene's confidential bond with audience members as he guides them through the 1937 world of Brighton Beach.

Inspired by Simon's experience in the military, Biloxi Blues follows Eugene, again played by Broderick, into army basic training during World War II, accentuating his coming of age. Six years older in 1943, Eugene has never been away from home before and must adjust to the rigors of army life. He is appalled by his fanatical drill sergeant, Merwin J. Toomey, who appears to go out of his way to torment the troops, and he is distressed by the anti-Semitism and homophobia evinced by his fellow recruits. When one of the soldiers, Arnold Epstein, becomes the victim of bigoted attacks, Eugene regrets not taking a stronger stand in defense of a friend and "a fellow Jew."

Eugene also matures through experiences outside the army barracks–having his initial sexual experience (with a prostitute named Rowena) and falling in love for the first time (with an innocent Catholic girl named Daisy Hannigan). Moreover, at the end of the play Eugene is no longer simply "scribbling" in his journal–he has been employed as a writer for the G.I. newspaper Stars and Stripes. He appears to have accomplished all three of the goals that he originally set for himself when he entered the military: "Become a writer, not get killed, and lose my virginity."

On its own, Biloxi Blues is a lesser play than the other two works in the Brighton Beach trilogy, but it should not be dismissed as a formulaic barracks-room comedy. Eugene is still a humorous, engaging character, and the problems that he encounters in the army are both real and compelling. Recognizing the solid material of the play, director Mike Nichols in 1988 turned Biloxi Blues into the most successful movie version of any of the Brighton Beach dramas.

Broadway Bound, the last play in the trilogy, is the most serious–and the most skillfully crafted–of the three comedies. Simon focuses on two main themes: the maturation of Eugene (evidenced by the launching of his comedy-writing career), and the breakup of the thirty-three-year marriage between Eugene's parents, Kate and Jack Jerome. Whereas the first theme is treated comedically (Simon even includes an early comedy sketch for radio that Eugene and his brother, Stanley, have written), the second is handled in a realistic, poignant manner. As Allan Wallach observed in *New York Newsday* (5 December 1986), "it is as though a familiar Simon comedy were intertwined with an Arthur Miller play."

Critics were particularly impressed in *Broadway Bound* by Simon's tribute to his mother. During a key scene in act 2, Kate Jerome (modeled after Mamie Simon) recalls a special night during her youth when she danced at the Primrose Ballroom with movie star George Raft. As Eugene listens to the story and then dances with Kate himself, he realizes how graceful and how vibrantly alive his mother once was. The play does not end happily for Kate, who has been abandoned by her husband and whose sons are also leaving the house for good. But Eugene assures the audience that his mother has experienced moments of pleasure in her life and, on the whole, counts herself a lucky woman: "After all," he explains, "she did once dance with George Raft." One of the best American plays of the 1980s, *Broadway Bound* provides an amusing, tender, and highly pleasing conclusion to Simon's Brighton Beach trilogy.

After three straight "serious" comedies, Simon wanted to try writing a full-length farce, something that he had never attempted before. He recognized the demands of the form—particularly the need for nonstop action and plenty of plot twists. *Rumors* (1988) presents a convoluted story involving four couples who have gathered for dinner at the home of the deputy New York mayor, Charley Brock, and his wife, Myra, in order to celebrate the pair's tenth wedding anniversary. When the guests discover that Charley has apparently attempted suicide (shooting himself through the earlobe) and that Myra is missing, they go to absurd lengths to cover up the situation, especially when the police finally arrive. The play is held together, to some extent, by the theme of rumors that destroy both friendships and marriages. But the fast-paced, laugh-a-minute action is what dominates this farce, in which one crisis comes after another. Although *Rumors* received some unfavorable critical reviews, it was a box-office hit, enjoying a Broadway run of 531 performances.

Set in 1942, Simon's Pulitzer Prize–winning play *Lost in Yonkers* (1991) is one of his darkest comedies, focusing on a dysfunctional Jewish family. The play describes the experiences of two teenage boys—Jay and Arty—who, after the death of their mother, are forced to live with their stern, intimidating Grandma Kurnitz for ten months and to contend with their Aunt Bella (who is emotionally arrested), their Uncle Louie (who is a bagman for the mob), and their Aunt Gert (who suffers from a speech impediment). A victim of anti-Semitism in Germany, Grandma Kurnitz believes that "You don't survive in dis world vitout being like steel." She has allowed herself to become emotionally hardened, has abused her children, and has become a monster in the eyes of her grandsons. As Jay tells Arty, "When I was five, I drew a picture of her and called it 'Frankenstein's Grandma.'"

Grandma Kurnitz's coldness is contrasted with the warm, affectionate nature of Aunt Bella, who, despite having a child's mentality, serves as a sort of surrogate mother for the two boys during their extended stay. Reviewers particularly applauded a key scene in act 2, in which Bella announces her plan to marry a mentally challenged theater usher, to open a restaurant, and to have children of her own. "Let me have my babies, Momma," she begs during a poignant monologue. "Because I have to love somebody. I have to love someone who'll love me back before I die." This scene, which actually begins in a comedic manner, demonstrates Simon's ability to move his audience from laughter to tears—even within the space of a few minutes.

Both a popular and critical success, *Lost in Yonkers* represents Simon at the pinnacle of his career. Although the play is not as openly autobiographical as some of his other works, it is true to life—offering a heartrending image of what can happen when human beings (and especially children) are deprived of love. As Frank Rich observed in *The New York Times* (22 February 1991), "the wounds run so deep that one feels it just may be his most honest" play.

Eschewing the conventions of realism in *Jake's Women* (1992), Simon takes the audience inside the mind of a writer, describing—in a series of scenes that are sometimes real and sometimes imagined—the protagonist's efforts to come to terms with the most significant women in his life: his first and second wives, his sister, his daughter, and his analyst. Speaking directly to the audience, Jake (played by Alan Alda in the premiere production) reveals that he is going through a midlife crisis; that his marriage to his second wife, Maggie, is breaking up; and that he is still trying to get over the death of his first wife, Julie. Many of Jake's problems are connected with his all-consuming career as a writer. Although his work gives him an exhilarating sense of control ("You don't get to play God, you get to *be* God!" he explains), Jake is emotionally isolated from others and is an observer of life rather than a participant. As Jack

Simon's office in Los Angeles (from Simon, The Play Goes On: A Memoir, *1999)*

Kroll noted in *Newsweek* (6 April 1992), "Jake's chief problem is that he'd rather write than live."

The play received a mixed response from the critics. Some, such as Barnes, praised Simon for his experimental blend of reality and illusion, finding this drama "an intricately devised, bizarrely convincing portrait of the artist as a hall of mirrors" (*New York Post,* 25 March 1992). But other reviewers were put off by a tendency in the play toward psychobabble, by Simon's failure to endear Jake to the audience (as he had done with Eugene Jerome in the Brighton Beach trilogy), and by a happy ending that struck them as contrived. It should be noted, however, that the final tableau, in which Jake and Maggie reach for each other on the stairs "like God and Adam reaching out in the Sistine Chapel," is perfectly in keeping with Simon's expressionistic approach as well as with his overall theme: the importance of human connection.

Simon explores this same theme of connection in *Laughter on the 23rd Floor* (1993), a comedy based on the playwright's early days in television, when he teamed up with talented writers such as Mel Brooks, Carl Reiner, and Larry Gelbart to create scripts for *Your Show of Shows*. Set in 1953 against the backdrop of McCarthyism, the play depicts seven writers—including the playwright's alter ego, Lucas Brickman—who meet each day in the Writers' Room to exchange wisecracks, to brainstorm about ideas for their weekly variety show, and to deal with their temperamental star, Max Prince (modeled on Sid Caesar and played by Nathan Lane). Although the plot focuses on a threat by NBC to cancel *The Max Prince Show,* the play is really about the need for community and about the ways that laughter can bring people together.

Critics were sharply divided in their response to this comedy. Some believed that the character of the narrator, Lucas Brickman, was bland and superficial and that Simon's plot was nothing more than a string of one-liners. Other reviewers, however, hailed the play as one of Simon's funniest, arguing that since the story centers on a group of comedy writers, the jokes, gags, and wisecracks are justified. *Laughter on the 23rd Floor* may lack the depth and poignancy of *The Sunshine Boys*, but it offers an amusing retrospective on the Golden Age of television comedy, sketching a portrait of that special group of writers whom Simon called "the funniest people in the world."

In a break from custom, Simon took his next comedy, *London Suite* (1995), to Off Broadway, where the play experienced only limited success. Returning to the sketch format of *Plaza Suite* and *California Suite*, Simon presents four playlets, all set at a luxury hotel in London. "Settling Accounts" describes a confrontation between writer Brian Cronin and his business manager, Billy Fox, who has absconded with Brian's life savings. The second sketch, "Going Home," focuses on Lauren Semple's matchmaking efforts for her widowed mother, Sheryl, and on the mother's account of her disastrous date with a wealthy Scotsman. The next playlet, "Diana and Sydney," describes an encounter between the long-divorced Diana and Sydney Nichols (the witty British pair from *California Suite*), during which Sydney asks Diana for financial help in caring for his dying male lover—ultimately revealing, however, that he is actually the one who is gravely ill. Finally, the farcical "Man on the Floor" depicts an American couple, Mark and Annie Ferris, who are frantic after misplacing their Wimbledon tickets and who experience further calamity when Mark throws his back out at the hotel.

On the whole, *London Suite* is weakened by its lack of memorable characters and a unifying theme. Nor are the one-liners and basic comedic situations as humorous as they were in *Plaza Suite* and *California Suite*. Still interested in the one-act format, however, Simon gathered his favorite playlets from each of these works and re-presented them as *Hotel Suite* (2000).

Proposals (1997), set in 1953, when Simon courted and married his first wife, Joan, breaks new ground for the author in several respects: the play is situated outdoors, a rarity for a dramatist who normally focuses on urban characters and locales; and for the first time in his career Simon presents a major character who is African American—the housekeeper, Clemma Diggins, who also serves as the narrator of the play and who actually recounts its events from beyond the grave. *Proposals* describes the personal and romantic relationships of the Hines family, as they enjoy their last summer together in the Pocono Mountains in Pennsylvania. Businessman Burt Hines is in poor health after suffering several heart attacks; his daughter, Josie, who has just broken off her engagement to law student Kenny Norman, is really in love with his best friend, Ray Dolenz; and Burt's former wife, Annie Robbins, has returned to the family cabin in an effort to repair her relationship with her daughter. Several minor characters also converge on the scene: Clemma's estranged husband, Lewis Barnett; Ray's new girlfriend, Sammii; and a flamboyant young mobster from Miami named Vinnie Bavasi. Like many other comedies by Simon, *Proposals* aims at a Chekhovian blend of humor and pathos—emphasizing the importance of loving relationships in a world where life is all too short. But the message of the play tends to get lost among its many characters, whose diverse stories—engaging as they may be—prevent any single character's story from being told in depth. A hit neither with the critics nor with the public, *Proposals* closed on Broadway after only a two-month run.

During his long-standing career Simon has received many honors, including the 1965 Tony Award for best dramatic author (*The Odd Couple*), the Sam S. Shubert Award (1968), the Cue Entertainer of the Year Award (1972), a special Tony Award for his overall contribution to the theater (1975), the New York Drama Critics Circle Award and the Outer Critics Circle Award for *Brighton Beach Memoirs* (1983), the Tony Award for best play and the Outer Critics Circle Award for *Biloxi Blues* (1985), the New York State Governor's Award (1986), a Lifetime Creative Achievement Award from the American Comedy Awards (1989), and the Tony Award for best play as well as the Pulitzer Prize for *Lost in Yonkers* (1991). The Alvin Theatre on West Fifty-second Street in New York was renamed the Neil Simon Theatre in June 1983, during the run of *Brighton Beach Memoirs*. In 1995 Simon received the Kennedy Center Honors in Washington, D.C., and the following year the William Inge Theatre Festival saluted him for Distinguished Achievement in the American Theater. In September 1999 he married actress Elaine Joyce.

Simon has shown no sign of slowing down. With a cast that included Henry Winkler and John Ritter, his comedy *The Dinner Party* (2000) enjoyed a healthy run on Broadway, and another play, *45 Seconds from Broadway*, opened in the fall of 2001. Set in an elegant Parisian restaurant, *The Dinner Party* offers a tragicomic look at three divorced couples who are brought together by the lawyer who handled their divorces. *45 Seconds from Broadway*, which features the proprietors of a popular theater hangout, is a lighthearted salute to the New York of Simon's heyday. As Simon explains in *The Play Goes On: A Memoir* (1999), "I still feel an intense desire to put pen to paper, to put words to use, to put ideas into stories and to wed new stories into even newer forms."

Interviews:

Stefan Kanfer, "Neil Simon: The Unshine Boy," *Time* (15 January 1973): 58–59;

Otis L. Guernsey Jr., "Everything You've Always Wanted to Know About . . . Neil Simon . . . But Never Had a Chance to Ask," in *Playwrights, Lyri-*

cists, *Composers On Theater,* edited by Guernsey (New York: Dodd, Mead, 1974), pp. 227–242;

Clive Hirschhorn, "Make 'em Laugh," *Plays and Players,* 24 (September 1977): 12–15;

Lawrence Linderman, "*Playboy* Interview: Neil Simon," *Playboy,* 26 (February 1979): 57–58, 60, 62, 66, 68, 73–76, 78;

Samuel G. Freedman and Michaela Williams, eds., "A Conversation between Neil Simon and David Rabe: The Craft of the Playwright," *New York Times Magazine* (26 May 1985): 37–38, 52, 56–57, 60–62;

Jackson R. Bryer, "An Interview with Neil Simon," *Studies in American Drama: 1945–Present,* 6 (1991): 153–176;

"Neil Simon," in *The Playwright's Art: Conversations with Contemporary American Dramatists,* edited by Bryer (New Brunswick: Rutgers University Press, 1995), pp. 221–240.

Bibliographies:

Kimball King, *Ten Modern American Playwrights: An Annotated Bibliography* (New York: Garland, 1982), pp. 215–233;

Laura Morrow, "Neil Simon," in *American Playwrights Since 1945: A Guide to Scholarship, Criticism, and Performance,* edited by Philip C. Kolin (Westport, Conn.: Greenwood Press, 1989), pp. 420–436.

References:

Peter L. Hays, "Neil Simon and the Funny Jewish Blues," in *Neil Simon: A Casebook,* edited by Gary Konas (New York: Garland, 1997), pp. 59–68;

Robert K. Johnson, *Neil Simon* (Boston: Twayne, 1983);

Susan Koprince, *Understanding Neil Simon* (Columbia: University of South Carolina Press, 2002);

Edythe M. McGovern, *Neil Simon: A Critical Study,* second edition (New York: Ungar, 1979);

Richard Meryman, "When the Funniest Writer in America Tried to Be Serious," *Life* (7 May 1971): 60B–60D, 64, 66–69, 71, 73, 75, 77, 79–80, 83;

David Richards, "The Last of the Red-Hot Playwrights," *New York Times Magazine* (17 February 1991): 30–32, 36, 57, 64;

Ellen Schiff, "Funny, He *Does* Look Jewish," in *Neil Simon: A Casebook,* edited by Konas (New York: Garland, 1997), pp. 47–58;

Daniel Walden, "Neil Simon's Jewish-Style Comedies," in *From Hester Street to Hollywood: The Jewish-American Stage and Screen,* edited by Sarah Blacher Cohen (Bloomington: Indiana University Press, 1983), pp. 152–166;

Michael Woolf, "Neil Simon," in *American Drama,* edited by Clive Bloom (New York: St. Martin's Press, 1995), pp. 117–130;

Paul D. Zimmerman, "Neil Simon: Up From Success," *Newsweek* (2 February 1970): 52–56.

Papers:

The Neil Simon Papers, including play drafts, final scripts, screenplays, and page proofs, are part of the Harvard Theatre Collection, Nathan Marsh Pusey Library, Harvard University.

Samuel Spewack

(16 September 1899 – 14 October 1971)

and

Bella Cohen Spewack

(25 March 1899 – 27 April 1990)

Donald E. Whittaker
Louisiana State University

PLAY PRODUCTIONS (BY SAMUEL SPEWACK): *Two Blind Mice,* New York, Cort Theatre, 2 March 1949;

The Golden State, New York, Fulton Theatre, 25 November 1950;

Under The Sycamore Tree, London, Aldwych Theatre, 23 April 1952; New York, Cricket Theatre, 7 March 1960;

Once There Was A Russian, New York, Music Box Theatre, 18 February 1961;

Pleasures and Palaces, book by Samuel Spewack, music and lyrics by Frank Loesser, Detroit, Fisher Theater, 11 March 1965.

PLAY PRODUCTIONS (BY SAMUEL SPEWACK AND BELLA COHEN SPEWACK): *The Solitaire Man,* Boston, 1926;

The War Song, by Samuel Spewack, Bella Cohen Spewack, and George Jessel, New York, National Theatre, 24 September 1928;

Poppa, New York, Biltmore Theatre, 24 December 1928; transferred to Hudson Theatre;

Clear All Wires! New York, Times Square Theatre, 14 September 1932;

Spring Song, New York, Morosco Theatre, 1 October 1934;

Boy Meets Girl, New York, Cort Theatre, 27 November 1935;

Leave It To Me! book by Samuel Spewack and Bella Cohen Spewack, music and lyrics by Cole Porter, New York, Imperial Theatre, 9 November 1938;

Miss Swan Expects, New York, Cort Theatre, 20 February 1939;

Woman Bites Dog, New York, Belasco Theatre, 17 April 1946;

Kiss Me, Kate, book by Samuel Spewack and Bella Cohen Spewack, music and lyrics by Porter, New York, New Century Theatre, 30 December 1948;

My 3 Angels, based on Albert Husson's *La Cuisine des Anges,* New York, Morosco Theatre, 11 March 1953;

Festival, New York, Longacre Theatre, 18 January 1955.

BOOKS (BY SAMUEL SPEWACK): *Red Russia Revealed: The Truth About the Soviet Government and Its Methods as Told by Samuel Spewack* (New York: World, 1923);

Mon Paul: The Private Life of a Privateer, as A. A. Abbott (New York: Macaulay, 1928);

The Skyscraper Murder (New York: Macaulay, 1928);

Murder in the Gilded Cage (New York: Simon & Schuster, 1929);

The Busy, Busy People (Boston: Houghton Mifflin, 1948);

Two Blind Mice (New York: Dramatists Play Service, 1949);

Under the Sycamore Tree (London: S. French, 1953; New York: Dramatists Play Service, 1960);

The Prince and Mr. Jones (New York: Dramatists Play Service, 1961).

BOOK (BY BELLA COHEN SPEWACK): *Streets: A Memoir of the Lower East Side,* introduction by Ruth Limmer, afterword by Lois Raeder Elias (New York: Feminist Press, 1995).

BOOKS (BY SAMUEL SPEWACK AND BELLA COHEN SPEWACK): *Poppa* (New York & London: S. French, 1929);

Clear All Wires! (New York, Los Angeles & London: S. French, 1932);

Bella Cohen Spewack and Samuel Spewack in 1924 (Sam and Bella Spewack Archive, Rare Book and Manuscript Library, Columbia University)

The Solitaire Man (New York, Los Angeles & London: S. French, 1934);

Boy Meets Girl; Spring Song (New York: Random House, 1936);

Trousers to Match (New York: Dramatists Play Service, 1941);

Woman Bites Dog (New York: Dramatists Play Service, 1947);

The Golden State (New York: Dramatists Play Service, 1951);

Kiss Me, Kate, book by Samuel Spewack and Bella Cohen Spewack, lyrics by Cole Porter (New York: Knopf, 1953);

My 3 Angels (New York: Random House, 1953; London: S. French, 1956);

Festival (New York: Dramatists Play Service, 1955).

PRODUCED SCRIPTS (BY SAMUEL SPEWACK): *Caught,* by Agnes Brand and Keene Thompson, additional dialogue by Samuel Spewack, motion picture, Paramount Pictures, 1931;

The Secret Witness, based on Spewack's novel *Murder in the Gilded Cage,* motion picture, Columbia Pictures, 1931;

The World at War, motion picture, U.S. Government, 1942.

PRODUCED SCRIPTS (BY SAMUEL SPEWACK AND BELLA COHEN SPEWACK): *Should Ladies Behave?* based on Paul Osborn's *The Vinegar Tree,* motion picture, M-G-M, 1933;

Clear All Wires! motion picture, M-G-M, 1933;

The Nuisance, based on Chandler Sprague and Howard Emmett Rogers's story, motion picture, M-G-M, 1933; remade as *The Chaser,* by Samuel Spewack, Bella Cohen Spewack, Everett Freeman, and Harry Ruskin, motion picture, M-G-M, 1938;

The Cat and the Fiddle, based on Jerome Kern and Otto Harbach's play, motion picture, M-G-M, 1934;

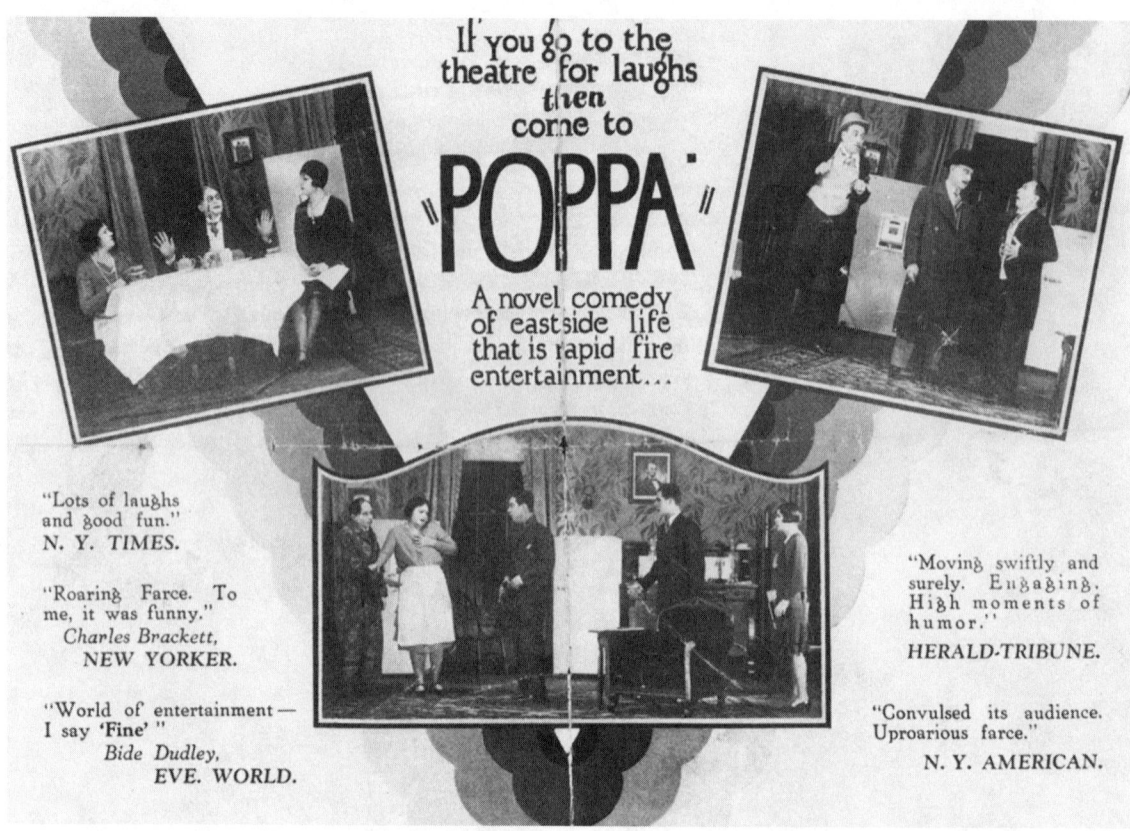

Publicity flier for the New York production of the Spewacks' 1928 play, after the production transferred from the Biltmore Theatre to the Hudson Theatre (Sam and Bella Spewack Archive, Rare Book and Manuscript Library, Columbia University)

The Gay Bride, based on Charles Francis Coe's story "Repeal," motion picture, M-G-M, 1934;

Rendezvous, by Samuel Spewack, Bella Cohen Spewack, P. J. Wolfson, and George Oppenheimer, based on Herbert O. Yardley's *American Black Chamber,* motion picture, M-G-M, 1935;

Vogues of 1938, motion picture, United Artists, 1937;

Boy Meets Girl, motion picture, Warner Bros., 1938;

Three Loves Has Nancy, by Samuel Spewack, Bella Cohen Spewack, Oppenheimer, and David Hertz, based on Lee Loeb and Mort Braus's story, motion picture, M-G-M, 1938;

My Favorite Wife, based on Leo McCarey's story, motion picture, RKO, 1940;

Week-End at the Waldorf, by Samuel Spewack, Bella Cohen Spewack, and Guy Bolton, based on Vicki Baum's *Grand Hotel,* motion picture, M-G-M, 1945;

Kiss Me, Kate, television, NBC, 20 November 1958;

My Three Angels, television, NBC, 8 December 1959;

The Enchanted Nutcracker, based on Pyotr Ilich Tchaikovsky's *The Nutcracker,* television, 23 December 1961.

Samuel and Bella Spewack were historians, reporters, novelists, screenwriters, social philanthropists, and dramatists. Their works crossed genres, altered literary expectations, and on occasion mapped out new areas in American literature by combining elements of their disparate interests into a single work. They were never afraid to branch out in new directions, nor were critical responses as important to them as the conviction of the worth of an idea. This characteristic held true for both, even before they married and began collaborating. Particularly in the field of drama, the Spewacks pushed accepted limits by including protofeminist themes and mixing styles within the same piece, as well as including simultaneously realistic and cynical portraits of many of their characters.

Bella Cohen was born on 25 March 1899 in the Transylvania region of what is now Romania to Adolph Loebel and Fanny Cohen Loebel. Two weeks after Bella's birth, her father abandoned the family, leaving her teenage mother to raise Bella alone; Bella kept her mother's maiden name. The two immigrated to America when the child was three years old, living in poverty on the Lower East Side of New York until Bella reached adulthood. Fanny Cohen remarried, although Bella never accepted her stepfather, Noonan Lang. The couple had two sons before Lang also left: Herschey Lang died at five years of age, but Daniel Lang, like his half sister, became a prizewinning writer, maintaining a forty-year career on the staff of *The New Yorker*.

Bella Cohen spent the majority of her early years "performing," often to keep neighborhood bullies from teasing her. This neighborhood also taught her strength and survival. She began writing early, publishing her first newspaper article in her high-school paper. After graduation she began work as a professional reporter, moving through smaller papers to *The Call*, a socialist paper, and eventually becoming the literary editor of the *New York Evening Mail*.

Samuel Spewack was born on 16 September 1899, in Bachmut in the Russian Ukraine, to Noel Spewack and Sema Zelavetski Spewack; his family moved to America in 1903. He attended Columbia University, leaving before graduation to take the job of police reporter on the *New York World* by the age of eighteen. He and Bella Cohen met while he was reporting for the *Evening World* and she for the *New York Call*. They were married in 1922, shortly after Spewack, who went by "Sam" and only used "Samuel" for his byline, covered the Geneva Conference earlier that year. The couple divided the next four years between America and Europe, where they worked as foreign correspondents. Samuel Spewack wired reports from Russia and Germany during this time, and these reports eventually culminated in his book *Red Russia Revealed: The Truth About the Soviet Government and Its Methods as Told by Samuel Spewack* (1923). In 1922 Bella Spewack recounted her early years in the autobiographical *Streets: A Memoir of the Lower East Side*; the work was published posthumously in 1995. In 1923 she wrote a series of articles on slum housing for the *Evening World*, which eventually resulted in the passage of rent laws in New York State. In 1926 she scooped the journalistic world with her story on Anna Anderson, who professed to be Anastasia Romanov, the last remaining member of the Romanov family. The article, published in *The New York Times*, made headlines around the world.

Their shared background as journalists contributed greatly to the couple's success as playwrights, giving them settings, characters, and plots. Their ability to report what they saw around them also helped them create convincing dramatic environments. It was Bella Spewack's idea that she and Samuel Spewack collaborate as playwrights, although she always maintained that he misunderstood her suggestion and proposed marriage to her instead. Their first play, *The Solitaire Man* (1926), closed in Boston tryouts. The plot concerned a gang of jewel thieves on a flight from London to Paris, with the discovery of double-dealing among the group as the flight continued. Despite its failure onstage, it was made into a movie in 1933, with a screenplay by James K. McGuinness.

Their first play to make it into New York was *The War Song* (1928), written in collaboration with George Jessel; it lasted eighty performances. The work concerns a young American songwriter drafted into World War I. An extremely unlucky young man, he loses his girlfriend and learns that his unmarried sister is pregnant. While following her seducer behind German lines, he is taken prisoner the same day he learns of his mother's death. The play was a comment on the situation of an individual caught up in the machinery of war and was an attempt to combine comedy and pathos, with the work primarily for laughs until the final moments. The review for *The New York Times* called it "an exceedingly interesting entertainment and an effective theatrical invention."

That same year, the Spewacks also premiered *Poppa*, their first show written with no outside collaboration to play on Broadway. The piece was the first of many to utilize their inside knowledge of politics. The title character, Poppa Schwitzsky, begins mixing in politics to the neglect of his insurance business. After the naive Poppa's election to alderman, another politician frames Poppa with charges of bribery in order to escape his own arrest. Poppa is only cleared of the charges at the last moment when his son uses a hidden dictaphone machine to tape the real culprit's confession. The play, the couple's first foray into the world of politics, earned Brooks Atkinson's comment that it was "neither fish nor fowl nor good red herring. It looks lively without being genuinely hilarious in its heart."

Clear All Wires! (1932) was the first play the couple wrote that drew on their newspaper experience, and it ran for ninety-four performances. Buckley Thomas, chief of the foreign news service for the *Chicago Press*, is relieved of his position when he becomes interested in the same woman his boss likes—a singer named Dolly Winslow. Buckley is reassigned to Moscow but foils the plot by taking Dolly with him, and the couple spends two weeks dodging telegrams intended to fire him. To regain his employer's confidence, he plots a fraudulent assassination attempt, ostensibly directed toward a Romanov; however, Buckley takes the bullet and is declared a hero until his eventual exposure. Revealed as a charlatan, he accepts a fresh newspaper position in China for William Randolph Hearst. This play is the first of the Spewacks' works in which a strong streak of metatheatricality appears. Buckley is one of their "interior directors," a character who will arrange the world around him in order to make things come out correctly.

Lobby poster for the Spewacks' 1933 movie adaptation of their 1932 play (Sam and Bella Spewack Archive, Rare Book and Manuscript Library, Columbia University)

M-G-M took particular notice of *Clear All Wires!* and offered the couple Hollywood writing contracts. The Spewacks spent the next six years writing screenplays in Hollywood, and they returned to writing for movies intermittently through the 1960s. Their screenplays included *The Nuisance* (1933), about an ambulance-chasing attorney, as well as its remake, *The Chaser* (1938). They also wrote *Rendezvous* (1935), which presented a realistic look at World War I code breakers couched within a witty, urbane comedy. The couple also adapted existing stage works for the screen, including *The Cat and the Fiddle* (1934) and their own *Clear All Wires!*, which reached movie screens in 1933. Their movies starred such luminaries as Ramon Novarro and Jeanette MacDonald (*The Cat and the Fiddle*), William Powell and Rosalind Russell (*Rendezvous*), and Carole Lombard (*The Gay Bride*, 1934). Their Hollywood experiences later served as fodder for one of their greatest stage hits, *Boy Meets Girl* (1935).

The couple turned again to the stage in 1934 with *Spring Song,* a play that represents a return to Bella's childhood experiences in East Side tenements. Florrie, the heroine, is lonely because her sweetheart, a traveling salesman, is often absent. She turns for company to her sister's fiancé, who is also restless and dissatisfied; Florrie discovers she is pregnant at the same time she realizes that she does not love him. Her mother insists on a marriage to satisfy propriety, but Florrie dies in childbirth. Atkinson stated that the Spewacks wrote of life on New York's East Side "out of an affectionate understanding, which is one of the qualities Broadway does not have in abundance," but termed the resulting play "pedestrian."

During the mid 1930s Bella Spewack, determined that the couple's plays would no longer be ignored by agents as not commercial enough, tackled New York theatrical offices herself. The success of their next play assured their fame. *Boy Meets Girl,* one of several theatrical Hollywood satires, is the longest running of any of them, amassing 669 performances. The story concerns Robert Law and J. Carlyle Benson, two screenwriters with little to no respect for the "serious" business they are in. They befriend a pregnant, unmarried commissary waitress, plotting to make her baby a colossal child star by pairing him with a dim-witted cowboy actor. As the cowboy finds himself upstaged by his new costar, he plots to marry the waitress and become the child's legal guardian, thereby gaining access to the infant's salary. Law and Benson foil this scheme by getting the young woman married to the right man (who is actually in love with her), managing to secure lifetime contracts for themselves in the process.

The characters of Law and Benson were popularly assumed to be modeled on Ben Hecht and Charles MacArthur. Although everyone connected with *Boy Meets Girl*—not to mention Hecht and MacArthur themselves—denied this rumor, it was never completely laid to rest. Obviously, the play was based heavily on the Spewacks' Hollywood experiences, including their aversion to the studio executives' idea of a sure-fire storyline—already a tired cliché—which gives the play its name: "Boy meets girl. Boy loses girl. Boy gets girl." George Abbott directed the play, also acting as producer for the first time in his career. Abbott said in the introduction to the published play (1936) that *Boy Meets Girl* was the best play ever written about Hollywood, adding that the Spewacks' wit and knowledge of the Hollywood milieu were what made the show so good.

Both audiences and critics loved the play, and it won the Roi Cooper Megrue Prize. After its Broadway run, *Boy Meets Girl* was made into a movie in 1938—despite its pointed ridicule of Hollywood—with the Spewacks adapting the play themselves. The movie

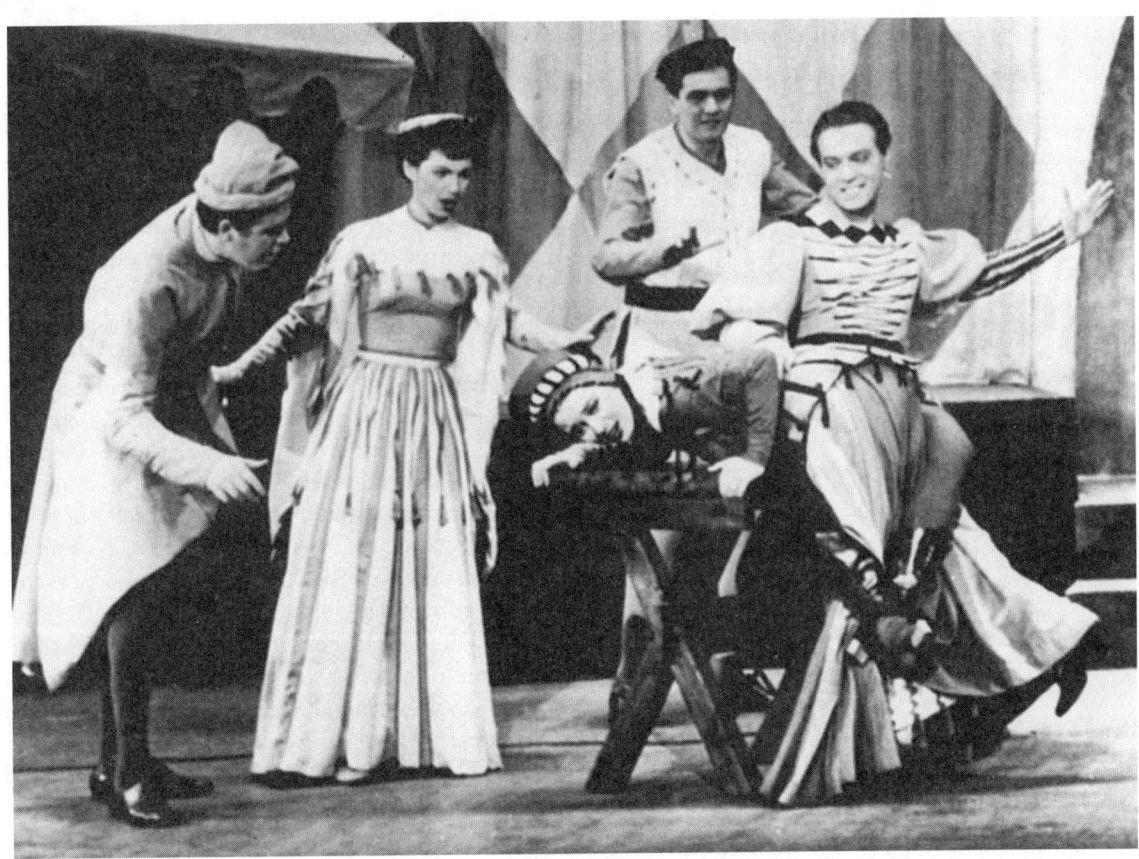

Scene from the 1948 New Century Theatre production of Kiss Me, Kate, *the Spewacks and Cole Porter's musical version of William Shakespeare's* The Taming of the Shrew *(Sam and Bella Spewack Archive, Rare Book and Manuscript Library, Columbia University)*

starred James Cagney and Pat O'Brien as the screenwriters, with future U.S. president Ronald Reagan in a minor role.

In 1938 Bella Spewack aided in the founding of the New York Girls' Scholarship Fund. That same year, the couple completed their first collaboration with Cole Porter, *Leave It To Me!* The show combined their knowledge of Soviet Russia with their journalistic experiences. *Leave It To Me!* also marked the beginning of Mary Martin's stardom as she performed a mild striptease to the song "My Heart Belongs to Daddy" in front of a male chorus, which included Gene Kelly. Samuel Spewack directed the play.

Leave it to Me! is often referred to as an adaptation of *Clear All Wires!* but simply shares common plot devices rather than the actual story. A reluctant Alonso P. Goodhue is made ambassador to the Soviet Republic through his wife's machinations. Alonso would rather stay in Kansas and remain horseshoe champion, so he teams up with a reporter to find a way to discredit himself. In pursuit of this goal, he kicks a Japanese ambassador, but the American government is pleased instead. He attempts to assassinate a Russian diplomat, but misses and instead hits a Trotskyite, so he becomes a national hero. Finally, he gives up and embraces his fate, deciding to do his job extremely well by doing at least one good deed a day. This course of action gets him in hot water with everyone, and he is recalled to Kansas. The show ran for 291 performances.

In *Miss Swan Expects* (1939) the title character is a pregnant proofreader. She borrows heavily against her husband's expected income when he is commissioned to write the biography of an important industrialist. When this industrialist decides against publishing the book, Miss Swan sneaks a woman into his home to persuade him to rethink his position (or to blackmail him if said persuasion does not work). She finally succeeds in reestablishing at least the expectation of a happy ending as the industrialist reconsiders. The show did not fare well, lasting only eight performances. A revised acting edition was published in 1941 as *Trousers to Match*.

During the next several years the couple was involved in a great deal of work concerning World War II. Samuel Spewack's next project began with an invitation from the Office of War Information, an organization established by presidential order to increase public

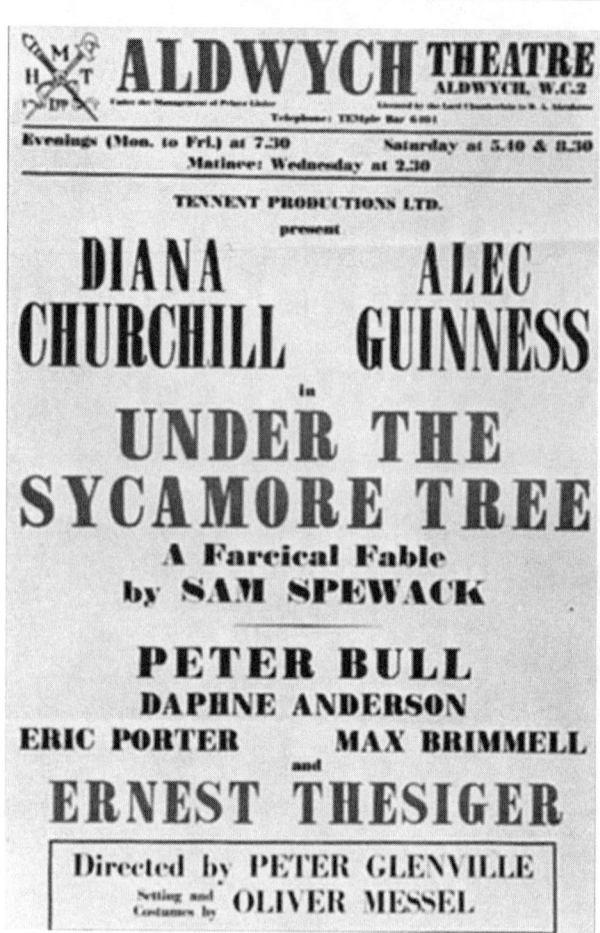

Poster for the 1952 London production of Samuel Spewack's social satire set in an ant colony (Sam and Bella Spewack Archive, Rare Book and Manuscript Library, Columbia University)

understanding of the war, both at home and abroad. Also, the government was asking that wartime motion pictures be intended to lift the spirits of Americans. As part of this effort, the Army Signal Corps commissioned Frank Capra to make a seven-part series of training movies about the origins and first years of the war. Samuel Spewack's contribution, *The World at War* (1942), was the only movie in the series that was released to public theaters and was extremely successful. In 1943 Samuel Spewack attended the Moscow Conference as press attaché for the United States embassy in Moscow. In 1946 Bella Spewack broadcast radio reports on her journey through Eastern Europe as a representative of the United Nations Relief and Rehabilitation Agency.

The Spewacks' first postwar play, *Woman Bites Dog* (1946), returned to the world of journalism that the couple knew so well. It ran only five performances but was always the couple's favorite show. The comedy concerns a family of newspaper publishers: the head of the family, the "Commander," spends his days dictating what his reporters will say (even when they tell him differently) and running their private lives. He is so worried about Communist infiltration of America that an enterprising young reporter named Hopkins tells him exactly what he wants to hear, hoping that the Commander will hang himself, given enough rope. Hopkins's story is that, having come back from defending his country in World War II, he has been appalled to discover that his entire hometown of Danville has become Socialist. The Commander swallows the story completely, with no regard for its plausibility. When Danville is outraged at the story, the Commander declares that the story was the result of a mechanical printing error—that the word "if" was left out of the sentence declaring the town to be Socialist. This public declaration may save the paper, but it also prevents him from prosecuting Hopkins.

The couple believed that they were offering a solution to the absence of restrictions imposed on newspapers. Some critics disliked the Spewacks' treatment of the subject within the outlines of a comedy, and at least one reviewer took their criticism of the media at home as a defense of Soviet Russia, because of the comic handling of the idea that publishers in both America and Russia "believe readers should know only what the owners of the papers decide is good for them." Samuel Spewack published a rather lengthy introduction to the 1947 printed edition of the play defending his and his wife's work, calling *Woman Bites Dog* an experiment "in the use of satiric farce as a means of exposing a social evil—in this case, irresponsible journalism."

Perhaps the Spewacks' best-known dramatic achievement is the creation of *Kiss Me, Kate* (1948). According to Porter biographer George Eells, when fledgling producers Lemuel Ayers and Arnold Saint Subber approached Bella Spewack about the show, her initial reaction was, "What did I think of the idea of *The Taming of the Shrew* as a musical? I said, 'It's a lousy play. I read it in high school. One of the worst Shakespeare wrote.'" After Saint Subber pleaded with her, she thought about the project for six weeks, deciding on the now-famous concept of a theatrical company whose private lives mirror the roles they portray in the William Shakespeare play, and she demanded that Porter write the score. By this time, Porter was considered to be washed up, his previous five shows having flopped. But Bella Spewack was adamant, saying that she could not (or would not) do the show without Porter.

Her next challenge was convincing Porter to join the production team. He thought the idea was far too esoteric and highbrow and that his own style was the farthest possible thing from Shakespeare. Bella

Spewack, having decided on Porter, nagged him for months, eventually convincing him that Shakespeare's work was really just "a Yiddish play at heart," as Porter biographer Charles Schwartz recounts. The basic concept of a younger sister being unable to marry until her older sister had done so was "a Jewish custom that was at the heart of many Yiddish shows that had played on Second Avenue." Porter thus went on to produce his greatest score, the one most closely resembling the type of integrated score popularized by Richard Rodgers and Oscar Hammerstein, and the Spewacks won the first Antoinette Perry (Tony) Award given for best book of a musical. *Kiss Me, Kate* was only the third musical ever to run more than 1,000 performances, lasting for 1,077. The Spewacks did not write the 1953 movie version themselves, but they subsequently adapted the work for both American and British television.

Two Blind Mice (1949) lasted 157 performances and was considered important enough to be included in *Burns Mantle Best Plays of 1948–1949*. The play concerns Mrs. Letitia Turnbull, who is still running her deceased husband's government office–Seeds and Standards–despite the government's having closed it. Since Letitia never received official notification, and since the office was her late husband's lifework, Letitia refuses to close it down. In order to make ends meet, she rents out the other rooms of the building to various people, including a dance teacher and an expectant mother. Into this mix are thrown Letitia's niece Karen Norwood, and in the best screwball-comedy tradition, Karen's former husband, Tommy Thurston, a newspaper reporter. Thurston is a wisecracking male in the tradition of Law and Benson from *Boy Meets Girl*. While Letitia and her friend Crystal receive notice that the U.S. government will be giving four offices in the building to another department, Thurston manages to win Karen away from her fiancé while simultaneously finding governmental positions for Letitia and Crystal as herb and plant experts.

Karen is introduced with stage directions indicating that "stage conventions demand that she be attractive. She is also intelligent." The word "intelligent" shows up frequently in reference to the Spewacks' heroines; the pair usually created female characters who were strong and self-sufficient, fighting resolutely against their lot in life.

My 3 Angels (1953) was based on a French play by Albert Husson, *La Cuisine des Anges* (1952). Husson's first play, it won the 1952 Tristan Bernard Prize in France. The Spewack adaptation ran for almost a year–344 performances–although *Variety* indicated that the English adaptation still lost money. The play takes place on Christmas Eve 1910 and the following morning, in a small general store in the penal colony of Cay-

The Spewacks, circa 1971 (photograph by Cookie Snyder)

enne, French Guiana. The store belongs to Felix Ducotel, a genial Frenchman who was cheated out of his Parisian department store many years before. Felix is so easygoing that he rarely manages to collect his customers' money, nor will he do anything about the endless petty thefts from the store. Three convicts from the nearby prison are repairing the Ducotels' roof: Joseph, a former forger; Jules, who killed his faithless wife; and Alfred, who murdered for money. The three take a liking to the Ducotels and aid the family in their various enterprises.

Daughter Marie Louise is informed that Paul, her fiancé, is to marry someone else; Alfred takes it upon himself to keep her from committing suicide at the news. Joseph is a smooth-talking salesman who helps in the selling of several items. Jules is the head of the trio. When Henri Trochard, who swindled Felix out of his Paris store, comes to visit, the three put a poisonous snake in his bedroom, neatly dispatching most of the family's problems. Henri had been keeping Paul, his nephew, tightly under his thumb; when Henri's death does not have the desired effect of renewing Paul's resolve to marry Marie Louise, the three convicts allow the snake to continue its work, ultimately resulting in Paul's death as well. In each case, the three concoct elaborate deathbed confessions effecting forgiveness from the wronged Ducotels. As the play ends, Marie Louise meets a young naval officer who seems genuinely interested in her, and the three men reascend their ladder to the roof. The 1955 Humphrey Bogart movie *We're No Angels* (only loosely related to the 1989 movie of the same title) was based again on the original French play. The Spewacks adapted their own version for American television in 1959.

The Golden State (1950) was written solely by Samuel Spewack but was produced by his wife; it ran only for twenty-five performances. The plot concerns Mrs. Moreno, a boardinghouse landlady of reduced circumstances, who believes that she is the rightful heir to current-day Beverly Hills through a Spanish ancestor. One of her tenants is a desert prospector, and when some of his ore is accidentally lost in Mrs. Moreno's backyard, everyone in the house catches gold fever.

Under The Sycamore Tree (1952) was an attempt at strong social satire and Samuel Spewack's most experimental play. It premiered in London, running for 189 performances and featuring Alec Guinness as the Ant Scientist, but in America it lasted slightly more than a month. The play is set in the queen's throne room of an ant colony and consists of various episodes in which the ants tried to solve their problems both with other ant colonies and with human beings.

In 1955 *Festival* signaled the Spewacks' attempt to return to the screwball-comedy genre that had characterized *Boy Meets Girl*. Sally Ann Peterson, a music teacher, and her child-prodigy pupil, Abbott Lee Ruskin, move into the life of Max Grenada, an important music impresario. By the end of the play, Sally has been rumored to have been Granada's mistress and Abbott their love child; simultaneously, Abbott's biological father begins to suspect his wife of infidelity. Meanwhile, Martova, an exotic female cellist, races through the play in an attempt to find a man—any man—to seduce. *Festival* ran for only twenty-three performances and was the last play the couple wrote together.

Once There Was A Russian (1961), written by Samuel Spewack, begins with the visit of John Paul Jones to the court of Catherine the Great in 1788, setting in motion several romantic entanglements between Jones, Catherine, and Grigory Aleksandrovich Potemkin. The work ran exactly one night, although it attracted the attention of Frank Loesser who, together with Samuel Spewack, set out to write a musical version. The result, *Pleasures and Palaces* (1965), closed on the road, despite the potent combination of Spewack, Loesser, and Bob Fosse.

The Spewacks' last work together was a 1961 television adaptation of Pyotr Ilich Tchaikovsky's *The Nutcracker* (1892) titled *The Enchanted Nutcracker*. They continued to work outside the worlds of theater and Hollywood, concentrating particularly on charitable organizations. In the 1960s the couple founded the Spewack Sports Club for the Handicapped in Israel. In 1963 Samuel Spewack received the Columbia School of Journalism Alumni Award.

Samuel Spewack died in 1971. Bella Spewack outlived him by nineteen years, although her writing career was mostly over. She continued to work occasionally as a freelance publicist; she was the one who suggested to the Girl Scouts of America that they should sell cookies to raise money. She also continued to manage her and her husband's published estate and enjoyed traveling and seeing productions of their plays. The couple had no children.

Creating their works from a detailed awareness of genre practices, Samuel and Bella Spewack knew how to breath new life into those practices and alter them meaningfully without betraying the original traditions. The Spewacks' works include a keen edge of satire and moral complexity, and their faults (notably in the area of structure) are overshadowed by the gifts of wit and intelligence that the playwrights bestow on their characters. Above all, the works are entertaining and funny while striking at the truths behind the stories.

References:

George Eells, *The Life That Late He Led: A Biography of Cole Porter* (New York: Putnam, 1967), pp. 238–455;

Rudolph Ellenbogen and Bradley D. Westbrook, comps., *From Russia to Kiss Me, Kate: The Careers of Sam and Bella Spewack* (New York: Columbia University Libraries, 1993);

Susan Loesser, *A Most Remarkable Fella: Frank Loesser and the Guys and Dolls in His Life* (New York: Donald I. Fine, 1993), pp. 240–245;

Charles Schwartz, *Cole Porter: A Biography* (New York: Dial, 1977), pp. 230–247;

John Russell Taylor, *Alec Guinness: A Celebration* (London: Pavilion Books, 1984), pp. 81–82.

Papers:

The major archive of Samuel and Bella Cohen Spewack's papers is at the Rare Book and Manuscript Library at Columbia University.

Cheryl L. West

(23 October 1957 –)

Tracey L. Walters
Stony Brook University

PLAY PRODUCTIONS: *Getting Right Behind Something Like That,* Champaign, University of Illinois, 1986;

Before It Hits Home, Champaign, Illinois, Parkland College, 1988; Seattle, Seattle Group Theatre, 1989; Washington, D.C., Arena Stage, January 1991; New York, Second Stage Theatre, 1992;

Jar the Floor, Seattle, Empty Space Theatre, 12 June 1991; San Diego, Old Globe Theatre, 1994; New York, Second Stage Theatre, 11 August 1999;

Puddin 'n Pete, Chicago, Goodman Theatre, 15 February 1993; San Diego, Old Globe Theatre, 1995;

Holiday Heart, Syracuse, N.Y., Syracuse Stage, 1994; New York, Manhattan Theatre Club, 31 January 1995;

Play On! book by West, adapted from William Shakespeare's *Twelfth Night,* music arranged by Luther Henderson, San Diego, Old Globe Theatre, 1996; New York, Brooks Atkinson Theatre, 20 March 1997.

BOOKS: *Before It Hits Home* (New York: Dramatists Play Service, 1993);

Jar the Floor (New York: Dramatists Play Service, 2002).

PRODUCED SCRIPTS: *Play On!* book by West, adapted from William Shakespeare's *Twelfth Night,* television, PBS, 21 June 2000;

Holiday Heart, television, Showtime, 10 December 2000.

OTHER: *Jar the Floor,* in *Women Playwrights: The Best Plays of 1992,* edited by Robyn Goodman and Marisa Smith (Newbury, Vt.: Smith & Kraus, 1992), pp. 54–96.

Cheryl L. West has written and directed several nationally produced plays, adapted two of her plays into screenplays, and received several prestigious theater awards and honors; yet, she is virtually unknown by those outside of the theater community.

Cheryl L. West (photograph by Joan Marcus)

The difficulty in obtaining the scripts and screenplays of West's productions is just one reason for the limited critical reception of her work by those in the literary and academic arenas. Most of West's plays have been staged in lesser-known theater houses, thus limiting her exposure to the general public. But West is one of the few contemporary African American female playwrights who is relentless in her presentation of controversial plays that force audiences to confront taboo issues such as incest, molestation, homosexuality, bisexuality, transvestitism, interracial relationships, AIDS, and drug addiction. Like her predecessors James Baldwin, August Wilson, Alice Walker, and Maya Angelou—individuals West holds as literary influences—West is consistent in her tackling of topics that are uncomfortable for audiences or deemed by critics as agitprop or "issue-laden." Most of West's plays center on the experiences of black characters. West admitted in a 2001 interview with Alexis Greene that when she begins to develop her plays, she writes for a black audience: "When I became a writer I really wanted to write for my community, and so I start there." While the plays focus on topics that impact the black community, the stories are by no means restricted to the black experience. Rather, they hold a universal appeal and highlight social issues dealing with race, class, and gender. An emphasis on family is one of West's major themes; in a 1996 interview with Everett Evans she noted, "I always write about family, about what we do to get a family, to maintain a family, about false images we build up of family. It can be blood family or a family we create."

Cheryl L. West was born in Chicago on 23 October 1957 and was raised by her mother along with her sister and brother first in the South Side of Chicago and later in the suburb of Markham. Before trying her hand at playwriting, West followed her mother's advice and sought a profession that would allow her to have something to "fall back on." She enrolled at Southern Illinois University-Carbondale, where she received a B.S. in administration of justice and a master's degree in rehabilitation in 1980. After graduation West worked as a social-services counselor but soon realized that her true passion was writing. She told Greene,

> I became a social worker because that seemed safe, and it was something I knew I could do well. But I still kept journals and did my little poetry. I was working at different part-time jobs, and I thought, "I really want to write." So I went to school to be legitimized. . . . I said, I'll go get a degree in journalism . . . because then I'll be a legitimate writer.

After completing her master's degree in journalism from the University of Illinois in Champaign-Urbana, West decided she really wanted to write plays. A friend told her if she wanted to be a writer she did not need to obtain a degree in drama; rather, she should watch as many plays as possible and then compose her own. One year after graduating, and while still working full-time as a social worker, West took her friend's advice and completed her first play, *Getting Right Behind Something Like That* (1986), which was staged at the University of Illinois Women's Conference. The play was never mounted professionally, but West gained the confidence necessary to consider playwriting as a serious vocation.

In 1987 West accepted an International Rotary Fellowship and traveled to the Caribbean to study at the Jamaican School of Drama. While in Jamaica, West was inspired to write her first successful play, *Before It Hits Home* (1988), a play about AIDS and its impact on the black community. In a March 1992 interview with Cathy Madison for *American Theatre* she recalled, "I knew right away that the repercussions of the disease in the black community would be terrible and that there would be denial on the part of some blacks." *Before It Hits Home* was first staged at Parkland College in Champaign, Illinois. As a novice playwright, West was forced to produce the play herself. The following year, West sent the play to the Seattle Group Theatre's Multicultural Playwrights' Festival; it was accepted, and she won an award and an opportunity to workshop the play. The Seattle mounting of *Before It Hits Home* was crucial for West's career. Tazewell Thompson, who was then an artistic associate for the Arena Stage in Washington, D.C., was highly impressed with the production. He offered West an Allen Lee Hughes Fellowship, which allowed her make the necessary revisions before introducing the play at Arena Stage in January 1991.

During the 1980s *Before It Hits Home* was one of only a few plays that approached the topics of bisexuality, homosexuality, and AIDS. The black community's hesitation to address such concerns prompted West to write this play. She told Evans: "There's the denial that we don't have bisexual people. The denial thinking gay people don't exist, or that they aren't active in our community or thinking, if you are married you're safe. Or if your partner looks healthy you're safe. We have had to learn that this virus doesn't choose only certain people. It can happen to anyone." As an artist, West desires not only to expose the social problems the black community chooses to ignore but also, as she said to Madison, to "open up discussions and challenge certain attitudes that might be hurtful or harmful." In *Before It Hits Home* West presents a telling example of how one black family's unwillingness to talk openly about AIDS leads to their dissolution.

Before It Hits Home centers on the life of Wendal Bailey, a bisexual jazz musician who, after denying and then accepting that he has AIDS, faces the challenge of informing those he loves that he has contracted the disease. When Wendal undertakes the task of telling his lovers—Douglass, a married, bisexual male, and Simone, a heterosexual woman—that he has AIDS, his separate conversations with each partner overlap so that the effect is a confusing exchange

Elain Graham as Maydee, Crystal Laws Green as Lola, and Irma P. Hall as MaDear in a 1995 Cincinnati Playhouse in the Park production of West's 1991 play, Jar the Floor *(photograph by Sandy Underwood)*

of dialogue that makes it difficult for him to be heard clearly. It is even more difficult for Wendal to tell his relatives. He is already estranged from his father, Bailey, a hardworking homophobe who rejects Wendal's career as a musician. Bailey would prefer that Wendal be more like his younger brother, Junior, a military man whom Bailey deems more responsible. Wendal and his father also stand in conflict because Bailey and Reba, Wendal's mother, are raising Wendal's twelve-year-old son, Dwayne. Furthermore, Wendal's task of revealing that he has AIDS will be complex, because his conversations with his parents are like those he has with Douglass and Simone—a muddled exchange in which his parents command the conversation and either ignore what Wendal has to say or do not give him a chance to say anything.

In act 2 West portrays the black community's negative views toward homosexuality and AIDS. Wendal returns home and endures homophobic statements made at dinner by his father, who tells Dwayne to take off the frilly apron he is wearing because he "looks like a sissy faggot," a remark that amuses everyone except Wendal. Dwayne responds by ripping off the apron and retorting with disdain, "I don't look like no fag." The homophobic sentiment is further displayed when Wendal tells Reba he has AIDS. Until this point, Reba has been the most supportive, constantly defending Wendal from Bailey's condemnation. But West reveals that even a mother's love can sour when she learns that her child might be gay and infected with AIDS. Reba appears to be more distraught that Wendal is "one of those people" and has contaminated her home and is less concerned with the news that her son is dying. When she discovers that Wendal did not contract the disease through a blood transfusion, but that he is gay, Reba is so devastated by the news that she shuns Wendal, moves out of the home with Dwayne, and refuses to see her son again.

When the other family members are told that Wendal has AIDS, they are equally upset. Junior cannot believe that Wendal is not the ideal brother he thought he was, and Dwayne is afraid to go near his father. At first, Bailey's reaction is as adverse as Reba's. Bailey is unwilling to accept that Wendal is gay and deduces that his son must be a drug addict. Surprisingly, though, in the end it is Bailey who takes care of Wendal. He places his fear and feelings of homophobia aside and accepts both Wendal's bisexuality and the fact that his son is dying of AIDS. West says earlier versions of the play depicted Reba as more understanding than Bailey, but she decided to change Reba's position because audience members expected Bailey to be less supportive.

To reinforce the fact that AIDS has not affected just Wendal and his immediate family, West concludes the play with a powerful image. In the last scene the audience learns that the consequences of Wendal's past have devastated one more life. Although Douglass is free of the virus, Simone is not as fortunate. Wendal was never able to tell Simone he was infected. As a result, Wendal has passed the disease not only to Simone but also to their unborn baby. Simone is depicted entering an AIDS clinic, pregnant and despondent. The message is obvious: people must be open and honest about AIDS because it affects everyone–young, old, black, white, straight, gay, male, and female.

The Arena Stage premiere of *Before It Hits Home* was so successful that one reporter noted on closing night that all seats were sold out. *Before It Hits Home* also ran in 1992 Off-Broadway on Second Stage and in 2001 in San Diego, California, at Urban Village Theatre. Critics gave the play mixed reviews. Some were uncomfortable with the themes of homosexuality; one reporter noted that during an Arena Stage performance, male audience members hissed and shouted disapproval at the intimate scenes between Wendal and Douglass. Others found the play to be "preachy" or melodramatic. West defended her play, stating to Madison that her work was no different from other plays dealing with social themes: "The white community . . . made several plays and movies about the AIDS crises. Once there are more artistic expressions of blacks with AIDS out there, one play won't be singled out as being 'preachy.'" Some critics praised the play. One reviewer described *Before It Hits Home* as a "mix of sitcom laughter, high-packed melodrama and emotional insight." Moreover, the awards West received were a testimony of the success of the play. In 1990 West became the first African American recipient of the Susan Smith Blackburn Prize, an international literary award given to a woman for an outstanding English-language play. In 1991 she was also presented with the AUDELCO Award for outstanding play and in 1992 received the Helen Hayes Charles MacArthur Award for outstanding new play.

Many who have analyzed West's work have been quick to assume that the inspiration for *Before It Hits Home* and other plays came from West's experiences as a social worker. West insists that is not the case. For example, she notes that she obtained her job as an HIV counselor only after she began working on *Before It Hits Home*. In addition, West advises critics to abstain from assuming that her works are semi-autobiographical.

A year after writing *Before It Hits Home,* West gained the necessary confidence to finally leave her fifteen-year tenure as a social services professional and concentrate full-time on playwriting. *Before It Hits Home* had solidified West's relationship with Arena Stage, and the company agreed to stage her second play, *Jar the Floor* (1991). This play is perhaps the best example of how West weaves lightening elements of humor into narratives that examine sobering topics. The title is based on a saying from West's Mississippi great-grandparents, who used to exclaim, "jar the floor"–meaning wake up and rattle the floorboards or make one's presence felt. In this play, one has no choice but to acknowledge the presence of these characters, who demand attention.

In *Jar the Floor* West addresses themes similar to those in *Before It Hits Home*. In addition to highlighting homosexuality and the effects of disease (in this case, cancer and senility instead of AIDS), she introduces molestation into the narrative. These topics, however, are overshadowed by the major motif: the conflict between mothers and their daughters. The adage "children pay for the sins of their parents" rings true for the characters in *Jar the Floor*. In this play three generations of failed motherhood prove that daughters who have been raised by mothers who hurt, neglect, condemn, and chastise them inevitably bear children who continue the cycle of dysfunctional parenting. West explained her motivation to Greene: "My idea with *Jar* is that until you know your mother's journey as a woman, you will never be able to understand her mistakes and forgive her. We tend to look at our mothers only as our mothers. If women were able to understand what our mothers' personal journeys were–what they had to give up, for instance–maybe we could have a different view of them."

The mother/daughter conflict is played out in a single day when MaDear (Viola), her daughter, Lola, granddaughter, Maydee, and great-granddaughter, Vennie, congregate at Maydee's home to celebrate MaDear's ninetieth birthday. Each mother/daughter dyad harbors resentment because of painful, unresolved past issues. None seems willing to forgive, forget, or even understand the actions of her predecessor. Each woman appears to be strikingly different from the others, and in terms of their use of language, dress, and mannerisms they are indeed dissimilar. MaDear is a senile, sassy, sexually aware, foul-mouthed matriarch. Lola is a bawdy, ostentatious, sixty-five-year-old grandmother who dates younger men and repudiates the idea of being a grandparent. Maydee is the highly etiquette-conscious, conservative, college-educated, soon-to-be-tenured professor. Finally, Vennie, the youngest member of the matrilineal line, is a bisexual

Maggie Rush as Wanda, Afi McClendon as Nikki, and Keith Randolph Smith in the title role in the 1995 Manhattan Theatre Club production of West's 1994 play, Holiday Heart *(photograph by Martha Swope)*

eccentric who refuses to speak proper English, rejects her mother's polite demeanor, and adopts the mannerisms of her grandmother Lola. In spite of these surface differences, however, the women share commonalities. As both mothers and daughters berate each other for their lack of attention and poor mothering skills, the audience sees that the women are more alike than they know.

The tension between the mothers and daughters is in part caused by past relationships with husbands, lovers, and fathers who in some way harmed the women of this story. MaDear's failed relationship with her philandering husband and his attention to Lola create feelings of rejection and jealousy. MaDear openly expresses her resentment of her daughter. She never refers to Lola by her name but instead calls her "split-tail" or "Sister." Furthermore, in her semidemented state, MaDear constantly suggests that Lola is sexually enticing her husband. At one point she says, "I should have killed you when you were born." Lola's obvious lack of affection and love from MaDear forced her to seek solace in male lovers. After many unsuccessful relationships, she found a man who gave her the love and support she craves. However, when this man ended up molesting her daughter, Maydee, Lola turned a blind eye to the abuse rather than leaving the relationship. After being sexually molested by her stepfather, Maydee was damaged emotionally and sexually. As a child she slept with knives to protect herself, and at thirteen she was still wetting the bed. Though Maydee has a child, it is implied that the pregnancy was unwanted. In an effort to control some aspect of her life, Maydee devotes her time to the development of her career, and these aspirations jeopardize her relationship with Vennie, for they have little free time to spend together. In turn, Vennie resents her mother's lack of affection.

All of the women have been emotionally scarred, but because they are unwilling to address what has happened to them, they are unable to heal. West makes it clear that the past experiences of these women are not relative only to black women. Vennie's white lover Raisa feuds with her mother in the same way that Vennie argues with Maydee. In addition, Raisa has been abandoned by her husband because he could not face the fact that she has had a mastectomy. Raisa's wounds are physical and emotional. Unlike the other characters, however, she does not allow the scars to dictate her actions. She refuses to wear a prosthesis and wears tight-fitting shirts so that she can proudly sport her single breast, proving that when one acknowledges or embraces a scar, it is easier to heal. MaDear applauds Raisa for confronting her pain; in act 2 MaDear tells Raisa, "You show me a woman dat ain't gotta scar somewhere an I'll show you a woman dat ain't lived nuttin' but a lie. It's dem inside scars, dem de ones you gotta watch out for. Dey'll tear you up tryin' to git loose. I know. But ours, it's breathin' good . . . yes, sir . . . breathin' real good." MaDear does not heed the advice she gives to Raisa.

Lola and Maydee believe they did the best they could for their daughters. Lola convinced herself that she was at least providing a father for her daughter, even though Maydee was being molested. In an effort to redeem themselves for their past actions, each woman behaves as caretaker of another's child or mother (Lola helped raise Vennie, and Maydee takes care of MaDear). The mothers also indulge in purchasing gifts that are unappreciated: Lola provides piano lessons for Maydee and a wheelchair to help with MaDear, and Maydee saves money for Vennie's college education and buys Vennie expensive outfits. But what each mother fails to learn is that love cannot be packaged in material goods. Their daughters do not want presents; rather, they want love. Thus, the daughters reject the gifts. Maydee hates the piano, and Vennie never completes her degree. Instead, Vennie requests the money so that she can go to Europe and pursue a singing career.

The climax of the play reveals the reason for the dissention among the mothers and daughters: it was MaDear's mother who began the cycle of bad parenting. She mistreated MaDear by rejecting her and calling her ugly. Thus, all of the women have had to pay for this legacy of maternal neglect. By the end of the play the women have expressed the reasons for their resentment, and MaDear's party continues. Nothing has been resolved, but at least all have finally confronted their past.

After its debut in Seattle, *Jar the Floor* was staged at the Old Globe Theatre in San Diego, the Arena Stage in Washington, D.C., the Cleveland Playhouse, and twice in Off-Broadway New York theaters before returning to Seattle in 2000. *Jar the Floor* also earned West the Beverly Hills/Hollywood NAACP Award for best play in 1995. Overall most critics praised *Jar the Floor* for its humor and meaningful story line. The *New York Times* gave the play a positive review. There were some who were put off by the explicit language and melodramatic nature of the play. During the New York run, a theater critic for *Variety* noted: "While there is much to enjoy in *Jar the Floor,* notably a heavy dose of tart humor . . . the play is dismayingly over-stuffed with conflict and contention and mechanical bursts of bitterness."

By 1993 West was working full-time as a writer based in Illinois, and *Puddin 'n Pete* premiered at the Goodman Theatre in Chicago on 15 February of that year. *Puddin 'n Pete,* her least-known play, is no less provocative than West's other works. Issues of molestation, incest, race, class, and gender are again brought to light. In *Puddin 'n Pete* the moral thesis is clear: marriages or relationships that are not based on trust and honesty are doomed to failure. The title characters are a newlywed couple who face the challenge of trying to make their marriage successful. From the onset of the narrative it is evident that the chances of this union surviving are bleak. Puddin and Pete both claim they are willing to accept each other for who they are, but neither is completely honest. Both have been married before; both were unhappy with how they were treated by their former spouses. Pete, a janitor, had a wife who put pressure on him to be more ambitious and do more than "clean up after others." Puddin had experiences with men who used her. Both resolve that things will be different this time. When Puddin and Pete each discover that the other does not live up to the ideal they have created in their own minds, they become disillusioned.

Puddin and Pete obviously have nothing in common. Their only shared interest is in lovemaking, but before long even this bond proves insufficient to keep them together. Puddin is a forty-year-old, educated, ambitious career woman who aspires to climb the corporate ladder and achieve middle-class status. The difference in class separates Puddin from Pete, who is content with his blue-collar job. The main things he desires in life are happiness and respect. Although he is respectful to all whom he encounters, he is constantly disrespected. Each day Pete's dignity is brought into question, inside and outside of the home. Puddin humiliates Pete by chastising him over his lack of skill at playing Scrabble and by complaining to her friends about his inability to hold an intelligent conversation with her. Outside of the home Pete is constantly reminded of "his place" as a black male in white society. At work he is constantly reminded that he is nothing more than the janitor; in one instance, when he is caught conversing with students, a teacher reminds them, "We don't pay Mr. Butler to fraternize with our students. He's a busy man." Only the chil-

Yvette Cason, Lawrence Hamilton, Larry Marshall, and Andre De Shields in the 1997 New York production of Play On!, *West's 1996 adaptation of William Shakespeare's* Twelfth Night *(photograph by Carol Rosegg)*

dren show Pete a level of respect. Although Pete says he can appreciate Puddin because she allows him to hold on to his manhood, he is lying. In fact, before long he has difficulty engaging in lovemaking.

Pete becomes consumed in the affairs of a white sixteen-year-old abused student, Ariel. Pete helps Ariel realize that despite the odds and her mother's alcoholism and abusiveness, Ariel is important. Pete's relationship with Ariel is the one relationship in which he does not feel socially or intellectually inferior—but the friendship has consequences. Although the relationship between the two is innocent, Ariel kisses Pete; the incident is witnessed by Ariel's aunt and a teacher, and it jeopardizes Pete's marriage and his job.

West also uses this play to raise questions about racism and prejudice. When Puddin's friends Dehlia and Rose Marie come to the house to console her, a conversation about Pete's innocence or guilt is presented. Dehlia (who is black) is convinced that because Pete is a black man, he will be presumed guilty. She suggests Ariel forced herself on Pete: "That girl knew what she was doing. I wouldn't be surprised if somebody put her up to it. They always ready, wanna bring a good man down every time." In response to Dehlia's comment, Rose Marie (who is white) presents her opinion: "Dehlia, nobody put Pete in this position. He put himself in this position. I happen to think he's innocent but don't think every white woman is the cause of bringing down every black man, nor do I think most women lie about being molested." Although Rose Marie's opinion does not have racist undertones, she is castigated by Dehlia for being racist. By presenting the view of both black and white females in the play, West underscores the universality of the issues on which she focuses.

After learning about the kiss, Puddin is not only upset because her husband might be a pedophile but also, more important, she is jealous of Pete's display of affection for another. Puddin had been fearful of investing her heart into a relationship because she was molested by her father. She felt Pete was the one person who would not hurt her, but he proved her wrong. Pete feels he is innocent and cannot believe that Puddin does not defend him. He goes home to the South, where he is given some sound advice from his mother. Alluding to the Adam and Eve story, Pete's mother tells him there is a snake lurking in every relationship. In order to protect the other from being bitten, one partner has to make sure the other also sees the snake. The snake in Puddin and Pete's relationship was not only the potential for infidelity but also the lack of honesty. Neither Puddin nor Pete was willing to admit their dissatisfaction with the other. Thus, the lesson for them both is that in order for their relationship to work they must be honest about what each expects from the other. At the end Puddin and Pete reconcile.

West and one of her first supporters, Thompson, collaborated on the production of *Holiday Heart,* which made its world premiere at the Syracuse Stage in 1994. With this play West continues to explore the dysfunctional or unconventional family. The maxim "Everyone has a story to tell" is just one of the many familiar lines quoted by the title character, Holiday Heart, an unforgettable six-foot-tall, loud-talking, unafraid, unashamed drag queen. Holiday sacrifices his own ambitions and dreams so that he can attempt to save the life of Wanda, a crack-addicted aspiring writer, and her preteen daughter, Nikki. West told Greene that the impetus for this play came when she read about a mother who shot and killed her crack-addicted daughter: "I was so moved: how could an older woman shoot her daughter?" In *Holiday Heart* the audience witnesses the grim realities of crack-cocaine addiction. Like *Before It Hits Home,* the play reveals how disease–in this case, drug addiction–affects not only the sick but also the family and friends who try in vain to save the addict and live their own lives.

West also draws again upon the theme of motherhood, showing that the ability to "mother" is not necessarily female. Although Holiday, as a man, cannot bear children, he assumes the self-proclaimed title of "mother" to both Wanda and Nikki. Unlike the women in *Jar the Floor,* Holiday is a nurturer who takes his role of motherhood seriously and is willing to make sacrifices for those in his care. Not only does he give up his privacy and his living space, but he also abandons his lifelong dream of traveling to Paris and even compromises his friendship with his best friend, Blue, another over-the-top drag queen. Like the women in *Jar the Floor,* Holiday has experienced pain. At sixteen he went to jail for killing a man who physically abused his mother. Rather than defend her son, his mother appealed to have Holiday placed in jail, where he was sodomized by the older male inmates. Holiday's lover Fisher dies, leaving Holiday alone with the faded hope of going to Paris with the man of his dreams. Despite his painful past, Holiday finds love enough in his heart to provide for Wanda and her child.

Wanda, on the other hand, displays a selfish attitude that is reminiscent of the women in *Jar the Floor.* Wanda places her own needs before Nikki's, and she is also ungracious when Holiday helps her. For example, after Holiday secures a safe place for her and Nikki to stay, she asks, "Why are you doing all of this for us? Just so you know, I don't do fags." Again, after Holiday finds a job for her, she takes in a flashy drug dealer, Silas, Nikki's father, and shuts Holiday out of the new family unit she creates.

While Wanda is desperate for the perfect family, her plan falters as drugs overtake her desire to remain a part of the family unit she constructs. However, just as West presents alternative definitions of motherhood, she also suggests new views of the conventional family. At the conclusion of this play Wanda dies, leaving Holiday to hold to his promise that he will raise Nikki. But Holiday will not be a single parent, as Silas intends to play a role in Nikki's life. A drag queen and a heterosexual raising Nikki is not a conventional family, but it is a social unit based on trust and honesty. West confided to Greene that her intention was to prove that the nuclear family is not the only concept of family that exists: "A mom and pop and two kids is the image many of us grow up thinking the average family looks like, but what a family is are people who are joined not necessarily by blood but by a willingness to love each other through the darkest hours."

Holiday Heart was given a lukewarm reception. A Seattle reporter suggested that West was "too obsessed with black pathology." A reviewer of the 1995 New York production accused West of "Working overtime in an effort to unsettle and subvert." Others delighted in what one reviewer described as the "honest portrayal of inner city life." After its Syracuse staging, the play ran through 1994 and 1995 in Cleveland, Seattle Repertory Theatre, Off-Broadway in New York, and in Washington, D.C. *Holiday Heart* was later adapted into a movie for the Showtime cable network, directed by Robert Townsend and featuring Ving Rhames and Alfre Woodard.

After *Holiday Heart,* West turned her attention to writing the libretto for *Play On!* (1996), a musical adaptation of William Shakespeare's *Twelfth Night* (circa 1602) conceived and directed by Sheldon Epps with choreography by Duke Ellington's granddaughter, Mercedes Ellington. Complete with a score of twenty of Duke Ellington's well-known songs, the play follows the experiences of Vy (Viola in *Twelfth Night*), a Mississippi songwriter who travels to Harlem during the 1940s with the intention of writing songs for the jazz great Duke Orsino. When Vy discovers that the songwriting industry is male-dominated, she is forced to disguise herself as a man and becomes Vy-man. True to the Shakespearean script, Vy's disguise leads to misunderstanding and mismatched lovers. Vy becomes the object of desire of Lady Liv, Duke Orsino's former lover, while Vy falls in love with the Duke. As is to be expected, though, all ends well. The play, which managed to reach Broadway, was not a favorite with New

York audiences; after sixty-one performances, the play was pulled. Many felt the attempt to blend Shakespeare and Ellington was futile. However, the play was received favorably in other parts of the country. *Play On!* was also successful enough to be picked up as part of a PBS miniseries, which ran in the summer of 2000.

West continues to hone her screenwriting and playwriting skills with projects that include an original movie for MTV and an adaptation of *Jar the Floor* into a movie for Paramount. Despite her success, she prefers to remain outside of the large cultural centers such as New York or California and instead keeps a low profile in Seattle, Washington, where she is raising her two children. West says living in the Pacific Northwest allows her to remain true to her art. Seattle has offered her access to the Seattle Repertory Theatre, which West claims is her artistic home. She believes that in Seattle she is free from the distractions of larger cities and is therefore able to work in a calmer environment. West has learned from her tenure as a playwright to ignore those critics who undermine her talent. She told Greene: "It takes a lot of courage to do theater, because you deal with critics, with the audience, with other artists, and every day you have to keep believing, 'I've got something to say that's unique.' It takes a lot to keep going, particularly if you do work that you believe in but nobody gets."

Interviews:

Cathy Madison, "West Probes Traumas–With No Flinching," *American Theatre* (March 1992): 46–47;

Carrie Kaufman, "Cheryl L. West On the Struggle of Success in Theatre," *Performink* (25 February 1993): 4–5;

Diane Haithman, "Hitting Home in the Heartland," *Los Angeles Times,* 23 October 1994, p. 50;

Everett Evans, "From 'What If?' to 'What Now?': Playwright Explores Denial That's Helped AIDS Gain Foothold," *Houston Chronicle,* 28 January 1996, p. 11;

Alexis Greene, "Cheryl West," in *Women Who Write Plays: Interviews with American Dramatists,* edited by Greene (Hanover, N.H.: Smith & Kraus, 2001), pp. 472–493.

References:

Paul Carter Harrison, "The Crisis of Black Theatre Identity," *African American Review,* 31, no. 4 (1997): 567–577;

Ann Russo, "Exploring AIDS in the Black Community," *Sojourner: The Women's Forum,* 15, no. 1 (1989): 38.

Elizabeth Wong
(6 June 1958 –)

Elizabeth Kim
University of Wisconsin–Whitewater

PLAY PRODUCTIONS: *Letters to a Student Revolutionary,* New York City, Pan Asian Repertory Theatre, 7 May 1991; Los Angeles, East/West Players, 5 May 1994;

Kimchee and Chitlins: A Serious Comedy about Getting Along, Chicago, Victory Gardens Theater, May 1993; Los Angeles, West Coast Ensemble, 29 July 1994;

China Doll, Brunswick, Me., Pickard Theatre, Bowdoin College, 14 November 1996; Salisbury, N.C., Hedrick Theatre, Catawba College, 22 February 2000; Seattle, Northwest Asian American Theatre, October 2001;

Let the Big Dog Eat, Louisville, Ky., Actors Theatre, 4 March 1998;

Prometheus, Denver, Co., Denver Center Theatre, 25 January 1999;

Boyd and Oskar: A Play Inspired by Oscar Wilde's The Happy Prince, Cincinnati, Ohio, Cincinnati Playhouse in the Park, 25 March 2000;

Amazing Adventures of the Marvelous Monkey King, Denver, Co., Denver Center Theatre, 31 January 2001; Honolulu, Hawaii, Honolulu Theatre For Youth, 5 October 2002;

Badass of the RIP Eternal, Louisville, Ky., Actors Theatre, 23 March 2001;

Punk Girls: On Divine Omnipotence and the Longstanding Nature of Evil, Los Angeles, Jewish Women's Theatre Project, 21 August 2001; New York, Shalimar Theatre Productions, 17 September 2001.

BOOKS: *Letters to a Student Revolutionary* (Woodstock, Ill.: Dramatic Publishing, 1994);

Kimchee and Chitlins: A Serious Comedy about Getting Along (Woodstock, Ill.: Dramatic Publishing, 1996).

PRODUCED SCRIPTS: "Yung at Heart," *All-American Girl,* television, ABC, 5 October 1994;

"The Apartment," *All-American Girl,* television, ABC, 11 January 1995.

Elizabeth Wong (photograph by Ruth Wong; courtesy of Elizabeth Wong)

OTHER: *Letters to a Student Revolutionary,* in *Women on the Verge: Seven Avant-Garde Playwrights,* edited by Rosette C. Lamont (New York: Applause Theatre Books, 1993); republished in *Unbroken Thread: An Anthology of Plays by Asian American Women,* edited by Roberta Uno (Amherst: University of Massachusetts Press, 1993); republished in *Multicultural Theatre II: Contemporary Hispanic, Asian and African-American Plays,* edited by

Roger Ellis (Colorado Springs: Meriwether Publishing, 1998);

China Doll, in *Contemporary Plays by Women of Color,* edited by Kathy Perkins and Uno (New York: Routledge, 1996);

Kimchee and Chitlins: A Serious Comedy about Getting Along, in *But Still, Like Air, I'll Rise: New Asian American Plays,* edited by Velina Hasu Houston (Philadelphia: Temple University Press, 1997);

Let the Big Dog Eat, in *Humana Festival '98: The Complete Plays,* edited by Michael Bigelow Dixon and Amy Wegener (Lyme, N.H.: Smith & Kraus, 1998); republished in *Ten-Minute Plays: Volume 5, Actors Theatre of Louisville,* edited by Dixon and Wegener (New York: S. French, 2000);

Punk Girls: On Divine Omnipotence and the Longstanding Nature of Evil, in *Contest Monologues* (Colorado Springs: Meriwether Publishing, 1999); republished in *Scenes and Monologues for Young Actors,* edited by Kent R. Brown (Woodstock, Ill.: Dramatic Publishing, 2000);

"For Maria Irene Fornes: The Tarot of Sarita," in *Conducting a Life: Reflections on the Theatre of Maria Irene Fornes,* edited by Maria M. Delgado and Caridad Svich (Lyme, N.H.: Smith & Kraus, 1999);

Inside a Red Envelope, in *Playwriting Master Class: The Personality of Process and the Art of Rewriting,* edited by Michael Wright (Portsmouth, N.H.: Heinemann, 2000);

"Return of the Prodigal: An Ongoing Theatrical/Art/Internet Installation/Conversation Between Playwright Elizabeth Wong of the United States and Painter Georges Pfruender of Switzerland," in *Transglobal Readings: Crossing Theatrical Boundaries,* edited by Svich (Manchester: Manchester University Press, forthcoming 2002).

SELECTED PERIODICAL PUBLICATIONS–UNCOLLECTED: "The Struggle to be an All-American Girl," *Los Angeles Times,* 7 September 1980, V: 5;

"A Present for Popo," *Los Angeles Times,* 30 December 1992, p. B7;

"Reflections on Outrage in the Street," *Los Angeles Times,* 14 April 1993, p. B7;

"In Search of the Monkey King: The Tricky Business of Adapting Myth for Children," *Headline Muse.com,* no. 8 (6 October 2000), <http://www.headlinemuse.com/archives/newarchives.htm>;

"Shopping With The Gods: Myth In Advertising," *Headline Muse.com,* no. 10 (6 December 2000); no. 11 (6 January 2001), <http://www.headlinemuse.com/Culture/mythinadvertising.htm>;

"Icarus Does An Ollie: Extreme Skateboarding," *Headline Muse.com,* no. 12 (6 February 2001), <http://www.headlinemuse.com/Culture/icarus.htm>;

"Golfing With the Gods: The Mysterious Allure of a Game and a Little White Ball," *Headline Muse.com,* no. 15 (5 May 2001); no. 16 (6 June 2001), <http://www.headlinemuse.com/Culture/golf.htm>;

"The Mists of Avalon: Return To The Goddess," *Headline Muse.com,* no. 17 (6 July 2001), <http://www.headlinemuse.com/Politics/mists.htm>.

For American playwright Elizabeth Wong, writing for the theater is, at its core, a mode of response. In her works she has responded to timely political crises such as the Tiananmen Square massacre of 1989 and the African American boycott of Korean American–owned businesses in Brooklyn in 1990 as well as more individually affecting topics such as the race- and gender-based struggles of pioneering Chinese American actress Anna May Wong in early Hollywood. Her engagement with these subjects is often a reflection of Wong's identity and experiences as a Chinese American living in multicultural urban America in the second half of the twentieth century. As a child of Chinese immigrant parents, Wong inevitably encountered the many tensions resulting from the collision of traditional Chinese expectations and values with culturally diverse American realities. And while most of the generational and cultural conflicts in her dramas do not settle into easy compromise or mutual accommodation, the process of negotiating difference, of engaging in dialogue, emerges as the central value in Wong's work.

Elizabeth Ann Wong was born on 6 June 1958 in Southgate, an industrial area of Los Angeles, California, and raised in Chinatown and later Monterey Park. She learned at a young age the necessity of successfully navigating cross-generational and cross-cultural minefields. Wong's parents, like many Asian American immigrants in the 1950s, 1960s, and 1970s, had to work long hours at labor-intensive jobs to provide for their family. Wong's father, James King Wong, owned a small family grocery store, although he was trained as a chemical engineer at the University of California at Berkeley. According to Wong's mother, Ruth Tsui-Wah Wong, racial discrimination kept her husband from working in his trained profession, a common situation for many college-educated Asian Americans of that era. After Wong's father died when the playwright was five, her mother worked in both blue- and white-collar jobs to support her two children. In such hard circumstances Wong treasured the solace and imaginative release provided by books: "Life in Chinatown was harsh for a chubby, non-athletic, non-achiever like

Promotional material for the 1991 New York and 1994 Los Angeles productions of Wong's first play, inspired by the 1989 political protests in Beijing (Collection of Elizabeth Wong)

myself. I was the geeky four-eyed kid anxious for the arrival of the bookmobile. I'd monopolize all the best books, checking out the maximum ten, all the Nancy Drew, anything in the fantasy section, anything on talking cats or magical closets or time travel."

In time Wong's passion for stories, coupled with her inquisitive nature, led her to study journalism at the University of Southern California, where she received her bachelor's degree in 1980. One of her professors, Jack Langguth, a former *New York Times* Saigon bureau chief, stirred Wong's interest in the field with his stories of life as a foreign correspondent. As a young person pondering a career in the mid 1970s, she was also inspired by the tenacity of journalists Bob Woodward and Carl Bernstein to get at the "truth" of the Watergate cover-up. Wong worked for ten years in journalism, starting her career as a production assistant for KNXT-TV Channel Two News in Los Angeles (1980–1983), then later as a reporter for *The San Diego Tribune* (1984–1986) and *The Hartford Courant* in Connecticut (1986–1988). Even after turning from journalism to writing for the theater, Wong was solicited by the *Los Angeles Times* to contribute regularly to its opinion pages, which she did from 1992 to 1996, offering editorials on various issues ranging from the aftermath of the Rodney King verdict to musings on vegetarianism or on the lack of varied and complex representations of people of color in American movies and on American television in the 1990s.

Wong's career shift from journalism to dramatic writing in the late 1980s was rooted in her desire for greater self-expression than conventional journalism allowed. While pondering this change, Wong also drew inspiration from the televised plays of Wakako Yamauchi, particularly the lyrical *And the Soul Shall Dance* (1976), and by the Broadway success of a high-school acquaintance, Chinese American playwright David Henry Hwang. If someone who shared her background could flourish as a playwright, Wong thought, then perhaps she could as well. About this relatively recent entry of Asian Americans into active literary production, Wong has said: "I think the Asian family in America has been at a station where they couldn't branch out into the arts, because they've always been at the survival-struggle level. My generation is starting to deal with the questions beyond just struggling to stabilize as immigrants." The other motivating factor in her career switch was the example of her self-reliant mother: "My mother was sort of a pioneer. She was widowed at the age of 25, she didn't speak much English, and she had to learn how to drive a car. I turned out to be independent, too. I struck out on my own and came East." Encouraged by these models, Wong enrolled in 1989 in the M.F.A. playwriting program at New York University's Tisch School of the Arts.

Wong's literary talents quickly surfaced at Tisch. Her first play, *Letters to a Student Revolutionary*, was written during her first year in the program and produced Off-Broadway by the Pan Asian Repertory Theatre under the artistic direction of Tisa Chang in 1991. Wong has described the play as a "creative opinion," a decided departure from the objective, politically neutral writing that marked her ten-year career as a journalist. *Letters to a Student Revolutionary* addresses the student-led political protests in Beijing in the summer of 1989 and the Chinese government's subsequent brutal crackdown on the resistance movement. Of the remarkable events of that summer, the playwright has said:

> I sat in front of the television set and was horrified by what I saw. It was ugly and disturbing and tragic. I felt a kind of overwhelming connection because I was Chinese, or thought I was Chinese. . . . I felt it on two levels. . . . One, I was aghast and appalled that a country could destroy its own children. . . . But on another level . . . being Chinese American, seeing people who looked like me, really made me feel endangered in some way. I made that leap across the miles.

Out of a sense of shared identity with the Chinese people, Wong felt compelled to write the play.

Wong's close identification with the subject of the play is evident in her use of autobiographical details as a central framing device. The friendship between the two central characters, Bibi and Karen, parallels Wong's real-life friendship with a young Chinese woman whom Wong met while visiting China with her family in 1984, five years after the normalization of diplomatic relations between the United States and the People's Republic of China. Bibi is a typical young American woman—hip to trendy American fashions, music, and attitudes—who eventually settles into a career in journalism. Karen is patterned after the Chinese woman with whom Wong had exchanged letters for several years until the June 1989 massacre. In the play Wong stretches this correspondence to ten years, the extended time frame allowing for a more comprehensive examination of the interplay of political and cultural events with the young women's rite-of-passage experiences.

Through the course of their decade-long epistolary friendship, the two women discover that their experiences and viewpoints diverge more than they connect. Bibi's passage through a young woman's life stages occurs within the context of 1980s America, while Karen's is markedly 1980s People's Republic of China. Karen, who, in her idealization of all things American, has even chosen an American name for herself, bemoans the doubly tiered cultural constraints upon her: one as a woman in a patriarchal social system, the other as a Chinese in a conformist, repressive regime. She confides in her American friend about her alienation, especially from the state-run socioeconomic machinery: "More and more, I feel bitter toward my life and my uselessness. I go to work, I have ideas to improve my job, and no one listens to me. I am a nobody. And I want to be a somebody." She longs for imagined freedoms and self-determination in America, and in the early stages of their correspondence she implores her American friend to send for her: "You live in a democracy, the individual can vote. You can count for something. . . . You have the luxury to be selfish. To think of only yourself. You live in Paradise. I live in hell. . . . I want Democracy. Democracy for me. Freedom of speech. Freedom to choose."

Karen's dichotomous view of the two countries is immediately rejected by Bibi, who questions the value of choices in America, a culture set adrift in hollow abundance and spiritual malaise. Dissatisfied with her work as a journalist and after having "changed newspapers five times in the past three years," Bibi retorts pointedly that in America one has the "freedom to be confused." Bibi further insists that unrestricted freedoms actually lead to a host of social ills, from unemployment and homelessness to sexual harassment, racism, and social alienation. And most Americans transcend these ills by engaging in "the national pastime" of "retail therapy," conducted "at the altar of The Church of Our Lady of Retail–Nordstroms, Lord and Taylor." When Karen rejects this conflation of democracy with capitalism, Bibi is allowed the final say: "Well . . . in America, we like to *think* we're a democracy, but we're definitely a nation of shoppers." What becomes apparent through this dialogue is that both characters hold gross misconceptions about the other's cultural realities. Wong uses this mutual misconception to underscore her rejection of people's uncritical embrace of either cultural situation and their binary notions about the two societies: American freedom versus Chinese oppression.

William Cain, Brian Keeler, William McNulty, and Fred Major in the 1998 Actors Theatre of Louisville production of Let the Big Dog Eat *(photograph by Richard Trigg)*

Critical reactions to *Letters to a Student Revolutionary* have been largely favorable. Aileen Jacobson, of the Long Island *Newsday* (21 May 1991), praised it as "a very fine play," and in the *Los Angeles Times* (13 May 1994) drama critic F. Kathleen Foley described it as "ultimately moving" despite its "broad black-and-white brush strokes." For its originality and promise, the play was awarded the 1990 Playwright Forum Award by TheatreWorks in Colorado Springs. The many performances attest to its widespread appeal; it was also the only American play invited to take part in the 1992 Singapore Arts Festival.

In her next major play, *Kimchee and Chitlins: A Serious Comedy about Getting Along* (1993), Wong again responds to another real-life conflict, although this one was much more regional in scope and decidedly late-twentieth-century American in nature. The African American boycott of stores owned by Korean Americans in Brooklyn in 1990 served as the real-life catalyst for this play. In a May 1993 interview with Jae-Ha Kim for the *Chicago Sun-Times*, Wong explained how her idea for the play was rooted in response: in 1990, as she was watching a news story about the Brooklyn boycott, she became frustrated by what she felt was the lack of substantive and unbiased reporting. She found similar flawed reporting on other stations: "The reporters talked to angry blacks who were shouting at the Koreans. But nobody talked to the Koreans. I thought, 'Somebody is falling down on the job.' Why did all these reporters across the board miss the boat? One of the reasons obviously is the language barrier, but no one even mentioned that. They just excluded one-half of the story." With her journalistic sense of fair play thus stirred, the playwright decided to provide a more fleshed-out and balanced dramatic treatment of the subject.

Described as a satire in the style of the motion picture *Rashomon* (1950), *Kimchee and Chitlins* examines the complications attendant upon the search for the "truth," especially within the context of a news-media probe of modern-day race relations in America. At the core of the news story is an alleged racial incident at the New Way Grocery Store in Brooklyn. Despite the truth-seeking efforts of Suzie Seeto, a Chinese American television reporter assigned to cover the story, the "truth" of what actually happened in the grocery store goes unanswered in the play. Seeto is instead left to sift through two sharply contradictory versions of the alleged incident, while having at the same time to juggle aversive newsroom politics that threaten to compromise her fair coverage of the story. According to the African American protesters, led by the opportunistic Reverend Lonnie Carter, a Haitian American customer named Matilda Duvet was beaten up by Key Chun Mak, the Korean American grocery-store owner who wrongly accused her of shoplifting. Mak, corroborated by his nephew and niece who work for him in the store, insists that Duvet fell mysteriously on the floor, perhaps suffering a heart attack or a fainting spell. But the Reverend Carter's version of the story resonates throughout the largely African American community, and local residents organize a boycott of the grocery store.

Deeply entrenched racial fears, prejudices, and hostilities soon erupt as media attention is directed at the boycott. The heated quarreling between the two groups obscures the truth of what happened in the grocery store, while it also makes clear how far apart the two groups are, separated by a chasm of misreadings, suspicions, and resentments. As Seeto begins her investigation, she hears the protesters' grievances. Joining the Reverend Carter in the boycott are neighborhood mainstays nurse Ruth Betty and barber James Brown, who complain that Mak disrespects his African American customers through several social etiquette breaches. Mak and his Korean employees avoid eye contact with their customers and, as if to imply that the customers have a "social disease," put their change on the counter instead of in their hands. Further, according to the protesters, Mak doggedly surveils his black customers in the store, believing them all to be thieves and shoplifters. Addressing these charges, Mak explains that direct eye contact and expressions of inappropriate familiarity such as touching a stranger's hand are considered signs of disrespect within Korean society. Thus, different cultural codes fuel the mutual grievances.

The play extends this theme of racial misunderstandings and resentments beyond the two feuding parties. Despite her well-intended but naive attempt to be a fair and impartial reporter, Seeto, at various points in the play, is accused by both parties of showing partiality for the other group. By the end of the play Seeto herself comes to realize that in a racially contentious society no individual may claim the luxury of exemption or dissociation. To drive this point home, Wong, in the closing scenes of the play, includes a fictionalized account of the real-life incident of a Vietnamese boy brutally assaulted by four African American teens who mistake the youth for a Korean. When Seeto witnesses this attack, she is faced with a sobering truth about American race relations and about her own illusions:

> Standing there, watching those boys and that kid. I wasn't hating them. No, no . . . I was too busy, too preoccupied with disassociating myself from that squirming, weak, yellow boy on the ground. Coolly, I hid behind my profession, thoroughly brainwashed by my complete-and-utter certainty that I could not and would not be hurt . . . because I was NOT like that kid. Those black boys with their baseball bat shattered my beautiful delusion once and forever. For if I wasn't yellow, then what color did I think I was?

The play asserts that professional dissociation in matters of race is impossible, for no American escapes involvement or implication in these issues. As the mediation efforts of the two groups degenerate into mutual name calling and fist fighting, the events reveal not only Seeto's racial angst but also the racial stereotyping and hostilities of her white news director, Mark Thompson. He views Seeto and Asian women in general as the "eroticized exotic," while his blatant disdain for African Americans leaks out in a moment of uncensored frustration with Seeto. The conclusion of the play offers no real reconciliation, as Mak is eventually defeated by the boycott and forced to close his business. Wong's offering of an alternative, "more cheerful" second ending perhaps underscores for many observers the sad realization that the racial divide defies bridging. In the alternative ending, Brown invites Mak to dinner at his house, where he promises to serve kimchee and chitlins, the signature foods of Koreans and African Americans, respectively.

Despite the implications of this contrived conclusion, one could argue that the play does at least gesture toward racial reconciliation as the two disputing parties are allowed to air their grievances, thereby having to contend with the other group's responses. But any progress in race relations is arguably located outside of the characters, in the raising of the audience's compassion for the characters. In a few tender moments, several of the characters are humanized for the audience, their daily struggles acknowledged. The audience learns, for example, that Matilda Duvet works long hours "sweeping and cleaning for some uptown people" and that she had been shopping for groceries to cook a consoling meal for her heartbroken sister, visiting from Port-au-Prince. Times are hard in Haiti, and the sister's husband has recently left her. Mak also carries enormous heartache; he has been separated for years from his wife, who lives in Korea and who refuses to join him in the United States until he can save enough

(MORE)
ANNA MAY (CONT'D)

I have indulged greatly in all my passions. ~~And dahling, it felt good,~~ every imaginable vice, felt richly and inhaled deeply. I know what it's like to be very very very very naughty. But let me tell you, ~~passion is like a Chinese finger puzzle. The more you indulge, or struggle against it, the more it entraps you, holds you slave. Passions get you into powerful trouble, leads you to lie next to liars and cheats and false prophets, causes terrible decisions that raise up lifelong regret, remorse, guilt. It leads you to drink and to sexual excess. Hear hear.~~ (raises her cup) ~~Wise up kiddo.~~ Passion leads to wrinkles ~~about the eyes, sallow complexion,~~ hair that turns gray prematurely. It makes the breasts sag and the lips of your secrets to part company with reason. ~~To indulge in one's passions is a sure road to ruination.~~ So I have wrestled the beast of my passions like a lion tamer with a whip (indicates cigarette), plus a little scotch with a tiny splash of water, a short bourbon chaser, and a quick shot of good Russian vodka. I ~~live quietly, wanting nothing more than to stay home. Here at Moongate, safely behind the round red gates. The serenity marred~~ only your ~~monthly visitations and my little brother~~ Richie. I have spent five years in this very chair, wanting nothing more than to sit with my thoughts of nothing. Such a relief, I tell you. To do nothing. To strive for nothing. To want nothing more than to sit and breath. I recommend it highly, the art of sitting still. When I was a child, I was impossibly squirmy. Mother used to play this game, bribe us with a nickel for every minute we could sit still.

CONRAD

Well by now, you must be a millionaire. Thanks for the tea, Anna May, I really gotta go. See you next month!

He exits.

ANNA MAY

A boy and a girl.

LOUD BUZZER. BELL. Lights up on Mother on the phone.

Pages from the revised typescript for Wong's 1996 play, China Doll *(Collection of Elizabeth Wong)*

MARLENE DIETRICH

But you have so much more than silks and brocades to give to the world.

ANNA MAY

Don't lie to me, Marlene.

MARLENE DIETRICH

But that's what we do best, darling. Reality is too confusing. Sometimes a beautiful lie can do more to reveal a truth or heal a hurt. Sometimes a splendid lie breaks open the mundane cocoon of our lives, transforming us, into butterflies. We lie to feel our greatest humanity. This is why we invent ourselves, why we invent stories. The abundance of love in your heart begs to be expressed. Anything less would be an affront to God. Anything less would be tantamount to suicide.

ANNA MAY

Brava Marlene, such a convincing performance. Brava! But I know all your tricks now, I've been your eager pupil. But no more. Let's not *lie* to one another. I couldn't bear it. I've been living in a fantasy, Marlene, more real to me than all the people in my life. I've been pursuing a stupid love, desiring an impossible union, driven by a ridiculous illusion, given to me by you. I was your dupe, your willing fool. Well, no more. Father was right. The world was made for you Marlene, not for me. What kind of daughter doesn't attend her own mother's funeral? Thirty five years old, and I have nothing. Except these silks and brocades. These are worth something.

MARLENE DIETRICH

When the war is over, you'll work again. I promise you. To quit would be a terrible tragedy. Trust me, liebshen. Mother Marlene will take *care of you*.

money to bring her entire family over. Like the lives of many immigrant shop owners, Mak's is tightly circumscribed, bound by the monotony of day-to-day existence: "I am too busy for friends. Wake up at five A.M., work until one A.M. Do it all over again next day. Seven days a week. Even Sunday." Such sympathetic glimpses into the hard lives of both African American and Korean American characters awaken in the audience an empathetic response. The audience is left to wonder at the social strides to be made if only that empathy were grasped by the characters in the play and, on a more ambitious scale, by American society as a whole.

Since its world premiere in 1993 at the Victory Gardens Theater in Chicago, Illinois, *Kimchee and Chitlins* has been performed many times in full-length theater productions and in workshops and readings. It has also been published in an anthology, *But Still, Like Air, I'll Rise: New Asian American Plays* (1997), edited by noted playwright Velina Hasu Houston. Reception of the play has been largely favorable, but a few critics have questioned Wong's choice of genre for exploring the serious and divisive subject matter of the Brooklyn boycott and more generally the state of African American and Korean American race relations. In her interview with Kim, Wong commented on this objection: "I wanted to make it a comedy because people often view race relations with fists clenched, minds closed and points of view narrowed. I think a comedy helps them unclench those fists and kind of relax a little bit. They get to laugh at themselves and step away from the issue enough to look at it and be willing to step into another person's shoes."

In the fall of 1991, after her graduation from Tisch, Wong was awarded a residency fellowship with Yaddo, the prestigious artist colony in Saratoga Springs, New York. The residency allowed Wong to meet artists from other media, including the visual artist Georges Pfruender of Switzerland, with whom Wong has collaborated on what Wong describes as "an ongoing, open-ended site-specific work, first installed in an abandoned hotel in Montreux, Switzerland." The collaboration involves Pfruender's creating visual art inspired by a locale, which he then sends to Wong for interpretation as a theatrical piece. According to Wong, "the advent of the Internet excited additional collaborations in other cities around the world. My positive experience with Georges led me to have a number of wonderfully creative and whimsical associations with other visual artists, notably Judy Gregory and Sharon Harper."

Other unforeseen career paths soon opened for Wong as a result of *Kimchee and Chitlins*. During a reading of the play at the Mark Taper Forum in Los Angeles in October 1992, Janet Blake, then head of the Disney Writing Fellowship, was so impressed by the comedy and television aspects of the play that she invited Wong to take up the coveted fellowship with Disney Studios. During her fellowship year Wong wrote a made-for-television movie, "Colors United," and scripts for popular television sitcoms such as *Seinfeld* and *Roseanne*. None of these scripts was ever produced. On a personal level the fellowship was welcome because it gave Wong the resources to leave New York City and move back to Los Angeles to be closer to home in the wake of her beloved grandmother's death.

The same reading of *Kimchee and Chitlins* at the Mark Taper Forum received the favorable notice of Gary Jacobs, who later became the executive producer of the groundbreaking ABC television sitcom *All-American Girl* (1994–1995). When Wong and her agent, Jason Fogelson, contacted Jacobs about a position as staff writer for the show, Jacobs agreed to an interview, after which he hired Wong. *All-American Girl* was the first network television series with a completely Asian American cast, headed by Margaret Cho, best known at that time for her stand-up comedy. During the early promotion of the show, Wong stressed that the primary aim of the show was to entertain, to persuade mainstream American audiences to accept an Asian American family comedy before tackling such hard issues as racism.

Response to the show, particularly within the Asian American community, ranged from celebration and enthusiastic support to vehement protest. Many delighted in the visibility of Asian Americans on network television, while others berated the show for perpetuating undesirable and damaging stereotypes of Asian Americans. Despite early public interest in the show, midseason ratings began to wane, and network executives decided not to renew the show for a second season. Of the experience, Wong says, "Any other show with our solid ratings would have gone on to another season. But we writers were told, unbelievably, that all the possible storylines for an Asian family had been exhausted and that the show had played itself to its natural conclusion. That is a sad commentary on the realities of Hollywood—the incredible narrowmindedness and fearfulness of the 'other.'"

The idea for Wong's next major play, *China Doll* (1996), a fictionalized account of the life of the pioneering Chinese American actress Anna May Wong, came to Wong in two separate moments. The first occurred while she was browsing in a Greenwich Village card shop in the late 1980s and found a black-and-white postcard image of an Asian woman dressed in a tuxedo, its caption reading "Anna May Wong, American actress." Intrigued by the image, Wong conducted some research and was surprised to find many surface parallels between herself and Anna May Wong. They both grew up in Chinatown in Los Angeles, and they both left the ghetto as soon as they could. But beyond retrieving a few basic facts on the actress, Wong found nothing substantive. The second moment of inspiration was prompted a few years later by the casting controversy surrounding the Broadway musical *Miss Saigon* (1991). Claiming that there were no suitable Asian actors to play the part of a Eurasian engineer, the producers cast a white actor in the role, sparking protests from many Asian Americans in the entertainment industry. Wong decided to respond to the controversy by writing a play about the race- and gender-based impediments faced by an Asian American actress of a past era. The subject of *China Doll* thereby invited implicit parallels to the *Miss Saigon* issue, and in doing so it drew attention to the fact that a lack of opportunities and recognition remains a vexing issue for many Asian American artists.

First conceived as a ten-minute work of response, *China Doll* was soon expanded into a full-length play encompassing more of the historical backdrop that shaped the lives of artists of color of Anna May Wong's era. In her artistic statement on the play, included with it in the anthology *Contemporary Plays by Women of Color* (1996), Wong explains:

> Anna May's life is a barometer for the advances, or lack thereof, in the artistic expression of minority artists, particularly during the halcyon heyday of the Hollywood studio system. The play presented an opportunity for me to discuss various high points in American history and the responses to them by artists of color, such as the then-unrepealed miscegenation laws, the House of Representatives Un-American Activities Committee hearings, and World War II.

Against this complex and shifting cultural landscape, Anna May Wong's life—as a woman and as a Chinese American woman and artist—commands center stage, albeit in a largely fictionalized treatment, and the play thus restores the actress's place in early movie history.

China Doll has received several awards, beginning with the 1998 Jane Chambers Award from the Association for Theatre in Higher Education, given annually to the best unproduced play by a woman playwright. In 2000 it received the Petersen Emerging Playwright Award from Catawba College, which allowed Wong to be in residence at Catawba to work with the director and cast in a rehearsal and production of the show. In 2001 *China Doll* won the Marc David Cohen Award from the Kennedy Center and was featured at Arena Stage in Washington, D.C., as part of the inaugural "Downstairs" reading series for new American plays.

The play has also benefited from development workshops with the Asian Theatre Workshop at the Mark Taper Forum and at Denver Center Theatre, Bowdoin College, and Harvard University.

Following the success of *China Doll,* Wong was commissioned by Actors Theatre of Louisville to write a play for its 1998 Humana Festival. The result was *Let the Big Dog Eat* (1998), which, like *China Doll,* brings to life public figures through imagined characterization and dialogue. This play was occasioned by Ted Turner's headline-making announcement in 1997 that he would donate $1 billion to United Nations programs over the course of ten years. Wong brings together well-known business magnates Turner, Bill Gates, Michael Eisner, and Warren Buffet and sets them on a golf course. A competitive game of golf and a spirited conversation ensue. By facilitating an atmosphere of lighthearted jesting, the casual setting of *Let the Big Dog Eat* counterbalances its serious discussion of class privilege and its attendant social responsibilities.

After *Let the Big Dog Eat* Wong's playwriting developed further through a series of commissions. In 1997 the late John Lion, former cofounder of the Magic Theatre, and the Kennedy Center for the Performing Arts invited Wong to fashion a classical adaptation of Oscar Wilde's short fairy tale "The Happy Prince" (1888) into a play for young audiences. Subsequently, the play was recommissioned in 2001 by the Kennedy Center to be adapted into an opera for children for production in its 2002–2003 season. A more contemporary version of the same play, renamed *Boyd and Oskar,* was also commissioned for the Cincinnati Playhouse in the Park by artistic director Ed Stern and education director Bert Goldstein. *Boyd and Oskar,* which premiered in spring 2000, offers a modern-day parable on the value of human compassion and self-sacrifice.

About the difficulties of adapting Wilde's tragic tale into a more lighthearted children's play, Wong has said:

> I was challenged by the idea of updating the story, and turning it into a comedy. To find comedic elements, in essentially a tragedy, yet staying attentive to Wilde's original tone and intent. The most important thing about adaptation is to preserve the integrity of the Author's intent, especially the ending of the story. I found the essential idea of the story to be very compelling. It basically asks the question: "Why do a good deed, even when there is no earthly reward?"

In *Boyd and Oskar* a talking sparrow and a human being magically turned into a rare showcase sports car (a 1956 Corvette convertible) are rendered into believable characters who experience the joys of friendship and giving and the sorrow of loss.

Following the Kennedy Center commission, Wong was invited to write additional plays for young audiences, including *Prometheus* (1999), an adaptation of Aeschylus's *Prometheus Bound* trilogy, by the Denver Center Theatre Academy and its artistic director, Donovan Marley. In *Prometheus* Wong uses the classical myth to celebrate not only the unspeakably costly sacrifice of Prometheus for humans (the "mudsticks") but the courage and self-sacrifice of the humans themselves for the god whose sacrificial gift to them has incurred the wrath of Zeus. The humans' demonstration of devotion to Prometheus in the end moves Zeus to release the lesser god. The play thus urges the virtues of mutual giving, loyalty, and sacrifice.

Next, Denver Center education director Daniel Renner asked Wong to write *Amazing Adventures of the Marvelous Monkey King* (2001), a martial-arts play and a modern adaptation of classical Chinese opera. After its world premiere at the Denver Center Theatre in January 2001, the play toured for four months in Colorado and Wyoming. In 2000 the Actors Theatre of Louisville, which had commissioned *Let the Big Dog Eat,* again commissioned Wong to write a play–this time on the subject of extreme skateboarding. *Badass of the RIP Eternal* was produced in the 2001 Humana Festival.

In a 2001 interview with fellow playwright Caridad Svich about her participation in children's playwriting, Wong has explained the rewards of the genre for her:

> Why do I love writing for this age group? Children are extraordinarily receptive to myth and mythmaking. They smartly intuit the job of myth, which is, to instruct them entertainingly on the nature of their own humanity. Consequently, this innate understanding makes them the most discerning and critical of all audiences. . . . Always, I am checking to make sure I do not succumb to antiquated notions about children's theater, that they are too delicate and cannot "handle" serious investigations into the heart of the human soul and experience.

Elizabeth Wong's belief in the importance of giving, of helping others, is not a mere abstraction dramatized in her plays for the benefit of young audiences. Beginning as a playwriting teacher for the David Hwang Institute in Los Angeles (1993–1994), and later as playwright-in-residence at Bowdoin College, Maine (1996–1997) and at the University of Southern Maine in 2001, Wong has shared her skills with budding writers. She continues to support rising playwrights by teaching drama and creative-writing courses at the University of Southern California and at the University of California, Santa Barbara, while working on her own projects. Wong sums up her purpose as a writer: "I am an American writer, of Chinese ancestry, blessed with a rich heritage of books and movies and food and people and languages from the world over, because, like it or not, that's the true inheritance, the true nature of America. And as a writer, I've drawn from all of those influences. . . . I am forever trying to live and write beautifully, and hoping to explore and illuminate what it means to be fully human."

Interviews:

Jae-Ha Kim, "Hated Hyphens: Playwright Discards Easy Definitions of Origin," *Chicago Sun-Times,* 6 May 1993;

Mai Li Munoz, "From the Heart to the Stage," *Salisbury Post,* 20 February 2000, p. B1;

Caridad Svich, "A Conversation with Elizabeth Wong," *Dramatist,* 4 (September–October 2001): 22–29.

Reference:

"Going Mainstream: U.S. Television Has Its First Asian-American Show," *Asiaweek,* 20, no. 41 (12 October 1994): 42.

Papers:

Elizabeth Wong's papers, including working drafts of plays, production records, reviews, and correspondence, are in the California Ethnic and Multicultural Archives of the Department of Special Collections, Davidson Library, University of California, Santa Barbara.

Books for Further Reading

Adler, Thomas P. *American Drama, 1940–1960: A Critical History*. New York: Twayne, 1994.

Adler. *Mirror on the Stage: The Pulitzer Play as an Approach to American Drama*. West Lafayette, Ind.: Purdue University Press, 1987.

Aronson, Arnold. *American Avant-Garde Theatre: A History*. London & New York: Routledge, 2000.

Bean, Annemarie, ed. *A Sourcebook on African-American Performance: Plays, People, Movements*. London & New York: Routledge, 1999.

Berkowitz, Gerald M. *American Drama of the Twentieth Century*. London & New York: Longman, 1992.

Berkowitz. *New Broadways: Theatre across America, 1950–1980*. Totowa, N.J.: Rowman & Littlefield, 1982.

Bigsby, Christopher. *Confrontation and Commitment: A Study of Contemporary American Drama, 1959–1966*. London: MacGibbon & Kee, 1967.

Bigsby. *A Critical Introduction to Twentieth-Century American Drama*. 3 volumes. Cambridge: Cambridge University Press, 1982–1985.

Bigsby. *Modern American Drama, 1945–1990*. Cambridge & New York: Cambridge University Press, 1992.

Bloom, Clive, ed. *American Drama*. New York: St. Martin's Press, 1995.

Bonin, Jane F. *Major Themes in Prize-Winning American Drama*. Metuchen, N.J.: Scarecrow Press, 1975.

Bryer, Jackson R. *The Playwright's Art: Conversations with Contemporary American Dramatists*. New Brunswick, N.J.: Rutgers University Press, 1995.

Cole, Susan Letzler. *Playwrights in Rehearsal: The Seduction of Company*. London & New York: Routledge, 2001.

Coven, Brenda. *American Women Dramatists of the Twentieth Century: A Bibliography*. Metuchen, N.J.: Scarecrow Press, 1982.

Coven and Christine E. King. *Joseph Papp and the New York Shakespeare Festival: An Annotated Bibliography*. New York: Garland, 1987.

Craig, Evelyn Quita. *Black Drama of the Federal Theatre Era: Beyond the Formal Horizons*. Amherst: University of Massachusetts Press, 1980.

Debusscher, Gilbert, and Henry I. Schvey, eds. *New Essays on American Drama*. Amsterdam & Atlanta: Rodopi, 1989.

Demastes, William W. *Beyond Naturalism: A New Realism in American Theatre*. Westport, Conn.: Greenwood Press, 1988.

Books for Further Reading

Demastes. *Theatre of Chaos: Beyond Absurdism, into Orderly Disorder.* Cambridge & New York: Cambridge University Press, 1998.

Demastes, ed. *Realism and the American Dramatic Tradition.* Tuscaloosa: University of Alabama Press, 1996.

DiGaetani, John L. *A Search for a Postmodern Theater: Interviews with Contemporary Playwrights.* New York: Greenwood Press, 1991.

Dukore, Bernard F. *American Dramatists, 1918–1945.* New York: Grove, 1984.

Esslin, Martin. *The Theatre of the Absurd,* third edition, revised. London & New York: Penguin, 1991.

Fearnow, Mark. *The American Stage and the Great Depression: A Cultural History of the Grotesque.* Cambridge & New York: Cambridge University Press, 1997.

Gardner, Bonnie Milne. *The Emergence of the Playwright-Director in American Theatre, 1960–1983.* Lewistown, N.Y.: E. Mellen Press, 2001.

Gassner, John. *Directions in Modern Theatre and Drama.* New York: Holt, Rinehart & Winston, 1965.

Gassner. *Dramatic Soundings: Evaluations and Retractions Culled from 30 Years of Dramatic Criticism,* edited by Glenn Loney. New York: Crown, 1968.

Gassner. *Theatre at the Crossroads: Plays and Playwrights of the Mid-Century American Stage.* New York: Holt, Rinehart & Winston, 1960.

Harris, Andrew B. *Broadway Theatre.* London & New York: Routledge, 1994.

Henderson, Cathy, comp. *Twentieth-Century American Playwrights: Views of a Changing Culture.* Austin: Harry Ransom Humanities Research Center, University of Texas at Austin, 1994.

Herman, William. *Understanding Contemporary American Drama.* Columbia: University of South Carolina Press, 1987.

Horn, Barbara Lee. *Ellen Stewart and La MaMa: A Bio-Bibliography.* Westport, Conn.: Greenwood Press, 1993.

Kolin, Philip C., ed. *American Playwrights Since 1945: A Guide to Scholarship, Criticism, and Performance.* New York: Greenwood Press, 1989.

Kolin and Colby H. Kullman, eds. *Speaking on Stage: Interviews with Contemporary American Playwrights.* Tuscaloosa: University of Alabama Press, 1996.

Laufe, Abe. *Anatomy of a Hit: Long Run Plays on Broadway from 1900 to the Present Day.* New York: Hawthorn Books, 1966.

Lawson, John Howard. *Theory and Technique of Playwriting.* New York: Putnam, 1936. Revised and enlarged as *Theory and Technique of Playwriting and Screenwriting.* New York: Putnam, 1949.

Lee, Josephine. *Performing Asian America: Race and Ethnicity on the Contemporary Stage.* Philadelphia: Temple University Press, 1997.

Miller, Jordan Yale. *American Drama Between the Wars: A Critical History.* Boston: Twayne, 1991.

Murphy, Brenda. *American Realism and American Drama, 1880–1940.* Cambridge & New York: Cambridge University Press, 1987.

Murphy, ed. *The Cambridge Companion to American Women Playwrights*. Cambridge & New York: Cambridge University Press, 1999.

Olauson, Judith. *The American Woman Playwright: A View of Criticism and Characterization*. Troy, N.Y.: Whitston, 1981.

Peterson, Jane T., and Suzanne Bennett, eds. *Women Playwrights of Diversity: A Bio-Bibliographical Sourcebook*. Westport, Conn.: Greenwood Press, 1997.

Price, Julia S. *The Off-Broadway Theater*. New York: Scarecrow Press, 1962.

Robinson, Marc. *The Other American Drama*. Cambridge & New York: Cambridge University Press, 1994.

Roudané, Matthew Charles. *American Drama Since 1960: A Critical History*. New York: Twayne, 1996.

Savran, David. *In Their Own Words: Contemporary American Playwrights*. New York: Theatre Communications Group, 1988.

Savran. *The Playwright's Voice: American Dramatists on Memory, Writing and the Politics of Culture*. New York: Theatre Communications Group, 1999.

Schanke, Robert A., and Kim Marra, eds. *Staging Desire: Queer Readings of American Theater History*. Ann Arbor: University of Michigan Press, 2002.

Scharine, Richard G. *From Class to Caste in American Drama: Political and Social Themes Since the 1930s*. New York: Greenwood Press, 1991.

Shank, Theodore. *American Alternative Theater*. New York: Grove, 1982.

Shiach, Don. *American Drama 1900–1990*. Cambridge: Cambridge University Press, 2000.

Stanton, Sarah, and Martin Banham, eds. *Cambridge Paperback Guide to Theatre*. Cambridge & New York: Cambridge University Press, 1996.

Williams, Mance. *Black Theatre in the 1960s and 1970s: A Historical-Critical Analysis of the Movement*. Westport, Conn.: Greenwood Press, 1985.

Wilmeth, Don B., and Tice L. Miller. *The Cambridge Guide to American Theatre*. Cambridge & New York: Cambridge University Press, 1996.

Wilmeth and Bigsby, eds. *The Cambridge History of American Theater*. 1 volume to date. Cambridge & New York: Cambridge University Press, 1998– .

Contributors

Brian M. Amend . . . . *Lynchburg College*
William C. Boles . . . . *Rollins College*
Bridget Brennan . . . . *Catholic University of America*
Angela Courtney . . . . *Fairfield University*
Mary L. Cutler . . . . *University of North Dakota*
Martha Greene Eads . . . . *Valparaiso University*
Colette Epplé . . . . *Catholic University of America*
James Fisher . . . . *Wabash College*
Sara J. Ford . . . . *Inver Hills Community College*
Glenda Frank . . . . *Fashion Institute of Technology, State University of New York*
Kathleen M. Gough . . . . *University of California, Berkeley*
Robert F. Gross . . . . *Hobart and William Smith Colleges*
Mark Hodin . . . . *Canisius College*
Elizabeth Kim . . . . *University of Wisconsin–Whitewater*
Lincoln Konkle . . . . *College of New Jersey*
Susan Koprince . . . . *University of North Dakota*
Jasmin L. Lambert . . . . *College of William and Mary*
Magdalena Mączyńska . . . . *Catholic University of America*
Stephen A. Marino . . . . *Saint Francis College*
Christina S. McGowan . . . . *Fairfield University*
Pamela Monaco . . . . *Mississippi Valley State University*
Jon D. Rossini . . . . *Texas Tech University*
Çiğdem Üsekes . . . . *Western Connecticut State University*
Tracey L. Walters . . . . *Stony Brook University*
Charles S. Watson . . . . *University of Alabama*
Donald E. Whittaker . . . . *Louisiana State University*

Cumulative Index

Dictionary of Literary Biography, Volumes 1-266
Dictionary of Literary Biography Yearbook, 1980-2001
Dictionary of Literary Biography Documentary Series, Volumes 1-19
Concise Dictionary of American Literary Biography, Volumes 1-7
Concise Dictionary of British Literary Biography, Volumes 1-8
Concise Dictionary of World Literary Biography, Volumes 1-4

Cumulative Index

DLB before number: *Dictionary of Literary Biography,* Volumes 1-266
Y before number: *Dictionary of Literary Biography Yearbook,* 1980-2001
DS before number: *Dictionary of Literary Biography Documentary Series,* Volumes 1-19
CDALB before number: *Concise Dictionary of American Literary Biography,* Volumes 1-7
CDBLB before number: *Concise Dictionary of British Literary Biography,* Volumes 1-8
CDWLB before number: *Concise Dictionary of World Literary Biography,* Volumes 1-4

A

Aakjær, Jeppe 1866-1930 ... DLB-214
Abbey, Edward 1927-1989 ... DLB-256
Abbey, Edwin Austin 1852-1911 ... DLB-188
Abbey, Maj. J. R. 1894-1969 ... DLB-201
Abbey Press ... DLB-49
The Abbey Theatre and Irish Drama, 1900-1945 ... DLB-10
Abbot, Willis J. 1863-1934 ... DLB-29
Abbott, Jacob 1803-1879 ... DLB-1, 42, 243
Abbott, Lee K. 1947- ... DLB-130
Abbott, Lyman 1835-1922 ... DLB-79
Abbott, Robert S. 1868-1940 ... DLB-29, 91
Abe Kōbō 1924-1993 ... DLB-182
Abelard, Peter circa 1079-1142? ... DLB-115, 208
Abelard-Schuman ... DLB-46
Abell, Arunah S. 1806-1888 ... DLB-43
Abell, Kjeld 1901-1961 ... DLB-214
Abercrombie, Lascelles 1881-1938 ... DLB-19
Aberdeen University Press Limited ... DLB-106
Abish, Walter 1931- ... DLB-130, 227
Ablesimov, Aleksandr Onisimovich 1742-1783 ... DLB-150
Abraham à Sancta Clara 1644-1709 ... DLB-168
Abrahams, Peter 1919- ... DLB-117, 225; CDWLB-3
Abrams, M. H. 1912- ... DLB-67
Abramson, Jesse 1904-1979 ... DLB-241
Abrogans circa 790-800 ... DLB-148
Abschatz, Hans Aßmann von 1646-1699 ... DLB-168
Abse, Dannie 1923- ... DLB-27, 245
Abutsu-ni 1221-1283 ... DLB-203
Academy Chicago Publishers ... DLB-46
Accius circa 170 B.C.-circa 80 B.C. ... DLB-211
Accrocca, Elio Filippo 1923- ... DLB-128
Ace Books ... DLB-46
Achebe, Chinua 1930- ... DLB-117; CDWLB-3
Achtenberg, Herbert 1938- ... DLB-124
Ackerman, Diane 1948- ... DLB-120
Ackroyd, Peter 1949- ... DLB-155, 231

Acorn, Milton 1923-1986 ... DLB-53
Acosta, Oscar Zeta 1935?- ... DLB-82
Acosta Torres, José 1925- ... DLB-209
Actors Theatre of Louisville ... DLB-7
Adair, Gilbert 1944- ... DLB-194
Adair, James 1709?-1783? ... DLB-30
Adam, Graeme Mercer 1839-1912 ... DLB-99
Adam, Robert Borthwick, II 1863-1940 ... DLB-187
Adame, Leonard 1947- ... DLB-82
Adameșteanu, Gabriel 1942- ... DLB-232
Adamic, Louis 1898-1951 ... DLB-9
Adams, Abigail 1744-1818 ... DLB-200
Adams, Alice 1926-1999 ... DLB-234; Y-86
Adams, Bertha Leith (Mrs. Leith Adams, Mrs. R. S. de Courcy Laffan) 1837?-1912 ... DLB-240
Adams, Brooks 1848-1927 ... DLB-47
Adams, Charles Francis, Jr. 1835-1915 ... DLB-47
Adams, Douglas 1952- ... DLB-261; Y-83
Adams, Franklin P. 1881-1960 ... DLB-29
Adams, Hannah 1755-1832 ... DLB-200
Adams, Henry 1838-1918 ... DLB-12, 47, 189
Adams, Herbert Baxter 1850-1901 ... DLB-47
Adams, J. S. and C. [publishing house] ... DLB-49
Adams, James Truslow 1878-1949 ... DLB-17; DS-17
Adams, John 1735-1826 ... DLB-31, 183
Adams, John 1735-1826 and Adams, Abigail 1744-1818 ... DLB-183
Adams, John Quincy 1767-1848 ... DLB-37
Adams, Léonie 1899-1988 ... DLB-48
Adams, Levi 1802-1832 ... DLB-99
Adams, Richard 1920- ... DLB-261
Adams, Samuel 1722-1803 ... DLB-31, 43
Adams, Sarah Fuller Flower 1805-1848 ... DLB-199
Adams, Thomas 1582 or 1583-1652 ... DLB-151
Adams, William Taylor 1822-1897 ... DLB-42
Adamson, Sir John 1867-1950 ... DLB-98
Adamson, Harold 1906-1980 ... DLB-265
Adcock, Arthur St. John 1864-1930 ... DLB-135
Adcock, Betty 1938- ... DLB-105

"Certain Gifts" ... DLB-105
Adcock, Fleur 1934- ... DLB-40
Addison, Joseph 1672-1719 ... DLB-101; CDBLB-2
Ade, George 1866-1944 ... DLB-11, 25
Adeler, Max (see Clark, Charles Heber)
Adlard, Mark 1932- ... DLB-261
Adler, Richard 1921- and Ross, Jerry 1926-1955 ... DLB-265
Adonias Filho 1915-1990 ... DLB-145
Adorno, Theodor W. 1903-1969 ... DLB-242
Advance Publishing Company ... DLB-49
Ady, Endre 1877-1919 ... DLB-215; CDWLB-4
AE 1867-1935 ... DLB-19; CDBLB-5
Ælfric circa 955-circa 1010 ... DLB-146
Aeschines circa 390 B.C.-circa 320 B.C. ... DLB-176
Aeschylus 525-524 B.C.-456-455 B.C. ... DLB-176; CDWLB-1
Afro-American Literary Critics: An Introduction ... DLB-33
After Dinner Opera Company ... Y-92
Agassiz, Elizabeth Cary 1822-1907 ... DLB-189
Agassiz, Louis 1807-1873 ... DLB-1, 235
Agee, James 1909-1955 ... DLB-2, 26, 152; CDALB-1
The Agee Legacy: A Conference at the University of Tennessee at Knoxville ... Y-89
Aguilera Malta, Demetrio 1909-1981 ... DLB-145
Ahlin, Lars 1915-1997 ... DLB-257
Ai 1947- ... DLB-120
Aichinger, Ilse 1921- ... DLB-85
Aickman, Robert 1914-1981 ... DLB-261
Aidoo, Ama Ata 1942- ... DLB-117; CDWLB-3
Aiken, Conrad 1889-1973 ... DLB-9, 45, 102; CDALB-5
Aiken, Joan 1924- ... DLB-161
Aikin, Lucy 1781-1864 ... DLB-144, 163
Ainsworth, William Harrison 1805-1882 ... DLB-21
Aistis, Jonas 1904-1973 ... DLB-220; CDWLB-4
Aitken, George A. 1860-1917 ... DLB-149
Aitken, Robert [publishing house] ... DLB-49
Akenside, Mark 1721-1770 ... DLB-109
Akins, Zoë 1886-1958 ... DLB-26

325

Cumulative Index

Aksahov, Sergei Timofeevich
    1791-1859..................... DLB-198

Akutagawa, Ryūnsuke 1892-1927 ...... DLB-180

Alabaster, William 1568-1640 .... DLB-132

Alain de Lille circa 1116-1202/1203 ..... DLB-208

Alain-Fournier 1886-1914............. DLB-65

Alanus de Insulis (see Alain de Lille)

Alarcón, Francisco X. 1954- DLB-122

Alarcón, Justo S. 1930- DLB-209

Alba, Nanina 1915-1968............... DLB-41

Albee, Edward 1928- ... DLB-7, 266; CDALB-1

Albert the Great circa 1200-1280 .... DLB-115

Albert, Octavia 1853-ca. 1889 .... DLB-221

Alberti, Rafael 1902-1999 .... DLB-108

Albertinus, Aegidius circa 1560-1620 .... DLB-164

Alcaeus born circa 620 B.C............DLB-176

Alcott, Bronson 1799-1888 .... DLB-1, 223

Alcott, Louisa May 1832-1888
    ... DLB-1, 42, 79, 223, 239; DS-14; CDALB-3

Alcott, William Andrus 1798-1859 .... DLB-1, 243

Alcuin circa 732-804 .... DLB-148

Alden, Beardsley and Company......... DLB-49

Alden, Henry Mills 1836-1919 .... DLB-79

Alden, Isabella 1841-1930.............. DLB-42

Alden, John B. [publishing house]........ DLB-49

Aldington, Richard
    1892-1962 ....DLB-20, 36, 100, 149

Aldis, Dorothy 1896-1966 .... DLB-22

Aldis, H. G. 1863-1919................ DLB-184

Aldiss, Brian W. 1925- DLB-14, 261

Aldrich, Thomas Bailey
    1836-1907................DLB-42, 71, 74, 79

Alegría, Ciro 1909-1967 .... DLB-113

Alegría, Claribel 1924- DLB-145

Aleixandre, Vicente 1898-1984......... DLB-108

Aleksandravičius, Jonas (see Aistis, Jonas)

Aleksandrov, Aleksandr Andreevich
    (see Durova, Nadezhda Andreevna)

Aleramo, Sibilla 1876-1960 .... DLB-114, 264

Alexander, Cecil Frances 1818-1895..... DLB-199

Alexander, Charles 1868-1923 .... DLB-91

Alexander, Charles Wesley
    [publishing house] DLB-49

Alexander, James 1691-1756............ DLB-24

Alexander, Lloyd 1924- DLB-52

Alexander, Sir William, Earl of Stirling
    1577?-1640................... DLB-121

Alexie, Sherman 1966- DLB-175, 206

Alexis, Willibald 1798-1871............ DLB-133

Alfred, King 849-899 .... DLB-146

Alger, Horatio, Jr. 1832-1899 .... DLB-42

Algonquin Books of Chapel Hill........ DLB-46

Algren, Nelson
    1909-1981 .....DLB-9; Y-81, Y-82; CDALB-1

Nelson Algren: An International
    Symposium Y-00

"All the Faults of Youth and Inexperience":
    A Reader's Report on
    Thomas Wolfe's *O Lost* Y-01

Allan, Andrew 1907-1974 .... DLB-88

Allan, Ted 1916-1995................. DLB-68

Allbeury, Ted 1917- DLB-87

Alldritt, Keith 1935- DLB-14

Allen, Ethan 1738-1789................ DLB-31

Allen, Frederick Lewis 1890-1954 ...... DLB-137

Allen, Gay Wilson 1903-1995 .....DLB-103; Y-95

Allen, George 1808-1876 .... DLB-59

Allen, George [publishing house] DLB-106

Allen, George, and Unwin Limited DLB-112

Allen, Grant 1848-1899 ....DLB-70, 92, 178

Allen, Henry W. 1912- Y-85

Allen, Hervey 1889-1949 .... DLB-9, 45

Allen, James 1739-1808................ DLB-31

Allen, James Lane 1849-1925 .... DLB-71

Allen, Jay Presson 1922- DLB-26

Allen, John, and Company............. DLB-49

Allen, Paula Gunn 1939- DLB-175

Allen, Samuel W. 1917- DLB-41

Allen, Woody 1935- DLB-44

Allende, Isabel 1942- DLB-145; CDWLB-3

Alline, Henry 1748-1784............... DLB-99

Allingham, Margery 1904-1966 .... DLB-77

Allingham, William 1824-1889.......... DLB-35

Allison, W. L. [publishing house]........ DLB-49

The *Alliterative Morte Arthure and the Stanzaic*
    Morte Arthur circa 1350-1400 .... DLB-146

Allott, Kenneth 1912-1973 .... DLB-20

Allston, Washington 1779-1843 ...... DLB-1, 235

Almon, John [publishing house] DLB-154

Alonzo, Dámaso 1898-1990 .... DLB-108

Alsop, George 1636-post 1673 .... DLB-24

Alsop, Richard 1761-1815.............. DLB-37

Altemus, Henry, and Company DLB-49

Altenberg, Peter 1885-1919 .... DLB-81

Althusser, Louis 1918-1990 .... DLB-242

Altolaguirre, Manuel 1905-1959........ DLB-108

Aluko, T. M. 1918- DLB-117

Alurista 1947- DLB-82

Alvarez, A. 1929- DLB-14, 40

Alvaro, Corrado 1895-1956 .... DLB-264

Alver, Betti 1906-1989 ..... DLB-220; CDWLB-4

Amadi, Elechi 1934- DLB-117

Amado, Jorge 1912- DLB-113

Ambler, Eric 1909-1998 .... DLB-77

American Conservatory Theatre DLB-7

American Fiction and the 1930s.......... DLB-9

American Humor: A Historical Survey
    East and Northeast
    South and Southwest
    Midwest
    West......................... DLB-11

The American Library in Paris............. Y-93

American News Company DLB-49

The American Poets' Corner: The First
    Three Years (1983-1986) Y-86

American Publishing Company DLB-49

American Stationers' Company DLB-49

American Sunday-School Union DLB-49

American Temperance Union DLB-49

American Tract Society DLB-49

The American Trust for the
    British Library.................... Y-96

The American Writers Congress
    (9-12 October 1981).................. Y-81

The American Writers Congress: A Report
    on Continuing Business............... Y-81

Ames, Fisher 1758-1808 .... DLB-37

Ames, Mary Clemmer 1831-1884 .... DLB-23

Amiel, Henri-Frédéric 1821-1881........DLB-217

Amini, Johari M. 1935- DLB-41

Amis, Kingsley 1922-1995
    .... DLB-15, 27, 100, 139, Y-96; CDBLB-7

Amis, Martin 1949- DLB-194

Ammianus Marcellinus
    circa A.D. 330-A.D. 395 .... DLB-211

Ammons, A. R. 1926- DLB-5, 165

Amory, Thomas 1691?-1788 .... DLB-39

Anania, Michael 1939- DLB-193

Anaya, Rudolfo A. 1937- DLB-82, 206

Ancrene Riwle circa 1200-1225 .... DLB-146

Andersch, Alfred 1914-1980............ DLB-69

Andersen, Benny 1929- DLB-214

Anderson, Alexander 1775-1870........ DLB-188

Anderson, David 1929- DLB-241

Anderson, Frederick Irving 1877-1947 ... DLB-202

Anderson, Margaret 1886-1973 .... DLB-4, 91

Anderson, Maxwell 1888-1959........DLB-7, 228

Anderson, Patrick 1915-1979 .... DLB-68

Anderson, Paul Y. 1893-1938........... DLB-29

Anderson, Poul 1926- DLB-8

Anderson, Robert 1750-1830 .... DLB-142

Anderson, Robert 1917- DLB-7

Anderson, Sherwood
    1876-1941...... DLB-4, 9, 86; DS-1; CDALB-4

Andreae, Johann Valentin 1586-1654.... DLB-164

Andreas Capellanus
    flourished circa 1185 .... DLB-208

Andreas-Salomé, Lou 1861-1937 .... DLB-66

Andres, Stefan 1906-1970.............. DLB-69

Andreu, Blanca 1959- DLB-134

Andrewes, Lancelot 1555-1626 ......DLB-151, 172

Andrews, Charles M. 1863-1943 ....DLB-17

Andrews, Miles Peter ?-1814 .... DLB-89

Andrews, Stephen Pearl 1812-1886 ..... DLB-250

Andrian, Leopold von 1875-1951........ DLB-81

Andrić, Ivo 1892-1975 ......DLB-147; CDWLB-4

Andrieux, Louis (see Aragon, Louis)

Andrus, Silas, and Son DLB-49

Andrzejewski, Jerzy 1909-1983......... DLB-215

Angell, James Burrill 1829-1916..........DLB-64
Angell, Roger 1920- DLB-171, 185
Angelou, Maya 1928- DLB-38; CDALB-7
Anger, Jane flourished 1589............DLB-136
Angers, Félicité (see Conan, Laure)
Anglo-Norman Literature in the Development
 of Middle English Literature........DLB-146
The Anglo-Saxon Chronicle circa 890-1154...DLB-146
The "Angry Young Men"..............DLB-15
Angus and Robertson (UK) Limited.....DLB-112
Anhalt, Edward 1914-2000 ....DLB-26
Anners, Henry F. [publishing house]......DLB-49
Annolied between 1077 and 1081.........DLB-148
Annual Awards for *Dictionary of Literary
 Biography* Editors
 and Contributors...... Y-98, Y-99, Y-00, Y-01
Anscombe, G. E. M. 1919-2001.........DLB-262
Anselm of Canterbury 1033-1109 ....DLB-115
Anstey, F. 1856-1934............ DLB-141, 178
Anthony, Michael 1932- DLB-125
Anthony, Piers 1934- DLB-8
Anthony, Susanna 1726-1791...........DLB-200
Antin, David 1932- DLB-169
Antin, Mary 1881-1949 .... DLB-221; Y-84
Anton Ulrich, Duke of Brunswick-Lüneburg
 1633-1714 ....DLB-168
Antschel, Paul (see Celan, Paul)
Anyidoho, Kofi 1947- DLB-157
Anzaldúa, Gloria 1942- DLB-122
Anzengruber, Ludwig 1839-1889 ....DLB-129
Apess, William 1798-1839 .... DLB-175, 243
Apodaca, Rudy S. 1939- DLB-82
Apollinaire, Guillaume 1880-1918.......DLB-258
Apollonius Rhodius third century B.C....DLB-176
Apple, Max 1941- DLB-130
Appleton, D., and Company DLB-49
Appleton-Century-Crofts...............DLB-46
Applewhite, James 1935- DLB-105
Applewood Books....................DLB-46
April, Jean-Pierre 1948- DLB-251
Apuleius circa A.D. 125-post A.D. 164
 .... DLB-211; CDWLB-1
Aquin, Hubert 1929-1977 ....DLB-53
Aquinas, Thomas 1224 or 1225-1274 ....DLB-115
Aragon, Louis 1897-1982... ....DLB-72, 258
Aralica, Ivan 1930- DLB-181
Aratus of Soli
 circa 315 B.C.-circa 239 B.C. DLB-176
Arbasino, Alberto 1930- DLB-196
Arbor House Publishing Company.......DLB-46
Arbuthnot, John 1667-1735 ....DLB-101
Arcadia House......................DLB-46
Arce, Julio G. (see Ulica, Jorge)
Archer, William 1856-1924.............DLB-10
Archilochhus
 mid seventh century B.C.E. DLB-176

The Archpoet circa 1130?-?............DLB-148
Archpriest Avvakum (Petrovich)
 1620?-1682 ....DLB-150
Arden, John 1930- DLB-13, 245
Arden of Faversham...................DLB-62
Ardis Publishers...................... Y-89
Ardizzone, Edward 1900-1979..........DLB-160
Arellano, Juan Estevan 1947- DLB-122
The Arena Publishing Company.........DLB-49
Arena Stage DLB-7
Arenas, Reinaldo 1943-1990 ....DLB-145
Arendt, Hannah 1906-1975 ....DLB-242
Arensberg, Ann 1937- Y-82
Arghezi, Tudor 1880-1967... DLB-220; CDWLB-4
Arguedas, José María 1911-1969........DLB-113
Argueta, Manilio 1936- DLB-145
Arias, Ron 1941- DLB-82
Arishima, Takeo 1878-1923............DLB-180
Aristophanes circa 446 B.C.-circa 386 B.C.
 .... DLB-176; CDWLB-1
Aristotle 384 B.C.-322 B.C.
 .... DLB-176; CDWLB-1
Ariyoshi Sawako 1931-1984 ....DLB-182
Arland, Marcel 1899-1986..............DLB-72
Arlen, Michael 1895-1956 .... DLB-36, 77, 162
Armah, Ayi Kwei 1939- ... DLB-117; CDWLB-3
Armantrout, Rae 1947- DLB-193
Der arme Hartmann ?-after 1150.......DLB-148
Armed Services Editions DLB-46
Armstrong, Martin Donisthorpe
 1882-1974 ....DLB-197
Armstrong, Richard 1903- DLB-160
Armstrong, Terence Ian Fytton (see Gawsworth, John)
Arndt, Ernst Moritz 1769-1860 ....DLB-90
Arnim, Achim von 1781-1831 ....DLB-90
Arnim, Bettina von 1785-1859..........DLB-90
Arnim, Elizabeth von (Countess Mary
 Annette Beauchamp Russell)
 1866-1941 ....DLB-197
Arno Press........................DLB-46
Arnold, Edward [publishing house]......DLB-112
Arnold, Edwin 1832-1904 ....DLB-35
Arnold, Edwin L. 1857-1935 ....DLB-178
Arnold, Matthew
 1822-1888 ....DLB-32, 57; CDBLB-4
Preface to *Poems* (1853) DLB-32
Arnold, Thomas 1795-1842............DLB-55
Arnott, Peter 1962- DLB-233
Arnow, Harriette Simpson 1908-1986......DLB-6
Arp, Bill (see Smith, Charles Henry)
Arpino, Giovanni 1927-1987 ....DLB-177
Arreola, Juan José 1918- DLB-113
Arrian circa 89-circa 155 ....DLB-176
Arrowsmith, J. W. [publishing house] DLB-106
The Art and Mystery of Publishing:
 Interviews Y-97
Artaud, Antonin 1896-1948............DLB-258

Arthur, Timothy Shay
 1809-1885........ DLB-3, 42, 79, 250; DS-13
The Arthurian Tradition and
 Its European Context DLB-138
Artmann, H. C. 1921-2000 ....DLB-85
Arvin, Newton 1900-1963 ....DLB-103
Asch, Nathan 1902-1964 ....DLB-4, 28
Ascham, Roger 1515 or 1516-1568......DLB-236
Ash, John 1948- DLB-40
Ashbery, John 1927- DLB-5, 165; Y-81
Ashbridge, Elizabeth 1713-1755.........DLB-200
Ashburnham, Bertram Lord
 1797-1878.....................DLB-184
Ashendene Press DLB-112
Asher, Sandy 1942- Y-83
Ashton, Winifred (see Dane, Clemence)
Asimov, Isaac 1920-1992........... DLB-8; Y-92
Askew, Anne circa 1521-1546..........DLB-136
Aspazija 1865-1943 .... DLB-220; CDWLB-4
Asselin, Olivar 1874-1937 ....DLB-92
The Association of American Publishers..... Y-99
The Association for Documentary Editing ... Y-00
Astell, Mary 1666-1731 ....DLB-252
Astley, William (see Warung, Price)
Asturias, Miguel Angel
 1899-1974 .... DLB-113; CDWLB-3
At Home with Albert Erskine Y-00
Atheneum Publishers..................DLB-46
Atherton, Gertrude 1857-1948..... DLB-9, 78, 186
Athlone Press......................DLB-112
Atkins, Josiah circa 1755-1781 ....DLB-31
Atkins, Russell 1926- DLB-41
Atkinson, Louisa 1834-1872 ....DLB-230
The Atlantic Monthly Press.............DLB-46
Attaway, William 1911-1986............DLB-76
Atwood, Margaret 1939- DLB-53, 251
Aubert, Alvin 1930- DLB-41
Aubert de Gaspé, Phillipe-Ignace-François
 1814-1841 ....DLB-99
Aubert de Gaspé, Phillipe-Joseph
 1786-1871 ....DLB-99
Aubin, Napoléon 1812-1890 ....DLB-99
Aubin, Penelope
 1685-circa 1731 ....DLB-39
Preface to *The Life of Charlotta
 du Pont* (1723) DLB-39
Aubrey-Fletcher, Henry Lancelot (see Wade, Henry)
Auchincloss, Louis 1917- DLB-2, 244; Y-80
Auction of Jack Kerouac's *On the Road* Scroll .. Y-01
Auden, W. H. 1907-1973 ...DLB-10, 20; CDBLB-6
Audio Art in America: A Personal Memoir... Y-85
Audubon, John James 1785-1851........DLB-248
Audubon, John Woodhouse
 1812-1862 ....DLB-183
Auerbach, Berthold 1812-1882 ....DLB-133
Auernheimer, Raoul 1876-1948 ....DLB-81
Augier, Emile 1820-1889 ....DLB-192

327

Cumulative Index

Augustine 354-430 .... DLB-115
Responses to Ken Auletta Y-97
Aulus Cellius
  circa A.D. 125-circa A.D. 180? DLB-211
Austen, Jane
  1775-1817 .... DLB-116; CDBLB-3
Auster, Paul 1947- DLB-227
Austin, Alfred 1835-1913 .... DLB-35
Austin, J. L. 1911-1960 .... DLB-262
Austin, Jane Goodwin 1831-1894 .... DLB-202
Austin, John 1790-1859 .... DLB-262
Austin, Mary 1868-1934 ...... DLB-9, 78, 206, 221
Austin, William 1778-1841 .... DLB-74
Australie (Emily Manning)
  1845-1890 .... DLB-230
Author-Printers, 1476–1599 .... DLB-167
Author Websites Y-97
Authors and Newspapers Association DLB-46
Authors' Publishing Company DLB-49
Avallone, Michael 1924-1999 .... Y-99
Avalon Books DLB-46
Avancini, Nicolaus 1611-1686 .... DLB-164
Avendaño, Fausto 1941- DLB-82
Averroëö 1126-1198 .... DLB-115
Avery, Gillian 1926- DLB-161
Avicenna 980-1037 .... DLB-115
Avison, Margaret 1918- DLB-53
Avon Books DLB-46
Avyžius, Jonas 1922-1999 .... DLB-220
Awdry, Wilbert Vere 1911-1997 .... DLB-160
Awoonor, Kofi 1935- DLB-117
Ayckbourn, Alan 1939- DLB-13, 245
Ayer, A. J. 1910-1989 .... DLB-262
Aymé, Marcel 1902-1967 .... DLB-72
Aytoun, Sir Robert 1570-1638 .... DLB-121
Aytoun, William Edmondstoune
  1813-1865 .... DLB-32, 159

B

B. V. (see Thomson, James)
Babbitt, Irving 1865-1933 .... DLB-63
Babbitt, Natalie 1932- DLB-52
Babcock, John [publishing house] DLB-49
Babits, Mihály 1883-1941 ... DLB-215; CDWLB-4
Babrius circa 150-200 .... DLB-176
Baca, Jimmy Santiago 1952- DLB-122
Bacchelli, Riccardo 1891-1985 .... DLB-264
Bache, Benjamin Franklin 1769-1798 ..... DLB-43
Bacheller, Irving 1859-1950 .... DLB-202
Bachmann, Ingeborg 1926-1973 .... DLB-85
Bačinskaitė-Bučienė, Salomėja (see Nėris, Salomėja)
Bacon, Delia 1811-1859 .... DLB-1, 243
Bacon, Francis
  1561-1626 .... DLB-151, 236, 252; CDBLB-1
Bacon, Sir Nicholas circa 1510-1579 ..... DLB-132
Bacon, Roger circa 1214/1220-1292 ..... DLB-115

Bacon, Thomas circa 1700-1768 .... DLB-31
Bacovia, George
  1881-1957 .... DLB-220; CDWLB-4
Badger, Richard G., and Company DLB-49
Bagaduce Music Lending Library Y-00
Bage, Robert 1728-1801 .... DLB-39
Bagehot, Walter 1826-1877 .... DLB-55
Bagley, Desmond 1923-1983 .... DLB-87
Bagley, Sarah G. 1806-1848 .... DLB-239
Bagnold, Enid 1889-1981 ... DLB-13, 160, 191, 245
Bagryana, Elisaveta
  1893-1991 .... DLB-147; CDWLB-4
Bahr, Hermann 1863-1934 .... DLB-81, 118
Bailey, Abigail Abbot 1746-1815 .... DLB-200
Bailey, Alfred Goldsworthy 1905- DLB-68
Bailey, Francis [publishing house] DLB-49
Bailey, H. C. 1878-1961 .... DLB-77
Bailey, Jacob 1731-1808 .... DLB-99
Bailey, Paul 1937- DLB-14
Bailey, Philip James 1816-1902 .... DLB-32
Baillargeon, Pierre 1916-1967 .... DLB-88
Baillie, Hugh 1890-1966 .... DLB-29
Baillie, Joanna 1762-1851 .... DLB-93
Bailyn, Bernard 1922- DLB-17
Bainbridge, Beryl 1933- DLB-14, 231
Baird, Irene 1901-1981 .... DLB-68
Baker, Augustine 1575-1641 .... DLB-151
Baker, Carlos 1909-1987 .... DLB-103
Baker, David 1954- DLB-120
Baker, George Pierce 1866-1935 .... DLB-266
Baker, Herschel C. 1914-1990 .... DLB-111
Baker, Houston A., Jr. 1943- DLB-67
Baker, Nicholson 1957- DLB-227
Baker, Samuel White 1821-1893 .... DLB-166
Baker, Thomas 1656-1740 .... DLB-213
Baker, Walter H., Company
  ("Baker's Plays") DLB-49
The Baker and Taylor Company DLB-49
Bakhtin, Mikhail Mikhailovich
  1895-1975 .... DLB-242
Balaban, John 1943- DLB-120
Bald, Wambly 1902- DLB-4
Balde, Jacob 1604-1668 .... DLB-164
Balderston, John 1889-1954 .... DLB-26
Baldwin, James 1924-1987
  .... DLB-2, 7, 33, 249; Y-87; CDALB-1
Baldwin, Joseph Glover
  1815-1864 .... DLB-3, 11, 248
Baldwin, Louisa (Mrs. Alfred Baldwin)
  1845-1925 .... DLB-240
Baldwin, Richard and Anne
  [publishing house] DLB-170
Baldwin, William circa 1515-1563 ..... DLB-132
Bale, John 1495-1563 .... DLB-132
Balestrini, Nanni 1935- DLB-128, 196
Balfour, Sir Andrew 1630-1694 .... DLB-213
Balfour, Arthur James 1848-1930 .... DLB-190

Balfour, Sir James 1600-1657 .... DLB-213
Ballantine Books DLB-46
Ballantyne, R. M. 1825-1894 .... DLB-163
Ballard, J. G. 1930- DLB-14, 207, 261
Ballard, Martha Moore 1735-1812 ..... DLB-200
Ballerini, Luigi 1940- DLB-128
Ballou, Maturin Murray
  1820-1895 .... DLB-79, 189
Ballou, Robert O. [publishing house] DLB-46
Balzac, Honoré de 1799-1855 .... DLB-119
Bambara, Toni Cade
  1939- DLB-38, 218; CDALB-7
Bamford, Samuel 1788-1872 .... DLB-190
Bancroft, A. L., and Company DLB-49
Bancroft, George 1800-1891 ... DLB-1, 30, 59, 243
Bancroft, Hubert Howe 1832-1918 ... DLB-47, 140
Bandelier, Adolph F. 1840-1914 .... DLB-186
Bangs, John Kendrick 1862-1922 ..... DLB-11, 79
Banim, John 1798-1842 .... DLB-116, 158, 159
Banim, Michael 1796-1874 .... DLB-158, 159
Banks, Iain 1954- DLB-194, 261
Banks, John circa 1653-1706 .... DLB-80
Banks, Russell 1940- DLB-130
Bannerman, Helen 1862-1946 .... DLB-141
Bantam Books DLB-46
Banti, Anna 1895-1985 .... DLB-177
Banville, John 1945- DLB-14
Banville, Théodore de 1823-1891 ..... DLB-217
Baraka, Amiri
  1934- DLB-5, 7, 16, 38; DS-8; CDALB-1
Barańczak, Stanisław 1946- DLB-232
Baratynsky, Evgenii Abramovich
  1800-1844 .... DLB-205
Barbauld, Anna Laetitia
  1743-1825 .... DLB-107, 109, 142, 158
Barbeau, Marius 1883-1969 .... DLB-92
Barber, John Warner 1798-1885 .... DLB-30
Bàrberi Squarotti, Giorgio 1929- DLB-128
Barbey d'Aurevilly, Jules-Amédée
  1808-1889 .... DLB-119
Barbier, Auguste 1805-1882 .... DLB-217
Barbilian, Dan (see Barbu, Ion)
Barbour, John circa 1316-1395 .... DLB-146
Barbour, Ralph Henry 1870-1944 .... DLB-22
Barbu, Ion 1895-1961 ...... DLB-220; CDWLB-4
Barbusse, Henri 1873-1935 .... DLB-65
Barclay, Alexander circa 1475-1552 ..... DLB-132
Barclay, E. E., and Company DLB-49
Bardeen, C. W. [publishing house] DLB-49
Barham, Richard Harris 1788-1845 ..... DLB-159
Barich, Bill 1943- DLB-185
Baring, Maurice 1874-1945 .... DLB-34
Baring-Gould, Sabine
  1834-1924 .... DLB-156, 190
Barker, A. L. 1918- DLB-14, 139
Barker, Arthur, Limited DLB-112

Barker, Clive 1952- DLB-261
Barker, George 1913-1991..............DLB-20
Barker, Harley Granville 1877-1946......DLB-10
Barker, Howard 1946- DLB-13, 233
Barker, James Nelson 1784-1858 ....DLB-37
Barker, Jane 1652-1727 ....DLB-39, 131
Barker, Lady Mary Anne 1831-1911.....DLB-166
Barker, William circa 1520-after 1576 ....DLB-132
Barkov, Ivan Semenovich 1732-1768.....DLB-150
Barks, Coleman 1937- DLB-5
Barlach, Ernst 1870-1938...........DLB-56, 118
Barlow, Joel 1754-1812.................DLB-37
The Prospect of Peace (1778)..............DLB-37
Barnard, John 1681-1770 ....DLB-24
Barnard, Marjorie 1879-1987 and Eldershaw, Flora (M. Barnard Eldershaw) 1897-1956...DLB-260
Barne, Kitty (Mary Catherine Barne) 1883-1957 ....DLB-160
Barnes, A. S., and Company DLB-49
Barnes, Barnabe 1571-1609 ....DLB-132
Barnes, Djuna 1892-1982..........DLB-4, 9, 45
Barnes, Jim 1933- DLB-175
Barnes, Julian 1946- DLB-194; Y-93
Julian Barnes Checklist Y-01
Barnes, Margaret Ayer 1886-1967 ....DLB-9
Barnes, Peter 1931- DLB-13, 233
Barnes, William 1801-1886 ....DLB-32
Barnes and Noble Books DLB-46
Barnet, Miguel 1940- DLB-145
Barney, Natalie 1876-1972 ....DLB-4
Barnfield, Richard 1574-1627............DLB-172
Baron, Richard W., Publishing Company................DLB-46
Barr, Amelia Edith Huddleston 1831-1919 ....DLB-202, 221
Barr, Robert 1850-1912..............DLB-70, 92
Barral, Carlos 1928-1989...............DLB-134
Barrax, Gerald William 1933- DLB-41, 120
Barrès, Maurice 1862-1923 ....DLB-123
Barrett, Eaton Stannard 1786-1820 ......DLB-116
Barrie, J. M. 1860-1937 ......DLB-10, 141, 156; CDBLB-5
Barrie and Jenkins DLB-112
Barrio, Raymond 1921- DLB-82
Barrios, Gregg 1945- DLB-122
Barry, Philip 1896-1949.............DLB-7, 228
Barry, Robertine (see Françoise)
Barry, Sebastian 1955- DLB-245
Barse and Hopkins....................DLB-46
Barstow, Stan 1928- DLB-14, 139
Barth, John 1930- DLB-2, 227
Barthelme, Donald 1931-1989 ....DLB-2, 234; Y-80, Y-89
Barthelme, Frederick 1943- DLB-244; Y-85
Bartholomew, Frank 1898-1985.........DLB-127
Bartlett, John 1820-1905 ....DLB-1, 235

Bartol, Cyrus Augustus 1813-1900 ....DLB-1, 235
Barton, Bernard 1784-1849 ....DLB-96
Barton, John ca. 1610-1675 ....DLB-236
Barton, Thomas Pennant 1803-1869.....DLB-140
Bartram, John 1699-1777 ....DLB-31
Bartram, William 1739-1823 ....DLB-37
Basic Books DLB-46
Basille, Theodore (see Becon, Thomas)
Bass, Rick 1958- DLB-212
Bass, T. J. 1932- Y-81
Bassani, Giorgio 1916- DLB-128, 177
Basse, William circa 1583-1653 ....DLB-121
Bassett, John Spencer 1867-1928 ....DLB-17
Bassler, Thomas Joseph (see Bass, T. J.)
Bate, Walter Jackson 1918-1999 .....DLB-67, 103
Bateman, Christopher [publishing house]................DLB-170
Bateman, Stephen circa 1510-1584 .....DLB-136
Bates, H. E. 1905-1974...........DLB-162, 191
Bates, Katharine Lee 1859-1929 ....DLB-71
Batiushkov, Konstantin Nikolaevich 1787-1855.....................DLB-205
Batsford, B. T. [publishing house] DLB-106
Battiscombe, Georgina 1905- DLB-155
The Battle of Maldon circa 1000 ....DLB-146
Baudelaire, Charles 1821-1867 ....DLB-217
Bauer, Bruno 1809-1882 ....DLB-133
Bauer, Wolfgang 1941- DLB-124
Baum, L. Frank 1856-1919 ....DLB-22
Baum, Vicki 1888-1960 ....DLB-85
Baumbach, Jonathan 1933- Y-80
Bausch, Richard 1945- DLB-130
Bausch, Robert 1945- DLB-218
Bawden, Nina 1925- DLB-14, 161, 207
Bax, Clifford 1886-1962 ....DLB-10, 100
Baxter, Charles 1947- DLB-130
Bayer, Eleanor (see Perry, Eleanor)
Bayer, Konrad 1932-1964 ....DLB-85
Bayley, Barrington J. 1937- DLB-261
Baynes, Pauline 1922- DLB-160
Baynton, Barbara 1857-1929 ....DLB-230
Bazin, Hervé 1911-1996................DLB-83
Beach, Sylvia 1887-1962..........DLB-4; DS-15
Beacon Press DLB-49
Beadle and Adams....................DLB-49
Beagle, Peter S. 1939- Y-80
Beal, M. F. 1937- Y-81
Beale, Howard K. 1899-1959............DLB-17
Beard, Charles A. 1874-1948 ....DLB-17
A Beat Chronology: The First Twenty-five Years, 1944-1969.................DLB-16
Periodicals of the Beat Generation........DLB-16
The Beats in New York City DLB-237
The Beats in the West DLB-237
Beattie, Ann 1947- DLB-218; Y-82

Beattie, James 1735-1803 ....DLB-109
Beatty, Chester 1875-1968.............DLB-201
Beauchemin, Nérée 1850-1931 ....DLB-92
Beauchemin, Yves 1941- DLB-60
Beaugrand, Honoré 1848-1906 ....DLB-99
Beaulieu, Victor-Lévy 1945- DLB-53
Beaumont, Francis circa 1584-1616 and Fletcher, John 1579-1625 ....DLB-58; CDBLB-1
Beaumont, Sir John 1583?-1627.........DLB-121
Beaumont, Joseph 1616-1699 ....DLB-126
Beauvoir, Simone de 1908-1986 ....DLB-72; Y-86
Becher, Ulrich 1910- DLB-69
Becker, Carl 1873-1945 ....DLB-17
Becker, Jurek 1937-1997................DLB-75
Becker, Jurgen 1932- DLB-75
Beckett, Samuel 1906-1989 ....DLB-13, 15, 233; Y-90; CDBLB-7
Beckford, William 1760-1844 ....DLB-39
Beckham, Barry 1944- DLB-33
Becon, Thomas circa 1512-1567 ....DLB-136
Becque, Henry 1837-1899 ....DLB-192
Beddoes, Thomas 1760-1808...........DLB-158
Beddoes, Thomas Lovell 1803-1849 ......DLB-96
Bede circa 673-735....................DLB-146
Bedford-Jones, H. 1887-1949 ....DLB-251
Beecher, Catharine Esther 1800-1878 ..DLB-1, 243
Beecher, Henry Ward 1813-1887 ..DLB-3, 43, 250
Beer, George L. 1872-1920 ....DLB-47
Beer, Johann 1655-1700 ....DLB-168
Beer, Patricia 1919-1999 ....DLB-40
Beerbohm, Max 1872-1956 ....DLB-34, 100
Beer-Hofmann, Richard 1866-1945.......DLB-81
Beers, Henry A. 1847-1926 ....DLB-71
Beeton, S. O. [publishing house] DLB-106
Bégon, Elisabeth 1696-1755 ....DLB-99
Behan, Brendan 1923-1964 ....DLB-13, 233; CDBLB-7
Behn, Aphra 1640?-1689........DLB-39, 80, 131
Behn, Harry 1898-1973 ....DLB-61
Behrman, S. N. 1893-1973............DLB-7, 44
Belaney, Archibald Stansfeld (see Grey Owl)
Belasco, David 1853-1931 ....DLB-7
Belford, Clarke and Company DLB-49
Belinksy, Vissarion Grigor'evich 1811-1848.....................DLB-198
Belitt, Ben 1911- DLB-5
Belknap, Jeremy 1744-1798 ....DLB-30, 37
Bell, Adrian 1901-1980 ....DLB-191
Bell, Clive 1881-1964..................DS-10
Bell, Daniel 1919- DLB-246
Bell, George, and Sons................DLB-106
Bell, Gertrude Margaret Lowthian 1868-1926.....................DLB-174
Bell, James Madison 1826-1902.........DLB-50
Bell, Madison Smartt 1957- DLB-218

Cumulative Index

Bell, Marvin 1937- DLB-5
Bell, Millicent 1919- DLB-111
Bell, Quentin 1910-1996 .... DLB-155
Bell, Robert [publishing house] DLB-49
Bell, Vanessa 1879-1961 .... DS-10
Bellamy, Edward 1850-1898 .... DLB-12
Bellamy, John [publishing house] DLB-170
Bellamy, Joseph 1719-1790 .... DLB-31
La Belle Assemblée 1806-1837 .... DLB-110
Bellezza, Dario 1944-1996 .... DLB-128
Belloc, Hilaire 1870-1953 .... DLB-19, 100, 141, 174
Belloc, Madame (see Parkes, Bessie Rayner)
Bellonci, Maria 1902-1986 .... DLB-196
Bellow, Saul
 1915- DLB-2, 28; Y-82; DS-3; CDALB-1
Belmont Productions DLB-46
Bels, Alberts 1938- DLB-232
Belševica, Vizma 1931- ... DLB-232; CDWLB-4
Bemelmans, Ludwig 1898-1962 .... DLB-22
Bemis, Samuel Flagg 1891-1973 .... DLB-17
Bemrose, William [publishing house] DLB-106
Ben no Naishi 1228?-1271? DLB-203
Benchley, Robert 1889-1945 .... DLB-11
Bencúr, Matej (see Kukučín, Martin)
Benedetti, Mario 1920- DLB-113
Benedict, Pinckney 1964- DLB-244
Benedict, Ruth 1887-1948 .... DLB-246
Benedictus, David 1938- DLB-14
Benedikt, Michael 1935- DLB-5
Benediktov, Vladimir Grigor'evich
 1807-1873 .... DLB-205
Benét, Stephen Vincent
 1898-1943 .... DLB-4, 48, 102, 249
Benét, William Rose 1886-1950 .... DLB-45
Benford, Gregory 1941- Y-82
Benjamin, Park 1809-1864 .... DLB-3, 59, 73, 250
Benjamin, S. G. W. 1837-1914 .... DLB-189
Benjamin, Walter 1892-1940 .... DLB-242
Benlowes, Edward 1602-1676 .... DLB-126
Benn Brothers Limited DLB-106
Benn, Gottfried 1886-1956 .... DLB-56
Bennett, Arnold
 1867-1931 .... DLB-10, 34, 98, 135; CDBLB-5
Bennett, Charles 1899-1995 .... DLB-44
Bennett, Emerson 1822-1905 .... DLB-202
Bennett, Gwendolyn 1902- DLB-51
Bennett, Hal 1930- DLB-33
Bennett, James Gordon 1795-1872 ..... DLB-43
Bennett, James Gordon, Jr. 1841-1918 .... DLB-23
Bennett, John 1865-1956 .... DLB-42
Bennett, Louise 1919- DLB-117; CDWLB-3
Benni, Stefano 1947- DLB-196
Benoit, Jacques 1941- DLB-60
Benson, A. C. 1862-1925 .... DLB-98
Benson, E. F. 1867-1940 .... DLB-135, 153

Benson, Jackson J. 1930- DLB-111
Benson, Robert Hugh 1871-1914 .... DLB-153
Benson, Stella 1892-1933 .... DLB-36, 162
Bent, James Theodore 1852-1897 ...... DLB-174
Bent, Mabel Virginia Anna ?-? DLB-174
Bentham, Jeremy 1748-1832 ... DLB-107, 158, 252
Bentley, E. C. 1875-1956 .... DLB-70
Bentley, Phyllis 1894-1977 .... DLB-191
Bentley, Richard 1662-1742 .... DLB-252
Bentley, Richard [publishing house] DLB-106
Benton, Robert 1932- and Newman,
 David 1937- DLB-44
Benziger Brothers DLB-49
Beowulf circa 900-1000 or 790-825
 .... DLB-146; CDBLB-1
Berent, Wacław 1873-1940 .... DLB-215
Beresford, Anne 1929- DLB-40
Beresford, John Davys
 1873-1947 .... DLB-162, 178, 197
"Experiment in the Novel" (1929) DLB-36
Beresford-Howe, Constance 1922- DLB-88
Berford, R. G., Company DLB-49
Berg, Stephen 1934- DLB-5
Bergengruen, Werner 1892-1964 .... DLB-56
Berger, John 1926- DLB-14, 207
Berger, Meyer 1898-1959 .... DLB-29
Berger, Thomas 1924- DLB-2; Y-80
Bergman, Hjalmar 1883-1931 .... DLB-259
Bergman, Ingmar 1918- DLB-257
Berkeley, Anthony 1893-1971 .... DLB-77
Berkeley, George 1685-1753 .... DLB-31, 101, 252
The Berkley Publishing Corporation DLB-46
Berlin, Irving 1888-1989 .... DLB-265
Berlin, Lucia 1936- DLB-130
Berman, Marshall 1940- DLB-246
Bernal, Vicente J. 1888-1915 .... DLB-82
Bernanos, Georges 1888-1948 .... DLB-72
Bernard, Harry 1898-1979 .... DLB-92
Bernard, John 1756-1828 .... DLB-37
Bernard of Chartres circa 1060-1124? ... DLB-115
Bernard of Clairvaux 1090-1153 .... DLB-208
The Bernard Malamud Archive at the
 Harry Ransom Humanities
 Research Center................... Y-00
Bernard Silvestris
 flourished circa 1130-1160 .... DLB-208
Bernari, Carlo 1909-1992 .... DLB-177
Bernhard, Thomas
 1931-1989 ....DLB-85, 124; CDWLB-2
Bernstein, Charles 1950- DLB-169
Berriault, Gina 1926-1999 .... DLB-130
Berrigan, Daniel 1921- DLB-5
Berrigan, Ted 1934-1983 .... DLB-5, 169
Berry, Wendell 1934- DLB-5, 6, 234
Berryman, John 1914-1972 .... DLB-48; CDALB-1
Bersianik, Louky 1930- DLB-60

Berthelet, Thomas [publishing house] DLB-170
Berto, Giuseppe 1914-1978.............DLB-177
Bertolucci, Attilio 1911- DLB-128
Berton, Pierre 1920- DLB-68
Bertrand, Louis "Aloysius"
 1807-1841......................DLB-217
Besant, Sir Walter 1836-1901...... DLB-135, 190
Bessette, Gerard 1920- DLB-53
Bessie, Alvah 1904-1985................ DLB-26
Bester, Alfred 1913-1987 .... DLB-8
Besterman, Theodore 1904-1976 .... DLB-201
The Bestseller Lists: An Assessment......... Y-84
Bestuzhev, Aleksandr Aleksandrovich
 (Marlinsky) 1797-1837 .... DLB-198
Bestuzhev, Nikolai Aleksandrovich
 1791-1855..................... DLB-198
Betham-Edwards, Matilda Barbara (see Edwards,
 Matilda Barbara Betham-)
Betjeman, John
 1906-1984 .... DLB-20; Y-84; CDBLB-7
Betocchi, Carlo 1899-1986............. DLB-128
Bettarini, Mariella 1942- DLB-128
Betts, Doris 1932- DLB-218; Y-82
Beúkoviù, Matija 1939- DLB-181
Beveridge, Albert J. 1862-1927 ....DLB-17
Beverley, Robert circa 1673-1722 ..... DLB-24, 30
Bevilacqua, Alberto 1934- DLB-196
Bevington, Louisa Sarah 1845-1895..... DLB-199
Beyle, Marie-Henri (see Stendhal)
Białoszewski, Miron 1922-1983 .... DLB-232
Bianco, Margery Williams 1881-1944 ... DLB-160
Bibaud, Adèle 1854-1941 .... DLB-92
Bibaud, Michel 1782-1857 .... DLB-99
Bibliographical and Textual Scholarship
 Since World War II................... Y-89
Bichsel, Peter 1935- DLB-75
Bickerstaff, Isaac John 1733-circa 1808.... DLB-89
Biddle, Drexel [publishing house]........ DLB-49
Bidermann, Jacob
 1577 or 1578-1639 .... DLB-164
Bidwell, Walter Hilliard 1798-1881 ...... DLB-79
Bienek, Horst 1930- DLB-75
Bierbaum, Otto Julius 1865-1910 .... DLB-66
Bierce, Ambrose 1842-1914?
 ....DLB-11, 12, 23, 71, 74, 186; CDALB-3
Bigelow, William F. 1879-1966 .... DLB-91
Biggle, Lloyd, Jr. 1923- DLB-8
Bigiaretti, Libero 1905-1993.............DLB-177
Bigland, Eileen 1898-1970 .... DLB-195
Biglow, Hosea (see Lowell, James Russell)
Bigongiari, Piero 1914- DLB-128
Bilenchi, Romano 1909-1989 .... DLB-264
Billinger, Richard 1890-1965 .... DLB-124
Billings, Hammatt 1818-1874 .... DLB-188
Billings, John Shaw 1898-1975 ....DLB-137
Billings, Josh (see Shaw, Henry Wheeler)
Binding, Rudolf G. 1867-1938 .... DLB-66

Bingay, Malcolm 1884-1953 ....DLB-241
Bingham, Caleb 1757-1817 ....DLB-42
Bingham, George Barry 1906-1988 ......DLB-127
Bingham, Sallie 1937- DLB-234
Bingley, William [publishing house] DLB-154
Binyon, Laurence 1869-1943 ....DLB-19
Biographia Brittanica DLB-142
Biographical Documents I Y-84
Biographical Documents II Y-85
Bioren, John [publishing house] DLB-49
Bioy Casares, Adolfo 1914- DLB-113
Bird, Isabella Lucy 1831-1904 ....DLB-166
Bird, Robert Montgomery 1806-1854 ....DLB-202
Bird, William 1888-1963 ....DLB-4; DS-15
Birken, Sigmund von 1626-1681 ....DLB-164
Birney, Earle 1904-1995 ....DLB-88
Birrell, Augustine 1850-1933 ....DLB-98
Bisher, Furman 1918- DLB-171
Bishop, Elizabeth
 1911-1979 ....DLB-5, 169; CDALB-6
Bishop, John Peale 1892-1944 ....DLB-4, 9, 45
Bismarck, Otto von 1815-1898 ....DLB-129
Bisset, Robert 1759-1805 ....DLB-142
Bissett, Bill 1939- DLB-53
Bitzius, Albert (see Gotthelf, Jeremias)
Bjørnvig, Thorkild 1918- DLB-214
Black, David (D. M.) 1941- DLB-40
Black, Walter J. [publishing house] DLB-46
Black, Winifred 1863-1936 ....DLB-25
The Black Aesthetic: Background DS-8
Black Theaters and Theater Organizations in
 America, 1961-1982:
 A Research List DLB-38
Black Theatre: A Forum [excerpts] DLB-38
Blackamore, Arthur 1679-? DLB-24, 39
Blackburn, Alexander L. 1929- Y-85
Blackburn, John 1923- DLB-261
Blackburn, Paul 1926-1971 ....DLB-16; Y-81
Blackburn, Thomas 1916-1977 ....DLB-27
Blackmore, R. D. 1825-1900 ....DLB-18
Blackmore, Sir Richard 1654-1729 ......DLB-131
Blackmur, R. P. 1904-1965 ....DLB-63
Blackwell, Basil, Publisher DLB-106
Blackwood, Algernon Henry
 1869-1951 .... DLB-153, 156, 178
Blackwood, Caroline 1931-1996 .....DLB-14, 207
Blackwood, William, and Sons, Ltd. DLB-154
Blackwood's Edinburgh Magazine
 1817-1980 ....DLB-110
Blades, William 1824-1890 ....DLB-184
Blaga, Lucian 1895-1961 ....DLB-220
Blagden, Isabella 1817?-1873 ....DLB-199
Blair, Eric Arthur (see Orwell, George)
Blair, Francis Preston 1791-1876 ....DLB-43
Blair, James circa 1655-1743 ....DLB-24
Blair, John Durburrow 1759-1823 ....DLB-37

Blais, Marie-Claire 1939- DLB-53
Blaise, Clark 1940- DLB-53
Blake, George 1893-1961 ....DLB-191
Blake, Lillie Devereux 1833-1913 ...DLB-202, 221
Blake, Nicholas 1904-1972 ....DLB-77
 (see Day Lewis, C.)
Blake, William
 1757-1827 ....DLB-93, 154, 163; CDBLB-3
The Blakiston Company DLB-49
Blandiana, Ana 1942- DLB-232; CDWLB-4
Blanchot, Maurice 1907- DLB-72
Blanckenburg, Christian Friedrich von
 1744-1796 ....DLB-94
Blaser, Robin 1925- DLB-165
Blaumanis, Rudolfs 1863-1908 ....DLB-220
Bleasdale, Alan 1946- DLB-245
Bledsoe, Albert Taylor 1809-1877 ..DLB-3, 79, 248
Bleecker, Ann Eliza 1752-1783 ....DLB-200
Blelock and Company DLB-49
Blennerhassett, Margaret Agnew
 1773-1842 ....DLB-99
Bles, Geoffrey [publishing house] DLB-112
Blessington, Marguerite, Countess of
 1789-1849 ....DLB-166
Blew, Mary Clearman 1939- DLB-256
The Blickling Homilies circa 971 ....DLB-146
Blind, Mathilde 1841-1896 ....DLB-199
Blish, James 1921-1975................DLB-8
Bliss, E., and E. White
 [publishing house] DLB-49
Bliven, Bruce 1889-1977 ....DLB-137
Blixen, Karen 1885-1962 ....DLB-214
Bloch, Robert 1917-1994 ....DLB-44
Block, Lawrence 1938- DLB-226
Block, Rudolph (see Lessing, Bruno)
Blondal, Patricia 1926-1959............DLB-88
Bloom, Harold 1930- DLB-67
Bloomer, Amelia 1818-1894 ....DLB-79
Bloomfield, Robert 1766-1823 ....DLB-93
Bloomsbury Group DS-10
Blotner, Joseph 1923- ,,,,,,,,,,,,,,,,DLB-111
Blount, Thomas 1618?-1679 ....DLB-236
Bloy, Léon 1846-1917 ....DLB-123
Blume, Judy 1938- DLB-52
Blunck, Hans Friedrich 1888-1961 ....DLB-66
Blunden, Edmund 1896-1974 ...DLB-20, 100, 155
Blundeville, Thomas 1522?-1606 ....DLB-236
Blunt, Lady Anne Isabella Noel
 1837-1917 ....DLB-174
Blunt, Wilfrid Scawen 1840-1922 .... DLB-19, 174
Bly, Nellie (see Cochrane, Elizabeth)
Bly, Robert 1926- DLB-5
Blyton, Enid 1897-1968 ....DLB-160
Boaden, James 1762-1839 ....DLB-89
Boas, Frederick S. 1862-1957 ....DLB-149
The Bobbs-Merrill Archive at the
 Lilly Library, Indiana University Y-90

Boborykin, Petr Dmitrievich 1836-1921 ..DLB-238
The Bobbs-Merrill Company DLB-46
Bobrov, Semen Sergeevich
 1763?-1810 ....DLB-150
Bobrowski, Johannes 1917-1965 ....DLB-75
The Elmer Holmes Bobst Awards in Arts
 and Letters Y-87
Bodenheim, Maxwell 1892-1954 ....DLB-9, 45
Bodenstedt, Friedrich von 1819-1892 ....DLB-129
Bodini, Vittorio 1914-1970...........DLB-128
Bodkin, M. McDonnell 1850-1933 ....DLB-70
Bodley, Sir Thomas 1545-1613 ....DLB-213
Bodley Head DLB-112
Bodmer, Johann Jakob 1698-1783 ....DLB-97
Bodmershof, Imma von 1895-1982 ....DLB-85
Bodsworth, Fred 1918- DLB-68
Boehm, Sydney 1908- DLB-44
Boer, Charles 1939- DLB-5
Boethius circa 480-circa 524 ....DLB-115
Boethius of Dacia circa 1240-? DLB-115
Bogan, Louise 1897-1970 ....DLB-45, 169
Bogarde, Dirk 1921- DLB-14
Bogdanovich, Ippolit Fedorovich
 circa 1743-1803 ....DLB-150
Bogue, David [publishing house] DLB-106
Böhme, Jakob 1575-1624 ....DLB-164
Bohn, H. G. [publishing house] DLB-106
Bohse, August 1661-1742 ....DLB-168
Boie, Heinrich Christian 1744-1806 ....DLB-94
Bok, Edward W. 1863-1930 ......DLB-91; DS-16
Boland, Eavan 1944- DLB-40
Boldrewood, Rolf (Thomas Alexander Browne)
 1826?-1915 ....DLB-230
Bolingbroke, Henry St. John, Viscount
 1678-1751 ....DLB-101
Böll, Heinrich
 1917-1985 ....DLB-69; Y-85; CDWLB-2
Bolling, Robert 1738-1775 ....DLB-31
Bolotov, Andrei Timofeevich
 1738-1833 ....DLB-150
Bolt, Carol 1941- DLB-60
Bolt, Robert 1924-1995 ....DLB-13, 233
Bolton, Herbert E. 1870-1953 ....DLB-17
Bonaventura DLB-90
Bonaventure circa 1217-1274 ....DLB-115
Boناviri, Giuseppe 1924- DLB-177
Bond, Edward 1934- DLB-13
Bond, Michael 1926- DLB-161
Boni, Albert and Charles
 [publishing house] DLB-46
Boni and Liveright....................DLB-46
Bonnefoy, Yves 1923- DLB-258
Bonner, Marita 1899-1971 ....DLB-228
Bonner, Paul Hyde 1893-1968............ DS-17
Bonner, Sherwood (see McDowell, Katharine
 Sherwood Bonner)
Robert Bonner's Sons DLB-49

Cumulative Index

Bonnin, Gertrude Simmons (see Zitkala-Ša)

Bonsanti, Alessandro 1904-1984 . . . . .DLB-177

Bontempelli, Massimo 1878-1960 . . . . . . DLB-264

Bontemps, Arna 1902-1973 . . . . DLB-48, 51

The Book Arts Press at the University
of Virginia Y-96

The Book League of America DLB-46

Book Publishing Accounting: Some Basic
Concepts Y-98

Book Reviewing in America: I Y-87

Book Reviewing in America: II Y-88

Book Reviewing in America: III. Y-89

Book Reviewing in America: IV. Y-90

Book Reviewing in America: V Y-91

Book Reviewing in America: VI. Y-92

Book Reviewing in America: VII Y-93

Book Reviewing in America: VIII Y-94

Book Reviewing in America and the
Literary Scene Y-95

Book Reviewing and the
Literary Scene Y-96, Y-97

Book Supply Company DLB-49

The Book Trade History Group Y-93

The Book Trade and the Internet Y-00

The Booker Prize Y-96

Address by Anthony Thwaite,
Chairman of the Booker Prize Judges
Comments from Former Booker
Prize Winners Y-86

The Books of George V. Higgins:
A Checklist of Editions and Printings Y-00

Boorde, Andrew circa 1490-1549 . . . . DLB-136

Boorstin, Daniel J. 1914- DLB-17

Booth, Franklin 1874-1948 . . . . DLB-188

Booth, Mary L. 1831-1889 . . . . DLB-79

Booth, Philip 1925- Y-82

Booth, Wayne C. 1921- DLB-67

Booth, William 1829-1912 . . . . DLB-190

Borchardt, Rudolf 1877-1945 . . . . DLB-66

Borchert, Wolfgang 1921-1947 . . . . . DLB-69, 124

Borel, Pétrus 1809-1859 . . . . DLB-119

Borges, Jorge Luis
1899-1986 . . . . . . .DLB-113; Y-86; CDWLB-3

Borgese, Giuseppe Antonio 1882-1952 . . . DLB-264

Börne, Ludwig 1786-1837 . . . . DLB-90

Bornstein, Miriam 1950- DLB-209

Borowski, Tadeusz
1922-1951 . . . . DLB-215; CDWLB-4

Borrow, George 1803-1881 . . . . . DLB-21, 55, 166

Bosanquet, Bernard 1848-1923 . . . . DLB-262

Bosch, Juan 1909- DLB-145

Bosco, Henri 1888-1976 . . . . DLB-72

Bosco, Monique 1927- DLB-53

Bosman, Herman Charles 1905-1951 . . . . DLB-225

Bostic, Joe 1908-1988 . . . . DLB-241

Boston, Lucy M. 1892-1990 . . . . DLB-161

Boswell, James
1740-1795 . . . . DLB-104, 142; CDBLB-2

Boswell, Robert 1953- DLB-234

Bote, Hermann
circa 1460-circa 1520 . . . . .DLB-179

Botev, Khristo 1847-1876 . . . . DLB-147

Botta, Anne C. Lynch 1815-1891 . . . . . DLB-3, 250

Botto, Ján (see Krasko, Ivan)

Bottome, Phyllis 1882-1963 . . . . DLB-197

Bottomley, Gordon 1874-1948 . . . . DLB-10

Bottoms, David 1949- DLB-120; Y-83

Bottrall, Ronald 1906- DLB-20

Bouchardy, Joseph 1810-1870 . . . . DLB-192

Boucher, Anthony 1911-1968 . . . . DLB-8

Boucher, Jonathan 1738-1804 . . . . DLB-31

Boucher de Boucherville, George
1814-1894 . . . . DLB-99

Boudreau, Daniel (see Coste, Donat)

Bourassa, Napoléon 1827-1916 . . . . DLB-99

Bourget, Paul 1852-1935 . . . . DLB-123

Bourinot, John George 1837-1902 . . . . . . DLB-99

Bourjaily, Vance 1922- DLB-2, 143

Bourne, Edward Gaylord
1860-1908 . . . . DLB-47

Bourne, Randolph 1886-1918 . . . . DLB-63

Bousoño, Carlos 1923- DLB-108

Bousquet, Joë 1897-1950 . . . . DLB-72

Bova, Ben 1932- Y-81

Bovard, Oliver K. 1872-1945 . . . . DLB-25

Bove, Emmanuel 1898-1945 . . . . DLB-72

Bowen, Elizabeth
1899-1973 . . . . DLB-15, 162; CDBLB-7

Bowen, Francis 1811-1890 . . . . . . DLB-1, 59, 235

Bowen, John 1924- DLB-13

Bowen, Marjorie 1886-1952 . . . . DLB-153

Bowen-Merrill Company DLB-49

Bowering, George 1935- DLB-53

Bowers, Bathsheba 1671-1718 . . . . DLB-200

Bowers, Claude G. 1878-1958 . . . . DLB-17

Bowers, Edgar 1924-2000 . . . . DLB-5

Bowers, Fredson Thayer
1905-1991 . . . . .DLB-140; Y-80, 91

Bowles, Paul 1910-1999 . . . . . .DLB-5, 6, 218; Y-99

Bowles, Samuel, III 1826-1878 . . . . DLB-43

Bowles, William Lisles 1762-1850 . . . . DLB-93

Bowman, Louise Morey 1882-1944 . . . . . . DLB-68

Boyd, James 1888-1944 . . . . DLB-9; DS-16

Boyd, John 1919- DLB-8

Boyd, Martin 1893-1972 . . . . DLB-260

Boyd, Thomas 1898-1935 . . . . DLB-9; DS-16

Boyd, William 1952- DLB-231

Boye, Karin 1900-1941 . . . . DLB-259

Boyesen, Hjalmar Hjorth
1848-1895 . . . . .DLB-12, 71; DS-13

Boyle, Kay 1902-1992 . . . . .DLB-4, 9, 48, 86; Y-93

Boyle, Roger, Earl of Orrery 1621-1679 . . . DLB-80

Boyle, T. Coraghessan 1948- DLB-218; Y-86

Božić, Mirko 1919- DLB-181

Brackenbury, Alison 1953- DLB-40

Brackenridge, Hugh Henry
1748-1816 .DLB-11, 37

Brackett, Charles 1892-1969 . . . . DLB-26

Brackett, Leigh 1915-1978 . . . . DLB-8, 26

Bradburn, John [publishing house] DLB-49

Bradbury, Malcolm 1932-2000 . . . . . . DLB-14, 207

Bradbury, Ray 1920- DLB-2, 8; CDALB-6

Bradbury and Evans DLB-106

Braddon, Mary Elizabeth
1835-1915 . . . . .DLB-18, 70, 156

Bradford, Andrew 1686-1742 . . . . DLB-43, 73

Bradford, Gamaliel 1863-1932 . . . . .DLB-17

Bradford, John 1749-1830 . . . . DLB-43

Bradford, Roark 1896-1948 . . . . DLB-86

Bradford, William 1590-1657 . . . . DLB-24, 30

Bradford, William, III 1719-1791 . . . . . DLB-43, 73

Bradlaugh, Charles 1833-1891 . . . . DLB-57

Bradley, David 1950- DLB-33

Bradley, F. H. 1846-1924 . . . . DLB-262

Bradley, Ira, and Company DLB-49

Bradley, J. W., and Company DLB-49

Bradley, Katherine Harris (see Field, Michael)

Bradley, Marion Zimmer 1930-1999 . . . . . . DLB-8

Bradley, William Aspenwall 1878-1939 . . . . DLB-4

Bradshaw, Henry 1831-1886 . . . . DLB-184

Bradstreet, Anne
1612 or 1613-1672 . . . . DLB-24; CDABL-2

Bradūnas, Kazys 1917- DLB-220

Bradwardine, Thomas circa
1295-1349 . . . . DLB-115

Brady, Frank 1924-1986 . . . . DLB-111

Brady, Frederic A. [publishing house] DLB-49

Bragg, Melvyn 1939- DLB-14

Brainard, Charles H. [publishing house] . . DLB-49

Braine, John 1922-1986 . DLB-15; Y-86; CDBLB-7

Braithwait, Richard 1588-1673 . . . . DLB-151

Braithwaite, William Stanley
1878-1962 .DLB-50, 54

Braker, Ulrich 1735-1798 . . . . DLB-94

Bramah, Ernest 1868-1942 . . . . DLB-70

Branagan, Thomas 1774-1843 . . . . DLB-37

Brancati, Vitaliano 1907-1954 . . . . DLB-264

Branch, William Blackwell 1927- DLB-76

Brand, Max (see Faust, Frederick Schiller)

Branden Press DLB-46

Branner, H.C. 1903-1966 . . . . DLB-214

Brant, Sebastian 1457-1521 . . . . .DLB-179

Brassey, Lady Annie (Allnutt)
1839-1887 . . . . DLB-166

Brathwaite, Edward Kamau
1930- DLB-125; CDWLB-3

Brault, Jacques 1933- DLB-53

Braun, Matt 1932- DLB-212

Braun, Volker 1939- DLB-75

Brautigan, Richard
1935-1984 . . . . .DLB-2, 5, 206; Y-80, Y-84

Braxton, Joanne M. 1950- DLB-41
Bray, Anne Eliza 1790-1883 .... DLB-116
Bray, Thomas 1656-1730 .... DLB-24
Brazdžionis, Bernardas 1907- DLB-220
Braziller, George [publishing house] DLB-46
The Bread Loaf Writers' Conference 1983 ... Y-84
Breasted, James Henry 1865-1935 .... DLB-47
Brecht, Bertolt
   1898-1956 .... DLB-56, 124; CDWLB-2
Bredel, Willi 1901-1964 .... DLB-56
Bregendahl, Marie 1867-1940 .... DLB-214
Breitinger, Johann Jakob 1701-1776 .... DLB-97
Bremser, Bonnie 1939- DLB-16
Bremser, Ray 1934- DLB-16
Brennan, Christopher 1870-1932 .... DLB-230
Brentano, Bernard von 1901-1964 .... DLB-56
Brentano, Clemens 1778-1842 .... DLB-90
Brentano's DLB-49
Brenton, Howard 1942- DLB-13
Breslin, Jimmy 1929-1996 .... DLB-185
Breton, André 1896-1966 .... DLB-65, 258
Breton, Nicholas circa 1555-circa 1626 ... DLB-136
The Breton Lays
   1300-early fifteenth century DLB-146
Brewer, Luther A. 1858-1933 .... DLB-187
Brewer, Warren and Putnam DLB-46
Brewster, Elizabeth 1922- DLB-60
Breytenbach, Breyten 1939- DLB-225
Bridge, Ann (Lady Mary Dolling Sanders
   O'Malley) 1889-1974 .... DLB-191
Bridge, Horatio 1806-1893 .... DLB-183
Bridgers, Sue Ellen 1942- DLB-52
Bridges, Robert
   1844-1930 .... DLB-19, 98; CDBLB-5
The Bridgewater Library DLB-213
Bridie, James 1888-1951 .... DLB-10
Brieux, Eugene 1858-1932 .... DLB-192
Brigadere, Anna 1861-1933 .... DLB-220
Briggs, Charles Frederick
   1804-1877 .... DLB-3, 250
Brighouse, Harold 1882-1958 .... DLB-10
Bright, Mary Chavelita Dunne (see Egerton, George)
Brimmer, B. J., Company DLB-46
Brines, Francisco 1932- DLB-134
Brink, André 1935- DLB-225
Brinley, George, Jr. 1817-1875 .... DLB-140
Brinnin, John Malcolm 1916-1998 .... DLB-48
Brisbane, Albert 1809-1890 .... DLB-3, 250
Brisbane, Arthur 1864-1936 .... DLB-25
British Academy DLB-112
The British Critic 1793-1843 .... DLB-110
The British Library and the Regular
   Readers' Group Y-91
British Literary Prizes Y-98
The British Review and London Critical
   Journal 1811-1825 .... DLB-110

British Travel Writing, 1940-1997 .... DLB-204
Brito, Aristeo 1942- DLB-122
Brittain, Vera 1893-1970 .... DLB-191
Brizeux, Auguste 1803-1858 .... DLB-217
Broadway Publishing Company DLB-46
Broch, Hermann
   1886-1951 .... DLB-85, 124; CDWLB-2
Brochu, André 1942- DLB-53
Brock, Edwin 1927- DLB-40
Brockes, Barthold Heinrich 1680-1747 ... DLB-168
Brod, Max 1884-1968 .... DLB-81
Brodber, Erna 1940- DLB-157
Brodhead, John R. 1814-1873 .... DLB-30
Brodkey, Harold 1930-1996 .... DLB-130
Brodsky, Joseph 1940-1996 .... Y-87
Brodsky, Michael 1948- DLB-244
Broeg, Bob 1918- DLB-171
Brøgger, Suzanne 1944- DLB-214
Brome, Richard circa 1590-1652 .... DLB-58
Brome, Vincent 1910- DLB-155
Bromfield, Louis 1896-1956 .... DLB-4, 9, 86
Bromige, David 1933- DLB-193
Broner, E. M. 1930- DLB-28
Bronk, William 1918-1999 .... DLB-165
Bronnen, Arnolt 1895-1959 .... DLB-124
Brontë, Anne 1820-1849 .... DLB-21, 199
Brontë, Charlotte
   1816-1855 ...... DLB-21, 159, 199; CDBLB-4
Brontë, Emily
   1818-1848 ...... DLB-21, 32, 199; CDBLB-4
Brook, Stephen 1947- DLB-204
Brook Farm 1841-1847 .... DLB-223
Brooke, Frances 1724-1789 .... DLB-39, 99
Brooke, Henry 1703?-1783 .... DLB-39
Brooke, L. Leslie 1862-1940 .... DLB-141
Brooke, Margaret, Ranee of Sarawak
   1849-1936 .... DLB-174
Brooke, Rupert
   1887-1915 .... DLB-19, 216; CDBLB-6
Brooker, Bertram 1888-1955 .... DLB-88
Brooke-Rose, Christine 1923- DLB-14, 231
Brookner, Anita 1928- DLB-194; Y-87
Brooks, Charles Timothy 1813-1883 ... DLB-1, 243
Brooks, Cleanth 1906-1994 .... DLB-63; Y-94
Brooks, Gwendolyn
   1917-2000 .... DLB-5, 76, 165; CDALB-1
Brooks, Jeremy 1926- DLB-14
Brooks, Mel 1926- DLB-26
Brooks, Noah 1830-1903 .... DLB-42; DS-13
Brooks, Richard 1912-1992 .... DLB-44
Brooks, Van Wyck
   1886-1963 .... DLB-45, 63, 103
Brophy, Brigid 1929-1995 .... DLB-14
Brophy, John 1899-1965 .... DLB-191
Brossard, Chandler 1922-1993 .... DLB-16
Brossard, Nicole 1943- DLB-53

Broster, Dorothy Kathleen 1877-1950 .... DLB-160
Brother Antoninus (see Everson, William)
Brotherton, Lord 1856-1930 .... DLB-184
Brougham and Vaux, Henry Peter Brougham,
   Baron 1778-1868 .... DLB-110, 158
Brougham, John 1810-1880 .... DLB-11
Broughton, James 1913-1999 .... DLB-5
Broughton, Rhoda 1840-1920 .... DLB-18
Broun, Heywood 1888-1939 .... DLB-29, 171
Brown, Alice 1856-1948 .... DLB-78
Brown, Bob 1886-1959 .... DLB-4, 45
Brown, Cecil 1943- DLB-33
Brown, Charles Brockden
   1771-1810 .... DLB-37, 59, 73; CDALB-2
Brown, Christy 1932-1981 .... DLB-14
Brown, Dee 1908- Y-80
Brown, Frank London 1927-1962 .... DLB-76
Brown, Fredric 1906-1972 .... DLB-8
Brown, George Mackay
   1921-1996 .... DLB-14, 27, 139
Brown, Harry 1917-1986 .... DLB-26
Brown, Larry 1951- DLB-234
Brown, Lew (see DeSylva, Buddy)
Brown, Marcia 1918- DLB-61
Brown, Margaret Wise 1910-1952 .... DLB-22
Brown, Morna Doris (see Ferrars, Elizabeth)
Brown, Oliver Madox 1855-1874 .... DLB-21
Brown, Sterling 1901-1989 .... DLB-48, 51, 63
Brown, T. E. 1830-1897 .... DLB-35
Brown, Thomas Alexander (see Boldrewood, Rolf)
Brown, Warren 1894-1978 .... DLB-241
Brown, William Hill 1765-1793 .... DLB-37
Brown, William Wells
   1815-1884 .... DLB-3, 50, 183, 248
Browne, Charles Farrar 1834-1867 .... DLB-11
Browne, Frances 1816-1879 .... DLB-199
Browne, Francis Fisher 1843-1913 .... DLB-79
Browne, Howard 1908-1999 .... DLB-226
Browne, J. Ross 1821-1875 .... DLB-202
Browne, Michael Dennis 1940- DLB-40
Browne, Sir Thomas 1605-1682 .... DLB-151
Browne, William, of Tavistock
   1590-1645 .... DLB-121
Browne, Wynyard 1911-1964 .... DLB-13, 233
Browne and Nolan DLB-106
Brownell, W. C. 1851-1928 .... DLB-71
Browning, Elizabeth Barrett
   1806-1861 .... DLB-32, 199; CDBLB-4
Browning, Robert
   1812-1889 .... DLB-32, 163; CDBLB-4
Introductory Essay: Letters of Percy
   Bysshe Shelley (1852) DLB-32
Brownjohn, Allan 1931- DLB-40
Brownson, Orestes Augustus
   1803-1876 .... DLB-1, 59, 73, 243
Bruccoli, Matthew J. 1931- DLB-103
Bruce, Charles 1906-1971 .... DLB-68

John Edward Bruce: Three Documents . . . DLB-50
Bruce, Leo 1903-1979 . . . . DLB-77
Bruce, Mary Grant 1878-1958 . . . . DLB-230
Bruce, Philip Alexander 1856-1933 . . . . . . DLB-47
Bruce Humphries [publishing house] DLB-46
Bruce-Novoa, Juan 1944- DLB-82
Bruckman, Clyde 1894-1955 . . . . DLB-26
Bruckner, Ferdinand 1891-1958 . . . . DLB-118
Brundage, John Herbert (see Herbert, John)
Brunner, John 1934-1995 . . . . DLB-261
Brutus, Dennis
  1924- DLB-117, 225; CDWLB-3
Bryan, C. D. B. 1936- DLB-185
Bryant, Arthur 1899-1985 . . . . DLB-149
Bryant, William Cullen 1794-1878
  . . . . DLB-3, 43, 59, 189, 250; CDALB-2
Bryce Echenique, Alfredo
  1939- DLB-145; CDWLB-3
Bryce, James 1838-1922 . . . . DLB-166, 190
Bryden, Bill 1942- DLB-233
Brydges, Sir Samuel Egerton 1762-1837 . . DLB-107
Bryskett, Lodowick 1546?-1612 . . . . DLB-167
Buchan, John 1875-1940 . . . . DLB-34, 70, 156
Buchanan, George 1506-1582 . . . . DLB-132
Buchanan, Robert 1841-1901 . . . . DLB-18, 35
"The Fleshly School of Poetry and Other
  Phenomena of the Day" (1872), by
  Robert Buchanan DLB-35
"The Fleshly School of Poetry: Mr. D. G.
  Rossetti" (1871), by Thomas Maitland
  (Robert Buchanan) DLB-35
Buchman, Sidney 1902-1975 . . . . DLB-26
Buchner, Augustus 1591-1661 . . . . DLB-164
Büchner, Georg 1813-1837 . . DLB-133; CDWLB-2
Bucholtz, Andreas Heinrich 1607-1671 . . . DLB-168
Buck, Pearl S. 1892-1973 . . DLB-9, 102; CDALB-7
Bucke, Charles 1781-1846 . . . . DLB-110
Bucke, Richard Maurice 1837-1902 . . . . . . DLB-99
Buckingham, Joseph Tinker 1779-1861 and
  Buckingham, Edwin 1810-1833 . . . . . . DLB-73
Buckler, Ernest 1908-1984 . . . . DLB-68
Buckley, William F., Jr. 1925- DLB-137; Y-80
Buckminster, Joseph Stevens
  1784-1812 . . . . DLB-37
Buckner, Robert 1906- DLB-26
Budd, Thomas ?-1698 . . . . DLB-24
Budrys, A. J. 1931- DLB-8
Buechner, Frederick 1926- Y-80
Buell, John 1927- DLB-53
Bufalino, Gesualdo 1920-1996 . . . . DLB-196
Buffum, Job [publishing house] DLB-49
Bugnet, Georges 1879-1981 . . . . DLB-92
Buies, Arthur 1840-1901 . . . . DLB-99
Building the New British Library
  at St Pancras Y-94
Bukowski, Charles 1920-1994 . . . DLB-5, 130, 169
Bulatović, Miodrag
  1930-1991 . . . . DLB-181; CDWLB-4

Bulgarin, Faddei Venediktovich
  1789-1859 . . . . DLB-198
Bulger, Bozeman 1877-1932 . . . . DLB-171
Bullein, William
  between 1520 and 1530-1576 . . . . DLB-167
Bullins, Ed 1935- DLB-7, 38, 249
Bulwer, John 1606-1656 . . . . DLB-236
Bulwer-Lytton, Edward (also Edward Bulwer)
  1803-1873 . . . . DLB-21
"On Art in Fiction" (1838) DLB-21
Bumpus, Jerry 1937- Y-81
Bunce and Brother DLB-49
Bunner, H. C. 1855-1896 . . . . DLB-78, 79
Bunting, Basil 1900-1985 . . . . DLB-20
Buntline, Ned (Edward Zane Carroll Judson)
  1821-1886 . . . . DLB-186
Bunyan, John 1628-1688 . . . . . DLB-39; CDBLB-2
Burch, Robert 1925- DLB-52
Burciaga, José Antonio 1940- DLB-82
Burdekin, Katharine 1896-1963 . . . . DLB-255
Bürger, Gottfried August 1747-1794 . . . . . DLB-94
Burgess, Anthony
  1917-1993 . . . . . . DLB-14, 194, 261; CDBLB-8
The Anthony Burgess Archive at
  the Harry Ransom Humanities
  Research Center Y-98
Anthony Burgess's 99 Novels:
  An Opinion Poll Y-84
Burgess, Gelett 1866-1951 . . . . DLB-11
Burgess, John W. 1844-1931 . . . . DLB-47
Burgess, Thornton W. 1874-1965 . . . . DLB-22
Burgess, Stringer and Company DLB-49
Burick, Si 1909-1986 . . . . DLB-171
Burk, John Daly circa 1772-1808 . . . . DLB-37
Burk, Ronnie 1955- DLB-209
Burke, Edmund 1729?-1797 . . . . DLB-104, 252
Burke, James Lee 1936- DLB-226
Burke, Johnny 1908-1964 . . . . DLB-265
Burke, Kenneth 1897-1993 . . . . DLB-45, 63
Burke, Thomas 1886-1945 . . . . DLB-197
Burley, Dan 1907-1962 . . . . DLB-241
Burlingame, Edward Livermore
  1848-1922 . . . . DLB-79
Burman, Carina 1960- DLB-257
Burnet, Gilbert 1643-1715 . . . . DLB-101
Burnett, Frances Hodgson
  1849-1924 . . . . DLB-42, 141; DS-13, 14
Burnett, W. R. 1899-1982 . . . . DLB-9, 226
Burnett, Whit 1899-1973 and
  Martha Foley 1897-1977 . . . . DLB-137
Burney, Fanny 1752-1840 . . . . DLB-39
Dedication, The Wanderer (1814) DLB-39
Preface to Evelina (1778) DLB-39
Burns, Alan 1929- DLB-14, 194
Burns, John Horne 1916-1953 . . . . Y-85
Burns, Robert 1759-1796 . . . . DLB-109; CDBLB-3
Burns and Oates DLB-106
Burnshaw, Stanley 1906- DLB-48

Burr, C. Chauncey 1815?-1883 . . . . DLB-79
Burr, Esther Edwards 1732-1758 . . . . DLB-200
Burroughs, Edgar Rice 1875-1950 . . . . DLB-8
Burroughs, John 1837-1921 . . . . DLB-64
Burroughs, Margaret T. G. 1917- DLB-41
Burroughs, William S., Jr. 1947-1981 . . . . DLB-16
Burroughs, William Seward 1914-1997
  . . . . DLB-2, 8, 16, 152, 237; Y-81, Y-97
Burroway, Janet 1936- DLB-6
Burt, Maxwell Struthers
  1882-1954 . . . . DLB-86; DS-16
Burt, A. L., and Company DLB-49
Burton, Hester 1913- DLB-161
Burton, Isabel Arundell 1831-1896 . . . . . . DLB-166
Burton, Miles (see Rhode, John)
Burton, Richard Francis
  1821-1890 . . . . DLB-55, 166, 184
Burton, Robert 1577-1640 . . . . DLB-151
Burton, Virginia Lee 1909-1968 . . . . DLB-22
Burton, William Evans 1804-1860 . . . . DLB-73
Burwell, Adam Hood 1790-1849 . . . . DLB-99
Bury, Lady Charlotte 1775-1861 . . . . DLB-116
Busch, Frederick 1941- DLB-6, 218
Busch, Niven 1903-1991 . . . . DLB-44
Bushnell, Horace 1802-1876 . . . . DS-13
Bussieres, Arthur de 1877-1913 . . . . DLB-92
Butler, Charles ca. 1560-1647 . . . . DLB-236
Butler, Guy 1918- DLB-225
Butler, E. H., and Company DLB-49
Butler, Joseph 1692-1752 . . . . DLB-252
Butler, Josephine Elizabeth
  1828-1906 . . . . DLB-190
Butler, Juan 1942-1981 . . . . DLB-53
Butler, Judith 1956- DLB-246
Butler, Octavia E. 1947- DLB-33
Butler, Pierce 1884-1953 . . . . DLB-187
Butler, Robert Olen 1945- DLB-173
Butler, Samuel 1613-1680 . . . . DLB-101, 126
Butler, Samuel 1835-1902 . . . . DLB-18, 57, 174
Butler, William Francis
  1838-1910 . . . . DLB-166
Butor, Michel 1926- DLB-83
Butter, Nathaniel [publishing house] DLB-170
Butterworth, Hezekiah 1839-1905 . . . . DLB-42
Buttitta, Ignazio 1899- DLB-114
Butts, Mary 1890-1937 . . . . DLB-240
Buzzati, Dino 1906-1972 . . . . DLB-177
Byars, Betsy 1928- DLB-52
Byatt, A. S. 1936- DLB-14, 194
Byles, Mather 1707-1788 . . . . DLB-24
Bynneman, Henry
  [publishing house] DLB-170
Bynner, Witter 1881-1968 . . . . DLB-54
Byrd, William circa 1543-1623 . . . . DLB-172
Byrd, William, II 1674-1744 . . . . DLB-24, 140
Byrne, John Keyes (see Leonard, Hugh)

Byron, George Gordon, Lord
 1788-1824 ....DLB-96, 110; CDBLB-3

Byron, Robert 1905-1941 ....DLB-195

C

Caballero Bonald, José Manuel
 1926- DLB-108

Cabañero, Eladio 1930- DLB-134

Cabell, James Branch 1879-1958 ....DLB-9, 78

Cabeza de Baca, Manuel 1853-1915 .....DLB-122

Cabeza de Baca Gilbert, Fabiola
 1898- DLB-122

Cable, George Washington
 1844-1925 ....DLB-12, 74; DS-13

Cable, Mildred 1878-1952 ....DLB-195

Cabrera, Lydia 1900-1991 ....DLB-145

Cabrera Infante, Guillermo
 1929- DLB-113; CDWLB-3

Cadell [publishing house]..............DLB-154

Cady, Edwin H. 1917- DLB-103

Caedmon flourished 658-680............DLB-146

Caedmon School circa 660-899..........DLB-146

Caesar, Irving 1895-1996...............DLB-265

Cafés, Brasseries, and Bistros..........DS-15

Cage, John 1912-1992..................DLB-193

Cahan, Abraham 1860-1951 ....DLB-9, 25, 28

Cahn, Sammy 1913-1993...............DLB-265

Cain, George 1943- DLB-33

Cain, James M. 1892-1977 ....DLB-226

Caird, Edward 1835-1908 ....DLB-262

Caird, Mona 1854-1932...............DLB-197

Čaks, Aleksandrs
 1901-1950 ....DLB-220; CDWLB-4

Caldecott, Randolph 1846-1886 ....DLB-163

Calder, John (Publishers), Limited.......DLB-112

Calderón de la Barca, Fanny
 1804-1882 ....DLB-183

Caldwell, Ben 1937- DLB-38

Caldwell, Erskine 1903-1987 ....DLB-9, 86

Caldwell, H. M., Company DLB-49

Caldwell, Taylor 1900-1985 ....DS-17

Calhoun, John C. 1782-1850 ....DLB-3, 248

Călinescu, George 1899-1965 ....DLB-220

Calisher, Hortense 1911- DLB-2, 218

A Call to Letters and an Invitation
 to the Electric Chair,
 by Siegfried Mandel DLB-75

Callaghan, Mary Rose 1944- DLB-207

Callaghan, Morley 1903-1990 ....DLB-68

Callahan, S. Alice 1868-1894 ......DLB-175, 221

Callaloo Y-87

Callimachus circa 305 B.C.-240 B.C.....DLB-176

Calmer, Edgar 1907- DLB-4

Calverley, C. S. 1831-1884 ....DLB-35

Calvert, George Henry
 1803-1889 ....DLB-1, 64, 248

Calvino, Italo 1923-1985 ....DLB-196

Cambridge, Ada 1844-1926..........DLB-230

Cambridge Press DLB-49

Cambridge Songs (Carmina Cantabrigensia)
 circa 1050 ....DLB-148

Cambridge University Press DLB-170

Camden, William 1551-1623..........DLB-172

Camden House: An Interview with
 James Hardin Y-92

Cameron, Eleanor 1912- DLB-52

Cameron, George Frederick
 1854-1885 ....DLB-99

Cameron, Lucy Lyttelton 1781-1858.....DLB-163

Cameron, Peter 1959- DLB-234

Cameron, William Bleasdell 1862-1951 ...DLB-99

Camm, John 1718-1778 ....DLB-31

Camon, Ferdinando 1935- DLB-196

Camp, Walter 1859-1925 ....DLB-241

Campana, Dino 1885-1932 ....DLB-114

Campbell, Bebe Moore 1950- DLB-227

Campbell, David 1915-1979...........DLB-260

Campbell, Gabrielle Margaret Vere
 (see Shearing, Joseph, and Bowen, Marjorie)

Campbell, James Dykes 1838-1895 ......DLB-144

Campbell, James Edwin 1867-1896 ......DLB-50

Campbell, John 1653-1728.............DLB-43

Campbell, John W., Jr. 1910-1971 ....DLB-8

Campbell, Ramsey 1946- DLB-261

Campbell, Roy 1901-1957 ....DLB-20, 225

Campbell, Thomas 1777-1844 ....DLB-93, 144

Campbell, William Wilfred 1858-1918 ....DLB-92

Campion, Edmund 1539-1581 ....DLB-167

Campion, Thomas
 1567-1620 ....DLB-58, 172; CDBLB-1

Campton, David 1924- DLB-245

Camus, Albert 1913-1960 ....DLB-72

The Canadian Publishers' Records
 Database Y-96

Canby, Henry Seidel 1878-1961 ....DLB-91

Candelaria, Cordelia 1943- DLB-82

Candelaria, Nash 1928- DLB-82

Canetti, Elias
 1905-1994 ....DLB-85, 124; CDWLB-2

Canham, Erwin Dain 1904-1982........DLB-127

Canitz, Friedrich Rudolph Ludwig von
 1654-1699 ....DLB-168

Cankar, Ivan 1876-1918 .....DLB-147; CDWLB-4

Cannan, Gilbert 1884-1955 ....DLB-10, 197

Cannan, Joanna 1896-1961 ....DLB-191

Cannell, Kathleen 1891-1974................DLB-4

Cannell, Skipwith 1887-1957 ....DLB-45

Canning, George 1770-1827 ....DLB-158

Cannon, Jimmy 1910-1973 ....DLB-171

Cano, Daniel 1947- DLB-209

Cantú, Norma Elia 1947- DLB-209

Cantwell, Robert 1908-1978 ....DLB-9

Cape, Jonathan, and Harrison Smith
 [publishing house]................DLB-46

Cape, Jonathan, Limited DLB-112

Čapek, Karel 1890-1938 ....DLB-215; CDWLB-4

Capen, Joseph 1658-1725...............DLB-24

Capes, Bernard 1854-1918 ....DLB-156

Capote, Truman 1924-1984
 .....DLB-2, 185, 227; Y-80, Y-84; CDALB-1

Capps, Benjamin 1922- DLB-256

Caproni, Giorgio 1912-1990 ....DLB-128

Caragiale, Mateiu Ioan 1885-1936.......DLB-220

Cardarelli, Vincenzo 1887-1959.........DLB-114

Cárdenas, Reyes 1948- DLB-122

Cardinal, Marie 1929- DLB-83

Carew, Jan 1920- DLB-157

Carew, Thomas 1594 or 1595-1640.....DLB-126

Carey, Henry circa 1687-1689-1743.......DLB-84

Carey, M., and Company DLB-49

Carey, Mathew 1760-1839..........DLB-37, 73

Carey and Hart DLB-49

Carlell, Lodowick 1602-1675............DLB-58

Carleton, William 1794-1869...........DLB-159

Carleton, G. W. [publishing house].......DLB-49

Carlile, Richard 1790-1843 ....DLB-110, 158

Carlson, Ron 1947- DLB-244

Carlyle, Jane Welsh 1801-1866.........DLB-55

Carlyle, Thomas
 1795-1881 ....DLB-55, 144; CDBLB-3

"The Hero as Man of Letters: Johnson,
 Rousseau, Burns" (1841) [excerpt] DLB-57

The Hero as Poet. Dante;
 Shakspeare (1841)...............DLB-32

Carman, Bliss 1861-1929...............DLB-92

Carmina Burana circa 1230 ....DLB-138

Carnero, Guillermo 1947- DLB-108

Carossa, Hans 1878-1956 ....DLB-66

Carpenter, Humphrey
 1946- DLB-155; Y-84, Y-99

The Practice of Biography III: An Interview
 with Humphrey Carpenter Y-84

Carpenter, Stephen Cullen ?-1820?........DLB-73

Carpentier, Alejo
 1904-1980 ....DLB-113; CDWLB-3

Carr, Marina 1961- DLB-245

Carrier, Roch 1937- DLB-53

Carrillo, Adolfo 1855-1926 ....DLB-122

Carroll, Gladys Hasty 1904- DLB-9

Carroll, John 1735-1815................DLB-37

Carroll, John 1809-1884 ....DLB-99

Carroll, Lewis
 1832-1898......DLB-18, 163, 178; CDBLB-4

The Lewis Carroll Centenary Y-98

Carroll, Paul 1927- DLB-16

Carroll, Paul Vincent 1900-1968.........DLB-10

Carroll and Graf Publishers DLB-46

Carruth, Hayden 1921- DLB-5, 165

Carryl, Charles E. 1841-1920 ....DLB-42

Carson, Anne 1950- DLB-193

Carswell, Catherine 1879-1946 ....DLB-36

Cărtărescu, Mirea 1956- DLB-232

Carter, Angela 1940-1992. ..... DLB-14, 207, 261

Carter, Elizabeth 1717-1806 .... DLB-109

Carter, Henry (see Leslie, Frank)

Carter, Hodding, Jr. 1907-1972. .... DLB-127

Carter, John 1905-1975. .... DLB-201

Carter, Landon 1710-1778. .... DLB-31

Carter, Lin 1930- Y-81

Carter, Martin 1927-1997 .... DLB-117; CDWLB-3

Carter, Robert, and Brothers DLB-49

Carter and Hendee. DLB-49

Cartwright, Jim 1958- DLB-245

Cartwright, John 1740-1824 .... DLB-158

Cartwright, William circa 1611-1643 .... DLB-126

Caruthers, William Alexander
  1802-1846 .... DLB-3, 248

Carver, Jonathan 1710-1780 .... DLB-31

Carver, Raymond
  1938-1988 .... DLB-130; Y-83, Y-88

First Strauss "Livings" Awarded to Cynthia
  Ozick and Raymond Carver
  An Interview with Raymond Carver Y-83

Cary, Alice 1820-1871. .... DLB-202

Cary, Joyce 1888-1957 ... DLB-15, 100; CDBLB-6

Cary, Patrick 1623?-1657 .... DLB-131

Casey, Gavin 1907-1964. .... DLB-260

Casey, Juanita 1925- DLB-14

Casey, Michael 1947- DLB-5

Cassady, Carolyn 1923- DLB-16

Cassady, Neal 1926-1968 .... DLB-16, 237

Cassell and Company. DLB-106

Cassell Publishing Company DLB-49

Cassill, R. V. 1919- DLB-6, 218

Cassity, Turner 1929- DLB-105

Cassius Dio circa 155/164-post 229 ..... DLB-176

Cassola, Carlo 1917-1987 .... DLB-177

The Castle of Perserverance circa 1400-1425 . DLB-146

Castellano, Olivia 1944- DLB-122

Castellanos, Rosario
  1925-1974. .... DLB-113; CDWLB-3

Castillo, Ana 1953- DLB-122, 227

Castillo, Rafael C. 1950- DLB-209

Castlemon, Harry (see Fosdick, Charles Austin)

Čašule, Kole 1921- DLB-181

Caswall, Edward 1814-1878 .... DLB-32

Catacalos, Rosemary 1944- DLB-122

Cather, Willa 1873-1947
  .... DLB-9, 54, 78, 256; DS-1; CDALB-3

Catherine II (Ekaterina Alekseevna), "The Great,"
  Empress of Russia 1729-1796. ...... DLB-150

Catherwood, Mary Hartwell 1847-1902... DLB-78

Catledge, Turner 1901-1983 .... DLB-127

Catlin, George 1796-1872 .... DLB-186, 189

Cato the Elder 234 B.C.-149 B.C. DLB-211

Cattafi, Bartolo 1922-1979 .... DLB-128

Catton, Bruce 1899-1978 .... DLB-17

Catullus circa 84 B.C.-54 B.C.
  .... DLB-211; CDWLB-1

Causley, Charles 1917- DLB-27

Caute, David 1936- DLB-14, 231

Cavendish, Duchess of Newcastle,
  Margaret Lucas 1623-1673 .... DLB-131, 252

Cawein, Madison 1865-1914 .... DLB-54

Caxton, William [publishing house]......DLB-170

The Caxton Printers, Limited DLB-46

Caylor, O. P. 1849-1897. .... DLB-241

Cayrol, Jean 1911- DLB-83

Cecil, Lord David 1902-1986 .... DLB-155

Cela, Camilo José 1916- Y-89

Celan, Paul 1920-1970 ...... DLB-69; CDWLB-2

Celati, Gianni 1937- DLB-196

Celaya, Gabriel 1911-1991 .... DLB-108

A Celebration of Literary Biography Y-98

Céline, Louis-Ferdinand 1894-1961 ...... DLB-72

The Celtic Background to Medieval English
  Literature DLB-146

Celtis, Conrad 1459-1508. .... DLB-179

Cendrars, Blaise 1887-1961. .... DLB-258

Center for Bibliographical Studies and
  Research at the University of
  California, Riverside Y-91

The Center for the Book in the Library
  of Congress Y-93

Center for the Book Research Y-84

Centlivre, Susanna 1669?-1723. .... DLB-84

The Centre for Writing, Publishing and
  Printing History at the University
  of Reading Y-00

The Century Company DLB-49

Cernuda, Luis 1902-1963............. DLB-134

Cervantes, Lorna Dee 1954- DLB-82

de Céspedes, Alba 1911-1997.......... DLB-264

Ch., T. (see Marchenko, Anastasiia Iakovlevna)

Chaadaev, Petr Iakovlevich
  1794-1856...................... DLB-198

Chacel, Rosa 1898- DLB-134

Chacón, Eusebio 1869-1948............ DLB-82

Chacón, Felipe Maximiliano 1873-? DLB-82

Chadwick, Henry 1824-1908 .... DLB-241

Chadwyck-Healey's Full-Text Literary Databases:
  Editing Commercial Databases of
  Primary Literary Texts Y-95

Challans, Eileen Mary (see Renault, Mary)

Chalmers, George 1742-1825 .... DLB-30

Chaloner, Sir Thomas 1520-1565 ...... DLB-167

Chamberlain, Samuel S. 1851-1916 ..... DLB-25

Chamberland, Paul 1939- DLB-60

Chamberlin, William Henry 1897-1969 ... DLB-29

Chambers, Charles Haddon 1860-1921 ... DLB-10

Chambers, María Cristina (see Mena, María Cristina)

Chambers, Robert W. 1865-1933 ...... DLB-202

Chambers, W. and R.
  [publishing house] DLB-106

Chamisso, Albert von 1781-1838 .... DLB-90

Champfleury 1821-1889............. DLB-119

Chandler, Harry 1864-1944........... DLB-29

Chandler, Norman 1899-1973 .... DLB-127

Chandler, Otis 1927- DLB-127

Chandler, Raymond
  1888-1959 ... DLB-226, 253; DS-6; CDALB-5

Raymond Chandler Centenary Tributes
  from Michael Avallone, James Ellroy,
  Joe Gores, and William F. Nolan........ Y-88

Channing, Edward 1856-1931 .... DLB-17

Channing, Edward Tyrrell
  1790-1856. .... DLB-1, 59, 235

Channing, William Ellery
  1780-1842. .... DLB-1, 59, 235

Channing, William Ellery, II
  1817-1901................... DLB-1, 223

Channing, William Henry
  1810-1884 .... DLB-1, 59, 243

Chaplin, Charlie 1889-1977 .... DLB-44

Chapman, George
  1559 or 1560-1634............ DLB-62, 121

Chapman, John DLB-106

Chapman, Olive Murray 1892-1977..... DLB-195

Chapman, R. W. 1881-1960 .... DLB-201

Chapman, William 1850-1917 .... DLB-99

Chapman and Hall. DLB-106

Chappell, Fred 1936- DLB-6, 105

"A Detail in a Poem" DLB-105

Chappell, William 1582-1649.......... DLB-236

Char, René 1907-1988 .... DLB-258

Charbonneau, Jean 1875-1960 .... DLB-92

Charbonneau, Robert 1911-1967........ DLB-68

Charles, Gerda 1914- DLB-14

Charles, William [publishing house]...... DLB-49

Charles d'Orléans 1394-1465 .... DLB-208

Charley (see Mann, Charles)

Charteris, Leslie 1907-1993............. DLB-77

Chartier, Alain circa 1385-1430 .... DLB-208

Charyn, Jerome 1937- Y-83

Chase, Borden 1900-1971 .... DLB-26

Chase, Edna Woolman 1877-1957 ...... DLB-91

Chase, Mary Coyle 1907-1981 .... DLB-228

Chase-Riboud, Barbara 1936- DLB-33

Chateaubriand, François-René de
  1768-1848..................... DLB-119

Chatterton, Thomas 1752-1770......... DLB-109

Essay on Chatterton (1842), by
  Robert Browning DLB-32

Chatto and Windus DLB-106

Chatwin, Bruce 1940-1989........ DLB-194, 204

Chaucer, Geoffrey
  1340?-1400............ DLB-146; CDBLB-1

Chauncy, Charles 1705-1787 .... DLB-24

Chauveau, Pierre-Joseph-Olivier
  1820-1890 .... DLB-99

Chávez, Denise 1948- DLB-122

Chávez, Fray Angélico 1910- DLB-82

Chayefsky, Paddy 1923-1981.....DLB-7, 44; Y-81

Cheesman, Evelyn 1881-1969 ....DLB-195

Cheever, Ezekiel 1615-1708............DLB-24

Cheever, George Barrell 1807-1890.......DLB-59

Cheever, John 1912-1982
..... DLB-2, 102, 227; Y-80, Y-82; CDALB-1

Cheever, Susan 1943- Y-82

Cheke, Sir John 1514-1557 ....DLB-132

Chelsea House....................DLB-46

Chênedollé, Charles de 1769-1833.......DLB-217

Cheney, Ednah Dow 1824-1904 ......DLB-1, 223

Cheney, Harriet Vaughn 1796-1889 ......DLB-99

Chénier, Marie-Joseph 1764-1811 ....DLB-192

Chernyshevsky, Nikolai Gavrilovich
1828-1889 ....DLB-238

Cherry, Kelly 1940 .... Y-83

Cherryh, C. J. 1942- Y-80

Chesebro', Caroline 1825-1873 ....DLB-202

Chesney, Sir George Tomkyns
1830-1895 ....DLB-190

Chesnut, Mary Boykin 1823-1886.......DLB-239

Chesnutt, Charles Waddell
1858-1932 .... DLB-12, 50, 78

Chesson, Mrs. Nora (see Hopper, Nora)

Chester, Alfred 1928-1971 ....DLB-130

Chester, George Randolph 1869-1924 ....DLB-78

The Chester Plays circa 1505-1532;
revisions until 1575 ....DLB-146

Chesterfield, Philip Dormer Stanhope,
Fourth Earl of 1694-1773............DLB-104

Chesterton, G. K. 1874-1936
.. DLB-10, 19, 34, 70, 98, 149, 178; CDBLB-6

Chettle, Henry circa 1560-circa 1607......DLB-136

Cheuse, Alan 1940- DLB-244

Chew, Ada Nield 1870-1945 ....DLB-135

Cheyney, Edward P. 1861-1947 ....DLB-47

Chiara, Piero 1913-1986 ....DLB-177

Chicano History DLB-82

Chicano Language..................DLB-82

Child, Francis James 1825-1896....DLB-1, 64, 235

Child, Lydia Maria 1802-1880 ....DLB-1, 74, 243

Child, Philip 1898-1978 ....DLB-68

Childers, Erskine 1870-1922 ....DLB-70

Children's Book Awards and Prizes.......DLB-61

Children's Illustrators, 1800-1880 ....DLB-163

Childress, Alice 1916-1994 ...... DLB-7, 38, 249

Childs, George W. 1829-1894..........DLB-23

Chilton Book Company DLB-46

Chin, Frank 1940- DLB-206

Chinweizu 1943- DLB-157

Chitham, Edward 1932- DLB-155

Chittenden, Hiram Martin 1858-1917 .....DLB-47

Chivers, Thomas Holley 1809-1858 ...DLB-3, 248

Cholmondeley, Mary 1859-1925 ....DLB-197

Chomsky, Noam 1928- DLB-246

Chopin, Kate 1850-1904 ...DLB-12, 78; CDALB-3

Chopin, Rene 1885-1953...............DLB-92

Choquette, Adrienne 1915-1973 ....DLB-68

Choquette, Robert 1905- DLB-68

Choyce, Lesley 1951- DLB-251

Chrétien de Troyes
circa 1140-circa 1190..............DLB-208

Christensen, Inger 1935- DLB-214

The Christian Publishing Company DLB-49

Christie, Agatha
1890-1976 .... DLB-13, 77, 245; CDBLB-6

Christine de Pizan
circa 1365-circa 1431..............DLB-208

Christopher, John 1922- DLB-255

Christus und die Samariterin circa 950 .....DLB-148

Christy, Howard Chandler 1873-1952 ...DLB-188

Chulkov, Mikhail Dmitrievich
1743?-1792 ....DLB-150

Church, Benjamin 1734-1778...........DLB-31

Church, Francis Pharcellus 1839-1906 ....DLB-79

Church, Peggy Pond 1903-1986 ....DLB-212

Church, Richard 1893-1972............DLB-191

Church, William Conant 1836-1917 .....DLB-79

Churchill, Caryl 1938- DLB-13

Churchill, Charles 1731-1764..........DLB-109

Churchill, Winston 1871-1947.........DLB-202

Churchill, Sir Winston
1874-1965 ....DLB-100; DS-16; CDBLB-5

Churchyard, Thomas 1520?-1604.......DLB-132

Churton, E., and Company............DLB-106

Chute, Marchette 1909-1994..........DLB-103

Ciardi, John 1916-1986 .... DLB-5; Y-86

Cibber, Colley 1671-1757..............DLB-84

Cicero
106 B.C.-43 B.C........ DLB-211, CDWLB-1

Cima, Annalisa 1941- DLB-128

Čingo, Živko 1935-1987 ....DLB-181

Cioran, E. M. 1911-1995..............DLB-220

Čipkus, Alfonsas (see Nyka-Niliūnas, Alfonsas)

Cirese, Eugenio 1884-1955 ....DLB-114

Cīrulis, Jānis (see Bels, Alberts)

Cisneros, Sandra 1954- DLB-122, 152

City Lights Books DLB-46

Cixous, Hélène 1937- DLB-83, 242

The Claims of Business and Literature:
An Undergraduate Essay by
Maxwell Perkins Y-01

Clampitt, Amy 1920-1994............DLB-105

Clancy, Tom 1947- DLB-227

Clapper, Raymond 1892-1944.........DLB-29

Clare, John 1793-1864............DLB-55, 96

Clarendon, Edward Hyde, Earl of
1609-1674 ....DLB-101

Clark, Alfred Alexander Gordon (see Hare, Cyril)

Clark, Ann Nolan 1896- DLB-52

Clark, C. E. Frazer, Jr. 1925- DLB-187; Y-01

Clark, C. M., Publishing Company.......DLB-46

Clark, Catherine Anthony 1892-1977 .....DLB-68

Clark, Charles Heber 1841-1915 ....DLB-11

Clark, Davis Wasgatt 1812-1871 ....DLB-79

Clark, Eleanor 1913- DLB-6

Clark, J. P. 1935- DLB-117; CDWLB-3

Clark, Lewis Gaylord
1808-1873 ....DLB-3, 64, 73, 250

Clark, Walter Van Tilburg
1909-1971 ....DLB-9, 206

Clark, William (see Lewis, Meriwether)

Clark, William Andrews, Jr. 1877-1934 ...DLB-187

Clarke, Sir Arthur C. 1917- DLB-261

Clarke, Austin 1896-1974 ....DLB-10, 20

Clarke, Austin C. 1934- DLB-53, 125

Clarke, Gillian 1937- DLB-40

Clarke, James Freeman
1810-1888 ....DLB-1, 59, 235

Clarke, Lindsay 1939- DLB-231

Clarke, Marcus 1846-1881 ....DLB-230

Clarke, Pauline 1921- DLB-161

Clarke, Rebecca Sophia 1833-1906 ....DLB-42

Clarke, Robert, and Company DLB-49

Clarke, Samuel 1675-1729 ....DLB-252

Clarkson, Thomas 1760-1846 ....DLB-158

Claudel, Paul 1868-1955 ....DLB-192, 258

Claudius, Matthias 1740-1815 ....DLB-97

Clausen, Andy 1943- DLB-16

Clawson, John L. 1865-1933 ....DLB-187

Claxton, Remsen and Haffelfinger DLB-49

Clay, Cassius Marcellus 1810-1903.......DLB-43

Cleage, Pearl 1948- DLB-228

Cleary, Beverly 1916- DLB-52

Cleary, Kate McPhelim 1863-1905 .....DLB-221

Cleaver, Vera 1919- and
Cleaver, Bill 1920-1981..............DLB-52

Cleland, John 1710-1789 ....DLB-39

Clemens, Samuel Langhorne (Mark Twain)
1835-1910 ....DLB-11, 12, 23, 64, 74,
186, 189; CDALB-3

Mark Twain on Perpetual Copyright Y-92

Clement, Hal 1922- DLB-8

Clemo, Jack 1916- DLB-27

Clephane, Elizabeth Cecilia
1830-1869 ....DLB-199

Cleveland, John 1613-1658 ....DLB-126

Cliff, Michelle 1946- DLB-157; CDWLB-3

Clifford, Lady Anne 1590-1676.........DLB-151

Clifford, James L. 1901-1978 ....DLB-103

Clifford, Lucy 1853?-1929..... DLB-135, 141, 197

Clift, Charmian 1923-1969 ....DLB-260

Clifton, Lucille 1936- DLB-5, 41

Clines, Francis X. 1938- DLB-185

Clive, Caroline (V) 1801-1873..........DLB-199

Clode, Edward J. [publishing house]......DLB-46

Clough, Arthur Hugh 1819-1861 ....DLB-32

Cloutier, Cécile 1930- DLB-60

Clouts, Sidney 1926-1982 ....DLB-225

Clutton-Brock, Arthur 1868-1924 ....DLB-98

Cumulative Index

Coates, Robert M. 1897-1973 . . . . . . DLB-4, 9, 102
Coatsworth, Elizabeth 1893- DLB-22
Cobb, Charles E., Jr. 1943- DLB-41
Cobb, Frank I. 1869-1923 . . . . DLB-25
Cobb, Irvin S. 1876-1944 . . . . DLB-11, 25, 86
Cobbe, Frances Power 1822-1904 . . . . . . DLB-190
Cobbett, William 1763-1835 . . . . DLB-43, 107
Cobbledick, Gordon 1898-1969 . . . . DLB-171
Cochran, Thomas C. 1902- DLB-17
Cochrane, Elizabeth 1867-1922 . . . . . DLB-25, 189
Cockerell, Sir Sydney 1867-1962 . . . . DLB-201
Cockerill, John A. 1845-1896 . . . . DLB-23
Cocteau, Jean 1889-1963 . . . . DLB-65, 258
Coderre, Emile (see Jean Narrache)
Coe, Jonathan 1961- DLB-231
Coetzee, J. M. 1940- DLB-225
Coffee, Lenore J. 1900?-1984 . . . . DLB-44
Coffin, Robert P. Tristram 1892-1955 . . . . DLB-45
Coghill, Mrs. Harry (see Walker, Anna Louisa)
Cogswell, Fred 1917- DLB-60
Cogswell, Mason Fitch 1761-1830 . . . . DLB-37
Cohan, George M. 1878-1942 . . . . DLB-249
Cohen, Arthur A. 1928-1986 . . . . DLB-28
Cohen, Leonard 1934- DLB-53
Cohen, Matt 1942- DLB-53
Colbeck, Norman 1903-1987 . . . . DLB-201
Colden, Cadwallader 1688-1776 . . . . . . DLB-24, 30
Colden, Jane 1724-1766 . . . . DLB-200
Cole, Barry 1936- DLB-14
Cole, George Watson 1850-1939 . . . . DLB-140
Colegate, Isabel 1931- DLB-14, 231
Coleman, Emily Holmes 1899-1974 . . . . . . DLB-4
Coleman, Wanda 1946- DLB-130
Coleridge, Hartley 1796-1849 . . . . DLB-96
Coleridge, Mary 1861-1907 . . . . DLB-19, 98
Coleridge, Samuel Taylor
 1772-1834 . . . . DLB-93, 107; CDBLB-3
Coleridge, Sara 1802-1852 . . . . DLB-199
Colet, John 1467-1519 . . . . DLB-132
Colette 1873-1954 . . . . DLB-65
Colette, Sidonie Gabrielle (see Colette)
Colinas, Antonio 1946- DLB-134
Coll, Joseph Clement 1881-1921 . . . . DLB-188
Collier, John 1901-1980 . . . . DLB-77, 255
Collier, John Payne 1789-1883 . . . . DLB-184
Collier, Mary 1690-1762 . . . . DLB-95
Collier, P. F. [publishing house] DLB-49
Collier, Robert J. 1876-1918 . . . . DLB-91
Collin and Small DLB-49
Collingwood, R. G. 1889-1943 . . . . DLB-262
Collingwood, W. G. 1854-1932 . . . . DLB-149
Collins, An floruit circa 1653 . . . . DLB-131
Collins, Anthony 1676-1729 . . . . DLB-252
Collins, Isaac [publishing house] DLB-49

Collins, Merle 1950- DLB-157
Collins, Mortimer 1827-1876 . . . . DLB-21, 35
Collins, Tom (see Furphy, Joseph)
Collins, Wilkie
 1824-1889 . . . . . . DLB-18, 70, 159; CDBLB-4
Collins, William 1721-1759 . . . . DLB-109
Collins, William, Sons and Company . . . DLB-154
Collis, Maurice 1889-1973 . . . . DLB-195
Collyer, Mary 1716?-1763? DLB-39
Colman, Benjamin 1673-1747 . . . . DLB-24
Colman, George, the Elder 1732-1794 . . . DLB-89
Colman, George, the Younger
 1762-1836 . . . . DLB-89
Colman, S. [publishing house] DLB-49
Colombo, John Robert 1936- DLB-53
Colquhoun, Patrick 1745-1820 . . . . DLB-158
Colter, Cyrus 1910- DLB-33
Colum, Padraic 1881-1972 . . . . DLB-19
Columella fl. first century A.D. DLB-211
Colvin, Sir Sidney 1845-1927 . . . . DLB-149
Colwin, Laurie 1944-1992 . . . . DLB-218; Y-80
Comden, Betty 1919- and
 Green, Adolph 1918- DLB-44, 265
Come to Papa Y-99
Comi, Girolamo 1890-1968 . . . . DLB-114
The Comic Tradition Continued
 [in the British Novel] DLB-15
Comisso, Giovanni 1895-1969 . . . . DLB-264
Commager, Henry Steele 1902-1998 . . . . DLB-17
The Commercialization of the Image of
 Revolt, by Kenneth Rexroth DLB-16
Community and Commentators: Black
 Theatre and Its Critics DLB-38
Commynes, Philippe de
 circa 1447-1511 . . . . DLB-208
Compton, D. G. 1930- DLB-261
Compton-Burnett, Ivy 1884?-1969 . . . . . . DLB-36
Conan, Laure 1845-1924 . . . . DLB-99
Concord History and Life DLB-223
Concord Literary History of a Town DLB-223
Conde, Carmen 1901- DLB-108
Conference on Modern Biography Y-85
Congreve, William
 1670-1729 . . . . DLB-39, 84; CDBLB-2
Preface to Incognita (1692) DLB-39
Conkey, W. B., Company DLB-49
Conn, Stewart 1936- DLB-233
Connell, Evan S., Jr. 1924- DLB-2; Y-81
Connelly, Marc 1890-1980 . . . . DLB-7; Y-80
Connolly, Cyril 1903-1974 . . . . DLB-98
Connolly, James B. 1868-1957 . . . . DLB-78
Connor, Ralph 1860-1937 . . . . DLB-92
Connor, Tony 1930- DLB-40
Conquest, Robert 1917- DLB-27
Conrad, John, and Company DLB-49
Conrad, Joseph
 1857-1924 . . . . DLB-10, 34, 98, 156; CDBLB-5

Conroy, Jack 1899-1990 . . . . Y-81
Conroy, Pat 1945- DLB-6
Considine, Bob 1906-1975 . . . . DLB-241
The Consolidation of Opinion: Critical
 Responses to the Modernists DLB-36
Consolo, Vincenzo 1933- DLB-196
Constable, Archibald, and Company DLB-154
Constable, Henry 1562-1613 . . . . DLB-136
Constable and Company Limited DLB-112
Constant, Benjamin 1767-1830 . . . . DLB-119
Constant de Rebecque, Henri-Benjamin de
 (see Constant, Benjamin)
Constantine, David 1944- DLB-40
Constantin-Weyer, Maurice 1881-1964 . . . DLB-92
Contempo Caravan: Kites in a Windstorm . . . Y-85
A Contemporary Flourescence of Chicano
 Literature Y-84
Continental European Rhetoricians,
 1400-1600 . . . . DLB-236
The Continental Publishing Company . . . DLB-49
Conversations with Editors Y-95
Conversations with Publishers I: An Interview
 with Patrick O'Connor Y-84
Conversations with Publishers II: An Interview
 with Charles Scribner III Y-94
Conversations with Publishers III: An Interview
 with Donald Lamm Y-95
Conversations with Publishers IV: An Interview
 with James Laughlin Y-96
Conversations with Rare Book Dealers I: An
 Interview with Glenn Horowitz Y-90
Conversations with Rare Book Dealers II: An
 Interview with Ralph Sipper Y-94
Conversations with Rare Book Dealers
 (Publishers) III: An Interview with
 Otto Penzler Y-96
The Conversion of an Unpolitical Man,
 by W. H. Bruford DLB-66
Conway, Anne 1631-1679 . . . . DLB-252
Conway, Moncure Daniel
 1832-1907 . . . . DLB-1, 223
Cook, David C., Publishing Company . . . DLB-49
Cook, Ebenezer circa 1667-circa 1732 . . . . DLB-24
Cook, Edward Tyas 1857-1919 . . . . DLB-149
Cook, Eliza 1818-1889 . . . . DLB-199
Cook, George Cram 1873-1924 . . . . DLB-266
Cook, Michael 1933-1994 . . . . DLB-53
Cooke, George Willis 1848-1923 . . . . DLB-71
Cooke, Increase, and Company DLB-49
Cooke, John Esten 1830-1886 . . . . DLB-3, 248
Cooke, Philip Pendleton
 1816-1850 . . . . DLB-3, 59, 248
Cooke, Rose Terry 1827-1892 . . . . DLB-12, 74
Cook-Lynn, Elizabeth 1930- DLB-175
Coolbrith, Ina 1841-1928 . . . . DLB-54, 186
Cooley, Peter 1940- DLB-105
"Into the Mirror" DLB-105
Coolidge, Clark 1939- DLB-193
Coolidge, George [publishing house] DLB-49

Coolidge, Susan (see Woolsey, Sarah Chauncy)
Cooper, Anna Julia 1858-1964..........DLB-221
Cooper, Edith Emma (see Field, Michael)
Cooper, Giles 1918-1966................DLB-13
Cooper, J. California 19??- DLB-212
Cooper, James Fenimore
  1789-1851.......DLB-3, 183, 250; CDALB-2
Cooper, Kent 1880-1965................DLB-29
Cooper, Susan 1935- DLB-161, 261
Cooper, Susan Fenimore 1813-1894.....DLB-239
Cooper, William [publishing house] DLB-170
Coote, J. [publishing house]............DLB-154
Coover, Robert 1932- DLB-2, 227; Y-81
Copeland and Day..................DLB-49
Ćopić, Branko 1915-1984..............DLB-181
Copland, Robert 1470?-1548............DLB-136
Coppard, A. E. 1878-1957.............DLB-162
Coppée, François 1842-1908...........DLB-217
Coppel, Alfred 1921- Y-83
Coppola, Francis Ford 1939- DLB-44
Copway, George (Kah-ge-ga-gah-bowh)
  1818-1869..................DLB-175, 183
Corazzini, Sergio 1886-1907...........DLB-114
Corbett, Richard 1582-1635...........DLB-121
Corbière, Tristan 1845-1875............DLB-217
Corcoran, Barbara 1911- DLB-52
Cordelli, Franco 1943- DLB-196
Corelli, Marie 1855-1924............DLB-34, 156
Corle, Edwin 1906-1956.................Y-85
Corman, Cid 1924- DLB-5, 193
Cormier, Robert 1925-2000....DLB-52; CDALB-6
Corn, Alfred 1943- DLB-120; Y-80
Cornford, Frances 1886-1960..........DLB-240
Cornish, Sam 1935- DLB-41
Cornish, William circa 1465-circa 1524...DLB-132
Cornwall, Barry (see Procter, Bryan Waller)
Cornwallis, Sir William, the Younger
  circa 1579-1614..................DLB-151
Cornwell, David John Moore (see le Carré, John)
Corpi, Lucha 1945- DLB-82
Corrington, John William
  1932-1988.....................DLB-6, 244
Corriveau, Monique 1927-1976.........DLB-251
Corrothers, James D. 1869-1917........DLB-50
Corso, Gregory 1930- DLB-5, 16, 237
Cortázar, Julio 1914-1984...DLB-113; CDWLB-3
Cortéz, Carlos 1923- DLB-209
Cortez, Jayne 1936- DLB-41
Corvinus, Gottlieb Siegmund
  1677-1746......................DLB-168
Corvo, Baron (see Rolfe, Frederick William)
Cory, Annie Sophie (see Cross, Victoria)
Cory, William Johnson 1823-1892.......DLB-35
Coryate, Thomas 1577?-1617 ......DLB-151, 172
Ćosić, Dobrica 1921- DLB-181; CDWLB-4
Cosin, John 1595-1672............DLB-151, 213

Cosmopolitan Book Corporation DLB-46
The Cost of *The Cantos:* William Bird
  to Ezra Pound....................Y-01
Costain, Thomas B. 1885-1965..........DLB-9
Coste, Donat 1912-1957...............DLB-88
Costello, Louisa Stuart 1799-1870......DLB-166
Cota-Cárdenas, Margarita 1941- DLB-122
Côté, Denis 1954- DLB-251
Cotten, Bruce 1873-1954..............DLB-187
Cotter, Joseph Seamon, Sr. 1861-1949.....DLB-50
Cotter, Joseph Seamon, Jr. 1895-1919....DLB-50
Cottle, Joseph [publishing house].......DLB-154
Cotton, Charles 1630-1687............DLB-131
Cotton, John 1584-1652...............DLB-24
Cotton, Sir Robert Bruce 1571-1631.....DLB-213
Coulter, John 1888-1980..............DLB-68
Cournos, John 1881-1966..............DLB-54
Courteline, Georges 1858-1929.........DLB-192
Cousins, Margaret 1905-1996..........DLB-137
Cousins, Norman 1915-1990...........DLB-137
Couvreur, Jessie (see Tasma)
Coventry, Francis 1725-1754...........DLB-39
Dedication, *The History of Pompey
  the Little* (1751).................DLB-39
Coverdale, Miles 1487 or 1488-1569.....DLB-167
Coverly, N. [publishing house]..........DLB-49
Covici-Friede......................DLB-46
Cowan, Peter 1914- DLB-260
Coward, Noel
  1899-1973..............DLB-10, 245; CDBLB-6
Coward, McCann and Geoghegan DLB-46
Cowles, Gardner 1861-1946...........DLB-29
Cowles, Gardner "Mike", Jr.
  1903-1985...................DLB-127, 137
Cowley, Abraham 1618-1667 ......DLB-131, 151
Cowley, Hannah 1743-1809............DLB-89
Cowley, Malcolm
  1898-1989......... DLB-4, 48; Y-81, Y-89
Cowper, Richard 1926-2002............DLB-261
Cowper, William 1731-1800 ....DLB-104, 109
Cox, A. B. (see Berkeley, Anthony)
Cox, James McMahon 1903-1974.......DLB-127
Cox, James Middleton 1870-1957.......DLB-127
Cox, Leonard ca. 1495-ca. 1550 ....DLB-236
Cox, Palmer 1840-1924...............DLB-42
Coxe, Louis 1918-1993.................DLB-5
Coxe, Tench 1755-1824................DLB-37
Cozzens, Frederick S. 1818-1869........DLB-202
Cozzens, James Gould
  1903-1978......DLB-9; Y-84; DS-2; CDALB-1
James Gould Cozzens–A View from Afar....Y-97
James Gould Cozzens Case Re-opened Y-97
James Gould Cozzens: How to Read Him....Y-97
Cozzens's *Michael Scarlett*.................Y-97
James Gould Cozzens Symposium and
  Exhibition at the University of
  South Carolina, Columbia Y-00

Crabbe, George 1754-1832 ....DLB-93
Crace, Jim 1946- DLB-231
Crackanthorpe, Hubert 1870-1896 ......DLB-135
Craddock, Charles Egbert (see Murfree, Mary N.)
Cradock, Thomas 1718-1770............DLB-31
Craig, Daniel H. 1811-1895..............DLB-43
Craik, Dinah Maria 1826-1887 ......DLB-35, 136
Cramer, Richard Ben 1950- DLB-185
Cranch, Christopher Pearse
  1813-1892..................DLB-1, 42, 243
Crane, Hart 1899-1932.....DLB-4, 48; CDALB-4
Crane, R. S. 1886-1967.................DLB-63
Crane, Stephen
  1871-1900........DLB-12, 54, 78; CDALB-3
Crane, Walter 1845-1915 ....DLB-163
Cranmer, Thomas 1489-1556......DLB-132, 213
Crapsey, Adelaide 1878-1914...........DLB-54
Crashaw, Richard 1612 or 1613-1649....DLB-126
Craven, Avery 1885-1980..............DLB-17
Crawford, Charles 1752-circa 1815 ....DLB-31
Crawford, F. Marion 1854-1909 ....DLB-71
Crawford, Isabel Valancy 1850-1887 .....DLB-92
Crawley, Alan 1887-1975...............DLB-68
Crayon, Geoffrey (see Irving, Washington)
Crayon, Porte (see Strother, David Hunter)
Creamer, Robert W. 1922- DLB-171
Creasey, John 1908-1973...............DLB-77
Creative Age Press.....................DLB-46
Creech, William [publishing house].....DLB-154
Creede, Thomas [publishing house] DLB-170
Creel, George 1876-1953 ....DLB-25
Creeley, Robert 1926- DLB-5, 16, 169; DS-17
Creelman, James 1859-1915 ....DLB-23
Cregan, David 1931- DLB-13
Creighton, Donald Grant 1902-1979......DLB-88
Cremazie, Octave 1827-1879............DLB-99
Crémer, Victoriano 1909?- DLB-108
Crescas, Hasdai circa 1340-1412?.......DLB-115
Crespo, Angel 1926- DLB-134
Cresset Press DLB-112
Cresswell, Helen 1934- DLB-161
Crèvecoeur, Michel Guillaume Jean de
  1735-1813......................DLB-37
Crewe, Candida 1964- DLB-207
Crews, Harry 1935- DLB-6, 143, 185
Crichton, Michael 1942- Y-81
A Crisis of Culture: The Changing Role
  of Religion in the New Republic......DLB-37
Crispin, Edmund 1921-1978.............DLB-87
Cristofer, Michael 1946- DLB-7
Crnjanski, Miloš
  1893-1977............DLB-147; CDWLB-4
Crocker, Hannah Mather 1752-1829.....DLB-200
Crockett, David (Davy)
  1786-1836............DLB-3, 11, 183, 248
Croft-Cooke, Rupert (see Bruce, Leo)

Crofts, Freeman Wills 1879-1957 .... DLB-77
Croker, John Wilson 1780-1857 .... DLB-110
Croly, George 1780-1860 .... DLB-159
Croly, Herbert 1869-1930 .... DLB-91
Croly, Jane Cunningham 1829-1901 ..... DLB-23
Crompton, Richmal 1890-1969 .... DLB-160
Cronin, A. J. 1896-1981 .... DLB-191
Cros, Charles 1842-1888 .... DLB-217
Crosby, Caresse 1892-1970 .... DLB-48
Crosby, Caresse 1892-1970
 and Crosby, Harry
 1898-1929 .... DLB-4; DS-15
Crosby, Harry 1898-1929 .... DLB-48
Crosland, Camilla Toulmin
 (Mrs. Newton Crosland)
 1812-1895 .... DLB-240
Cross, Gillian 1945- DLB-161
Cross, Victoria 1868-1952 .... DLB-135, 197
Crossley-Holland, Kevin 1941- DLB-40, 161
Crothers, Rachel 1870-1958 .... DLB-7, 266
Crowell, Thomas Y., Company DLB-49
Crowley, John 1942- Y-82
Crowley, Mart 1935- DLB-7, 266
Crown Publishers DLB-46
Crowne, John 1641-1712 .... DLB-80
Crowninshield, Edward Augustus
 1817-1859 .... DLB-140
Crowninshield, Frank 1872-1947 .... DLB-91
Croy, Homer 1883-1965 .... DLB-4
Crumley, James 1939- DLB-226; Y-84
Cruse, Mary Anne 1825?-1910 .... DLB-239
Cruz, Migdalia 1958- DLB-249
Cruz, Victor Hernández 1949- DLB-41
Csokor, Franz Theodor 1885-1969 ..... DLB-81
Csoóri, Sándor 1930- DLB-232; CDWLB-4
Cuala Press DLB-112
Cudworth, Ralph 1617-1688 .... DLB-252
Cullen, Countee
 1903-1946 .... DLB-4, 48, 51; CDALB-4
Culler, Jonathan D. 1944- DLB-67, 246
Cullinan, Elizabeth 1933- DLB-234
The Cult of Biography
 Excerpts from the Second Folio Debate:
 "Biographies are generally a disease of
 English Literature" – Germaine Greer,
 Victoria Glendinning, Auberon Waugh,
 and Richard Holmes Y-86
Culverwel, Nathaniel 1619?-1651? DLB-252
Cumberland, Richard 1732-1811 .... DLB-89
Cummings, Constance Gordon
 1837-1924 .... DLB-174
Cummings, E. E.
 1894-1962 .... DLB-4, 48; CDALB-5
Cummings, Ray 1887-1957 .... DLB-8
Cummings and Hilliard DLB-49
Cummins, Maria Susanna
 1827-1866 .... DLB-42
Cumpián, Carlos 1953- DLB-209
Cunard, Nancy 1896-1965 .... DLB-240

Cundall, Joseph [publishing house] DLB-106
Cuney, Waring 1906-1976 .... DLB-51
Cuney-Hare, Maude 1874-1936 .... DLB-52
Cunningham, Allan 1784-1842 ..... DLB-116, 144
Cunningham, J. V. 1911- DLB-5
Cunningham, Peter F.
 [publishing house] DLB-49
Cunqueiro, Alvaro 1911-1981 .... DLB-134
Cuomo, George 1929- Y-80
Cupples, Upham and Company DLB-49
Cupples and Leon DLB-46
Cuppy, Will 1884-1949 .... DLB-11
Curiel, Barbara Brinson 1956- DLB-209
Curll, Edmund [publishing house] DLB-154
Currie, James 1756-1805 .... DLB-142
Currie, Mary Montgomerie Lamb Singleton,
 Lady Currie
 (see Fane, Violet)
Cursor Mundi circa 1300 .... DLB-146
Curti, Merle E. 1897- DLB-17
Curtis, Anthony 1926- DLB-155
Curtis, Cyrus H. K. 1850-1933 .... DLB-91
Curtis, George William
 1824-1892 .... DLB-1, 43, 223
Curzon, Robert 1810-1873 .... DLB-166
Curzon, Sarah Anne 1833-1898 .... DLB-99
Cusack, Dymphna 1902-1981 .... DLB-260
Cushing, Harvey 1869-1939 .... DLB-187
Custance, Olive (Lady Alfred Douglas)
 1874-1944 .... DLB-240
Cynewulf circa 770-840 .... DLB-146
Czepko, Daniel 1605-1660 .... DLB-164
Czerniawski, Adam 1934- DLB-232

D

Dabit, Eugène 1898-1936 .... DLB-65
Daborne, Robert circa 1580-1628 ..... DLB-58
Dąbrowska, Maria
 1889-1965 .... DLB-215; CDWLB-4
Dacey, Philip 1939- DLB-105
"Eyes Across Centuries: Contemporary
 Poetry and 'That Vision Thing,'" ... DLB-105
Dach, Simon 1605-1659 .... DLB-164
Dagerman, Stig 1923-1954 .... DLB-259
Daggett, Rollin M. 1831-1901 .... DLB-79
D'Aguiar, Fred 1960- DLB-157
Dahl, Roald 1916-1990 .... DLB-139, 255
Dahlberg, Edward 1900-1977 .... DLB-48
Dahn, Felix 1834-1912 .... DLB-129
Dal', Vladimir Ivanovich (Kazak Vladimir
 Lugansky) 1801-1872 .... DLB-198
Dale, Peter 1938- DLB-40
Daley, Arthur 1904-1974 .... DLB-171
Dall, Caroline Healey 1822-1912 ..... DLB-1, 235
Dallas, E. S. 1828-1879 .... DLB-55
From The Gay Science (1866) DLB-21
The Dallas Theater Center DLB-7

D'Alton, Louis 1900-1951 .... DLB-10
Daly, Carroll John 1889-1958 .... DLB-226
Daly, T. A. 1871-1948 .... DLB-11
Damon, S. Foster 1893-1971 .... DLB-45
Damrell, William S. [publishing house] ... DLB-49
Dana, Charles A. 1819-1897 ..... DLB-3, 23, 250
Dana, Richard Henry, Jr.
 1815-1882 .... DLB-1, 183, 235
Dandridge, Ray Garfield DLB-51
Dane, Clemence 1887-1965 .... DLB-10, 197
Danforth, John 1660-1730 .... DLB-24
Danforth, Samuel, I 1626-1674 .... DLB-24
Danforth, Samuel, II 1666-1727 .... DLB-24
Dangerous Years: London Theater,
 1939-1945 .... DLB-10
Daniel, John M. 1825-1865 .... DLB-43
Daniel, Samuel 1562 or 1563-1619 ..... DLB-62
Daniel Press DLB-106
Daniells, Roy 1902-1979 .... DLB-68
Daniels, Jim 1956- DLB-120
Daniels, Jonathan 1902-1981 .... DLB-127
Daniels, Josephus 1862-1948 .... DLB-29
Daniels, Sarah 1957- DLB-245
Danilevsky, Grigorii Petrovich
 1829-1890 .... DLB-238
Dannay, Frederic 1905-1982 and
 Manfred B. Lee 1905-1971 .... DLB-137
Danner, Margaret Esse 1915- DLB-41
Danter, John [publishing house] DLB-170
Dantin, Louis 1865-1945 .... DLB-92
Danzig, Allison 1898-1987 .... DLB-171
D'Arcy, Ella circa 1857-1937 .... DLB-135
Dark, Eleanor 1901-1985 .... DLB-260
Darke, Nick 1948- DLB-233
Darley, Felix Octavious Carr 1822-1888 . DLB-188
Darley, George 1795-1846 .... DLB-96
Darmesteter, Madame James
 (see Robinson, A. Mary F.)
Darwin, Charles 1809-1882 .... DLB-57, 166
Darwin, Erasmus 1731-1802 .... DLB-93
Daryush, Elizabeth 1887-1977 .... DLB-20
Dashkova, Ekaterina Romanovna
 (née Vorontsova) 1743-1810 .... DLB-150
Dashwood, Edmée Elizabeth Monica de la Pasture
 (see Delafield, E. M.)
Daudet, Alphonse 1840-1897 .... DLB-123
d'Aulaire, Edgar Parin 1898- and
 d'Aulaire, Ingri 1904- DLB-22
Davenant, Sir William 1606-1668 ... DLB-58, 126
Davenport, Guy 1927- DLB-130
Davenport, Marcia 1903-1996 .... DS-17
Davenport, Robert ?-? DLB-58
Daves, Delmer 1904-1977 .... DLB-26
Davey, Frank 1940- DLB-53
Davidson, Avram 1923-1993 .... DLB-8
Davidson, Donald 1893-1968 .... DLB-45
Davidson, John 1857-1909 .... DLB-19

Davidson, Lionel 1922- DLB-14	Dazai Osamu 1909-1948 ....DLB-182	Del Giudice, Daniele 1949- DLB-196
Davidson, Robyn 1950- DLB-204	Deacon, William Arthur 1890-1977.......DLB-68	De Libero, Libero 1906-1981 ....DLB-114
Davidson, Sara 1943- DLB-185	Deal, Borden 1922-1985 ....DLB-6	DeLillo, Don 1936- DLB-6, 173
Davie, Donald 1922- DLB-27	de Angeli, Marguerite 1889-1987.......DLB-22	de Lint, Charles 1951- DLB-251
Davie, Elspeth 1919- DLB-139	De Angelis, Milo 1951- DLB-128	de Lisser H. G. 1878-1944..............DLB-117
Davies, Sir John 1569-1626 ....DLB-172	De Bow, J. D. B. 1820-1867 ....DLB-3, 79, 248	Dell, Floyd 1887-1969 ....DLB-9
Davies, John, of Hereford 1565?-1618....DLB-121		Dell Publishing Company DLB-46
Davies, Peter, Limited DLB-112	de Bruyn, Günter 1926- DLB-75	delle Grazie, Marie Eugene 1864-1931 ....DLB-81
Davies, Rhys 1901-1978.........DLB-139, 191	de Camp, L. Sprague 1907-2000 ....DLB-8	Deloney, Thomas died 1600 ....DLB-167
Davies, Robertson 1913-1995 ....DLB-68	De Carlo, Andrea 1952- DLB-196	Deloria, Ella C. 1889-1971..............DLB-175
Davies, Samuel 1723-1761 ....DLB-31	De Casas, Celso A. 1944- DLB-209	Deloria, Vine, Jr. 1933- DLB-175
Davies, Thomas 1712?-1785. ....DLB-142, 154	Dechert, Robert 1895-1975 ....DLB-187	del Rey, Lester 1915-1993 ....DLB-8
Davies, W. H. 1871-1940...........DLB-19, 174	Dedications, Inscriptions, and Annotations ... Y-01	Del Vecchio, John M. 1947- DS-9
Daviot, Gordon 1896?-1952 ....DLB-10 (see also Tey, Josephine)	Dee, John 1527-1608 or 1609.......DLB-136, 213	Del'vig, Anton Antonovich 1798-1831 ...DLB-205
	Deeping, George Warwick 1877-1950 ....DLB 153	de Man, Paul 1919-1983 ....DLB-67
Davis, Arthur Hoey (see Rudd, Steele)	Defoe, Daniel 1660-1731 ....DLB-39, 95, 101; CDBLB-2	DeMarinis, Rick 1934- DLB-218
Davis, Charles A. 1795-1867 ....DLB-11		Demby, William 1922- DLB-33
Davis, Clyde Brion 1894-1962............DLB-9	Preface to *Colonel Jack* (1722) DLB-39	De Mille, James 1833-1880 ....DLB-251
Davis, Dick 1945- DLB-40	Preface to *The Farther Adventures of Robinson Crusoe* (1719)..............DLB-39	de Mille, William 1878-1955 ....DLB-266
Davis, Frank Marshall 1905-? DLB-51		Deming, Philander 1829-1915 ....DLB-74
Davis, H. L. 1894-1960 ....DLB-9, 206	Preface to *Moll Flanders* (1722) DLB-39	Deml, Jakub 1878-1961 ....DLB-215
Davis, John 1774-1854 ....DLB-37	Preface to *Robinson Crusoe* (1719) DLB-39	Demorest, William Jennings 1822-1895 ...DLB-79
Davis, Lydia 1947- DLB-130	Preface to *Roxana* (1724).................DLB-39	De Morgan, William 1839-1917 ....DLB-153
Davis, Margaret Thomson 1926- DLB-14	de Fontaine, Felix Gregory 1834-1896.....DLB-43	Demosthenes 384 B.C.-322 B.C.........DLB-176
Davis, Ossie 1917- DLB-7, 38, 249	De Forest, John William 1826-1906...DLB-12, 189	Denham, Henry [publishing house]......DLB-170
Davis, Owen 1874-1956..............DLB-249	DeFrees, Madeline 1919- DLB-105	Denham, Sir John 1615-1669........DLB-58, 126
Davis, Paxton 1925-1994................ Y-89	"The Poet's Kaleidoscope: The Element of Surprise in the Making of the Poem" DLB-105	Denison, Merrill 1893-1975 ....DLB-92
Davis, Rebecca Harding 1831-1910...DLB-74, 239		Denison, T. S., and Company..........DLB-49
Davis, Richard Harding 1864-1916 ....DLB-12, 23, 78, 79, 189; DS-13	DeGolyer, Everette Lee 1886-1956 ......DLB-187	Dennery, Adolphe Philippe 1811-1899 ...DLB-192
	de Graff, Robert 1895-1981............... Y-81	Dennie, Joseph 1768-1812 ..... DLB-37, 43, 59, 73
Davis, Samuel Cole 1764-1809 ....DLB-37	de Graft, Joe 1924-1978 ....DLB-117	Dennis, C. J. 1876-1938..............DLB-260
Davis, Samuel Post 1850-1918...........DLB-202	*De Heinrico* circa 980?..................DLB-148	Dennis, John 1658-1734................DLB-101
Davison, Frank Dalby 1893-1970 ....DLB-260	Deighton, Len 1929- DLB-87; CDBLB-8	Dennis, Nigel 1912-1989 ..... DLB-13, 15, 233
Davison, Peter 1928- DLB-5	DeJong, Meindert 1906-1991...........DLB-52	Denslow, W. W. 1856-1915 ....DLB-188
Davydov, Denis Vasil'evich 1784-1839 ....DLB-205	Dekker, Thomas circa 1572-1632 ....DLB-62, 172; CDBLB-1	Dent, J. M., and Sons................DLB-112
		Dent, Tom 1932-1998 ....DLB-38
Davys, Mary 1674-1732................DLB-39	Delacorte, George T., Jr. 1894-1991 ......DLB-91	Denton, Daniel circa 1626-1703..........DLB-24
Preface to *The Works of Mrs. Davys* (1725)..................DLB-39	Delafield, E. M. 1890-1943 ....DLB-34	DePaola, Tomie 1934- DLB-61
	Delahaye, Guy 1888-1969 ....DLB-92	Department of Library, Archives, and Institutional Research, American Bible Society........Y-97
DAW Books........................DLB-46	de la Mare, Walter 1873-1956 ....DLB-19, 153, 162, 255; CDBLB-6	
Dawson, Ernest 1882-1947 ....DLB-140		De Quille, Dan 1829-1898..............DLB-186
Dawson, Fielding 1930- DLB-130	Deland, Margaret 1857-1945 ....DLB-78	De Quincey, Thomas 1785-1859 ....DLB-110, 144; CDBLB-3
Dawson, Sarah Morgan 1842-1909 ......DLB-239	Delaney, Shelagh 1939- DLB-13; CDBLB-8	
Dawson, William 1704-1752 ....DLB-31	Delano, Amasa 1763-1823 ....DLB-183	"Rhetoric" (1828; revised, 1859) [excerpt] DLB-57
Day, Angel flourished 1583-1599 .... DLB-167, 236	Delany, Martin Robinson 1812-1885 .....DLB-50	
Day, Benjamin Henry 1810-1889 ....DLB-43	Delany, Samuel R. 1942- DLB-8, 33	Derby, George Horatio 1823-1861 ....DLB-11
Day, Clarence 1874-1935...............DLB-11	de la Roche, Mazo 1879-1961 ....DLB-68	Derby, J. C., and Company.............DLB-49
Day, Dorothy 1897-1980 ....DLB-29	Delavigne, Jean François Casimir 1793-1843 ....DLB-192	Derby and Miller..................DLB-49
Day, Frank Parker 1881-1950 ....DLB-92		De Ricci, Seymour 1881-1942 ....DLB-201
Day, John circa 1574-circa 1640...........DLB-62	Delbanco, Nicholas 1942- DLB-6, 234	Derleth, August 1909-1971 .... DLB-9; DS-17
Day, John [publishing house]...........DLB-170	Delblanc, Sven 1931-1992 ....DLB-257	Derrida, Jacques 1930- DLB-242
Day, The John, Company.............DLB-46	Del Castillo, Ramón 1949- DLB-209	The Derrydale Press DLB-46
Day Lewis, C. 1904-1972.........DLB-15, 20 (see also Blake, Nicholas)	Deledda, Grazia 1871-1936 ....DLB-264	Derzhavin, Gavriil Romanovich 1743-1816 ....DLB-150
	De León, Nephtal 1945- DLB-82	
Day, Mahlon [publishing house] DLB-49	Delfini, Antonio 1907-1963 ....DLB-264	
Day, Thomas 1748-1789 ....DLB-39	Delgado, Abelardo Barrientos 1931- DLB-82	Desaulniers, Gonsalve 1863-1934 ....DLB-92

Desbordes-Valmore, Marceline
  1786-1859 .... DLB-217
Deschamps, Emile 1791-1871 .... DLB-217
Deschamps, Eustache 1340?-1404 ...... DLB-208
Desbiens, Jean-Paul 1927- DLB-53
des Forêts, Louis-Rene 1918- DLB-83
Desiato, Luca 1941- DLB-196
Desnica, Vladan 1905-1967 .... DLB-181
Desnos, Robert 1900-1945 .... DLB-258
DesRochers, Alfred 1901-1978 .... DLB-68
Desrosiers, Léo-Paul 1896-1967 .... DLB-68
Dessì, Giuseppe 1909-1977 .... DLB-177
Destouches, Louis-Ferdinand
  (see Céline, Louis-Ferdinand)
DeSylva, Buddy 1895-1950 and
  Brown, Lew 1893-1958 .... DLB-265
De Tabley, Lord 1835-1895 .... DLB-35
Deutsch, André, Limited DLB-112
Deutsch, Babette 1895-1982 .... DLB-45
Deutsch, Niklaus Manuel (see Manuel, Niklaus)
Devanny, Jean 1894-1962 .... DLB-260
Deveaux, Alexis 1948- DLB-38
The Development of the Author's Copyright
  in Britain DLB-154
The Development of Lighting in the Staging
  of Drama, 1900-1945 .... DLB-10
"The Development of Meiji Japan" DLB-180
De Vere, Aubrey 1814-1902 .... DLB-35
Devereux, second Earl of Essex, Robert
  1565-1601 .... DLB-136
The Devin-Adair Company DLB-46
De Vinne, Theodore Low 1828-1914 .... DLB-187
Devlin, Anne 1951- DLB-245
De Voto, Bernard 1897-1955 .... DLB-9, 256
De Vries, Peter 1910-1993 .... DLB-6; Y-82
Dewdney, Christopher 1951- DLB-60
Dewdney, Selwyn 1909-1979 .... DLB-68
Dewey, John 1859-1952 .... DLB-246
Dewey, Orville 1794-1882 .... DLB-243
Dewey, Thomas B. 1915-1981 .... DLB-226
DeWitt, Robert M., Publisher DLB-49
DeWolfe, Fiske and Company DLB-49
Dexter, Colin 1930- DLB-87
de Young, M. H. 1849-1925 .... DLB-25
Dhlomo, H. I. E. 1903-1956 .... DLB-157, 225
Dhuoda circa 803-after 843 .... DLB-148
The Dial 1840-1844 .... DLB-223
The Dial Press DLB-46
Diamond, I. A. L. 1920-1988 .... DLB-26
Dibble, L. Grace 1902-1998 .... DLB-204
Dibdin, Thomas Frognall 1776-1847 ..... DLB-184
Di Cicco, Pier Giorgio 1949- DLB-60
Dick, Philip K. 1928-1982 .... DLB-8
Dick and Fitzgerald DLB-49
Dickens, Charles 1812-1870
  .... DLB-21, 55, 70, 159, 166; CDBLB-4

Dickey, James 1923-1997
  .... DLB-5, 193; Y-82, Y-93, Y-96;
                      DS-7, DS-19; CDALB-6
James Dickey Tributes Y-97
The Life of James Dickey: A Lecture to
  the Friends of the Emory Libraries,
  by Henry Hart..................... Y-98
Dickey, William 1928-1994 .... DLB-5
Dickinson, Emily
  1830-1886 .... DLB-1, 243; CDWLB-3
Dickinson, John 1732-1808............. DLB-31
Dickinson, Jonathan 1688-1747 .... DLB-24
Dickinson, Patric 1914- DLB-27
Dickinson, Peter 1927- DLB-87, 161
Dicks, John [publishing house]........ DLB-106
Dickson, Gordon R. 1923- DLB-8
Dictionary of Literary Biography Yearbook Awards
  ..... Y-92, Y-93, Y-97, Y-98, Y-99, Y-00, Y-01
The Dictionary of National Biography DLB-144
Didion, Joan 1934-
  ...... DLB-2, 173, 185; Y-81, Y-86; CDALB-6
Di Donato, Pietro 1911- DLB-9
Die Fürstliche Bibliothek Corvey........... Y-96
Diego, Gerardo 1896-1987 .... DLB-134
Dietz, Howard 1896-1983 .... DLB-265
Digges, Thomas circa 1546-1595 .... DLB-136
The Digital Millennium Copyright Act:
  Expanding Copyright Protection in
  Cyberspace and Beyond Y-98
Diktonius, Elmer 1896-1961........... DLB-259
Dillard, Annie 1945- Y-80
Dillard, R. H. W. 1937- DLB-5, 244
Dillingham, Charles T., Company....... DLB-49
The Dillingham, G. W., Company DLB-49
Dilly, Edward and Charles
  [publishing house] DLB-154
Dilthey, Wilhelm 1833-1911 .... DLB-129
Dimitrova, Blaga 1922- ... DLB-181; CDWLB-4
Dimov, Dimitr 1909-1966 .... DLB-181
Dimsdale, Thomas J. 1831?-1866...... DLB-186
Dinescu, Mircea 1950- DLB-232
Dinesen, Isak (see Blixen, Karen)
Dingelstedt, Franz von 1814-1881 ..... DLB-133
Dintenfass, Mark 1941- Y-84
Diogenes, Jr. (see Brougham, John)
Diogenes Laertius circa 200 .... DLB-176
DiPrima, Diane 1934- DLB-5, 16
Disch, Thomas M. 1940- DLB-8
Disney, Walt 1901-1966 .... DLB-22
Disraeli, Benjamin 1804-1881........ DLB-21, 55
D'Israeli, Isaac 1766-1848............. DLB-107
Ditlevsen, Tove 1917-1976 .... DLB-214
Ditzen, Rudolf (see Fallada, Hans)
Dix, Dorothea Lynde 1802-1887 ..... DLB-1, 235
Dix, Dorothy (see Gilmer, Elizabeth Meriwether)
Dix, Edwards and Company DLB-49
Dix, Gertrude circa 1874-? DLB-197

Dixie, Florence Douglas 1857-1905 ...... DLB-174
Dixon, Ella Hepworth
  1855 or 1857-1932 .... DLB-197
Dixon, Paige (see Corcoran, Barbara)
Dixon, Richard Watson 1833-1900 ...... DLB-19
Dixon, Stephen 1936- DLB-130
Dmitriev, Ivan Ivanovich 1760-1837..... DLB-150
Do They Or Don't They?
  Writers Reading Book Reviews......... Y-01
Dobell, Bertram 1842-1914 .... DLB-184
Dobell, Sydney 1824-1874 .... DLB-32
Dobie, J. Frank 1888-1964 .... DLB-212
Döblin, Alfred 1878-1957 .... DLB-66; CDWLB-2
Dobson, Austin 1840-1921......... DLB-35, 144
Dobson, Rosemary 1920- DLB-260
Doctorow, E. L.
  1931- DLB-2, 28, 173; Y-80; CDALB-6
Documents on Sixteenth-Century
  Literature DLB-167, 172
Dodd, Anne [publishing house] DLB-154
Dodd, Mead and Company DLB-49
Dodd, Susan M. 1946- DLB-244
Dodd, William E. 1869-1940 .... DLB-17
Doderer, Heimito von 1896-1968 .... DLB-85
Dodge, B. W., and Company........... DLB-46
Dodge, Mary Abigail 1833-1896 .... DLB-221
Dodge, Mary Mapes
  1831?-1905.............. DLB-42, 79; DS-13
Dodge Publishing Company DLB-49
Dodgson, Charles Lutwidge (see Carroll, Lewis)
Dodsley, R. [publishing house] DLB-154
Dodsley, Robert 1703-1764 .... DLB-95
Dodson, Owen 1914-1983 .... DLB-76
Dodwell, Christina 1951- DLB-204
Doesticks, Q. K. Philander, P. B.
  (see Thomson, Mortimer)
Doheny, Carrie Estelle 1875-1958 ...... DLB-140
Doherty, John 1798?-1854 .... DLB-190
Doig, Ivan 1939- DLB-206
Doinaş, Ştefan Augustin 1922- DLB-232
Domínguez, Sylvia Maida 1935- DLB-122
Donahoe, Patrick [publishing house] DLB-49
Donald, David H. 1920- DLB-17
The Practice of Biography VI: An
  Interview with David Herbert Donald.... Y-87
Donaldson, Scott 1928- DLB-111
Doni, Rodolfo 1919- DLB-177
Donleavy, J. P. 1926- DLB-6, 173
Donnadieu, Marguerite (see Duras, Marguerite)
Donne, John
  1572-1631........ DLB-121, 151; CDBLB-1
Donnelley, R. R., and Sons Company DLB-49
Donnelly, Ignatius 1831-1901.......... DLB-12
Donohue and Henneberry DLB-49
Donoso, José 1924-1996.... DLB-113; CDWLB-3
Doolady, M. [publishing house] DLB-49
Dooley, Ebon (see Ebon)

Doolittle, Hilda 1886-1961............DLB-4, 45

Doplicher, Fabio 1938- DLB-128

Dor, Milo 1923- DLB-85

Doran, George H., Company DLB-46

Dorgelès, Roland 1886-1973 ....DLB-65

Dorn, Edward 1929-1999 ....DLB-5

Dorr, Rheta Childe 1866-1948 ....DLB-25

Dorris, Michael 1945-1997............DLB-175

Dorset and Middlesex, Charles Sackville,
  Lord Buckhurst, Earl of 1643-1706....DLB-131

Dorsey, Candas Jane 1952- DLB-251

Dorst, Tankred 1925- DLB-75, 124

Dos Passos, John 1896-1970
  ....DLB-4, 9; DS-1, DS-15; CDALB-5

John Dos Passos: Artist Y-99

John Dos Passos: A Centennial
  Commemoration...................Y-96

Dostoevsky, Fyodor 1821-1881.........DLB-238

Doubleday and Company DLB-49

Dougall, Lily 1858-1923 ....DLB-92

Doughty, Charles M.
  1843-1926................ DLB-19, 57, 174

Douglas, Lady Alfred (see Custance, Olive)

Douglas, Gavin 1476-1522.............DLB-132

Douglas, Keith 1920-1944 ....DLB-27

Douglas, Norman 1868-1952.........DLB-34, 195

Douglass, Frederick 1818-1895
  ....DLB-1, 43, 50, 79, 243; CDALB-2

Frederick Douglass Creative Arts Center Y-01

Douglass, William circa 1691-1752 ....DLB-24

Dourado, Autran 1926- DLB-145

Dove, Arthur G. 1880-1946............DLB-188

Dove, Rita 1952- DLB-120; CDALB-7

Dover Publications...................DLB-46

Doves Press........................DLB-112

Dowden, Edward 1843-1913........DLB-35, 149

Dowell, Coleman 1925-1985............DLB-130

Dowland, John 1563-1626..............DLB-172

Downes, Gwladys 1915- DLB-88

Downing, J., Major (see Davis, Charles A.)

Downing, Major Jack (see Smith, Seba)

Dowriche, Anne
  before 1560-after 1613...............DLB-172

Dowson, Ernest 1867-1900 ....DLB-19, 135

Doxey, William [publishing house] DLB-49

Doyle, Sir Arthur Conan
  1859-1930 ... DLB-18, 70, 156, 178; CDBLB-5

Doyle, Kirby 1932- DLB-16

Doyle, Roddy 1958- DLB-194

Drabble, Margaret
  1939- DLB-14, 155, 231; CDBLB-8

Drach, Albert 1902- DLB-85

Dragojević, Danijel 1934- DLB-181

Drake, Samuel Gardner 1798-1875 .....DLB-187

The Dramatic Publishing Company DLB-49

Dramatists Play Service DLB-46

Drant, Thomas early 1540s?-1578.......DLB-167

Draper, John W. 1811-1882 ....DLB-30

Draper, Lyman C. 1815-1891 ....DLB-30

Drayton, Michael 1563-1631...........DLB-121

Dreiser, Theodore 1871-1945
  ....DLB-9, 12, 102, 137; DS-1; CDALB-3

Dresser, Davis 1904-1977 ....DLB-226

Drewitz, Ingeborg 1923-1986 ....DLB-75

Drieu La Rochelle, Pierre 1893-1945......DLB-72

Drinker, Elizabeth 1735-1807...........DLB-200

Drinkwater, John
  1882-1937.................DLB-10, 19, 149

Droste-Hülshoff, Annette von
  1797-1848............DLB-133; CDWLB-2

The Drue Heinz Literature Prize
  Excerpt from "Excerpts from a Report
  of the Commission," in David
  Bosworth's The Death of Descartes
  An Interview with David Bosworth Y-82

Drummond, William, of Hawthornden
  1585-1649 ....DLB-121, 213

Drummond, William Henry
  1854-1907 ....DLB-92

Druzhinin, Aleksandr Vasil'evich
  1824-1864 ....DLB-238

Dryden, Charles 1860?-1931...........DLB-171

Dryden, John
  1631-1700 ......DLB-80, 101, 131; CDBLB-2

Držić, Marin
  circa 1508-1567........DLB-147; CDWLB-4

Duane, William 1760-1835 ....DLB-43

Dubé, Marcel 1930- DLB-53

Dubé, Rodolphe (see Hertel, François)

Dubie, Norman 1945- DLB-120

Dubin, Al 1891-1945 ....DLB-265

Dubois, Silvia
  1788 or 1789?-1889 ....DLB-239

Du Bois, W. E. B.
  1868-1963 .... DLB-47, 50, 91, 246; CDALB-3

Du Bois, William Pène 1916-1993.........DLB-61

Dubrovina, Ekaterina Oskarovna
  1846-1913 ....DLB-238

Dubus, Andre 1936-1999..............DLB-130

Ducange, Victor 1783-1833 ....DLB-192

Du Chaillu, Paul Belloni 1831?-1903.....DLB-189

Ducharme, Réjean 1941- DLB-60

Dučić, Jovan
  1871-1943 ....DLB-147; CDWLB-4

Duck, Stephen 1705?-1756..............DLB-95

Duckworth, Gerald, and Company
  Limited DLB-112

Duclaux, Madame Mary (see Robinson, A. Mary F.)

Dudek, Louis 1918- DLB-88

Duell, Sloan and Pearce..............DLB-46

Duerer, Albrecht 1471-1528........... DLB-179

Duff Gordon, Lucie 1821-1869 ....DLB-166

Dufferin, Helen Lady, Countess of Gifford
  1807-1867 ....DLB-199

Duffield and Green DLB-46

Duffy, Maureen 1933- DLB-14

Dufief, Nicholas Gouin 1776-1834.......DLB-187

Dugan, Alan 1923- DLB-5

Dugard, William [publishing house] DLB-170

Dugas, Marcel 1883-1947 ....DLB-92

Dugdale, William [publishing house].....DLB-106

Duhamel, Georges 1884-1966..........DLB-65

Dujardin, Edouard 1861-1949..........DLB-123

Dukes, Ashley 1885-1959 ....DLB-10

Dumas, Alexandre père 1802-1870.....DLB-119, 192

Dumas, Alexandre fils
  1824-1895 ....DLB-192

Dumas, Henry 1934-1968 ....DLB-41

du Maurier, Daphne 1907-1989.........DLB-191

Du Maurier, George
  1834-1896 ....DLB-153, 178

Dummett, Michael 1925- DLB-262

Dunbar, Paul Laurence
  1872-1906 ....DLB-50, 54, 78; CDALB-3

Dunbar, William
  circa 1460-circa 1522..........DLB-132, 146

Duncan, Dave 1933- DLB-251

Duncan, David James 1952- DLB-256

Duncan, Norman 1871-1916 ....DLB-92

Duncan, Quince 1940- DLB-145

Duncan, Robert 1919-1988 ....DLB-5, 16, 193

Duncan, Ronald 1914-1982............DLB-13

Duncan, Sara Jeannette 1861-1922 ......DLB-92

Dunigan, Edward, and Brother DLB-49

Dunlap, John 1747-1812...............DLB-43

Dunlap, William 1766-1839....... DLB-30, 37, 59

Dunn, Douglas 1942- DLB-40

Dunn, Harvey Thomas 1884-1952 ......DLB-188

Dunn, Stephen 1939- DLB-105

"The Good, The Not So Good" DLB-105

Dunne, Finley Peter 1867-1936 ....DLB-11, 23

Dunne, John Gregory 1932- Y-80

Dunne, Philip 1908-1992...............DLB-26

Dunning, Ralph Cheever 1878-1930 ....DLB-4

Dunning, William A. 1857-1922 ....DLB-17

Dunsany, Lord (Edward John Moreton
  Drax Plunkett, Baron Dunsany)
  1878-1957 ....DLB-10, 77, 153, 156, 255

Duns Scotus, John
  circa 1266-1308..................DLB-115

Dunton, John [publishing house].......DLB-170

Dunton, W. Herbert 1878-1936........DLB-188

Dupin, Amantine-Aurore-Lucile (see Sand, George)

Dupuy, Eliza Ann 1814-1880 ....DLB-248

Durack, Mary 1913-1994 ....DLB-260

Durand, Lucile (see Bersianik, Louky)

Duranti, Francesca 1935- DLB-196

Duranty, Walter 1884-1957............DLB-29

Duras, Marguerite 1914-1996 ....DLB-83

Durfey, Thomas 1653-1723.............DLB-80

Durova, Nadezhda Andreevna
  (Aleksandr Andreevich Aleksandrov)
  1783-1866 ....DLB-198

Cumulative Index

Durrell, Lawrence 1912-1990
..........DLB-15, 27, 204; Y-90; CDBLB-7
Durrell, William [publishing house] DLB-49
Dürrenmatt, Friedrich
  1921-1990 .... DLB-69, 124; CDWLB-2
Duston, Hannah 1657-1737............ DLB-200
Dutt, Toru 1856-1877................ DLB-240
Dutton, E. P., and Company DLB-49
Duvoisin, Roger 1904-1980 .... DLB-61
Duyckinck, Evert Augustus
  1816-1878................ DLB-3, 64, 250
Duyckinck, George L.
  1823-1863 .... DLB-3, 250
Duyckinck and Company............. DLB-49
Dwight, John Sullivan 1813-1893..... DLB-1, 235
Dwight, Timothy 1752-1817............ DLB-37
Dybek, Stuart 1942- DLB-130
Dyer, Charles 1928- DLB-13
Dyer, Sir Edward 1543-1607 .... DLB-136
Dyer, George 1755-1841............... DLB-93
Dyer, John 1699-1757................. DLB-95
Dyk, Viktor 1877-1931................ DLB-215
Dylan, Bob 1941- DLB-16

E

Eager, Edward 1911-1964 .... DLB-22
Eagleton, Terry 1943- DLB-242
Eames, Wilberforce 1855-1937........ DLB-140
Earle, Alice Morse 1853-1911......... DLB-221
Earle, James H., and Company DLB-49
Earle, John 1600 or 1601-1665........ DLB-151
Early American Book Illustration,
  by Sinclair Hamilton DLB-49
Eastlake, William 1917-1997......... DLB-6, 206
Eastman, Carol ?- DLB-44
Eastman, Charles A. (Ohiyesa)
  1858-1939................DLB-175
Eastman, Max 1883-1969.............. DLB-91
Eaton, Daniel Isaac 1753-1814 .... DLB-158
Eaton, Edith Maude 1865-1914 ..... DLB-221
Eaton, Winnifred 1875-1954.......... DLB-221
Eberhart, Richard 1904- DLB-48; CDALB-1
Ebner, Jeannie 1918- DLB-85
Ebner-Eschenbach, Marie von
  1830-1916................. DLB-81
Ebon 1942- DLB-41
E-Books Turn the Corner.................Y-98
Ecbasis Captivi circa 1045 .... DLB-148
Ecco Press........................ DLB-46
Eckhart, Meister circa 1260-circa 1328... DLB-115
The Eclectic Review 1805-1868........... DLB-110
Eco, Umberto 1932- DLB-196, 242
Eddison, E. R. 1882-1945............. DLB-255
Edel, Leon 1907-1997................ DLB-103
Edelfeldt, Inger 1956- DLB-257
Edes, Benjamin 1732-1803 .... DLB-43

Edgar, David 1948- DLB-13, 233
Edgeworth, Maria
  1768-1849...............DLB-116, 159, 163
The Edinburgh Review 1802-1929 .... DLB-110
Edinburgh University Press DLB-112
The Editor Publishing Company DLB-49
Editorial Institute at Boston University Y-00
Editorial Statements DLB-137
Edmonds, Randolph 1900- DLB-51
Edmonds, Walter D. 1903-1998......... DLB-9
Edschmid, Kasimir 1890-1966 .... DLB-56
Edson, Margaret 1961- DLB-266
Edson, Russell 1935- DLB-244
Edwards, Amelia Anne Blandford
  1831-1892 ....DLB-174
Edwards, Dic 1953- DLB-245
Edwards, Edward 1812-1886 .... DLB-184
Edwards, James [publishing house]...... DLB-154
Edwards, Jonathan 1703-1758......... DLB-24
Edwards, Jonathan, Jr. 1745-1801....... DLB-37
Edwards, Junius 1929- DLB-33
Edwards, Matilda Barbara Betham
  1836-1919 ....DLB-174
Edwards, Richard 1524-1566.......... DLB-62
Edwards, Sarah Pierpont 1710-1758 ..... DLB-200
Effinger, George Alec 1947- DLB-8
Egerton, George 1859-1945 .... DLB-135
Eggleston, Edward 1837-1902......... DLB-12
Eggleston, Wilfred 1901-1986 .... DLB-92
Eglītis, Anšlavs 1906-1993 .... DLB-220
Ehrenreich, Barbara 1941- DLB-246
Ehrenstein, Albert 1886-1950.......... DLB-81
Ehrhart, W. D. 1948- DS-9
Ehrlich, Gretel 1946- DLB-212
Eich, Günter 1907-1972.......... DLB-69, 124
Eichendorff, Joseph Freiherr von
  1788-1857..................... DLB-90
Eifukumon'in 1271-1342.............. DLB-203
1873 Publishers' Catalogues DLB-49
Eighteenth-Century Aesthetic
  Theories...................... DLB-31
Eighteenth-Century Philosophical
  Background DLB-31
Eigner, Larry 1926-1996 .... DLB-5, 193
Eikon Basilike 1649.................. DLB-151
Eilhart von Oberge
  circa 1140-circa 1195 .... DLB-148
Einhard circa 770-840 .... DLB-148
Eiseley, Loren 1907-1977 .... DS-17
Eisenberg, Deborah 1945- DLB-244
Eisenreich, Herbert 1925-1986......... DLB-85
Eisner, Kurt 1867-1919 .... DLB-66
Ekelöf, Gunnar 1907-1968 .... DLB-259
Eklund, Gordon 1945- Y-83
Ekman, Kerstin 1933- DLB-257
Ekwensi, Cyprian
  1921- DLB-117; CDWLB-3

Elaw, Zilpha circa 1790-? DLB-239
Eld, George [publishing house]..........DLB-170
Elder, Lonne, III 1931- DLB-7, 38, 44
Elder, Paul, and Company............ DLB-49
The Electronic Text Center and the Electronic
  Archive of Early American Fiction at the
  University of Virginia Library......... Y-98
Eliade, Mircea 1907-1986 ... DLB-220; CDWLB-4
Elie, Robert 1915-1973 .... DLB-88
Elin Pelin 1877-1949 ....DLB-147; CDWLB-4
Eliot, George
  1819-1880 .... DLB-21, 35, 55; CDBLB-4
Eliot, John 1604-1690................ DLB-24
Eliot, T. S. 1888-1965
  ....DLB-7, 10, 45, 63, 245; CDALB-5
T. S. Eliot Centennial................. Y-88
Eliot's Court Press DLB-170
Elizabeth I 1533-1603 .... DLB-136
Elizabeth of Nassau-Saarbrücken
  after 1393-1456 ....DLB-179
Elizondo, Salvador 1932- DLB-145
Elizondo, Sergio 1930- DLB-82
Elkin, Stanley 1930-1995 ....DLB-2, 28, 218; Y-80
Elles, Dora Amy (see Wentworth, Patricia)
Ellet, Elizabeth F. 1818?-1877........... DLB-30
Elliot, Ebenezer 1781-1849 .... DLB-96, 190
Elliot, Frances Minto (Dickinson)
  1820-1898 .... DLB-166
Elliott, Charlotte 1789-1871 .... DLB-199
Elliott, George 1923- DLB-68
Elliott, George P. 1918-1980........... DLB-244
Elliott, Janice 1931- DLB-14
Elliott, Sarah Barnwell 1848-1928 ...... DLB-221
Elliott, Thomes and Talbot DLB-49
Elliott, William, III 1788-1863 .... DLB-3, 248
Ellis, Alice Thomas (Anna Margaret Haycraft)
  1932- DLB-194
Ellis, Edward S. 1840-1916........... DLB-42
Ellis, Frederick Staridge
  [publishing house] DLB-106
The George H. Ellis Company.......... DLB-49
Ellis, Havelock 1859-1939 .... DLB-190
Ellison, Harlan 1934- DLB-8
Ellison, Ralph
  1914-1994 ...DLB-2, 76, 227; Y-94; CDALB-1
Ellmann, Richard 1918-1987 ....DLB-103; Y-87
Ellroy, James 1948- DLB-226; Y-91
Eluard, Paul 1895-1952 .... DLB-258
Elyot, Thomas 1490?-1546 .... DLB-136
Emanuel, James Andrew 1921- DLB-41
Emecheta, Buchi 1944- DLB-117; CDWLB-3
Emendations for Look Homeward, Angel....... Y-00
The Emergence of Black Women Writers....DS-8
Emerson, Ralph Waldo 1803-1882
  .... DLB-1, 59, 73, 183, 223; CDALB-2
Ralph Waldo Emerson in 1982 .... Y-82
Emerson, William 1769-1811 .... DLB-37

Emerson, William 1923-1997 . . . . Y-97

Emin, Fedor Aleksandrovich
circa 1735-1770 . . . . DLB-150

Emmanuel, Pierre 1916-1984. . . . . DLB-258

Empedocles fifth century B.C. DLB-176

Empson, William 1906-1984 . . . . .DLB-20

Enchi Fumiko 1905-1986. . . . . DLB-182

"Encounter with the West" DLB-180

The End of English Stage Censorship,
1945-1968 . . . . .DLB-13

Ende, Michael 1929-1995 . . . . DLB-75

Endō Shūsaku 1923-1996. . . . . DLB-182

Engel, Marian 1933-1985. . . . . DLB-53

Engels, Friedrich 1820-1895. . . . . .DLB-129

Engle, Paul 1908- DLB-48

English, Thomas Dunn 1819-1902 . . . . . . DLB-202

English Composition and Rhetoric (1866),
by Alexander Bain [excerpt] DLB-57

The English Language: 410 to 1500 . . . . . DLB-146

Ennius 239 B.C.-169 B.C. DLB-211

Enquist, Per Olov 1934- DLB-257

Enright, D. J. 1920- DLB-27

Enright, Elizabeth 1909-1968. . . . . DLB-22

Epic and Beast Epic DLB-208

Epictetus circa 55-circa 125-130 . . . . DLB-176

Epicurus 342/341 B.C.-271/270 B.C. DLB-176

Epps, Bernard 1936- DLB-53

Epstein, Julius 1909- and
Epstein, Philip 1909-1952 . . . . DLB-26

Equiano, Olaudah
circa 1745-1797 . . . . DLB-37, 50; DWLB-3

Olaudah Equiano and Unfinished Journeys:
The Slave-Narrative Tradition and
Twentieth-Century Continuities, by
Paul Edwards and Pauline T.
Wangman DLB-117

The E-Researcher: Possibilities and Pitfalls . . . Y-00

Eragny Press DLB-112

Erasmus, Desiderius 1467-1536 . . . . DLB-136

Erba, Luciano 1922- DLB-128

Erdrich, Louise
1954- DLB-152, 175, 206; CDALB-7

Erichsen-Brown, Gwethalyn Graham
(see Graham, Gwethalyn)

Eriugena, John Scottus circa 810-877 . . . . DLB-115

Ernst, Paul 1866-1933 . . . . DLB-66, 118

Ershov, Petr Pavlovich 1815-1869. . . . . . . DLB-205

Erskine, Albert 1911-1993 . . . . Y-93

Erskine, John 1879-1951 . . . . DLB-9, 102

Erskine, Mrs. Steuart ?-1948 . . . . DLB-195

Ertel', Aleksandr Ivanovich
1855-1908. . . . . DLB-238

Ervine, St. John Greer 1883-1971 . . . . DLB-10

Eschenburg, Johann Joachim 1743-1820 . . . DLB-97

Escoto, Julio 1944- DLB-145

Esdaile, Arundell 1880-1956 . . . . DLB-201

Eshleman, Clayton 1935- DLB-5

Espriu, Salvador 1913-1985 . . . . DLB-134

Ess Ess Publishing Company. DLB-49

Essex House Press DLB-112

Esson, Louis 1878-1993 . . . . DLB-260

Essop, Ahmed 1931- DLB-225

Esterházy, Péter 1950- DLB-232; CDWLB-4

Estes, Eleanor 1906-1988 . . . . DLB-22

Estes and Lauriat. DLB-49

Estleman, Loren D. 1952- DLB-226

Eszterhas, Joe 1944- DLB-185

Etherege, George 1636-circa 1692 . . . . DLB-80

Ethridge, Mark, Sr. 1896-1981 . . . . DLB-127

Ets, Marie Hall 1893- DLB-22

Etter, David 1928- DLB-105

Ettner, Johann Christoph 1654-1724 . . . . DLB-168

Eugene Gant's Projected Works Y-01

Eupolemius flourished circa 1095 . . . . DLB-148

Euripides circa 484 B.C.-407/406 B.C.
. . . . DLB-176; CDWLB-1

Evans, Augusta Jane 1835-1909 . . . . DLB-239

Evans, Caradoc 1878-1945 . . . . DLB-162

Evans, Charles 1850-1935 . . . . DLB-187

Evans, Donald 1884-1921 . . . . DLB-54

Evans, George Henry 1805-1856 . . . . DLB-43

Evans, Hubert 1892-1986 . . . . DLB-92

Evans, M., and Company DLB-46

Evans, Mari 1923- DLB-41

Evans, Mary Ann (see Eliot, George)

Evans, Nathaniel 1742-1767 . . . . DLB-31

Evans, Sebastian 1830-1909 . . . . DLB-35

Evans, Ray 1915- and
Livingston, Jay 1915-2001 . . . . DLB-265

Evaristi, Marcella 1953- DLB-233

Everett, Alexander Hill 1790-1847 . . . . DLB-59

Everett, Edward 1794-1865 . . . . DLB-1, 59, 235

Everson, R. G. 1903- DLB-88

Everson, William 1912-1994 . . . . . . DLB-5, 16, 212

Ewart, Gavin 1916-1995 . . . . DLB-40

Ewing, Juliana Horatia 1841-1885 . . . . DLB-21, 163

The Examiner 1808-1881 . . . . DLB-110

Exley, Frederick 1929-1992 . . . . DLB-143, Y-81

von Eyb, Albrecht 1420-1475. . . . . DLB-179

Eyre and Spottiswoode DLB-106

Ezera, Regīna 1930- DLB-232

Ezzo ?-after 1065 . . . . DLB-148

F

Faber, Frederick William 1814-1863 . . . . . . DLB-32

Faber and Faber Limited DLB-112

Faccio, Rena (see Aleramo, Sibilla)

Fagundo, Ana María 1938- DLB-134

Fair, Ronald L. 1932- DLB-33

Fairfax, Beatrice (see Manning, Marie)

Fairlie, Gerard 1899-1983 . . . . DLB-77

Fallada, Hans 1893-1947 . . . . .DLB-56

Fancher, Betsy 1928- Y-83

Fane, Violet 1843-1905 . . . . DLB-35

Fanfrolico Press DLB-112

Fanning, Katherine 1927 . . . . DLB-127

Fanshawe, Sir Richard 1608-1666 . . . . . . .DLB-126

Fantasy Press Publishers DLB-46

Fante, John 1909-1983 . . . . DLB-130; Y-83

Al-Farabi circa 870-950 . . . . DLB-115

Farabough, Laura 1949- DLB-228

Farah, Nuruddin 1945- . . . DLB-125; CDWLB-3

Farber, Norma 1909-1984 . . . . DLB-61

Fargue, Léon-Paul 1876-1947 . . . . DLB-258

Farigoule, Louis (see Romains, Jules)

Farjeon, Eleanor 1881-1965 . . . . DLB-160

Farley, Harriet 1812-1907 . . . . DLB-239

Farley, Walter 1920-1989 . . . . DLB-22

Farmborough, Florence 1887-1978 . . . . . . DLB-204

Farmer, Penelope 1939- DLB-161

Farmer, Philip José 1918- DLB-8

Farnaby, Thomas 1575?-1647 . . . . DLB-236

Farningham, Marianne (see Hearn, Mary Anne)

Farquhar, George circa 1677-1707 . . . . DLB-84

Farquharson, Martha (see Finley, Martha)

Farrar, Frederic William 1831-1903 . . . . . DLB-163

Farrar and Rinehart DLB-46

Farrar, Straus and Giroux DLB-46

Farrell, J. G. 1935-1979 . . . . DLB-14

Farrell, James T. 1904-1979 . . . . DLB-4, 9, 86; DS-2

Fast, Howard 1914- DLB-9

Faulkner, George [publishing house] DLB-154

Faulkner, William 1897-1962
. . . DLB-9, 11, 44, 102; DS-2; Y-86; CDALB-5

William Faulkner Centenary Y-97

"Faulkner 100–Celebrating the Work,"
University of South Carolina, Columbia . . Y-97

Impressions of William Faulkner Y-97

Faulkner and Yoknapatawpha Conference,
Oxford, Mississippi Y-97

Faulks, Sebastian 1953- DLB-207

Fauset, Jessie Redmon 1882-1961 . . . . DLB-51

Faust, Frederick Schiller (Max Brand)
1892-1944 . . . . DLB-256

Faust, Irvin 1924- DLB-2, 28, 218; Y-80

Fawcett, Edgar 1847-1904 . . . . DLB-202

Fawcett, Millicent Garrett 1847-1929 . . . . . DLB-190

Fawcett Books DLB-46

Fay, Theodore Sedgwick 1807-1898 . . . . . DLB-202

Fearing, Kenneth 1902-1961 . . . . DLB-9

Federal Writers' Project DLB-46

Federman, Raymond 1928- Y-80

Fedorov, Innokentii Vasil'evich
(see Omulevsky, Innokentii Vasil'evich)

Feiffer, Jules 1929- DLB-7, 44

Feinberg, Charles E. 1899-1988 . . . . DLB-187; Y-88

Feind, Barthold 1678-1721 . . . . DLB-168

Feinstein, Elaine 1930- DLB-14, 40

Feiss, Paul Louis 1875-1952 . . . . DLB-187

Cumulative Index   DLB 266

Feldman, Irving 1928- DLB-169
Felipe, Léon 1884-1968............... DLB-108
Fell, Frederick, Publishers.............. DLB-46
Felltham, Owen 1602?-1668....... DLB-126, 151
Felman, Soshana 1942- DLB-246
Fels, Ludwig 1946- DLB-75
Felton, Cornelius Conway 1807-1862.. DLB-1, 235
Fenn, Harry 1837-1911.............. DLB-188
Fennario, David 1947- DLB-60
Fenner, Dudley 1558?-1587? DLB-236
Fenno, Jenny 1765?-1803 .... DLB-200
Fenno, John 1751-1798 .... DLB-43
Fenno, R. F., and Company DLB-49
Fenoglio, Beppe 1922-1963...........DLB-177
Fenton, Geoffrey 1539?-1608 .... DLB-136
Fenton, James 1949- DLB-40
Ferber, Edna 1885-1968....... DLB-9, 28, 86, 266
Ferdinand, Vallery, III (see Salaam, Kalamu ya)
Ferguson, Sir Samuel 1810-1886......... DLB-32
Ferguson, William Scott 1875-1954 ...... DLB-47
Fergusson, Robert 1750-1774 .... DLB-109
Ferland, Albert 1872-1943............. DLB-92
Ferlinghetti, Lawrence
    1919- DLB-5, 16; CDALB-1
Fermor, Patrick Leigh 1915- DLB-204
Fern, Fanny (see Parton, Sara Payson Willis)
Ferrars, Elizabeth 1907- DLB-87
Ferré, Rosario 1942- DLB-145
Ferret, E., and Company DLB-49
Ferrier, Susan 1782-1854.............. DLB-116
Ferril, Thomas Hornsby 1896-1988..... DLB-206
Ferrini, Vincent 1913- DLB-48
Ferron, Jacques 1921-1985 .... DLB-60
Ferron, Madeleine 1922- DLB-53
Ferrucci, Franco 1936- DLB-196
Fetridge and Company................ DLB-49
Feuchtersleben, Ernst Freiherr von
    1806-1849 .... DLB-133
Feuchtwanger, Lion 1884-1958.......... DLB-66
Feuerbach, Ludwig 1804-1872 .... DLB-133
Feuillet, Octave 1821-1890............ DLB-192
Feydeau, Georges 1862-1921 .... DLB-192
Fichte, Johann Gottlieb 1762-1814 .... DLB-90
Ficke, Arthur Davison 1883-1945........ DLB-54
Fiction Best-Sellers, 1910-1945 .... DLB-9
Fiction into Film, 1928-1975: A List of Movies
    Based on the Works of Authors in
    British Novelists, 1930-1959 .... DLB-15
Fiedler, Leslie A. 1917- DLB-28, 67
Field, Barron 1789-1846 .... DLB-230
Field, Edward 1924- DLB-105
Field, Joseph M. 1810-1856 .... DLB-248
Field, Michael
    (Katherine Harris Bradley [1846-1914]
    and Edith Emma Cooper
    [1862-1913]).................... DLB-240

"The Poetry File" DLB-105
Field, Eugene
    1850-1895 .... DLB-23, 42, 140; DS-13
Field, John 1545?-1588................ DLB-167
Field, Marshall, III 1893-1956 .... DLB-127
Field, Marshall, IV 1916-1965 .... DLB-127
Field, Marshall, V 1941- DLB-127
Field, Nathan 1587-1619 or 1620 .... DLB-58
Field, Rachel 1894-1942 .... DLB-9, 22
A Field Guide to Recent Schools of American
    Poetry......................... Y-86
Fielding, Helen 1958- DLB-231
Fielding, Henry
    1707-1754 .... DLB-39, 84, 101; CDBLB-2
"Defense of *Amelia*" (1752) DLB-39
From *The History of the Adventures of
    Joseph Andrews* (1742) DLB-39
Preface to *Joseph Andrews* (1742) DLB-39
Preface to Sarah Fielding's *The Adventures
    of David Simple* (1744) DLB-39
Preface to Sarah Fielding's *Familiar Letters*
    (1747) [excerpt].................... DLB-39
Fielding, Sarah 1710-1768 .... DLB-39
Preface to *The Cry* (1754)............. DLB-39
Fields, Annie Adams 1834-1915........ DLB-221
Fields, Dorothy 1905-1974 .... DLB-265
Fields, James T. 1817-1881 .... DLB-1, 235
Fields, Julia 1938- DLB-41
Fields, Osgood and Company DLB-49
Fields, W. C. 1880-1946............... DLB-44
Fierstein, Harvey 1954- DLB-266
Fifty Penguin Years Y-85
Figes, Eva 1932- DLB-14
Figuera, Angela 1902-1984............ DLB-108
Filmer, Sir Robert 1586-1653 .... DLB-151
Filson, John circa 1753-1788 .... DLB-37
Finch, Anne, Countess of Winchilsea
    1661-1720..................... DLB-95
Finch, Robert 1900- DLB-88
Findley, Timothy 1930- DLB-53
Finlay, Ian Hamilton 1925- DLB-40
Finley, Martha 1828-1909 .... DLB-42
Finn, Elizabeth Anne (McCaul)
    1825-1921 .... DLB-166
Finnegan, Seamus 1949- DLB-245
Finney, Jack 1911-1995................. DLB-8
Finney, Walter Braden (see Finney, Jack)
Firbank, Ronald 1886-1926 .... DLB-36
Firmin, Giles 1615-1697 .... DLB-24
First Edition Library/Collectors'
    Reprints, Inc...................... Y-91
Fischart, Johann
    1546 or 1547-1590 or 1591 ....DLB-179
Fischer, Karoline Auguste Fernandine
    1764-1842..................... DLB-94
Fischer, Tibor 1959- DLB-231
Fish, Stanley 1938- DLB-67
Fishacre, Richard 1205-1248 .... DLB-115

Fisher, Clay (see Allen, Henry W.)
Fisher, Dorothy Canfield 1879-1958... DLB-9, 102
Fisher, Leonard Everett 1924- DLB-61
Fisher, Roy 1930- DLB-40
Fisher, Rudolph 1897-1934.......... DLB-51, 102
Fisher, Steve 1913-1980 .... DLB-226
Fisher, Sydney George 1856-1927 .... DLB-47
Fisher, Vardis 1895-1968 .... DLB-9, 206
Fiske, John 1608-1677................. DLB-24
Fiske, John 1842-1901 .... DLB-47, 64
Fitch, Thomas circa 1700-1774 .... DLB-31
Fitch, William Clyde 1865-1909.......... DLB-7
FitzGerald, Edward 1809-1883.......... DLB-32
Fitzgerald, F. Scott 1896-1940
    .... DLB-4, 9, 86, 219; Y-81, Y-92;
    DS-1, 15, 16; CDALB-4
F. Scott Fitzgerald Centenary
    Celebrations..................... Y-96
F. Scott Fitzgerald: A Descriptive Bibliography,
    Supplement (2001).................. Y-01
F. Scott Fitzgerald Inducted into the American
    Poets' Corner at St. John the Divine;
    Ezra Pound Banned................. Y-99
"F. Scott Fitzgerald: St. Paul's Native Son
    and Distinguished American Writer":
    University of Minnesota Conference,
    29-31 October 1982................. Y-82
First International F. Scott Fitzgerald
    Conference...................... Y-92
Fitzgerald, Penelope 1916- DLB-14, 194
Fitzgerald, Robert 1910-1985 .... Y-80
FitzGerald, Robert D. 1902-1987 .... DLB-260
Fitzgerald, Thomas 1819-1891.......... DLB-23
Fitzgerald, Zelda Sayre 1900-1948 .... Y-84
Fitzhugh, Louise 1928-1974 .... DLB-52
Fitzhugh, William circa 1651-1701 ...... DLB-24
Flagg, James Montgomery 1877-1960.... DLB-188
Flanagan, Thomas 1923- Y-80
Flanner, Hildegarde 1899-1987 .... DLB-48
Flanner, Janet 1892-1978 .... DLB-4
Flannery, Peter 1951- DLB-233
Flaubert, Gustave 1821-1880 .... DLB-119
Flavin, Martin 1883-1967............... DLB-9
Fleck, Konrad
    (flourished circa 1220) DLB-138
Flecker, James Elroy 1884-1915........DLB-10, 19
Fleeson, Doris 1901-1970 .... DLB-29
Fleißer, Marieluise 1901-1974........ DLB-56, 124
Fleischer, Nat 1887-1972............... DLB-241
Fleming, Abraham 1552?-1607......... DLB-236
Fleming, Ian 1908-1964 ...DLB-87, 201; CDBLB-7
Fleming, Paul 1609-1640 .... DLB-164
Fleming, Peter 1907-1971 .... DLB-195
Fletcher, Giles, the Elder 1546-1611..... DLB-136
Fletcher, Giles, the Younger
    1585 or 1586-1623................ DLB-121
Fletcher, J. S. 1863-1935.............. DLB-70
Fletcher, John (see Beaumont, Francis)

Fletcher, John Gould 1886-1950 . . . . . . .DLB-4, 45
Fletcher, Phineas 1582-1650 . . . . .DLB-121
Flieg, Helmut (see Heym, Stefan)
Flint, F. S. 1885-1960. . . . . .DLB-19
Flint, Timothy 1780-1840 . . . . .DLB-73, 186
Flores-Williams, Jason 1969- DLB-209
Florio, John 1553?-1625. . . . . .DLB-172
Fo, Dario 1926- Y-97
Foix, J. V. 1893-1987 . . . . .DLB-134
Foley, Martha (see Burnett, Whit, and Martha Foley)
Folger, Henry Clay 1857-1930 . . . . .DLB-140
Folio Society. DLB-112
Follain, Jean 1903-1971 . . . . .DLB-258
Follen, Charles 1796-1840 . . . . .DLB-235
Follen, Eliza Lee (Cabot) 1787-1860. . . .DLB-1, 235
Follett, Ken 1949- DLB-87; Y-81
Follett Publishing Company. DLB-46
Folsom, John West [publishing house]. DLB-49
Folz, Hans between 1435 and 1440-1513 . . . . . . .DLB-179
Fontane, Theodor 1819-1898 . . . . .DLB-129; CDWLB-2
Fontes, Montserrat 1940- DLB-209
Fonvisin, Denis Ivanovich 1744 or 1745-1792 . . . . .DLB-150
Foote, Horton 1916- DLB-26, 266
Foote, Mary Hallock 1847-1938 . . . . .DLB-186, 188, 202, 221
Foote, Samuel 1721-1777 . . . . .DLB-89
Foote, Shelby 1916- DLB-2, 17
Forbes, Calvin 1945- DLB-41
Forbes, Ester 1891-1967. . . . . .DLB-22
Forbes, Rosita 1893?-1967. . . . . .DLB-195
Forbes and Company. DLB-49
Force, Peter 1790-1868. . . . . .DLB-30
Forché, Carolyn 1950- DLB-5, 193
Ford, Charles Henri 1913- DLB-4, 48
Ford, Corey 1902-1969 . . . . .DLB-11
Ford, Ford Madox 1873-1939 . . . . . . .DLB-34, 98, 162; CDBLB-6
Ford, J. B., and Company DLB-49
Ford, Jesse Hill 1928-1996. . . . . .DLB-6
Ford, John 1586-? DLB-58; CDBLB-1
Ford, R. A. D. 1915- DLB-88
Ford, Richard 1944- DLB-227
Ford, Worthington C. 1858-1941 . . . . . . .DLB-47
Fords, Howard, and Hulbert DLB-49
Foreman, Carl 1914-1984 . . . . .DLB-26
Forester, C. S. 1899-1966. . . . . .DLB-191
Forester, Frank (see Herbert, Henry William)
Forman, Harry Buxton 1842-1917. . . . . . .DLB-184
Fornés, María Irene 1930- DLB-7
Forrest, Leon 1937-1997. . . . . .DLB-33
Forster, E. M. 1879-1970 . . . . . . .DLB-34, 98, 162, 178, 195; DS-10; CDBLB-6

Forster, Georg 1754-1794. . . . . .DLB-94
Forster, John 1812-1876 . . . . .DLB-144
Forster, Margaret 1938- DLB-155
Forsyth, Frederick 1938- DLB-87
Forten, Charlotte L. 1837-1914 . . . . . .DLB-50, 239
Charlotte Forten: Pages from her Diary. DLB-50
Fortini, Franco 1917- DLB-128
Fortune, Mary ca. 1833-ca. 1910 . . . . . . .DLB-230
Fortune, T. Thomas 1856-1928. . . . . .DLB-23
Fosdick, Charles Austin 1842-1915 . . . . . .DLB-42
Foster, Genevieve 1893-1979 . . . . .DLB-61
Foster, Hannah Webster 1758-1840. . . DLB-37, 200
Foster, John 1648-1681 . . . . .DLB-24
Foster, Michael 1904-1956. . . . . .DLB-9
Foster, Myles Birket 1825-1899. . . . . .DLB-184
Foucault, Michel 1926-1984. . . . . .DLB-242
Foulis, Robert and Andrew / R. and A. [publishing house] DLB-154
Fouqué, Caroline de la Motte 1774-1831 . . . . .DLB-90
Fouqué, Friedrich de la Motte 1777-1843. . . . . .DLB-90
Four Seas Company. DLB-46
Four Winds Press DLB-46
Fournier, Henri Alban (see Alain-Fournier)
Fowler and Wells Company DLB-49
Fowles, John 1926- DLB-14, 139, 207; CDBLB-8
Fox, John 1939- DLB-245
Fox, John, Jr. 1862 or 1863-1919. . . .DLB-9; DS-13
Fox, Paula 1923- DLB-52
Fox, Richard K. [publishing house] DLB-49
Fox, Richard Kyle 1846-1922 . . . . .DLB-79
Fox, William Price 1926- DLB-2; Y-81
Foxe, John 1517-1587 . . . . .DLB-132
Fraenkel, Michael 1896-1957. . . . . .DLB-4
France, Anatole 1844-1924 . . . . .DLB-123
France, Richard 1938- DLB-7
Francis, C. S. [publishing house] DLB-49
Francis, Convers 1795-1863. . . . . .DLB 1, 235
Francis, Dick 1920- DLB-87
Francis, Sir Frank 1901-1988 . . . . .DLB-201
Francis, Jeffrey, Lord 1773-1850 . . . . . . .DLB-107
François 1863-1910 . . . . .DLB-92
François, Louise von 1817-1893. . . . . . . .DLB-129
Franck, Sebastian 1499-1542 . . . . .DLB-179
Francke, Kuno 1855-1930 . . . . .DLB-71
Frank, Bruno 1887-1945 . . . . .DLB-118
Frank, Leonhard 1882-1961 . . . . . . .DLB-56, 118
Frank, Melvin (see Panama, Norman)
Frank, Waldo 1889-1967 . . . . .DLB-9, 63
Franken, Rose 1895?-1988 . . . . . .DLB-228, Y-84
Franklin, Benjamin 1706-1790 . . . . . . .DLB-24, 43, 73, 183; CDALB-2
Franklin, James 1697-1735 . . . . .DLB-43

Franklin, Miles 1879-1954 . . . . .DLB-230
Franklin Library .DLB-46
Frantz, Ralph Jules 1902-1979 . . . . .DLB-4
Franzos, Karl Emil 1848-1904 . . . . .DLB-129
Fraser, G. S. 1915-1980 . . . . .DLB-27
Fraser, Kathleen 1935- DLB-169
Frattini, Alberto 1922- DLB-128
Frau Ava ?-1127 .DLB-148
Fraunce, Abraham 1558?-1592 or 1593. . .DLB-236
Frayn, Michael 1933- DLB-13, 14, 194, 245
Frederic, Harold 1856-1898 . . . . .DLB-12, 23; DS-13
Freed, Arthur 1894-1973 . . . . .DLB-265
Freeling, Nicolas 1927- DLB-87
Freeman, Douglas Southall 1886-1953 . . . . .DLB-17; DS-17
Freeman, Judith 1946- DLB-256
Freeman, Legh Richmond 1842-1915 . . . . .DLB-23
Freeman, Mary E. Wilkins 1852-1930 . . . . .DLB-12, 78, 221
Freeman, R. Austin 1862-1943 . . . . .DLB-70
Freidank circa 1170-circa 1233. . . . . .DLB-138
Freiligrath, Ferdinand 1810-1876 . . . . . . .DLB-133
Frémont, John Charles 1813-1890 . . . . . .DLB-186
Frémont, John Charles 1813-1890 and Frémont, Jessie Benton 1834-1902 . . .DLB-183
French, Alice 1850-1934 . . . . .DLB-74; DS-13
French Arthurian Literature DLB-208
French, David 1939- DLB-53
French, Evangeline 1869-1960. . . . . .DLB-195
French, Francesca 1871-1960 . . . . .DLB-195
French, James [publishing house]. DLB-49
French, Samuel [publishing house] DLB-49
Samuel French, Limited. DLB-106
Freneau, Philip 1752-1832 . . . . .DLB-37, 43
Freni, Melo 1934- DLB-128
Freshfield, Douglas W. 1845-1934 . . . . . .DLB-174
Freytag, Gustav 1816-1895 . . . . .DLB-129
Fridegård, Jan 1897-1968 . . . . .DLB-259
Fried, Erich 1921-1988 . . . . .DLB-85
Friedan, Betty 1921- DLB-246
Friedman, Bruce Jay 1930- DLB-2, 28, 244
Friedrich von Hausen circa 1171-1190. . . .DLB-138
Friel, Brian 1929- DLB-13
Friend, Krebs 1895?-1967? DLB-4
Fries, Fritz Rudolf 1935- DLB-75
Fringe and Alternative Theater in Great Britain DLB-13
Frisch, Max 1911-1991 . . . . .DLB-69, 124; CDWLB-2
Frischlin, Nicodemus 1547-1590 . . . . . . .DLB-179
Frischmuth, Barbara 1941- DLB-85
Fritz, Jean 1915- DLB-52
Froissart, Jean circa 1337-circa 1404. . . . .DLB-208
From John Hall Wheelock's Oral Memoir . . . Y-01
Fromentin, Eugene 1820-1876 . . . . .DLB-123

347

Frontinus circa A.D. 35-A.D. 103/104 ... DLB-211
Frost, A. B. 1851-1928 .... DLB-188; DS-13
Frost, Robert
 1874-1963......... DLB-54; DS-7; CDALB-4
Frostenson, Katarina 1953- DLB-257
Frothingham, Octavius Brooks
 1822-1895 .... DLB-1, 243
Froude, James Anthony
 1818-1894.................DLB-18, 57, 144
Fruitlands 1843-1844 .... DLB-223
Fry, Christopher 1907- DLB-13
Fry, Roger 1866-1934.................... DS-10
Fry, Stephen 1957- DLB-207
Frye, Northrop 1912-1991 .... DLB-67, 68, 246
Fuchs, Daniel 1909-1993 .....DLB-9, 26, 28; Y-93
Fuentes, Carlos 1928- DLB-113; CDWLB-3
Fuertes, Gloria 1918- DLB-108
Fugard, Athol 1932- DLB-225
The Fugitives and the Agrarians:
 The First Exhibition................ Y-85
Fujiwara no Shunzei 1114-1204 ...... DLB-203
Fujiwara no Tameaki 1230s?-1290s? DLB-203
Fujiwara no Tameie 1198-1275....... DLB-203
Fujiwara no Teika 1162-1241........ DLB-203
Fulbecke, William 1560-1603?.........DLB-172
Fuller, Charles H., Jr. 1939- DLB-38, 266
Fuller, Henry Blake 1857-1929 .... DLB-12
Fuller, John 1937- DLB-40
Fuller, Margaret (see Fuller, Sarah)
Fuller, Roy 1912-1991 .... DLB-15, 20
Fuller, Samuel 1912- DLB-26
Fuller, Sarah 1810-1850
 ..... DLB-1, 59, 73, 183, 223, 239; CDALB-2
Fuller, Thomas 1608-1661 .... DLB-151
Fullerton, Hugh 1873-1945.............DLB-171
Fullwood, William flourished 1568 ..... DLB-236
Fulton, Alice 1952- DLB-193
Fulton, Len 1934- Y-86
Fulton, Robin 1937- DLB-40
Furbank, P. N. 1920- DLB-155
Furman, Laura 1945- Y-86
Furness, Horace Howard
 1833-1912....................... DLB-64
Furness, William Henry
 1802-1896 .... DLB-1, 235
Furnivall, Frederick James
 1825-1910....................... DLB-184
Furphy, Joseph
 (Tom Collins) 1843-1912.......... DLB-230
Furthman, Jules 1888-1966............ DLB-26
Furui Yoshikichi 1937- DLB-182
Fushimi, Emperor 1265-1317 .... DLB-203
Futabatei, Shimei
 (Hasegawa Tatsunosuke)
 1864-1909 .... DLB-180
The Future of the Novel (1899), by
 Henry James.................... DLB-18
Fyleman, Rose 1877-1957 .... DLB-160

G

Gadallah, Leslie 1939- DLB-251
Gadda, Carlo Emilio 1893-1973.........DLB-177
Gaddis, William 1922-1998 ....DLB-2, Y-99
Gág, Wanda 1893-1946 .... DLB-22
Gagarin, Ivan Sergeevich 1814-1882 .... DLB-198
Gagnon, Madeleine 1938- DLB-60
Gaiman, Neil 1960- DLB-261
Gaine, Hugh 1726-1807 .... DLB-43
Gaine, Hugh [publishing house]......... DLB-49
Gaines, Ernest J.
 1933- DLB-2, 33, 152; Y-80; CDALB-6
Gaiser, Gerd 1908-1976 .... DLB-69
Gaitskill, Mary 1954- DLB-244
Galarza, Ernesto 1905-1984 .... DLB-122
Galaxy Science Fiction Novels DLB-46
Gale, Zona 1874-1938............DLB-9, 228, 78
Galen of Pergamon 129-after 210........DLB-176
Gales, Winifred Marshall 1761-1839 .... DLB-200
Gall, Louise von 1815-1855 .... DLB-133
Gallagher, Tess 1943- DLB-120, 212, 244
Gallagher, Wes 1911- DLB-127
Gallagher, William Davis 1808-1894 .... DLB-73
Gallant, Mavis 1922- DLB-53
Gallegos, María Magdalena 1935- DLB-209
Gallico, Paul 1897-1976..............DLB-9, 171
Gallop, Jane 1952- DLB-246
Galloway, Grace Growden 1727-1782.... DLB-200
Gallup, Donald 1913- DLB-187
Galsworthy, John 1867-1933
 ...... DLB-10, 34, 98, 162; DS-16; CDBLB-5
Galt, John 1779-1839 .... DLB-99, 116
Galton, Sir Francis 1822-1911 .... DLB-166
Galvin, Brendan 1938- DLB-5
Gambit DLB-46
Gamboa, Reymundo 1948- DLB-122
Gammer Gurton's Needle................ DLB-62
Gan, Elena Andreevna (Zeneida R-va)
 1814-1842 .... DLB-198
Gannett, Frank E. 1876-1957 .... DLB-29
Gao Xingjian 1940- Y-00
Gaos, Vicente 1919-1980 .... DLB-134
García, Andrew 1854?-1943............ DLB-209
García, Lionel G. 1935- DLB-82
García, Richard 1941- DLB-209
García-Camarillo, Cecilio 1943- DLB-209
García Lorca, Federico 1898-1936 ..... DLB-108
García Márquez, Gabriel
 1928- DLB-113; Y-82; CDWLB-3
Gardam, Jane 1928- DLB-14, 161, 231
Gardell, Jonas 1963- DLB-257
Garden, Alexander circa 1685-1756 ...... DLB-31
Gardiner, John Rolfe 1936- DLB-244
Gardiner, Margaret Power Farmer
 (see Blessington, Marguerite, Countess of)

Gardner, John
 1933-1982 .... DLB-2; Y-82; CDALB-7
Garfield, Leon 1921-1996............ DLB-161
Garis, Howard R. 1873-1962 .... DLB-22
Garland, Hamlin 1860-1940...DLB-12, 71, 78, 186
Garneau, Francis-Xavier 1809-1866...... DLB-99
Garneau, Hector de Saint-Denys
 1912-1943 .... DLB-88
Garneau, Michel 1939- DLB-53
Garner, Alan 1934- DLB-161, 261
Garner, Hugh 1913-1979 .... DLB-68
Garnett, David 1892-1981 .... DLB-34
Garnett, Eve 1900-1991 .... DLB-160
Garnett, Richard 1835-1906 .... DLB-184
Garrard, Lewis H. 1829-1887............ DLB-186
Garraty, John A. 1920- DLB-17
Garrett, George
 1929- DLB-2, 5, 130, 152; Y-83
Fellowship of Southern Writers Y-98
Garrett, John Work 1872-1942.........DLB-187
Garrick, David 1717-1779 .... DLB-84, 213
Garrison, William Lloyd
 1805-1879....... DLB-1, 43, 235; CDALB-2
Garro, Elena 1920-1998 .... DLB-145
Garth, Samuel 1661-1719 .... DLB-95
Garve, Andrew 1908- DLB-87
Gary, Romain 1914-1980............. DLB-83
Gascoigne, George 1539?-1577......... DLB-136
Gascoyne, David 1916- DLB-20
Gaskell, Elizabeth Cleghorn
 1810-1865 ..... DLB-21, 144, 159; CDBLB-4
Gaskell, Jane 1941- DLB-261
Gaspey, Thomas 1788-1871 .... DLB-116
Gass, William H. 1924- DLB-2, 227
Gates, Doris 1901- DLB-22
Gates, Henry Louis, Jr. 1950- DLB-67
Gates, Lewis E. 1860-1924............ DLB-71
Gatto, Alfonso 1909-1976.............. DLB-114
Gault, William Campbell 1910-1995 .... DLB-226
Gaunt, Mary 1861-1942...........DLB-174, 230
Gautier, Théophile 1811-1872 .... DLB-119
Gauvreau, Claude 1925-1971........... DLB-88
The Gawain-Poet
 flourished circa 1350-1400......... DLB-146
Gawsworth, John (Terence Ian Fytton Armstrong)
 1912-1970..................... DLB-255
Gay, Ebenezer 1696-1787............. DLB-24
Gay, John 1685-1732 .... DLB-84, 95
Gayarré, Charles E. A. 1805-1895 .... DLB-30
Gaylord, Charles [publishing house] DLB-49
Gaylord, Edward King 1873-1974 .....DLB-127
Gaylord, Edward Lewis 1919- DLB-127
Geda, Sigitas 1943- DLB-232
Geddes, Gary 1940- DLB-60
Geddes, Virgil 1897- DLB-4
Gedeon (Georgii Andreevich Krinovsky)
 circa 1730-1763.................. DLB-150

Gee, Maggie 1948- DLB-207
Gee, Shirley 1932- DLB-245
Geßner, Salomon 1730-1788 ....DLB-97
Geibel, Emanuel 1815-1884...........DLB-129
Geiogamah, Hanay 1945- DLB-175
Geis, Bernard, Associates.............DLB-46
Geisel, Theodor Seuss 1904-1991 ...DLB-61; Y-91
Gelb, Arthur 1924- DLB-103
Gelb, Barbara 1926- DLB-103
Gelber, Jack 1932- DLB-7, 228
Gelinas, Gratien 1909- DLB-88
Gellert, Christian Füerchtegott
    1715-1769..........................DLB-97
Gellhorn, Martha 1908-1998.........Y-82, Y-98
Gems, Pam 1925- DLB-13
Genet, Jean 1910-1986............ DLB-72; Y-86
Genette, Gérard 1930- DLB-242
Genevoix, Maurice 1890-1980..........DLB-65
Genovese, Eugene D. 1930- DLB-17
Gent, Peter 1942- Y-82
Geoffrey of Monmouth
    circa 1100-1155....................DLB-146
George, Henry 1839-1897 ....DLB-23
George, Jean Craighead 1919- DLB-52
George, W. L. 1882-1926 ....DLB-197
George III, King of Great Britain and Ireland
    1738-1820 ....DLB-213
George V. Higgins to Julian Symons........ Y-99
Georgslied 896?....................DLB-148
Gerber, Merrill Joan 1938- DLB-218
Gerhardie, William 1895-1977..........DLB-36
Gerhardt, Paul 1607-1676.............DLB-164
Gérin, Winifred 1901-1981 ....DLB-155
Gérin-Lajoie, Antoine 1824-1882........DLB-99
German Drama 800-1280 ....DLB-138
German Drama from Naturalism
    to Fascism: 1889-1933.............DLB-118
German Literature and Culture from Charlemagne
    to the Early Courtly Period
    ....DLB-148; CDWLB-2
German Radio Play, The..............DLB-124
German Transformation from the Baroque
    to the Enlightenment, The DLB-97
The Germanic Epic and Old English
    Heroic Poetry: *Widsith*, *Waldere*,
    and *The Fight at Finnsburg*..........DLB-146
Germanophilism, by Hans Kohn........DLB-66
Gernsback, Hugo 1884-1967........DLB-8, 137
Gerould, Katharine Fullerton
    1879-1944 ....DLB-78
Gerrish, Samuel [publishing house] DLB-49
Gerrold, David 1944- DLB-8
Gershwin, Ira 1896-1983..............DLB-265
The Ira Gershwin Centenary............... Y-96
Gerson, Jean 1363-1429...............DLB-208
Gersonides 1288-1344 ....DLB-115
Gerstäcker, Friedrich 1816-1872 ....DLB-129

Gerstenberg, Heinrich Wilhelm von
    1737-1823......................DLB-97
Gervinus, Georg Gottfried
    1805-1871 ....DLB-133
Geston, Mark S. 1946- DLB-8
Al-Ghazali 1058-1111.................DLB-115
Gibbings, Robert 1889-1958 ....DLB-195
Gibbon, Edward 1737-1794 ....DLB-104
Gibbon, John Murray 1875-1952........DLB-92
Gibbon, Lewis Grassic (see Mitchell, James Leslie)
Gibbons, Floyd 1887-1939 ....DLB-25
Gibbons, Reginald 1947- DLB-120
Gibbons, William ?-?..................DLB-73
Gibson, Charles Dana
    1867-1944 ....DLB-188; DS-13
Gibson, Graeme 1934- DLB-53
Gibson, Margaret 1944- DLB-120
Gibson, Margaret Dunlop 1843-1920 ....DLB-174
Gibson, Wilfrid 1878-1962.............DLB-19
Gibson, William 1914- DLB-7
Gibson, William 1948- DLB-251
Gide, André 1869-1951 ....DLB-65
Giguère, Diane 1937- DLB-53
Giguère, Roland 1929- DLB-60
Gil de Biedma, Jaime 1929-1990 ....DLB-108
Gil-Albert, Juan 1906- DLB-134
Gilbert, Anthony 1899-1973 ....DLB-77
Gilbert, Sir Humphrey 1537-1583 ....DLB-136
Gilbert, Michael 1912- DLB-87
Gilbert, Sandra M. 1936- DLB-120, 246
Gilchrist, Alexander 1828-1861 ....DLB-144
Gilchrist, Ellen 1935- DLB-130
Gilder, Jeannette L. 1849-1916 ....DLB-79
Gilder, Richard Watson 1844-1909.... DLB-64, 79
Gildersleeve, Basil 1831-1924 ....DLB-71
Giles of Rome circa 1243-1316 ....DLB-115
Giles, Henry 1809-1882................DLB-64
Gilfillan, George 1813-1878 ....DLB-144
Gill, Eric 1882-1940..................DLB-98
Gill, Sarah Prince 1728-1771 ....DLB-200
Gill, William F., Company DLB-49
Gillespie, A. Lincoln, Jr. 1895-1950........DLB-4
Gillespie, Haven 1883-1975 ....DLB-265
Gilliam, Florence ?-? DLB-4
Gilliatt, Penelope 1932-1993 ....DLB-14
Gillott, Jacky 1939-1980 ....DLB-14
Gilman, Caroline H. 1794-1888........DLB-3, 73
Gilman, Charlotte Perkins 1860-1935....DLB-221
Gilman, W. and J. [publishing house] DLB-49
Gilmer, Elizabeth Meriwether 1861-1951 ..DLB-29
Gilmer, Francis Walker 1790-1826 ....DLB-37
Gilmore, Mary 1865-1962 ....DLB-260
Gilroy, Frank D. 1925- DLB-7
Gimferrer, Pere (Pedro) 1945- DLB-134
Gingrich, Arnold 1903-1976 ....DLB-137

Ginsberg, Allen
    1926-1997 .... DLB-5, 16, 169, 237; CDALB-1
Ginzburg, Natalia 1916-1991..........DLB-177
Ginzkey, Franz Karl 1871-1963 ....DLB-81
Gioia, Dana 1950- DLB-120
Giono, Jean 1895-1970.................DLB-72
Giotti, Virgilio 1885-1957 ....DLB-114
Giovanni, Nikki 1943- DLB-5, 41; CDALB-7
Gipson, Lawrence Henry 1880-1971 ......DLB-17
Girard, Rodolphe 1879-1956 ....DLB-92
Giraudoux, Jean 1882-1944.............DLB-65
Gissing, George 1857-1903 ..... DLB-18, 135, 184
The Place of Realism in Fiction (1895) DLB-18
Giudici, Giovanni 1924- DLB-128
Giuliani, Alfredo 1924- DLB-128
Glackens, William J. 1870-1938..........DLB-188
Gladstone, William Ewart
    1809-1898 .... DLB-57, 184
Glaeser, Ernst 1902-1963...............DLB-69
Glancy, Diane 1941- DLB-175
Glanvill, Joseph 1636-1680 ....DLB-252
Glanville, Brian 1931- DLB-15, 139
Glapthorne, Henry 1610-1643?..........DLB-58
Glasgow, Ellen 1873-1945 ....DLB-9, 12
Glasier, Katharine Bruce 1867-1950......DLB-190
Glaspell, Susan 1876-1948 ...... DLB-7, 9, 78, 228
Glass, Montague 1877-1934.............DLB-11
Glassco, John 1909-1981 ....DLB-68
Glauser, Friedrich 1896-1938 ....DLB-56
F. Gleason's Publishing Hall DLB-49
Gleim, Johann Wilhelm Ludwig
    1719-1803 ....DLB-97
Glendinning, Victoria 1937- DLB-155
The Cult of Biography
    Excerpts from the Second Folio Debate:
    "Biographies are generally a disease of
    English Literature" Y-86
Glidden, Frederick Dilley (Luke Short)
    1908-1975 ....DLB-256
Glinka, Fedor Nikolaevich 1786-1880 ....DLB-205
Glover, Keith 1966- DLB-249
Glover, Richard 1712-1785 ....DLB-95
Glück, Louise 1943- DLB-5
Glyn, Elinor 1864-1943................DLB-153
Gnedich, Nikolai Ivanovich 1784-1833 ...DLB-205
Gobineau, Joseph-Arthur de
    1816-1882 ....DLB-123
Godber, John 1956- DLB-233
Godbout, Jacques 1933- DLB-53
Goddard, Morrill 1865-1937 ....DLB-25
Goddard, William 1740-1817............DLB-43
Godden, Rumer 1907-1998 ....DLB-161
Godey, Louis A. 1804-1878 ....DLB-73
Godey and McMichael DLB-49
Godfrey, Dave 1938- DLB-60
Godfrey, Thomas 1736-1763 ....DLB-31
Godine, David R., Publisher DLB-46

Cumulative Index

Godkin, E. L. 1831-1902 . . . . DLB-79
Godolphin, Sidney 1610-1643 . . . . DLB-126
Godwin, Gail 1937- DLB-6, 234
Godwin, M. J., and Company DLB-154
Godwin, Mary Jane Clairmont
    1766-1841 . . . . DLB-163
Godwin, Parke 1816-1904 . . . . DLB-3, 64, 250
Godwin, William 1756-1836 . . . . DLB-39, 104,
    . . . . 142, 158, 163, 262; CDBLB-3
    Preface to *St. Leon* (1799) DLB-39
Goering, Reinhard 1887-1936 . . . . DLB-118
Goes, Albrecht 1908- DLB-69
Goethe, Johann Wolfgang von
    1749-1832 . . . . DLB-94; CDWLB-2
Goetz, Curt 1888-1960 . . . . DLB-124
Goffe, Thomas circa 1592-1629 . . . . DLB-58
Goffstein, M. B. 1940- DLB-61
Gogarty, Oliver St. John 1878-1957 . . . DLB-15, 19
Gogol, Nikolai Vasil'evich 1809-1852 . . . DLB-198
Goines, Donald 1937-1974 . . . . DLB-33
Gold, Herbert 1924- DLB-2; Y-81
Gold, Michael 1893-1967 . . . . DLB-9, 28
Goldbarth, Albert 1948- DLB-120
Goldberg, Dick 1947- DLB-7
Golden Cockerel Press DLB-112
Golding, Arthur 1536-1606 . . . . DLB-136
Golding, Louis 1895-1958 . . . . DLB-195
Golding, William 1911-1993
    . . . . DLB-15, 100, 255; Y-83; CDBLB-7
Goldman, Emma 1869-1940 . . . . DLB-221
Goldman, William 1931- DLB-44
Goldring, Douglas 1887-1960 . . . . DLB-197
Goldsmith, Oliver 1730?-1774
    . . . . DLB-39, 89, 104, 109, 142; CDBLB-2
Goldsmith, Oliver 1794-1861 . . . . DLB-99
Goldsmith Publishing Company DLB-46
Goldstein, Richard 1944- DLB-185
Gollancz, Sir Israel 1864-1930 . . . . DLB-201
Gollancz, Victor, Limited DLB-112
Gombrowicz, Witold
    1904-1969 . . . . DLB-215; CDWLB-4
Gómez-Quiñones, Juan 1942- DLB-122
Gomme, Laurence James
    [publishing house] DLB-46
Goncharov, Ivan Aleksandrovich
    1812-1891 . . . . DLB-238
Goncourt, Edmond de 1822-1896 . . . . DLB-123
Goncourt, Jules de 1830-1870 . . . . DLB-123
Gonzales, Rodolfo "Corky" 1928- DLB-122
González, Angel 1925- DLB-108
Gonzalez, Genaro 1949- DLB-122
Gonzalez, Ray 1952- DLB-122
Gonzales-Berry, Erlinda 1942- DLB-209
    "Chicano Language" DLB-82
González de Mireles, Jovita
    1899-1983 . . . . DLB-122
González-T., César A. 1931- DLB-82

Goodbye, Gutenberg? A Lecture at the
    New York Public Library,
    18 April 1995, by Donald Lamm Y-95
Goodis, David 1917-1967 . . . . DLB-226
Goodison, Lorna 1947- DLB-157
Goodman, Allegra 1967- DLB-244
Goodman, Paul 1911-1972 . . . . DLB-130, 246
The Goodman Theatre DLB-7
Goodrich, Frances 1891-1984 and
    Hackett, Albert 1900-1995 . . . . DLB-26
Goodrich, Samuel Griswold
    1793-1860 . . . . DLB-1, 42, 73, 243
Goodrich, S. G. [publishing house] DLB-49
Goodspeed, C. E., and Company DLB-49
Goodwin, Stephen 1943- Y-82
Googe, Barnabe 1540-1594 . . . . DLB-132
Gookin, Daniel 1612-1687 . . . . DLB-24
Goran, Lester 1928- DLB-244
Gordimer, Nadine 1923- DLB-225; Y-91
Gordon, Adam Lindsay 1833-1870 . . . . . . DLB-230
Gordon, Caroline
    1895-1981 . . . . DLB-4, 9, 102; DS-17; Y-81
Gordon, Charles F. (see OyamO)
Gordon, Giles 1940- DLB-14, 139, 207
Gordon, Helen Cameron, Lady Russell
    1867-1949 . . . . DLB-195
Gordon, Lyndall 1941- DLB-155
Gordon, Mack 1904-1959 . . . . DLB-265
Gordon, Mary 1949- DLB-6; Y-81
Gordone, Charles 1925-1995 . . . . DLB-7
Gore, Catherine 1800-1861 . . . . DLB-116
Gore-Booth, Eva 1870-1926 . . . . DLB-240
Gores, Joe 1931- DLB-226
Gorey, Edward 1925-2000 . . . . DLB-61
Gorgias of Leontini
    circa 485 B.C.-376 B.C. DLB-176
Görres, Joseph 1776-1848 . . . . DLB-90
Gosse, Edmund 1849-1928 . . . . . DLB-57, 144, 184
Gosson, Stephen 1554-1624 . . . . DLB-172
    The Schoole of Abuse (1579) DLB-172
Gotanda, Philip Kan 1951- DLB-266
Gotlieb, Phyllis 1926- DLB-88, 251
Go-Toba 1180-1239 . . . . DLB-203
Gottfried von Straßburg
    died before 1230 . . . . . . DLB-138; CDWLB-2
Gotthelf, Jeremias 1797-1854 . . . . DLB-133
Gottschalk circa 804/808-869 . . . . DLB-148
Gottsched, Johann Christoph
    1700-1766 . . . . DLB-97
Götz, Johann Nikolaus 1721-1781 . . . . DLB-97
Goudge, Elizabeth 1900-1984 . . . . DLB-191
Gough, John B. 1817-1886 . . . . DLB-243
Gould, Wallace 1882-1940 . . . . DLB-54
Govoni, Corrado 1884-1965 . . . . DLB-114
Gower, John circa 1330-1408 . . . . DLB-146
Goyen, William 1915-1983 . . . . . DLB-2, 218; Y-83
Goytisolo, José Augustín 1928- DLB-134

Gozzano, Guido 1883-1916 . . . . DLB-114
Grabbe, Christian Dietrich 1801-1836 . . . DLB-133
Gracq, Julien 1910- DLB-83
Grady, Henry W. 1850-1889 . . . . DLB-23
Graf, Oskar Maria 1894-1967 . . . . DLB-56
Graf Rudolf
    between circa 1170 and circa 1185 . . . DLB-148
Graff, Gerald 1937- DLB-246
Grafton, Richard [publishing house] DLB-170
Grafton, Sue 1940- DLB-226
Graham, Frank 1893-1965 . . . . DLB-241
Graham, George Rex 1813-1894 . . . . DLB-73
Graham, Gwethalyn 1913-1965 . . . . DLB-88
Graham, Jorie 1951- DLB-120
Graham, Katharine 1917- DLB-127
Graham, Lorenz 1902-1989 . . . . DLB-76
Graham, Philip 1915-1963 . . . . DLB-127
Graham, R. B. Cunninghame
    1852-1936 . . . . DLB-98, 135, 174
Graham, Shirley 1896-1977 . . . . DLB-76
Graham, Stephen 1884-1975 . . . . DLB-195
Graham, W. S. 1918- DLB-20
Graham, William H. [publishing house] . . . DLB-49
Graham, Winston 1910- DLB-77
Grahame, Kenneth
    1859-1932 . . . . DLB-34, 141, 178
Grainger, Martin Allerdale 1874-1941 . . . DLB-92
Gramatky, Hardie 1907-1979 . . . . DLB-22
Grand, Sarah 1854-1943 . . . . DLB-135, 197
Grandbois, Alain 1900-1975 . . . . DLB-92
Grandson, Oton de circa 1345-1397 . . . . . DLB-208
Grange, John circa 1556-? DLB-136
Granich, Irwin (see Gold, Michael)
Granovsky, Timofei Nikolaevich
    1813-1855 . . . . DLB-198
Grant, Anne MacVicar 1755-1838 . . . . . . DLB-200
Grant, Duncan 1885-1978 . . . . DS-10
Grant, George 1918-1988 . . . . DLB-88
Grant, George Monro 1835-1902 . . . . DLB-99
Grant, Harry J. 1881-1963 . . . . DLB-29
Grant, James Edward 1905-1966 . . . . DLB-26
Grass, Günter 1927- . . . DLB-75, 124; CDWLB-2
Grasty, Charles H. 1863-1924 . . . . DLB-25
Grau, Shirley Ann 1929- DLB-2, 218
Graves, John 1920- Y-83
Graves, Richard 1715-1804 . . . . DLB-39
Graves, Robert 1895-1985
    . . . DLB-20, 100, 191; DS-18; Y-85; CDBLB-6
Gray, Alasdair 1934- DLB-194, 261
Gray, Asa 1810-1888 . . . . DLB-1, 235
Gray, David 1838-1861 . . . . DLB-32
Gray, Simon 1936- DLB-13
Gray, Thomas 1716-1771 . . . . DLB-109; CDBLB-2
Grayson, Richard 1951- DLB-234
Grayson, William J. 1788-1863 . . . . DLB-3, 64, 248
The Great Bibliographers Series Y-93

The Great Modern Library Scam Y-98

The Great War and the Theater, 1914-1918
[Great Britain] DLB-10

The Great War Exhibition and Symposium at
the University of South Carolina Y-97

Grech, Nikolai Ivanovich 1787-1867 ..... DLB-198

Greeley, Horace 1811-1872 ... DLB-3, 43, 189, 250

Green, Adolph (see Comden, Betty)

Green, Anna Katharine
1846-1935 .... DLB-202, 221

Green, Duff 1791-1875 .... DLB-43

Green, Elizabeth Shippen 1871-1954 ..... DLB-188

Green, Gerald 1922- DLB-28

Green, Henry 1905-1973 .... DLB-15

Green, Jonas 1712-1767 .... DLB-31

Green, Joseph 1706-1780 .... DLB-31

Green, Julien 1900-1998 .... DLB-4, 72

Green, Paul 1894-1981 ...... DLB-7, 9, 249; Y-81

Green, T. and S. [publishing house] DLB-49

Green, T. H. 1836-1882 .... DLB-262

Green, Terence M. 1947- DLB-251

Green, Thomas Hill 1836-1882 ..... DLB-190, 262

Green, Timothy [publishing house] DLB-49

Greenaway, Kate 1846-1901 .... DLB-141

Greenberg: Publisher DLB-46

Green Tiger Press DLB-46

Greene, Asa 1789-1838 .... DLB-11

Greene, Belle da Costa 1883-1950 .... DLB-187

Greene, Benjamin H.
[publishing house] DLB-49

Greene, Graham 1904-1991
.... DLB-13, 15, 77, 100, 162, 201, 204;
Y-85, Y-91; CDBLB-7

Greene, Robert 1558-1592 .... DLB-62, 167

Greene, Robert Bernard (Bob), Jr.
1947- DLB-185

Greenfield, George 1917-2000 .... Y-00

Greenhow, Robert 1800-1854 .... DLB-30

Greenlee, William B. 1872-1953 .... DLB-187

Greenough, Horatio 1805-1852 .... DLB-1, 235

Greenwell, Dora 1821-1882 .... DLB-35, 199

Greenwillow Books DLB-46

Greenwood, Grace (see Lippincott, Sara Jane Clarke)

Greenwood, Walter 1903-1974 ...... DLB-10, 191

Greer, Ben 1948- DLB-6

Greflinger, Georg 1620?-1677 .... DLB-164

Greg, W. R. 1809-1881 .... DLB-55

Greg, W. W. 1875-1959 .... DLB-201

Gregg, Josiah 1806-1850 .... DLB-183, 186

Gregg Press DLB-46

Gregory, Isabella Augusta Persse, Lady
1852-1932 .... DLB-10

Gregory, Horace 1898-1982 .... DLB-48

Gregory of Rimini circa 1300-1358 ...... DLB-115

Gregynog Press DLB-112

Greiffenberg, Catharina Regina von
1633-1694 .... DLB-168

Greig, Noël 1944- DLB-245

Grenfell, Wilfred Thomason
1865-1940 .... DLB-92

Gress, Elsa 1919-1988 .... DLB-214

Greve, Felix Paul (see Grove, Frederick Philip)

Greville, Fulke, First Lord Brooke
1554-1628 .... DLB-62, 172

Grey, Sir George, K.C.B. 1812-1898 ..... DLB-184

Grey, Lady Jane 1537-1554 .... DLB-132

Grey Owl 1888-1938 .... DLB-92; DS-17

Grey, Zane 1872-1939 .... DLB-9, 212

Grey Walls Press DLB-112

Griboedov, Aleksandr Sergeevich
1795?-1829 .... DLB-205

Grier, Eldon 1917- DLB-88

Grieve, C. M. (see MacDiarmid, Hugh)

Griffin, Bartholomew flourished 1596 .... DLB-172

Griffin, Gerald 1803-1840 .... DLB-159

The Griffin Poetry Prize Y-00

Griffith, Elizabeth 1727?-1793 .... DLB-39, 89

Preface to *The Delicate Distress* (1769) DLB-39

Griffith, George 1857-1906 .... DLB-178

Griffiths, Ralph [publishing house] DLB-154

Griffiths, Trevor 1935- DLB-13, 245

Griggs, S. C., and Company DLB-49

Griggs, Sutton Elbert 1872-1930 .... DLB-50

Grignon, Claude-Henri 1894-1976 .... DLB-68

Grigorovich, Dmitrii Vasil'evich
1822-1899 .... DLB-238

Grigson, Geoffrey 1905- DLB-27

Grillparzer, Franz
1791-1872 .... DLB-133; CDWLB-2

Grimald, Nicholas
circa 1519-circa 1562 .... DLB-136

Grimké, Angelina Weld 1880-1958 .... DLB-50, 54

Grimké, Sarah Moore 1792-1873 .... DLB-239

Grimm, Hans 1875-1959 .... DLB-66

Grimm, Jacob 1785-1863 .... DLB-90

Grimm, Wilhelm
1786-1859 .... DLB-90; CDWLB-2

Grimmelshausen, Johann Jacob Christoffel von
1621 or 1622-1676 ...... DLB-168; CDWLB-2

Grimshaw, Beatrice Ethel 1871-1953 ..... DLB-174

Grindal, Edmund 1519 or 1520-1583 .... DLB-132

Gripe, Maria (Kristina) 1923- DLB-257

Griswold, Rufus Wilmot
1815-1857 .... DLB-3, 59, 250

Grosart, Alexander Balloch 1827-1899 ... DLB-184

Gross, Milt 1895-1953 .... DLB-11

Grosset and Dunlap DLB-49

Grossman, Allen 1932- DLB-193

Grossman Publishers DLB-46

Grosseteste, Robert circa 1160-1253 ..... DLB-115

Grosvenor, Gilbert H. 1875-1966 .... DLB-91

Groth, Klaus 1819-1899 .... DLB-129

Groulx, Lionel 1878-1967 .... DLB-68

Grove, Frederick Philip 1879-1949 .... DLB-92

Grove Press DLB-46

Grubb, Davis 1919-1980 .... DLB-6

Gruelle, Johnny 1880-1938 .... DLB-22

von Grumbach, Argula
1492-after 1563? DLB-179

Grymeston, Elizabeth
before 1563-before 1604 .... DLB-136

Gryphius, Andreas
1616-1664 .... DLB-164; CDWLB-2

Gryphius, Christian 1649-1706 .... DLB-168

Guare, John 1938- DLB-7, 249

Guerra, Tonino 1920- DLB-128

Guest, Barbara 1920- DLB-5, 193

Guèvremont, Germaine 1893-1968 .... DLB-68

Guglielminetti, Amalia 1881-1941 .... DLB-264

Guidacci, Margherita 1921-1992 .... DLB-128

Guide to the Archives of Publishers, Journals,
and Literary Agents in North American
Libraries Y-93

Guillén, Jorge 1893-1984 .... DLB-108

Guilloux, Louis 1899-1980 .... DLB-72

Guilpin, Everard
circa 1572-after 1608? DLB-136

Guiney, Louise Imogen 1861-1920 .... DLB-54

Guiterman, Arthur 1871-1943 .... DLB-11

Günderrode, Caroline von
1780-1806 .... DLB-90

Gundulić, Ivan
1589-1638 .... DLB-147; CDWLB-4

Gunn, Bill 1934-1989 .... DLB-38

Gunn, James E. 1923- DLB-8

Gunn, Neil M. 1891-1973 .... DLB-15

Gunn, Thom 1929- DLB-27; CDBLB-8

Gunnars, Kristjana 1948- DLB-60

Günther, Johann Christian
1695-1723 .... DLB-168

Gurik, Robert 1932- DLB-60

Gurney, A. R. 1930- DLB-266

Gustafson, Ralph 1909-1995 .... DLB-88

Gustafsson, Lars 1936- DLB-257

Gütersloh, Albert Paris 1887-1973 ...... DLB-81

Guthrie, A. B., Jr. 1901-1991 .... DLB-6, 212

Guthrie, Ramon 1896-1973 .... DLB-4

The Guthrie Theater DLB-7

Guthrie, Thomas Anstey (see Anstey, FC)

Gutzkow, Karl 1811-1878 .... DLB-133

Guy, Ray 1939- DLB-60

Guy, Rosa 1925- DLB-33

Guyot, Arnold 1807-1884 .... DS-13

Gwynne, Erskine 1898-1948 .... DLB-4

Gyles, John 1680-1755 .... DLB-99

Gyllensten, Lars 1921- DLB-257

Gysin, Brion 1916- DLB-16

H

H.D. (see Doolittle, Hilda)

Habermas, Jürgen 1929- DLB-242

Cumulative Index

Habington, William 1605-1654 .... DLB-126

Hacker, Marilyn 1942- DLB-120

Hackett, Albert (see Goodrich, Frances)

Hacks, Peter 1928- DLB-124

Hadas, Rachel 1948- DLB-120

Hadden, Briton 1898-1929 .... DLB-91

Hagedorn, Friedrich von 1708-1754 ..... DLB-168

Hagelstange, Rudolf 1912-1984 .... DLB-69

Haggard, H. Rider
1856-1925 .... DLB-70, 156, 174, 178

Haggard, William 1907-1993 .... Y-93

Hagy, Alyson 1960- DLB-244

Hahn-Hahn, Ida Gräfin von
1805-1880 .... DLB-133

Haig-Brown, Roderick 1908-1976....... DLB-88

Haight, Gordon S. 1901-1985.......... DLB-103

Hailey, Arthur 1920- DLB-88; Y-82

Haines, John 1924- DLB-5, 212

Hake, Edward flourished 1566-1604 .... DLB-136

Hake, Thomas Gordon 1809-1895....... DLB-32

Hakluyt, Richard 1552?-1616.......... DLB-136

Halas, František 1901-1949 .... DLB-215

Halbe, Max 1865-1944............... DLB-118

Halberstam, David 1934- DLB-241

Haldane, J. B. S. 1892-1964 .... DLB-160

Haldeman, Joe 1943- DLB-8

Haldeman-Julius Company............. DLB-46

Haldone, Charlotte 1894-1969 .... DLB-191

Hale, E. J., and Son................... DLB-49

Hale, Edward Everett
1822-1909 ....DLB-1, 42, 74, 235

Hale, Janet Campbell 1946- DLB-175

Hale, Kathleen 1898- DLB-160

Hale, Leo Thomas (see Ebon)

Hale, Lucretia Peabody 1820-1900....... DLB-42

Hale, Nancy
1908-1988 .... DLB-86; DS-17; Y-80, Y-88

Hale, Sarah Josepha (Buell)
1788-1879............. DLB-1, 42, 73, 243

Hale, Susan 1833-1910................ DLB-221

Hales, John 1584-1656 .... DLB-151

Halévy, Ludovic 1834-1908 .... DLB-192

Haley, Alex 1921-1992....... DLB-38; CDALB-7

Haliburton, Thomas Chandler
1796-1865.................. DLB-11, 99

Hall, Anna Maria 1800-1881 .... DLB-159

Hall, Donald 1928- DLB-5

Hall, Edward 1497-1547 .... DLB-132

Hall, Halsey 1898-1977................ DLB-241

Hall, James 1793-1868 ....DLB-73, 74

Hall, Joseph 1574-1656........... DLB-121, 151

Hall, Radclyffe 1880-1943 .... DLB-191

Hall, Samuel [publishing house] DLB-49

Hall, Sarah Ewing 1761-1830 .... DLB-200

Hall, Stuart 1932- DLB-242

Hallam, Arthur Henry 1811-1833 .... DLB-32

On Some of the Characteristics of Modern
Poetry and On the Lyrical Poems of
Alfred Tennyson (1831)............ DLB-32

Halleck, Fitz-Greene 1790-1867 ...... DLB-3, 250

Haller, Albrecht von 1708-1777........ DLB-168

Halliday, Brett (see Dresser, Davis)

Halliwell-Phillipps, James Orchard
1820-1889 .... DLB-184

Hallmann, Johann Christian
1640-1704 or 1716? DLB-168

Hallmark Editions DLB-46

Halper, Albert 1904-1984............... DLB-9

Halperin, John William 1941- DLB-111

Halstead, Murat 1829-1908 .... DLB-23

Hamann, Johann Georg 1730-1788....... DLB-97

Hamburger, Michael 1924- DLB-27

Hamilton, Alexander 1712-1756 .... DLB-31

Hamilton, Alexander 1755?-1804 .... DLB-37

Hamilton, Cicely 1872-1952.........DLB-10, 197

Hamilton, Edmond 1904-1977 .... DLB-8

Hamilton, Elizabeth 1758-1816..... DLB-116, 158

Hamilton, Gail (see Corcoran, Barbara)

Hamilton, Gail (see Dodge, Mary Abigail)

Hamilton, Hamish, Limited DLB-112

Hamilton, Ian 1938- DLB-40, 155

Hamilton, Janet 1795-1873 .... DLB-199

Hamilton, Mary Agnes 1884-1962...... DLB-197

Hamilton, Patrick 1904-1962 .... DLB-10, 191

Hamilton, Virginia 1936- DLB-33, 52

Hamilton, Sir William 1788-1856....... DLB-262

Hammerstein, Oscar, II 1895-1960 ..... DLB-265

Hammett, Dashiell
1894-1961 .... DLB-226; DS-6; CDALB-5

The Glass Key and Other Dashiell Hammett
Mysteries......................... Y-96

Dashiell Hammett: An Appeal in TAC....... Y-91

Hammon, Jupiter 1711-died between
1790 and 1806 .... DLB-31, 50

Hammond, John ?-1663 .... DLB-24

Hamner, Earl 1923- DLB-6

Hampson, John 1901-1955............. DLB-191

Hampton, Christopher 1946- DLB-13

Handel-Mazzetti, Enrica von 1871-1955... DLB-81

Handke, Peter 1942- DLB-85, 124

Handlin, Oscar 1915- DLB-17

Hankin, St. John 1869-1909 .... DLB-10

Hanley, Clifford 1922- DLB-14

Hanley, James 1901-1985............. DLB-191

Hannah, Barry 1942- DLB-6, 234

Hannay, James 1827-1873............. DLB-21

Hano, Arnold 1922- DLB-241

Hansberry, Lorraine
1930-1965 .... DLB-7, 38; CDALB-1

Hansen, Martin A. 1909-1955 .... DLB-214

Hansen, Thorkild 1927-1989 .... DLB-214

Hanson, Elizabeth 1684-1737 .... DLB-200

Hapgood, Norman 1868-1937 .... DLB-91

Happel, Eberhard Werner 1647-1690.... DLB-168

Harbach, Otto 1873-1963............. DLB-265

The Harbinger 1845-1849.............. DLB-223

Harburg, E. Y. "Yip" 1896-1981 .... DLB-265

Harcourt Brace Jovanovich DLB-46

Hardenberg, Friedrich von (see Novalis)

Harding, Walter 1917- DLB-111

Hardwick, Elizabeth 1916- DLB-6

Hardy, Frank 1917-1994............. DLB-260

Hardy, Thomas
1840-1928 .... DLB-18, 19, 135; CDBLB-5

"Candour in English Fiction" (1890) DLB-18

Hare, Cyril 1900-1958 .... DLB-77

Hare, David 1947- DLB-13

Hare, R. M. 1919-2002................ DLB-262

Hargrove, Marion 1919- DLB-11

Häring, Georg Wilhelm Heinrich
(see Alexis, Willibald)

Harington, Donald 1935- DLB-152

Harington, Sir John 1560-1612......... DLB-136

Harjo, Joy 1951- DLB-120, 175

Harkness, Margaret (John Law)
1854-1923 ....DLB-197

Harley, Edward, second Earl of Oxford
1689-1741..................... DLB-213

Harley, Robert, first Earl of Oxford
1661-1724..................... DLB-213

Harlow, Robert 1923- DLB-60

Harman, Thomas flourished 1566-1573.. DLB-136

Harness, Charles L. 1915- DLB-8

Harnett, Cynthia 1893-1981........... DLB-161

Harnick, Sheldon 1924- DLB-265

Harper, Edith Alice Mary (see Wickham, Anna)

Harper, Fletcher 1806-1877 .... DLB-79

Harper, Frances Ellen Watkins
1825-1911 .... DLB-50, 221

Harper, Michael S. 1938- DLB-41

Harper and Brothers DLB-49

Harpur, Charles 1813-1868 .... DLB-230

Harraden, Beatrice 1864-1943 .... DLB-153

Harrap, George G., and Company
Limited..................... DLB-112

Harriot, Thomas 1560-1621............ DLB-136

Harris, Alexander 1805-1874 .... DLB-230

Harris, Benjamin ?-circa 1720........ DLB-42, 43

Harris, Christie 1907- DLB-88

Harris, Frank 1856-1931 ....DLB-156, 197

Harris, George Washington
1814-1869 .... DLB-3, 11, 248

Harris, Joel Chandler
1848-1908 ....DLB-11, 23, 42, 78, 91

Harris, Mark 1922- DLB-2; Y-80

Harris, Wilson 1921- DLB-117; CDWLB-3

Harrison, Mrs. Burton
(see Harrison, Constance Cary)

Harrison, Charles Yale 1898-1954....... DLB-68

Harrison, Constance Cary 1843-1920 ... DLB-221

Harrison, Frederic 1831-1923 . . . . DLB-57, 190
"On Style in English Prose" (1898) DLB-57
Harrison, Harry 1925- DLB-8
Harrison, James P., Company DLB-49
Harrison, Jim 1937- Y-82
Harrison, M. John 1945- DLB-261
Harrison, Mary St. Leger Kingsley
 (see Malet, Lucas)
Harrison, Paul Carter 1936- DLB-38
Harrison, Susan Frances 1859-1935. . . . . . DLB-99
Harrison, Tony 1937- DLB-40, 245
Harrison, William 1535-1593 . . . . DLB-136
Harrison, William 1933- DLB-234
Harrisse, Henry 1829-1910 . . . . DLB-47
The Harry Ransom Humanities
 Research Center at the University
 of Texas at Austin Y-00
Harryman, Carla 1952- DLB-193
Harsdörffer, Georg Philipp 1607-1658 . . . . DLB-164
Harsent, David 1942- DLB-40
Hart, Albert Bushnell 1854-1943 . . . . DLB-17
Hart, Anne 1768-1834 . . . . DLB-200
Hart, Elizabeth 1771-1833 . . . . DLB-200
Hart, Julia Catherine 1796-1867 . . . . DLB-99
Hart, Lorenz 1895-1943 . . . . DLB-265
The Lorenz Hart Centenary Y-95
Hart, Moss 1904-1961 . . . . DLB-7, 266
Hart, Oliver 1723-1795 . . . . DLB-31
Hart-Davis, Rupert, Limited DLB-112
Harte, Bret 1836-1902
 . . . . DLB-12, 64, 74, 79, 186; CDALB-3
Harte, Edward Holmead 1922- DLB-127
Harte, Houston Harriman 1927- DLB-127
Hartlaub, Felix 1913-1945 . . . . DLB-56
Hartleben, Otto Erich 1864-1905 . . . . . . DLB-118
Hartley, David 1705-1757 . . . . DLB-252
Hartley, L. P. 1895-1972 . . . . DLB-15, 139
Hartley, Marsden 1877-1943 . . . . DLB-54
Hartling, Peter 1933- DLB-75
Hartman, Geoffrey H. 1929- DLB-67
Hartmann, Sadakichi 1867-1944 . . . . DLB-54
Hartmann von Aue
 circa 1160-circa 1205 . . . . DLB-138; CDWLB-2
Harvey, Gabriel 1550?-1631 . . . DLB-167, 213, 236
Harvey, Jean-Charles 1891-1967 . . . . DLB-88
Harvill Press Limited DLB-112
Harwood, Lee 1939- DLB-40
Harwood, Ronald 1934- DLB-13
Hašek, Jaroslav 1883-1923 . . . DLB-215; CDWLB-4
Haskins, Charles Homer 1870-1937 . . . . . DLB-47
Haslam, Gerald 1937- DLB-212
Hass, Robert 1941- DLB-105, 206
Hasselstrom, Linda M. 1943- DLB-256
Hastings, Michael 1938- DLB-233
Hatar, Győző 1914- DLB-215
The Hatch-Billops Collection DLB-76

Hathaway, William 1944- DLB-120
Hauff, Wilhelm 1802-1827 . . . . DLB-90
A Haughty and Proud Generation (1922),
 by Ford Madox Hueffer DLB-36
Haugwitz, August Adolph von
 1647-1706 . . . . DLB-168
Hauptmann, Carl 1858-1921 . . . . DLB-66, 118
Hauptmann, Gerhart
 1862-1946 . . . . DLB-66, 118; CDWLB-2
Hauser, Marianne 1910- Y-83
Havel, Václav 1936- DLB-232; CDWLB-4
Haven, Alice B. Neal 1827-1863 . . . . DLB-260
Havergal, Frances Ridley 1836-1879 . . . . . DLB-199
Hawes, Stephen 1475?-before 1529 . . . . . . DLB-132
Hawker, Robert Stephen 1803-1875 . . . . . . DLB-32
Hawkes, John
 1925-1998 . . . . DLB-2, 7, 227; Y-80, Y-98
John Hawkes: A Tribute Y-98
Hawkesworth, John 1720-1773 . . . . DLB-142
Hawkins, Sir Anthony Hope (see Hope, Anthony)
Hawkins, Sir John 1719-1789 . . . . DLB-104, 142
Hawkins, Walter Everette 1883-? DLB-50
Hawthorne, Nathaniel
 1804-1864 . . . . DLB-1, 74, 183, 223; CDALB-2
Hawthorne, Nathaniel 1804-1864 and
 Hawthorne, Sophia Peabody
 1809-1871 . . . . DLB-183
Hawthorne, Sophia Peabody
 1809-1871 . . . . DLB-183, 239
Hay, John 1835-1905 . . . . DLB-12, 47, 189
Hayashi, Fumiko 1903-1951 . . . . DLB-180
Haycox, Ernest 1899-1950 . . . . DLB-206
Haycraft, Anna Margaret (see Ellis, Alice Thomas)
Hayden, Robert
 1913-1980 . . . . DLB-5, 76; CDALB-1
Haydon, Benjamin Robert
 1786-1846 . . . . DLB-110
Hayes, John Michael 1919- DLB-26
Hayley, William 1745-1820 . . . . DLB-93, 142
Haym, Rudolf 1821-1901 . . . . DLB-129
Hayman, Robert 1575-1629 . . . . DLB-99
Hayman, Ronald 1932- DLB-155
Hayne, Paul Hamilton
 1830-1886 . . . . DLB-3, 64, 79, 248
Hays, Mary 1760-1843 . . . . DLB-142, 158
Hayward, John 1905-1965 . . . . DLB-201
Haywood, Eliza 1693?-1756 . . . . DLB-39
From the Dedication, Lasselia (1723) DLB-39
From The Tea-Table DLB-39
From the Preface to The Disguis'd
 Prince (1723) DLB-39
Hazard, Willis P. [publishing house] DLB-49
Hazlitt, William 1778-1830 . . . . DLB-110, 158
Hazzard, Shirley 1931- Y-82
Head, Bessie
 1937-1986 . . . . . . DLB-117, 225; CDWLB-3
Headley, Joel T. 1813-1897 . . . DLB-30, 183; DS-13
Heaney, Seamus
 1939- DLB-40; Y-95; CDBLB-8

Heard, Nathan C. 1936- DLB-33
Hearn, Lafcadio 1850-1904 . . . . . DLB-12, 78, 189
Hearn, Mary Anne (Marianne Farningham,
 Eva Hope) 1834-1909 . . . . DLB-240
Hearne, John 1926- DLB-117
Hearne, Samuel 1745-1792 . . . . DLB-99
Hearne, Thomas 1678?-1735 . . . . DLB-213
Hearst, William Randolph 1863-1951 . . . . . DLB-25
Hearst, William Randolph, Jr.
 1908-1993 . . . . DLB-127
Heartman, Charles Frederick
 1883-1953 . . . . DLB-187
Heath, Catherine 1924- DLB-14
Heath, James Ewell 1792-1862 . . . . DLB-248
Heath, Roy A. K. 1926- DLB-117
Heath-Stubbs, John 1918- DLB-27
Heavysege, Charles 1816-1876 . . . . DLB-99
Hebbel, Friedrich
 1813-1863 . . . . DLB-129; CDWLB-2
Hebel, Johann Peter 1760-1826 . . . . DLB-90
Heber, Richard 1774-1833 . . . . DLB-184
Hébert, Anne 1916-2000 . . . . DLB-68
Hébert, Jacques 1923- DLB-53
Hecht, Anthony 1923- DLB-5, 169
Hecht, Ben 1894-1964 . . . DLB-7, 9, 25, 26, 28, 86
Hecker, Isaac Thomas 1819-1888 . . . . . DLB-1, 243
Hedge, Frederic Henry
 1805-1890 . . . . DLB-1, 59, 243
Hefner, Hugh M. 1926- DLB-137
Hegel, Georg Wilhelm Friedrich
 1770-1831 . . . . DLB-90
Heide, Robert 1939- DLB-249
Heidish, Marcy 1947- Y-82
Heißenbüttel, Helmut 1921-1996 . . . . DLB-75
Heike monogatari DLB-203
Hein, Christoph 1944- DLB-124; CDWLB-2
Hein, Piet 1905-1996 . . . . DLB-214
Heine, Heinrich 1797-1856 . . . . DLB-90; CDWLB-2
Heinemann, Larry 1944- DS-9
Heinemann, William, Limited DLB-112
Heinesen, William 1900-1991 . . . . DLB-214
Heinlein, Robert A. 1907-1988 . . . . DLB-8
Heinrich Julius of Brunswick
 1564-1613 . . . . DLB-164
Heinrich von dem Türlîn
 flourished circa 1230 . . . . DLB-138
Heinrich von Melk
 flourished after 1160 . . . . DLB-148
Heinrich von Veldeke
 circa 1145-circa 1190 . . . . DLB-138
Heinrich, Willi 1920- DLB-75
Heinse, Wilhelm 1746-1803 . . . . DLB-94
Heinz, W. C. 1915- DLB-171
Heiskell, John 1872-1972 . . . . DLB-127
Hejinian, Lyn 1941- DLB-165
Heliand circa 850 . . . . DLB-148
Heller, Joseph
 1923-1999 . . . . . . DLB-2, 28, 227; Y-80, Y-99

Heller, Michael 1937- DLB-165
Hellman, Lillian 1906-1984 ..... DLB-7, 228; Y-84
Hellwig, Johann 1609-1674 .... DLB-164
Helprin, Mark 1947- Y-85; CDALB-7
Helwig, David 1938- DLB-60
Hemans, Felicia 1793-1835 .... DLB-96
Hemenway, Abby Maria 1828-1890 ..... DLB-243
Hemingway, Ernest 1899-1961
 ..... DLB-4, 9, 102, 210; Y-81, Y-87, Y-99;
 DS-1, DS-15, DS-16; CDALB-4
The Hemingway Centenary Celebration at the
 JFK Library Y-99
Ernest Hemingway: A Centennial
 Celebration Y-99
The Ernest Hemingway Collection at the
 John F. Kennedy Library Y-99
Ernest Hemingway Declines to Introduce
 War and Peace Y-01
Ernest Hemingway's Reaction to James Gould
 Cozzens Y-98
Ernest Hemingway's Toronto Journalism
 Revisited: With Three Previously
 Unrecorded Stories Y-92
Falsifying Hemingway Y-96
Hemingway: Twenty-Five Years Later Y-85
Not Immediately Discernible . . . but Eventually
 Quite Clear: The *First Light* and *Final Years*
 of Hemingway's Centenary Y-99
Hemingway Salesmen's Dummies Y-00
Second International Hemingway Colloquium:
 Cuba Y-98
Hémon, Louis 1880-1913 .... DLB-92
Hempel, Amy 1951- DLB-218
Hemphill, Paul 1936- Y-87
Hénault, Gilles 1920- DLB-88
Henchman, Daniel 1689-1761 .... DLB-24
Henderson, Alice Corbin 1881-1949 ..... DLB-54
Henderson, Archibald 1877-1963 .... DLB-103
Henderson, David 1942- DLB-41
Henderson, George Wylie 1904- DLB-51
Henderson, Zenna 1917-1983 .... DLB-8
Henighan, Tom 1934- DLB-251
Henisch, Peter 1943- DLB-85
Henley, Beth 1952- Y-86
Henley, William Ernest 1849-1903 ...... DLB-19
Henning, Rachel 1826-1914 .... DLB-230
Henningsen, Agnes 1868-1962 .... DLB-214
Henniker, Florence 1855-1923 .... DLB-135
Henry, Alexander 1739-1824 .... DLB-99
Henry, Buck 1930- DLB-26
Henry VIII of England 1491-1547 ...... DLB-132
Henry of Ghent
 circa 1217-1229 - 1293 .... DLB-115
Henry, Marguerite 1902-1997 .... DLB-22
Henry, O. (see Porter, William Sydney)
Henry, Robert Selph 1889-1970 .... DLB-17
Henry, Will (see Allen, Henry W.)
Henryson, Robert
 1420s or 1430s-circa 1505 .... DLB-146

Henschke, Alfred (see Klabund)
Hensley, Sophie Almon 1866-1946 ...... DLB-99
Henson, Lance 1944- DLB-175
Henty, G. A. 1832?-1902 .... DLB-18, 141
Hentz, Caroline Lee 1800-1856 ...... DLB-3, 248
Heraclitus
 flourished circa 500 B.C. DLB-176
Herbert, Agnes circa 1880-1960 ....DLB-174
Herbert, Alan Patrick 1890-1971 .... DLB-10, 191
Herbert, Edward, Lord, of Cherbury
 1582-1648 .... DLB-121, 151, 252
Herbert, Frank 1920-1986 ..... DLB-8; CDALB-7
Herbert, George 1593-1633 .. DLB-126; CDBLB-1
Herbert, Henry William 1807-1858 .... DLB-3, 73
Herbert, John 1926- DLB-53
Herbert, Mary Sidney, Countess of Pembroke
 (see Sidney, Mary)
Herbert, Xavier 1901-1984 .... DLB-260
Herbert, Zbigniew
 1924-1998 .... DLB-232; CDWLB-4
Herbst, Josephine 1892-1969 .... DLB-9
Herburger, Gunter 1932- DLB-75, 124
Hercules, Frank E. M. 1917-1996 .... DLB-33
Herder, Johann Gottfried 1744-1803 ..... DLB-97
Herder, B., Book Company DLB-49
Heredia, José-María de 1842-1905 ...... DLB-217
Herford, Charles Harold 1853-1931 .... DLB-149
Hergesheimer, Joseph 1880-1954 ..... DLB-9, 102
Heritage Press DLB-46
Hermann the Lame 1013-1054 .... DLB-148
Hermes, Johann Timotheus
 1738-1821 .... DLB-97
Hermlin, Stephan 1915-1997 .... DLB-69
Hernández, Alfonso C. 1938- DLB-122
Hernández, Inés 1947- DLB-122
Hernández, Miguel 1910-1942 .... DLB-134
Hernton, Calvin C. 1932- DLB-38
Herodotus circa 484 B.C.-circa 420 B.C.
 ....DLB-176; CDWLB-1
Heron, Robert 1764-1807 .... DLB-142
Herr, Michael 1940- DLB-185
Herrera, Juan Felipe 1948- DLB-122
Herrick, E. R., and Company DLB-49
Herrick, Robert 1591-1674 .... DLB-126
Herrick, Robert 1868-1938 ....DLB-9, 12, 78
Herrick, William 1915- Y-83
Herrmann, John 1900-1959 .... DLB-4
Hersey, John 1914-1993 ... DLB-6, 185; CDALB-7
Hertel, François 1905-1985 .... DLB-68
Hervé-Bazin, Jean Pierre Marie (see Bazin, Hervé)
Hervey, John, Lord 1696-1743 .... DLB-101
Herwig, Georg 1817-1875 .... DLB-133
Herzog, Emile Salomon Wilhelm
 (see Maurois, André)
Hesiod eighth century B.C. DLB-176
Hesse, Hermann
 1877-1962 .... DLB-66; CDWLB-2

Hessus, Helius Eobanus 1488-1540 ......DLB-179
Hewat, Alexander circa 1743-circa 1824 ... DLB-30
Hewitt, John 1907- DLB-27
Hewlett, Maurice 1861-1923 ...... DLB-34, 156
Heyen, William 1940- DLB-5
Heyer, Georgette 1902-1974 ....DLB-77, 191
Heym, Stefan 1913- DLB-69
Heyse, Paul 1830-1914 .... DLB-129
Heytesbury, William
 circa 1310-1372 or 1373 .... DLB-115
Heyward, Dorothy 1890-1961 ....DLB-7, 249
Heyward, DuBose 1885-1940 ...DLB-7, 9, 45, 249
Heywood, John 1497?-1580? DLB-136
Heywood, Thomas
 1573 or 1574-1641 .... DLB-62
Hibbs, Ben 1901-1975 ....DLB-137
Hichens, Robert S. 1864-1950 .... DLB-153
Hickey, Emily 1845-1924 .... DLB-199
Hickman, William Albert 1877-1957 ...... DLB-92
Hicks, Granville 1901-1982 .... DLB-246
Hidalgo, José Luis 1919-1947 .... DLB-108
Hiebert, Paul 1892-1987 .... DLB-68
Hieng, Andrej 1925- DLB-181
Hierro, José 1922- DLB-108
Higgins, Aidan 1927- DLB-14
Higgins, Colin 1941-1988 .... DLB-26
Higgins, George V.
 1939-1999 .... DLB-2; Y-81, Y-98, Y-99
George V. Higgins to Julian Symons Y-99
Higginson, Thomas Wentworth
 1823-1911 .... DLB-1, 64, 243
Highwater, Jamake 1942?- DLB-52; Y-85
Hijuelos, Oscar 1951- DLB-145
Hildegard von Bingen 1098-1179 .... DLB-148
Das Hildebrandslied
 circa 820 ....DLB-148; CDWLB-2
Hildesheimer, Wolfgang
 1916-1991 .... DLB-69, 124
Hildreth, Richard 1807-1865 .. DLB-1, 30, 59, 235
Hill, Aaron 1685-1750 .... DLB-84
Hill, Geoffrey 1932- DLB-40; CDBLB-8
Hill, George M., Company DLB-49
Hill, "Sir" John 1714?-1775 .... DLB-39
Hill, Lawrence, and Company,
 Publishers DLB-46
Hill, Leslie 1880-1960 .... DLB-51
Hill, Susan 1942- DLB-14, 139
Hill, Walter 1942- DLB-44
Hill and Wang DLB-46
Hillberry, Conrad 1928- DLB-120
Hillerman, Tony 1925- DLB-206
Hilliard, Gray and Company DLB-49
Hills, Lee 1906- DLB-127
Hillyer, Robert 1895-1961 .... DLB-54
Hilton, James 1900-1954 ....DLB-34, 77
Hilton, Walter died 1396 .... DLB-146

Hilton and Company................DLB-49

Himes, Chester 1909-1984....DLB-2, 76, 143, 226

Hindmarsh, Joseph [publishing house]....DLB-170

Hine, Daryl 1936- DLB-60

Hingley, Ronald 1920- DLB-155

Hinojosa-Smith, Rolando 1929- DLB-82

Hinton, S. E. 1948- CDALB-7

Hippel, Theodor Gottlieb von
  1741-1796......................DLB-97

Hippocrates of Cos flourished circa 425 B.C.
  ....DLB-176; CDWLB-1

Hirabayashi, Taiko 1905-1972.........DLB-180

Hirsch, E. D., Jr. 1928- DLB-67

Hirsch, Edward 1950- DLB-120

Hoagland, Edward 1932- DLB-6

Hoagland, Everett H., III 1942- DLB-41

Hoban, Russell 1925- DLB-52; Y-90

Hobbes, Thomas 1588-1679 ....DLB-151, 252

Hobby, Oveta 1905- DLB-127

Hobby, William 1878-1964 ....DLB-127

Hobsbaum, Philip 1932- DLB-40

Hobson, Laura Z. 1900- DLB-28

Hobson, Sarah 1947- DLB-204

Hoby, Thomas 1530-1566..............DLB-132

Hoccleve, Thomas
  circa 1368-circa 1437..............DLB-146

Hochhuth, Rolf 1931- DLB-124

Hochman, Sandra 1936- DLB-5

Hocken, Thomas Morland
  1836-1910 ....DLB-184

Hodder and Stoughton, Limited........DLB-106

Hodgins, Jack 1938- DLB-60

Hodgman, Helen 1945- DLB-14

Hodgskin, Thomas 1787-1869 ....DLB-158

Hodgson, Ralph 1871-1962 ....DLB-19

Hodgson, William Hope
  1877-1918............ DLB-70, 153, 156, 178

Hoe, Robert, III 1839-1909...............DLB-187

Høeg, Peter 1957- DLB-214

Højholt, Per 1928- DLB-214

Hoffenstein, Samuel 1890-1947 ....DLB-11

Hoffman, Charles Fenno 1806-1884 ...DLB-3, 250

Hoffman, Daniel 1923- DLB-5

Hoffmann, E. T. A.
  1776-1822............DLB-90; CDWLB-2

Hoffman, Frank B. 1888-1958.........DLB-188

Hoffman, William 1925- DLB-234

Hoffmanswaldau, Christian Hoffman von
  1616-1679 ....DLB-168

Hofmann, Michael 1957- DLB-40

Hofmannsthal, Hugo von
  1874-1929.........DLB-81, 118; CDWLB-2

Hofstadter, Richard 1916-1970 ...... DLB-17, 246

Hogan, Desmond 1950- DLB-14

Hogan, Linda 1947- DLB-175

Hogan and Thompson................DLB-49

Hogarth Press DLB-112

Hogg, James 1770-1835 ....DLB-93, 116, 159

Hohberg, Wolfgang Helmhard Freiherr von
  1612-1688....................DLB-168

von Hohenheim, Philippus Aureolus
  Theophrastus Bombastus (see Paracelsus)

Hohl, Ludwig 1904-1980...............DLB-56

Holbrook, David 1923- DLB-14, 40

Holcroft, Thomas 1745-1809.....DLB-39, 89, 158

Preface to *Alwyn* (1780) DLB-39

Holden, Jonathan 1941- DLB-105

"Contemporary Verse Story-telling" DLB-105

Holden, Molly 1927-1981 ....DLB-40

Hölderlin, Friedrich 1770-1843 DLB-90; CDWLB-2

Holdstock, Robert 1948- DLB-261

Holiday House......................DLB-46

Holinshed, Raphael died 1580..........DLB-167

Holland, J. G. 1819-1881................DS-13

Holland, Norman N. 1927- DLB-67

Hollander, John 1929- DLB-5

Holley, Marietta 1836-1926..............DLB-11

Hollinghurst, Alan 1954- DLB-207

Hollingsworth, Margaret 1940- DLB-60

Hollo, Anselm 1934- DLB-40

Holloway, Emory 1885-1977...........DLB-103

Holloway, John 1920- DLB-27

Holloway House Publishing Company....DLB-46

Holme, Constance 1880-1955 ....DLB-34

Holmes, Abraham S. 1821?-1908 ....DLB-99

Holmes, John Clellon 1926-1988......DLB-16, 237

"Four Essays on the Beat Generation".....DLB-16

Holmes, Mary Jane 1825-1907 .....DLB-202, 221

Holmes, Oliver Wendell
  1809-1894.......DLB-1, 189, 235; CDALB-2

Holmes, Richard 1945- DLB-155

The Cult of Biography
  Excerpts from the Second Folio Debate:
  "Biographies are generally a disease of
  English Literature" Y-86

Holmes, Thomas James 1874-1959 ....DLB-187

Holroyd, Michael 1935- DLB-155, Y-99

Holst, Hermann E. von 1841-1904 ....DLB-47

Holt, Henry, and Company DLB-49

Holt, John 1721-1784 ....DLB-43

Holt, Rinehart and Winston DLB-46

Holtby, Winifred 1898-1935......,..DLB-191

Holthusen, Hans Egon 1913- DLB-69

Hölty, Ludwig Christoph Heinrich
  1748-1776.......................DLB-94

Holub, Miroslav
  1923-1998............DLB-232; CDWLB-4

Holz, Arno 1863-1929...............DLB-118

Home, Henry, Lord Kames
  (see Kames, Henry Home, Lord)

Home, John 1722-1808 ....DLB-84

Home, William Douglas 1912- DLB-13

Home Publishing Company DLB-49

Homer circa eighth-seventh centuries B.C.
  ....DLB-176; CDWLB-1

Homer, Winslow 1836-1910 ....DLB-188

Homes, Geoffrey (see Mainwaring, Daniel)

Honan, Park 1928- DLB-111

Hone, William 1780-1842 .... DLB-110, 158

Hongo, Garrett Kaoru 1951- DLB-120

Honig, Edwin 1919- DLB-5

Hood, Hugh 1928- DLB-53

Hood, Mary 1946- DLB-234

Hood, Thomas 1799-1845..............DLB-96

Hook, Theodore 1788-1841.............DLB-116

Hooker, Jeremy 1941- DLB-40

Hooker, Richard 1554-1600 ....DLB-132

Hooker, Thomas 1586-1647 ....DLB-24

hooks, bell 1952- DLB-246

Hooper, Johnson Jones
  1815-1862................DLB-3, 11, 248

Hope, Anthony 1863-1933 ....DLB-153, 156

Hope, Christopher 1944- DLB-225

Hope, Eva (see Hearn, Mary Anne)

Hope, Laurence (Adela Florence
  Cory Nicolson) 1865-1904 ....DLB-240

Hopkins, Ellice 1836-1904..............DLB-190

Hopkins, Gerard Manley
  1844-1889..........DLB-35, 57; CDBLB-5

Hopkins, John (see Sternhold, Thomas)

Hopkins, John H., and Son DLB-46

Hopkins, Lemuel 1750-1801 ....DLB-37

Hopkins, Pauline Elizabeth 1859-1930 ....DLB-50

Hopkins, Samuel 1721-1803 ....DLB-31

Hopkinson, Francis 1737-1791 ....DLB-31

Hopkinson, Nalo 1960- DLB-251

Hopper, Nora (Mrs. Nora Chesson)
  1871-1906 ....DLB-240

Hoppin, Augustus 1828-1896 ....DLB-188

Hora, Josef 1891-1945......DLB-215; CDWLB-4

Horace 65 B.C.-8 B.C.......DLB-211; CDWLB-1

Horgan, Paul 1903-1995 ..... DLB-102, 212; Y-85

Horizon Press DLB-46

Hornby, C. H. St. John 1867-1946 ....DLB-201

Hornby, Nick 1957- DLB-207

Horne, Frank 1899-1974 ....DLB-51

Horne, Richard Henry (Hengist)
  1802 or 1803-1884 ....DLB-32

Horney, Karen 1885-1952 ....DLB-246

Hornung, E. W. 1866-1921...............DLB 70

Horovitz, Israel 1939- DLB-7

Horton, George Moses 1797?-1883? DLB-50

Horváth, Ödön von 1901-1938......DLB-85, 124

Horwood, Harold 1923- DLB-60

Hosford, E. and E. [publishing house].....DLB-49

Hoskens, Jane Fenn 1693-1770?.........DLB-200

Hoskyns, John 1566-1638 ....DLB-121

Hosokawa Yūsai 1535-1610 ....DLB-203

Hostovský, Egon 1908-1973 ....DLB-215

Hotchkiss and Company DLB-49
Hough, Emerson 1857-1923 .... DLB-9, 212
Houghton, Stanley 1881-1913 .... DLB-10
Houghton Mifflin Company............ DLB-49
Household, Geoffrey 1900-1988......... DLB-87
Housman, A. E. 1859-1936 ... DLB-19; CDBLB-5
Housman, Laurence 1865-1959 .... DLB-10
Houston, Pam 1962- DLB-244
Houwald, Ernst von 1778-1845 .... DLB-90
Hovey, Richard 1864-1900............ DLB-54
Howard, Donald R. 1927-1987 .... DLB-111
Howard, Maureen 1930- Y-83
Howard, Richard 1929- DLB-5
Howard, Roy W. 1883-1964 .... DLB-29
Howard, Sidney 1891-1939 ....DLB-7, 26, 249
Howard, Thomas, second Earl of Arundel
  1585-1646 .... DLB-213
Howe, E. W. 1853-1937............. DLB-12, 25
Howe, Henry 1816-1893 .... DLB-30
Howe, Irving 1920-1993 .... DLB-67
Howe, Joseph 1804-1873 .... DLB-99
Howe, Julia Ward 1819-1910 .... DLB-1, 189, 235
Howe, Percival Presland 1886-1944..... DLB-149
Howe, Susan 1937- DLB-120
Howell, Clark, Sr. 1863-1936.......... DLB-25
Howell, Evan P. 1839-1905 .... DLB-23
Howell, James 1594?-1666 .... DLB-151
Howell, Soskin and Company DLB-46
Howell, Warren Richardson
  1912-1984...................... DLB-140
Howells, William Dean 1837-1920
  ....DLB-12, 64, 74, 79, 189; CDALB-3
Introduction to Paul Laurence Dunbar,
  Lyrics of Lowly Life (1896) DLB-50
Howitt, Mary 1799-1888.......... DLB-110, 199
Howitt, William 1792-1879 and
  Howitt, Mary 1799-1888 .... DLB-110
Hoyem, Andrew 1935- DLB-5
Hoyers, Anna Ovena 1584-1655 .... DLB-164
Hoyle, Fred 1915-2001............... DLB-261
Hoyos, Angela de 1940- DLB-82
Hoyt, Henry [publishing house]........ DLB-49
Hoyt, Palmer 1897-1979 .... DLB-127
Hrabal, Bohumil 1914-1997 .... DLB-232
Hrabanus Maurus 776?-856 .... DLB-148
Hronský, Josef Cíger 1896-1960........ DLB-215
Hrotsvit of Gandersheim
  circa 935-circa 1000 .... DLB-148
Hubbard, Elbert 1856-1915 .... DLB-91
Hubbard, Kin 1868-1930 .... DLB-11
Hubbard, William circa 1621-1704 ..... DLB-24
Huber, Therese 1764-1829 .... DLB-90
Huch, Friedrich 1873-1913 .... DLB-66
Huch, Ricarda 1864-1947............. DLB-66
Huck at 100: How Old Is
  Huckleberry Finn?................... Y-85

Huddle, David 1942- DLB-130
Hudgins, Andrew 1951- DLB-120
Hudson, Henry Norman 1814-1886 ..... DLB-64
Hudson, Stephen 1868?-1944.......... DLB-197
Hudson, W. H. 1841-1922......DLB-98, 153, 174
Hudson and Goodwin DLB-49
Huebsch, B. W. [publishing house] DLB-46
Oral History: B. W. Huebsch.............. Y-99
Hueffer, Oliver Madox 1876-1931 ...... DLB-197
Hugh of St. Victor circa 1096-1141 ..... DLB-208
Hughes, David 1930- DLB-14
Hughes, Dusty 1947- DLB-233
Hughes, Hatcher 1881-1945........... DLB-249
Hughes, John 1677-1720 .... DLB-84
Hughes, Langston 1902-1967
  ....DLB-4, 7, 48, 51, 86, 228; CDALB-5
Hughes, Richard 1900-1976 .... DLB-15, 161
Hughes, Ted 1930-1998............ DLB-40, 161
Hughes, Thomas 1822-1896 .... DLB-18, 163
Hugo, Richard 1923-1982 .... DLB-5, 206
Hugo, Victor 1802-1885........DLB-119, 192, 217
Hugo Awards and Nebula Awards DLB-8
Hull, Richard 1896-1973.............. DLB-77
Hulme, T. E. 1883-1917............... DLB-19
Hulton, Anne ?-1779? DLB-200
Humboldt, Alexander von 1769-1859 .... DLB-90
Humboldt, Wilhelm von 1767-1835 ...... DLB-90
Hume, David 1711-1776 .... DLB-104, 252
Hume, Fergus 1859-1932 .... DLB-70
Hume, Sophia 1702-1774 .... DLB-200
Hume-Rothery, Mary Catherine
  1824-1885 .... DLB-240
Humishuma (see Mourning Dove)
Hummer, T. R. 1950- DLB-120
Humorous Book Illustration............ DLB-11
Humphrey, Duke of Gloucester
  1391-1447...................... DLB-213
Humphrey, William 1924-1997 .. DLB-6, 212, 234
Humphreys, David 1752-1818 .... DLB-37
Humphreys, Emyr 1919- DLB-15
Huncke, Herbert 1915-1996............ DLB-16
Huneker, James Gibbons 1857-1921...... DLB-71
Hunold, Christian Friedrich 1681-1721 .. DLB-168
Hunt, Irene 1907- DLB-52
Hunt, Leigh 1784-1859.........DLB-96, 110, 144
Hunt, Violet 1862-1942 ....DLB-162, 197
Hunt, William Gibbes 1791-1833 .... DLB-73
Hunter, Evan 1926- Y-82
Hunter, Jim 1939- DLB-14
Hunter, Kristin 1931- DLB-33
Hunter, Mollie 1922- DLB-161
Hunter, N. C. 1908-1971 .... DLB-10
Hunter-Duvar, John 1821-1899 .... DLB-99
Huntington, Henry E. 1850-1927....... DLB-140

Huntington, Susan Mansfield
  1791-1823..................... DLB-200
Hurd and Houghton DLB-49
Hurst, Fannie 1889-1968 .... DLB-86
Hurst and Blackett DLB-106
Hurst and Company DLB-49
Hurston, Zora Neale
  1901?-1960.......... DLB-51, 86; CDALB-7
Husson, Jules-François-Félix (see Champfleury)
Huston, John 1906-1987 .... DLB-26
Hutcheson, Francis 1694-1746 ...... DLB-31, 252
Hutchinson, Ron 1947- DLB-245
Hutchinson, R. C. 1907-1975 .... DLB-191
Hutchinson, Thomas 1711-1780
  .... DLB-30, 31
Hutchinson and Company
  (Publishers) Limited.............. DLB-112
Hutton, Richard Holt 1826-1897 .... DLB-57
von Hutton, Ulrich 1488-1523..........DLB-179
Huxley, Aldous 1894-1963
  ...... DLB-36, 100, 162, 195, 255; CDBLB-6
Huxley, Elspeth Josceline
  1907-1997...................DLB-77, 204
Huxley, T. H. 1825-1895.............. DLB-57
Huyghue, Douglas Smith 1816-1891 ..... DLB-99
Huysmans, Joris-Karl 1848-1907 .... DLB-123
Hwang, David Henry
  1957- DLB-212, 228
Hyde, Donald 1909-1966 and
  Hyde, Mary 1912- DLB-187
Hyman, Trina Schart 1939- DLB-61

I

Iavorsky, Stefan 1658-1722............ DLB-150
Iazykov, Nikolai Mikhailovich
  1803-1846 .... DLB-205
Ibáñez, Armando P. 1949- DLB-209
Ibn Bajja circa 1077-1138 .... DLB-115
Ibn Gabirol, Solomon
  circa 1021-circa 1058 .... DLB-115
Ibuse, Masuji 1898-1993.............. DLB-180
Ichijō Kanera
  (see Ichijō Kaneyoshi)
Ichijō Kaneyoshi (Ichijō Kanera)
  1402-1481 .... DLB-203
The Iconography of Science-Fiction Art.... DLB-8
Iffland, August Wilhelm 1759-1814 ...... DLB-94
Ignatow, David 1914-1997 .... DLB-5
Ike, Chukwuemeka 1931- DLB-157
Ikkyū Sōjun 1394-1481 .... DLB-203
Iles, Francis (see Berkeley, Anthony)
Illich, Ivan 1926- DLB-242
The Illustration of Early German Literar
  Manuscripts, circa 1150-circa 1300 .. DLB-148
Illyés, Gyula 1902-1983 .....DLB-215; CDWLB-4
Imbs, Bravig 1904-1946 .... DLB-4
Imbuga, Francis D. 1947- DLB-157
Immermann, Karl 1796-1840 .... DLB-133

Inchbald, Elizabeth 1753-1821 . . . . DLB-39, 89	Iggulden, John Y-01	Irving, Washington 1783-1859 . . . . DLB-3, 11, 30, 59, 73, 74, 183, 186, 250; CDALB-2
Ingamells, Rex 1913-1955 . . . . DLB-260	Jakes, John Y-83	
Inge, William 1913-1973 . . . DLB-7, 249; CDALB-1	Jenkinson, Edward B. Y-82	Irwin, Grace 1907- DLB-68
Ingelow, Jean 1820-1897 . . . . DLB-35, 163	Jenks, Tom Y-86	Irwin, Will 1873-1948 . . . . DLB-25
Ingersoll, Ralph 1900-1985 . . . . DLB-127	Kaplan, Justin Y-86	Isaksson, Ulla 1916-2000 . . . . DLB-257
The Ingersoll Prizes Y-84	King, Florence Y-85	Iser, Wolfgang 1926- DLB-242
Ingoldsby, Thomas (see Barham, Richard Harris)	Klopfer, Donald S. Y-97	Isherwood, Christopher 1904-1986 . . . . DLB-15, 195; Y-86
Ingraham, Joseph Holt 1809-1860 . . . . . DLB-3, 248	Krug, Judith Y-82	
Inman, John 1805-1850 . . . . DLB-73	Lamm, Donald Y-95	The Christopher Isherwood Archive, The Huntington Library Y-99
Innerhofer, Franz 1944- DLB-85	Laughlin, James Y-96	
Innis, Harold Adams 1894-1952 . . . . DLB-88	Lindsay, Jack Y-84	Ishiguro, Kazuo 1954- DLB-194
Innis, Mary Quayle 1899-1972 . . . . DLB-88	Mailer, Norman Y-97	
Inō Sōgi 1421-1502 . . . . DLB-203	Manchester, William Y-85	Ishikawa Jun 1899-1987 . . . . DLB-182
Inoue Yasushi 1907-1991 . . . . DLB-181	McCormack, Thomas Y-98	
International Publishers Company DLB-46	McNamara, Katherine Y-97	The Island Trees Case: A Symposium on School Library Censorship An Interview with Judith Krug An Interview with Phyllis Schlafly An Interview with Edward B. Jenkinson An Interview with Lamarr Mooneyham An Interview with Harriet Bernstein Y-82
Interviews:	McTaggart, J. M. E. 1866-1925 . . . . DLB-262	
Adoff, Arnold and Virginia Hamilton Y-01	Mellen, Joan Y-94	
Anastas, Benjamin Y-98	Menaher, Daniel Y-97	
Baker, Nicholson Y-00	Mooneyham, Lamarr. Y-82	
Bank, Melissa Y-98	Murray, Les Y-01	Islas, Arturo 1938-1991 . . . . DLB-122
Bernstein, Harriet Y-82	Nosworth, David Y-82	
Betts, Doris Y-82	O'Connor, Patrick Y-84, Y-99	Issit, Debbie 1966- DLB-233
Bosworth, David Y-82	Ozick, Cynthia Y-83	Ivanišević, Drago |1907-1981 . . . . DLB-181
Bottoms, David Y-83	Penner, Jonathan Y-83	
Bowers, Fredson Y-80	Pennington, Lee Y-82	Ivaska, Astrīde 1926- DLB-232
Burnshaw, Stanley Y-97	Penzler, Otto Y-96	Ivers, M. J., and Company DLB-49
Carpenter, Humphrey Y-84, Y-99	Plimpton, George Y-99	Iwaniuk, Wacław 1915- DLB-215
Carr, Virginia Spencer Y-00	Potok, Chaim Y-84	Iwano, Hōmei 1873-1920. . . . . DLB-180
Carver, Raymond Y-83	Powell, Padgett Y-01	Iwaszkiewicz, Jarosław 1894-1980 . . . . . . DLB-215
Cherry, Kelly Y-83	Prescott, Peter S. Y-86	Iyayi, Festus 1947- DLB-157
Coppel, Alfred Y-83	Rabe, David Y-91	Izumi, Kyōka 1873-1939 . . . . DLB-180
Cowley, Malcolm Y-81	Rallyson, Carl Y-97	
Davis, Paxton Y-89	Rechy, John Y-82	# J
De Vries, Peter Y-82	Reid, B. L. Y-83	
Dickey, James Y-82	Reynolds, Michael Y-95, Y-99	Jackmon, Marvin E. (see Marvin X)
Donald, David Herbert Y-87	Schlafly, Phyllis Y-82	Jacks, L. P. 1860-1955 . . . . DLB-135
Ellroy, James Y-91	Schroeder, Patricia Y-99	Jackson, Angela 1951- DLB-41
Fancher, Betsy Y-83	Schulberg, Budd Y-81, Y-01	Jackson, Charles 1903-1968 . . . . DLB-234
Faust, Irvin Y-00	Scribner, Charles, III Y-94	Jackson, Helen Hunt 1830-1885 . . . . DLB-42, 47, 186, 189
Fulton, Len Y-86	Sipper, Ralph Y-94	
Furst, Alan Y-01	Staley, Thomas F. Y-00	Jackson, Holbrook 1874-1948 . . . . DLB-98
Garrett, George Y-83	Styron, William Y-80	Jackson, Laura Riding 1901-1991 . . . . DLB-48
Greenfield, George Y-91	Toth, Susan Allen Y-86	Jackson, Shirley 1916-1965 . . . . DLB-6, 234; CDALB-1
Griffin, Bryan Y-81	Tyler, Anne Y-82	
Groom, Winston Y-01	Vaughan, Samuel Y-97	Jacob, Max 1876-1944 . . . . DLB-258
Guilds, John Caldwell Y-92	Von Ogtrop, Kristin Y-92	Jacob, Naomi 1884?-1964 . . . . DLB-191
Hardin, James Y-92	Wallenstein, Barry Y-92	Jacob, Piers Anthony Dillingham (see Anthony, Piers)
Harrison, Jim Y-82	Weintraub, Stanley Y-82	
Hazzard, Shirley Y-82	Williams, J. Chamberlain Y-84	Jacob, Violet 1863-1946 . . . . DLB-240
Herrick, William Y-01	Editors, Conversations with Y-95	Jacobi, Friedrich Heinrich 1743-1819 . . . . . DLB-94
Higgins, George V. Y-98	Interviews on E-Publishing Y-00	Jacobi, Johann Georg 1740-1841 . . . . DLB-97
Hoban, Russell Y-90	Into the Past: William Jovanovich's Reflections in Publishing Y-01	Jacobs, George W., and Company DLB-49
Holroyd, Michael Y-99		Jacobs, Harriet 1813-1897 . . . . DLB-239
Horowitz, Glen Y-90	Irving, John 1942- DLB-6; Y-82	Jacobs, Joseph 1854-1916 . . . . DLB-141
		Jacobs, W. W. 1863-1943 . . . . DLB-135
		Jacobsen, Jørgen-Frantz 1900-1938 . . . . . . DLB-214
		Jacobsen, Josephine 1908- DLB-244
		Jacobson, Dan 1929- DLB-14, 207, 225

Cumulative Index

Jacobson, Howard 1942- DLB-207

Jacques de Vitry circa 1160/1170-1240 ... DLB-208

Jæger, Frank 1926-1977 .... DLB-214

Jaggard, William [publishing house] DLB-170

Jahier, Piero 1884-1966 .... DLB-114, 264

Jahnn, Hans Henny 1894-1959 ..... DLB-56, 124

Jakes, John 1932- Y-83

Jakobson, Roman 1896-1982 .... DLB-242

James, Alice 1848-1892 .... DLB-221

James, C. L. R. 1901-1989 .... DLB-125

James, George P. R. 1801-1860 .... DLB-116

James, Henry 1843-1916
.......DLB-12, 71, 74, 189; DS-13; CDALB-3

James, John circa 1633-1729 .... DLB-24

James, M. R. 1862-1936 .... DLB-156, 201

James, Naomi 1949- DLB-204

James, P. D. 1920- ... DLB-87; DS-17; CDBLB-8

James VI of Scotland, I of England
1566-1625 ....DLB-151, 172

*Ane Schort Treatise Conteining Some Revlis
and Cautelis to Be Obseruit and Eschewit
in Scottis Poesi* (1584) DLB-172

James, Thomas 1572?-1629 .... DLB-213

James, U. P. [publishing house] DLB-49

James, Will 1892-1942 ....DS-16

Jameson, Anna 1794-1860 .... DLB-99, 166

Jameson, Fredric 1934- DLB-67

Jameson, J. Franklin 1859-1937 .... DLB-17

Jameson, Storm 1891-1986 .... DLB-36

Jančar, Drago 1948- DLB-181

Janés, Clara 1940- DLB-134

Janevski, Slavko 1920- ... DLB-181; CDWLB-4

Jansson, Tove 1914-2001 .... DLB-257

Janvier, Thomas 1849-1913 .... DLB-202

Jaramillo, Cleofas M. 1878-1956 .... DLB-122

Jarman, Mark 1952- DLB-120

Jarrell, Randall 1914-1965 . DLB-48, 52; CDALB-1

Jarrold and Sons DLB-106

Jarry, Alfred 1873-1907 .... DLB-192, 258

Jarves, James Jackson 1818-1888 .... DLB-189

Jasmin, Claude 1930- DLB-60

Jaunsudrabiņš, Jānis 1877-1962 .... DLB-220

Jay, John 1745-1829 .... DLB-31

Jean de Garlande (see John of Garland)

Jefferies, Richard 1848-1887 .... DLB-98, 141

Jeffers, Lance 1919-1985 .... DLB-41

Jeffers, Robinson
1887-1962 .... DLB-45, 212; CDALB-4

Jefferson, Thomas
1743-1826 .... DLB-31, 183; CDALB-2

Jégé 1866-1940 .... DLB-215

Jelinek, Elfriede 1946- DLB-85

Jellicoe, Ann 1927- DLB-13, 233

Jemison, Mary circa 1742-1833 .... DLB-239

Jenkins, Dan 1929- DLB-241

Jenkins, Elizabeth 1905- DLB-155

Jenkins, Robin 1912- DLB-14

Jenkins, William Fitzgerald (see Leinster, Murray)

Jenkins, Herbert, Limited DLB-112

Jennings, Elizabeth 1926- DLB-27

Jens, Walter 1923- DLB-69

Jensen, Johannes V. 1873-1950 .... DLB-214

Jensen, Merrill 1905-1980 .... DLB-17

Jensen, Thit 1876-1957 .... DLB-214

Jephson, Robert 1736-1803 .... DLB-89

Jerome, Jerome K. 1859-1927 ..... DLB-10, 34, 135

Jerome, Judson 1927-1991 .... DLB-105

Jerrold, Douglas 1803-1857 .... DLB-158, 159

Jersild, Per Christian 1935- DLB-257

Jesse, F. Tennyson 1888-1958 .... DLB-77

Jewel, John 1522-1571 .... DLB-236

Jewett, John P., and Company DLB-49

Jewett, Sarah Orne 1849-1909 ....DLB-12, 74, 221

The Jewish Publication Society DLB-49

Jewitt, John Rodgers 1783-1821 .... DLB-99

Jewsbury, Geraldine 1812-1880 .... DLB-21

Jewsbury, Maria Jane 1800-1833 .... DLB-199

Jhabvala, Ruth Prawer 1927- DLB-139, 194

Jiménez, Juan Ramón 1881-1958 .... DLB-134

Jimmy, Red, and Others: Harold Rosenthal
Remembers the Stars of the Press Box.... Y-01

Jin, Ha 1956- DLB-244

Joans, Ted 1928- DLB-16, 41

Jōha 1525-1602 .... DLB-203

Johannis de Garlandia (see John of Garland)

John, Errol 1924-1988 .... DLB-233

John, Eugenie (see Marlitt, E.)

John of Dumbleton
circa 1310-circa 1349 .... DLB-115

John of Garland (Jean de Garlande, Johannis de
Garlandia) circa 1195-circa 1272 .... DLB-208

Johns, Captain W. E. 1893-1968 .... DLB-160

Johnson, Mrs. A. E. ca. 1858-1922...... DLB-221

Johnson, Amelia (see Johnson, Mrs. A. E.)

Johnson, B. S. 1933-1973 .... DLB-14, 40

Johnson, Benjamin [publishing house] DLB-49

Johnson, Benjamin, Jacob, and
Robert [publishing house] DLB-49

Johnson, Charles 1679-1748 .... DLB-84

Johnson, Charles R. 1948- DLB-33

Johnson, Charles S. 1893-1956 .... DLB-51, 91

Johnson, Denis 1949- DLB-120

Johnson, Diane 1934- Y-80

Johnson, Dorothy M. 1905–1984 .... DLB-206

Johnson, E. Pauline (Tekahionwake)
1861-1913 ....DLB-175

Johnson, Edgar 1901-1995 .... DLB-103

Johnson, Edward 1598-1672............ DLB-24

Johnson, Eyvind 1900-1976 .... DLB-259

Johnson, Fenton 1888-1958 .... DLB-45, 50

Johnson, Georgia Douglas
1877?-1966 .... DLB-51, 249

Johnson, Gerald W. 1890-1980 .... DLB-29

Johnson, Greg 1953- DLB-234

Johnson, Helene 1907-1995 .... DLB-51

Johnson, Jacob, and Company DLB-49

Johnson, James Weldon
1871-1938.............. DLB-51; CDALB-4

Johnson, John H. 1918- DLB-137

Johnson, Joseph [publishing house] DLB-154

Johnson, Linton Kwesi 1952- DLB-157

Johnson, Lionel 1867-1902 .... DLB-19

Johnson, Nunnally 1897-1977 .... DLB-26

Johnson, Owen 1878-1952 .... Y-87

Johnson, Pamela Hansford 1912- DLB-15

Johnson, Pauline 1861-1913 .... DLB-92

Johnson, Ronald 1935-1998 .... DLB-169

Johnson, Samuel 1696-1772 ... DLB-24; CDBLB-2

Johnson, Samuel
1709-1784........DLB-39, 95, 104, 142, 213

Johnson, Samuel 1822-1882 .... DLB-1, 243

Johnson, Susanna 1730-1810 .... DLB-200

Johnson, Terry 1955- DLB-233

Johnson, Uwe 1934-1984.....DLB-75; CDWLB-2

Johnston, Annie Fellows 1863-1931 ...... DLB-42

Johnston, Basil H. 1929- DLB-60

Johnston, David Claypole 1798?-1865 ... DLB-188

Johnston, Denis 1901-1984............. DLB-10

Johnston, Ellen 1835-1873 .... DLB-199

Johnston, George 1912-1970............ DLB-260

Johnston, George 1913- DLB-88

Johnston, Sir Harry 1858-1927..........DLB-174

Johnston, Jennifer 1930- DLB-14

Johnston, Mary 1870-1936 .... DLB-9

Johnston, Richard Malcolm 1822-1898 ... DLB-74

Johnstone, Charles 1719?-1800?......... DLB-39

Johst, Hanns 1890-1978 .... DLB-124

Jolas, Eugene 1894-1952............. DLB-4, 45

Jones, Alice C. 1853-1933............. DLB-92

Jones, Charles C., Jr. 1831-1893......... DLB-30

Jones, D. G. 1929- DLB-53

Jones, David 1895-1974 .. DLB-20, 100; CDBLB-7

Jones, Diana Wynne 1934- DLB-161

Jones, Ebenezer 1820-1860 .... DLB-32

Jones, Ernest 1819-1868................ DLB-32

Jones, Gayl 1949- DLB-33

Jones, George 1800-1870 .... DLB-183

Jones, Glyn 1905- DLB-15

Jones, Gwyn 1907- DLB-15, 139

Jones, Henry Arthur 1851-1929......... DLB-10

Jones, Hugh circa 1692-1760 .... DLB-24

Jones, James 1921-1977........DLB-2, 143; DS-17

James Jones Papers in the Handy Writers'
Colony Collection at the University of
Illinois at Springfield Y-98

The James Jones Society.................. Y-92

Jones, Jenkin Lloyd 1911- DLB-127

358

Jones, John Beauchamp 1810-1866 . . . . . . DLB-202

Jones, LeRoi (see Baraka, Amiri)

Jones, Lewis 1897-1939 . . . . DLB-15

Jones, Madison 1925- DLB-152

Jones, Major Joseph (see Thompson, William Tappan)

Jones, Marie 1955- DLB-233

Jones, Preston 1936-1979 . . . . DLB-7

Jones, Rodney 1950- DLB-120

Jones, Thom 1945- DLB-244

Jones, Sir William 1746-1794 . . . . DLB-109

Jones, William Alfred 1817-1900 . . . . DLB-59

Jones's Publishing House DLB-49

Jong, Erica 1942- DLB-2, 5, 28, 152

Jonke, Gert F. 1946- DLB-85

Jonson, Ben 1572?-1637 . . . . DLB-62, 121; CDBLB-1

Jordan, June 1936- DLB-38

Joseph and George Y-99

Joseph, Jenny 1932- DLB-40

Joseph, Michael, Limited DLB-112

Josephson, Matthew 1899-1978 . . . . DLB-4

Josephus, Flavius 37-100 . . . . DLB-176

Josiah Allen's Wife (see Holley, Marietta)

Josipovici, Gabriel 1940- DLB-14

Josselyn, John ?-1675 . . . . DLB-24

Joudry, Patricia 1921- DLB-88

Jouve, Pierre-Jean 1887-1976 . . . . DLB-258

Jovanovich, William 1920-2001 . . . . Y-01

Into the Past: William Jovanovich's Reflections on Publishing Y-01

Jovine, Francesco 1902-1950 . . . . DLB-264

Jovine, Giuseppe 1922- DLB-128

Joyaux, Philippe (see Sollers, Philippe)

Joyce, Adrien (see Eastman, Carol)

Joyce, James 1882-1941
. . . . DLB-10, 19, 36, 162, 247; CDBLB-6

James Joyce Centenary: Dublin, 1982 . . . . . . Y-82

James Joyce Conference Y-85

A Joyce (Con)Text: Danis Rose and the Remaking of *Ulysses* Y-97

The New *Ulysses* Y-84

Jozsef, Attila 1905-1937 . . . . DLB-215; CDWLB-4

Judd, Orange, Publishing Company DLB-49

Judd, Sylvester 1813-1853 . . . . DLB-1, 243

Judith circa 930 . . . . DLB-146

Julian Barnes Checklist Y-01

Julian of Norwich 1342-circa 1420 . . . . DLB-1146

Julius Caesar 100 B.C.-44 B.C. DLB-211; CDWLB-1

June, Jennie (see Croly, Jane Cunningham)

Jung, Franz 1888-1963 . . . . DLB-118

Jünger, Ernst 1895- DLB-56; CDWLB-2

Der jüngere Titurel circa 1275 . . . . DLB-138

Jung-Stilling, Johann Heinrich 1740-1817 . . . . DLB-94

Justice, Donald 1925- Y-83

Juvenal circa A.D. 60-circa A.D. 130
. . . . DLB-211; CDWLB-1

The Juvenile Library (see Godwin, M. J., and Company)

K

Kacew, Romain (see Gary, Romain)

Kafka, Franz 1883-1924 . . . . . . DLB-81; CDWLB-2

Kahn, Gus 1886-1941 . . . . DLB-265

Kahn, Roger 1927- DLB-171

Kaikō Takeshi 1939-1989 . . . . DLB-182

Kaiser, Georg 1878-1945 . . . . DLB-124; CDWLB-2

Kaiserchronik circca 1147 . . . . DLB-148

Kaleb, Vjekoslav 1905- DLB-181

Kalechofsky, Roberta 1931- DLB-28

Kaler, James Otis 1848-1912 . . . . DLB-12

Kalmar, Bert 1884-1947 . . . . DLB-265

Kames, Henry Home, Lord 1696-1782 . . . . DLB-31, 104

Kamo no Chōmei (Kamo no Nagaakira) 1153 or 1155-1216 . . . . DLB-203

Kamo no Nagaakira (see Kamo no Chōmei)

Kampmann, Christian 1939-1988 . . . . DLB-214

Kandel, Lenore 1932- DLB-16

Kanin, Garson 1912-1999 . . . . DLB-7

Kant, Hermann 1926- DLB-75

Kant, Immanuel 1724-1804 . . . . DLB-94

Kantemir, Antiokh Dmitrievich 1708-1744 . . . . DLB-150

Kantor, MacKinlay 1904-1977 . . . . DLB-9, 102

Kanze Kōjirō Nobumitsu 1435-1516 . . . . . DLB-203

Kanze Motokiyo (see Zeimi)

Kaplan, Fred 1937- DLB-111

Kaplan, Johanna 1942- DLB-28

Kaplan, Justin 1925- DLB-111; Y-86

The Practice of Biography V: An Interview with Justin Kaplan Y-86

Kaplinski, Jaan 1941- DLB-232

Kapnist, Vasilii Vasilevich 1758?-1823 . . . DLB-150

Karadžić, Vuk Stefanović 1787-1864 . . . . DLB-147; CDWLB-4

Karamzin, Nikolai Mikhailovich 1766-1826 . . . . DLB-150

Karinthy, Frigyes 1887-1938 . . . . DLB-215

Karsch, Anna Louisa 1722-1791 . . . . DLB-97

Kasack, Hermann 1896-1966 . . . . DLB-69

Kasai, Zenzō 1887-1927 . . . . DLB-180

Kaschnitz, Marie Luise 1901-1974 . . . . . . DLB-69

Kassák, Lajos 1887-1967 . . . . DLB-215

Kaštelan, Jure 1919-1990 . . . . DLB-147

Kästner, Erich 1899-1974 . . . . DLB-56

Katenin, Pavel Aleksandrovich 1792-1853 . . . . DLB-205

Kattan, Naim 1928- DLB-53

Katz, Steve 1935- Y-83

Kauffman, Janet 1945- DLB-218; Y-86

Kauffmann, Samuel 1898-1971 . . . . DLB-127

Kaufman, Bob 1925- DLB-16, 41

Kaufman, George S. 1889-1961 . . . . DLB-7

Kavan, Anna 1901-1968 . . . . DLB-255

Kavanagh, P. J. 1931- DLB-40

Kavanagh, Patrick 1904-1967 . . . . DLB-15, 20

Kawabata, Yasunari 1899-1972 . . . . DLB-180

Kay, Guy Gavriel 1954- DLB-251

Kaye-Smith, Sheila 1887-1956 . . . . DLB-36

Kazin, Alfred 1915-1998 . . . . DLB-67

Keane, John B. 1928- DLB-13

Keary, Annie 1825-1879 . . . . DLB-163

Keary, Eliza 1827-1918 . . . . DLB-240

Keating, H. R. F. 1926- DLB-87

Keatley, Charlotte 1960- DLB-245

Keats, Ezra Jack 1916-1983 . . . . DLB-61

Keats, John 1795-1821 . . . . DLB-96, 110; CDBLB-3

Keble, John 1792-1866 . . . . DLB-32, 55

Keckley, Elizabeth 1818?-1907 . . . . DLB-239

Keeble, John 1944- Y-83

Keeffe, Barrie 1945- DLB-13, 245

Keeley, James 1867-1934 . . . . DLB-25

W. B. Keen, Cooke and Company DLB-49

Keillor, Garrison 1942- Y-87

Keith, Marian 1874?-1961 . . . . DLB-92

Keller, Gary D. 1943- DLB-82

Keller, Gottfried 1819-1890 . . . . DLB-129; CDWLB-2

Kelley, Edith Summers 1884-1956 . . . . DLB-9

Kelley, Emma Dunham ?-? DLB-221

Kelley, William Melvin 1937- DLB-33

Kellogg, Ansel Nash 1832-1886 . . . . DLB-23

Kellogg, Steven 1941- DLB-61

Kelly, George E. 1887-1974 . . . . DLB-7, 249

Kelly, Hugh 1739-1777 . . . . DLB-89

Kelly, Piet and Company DLB-49

Kelly, Robert 1935- DLB-5, 130, 165

Kelman, James 1946- DLB-194

Kelmscott Press DLB-112

Kelton, Elmer 1926- DLB-256

Kemble, E. W. 1861-1933 . . . . DLB-188

Kemble, Fanny 1809-1893 . . . . DLB-32

Kemelman, Harry 1908- DLB-28

Kempe, Margery circa 1373-1438 . . . . DLB-146

Kempner, Friederike 1836-1904 . . . . DLB-129

Kempowski, Walter 1929- DLB-75

Kendall, Claude [publishing company] DLB-46

Kendall, Henry 1839-1882 . . . . DLB-230

Kendall, May 1861-1943 . . . . DLB-240

Kendell, George 1809-1867 . . . . DLB-43

Kenedy, P. J., and Sons DLB-49

Kenkō circa 1283-circa 1352.......... DLB-203
Kennan, George 1845-1924 .... DLB-189
Kennedy, Adrienne 1931- DLB-38
Kennedy, John Pendleton 1795-1870 .. DLB-3, 248
Kennedy, Leo 1907- DLB-88
Kennedy, Margaret 1896-1967......... DLB-36
Kennedy, Patrick 1801-1873........... DLB-159
Kennedy, Richard S. 1920- DLB-111
Kennedy, William 1928- DLB-143; Y-85
Kennedy, X. J. 1929- DLB-5
Kennelly, Brendan 1936- DLB-40
Kenner, Hugh 1923- DLB-67
Kennerley, Mitchell [publishing house] ... DLB-46
Kenny, Maurice 1929- DLB-175
Kent, Frank R. 1877-1958............. DLB-29
Kenyon, Jane 1947-1995.............. DLB-120
Keough, Hugh Edmund 1864-1912 .....DLB-171
Keppler and Schwartzmann DLB-49
Ker, John, third Duke of Roxburghe
  1740-1804..................... DLB-213
Ker, N. R. 1908-1982................. DLB-201
Kerlan, Irvin 1912-1963 .... DLB-187
Kermode, Frank 1919- DLB-242
Kern, Jerome 1885-1945.............. DLB-187
Kernaghan, Eileen 1939- DLB-251
Kerner, Justinus 1776-1862 .... DLB-90
Kerouac, Jack
  1922-1969 .. DLB-2, 16, 237; DS-3; CDALB-1
The Jack Kerouac Revival Y-95
"Re-meeting of Old Friends":
  The Jack Kerouac Conference Y-82
Auction of Jack Kerouac's On the Road Scroll .. Y-01
Kerouac, Jan 1952-1996 .... DLB-16
Kerr, Charles H., and Company DLB-49
Kerr, Orpheus C. (see Newell, Robert Henry)
Kersh, Gerald 1911-1968 .... DLB-255
Kesey, Ken
  1935-2001 .... DLB-2, 16, 206; CDALB-6
Kessel, Joseph 1898-1979 .... DLB-72
Kessel, Martin 1901- DLB-56
Kesten, Hermann 1900- DLB-56
Keun, Irmgard 1905-1982 .... DLB-69
Key, Ellen 1849-1926 .... DLB-259
Key and Biddle..................... DLB-49
Keynes, Sir Geoffrey 1887-1982 .... DLB-201
Keynes, John Maynard 1883-1946.........DS-10
Keyserling, Eduard von 1855-1918 ...... DLB-66
Khan, Ismith 1925- DLB-125
Khaytov, Nikolay 1919- DLB-181
Khemnitser, Ivan Ivanovich
  1745-1784..................... DLB-150
Kheraskov, Mikhail Matveevich
  1733-1807..................... DLB-150
Khomiakov, Aleksei Stepanovich
  1804-1860..................... DLB-205
Khristov, Boris 1945- DLB-181

Khvoshchinskaia, Nadezhda Dmitrievna
  1824-1889 .... DLB-238
Khvostov, Dmitrii Ivanovich
  1757-1835 .... DLB-150
Kidd, Adam 1802?-1831............. DLB-99
Kidd, William [publishing house]....... DLB-106
Kidder, Tracy 1945- DLB-185
Kiely, Benedict 1919- DLB-15
Kieran, John 1892-1981 ....DLB-171
Kiggins and Kellogg DLB-49
Kiley, Jed 1889-1962................. DLB-4
Kilgore, Bernard 1908-1967 .... DLB-127
Kilian, Crawford 1941- DLB-251
Killens, John Oliver 1916- DLB-33
Killigrew, Anne 1660-1685 .... DLB-131
Killigrew, Thomas 1612-1683 .... DLB-58
Kilmer, Joyce 1886-1918............. DLB-45
Kilroy, Thomas 1934- DLB-233
Kilwardby, Robert circa 1215-1279 .... DLB-115
Kilworth, Garry 1941- DLB-261
Kimball, Richard Burleigh 1816-1892 ... DLB-202
Kincaid, Jamaica 1949-
  .... DLB-157, 227; CDALB-7; CDWLB-3
King, Charles 1844-1933 .... DLB-186
King, Clarence 1842-1901 .... DLB-12
King, Florence 1936 .... Y-85
King, Francis 1923- DLB-15, 139
King, Grace 1852-1932..............DLB-12, 78
King, Harriet Hamilton 1840-1920...... DLB-199
King, Henry 1592-1669 .... DLB-126
King, Solomon [publishing house] DLB-49
King, Stephen 1947- DLB-143; Y-80
King, Susan Petigru 1824-1875......... DLB-239
King, Thomas 1943- DLB-175
King, Woodie, Jr. 1937- DLB-38
Kinglake, Alexander William
  1809-1891 .... DLB-55, 166
Kingsbury, Donald 1929- DLB-251
Kingsley, Charles
  1819-1875.........DLB-21, 32, 163, 178, 190
Kingsley, Henry 1830-1876 .... DLB-21, 230
Kingsley, Mary Henrietta 1862-1900 .....DLB-174
Kingsley, Sidney 1906- DLB-7
Kingsmill, Hugh 1889-1949 .... DLB-149
Kingsolver, Barbara
  1955- DLB-206; CDALB-7
Kingston, Maxine Hong
  1940- DLB-173, 212; Y-80; CDALB-7
Kingston, William Henry Giles
  1814-1880 .... DLB-163
Kinnan, Mary Lewis 1763-1848 .... DLB-200
Kinnell, Galway 1927- DLB-5; Y-87
Kinsella, Thomas 1928- DLB-27
Kipling, Rudyard 1865-1936
  .... DLB-19, 34, 141, 156; CDBLB-5
Kipphardt, Heinar 1922-1982.......... DLB-124
Kirby, William 1817-1906............. DLB-99

Kircher, Athanasius 1602-1680 .... DLB-164
Kireevsky, Ivan Vasil'evich 1806-1856 .. DLB-198
Kireevsky, Petr Vasil'evich 1808-1856... DLB-205
Kirk, Hans 1898-1962 .... DLB-214
Kirk, John Foster 1824-1904........... DLB-79
Kirkconnell, Watson 1895-1977 .... DLB-68
Kirkland, Caroline M.
  1801-1864.......DLB-3, 73, 74, 250; DS-13
Kirkland, Joseph 1830-1893 .... DLB-12
Kirkman, Francis [publishing house] DLB-170
Kirkpatrick, Clayton 1915- DLB-127
Kirkup, James 1918- DLB-27
Kirouac, Conrad (see Marie-Victorin, Frère)
Kirsch, Sarah 1935- DLB-75
Kirst, Hans Hellmut 1914-1989 .... DLB-69
Kiš, Danilo 1935-1989 ......DLB-181; CDWLB-4
Kita Morio 1927- DLB-182
Kitcat, Mabel Greenhow 1859-1922..... DLB-135
Kitchin, C. H. B. 1895-1967........... DLB-77
Kittredge, William 1932- DLB-212, 244
Kiukhel'beker, Vil'gel'm Karlovich
  1797-1846 .... DLB-205
Kizer, Carolyn 1925- DLB-5, 169
Klabund 1890-1928 .... DLB-66
Klaj, Johann 1616-1656 .... DLB-164
Klappert, Peter 1942- DLB-5
Klass, Philip (see Tenn, William)
Klein, A. M. 1909-1972 .... DLB-68
Kleist, Ewald von 1715-1759........... DLB-97
Kleist, Heinrich von
  1777-1811 .... DLB-90; CDWLB-2
Klinger, Friedrich Maximilian
  1752-1831 .... DLB-94
Klíma, Ivan 1931- DLB-232; CDWLB-4
Kliushnikov, Viktor Petrovich
  1841-1892 .... DLB-238
Oral History Interview with Donald S.
  Klopfer......................... Y-97
Klopstock, Friedrich Gottlieb
  1724-1803 .... DLB-97
Klopstock, Meta 1728-1758........... DLB-97
Kluge, Alexander 1932- DLB-75
Knapp, Joseph Palmer 1864-1951........ DLB-91
Knapp, Samuel Lorenzo 1783-1838 ...... DLB-59
Knapton, J. J. and P.
  [publishing house] DLB-154
Kniazhnin, Iakov Borisovich
  1740-1791 .... DLB-150
Knickerbocker, Diedrich (see Irving, Washington)
Knigge, Adolph Franz Friedrich Ludwig,
  Freiherr von 1752-1796 .... DLB-94
Knight, Charles, and Company DLB-106
Knight, Damon 1922- DLB-8
Knight, Etheridge 1931-1992 .... DLB-41
Knight, John S. 1894-1981 .... DLB-29
Knight, Sarah Kemble 1666-1727 .... DLB-24, 200
Knight-Bruce, G. W. H. 1852-1896 ......DLB-174

Knister, Raymond 1899-1932 . . . . .DLB-68

Knoblock, Edward 1874-1945 . . . . .DLB-10

Knopf, Alfred A. 1892-1984. . . . . Y-84

Knopf, Alfred A. [publishing house] DLB-46

Knopf to Hammett: The Editoral Correspondence Y-00

Knorr von Rosenroth, Christian 1636-1689 . . . . .DLB-168

"Knots into Webs: Some Autobiographical Sources," by Dabney Stuart DLB-105

Knowles, John 1926- DLB-6; CDALB-6

Knox, Frank 1874-1944 . . . . .DLB-29

Knox, John circa 1514-1572 . . . . .DLB-132

Knox, John Armoy 1850-1906. . . . . .DLB-23

Knox, Lucy 1845-1884 . . . . .DLB-240

Knox, Ronald Arbuthnott 1888-1957 . . . . .DLB-77

Knox, Thomas Wallace 1835-1896 . . . . . .DLB-189

Kobayashi Takiji 1903-1933 . . . . .DLB-180

Kober, Arthur 1900-1975 . . . . .DLB-11

Kobiakova, Aleksandra Petrovna 1823-1892 . . . . .DLB-238

Kocbek, Edvard 1904-1981 . . . DLB-147; CDWB-4

Koch, Howard 1902- DLB-26

Koch, Kenneth 1925- DLB-5

Kōda, Rohan 1867-1947 . . . . .DLB-180

Koehler, Ted 1894-1973 . . . . .DLB-265

Koenigsberg, Moses 1879-1945 . . . . .DLB-25

Koeppen, Wolfgang 1906-1996 . . . . .DLB-69

Koertge, Ronald 1940- DLB-105

Koestler, Arthur 1905-1983 . . . . . . Y-83; CDBLB-7

Kohn, John S. Van E. 1906-1976 and Papantonio, Michael 1907-1978 . . . . . .DLB-187

Kokoschka, Oskar 1886-1980 . . . . .DLB-124

Kolb, Annette 1870-1967 . . . . .DLB-66

Kolbenheyer, Erwin Guido 1878-1962 .DLB-66, 124

Kolleritsch, Alfred 1931- DLB-85

Kolodny, Annette 1941- DLB-67

Kol'tsov, Aleksei Vasil'evich 1809-1842 . . . . .DLB-205

Komarov, Matvei circa 1730-1812 . . . . . . .DLB-150

Komroff, Manuel 1890-1974 . . . . .DLB-4

Komunyakaa, Yusef 1947- DLB-120

Kondoleon, Harry 1955-1994 . . . . .DLB-266

Koneski, Blaže 1921-1993 . . .DLB-181; CDWLB-4

Konigsburg, E. L. 1930- DLB-52

Konparu Zenchiku 1405-1468? DLB-203

Konrád, György 1933- DLB-232; CDWLB-4

Konrad von Würzburg circa 1230-1287 . . . . .DLB-138

Konstantinov, Aleko 1863-1897 . . . . .DLB-147

Konwicki, Tadeusz 1926- DLB-232

Kooser, Ted 1939- DLB-105

Kopit, Arthur 1937- DLB-7

Kops, Bernard 1926?- DLB-13

Kornbluth, C. M. 1923-1958 . . . . .DLB-8

Körner, Theodor 1791-1813 . . . . .DLB-90

Kornfeld, Paul 1889-1942 . . . . .DLB-118

Kosinski, Jerzy 1933-1991 . . . . DLB-2; Y-82

Kosmač, Ciril 1910-1980 . . . . .DLB-181

Kosovel, Srečko 1904-1926 . . . . .DLB-147

Kostrov, Ermil Ivanovich 1755-1796 . . . . .DLB-150

Kotzebue, August von 1761-1819 . . . . . . .DLB-94

Kotzwinkle, William 1938- DLB-173

Kovačić, Ante 1854-1889 . . . . .DLB-147

Kovič, Kajetan 1931- DLB-181

Kozlov, Ivan Ivanovich 1779-1840 . . . . . . .DLB-205

Kraf, Elaine 1946- Y-81

Kramer, Jane 1938- DLB-185

Kramer, Larry 1935- DLB-249

Kramer, Mark 1944- DLB-185

Kranjčević, Silvije Strahimir 1865-1908 . . . . .DLB-147

Krasko, Ivan 1876-1958 . . . . .DLB-215

Krasna, Norman 1909-1984 . . . . .DLB-26

Kraus, Hans Peter 1907-1988 . . . . .DLB-187

Kraus, Karl 1874-1936 . . . . .DLB-118

Krause, Herbert 1905-1976 . . . . .DLB-256

Krauss, Ruth 1911-1993 . . . . .DLB-52

Kreisel, Henry 1922- DLB-88

Krestovsky V. (see Khvoshchinskaia, Nadezhda Dmitrievna)

Krestovsky, Vsevolod Vladimirovich 1839-1895 . . . . .DLB-238

Kreuder, Ernst 1903-1972 . . . . .DLB-69

Krėvė-Mickevičius, Vincas 1882-1954 . . . .DLB-220

Kreymborg, Alfred 1883-1966 . . . . .DLB-4, 54

Krieger, Murray 1923- DLB-67

Krim, Seymour 1922-1989 . . . . .DLB-16

Kristensen, Tom 1893-1974 . . . . .DLB-214

Kristeva, Julia 1941- DLB-242

Krleža, Miroslav 1893-1981 . . DLB-147; CDWLB-4

Krock, Arthur 1886-1974 . . . . .DLB-29

Kroetsch, Robert 1927- DLB-53

Kross, Jaan 1920- DLB-232

Krúdy, Gyula 1878-1933 . . . . .DLB-215

Krutch, Joseph Wood 1893-1970 . . . . .DLB-63, 206

Krylov, Ivan Andreevich 1769-1844 . . . . .DLB-150

Kubin, Alfred 1877-1959 . . . . .DLB-81

Kubrick, Stanley 1928-1999 . . . . .DLB-26

Kudrun circa 1230-1240 . . . . .DLB-138

Kuffstein, Hans Ludwig von 1582-1656 . . . . .DLB-164

Kuhlmann, Quirinus 1651-1689 . . . . .DLB-168

Kuhnau, Johann 1660-1722 . . . . .DLB-168

Kukol'nik, Nestor Vasil'evich 1809-1868 . . . . .DLB-205

Kukučín, Martin 1860-1928 . . . . DLB-215; CDWLB-4

Kumin, Maxine 1925- DLB-5

Kuncewicz, Maria 1895-1989 . . . . .DLB-215

Kundera, Milan 1929- DLB-232; CDWLB-4

Kunene, Mazisi 1930- DLB-117

Kunikida, Doppo 1869-1908 . . . . .DLB-180

Kunitz, Stanley 1905- DLB-48

Kunjufu, Johari M. (see Amini, Johari M.)

Kunnert, Gunter 1929- DLB-75

Kunze, Reiner 1933- DLB-75

Kupferberg, Tuli 1923- DLB-16

Kurahashi Yumiko 1935- DLB-182

Kureishi, Hanif 1954- DLB-194, 245

Kürnberger, Ferdinand 1821-1879 . . . . . .DLB-129

Kurz, Isolde 1853-1944 . . . . .DLB-66

Kusenberg, Kurt 1904-1983 . . . . .DLB-69

Kushchevsky, Ivan Afanas'evich 1847-1876 . . . . .DLB-238

Kushner, Tony 1956- DLB-228

Kuttner, Henry 1915-1958 . . . . .DLB-8

Kyd, Thomas 1558-1594 . . . . .DLB-62

Kyffin, Maurice circa 1560?-1598 . . . . . . .DLB-136

Kyger, Joanne 1934- DLB-16

Kyne, Peter B. 1880-1957 . . . . .DLB-78

Kyōgoku Tamekane 1254-1332 . . . . .DLB-203

Kyrklund, Willy 1921- DLB-257

L

L. E. L. (see Landon, Letitia Elizabeth)

Laberge, Albert 1871-1960 . . . . .DLB-68

Laberge, Marie 1950- DLB-60

Labiche, Eugène 1815-1888 . . . . .DLB-192

Labrunie, Gerard (see Nerval, Gerard de)

La Capria, Raffaele 1922- DLB-196

Lacombe, Patrice (see Trullier-Lacombe, Joseph Patrice)

Lacretelle, Jacques de 1888-1985 . . . . .DLB-65

Lacy, Ed 1911-1968 . . . . .DLB-226

Lacy, Sam 1903- DLB-171

Ladd, Joseph Brown 1764-1786 . . . . .DLB-37

La Farge, Oliver 1901-1963 . . . . .DLB-9

Laffan, Mrs. R. S. de Courcy (see Adams, Bertha Leith)

Lafferty, R. A. 1914- DLB-8

La Flesche, Francis 1857-1932 . . . . .DLB-175

Laforge, Jules 1860-1887 . . . . .DLB-217

Lagerkvist, Pär 1891-1974 . . . . .DLB-259

Lagerlöf, Selma 1858-1940 . . . . .DLB-259

Lagorio, Gina 1922- DLB-196

La Guma, Alex 1925-1985 . . . . DLB-117, 225; CDWLB-3

Lahaise, Guillaume (see Delahaye, Guy)

Lahontan, Louis-Armand de Lom d'Arce, Baron de 1666-1715? DLB-99

Laing, Kojo 1946- DLB-157

Laird, Carobeth 1895- Y-82

Laird and Lee DLB-49

Lalić, Ivan V. 1931-1996 . . . . .DLB-181

Lalić, Mihailo 1914-1992 . . . . .DLB-181

Lalonde, Michèle 1937- DLB-60

Cumulative Index

Lamantia, Philip 1927- DLB-16

Lamartine, Alphonse de 1790-1869 ..... DLB-217

Lamb, Lady Caroline 1785-1828 .... DLB-116

Lamb, Charles
  1775-1834....... DLB-93, 107, 163; CDBLB-3

Lamb, Mary 1764-1874................ DLB-163

Lambert, Betty 1933-1983 .... DLB-60

Lamming, George 1927- .. DLB-125; CDWLB-3

L'Amour, Louis 1908-1988 ..... DLB-206; Y-80

Lampman, Archibald 1861-1899 .... DLB-92

Lamson, Wolffe and Company DLB-49

Lancer Books DLB-46

Landesman, Jay 1919- and
  Landesman, Fran 1927- DLB-16

Landolfi, Tommaso 1908-1979......... DLB-177

Landon, Letitia Elizabeth 1802-1838 ..... DLB-96

Landor, Walter Savage 1775-1864 .... DLB-93, 107

Landry, Napoléon-P. 1884-1956......... DLB-92

Lane, Charles 1800-1870 .... DLB-1, 223

Lane, F. C. 1885-1984 .... DLB-241

Lane, John, Company................. DLB-49

Lane, Laurence W. 1890-1967 .... DLB-91

Lane, M. Travis 1934- DLB-60

Lane, Patrick 1939- DLB-53

Lane, Pinkie Gordon 1923- DLB-41

Laney, Al 1896-1988 .... DLB-4, 171

Lang, Andrew 1844-1912...... DLB-98, 141, 184

Langevin, André 1927- DLB-60

Langford, David 1953- DLB-261

Langgässer, Elisabeth 1899-1950 ..... DLB-69

Langhorne, John 1735-1779 .... DLB-109

Langland, William
  circa 1330-circa 1400 .... DLB-146

Langton, Anna 1804-1893 .... DLB-99

Lanham, Edwin 1904-1979............ DLB-4

Lanier, Sidney 1842-1881........ DLB-64; DS-13

Lanyer, Aemilia 1569-1645........... DLB-121

Lapointe, Gatien 1931-1983 .... DLB-88

Lapointe, Paul-Marie 1929- DLB-88

Larcom, Lucy 1824-1893 .... DLB-221, 243

Lardner, John 1912-1960 .... DLB-171

Lardner, Ring 1885-1933
  .... DLB-11, 25, 86, 171; DS-16; CDALB-4

Lardner 100: Ring Lardner
  Centennial Symposium Y-85

Lardner, Ring, Jr. 1915-2000 .... DLB-26, Y-00

Larkin, Philip 1922-1985 ..... DLB-27; CDBLB-8

La Roche, Sophie von 1730-1807 ..... DLB-94

La Rocque, Gilbert 1943-1984 .... DLB-60

Laroque de Roquebrune, Robert
  (see Roquebrune, Robert de)

Larrick, Nancy 1910- DLB-61

Larsen, Nella 1893-1964............. DLB-51

Larson, Clinton F. 1919-1994........ DLB-256

La Sale, Antoine de
  circa 1386-1460/1467 .... DLB-208

Lasch, Christopher 1932-1994 .... DLB-246

Lasker-Schüler, Else 1869-1945 ..... DLB-66, 124

Lasnier, Rina 1915- DLB-88

Lassalle, Ferdinand 1825-1864 .... DLB-129

Latham, Robert 1912-1995............ DLB-201

Lathrop, Dorothy P. 1891-1980 .... DLB-22

Lathrop, George Parsons 1851-1898 ..... DLB-71

Lathrop, John, Jr. 1772-1820......... DLB-37

Latimer, Hugh 1492?-1555............ DLB-136

Latimore, Jewel Christine McLawler
  (see Amini, Johari M.)

La Tour du Pin, Patrice de 1911-1975 ... DLB-258

Latymer, William 1498-1583 .... DLB-132

Laube, Heinrich 1806-1884 .... DLB-133

Laud, William 1573-1645............ DLB-213

Laughlin, James 1914-1997......... DLB-48; Y-96

James Laughlin Tributes............... Y-97

Conversations with Publishers IV:
  An Interview with James Laughlin....... Y-96

Laumer, Keith 1925- DLB-8

Lauremberg, Johann 1590-1658 .... DLB-164

Laurence, Margaret 1926-1987........ DLB-53

Laurentius von Schnüffis 1633-1702..... DLB-168

Laurents, Arthur 1918- DLB-26

Laurie, Annie (see Black, Winifred)

Laut, Agnes Christiana 1871-1936 .... DLB-92

Lauterbach, Ann 1942- DLB-193

Lautreamont, Isidore Lucien Ducasse, Comte de
  1846-1870...................... DLB-217

Lavater, Johann Kaspar 1741-1801 ..... DLB-97

Lavin, Mary 1912-1996 .... DLB-15

Law, John (see Harkness, Margaret)

Lawes, Henry 1596-1662 .... DLB-126

Lawless, Anthony (see MacDonald, Philip)

Lawless, Emily (The Hon. Emily Lawless) 1845-1913
  DLB-240

Lawrence, D. H. 1885-1930
  ..... DLB-10, 19, 36, 98, 162, 195; CDBLB-6

Lawrence, David 1888-1973........... DLB-29

Lawrence, Jerome 1915- and
  Lee, Robert E. 1918-1994.......... DLB-228

Lawrence, Seymour 1926-1994 .... Y-94

Lawrence, T. E. 1888-1935 .... DLB-195

Lawson, George 1598-1678 .... DLB-213

Lawson, Henry 1867-1922 .... DLB-230

Lawson, John ?-1711................. DLB-24

Lawson, John Howard 1894-1977 ...... DLB-228

Lawson, Louisa Albury 1848-1920...... DLB-230

Lawson, Robert 1892-1957............ DLB-22

Lawson, Victor F. 1850-1925 .... DLB-25

Layard, Sir Austen Henry
  1817-1894...................... DLB-166

Layton, Irving 1912- DLB-88

LaZamon flourished circa 1200 .... DLB-146

Lazarević, Laza K. 1851-1890......... DLB-147

Lazarus, George 1904-1997 .... DLB-201

Lazhechnikov, Ivan Ivanovich
  1792-1869...................... DLB-198

Lea, Henry Charles 1825-1909 .... DLB-47

Lea, Sydney 1942- DLB-120

Lea, Tom 1907- DLB-6

Leacock, John 1729-1802 .... DLB-31

Leacock, Stephen 1869-1944 .... DLB-92

Lead, Jane Ward 1623-1704.......... DLB-131

Leadenhall Press................... DLB-106

Leakey, Caroline Woolmer 1827-1881... DLB-230

Leapor, Mary 1722-1746............. DLB-109

Lear, Edward 1812-1888 .... DLB-32, 163, 166

Leary, Timothy 1920-1996 .... DLB-16

Leary, W. A., and Company DLB-49

Léautaud, Paul 1872-1956 .... DLB-65

Leavis, F. R. 1895-1978............. DLB-242

Leavitt, David 1961- DLB-130

Leavitt and Allen DLB-49

Le Blond, Mrs. Aubrey 1861-1934...... DLB-174

le Carré, John 1931- DLB-87; CDBLB-8

Lécavelé, Roland (see Dorgeles, Roland)

Lechlitner, Ruth 1901- DLB-48

Leclerc, Félix 1914- DLB-60

Le Clézio, J. M. G. 1940- DLB-83

Lectures on Rhetoric and Belles Lettres (1783),
  by Hugh Blair [excerpts] DLB-31

Leder, Rudolf (see Hermlin, Stephan)

Lederer, Charles 1910-1976 .... DLB-26

Ledwidge, Francis 1887-1917 .... DLB-20

Lee, Dennis 1939- DLB-53

Lee, Don L. (see Madhubuti, Haki R.)

Lee, George W. 1894-1976 .... DLB-51

Lee, Harper 1926- DLB-6; CDALB-1

Lee, Harriet (1757-1851) and
  Lee, Sophia (1750-1824)........... DLB-39

Lee, Laurie 1914-1997 .... DLB-27

Lee, Leslie 1935- DLB-266

Lee, Li-Young 1957- DLB-165

Lee, Manfred B. (see Dannay, Frederic, and
  Manfred B. Lee)

Lee, Nathaniel circa 1645-1692 .... DLB-80

Lee, Sir Sidney 1859-1926 .... DLB-149, 184

Lee, Sir Sidney, "Principles of Biography," in
  Elizabethan and Other Essays DLB-149

Lee, Tanith 1947- DLB-261

Lee, Vernon
  1856-1935....... DLB-57, 153, 156, 174, 178

Lee and Shepard................... DLB-49

Le Fanu, Joseph Sheridan
  1814-1873............. DLB-21, 70, 159, 178

Leffland, Ella 1931- Y-84

le Fort, Gertrud von 1876-1971......... DLB-66

Le Gallienne, Richard 1866-1947......... DLB-4

Legaré, Hugh Swinton
  1797-1843............. DLB-3, 59, 73, 248

Legaré, James Mathewes 1823-1859... DLB-3, 248

The Legends of the Saints and a Medieval
 Christian Worldview DLB-148
Léger, Antoine-J. 1880-1950 ....DLB-88
Leggett, William 1801-1839............DLB-250
Le Guin, Ursula K.
 1929- DLB-8, 52, 256; CDALB-6
Lehman, Ernest 1920- DLB-44
Lehmann, John 1907- DLB-27, 100
Lehmann, John, Limited DLB-112
Lehmann, Rosamond 1901-1990.........DLB-15
Lehmann, Wilhelm 1882-1968 ....DLB-56
Leiber, Fritz 1910-1992 ....DLB-8
Leibniz, Gottfried Wilhelm 1646-1716....DLB-168
Leicester University Press DLB-112
Leigh, Carolyn 1926-1983 ....DLB-265
Leigh, W. R. 1866-1955 ....DLB-188
Leinster, Murray 1896-1975..............DLB-8
Leiser, Bill 1898-1965 ....DLB-241
Leisewitz, Johann Anton 1752-1806.......DLB-94
Leitch, Maurice 1933- DLB-14
Leithauser, Brad 1943- DLB-120
Leland, Charles G. 1824-1903 ....DLB-11
Leland, John 1503?-1552................DLB-136
Lemay, Pamphile 1837-1918 ....DLB-99
Lemelin, Roger 1919-1992...............DLB-88
Lemercier, Louis-Jean-Népomucène
 1771-1840 ....DLB-192
Le Moine, James MacPherson
 1825-1912 ....DLB-99
Lemon, Mark 1809-1870 ....DLB-163
Le Moyne, Jean 1913-1996 ....DLB-88
Lemperly, Paul 1858-1939.............DLB-187
L'Engle, Madeleine 1918- DLB-52
Lennart, Isobel 1915-1971 ....DLB-44
Lennox, Charlotte
 1729 or 1730-1804..................DLB-39
Lenox, James 1800-1880 ....DLB-140
Lenski, Lois 1893-1974 ....DLB-22
Lentricchia, Frank 1940- DLB-246
Lenz, Hermann 1913-1998 ....DLB-69
Lenz, J. M. R. 1751-1792 ....DLB-94
Lenz, Siegfried 1926- DLB-75
Leonard, Elmore 1925- DLB-173, 226
Leonard, Hugh 1926- DLB-13
Leonard, William Ellery 1876-1944.......DLB-54
Leonowens, Anna 1834-1914 .....DLB-99, 166
LePan, Douglas 1914- DLB-88
Lepik, Kalju 1920-1999 ....DLB-232
Leprohon, Rosanna Eleanor 1829-1879....DLB-99
Le Queux, William 1864-1927............DLB-70
Lermontov, Mikhail Iur'evich
 1814-1841 ....DLB-205
Lerner, Alan Jay 1918-1986............DLB-265
Lerner, Max 1902-1992 ....DLB-29
Lernet-Holenia, Alexander 1897-1976 .....DLB-85
Le Rossignol, James 1866-1969 ....DLB-92

Lescarbot, Marc circa 1570-1642.........DLB-99
LeSeur, William Dawson 1840-1917......DLB-92
LeSieg, Theo. (see Geisel, Theodor Seuss)
Leskov, Nikolai Semenovich 1831-1895 ..DLB-238
Leslie, Doris before 1902-1982 ....DLB-191
Leslie, Eliza 1787-1858 ....DLB-202
Leslie, Frank 1821-1880..............DLB-43, 79
Leslie, Frank, Publishing House DLB-49
Leśmian, Bolesław 1878-1937 ....DLB-215
Lesperance, John 1835?-1891 ....DLB-99
Lessing, Bruno 1870-1940 ....DLB-28
Lessing, Doris
 1919- DLB-15, 139; Y-85; CDBLB-8
Lessing, Gotthold Ephraim
 1729-1781 ....DLB-97; CDWLB-2
Lettau, Reinhard 1929- DLB-75
Letter from Japan.................Y-94, Y-98
Letter from London................. Y-96
Letter to [Samuel] Richardson on *Clarissa*
 (1748), by Henry Fielding..........DLB-39
A Letter to the Editor of *The Irish Times*...... Y-97
Lever, Charles 1806-1872 ....DLB-21
Lever, Ralph ca. 1527-1585 ....DLB-236
Leverson, Ada 1862-1933 ....DLB-153
Levertov, Denise
 1923-1997 ....DLB-5, 165; CDALB-7
Levi, Peter 1931- DLB-40
Levi, Primo 1919-1987................DLB-177
Lévi-Strauss, Claude 1908- DLB-242
Levien, Sonya 1888-1960...............DLB-44
Levin, Meyer 1905-1981 ....DLB-9, 28; Y-81
Levine, Norman 1923- DLB-88
Levine, Philip 1928- DLB-5
Levis, Larry 1946- DLB-120
Levy, Amy 1861-1889............DLB-156, 240
Levy, Benn Wolfe 1900-1973 ......DLB-13; Y-81
Lewald, Fanny 1811-1889 ....DLB-129
Lewes, George Henry 1817-1878.....DLB-55, 144
"Criticism In Relation To
 Novels" (1863) DLB-21
The Principles of Success in Literature
 (1865) [excerpt]....................DLB-57
Lewis, Agnes Smith 1843-1926 ....DLB-174
Lewis, Alfred H. 1857-1914 ....DLB-25, 186
Lewis, Alun 1915-1944 ....DLB-20, 162
Lewis, C. Day (see Day Lewis, C.)
Lewis, C. S. 1898-1963
 ....DLB-15, 100, 160, 255; CDBLB-7
Lewis, Charles B. 1842-1924............DLB-11
Lewis, Henry Clay 1825-1850........DLB-3, 248
Lewis, Janet 1899-1999 ....Y-87
Lewis, Matthew Gregory
 1775-1818 .... DLB-39, 158, 178
Lewis, Meriwether 1774-1809 and
 Clark, William 1770-1838.......DLB-183, 186
Lewis, Norman 1908- DLB-204
Lewis, R. W. B. 1917- DLB-111

Lewis, Richard circa 1700-1734 ....DLB-24
Lewis, Sinclair
 1885-1951 ......DLB-9, 102; DS-1; CDALB-4
Sinclair Lewis Centennial Conference........ Y-85
Lewis, Wilmarth Sheldon 1895-1979.....DLB-140
Lewis, Wyndham 1882-1957............DLB-15
Lewisohn, Ludwig 1882-1955 ...DLB-4, 9, 28, 102
Leyendecker, J. C. 1874-1951 ....DLB-188
Lezama Lima, José 1910-1976 ....DLB-113
L'Heureux, John 1934- DLB-244
Libbey, Laura Jean 1862-1924..........DLB-221
The Library of America.................DLB-46
Library History Group Y-01
The Licensing Act of 1737 ....DLB-84
Lichfield, Leonard I [publishing house]...DLB-170
Lichtenberg, Georg Christoph 1742-1799 ..DLB-94
The Liddle Collection Y-97
Lidman, Sara 1923- DLB-257
Lieb, Fred 1888-1980.................DLB-171
Liebling, A. J. 1904-1963 ....DLB-4, 171
Lieutenant Murray (see Ballou, Maturin Murray)
Lighthall, William Douw 1857-1954 ......DLB-92
Lilar, Françoise (see Mallet-Joris, Françoise)
Lili'uokalani, Queen 1838-1917.........DLB-221
Lillo, George 1691-1739.................DLB-84
Lilly, J. K., Jr. 1893-1966 ....DLB-140
Lilly, Wait and Company DLB-49
Lily, William circa 1468-1522 ....DLB-132
Limited Editions Club DLB-46
Limón, Graciela 1938- DLB-209
Lincoln and Edmands DLB-49
Lindesay, Ethel Forence
 (see Richardson, Henry Handel)
Lindgren, Astrid 1907-2002 ....DLB-257
Lindgren, Torgny 1938- DLB-257
Lindsay, Alexander William, Twenty-fifth Earl
 of Crawford 1812-1880............DLB-184
Lindsay, Sir David circa 1485-1555......DLB-132
Lindsay, David 1878-1945.............DLB-255
Lindsay, Jack 1900- Y-84
Lindsay, Lady (Caroline Blanche Elizabeth Fitzroy
 Lindsay) 1844-1912................DLB-199
Lindsay, Norman 1879-1969 ....DLB-260
Lindsay, Vachel 1879-1931 ....DLB-54; CDALB-3
Linebarger, Paul Myron Anthony
 (see Smith, Cordwainer)
Link, Arthur S. 1920-1998................DLB-17
Linn, Ed 1922-2000...................DLB-241
Linn, John Blair 1777-1804..............DLB-37
Lins, Osman 1924-1978................DLB-145
Linton, Eliza Lynn 1822-1898...........DLB-18
Linton, William James 1812-1897 ....DLB-32
Lintot, Barnaby Bernard
 [publishing house]................DLB-170
Lion Books DLB-46
Lionni, Leo 1910-1999................DLB-61

Cumulative Index

Lippard, George 1822-1854 . . . . DLB-202
Lippincott, J. B., Company DLB-49
Lippincott, Sara Jane Clarke 1823-1904 . . . DLB-43
Lippmann, Walter 1889-1974 . . . . DLB-29
Lipton, Lawrence 1898-1975 . . . . DLB-16
Liscow, Christian Ludwig 1701-1760 . . . . . DLB-97
Lish, Gordon 1934- DLB-130
Lisle, Charles-Marie-René Leconte de 1818-1894 . . . . DLB-217
Lispector, Clarice 1925-1977 . . . . DLB-113; CDWLB-3
LitCheck Website Y-01
A Literary Archaelogist Digs On: A Brief Interview with Michael Reynolds by Michael Rogers Y-99
The Literary Chronicle and Weekly Review 1819-1828 . . . . DLB-110
Literary Documents: William Faulkner and the People-to-People Program Y-86
Literary Documents II: *Library Journal* Statements and Questionnaires from First Novelists Y-87
Literary Effects of World War II [British novel] DLB-15
Literary Prizes Y-00
Literary Prizes [British] DLB-15
Literary Research Archives: The Humanities Research Center, University of Texas Y-82
Literary Research Archives II: Berg Collection of English and American Literature of the New York Public Library Y-83
Literary Research Archives III: The Lilly Library Y-84
Literary Research Archives IV: The John Carter Brown Library Y-85
Literary Research Archives V: Kent State Special Collections Y-86
Literary Research Archives VI: The Modern Literary Manuscripts Collection in the Special Collections of the Washington University Libraries Y-87
Literary Research Archives VII: The University of Virginia Libraries Y-91
Literary Research Archives VIII: The Henry E. Huntington Library Y-92
Literary Research Archives IX: Special Collections at Boston University . . Y-99
The Literary Scene and Situation and . . . Who (Besides Oprah) Really Runs American Literature? Y-99
Literary Societies Y-98, Y-99, Y-00, Y-01
"Literary Style" (1857), by William Forsyth [excerpt] DLB-57
Literatura Chicanesca: The View From Without DLB-82
Literature at Nurse, or Circulating Morals (1885), by George Moore DLB-18
The Literature of Boxing in England through Arthur Conan Doyle Y-01
The Literature of the Modern Breakthrough DLB-259
Littell, Eliakim 1797-1870 . . . . DLB-79
Littell, Robert S. 1831-1896 . . . . DLB-79

Little, Brown and Company DLB-49
Little Magazines and Newspapers DS-15
The Little Review 1914-1929 . . . . DS-15
Littlewood, Joan 1914- DLB-13
Lively, Penelope 1933- DLB-14, 161, 207
Liverpool University Press DLB-112
The Lives of the Poets DLB-142
Livesay, Dorothy 1909- DLB-68
Livesay, Florence Randal 1874-1953 . . . . . DLB-92
"Living in Ruin," by Gerald Stern DLB-105
Livings, Henry 1929-1998 . . . . DLB-13
Livingston, Anne Howe 1763-1841 . . . DLB-37, 200
Livingston, Jay (see Evans, Ray)
Livingston, Myra Cohn 1926-1996 . . . . . . DLB-61
Livingston, William 1723-1790 . . . . DLB-31
Livingstone, David 1813-1873 . . . . DLB-166
Livingstone, Douglas 1932-1996 . . . . DLB-225
Livy 59 B.C.-A.D. 17 . . . . . . DLB-211; CDWLB-1
Liyong, Taban lo (see Taban lo Liyong)
Lizárraga, Sylvia S. 1925- DLB-82
Llewellyn, Richard 1906-1983 . . . . DLB-15
Lloyd, Edward [publishing house] DLB-106
Lobel, Arnold 1933- DLB-61
Lochridge, Betsy Hopkins (see Fancher, Betsy)
Locke, David Ross 1833-1888 . . . . DLB-11, 23
Locke, John 1632-1704 . . . . . DLB-31, 101, 213, 252
Locke, Richard Adams 1800-1871 . . . . DLB-43
Locker-Lampson, Frederick 1821-1895 . . . . DLB-35, 184
Lockhart, John Gibson 1794-1854 . . . . DLB-110, 116 144
Lockridge, Ross, Jr. 1914-1948 . . . . . DLB-143; Y-80
Locrine and Selimus DLB-62
Lodge, David 1935- DLB-14, 194
Lodge, George Cabot 1873-1909 . . . . DLB-54
Lodge, Henry Cabot 1850-1924 . . . . DLB-47
Lodge, Thomas 1558-1625 . . . . DLB-172
From *Defence of Poetry* (1579) DLB-172
Loeb, Harold 1891-1974 . . . . DLB-4
Loeb, William 1905-1981 . . . . DLB-127
Loesser, Frank 1919-1986 . . . . DLB-265
Lofting, Hugh 1886-1947 . . . . DLB-160
Logan, Deborah Norris 1761-1839 . . . . . . DLB-200
Logan, James 1674-1751 . . . . DLB-24, 140
Logan, John 1923- DLB-5
Logan, Martha Daniell 1704?-1779 . . . . . . DLB-200
Logan, William 1950- DLB-120
Logau, Friedrich von 1605-1655 . . . . DLB-164
Logue, Christopher 1926- DLB-27
Lohenstein, Daniel Casper von 1635-1683 . . . . DLB-168
Lo-Johansson, Ivar 1901-1990 . . . . DLB-259
Lomonosov, Mikhail Vasil'evich 1711-1765 . . . . DLB-150
London, Jack 1876-1916 . . . . . DLB-8, 12, 78, 212; CDALB-3

The London Magazine 1820-1829 . . . . DLB-110
Long, David 1948- DLB-244
Long, H., and Brother DLB-49
Long, Haniel 1888-1956 . . . . DLB-45
Long, Ray 1878-1935 . . . . DLB-137
Longfellow, Henry Wadsworth 1807-1882 . . . . DLB-1, 59, 235; CDALB-2
Longfellow, Samuel 1819-1892 . . . . DLB-1
Longford, Elizabeth 1906- DLB-155
Longinus circa first century DLB-176
Longley, Michael 1939- DLB-40
Longman, T. [publishing house] DLB-154
Longmans, Green and Company DLB-49
Longmore, George 1793?-1867 . . . . DLB-99
Longstreet, Augustus Baldwin 1790-1870 . . . . DLB-3, 11, 74, 248
Longworth, D. [publishing house] DLB-49
Lonsdale, Frederick 1881-1954 . . . . DLB-10
A Look at the Contemporary Black Theatre Movement DLB-38
Loos, Anita 1893-1981 . . . . . DLB-11, 26, 228; Y-81
Lopate, Phillip 1943- Y-80
Lopez, Barry 1945- DLB-256
López, Diana (see Isabella, Ríos)
López, Josefina 1969- DLB-209
Loranger, Jean-Aubert 1896-1942 . . . . DLB-92
Lorca, Federico García 1898-1936 . . . . . . DLB-108
Lord, John Keast 1818-1872 . . . . DLB-99
The Lord Chamberlain's Office and Stage Censorship in England DLB-10
Lorde, Audre 1934-1992 . . . . DLB-41
Lorimer, George Horace 1867-1939 . . . . . . DLB-91
Loring, A. K. [publishing house] DLB-49
Loring and Mussey DLB-46
Lorris, Guillaume de (see *Roman de la Rose*)
Lossing, Benson J. 1813-1891 . . . . DLB-30
Lothar, Ernst 1890-1974 . . . . DLB-81
Lothrop, D., and Company DLB-49
Lothrop, Harriet M. 1844-1924 . . . . DLB-42
Loti, Pierre 1850-1923 . . . . DLB-123
Lotichius Secundus, Petrus 1528-1560 . . . . DLB-179
Lott, Emeline ?-? DLB-166
Louisiana State University Press Y-97
The Lounger, no. 20 (1785), by Henry Mackenzie DLB-39
Lounsbury, Thomas R. 1838-1915 . . . . DLB-71
Louÿs, Pierre 1870-1925 . . . . DLB-123
Lovelace, Earl 1935- DLB-125; CDWLB-3
Lovelace, Richard 1618-1657 . . . . DLB-131
Lovell, Coryell and Company DLB-49
Lovell, John W., Company DLB-49
Lover, Samuel 1797-1868 . . . . DLB-159, 190
Lovesey, Peter 1936- DLB-87
Lovinescu, Eugen 1881-1943 . . . . DLB-220; CDWLB-4

Lovingood, Sut (see Harris, George Washington)
Low, Samuel 1765-? DLB-37
Lowell, Amy 1874-1925...........DLB-54, 140
Lowell, James Russell 1819-1891
......DLB-1, 11, 64, 79, 189, 235; CDALB-2
Lowell, Robert 1917-1977...DLB-5, 169; CDALB-7
Lowenfels, Walter 1897-1976............DLB-4
Lowndes, Marie Belloc 1868-1947.......DLB-70
Lowndes, William Thomas 1798-1843...DLB-184
Lownes, Humphrey [publishing house]...DLB-170
Lowry, Lois 1937- DLB-52
Lowry, Malcolm 1909-1957... DLB-15; CDBLB-7
Lowther, Pat 1935-1975................DLB-53
Loy, Mina 1882-1966...............DLB-4, 54
Lozeau, Albert 1878-1924 ....DLB-92
Lubbock, Percy 1879-1965.............DLB-149
Lucan A.D. 39-A.D. 65 ....DLB-211
Lucas, E. V. 1868-1938........DLB-98, 149, 153
Lucas, Fielding, Jr. [publishing house].....DLB-49
Luce, Clare Booth 1903-1987 ....DLB-228
Luce, Henry R. 1898-1967..............DLB-91
Luce, John W., and Company..........DLB-46
Lucian circa 120-180 ....DLB-176
Lucie-Smith, Edward 1933- DLB-40
Lucilius circa 180 B.C.-102/101 B.C......DLB-211
Lucini, Gian Pietro 1867-1914 ....DLB-114
Lucretius circa 94 B.C.-circa 49 B.C.
...................DLB-211; CDWLB-1
Luder, Peter circa 1415-1472 ....DLB-179
Ludlam, Charles 1943-1987............DLB-266
Ludlum, Robert 1927- Y-82
Ludus de Antichristo circa 1160............DLB-148
Ludvigson, Susan 1942- DLB-120
Ludwig, Jack 1922- DLB-60
Ludwig, Otto 1813-1865 ....DLB-129
Ludwigslied 881 or 882 ....DLB-148
Luera, Yolanda 1953- DLB-122
Luft, Lya 1938- DLB-145
Lugansky, Kazak Vladimir (see Dal', Vladimir Ivanovich)
Lugn, Kristina 1948- DLB-257
Lukács, Georg (see Lukács, György)
Lukács, György 1885-1971........DLB 215, 242; CDWLB-4
Luke, Peter 1919- DLB-13
Lummis, Charles F. 1859-1928 ....DLB-186
Lundkvist, Artur 1906-1991 ....DLB-259
Lupton, F. M., Company.............DLB-49
Lupus of Ferrières circa 805-circa 862...............DLB-148
Lurie, Alison 1926- DLB-2
Lussu, Emilio 1890-1975 ....DLB-264
Lustig, Arnošt 1926- DLB-232
Luther, Martin 1483-1546... DLB-179; CDWLB-2
Luzi, Mario 1914- DLB-128

L'vov, Nikolai Aleksandrovich 1751-1803..DLB-150
Lyall, Gavin 1932- DLB-87
Lydgate, John circa 1370-1450.........DLB-146
Lyly, John circa 1554-1606 ....DLB-62, 167
Lynch, Patricia 1898-1972 ....DLB-160
Lynch, Richard flourished 1596-1601....DLB-172
Lynd, Robert 1879-1949 ....DLB-98
Lyon, Matthew 1749-1822...............DLB-43
Lyotard, Jean-François 1924-1998.......DLB-242
Lysias circa 459 B.C.-circa 380 B.C.......DLB-176
Lytle, Andrew 1902-1995 ....DLB-6; Y-95
Lytton, Edward (see Bulwer-Lytton, Edward)
Lytton, Edward Robert Bulwer 1831-1891 ....DLB-32

M

Maass, Joachim 1901-1972...............DLB-69
Mabie, Hamilton Wright 1845-1916......DLB-71
Mac A'Ghobhainn, Iain (see Smith, Iain Crichton)
MacArthur, Charles 1895-1956.....DLB-7, 25, 44
Macaulay, Catherine 1731-1791.........DLB-104
Macaulay, David 1945- DLB-61
Macaulay, Rose 1881-1958 ....DLB-36
Macaulay, Thomas Babington 1800-1859 ....DLB-32, 55; CDBLB-4
Macaulay Company DLB-46
MacBeth, George 1932- DLB-40
Macbeth, Madge 1880-1965 ....DLB-92
MacCaig, Norman 1910-1996 ....DLB-27
MacDiarmid, Hugh 1892-1978 ....DLB-20; CDBLB-7
MacDonald, Cynthia 1928- DLB-105
MacDonald, George 1824-1905....DLB-18, 163, 178
MacDonald, John D. 1916-1986 .....DLB-8; Y-86
MacDonald, Philip 1899?-1980 ....DLB-77
Macdonald, Ross (see Millar, Kenneth)
Macdonald, Sharman 1951- DLB-245
MacDonald, Wilson 1880-1967..........DLB-92
Macdonald and Company (Publishers)...DLB-112
MacEwen, Gwendolyn 1941-1987....DLB-53, 251
Macfadden, Bernarr 1868-1955........DLB-25, 91
MacGregor, John 1825-1892 ....DLB-166
MacGregor, Mary Esther (see Keith, Marian)
Machado, Antonio 1875-1939 ....DLB-108
Machado, Manuel 1874-1947............DLB-108
Machar, Agnes Maule 1837-1927........DLB-92
Machaut, Guillaume de circa 1300-1377 ....DLB-208
Machen, Arthur Llewelyn Jones 1863-1947............... DLB-36, 156, 178
MacInnes, Colin 1914-1976.............DLB-14
MacInnes, Helen 1907-1985............DLB-87
Mac Intyre, Tom 1931- DLB-245
Mačiulis, Jonas (see Maironis, Jonas)
Mack, Maynard 1909- DLB-111

Mackall, Leonard L. 1879-1937........DLB-140
MacKaye, Percy 1875-1956.............DLB-54
Macken, Walter 1915-1967..............DLB-13
Mackenzie, Alexander 1763-1820.......DLB-99
Mackenzie, Alexander Slidell 1803-1848.....................DLB-183
Mackenzie, Compton 1883-1972.....DLB-34, 100
Mackenzie, Henry 1745-1831 ....DLB-39
Mackenzie, Kenneth (Seaforth) 1913-1955....................DLB-260
Mackenzie, William 1758-1828 ....DLB-187
Mackey, Nathaniel 1947- DLB-169
Mackey, Shena 1944- DLB-231
Mackey, William Wellington 1937- DLB-38
Mackintosh, Elizabeth (see Tey, Josephine)
Mackintosh, Sir James 1765-1832.......DLB-158
Maclaren, Ian (see Watson, John)
Macklin, Charles 1699-1797............DLB-89
MacLean, Katherine Anne 1925- DLB-8
Maclean, Norman 1902-1990 ....DLB-206
MacLeish, Archibald 1892-1982 ....DLB-4, 7, 45, 228; Y-82; CDALB-7
MacLennan, Hugh 1907-1990 ....DLB-68
MacLeod, Alistair 1936- DLB-60
Macleod, Fiona (see Sharp, William)
Macleod, Norman 1906-1985 ....DLB-4
Mac Low, Jackson 1922- DLB-193
Macmillan and Company DLB-106
The Macmillan Company DLB-49
Macmillan's English Men of Letters, First Series (1878-1892) DLB-144
MacNamara, Brinsley 1890-1963 ....DLB-10
MacNeice, Louis 1907-1963..........DLB-10, 20
MacPhail, Andrew 1864-1938 ....DLB-92
Macpherson, James 1736-1796..........DLB-109
Macpherson, Jay 1931- DLB-53
Macpherson, Jeanie 1884-1946 ....DLB-44
Macrae Smith Company DLB-46
MacRaye, Lucy Betty (see Webling, Lucy)
Macrone, John [publishing house]........DLB-106
MacShane, Frank 1927-1999 ....DLB-111
Macy-Masius DLB-46
Madden, David 1933- DLB-6
Madden, Sir Frederic 1801-1873 ....DLB-184
Maddow, Ben 1909-1992...............DLB-44
Maddux, Rachel 1912-1983.......DLB-234; Y-93
Madgett, Naomi Long 1923- DLB-76
Madhubuti, Haki R. 1942- DLB-5, 41; DS-8
Madison, James 1751-1836 ....DLB-37
Madsen, Svend Åge 1939- DLB-214
Maeterlinck, Maurice 1862-1949........DLB-192
Mafūz, Najīb 1911- Y-88
Magee, David 1905-1977..............DLB-187
Maginn, William 1794-1842 ....DLB-110, 159
Magoffin, Susan Shelby 1827-1855......DLB-239

Mahan, Alfred Thayer 1840-1914 .... DLB-47
Maheux-Forcier, Louise 1929- DLB-60
Mahin, John Lee 1902-1984 .... DLB-44
Mahon, Derek 1941- DLB-40
Maikov, Vasilii Ivanovich 1728-1778 .... DLB-150
Mailer, Norman 1923-
.... DLB-2, 16, 28, 185; Y-80, Y-83, Y-97;
DS-3; CDALB-6
Maillart, Ella 1903-1997 .... DLB-195
Maillet, Adrienne 1885-1963 .... DLB-68
Maillet, Antonine 1929- DLB-60
Maillu, David G. 1939- DLB-157
Maimonides, Moses 1138-1204 .... DLB-115
Main Selections of the Book-of-the-Month
Club, 1926-1945.................. DLB-9
Main Trends in Twentieth-Century Book
Clubs DLB-46
Mainwaring, Daniel 1902-1977 .... DLB-44
Mair, Charles 1838-1927 .... DLB-99
Maironis, Jonas
1862-1932 .... DLB-220; CDWLB-4
Mais, Roger 1905-1955..... DLB-125; CDWLB-3
Major, Andre 1942- DLB-60
Major, Charles 1856-1913 .... DLB-202
Major, Clarence 1936- DLB-33
Major, Kevin 1949- DLB-60
Major Books..................... DLB-46
Makemie, Francis circa 1658-1708 .... DLB-24
The Making of Americans Contract............ Y-98
The Making of a People, by
J. M. Ritchie.................... DLB-66
Maksimović, Desanka
1898-1993 ....DLB-147; CDWLB-4
Malamud, Bernard 1914-1986
.... DLB-2, 28, 152; Y-80, Y-86; CDALB-1
Mălăncioiu, Ileana 1940- DLB-232
Malaparte, Curzio 1898-1957 .... DLB-264
Malerba, Luigi 1927- DLB-196
Malet, Lucas 1852-1931 .... DLB-153
Mallarmé, Stéphane 1842-1898 .... DLB-217
Malleson, Lucy Beatrice (see Gilbert, Anthony)
Mallet-Joris, Françoise 1930- DLB-83
Mallock, W. H. 1849-1923......... DLB-18, 57
"Every Man His Own Poet; or,
The Inspired Singer's Recipe
Book" (1877) DLB-35
Malone, Dumas 1892-1986............. DLB-17
Malone, Edmond 1741-1812.......... DLB-142
Malory, Sir Thomas
circa 1400-1410 - 1471 ... DLB-146; CDBLB-1
Malpede, Karen 1945- DLB-249
Malraux, André 1901-1976........... DLB-72
Malthus, Thomas Robert
1766-1834..................DLB-107, 158
Maltz, Albert 1908-1985.............. DLB-102
Malzberg, Barry N. 1939- DLB-8
Mamet, David 1947- DLB-7
Mamin, Dmitrii Narkisovich 1852-1912.. DLB-238

Manaka, Matsemela 1956- DLB-157
Manchester University Press DLB-112
Mandel, Eli 1922-1992 .... DLB-53
Mandeville, Bernard 1670-1733 .... DLB-101
Mandeville, Sir John
mid fourteenth century DLB-146
Mandiargues, André Pieyre de 1909- ... DLB-83
Manea, Norman 1936- DLB-232
Manfred, Frederick 1912-1994 ....DLB-6, 212, 227
Manfredi, Gianfranco 1948- DLB-196
Mangan, Sherry 1904-1961 .... DLB-4
Manganelli, Giorgio 1922-1990 .... DLB-196
Manilius fl. first century A.D............ DLB-211
Mankiewicz, Herman 1897-1953 .... DLB-26
Mankiewicz, Joseph L. 1909-1993 ...... DLB-44
Mankowitz, Wolf 1924-1998 .... DLB-15
Manley, Delarivière 1672?-1724 ...... DLB-39, 80
Preface to The Secret History, of Queen Zarah,
and the Zarazians (1705) DLB-39
Mann, Abby 1927- DLB-44
Mann, Charles 1929-1998 ....Y-98
Mann, Emily 1952- DLB-266
Mann, Heinrich 1871-1950 .... DLB-66, 118
Mann, Horace 1796-1859........... DLB-1, 235
Mann, Klaus 1906-1949 .... DLB-56
Mann, Mary Peabody 1806-1887....... DLB-239
Mann, Thomas 1875-1955 ... DLB-66; CDWLB-2
Mann, William D'Alton 1839-1920 ..... DLB-137
Mannin, Ethel 1900-1984......... DLB-191, 195
Manning, Emily (see Australie)
Manning, Frederic 1882-1935.......... DLB-260
Manning, Laurence 1899-1972......... DLB-251
Manning, Marie 1873?-1945............ DLB-29
Manning and Loring DLB-49
Mannyng, Robert
flourished 1303-1338 .... DLB-146
Mano, D. Keith 1942- DLB-6
Manor Books DLB-46
Mansfield, Katherine 1888-1923........ DLB-162
Manuel, Niklaus circa 1484-1530 .....DLB-179
Manzini, Gianna 1896-1974 ....DLB-177
Mapanje, Jack 1944- DLB-157
Maraini, Dacia 1936- DLB-196
Marcel Proust at 129 and the Proust Society
of America Y-00
Marcel Proust's Remembrance of Things Past:
The Rediscovered Galley Proofs Y-00
March, William 1893-1954............ DLB-9, 86
Marchand, Leslie A. 1900-1999 .... DLB-103
Marchant, Bessie 1862-1941.......... DLB-160
Marchant, Tony 1959- DLB-245
Marchenko, Anastasiia Iakovlevna
1830-1880 .... DLB-238
Marchessault, Jovette 1938- DLB-60
Marcinkevičius, Justinas 1930- DLB-232
Marcus, Frank 1928- DLB-13

Marcuse, Herbert 1898-1979 .... DLB-242
Marden, Orison Swett 1850-1924 ......DLB-137
Marechera, Dambudzo 1952-1987 ....DLB-157
Marek, Richard, Books................ DLB-46
Mares, E. A. 1938- DLB-122
Margulies, Donald 1954- DLB-228
Mariani, Paul 1940- DLB-111
Marie de France flourished 1160-1178 ... DLB-208
Marie-Victorin, Frère 1885-1944 .... DLB-92
Marin, Biagio 1891-1985 .... DLB-128
Marincovič, Ranko
1913- DLB-147; CDWLB-4
Marinetti, Filippo Tommaso
1876-1944................. DLB-114, 264
Marion, Frances 1886-1973 .... DLB-44
Marius, Richard C. 1933-1999............Y-85
Markevich, Boleslav Mikhailovich
1822-1884 .... DLB-238
Markfield, Wallace 1926- DLB-2, 28
Markham, Edwin 1852-1940 .... DLB-54, 186
Markle, Fletcher 1921-1991 ....DLB-68; Y-91
Marlatt, Daphne 1942- DLB-60
Marlitt, E. 1825-1887 .... DLB-129
Marlowe, Christopher
1564-1593 .... DLB-62; CDBLB-1
Marlyn, John 1912- DLB-88
Marmion, Shakerley 1603-1639......... DLB-58
Der Marner before 1230-circa 1287 ..... DLB-138
Marnham, Patrick 1943- DLB-204
The Marprelate Tracts 1588-1589 .... DLB-132
Marquand, John P. 1893-1960 ...... DLB-9, 102
Marqués, René 1919-1979 .... DLB-113
Marquis, Don 1878-1937 .... DLB-11, 25
Marriott, Anne 1913- DLB-68
Marryat, Frederick 1792-1848 ..... DLB-21, 163
Marsh, Capen, Lyon and Webb........ DLB-49
Marsh, George Perkins
1801-1882 .... DLB-1, 64, 243
Marsh, James 1794-1842............. DLB-1, 59
Marsh, Narcissus 1638-1713........... DLB-213
Marsh, Ngaio 1899-1982 .... DLB-77
Marshall, Alan 1902-1984 .... DLB-260
Marshall, Edison 1894-1967........... DLB-102
Marshall, Edward 1932- DLB-16
Marshall, Emma 1828-1899 .... DLB-163
Marshall, James 1942-1992........... DLB-61
Marshall, Joyce 1913- DLB-88
Marshall, Paule 1929- DLB-33, 157, 227
Marshall, Tom 1938-1993 .... DLB-60
Marsilius of Padua
circa 1275-circa 1342 .... DLB-115
Mars-Jones, Adam 1954- DLB-207
Marson, Una 1905-1965............DLB-157
Marston, John 1576-1634 ....DLB-58, 172
Marston, Philip Bourke 1850-1887....... DLB-35
Martens, Kurt 1870-1945 .... DLB-66

Martial circa A.D. 40-circa A.D. 103 .... DLB-211; CDWLB-1	Mathias, Roland 1915- DLB-27	McAuley, James 1917-1976 .... DLB-260
Martien, William S. [publishing house] DLB-49	Mathis, June 1892-1927 .... DLB-44	McBride, Robert M., and Company DLB-46
Martin, Abe (see Hubbard, Kin)	Mathis, Sharon Bell 1937- DLB-33	McCabe, Patrick 1955- DLB-194
Martin, Catherine ca. 1847-1937 .... DLB-230	Matković, Marijan 1915-1985 .... DLB-181	McCaffrey, Anne 1926- DLB-8
Martin, Charles 1942- DLB-120	Matoš, Antun Gustav 1873-1914 .... DLB-147	McCarthy, Cormac 1933- DLB-6, 143, 256
Martin, Claire 1914- DLB-60	Matsumoto Seichō 1909-1992 .... DLB-182	McCarthy, Mary 1912-1989 .... DLB-2; Y-81
Martin, David 1915-1997 .... DLB-260	The Matter of England 1240-1400 ...... DLB-146	McCay, Winsor 1871-1934 .... DLB-22
Martin, Jay 1935- DLB-111	The Matter of Rome early twelfth to late fifteenth century DLB-146	McClane, Albert Jules 1922-1991 .... DLB-171
Martin, Johann (see Laurentius von Schnüffis)	Matthew of Vendôme circa 1130-circa 1200 .... DLB-208	McClatchy, C. K. 1858-1936 .... DLB-25
Martin, Thomas 1696-1771 .... DLB-213		McClellan, George Marion 1860-1934 .... DLB-50
Martin, Violet Florence (see Ross, Martin)	Matthews, Brander 1852-1929 .... DLB-71, 78; DS-13	McCloskey, Robert 1914- DLB-22
Martin du Gard, Roger 1881-1958 .... DLB-65	Matthews, Jack 1925- DLB-6	McClung, Nellie Letitia 1873-1951 .... DLB-92
Martineau, Harriet 1802-1876 .... DLB-21, 55, 159, 163, 166, 190	Matthews, Victoria Earle 1861-1907 ..... DLB-221	McClure, Joanna 1930- DLB-16
Martínez, Demetria 1960- DLB-209	Matthews, William 1942-1997 .... DLB-5	McClure, Michael 1932- DLB-16
Martínez, Eliud 1935- DLB-122	Matthiessen, F. O. 1902-1950 .... DLB-63	McClure, Phillips and Company DLB-46
Martínez, Max 1943- DLB-82	Matthiessen, Peter 1927- DLB-6, 173	McClure, S. S. 1857-1949 .... DLB-91
Martínez, Rubén 1962- DLB-209	Maturin, Charles Robert 1780-1824 ..... DLB-178	McClurg, A. C., and Company DLB-49
Martinson, Harry 1904-1978 .... DLB-259	Maugham, W. Somerset 1874-1965 .... DLB-10, 36, 77, 100, 162, 195; CDBLB-6	McCluskey, John A., Jr. 1944- DLB-33
Martinson, Moa 1890-1964 .... DLB-259	Maupassant, Guy de 1850-1893 .... DLB-123	McCollum, Michael A. 1946 .... Y-87
Martone, Michael 1955- DLB-218	Mauriac, Claude 1914-1996 .... DLB-83	McConnell, William C. 1917- DLB-88
Martyn, Edward 1859-1923 .... DLB-10	Mauriac, François 1885-1970 .... DLB-65	McCord, David 1897-1997 .... DLB-61
Marvell, Andrew 1621-1678 .... DLB-131; CDBLB-2	Maurice, Frederick Denison 1805-1872 .... DLB-55	McCord, Louisa S. 1810-1879 .... DLB-248
Marvin X 1944- DLB-38		McCorkle, Jill 1958- DLB-234; Y-87
Marx, Karl 1818-1883 .... DLB-129	Maurois, André 1885-1967 .... DLB-65	McCorkle, Samuel Eusebius 1746-1811 .... DLB-37
Marzials, Theo 1850-1920 .... DLB-35	Maury, James 1718-1769 .... DLB-31	McCormick, Anne O'Hare 1880-1954 .... DLB-29
Masefield, John 1878-1967 ... DLB-10, 19, 153, 160; CDBLB-5	Mavor, Elizabeth 1927- DLB-14	Kenneth Dale McCormick Tributes Y-97
Masham, Damaris Cudworth Lady 1659-1708 .... DLB-252	Mavor, Osborne Henry (see Bridie, James)	McCormick, Robert R. 1880-1955 .... DLB-29
	Maxwell, Gavin 1914-1969 .... DLB-204	McCourt, Edward 1907-1972 .... DLB-88
Masino, Paola 1908-1989 .... DLB-264	Maxwell, H. [publishing house] DLB-49	McCoy, Horace 1897-1955 .... DLB-9
Mason, A. E. W. 1865-1948 .... DLB-70	Maxwell, John [publishing house] DLB-106	McCrae, Hugh 1876-1958 .... DLB-260
Mason, Bobbie Ann 1940- DLB-173; Y-87; CDALB-7	Maxwell, William 1908- DLB-218; Y-80	McCrae, John 1872-1918 .... DLB-92
Mason, William 1725-1797 .... DLB-142	May, Elaine 1932- DLB-44	McCullagh, Joseph B. 1842-1896 .... DLB-23
Mason Brothers DLB-49	May, Karl 1842-1912 .... DLB-129	McCullers, Carson 1917-1967 ..... DLB-2, 7, 173, 228; CDALB-1
Massey, Gerald 1828-1907 .... DLB-32	May, Thomas 1595 or 1596-1650 .... DLB-58	McCulloch, Thomas 1776-1843 .... DLB-99
Massey, Linton R. 1900-1974 .... DLB-187	Mayer, Bernadette 1945- DLB-165	McDonald, Forrest 1927- DLB-17
Massinger, Philip 1583-1640 .... DLB-58	Mayer, Mercer 1943- DLB-61	McDonald, Walter 1934- DLB-105, DS-9
Masson, David 1822-1907 .... DLB-144	Mayer, O. B. 1818-1891 .... DLB-3, 248	"Getting Started: Accepting the Regions You Own–or Which Own You," DLB-105
Masters, Edgar Lee 1868-1950 .... DLB-54; CDALB-3	Mayes, Herbert R. 1900-1987 .... DLB-137	McDougall, Colin 1917-1984 .... DLB-68
	Mayes, Wendell 1919-1992 .... DLB-26	McDowell, Katharine Sherwood Bonner 1849-1883 .... DLB-202, 239
Masters, Hilary 1928- DLB-244	Mayfield, Julian 1928-1984 .... DLB-33; Y-84	
Mastronardi, Lucio 1930-1979 .... DLB-177	Mayhew, Henry 1812-1887 ...... DLB-18, 55, 190	McDowell, Obolensky DLB-46
Matevski, Mateja 1929- ... DLB-181; CDWLB-4	Mayhew, Jonathan 1720-1766 .... DLB-31	McEwan, Ian 1948- DLB-14, 194
Mather, Cotton 1663-1728 .... DLB-24, 30, 140; CDALB-2	Mayne, Ethel Colburn 1865-1941 .... DLB-197	McFadden, David 1940- DLB-60
	Mayne, Jasper 1604-1672 .... DLB-126	McFall, Frances Elizabeth Clarke (see Grand, Sarah)
Mather, Increase 1639-1723 .... DLB-24	Mayne, Seymour 1944- DLB-60	
Mather, Richard 1596-1669 .... DLB-24	Mayor, Flora Macdonald 1872-1932 ..... DLB-36	McFarlane, Leslie 1902-1977 .... DLB-88
Matheson, Annie 1853-1924 .... DLB-240	Mayrocker, Friederike 1924- DLB-85	McFarland, Ronald 1942- DLB-256
Matheson, Richard 1926- DLB-8, 44	Mazrui, Ali A. 1933- DLB-125	McFee, William 1881-1966 .... DLB-153
Matheus, John F. 1887- DLB-51	Mažuranić, Ivan 1814-1890 .... DLB-147	McGahern, John 1934- DLB-14, 231
Mathews, Cornelius 1817?-1889 ... DLB-3, 64, 250	Mazursky, Paul 1930- DLB-44	McGee, Thomas D'Arcy 1825-1868 ...... DLB-99
Mathews, Elkin [publishing house] DLB-112	McAlmon, Robert 1896-1956 ... DLB-4, 45; DS-15	McGeehan, W. O. 1879-1933 .... DLB-25, 171
Mathews, John Joseph 1894-1979 .... DLB-175	Robert McAlmon's "A Night at Bricktop's" .. Y-01	McGill, Ralph 1898-1969 .... DLB-29
	McArthur, Peter 1866-1924 .... DLB-92	McGinley, Phyllis 1905-1978 .... DLB-11, 48

Cumulative Index

McGinniss, Joe 1942- DLB-185
McGirt, James E. 1874-1930 .... DLB-50
McGlashan and Gill DLB-106
McGough, Roger 1937- DLB-40
McGrath, John 1935- DLB-233
McGrath, Patrick 1950- DLB-231
McGraw-Hill DLB-46
McGuane, Thomas 1939- DLB-2, 212; Y-80
McGuckian, Medbh 1950- DLB-40
McGuffey, William Holmes 1800-1873 ... DLB-42
McGuinness, Frank 1953- DLB-245
McHenry, James 1785-1845 .... DLB-202
McIlvanney, William 1936- DLB-14, 207
McIlwraith, Jean Newton 1859-1938 ..... DLB-92
McIntosh, Maria Jane 1803-1878 ... DLB-239, 248
McIntyre, James 1827-1906 .... DLB-99
McIntyre, O. O. 1884-1938 .... CDALB-25
McKay, Claude 1889-1948 ..... DLB-4, 45, 51, 117
The David McKay Company DLB-49
McKean, William V. 1820-1903 .... DLB-23
McKenna, Stephen 1888-1967 .... DLB-197
The McKenzie Trust Y-96
McKerrow, R. B. 1872-1940 .... DLB-201
McKinley, Robin 1952- DLB-52
McKnight, Reginald 1956- DLB-234
McLachlan, Alexander 1818-1896 .... DLB-99
McLaren, Floris Clark 1904-1978 .... DLB-68
McLaverty, Michael 1907- DLB-15
McLean, John R. 1848-1916 .... DLB-23
McLean, William L. 1852-1931 .... DLB-25
McLennan, William 1856-1904 .... DLB-92
McLoughlin Brothers DLB-49
McLuhan, Marshall 1911-1980 .... DLB-88
McMaster, John Bach 1852-1932 .... DLB-47
McMurtry, Larry 1936-
...... DLB-2, 143, 256; Y-80, Y-87; CDALB-6
McNally, Terrence 1939- DLB-7, 249
McNeil, Florence 1937- DLB-60
McNeile, Herman Cyril 1888-1937 .... DLB-77
McNickle, D'Arcy 1904-1977 .... DLB-175, 212
McPhee, John 1931- DLB-185
McPherson, James Alan 1943- DLB-38, 244
McPherson, Sandra 1943- Y-86
McTaggart, J. M. E. 1866-1925 .... DLB-262
McWhirter, George 1939- DLB-60
McWilliams, Carey 1905-1980 .... DLB-137
Mda, Zakes 1948- DLB-225
Mead, L. T. 1844-1914 .... DLB-141
Mead, Matthew 1924- DLB-40
Mead, Taylor ?- DLB-16
Meany, Tom 1903-1964 .... DLB-171
Mechthild von Magdeburg
    circa 1207-circa 1282 .... DLB-138
Medieval French Drama DLB-208
Medieval Travel Diaries DLB-203

Medill, Joseph 1823-1899 .... DLB-43
Medoff, Mark 1940- DLB-7
Meek, Alexander Beaufort
    1814-1865 .... DLB-3, 248
Meeke, Mary ?-1816? DLB-116
Meinke, Peter 1932- DLB-5
Mejia Vallejo, Manuel 1923- DLB-113
Melanchthon, Philipp 1497-1560 ...... DLB-179
Melançon, Robert 1947- DLB-60
Mell, Max 1882-1971 .... DLB-81, 124
Mellow, James R. 1926-1997 .... DLB-111
Mel'nikov, Pavel Ivanovich 1818-1883 .. DLB-238
Meltzer, David 1937- DLB-16
Meltzer, Milton 1915- DLB-61
Melville, Elizabeth, Lady Culross
    circa 1585-1640 .... DLB-172
Melville, Herman
    1819-1891 ...... DLB-3, 74, 250; CDALB-2
Memoirs of Life and Literature (1920),
    by W. H. Mallock [excerpt] DLB-57
Mena, María Cristina 1893-1965 ... DLB-209, 221
Menander 342-341 B.C.-circa 292-291 B.C.
    .... DLB-176; CDWLB-1
Menantes (see Hunold, Christian Friedrich)
Mencke, Johann Burckhard
    1674-1732 .... DLB-168
Mencken, H. L. 1880-1956
    .... DLB-11, 29, 63, 137, 222; CDALB-4
H. L. Mencken's "Berlin, February, 1917" Y-00
Mencken and Nietzsche: An Unpublished
    Excerpt from H. L. Mencken's *My Life
    as Author and Editor* Y-93
Mendelssohn, Moses 1729-1786 .... DLB-97
Mendes, Catulle 1841-1909 .... DLB-217
Méndez M., Miguel 1930- DLB-82
Mens Rea (or Something) Y-97
The Mercantile Library of New York Y-96
Mercer, Cecil William (see Yates, Dornford)
Mercer, David 1928-1980 .... DLB-13
Mercer, John 1704-1768 .... DLB-31
Mercer, Johnny 1909?-1976 .... DLB-265
Meredith, George
    1828-1909 .... DLB-18, 35, 57, 159; CDBLB-4
Meredith, Louisa Anne 1812-1895 .. DLB-166, 230
Meredith, Owen
    (see Lytton, Edward Robert Bulwer)
Meredith, William 1919- DLB-5
Mergerle, Johann Ulrich
    (see Abraham ä Sancta Clara)
Mérimée, Prosper 1803-1870 ...... DLB-119, 192
Merivale, John Herman 1779-1844 ..... DLB-96
Meriwether, Louise 1923- DLB-33
Merlin Press DLB-112
Merriam, Eve 1916-1992 .... DLB-61
The Merriam Company DLB-49
Merril, Judith 1923-1997 .... DLB-251
Merrill, James 1926-1995 ...... DLB-5, 165; Y-85
Merrill and Baker DLB-49

The Mershon Company DLB-49
Merton, Thomas 1915-1968 .... DLB-48; Y-81
Merwin, W. S. 1927- DLB-5, 169
Messner, Julian [publishing house] DLB-46
Mészöly, Miklós 1921- DLB-232
Metcalf, J. [publishing house] DLB-49
Metcalf, John 1938- DLB-60
The Methodist Book Concern DLB-49
Methuen and Company DLB-112
Meun, Jean de (see *Roman de la Rose*)
Mew, Charlotte 1869-1928 .... DLB-19, 135
Mewshaw, Michael 1943- Y-80
Meyer, Conrad Ferdinand 1825-1898 ... DLB-129
Meyer, E. Y. 1946- DLB-75
Meyer, Eugene 1875-1959 .... DLB-29
Meyer, Michael 1921-2000 .... DLB-155
Meyers, Jeffrey 1939- DLB-111
Meynell, Alice 1847-1922 .... DLB-19, 98
Meynell, Viola 1885-1956 .... DLB-153
Meyrink, Gustav 1868-1932 .... DLB-81
Mézières, Philipe de circa 1327-1405 .... DLB-208
Michael, Ib 1945- DLB-214
Michaëlis, Karen 1872-1950 .... DLB-214
Michaels, Leonard 1933- DLB-130
Michaux, Henri 1899-1984 .... DLB-258
Micheaux, Oscar 1884-1951 .... DLB-50
Michel of Northgate, Dan
    circa 1265-circa 1340 .... DLB-146
Micheline, Jack 1929-1998 .... DLB-16
Michener, James A. 1907?-1997 .... DLB-6
Micklejohn, George
    circa 1717-1818 .... DLB-31
Middle English Literature:
    An Introduction DLB-146
The Middle English Lyric DLB-146
Middle Hill Press DLB-106
Middleton, Christopher 1926- DLB-40
Middleton, Richard 1882-1911 .... DLB-156
Middleton, Stanley 1919- DLB-14
Middleton, Thomas 1580-1627 .... DLB-58
Miegel, Agnes 1879-1964 .... DLB-56
Mieželaitis, Eduardas 1919-1997 ...... DLB-220
Mihailović, Dragoslav 1930- DLB-181
Mihalić, Slavko 1928- DLB-181
Mikhailov, A. (see Sheller, Aleksandr
    Konstantinovich)
Mikhailov, Mikhail Larionovich
    1829-1865 .... DLB-238
Miles, Josephine 1911-1985 .... DLB-48
Miles, Susan (Ursula Wyllie Roberts)
    1888-1975 .... DLB-240
Miliković, Branko 1934-1961 .... DLB-181
Milius, John 1944- DLB-44
Mill, James 1773-1836 .... DLB-107, 158, 262
Mill, John Stuart
    1806-1873 ...... DLB-55, 190, 262; CDBLB-4

Millar, Andrew [publishing house]......DLB-154
Millar, Kenneth
    1915-1983.........DLB-2, 226; Y-83; DS-6
Millay, Edna St. Vincent
    1892-1950........DLB-45, 249; CDALB-4
Millen, Sarah Gertrude 1888-1968......DLB-225
Miller, Arthur
    1915-............DLB-7, 266; CDALB-1
Miller, Caroline 1903-1992..............DLB-9
Miller, Eugene Ethelbert 1950-........DLB-41
Miller, Heather Ross 1939-............DLB-120
Miller, Henry
    1891-1980........DLB-4, 9; Y-80; CDALB-5
Miller, Hugh 1802-1856.................DLB-190
Miller, J. Hillis 1928-.................DLB-67
Miller, James [publishing house]........DLB-49
Miller, Jason 1939-....................DLB-7
Miller, Joaquin 1839-1913..............DLB-186
Miller, May 1899-......................DLB-41
Miller, Paul 1906-1991.................DLB-127
Miller, Perry 1905-1963.............DLB-17, 63
Miller, Sue 1943-......................DLB-143
Miller, Vassar 1924-1998...............DLB-105
Miller, Walter M., Jr. 1923-...........DLB-8
Miller, Webb 1892-1940.................DLB-29
Millett, Kate 1934-....................DLB-246
Millhauser, Steven 1943-...............DLB-2
Millican, Arthenia J. Bates 1920-......DLB-38
Milligan, Alice 1866-1953..............DLB-240
Mills and Boon.........................DLB-112
Milman, Henry Hart 1796-1868...........DLB-96
Milne, A. A. 1882-1956.....DLB-10, 77, 100, 160
Milner, Ron 1938-......................DLB-38
Milner, William [publishing house]......DLB-106
Milnes, Richard Monckton (Lord Houghton)
    1809-1885....................DLB-32, 184
Milton, John
    1608-1674.........DLB-131, 151; CDBLB-2
Miłosz, Czesław 1911-....DLB-215; CDWLB-4
Minakami Tsutomu 1919-.................DLB-182
Minamoto no Sanetomo 1192-1219........DLB-203
The Minerva Press......................DLB-154
Minnesang circa 1150-1280............DLB-138
Minns, Susan 1839-1938.................DLB-140
Minor Illustrators, 1880-1914..........DLB-141
Minor Poets of the Earlier Seventeenth
    Century..........................DLB-121
Minton, Balch and Company..............DLB-46
Mirbeau, Octave 1848-1917..........DLB-123, 192
Mirk, John died after 1414?............DLB-146
Miron, Gaston 1928-....................DLB-60
A Mirror for Magistrates.............DLB-167
Mishima Yukio 1925-1970................DLB-182
Mitchel, Jonathan 1624-1668............DLB-24
Mitchell, Adrian 1932-.................DLB-40
Mitchell, Donald Grant
    1822-1908....................DLB-1, 243; DS-13

Mitchell, Gladys 1901-1983.............DLB-77
Mitchell, James Leslie 1901-1935.......DLB-15
Mitchell, John (see Slater, Patrick)
Mitchell, John Ames 1845-1918..........DLB-79
Mitchell, Joseph 1908-1996.........DLB-185; Y-96
Mitchell, Julian 1935-.................DLB-14
Mitchell, Ken 1940-....................DLB-60
Mitchell, Langdon 1862-1935............DLB-7
Mitchell, Loften 1919-.................DLB-38
Mitchell, Margaret 1900-1949...DLB-9; CDALB-7
Mitchell, S. Weir 1829-1914............DLB-202
Mitchell, W. J. T. 1942-...............DLB-246
Mitchell, W. O. 1914-..................DLB-88
Mitchison, Naomi Margaret (Haldane)
    1897-1999...............DLB-160, 191, 255
Mitford, Mary Russell 1787-1855...DLB-110, 116
Mitford, Nancy 1904-1973...............DLB-191
Mittelholzer, Edgar
    1909-1965.............DLB-117; CDWLB-3
Mitterer, Erika 1906-..................DLB-85
Mitterer, Felix 1948-..................DLB-124
Mitternacht, Johann Sebastian
    1613-1679.......................DLB-168
Miyamoto, Yuriko 1899-1951.............DLB-180
Mizener, Arthur 1907-1988..............DLB-103
Mo, Timothy 1950-......................DLB-194
Moberg, Vilhelm 1898-1973..............DLB-259
Modern Age Books.......................DLB-46
"Modern English Prose" (1876),
    by George Saintsbury.............DLB-57
The Modern Language Association of America
    Celebrates Its Centennial..........Y-84
The Modern Library.....................DLB-46
"Modern Novelists – Great and Small" (1855),
    by Margaret Oliphant.............DLB-21
"Modern Style" (1857), by Cockburn
    Thomson [excerpt]................DLB-57
The Modernists (1932),
    by Joseph Warren Beach...........DLB-36
Modiano, Patrick 1945-.................DLB-83
Moffat, Yard and Company...............DLB-46
Moffet, Thomas 1553-1604...............DLB-136
Mohr, Nicholasa 1938-..................DLB-145
Moix, Ana María 1947-..................DLB-134
Molesworth, Louisa 1839-1921...........DLB-135
Möllhausen, Balduin 1825-1905..........DLB-129
Molnár, Ferenc
    1878-1952.............DLB-215; CDWLB-4
Molnár, Miklós (see Mészöly, Miklós)
Momaday, N. Scott
    1934-........DLB-143, 175, 256; CDALB-7
Monkhouse, Allan 1858-1936.............DLB-10
Monro, Harold 1879-1932................DLB-19
Monroe, Harriet 1860-1936..........DLB-54, 91
Monsarrat, Nicholas 1910-1979..........DLB-15
Montagu, Lady Mary Wortley
    1689-1762....................DLB-95, 101
Montague, C. E. 1867-1928..............DLB-197

Montague, John 1929-...................DLB-40
Montale, Eugenio 1896-1981.............DLB-114
Montalvo, José 1946-1994...............DLB-209
Monterroso, Augusto 1921-..............DLB-145
Montesquiou, Robert de 1855-1921......DLB-217
Montgomerie, Alexander
    circa 1550?-1598.................DLB-167
Montgomery, James 1771-1854.......DLB-93, 158
Montgomery, John 1919-.................DLB-16
Montgomery, Lucy Maud
    1874-1942...................DLB-92; DS-14
Montgomery, Marion 1925-...............DLB-6
Montgomery, Robert Bruce (see Crispin, Edmund)
Montherlant, Henry de 1896-1972........DLB-72
The Monthly Review 1749-1844...........DLB-110
Montigny, Louvigny de 1876-1955........DLB-92
Montoya, José 1932-....................DLB-122
Moodie, John Wedderburn Dunbar
    1797-1869........................DLB-99
Moodie, Susanna 1803-1885..............DLB-99
Moody, Joshua circa 1633-1697..........DLB-24
Moody, William Vaughn 1869-1910....DLB-7, 54
Moorcock, Michael 1939-....DLB-14, 231, 261
Moore, Alan 1953-......................DLB-261
Moore, Brian 1921-1999.................DLB-251
Moore, Catherine L. 1911-..............DLB-8
Moore, Clement Clarke 1779-1863........DLB-42
Moore, Dora Mavor 1888-1979............DLB-92
Moore, G. E. 1873-1958.................DLB-262
Moore, George 1852-1933....DLB-10, 18, 57, 135
Moore, Lorrie 1957-....................DLB-234
Moore, Marianne
    1887-1972.........DLB-45; DS-7; CDALB-5
Moore, Mavor 1919-.....................DLB-88
Moore, Richard 1927-...................DLB-105
Moore, T. Sturge 1870-1944.............DLB-19
Moore, Thomas 1779-1852............DLB-96, 144
Moore, Ward 1903-1978..................DLB-8
Moore, Wilstach, Keys and Company.....DLB-49
Moorehead, Alan 1901-1983..............DLB-204
Moorhouse, Geoffrey 1931-..............DLB-204
The Moorland-Spingarn Research
    Center...........................DLB-76
Moorman, Mary C. 1905-1994.............DLB-155
Mora, Pat 1942-........................DLB-209
Moraga, Cherríe 1952-..............DLB-82, 249
Morales, Alejandro 1944-...............DLB-82
Morales, Mario Roberto 1947-...........DLB-145
Morales, Rafael 1919-..................DLB-108
Morality Plays: *Mankind* circa 1450-1500 and
    Everyman circa 1500............DLB-146
Morante, Elsa 1912-1985................DLB-177
Morata, Olympia Fulvia 1526-1555......DLB-179
Moravia, Alberto 1907-1990.............DLB-177
Mordaunt, Elinor 1872-1942.............DLB-174
Mordovtsev, Daniil Lukich 1830-1905...DLB-238

Cumulative Index

More, Hannah 1745-1833 .... DLB-107, 109, 116, 158
More, Henry 1614-1687 .... DLB-126, 252
More, Sir Thomas 1477 or 1478-1535 .... DLB-136
Moreno, Dorinda 1939- DLB-122
Morency, Pierre 1942- DLB-60
Moretti, Marino 1885-1979 .... DLB-114, 264
Morgan, Berry 1919- DLB-6
Morgan, Charles 1894-1958 .... DLB-34, 100
Morgan, Edmund S. 1916- DLB-17
Morgan, Edwin 1920- DLB-27
Morgan, John Pierpont 1837-1913 .... DLB-140
Morgan, John Pierpont, Jr. 1867-1943 ... DLB-140
Morgan, Robert 1944- DLB-120
Morgan, Sydney Owenson, Lady 1776?-1859 .... DLB-116, 158
Morgner, Irmtraud 1933- DLB-75
Morhof, Daniel Georg 1639-1691 ...... DLB-164
Mori, Ōgai 1862-1922 .... DLB-180
Móricz, Zsigmond 1879-1942 .... DLB-215
Morier, James Justinian 1782 or 1783?-1849 .... DLB-116
Mörike, Eduard 1804-1875 .... DLB-133
Morin, Paul 1889-1963 .... DLB-92
Morison, Richard 1514?-1556 .... DLB-136
Morison, Samuel Eliot 1887-1976 .... DLB-17
Morison, Stanley 1889-1967 .... DLB-201
Moritz, Karl Philipp 1756-1793 ...... DLB-94
Moriz von Craûn circa 1220-1230 ... DLB-138
Morley, Christopher 1890-1957 .... DLB-9
Morley, John 1838-1923 .... DLB-57, 144, 190
Morris, George Pope 1802-1864 .... DLB-73
Morris, James Humphrey (see Morris, Jan)
Morris, Jan 1926- DLB-204
Morris, Lewis 1833-1907 .... DLB-35
Morris, Margaret 1737-1816 .... DLB-200
Morris, Richard B. 1904-1989 .... DLB-17
Morris, William 1834-1896 ..... DLB-18, 35, 57, 156, 178, 184; CDBLB-4
Morris, Willie 1934-1999 .... Y-80
Morris, Wright 1910-1998 .... DLB-2, 206, 218; Y-81
Morrison, Arthur 1863-1945 .... DLB-70, 135, 197
Morrison, Charles Clayton 1874-1966 .... DLB-91
Morrison, John 1904-1988 .... DLB-260
Morrison, Toni 1931- DLB-6, 33, 143; Y-81, Y-93; CDALB-6
Morrow, William, and Company DLB-46
Morse, James Herbert 1841-1923 .... DLB-71
Morse, Jedidiah 1761-1826 .... DLB-37
Morse, John T., Jr. 1840-1937 ...... DLB-47
Morselli, Guido 1912-1973 .... DLB-177
Mortimer, Favell Lee 1802-1878 ...... DLB-163
Mortimer, John 1923- DLB-13, 245; CDBLB-8
Morton, Carlos 1942- DLB-122

Morton, H. V. 1892-1979 .... DLB-195
Morton, John P., and Company DLB-49
Morton, Nathaniel 1613-1685 .... DLB-24
Morton, Sarah Wentworth 1759-1846 .... DLB-37
Morton, Thomas circa 1579-circa 1647 ... DLB-24
Moscherosch, Johann Michael 1601-1669 .... DLB-164
Moseley, Humphrey [publishing house] DLB-170
Möser, Justus 1720-1794 .... DLB-97
Mosley, Nicholas 1923- DLB-14, 207
Moss, Arthur 1889-1969 .... DLB-4
Moss, Howard 1922-1987 .... DLB-5
Moss, Thylias 1954- DLB-120
The Most Powerful Book Review in America [*New York Times Book Review*] Y-82
Motion, Andrew 1952- DLB-40
Motley, John Lothrop 1814-1877 .... DLB-1, 30, 59, 235
Motley, Willard 1909-1965 .... DLB-76, 143
Mott, Lucretia 1793-1880 .... DLB-239
Motte, Benjamin, Jr. [publishing house] .. DLB-154
Motteux, Peter Anthony 1663-1718 ...... DLB-80
Mottram, R. H. 1883-1971 .... DLB-36
Mount, Ferdinand 1939- DLB-231
Mouré, Erin 1955- DLB-60
Mourning Dove (Humishuma) between 1882 and 1888?-1936 .... DLB-175, 221
Movies from Books, 1920-1974 .... DLB-9
Mowat, Farley 1921- DLB-68
Mowbray, A. R., and Company, Limited DLB-106
Mowrer, Edgar Ansel 1892-1977 .... DLB-29
Mowrer, Paul Scott 1887-1971 .... DLB-29
Moxon, Edward [publishing house] DLB-106
Moxon, Joseph [publishing house] DLB-170
Mphahlele, Es'kia (Ezekiel) 1919- DLB-125; CDWLB-3
Mrożek, Sławomir 1930- .. DLB-232; CDWLB-4
Mtshali, Oswald Mbuyiseni 1940- DLB-125
Mucedorus DLB-62
Mudford, William 1782-1848 .... DLB-159
Mueller, Lisel 1924- DLB-105
Muhajir, El (see Marvin X)
Muhajir, Nazzam Al Fitnah (see Marvin X)
Mühlbach, Luise 1814-1873 .... DLB-133
Muir, Edwin 1887-1959 .... DLB-20, 100, 191
Muir, Helen 1937- DLB-14
Muir, John 1838-1914 .... DLB-186
Muir, Percy 1894-1979 .... DLB-201
Mujū Ichien 1226-1312 .... DLB-203
Mukherjee, Bharati 1940- DLB-60, 218
Mulcaster, Richard 1531 or 1532-1611 .... DLB-167
Muldoon, Paul 1951- DLB-40
Müller, Friedrich (see Müller, Maler)

Müller, Heiner 1929-1995 .... DLB-124
Müller, Maler 1749-1825 .... DLB-94
Muller, Marcia 1944- DLB-226
Müller, Wilhelm 1794-1827 .... DLB-90
Mumford, Lewis 1895-1990 .... DLB-63
Munby, A. N. L. 1913-1974 .... DLB-201
Munby, Arthur Joseph 1828-1910 ...... DLB-35
Munday, Anthony 1560-1633 .... DLB-62, 172
Mundt, Clara (see Mühlbach, Luise)
Mundt, Theodore 1808-1861 .... DLB-133
Munford, Robert circa 1737-1783 ..... DLB-31
Mungoshi, Charles 1947- DLB-157
Munk, Kaj 1898-1944 .... DLB-214
Munonye, John 1929- DLB-117
Munro, Alice 1931- DLB-53
Munro, George [publishing house] DLB-49
Munro, H. H. 1870-1916 .... DLB-34, 162; CDBLB-5
Munro, Neil 1864-1930 .... DLB-156
Munro, Norman L. [publishing house] DLB-49
Munroe, James, and Company DLB-49
Munroe, Kirk 1850-1930 .... DLB-42
Munroe and Francis DLB-49
Munsell, Joel [publishing house] DLB-49
Munsey, Frank A. 1854-1925 ...... DLB-25, 91
Munsey, Frank A., and Company DLB-49
Murakami Haruki 1949- DLB-182
Murav'ev, Mikhail Nikitich 1757-1807 .... DLB-150
Murdoch, Iris 1919-1999 .... DLB-14, 194, 233; CDBLB-8
Murdoch, Rupert 1931- DLB-127
Murfree, Mary N. 1850-1922 .... DLB-12, 74
Murger, Henry 1822-1861 .... DLB-119
Murger, Louis-Henri (see Murger, Henry)
Murner, Thomas 1475-1537 .... DLB-179
Muro, Amado 1915-1971 .... DLB-82
Murphy, Arthur 1727-1805 .... DLB-89, 142
Murphy, Beatrice M. 1908- DLB-76
Murphy, Dervla 1931- DLB-204
Murphy, Emily 1868-1933 .... DLB-99
Murphy, Jack 1923-1980 .... DLB-241
Murphy, John, and Company DLB-49
Murphy, John H., III 1916- DLB-127
Murphy, Richard 1927-1993 .... DLB-40
Murray, Albert L. 1916- DLB-38
Murray, Gilbert 1866-1957 .... DLB-10
Murray, Jim 1919-1998 .... DLB-241
Murray, John [publishing house] DLB-154
Murry, John Middleton 1889-1957 ..... DLB-149
"The Break-Up of the Novel" (1922) DLB-36
Murray, Judith Sargent 1751-1820 .... DLB-37, 200
Murray, Pauli 1910-1985 .... DLB-41
Musäus, Johann Karl August 1735-1787 ... DLB-97

Muschg, Adolf 1934- DLB-75

The Music of *Minnesang* DLB-138

Musil, Robert 1880-1942 .... DLB-81, 124; CDWLB-2

Muspilli circa 790-circa 850 .... DLB-148

Musset, Alfred de 1810-1857 .... DLB-192, 217

Mussey, Benjamin B., and Company DLB-49

Mutafchieva, Vera 1929- DLB-181

Mwangi, Meja 1948- DLB-125

My Summer Reading Orgy: Reading for Fun and Games: One Reader's Report on the Summer of 2001 .... Y-01

Myers, Frederic W. H. 1843-1901 .... DLB-190

Myers, Gustavus 1872-1942 .... DLB-47

Myers, L. H. 1881-1944 .... DLB-15

Myers, Walter Dean 1937- DLB-33

Mykolaitis-Putinas, Vincas 1893-1967 .... DLB-220

Myles, Eileen 1949- DLB-193

Myrdal, Jan 1927- DLB-257

N

Na Prous Boneta circa 1296-1328 .... DLB-208

Nabl, Franz 1883-1974 .... DLB-81

Nabokov, Vladimir 1899-1977 .... DLB-2, 244; Y-80, Y-91; DS-3; CDALB-1

The Vladimir Nabokov Archive in the Berg Collection Y-91

Nabokov Festival at Cornell Y-83

Nádaši, Ladislav (see Jégé)

Naden, Constance 1858-1889 .... DLB-199

Nadezhdin, Nikolai Ivanovich 1804-1856 .... DLB-198

Naevius circa 265 B.C.-201 B.C. DLB-211

Nafis and Cornish DLB-49

Nagai, Kafū 1879-1959 .... DLB-180

Naipaul, Shiva 1945-1985 .... DLB-157; Y-85

Naipaul, V. S. 1932- DLB-125, 204, 207; Y-85, Y-01; CDBLB-8; CDWLB-3

Nakagami Kenji 1946-1992 .... DLB-182

Nakano-in Masatada no Musume (see Nijō, Lady)

Nałkowska, Zofia 1884-1954 .... DLB-215

Nancrede, Joseph [publishing house] DLB-49

Naranjo, Carmen 1930- DLB-145

Narezhny, Vasilii Trofimovich 1780-1825 .... DLB-198

Narrache, Jean 1893-1970 .... DLB-92

Nasby, Petroleum Vesuvius (see Locke, David Ross)

Nash, Eveleigh [publishing house] DLB-112

Nash, Ogden 1902-1971 .... DLB-11

Nashe, Thomas 1567-1601? DLB-167

Nason, Jerry 1910-1986 .... DLB-241

Nast, Conde 1873-1942 .... DLB-91

Nast, Thomas 1840-1902 .... DLB-188

Nastasijević, Momčilo 1894-1938 .... DLB-147

Nathan, George Jean 1882-1958 .... DLB-137

Nathan, Robert 1894-1985 .... DLB-9

National Book Critics Circle Awards Y-00; Y-01

The National Jewish Book Awards Y-85

The National Theatre and the Royal Shakespeare Company: The National Companies DLB-13

Natsume, Sōseki 1867-1916 .... DLB-180

Naughton, Bill 1910- DLB-13

Navarro, Joe 1953- DLB-209

Naylor, Gloria 1950- DLB-173

Nazor, Vladimir 1876-1949 .... DLB-147

Ndebele, Njabulo 1948- DLB-157

Neagoe, Peter 1881-1960 .... DLB-4

Neal, John 1793-1876 .... DLB-1, 59, 243

Neal, Joseph C. 1807-1847 .... DLB-11

Neal, Larry 1937-1981 .... DLB-38

The Neale Publishing Company DLB-49

Nebel, Frederick 1903-1967 .... DLB-226

Neely, F. Tennyson [publishing house] DLB-49

Negoițescu, Ion 1921-1993 .... DLB-220

Negri, Ada 1870-1945 .... DLB-114

"The Negro as a Writer," by G. M. McClellan DLB-50

"Negro Poets and Their Poetry," by Wallace Thurman DLB-50

Neidhart von Reuental circa 1185-circa 1240 .... DLB-138

Neihardt, John G. 1881-1973 ..... DLB-9, 54, 256

Neilson, John Shaw 1872-1942 .... DLB-230

Neledinsky-Meletsky, Iurii Aleksandrovich 1752-1828 .... DLB-150

Nelligan, Emile 1879-1941 .... DLB-92

Nelson, Alice Moore Dunbar 1875-1935 ... DLB-50

Nelson, Antonya 1961- DLB-244

Nelson, Kent 1943- DLB-234

Nelson, Thomas, and Sons [U.K.] DLB-106

Nelson, Thomas, and Sons [U.S.] DLB-49

Nelson, William 1908-1978 .... DLB-103

Nelson, William Rockhill 1841-1915 ..... DLB-23

Nemerov, Howard 1920-1991 ..... DLB-5, 6; Y-83

Németh, László 1901-1975 .... DLB-215

Nepos circa 100 B.C.-post 27 B.C. DLB-211

Nėris, Salomėja 1904-1945 .... DLB-220; CDWLB-4

Nerval, Gerard de 1808-1855 .... DLB-217

Nesbit, E. 1858-1924 .... DLB-141, 153, 178

Ness, Evaline 1911-1986 .... DLB-61

Nestroy, Johann 1801-1862 .... DLB-133

Nettleship, R. L. 1846-1892 .... DLB-262

Neugeboren, Jay 1938- DLB-28

Neukirch, Benjamin 1655-1729 .... DLB-168

Neumann, Alfred 1895-1952 .... DLB-56

Neumann, Ferenc (see Molnár, Ferenc)

Neumark, Georg 1621-1681 .... DLB-164

Neumeister, Erdmann 1671-1756 .... DLB-168

Nevins, Allan 1890-1971 .... DLB-17; DS-17

Nevinson, Henry Woodd 1856-1941 .... DLB-135

The New American Library DLB-46

New Approaches to Biography: Challenges from Critical Theory, USC Conference on Literary Studies, 1990 .... Y-90

New Directions Publishing Corporation ... DLB-46

A New Edition of *Huck Finn* Y-85

New Forces at Work in the American Theatre: 1915-1925 .... DLB-7

New Literary Periodicals: A Report for 1987 .... Y-87

New Literary Periodicals: A Report for 1988 .... Y-88

New Literary Periodicals: A Report for 1989 .... Y-89

New Literary Periodicals: A Report for 1990 .... Y-90

New Literary Periodicals: A Report for 1991 .... Y-91

New Literary Periodicals: A Report for 1992 .... Y-92

New Literary Periodicals: A Report for 1993 .... Y-93

The New Monthly Magazine 1814-1884 .... DLB-110

The New Variorum Shakespeare Y-85

A New Voice: The Center for the Book's First Five Years Y-83

The New Wave [Science Fiction] DLB-8

New York City Bookshops in the 1930s and 1940s: The Recollections of Walter Goldwater .. Y-93

Newbery, John [publishing house] DLB-154

Newbolt, Henry 1862-1938 .... DLB-19

Newbound, Bernard Slade (see Slade, Bernard)

Newby, Eric 1919- DLB-204

Newby, P. H. 1918- DLB-15

Newby, Thomas Cautley [publishing house] DLB-106

Newcomb, Charles King 1820-1894 ... DLB-1, 223

Newell, Peter 1862-1924 .... DLB-42

Newell, Robert Henry 1836-1901 .... DLB-11

Newhouse, Samuel I. 1895-1979 .... DLB-127

Newman, Cecil Earl 1903-1976 .... DLB-127

Newman, David (see Benton, Robert)

Newman, Frances 1883-1928 .... Y-80

Newman, Francis William 1805-1897 .... DLB-190

Newman, John Henry 1801-1890 .... DLB-18, 32, 55

Newman, Mark [publishing house] DLB-49

Newmarch, Rosa Harriet 1857-1940 ..... DLB-240

Newnes, George, Limited DLB-112

Newsome, Effie Lee 1885-1979 .... DLB-76

Newspaper Syndication of American Humor DLB-11

Newton, A. Edward 1864-1940 .... DLB-140

Newton, Sir Isaac 1642-1727 .... DLB-252

Nexø, Martin Andersen 1869-1954 ...... DLB-214

Nezval, Vítěslav 1900-1958 .... DLB-215; CDWLB-4

Ngugi wa Thiong'o 1938- DLB-125; CDWLB-3

Niatum, Duane 1938- DLB-175	Njegoš, Petar II Petrović 1813-1851 .... DLB-147; CDWLB-4	Noonday Press DLB-46
The *Nibelungenlied* and the *Klage* circa 1200 .... DLB-138	Nkosi, Lewis 1936- DLB-157	Noone, John 1936- DLB-14
Nichol, B. P. 1944-1988 .... DLB-53	"The No Self, the Little Self, and the Poets," by Richard Moore DLB-105	Nora, Eugenio de 1923- DLB-134
Nicholas of Cusa 1401-1464 .... DLB-115	Noah, Mordecai M. 1785-1851 .... DLB-250	Nordan, Lewis 1939- DLB-234
Nichols, Ann 1891?-1966 .... DLB-249	Noailles, Anna de 1876-1933 .... DLB-258	Nordbrandt, Henrik 1945- DLB-214
Nichols, Beverly 1898-1983 .... DLB-191	Nobel Peace Prize	Nordhoff, Charles 1887-1947 .... DLB-9
Nichols, Dudley 1895-1960 .... DLB-26	The 1986 Nobel Peace Prize: Elie Wiesel Y-86	Norén, Lars 1944- DLB-257
Nichols, Grace 1950- DLB-157	The Nobel Prize and Literary Politics Y-86	Norman, Charles 1904-1996 .... DLB-111
Nichols, John 1940- Y-82	Nobel Prize in Literature	Norman, Marsha 1947- DLB-266; Y-84
Nichols, Mary Sargeant (Neal) Gove 1810-1884 .... DLB-1, 243	The 1982 Nobel Prize in Literature: Gabriel García Márquez Y-82	Norris, Charles G. 1881-1945 .... DLB-9
Nichols, Peter 1927- DLB-13, 245	The 1983 Nobel Prize in Literature: William Golding Y-83	Norris, Frank 1870-1902 .... DLB-12, 71, 186; CDALB-3
Nichols, Roy F. 1896-1973 .... DLB-17	The 1984 Nobel Prize in Literature: Jaroslav Seifert Y-84	Norris, John 1657-1712 .... DLB-252
Nichols, Ruth 1948- DLB-60	The 1985 Nobel Prize in Literature: Claude Simon Y-85	Norris, Leslie 1921- DLB-27, 256
Nicholson, Edward Williams Byron 1849-1912 .... DLB-184	The 1986 Nobel Prize in Literature: Wole Soyinka Y-86	Norse, Harold 1916- DLB-16
Nicholson, Norman 1914- DLB-27	The 1987 Nobel Prize in Literature: Joseph Brodsky Y-87	Norte, Marisela 1955- DLB-209
Nicholson, William 1872-1949 .... DLB-141	The 1988 Nobel Prize in Literature: Najīb Mahfūz Y-88	North, Marianne 1830-1890 .... DLB-174
Ní Chuilleanáin, Eiléan 1942- DLB-40	The 1989 Nobel Prize in Literature: Camilo José Cela Y-89	North Point Press DLB-46
Nicol, Eric 1919- DLB-68	The 1990 Nobel Prize in Literature: Octavio Paz Y-90	Nortje, Arthur 1942-1970 .... DLB-125
Nicolai, Friedrich 1733-1811 .... DLB-97	The 1991 Nobel Prize in Literature: Nadine Gordimer Y-91	Norton, Alice Mary (see Norton, Andre)
Nicolas de Clamanges circa 1363-1437 .... DLB-208	The 1992 Nobel Prize in Literature: Derek Walcott Y-92	Norton, Andre 1912- DLB-8, 52
Nicolay, John G. 1832-1901 and Hay, John 1838-1905 .... DLB-47	The 1993 Nobel Prize in Literature: Toni Morrison Y-93	Norton, Andrews 1786-1853 .... DLB-1, 235
Nicolson, Adela Florence Cory (see Hope, Laurence)	The 1994 Nobel Prize in Literature: Kenzaburō Ōe Y-94	Norton, Caroline 1808-1877 .... DLB-21, 159, 199
Nicolson, Harold 1886-1968 .... DLB-100, 149	The 1995 Nobel Prize in Literature: Seamus Heaney Y-95	Norton, Charles Eliot 1827-1908 .... DLB-1, 64, 235
Nicolson, Harold, "The Practice of Biography," in *The English Sense of Humour and Other Essays* DLB-149	The 1996 Nobel Prize in Literature: Wisława Szymborska Y-96	Norton, John 1606-1663 .... DLB-24
Nicolson, Nigel 1917- DLB-155	The 1997 Nobel Prize in Literature: Dario Fo Y-97	Norton, Mary 1903-1992 .... DLB-160
Niebuhr, Reinhold 1892-1971 .... DLB-17; DS-17	The 1998 Nobel Prize in Literature: José Saramago Y-98	Norton, Thomas (see Sackville, Thomas)
Niedecker, Lorine 1903-1970 .... DLB-48	The 1999 Nobel Prize in Literature: Günter Grass Y-99	Norton, W. W., and Company DLB-46
Nieman, Lucius W. 1857-1935 .... DLB-25	The 2000 Nobel Prize in Literature: Gao Xingjian Y-00	Norwood, Robert 1874-1932 .... DLB-92
Nietzsche, Friedrich 1844-1900 .... DLB-129; CDWLB-2	The 2001 Nobel Prize in Literature: V. S. Naipaul Y-01	Nosaka Akiyuki 1930- DLB-182
Nievo, Stanislao 1928- DLB-196	Nodier, Charles 1780-1844 .... DLB-119	Nossack, Hans Erich 1901-1977 .... DLB-69
Niggli, Josefina 1910- Y-80	Noël, Marie 1883-1967 .... DLB-258	Not Immediately Discernible . . . but Eventually Quite Clear: The *First Light* and *Final Years* of Hemingway's Centenary Y-99
Nightingale, Florence 1820-1910 .... DLB-166	Noel, Roden 1834-1894 .... DLB-35	A Note on Technique (1926), by Elizabeth A. Drew [excerpts] DLB-36
Nijō, Lady (Nakano-in Masatada no Musume) 1258-after 1306 .... DLB-203	Nogami, Yaeko 1885-1985 .... DLB-180	Notes from the Underground of *Sister Carrie* Y-01
Nijō Yoshimoto 1320-1388 .... DLB-203	Nogo, Rajko Petrov 1945- DLB-181	Notker Balbulus circa 840-912 .... DLB-148
Nikolev, Nikolai Petrovich 1758-1815 .... DLB-150	Nolan, William F. 1928- DLB-8	Notker III of Saint Gall circa 950-1022 .... DLB-148
Niles, Hezekiah 1777-1839 .... DLB-43	Noland, C. F. M. 1810?-1858 .... DLB-11	Notker von Zweifalten ?-1095 .... DLB-148
Nims, John Frederick 1913-1999 .... DLB-5	Noma Hiroshi 1915-1991 .... DLB-182	Nourse, Alan E. 1928- DLB-8
Nin, Anaïs 1903-1977 .... DLB-2, 4, 152	Nonesuch Press DLB-112	Novak, Slobodan 1924- DLB-181
1985: The Year of the Mystery: A Symposium Y-85	Noonan, Robert Phillipe (see Tressell, Robert)	Novak, Vjenceslav 1859-1905 .... DLB-147
The 1997 Booker Prize Y-97		Novakovich, Josip 1956- DLB-244
The 1998 Booker Prize Y-98		Novalis 1772-1801 .... DLB-90; CDWLB-2
Niño, Raúl 1961- DLB-209		Novaro, Mario 1868-1944 .... DLB-114
Nissenson, Hugh 1933- DLB-28		Novás Calvo, Lino 1903-1983 .... DLB-145
Niven, Frederick John 1878-1944 .... DLB-92		"The Novel in [Robert Browning's] 'The Ring and the Book'" (1912), by Henry James DLB-32
Niven, Larry 1938- DLB-8		The Novel of Impressionism, by Jethro Bithell DLB-66
Nixon, Howard M. 1909-1983 .... DLB-201		Novel-Reading: *The Works of Charles Dickens, The Works of*
Nizan, Paul 1905-1940 .... DLB-72		

W. Makepeace Thackeray (1879), by Anthony Trollope........DLB-21

Novels for Grown-Ups Y-97

The Novels of Dorothy Richardson (1918), by May Sinclair DLB-36

Novels with a Purpose (1864), by Justin M'Carthy DLB-21

Noventa, Giacomo 1898-1960..........DLB-114

Novikov, Nikolai Ivanovich 1744-1818 ....DLB-150

Novomeský, Laco 1904-1976..........DLB-215

Nowlan, Alden 1933-1983..............DLB-53

Noyes, Alfred 1880-1958...............DLB-20

Noyes, Crosby S. 1825-1908............DLB-23

Noyes, Nicholas 1647-1717.............DLB-24

Noyes, Theodore W. 1858-1946........DLB-29

N-Town Plays circa 1468 to early sixteenth century DLB-146

Nugent, Frank 1908-1965 ....DLB-44

Nugent, Richard Bruce 1906- DLB-151

Nušić, Branislav 1864-1938 . . DLB-147; CDWLB-4

Nutt, David [publishing house] DLB-106

Nwapa, Flora 1931-1993 ....DLB-125; CDWLB-3

Nye, Bill 1850-1896....................DLB-186

Nye, Edgar Wilson (Bill) 1850-1896 ....DLB-11, 23

Nye, Naomi Shihab 1952- DLB-120

Nye, Robert 1939- DLB-14

Nyka-Niliūnas, Alfonsas 1919- DLB-220

O

Oakes Smith, Elizabeth 1806-1893 ....DLB-1, 239, 243

Oakes, Urian circa 1631-1681 ....DLB-24

Oakley, Violet 1874-1961 ....DLB-188

Oates, Joyce Carol 1938- ... DLB-2, 5, 130; Y-81

Ōba Minako 1930- DLB-182

Ober, Frederick Albion 1849-1913 ......DLB-189

Ober, William 1920-1993 .... Y-93

Oberholtzer, Ellis Paxson 1868-1936......DLB-47

Obradović, Dositej 1740?-1811 ....DLB-147

O'Brien, Charlotte Grace 1845-1909.....DLB-240

O'Brien, Edna 1932- ...DLB-14, 231; CDBLB-8

O'Brien, Fitz-James 1828-1862...........DLB-74

O'Brien, Flann (see O'Nolan, Brian)

O'Brien, Kate 1897-1974 ....DLB-15

O'Brien, Tim 1946- DLB-152; Y-80; DS-9; CDALB-7

O'Casey, Sean 1880-1964 .....DLB-10; CDBLB-6

Occom, Samson 1723-1792 ....DLB-175

Ochs, Adolph S. 1858-1935.............DLB-25

Ochs-Oakes, George Washington 1861-1931 ....DLB-137

O'Connor, Flannery 1925-1964 ....DLB-2, 152; Y-80; DS-12; CDALB-1

O'Connor, Frank 1903-1966 ....DLB-162

Octopus Publishing Group DLB-112

Oda Sakunosuke 1913-1947 ....DLB-182

Odell, Jonathan 1737-1818..........DLB-31, 99

O'Dell, Scott 1903-1989................DLB-52

Odets, Clifford 1906-1963 .... DLB-7, 26

Odhams Press Limited................DLB-112

Odoevsky, Aleksandr Ivanovich 1802-1839..................DLB-205

Odoevsky, Vladimir Fedorovich 1804 or 1803-1869 ....DLB-198

O'Donnell, Peter 1920- DLB-87

O'Donovan, Michael (see O'Connor, Frank)

O'Dowd, Bernard 1866-1953 ....DLB-230

Ōe Kenzaburō 1935- DLB-182; Y-94

O'Faolain, Julia 1932- DLB-14, 231

O'Faolain, Sean 1900- DLB-15, 162

Off Broadway and Off-Off Broadway......DLB-7

Off-Loop Theatres.....................DLB-7

Offord, Carl Ruthven 1910- DLB-76

O'Flaherty, Liam 1896-1984 . . . DLB-36, 162; Y-84

Ogilvie, J. S., and Company DLB-49

Ogilvy, Eliza 1822-1912................DLB-199

Ogot, Grace 1930- DLB-125

O'Grady, Desmond 1935- DLB-40

Ogunyemi, Wale 1939- DLB-157

O'Hagan, Howard 1902-1982 ....DLB-68

O'Hara, Frank 1926-1966 .... DLB-5, 16, 193

O'Hara, John 1905-1970 ....DLB-9, 86; DS-2; CDALB-5

John O'Hara's Pottsville Journalism Y-88

O'Hegarty, P. S. 1879-1955 ....DLB-201

Okara, Gabriel 1921- DLB-125; CDWLB-3

O'Keeffe, John 1747-1833...............DLB-89

Okes, Nicholas [publishing house]....... DLB-170

Okigbo, Christopher 1930-1967 .... DLB-125; CDWLB-3

Okot p'Bitek 1931-1982...... DLB-125; CDWLB-3

Okpewho, Isidore 1941- DLB-157

Okri, Ben 1959- DLB-157, 231

Olaudah Equiano and Unfinished Journeys: The Slave-Narrative Tradition and Twentieth-Century Continuities, by Paul Edwards and Pauline T. Wangman......................DLB-117

Old English Literature: An Introduction DLB-146

Old English Riddles eighth to tenth centuries DLB-146

Old Franklin Publishing House..........DLB-49

Old German Genesis and *Old German Exodus* circa 1050-circa 1130..............DLB-148

Old High German Charms and Blessings DLB-148; CDWLB-2

The *Old High German Isidor* circa 790-800 ....DLB-148

The Old Manse DLB-223

Older, Fremont 1856-1935 ....DLB-25

Oldham, John 1653-1683...............DLB-131

Oldman, C. B. 1894-1969 ....DLB-201

Olds, Sharon 1942- DLB-120

Olearius, Adam 1599-1671 ....DLB-164

O'Leary, Ellen 1831-1889 ....DLB-240

Oliphant, Laurence 1829?-1888.......DLB-18, 166

Oliphant, Margaret 1828-1897... DLB-18, 159, 190

Oliver, Chad 1928- DLB-8

Oliver, Mary 1935- DLB-5, 193

Ollier, Claude 1922- DLB-83

Olsen, Tillie 1912 or 1913-
...........DLB-28, 206; Y-80; CDALB-7

Olson, Charles 1910-1970 .... DLB-5, 16, 193

Olson, Elder 1909- DLB-48, 63

Omotoso, Kole 1943- DLB-125

Omulevsky, Innokentii Vasil'evich 1836 [or 1837]-1883 ....DLB-238

On Learning to Write Y-88

Ondaatje, Michael 1943- DLB-60

O'Neill, Eugene 1888-1953 .....DLB-7; CDALB-5

Eugene O'Neill Memorial Theater Center DLB-7

Eugene O'Neill's Letters: A Review Y-88

Onetti, Juan Carlos 1909-1994 .... DLB-113; CDWLB-3

Onions, George Oliver 1872-1961.......DLB-153

Onofri, Arturo 1885-1928 ....DLB-114

O'Nolan, Brian 1911-1966.............DLB-231

Opie, Amelia 1769-1853...........DLB-116, 159

Opitz, Martin 1597-1639 ....DLB-164

Oppen, George 1908-1984...........DLB-5, 165

Oppenheim, E. Phillips 1866-1946 ......DLB-70

Oppenheim, James 1882-1932...........DLB-28

Oppenheimer, Joel 1930-1988........DLB-5, 193

Optic, Oliver (see Adams, William Taylor)

Oral History: B. W. Huebsch Y-99

Oral History Interview with Donald S. Klopfer Y-97

Orczy, Emma, Baroness 1865-1947.......DLB-70

Oregon Shakespeare Festival............. Y-00

Origo, Iris 1902-1988.................DLB-155

Orlovitz, Gil 1918-1973 ....DLB-2, 5

Orlovsky, Peter 1933- DLB-16

Ormond, John 1923- DLB-27

Ornitz, Samuel 1890-1957 ....DLB-28, 44

O'Rourke, P. J. 1947- DLB-185

Orten, Jiří 1919-1941 ....DLB-215

Ortese, Anna Maria 1914- DLB-177

Ortiz, Simon J. 1941- DLB-120, 175, 256

Ortnit and *Wolfdietrich* circa 1225-1250 ....DLB-138

Orton, Joe 1933-1967 ....DLB-13; CDBLB-8

Orwell, George (Eric Arthur Blair) 1903-1950 ...DLB-15, 98, 195, 255; CDBLB-7

The Orwell Year Y-84

(Re-)Publishing Orwell Y-86

Ory, Carlos Edmundo de 1923- DLB-134

Osbey, Brenda Marie 1957- DLB-120

Osbon, B. S. 1827-1912................DLB-43
Osborn, Sarah 1714-1796............DLB-200
Osborne, John 1929-1994.....DLB-13; CDBLB-7
Osgood, Frances Sargent 1811-1850.....DLB-250
Osgood, Herbert L. 1855-1918.........DLB-47
Osgood, James R., and Company.......DLB-49
Osgood, McIlvaine and Company......DLB-112
O'Shaughnessy, Arthur 1844-1881.......DLB-35
O'Shea, Patrick [publishing house].....DLB-49
Osipov, Nikolai Petrovich
  1751-1799.....................DLB-150
Oskison, John Milton 1879-1947........DLB-175
Osler, Sir William 1849-1919..........DLB-184
Osofisan, Femi 1946-.....DLB-125; CDWLB-3
Ostenso, Martha 1900-1963............DLB-92
Ostrauskas, Kostas 1926-.............DLB-232
Ostriker, Alicia 1937-................DLB-120
Osundare, Niyi 1947-.....DLB-157; CDWLB-3
Oswald, Eleazer 1755-1795............DLB-43
Oswald von Wolkenstein
  1376 or 1377-1445.............DLB-179
Otero, Blas de 1916-1979.............DLB-134
Otero, Miguel Antonio 1859-1944.......DLB-82
Otero, Nina 1881-1965................DLB-209
Otero Silva, Miguel 1908-1985..........DLB-145
Otfried von Weißenburg
  circa 800-circa 875?.............DLB-148
Otis, Broaders and Company...........DLB-49
Otis, James (see Kaler, James Otis)
Otis, James, Jr. 1725-1783..............DLB-31
Ottaway, James 1911-...............DLB-127
Ottendorfer, Oswald 1826-1900........DLB-23
Ottieri, Ottiero 1924-.................DLB-177
Otto-Peters, Louise 1819-1895.........DLB-129
Otway, Thomas 1652-1685.............DLB-80
Ouellette, Fernand 1930-..............DLB-60
Ouida 1839-1908................DLB-18, 156
Outing Publishing Company...........DLB-46
Outlaw Days, by Joyce Johnson........DLB-16
Overbury, Sir Thomas
  circa 1581-1613.................DLB-151
The Overlook Press...................DLB-46
Overview of U.S. Book Publishing,
  1910-1945........................DLB-9
Ovid 43 B.C.-A.D. 17......DLB-211; CDWLB-1
Owen, Guy 1925-....................DLB-5
Owen, John 1564-1622...............DLB-121
Owen, John [publishing house].........DLB-49
Owen, Peter, Limited.................DLB-112
Owen, Robert 1771-1858........DLB-107, 158
Owen, Wilfred
  1893-1918.......DLB-20, DS-18; CDBLB-6
The Owl and the Nightingale
  circa 1189-1199.................DLB-146
Owsley, Frank L. 1890-1956............DLB-17
Oxford, Seventeenth Earl of, Edward
  de Vere 1550-1604................DLB-172

OyamO (Charles F. Gordon) 1943-....DLB-266
Ozerov, Vladislav Aleksandrovich
  1769-1816......................DLB-150
Ozick, Cynthia 1928-.......DLB-28, 152; Y-83
First Strauss "Livings" Awarded to Cynthia
  Ozick and Raymond Carver
  An Interview with Cynthia Ozick.......Y-83

P

Pace, Richard 1482?-1536............DLB-167
Pacey, Desmond 1917-1975............DLB-88
Pack, Robert 1929-....................DLB-5
Packaging Papa: *The Garden of Eden*.........Y-86
Padell Publishing Company............DLB-46
Padgett, Ron 1942-....................DLB-5
Padilla, Ernesto Chávez 1944-.........DLB-122
Page, L. C., and Company.............DLB-49
Page, Louise 1955-..................DLB-233
Page, P. K. 1916-....................DLB-68
Page, Thomas Nelson
  1853-1922..............DLB-12, 78; DS-13
Page, Walter Hines 1855-1918......DLB-71, 91
Paget, Francis Edward 1806-1882......DLB-163
Paget, Violet (see Lee, Vernon)
Pagliarani, Elio 1927-................DLB-128
Pain, Barry 1864-1928............DLB-135, 197
Pain, Philip ?-circa 1666..............DLB-24
Paine, Robert Treat, Jr. 1773-1811......DLB-37
Paine, Thomas
  1737-1809....DLB-31, 43, 73, 158; CDALB-2
Painter, George D. 1914-............DLB-155
Painter, William 1540?-1594..........DLB-136
Palazzeschi, Aldo 1885-1974......DLB-114, 264
Paley, Grace 1922-..............DLB-28, 218
Paley, William 1743-1805.............DLB-251
Palfrey, John Gorham 1796-1881..DLB-1, 30, 235
Palgrave, Francis Turner 1824-1897......DLB-35
Palmer, Joe H. 1904-1952.............DLB-171
Palmer, Michael 1943-...............DLB-169
Palmer, Nettie 1885-1964.............DLB-260
Palmer, Vance 1885-1959.............DLB-260
Paltock, Robert 1697-1767............DLB-39
Paludan, Jacob 1896-1975............DLB-214
Pan Books Limited..................DLB-112
Panama, Norman 1914- and
  Frank, Melvin 1913-1988.........DLB-26
Panaev, Ivan Ivanovich 1812-1862......DLB-198
Panaeva, Avdot'ia Iakovlevna
  1820-1893.....................DLB-238
Pancake, Breece D'J 1952-1979........DLB-130
Panduro, Leif 1923-1977..............DLB-214
Panero, Leopoldo 1909-1962..........DLB-108
Pangborn, Edgar 1909-1976............DLB-8
"Panic Among the Philistines": A Postscript,
  An Interview with Bryan Griffin.......Y-81
Panizzi, Sir Anthony 1797-1879........DLB-184
Panneton, Philippe (see Ringuet)

Panshin, Alexei 1940-.................DLB-8
Pansy (see Alden, Isabella)
Pantheon Books.....................DLB-46
Papadat-Bengescu, Hortensia
  1876-1955......................DLB-220
Papantonio, Michael (see Kohn, John S. Van E.)
Paperback Library...................DLB-46
Paperback Science Fiction..............DLB-8
Papini, Giovanni 1881-1956...........DLB-264
Paquet, Alfons 1881-1944.............DLB-66
Paracelsus 1493-1541.................DLB-179
Paradis, Suzanne 1936-...............DLB-53
Páral, Vladimír, 1932-................DLB-232
Pardoe, Julia 1804-1862..............DLB-166
Paredes, Américo 1915-1999..........DLB-209
Pareja Diezcanseco, Alfredo 1908-1993..DLB-145
Parents' Magazine Press..............DLB-46
Parfit, Derek 1942-..................DLB-262
Parise, Goffredo 1929-1986...........DLB-177
Parisian Theater, Fall 1984: Toward
  A New Baroque..................Y-85
Parish, Mitchell 1900-1993...........DLB-265
Parizeau, Alice 1930-.................DLB-60
Park, Ruth 1923-...................DLB-260
Parke, John 1754-1789................DLB-31
Parker, Dan 1893-1967...............DLB-241
Parker, Dorothy 1893-1967......DLB-11, 45, 86
Parker, Gilbert 1860-1932.............DLB-99
Parker, J. H. [publishing house].......DLB-106
Parker, James 1714-1770..............DLB-43
Parker, John [publishing house].......DLB-106
Parker, Matthew 1504-1575...........DLB-213
Parker, Stewart 1941-1988............DLB-245
Parker, Theodore 1810-1860.......DLB-1, 235
Parker, William Riley 1906-1968.......DLB-103
Parkes, Bessie Rayner (Madame Belloc)
  1829-1925.....................DLB-240
Parkman, Francis
  1823-1893........DLB-1, 30, 183, 186, 235
Parks, Gordon 1912-.................DLB-33
Parks, Tim 1954-...................DLB-231
Parks, William 1698-1750..............DLB-43
Parks, William [publishing house].......DLB-49
Parley, Peter (see Goodrich, Samuel Griswold)
Parmenides
  late sixth-fifth century B.C.........DLB-176
Parnell, Thomas 1679-1718...........DLB-95
Parnicki, Teodor 1908-1988...........DLB-215
Parr, Catherine 1513?-1548...........DLB-136
Parrington, Vernon L. 1871-1929.....DLB-17, 63
Parrish, Maxfield 1870-1966..........DLB-188
Parronchi, Alessandro 1914-..........DLB-128
Parton, James 1822-1891..............DLB-30
Parton, Sara Payson Willis
  1811-1872................DLB-43, 74, 239
Partridge, S. W., and Company........DLB-106

Parun, Vesna 1922- DLB-181; CDWLB-4
Pasinetti, Pier Maria 1913- DLB-177
Pasolini, Pier Paolo 1922- DLB-128, 177
Pastan, Linda 1932- DLB-5
Paston, George (Emily Morse Symonds)
  1860-1936.................DLB-149, 197
The Paston Letters 1422-1509 ....DLB-146
Pastorius, Francis Daniel
  1651-circa 1720 ....DLB-24
Patchen, Kenneth 1911-1972 ....DLB-16, 48
Pater, Walter
  1839-1894.........DLB-57, 156; CDBLB-4
  Aesthetic Poetry (1873) DLB-35
Paterson, A. B. "Banjo" 1864-1941 ......DLB-230
Paterson, Katherine 1932- DLB-52
Patmore, Coventry 1823-1896........DLB-35, 98
Paton, Alan 1903-1988..................DS-17
Paton, Joseph Noel 1821-1901..........DLB-35
Paton Walsh, Jill 1937- DLB-161
Patrick, Edwin Hill ("Ted") 1901-1964...DLB-137
Patrick, John 1906-1995................DLB-7
Pattee, Fred Lewis 1863-1950 ....DLB-71
Pattern and Paradigm: History as
  Design, by Judith Ryan.............DLB-75
Patterson, Alicia 1906-1963 ....DLB-127
Patterson, Eleanor Medill 1881-1948......DLB-29
Patterson, Eugene 1923- DLB-127
Patterson, Joseph Medill 1879-1946......DLB-29
Pattillo, Henry 1726-1801 ....DLB-37
Paul, Elliot 1891-1958 ....DLB-4
Paul, Jean (see Richter, Johann Paul Friedrich)
Paul, Kegan, Trench, Trubner and
  Company Limited................DLB-106
Paul, Peter, Book Company DLB-49
Paul, Stanley, and Company Limited DLB-112
Paulding, James Kirke
  1778-1860 ....DLB-3, 59, 74, 250
Paulin, Tom 1949- DLB-40
Pauper, Peter, Press DLB-46
Pavese, Cesare 1908-1950 ....DLB-128, 177
Pavić, Milorad 1929- DLB-181; CDWLB-4
Pavlov, Konstantin 1933- DLB-181
Pavlov, Nikolai Filippovich 1803-1864.....DLB-198
Pavlova, Karolina Karlovna 1807-1893 ....DLB-205
Pavlović, Miodrag
  1928- DLB-181; CDWLB-4
Paxton, John 1911-1985................DLB-44
Payn, James 1830-1898 ....DLB-18
Payne, John 1842-1916 ....DLB-35
Payne, John Howard 1791-1852 ....DLB-37
Payson and Clarke.....................DLB-46
Paz, Octavio 1914-1998 ....Y-90, Y-98
Pazzi, Roberto 1946- DLB-196
Pea, Enrico 1881-1958..................DLB-264
Peabody, Elizabeth Palmer 1804-1894..DLB-1, 223
Peabody, Elizabeth Palmer
  [publishing house]....................DLB-49

Peabody, Josephine Preston 1874-1922 ...DLB-249
Peabody, Oliver William Bourn
  1799-1848 ....DLB-59
Peace, Roger 1899-1968 ....DLB-127
Peacham, Henry 1578-1644?...........DLB-151
Peacham, Henry, the Elder
  1547-1634 ....DLB-172, 236
Peachtree Publishers, Limited DLB-46
Peacock, Molly 1947- DLB-120
Peacock, Thomas Love 1785-1866 ...DLB-96, 116
Pead, Deuel ?-1727....................DLB-24
Peake, Mervyn 1911-1968......DLB-15, 160, 255
Peale, Rembrandt 1778-1860 ....DLB-183
Pear Tree Press DLB-112
Pearce, Philippa 1920- DLB-161
Pearson, H. B. [publishing house] DLB-49
Pearson, Hesketh 1887-1964 ....DLB-149
Pechersky, Andrei (see Mel'nikov, Pavel Ivanovich)
Peck, George W. 1840-1916 ....DLB-23, 42
Peck, H. C., and Theo. Bliss
  [publishing house]..................DLB-49
Peck, Harry Thurston 1856-1914 .....DLB-71, 91
Peden, William 1913-1999.............DLB-234
Peele, George 1556-1596 ....DLB-62, 167
Pegler, Westbrook 1894-1969 ....DLB-171
Péguy, Charles Pierre 1873-1914........DLB-258
Pekić, Borislav 1930-1992 ...DLB-181; CDWLB-4
Pellegrini and Cudahy..................DLB-46
Pelletier, Aimé (see Vac, Bertrand)
Pelletier, Francine 1959- DLB-251
Pemberton, Sir Max 1863-1950 ....DLB-70
de la Peña, Terri 1947- DLB-209
Penfield, Edward 1866-1925 ....DLB-188
Penguin Books [U.K.] DLB-112
Penguin Books [U.S.]..................DLB-46
Penn Publishing Company DLB-49
Penn, William 1644-1718...............DLB-24
Penna, Sandro 1906-1977 ....DLB-114
Pennell, Joseph 1857-1926 ... .DLB-188
Penner, Jonathan 1940- Y-83
Pennington, Lee 1939- Y-82
Penton, Brian 1904-1951 ....DLB-260
Pepys, Samuel
  1633-1703 ....DLB-101, 213; CDBLB-2
Percy, Thomas 1729-1811 ....DLB-104
Percy, Walker 1916-1990 .....DLB-2; Y-80, Y-90
Percy, William 1575-1648 ....DLB-172
Perec, Georges 1936-1982 ....DLB-83
Perelman, Bob 1947- DLB-193
Perelman, S. J. 1904-1979............DLB-11, 44
Perez, Raymundo "Tigre" 1946- DLB-122
Peri Rossi, Cristina 1941- DLB-145
Perkins, Eugene 1932- DLB-41
Perkoff, Stuart Z. 1930-1974 ....DLB-16
Perley, Moses Henry 1804-1862 ....DLB-99

Permabooks.........................DLB-46
Perovsky, Aleksei Alekseevich
  (Antonii Pogorel'sky) 1787-1836 .....DLB-198
Perri, Henry 1561-1617...............DLB-236
Perrin, Alice 1867-1934 ....DLB-156
Perry, Bliss 1860-1954..................DLB-71
Perry, Eleanor 1915-1981 ....DLB-44
Perry, Henry (see Perri, Henry)
Perry, Matthew 1794-1858..............DLB-183
Perry, Sampson 1747-1823.............DLB-158
Perse, Saint-John 1887-1975 ....DLB-258
Persius A.D. 34-A.D. 62 ....DLB-211
Perutz, Leo 1882-1957.................DLB-81
Pesetsky, Bette 1932- DLB-130
Pestalozzi, Johann Heinrich 1746-1827 ....DLB-94
Peter, Laurence J. 1919-1990...........DLB-53
Peter of Spain circa 1205-1277..........DLB-115
Peterkin, Julia 1880-1961................DLB-9
Peters, Lenrie 1932- DLB-117
Peters, Robert 1924- DLB-105
  "Foreword to *Ludwig of Baviria*".........DLB-105
Petersham, Maud 1889-1971 and
  Petersham, Miska 1888-1960 ....DLB-22
Peterson, Charles Jacobs 1819-1887 ......DLB-79
Peterson, Len 1917- DLB-88
Peterson, Levi S. 1933- DLB-206
Peterson, Louis 1922-1998 ....DLB-76
Peterson, T. B., and Brothers DLB-49
Petitclair, Pierre 1813-1860 ....DLB-99
Petrescu, Camil 1894-1957 ....DLB-220
Petronius circa A.D. 20-A.D. 66
  ....DLB-211; CDWLB-1
Petrov, Aleksandar 1938- DLB-181
Petrov, Gavriil 1730-1801 ....DLB-150
Petrov, Valeri 1920- DLB-181
Petrov, Vasilii Petrovich 1736-1799......DLB-150
Petrović, Rastko
  1898-1949............DLB-147; CDWLB-4
Petruslied circa 854? DLB-148
Petry, Ann 1908-1997 ....DLB-76
Pettie, George circa 1548-1589 ....DLB-136
Peyton, K. M. 1929- DLB-161
Pfaffe Konrad flourished circa 1172......DLB-148
Pfaffe Lamprecht flourished circa 1150...DLB-148
Pfeiffer, Emily 1827-1890.............DLB-199
Pforzheimer, Carl H. 1879-1957 ....DLB-140
Phaedrus circa 18 B.C.-circa A.D. 50 ....DLB-211
Phaer, Thomas 1510?-1560............DLB-167
Phaidon Press Limited.................DLB-112
Pharr, Robert Deane 1916-1992 ....DLB-33
Phelps, Elizabeth Stuart 1815-1852 .....DLB-202
Phelps, Elizabeth Stuart 1844-1911 ...DLB-74, 221
Philander von der Linde
  (see Mencke, Johann Burckhard)
Philby, H. St. John B. 1885-1960........DLB-195
Philip, Marlene Nourbese 1947- DLB-157

Cumulative Index

Philippe, Charles-Louis 1874-1909 . . . . DLB-65
Philips, John 1676-1708. . . . . DLB-95
Philips, Katherine 1632-1664 . . . . DLB-131
Phillipps, Sir Thomas 1792-1872. . . . . . . DLB-184
Phillips, Caryl 1958- DLB-157
Phillips, David Graham 1867-1911 . . . . . DLB-9, 12
Phillips, Jayne Anne 1952- Y-80
Phillips, Robert 1938- DLB-105
 "Finding, Losing, Reclaiming: A Note
  on My Poems" DLB-105
Phillips, Sampson and Company DLB-49
Phillips, Stephen 1864-1915 . . . . DLB-10
Phillips, Ulrich B. 1877-1934. . . . . DLB-17
Phillips, Wendell 1811-1884. . . . . DLB-235
Phillips, Willard 1784-1873 . . . . DLB-59
Phillips, William 1907- DLB-137
Phillpotts, Adelaide Eden (Adelaide Ross)
  1896-1993 . . . . DLB-191
Phillpotts, Eden 1862-1960. . . DLB-10, 70, 135, 153
Philo circa 20-15 B.C.-circa A.D. 50 . . . . . .DLB-176
Philosophical Library DLB-46
Phinney, Elihu [publishing house] DLB-49
Phoenix, John (see Derby, George Horatio)
PHYLON (Fourth Quarter, 1950),
  The Negro in Literature:
  The Current Scene. DLB-76
Physiologus circa 1070-circa 1150 . . . . DLB-148
Piccolo, Lucio 1903-1969 . . . . DLB-114
Pickard, Tom 1946- DLB-40
Pickering, William [publishing house] . . . DLB-106
Pickthall, Marjorie 1883-1922. . . . . DLB-92
Pictorial Printing Company DLB-49
Pielmeier, John 1949- DLB-266
Piercy, Marge 1936- DLB-120, 227
Pierro, Albino 1916- DLB-128
Pignotti, Lamberto 1926- DLB-128
Pike, Albert 1809-1891 . . . . DLB-74
Pike, Zebulon Montgomery
  1779-1813. DLB-183
Pillat, Ion 1891-1945. . . . . DLB-220
Pilon, Jean-Guy 1930- DLB-60
Pinckney, Eliza Lucas 1722-1793 . . . . . . DLB-200
Pinckney, Josephine 1895-1957 . . . . DLB-6
Pindar circa 518 B.C.-circa 438 B.C.
  . . . . DLB-176; CDWLB-1
Pindar, Peter (see Wolcot, John)
Pineda, Cecile 1942- DLB-209
Pinero, Arthur Wing 1855-1934. . . . . DLB-10
Piñero, Miguel 1946-1988 . . . . DLB-266
Pinget, Robert 1919-1997 . . . . DLB-83
Pinkney, Edward Coote 1802-1828 . . . . . DLB-248
Pinnacle Books DLB-46
Piñon, Nélida 1935- DLB-145
Pinsky, Robert 1940- Y-82
 Robert Pinsky Reappointed Poet Laureate. . . . Y-98
Pinter, Harold 1930- DLB-13; CDBLB-8

Piontek, Heinz 1925- DLB-75
Piozzi, Hester Lynch [Thrale]
  1741-1821. . . . . DLB-104, 142
Piper, H. Beam 1904-1964 . . . . DLB-8
Piper, Watty DLB-22
Pirandello, Luigi 1868-1936 . . . . DLB-264
Pirckheimer, Caritas 1467-1532 . . . . .DLB-179
Pirckheimer, Willibald 1470-1530 . . . . . .DLB-179
Pisar, Samuel 1929- Y-83
Pisemsky, Aleksei Feofilaktovich
  1821-1881 . . . . DLB-238
Pitkin, Timothy 1766-1847 . . . . DLB-30
The Pitt Poetry Series: Poetry Publishing
  Today Y-85
Pitter, Ruth 1897- DLB-20
Pix, Mary 1666-1709 . . . . DLB-80
Pixérécourt, René Charles Guilbert de
  1773-1844. DLB-192
Plaatje, Sol T. 1876-1932 . . . . DLB-125, 225
Plante, David 1940- Y-83
Platen, August von 1796-1835 . . . . DLB-90
Plath, Sylvia
  1932-1963 . . . . DLB-5, 6, 152; CDALB-1
Plato circa 428 B.C.-348-347 B.C.
  . . . . DLB-176; CDWLB-1
Plato, Ann 1824?-? DLB-239
Platon 1737-1812. . . . . DLB-150
Platt, Charles 1945- DLB-261
Platt and Munk Company DLB-46
Plautus circa 254 B.C.-184 B.C.
  . . . . DLB-211; CDWLB-1
Playboy Press DLB-46
Playford, John [publishing house]. DLB-170
Plays, Playwrights, and Playgoers DLB-84
Playwrights on the Theater DLB-80
Der Pleier flourished circa 1250 . . . . DLB-138
Pleijel, Agneta 1940- DLB-257
Plenzdorf, Ulrich 1934- DLB-75
Plessen, Elizabeth 1944- DLB-75
Pletnev, Petr Aleksandrovich
  1792-1865. DLB-205
Pliekšāne, Elza Rozenberga (see Aspazija)
Pliekšāns, Jānis (see Rainis, Jānis)
Plievier, Theodor 1892-1955 . . . . DLB-69
Plimpton, George 1927- DLB-185, 241; Y-99
Pliny the Elder A.D. 23/24-A.D. 79 . . . . . DLB-211
Pliny the Younger
  circa A.D. 61-A.D. 112 . . . . DLB-211
Plomer, William
  1903-1973. . . . . .DLB-20, 162, 191, 225
Plotinus 204-270 . . . . DLB-176; CDWLB-1
Plowright, Teresa 1952- DLB-251
Plume, Thomas 1630-1704. . . . . DLB-213
Plumly, Stanley 1939- DLB-5, 193
Plumpp, Sterling D. 1940- DLB-41
Plunkett, James 1920- DLB-14
Plutarch
  circa 46-circa 120 . . . . . . .DLB-176; CDWLB-1

Plymell, Charles 1935- DLB-16
Pocket Books DLB-46
Poe, Edgar Allan 1809-1849
  . . . . .DLB-3, 59, 73, 74, 248; CDALB-2
Poe, James 1921-1980. . . . . DLB-44
The Poet Laureate of the United States
  Statements from Former Consultants
  in Poetry Y-86
Pogodin, Mikhail Petrovich
  1800-1875. DLB-198
Pogorel'sky, Antonii
  (see Perovsky, Aleksei Alekseevich)
Pohl, Frederik 1919- DLB-8
Poirier, Louis (see Gracq, Julien)
Poláček, Karel 1892-1945. . . .DLB-215; CDWLB-4
Polanyi, Michael 1891-1976 . . . . DLB-100
Pole, Reginald 1500-1558. . . . . DLB-132
Polevoi, Nikolai Alekseevich
  1796-1846. DLB-198
Polezhaev, Aleksandr Ivanovich
  1804-1838 . . . . DLB-205
Poliakoff, Stephen 1952- DLB-13
Polidori, John William 1795-1821 . . . . . . DLB-116
Polite, Carlene Hatcher 1932- DLB-33
Pollard, Alfred W. 1859-1944 . . . . DLB-201
Pollard, Edward A. 1832-1872 . . . . DLB-30
Pollard, Graham 1903-1976 . . . . DLB-201
Pollard, Percival 1869-1911 . . . . DLB-71
Pollard and Moss DLB-49
Pollock, Sharon 1936- DLB-60
Polonsky, Abraham 1910-1999 . . . . DLB-26
Polotsky, Simeon 1629-1680 . . . . DLB-150
Polybius circa 200 B.C.-118 B.C.. . . . . . .DLB-176
Pomialovsky, Nikolai Gerasimovich
  1835-1863 . . . . DLB-238
Pomilio, Mario 1921-1990 . . . . .DLB-177
Ponce, Mary Helen 1938- DLB-122
Ponce-Montoya, Juanita 1949- DLB-122
Ponet, John 1516?-1556 . . . . DLB-132
Ponge, Francis 1899-1988. . . . . DLB-258
Poniatowski, Elena
  1933- DLB-113; CDWLB-3
Ponsard, François 1814-1867 . . . . DLB-192
Ponsonby, William [publishing house] DLB-170
Pontiggia, Giuseppe 1934- DLB-196
Pony Stories DLB-160
Poole, Ernest 1880-1950. . . . . DLB-9
Poole, Sophia 1804-1891 . . . . DLB-166
Poore, Benjamin Perley 1820-1887. . . . . . DLB-23
Popa, Vasko 1922-1991 . . . . .DLB-181; CDWLB-4
Pope, Abbie Hanscom 1858-1894 . . . . . . DLB-140
Pope, Alexander
  1688-1744. . . . . . . DLB-95, 101, 213; CDBLB-2
Popov, Mikhail Ivanovich
  1742-circa 1790. . . . . DLB-150
Popović, Aleksandar 1929-1996. . . . . DLB-181
Popper, Sir Karl R. 1902-1994 . . . . DLB-262
Popular Library DLB-46

376

Porete, Marguerite ?-1310 . . . . .DLB-208

Porlock, Martin (see MacDonald, Philip)

Porpoise Press DLB-112

Porta, Antonio 1935-1989 . . . . .DLB-128

Porter, Anna Maria 1780-1832. . . . . . DLB-116, 159

Porter, Cole 1891-1964 . . . . .DLB-265

Porter, David 1780-1843 . . . . .DLB-183

Porter, Eleanor H. 1868-1920 . . . . .DLB-9

Porter, Gene Stratton (see Stratton-Porter, Gene)

Porter, Hal 1911-1984 . . . . .DLB-260

Porter, Henry ?-? DLB-62

Porter, Jane 1776-1850 . . . . DLB-116, 159

Porter, Katherine Anne 1890-1980
. . . . . . DLB-4, 9, 102; Y-80; DS-12; CDALB-7

Porter, Peter 1929- DLB-40

Porter, William Sydney
1862-1910 . . . . .DLB-12, 78, 79; CDALB-3

Porter, William T. 1809-1858 . . . . .DLB-3, 43, 250

Porter and Coates .DLB-49

Portillo Trambley, Estela 1927-1998 . . . . .DLB-209

Portis, Charles 1933- DLB-6

Posey, Alexander 1873-1908 . . . . .DLB-175

Postans, Marianne circa 1810-1865 . . . . . .DLB-166

Postl, Carl (see Sealsfield, Carl)

Poston, Ted 1906-1974 . . . . .DLB-51

Potekhin, Aleksei Antipovich 1829-1908 . .DLB-238

Potok, Chaim 1929- DLB-28, 152

A Conversation with Chaim Potok Y-84

Potter, Beatrix 1866-1943 . . . . .DLB-141

Potter, David M. 1910-1971 . . . . .DLB-17

Potter, Dennis 1935-1994 . . . . .DLB-233

The Harry Potter Phenomenon Y-99

Potter, John E., and Company DLB-49

Pottle, Frederick A. 1897-1987 . . . . . DLB-103; Y-87

Poulin, Jacques 1937- DLB-60

Pound, Ezra 1885-1972
. . . . .DLB-4, 45, 63; DS-15; CDALB-4

Poverman, C. E. 1944- DLB-234

Povich, Shirley 1905-1998 . . . . .DLB-171

Powell, Anthony 1905-2000 . . .DLB-15; CDBLB-7

The Anthony Powell Society: Powell and
the First Biennial Conference Y-01

Dawn Powell, Where Have You Been All
Our Lives? Y-97

Powell, John Wesley 1834-1902 . . . . .DLB-186

Powell, Padgett 1952- DLB-234

Powers, J. F. 1917-1999 . . . . .DLB-130

Powers, Jimmy 1903-1995 . . . . .DLB-241

Pownall, David 1938- DLB-14

Powys, John Cowper 1872-1963 . . . . .DLB-15, 255

Powys, Llewelyn 1884-1939 . . . . .DLB-98

Powys, T. F. 1875-1953 . . . . .DLB-36, 162

Poynter, Nelson 1903-1978 . . . . .DLB-127

The Practice of Biography: An Interview
with Stanley Weintraub Y-82

The Practice of Biography II: An Interview
with B. L. Reid Y-83

The Practice of Biography III: An Interview
with Humphrey Carpenter Y-84

The Practice of Biography IV: An Interview with
William Manchester Y-85

The Practice of Biography VI: An Interview with
David Herbert Donald Y-87

The Practice of Biography VII: An Interview with
John Caldwell Guilds Y-92

The Practice of Biography VIII: An Interview
with Joan Mellen Y-94

The Practice of Biography IX: An Interview
with Michael Reynolds Y-95

Prados, Emilio 1899-1962 . . . . .DLB-134

Praed, Mrs. Caroline (see Praed, Rosa)

Praed, Rosa (Mrs. Caroline Praed)
1851-1935 .DLB-230

Praed, Winthrop Mackworth 1802-1839 . . .DLB-96

Praeger Publishers .DLB-46

Praetorius, Johannes 1630-1680 . . . . .DLB-168

Pratolini, Vasco 1913-1991 . . . . .DLB-177

Pratt, E. J. 1882-1964 . . . . .DLB-92

Pratt, Samuel Jackson 1749-1814 . . . . .DLB-39

Preciado Martin, Patricia 1939- DLB-209

Preface to The History of Romances (1715), by
Pierre Daniel Huet [excerpts] DLB-39

Préfontaine, Yves 1937- DLB-53

Prelutsky, Jack 1940- DLB-61

Premisses, by Michael Hamburger DLB-66

Prentice, George D. 1802-1870 . . . . .DLB-43

Prentice-Hall DLB-46

Prescott, Orville 1906-1996 . . . . Y-96

Prescott, William Hickling
1796-1859 . . . . .DLB-1, 30, 59, 235

The Present State of the English Novel (1892),
by George Saintsbury DLB-18

Preseren, France
1800-1849 . . . . .DLB-147; CDWLB-4

Preston, Margaret Junkin
1820-1897 . . . . .DLB-239, 248

Preston, May Wilson 1873-1949 . . . . .DLB-188

Preston, Thomas 1537-1598 . . . . .DLB-62

Prévert, Jacques 1900-1977 . . . . .DLB-258

Prichard, Katharine Susannah
1883-1969 .DLB-260

Price, Reynolds 1933- DLB-2, 218

Price, Richard 1723-1791 . . . . .DLB-158

Price, Richard 1949- Y-81

Prideaux, John 1578-1650 . . . . .DLB-236

Priest, Christopher 1943- DLB-14, 207, 261

Priestley, J. B. 1894-1984
. . . DLB-10, 34, 77, 100, 139; Y-84; CDBLB-6

Priestley, Joseph 1733-1804 . . . . .DLB-252

Primary Bibliography: A Retrospective Y-95

Prime, Benjamin Young 1733-1791 . . . . . . .DLB-31

Primrose, Diana floruit circa 1630 . . . . . . .DLB-126

Prince, F. T. 1912- DLB-20

Prince, Nancy Gardner 1799-? DLB-239

Prince, Thomas 1687-1758 . . . . .DLB-24, 140

Pringle, Thomas 1789-1834 . . . . .DLB-225

Printz, Wolfgang Casper 1641-1717 . . . . . .DLB-168

Prior, Matthew 1664-1721 . . . . .DLB-95

Prisco, Michele 1920- DLB-177

Pritchard, William H. 1932- DLB-111

Pritchett, V. S. 1900-1997 . . . . .DLB-15, 139

Probyn, May 1856 or 1857-1909 . . . . .DLB-199

Procter, Adelaide Anne 1825-1864 . . .DLB-32, 199

Procter, Bryan Waller 1787-1874 . . . . .DLB-96, 144

Proctor, Robert 1868-1903 . . . . .DLB-184

Producing Dear Bunny, Dear Volodya: The Friendship
and the Feud Y-97

The Profession of Authorship:
Scribblers for Bread Y-89

Prokopovich, Feofan 1681?-1736 . . . . .DLB-150

Prokosch, Frederic 1906-1989 . . . . .DLB-48

The Proletarian Novel DLB-9

Pronzini, Bill 1943- DLB-226

Propertius circa 50 B.C.-post 16 B.C.
. . . . .DLB-211; CDWLB-1

Propper, Dan 1937- DLB-16

Prose, Francine 1947- DLB-234

Protagoras circa 490 B.C.-420 B.C. DLB-176

Proud, Robert 1728-1813 . . . . .DLB-30

Proust, Marcel 1871-1922 . . . . .DLB-65

Prynne, J. H. 1936- DLB-40

Przybyszewski, Stanislaw 1868-1927 . . . . . .DLB-66

Pseudo-Dionysius the Areopagite floruit
circa 500 . . . . .DLB-115

Public Domain and the Violation of Texts Y-97

The Public Lending Right in America Statement by
Sen. Charles McC. Mathias, Jr. PLR and the
Meaning of Literary Property Statements on
PLR by American Writers Y-83

The Public Lending Right in the United Kingdom
Public Lending Right: The First Year in the
United Kingdom Y-83

The Publication of English
Renaissance Plays DLB-62

Publications and Social Movements
[Transcendentalism] DLB-1

Publishers and Agents: The Columbia
Connection Y-87

Publishing Fiction at LSU Press Y-87

The Publishing Industry in 1998:
Sturm-und-drang.com Y-98

The Publishing Industry in 1999 . . . . Y-99

Pückler-Muskau, Hermann von
1785-1871 . . . . .DLB-133

Pufendorf, Samuel von 1632-1694 . . . . . . .DLB-168

Pugh, Edwin William 1874-1930 . . . . .DLB-135

Pugin, A. Welby 1812-1852 . . . . .DLB-55

Puig, Manuel 1932-1990 . . . . .DLB-113; CDWLB-3

Pulitzer, Joseph 1847-1911 . . . . .DLB-23

Pulitzer, Joseph, Jr. 1885-1955 . . . . .DLB-29

Pulitzer Prizes for the Novel,
1917-1945 . . . . .DLB-9

Pulliam, Eugene 1889-1975 . . . . .DLB-127

Cumulative Index

Purchas, Samuel 1577?-1626 . . . . DLB-151

Purdy, Al 1918-2000 . . . . DLB-88

Purdy, James 1923- DLB-2, 218

Purdy, Ken W. 1913-1972 . . . . DLB-137

Pusey, Edward Bouverie 1800-1882 . . . . . . DLB-55

Pushkin, Aleksandr Sergeevich
1799-1837 . . . . DLB-205

Pushkin, Vasilii L'vovich
1766-1830 . . . . DLB-205

Putnam, George Palmer
1814-1872 . . . . DLB-3, 79, 250, 254

G. P. Putnam [publishing house] DLB-254

G. P. Putnam's Sons [U.K.] DLB-106

G. P. Putnam's Sons [U.S.] DLB-49

A Publisher's Archives: G. P. Putnam Y-92

Putnam, Samuel 1892-1950 . . . . DLB-4

Puzo, Mario 1920-1999 . . . . DLB-6

Pyle, Ernie 1900-1945 . . . . DLB-29

Pyle, Howard
1853-1911 . . . . DLB-42, 188; DS-13

Pym, Barbara 1913-1980 . . . . . DLB-14, 207; Y-87

Pynchon, Thomas 1937- DLB-2, 173

Pyramid Books DLB-46

Pyrnelle, Louise-Clarke 1850-1907 . . . . . . DLB-42

Pythagoras circa 570 B.C.-? DLB-176

Q

Quad, M. (see Lewis, Charles B.)

Quaritch, Bernard 1819-1899 . . . . DLB-184

Quarles, Francis 1592-1644 . . . . DLB-126

The Quarterly Review 1809-1967 . . . . . . DLB-110

Quasimodo, Salvatore 1901-1968 . . . . . . DLB-114

Queen, Ellery (see Dannay, Frederic, and
Manfred B. Lee)

Queen, Frank 1822-1882 . . . . DLB-241

The Queen City Publishing House DLB-49

Queneau, Raymond 1903-1976 . . . . . DLB-72, 258

Quennell, Sir Peter 1905-1993 . . . . . DLB-155, 195

Quesnel, Joseph 1746-1809 . . . . DLB-99

The Question of American Copyright
in the Nineteenth Century
Preface, by George Haven Putnam
The Evolution of Copyright, by
Brander Matthews
Summary of Copyright Legislation in
the United States, by R. R. Bowker
Analysis of the Provisions of the
Copyright Law of 1891, by
George Haven Putnam
The Contest for International Copyright,
by George Haven Putnam
Cheap Books and Good Books,
by Brander Matthews DLB-49

Quiller-Couch, Sir Arthur Thomas
1863-1944 . . . . DLB-135, 153, 190

Quin, Ann 1936-1973 . . . . DLB-14, 231

Quincy, Samuel, of Georgia ?-? DLB-31

Quincy, Samuel, of Massachusetts
1734-1789 . . . . DLB-31

Quinn, Anthony 1915- DLB-122

The Quinn Draft of James Joyce's
Circe Manuscript Y-00

Quinn, John 1870-1924 . . . . DLB-187

Quiñónez, Naomi 1951- DLB-209

Quintana, Leroy V. 1944- DLB-82

Quintana, Miguel de 1671-1748
A Forerunner of Chicano Literature . DLB-122

Quintillian
circa A.D. 40-circa A.D. 96 . . . . DLB-211

Quintus Curtius Rufus fl. A.D. 35 . . . . . . DLB-211

Quist, Harlin, Books DLB-46

Quoirez, Françoise (see Sagan, Françoise)

R

R-va, Zeneida (see Gan, Elena Andreevna)

Raabe, Wilhelm 1831-1910 . . . . DLB-129

Raban, Jonathan 1942- DLB-204

Rabe, David 1940- DLB-7, 228

Raboni, Giovanni 1932- DLB-128

Rachilde 1860-1953 . . . . DLB-123, 192

Racin, Kočo 1908-1943 . . . . DLB-147

Rackham, Arthur 1867-1939 . . . . DLB-141

Radauskas, Henrikas
1910-1970 . . . . DLB-220; CDWLB-4

Radcliffe, Ann 1764-1823 . . . . DLB-39, 178

Raddall, Thomas 1903-1994 . . . . DLB-68

Radford, Dollie 1858-1920 . . . . DLB-240

Radichkov, Yordan 1929- DLB-181

Radiguet, Raymond 1903-1923 . . . . DLB-65

Radishchev, Aleksandr Nikolaevich
1749-1802 . . . . DLB-150

Radnóti, Miklós
1909-1944 . . . . DLB-215; CDWLB-4

Radványi, Netty Reiling (see Seghers, Anna)

Rahv, Philip 1908-1973 . . . . DLB-137

Raich, Semen Egorovich 1792-1855 . . . . . DLB-205

Raičković, Stevan 1928- DLB-181

Raimund, Ferdinand Jakob 1790-1836 . . . . DLB-90

Raine, Craig 1944- DLB-40

Raine, Kathleen 1908- DLB-20

Rainis, Jānis 1865-1929 . . . . . DLB-220; CDWLB-4

Rainolde, Richard
circa 1530-1606 . . . . DLB-136, 236

Rakić, Milan 1876-1938 . . . . . DLB-147; CDWLB-4

Rakosi, Carl 1903- DLB-193

Ralegh, Sir Walter
1554?-1618 . . . . DLB-172; CDBLB-1

Ralin, Radoy 1923- DLB-181

Ralph, Julian 1853-1903 . . . . DLB-23

Ramat, Silvio 1939- DLB-128

Rambler, no. 4 (1750), by Samuel Johnson
[excerpt] DLB-39

Ramée, Marie Louise de la (see Ouida)

Ramírez, Sergío 1942- DLB-145

Ramke, Bin 1947- DLB-120

Ramler, Karl Wilhelm 1725-1798 . . . . DLB-97

Ramon Ribeyro, Julio 1929- DLB-145

Ramos, Manuel 1948- DLB-209

Ramous, Mario 1924- DLB-128

Rampersad, Arnold 1941- DLB-111

Ramsay, Allan 1684 or 1685-1758 . . . . DLB-95

Ramsay, David 1749-1815 . . . . DLB-30

Ramsay, Martha Laurens 1759-1811 . . . . DLB-200

Ramsey, Frank P. 1903-1930 . . . . DLB-262

Ranck, Katherine Quintana 1942- DLB-122

Rand, Avery and Company DLB-49

Rand, Ayn 1905-1982 . . . . DLB-227; CDALB-7

Rand McNally and Company DLB-49

Randall, David Anton 1905-1975 . . . . DLB-140

Randall, Dudley 1914- DLB-41

Randall, Henry S. 1811-1876 . . . . DLB-30

Randall, James G. 1881-1953 . . . . DLB-17

The Randall Jarrell Symposium:
A Small Collection of Randall Jarrells
Excerpts From Papers Delivered at the
Randall Jarrel Symposium Y-86

Randolph, A. Philip 1889-1979 . . . . DLB-91

Randolph, Anson D. F.
[publishing house] DLB-49

Randolph, Thomas 1605-1635 . . . . . . DLB-58, 126

Random House DLB-46

Ranlet, Henry [publishing house] DLB-49

Ransom, Harry 1908-1976 . . . . DLB-187

Ransom, John Crowe
1888-1974 . . . . DLB-45, 63; CDALB-7

Ransome, Arthur 1884-1967 . . . . DLB-160

Raphael, Frederic 1931- DLB-14

Raphaelson, Samson 1896-1983 . . . . DLB-44

Rashi circa 1040-1105 . . . . DLB-208

Raskin, Ellen 1928-1984 . . . . DLB-52

Rastell, John 1475?-1536 . . . . DLB-136, 170

Rattigan, Terence
1911-1977 . . . . DLB-13; CDBLB-7

Rawlings, Marjorie Kinnan 1896-1953
. . . . DLB-9, 22, 102; DS-17; CDALB-7

Rawlinson, Richard 1690-1755 . . . . DLB-213

Rawlinson, Thomas 1681-1725 . . . . DLB-213

Raworth, Tom 1938- DLB-40

Ray, David 1932- DLB-5

Ray, Gordon Norton 1915-1986 . . . . DLB-103, 140

Ray, Henrietta Cordelia 1849-1916 . . . . . . DLB-50

Raymond, Ernest 1888-1974 . . . . DLB-191

Raymond, Henry J. 1820-1869 . . . . DLB-43, 79

Razaf, Andy 1895-1973 . . . . DLB-265

Michael M. Rea and the Rea Award for the
Short Story Y-97

Reach, Angus 1821-1856 . . . . DLB-70

Read, Herbert 1893-1968 . . . . DLB-20, 149

Read, Martha Meredith DLB-200

Read, Opie 1852-1939 . . . . DLB-23

Read, Piers Paul 1941- DLB-14

Reade, Charles 1814-1884 . . . . DLB-21

Reader's Digest Condensed Books DLB-46

Readers Ulysses Symposium Y-97

Reading, Peter 1946- DLB-40

Reading Series in New York City Y-96

The Reality of One Woman's Dream:
  The de Grummond Children's
  Literature Collection Y-99

Reaney, James 1926- DLB-68

Rebhun, Paul 1500?-1546 ....DLB-179

Rèbora, Clemente 1885-1957..........DLB-114

Rebreanu, Liviu 1885-1944 ....DLB-220

Rechy, John 1934- DLB-122; Y-82

The Recovery of Literature:
  Criticism in the 1990s: A Symposium.... Y-91

Redding, J. Saunders 1906-1988 ......DLB-63, 76

Redfield, J. S. [publishing house] DLB-49

Redgrove, Peter 1932- DLB-40

Redmon, Anne 1943- Y-86

Redmond, Eugene B. 1937- DLB-41

Redpath, James [publishing house] DLB-49

Reed, Henry 1808-1854...............DLB-59

Reed, Henry 1914- DLB-27

Reed, Ishmael
  1938- DLB-2, 5, 33, 169, 227; DS-8

Reed, Rex 1938- DLB-185

Reed, Sampson 1800-1880...........DLB-1, 235

Reed, Talbot Baines 1852-1893........DLB-141

Reedy, William Marion 1862-1920.......DLB-91

Reese, Lizette Woodworth 1856-1935.....DLB-54

Reese, Thomas 1742-1796 ....DLB-37

Reeve, Clara 1729-1807 ....DLB-39

Preface to The Old English Baron (1778) DLB-39

The Progress of Romance (1785) [excerpt].....DLB-39

Reeves, James 1909-1978 ....DLB-161

Reeves, John 1926- DLB-88

Reeves-Stevens, Garfield 1953- DLB-251

"Reflections: After a Tornado,"
  by Judson Jerome DLB-105

Regnery, Henry, Company DLB-46

Rehberg, Hans 1901-1963 ....DLB-124

Rehfisch, Hans José 1891-1960 ....DLB-124

Reich, Ebbe Kløvedal 1940- DLB-214

Reid, Alastair 1926- DLB-27

Reid, B. L. 1918-1990 ....DLB-111; Y-83

The Practice of Biography II:
  An Interview with B. L. Reid Y-83

Reid, Christopher 1949- DLB-40

Reid, Forrest 1875-1947 ....DLB-153

Reid, Helen Rogers 1882-1970.........DLB-29

Reid, James ?-?....................DLB-31

Reid, Mayne 1818-1883.............DLB-21, 163

Reid, Thomas 1710-1796 ....DLB-31, 252

Reid, V. S. (Vic) 1913-1987............DLB-125

Reid, Whitelaw 1837-1912.............DLB-23

Reilly and Lee Publishing Company DLB-46

Reimann, Brigitte 1933-1973............DLB-75

Reinmar der Alte
  circa 1165-circa 1205...............DLB-138

Reinmar von Zweter
  circa 1200-circa 1250...............DLB-138

Reisch, Walter 1903-1983 ....DLB-44

Reizei Family DLB-203

Remarks at the Opening of "The Biographical
  Part of Literature" Exhibition, by
  William R. Cagle Y-98

Remarque, Erich Maria
  1898-1970 ....DLB-56; CDWLB-2

Remington, Frederic
  1861-1909 ....DLB-12, 186, 188

Reminiscences, by Charles Scribner, Jr...... DS-17

Renaud, Jacques 1943- DLB-60

Renault, Mary 1905-1983 .... Y-83

Rendell, Ruth 1930- DLB-87

Rensselaer, Maria van Cortlandt van
  1645-1689 ....DLB-200

Repplier, Agnes 1855-1950 ....DLB-221

Representative Men and Women: A Historical
  Perspective on the British Novel,
  1930-1960 ....DLB-15

Research in the American Antiquarian Book
  Trade Y-97

Reshetnikov, Fedor Mikhailovich
  1841-1871 ....DLB-238

Rettenbacher, Simon 1634-1706........DLB-168

Reuchlin, Johannes 1455-1522.........DLB-179

Reuter, Christian 1665-after 1712 ......DLB-168

Revell, Fleming H., Company DLB-49

Reverdy, Pierre 1889-1960 ....DLB-258

Reuter, Fritz 1810-1874 ....DLB-129

Reuter, Gabriele 1859-1941 ....DLB-66

Reventlow, Franziska Gräfin zu
  1871-1918 ....DLB-66

Review of Nicholson Baker's Double Fold:
  Libraries and the Assault on Paper.......... Y-00

Review of Reviews Office DLB-112

Review of [Samuel Richardson's] Clarissa (1748),
  by Henry Fielding..................DLB-39

The Revolt (1937), by Mary Colum
  [excerpts] DLB-36

Rexroth, Kenneth 1905-1982
  ..... DLB-16, 48, 165, 212; Y-82; CDALB-1

Rey, H. A. 1898-1977 ....DLB-22

Reynal and Hitchcock DLB-46

Reynolds, G. W. M. 1814-1879..........DLB-21

Reynolds, John Hamilton 1794-1852......DLB-96

Reynolds, Sir Joshua 1723-1792........DLB-104

Reynolds, Mack 1917- DLB-8

A Literary Archaeologist Digs On: A Brief
  Interview with Michael Reynolds by
  Michael Rogers.................... Y-99

Reznikoff, Charles 1894-1976 ....DLB-28, 45

Rhett, Robert Barnwell 1800-1876........DLB-43

Rhode, John 1884-1964 ....DLB-77

Rhodes, Eugene Manlove 1869-1934 ....DLB-256

Rhodes, James Ford 1848-1927 ....DLB-47

Rhodes, Richard 1937- DLB-185

Rhys, Jean 1890-1979
  .... DLB-36, 117, 162; CDBLB-7; CDWLB-3

Ricardo, David 1772-1823 .... DLB-107, 158

Ricardou, Jean 1932- DLB-83

Rice, Elmer 1892-1967................DLB-4, 7

Rice, Grantland 1880-1954 .... DLB-29, 171

Rich, Adrienne 1929- DLB-5, 67; CDALB-7

Richard de Fournival
  1201-1259 or 1260 ....DLB-208

Richard, Mark 1955- DLB-234

Richards, David Adams 1950- DLB-53

Richards, George circa 1760-1814 ......DLB-37

Richards, Grant [publishing house] DLB-112

Richards, I. A. 1893-1979 ....DLB-27

Richards, Laura E. 1850-1943.........DLB-42

Richards, William Carey 1818-1892......DLB-73

Richardson, Charles F. 1851-1913.......DLB-71

Richardson, Dorothy M. 1873-1957 ......DLB-36

Richardson, Henry Handel
  (Ethel Florence Lindesay
  Robertson) 1870-1946......... DLB-197, 230

Richardson, Jack 1935- DLB-7

Richardson, John 1796-1852 ....DLB-99

Richardson, Samuel
  1689-1761 ....DLB-39, 154; CDBLB-2

Introductory Letters from the Second
  Edition of Pamela (1741) DLB-39

Postscript to [the Third Edition of]
  Clarissa (1751) DLB-39

Preface to the First Edition of
  Pamela (1740) DLB-39

Preface to the Third Edition of
  Clarissa (1751) [excerpt] DLB-39

Preface to Volume 1 of Clarissa (1747).....DLB-39

Preface to Volume 3 of Clarissa (1748).....DLB-39

Richardson, Willis 1889-1977 ....DLB-51

Riche, Barnabe 1542-1617 ....DLB-136

Richepin, Jean 1849-1926 ....DLB-192

Richler, Mordecai 1931- DLB-53

Richter, Conrad 1890-1968..........DLB-9, 212

Richter, Hans Werner 1908- DLB-69

Richter, Johann Paul Friedrich
  1763-1825 ....DLB-94; CDWLB-2

Rickerby, Joseph [publishing house] DLB-106

Rickword, Edgell 1898-1982 ....DLB-20

Riddell, Charlotte 1832-1906..........DLB-156

Riddell, John (see Ford, Corey)

Ridge, John Rollin 1827-1867 ....DLB-175

Ridge, Lola 1873-1941................DLB-54

Ridge, William Pett 1859-1930 ....DLB-135

Riding, Laura (see Jackson, Laura Riding)

Ridler, Anne 1912- DLB-27

Ridruego, Dionisio 1912-1975 ....DLB-108

Riel, Louis 1844-1885 ....DLB-99

Riemer, Johannes 1648-1714 ....DLB-168

Rifbjerg, Klaus 1931- DLB-214

Riffaterre, Michael 1924- DLB-67

Riggs, Lynn 1899-1954 ....DLB-175

Riis, Jacob 1849-1914 ....DLB-23

Riker, John C. [publishing house]........ DLB-49
Riley, James 1777-1840 .... DLB-183
Riley, John 1938-1978................. DLB-40
Rilke, Rainer Maria
  1875-1926............. DLB-81; CDWLB-2
Rimanelli, Giose 1926- DLB-177
Rimbaud, Jean-Nicolas-Arthur
  1854-1891 .... DLB-217
Rinehart and Company DLB-46
Ringuet 1895-1960 .... DLB-68
Ringwood, Gwen Pharis 1910-1984 ...... DLB-88
Rinser, Luise 1911- DLB-69
Ríos, Alberto 1952- DLB-122
Ríos, Isabella 1948- DLB-82
Ripley, Arthur 1895-1961............... DLB-44
Ripley, George 1802-1880 .... DLB-1, 64, 73, 235
The Rising Glory of America:
  Three Poems DLB-37
The Rising Glory of America:
  Written in 1771 (1786),
  by Hugh Henry Brackenridge and
  Philip Freneau DLB-37
Riskin, Robert 1897-1955 .... DLB-26
Risse, Heinz 1898- DLB-69
Rist, Johann 1607-1667 .... DLB-164
Ristikivi, Karl 1912-1977............... DLB-220
Ritchie, Anna Mowatt 1819-1870 ..... DLB-3, 250
Ritchie, Anne Thackeray 1837-1919...... DLB-18
Ritchie, Thomas 1778-1854 .... DLB-43
Rites of Passage [on William Saroyan] Y-83
The Ritz Paris Hemingway Award......... Y-85
Rivard, Adjutor 1868-1945............. DLB-92
Rive, Richard 1931-1989 .... DLB-125, 225
Rivera, José 1955- DLB-249
Rivera, Marina 1942- DLB-122
Rivera, Tomás 1935-1984 .... DLB-82
Rivers, Conrad Kent 1933-1968......... DLB-41
Riverside Press...................... DLB-49
Rivington, Charles [publishing house] ... DLB-154
Rivington, James circa 1724-1802....... DLB-43
Rivkin, Allen 1903-1990................ DLB-26
Roa Bastos, Augusto 1917- DLB-113
Robbe-Grillet, Alain 1922- DLB-83
Robbins, Tom 1936- Y-80
Roberts, Charles G. D. 1860-1943 .... DLB-92
Roberts, Dorothy 1906-1993 .... DLB-88
Roberts, Elizabeth Madox
  1881-1941 .... DLB-9, 54, 102
Roberts, James [publishing house] DLB-154
Roberts, Keith 1935-2000............. DLB-261
Roberts, Kenneth 1885-1957 .... DLB-9
Roberts, Michèle 1949- DLB-231
Roberts, Ursula Wyllie (see Miles, Susan)
Roberts, William 1767-1849 .... DLB-142
Roberts Brothers..................... DLB-49
Robertson, A. M., and Company........ DLB-49

Robertson, Ethel Florence Lindesay
  (see Richardson, Henry Handel)
Robertson, William 1721-1793 .... DLB-104
Robin, Leo 1895-1984 .... DLB-265
Robins, Elizabeth 1862-1952 .... DLB-197
Robinson, A. Mary F. (Madame James
  Darmesteter, Madame Mary
  Duclaux) 1857-1944 .... DLB-240
Robinson, Casey 1903-1979 .... DLB-44
Robinson, Edwin Arlington
  1869-1935 .... DLB-54; CDALB-3
Robinson, Henry Crabb 1775-1867 ......DLB-107
Robinson, James Harvey 1863-1936 ..... DLB-47
Robinson, Lennox 1886-1958 .... DLB-10
Robinson, Mabel Louise 1874-1962 ...... DLB-22
Robinson, Marilynne 1943- DLB-206
Robinson, Mary 1758-1800 .... DLB-158
Robinson, Richard circa 1545-1607 ..... DLB-167
Robinson, Therese 1797-1870 .... DLB-59, 133
Robison, Mary 1949- DLB-130
Roblès, Emmanuel 1914-1995 .... DLB-83
Roccatagliata Ceccardi, Ceccardo
  1871-1919..................... DLB-114
Roche, Billy 1949- DLB-233
Rochester, John Wilmot, Earl of
  1647-1680..................... DLB-131
Rochon, Esther 1948- DLB-251
Rock, Howard 1911-1976............. DLB-127
Rockwell, Norman Perceval 1894-1978 .. DLB-188
Rodgers, Carolyn M. 1945- DLB-41
Rodgers, W. R. 1909-1969............. DLB-20
Rodney, Lester 1911- DLB-241
Rodríguez, Claudio 1934-1999 .... DLB-134
Rodríguez, Joe D. 1943- DLB-209
Rodríguez, Luis J. 1954- DLB-209
Rodriguez, Richard 1944- DLB-82, 256
Rodríguez Julia, Edgardo 1946- DLB-145
Roe, E. P. 1838-1888 .... DLB-202
Roethke, Theodore
  1908-1963 .... DLB-5, 206; CDALB-1
Rogers, Jane 1952- DLB-194
Rogers, Pattiann 1940- DLB-105
Rogers, Samuel 1763-1855 .... DLB-93
Rogers, Will 1879-1935 .... DLB-11
Rohmer, Sax 1883-1959............... DLB-70
Roiphe, Anne 1935- Y-80
Rojas, Arnold R. 1896-1988 .... DLB-82
Rolfe, Frederick William
  1860-1913 .... DLB-34, 156
Rolland, Romain 1866-1944............ DLB-65
Rolle, Richard circa 1290-1300 - 1340 ... DLB-146
Rölvaag, O. E. 1876-1931........... DLB-9, 212
Romains, Jules 1885-1972.............. DLB-65
Roman, A., and Company DLB-49
Roman de la Rose: Guillaume de Lorris
  1200 to 1205-circa 1230, Jean de Meun
  1235-1240-circa 1305 .... DLB-208

Romano, Lalla 1906- DLB-177
Romano, Octavio 1923- DLB-122
Rome, Harold 1908-1993............. DLB-265
Romero, Leo 1950- DLB-122
Romero, Lin 1947- DLB-122
Romero, Orlando 1945- DLB-82
Rook, Clarence 1863-1915 .... DLB-135
Roosevelt, Theodore 1858-1919......DLB-47, 186
Root, Waverley 1903-1982 .... DLB-4
Root, William Pitt 1941- DLB-120
Roquebrune, Robert de 1889-1978....... DLB-68
Rorty, Richard 1931- DLB-246
Rosa, João Guimarães 1908-1967 ...... DLB-113
Rosales, Luis 1910-1992............. DLB-134
Roscoe, William 1753-1831 .... DLB-163
Danis Rose and the Rendering of Ulysses Y-97
Rose, Reginald 1920- DLB-26
Rose, Wendy 1948- DLB-175
Rosegger, Peter 1843-1918 .... DLB-129
Rosei, Peter 1946- DLB-85
Rosen, Norma 1925- DLB-28
Rosenbach, A. S. W. 1876-1952........ DLB-140
Rosenbaum, Ron 1946- DLB-185
Rosenberg, Isaac 1890-1918........ DLB-20, 216
Rosenfeld, Isaac 1918-1956 .... DLB-28
Rosenthal, Harold 1914-1999 .... DLB-241
Jimmy, Red, and Others: Harold Rosenthal
  Remembers the Stars of the Press Box ... Y-01
Rosenthal, M. L. 1917-1996 .... DLB-5
Rosenwald, Lessing J. 1891-1979 ....DLB-187
Ross, Alexander 1591-1654 .... DLB-151
Ross, Harold 1892-1951..............DLB-137
Ross, Jerry (see Adler, Richard)
Ross, Leonard Q. (see Rosten, Leo)
Ross, Lillian 1927- DLB-185
Ross, Martin 1862-1915 .... DLB-135
Ross, Sinclair 1908-1996............. DLB-88
Ross, W. W. E. 1894-1966............. DLB-88
Rosselli, Amelia 1930-1996 .... DLB-128
Rossen, Robert 1908-1966 .... DLB-26
Rossetti, Christina 1830-1894... DLB-35, 163, 240
Rossetti, Dante Gabriel
  1828-1882 .... DLB-35; CDBLB-4
Rossner, Judith 1935- DLB-6
Rostand, Edmond 1868-1918.......... DLB-192
Rosten, Leo 1908-1997................ DLB-11
Rostenberg, Leona 1908- DLB-140
Rostopchina, Evdokiia Petrovna
  1811-1858 .... DLB-205
Rostovsky, Dimitrii 1651-1709......... DLB-150
Rota, Bertram 1903-1966 .... DLB-201
  Bertram Rota and His Bookshop Y-91
Roth, Gerhard 1942- DLB-85, 124
Roth, Henry 1906?-1995 .... DLB-28
Roth, Joseph 1894-1939 .... DLB-85

Roth, Philip 1933- DLB-2, 28, 173; Y-82; CDALB-6
Rothenberg, Jerome 1931- DLB-5, 193
Rothschild Family DLB-184
Rotimi, Ola 1938- DLB-125
Routhier, Adolphe-Basile 1839-1920 ......DLB-99
Routier, Simone 1901-1987 ....DLB-88
Routledge, George, and Sons..........DLB-106
Roversi, Roberto 1923- DLB-128
Rowe, Elizabeth Singer 1674-1737 .....DLB-39, 95
Rowe, Nicholas 1674-1718............DLB-84
Rowlands, Samuel circa 1570-1630 ......DLB-121
Rowlandson, Mary circa 1637-circa 1711 ....DLB-24, 200
Rowley, William circa 1585-1626 ....DLB-58
Rowse, A. L. 1903-1997..............DLB-155
Rowson, Susanna Haswell circa 1762-1824 .... DLB-37, 200
Roy, Camille 1870-1943..............DLB-92
Roy, Gabrielle 1909-1983 ....DLB-68
Roy, Jules 1907- DLB-83
The G. Ross Roy Scottish Poetry Collection at the University of South Carolina Y-89
The Royal Court Theatre and the English Stage Company..................DLB-13
The Royal Court Theatre and the New Drama......................DLB-10
The Royal Shakespeare Company at the Swan Y-88
Royall, Anne Newport 1769-1854 ....DLB-43, 248
The Roycroft Printing Shop DLB-49
Royde-Smith, Naomi 1875-1964 ....DLB-191
Royster, Vermont 1914- DLB-127
Royston, Richard [publishing house].....DLB-170
Różewicz, Tadeusz 1921- DLB-232
Ruark, Gibbons 1941- DLB-120
Ruban, Vasilii Grigorevich 1742-1795 ....DLB-150
Rubens, Bernice 1928- DLB-14, 207
Rudd and Carleton DLB-49
Rudd, Steele (Arthur Hoey Davis)...... DLB-230
Rudkin, David 1936- DLB-13
Rudnick, Paul 1957- DLB-266
Rudolf von Ems circa 1200-circa 1254 ...DLB-138
Ruffin, Josephine St. Pierre 1842-1924 ....DLB-79
Ruganda, John 1941- DLB-157
Ruggles, Henry Joseph 1813-1906........DLB-64
Ruiz de Burton, María Amparo 1832-1895 ....DLB-209, 221
Rukeyser, Muriel 1913-1980 ....DLB-48
Rule, Jane 1931- DLB-60
Rulfo, Juan 1918-1986......DLB-113; CDWLB-3
Rumaker, Michael 1932- DLB-16
Rumens, Carol 1944- DLB-40
Rummo, Paul-Eerik 1942- DLB-232
Runyon, Damon 1880-1946 ..... DLB-11, 86, 171
Ruodlieb circa 1050-1075.............DLB-148

Rush, Benjamin 1746-1813 ....DLB-37
Rush, Rebecca 1779-?................DLB-200
Rushdie, Salman 1947- DLB-194
Rusk, Ralph L. 1888-1962.............DLB-103
Ruskin, John 1819-1900 ......DLB-55, 163, 190; CDBLB-4
Russ, Joanna 1937- DLB-8
Russell, B. B., and Company...........DLB-49
Russell, Benjamin 1761-1845 ....DLB-43
Russell, Bertrand 1872-1970.........DLB-100, 262
Russell, Charles Edward 1860-1941 .....DLB-25
Russell, Charles M. 1864-1926 ....DLB-188
Russell, Eric Frank 1905-1978 ....DLB-255
Russell, Fred 1906- DLB-241
Russell, George William (see AE)
Russell, Countess Mary Annette Beauchamp (see Arnim, Elizabeth von)
Russell, R. H., and Son DLB-49
Russell, Willy 1947- DLB-233
Rutebeuf flourished 1249-1277 ....DLB-208
Rutherford, Mark 1831-1913..........DLB-18
Ruxton, George Frederick 1821-1848 ....DLB-186
Ryan, Michael 1946- Y-82
Ryan, Oscar 1904- DLB-68
Ryder, Jack 1871-1936................DLB-241
Ryga, George 1932- DLB-60
Rylands, Enriqueta Augustina Tennant 1843-1908 ....DLB-184
Rylands, John 1801-1888..............DLB-184
Ryle, Gilbert 1900-1976...............DLB-262
Ryleev, Kondratii Fedorovich 1795-1826 ....DLB-205
Rymer, Thomas 1643?-1713 ....DLB-101
Ryskind, Morrie 1895-1985............DLB-26
Rzhevsky, Aleksei Andreevich 1737-1804....................DLB-150

S

The Saalfield Publishing Company DLB-46
Saba, Umberto 1883-1957 ....DLB-114
Sábato, Ernesto 1911- DLB-145; CDWLB-3
Saberhagen, Fred 1930- DLB-8
Sabin, Joseph 1821-1881 ....DLB-187
Sacer, Gottfried Wilhelm 1635-1699 .....DLB-168
Sachs, Hans 1494-1576 ..... DLB-179; CDWLB-2
Sack, John 1930- DLB-185
Sackler, Howard 1929-1982.............DLB-7
Sackville, Lady Margaret 1881-1963 .....DLB-240
Sackville, Thomas 1536-1608 ....DLB-132
Sackville, Thomas 1536-1608 and Norton, Thomas 1532-1584......DLB-62
Sackville-West, Edward 1901-1965 .....DLB-191
Sackville-West, V. 1892-1962 ......DLB-34, 195
Sadlier, D. and J., and Company........DLB-49
Sadlier, Mary Anne 1820-1903 ....DLB-99

Sadoff, Ira 1945- DLB-120
Sadoveanu, Mihail 1880-1961 ....DLB-220
Sáenz, Benjamin Alire 1954- DLB-209
Saenz, Jaime 1921-1986...............DLB-145
Saffin, John circa 1626-1710............DLB-24
Sagan, Françoise 1935- DLB-83
Sage, Robert 1899-1962................DLB-4
Sagel, Jim 1947- DLB-82
Sagendorph, Robb Hansell 1900-1970....DLB-137
Sahagún, Carlos 1938- DLB-108
Sahkomaapii, Piitai (see Highwater, Jamake)
Sahl, Hans 1902- DLB-69
Said, Edward W. 1935- DLB-67
Saigyō 1118-1190....................DLB-203
Saiko, George 1892-1962..............DLB-85
St. Dominic's Press DLB-112
Saint-Exupéry, Antoine de 1900-1944.....DLB-72
St. John, J. Allen 1872-1957 ....DLB-188
St. Johns, Adela Rogers 1894-1988 ......DLB-29
The St. John's College Robert Graves Trust.. Y-96
St. Martin's Press....................DLB-46
St. Omer, Garth 1931- DLB-117
Saint Pierre, Michel de 1916-1987 ....DLB-83
Sainte-Beuve, Charles-Augustin 1804-1869 ....DLB-217
Saints' Lives.......................DLB-208
Saintsbury, George 1845-1933....... DLB-57, 149
Saiokuken Sōchō 1448-1532 ....DLB-203
Saki (see Munro, H. H.)
Salaam, Kalamu ya 1947- DLB-38
Šalamun, Tomaž 1941- ... DLB-181; CDWLB-4
Salas, Floyd 1931- DLB-82
Sálaz-Marquez, Rubén 1935- DLB-122
Salemson, Harold J. 1910-1988 ....DLB-4
Salinas, Luis Omar 1937- DLB-82
Salinas, Pedro 1891-1951..............DLB-134
Salinger, J. D. 1919- DLB-2, 102, 173; CDALB-1
Salkey, Andrew 1928- DLB-125
Sallust circa 86 B.C.-35 B.C. DLB-211; CDWLB-1
Salt, Waldo 1914- DLB-44
Salter, James 1925- DLB-130
Salter, Mary Jo 1954- DLB-120
Saltus, Edgar 1855-1921 ....DLB-202
Saltykov, Mikhail Evgrafovich 1826-1889 ....DLB-238
Salustri, Carlo Alberto (see Trilussa)
Salverson, Laura Goodman 1890-1970 ....DLB-92
Samain, Albert 1858-1900 ....DLB-217
Sampson, Richard Henry (see Hull, Richard)
Samuels, Ernest 1903-1996 ....DLB-111
Sanborn, Franklin Benjamin 1831-1917 ....DLB-1, 223
Sánchez, Luis Rafael 1936- DLB-145
Sánchez, Philomeno "Phil" 1917- DLB-122

Sánchez, Ricardo 1941-1995 . . . . DLB-82

Sánchez, Saúl 1943- DLB-209

Sanchez, Sonia 1934- DLB-41; DS-8

Sand, George 1804-1876 . . . . DLB-119, 192

Sandburg, Carl
1878-1967 . . . . DLB-17, 54; CDALB-3

Sanders, Edward 1939- DLB-16, 244

Sandoz, Mari 1896-1966 . . . . DLB-9, 212

Sandwell, B. K. 1876-1954 . . . . DLB-92

Sandy, Stephen 1934- DLB-165

Sandys, George 1578-1644 . . . . DLB-24, 121

Sangster, Charles 1822-1893 . . . . DLB-99

Sanguineti, Edoardo 1930- DLB-128

Sanjōnishi Sanetaka 1455-1537 . . . . DLB-203

Sansay, Leonora ?-after 1823 . . . . DLB-200

Sansom, William 1912-1976 . . . . DLB-139

Santayana, George
1863-1952 . . . . DLB-54, 71, 246; DS-13

Santiago, Danny 1911-1988 . . . . DLB-122

Santmyer, Helen Hooven 1895-1986 . . . . Y-84

Sanvitale, Francesca 1928- DLB-196

Sapidus, Joannes 1490-1561 . . . . DLB-179

Sapir, Edward 1884-1939 . . . . DLB-92

Sapper (see McNeile, Herman Cyril)

Sappho circa 620 B.C.-circa 550 B.C.
. . . . DLB-176; CDWLB-1

Saramago, José 1922- Y-98

Sarban (John F. Wall) 1910-1989 . . . . DLB-255

Sardou, Victorien 1831-1908 . . . . DLB-192

Sarduy, Severo 1937- DLB-113

Sargent, Pamela 1948- DLB-8

Saro-Wiwa, Ken 1941- DLB-157

Saroyan, William
1908-1981 . . . . . DLB-7, 9, 86; Y-81; CDALB-7

Sarraute, Nathalie 1900-1999 . . . . DLB-83

Sarrazin, Albertine 1937-1967 . . . . DLB-83

Sarris, Greg 1952- DLB-175

Sarton, May 1912-1995 . . . . DLB-48; Y-81

Sartre, Jean-Paul 1905-1980 . . . . DLB-72

Sassoon, Siegfried
1886-1967 . . . . DLB-20, 191; DS-18

Siegfried Loraine Sassoon:
A Centenary Essay
Tributes from Vivien F. Clarke and
Michael Thorpe Y-86

Sata, Ineko 1904- DLB-180

Saturday Review Press DLB-46

Saunders, James 1925- DLB-13

Saunders, John Monk 1897-1940 . . . . DLB-26

Saunders, Margaret Marshall
1861-1947 . . . . DLB-92

Saunders and Otley DLB-106

Saussure, Ferdinand de 1857-1913 . . . . . . DLB-242

Savage, James 1784-1873 . . . . DLB-30

Savage, Marmion W. 1803?-1872 . . . . DLB-21

Savage, Richard 1697?-1743 . . . . DLB-95

Savard, Félix-Antoine 1896-1982 . . . . DLB-68

Savery, Henry 1791-1842 . . . . DLB-230

Saville, (Leonard) Malcolm 1901-1982 . . . DLB-160

Savinio, Alberto 1891-1952 . . . . DLB-264

Sawyer, Robert J. 1960- DLB-251

Sawyer, Ruth 1880-1970 . . . . DLB-22

Sayers, Dorothy L.
1893-1957 . . . . . DLB-10, 36, 77, 100; CDBLB-6

Sayle, Charles Edward 1864-1924 . . . . . . DLB-184

Sayles, John Thomas 1950- DLB-44

Sbarbaro, Camillo 1888-1967 . . . . DLB-114

Scalapino, Leslie 1947- DLB-193

Scannell, Vernon 1922- DLB-27

Scarry, Richard 1919-1994 . . . . DLB-61

Schaefer, Jack 1907-1991 . . . . DLB-212

Schaeffer, Albrecht 1885-1950 . . . . DLB-66

Schaeffer, Susan Fromberg 1941- DLB-28

Schaff, Philip 1819-1893 . . . . DS-13

Schaper, Edzard 1908-1984 . . . . DLB-69

Scharf, J. Thomas 1843-1898 . . . . DLB-47

Schede, Paul Melissus 1539-1602 . . . . DLB-179

Scheffel, Joseph Viktor von 1826-1886 . . . DLB-129

Scheffler, Johann 1624-1677 . . . . DLB-164

Schelling, Friedrich Wilhelm Joseph von
1775-1854 . . . . DLB-90

Scherer, Wilhelm 1841-1886 . . . . DLB-129

Scherfig, Hans 1905-1979 . . . . DLB-214

Schickele, René 1883-1940 . . . . DLB-66

Schiff, Dorothy 1903-1989 . . . . DLB-127

Schiller, Friedrich
1759-1805 . . . . DLB-94; CDWLB-2

Schirmer, David 1623-1687 . . . . DLB-164

Schlaf, Johannes 1862-1941 . . . . DLB-118

Schlegel, August Wilhelm 1767-1845 . . . . . DLB-94

Schlegel, Dorothea 1763-1839 . . . . DLB-90

Schlegel, Friedrich 1772-1829 . . . . DLB-90

Schleiermacher, Friedrich 1768-1834 . . . . . DLB-90

Schlesinger, Arthur M., Jr. 1917- DLB-17

Schlumberger, Jean 1877-1968 . . . . DLB-65

Schmid, Eduard Hermann Wilhelm
(see Edschmid, Kasimir)

Schmidt, Arno 1914-1979 . . . . DLB-69

Schmidt, Johann Kaspar (see Stirner, Max)

Schmidt, Michael 1947- DLB-40

Schmidtbonn, Wilhelm August
1876-1952 . . . . DLB-118

Schmitz, Aron Hector (see Svevo, Italo)

Schmitz, James H. 1911- DLB-8

Schnabel, Johann Gottfried
1692-1760 . . . . DLB-168

Schnackenberg, Gjertrud 1953- DLB-120

Schnitzler, Arthur
1862-1931 . . . . DLB-81, 118; CDWLB-2

Schnurre, Wolfdietrich 1920-1989 . . . . . . DLB-69

Schocken Books DLB-46

Scholartis Press DLB-112

Scholderer, Victor 1880-1971 . . . . DLB-201

The Schomburg Center for Research
in Black Culture DLB-76

Schönbeck, Virgilio (see Giotti, Virgilio)

Schönherr, Karl 1867-1943 . . . . DLB-118

Schoolcraft, Jane Johnston 1800-1841 . . . . DLB-175

School Stories, 1914-1960 . . . . DLB-160

Schopenhauer, Arthur 1788-1860 . . . . DLB-90

Schopenhauer, Johanna 1766-1838 . . . . . . DLB-90

Schorer, Mark 1908-1977 . . . . DLB-103

Schottelius, Justus Georg 1612-1676 . . . . . DLB-164

Schouler, James 1839-1920 . . . . DLB-47

Schoultz, Solveig von 1907-1996 . . . . DLB-259

Schrader, Paul 1946- DLB-44

Schreiner, Olive
1855-1920 . . . . DLB-18, 156, 190, 225

Schroeder, Andreas 1946- DLB-53

Schubart, Christian Friedrich Daniel
1739-1791 . . . . DLB-97

Schubert, Gotthilf Heinrich 1780-1860 . . . . DLB-90

Schücking, Levin 1814-1883 . . . . DLB-133

Schulberg, Budd 1914- DLB-6, 26, 28; Y-81

Schulte, F. J., and Company DLB-49

Schulz, Bruno 1892-1942 . . . . DLB-215; CDWLB-4

Schulze, Hans (see Praetorius, Johannes)

Schupp, Johann Balthasar 1610-1661 . . . . DLB-164

Schurz, Carl 1829-1906 . . . . DLB-23

Schuyler, George S. 1895-1977 . . . . . . DLB-29, 51

Schuyler, James 1923-1991 . . . . DLB-5, 169

Schwartz, Delmore 1913-1966 . . . . . . DLB-28, 48

Schwartz, Jonathan 1938- Y-82

Schwartz, Lynne Sharon 1939- DLB-218

Schwarz, Sibylle 1621-1638 . . . . DLB-164

Schwerner, Armand 1927-1999 . . . . DLB-165

Schwob, Marcel 1867-1905 . . . . DLB-123

Sciascia, Leonardo 1921-1989 . . . . DLB-177

Science Fantasy DLB-8

Science-Fiction Fandom and Conventions . . DLB-8

Science-Fiction Fanzines: The Time
Binders DLB-8

Science-Fiction Films DLB-8

Science Fiction Writers of America and the
Nebula Awards DLB-8

Scot, Reginald circa 1538-1599 . . . . DLB-136

Scotellaro, Rocco 1923-1953 . . . . DLB-128

Scott, Alicia Anne (Lady John Scott)
1810-1900 . . . . DLB-240

Scott, Catharine Amy Dawson
1865-1934 . . . . DLB-240

Scott, Dennis 1939-1991 . . . . DLB-125

Scott, Dixon 1881-1915 . . . . DLB-98

Scott, Duncan Campbell 1862-1947 . . . . . DLB-92

Scott, Evelyn 1893-1963 . . . . DLB-9, 48

Scott, F. R. 1899-1985 . . . . DLB-88

Scott, Frederick George 1861-1944 . . . . . . DLB-92

Scott, Geoffrey 1884-1929 . . . . DLB-149

Scott, Harvey W. 1838-1910 . . . . DLB-23

Scott, Lady Jane (see Scott, Alicia Anne)

Scott, Paul 1920-1978..............DLB-14, 207

Scott, Sarah 1723-1795................DLB-39

Scott, Tom 1918- DLB-27

Scott, Sir Walter 1771-1832
......DLB-93, 107, 116, 144, 159; CDBLB-3

Scott, Walter, Publishing
Company Limited.................DLB-112

Scott, William Bell 1811-1890..........DLB-32

Scott, William R. [publishing house]......DLB-46

Scott-Heron, Gil 1949- DLB-41

Scribe, Eugene 1791-1861 ....DLB-192

Scribner, Arthur Hawley 1859-1932 ....DS-13, 16

Scribner, Charles 1854-1930 ....DS-13, 16

Scribner, Charles, Jr. 1921-1995 ....Y-95

Reminiscences DS-17

Charles Scribner's Sons DLB-49; DS-13, 16, 17

Scripps, E. W. 1854-1926 ....DLB-25

Scudder, Horace Elisha 1838-1902 ....DLB-42, 71

Scudder, Vida Dutton 1861-1954 ....DLB-71

Scupham, Peter 1933- DLB-40

Seabrook, William 1886-1945 ....DLB-4

Seabury, Samuel 1729-1796 ....DLB-31

Seacole, Mary Jane Grant 1805-1881.....DLB-166

The Seafarer circa 970 ....DLB-146

Sealsfield, Charles (Carl Postl)
1793-1864 ....DLB-133, 186

Sears, Edward I. 1819?-1876 ....DLB-79

Sears Publishing Company DLB-46

Seaton, George 1911-1979 ....DLB-44

Seaton, William Winston 1785-1866 .....DLB-43

Secker, Martin [publishing house].......DLB-112

Secker, Martin, and Warburg Limited....DLB-112

The Second Annual New York Festival
of Mystery........................Y-00

Second-Generation Minor Poets of the
Seventeenth Century DLB-126

Sedgwick, Arthur George 1844-1915......DLB-64

Sedgwick, Catharine Maria
1789-1867 ....DLB-1, 74, 183, 239, 243

Sedgwick, Ellery 1872-1930 ....DLB-91

Sedgwick, Eve Kosofsky 1950- DLB-246

Sedley, Sir Charles 1639-1701 ....DLB-131

Seeberg, Peter 1925-1999................DLB-214

Seeger, Alan 1888-1916 ....DLB-45

Seers, Eugene (see Dantin, Louis)

Segal, Erich 1937- Y-86

Šegedin, Petar 1909- DLB-181

Seghers, Anna 1900-1983.....DLB-69; CDWLB-2

Seid, Ruth (see Sinclair, Jo)

Seidel, Frederick Lewis 1936- Y-84

Seidel, Ina 1885-1974...................DLB-56

Seifert, Jaroslav
1901-1986 ....DLB-215; Y-84; CDWLB-4

Seigenthaler, John 1927- DLB-127

Seizin Press DLB-112

Séjour, Victor 1817-1874 ....DLB-50

Séjour Marcou et Ferrand, Juan Victor
(see Séjour, Victor)

Sekowski, Józef-Julian, Baron Brambeus
(see Senkovsky, Osip Ivanovich)

Selby, Bettina 1934- DLB-204

Selby, Hubert, Jr. 1928- DLB-2, 227

Selden, George 1929-1989..............DLB-52

Selden, John 1584-1654................DLB-213

Selected English-Language Little Magazines
and Newspapers [France, 1920-1939] ...DLB-4

Selected Humorous Magazines
(1820-1950).......................DLB-11

Selected Science-Fiction Magazines and
Anthologies......................DLB-8

Selenić, Slobodan 1933-1995 ....DLB-181

Self, Edwin F. 1920- DLB-137

Self, Will 1961- DLB-207

Seligman, Edwin R. A. 1861-1939........DLB-47

Selimović, Meša
1910-1982..............DLB-181; CDWLB-4

Sellings, Arthur 1911-1968 ....DLB-261

Selous, Frederick Courteney
1851-1917 ....DLB-174

Seltzer, Chester E. (see Muro, Amado)

Seltzer, Thomas [publishing house].......DLB-46

Selvon, Sam 1923-1994 .....DLB-125; CDWLB-3

Semmes, Raphael 1809-1877 ....DLB-189

Senancour, Etienne de 1770-1846 ......DLB-119

Sendak, Maurice 1928- DLB-61

Seneca the Elder
circa 54 B.C.-circa A.D. 40 ....DLB-211

Seneca the Younger
circa 1 B.C.-A.D. 65 ....DLB-211; CDWLB-1

Senécal, Eva 1905- DLB-92

Sengstacke, John 1912- DLB-127

Senior, Olive 1941- DLB-157

Senkovsky, Osip Ivanovich
(Józef-Julian Sekowski, Baron Brambeus)
1800-1858 ....DLB-198

Šenoa, August 1838-1881 ...DLB-147; CDWLB-4

"Sensation Novels" (1863), by
H. L. Manse DLB-21

Sepamla, Sipho 1932- DLB-157, 225

Serao, Matilde 1856-1927 ....DLB-264

Seredy, Kate 1899-1975 ....DLB-22

Sereni, Vittorio 1913-1983..............DLB-128

Seres, William [publishing house].......DLB-170

Serling, Rod 1924-1975 ....DLB-26

Sernine, Daniel 1955- DLB-251

Serote, Mongane Wally 1944- DLB-125, 225

Serraillier, Ian 1912-1994................DLB-161

Serrano, Nina 1934- DLB-122

Service, Robert 1874-1958 ....DLB-92

Sessler, Charles 1854-1935 ....DLB-187

Seth, Vikram 1952- DLB-120

Seton, Elizabeth Ann 1774-1821........DLB-200

Seton, Ernest Thompson
1860-1942 ....DLB-92; DS-13

Setouchi Harumi 1922- DLB-182

Settle, Mary Lee 1918- DLB-6

Seume, Johann Gottfried 1763-1810 ......DLB-94

Seuse, Heinrich 1295?-1366............DLB-179

Seuss, Dr. (see Geisel, Theodor Seuss)

The Seventy-fifth Anniversary of the Armistice:
The Wilfred Owen Centenary and
the Great War Exhibit
at the University of Virginia Y-93

Severin, Timothy 1940- DLB-204

Sewall, Joseph 1688-1769................DLB-24

Sewall, Richard B. 1908- DLB-111

Sewell, Anna 1820-1878................DLB-163

Sewell, Samuel 1652-1730 ....DLB-24

Sex, Class, Politics, and Religion [in the
British Novel, 1930-1959]...........DLB-15

Sexton, Anne 1928-1974 ...DLB-5, 169; CDALB-1

Seymour-Smith, Martin 1928-1998......DLB-155

Sgorlon, Carlo 1930- DLB-196

Shaara, Michael 1929-1988 ....Y-83

Shabel'skaia, Aleksandra Stanislavovna
1845-1921......................DLB-238

Shadwell, Thomas 1641?-1692 ....DLB-80

Shaffer, Anthony 1926- DLB-13

Shaffer, Peter 1926- DLB-13, 233; CDBLB-8

Shaftesbury, Anthony Ashley Cooper,
Third Earl of 1671-1713 ....DLB-101

Shairp, Mordaunt 1887-1939............DLB-10

Shakespeare, Nicholas 1957- DLB-231

Shakespeare, William
1564-1616......DLB-62, 172, 263; CDBLB-1

$6,166,000 for a Book! Observations on
The Shakespeare First Folio: The History
of the Book.......................Y-01

The Shakespeare Globe Trust.............Y-93

Shakespeare Head Press DLB-112

Shakhovskoi, Aleksandr Aleksandrovich
1777-1846......................DLB-150

Shange, Ntozake 1948- DLB-38, 249

Shapiro, Karl 1913-2000 ....DLB-48

Sharon Publications....................DLB-46

Sharp, Margery 1905-1991 ....DLB-161

Sharp, William 1855-1905 ....DLB-156

Sharpe, Tom 1928- DLB-14, 231

Shaw, Albert 1857-1947 ....DLB-91

Shaw, George Bernard
1856-1950........DLB-10, 57, 190, CDBLB-6

Shaw, Henry Wheeler 1818-1885 ....DLB-11

Shaw, Joseph T. 1874-1952 ....DLB-137

Shaw, Irwin
1913-1984.......DLB-6, 102; Y-84; CDALB-1

Shaw, Mary 1854-1929 ....DLB-228

Shaw, Robert 1927-1978.............DLB-13, 14

Shaw, Robert B. 1947- DLB-120

Shawn, Wallace 1943- DLB-266

Shawn, William 1907-1992 ....DLB-137

Shay, Frank [publishing house].........DLB-46
Shchedrin, N. (see Saltykov, Mikhail Evgrafovich)
Shea, John Gilmary 1824-1892.........DLB-30
Sheaffer, Louis 1912-1993............DLB-103
Shearing, Joseph 1886-1952...........DLB-70
Shebbeare, John 1709-1788............DLB-39
Sheckley, Robert 1928-................DLB-8
Shedd, William G. T. 1820-1894.......DLB-64
Sheed, Wilfred 1930-.................DLB-6
Sheed and Ward [U.S.]................DLB-46
Sheed and Ward Limited [U.K.].......DLB-112
Sheldon, Alice B. (see Tiptree, James, Jr.)
Sheldon, Edward 1886-1946............DLB-7
Sheldon and Company..................DLB-49
Sheller, Aleksandr Konstantinovich
  1838-1900........................DLB-238
Shelley, Mary Wollstonecraft 1797-1851
  ....DLB-110, 116, 159, 178; CDBLB-3
Shelley, Percy Bysshe
  1792-1822......DLB-96, 110, 158; CDBLB-3
Shelnutt, Eve 1941-..................DLB-130
Shenstone, William 1714-1763.........DLB-95
Shepard, Clark and Brown.............DLB-49
Shepard, Ernest Howard 1879-1976.....DLB-160
Shepard, Sam 1943-................DLB-7, 212
Shepard, Thomas I, 1604 or 1605-1649...DLB-24
Shepard, Thomas, II, 1635-1677.......DLB-24
Shepherd, Luke
  flourished 1547-1554................DLB-136
Sherburne, Edward 1616-1702..........DLB-131
Sheridan, Frances 1724-1766........DLB-39, 84
Sheridan, Richard Brinsley
  1751-1816................DLB-89; CDBLB-2
Sherman, Francis 1871-1926...........DLB-92
Sherman, Martin 1938-................DLB-228
Sherriff, R. C. 1896-1975......DLB-10, 191, 233
Sherrod, Blackie 1919-...............DLB-241
Sherry, Norman 1935-.................DLB-155
Sherry, Richard 1506-1551 or 1555....DLB-236
Sherwood, Mary Martha 1775-1851.....DLB-163
Sherwood, Robert E. 1896-1955....DLB-7, 26, 249
Shevyrev, Stepan Petrovich
  1806-1864........................DLB-205
Shiel, M. P. 1865-1947...............DLB-153
Shiels, George 1886-1949.............DLB-10
Shiga, Naoya 1883-1971...............DLB-180
Shiina Rinzō 1911-1973...............DLB-182
Shikishi Naishinnō 1153?-1201........DLB-203
Shillaber, Benjamin Penhallow
  1814-1890..................DLB-1, 11, 235
Shimao Toshio 1917-1986..............DLB-182
Shimazaki, Tōson 1872-1943...........DLB-180
Shine, Ted 1931-.....................DLB-38
Shinkei 1406-1475....................DLB-203
Ship, Reuben 1915-1975...............DLB-88
Shirer, William L. 1904-1993.........DLB-4

Shirinsky-Shikhmatov, Sergii Aleksandrovich
  1783-1837........................DLB-150
Shirley, James 1596-1666.............DLB-58
Shishkov, Aleksandr Semenovich
  1753-1841........................DLB-150
Shockley, Ann Allen 1927-............DLB-33
Shōno Junzō 1921-....................DLB-182
Shore, Arabella 1820?-1901 and
  Shore, Louisa 1824-1895...........DLB-199
Short, Luke (see Glidden, Frederick Dilley)
Short, Peter [publishing house].........DLB-170
Shorter, Dora Sigerson 1866-1918.....DLB-240
Shorthouse, Joseph Henry 1834-1903...DLB-18
Shōtetsu 1381-1459...................DLB-203
Showalter, Elaine 1941-..............DLB-67
Shulevitz, Uri 1935-.................DLB-61
Shulman, Max 1919-1988...............DLB-11
Shute, Henry A. 1856-1943............DLB-9
Shute, Nevil 1899-1960...............DLB-255
Shuttle, Penelope 1947-............DLB-14, 40
Sibbes, Richard 1577-1635............DLB-151
Sibiriak, D. (see Mamin, Dmitrii Narkisovich)
Siddal, Elizabeth Eleanor 1829-1862....DLB-199
Sidgwick, Ethel 1877-1970............DLB-197
Sidgwick, Henry 1838-1900............DLB-262
Sidgwick and Jackson Limited.........DLB-112
Sidney, Margaret (see Lothrop, Harriet M.)
Sidney, Mary 1561-1621...............DLB-167
Sidney, Sir Philip
  1554-1586................DLB-167; CDBLB-1
An Apologie for Poetrie (the Olney
  edition, 1595, of Defence of Poesie)....DLB-167
Sidney's Press.......................DLB-49
Sierra, Rubén 1946-..................DLB-122
Sierra Club Books....................DLB-49
Siger of Brabant circa 1240-circa 1284...DLB-115
Sigourney, Lydia Huntley
  1791-1865........DLB-1, 42, 73, 183, 239, 243
Silkin, Jon 1930-....................DLB-27
Silko, Leslie Marmon 1948-......DLB-143, 175, 256
Silliman, Benjamin 1779-1864.........DLB-183
Silliman, Ron 1946-..................DLB-169
Silliphant, Stirling 1918-...........DLB-26
Sillitoe, Alan 1928-......DLB-14, 139; CDBLB-8
Silman, Roberta 1934-................DLB-28
Silone, Ignazio (Secondino Tranquilli)
  1900-1978........................DLB-264
Silva, Beverly 1930-.................DLB-122
Silverberg, Robert 1935-.............DLB-8
Silverman, Kaja 1947-................DLB-246
Silverman, Kenneth 1936-.............DLB-111
Simak, Clifford D. 1904-1988.........DLB-8
Simcoe, Elizabeth 1762-1850..........DLB-99
Simcox, Edith Jemima 1844-1901.......DLB-190
Simcox, George Augustus 1841-1905....DLB-35
Sime, Jessie Georgina 1868-1958......DLB-92

Simenon, Georges 1903-1989........DLB-72; Y-89
Simic, Charles 1938-.................DLB-105
  "Images and 'Images,'"...............DLB-105
Simionescu, Mircea Horia 1928-.......DLB-232
Simmel, Johannes Mario 1924-.........DLB-69
Simmes, Valentine [publishing house]....DLB-170
Simmons, Ernest J. 1903-1972.........DLB-103
Simmons, Herbert Alfred 1930-........DLB-33
Simmons, James 1933-.................DLB-40
Simms, William Gilmore
  1806-1870............DLB-3, 30, 59, 73, 248
Simms and M'Intyre...................DLB-106
Simon, Claude 1913-..............DLB-83; Y-85
Simon, Neil 1927-................DLB-7, 266
Simon and Schuster...................DLB-46
Simons, Katherine Drayton Mayrant
  1890-1969.........................Y-83
Simović, Ljubomir 1935-..............DLB-181
Simpkin and Marshall
  [publishing house]................DLB-154
Simpson, Helen 1897-1940.............DLB-77
Simpson, Louis 1923-.................DLB-5
Simpson, N. F. 1919-.................DLB-13
Sims, George 1923-..............DLB-87; Y-99
Sims, George Robert 1847-1922....DLB-35, 70, 135
Sinán, Rogelio 1904-.................DLB-145
Sinclair, Andrew 1935-...............DLB-14
Sinclair, Bertrand William 1881-1972....DLB-92
Sinclair, Catherine 1800-1864........DLB-163
Sinclair, Jo 1913-1995...............DLB-28
Sinclair, Lister 1921-...............DLB-88
Sinclair, May 1863-1946............DLB-36, 135
Sinclair, Upton 1878-1968......DLB-9; CDALB-5
Sinclair, Upton [publishing house]......DLB-46
Singer, Isaac Bashevis
  1904-1991...DLB-6, 28, 52; Y-91; CDALB-1
Singer, Mark 1950-...................DLB-185
Singmaster, Elsie 1879-1958..........DLB-9
Sinisgalli, Leonardo 1908-1981.......DLB-114
Siodmak, Curt 1902-2000..............DLB-44
Sîrbu, Ion D. 1919-1989..............DLB-232
Siringo, Charles A. 1855-1928........DLB-186
Sissman, L. E. 1928-1976.............DLB-5
Sisson, C. H. 1914-..................DLB-27
Sitwell, Edith 1887-1964........DLB-20; CDBLB-7
Sitwell, Osbert 1892-1969.........DLB-100, 195
Skácel, Jan 1922-1989................DLB-232
Skalbe, Kārlis 1879-1945.............DLB-220
Skármeta, Antonio
  1940-....................DLB-145; CDWLB-3
Skavronsky, A. (see Danilevsky, Grigorii Petrovich)
Skeat, Walter W. 1835-1912...........DLB-184
Skeffington, William
  [publishing house]................DLB-106
Skelton, John 1463-1529..............DLB-136
Skelton, Robin 1925-..............DLB-27, 53

Škėma, Antanas 1910-1961 ....DLB-220
Skinner, Constance Lindsay
 1877-1939 ....DLB-92
Skinner, John Stuart 1788-1851 ....DLB-73
Skipsey, Joseph 1832-1903..............DLB-35
Skou-Hansen, Tage 1925- DLB-214
Škvorecký, Josef 1924- DLB-232; CDWLB-4
Slade, Bernard 1930- DLB-53
Slamnig, Ivan 1930- DLB-181
Slančeková, Božena (see Timrava)
Slataper, Scipio 1888-1915.............DLB-264
Slater, Patrick 1880-1951...............DLB-68
Slaveykov, Pencho 1866-1912..........DLB-147
Slaviček, Milivoj 1929- DLB-181
Slavitt, David 1935- DLB-5, 6
Sleigh, Burrows Willcocks Arthur
 1821-1869 ....DLB-99
A Slender Thread of Hope:
 The Kennedy Center Black
 Theatre Project DLB-38
Slesinger, Tess 1905-1945 ....DLB-102
Slessor, Kenneth 1901-1971 ....DLB-260
Slick, Sam (see Haliburton, Thomas Chandler)
Sloan, John 1871-1951 ....DLB-188
Sloane, William, Associates DLB-46
Small, Maynard and Company DLB-49
Small Presses in Great Britain and Ireland,
 1960-1985 ....DLB-40
Small Presses I: Jargon Society............Y-84
Small Presses II: The Spirit That Moves
 Us Press Y-85
Small Presses III: Pushcart Press Y-87
Smart, Christopher 1722-1771 ....DLB-109
Smart, David A. 1892-1957 ....DLB-137
Smart, Elizabeth 1913-1986 ....DLB-88
Smart, J. J. C. 1920- DLB-262
Smedley, Menella Bute 1820?-1877 ......DLB-199
Smellie, William [publishing house] DLB-154
Smiles, Samuel 1812-1904 ....DLB-55
Smiley, Jane 1949- DLB-227, 234
Smith, A. J. M. 1902-1980 ....DLB-88
Smith, Adam 1723-1790 ....DLB-104, 252
Smith, Adam (George Jerome Waldo Goodman)
 1930- DLB-185
Smith, Alexander 1829-1867 ....DLB-32, 55
 "On the Writing of Essays" (1862) DLB-57
Smith, Amanda 1837-1915............DLB-221
Smith, Betty 1896-1972 ....Y-82
Smith, Carol Sturm 1938- Y-81
Smith, Charles Henry 1826-1903 ....DLB-11
Smith, Charlotte 1749-1806 ......DLB-39, 109
Smith, Chet 1899-1973................DLB-171
Smith, Cordwainer 1913-1966............DLB-8
Smith, Dave 1942- DLB-5
Smith, Dodie 1896- DLB-10
Smith, Doris Buchanan 1934- DLB-52

Smith, E. E. 1890-1965 ....DLB-8
Smith, Elder and Company...........DLB-154
Smith, Elihu Hubbard 1771-1798.........DLB-37
Smith, Elizabeth Oakes (Prince)
 (see Oakes Smith, Elizabeth)
Smith, Eunice 1757-1823 ....DLB-200
Smith, F. Hopkinson 1838-1915 ....DS-13
Smith, George D. 1870-1920 ....DLB-140
Smith, George O. 1911-1981 ....DLB-8
Smith, Goldwin 1823-1910 ....DLB-99
Smith, H. Allen 1907-1976 ....DLB-11, 29
Smith, Harrison, and Robert Haas
 [publishing house] DLB-46
Smith, Harry B. 1860-1936 ....DLB-187
Smith, Hazel Brannon 1914- DLB-127
Smith, Henry circa 1560-circa 1591 .....DLB-136
Smith, Horatio (Horace) 1779-1849 .....DLB-116
Smith, Horatio (Horace) 1779-1849 and
 James Smith 1775-1839 ....DLB-96
Smith, Iain Crichton 1928- DLB-40, 139
Smith, J. Allen 1860-1924 ....DLB-47
Smith, J. Stilman, and Company DLB-49
Smith, Jessie Willcox 1863-1935 ....DLB-188
Smith, John 1580-1631..............DLB-24, 30
Smith, John 1618-1652................DLB-252
Smith, Josiah 1704-1781 ....DLB-24
Smith, Ken 1938- DLB-40
Smith, Lee 1944- DLB-143; Y-83
Smith, Logan Pearsall 1865-1946........DLB-98
Smith, Margaret Bayard 1778-1844 .....DLB-248
Smith, Mark 1935- Y-82
Smith, Michael 1698-circa 1771 ....DLB-31
Smith, Pauline 1882-1959 ....DLB-225
Smith, Red 1905-1982 ....DLB-29, 171
Smith, Roswell 1829-1892 ....DLB-79
Smith, Samuel Harrison 1772-1845 ......DLB-43
Smith, Samuel Stanhope 1751-1819 ......DLB-37
Smith, Sarah (see Stretton, Hesba)
Smith, Sarah Pogson 1774-1870 ....DLB-200
Smith, Seba 1792-1868..........DLB-1, 11, 243
Smith, Stevie 1902-1971...............DLB-20
Smith, Sydney 1771-1845..............DLB-107
Smith, Sydney Goodsir 1915-1975 ....DLB-27
Smith, Sir Thomas 1513-1577 ....DLB-132
Smith, W. B., and Company DLB-49
Smith, W. H., and Son DLB-106
Smith, Wendell 1914-1972.............DLB-171
Smith, William flourished 1595-1597 ....DLB-136
Smith, William 1727-1803 ....DLB-31
A General Idea of the College of Mirania
 (1753) [excerpts] DLB-31
Smith, William 1728-1793 ....DLB-30
Smith, William Gardner 1927-1974 ......DLB-76
Smith, William Henry 1808-1872 ....DLB-159
Smith, William Jay 1918- DLB-5

Smithers, Leonard [publishing house] DLB-112
Smollett, Tobias
 1721-1771............DLB-39, 104; CDBLB-2
 Dedication, Ferdinand Count
  Fathom (1753) DLB-39
 Preface to Ferdinand Count Fathom (1753)....DLB-39
 Preface to Roderick Random (1748).........DLB-39
Smythe, Francis Sydney 1900-1949......DLB-195
Snelling, William Joseph 1804-1848 .....DLB-202
Snellings, Rolland (see Touré, Askia Muhammad)
Snodgrass, W. D. 1926- DLB-5
Snow, C. P.
 1905-1980.....DLB-15, 77; DS-17; CDBLB-7
Snyder, Gary 1930- ...DLB-5, 16, 165, 212, 237
Sobiloff, Hy 1912-1970.................DLB-48
The Society for Textual Scholarship and
 TEXT Y-87
The Society for the History of Authorship,
 Reading and Publishing Y-92
Söderberg, Hjalmar 1869-1941 ....DLB-259
Södergran, Edith 1892-1923 ....DLB-259
Soffici, Ardengo 1879-1964 ....DLB-114, 264
Sofola, 'Zulu 1938- DLB-157
Solano, Solita 1888-1975 ....DLB-4
Soldati, Mario 1906-1999 ....DLB-177
Šoljan, Antun 1932-1993 ....DLB-181
Sollers, Philippe 1936- DLB-83
Sollogub, Vladimir Aleksandrovich
 1813-1882 ....DLB-198
Sollors, Werner 1943- DBL-246
Solmi, Sergio 1899-1981 ....DLB-114
Solomon, Carl 1928- DLB-16
Solway, David 1941- DLB-53
Solzhenitsyn and America Y-85
Somerville, Edith Œnone 1858-1949.....DLB-135
Somov, Orest Mikhailovich
 1793-1833 ....DLB-198
Sønderby, Knud 1909-1966............DLB-214
Song, Cathy 1955- DLB-169
Sonnevi, Göran 1939- DLB-257
Sono Ayako 1931- DLB-182
Sontag, Susan 1933- DLB-2, 67
Sophocles 497/496 B.C.-406/405 B.C.
 ....DLB-176; CDWLB-1
Šopov, Aco 1923-1982 ....DLB-181
Sørensen, Villy 1929- DLB-214
Sorensen, Virginia 1912-1991 ....DLB-206
Sorge, Reinhard Johannes 1892-1916 ....DLB-118
Sorrentino, Gilbert 1929- DLB-5, 173; Y-80
Sotheby, James 1682-1742 ....DLB-213
Sotheby, John 1740-1807 ....DLB-213
Sotheby, Samuel 1771-1842 ....DLB-213
Sotheby, Samuel Leigh 1805-1861.......DLB-213
Sotheby, William 1757-1833.........DLB-93, 213
Soto, Gary 1952- DLB-82
Sources for the Study of Tudor and Stuart
 Drama.........................DLB-62

Souster, Raymond 1921- DLB-88

The *South English Legendary circa thirteenth-fifteenth centuries* DLB-146

Southerland, Ellease 1943- DLB-33

Southern, Terry 1924-1995 .... DLB-2

Southern Illinois University Press Y-95

Southern Writers Between the Wars DLB-9

Southerne, Thomas 1659-1746 .... DLB-80

Southey, Caroline Anne Bowles 1786-1854 .... DLB-116

Southey, Robert 1774-1843 ...... DLB-93, 107, 142

Southwell, Robert 1561?-1595 .... DLB-167

Southworth, E. D. E. N. 1819-1899 ...... DLB-239

Sowande, Bode 1948- DLB-157

Sowle, Tace [publishing house] DLB-170

Soyfer, Jura 1912-1939 .... DLB-124

Soyinka, Wole 1934- DLB-125; Y-86, Y-87; CDWLB-3

Spacks, Barry 1931- DLB-105

Spalding, Frances 1950- DLB-155

Spark, Muriel 1918- ... DLB-15, 139; CDBLB-7

Sparke, Michael [publishing house] DLB-170

Sparks, Jared 1789-1866 .... DLB-1, 30, 235

Sparshott, Francis 1926- DLB-60

Späth, Gerold 1939- DLB-75

Spatola, Adriano 1941-1988 .... DLB-128

Spaziani, Maria Luisa 1924- DLB-128

Special Collections at the University of Colorado at Boulder Y-98

The Spectator 1828- DLB-110

Spedding, James 1808-1881 .... DLB-144

Spee von Langenfeld, Friedrich 1591-1635 .... DLB-164

Speght, Rachel 1597-after 1630 .... DLB-126

Speke, John Hanning 1827-1864 .... DLB-166

Spellman, A. B. 1935- DLB-41

Spence, Catherine Helen 1825-1910 ..... DLB-230

Spence, Thomas 1750-1814 .... DLB-158

Spencer, Anne 1882-1975 .... DLB-51, 54

Spencer, Charles, third Earl of Sunderland 1674-1722 .... DLB-213

Spencer, Elizabeth 1921- DLB-6, 218

Spencer, George John, Second Earl Spencer 1758-1834 .... DLB-184

Spencer, Herbert 1820-1903 .... DLB-57, 262

"The Philosophy of Style" (1852) DLB-57

Spencer, Scott 1945- Y-86

Spender, J. A. 1862-1942 .... DLB-98

Spender, Stephen 1909-1995 ... DLB-20; CDBLB-7

Spener, Philipp Jakob 1635-1705 .... DLB-164

Spenser, Edmund circa 1552-1599 .... DLB-167; CDBLB-1

Envoy from *The Shepheardes Calender* DLB-167

"The Generall Argument of the Whole Booke," from *The Shepheardes Calender* DLB-167

"A Letter of the Authors Expounding His Whole Intention in the Course of this Worke: Which for that It Giueth Great Light to the Reader, for the Better Vnderstanding Is Hereunto Annexed," from *The Faerie Queene* (1590) DLB-167

"To His Booke," from *The Shepheardes Calender* (1579) DLB-167

"To the Most Excellent and Learned Both Orator and Poete, Mayster Gabriell Haruey, His Verie Special and Singular Good Frend E. K. Commendeth the Good Lyking of This His Labour, and the Patronage of the New Poete," from *The Shepheardes Calender* DLB-167

Sperr, Martin 1944- DLB-124

Spewack, Samuel 1899-1971 and Bella 1899-1990 .... DLB-266

Spicer, Jack 1925-1965 .... DLB-5, 16, 193

Spielberg, Peter 1929- Y-81

Spielhagen, Friedrich 1829-1911 .... DLB-129

"*Spielmannsepen*" (circa 1152-circa 1500) .. DLB-148

Spier, Peter 1927- DLB-61

Spillane, Mickey 1918- DLB-226

Spink, J. G. Taylor 1888-1962 .... DLB-241

Spinrad, Norman 1940- DLB-8

Spires, Elizabeth 1952- DLB-120

Spitteler, Carl 1845-1924 .... DLB-129

Spivak, Lawrence E. 1900- DLB-137

Spofford, Harriet Prescott 1835-1921 .... DLB-74, 221

Sprigge, T. L. S. 1932- DLB-262

Spring, Howard 1889-1965 .... DLB-191

Squibob (see Derby, George Horatio)

Squier, E. G. 1821-1888 .... DLB-189

Stableford, Brian 1948- DLB-261

Stacpoole, H. de Vere 1863-1951 .... DLB-153

Staël, Germaine de 1766-1817 ...... DLB-119, 192

Staël-Holstein, Anne-Louise Germaine de (see Staël, Germaine de)

Stafford, Jean 1915-1979 .... DLB-2, 173

Stafford, William 1914-1993 .... DLB-5, 206

Stage Censorship: "The Rejected Statement" (1911), by Bernard Shaw [excerpts] ... DLB-10

Stallings, Laurence 1894-1968 .... DLB-7, 44

Stallworthy, Jon 1935- DLB-40

Stampp, Kenneth M. 1912- DLB-17

Stănescu, Nichita 1933-1983 .... DLB-232

Stanev, Emiliyan 1907-1979 .... DLB-181

Stanford, Ann 1916- DLB-5

Stangerup, Henrik 1937-1998 .... DLB-214

Stanitsky, N. (see Panaeva, Avdot'ia Iakovlevna)

Stankevich, Nikolai Vladimirovich 1813-1840 .... DLB-198

Stanković, Borisav ("Bora") 1876-1927 .... DLB-147; CDWLB-4

Stanley, Henry M. 1841-1904 ... DLB-189; DS-13

Stanley, Thomas 1625-1678 .... DLB-131

Stannard, Martin 1947- DLB-155

Stansby, William [publishing house] DLB-170

Stanton, Elizabeth Cady 1815-1902 ...... DLB-79

Stanton, Frank L. 1857-1927 .... DLB-25

Stanton, Maura 1946- DLB-120

Stapledon, Olaf 1886-1950 .... DLB-15, 255

Star Spangled Banner Office DLB-49

Stark, Freya 1893-1993 .... DLB-195

Starkey, Thomas circa 1499-1538 ...... DLB-132

Starkie, Walter 1894-1976 .... DLB-195

Starkweather, David 1935- DLB-7

Starrett, Vincent 1886-1974 .... DLB-187

The State of Publishing Y-97

Statements on the Art of Poetry DLB-54

Stationers' Company of London, The DLB-170

Statius circa A.D. 45-A.D. 96 .... DLB-211

Stead, Christina 1902-1983 .... DLB-260

Stead, Robert J. C. 1880-1959 .... DLB-92

Steadman, Mark 1930- DLB-6

The Stealthy School of Criticism (1871), by Dante Gabriel Rossetti DLB-35

Stearns, Harold E. 1891-1943 .... DLB-4

Stebnitsky, M. (see Leskov, Nikolai Semenovich)

Stedman, Edmund Clarence 1833-1908 ... DLB-64

Steegmuller, Francis 1906-1994 .... DLB-111

Steel, Flora Annie 1847-1929 ...... DLB-153, 156

Steele, Max 1922- Y-80

Steele, Richard 1672-1729 .... DLB-84, 101; CDBLB-2

Steele, Timothy 1948- DLB-120

Steele, Wilbur Daniel 1886-1970 ...... DLB-86

Steere, Richard circa 1643-1721 .... DLB-24

Stefanovski, Goran 1952- DLB-181

Stegner, Wallace 1909-1993 ..... DLB-9, 206; Y-93

Stehr, Hermann 1864-1940 .... DLB-66

Steig, William 1907- DLB-61

Stein, Gertrude 1874-1946 .... DLB-4, 54, 86, 228; DS-15; CDALB-4

Stein, Leo 1872-1947 .... DLB-4

Stein and Day Publishers DLB-46

Steinbeck, John 1902-1968 .... DLB-7, 9, 212; DS-2; CDALB-5

John Steinbeck Research Center Y-85

Steinem, Gloria 1934- DLB-246

Steiner, George 1929- DLB-67

Steinhoewel, Heinrich 1411/1412-1479 ... DLB-179

Steloff, Ida Frances 1887-1989 .... DLB-187

Stendhal 1783-1842 .... DLB-119

Stephen Crane: A Revaluation Virginia Tech Conference, 1989 .... Y-89

Stephen, Leslie 1832-1904 ..... DLB-57, 144, 190

Stephen Vincent Benét Centenary Y-97

Stephens, A. G. 1865-1933 .... DLB-230

Stephens, Alexander H. 1812-1883 ...... DLB-47

Stephens, Alice Barber 1858-1932 ...... DLB-188

Stephens, Ann 1810-1886 .... DLB-3, 73, 250

Stephens, Charles Asbury 1844?-1931 .... DLB-42

Stephens, James 1882?-1950 ..... DLB-19, 153, 162

Stephens, John Lloyd 1805-1852 ... DLB-183, 250

Stephens, Michael 1946- DLB-234

Stephenson, P. R. 1901-1965..........DLB-260

Sterling, George 1869-1926 ....DLB-54

Sterling, James 1701-1763................DLB-24

Sterling, John 1806-1844 ....DLB-116

Stern, Gerald 1925- DLB-105

Stern, Gladys B. 1890-1973 ....DLB-197

Stern, Madeleine B. 1912- DLB-111, 140

Stern, Richard 1928- DLB-218; Y-87

Stern, Stewart 1922- DLB-26

Sterne, Laurence
 1713-1768.............. DLB-39; CDBLB-2

Sternheim, Carl 1878-1942..........DLB-56, 118

Sternhold, Thomas ?-1549 and
 John Hopkins ?-1570..............DLB-132

Steuart, David 1747-1824................DLB-213

Stevens, Henry 1819-1886..............DLB-140

Stevens, Wallace 1879-1955.....DLB-54; CDALB-5

Stevenson, Anne 1933- DLB-40

Stevenson, D. E. 1892-1973 ....DLB-191

Stevenson, Lionel 1902-1973 ....DLB-155

Stevenson, Robert Louis
 1850-1894 .... DLB-18, 57, 141, 156, 174;
 DS-13; CDBLB-5

"On Style in Literature:
 Its Technical Elements" (1885).......DLB-57

Stewart, Donald Ogden
 1894-1980 ....DLB-4, 11, 26

Stewart, Douglas 1913-1985 ....DLB-260

Stewart, Dugald 1753-1828 ....DLB-31

Stewart, George, Jr. 1848-1906 ....DLB-99

Stewart, George R. 1895-1980............DLB-8

Stewart, Harold 1916-1995 ....DLB-260

Stewart, Maria W. 1803?-1879..........DLB-239

Stewart, Randall 1896-1964 ....DLB-103

Stewart, Sean 1965- DLB-251

Stewart and Kidd Company DLB-46

Stickney, Trumbull 1874-1904..........DLB-54

Stieler, Caspar 1632-1707..............DLB-164

Stifter, Adalbert
 1805-1868 ....DLB-133; CDWLB-2

Stiles, Ezra 1727-1795 ....DLB-31

Still, James 1906- DLB-9; Y01

Stirling, S. M. 1954- DLB-251

Stirner, Max 1806-1856................DLB-129

Stith, William 1707-1755................DLB-31

Stock, Elliot [publishing house] DLB-106

Stockton, Frank R.
 1834-1902................DLB-42, 74; DS-13

Stockton, J. Roy 1892-1972 ....DLB-241

Stoddard, Ashbel [publishing house] DLB-49

Stoddard, Charles Warren
 1843-1909......................DLB-186

Stoddard, Elizabeth 1823-1902 ....DLB-202

Stoddard, Richard Henry
 1825-1903 ....DLB-3, 64, 250; DS-13

Stoddard, Solomon 1643-1729...........DLB-24

Stoker, Bram
 1847-1912 .... DLB-36, 70, 178; CDBLB-5

Stokes, Frederick A., Company..........DLB-49

Stokes, Thomas L. 1898-1958 ....DLB-29

Stokesbury, Leon 1945- DLB-120

Stolberg, Christian Graf zu 1748-1821.....DLB-94

Stolberg, Friedrich Leopold Graf zu
 1750-1819 ....DLB-94

Stone, Herbert S., and Company........DLB-49

Stone, Lucy 1818-1893 ....DLB-79, 239

Stone, Melville 1848-1929 ....DLB-25

Stone, Robert 1937- DLB-152

Stone, Ruth 1915- DLB-105

Stone, Samuel 1602-1663................DLB-24

Stone, William Leete 1792-1844 ....DLB-202

Stone and Kimball DLB-49

Stoppard, Tom
 1937- DLB-13, 233; Y-85; CDBLB-8

Playwrights and Professors DLB-13

Storey, Anthony 1928- DLB-14

Storey, David 1933- DLB-13, 14, 207, 245

Storm, Theodor 1817-1888 ..DLB-129; CDWLB-2

Story, Thomas circa 1670-1742 ....DLB-31

Story, William Wetmore 1819-1895 ...DLB-1, 235

Storytelling: A Contemporary Renaissance...Y-84

Stoughton, William 1631-1701..........DLB-24

Stow, John 1525-1605 ....DLB-132

Stow, Randolph 1935- DLB-260

Stowe, Harriet Beecher 1811-1896
 ..DLB-1, 12, 42, 74, 189, 239, 243; CDALB-3

Stowe, Leland 1899- DLB-29

Stoyanov, Dimitr Ivanov (see Elin Pelin)

Strabo 64 or 63 B.C.-circa A.D. 25 ......DLB-176

Strachey, Lytton 1880-1932......DLB-149; DS-10

Strachey, Lytton, Preface to Eminent
 Victorians DLB-149

Strahan, William [publishing house] DLB-154

Strahan and Company................DLB-106

Strand, Mark 1934- DLB-5

The Strasbourg Oaths 842.............DLB-148

Stratemeyer, Edward 1862-1930 ....DLB-42

Strati, Saverio 1924- DLB-177

Stratton and Barnard....................DLB-49

Stratton-Porter, Gene
 1863-1924.................DLB-221; DS-14

Straub, Peter 1943- Y-84

Strauß, Botho 1944- DLB-124

Strauß, David Friedrich 1808-1874 ......DLB-133

The Strawberry Hill Press DLB-154

Strawson, P. F. 1919- DLB-262

Streatfeild, Noel 1895-1986 ....DLB-160

Street, Cecil John Charles (see Rhode, John)

Street, G. S. 1867-1936................DLB-135

Street and Smith.....................DLB-49

Streeter, Edward 1891-1976 ....DLB-11

Streeter, Thomas Winthrop 1883-1965...DLB-140

Stretton, Hesba 1832-1911.........DLB-163, 190

Stribling, T. S. 1881-1965 ....DLB-9

Der Stricker circa 1190-circa 1250.......DLB-138

Strickland, Samuel 1804-1867 ....DLB-99

Strindberg, August 1849-1912..........DLB-259

Stringer, Arthur 1874-1950 ....DLB-92

Stringer and Townsend.................DLB-49

Strittmatter, Erwin 1912- DLB-69

Strniša, Gregor 1930-1987 ....DLB-181

Strode, William 1630-1645 ....DLB-126

Strong, L. A. G. 1896-1958 ....DLB-191

Strother, David Hunter (Porte Crayon)
 1816-1888....................DLB-3, 248

Strouse, Jean 1945- DLB-111

Stuart, Dabney 1937- DLB-105

Stuart, Jesse 1906-1984 .....DLB-9, 48, 102; Y-84

Stuart, Lyle [publishing house] DLB-46

Stuart, Ruth McEnery 1849?-1917 ......DLB-202

Stubbs, Harry Clement (see Clement, Hal)

Stubenberg, Johann Wilhelm von
 1619-1663......................DLB-164

Studebaker, William V. 1947- DLB-256

Studio.............................DLB-112

The Study of Poetry (1880), by
 Matthew Arnold DLB-35

Stump, Al 1916-1995.................DLB-241

Sturgeon, Theodore 1918-1985......DLB-8; Y-85

Sturges, Preston 1898-1959 ....DLB-26

"Style" (1840; revised, 1859), by
 Thomas de Quincey [excerpt].........DLB-57

"Style" (1888), by Walter Pater..........DLB-57

Style (1897), by Walter Raleigh
 [excerpt] DLB-57

"Style" (1877), by T. H. Wright
 [excerpt] DLB-57

"Le Style c'est l'homme" (1892), by
 W. H. Mallock DLB-57

Styron, William
 1925- DLB-2, 143; Y-80; CDALB-6

Suárez, Mario 1925- DLB-82

Such, Peter 1939- DLB-60

Suckling, Sir John 1609-1641?........DLB-58, 126

Suckow, Ruth 1892-1960............DLB-9, 102

Sudermann, Hermann 1857-1928 ....DLB-118

Sue, Eugène 1804-1857 ....DLB-119

Sue, Marie-Joseph (see Sue, Eugène)

Suetonius circa A.D. 69-post A.D. 122 ...DLB-211

Suggs, Simon (see Hooper, Johnson Jones)

Sui Sin Far (see Eaton, Edith Maude)

Suits, Gustav 1883-1956 .....DLB-220; CDWLB-4

Sukenick, Ronald 1932- DLB-173; Y-81

Suknaski, Andrew 1942- DLB-53

Sullivan, Alan 1868-1947...............DLB-92

Sullivan, C. Gardner 1886-1965 ....DLB-26

Sullivan, Frank 1892-1976 ....DLB-11

Sulte, Benjamin 1841-1923 ....DLB-99

Sulzberger, Arthur Hays 1891-1968 .....DLB-127

Sulzberger, Arthur Ochs 1926- DLB-127
Sulzer, Johann Georg 1720-1779 .... DLB-97
Sumarokov, Aleksandr Petrovich
  1717-1777 .... DLB-150
Summers, Hollis 1916- DLB-6
A Summing Up at Century's End Y-99
Sumner, Charles 1811-1874 .... DLB-235
Sumner, Henry A. [publishing house] DLB-49
Sundman, Per Olof 1922-1992 .... DLB-257
Supervielle, Jules 1884-1960 .... DLB-258
Surtees, Robert Smith 1803-1864 .... DLB-21
Survey of Literary Biographies Y-00
A Survey of Poetry Anthologies,
  1879-1960 .... DLB-54
Surveys: Japanese Literature,
  1987-1995 .... DLB-182
Sutherland, Efua Theodora
  1924-1996 .... DLB-117
Sutherland, John 1919-1956 .... DLB-68
Sutro, Alfred 1863-1933 .... DLB-10
Svendsen, Hanne Marie 1933- DLB-214
Svevo, Italo (Aron Hector Schmitz)
  1861-1928 .... DLB-264
Swados, Harvey 1920-1972 .... DLB-2
Swain, Charles 1801-1874 .... DLB-32
Swallow Press DLB-46
Swan Sonnenschein Limited DLB-106
Swanberg, W. A. 1907- DLB-103
Swenson, May 1919-1989 .... DLB-5
Swerling, Jo 1897- DLB-44
Swift, Graham 1949- DLB-194
Swift, Jonathan
  1667-1745 .... DLB-39, 95, 101; CDBLB-2
Swinburne, A. C.
  1837-1909 .... DLB-35, 57; CDBLB-4
Swineshead, Richard
  floruit circa 1350 .... DLB-115
Swinnerton, Frank 1884-1982 .... DLB-34
Swisshelm, Jane Grey 1815-1884 ..... DLB-43
Swope, Herbert Bayard 1882-1958 ..... DLB-25
Swords, T. and J., and Company DLB-49
Swords, Thomas 1763-1843 and
  Swords, James ?-1844 .... DLB-73
Sykes, Ella C. ?-1939 .... DLB-174
Sylvester, Josuah
  1562 or 1563-1618 .... DLB-121
Symonds, Emily Morse (see Paston, George)
Symonds, John Addington
  1840-1893 .... DLB-57, 144
"Personal Style" (1890) DLB-57
Symons, A. J. A. 1900-1941 .... DLB-149
Symons, Arthur 1865-1945 ... DLB-19, 57, 149
Symons, Julian
  1912-1994 .... DLB-87, 155; Y-92
Julian Symons at Eighty Y-92
Symons, Scott 1933- DLB-53
A Symposium on *The Columbia History of
  the Novel* Y-92

Synge, John Millington
  1871-1909 .... DLB-10, 19; CDBLB-5
Synge Summer School: J. M. Synge and the
  Irish Theater, Rathdrum, County Wiclow,
  Ireland Y-93
Syrett, Netta 1865-1943 .... DLB-135, 197
Szabó, Lőrinc 1900-1957 .... DLB-215
Szabó, Magda 1917- DLB-215
Szymborska, Wisława
  1923- DLB-232, Y-96; CDWLB-4

T

Taban lo Liyong 1939?- DLB-125
Tabori, George 1914- DLB-245
Tabucchi, Antonio 1943- DLB-196
Taché, Joseph-Charles 1820-1894 ...... DLB-99
Tachihara Masaaki 1926-1980 .... DLB-182
Tacitus circa A.D. 55-circa A.D. 117
  .... DLB-211; CDWLB-1
Tadijanović, Dragutin 1905- DLB-181
Tafdrup, Pia 1952- DLB-214
Tafolla, Carmen 1951- DLB-82
Taggard, Genevieve 1894-1948 .... DLB-45
Taggart, John 1942- DLB-193
Tagger, Theodor (see Bruckner, Ferdinand)
Taiheiki late fourteenth century DLB-203
Tait, J. Selwin, and Sons DLB-49
Tait's Edinburgh Magazine 1832-1861 ..... DLB-110
The Takarazuka Revue Company Y-91
Talander (see Bohse, August)
Talese, Gay 1932- DLB-185
Talev, Dimitr 1898-1966 .... DLB-181
Taliaferro, H. E. 1811-1875 .... DLB-202
Tallent, Elizabeth 1954- DLB-130
TallMountain, Mary 1918-1994 .... DLB-193
Talvj 1797-1870 .... DLB-59, 133
Tamási, Áron 1897-1966 .... DLB-215
Tammsaare, A. H.
  1878-1940 .... DLB-220; CDWLB-4
Tan, Amy 1952- DLB-173; CDALB-7
Tandori, Dezső 1938- DLB-232
Tanner, Thomas 1673/1674-1735 ...... DLB-213
Tanizaki Jun'ichirō 1886-1965 .... DLB-180
Tapahonso, Luci 1953- DLB-175
The Mark Taper Forum DLB-7
Taradash, Daniel 1913- DLB-44
Tarbell, Ida M. 1857-1944 .... DLB-47
Tardivel, Jules-Paul 1851-1905 .... DLB-99
Targan, Barry 1932- DLB-130
Tarkington, Booth 1869-1946 .... DLB-9, 102
Tashlin, Frank 1913-1972 .... DLB-44
Tasma (Jessie Couvreur) 1848-1897 .... DLB-230
Tate, Allen 1899-1979 .... DLB-4, 45, 63; DS-17
Tate, James 1943- DLB-5, 169
Tate, Nahum circa 1652-1715 .... DLB-80
Tatian circa 830 .... DLB-148

Taufer, Veno 1933- DLB-181
Tauler, Johannes circa 1300-1361 ...... DLB-179
Tavčar, Ivan 1851-1923 .... DLB-147
Taverner, Richard ca. 1505-1575 ...... DLB-236
Taylor, Ann 1782-1866 .... DLB-163
Taylor, Bayard 1825-1878 ...... DLB-3, 189, 250
Taylor, Bert Leston 1866-1921 .... DLB-25
Taylor, Charles H. 1846-1921 .... DLB-25
Taylor, Edward circa 1642-1729 .... DLB-24
Taylor, Elizabeth 1912-1975 .... DLB-139
Taylor, Henry 1942- DLB-5
Taylor, Sir Henry 1800-1886 .... DLB-32
Taylor, Jane 1783-1824 .... DLB-163
Taylor, Jeremy circa 1613-1667 .... DLB-151
Taylor, John 1577 or 1578 - 1653 ..... DLB-121
Taylor, Mildred D. ?- DLB-52
Taylor, Peter 1917-1994 ..... DLB-218; Y-81, Y-94
Taylor, Susie King 1848-1912 .... DLB-221
Taylor, William Howland 1901-1966 ... DLB-241
Taylor, William, and Company DLB-49
Taylor-Made Shakespeare? Or Is "Shall I Die?" the
  Long-Lost Text of Bottom's Dream? Y-85
Teasdale, Sara 1884-1933 .... DLB-45
Telles, Lygia Fagundes 1924- DLB-113
Temple, Sir William 1628-1699 .... DLB-101
Temple, William F. 1914-1989 .... DLB-255
Temrizov, A. (see Marchenko, Anastasia Iakovlevna)
Tench, Watkin ca. 1758-1833 .... DLB-230
Tenn, William 1919- DLB-8
Tennant, Emma 1937- DLB-14
Tenney, Tabitha Gilman
  1762-1837 .... DLB-37, 200
Tennyson, Alfred
  1809-1892 .... DLB-32; CDBLB-4
Tennyson, Frederick 1807-1898 .... DLB-32
Tenorio, Arthur 1924- DLB-209
Tepliakov, Viktor Grigor'evich
  1804-1842 .... DLB-205
Terence circa 184 B.C.-159 B.C. or after
  .... DLB-211; CDWLB-1
Terhune, Albert Payson 1872-1942 ..... DLB-9
Terhune, Mary Virginia
  1830-1922 .... DS-13, DS-16
Terry, Megan 1932- DLB-7, 249
Terson, Peter 1932- DLB-13
Tesich, Steve 1943-1996 .... Y-83
Tessa, Delio 1886-1939 .... DLB-114
Testori, Giovanni 1923-1993 .... DLB-128, 177
Tey, Josephine 1896?-1952 .... DLB-77
Thacher, James 1754-1844 .... DLB-37
Thackeray, William Makepeace
  1811-1863 .. DLB-21, 55, 159, 163; CDBLB-4
Thames and Hudson Limited DLB-112
Thanet, Octave (see French, Alice)
Thatcher, John Boyd 1847-1909 .... DLB-187
Thaxter, Celia Laighton 1835-1894 .... DLB-239

Thayer, Caroline Matilda Warren 1785-1844 .... DLB-200

Thayer, Douglas 1929- DLB-256

The Theatre Guild................. DLB-7

The Theater in Shakespeare's Time DLB-62

Thegan and the Astronomer flourished circa 850............... DLB-148

Thelwall, John 1764-1834 .... DLB-93, 158

Theocritus circa 300 B.C.-260 B.C....... DLB-176

Theodorescu, Ion N. (see Arghezi, Tudor)

Theodulf circa 760-circa 821 .... DLB-148

Theophrastus circa 371 B.C.-287 B.C..... DLB-176

Theriault, Yves 1915-1983............ DLB-88

Thério, Adrien 1925- DLB-53

Theroux, Paul 1941- DLB-2, 218; CDALB-7

Thesiger, Wilfred 1910- DLB-204

They All Came to Paris................ DS-16

Thibaudeau, Colleen 1925- DLB-88

Thielen, Benedict 1903-1965........... DLB-102

Thiong'o Ngugi wa (see Ngugi wa Thiong'o)

Third-Generation Minor Poets of the Seventeenth Century............. DLB-131

This Quarter 1925-1927, 1929-1932 ...... DS-15

Thoma, Ludwig 1867-1921 .... DLB-66

Thoma, Richard 1902- DLB-4

Thomas, Audrey 1935- DLB-60

Thomas, D. M. 1935- ..DLB-40, 207; CDBLB-8

D. M. Thomas: The Plagiarism Controversy Y-82

Thomas, Dylan 1914-1953 ......DLB-13, 20, 139; CDBLB-7

The Dylan Thomas Celebration Y-99

Thomas, Edward 1878-1917 .... DLB-19, 98, 156, 216

Thomas, Frederick William 1806-1866...DLB-202

Thomas, Gwyn 1913-1981 .... DLB-15, 245

Thomas, Isaiah 1750-1831 .... DLB-43, 73, 187

Thomas, Isaiah [publishing house]....... DLB-49

Thomas, Johann 1624-1679 .... DLB-168

Thomas, John 1900-1932............. DLB-4

Thomas, Joyce Carol 1938- DLB-33

Thomas, Lorenzo 1944- DLB-41

Thomas, R. S. 1915-2000......DLB-27; CDBLB-8

Thomasîn von Zerclære circa 1186-circa 1259.............. DLB-138

Thomasius, Christian 1655-1728....... DLB-168

Thompson, Daniel Pierce 1795-1868.....DLB-202

Thompson, David 1770-1857........... DLB-99

Thompson, Dorothy 1893-1961......... DLB-29

Thompson, E. P. 1924-1993........... DLB-242

Thompson, Flora 1876-1947 .... DLB-240

Thompson, Francis 1859-1907 .... DLB-19; CDBLB-5

Thompson, George Selden (see Selden, George)

Thompson, Henry Yates 1838-1928 ..... DLB-184

Thompson, Hunter S. 1939- DLB-185

Thompson, Jim 1906-1977............DLB-226

Thompson, John 1938-1976............DLB-60

Thompson, John R. 1823-1873 ....DLB-3, 73, 248

Thompson, Lawrance 1906-1973 .... DLB-103

Thompson, Maurice 1844-1901 ..... DLB-71, 74

Thompson, Ruth Plumly 1891-1976....... DLB-22

Thompson, Thomas Phillips 1843-1933 ...DLB-99

Thompson, William 1775-1833 .... DLB-158

Thompson, William Tappan 1812-1882.............DLB-3, 11, 248

Thomson, Edward William 1849-1924....DLB-92

Thomson, James 1700-1748 .... DLB-95

Thomson, James 1834-1882 .... DLB-35

Thomson, Joseph 1858-1895........... DLB-174

Thomson, Mortimer 1831-1875......... DLB-11

Thon, Melanie Rae 1957- DLB-244

Thoreau, Henry David 1817-1862 ......DLB-1, 183, 223; CDALB-2

The Thoreauvian Pilgrimage: The Structure of an American Cult.................. DLB-223

Thorpe, Adam 1956- DLB-231

Thorpe, Thomas Bangs 1815-1878 ....DLB-3, 11, 248

Thorup, Kirsten 1942- DLB-214

Thoughts on Poetry and Its Varieties (1833), by John Stuart Mill DLB-32

Thrale, Hester Lynch (see Piozzi, Hester Lynch [Thrale])

Thubron, Colin 1939- DLB-204, 231

Thucydides circa 455 B.C.-circa 395 B.C. DLB-176

Thulstrup, Thure de 1848-1930 .... DLB-188

Thümmel, Moritz August von 1738-1817 .... DLB-97

Thurber, James 1894-1961 .....DLB-4, 11, 22, 102; CDALB-5

Thurman, Wallace 1902-1934........... DLB-51

Thwaite, Anthony 1930- DLB-40

The Booker Prize Address by Anthony Thwaite, Chairman of the Booker Prize Judges Comments from Former Booker Prize Winners Y-86

Thwaites, Reuben Gold 1853-1913 .... DLB-47

Tibullus circa 54 B.C.-circa 19 B.C. DLB-211

Ticknor, George 1791-1871 ...DLB-1, 59, 140, 235

Ticknor and Fields.................. DLB-49

Ticknor and Fields (revived) DLB-46

Tieck, Ludwig 1773-1853..... DLB-90; CDWLB-2

Tietjens, Eunice 1884-1944 .... DLB-54

Tikkanen, Märta 1935- DLB-257

Tilghman, Christopher circa 1948-..... DLB-244

Tilney, Edmund circa 1536-1610....... DLB-136

Tilt, Charles [publishing house]........ DLB-106

Tilton, J. E., and Company DLB-49

Time and Western Man (1927), by Wyndham Lewis [excerpts]................. DLB-36

Time-Life Books DLB-46

Times Books DLB-46

Timothy, Peter circa 1725-1782 ....DLB-43

Timrava 1867-1951 .... DLB-215

Timrod, Henry 1828-1867 .... DLB-3, 248

Tindal, Henrietta 1818?-1879 ....DLB-199

Tinker, Chauncey Brewster 1876-1963 ...DLB-140

Tinsley Brothers DLB-106

Tiptree, James, Jr. 1915-1987............DLB-8

Tišma, Aleksandar 1924- DLB-181

Titus, Edward William 1870-1952 ....DLB-4; DS-15

Tiutchev, Fedor Ivanovich 1803-1873 ....DLB-205

Tlali, Miriam 1933- DLB-157, 225

Todd, Barbara Euphan 1890-1976.......DLB-160

Todorov, Tzvetan 1939- DLB-242

Tofte, Robert 1561 or 1562-1619 or 1620......... DLB-172

Toklas, Alice B. 1877-1967................DLB-4

Tokuda, Shūsei 1872-1943............ DLB-180

Toland, John 1670-1722................DLB-252

Tolkien, J. R. R. 1892-1973 ......DLB-15, 160, 255; CDBLB-6

Toller, Ernst 1893-1939................ DLB-124

Tollet, Elizabeth 1694-1754 ....DLB-95

Tolson, Melvin B. 1898-1966 .... DLB-48, 76

Tolstoy, Aleksei Konstantinovich 1817-1875................. DLB-238

Tolstoy, Leo 1828-1910................DLB-238

Tom Jones (1749), by Henry Fielding [excerpt] DLB-39

Tomalin, Claire 1933- DLB-155

Tomasi di Lampedusa, Giuseppe 1896-1957 .... DLB-177

Tomlinson, Charles 1927- DLB-40

Tomlinson, H. M. 1873-1958 ... DLB-36, 100, 195

Tompkins, Abel [publishing house]....... DLB-49

Tompson, Benjamin 1642-1714 .... DLB-24

Tomson, Graham R. (see Watson, Rosamund Marriott)

Ton'a 1289-1372 .... DLB-203

Tondelli, Pier Vittorio 1955-1991 .... DLB-196

Tonks, Rosemary 1932- DLB-14, 207

Tonna, Charlotte Elizabeth 1790-1846 ...DLB-163

Tonson, Jacob the Elder [publishing house] DLB-170

Toole, John Kennedy 1937-1969 .... Y-81

Toomer, Jean 1894-1967 ...DLB-45, 51; CDALB-4

Tor Books DLB-46

Torberg, Friedrich 1908-1979 .... DLB-85

Torrence, Ridgely 1874-1950........ DLB-54, 249

Torres-Metzger, Joseph V. 1933- DLB-122

Toth, Susan Allen 1940- Y-86

Tottell, Richard [publishing house] DLB-170

"The Printer to the Reader," (1557) by Richard Tottell................. DLB-167

Tough-Guy Literature.................. DLB-9

Touré, Askia Muhammad 1938- DLB-41

Tourgée, Albion W. 1838-1905.......... DLB-79

Tournemir, Elizaveta Sailhas de (see Tur, Evgeniia)

Cumulative Index

Tourneur, Cyril circa 1580-1626 . . . . DLB-58

Tournier, Michel 1924- DLB-83

Tousey, Frank [publishing house] DLB-49

Tower Publications DLB-46

Towne, Benjamin circa 1740-1793 . . . . . . DLB-43

Towne, Robert 1936- DLB-44

The Townely Plays fifteenth and sixteenth centuries DLB-146

Townshend, Aurelian by 1583-circa 1651 . . . . DLB-121

Toy, Barbara 1908- DLB-204

Tozzi, Federigo 1883-1920 . . . . DLB-264

Tracy, Honor 1913- DLB-15

Traherne, Thomas 1637?-1674 . . . . DLB-131

Traill, Catharine Parr 1802-1899 . . . . . . DLB-99

Train, Arthur 1875-1945 . . . . DLB-86; DS-16

Tranquilli, Secondino (see Silone, Ignazio)

The Transatlantic Publishing Company . . . DLB-49

The Transatlantic Review 1924-1925 . . . . DS-15

The Transcendental Club 1836-1840 . . . . DLB-223

Transcendentalism DLB-223

Transcendentalists, American DS-5

A Transit of Poets and Others: American Biography in 1982 . . . . Y-82

transition 1927-1938 . . . . DS-15

Translators of the Twelfth Century: Literary Issues Raised and Impact Created DLB-115

Tranströmer, Tomas 1931- DLB-257

Travel Writing, 1837-1875 . . . . DLB-166

Travel Writing, 1876-1909 . . . . DLB-174

Travel Writing, 1910-1939 . . . . DLB-195

Traven, B. 1882? or 1890?-1969? DLB-9, 56

Travers, Ben 1886-1980 . . . . DLB-10, 233

Travers, P. L. (Pamela Lyndon) 1899-1996 . . . . DLB-160

Trediakovsky, Vasilii Kirillovich 1703-1769 . . . . DLB-150

Treece, Henry 1911-1966 . . . . DLB-160

Trejo, Ernesto 1950- DLB-122

Trelawny, Edward John 1792-1881 . . . . DLB-110, 116, 144

Tremain, Rose 1943- DLB-14

Tremblay, Michel 1942- DLB-60

Trends in Twentieth-Century Mass Market Publishing DLB-46

Trent, William P. 1862-1939 . . . . DLB-47

Trescot, William Henry 1822-1898 . . . . . . DLB-30

Tressell, Robert (Robert Phillipe Noonan) 1870-1911 . . . . DLB-197

Trevelyan, Sir George Otto 1838-1928 . . . . DLB-144

Trevisa, John circa 1342-circa 1402 . . . . . DLB-146

Trevor, William 1928- DLB-14, 139

Trierer Floyris circa 1170-1180 . . . . DLB-138

Trillin, Calvin 1935- DLB-185

Trilling, Lionel 1905-1975 . . . . DLB-28, 63

Trilussa 1871-1950 . . . . DLB-114

Trimmer, Sarah 1741-1810 . . . . DLB-158

Triolet, Elsa 1896-1970 . . . . DLB-72

Tripp, John 1927- DLB-40

Trocchi, Alexander 1925- DLB-15

Troisi, Dante 1920-1989 . . . . DLB-196

Trollope, Anthony 1815-1882 . . . . DLB-21, 57, 159; CDBLB-4

Trollope, Frances 1779-1863 . . . . DLB-21, 166

Trollope, Joanna 1943- DLB-207

Troop, Elizabeth 1931- DLB-14

Trotter, Catharine 1679-1749 . . . . DLB-84, 252

Trotti, Lamar 1898-1952 . . . . DLB-44

Trottier, Pierre 1925- DLB-60

Trotzig, Birgitta 1929- DLB-257

Troubadours, *Trobaíritz*, and Trouvères . . . DLB-208

Troupe, Quincy Thomas, Jr. 1943- DLB-41

Trow, John F., and Company DLB-49

Trowbridge, John Townsend 1827-1916 . . . DLB-202

Trudel, Jean-Louis 1967- DLB-251

Truillier-Lacombe, Joseph-Patrice 1807-1863 . . . . DLB-99

Trumbo, Dalton 1905-1976 . . . . DLB-26

Trumbull, Benjamin 1735-1820 . . . . DLB-30

Trumbull, John 1750-1831 . . . . DLB-31

Trumbull, John 1756-1843 . . . . DLB-183

Truth, Sojourner 1797?-1883 . . . . DLB-239

Tscherning, Andreas 1611-1659 . . . . DLB-164

Tsubouchi, Shōyō 1859-1935 . . . . DLB-180

Tucholsky, Kurt 1890-1935 . . . . DLB-56

Tucker, Charlotte Maria 1821-1893 . . . . DLB-163, 190

Tucker, George 1775-1861 . . . . DLB-3, 30, 248

Tucker, James 1808?-1866? DLB-230

Tucker, Nathaniel Beverley 1784-1851 . . . . DLB-3, 248

Tucker, St. George 1752-1827 . . . . DLB-37

Tuckerman, Frederick Goddard 1821-1873 . . . . DLB-243

Tuckerman, Henry Theodore 1813-1871 . . . DLB-64

Tumas, Juozas (see Vaizgantas)

Tunis, John R. 1889-1975 . . . . DLB-22, 171

Tunstall, Cuthbert 1474-1559 . . . . DLB-132

Tunström, Göran 1937-2000 . . . . DLB-257

Tuohy, Frank 1925- DLB-14, 139

Tupper, Martin F. 1810-1889 . . . . DLB-32

Tur, Evgeniia 1815-1892 . . . . DLB-238

Turbyfill, Mark 1896- DLB-45

Turco, Lewis 1934- Y-84

Turgenev, Aleksandr Ivanovich 1784-1845 . . . . DLB-198

Turgenev, Ivan Sergeevich 1818-1883 . . . DLB-238

Turnball, Alexander H. 1868-1918 . . . . . . DLB-184

Turnbull, Andrew 1921-1970 . . . . DLB-103

Turnbull, Gael 1928- DLB-40

Turner, Arlin 1909-1980 . . . . DLB-103

Turner, Charles (Tennyson) 1808-1879 . . . . DLB-32

Turner, Ethel 1872-1958 . . . . DLB-230

Turner, Frederick 1943- DLB-40

Turner, Frederick Jackson 1861-1932 . . . . DLB-17, 186

Turner, Joseph Addison 1826-1868 . . . . . . DLB-79

Turpin, Waters Edward 1910-1968 . . . . . DLB-51

Turrini, Peter 1944- DLB-124

Tutuola, Amos 1920-1997 . . . DLB-125; CDWLB-3

Twain, Mark (see Clemens, Samuel Langhorne)

Tweedie, Ethel Brilliana circa 1860-1940 . . . DLB-174

The 'Twenties and Berlin, by Alex Natan . . DLB-66

Two Hundred Years of Rare Books and Literary Collections at the University of South Carolina Y-00

Twombly, Wells 1935-1977 . . . . DLB-241

Twysden, Sir Roger 1597-1672 . . . . DLB-213

Tyler, Anne 1941- DLB-6, 143; Y-82; CDALB-7

Tyler, Mary Palmer 1775-1866 . . . . DLB-200

Tyler, Moses Coit 1835-1900 . . . . DLB-47, 64

Tyler, Royall 1757-1826 . . . . DLB-37

Tylor, Edward Burnett 1832-1917 . . . . . . DLB-57

Tynan, Katharine 1861-1931 . . . . DLB-153, 240

Tyndale, William circa 1494-1536 . . . . . . DLB-132

U

Uchida, Yoshika 1921-1992 . . . . CDALB-7

Udall, Nicholas 1504-1556 . . . . DLB-62

Ugrêsic, Dubravka 1949- DLB-181

Uhland, Ludwig 1787-1862 . . . . DLB-90

Uhse, Bodo 1904-1963 . . . . DLB-69

Ujević, Augustin ("Tin") 1891-1955 . . . . . DLB-147

Ulenhart, Niclas flourished circa 1600 . . . DLB-164

Ulibarrí, Sabine R. 1919- DLB-82

Ulica, Jorge 1870-1926 . . . . DLB-82

Ulivi, Ferruccio 1912- DLB-196

Ulizio, B. George 1889-1969 . . . . DLB-140

Ulrich von Liechtenstein circa 1200-circa 1275 . . . . DLB-138

Ulrich von Zatzikhoven before 1194-after 1214 . . . . DLB-138

Ulysses, Reader's Edition Y-97

Unaipon, David 1872-1967 . . . . DLB-230

Unamuno, Miguel de 1864-1936 . . . . DLB-108

Under, Marie 1883-1980 . . . . DLB-220; CDWLB-4

Under the Microscope (1872), by A. C. Swinburne DLB-35

Underhill, Evelyn 1875-1941 . . . . DLB-240

Ungaretti, Giuseppe 1888-1970 . . . . DLB-114

Unger, Friederike Helene 1741-1813 . . . . DLB-94

United States Book Company DLB-49

Universal Publishing and Distributing Corporation DLB-46

The University of Iowa
  Writers' Workshop
  Golden Jubilee.................... Y-86
University of Missouri Press Y-01
The University of South Carolina Press Y-94
University of Wales Press DLB-112
University Press of Florida Y-00
University Press of Kansas Y-98
University Press of Mississippi Y-99
"The Unknown Public" (1858), by
  Wilkie Collins [excerpt]...........DLB-57
Uno, Chiyo 1897-1996................DLB-180
Unruh, Fritz von 1885-1970......DLB-56, 118
Unspeakable Practices II:
  The Festival of Vanguard
  Narrative at Brown University Y-93
Unsworth, Barry 1930- DLB-194
Unt, Mati 1944- DLB-232
The Unterberg Poetry Center of the
  92nd Street Y...................... Y-98
Unwin, T. Fisher [publishing house] DLB-106
Upchurch, Boyd B. (see Boyd, John)
Updike, John 1932-
  ....DLB-2, 5, 143, 218, 227; Y-80, Y-82;
                       DS-3; CDALB-6
John Updike on the Internet Y-97
Upīts, Andrejs 1877-1970..............DLB-220
Upton, Bertha 1849-1912 ....DLB-141
Upton, Charles 1948- DLB-16
Upton, Florence K. 1873-1922.........DLB-141
Upward, Allen 1863-1926 ....DLB-36
Urban, Milo 1904-1982................DLB-215
Urista, Alberto Baltazar (see Alurista)
Urquhart, Fred 1912- DLB-139
Urrea, Luis Alberto 1955- DLB-209
Urzidil, Johannes 1896-1976 ....DLB-85
The Uses of Facsimile Y-90
Usk, Thomas died 1388 ....DLB-146
Uslar Pietri, Arturo 1906- DLB-113
Ussher, James 1581-1656..............DLB-213
Ustinov, Peter 1921 ....DLB-13
Uttley, Alison 1884-1976 ....DLB-160
Uz, Johann Peter 1720-1796............DLB-97

V

Vac, Bertrand 1914- DLB-88
Vācietis, Ojārs 1933-1983 ....DLB-232
Vaičiulaitis, Antanas 1906-1992 ....DLB-220
Vaculík, Ludvík 1926- DLB-232
Vaičiūnaite, Judita 1937- DLB-232
Vail, Laurence 1891-1968 ....DLB-4
Vailland, Roger 1907-1965............DLB-83
Vaižgantas 1869-1933 ....DLB-220
Vajda, Ernest 1887-1954 ....DLB-44
Valdés, Gina 1943- DLB-122
Valdez, Luis Miguel 1940- DLB-122
Valduga, Patrizia 1953- DLB-128

Valente, José Angel 1929-2000 ....DLB-108
Valenzuela, Luisa 1938- ...DLB-113; CDWLB-3
Valeri, Diego 1887-1976...............DLB-128
Valerius Flaccus fl. circa A.D. 92........DLB-211
Valerius Maximus fl. circa A.D. 31 ......DLB-211
Valéry, Paul 1871-1945 ....DLB-258
Valesio, Paolo 1939- DLB-196
Valgardson, W. D. 1939- DLB-60
Valle, Víctor Manuel 1950- DLB-122
Valle-Inclán, Ramón del 1866-1936......DLB-134
Vallejo, Armando 1949- DLB-122
Vallès, Jules 1832-1885 ....DLB-123
Vallette, Marguerite Eymery (see Rachilde)
Valverde, José María 1926-1996 ....DLB-108
Van Allsburg, Chris 1949- DLB-61
Van Anda, Carr 1864-1945.............DLB-25
van der Post, Laurens 1906-1996 ....DLB-204
Van Dine, S. S. (see Wright, Williard Huntington)
Van Doren, Mark 1894-1972............DLB-45
van Druten, John 1901-1957 ....DLB-10
Van Duyn, Mona 1921- DLB-5
Van Dyke, Henry 1852-1933 .....DLB-71; DS-13
Van Dyke, Henry 1928- DLB-33
Van Dyke, John C. 1856-1932 ....DLB-186
van Gulik, Robert Hans 1910-1967........ DS-17
van Itallie, Jean-Claude 1936- DLB-7
Van Loan, Charles E. 1876-1919........DLB-171
Van Rensselaer, Mariana Griswold
  1851-1934 ....DLB-47
Van Rensselaer, Mrs. Schuyler
  (see Van Rensselaer, Mariana Griswold)
Van Vechten, Carl 1880-1964..........DLB-4, 9
van Vogt, A. E. 1912-2000 ....DLB-8, 251
Vanbrugh, Sir John 1664-1726.........DLB-80
Vance, Jack 1916?- DLB-8
Vančura, Vladislav
  1891-1942 ....DLB-215; CDWLB-4
Vane, Sutton 1888-1963 ....DLB-10
Vanguard Press DLB-46
Vann, Robert L. 1879-1940 ....DLB-29
Vargas Llosa, Mario
  1936- DLB-145; CDWLB-3
Varley, John 1947- Y-81
Varnhagen von Ense, Karl August
  1785-1858 ....DLB-90
Varnhagen von Ense, Rahel
  1771-1833 ....DLB-90
Varro 116 B.C.-27 B.C..................DLB-211
Vasiliu, George (see Bacovia, George)
Vásquez, Richard 1928- DLB-209
Vásquez Montalbán, Manuel 1939- DLB-134
Vassa, Gustavus (see Equiano, Olaudah)
Vassalli, Sebastiano 1941- DLB-128, 196
Vaughan, Henry 1621-1695 ....DLB-131
Vaughan, Thomas 1621-1666 ....DLB-131
Vaughn, Robert 1592?-1667 ....DLB-213

Vaux, Thomas, Lord 1509-1556........DLB-132
Vazov, Ivan 1850-1921 .....DLB-147; CDWLB-4
Véa, Alfredo, Jr. 1950- DLB-209
Veblen, Thorstein 1857-1929...........DLB-246
Vega, Janine Pommy 1942- DLB-16
Veiller, Anthony 1903-1965 ....DLB-44
Velásquez-Trevino, Gloria 1949- DLB-122
Veley, Margaret 1843-1887 ....DLB-199
Velleius Paterculus
  circa 20 B.C.-circa A.D. 30 ....DLB-211
Veloz Maggiolo, Marcio 1936- DLB-145
Vel'tman Aleksandr Fomich
  1800-1870 ....DLB-198
Venegas, Daniel ?-? DLB-82
Venevitinov, Dmitrii Vladimirovich
  1805-1827 ....DLB-205
Vergil, Polydore circa 1470-1555........DLB-132
Veríssimo, Erico 1905-1975............DLB-145
Verlaine, Paul 1844-1896 ....DLB-217
Verne, Jules 1828-1905 ....DLB-123
Verplanck, Gulian C. 1786-1870 ....DLB-59
Very, Jones 1813-1880................DLB-1, 243
Vian, Boris 1920-1959 ....DLB-72
Viazemsky, Petr Andreevich
  1792-1878 ....DLB-205
Vicars, Thomas 1591-1638 ....DLB-236
Vickers, Roy 1888?-1965..............DLB-77
Vickery, Sukey 1779-1821 ....DLB-200
Victoria 1819-1901 ....DLB-55
Victoria Press........................DLB-106
Vidal, Gore 1925- DLB-6, 152; CDALB-7
Vidal, Mary Theresa 1815-1873 ....DLB-230
Vidmer, Richards 1898-1978...........DLB-241
Viebig, Clara 1860-1952 ....DLB-66
Viereck, George Sylvester
  1884-1962 ....DLB-54
Viereck, Peter 1916- DLB-5
Viets, Roger 1738-1811 ....DLB-99
Viewpoint: Politics and Performance, by
  David Edgar DLB-13
Vigil-Piñon, Evangelina 1949- DLB-122
Vigneault, Gilles 1928- DLB-60
Vigny, Alfred de
  1797-1863..............DLB-119, 192, 217
Vigolo, Giorgio 1894-1983 ....DLB-114
The Viking Press....................DLB-46
Vilde, Eduard 1865-1933..............DLB-220
Vilinskaia, Mariia Aleksandrovna
  (see Vovchok, Marko)
Villanueva, Alma Luz 1944- DLB-122
Villanueva, Tino 1941- DLB-82
Villard, Henry 1835-1900 ....DLB-23
Villard, Oswald Garrison
  1872-1949 ....DLB-25, 91
Villarreal, Edit 1944- DLB-209
Villarreal, José Antonio 1924- DLB-82
Villaseñor, Victor 1940- DLB-209

Villegas de Magnón, Leonor 1876-1955 ..... DLB-122
Villehardouin, Geoffroi de circa 1150-1215 ..... DLB-208
Villemaire, Yolande 1949- DLB-60
Villena, Luis Antonio de 1951- DLB-134
Villiers, George, Second Duke of Buckingham 1628-1687 ..... DLB-80
Villiers de l'Isle-Adam, Jean-Marie Mathias Philippe-Auguste, Comte de 1838-1889 ..... DLB-123, 192
Villon, François 1431-circa 1463? DLB-208
Vine Press DLB-112
Viorst, Judith ?- DLB-52
Vipont, Elfrida (Elfrida Vipont Foulds, Charles Vipont) 1902-1992 ..... DLB-160
Viramontes, Helena María 1954- DLB-122
Virgil 70 B.C.-19 B.C. DLB-211; CDWLB-1
Virtual Books and Enemies of Books Y-00
Vischer, Friedrich Theodor 1807-1887 ..... DLB-133
Vitruvius circa 85 B.C.-circa 15 B.C. DLB-211
Vitry, Philippe de 1291-1361 ..... DLB-208
Vittorini, Elio 1908-1966 ..... DLB-264
Vivanco, Luis Felipe 1907-1975 ..... DLB-108
Vivian, E. Charles 1882-1947 ..... DLB-255
Viviani, Cesare 1947- DLB-128
Vivien, Renée 1877-1909 ..... DLB-217
Vizenor, Gerald 1934- DLB-175, 227
Vizetelly and Company DLB-106
Voaden, Herman 1903- DLB-88
Voß, Johann Heinrich 1751-1826 ..... DLB-90
Voigt, Ellen Bryant 1943- DLB-120
Vojnović, Ivo 1857-1929 ..... DLB-147; CDWLB-4
Volkoff, Vladimir 1932- DLB-83
Volland, P. F., Company DLB-46
Vollbehr, Otto H. F. 1872?-1945 or 1946 ..... DLB-187
Vologdin (see Zasodimsky, Pavel Vladimirovich)
Volponi, Paolo 1924- DLB-177
Vonarburg, Élisabeth 1947- DLB-251
von der Grün, Max 1926- DLB-75
Vonnegut, Kurt 1922- DLB-2, 8, 152; Y-80; DS-3; CDALB-6
Voranc, Prežihov 1893-1950 ..... DLB-147
Vovchok, Marko 1833-1907 ..... DLB-238
Voynich, E. L. 1864-1960 ..... DLB-197
Vroman, Mary Elizabeth circa 1924-1967 ..... DLB-33

W

Wace, Robert ("Maistre") circa 1100-circa 1175 ..... DLB-146
Wackenroder, Wilhelm Heinrich 1773-1798 ..... DLB-90
Wackernagel, Wilhelm 1806-1869 ..... DLB-133
Waddell, Helen 1889-1965 ..... DLB-240
Waddington, Miriam 1917- DLB-68
Wade, Henry 1887-1969 ..... DLB-77
Wagenknecht, Edward 1900- DLB-103
Wägner, Elin 1882-1949 ..... DLB-259
Wagner, Heinrich Leopold 1747-1779 ..... DLB-94
Wagner, Henry R. 1862-1957 ..... DLB-140
Wagner, Richard 1813-1883 ..... DLB-129
Wagoner, David 1926- DLB-5, 256
Wah, Fred 1939- DLB-60
Waiblinger, Wilhelm 1804-1830 ..... DLB-90
Wain, John 1925-1994 ..... DLB-15, 27, 139, 155; CDBLB-8
Wainwright, Jeffrey 1944- DLB-40
Waite, Peirce and Company DLB-49
Wakeman, Stephen H. 1859-1924 ..... DLB-187
Wakoski, Diane 1937- DLB-5
Walahfrid Strabo circa 808-849 ..... DLB-148
Walck, Henry Z. DLB-46
Walcott, Derek 1930- DLB-117; Y-81, Y-92; CDWLB-3
Waldegrave, Robert [publishing house] DLB-170
Waldman, Anne 1945- DLB-16
Waldrop, Rosmarie 1935- DLB-169
Walker, Alice 1900-1982 ..... DLB-201
Walker, Alice 1944- DLB-6, 33, 143; CDALB-6
Walker, Annie Louisa (Mrs. Harry Coghill) circa 1836-1907 ..... DLB-240
Walker, George F. 1947- DLB-60
Walker, John Brisben 1847-1931 ..... DLB-79
Walker, Joseph A. 1935- DLB-38
Walker, Margaret 1915- DLB-76, 152
Walker, Ted 1934- DLB-40
Walker and Company DLB-49
Walker, Evans and Cogswell Company DLB-49
Wall, John F. (see Sarban)
Wallace, Alfred Russel 1823-1913 ..... DLB-190
Wallace, Dewitt 1889-1981 and Lila Acheson Wallace 1889-1984 ..... DLB-137
Wallace, Edgar 1875-1932 ..... DLB-70
Wallace, Lew 1827-1905 ..... DLB-202
Wallace, Lila Acheson (see Wallace, Dewitt, and Lila Acheson Wallace)
Wallace, Naomi 1960- DLB-249
Wallant, Edward Lewis 1926-1962 ..... DLB-2, 28, 143
Waller, Edmund 1606-1687 ..... DLB-126
Walpole, Horace 1717-1797 ..... DLB-39, 104, 213
Preface to the First Edition of *The Castle of Otranto* (1764) DLB-39
Preface to the Second Edition of *The Castle of Otranto* (1765) DLB-39
Walpole, Hugh 1884-1941 ..... DLB-34
Walrond, Eric 1898-1966 ..... DLB-51
Walser, Martin 1927- DLB-75, 124
Walser, Robert 1878-1956 ..... DLB-66
Walsh, Ernest 1895-1926 ..... DLB-4, 45
Walsh, Robert 1784-1859 ..... DLB-59
Walters, Henry 1848-1931 ..... DLB-140
Waltharius circa 825 ..... DLB-148
Walther von der Vogelweide circa 1170-circa 1230 ..... DLB-138
Walton, Izaak 1593-1683 ..... DLB-151, 213; CDBLB-1
Wambaugh, Joseph 1937- DLB-6; Y-83
Wand, Alfred Rudolph 1828-1891 ..... DLB-188
Waniek, Marilyn Nelson 1946- DLB-120
Wanley, Humphrey 1672-1726 ..... DLB-213
Warburton, William 1698-1779 ..... DLB-104
Ward, Aileen 1919- DLB-111
Ward, Artemus (see Browne, Charles Farrar)
Ward, Arthur Henry Sarsfield (see Rohmer, Sax)
Ward, Douglas Turner 1930- DLB-7, 38
Ward, Mrs. Humphry 1851-1920 ..... DLB-18
Ward, James 1843-1925 ..... DLB-262
Ward, Lynd 1905-1985 ..... DLB-22
Ward, Lock and Company DLB-106
Ward, Nathaniel circa 1578-1652 ..... DLB-24
Ward, Theodore 1902-1983 ..... DLB-76
Wardle, Ralph 1909-1988 ..... DLB-103
Ware, Henry, Jr. 1794-1843 ..... DLB-235
Ware, William 1797-1852 ..... DLB-1, 235
Warfield, Catherine Ann 1816-1877 ..... DLB-248
Waring, Anna Letitia 1823-1910 ..... DLB-240
Warne, Frederick, and Company [U.K.] DLB-106
Warne, Frederick, and Company [U.S.] DLB-49
Warner, Anne 1869-1913 ..... DLB-202
Warner, Charles Dudley 1829-1900 ..... DLB-64
Warner, Marina 1946- DLB-194
Warner, Rex 1905- DLB-15
Warner, Susan 1819-1885 ..... DLB-3, 42, 239, 250
Warner, Sylvia Townsend 1893-1978 ..... DLB-34, 139
Warner, William 1558-1609 ..... DLB-172
Warner Books DLB-46
Warr, Bertram 1917-1943 ..... DLB-88
Warren, John Byrne Leicester (see De Tabley, Lord)
Warren, Lella 1899-1982 ..... Y-83
Warren, Mercy Otis 1728-1814 ..... DLB-31, 200
Warren, Robert Penn 1905-1989 ..... DLB-2, 48, 152; Y-80, Y-89; CDALB-6
Warren, Samuel 1807-1877 ..... DLB-190
Die Wartburgkrieg circa 1230-circa 1280 ..... DLB-138
Warton, Joseph 1722-1800 ..... DLB-104, 109
Warton, Thomas 1728-1790 ..... DLB-104, 109
Warung, Price (William Astley) 1855-1911 ..... DLB-230
Washington, George 1732-1799 ..... DLB-31
Washington, Ned 1901-1976 ..... DLB-265
Wassermann, Jakob 1873-1934 ..... DLB-66
Wasserstein, Wendy 1950- DLB-228
Wasson, David Atwood 1823-1887 ..... DLB-1, 223
Watanna, Onoto (see Eaton, Winnifred)
Waterhouse, Keith 1929- DLB-13, 15
Waterman, Andrew 1940- DLB-40

Waters, Frank 1902-1995 . . . . DLB-212; Y-86
Waters, Michael 1949- DLB-120
Watkins, Tobias 1780-1855 . . . . DLB-73
Watkins, Vernon 1906-1967 . . . . DLB-20
Watmough, David 1926- DLB-53
Watson, Ian 1943- DLB-261
Watson, James Wreford (see Wreford, James)
Watson, John 1850-1907 . . . . DLB-156
Watson, Rosamund Marriott
 (Graham R. Tomson) 1860-1911 . . . . DLB-240
Watson, Sheila 1909- DLB-60
Watson, Thomas 1545?-1592 . . . . DLB-132
Watson, Wilfred 1911- DLB-60
Watt, W. J., and Company DLB-46
Watten, Barrett 1948- DLB-193
Watterson, Henry 1840-1921 . . . . DLB-25
Watts, Alan 1915-1973 . . . . DLB-16
Watts, Franklin [publishing house] DLB-46
Watts, Isaac 1674-1748 . . . . DLB-95
Waugh, Alec 1898-1981 . . . . DLB-191
Waugh, Auberon 1939-2000 . . . DLB-14, 194; Y-00
The Cult of Biography
 Excerpts from the Second Folio Debate:
 "Biographies are generally a disease of
 English Literature" Y-86
Waugh, Evelyn
 1903-1966 . . . . . . DLB-15, 162, 195; CDBLB-6
Way and Williams DLB-49
Wayman, Tom 1945- DLB-53
We See the Editor at Work Y-97
Weatherly, Tom 1942- DLB-41
Weaver, Gordon 1937- DLB-130
Weaver, Robert 1921- DLB-88
Webb, Beatrice 1858-1943 and
 Webb, Sidney 1859-1947 . . . . DLB-190
Webb, Francis 1925-1973 . . . . DLB-260
Webb, Frank J. ?-? DLB-50
Webb, James Watson 1802-1884 . . . . DLB-43
Webb, Mary 1881-1927 . . . . DLB-34
Webb, Phyllis 1927- DLB-53
Webb, Walter Prescott 1888-1963 . . . . DLB-17
Webbe, William ?-1591 . . . . DLB-132
Webber, Charles Wilkins 1819-1856? DLB-202
Webling, Lucy (Lucy Betty MacRaye)
 1877-1952 . . . . DLB-240
Webling, Peggy (Arthur Weston)
 1871-1949 . . . . DLB-240
Webster, Augusta 1837-1894 . . . . DLB-35, 240
Webster, Charles L., and Company DLB-49
Webster, John
 1579 or 1580-1634? DLB-58; CDBLB-1
John Webster: The Melbourne
 Manuscript Y-86
Webster, Noah
 1758-1843 . . . . . . DLB-1, 37, 42, 43, 73, 243
Webster, Paul Francis 1907-1984 . . . . DLB-265
Weckherlin, Georg Rodolf 1584-1653 . . . . DLB-164

Wedekind, Frank
 1864-1918 . . . . DLB-118; CDBLB-2
Weeks, Edward Augustus, Jr.
 1898-1989 . . . . DLB-137
Weeks, Stephen B. 1865-1918 . . . . DLB-187
Weems, Mason Locke 1759-1825 . . DLB-30, 37, 42
Weerth, Georg 1822-1856 . . . . DLB-129
Weidenfeld and Nicolson DLB-112
Weidman, Jerome 1913-1998 . . . . DLB-28
Weiß, Ernst 1882-1940 . . . . DLB-81
Weigl, Bruce 1949- DLB-120
Weinbaum, Stanley Grauman 1902-1935 . . DLB-8
Weiner, Andrew 1949- DLB-251
Weintraub, Stanley 1929- DLB-111; Y82
The Practice of Biography: An Interview
 with Stanley Weintraub Y-82
Weise, Christian 1642-1708 . . . . DLB-168
Weisenborn, Gunther 1902-1969 . . . . DLB-69, 124
Weiss, John 1818-1879 . . . . DLB-1, 243
Weiss, Peter 1916-1982 . . . . DLB-69, 124
Weiss, Theodore 1916- DLB-5
Weisse, Christian Felix 1726-1804 . . . . DLB-97
Weitling, Wilhelm 1808-1871 . . . . DLB-129
Welch, James 1940- DLB-175, 256
Welch, Lew 1926-1971? DLB-16
Weldon, Fay 1931- DLB-14, 194; CDBLB-8
Wellek, René 1903-1995 . . . . DLB-63
Wells, Carolyn 1862-1942 . . . . DLB-11
Wells, Charles Jeremiah circa 1800-1879 . . . DLB-32
Wells, Gabriel 1862-1946 . . . . DLB-140
Wells, H. G.
 1866-1946 . . . DLB-34, 70, 156, 178; CDBLB-6
Wells, Helena 1758?-1824 . . . . DLB-200
Wells, Robert 1947- DLB-40
Wells-Barnett, Ida B. 1862-1931 . . . . . DLB-23, 221
Welty, Eudora 1909- DLB-2, 102, 143;
  . . . . Y-87, Y-01; DS-12; CDALB-1
Eudora Welty: Eye of the Storyteller Y-87
Eudora Welty Newsletter Y-99
Eudora Welty's Funeral Y-01
Eudora Welty's Ninetieth Birthday Y-99
Wendell, Barrett 1855-1921 . . . . DLB-71
Wentworth, Patricia 1878-1961 . . . . DLB-77
Wentworth, William Charles
 1790-1872 . . . . DLB-230
Werder, Diederich von dem 1584-1657 . . . DLB-164
Werfel, Franz 1890-1945 . . . . DLB-81, 124
Werner, Zacharias 1768-1823 . . . . DLB-94
The Werner Company DLB-49
Wersba, Barbara 1932- DLB-52
Wescott, Glenway 1901- DLB-4, 9, 102
Wesker, Arnold 1932- DLB-13; CDBLB-8
Wesley, Charles 1707-1788 . . . . DLB-95
Wesley, John 1703-1791 . . . . DLB-104
Wesley, Mary 1912- DLB-231
Wesley, Richard 1945- DLB-38

Wessels, A., and Company DLB-46
Wessobrunner Gebet circa 787-815 . . . . DLB-148
West, Anthony 1914-1988 . . . . DLB-15
West, Cheryl L. 1957- DLB-266
West, Cornel 1953- DLB-246
West, Dorothy 1907-1998 . . . . DLB-76
West, Jessamyn 1902-1984 . . . . DLB-6; Y-84
West, Mae 1892-1980 . . . . DLB-44
West, Michelle Sagara 1963- DLB-251
West, Nathanael
 1903-1940 . . . . DLB-4, 9, 28; CDALB-5
West, Paul 1930- DLB-14
West, Rebecca 1892-1983 . . . . DLB-36; Y-83
West, Richard 1941- DLB-185
West and Johnson DLB-49
Westcott, Edward Noyes 1846-1898 . . . . . DLB-202
The Western Messenger 1835-1841 . . . . DLB-223
Western Publishing Company DLB-46
Western Writers of America Y-99
The Westminster Review 1824-1914 . . . . DLB-110
Weston, Arthur (see Webling, Peggy)
Weston, Elizabeth Jane circa 1582-1612 . . DLB-172
Wetherald, Agnes Ethelwyn 1857-1940 . . . DLB-99
Wetherell, Elizabeth (see Warner, Susan)
Wetherell, W. D. 1948- DLB-234
Wetzel, Friedrich Gottlob 1779-1819 . . . . . DLB-90
Weyman, Stanley J. 1855-1928 . . . . . DLB-141, 156
Wezel, Johann Karl 1747-1819 . . . . DLB-94
Whalen, Philip 1923- DLB-16
Whalley, George 1915-1983 . . . . DLB-88
Wharton, Edith 1862-1937
 . . . . . DLB-4, 9, 12, 78, 189; DS-13; CDALB-3
Wharton, William 1920s?- Y-80
"What You Lose on the Swings You Make Up
 on the Merry-Go-Round" Y-99
Whately, Mary Louisa 1824-1889 . . . . DLB-166
Whately, Richard 1787-1863 . . . . DLB-190
From Elements of Rhetoric (1828;
 revised, 1846) DLB-57
What's Really Wrong With Bestseller Lists . . Y-84
Wheatley, Dennis 1897-1977 . . . . . . DLB-77, 255
Wheatley, Phillis
 circa 1754-1784 . . . . DLB-31, 50; CDALB-2
Wheeler, Anna Doyle 1785-1848? DLB-158
Wheeler, Charles Stearns 1816-1843 . . . DLB-1, 223
Wheeler, Monroe 1900-1988 . . . . DLB-4
Wheelock, John Hall 1886-1978 . . . . DLB-45
From John Hall Wheelock's Oral Memoir . . . Y-01
Wheelwright, J. B. 1897-1940 . . . . DLB-45
Wheelwright, John circa 1592-1679 . . . . . . DLB-24
Whetstone, George 1550-1587 . . . . DLB-136
Whetstone, Colonel Pete (see Noland, C. F. M.)
Whewell, William 1794-1866 . . . . DLB-262
Whichcote, Benjamin 1609?-1683 . . . . DLB-252
Whicher, Stephen E. 1915-1961 . . . . DLB-111
Whipple, Edwin Percy 1819-1886 . . . . . . DLB-1, 64

Cumulative Index

Whitaker, Alexander 1585-1617 .... DLB-24
Whitaker, Daniel K. 1801-1881 .... DLB-73
Whitcher, Frances Miriam
   1812-1852. .... DLB-11, 202
White, Andrew 1579-1656 .... DLB-24
White, Andrew Dickson 1832-1918 ...... DLB-47
White, E. B. 1899-1985 ... DLB-11, 22; CDALB-7
White, Edgar B. 1947- DLB-38
White, Edmund 1940- DLB-227
White, Ethel Lina 1887-1944 .... DLB-77
White, Hayden V. 1928- DLB-246
White, Henry Kirke 1785-1806 ...... DLB-96
White, Horace 1834-1916. .... DLB-23
White, James 1928-1999. .... DLB-261
White, Patrick 1912-1990. .... DLB-260
White, Phyllis Dorothy James (see James, P. D.)
White, Richard Grant 1821-1885 .... DLB-64
White, T. H. 1906-1964 .... DLB-160, 255
White, Walter 1893-1955. .... DLB-51
White, William, and Company DLB-49
White, William Allen 1868-1944 ...... DLB-9, 25
White, William Anthony Parker
   (see Boucher, Anthony)
White, William Hale (see Rutherford, Mark)
Whitechurch, Victor L. 1868-1933 ...... DLB-70
Whitehead, Alfred North 1861-1947 .... DLB-100
Whitehead, James 1936- Y-81
Whitehead, William 1715-1785 ...... DLB-84, 109
Whitfield, James Monroe 1822-1871 ..... DLB-50
Whitfield, Raoul 1898-1945 .... DLB-226
Whitgift, John circa 1533-1604. .... DLB-132
Whiting, John 1917-1963 .... DLB-13
Whiting, Samuel 1597-1679 .... DLB-24
Whitlock, Brand 1869-1934 .... DLB-12
Whitman, Albert, and Company DLB-46
Whitman, Albery Allson 1851-1901 ..... DLB-50
Whitman, Alden 1913-1990 .... Y-91
Whitman, Sarah Helen (Power)
   1803-1878. .... DLB-1, 243
Whitman, Walt
   1819-1892.... DLB-3, 64, 224, 250; CDALB-2
Whitman Publishing Company DLB-46
Whitney, Geoffrey 1548 or 1552?-1601.. DLB-136
Whitney, Isabella flourished 1566-1573.. DLB-136
Whitney, John Hay 1904-1982. .... DLB-127
Whittemore, Reed 1919-1995. .... DLB-5
Whittier, John Greenleaf
   1807-1892. .... DLB-1, 243; CDALB-2
Whittlesey House DLB-46
Who Runs American Literature? Y-94
Whose *Ulysses*? The Function of Editing Y-97
Wickham, Anna (Edith Alice Mary Harper)
   1884-1947. .... DLB-240
Wicomb, Zoë 1948- DLB-225
Wideman, John Edgar 1941- DLB-33, 143
Widener, Harry Elkins 1885-1912 ...... DLB-140

Wiebe, Rudy 1934- DLB-60
Wiechert, Ernst 1887-1950 .... DLB-56
Wied, Martina 1882-1957. .... DLB-85
Wiehe, Evelyn May Clowes (see Mordaunt, Elinor)
Wieland, Christoph Martin 1733-1813.... DLB-97
Wienbarg, Ludolf 1802-1872 .... DLB-133
Wieners, John 1934- DLB-16
Wier, Ester 1910- DLB-52
Wiesel, Elie
   1928- DLB-83; Y-86, 87; CDALB-7
Wiggin, Kate Douglas 1856-1923 .... DLB-42
Wigglesworth, Michael 1631-1705 ...... DLB-24
Wilberforce, William 1759-1833 .... DLB-158
Wilbrandt, Adolf 1837-1911 .... DLB-129
Wilbur, Richard
   1921- DLB-5, 169; CDALB-7
Wild, Peter 1940- DLB-5
Wilde, Lady Jane Francesca Elgee
   1821?-1896. .... DLB-199
Wilde, Oscar 1854-1900
   .... DLB-10, 19, 34, 57, 141, 156, 190; CDBLB-5
"The Critic as Artist" (1891) DLB-57
Oscar Wilde Conference at Hofstra
   University Y-00
From "The Decay of Lying" (1889) DLB-18
"The English Renaissance of
   Art" (1908). DLB-35
"L'Envoi" (1882) DLB-35
Wilde, Richard Henry 1789-1847 ...... DLB-3, 59
Wilde, W. A., Company DLB-49
Wilder, Billy 1906- DLB-26
Wilder, Laura Ingalls 1867-1957 ..... DLB-22, 256
Wilder, Thornton
   1897-1975 ....DLB-4, 7, 9, 228; CDALB-7
Thornton Wilder Centenary at Yale Y-97
Wildgans, Anton 1881-1932. .... DLB-118
Wiley, Bell Irvin 1906-1980 .... DLB-17
Wiley, John, and Sons DLB-49
Wilhelm, Kate 1928- DLB-8
Wilkes, Charles 1798-1877 .... DLB-183
Wilkes, George 1817-1885 .... DLB-79
Wilkins, John 1614-1672 .... DLB-236
Wilkinson, Anne 1910-1961. .... DLB-88
Wilkinson, Eliza Yonge
   1757-circa 1813. .... DLB-200
Wilkinson, Sylvia 1940- Y-86
Wilkinson, William Cleaver 1833-1920... DLB-71
Willard, Barbara 1909-1994 .... DLB-161
Willard, Emma 1787-1870 .... DLB-239
Willard, Frances E. 1839-1898 .... DLB-221
Willard, L. [publishing house] DLB-49
Willard, Nancy 1936- DLB-5, 52
Willard, Samuel 1640-1707. .... DLB-24
Willeford, Charles 1919-1988 .... DLB-226
William of Auvergne 1190-1249. ...... DLB-115

William of Conches
   circa 1090-circa 1154 .... DLB-115
William of Ockham circa 1285-1347 .... DLB-115
William of Sherwood
   1200/1205-1266/1271 .... DLB-115
The William Chavrat American Fiction Collection
   at the Ohio State University Libraries Y-92
Williams, A., and Company. DLB-49
Williams, Ben Ames 1889-1953 .... DLB-102
Williams, C. K. 1936- DLB-5
Williams, Chancellor 1905- DLB-76
Williams, Charles 1886-1945 ...DLB-100, 153, 255
Williams, Denis 1923-1998 ....DLB-117
Williams, Emlyn 1905-1987 ....DLB-10, 77
Williams, Garth 1912-1996 .... DLB-22
Williams, George Washington
   1849-1891 .... DLB-47
Williams, Heathcote 1941- DLB-13
Williams, Helen Maria 1761-1827 ...... DLB-158
Williams, Hugo 1942- DLB-40
Williams, Isaac 1802-1865 .... DLB-32
Williams, Joan 1928- DLB-6
Williams, Joe 1889-1972. .... DLB-241
Williams, John A. 1925- DLB-2, 33
Williams, John E. 1922-1994 .... DLB-6
Williams, Jonathan 1929- DLB-5
Williams, Miller 1930- DLB-105
Williams, Nigel 1948- DLB-231
Williams, Raymond 1921- ... DLB-14, 231, 242
Williams, Roger circa 1603-1683 .... DLB-24
Williams, Rowland 1817-1870 .... DLB-184
Williams, Samm-Art 1946- DLB-38
Williams, Sherley Anne 1944-1999 ...... DLB-41
Williams, T. Harry 1909-1979 ....DLB-17
Williams, Tennessee
   1911-1983 .... DLB-7; Y-83; DS-4; CDALB-1
Williams, Terry Tempest 1955- DLB-206
Williams, Ursula Moray 1911- DLB-160
Williams, Valentine 1883-1946 .... DLB-77
Williams, William Appleman 1921- DLB-17
Williams, William Carlos
   1883-1963 ...... DLB-4, 16, 54, 86; CDALB-4
Williams, Wirt 1921- DLB-6
Williams Brothers. DLB-49
Williamson, Henry 1895-1977 .... DLB-191
Williamson, Jack 1908- DLB-8
Willingham, Calder Baynard, Jr.
   1922-1995 .... DLB-2, 44
Williram of Ebersberg circa 1020-1085 .. DLB-148
Willis, Nathaniel Parker 1806-1867
   .... DLB-3, 59, 73, 74, 183, 250; DS-13
Willkomm, Ernst 1810-1886 .... DLB-133
Willumsen, Dorrit 1940- DLB-214
Wills, Garry 1934- DLB-246
Willson, Meredith 1902-1984. .... DLB-265
Wilmer, Clive 1945- DLB-40
Wilson, A. N. 1950- DLB-14, 155, 194

Wilson, Angus 1913-1991 . . . . . . DLB-15, 139, 155
Wilson, Arthur 1595-1652. . . . . DLB-58
Wilson, August 1945- DLB-228
Wilson, Augusta Jane Evans 1835-1909 . . . DLB-42
Wilson, Colin 1931- DLB-14, 194
Wilson, Edmund 1895-1972 . . . . DLB-63
Wilson, Effingham [publishing house] DLB-154
Wilson, Ethel 1888-1980 . . . . DLB-68
Wilson, F. P. 1889-1963 . . . . DLB-201
Wilson, Harriet E.
   1827/1828?-1863? DLB-50, 239, 243
Wilson, Harry Leon 1867-1939 . . . . DLB-9
Wilson, John 1588-1667 . . . . DLB-24
Wilson, John 1785-1854 . . . . DLB-110
Wilson, John Dover 1881-1969 . . . . DLB-201
Wilson, Lanford 1937- DLB-7
Wilson, Margaret 1882-1973 . . . . DLB-9
Wilson, Michael 1914-1978 . . . . DLB-44
Wilson, Mona 1872-1954 . . . . DLB-149
Wilson, Robert Charles 1953- DLB-251
Wilson, Robley 1930- DLB-218
Wilson, Romer 1891-1930 . . . . DLB-191
Wilson, Thomas 1524-1581 . . . . DLB-132, 236
Wilson, Woodrow 1856-1924 . . . . DLB-47
Wimsatt, William K., Jr. 1907-1975 . . . . . . DLB-63
Winchell, Walter 1897-1972 . . . . DLB-29
Winchester, J. [publishing house] DLB-49
Winckelmann, Johann Joachim
   1717-1768 . . . . DLB-97
Winckler, Paul 1630-1686 . . . . DLB-164
Wind, Herbert Warren 1916- DLB-171
Windet, John [publishing house] DLB-170
Windham, Donald 1920- DLB-6
Wing, Donald Goddard 1904-1972 . . . . . . DLB-187
Wing, John M. 1844-1917 . . . . DLB-187
Wingate, Allan [publishing house] DLB-112
Winnemucca, Sarah 1844-1921 . . . . DLB-175
Winnifrith, Tom 1938- DLB-155
Winning an Edgar Y-98
Winsloe, Christa 1888-1944 . . . . DLB-124
Winslow, Anna Green 1759-1780 . . . . DLB-200
Winsor, Justin 1831-1897 . . . . DLB-47
John C. Winston Company DLB-49
Winters, Yvor 1900-1968 . . . . DLB-48
Winterson, Jeanette 1959- DLB-207, 261
Winthrop, John 1588-1649 . . . . DLB-24, 30
Winthrop, John, Jr. 1606-1676 . . . . DLB-24
Winthrop, Margaret Tyndal 1591-1647 . . DLB-200
Winthrop, Theodore 1828-1861 . . . . DLB-202
Wirt, William 1772-1834 . . . . DLB-37
Wise, John 1652-1725 . . . . DLB-24
Wise, Thomas James 1859-1937 . . . . DLB-184
Wiseman, Adele 1928-1992 . . . . DLB-88
Wishart and Company DLB-112
Wisner, George 1812-1849 . . . . DLB-43

Wister, Owen 1860-1938 . . . . DLB-9, 78, 186
Wister, Sarah 1761-1804 . . . . DLB-200
Wither, George 1588-1667 . . . . DLB-121
Witherspoon, John 1723-1794 . . . . DLB-31
Withrow, William Henry 1839-1908 . . . . . DLB-99
Witkacy (see Witkiewicz, Stanisław Ignacy)
Witkiewicz, Stanisław Ignacy
   1885-1939 . . . . DLB-215; CDWLB-4
Wittgenstein, Ludwig 1889-1951 . . . . DLB-262
Wittig, Monique 1935- DLB-83
Wodehouse, P. G.
   1881-1975 . . . . DLB-34, 162; CDBLB-6
Wohmann, Gabriele 1932- DLB-75
Woiwode, Larry 1941- DLB-6
Wolcot, John 1738-1819 . . . . DLB-109
Wolcott, Roger 1679-1767 . . . . DLB-24
Wolf, Christa 1929- DLB-75; CDWLB-2
Wolf, Friedrich 1888-1953 . . . . DLB-124
Wolfe, Gene 1931- DLB-8
Wolfe, John [publishing house] DLB-170
Wolfe, Reyner (Reginald)
   [publishing house] DLB-170
Wolfe, Thomas
   1900-1938 . . . . DLB-9, 102, 229; Y-85;
                     DS-2, DS-16; CDALB-5
"All the Faults of Youth and Inexperience":
   A Reader's Report on
   Thomas Wolfe's *O Lost* Y-01
Eugene Gant's Projected Works Y-01
The Thomas Wolfe Collection at the University
   of North Carolina at Chapel Hill Y-97
Thomas Wolfe Centennial
   Celebration in Asheville Y-00
Fire at Thomas Wolfe Memorial Y-98
The Thomas Wolfe Society Y-97
Wolfe, Tom 1931- DLB-152, 185
Wolfenstein, Martha 1869-1906 . . . . DLB-221
Wolff, Helen 1906-1994 . . . . Y-94
Wolff, Tobias 1945- DLB-130
Wolfram von Eschenbach
   circa 1170-after 1220 . . . . DLB-138; CDWLB-2
Wolfram von Eschenbach's *Parzival*:
   Prologue and Book 3 . . . . DLB-138
Wolker, Jiří 1900-1924 . . . . DLB-215
Wollstonecraft, Mary 1759-1797
        . . . . DLB-39, 104, 158, 252; CDBLB-3
Wondratschek, Wolf 1943- DLB-75
Wong, Elizabeth 1958- DLB-266
Wood, Anthony à 1632-1695 . . . . DLB-213
Wood, Benjamin 1820-1900 . . . . DLB-23
Wood, Charles 1932- DLB-13
Wood, Mrs. Henry 1814-1887 . . . . DLB-18
Wood, Joanna E. 1867-1927 . . . . DLB-92
Wood, Sally Sayward Barrell Keating
   1759-1855 . . . . DLB-200
Wood, Samuel [publishing house] DLB-49
Wood, William ?-? DLB-24
The Charles Wood Affair:
   A Playwright Revived Y-83

Woodberry, George Edward
   1855-1930 . . . . DLB-71, 103
Woodbridge, Benjamin 1622-1684 . . . . . . DLB-24
Woodcock, George 1912-1995 . . . . DLB-88
Woodhull, Victoria C. 1838-1927 . . . . DLB-79
Woodmason, Charles circa 1720-? DLB-31
Woodress, Jr., James Leslie 1916- DLB-111
Woods, Margaret L. 1855-1945 . . . . DLB-240
Woodson, Carter G. 1875-1950 . . . . DLB-17
Woodward, C. Vann 1908-1999 . . . . DLB-17
Woodward, Stanley 1895-1965 . . . . DLB-171
Woodworth, Samuel 1785-1842 . . . . DLB-260
Wooler, Thomas 1785 or 1786-1853 . . . . . DLB-158
Woolf, David (see Maddow, Ben)
Woolf, Douglas 1922-1992 . . . . DLB-244
Woolf, Leonard 1880-1969 . . . . . . DLB-100; DS-10
Woolf, Virginia 1882-1941
   . . . . DLB-36, 100, 162; DS-10; CDBLB-6
Woolf, Virginia, "The New Biography," *New York
   Herald Tribune*, 30 October 1927 . . . . . DLB-149
Woollcott, Alexander 1887-1943 . . . . DLB-29
Woolman, John 1720-1772 . . . . DLB-31
Woolner, Thomas 1825-1892 . . . . DLB-35
Woolrich, Cornell 1903-1968 . . . . DLB-226
Woolsey, Sarah Chauncy 1835-1905 . . . . . DLB-42
Woolson, Constance Fenimore
   1840-1894 . . . . DLB-12, 74, 189, 221
Worcester, Joseph Emerson
   1784-1865 . . . . DLB-1, 235
Worde, Wynkyn de [publishing house] . . . DLB-170
Wordsworth, Christopher 1807-1885 . . . . DLB-166
Wordsworth, Dorothy 1771-1855 . . . . DLB-107
Wordsworth, Elizabeth 1840-1932 . . . . . . DLB-98
Wordsworth, William
   1770-1850 . . . . DLB-93, 107; CDBLB-3
Workman, Fanny Bullock 1859-1925 . . . . DLB-189
The Works of the Rev. John Witherspoon
   (1800-1801) [excerpts] DLB-31
A World Chronology of Important Science
   Fiction Works (1818-1979) DLB-8
World Literatue Today: A Journal for the
   New Millennium Y-01
World Publishing Company DLB-46
World War II Writers Symposium
   at the University of South Carolina,
   12–14 April 1995 . . . . Y-95
Worthington, R., and Company DLB-49
Wotton, Sir Henry 1568-1639 . . . . DLB-121
Wouk, Herman 1915- Y-82; CDALB-7
Wreford, James 1915- DLB-88
Wren, Sir Christopher 1632-1723 . . . . . . DLB-213
Wren, Percival Christopher
   1885-1941 . . . . DLB-153
Wrenn, John Henry 1841-1911 . . . . DLB-140
Wright, C. D. 1949- DLB-120
Wright, Charles 1935- DLB-165; Y-82
Wright, Charles Stevenson 1932- DLB-33
Wright, Frances 1795-1852 . . . . DLB-73
Wright, Harold Bell 1872-1944 . . . . DLB-9

Cumulative Index

Wright, James 1927-1980 .... DLB-5, 169; CDALB-7
Wright, Jay 1935- DLB-41
Wright, Judith 1915-2000 .... DLB-260
Wright, Louis B. 1899-1984 .... DLB-17
Wright, Richard 1908-1960 .... DLB-76, 102; DS-2; CDALB-5
Wright, Richard B. 1937- DLB-53
Wright, S. Fowler 1874-1965 .... DLB-255
Wright, Sarah Elizabeth 1928- DLB-33
Wright, Willard Huntington ("S. S. Van Dine") 1888-1939 .... DS-16
Wrigley, Robert 1951- DLB-256
A Writer Talking: A Collage Y-00
Writers and Politics: 1871-1918, by Ronald Gray DLB-66
Writers and their Copyright Holders: the WATCH Project Y-94
Writers' Forum Y-85
Writing for the Theatre, by Harold Pinter DLB-13
Wroth, Lawrence C. 1884-1970 .... DLB-187
Wroth, Lady Mary 1587-1653 .... DLB-121
Wurlitzer, Rudolph 1937- DLB-173
Wyatt, Sir Thomas circa 1503-1542 ..... DLB-132
Wycherley, William 1641-1715 .... DLB-80; CDBLB-2
Wyclif, John circa 1335-31 December 1384 ...... DLB-146
Wyeth, N. C. 1882-1945 .... DLB-188; DS-16
Wylie, Elinor 1885-1928 .... DLB-9, 45
Wylie, Philip 1902-1971 .... DLB-9
Wyllie, John Cook 1908-1968 .... DLB-140
Wyman, Lillie Buffum Chace 1847-1929 .... DLB-202
Wymark, Olwen 1934- DLB-233
Wyndham, John 1903-1969 .... DLB-255
Wynne-Tyson, Esmé 1898-1972 .... DLB-191

X

Xenophon circa 430 B.C.-circa 356 B.C. ... DLB-176

Y

Yasuoka Shōtarō 1920- DLB-182
Yates, Dornford 1885-1960 .... DLB-77, 153
Yates, J. Michael 1938- DLB-60
Yates, Richard 1926-1992 .... DLB-2, 234; Y-81, Y-92
Yau, John 1950- DLB-234
Yavorov, Peyo 1878-1914 .... DLB-147
The Year in Book Publishing Y-86
The Year in Book Reviewing and the Literary Situation Y-98
The Year in British Drama Y-99, Y-00, Y-01
The Year in British Fiction Y-99, Y-00, Y-01
The Year in Children's Books Y-92–Y-96, Y-98, Y-99, Y-00, Y-01

The Year in Children's Literature Y-97
The Year in Drama Y-82-Y-85, Y-87–Y-96
The Year in Fiction .. Y-84–Y-86, Y-89, Y-94–Y-99
The Year in Fiction: A Biased View Y-83
The Year in Literary Biography Y-83–Y-98, Y-00, Y-01
The Year in Literary Theory Y-92–Y-93
The Year in London Theatre Y-92
The Year in the Novel Y-87, Y-88, Y-90–Y-93
The Year in Poetry .. Y-83–Y-92, Y-94, Y-95, Y-96, ... Y-97, Y-98, Y-99, Y-00, Y-01
The Year in Science Fiction and Fantasy Y-00, Y-01
The Year in Short Stories Y-87
The Year in the Short Story Y-88, Y-90–Y-93
The Year in Texas Literature Y-98
The Year in U.S. Drama Y-00
The Year in U.S. Fiction Y-00, Y-01
The Year's Work in American Poetry Y-82
The Year's Work in Fiction: A Survey Y-82
Yearsley, Ann 1753-1806 .... DLB-109
Yeats, William Butler 1865-1939 ... DLB-10, 19, 98, 156; CDBLB-5
Yellen, Jack 1892-1991 .... DLB-265
Yep, Laurence 1948- DLB-52
Yerby, Frank 1916-1991 .... DLB-76
Yezierska, Anzia 1880-1970 .... DLB-28, 221
Yolen, Jane 1939- DLB-52
Yonge, Charlotte Mary 1823-1901 .... DLB-18, 163
The York Cycle circa 1376-circa 1569 ... DLB-146
A Yorkshire Tragedy DLB-58
Yoseloff, Thomas [publishing house] DLB-46
Young, A. S. "Doc" 1919-1996 .... DLB-241
Young, Al 1939- DLB-33
Young, Arthur 1741-1820 .... DLB-158
Young, Dick 1917 or 1918 - 1987 .... DLB-171
Young, Edward 1683-1765 .... DLB-95
Young, Frank A. "Fay" 1884-1957 ...... DLB-241
Young, Francis Brett 1884-1954 .... DLB-191
Young, Gavin 1928- DLB-204
Young, Stark 1881-1963 ...... DLB-9, 102; DS-16
Young, Waldeman 1880-1938 .... DLB-26
Young, William [publishing house] DLB-49
Young Bear, Ray A. 1950- DLB-175
Yourcenar, Marguerite 1903-1987 .... DLB-72; Y-88
"You've Never Had It So Good," Gusted by "Winds of Change": British Fiction in the 1950s, 1960s, and After DLB-14
Yovkov, Yordan 1880-1937 ..DLB-147; CDWLB-4

Z

Zachariä, Friedrich Wilhelm 1726-1777 ... DLB-97

Zagajewski, Adam 1945- DLB-232
Zagoskin, Mikhail Nikolaevich 1789-1852 .... DLB-198
Zajc, Dane 1929- DLB-181
Zālīte, Māra 1952- DLB-232
Zamora, Bernice 1938- DLB-82
Zand, Herbert 1923-1970 .... DLB-85
Zangwill, Israel 1864-1926 ..... DLB-10, 135, 197
Zanzotto, Andrea 1921- DLB-128
Zapata Olivella, Manuel 1920- DLB-113
Zasodimsky, Pavel Vladimirovich 1843-1912 .... DLB-238
Zebra Books DLB-46
Zebrowski, George 1945- DLB-8
Zech, Paul 1881-1946 .... DLB-56
Zeidner, Lisa 1955- DLB-120
Zeidonis, Imants 1933- DLB-232
Zeimi (Kanze Motokiyo) 1363-1443 ..... DLB-203
Zelazny, Roger 1937-1995 .... DLB-8
Zenger, John Peter 1697-1746 .... DLB-24, 43
Zepheria DLB-172
Zesen, Philipp von 1619-1689 .... DLB-164
Zhukovsky, Vasilii Andreevich 1783-1852 .... DLB-205
Zieber, G. B., and Company DLB-49
Ziedonis, Imants 1933- CDWLB-4
Zieroth, Dale 1946- DLB-60
Zigler und Kliphausen, Heinrich Anshelm von 1663-1697 .... DLB-168
Zimmer, Paul 1934- DLB-5
Zinberg, Len (see Lacy, Ed)
Zindel, Paul 1936- DLB-7, 52; CDALB-7
Zingref, Julius Wilhelm 1591-1635 ...... DLB-164
Zinnes, Harriet 1919- DLB-193
Zinzendorf, Nikolaus Ludwig von 1700-1760 .... DLB-168
Zitkala-Ša 1876-1938 .... DLB-175
Zīverts, Mārtiņš 1903-1990 .... DLB-220
Zlatovratsky, Nikolai Nikolaevich 1845-1911 .... DLB-238
Zola, Emile 1840-1902 .... DLB-123
Zolla, Elémire 1926- DLB-196
Zolotow, Charlotte 1915- DLB-52
Zschokke, Heinrich 1771-1848 .... DLB-94
Zubly, John Joachim 1724-1781 .... DLB-31
Zu-Bolton, Ahmos, II 1936- DLB-41
Zuckmayer, Carl 1896-1977 .... DLB-56, 124
Zukofsky, Louis 1904-1978 .... DLB-5, 165
Zupan, Vitomil 1914-1987 .... DLB-181
Župančič, Oton 1878-1949 ...DLB-147; CDWLB-4
zur Mühlen, Hermynia 1883-1951 ...... DLB-56
Zweig, Arnold 1887-1968 .... DLB-66
Zweig, Stefan 1881-1942 .... DLB-81, 118

ISBN 0-7876-6010-8